BARRON'S

GUIDE TO LAW SCHOOLS

20TH EDITION

Introduction by

Gary A. Munneke

Professor of Law, Pace University School of Law

The model LSAT Exam contained in this book is reprinted from *Barron's LSAT*, by Jerry Bobrow, rev. by Bernard V. Zandy, 2009. Chapter 9, "What Should I Expect in Law School?" contained in this book is reprinted from *Barron's How to Succeed in Law School*, by Gary A. Munneke, 2010.

All inquiries should be addressed to:
Barron's Educational Series, Inc.
250 Wireless Boulevard
Hauppauge, New York 11788
www.barronseduc.com

Every effort has been made to ensure the accuracy
of the information in this book. Because costs and
statistics change from year to year, prospective
students should contact the schools to verify this
information.

ISBN-13: 978-0-7641-4750-0

International Standard Serial Number 1062-2489

10%
**POST-CONSUMER
WASTE**
Paper contains a minimum
of 10% post-consumer
waste (PCW). Paper used
in this book was derived
from certified, sustainable
forestlands.

PRINTED IN THE UNITED STATES OF AMERICA
987654321

Contents

Abbreviations and Degrees

ABBREVIATIONS

AALL—American Association of Law Libraries
AALS—Association of American Law Schools
ABA—American Bar Association
ALAS—Auxiliary Loans to Assist Students
CAS—Credit Assembly Service
CCRAA—College Cost Reduction and Access Act
CLEO—Council on Legal Education Opportunity
CPPVE—Council for Private Postsecondary and Vocational Education
CRS—Candidate Referral Service
CSS—College Scholarship Service
CWSP—College Work-Study Program
FAFSA—Free Application for Federal Student Aid
FFS—Family Financial Statement
FWS—Federal Work Study Program
GAPSFAS—Graduate and Professional School Financial Aid Service
GBBE—Georgia Board of Bar Examiners
GPA—Grade Point Average
GSL—Guaranteed Student Loans
LSAT—Law School Admission Test
LSAC—Law School Admissions Council
MBR—Massachusetts Board of Regents
MSA—Middle States Association
NALP—National Association for Law Placement
NCA—North Central Association of Colleges and Schools
NDSL—National Direct Student Loan
NEASC—New England Association of Schools and Colleges
NWCCU—Northwest Commission on Colleges and Universities
SAAC—Student Aid Application for California
SACS—Southern Association of Colleges and Schools
SBC—State Bar of California
WASC—Western Association of Schools and Colleges
UGPA—Undergraduate Grade Point Average

DEGREES

D.C.L.—Doctor of Civil Law
D.C.L.—Doctor of Comparative Law

J.D.—Doctor of Jurisprudence
J.D./M.B.A.—Juris Doctor/Master of Business Administration
J.M.—Master of Jurisprudence
J.S.D.—Doctor of the Science of Law
J.S.M.—Master of the Science of Law
LL.B.—Bachelor of Laws
LL.M.—Master of Laws
M.A.—Master of Arts
M.Acc.—Master of Accountancy
M.A.L.I.R.—Master of Arts in Labor and Industrial Relations
M.A.P.A.—Master of Arts in Public Administration
M.A.S.—Master of Accounting Science
M.B.A.—Master of Business Administration
M.B.T.—Master of Business Taxation
M.C.J.—Master of Criminal Justice
M.C.L.—Master of Comparative Law
M.C.P.—Master of City Planning
M.C.P.—Master of Community Planning
M.C.R.P.—Master of City and Regional Planning
M.D.—Doctor of Medicine
M.H.A.—Master of Health Administration
M.I.L.R.—Master of Industrial and Labor Relations
M.L.S.—Master of Legal Studies
M.L.S.—Master of Library Science
M.L. & T.—Master of Law and Taxation
M.M.—Master of Management
M.O.B.—Master of Organizational Behavior
M.P.A.—Master of Public Administration
M.P.H.—Master of Public Health
M.P.P.A.—Master of Public Policy Administration
M.P.P.M.—Master of Public and Private Management
M.R.P.—Master of Regional Planning
M.S.—Master of Science
M.S.L.—Master of Studies in Law
M.S.S.A.—Master of Science in Social Administration
M.S.W.—Master of Social Work
M.U.P.—Master of Urban Planning
M.U.R.P.—Master of Urban and Regional Planning
Ph.D.—Doctor of Philosophy
S.J.D.—Doctor of the Science of Law

PART I

Choosing a Law School

CHAPTER 1

Introduction to Law Schools

Legal problems are pervasive in modern society. Virtually every day, news stories track legal issues, from laws that affect the way we live, to notorious cases that intrigue and even disgust us. The summer of 2011 provided television voyeurs with a live legal drama in the guise of the Casey Anthony murder trial. Whether viewers believed that the legal system worked or failed, it was hard not to get caught up in the legal chess game between prosecution and defense lawyers. Dramatizations of legal disputes and high-profile prosecutions capture the imaginations of viewers in a cycle of never-ending pathos. We live, in short, in a world of law and lawyers.

It is easy to forget that law is an ancient and traditional profession. One can go back to Greek and Roman times to find records of a class of people who represented other citizens before judicial tribunals. Our American brand of legal representation emerged in the wake of the Norman Conquest of England in 1066, when Anglo-Saxon-speaking peasants needed a voice in the French-speaking Norman courts. For a thousand years, lawyers in the British Commonwealth of nations and in the United States have continued the tradition of standing up for the accused and injured, and guiding them through the arcane labyrinth of the judicial system.

Conflict is at the heart of legal problems. If we did not have disputes, we would not need a legal system. But we do. Over the centuries, various utopian theorists have sought to create societies where people got along, where conflict was eliminated, and where a system for resolving disputes was unnecessary. These efforts have been uniformly unsuccessful, and in the absence of utopia, lawyers and a legal system remain essential to civilized society.

Lawyers and the Rule of Law are the last bastion of order as an alternative to anarchy and chaos. No corner of the globe is immune from breakdowns in the Rule of Law, which simply put is societal reliance on the orderly and peaceful resolution of disputes, in contrast to violence and mayhem as the dominant form of problem solving.

The law is nothing less than a substitute for violence as a means of resolving disputes. In a world where terrorism, ethnic cleansing, genocide, drive-by shootings, and domestic violence are all too commonplace, lawyers provide access to a peaceful option for resolving problems. Ironically, the oft-quoted Shakespearean line, "The first thing we do, we'll kill all the lawyers," was spoken by a character, Jack the Butcher, who was an avowed anarchist determined to overthrow the King. Without lawyers, he reasoned, his aims were more easily attainable.

Critics of lawyers and the judicial system complain about a litany of injustices, procedural loopholes, outrageous damage awards, and disparate treatment of the rich and poor. Yet, even recognizing that the legal system has room for improvement, few people are willing to scrap an institution that keeps the barbarians, like Jack the Butcher, at bay.

Lawyers are sometimes accused of greed for charging exorbitant fees for their services. The truth is that lawyers are compensated well for their work, but lawyer incomes are not out of line with incomes for other professionals with comparable education and training.

Lawyers are encouraged to provide a portion of their legal work to persons who cannot afford the fees, and many, if not all, lawyers take this admonition seriously. Other lawyers volunteer their time in community service to legislative bodies, councils, boards, and commissions. This tradition of public service goes back to the earliest days of the profession.

A small percentage of lawyers earn significantly more than the average $150,000 for all lawyers, and many, including most younger lawyers, earn less. News stories reporting that law graduates earn as much as $160,000, or more with bonuses, refer to the highest starting salaries, not the lower or even mid-range rates.

Considerable media attention has focused on the less than rosy job market for law school graduates. These stories began to emerge in

3

2008–09, at the height of the economic recession of those years, but they have continued—even intensified—in the years since, perhaps because the recovery has been particularly slow, perhaps because the 20th century economic model for law firms is proving less sustainable in the 21st century, perhaps because a law degree no longer seems like a guaranteed path to success, and perhaps all three of these reasons at the same time. In recent years, some commentators have questioned the benefit of obtaining a law degree in light of the cost of legal education. Others have questioned the efficacy of law school training to prepare students for the practice of law. These questions and others are dealt with in more detail in Chapter 10, page 83 of this guide. A few preliminary points deserve to be mentioned at the outset:

- A legal education is expensive; even at a state law school, tuition, books, living expenses, and forgone income require an investment of tens of thousands of dollars, and private schools invariably cost well into six figures. All but the wealthiest students must secure financial aid, or work while attending law school part-time.
- For a variety of reasons, the number of entry-level positions at the largest (best-paying) law firms has declined. This means that more graduates must accept positions in smaller firms, government, public service, or solo practice positions that do not pay as well.
- More graduates appear to be opting for law-related and nonlegal positions, for which their law degrees have prepared them, but bar admission is not required, because these positions pay better (and make better sense economically) than many legal positions.

- Job applicants who are flexible, both as to the types of positions and the geographic locations they are willing to consider, generally fare better in the employment market than those with rigid requirements and unreasonably high expectations.
- Although there is little indication that law graduates do not get jobs, there is ample evidence that fewer of them get their first or even second choices, and that it may take longer to find a good fit than in the past. In this regard, solid career assessment and job search skills are critical.
- It makes a difference where you go to law school, although success may not depend on the specific "rank" of your school. Other factors, like the number of graduates practicing in the city or area you want to work, particular course concentrations, clinical programs and internships, law school performance, as well as other factors, can be just as important as the law school's "tier" in determining what opportunities you have and choices you make.

As you read the ensuing chapters, keep in mind that you are not just choosing an advanced degree program that will land you a job and pay your bills; you are assuming a unique professional identity and following a long line of predecessors in service to society. In all likelihood, you will earn a good living as a lawyer, but more importantly, you will do some good for society along the way. You are choosing a career whose practitioners are proud of what they do and welcome recent law school graduates who bring enthusiasm, idealism, and energy to the practice of law.

by Gary A. Munneke, Professor of Law at Pace University School of Law, where he teaches Professional Responsibility and Law Practice Management. Prior to joining the Pace faculty in 1988, he served on the faculty of the Widener University School of Law, and as Assistant Dean at the University of Texas School of Law. Professor Munneke is the author of 20 books and numerous articles about current issues in the legal profession. His other books provide information about choosing law as a career (*Careers in Law* [2003] and *Opportunities in Law Careers* [2002], VGM Career Horizons, Lincolnwood, IL), what to do after you enter law school (*How to Succeed in Law School,* Barron's, NY, 2008), and what to do after you graduate from law school (*The Legal Career Guide: From Law Student to Lawyer* [2002], and *Nonlegal Careers for Lawyers* [2006], American Bar Association, Chicago). In addition, he has lectured extensively on these topics. Professor Munneke is Past Chair of the American Bar Association Law Practice Management Section and a former member of the ABA Board of Governors. He has served as President and Research Chair of the National Association for Law Placement as well as Chair of the ABA Standing Committee on Professional Utilizational and Career Development. Professor Munneke received his J.D. from the University of Texas Law School in 1973 and is licensed to practice law in Texas and Pennsylvania. He is a Fellow of the American Bar Foundation, and the College of Law Practice Management.

CHAPTER 2

Should I Go to Law School?

You picked up this book because you have given some thought to the question of going to law school, or else someone you know is thinking about going to law school. Each year, more than 40,000 students in the United States begin the long and arduous journey associated with law school. There was a time when large numbers of attorneys received their legal training by studying law books at home until they were knowledgeable enough to pass an oral examination to become a lawyer. Today, almost all lawyers attend a law school before taking a standardized written bar exam. The educational process takes three or four years, depending on whether the curriculum is full- or part-time, and whether it is obtained at one of the law schools approved by the American Bar Association, or a handful of other law schools approved in the state where they are located. Chapters 15–16 of this Guide provide detailed descriptions of these law schools, in order to help you decide which school is right for you. Chapter 7 offers a variety of thoughts on how to make this decision.

Law school is not for everyone. Some individuals cannot cope with the intellectual demands, while others find the psychological stress associated with the study and practice of law to be suffocating. Many bright and ambitious people do not succeed at law because they find other activities more rewarding and challenging. However, many college graduates will find law school to be the most stimulating experience of their lives.

There is a great deal of popular mythology about law school and the legal profession. This book attempts to get past much of the confusing rhetoric facing individuals contemplating a legal education. *Barron's Guide to Law Schools* is full of factual information about law schools and no nonsense advice on the application process, the LSAT, and the decision-making process. The rest of this chapter explains why the decision to go to law school is so complex and gives reasons why people make this important decision.

A COMPLEX DECISION

The process of choosing a law school is a complex one, and there are no easy answers along the way. Accordingly, this Guide should be viewed more as a road map to your destination than as the answer to all your questions. A road map may help you find your way, but it cannot replace the experience of getting there yourself.

This book focuses on the choices that each law school applicant must make during the admission process. As you are considering whether and where to attend law school, you will spend considerable energy weighing various options. The fact that you will feel confused (and at times overwhelmed) is normal. Regardless of your background, you cannot escape facing tough decisions that will affect the rest of your life. If you struggle with the choices, it is a sign that you appreciate the importance of the process.

The two basic problems (Which school is best for you? and Can you get admitted?) are the same for every applicant. Regardless of whether you have many choices or a single acceptance, so much rests on your decision that it is impossible not to feel the pressure. Most important decisions in life are fraught with stress; this is no exception.

The publisher and authors of this text have no ax to grind and no personal investment in whether you attend law school or not. Our aim is to provide objective information that will help you make an informed choice about a tough decision. We encourage you to listen to other voices who have opinions on this subject. There certainly is room for divergence of viewpoints on many of the subjects addressed here. One person will tell you that you have to be a lawyer, and the next person will tell you that nobody should be a lawyer. In the end, only you can decide on your best course of action. The best way to assure that your final decision will be the right one for you is to become fully informed on all the issues.

WHY GO TO LAW SCHOOL?

You might choose to go to law school for a number of different reasons. In fact, many lawyers were influenced by a variety of factors:

- They wanted the prestige, power, and panache that a degree in law provides;

- They wanted a professional career in which they could make enough money to establish and maintain a comfortable lifestyle;
- They wanted to change the world in order to make it a little better than it was when they arrived;
- They wanted to pursue a long family tradition;
- They wanted to do something different from anyone else in their family;
- They took an aptitude test during college and the career counselor said that they should become a lawyer; or
- They went to a prelaw association meeting as a favor to a roommate, got elected president, and couldn't back out (my personal reason for attending law school).

Everyone arrives at the law school door for different reasons. Some of these are more valid than others. Here are a few of the wrong reasons to go to law school:

- *Don't* go to law school because other people expect you to. Spouses, family, friends, and advisors seem perpetually willing to push their loved one, associate, or advisee in this direction. While these people almost always want what is best for you, their personal motives are inevitably more complex. Look at the source and weigh the advice accordingly. Ask yourself what these other people have to gain (or lose) if you go to law school. What will they contribute along the way to your success (or failure)? Can you listen to these voices and still make your own decision?

- *Don't* go to law school because of what you see on television or read in the newspapers about lawyers. Media coverage of high profile cases such as the David Goldman case, where an American father spent five years regaining custody from his former wife's new husband's family in Brazil, may present a skewed picture of what practicing law is all about. Popular television shows such as *Boston Legal* inevitably portray lawyers in a very different light than most lawyers experience in their daily lives. Lawyers are neither as rich, good-looking, and fast-talking, or as weasly, manipulative, and grasping as the stereotypes suggest. Most practicing lawyers will tell you that these images have little in common with their real lives. We smile bemusedly at the antics of the characters on popular television series, but in our hearts we know that they could never exist in the flesh.

If you want to discover how real-life lawyers work and live, ask them. Visit a law firm, or better yet, get a job in one. Look for lawyers outside the world of work; find out about lawyers in their neighborhoods and communities. Investigate how they live and play when they go home at night. You will probably discover that lawyers are a well-educated and intense (but diverse) lot, who give as much to the community as they do to their jobs.

• *Don't* go to law school because you can't figure out what to do with your life, or because you can't find anything else that interests you. Law school is not the place to go to find yourself. Law school is a significant investment of your time and money. Legal education is no place to buy more time to make a decision because you just can't bear to face the real world.

Whatever other motives may influence your decision to attend law school, make certain that a major consideration is your genuine desire to study law. If you have doubts about whether you want to *study* law (as opposed to *practice* law), do something else for a year or two. Work in a law firm, or join the Peace Corps. If you find you can't get the idea of law school out of your mind, that should be a sign to you. If, on the other hand, you forget about it, forget about it.

These admonitions may fall on deaf ears, but at least you've been warned. Many people find law school to be the most interesting, intellectually stimulating, and challenging experience of their educational lives (despite its many aggravations); others hate it almost more than they can bear. If you find that you fit into the latter group and not the former, don't put yourself through the misery of sitting through three years or more of law school classes, unless you are prepared to do so regardless of the outcome.

The question of whether to go to law school is sometimes confused with the question of which law school to choose. A person may thrive at one law school and wither at another. To the extent that the decision to attend law school is influenced by the choice of which law school to attend, applicants need to look closely at both sets of considerations. The issue of which law school to attend is covered in greater depth in Chapter 7, but for now it is sufficient to link these two areas of inquiry.

CHAPTER 3

Where Can I Find Information About Law School?

There is both a wealth and paucity of information about law schools. Books and guides of various sorts abound on the shelves of libraries and bookstores. A considerable amount of information is available in electronic formats. Information in the form of advice from well-meaning advisors is also easily accessible. If you are thinking about attending law school, the one thing you will find in abundance is advice. What is often in short supply is any way to tell whether the advice you get is good or not. This informational paradox was apparent to the developers of this Guide. The result is a Guide that is easy to use and understand, containing up-to-the-minute information about law schools.

In addition to the *Guide to Law Schools,* Barron's offers *Barron's LSAT* by Jerry Bobrow and revised by Bernard V. Zandy, an in-depth preparation guide for the law school admission test. A smaller version of the LSAT book, *Pass Key to the LSAT*, is also available. These books should provide you with enough information to tackle the law school challenge. Many readers, however, will want more. For those with the time, energy, and inclination, the following paragraphs discuss many other sources of information.

Web Sites

The Internet makes it easy to find information about law schools, legal education, and the practice of law (see Chart, page 9). Law schools provide web sites not only for their own students, but also for prospective students, alumni, and the public. These web sites are easily accessible to anyone seeking information.

The problem with online research is that often there is too much information, rather than too little. Locating the specific information you want can require persistence. When looking at law school sites, you may be able to find in-depth profiles of faculty members, courses, activities, and services beyond the superficial treatment in catalogs and other marketing pieces published by the school. Remember, however, that many law schools are sophisticated enough to create their web sites as marketing tools, and like other promotional materials, they provide you with a picture of the institution that is carefully painted.

What everyone is looking for is unbiased comparative information, isn't it? Much of the information you need appears right here in *Barron's Guide to Law Schools*, in a format that is easy to use and understand. There are a number of electronic resources that contain interesting compilations of data and commentary that go beyond the scope of this book. By using Google, Bing, or some other search engine, you might be able to drill down through layers of information to discover facts that will help you in making your decision. No matter how much time you spend on the Internet, however, your final decision may come down to intangible factors, such as how you feel about a law school through dealing with representatives or visiting in person.

Prelaw Advisors

Most colleges and universities designate one or more professors as prelaw advisors. Students thinking about law school are routinely funneled to these professors and administrators for guidance. The question of prelaw school education is addressed in more depth in the next chapter: The comments here are aimed more at assessing the pros and cons of utilizing a prelaw advisor at school.

First of all, it is very difficult to make generalizations about the type of individuals who become prelaw advisors or the quality of advice they dispense. Prelaw advisors may come from almost any discipline, although it seems that a high percentage are political science professors.

Web Site	Sponsor	Subject Matter
http://lsac.org	Law School Admissions Council	Provides information on preparing for law school, choosing a law school, taking the LSAT, applying to law school, and financing law school.
www.abanet.org/home.cfm	American Bar Association	A detailed web site offering information on everything you always wanted to know about law and the legal profession
www.abanet.org/legaled/ home.html	ABA Section of Legal Education and Admissions to the Bar	
www.abanet.org/cpr/	ABA Center for Professional Responsibility	
www.abanet.org/lsd/home.html	ABA Law Student Division	
www.abanet.org/journal/ redesign/home.html	*ABA Journal*	
www.alm.com/	American Lawyer Media	An expansive online source for lawyers, law managers, and in-house counsels regarding news, trends, and market intelligence
www.americanlawyer.com/	*American Lawyer Magazine*	An online magazine that features articles on the legal community both nationally and internationally and discusses lawyers and their work
www.law.com/index.shtml	*Law.com* information services	Offers information regarding recent changes in the law and reports regional and local news
http://nalp.org/	National Association for Law Placement	A web site designed to promote legal careers by posting opportunities
http://www.lawschool.com	*Lawschool.com*	Provides law school ranks, information on moot court, law review, and bar exam information on each US state
http://grad-schools.usnews. rankingsandreview.com/ best-graduate-schools/ top-law-schools/rankings	*U. S. News & World Report*	Provides annual law school ranks and an A–Z law school directory
http://jurist.law.pitt.edu/ admissions.htm	JURIST	Provides prelaw guidance and explains the ins and outs of law school
http://www.ilrg.com/	PublicLegal, a product of the Internet Legal Research Group (ILRG)	A comprehensive one-stop-shopping resource of information concerning law and the legal profession that offers a categorized index of more than 4000 links

Many, but certainly not all, possess a law degree themselves, in addition to professional credentials in their teaching field. They may be young professors, barely out of school themselves, or wizened veterans who have been advising generations of prospective law students.

Prelaw advisors often come to the table with a distinct set of biases in favor of or against certain law schools, approaches to the application process, and the qualities that are needed to succeed in law school. Keep in mind, however, that the more definite the advisor is in his or her opinions, the more likely it is that there are differing points of view that make as much sense. Some prelaw advisors diligently collect information about law schools, such as law school catalogs or information about former students who have attended certain law schools. Other advisors may have little in the way of written materials, but willingly commit many hours to give to those who want to talk.

Whether or not you should take the advice of your prelaw advisor is a very personal question. Just as it is with doctors, dentists, psychologists, and other professionals, chemistry is important. You need to find someone with whom it is easy to carry on a conversation, someone whose opinion you value, and someone who strikes you as well-informed and objective. The same prelaw advisor might hit it off with one student and turn off another. For this reason, it makes sense to get in to talk to your prelaw advisor as early as you can during your college career. If you have already graduated from college, you may be able to contact the prelaw advisor at your college anyway. And if you are in grad school, you may be able to talk to the prelaw advisor there.

If you are not happy with the advice you get, or not comfortable talking to the advisor, you have an opportunity to find another person to fill this role. You may find that advice from a trusted faculty mentor, such as a club sponsor, academic advisor, or favorite teacher who may work just as well for you as the school's official prelaw advisor. While this mentor may not be as well-versed on law schools as the regular prelaw advisor, the benefit that you will derive from being able to speak openly and candidly can be invaluable.

Prelaw Associations

Many colleges and universities have a prelaw association or club committed to supporting prelaw students at those institutions. These student organizations may sponsor programs, collect information, and at universities affiliated with a law school, provide opportunities for direct contact with law school faculty and students.

Career Counselors

At some institutions, the office of career services provides information and advice about law schools and legal education. Because career counselors have training and experience in helping people to make career decisions, they may be able to assist you in ways that a faculty member could not. Some career services offices offer testing programs, which attempt to identify things like work values, personality types, and vocational interests. These tests are often validated by comparison to control groups of individuals from particular professions. Thus, you can determine whether your personality type or professional values are similar to the values or personality of other people who have chosen to go into law. Such tests can lay a trap for those who do not interpret the results with a critical eye. It is one thing to say that you are like other members of a group; it does not necessarily follow that you have to have those traits in order to be successful in a given field. In reality, successful lawyers are as diverse in terms of personality and values as the general population, and while it may be possible to identify characteristics common among typical lawyers, it is not uncommon to find lawyers who do not fit into the mold. For example, tests may tell you that you should be a trial lawyer, but if you hate trial work, the test results do not matter.

Other Advisors

It is not necessary to limit the universe of potential advisors to educational settings. Well-informed family members, work supervisors, friends, and business associates all may have qualities that make them good advisors for you. If you know a practicing lawyer personally, you can seek guidance from him or her. In fact, nowhere is it written that you can seek advice from only one person. You may want to take a sampling of opinions from various people and reach your own decisions.

Law School Career Days

One of the best ways to get information about law schools is to attend a law school career day. These events come in a variety of forms, from those sponsored by a single university, attended by as few as a single law school, to those sponsored by Law Services in major U.S. cities, sometimes attended by more than one hundred law schools. Law schools typically send representatives to these events, in areas where they hope to draw their students. Individual law schools may schedule a day of interviews through the career services office, or the prelaw advisor. Several colleges may join together to schedule panels or career fairs of law school representatives. The Law Services annual law forums are regional fairs in major cities attended by a large number of American law schools. Law school forums allow you to visit a number of law school representatives in person and in close proximity for easy comparison. The law schools usually bring catalogs, applications, and other literature for you to take, thus providing a quick way to receive materials.

Law School Forums in 2012*

If you're considering law school, come to a Law School Forum. Free admission. Registration is easy. Register at the forum or avoid the wait and register online at *www.LSAC.org*.

- talk with representatives of LSAC-member law schools from across the United States and Canada;
- obtain admission materials, catalogs, and financial aid information;
- view video programs about the law school admission process, legal education and careers, minority perspectives on legal education, and gay and lesbian issues;
- attend informational sessions on the law school admission process, financing a legal education, and issues of importance to minority applicants; and
- review LSAC publications, videos, software, and LSAT® preparation materials.

Miami, FL	September 15, 2012 Hyatt Regency Miami
Los Angeles, CA	November 12, 2012 Millennium Biltmore Hotel Los Angeles
New York, NY	October 12, 2012 Hilton New York
Boston, MA	November 17, 2012 Renaissance Boston Waterfront Hotel
Chicago, IL	July 14, 2012 Palmer House Hilton
Atlanta, GA	September 8, 2012 Marriott Marquis
Houston, TX	September 29, 2012 JW Marriott Houston

For further information contact: *LSACinfo@lsac.org*

Law School Visits

If you have narrowed the number of law schools to which you plan to apply to two or three, it may make sense for you to visit the schools in person. When you applied to undergraduate schools, you probably visited campuses before you made your final choice. What you learned about the setting, ambiance, and facilities undoubtedly contributed to your final decision. It is no different with the decision to attend law school. Some law schools encourage on-site visits through open houses on specific dates. Most law schools, however, are happy to arrange for a campus visit at any time. It makes sense to try to schedule your visit at a time when classes are in session in order to get a sense of what law school life is like at the school. You may be able to visit classes, talk to students and faculty, and meet with officials about such matters as applications and financial aid. See the checklist on page 12 to guide you on campus visits.

Interviews

Some law schools incorporate personal interviews into the application process. A few schools utilize interviews as a formal part of the selection process. Some other schools encourage, but do not require, applicants to interview with a representative of the law school as a means of gathering more data about the candidate. An interview is typically a one- or two-on-one process, not unlike a job interview, as distinguished from more informal visits with law school personnel in conjunction with law forums or campus visits. Find out if the schools to which you plan to apply provide for interviews. If they

*Check for updated dates and locations for 2013 and beyond, as they become available at *www.lsac.org*.

CHECKLIST FOR CAMPUS VISIT

☐ Were the arrangements professionally and accurately made?

☐ Was it easy to get to the campus for your visit?
  ☐ Directions
  ☐ Traffic (for automobile visitors)
  ☐ Public transportation

☐ Were the law school staff who greeted you friendly and accommodating?

☐ Did you visit one or more class(es) during your visit?
  ☐ Did you enjoy the class?
  ☐ Did the students in the class seem to enjoy the class?
  ☐ Did the professor seem interesting?

☐ Did you attend a formal program on campus?
  ☐ Did speakers provide useful information about the law school?
  ☐ Did you gain insights into the application/admission process?
  ☐ Did you have an opportunity to talk to faculty and students?

☐ Did you take a tour of the law school facilities?
  ☐ Were the facilities clean, attractive, and appealing?
  ☐ Did there appear to be enough space for the programs of the law school?

☐ Did the law school share space with other university activities?

☐ Did you check out the adequacy of parking, housing, food services?

☐ Were the facilities adequate to accommodate your physical disabilities?

☐ Were there places for students to study, meet in small groups, and talk?

☐ What kind of technology support does the law school provide?

☐ Did the people you encountered on the tour seem to be having a good time?

☐ Did you have a formal interview while you were on campus?
  ☐ Was the interview for information purposes only?
  ☐ Was the interview a part of the admission process?
  ☐ Were the interviewers faculty, staff, students, alumni, or a combination?
  ☐ Were the evaluation criteria used in the interview explained to you?
  ☐ Did you have a chance to make your case for admission?

do, decide whether you want to avail yourself of this opportunity. Most applicants welcome the chance to sell themselves directly to the school.

Law-Related Jobs

Part of the information gathering process may include finding out more about what lawyers do. If you grew up in a family of one or more lawyers, you probably learned a great deal about the legal profession and the practice of law through contact with these family members. You probably learned more about lawyers than you realized at the time. The fact that you remain interested in a career in law suggests that something about the lifestyle of a lawyer appeals to you.

If you did not grow up in such a family, or if you did and you want to learn more, one of the best ways to find out whether you want to practice law is to work in a law firm or other legal organization. Even if you visited a law office as part of a career day in high school or college, nothing will give you a first-hand view of legal work better than a job in the law. You might be surprised at how many opportunities

there are in the law firms, corporate law departments, government law departments, district attorney and public defender offices, and public service organizations. Even in a weak economy opportunities abound for talented individuals. These organizations include, in addition to the legal staff, a support staff of people who have not attended law school, such as legal assistants, legal secretaries, and file clerks.

The jobs may be full time or part time, depending on the needs of the employer, and the pay may vary widely depending on the qualifications for the job and the marketplace for workers in the area. You may be able to find a job with a law firm or other employer for the summer, or as part of a school-sponsored internship. If you are already working for a company, you may be able to arrange for temporary assignments with the company's legal department, or to take on other law-related tasks.

The greatest number of opportunities in the legal marketplace is probably for permanent support staff positions. For paralegals or legal secretaries, training or experience in the field will be helpful; however, there are no state or national standards for these positions such as there would be for becoming a lawyer in the organization. Some firms try to hire highly intelligent and motivated people, who possess basic skills such as keyboarding, word processing, and other computer skills, and provide the training to these individuals themselves.

Over the past two decades, law firms have delegated more work to staff in order to devote themselves more fully to the practice of law. This phenomenon has been most pronounced in larger law firms, but has slowly filtered down to smaller organizations. Here are a few of the areas where prelaw students may find employment, which many continue throughout law school. The common though not exclusive undergraduate and graduate degree programs are listed in parentheses.

- General management (BBA, MBA)
- Librarian (MLS)
- Information Technology (computer sciences)
- Human Resources (BBA, MBA)
- Accounting, Finance (accounting, CPA)
- Paralegal work (paralegal studies, bachelor's degree)
- Investigation, security (criminal justice)
- Economic modeling, research (economics)
- Jury selection (psychology, social science)
- Marketing (BBA, MBA)
- Writing, editing (English, journalism)
- Translation (foreign languages)
- Secretarial (secretarial training or experience)

It is not uncommon for law students today to have spent two to three years, or more, working in a law firm or other organization, before coming to law school. Many law students continue these prelegal positions while they go to law school, either cutting back on their work hours to part-time status while they are in school, or continuing to work full time, but attending law school part time in the evening. ABA accreditation standards limit full time students to 20 hours of work per week; part time students are not limited as to the number of hours they may work. One potential advantage of working in a law-related position before or during law school, is that there may be an increased probability of obtaining employment with that organization as a lawyer after graduation. Even more important, however, employment in a legal setting may help you to decide whether you want to work in law at all. You will see up close that the practice of law is very different from the images of legal work garnered from books, television, and second-hand anecdotal information.

LITERATURE AND THE MEDIA

Lawyers are portrayed in a variety of lights in literature and the media. Many of the images of lawyers in television and film, as well as in books and the news, are exaggerated, distorted, and stereotypical. It is very difficult to capture the essence of legal work through a literary or cinematic eye. Notwithstanding this limitation, the pervasiveness of media images of lawyers makes it inevitable that we are influenced by these images. Even lawyers themselves are sometimes influenced by their own media hype.

There are a number of excellent books and films on the legal profession, and regular viewing of court proceedings and discussion of legal issues on CNN, C-SPAN, and other news channels can be highly illuminating. Here are a few specific recommendations on books and films:

- *The Bramble Bush* by Carl Llewellyn, read by generations of law students.

- *The Paper Chase* by John Jay Osborne. The book (or the movie with John Houseman) presents a fictitious first year with the quintessential law professor who does intellectual battle with his less-than-equal student nemesis, Hart.

- *One L* by Scott Turow. Probably a more realistic picture of law school, this book is based on Turow's school notes about the first year of law school.

- *A Civil Action* by Jonathan Harr is a riveting account of the colossal battle between a brash, aggressive plaintiff lawyer and an icon of the Boston legal establishment in an environmental pollution case in the town of Woburn, Massachusetts—a true story.

- *Michael Clayton.* The sad story of a lawyer (George Clooney) who was passed over for partnership in a big law firm and carries out all the mundane grunt work and unseemly tasks for his more successful counterparts.

- *Inherit the Wind.* The book, the play, and the movie present a fictionalization of the Scopes Monkey Trial, in which a Tennessee science teacher was prosecuted for teaching evolution. The lawyers in the real case were three-time presidential candidate William Jennings Bryan and famed defense counsel Clarence Darrow.

- *A Few Good Men,* with Jack Nicholson and Tom Cruise, tells the story of military justice, after a commander's rigid discipline leads to a soldier's death. We all know that the villain doesn't usually break down on the stand in real life, but Jack makes us believe anyway.

- *Gideon's Trumpet* by Anthony Lewis. If ever you wanted a reason to become a lawyer, this is it: indigent man fights to the Supreme Court for the right to be represented by counsel.

- *To Kill a Mockingbird* by Harper Lee, or the movie with Gregory Peck. A classic in print or film: small town Southern lawyer faces the challenges of practicing law, while standing up for truth, justice, and the American way of life, with dignity and courage.

- Anything by John Grisham. Sure, the plots are far-fetched, and the dialogue hardly Hemingway, but each one of Grisham's tales provides great imagery on different practice settings from personal injury practice (*The Rainmaker*), to elite corporate work (*The Firm*), to high profile criminal cases (*A Time to Kill*).

- *Kramer v. Kramer.* Dustin Hoffman and Meryl Streep fight for custody in a courtroom drama that demonstrates how justice isn't always easy to find in the courtroom.

- *Erin Brockovich.* A feisty paralegal played by Julia Roberts helps expose Pacific Gas & Electric pollution coverup. Based on a true story.

The list could go on and on, because lawyers, trials, and the stories of people who encounter the justice system provide such fertile soil for intriguing plotlines. Whether the source is books, movies, or TV (depictions of lawyers on the small screen are legion), it is possible to learn about the work of lawyers by watching how they are depicted in various media. What you learn may not dictate your choices about law school, but it may provide useful clues to help you answer your questions. See also Richard Burst, "The 25 Greatest Legal Movies," ABA Journal (August 2008).

A Variety of Sources

It should be apparent to you that in order for you to gather information about law schools, you need to evaluate information from a variety of sources in light of your own aspirations. The decision to attend law school may involve the outlay of one hundred thousand dollars, or more, in direct costs, and require you to forego other income for a period of three or four years. For this reason, the decision to go to law school should not be made lightly. This chapter has provided an overview of the primary sources of information available to help you make this decision. The rest is up to you.

CHAPTER 4

What Course of Prelaw Study Should I Take?

There is no standard prelaw curriculum. Law schools do not require any particular undergraduate degree, course of study, or particular courses in order to gain admission. Statistics on the entering class of every law school will demonstrate that students come from a wide variety of backgrounds. Perhaps the largest number of law students started out as political science majors, but other majors from the arts and social sciences are well represented, including history, English, psychology, and sociology. Law schools generally have a high concentration of business majors, including tax and accounting, general business, economics, criminal justice, and international relations. There are usually smaller but significant numbers from the hard sciences like physics, chemistry, and biology, or engineering. Other majors, such as journalism, environmental science, art, music, or drama, are likely to be found in a typical first-year class. Included in this group may be a variety of other professionals including doctors, psychologists, CPAs, professors, and even members of the clergy. You should not be surprised in your first year law school class to find yourself sitting between an anesthesiologist and a history professor. You may have obtained a graduate degree yourself, and wondered if there is room in law school for someone like you. The answer is yes.

Because law schools only require that you complete an undergraduate degree, every degree program is equal, at least in theory. In practice, law schools may find that they have had better success with graduates from certain degree programs at certain universities than others. Individual admissions committee members at different schools may have their own ideas about what kind of prelaw training will prepare students best for law school. Undergraduate advisors may channel prelaw students into certain majors that they perceive to have a nexus with law school. If your research discloses that certain concentrations or degree programs are likely to receive favorable treatment in the admissions process of schools where you plan to apply, you would be wise to pursue such a course of study.

Otherwise, the best advice for your prelegal education is to follow a curriculum that you enjoy. It is important for you to possess an interest independent of law school. There are two important reasons for this: First, chances are that you will do better in a subject area that you enjoy than you will in one that you hate. If you have to struggle each day to get up and go to class, it will undoubtedly be reflected in your grades, and a poor showing will adversely affect your chances to be admitted to law school. Second, if you do not get into law school or decide not to go to law school, you will have pursued a course of study that will help you in some alternative career path.

Much the same advice can be said about specific courses. Take courses that you like, that provide an intellectual challenge for you personally. Study under professors who are interesting and exciting, rather than those who put you to sleep. Take classes that make you want to learn, rather than those that fit into a convenient schedule or guarantee an "A."

There is no washout course for prelaw, like Organic Chemistry for premed majors. There is no one course that every law school applicant must complete. Yet, prelaw students continue to pose the question: What courses will help me most in law school? At the risk of negating the advice of take what you like, the following are this author's personal suggestions for courses that may help you to develop skills you can use in law school:

1. **Research and writing.** Any course that imposes a demanding regimen of critiqued writing based upon academic research will help you in law school. All law students are required to complete research and writing assignments during law school—

an activity that does not end with graduation, because much of lawyering involves research and writing. In addition, many law school exams are essay tests, which favor effective writers. The more writing experience you get, the better off you will be in law school. If your high school preparation for research and writing was poor, you may want to impose a remedial curriculum on yourself during college or graduate school. If your writing skills are strong, you can always do more to enhance them.

2. **Logic or reasoning.** Much of law school centers on legal analysis, which is fundamentally deductive logic. Learning about logic and reasoning can help to prepare you for the kind of thinking you will be required to do in law school.

3. **Legal history.** Although you will read historical cases in law school, law professors give scant attention to the roots of our legal system. A course that traces the development of the law, particularly Anglo-American jurisprudence, will provide you with a useful background throughout your legal career.

4. **Public speaking.** You will be required to speak when called on in class, and you will need to be able to make oral arguments throughout law school. Courses that polish your speaking ability and the skill of thinking on your feet will make the inevitable speaking requirements of law school more palatable. A course like this might be particularly valuable for someone who is not accustomed to, or afraid of, standing up and speaking publicly. Many high schools and colleges also sponsor extra-curricular programs in speech, drama, and debate, which provide preparation for oral advocacy in law school.

5. **Basic accounting.** Certain law school courses in the areas of contracts, business and tax, assume a fundamental understanding of financial and accounting terms and principles. Legal practitioners are constantly required to deal with their clients' money, as well as their own. Understanding the basics of accounting and business will prove invaluable.

6. **Speed reading.** You will probably be required to do more reading in law school than you ever have before. You will also be expected to understand the material in greater depth than in the past. Accordingly, the ability to pore over a great amount of reading with a high level of retention is important. Many universities offer such courses on either a credit or noncredit basis; if yours does not, consider taking such a course outside of school.

Here are a few other suggestions for course selection in undergraduate school:

• Do not be afraid of courses that are intellectually demanding; these classes will train your mind for the rigors of a legal education.

• Get a well-rounded education; take courses outside your major. Legal problems draw from the experience of humankind, and so lawyers inevitably must be renaissance people in order to understand these legal problems.

• Master technology; universities provide wired (or wireless) environments, and college students use computers in a variety of ways. This will not change.

• Do more than go to classes; get involved in extracurricular activities as well. Evidence of learning is found in more places than transcripts.

If it has been several years since you were in school, you may find yourself experiencing some uneasiness about returning to the world of education. Some of this malaise you should discount out of hand. You will find that your reacclimation to school comes quickly. You will also discover that life experiences gained since college give you valuable perspectives that you will use in the law. The discipline of managing life in the real world will undoubtedly help you to organize your time and maximize your performance in law school. If you have been out of school for a long time, or remain nervous about returning to school for any other reason, then take courses before you apply to law school. These might be undergraduate courses at a local community college or a university, or they might be graduate level courses offered through your employer. Such experiences may help to make the transition go more smoothly.

Although the bulk of this section has dealt with undergraduate education, it is worth noting that a significant number of law school entrants possess advanced degrees, including MBAs, CPAs, master's degrees in a variety of other fields, Ph.D.s, MDs, and other medical degrees. People who come to law school with professional degree certification usually fall into one of two groups: those who hope to build upon their prior training with a degree in law, and those who hope to make a complete career change because they are not satisfied with their chosen occupation. Both groups are well represented in law school. Graduate level training can be a useful credential for law school admission and an excellent preparation for the study of law. However, because the admission process typically focuses on undergraduate grades, A's in graduate school will not wipe out C's in college.

Finally, a word about *which* college. Law schools take into consideration the reputations of undergraduate institutions just as other graduate programs do. If you went to a school with an excellent reputation, or a highly regarded degree program, it will help you in the application process. Because law schools are able to compare the performance of admitted students with their undergraduate institutions, they may have evidence to show that students from a particular school or college perform above or below the average of admitted students. This may be because the undergraduate school recommends more or fewer of its better students to a particular law school. It may be that a larger number of applicants coming from a particular university (say a local one) means that admitted students fall within the full range of qualifications in the entering class. Whatever the reasons, your school does make a difference. If you think that law schools may not know enough about your prelegal schools or degree programs to be able to make an accurate assessment of these institutions, send informational material about the school or program with your application.

In the final analysis, your prelegal education can help you in a variety of ways to prepare for the rigors of law school. The absence of specific requirements gives you a great deal of freedom in choosing a path. Select one that builds the skills you will need in law school, that is simultaneously interesting and fulfilling on its own.

CHAPTER 5

How Do I Apply to Law School?

The law school application process that you will complete as an applicant is somewhat analogous to what you will be doing as a law student. You will research the issue, you will analyze the results of your research, and you will reach a conclusion.

The application process must be taken seriously and applicants should investigate all options available to them. Fortunately, there are many sources of information for prospective law students to use. See Chapter 3, particularly the schedule of Law School Forums for 2012.

GRADES

Unlike the LSAT, which represents a straightforward index of performance, grades represent a murky and sometimes unfathomable representation of law school applicants' capabilities. Rather than a single test that compares all test takers to all others at discrete points in time, grades represent hundreds of tests, papers, projects, objective and subjective assessments, and other considerations accumulated over a period of years. Grading standards vary by institution, and even within schools, colleges, and departments within institutions. Grades are affected by myriad variables, from time available to devote to schoolwork, test taking, and writing skills, to personal commitment to learning, health, and lifestyle. Grades can cover a four-year undergraduate curriculum, a degree earned over an extended number of years, graduate and professional school attendance, and even non-degree course work. Grades may represent a candidate's performance over the past four or five years, or educational accomplishments that may be decades old.

The illusiveness of attaching meaning to grades can be as confusing to applicants as it is to the law schools, which vary from school to school as to how they treat grades. Some basic considerations are worth noting. Law schools *do* look at grades, and a dismal academic performance may preclude admission to any law school. You may be able to cite chapter and verse to explain why your grades do not represent your ability to do law school work. In fact, grades may not reflect as much about your innate intellect as they do about your ability to withstand the demands of a legal education. Grades reflect some level of discipline, commitment, and skill in mastering a course of instruction over an extended period of time, in addition to substantive knowledge.

Law School Admissions Council (LSAC) will take your transcripts and produce a report to the law schools to which you apply summarizing your undergraduate grades. Relying on information from hundreds of institutions, LSAC attempts to give the law schools information that they can interpret with some degree of reliability. Thus, your report will include an undergraduate grade point average (UGPA) that may differ from your actual GPA at the school from which you graduated. This is because the UGPA reported to the law schools includes all the undergraduate courses you took from all the universities you attended. So, if you attended summer school at a university in your hometown, the grades from summer may be recorded as a "Pass" by your home university, but they will be recorded with actual grades by LSAC. If your college uses a different grading system—for instance, reporting all grades on a 100-point scale instead of a 4.0 scale—LSAC will convert the grades to a standard 4.0 scale.

If your school's grading system is different from the norm, you should be prepared to explain to the law schools considering your application what your GPA means. If your actual GPA includes anomalies, such as one terrible semester when you had health problems or changed majors, you should explain candidly, without being apologetic, about what happened. If your grades have shown improvement over the course of time, be sure to point out the improvement. If you have participated in special programs or received academic awards that may not be apparent on standard reports, describe what these honors mean.

Graduate School Grades

One area that surprises many applicants is the way that law schools treat graduate education. As a rule, graduate level grades are not included in the calculation of your undergraduate GPA. This is because undergraduate and graduate schools are not the same. Graduate school often requires the same kind of competitive application process that it takes to get into law school, so acceptance into a graduate program merely says that an applicant possesses the requisite qualifications that the law school is considering. Graduate level grades are often considerably higher than undergraduate grades, and may not reflect the same range of performance as undergraduate grades. Although law schools do not incorporate graduate school grades into the UGPA, admissions committees typically are very interested in post-baccalaureate educational experiences. Thus, if you have attended graduate or professional school, do not hesitate to mention these experiences.

In the final analysis, law schools want to know how well you have done in school in the past, because they believe that your past performance gives some indication of how you will do in law school. Despite the fact that interpretation of academic performance is challenging, law schools do learn valuable information about you. Combined with the LSAT, the UGPA provides a strong indicator of future success in law school.

THE LSAT

Each applicant to law school is required to take the Law School Admission Test (LSAT). The LSAT is administered four times per year, typically June, October, December, and February. (See page 42 for 2012–13 test dates.) For most law schools, the LSAT is one of the most important factors in making admission decisions, as it is a common denominator for every applicant

In determining whether a particular application is appropriate, law school representatives will release median numbers. Applicants should know that a median means the middle score in a series. At any given school, there are students with numbers above and below the median undergraduate GPA and LSAT scores. Some schools may also release the 25th and 75th percentile scores, which represent the score range of the middle of the class. Applicants should also be aware that the LSAT and GPA medians are not the same for the total applicant pool, admitted students, and enrolled students. The admitted pool is higher than the total pool, because schools admit the best applicants, but the enrolled pool is lower than the admitted pool, because some good students choose to go to other schools.

To see how this might work in practice, let's take a look at three law schools and six students. Assume that School A is a highly competitive, elite school; School B is a mid-range state school; and School C is a less competitive, new private school. Chart A illustrates where the median UGPA and LSAT scores fall:

Chart A
GPA and LSAT Medians for Three Hypothetical Law Schools

LSAT	UGPA	SCHOOL A LSAT	SCHOOL A GPA	SCHOOL B LSAT	SCHOOL B GPA	SCHOOL C LSAT	SCHOOL C GPA
175–180	3.9–4.0						
170–174	3.7–3.8	172	3.8				
165–169	3.5–3.6				3.6		
160–164	3.3–3.4						
155–159	3.1–3.2			158			
150–154	2.9–3.0						3.0
145–149	2.7–2.8					148	
140–144	2.6–2.7						
Below 140	2.5–2.6						
	Below 2.5						

Now let's look at six students, each with different UGPA and LSAT scores, some higher or lower on one, and others high or low on both:

Chart B
LSAT and GPA Scores for Six Hypothetical Students

LSAT	UGPA	Student 1	Student 2	Student 3	Student 4	Student 5	Student 6
175–180	3.9–4.0		3.9				
170–174	3.7–3.8	174			170		
165–169	3.5–3.6	3.5				3.6	
160–164	3.3–3.4			162/3.4			
155–159	3.1–3.2						
150–154	2.9–3.0		150				
145–149	2.7–2.8						
140–144	2.6–2.7					144	
Below 140	2.5–2.6				2.2		140/2.5
	Below 2.5						

With the caveat that medians can be deceiving and that the number of students competing for seats may affect who is selected from the applicant pool, these charts show, in general terms, how each of six students will fare at the three schools described above.

- Student 1 will easily get into Schools B and C, but is marginal at A, where her LSAT is in the ballpark, but her GPA is a little low. If School A looks at a variety of factors, such as where she went to school, her major, her GPA improvement over four years, and her extracurricular activities, she may have a chance. If they rely on a formula, she may be in trouble.
- Although student 2 has excellent grades, his LSAT is probably too low for School A. Although he is a little below the median for the LSAT at B, if the rest of the application is strong, he has a reasonably good chance. School C will be glad to get him.
- Student 3 with solid LSAT and GPA scores is also out of the picture at School A but a pretty sure bet at B. School C will offer scholarship money.
- Student 4 has really great LSAT and a disastrous GPA. For this student, School B is likely to be very nervous but may want to look behind the numbers; even School A may be curious to see if there is some reason for the low GPA, but this is a long shot. This is an ideal candidate for School C with

great potential and a significant risk of failure (if whatever happened in undergraduate school happens again in law school). All three schools will want to see what Student 4 has done to turn his life around.
- Student 5 has a solid GPA, but a weak LSAT. Neither A nor B will give her much of a shot, but School C will find the good grades appealing, and depending on the overall applicant pool, the LSAT is not dramatically below the school's median LSAT. Depending on other factors, she has a fair chance of admission at School C.
- Student 6 is out of bounds at all three schools. His LSAT is a big risk factor. There is a relationship between LSAT score and bar passage, so any school is going to expect a strong academic record to offset the weak LSAT. Even retaking the LSAT is not likely to help. Student 6 may want to look at admission to a law school not approved by the American Bar Association, or acceptance in a summer trial admission program.

It would appear to be a rather simple matter to compare law schools based on their medians if that were the only criteria used in admission. However, an applicant's undergraduate career typically plays an equally important role in the decision process. A student's academic record must be analyzed very carefully. Factors such as school(s) attended, classes taken, major, minor, number of hours worked while in school, as well as grade progression are all important factors. Therefore, applicants should acknowledge particular strengths in their academic performance, and point out events such as a change of major that may have had a significant impact on the progression of grades.

FACTORS TO CONSIDER

Choosing a law school is a complex process that requires a great deal of thought. The preceding chapters have given you a sense of the considerations that will go into your decision. It is worth noting that all the charts and lists will not answer the intangible questions about which law school is best for you. Where will you be most comfortable? Where are you most likely to be successful? What law school is most likely to further your long-term career aspirations? Where will you be happiest in your personal life?

The answers to these questions are not easy, and in fact may not lend themselves to clear answers at all; but they do bring into play subjective feelings that are very important. Gut feeling, instinct, intuition, prescience, whatever you want to call it, plays a role. All your logical analysis may tell you to go to school X, but your heart tells you to go to school Y. What do you do?

For many applicants, a visit to campus can help to clarify the decision. Taking the time to meet the admissions staff, faculty, students, and even alumni may help you to confirm or clarify your feelings. Imagining yourself in the environment and culture of a particular law school may provide insights that do not appear in any of your charts or logical analyses. Sometimes, as it is in your personal life, your heart is your best guide. If you feel good about one particular law school and kind of creepy about another, go with the one that makes you feel good. In the end, assuming you have choices, you will involve some combination of objective evaluation and subjective guesswork to reach a decision. As long as you have done your homework, and invested your time and energy into the process, your decision will probably be the best one for you.

What you want to avoid is not doing your homework, procrastinating until you foreclose desirable outcomes, delude yourself into thinking that one choice is right for you when in your heart of hearts you know it isn't, and listening to friends, family, and advisors who are pushing their own agendas for you. If you can avoid these pitfalls, you are more likely to end up in a law school that works for you. And if you hate your law school, you can consider transferring after the first year, or getting out of law school altogether.

At this point, the key is to complete the application process in a timely fashion, and to present the best possible case to the law schools you have chosen. If you do this, you can maximize the options that are open to you and the likelihood of making a sound decision.

The number of law schools remaining after this cursory review is probably still too large a number for you to consider applying to all, not only because of the time associated with filling out the applications, but also because of the fees associated with each one. Therefore, look closely at the schools that meet your needs, based on the preliminary information you have gathered. How well do you match up with the profile of these law schools' most recent incoming class? What are the medians of the schools in which you are interested and how do your numerical predictors match up with their numbers?

It may appear that applicants are judged only on the numbers; to the extent that strong or weak scores affect your admissibility, this is true. However, most law schools consider many other aspects of the application as discussed earlier. Applicants must recognize that the LSAT and GPA are the most common factors to each applicant, thus placing everyone at a starting point or on a level playing field. Other factors then become important, such as major, undergraduate institution, advanced degrees, leadership roles in community or within extracurricular activities, letters of recommendation, and the personal essay.

Most applicants submit anywhere from seven to nine applications to various law schools. Applying to one law school is probably unwise; likewise, applying to 100 law schools is not necessary and is very expensive.

It might make sense to use a technique that is common among college applicants: to identify a dream school, one of stronger possibilities, and one safe school. The dream school might be one where you are on the low side of the admission criteria, but you think you have some chance for admission. (If you have no chance of being admitted to a school, don't bother.) The strong school would include institutions where your credentials are competitive with other applicants, but because of the competition for seats, admission is no guarantee. The safe school is one where your credentials are such that you have a very high likelihood of being admitted.

Some students may find that their credentials are not strong enough to use this approach;

other students may have a limited number of choices because of geographic limitations. Many applicants live and/or work in a city where there is only one law school, and they have to gain admission to that school or forego law school altogether. However, if you are in a position where you have options, do not fail to reach for the sky, as long as you keep a safety net if you fall.

DIVERSITY IN THE ADMISSIONS PROCESS

Law schools seek to enroll a diverse student body. In part, this reflects a desire to create opportunities for all Americans to obtain professional education and to gain a degree of upward economic and social mobility. This model has worked for over two centuries in the United States, where generations of children of immigrants have sought and achieved the American Dream as lawyers. And immigrant parents, aspiring to a better life for their children than they experienced themselves, have pushed their children to pursue a career in the law. Today, however, there is another reason to foster diversity: demographers report that by the year 2050, Caucasians of Western European backgrounds will constitute less than 50 percent of the population of the United States. At the current rates of graduation, however, only about 10 percent of lawyers will come from ethnically diverse backgrounds. This gap leads many leaders in the legal profession to support efforts to increase the representation of diverse lawyers in this country.

The American Bar Association Standards for the Approval of Law Schools call upon all approved law schools to seek diversity in the student body and faculty of the institution. This policy has created a considerable amount of controversy because there are not enough seats for everyone who wants to go to law school to be admitted to law school, and some of those denied admission believed that they were more qualified than students admitted under so-called affirmative action plans. Lawsuits going all the way to the U.S. Supreme Court have produced holdings that have forced law schools to rethink admission criteria and procedures.

A short version of what the Supreme Court said is that it is not inappropriate for law schools and other educational institutions to seek to enroll a diverse student body, as long as the criteria for achieving such diversity are narrowly tailored. Thus, schools could not create quotas for minority students, or give minority applicants "bonus" points in admission formulas. Law schools may employ a race-conscious admissions program in order to attain their diversity goals. What this means is that law schools can look at a variety of factors, including those which might be useful in identifying qualified diversity applicants, but if the criteria go too far and create de facto quotas, they are subject to challenge and are likely to be struck down.

For diverse applicants, it will be important to describe your ethnic background in a way that admissions committees understand background. It may not be enough just to check a box on the law school application identifying yourself as a diverse applicant. Your personal statement, letters of reference, and other materials should describe your experience. Whether your diversity is based upon race, ethnicity, religious background, or culture, you should paint a picture of yourself that features your uniqueness.

- Was English a second language for you?
- Were you born outside the United States or a victim of political oppression in your native country?
- Is your diversity also related to socioeconomic disadvantage, which affected your educational or other opportunities growing up?
- How have you personally succeeded in overcoming adversity to get to where you are today?
- What contributions have you made to your home community, and what plans do you have in this regard for the future?
- Are you a Native American who needs to demonstrate your lineage or membership in a particular tribe?
- If your background is not apparent from your name (e.g., you are a Puerto Rican Latino named George Smith), how do you assure that your status is effectively communicated on your application?
- Are there other aspects of your diversity that will need to be clarified to those who will be reading your application?

These points reflect the fluid nature of the admissions process at most schools, which is governed by an assessment of an applicant's entire file, not a simple inclusion in a preferred or nonpreferred group. Likewise, members of other diverse groups, such as individuals protected under the Americans with Disabilities Act (ADA) or the LGBT community, should consider sharing the elements of their backgrounds, which make them diverse. Law schools will respect your right to privacy about personal information, so the decision to include such facts is yours, but you may be able to help your candidacy by incorporating your diversity into your application.

FILLING OUT THE APPLICATION

Once you have identified the schools you will be applying to, you must complete the applications in a timely manner. Applicants must read the instructions for each school carefully. Complete all questions that are not identified as optional and provide explanations where necessary. Any questions labeled "optional" may be left blank. (The sample application for Pace Law School on p. 24 is typical of, if not identical to, other law school applications. Students should go to the web sites of schools to which they wish to apply to access the application forms for those schools.)

Applications may be completed by utilizing school specific online applications or the LSAC web site (*www./lsac.org*). All ABA-approved law schools are included in the LSAC's fully searchable database and easy-to-use application forms. Most applications at many schools are processed through the LSAC site. Most law schools also allow you to apply online through their web sites. See individual school profiles for web site addresses. Although almost all students apply online, either through the LSAC or a law school site, if you do not have access to the Internet, contact the schools where you want to apply to obtain a printed application form. Remember to make copies of each application that is submitted.

The Personal Statement

Because most law schools in the country do not interview candidates for admission, your personal statement is the only place in which you are able to sell yourself to the law school. This may be the only opportunity that the admissions committee has to get to know the person behind the application. It is an opportunity for you to respond to questions you think the committee members may have when they review your application and academic record. It is the place to express who you are and what is important to you. You may wish to emphasize any personal or professional experiences and how they have contributed to your growth and/or personal development. Examples of items that applicants might consider including are:

- a description of work experience and extracurricular activities;

- an explanation of distinct trends or discrepancies among grades;

- a description of substantial time commitments while attending school;

- verification that standardized tests have underpredicted academic performance in the past (prior test scores should be provided);

- cultural, ethnic, educational, or other factors that might cause the LSAT score or GPA to be an inaccurate measure of potential for law study.

In addition, you may wish to mention the fact that you are the first member of the family to graduate from college, or you may wish to explain hardships or handicaps that you have overcome in order to achieve your degree. Whereas test scores place all applicants in a standardized light, the personal statement focuses on the uniqueness of the applicant. If you can paint a favorable picture of yourself, you may be able to stand out among a group of similarly credentialed applicants.

In sum, the personal statement is a case that you have made for yourself to the admissions committee. Correct spelling and grammar are essential. If you tell a great story poorly, you might as well not tell it at all.

Letters of Recommendation

Letters of recommendation can be very helpful to the admissions committee. For recent graduates (within two years), most schools prefer at least one faculty appraisal. Other applicants who would find it difficult to obtain faculty appraisals may request recommendations from individuals who can appraise their ability to perform in law school. Where an institution has a central file for appraisals that are duplicated as needed, or where a committee provides a composite appraisal, typically these alternative procedures are acceptable.

Applicants who have been out of school for a number of years should seek letters of recommendation from individuals who can speak to the applicant's character, leadership abilities, and analytical skills. The quality of the recommendation and content are more important than who writes the letter. It is generally better to use only enthusiastic recommendations; being cursed by faint praise is worse than no praise at all.

Letters of recommendation are additional pieces of evidence that support your case for admission. Many law schools utilize standard recommendation forms in lieu of or in addition to letters. If the school provides such forms, make sure that your references are complete, then return them.

(go to page 39)

Pace University School of Law
JD Application
Page 1 of 15

Application Instructions

The Admissions Committee Requires the Following Documents:

1. Electronic Application Form and Certification Statement

2.

   Personal Statement — The Admissions Committee requires each applicant to submit a brief, typed, double-spaced personal statement, typically not to exceed 500 words, as part of the application. The statement should describe any personal attributes that you consider to be an asset and which will serve to your advantage in law school. We are particularly interested in aspects of your background that may not be evident from other parts of your application, which have prepared you to succesfully undertake a rigorous program of law study. You may also provide a perspective on your career objectives and goals.

3. Two Letters of Recommendation — submitted to the LSAC Letter of Recommendation Service that serves all member schools. — This service is included in your Credential Assembly Service registration. Your letters will be copied and sent to us along with your LSAC Law School Report or as received. Therefore, we will receive any new letters for an applicant's file whenever a report update is produced. The Admissions Committee wishes to assure you that no additional weight is placed on appraisals for which the student has waived his or her right. Please note that at least one faculty appraisal is preferred for recent college graduates. Other applicants who would find it difficult to obtain faculty appraisals may request recommendations from individuals who can appraise their ability to perform in law school.

4. Official LSAC Law School Report, including transcripts of all college academic records, letters of recommendation, and a report of the candidate's score(s) on the LSAT.

5. $65.00 Application Fee — Applicants may pay the fee online through LSAC. If you require an application fee waiver, you must contact the Office of Admissions for a fee waiver form.

   Applicants will be notified of application completion and updates by e-mail only.

DIVERSITY STATEMENT (OPTIONAL)

Pace Law School is committed to diversity in legal education and to ensuring that the profession, and ultimately the judiciary, is representative of the American public. In an effort to ensure diversity, the law school offers potential students the opportunity to provide a diversity statement. This statement should demonstrate a candidate's potential to contribute meaningfully to the diversity of the Law School community and the legal profession. The committee shall take into account all factors that indicate that the candidate will contribute to diversity, including, but not limited to, a history of overcoming socioeconomic hardship; family background with little or no formal higher education; membership in a group that has historically been underrepresented in the legal community, including, but not limited to, groups based on race, nationality, ethnicity, gender, sexual orientation, religion, disability, veteran status, or age; geographic diversity; or service employment in furtherance of the goal of diversity.

ADDENDUM(S):

Applicants may wish to include an addendum explanation of any inconsistencies in their application and provide answers to questions that they think the committee might raise when reviewing their application. Examples of items that applicants might consider including are a description of work experience and extracurricular or other voluntary activities; an explanation of distinct trends or discrepancies among grades; and a description of substantial time commitments while attending school.

ENTRANCE DATES AND DEADLINES

March 1, 2012   Priority Deadline for Fall Admission
June 1, 2012   Priority Deadline for Transfer/Visiting Students

First-year full-time students may enter the Law School in the fall or spring semester. Part-time, day students may only start in the fall semester. Transfer and visiting students that have completed the first year of a law school approved by the American Bar Association or a state-approved law school may enter at the beginning of any semester after admission if all grades are available prior to the start of the semester.

Pace University School of Law
JD Application
Page 2 of 15

ROLLING ADMISSIONS

While the Law School has no formal deadline for submission of applications, no assurance of consideration can be given to applicants who present incomplete applications after the priority deadlines, since the bulk of the decisions in the entering class will be made from those applications already completed. The Admissions Committee will begin to notify applicants of decisions at the beginning of the calendar year and will continue to do so until the school year commences.

GENERAL ADMISSION INFORMATION (JD)

A person who has attained the age of 18 years and who holds a bachelor's degree is eligible for admission to the Law School as a candidate for the JD degree. Students who have earned degrees from most accredited institutions of collegiate rank automatically meet the requirements of the New York State Department of Education for consideration for admission to professional study in New York. At Pace, as at many law schools, the most important admissions criteria are the undergraduate grade point average (GPA) and the Law School Admission Test (LSAT) score. Reliance on these purely academic criteria is appropriate in making many decisions, particularly those involving candidates either clearly admissible, or clearly inadmissible. However, other factors can become important within the middle range of applications. For instance, the applicant's GPA may be interpreted by carefully evaluating his or her transcript. Judgment may be made regarding the strength of the curriculum undertaken or the quality of the institution at which undergraduate work was done. Class rank and the progression of grades may be significant. Where there has been an interval of some years between college graduation and application to law school, especially where the candidate presents a strong recent LSAT score, better law school performance may be predicted than undergraduate grades would suggest. Writing, grammar, and spelling skills are also extremely important. In addition, proven capacity for leadership, dedication to community service, excellence in a particular field, diversity, motivation, graduate study in another discipline, work experience, and extracurricular activities all receive careful consideration in appropriate cases.

Approximately 200 students enter the three-year day division program and 15 to 20 enter the part-time day division each fall. The average LSAT and GPA for the students offered admission for fall 2011 are approximately 156 and 3.40, respectively. Candidates concerned about the appropriateness of an application may call the Law School and speak with a counselor. Application to law school is not a passive process, and it requires investigation and care. Should you have any questions or require assistance, please feel free to contact us.

Pace University admits, and will continue to admit, students of any gender, disability, race, sexual orientation, color, or national and ethnic origin to all rights, privileges, programs, and activities generally accorded or made available to students at the school. It does not, and will not, discriminate on the basis of gender, age, religion, disability, race, sexual orientation, color, or national and ethnic origin in administration of its educational policies, admissions policies, scholarships and loan programs, and athletic and other school-administered programs. Inquiries regarding compliance with related federal regulations may be directed to Affirmative Action Officer, Pace University, Pace Plaza, New York, NY 10038, 212.346.1310, or to the Director of the Office of Civil Rights, Department of Health and Human Services, Washington, DC 20201, 202.619.0257.

LAW SCHOOL ADMISSION TEST AND CREDENTIAL ASSEMBLY SERVICE

Each applicant is required to take the LSAT and to register with the LSAC Credential Assembly Service. Application and registration forms for both the LSAT and Credential Assembly Service may be obtained from the Law School Admission Council, PO Box 2000, Newtown, Pennsylvania 18940-0998; (215.968.1001); or LSAC.org; and from prelaw advisors at most undergraduate schools. The LSAT is administered by the Law School Admission Council four times per year--typically in October, December, February, and June--at various test centers throughout the United States, as well as in international locations. An applicant should take the LSAT no later than the February test date to guarantee equal consideration for admission the following fall. Applicants who have taken the test more than five years before the entrance date must retake the test. Each applicant who attended college in the US or Canada must arrange to have transcripts of his or her academic record (all undergraduate and any graduate-level studies) sent directly to LSAC in Newtown. The Law School will request a summary of the applicant's academic record, copies of college transcripts, and the LSAT scores. The Credential Assembly Service code number for the Pace Law School is 2644. Students who did not attend college in the US or Canada must register for the Credential Assembly Service and register for and take the LSAT. An official LSAT report will then be sent to the Law School.

APPLICANTS WITH INTERNATIONAL CREDENTIALS AND/OR NON-IMMIGRANT VISAS MUST NOTE:

Applicants who have completed most or all of their education outside the US or Canada must submit their transcripts to the LSAC Credential Assembly Service for the evaluation of international transcripts. The one exception to this requirement is international work through a study-abroad, consortium, or exchange program sponsored by a US or Canadian institution if the work is clearly indicated as such on the home campus transcript. This service is included in the Credential Assembly Service registration fee. An International Credential Evaluation will be completed by the American Association of Collegiate Registrars and Admissions Officers (AACRAO), which will be incorporated into the LSAC Law School Report.

Questions about the Credential Assembly Service can be directed to LSAC at 215.968.1001, or LSACinfo@LSAC.org.

Aside from the US, Canada, Great Britain, and Australia, applicants educated in non-English-speaking countries must take the TOEFL (Test of English as a Foreign Language) and submit the results before their applications can be reviewed. A minimum score of 250 on the written exam or 100 on the Internet exam is required. All other applicants with nonimmigrant visas, regardless of where they were educated, should contact the admissions office to determine if they too must take the TOEFL.

APPLICANTS WHO HAVE ATTENDED OTHER LAW SCHOOLS

Regardless of whether transfer credit is sought, applicants who have previously attended another law school must provide, in addition to the application and fee, (1) a letter from the dean or registrar of the law school, which indicates whether or not the student withdrew in good academic standing and any conditions as to eligibility to return, and (2) an official transcript of the applicant's law school academic record reflecting all courses taken and grades.

TRANSFER STUDENTS WITH ADVANCED STANDING

Transfer students who have completed acceptable work at law schools approved by the American Bar Association or at state-approved law schools may be eligible for admission to the Law School with advanced standing. Transfer credit will be determined in accordance with Law School procedures. Transfer students with advanced standing must submit, in addition to the application and items (1) and (2) in the previous section, the following: a $65 application fee, a copy of your LSAC Law School Report, a personal statement that includes the reason(s) you wish to transfer, a copy of your law school catalogue or copies of the pages that list and describe all courses and course content for which the student registered, and one letter of recommendation from law faculty.

VISITING STUDENTS

A limited number of students who are matriculated at law schools approved by the American Bar Association or state-approved law schools may study at the Law School as visiting students. Such students must submit an application, fee, and personal statement that includes their reason(s) for requesting visiting student status, and a letter from the dean of the law school in which they are enrolled certifying that the student is a degree candidate in good standing, certifying that credit earned at the Law School will be counted toward the degree to be conferred upon the student, and stating any specific requirements that must be completed while attending Pace.

TWENTY-CREDIT PROGRAM

A limited number of international lawyers who wish to be certified to sit for the New York State Bar Exam may study at the Law School in the 20-credit program. Such students must submit an application; fee; personal statement; a letter from the Board of Law Examiners of the State of New York certifying that the candidate is eligible for enrollment in such a program; certified, translated copies of all academic work; two letters of recommendation; and a TOEFL score. The Law School requires a 100 minimum score on the Internet-based TOEFL exam.

Please note that the 20-credit program is a nondegree-granting program. Students interested in obtaining a degree may wish to apply for entrance to one of the graduate law programs.

REAPPLICATION PROCEDURES

If an applicant has applied within the last year, all materials previously submitted have been retained. You may use any appraisals already on file. You must file a new application, application fee, and personal statement. A new LSAC Law School Report is required. All other requirements remain the same.

DEPOSIT

In order to reserve a place in the entering class, each accepted applicant must pay the Law School a nonrefundable deposit of $300, which will be applied against tuition for the first semester. A second nonrefundable deposit of $100 to confirm enrollment is due at a later date. Students who are awarded a merit scholarship will be required to submit a deposit to confirm acceptance of the scholarship. The first deposits are required by April 1 for fall admission or two weeks after the letter of

Pace University School of Law
JD Application
Page 4 of 15

admission, whichever is later. The request for a deposit deadline extension while waiting for a financial aid award notice must be received by the specified deposit date.

DEFERRED ENTRANCE

Students who are admitted to the full- or part-time classes and wish to defer entry should contact the admissions office for further information. While all deferred requests are considered on an individual basis, deferrals will be granted only if there is no reservation that the student will meet the succeeding year's admission criteria.

FIRST-YEAR CLASS VISITS

Opportunities for individual visits and to view a law class are available throughout the academic year. Arrangements may be made by calling the admissions office at 914.422.4210.

Applicant Status

APPLICATION AS (only check one):

____ 1st Time

____ Visitor

____ Transfer

____ 20 Credit

Division (only select one):

____ Part Time Day

____ Full Time Day

Biographical

Prefix: _____

First name: _____

Middle name: _____

Last name: _____

Suffix: _____

Previous (other) name _____

Preferred first name: _____

Date of birth _____

Place of birth: City: _____

Place of birth: Country _____

Place of birth: State/Province: _____

Social security number (last 4 digits) _____

LSAC account number: _____

Demographics

1. Citizenship

Citizenship

____ empty

____ Non-Resident Alien

____ US Citizen

____ US Permanent Resident

Country of citizenship _____

Visa number _____

Permanent resident number _____

Country of citizenship _____

Permanent city _____

Permanent state/province _____

Permanent country _____

Pace University School of Law
JD Application
Page 6 of 15

Contact Information

Current Address

Country _____

Street address--line 1 _____

Street address--line 2 _____

Street address--line 3 _____

City _____

State/province _____

Zip/postal code _____

Current address good until date _____

Day phone _____

Evening phone _____

Permanent Address

Country _____

Street address--line 1 _____

Street address--line 2 _____

Street address--line 3 _____

City _____

State/province _____

Zip/postal code _____

Permanent address good until date _____

Day phone _____

Evening phone _____

Other Contact Information

Primary e-mail _____

Secondary e-mail _____

Mobile phone _____

Pace University School of Law can send text messages to my mobile phone

_____ Yes

_____ No

Pace University School of Law
JD Application
Page 7 of 15

Standardized Testing

LSAT

Test Date   Test Score

_____   _____

_____   _____

_____   _____

Character and Fitness

Note: Admission to law school does not mean you will meet the character and fitness requirements for admission to the bar of any state. If you are concerned as to whether an event in your life will affect your eligibility for a license to practice law, you should discuss the matter with the Board of Bar Examiners in the state(s) where you plan to practice.

Have you ever been placed on probation or dismissed from any college, university, graduate, or professional educational institution for academic reasons or otherwise?

_____ Yes

_____ No

Have you ever been placed on academic and/or disciplinary probation for actions arising from allegations of academic dishonesty, plagiarism, or cheating during your college, university, graduate, or professional coursework?

_____ Yes

_____ No

Are there any disciplinary charges pending against you?

_____ Yes

_____ No

Have you ever been convicted of a crime other than a minor traffic violation? If so, describe the nature of the charge and sentence/punishment on a supplemental sheet or electronic attachment.

_____ Yes

_____ No

Are there any criminal charges pending against you?

_____ Yes

_____ No

Have you ever been disciplined, reprimanded, suspended, or discharged from any job for conduct involving dishonesty, fraud, misrepresentation, deceit, or any violation of Federal or State laws or regulations?

_____ Yes

_____ No

Pace University School of Law
JD Application
Page 8 of 15

Character and Fitness continued

Have you ever resigned or quit a job when you were under investigation or inquiry for conduct that could have been considered as involving dishonesty, fraud, misrepresentation, deceit, or violation of Federal or State laws or regulations, or after receiving notice or being advised of possible investigation, inquiry, or disciplinary action for such conduct?

_____ Yes
_____ No

Education

List ALL educational institutions attended.

Institution name _____

Major _____   Country _____

Start date _____   State/Province _____

End date _____   City _____

Degree _____   GPA _____

Date degree granted _____   Rank _____

Institution name _____

Major _____   Country _____

Start date _____   State/Province _____

End date _____   City _____

Degree _____   GPA _____

Date degree granted _____   Rank _____

Institution name _____

Major _____   Country _____

Start date _____   State/Province _____

End date _____   City _____

Degree _____   GPA _____

Date degree granted _____   Rank _____

Education continued

Institution name _____

Major _____   Country _____

Start date _____   State/Province _____

End date _____   City _____

Degree _____   GPA _____

Date degree granted _____   Rank _____

Have you ever attended any law school?
_____ Yes
_____ No

Did you leave the law school in good standing?
_____ Yes
_____ No

Has your education in college, university, or professional school been interrupted for one term or more for any reason?
_____ Yes
_____ No

List the academic honors, awards, or other recognitions you have received and explain the reason(s) upon which awards were made.

_____

_____

_____

_____

Application Information

Please complete. Information regarding the status of my application may be released to the following individual. If this section is left blank, information will not be released to anyone except the applicant. Final decisions are not released over the telephone to anyone.

Name:

_____

Relationship:

_____

Pace University School of Law
JD Application
Page 10 of 15

Areas of Interest

If you are interested in information concerning a specific area of law, indicate below the area of interest:

____ Corporate and Securities Law

____ Criminal Law

____ Environmental Law

____ Women's Justice

____ International Law

____ Public Interest Law

____ Real Estate/Land Use Planning

____ Intellectual Property Law

Military

Have you served or are you now serving on full-time, active US military duty?

____ Yes

____ No

Date of entrance (month/year) _____

Date of discharge (month/year) _____

Rank _____

Expected military reserve or National Guard status during law school

_____

Branch _____

Discharge type _____

Have you ever been separated from any branch of the US armed forces under less than honorable conditions?

____ Yes

____ No

If you have been separated from any branch of the US armed forces under less than honorable conditions, explain the circumstances.

_____

_____

_____

_____

Pace University School of Law
JD Application
Page 11 of 15

Law School Interest

What prompted you to apply to this law school?

Internet

____ Law school

____ LSAC

____ ABA

____ Other

Faculty/Alumni/Professional

____ Faculty/acquaintance

____ Law school faculty member

____ Admissions recruiter

____ University/college faculty member

____ Legal professional

____ Prelaw advisor

Publications

____ US News & World Report

____ Law school publication

____ ABA-LSAC Official Guide

____ Princeton Review

____ Other advertisement

Recruiting Events

____ LSAC Forum

____ Law school fair

____ International forum

____ Campus event

____ Law school direct mail/e-mail

____ Current student

If you attended any events mentioned in the Recruiting Events section, please list them below:

_____

_____

_____

_____

If you applied previously, what year was the application for?   _____

Where you offered admission?

____ Yes

____ No

Are you applying, or have you applied, to other law schools? If so, please list them.

_____

_____

_____

_____

Pace University School of Law
JD Application
Page 12 of 15

Family

1. Next of Kin/Emergency Contact

First (given) name _____

Middle name/initial _____

Last (family) name _____

Telephone (include area code) _____

Country _____

Street address--line 1 _____

Street address--line 2 _____

Street address--line 3 _____

City _____

State/province _____

Zip/postal code _____

2. If you have any close relatives who have been students at this university, please provide the following information.

Relative 1

First (given) name _____

Middle name/initial _____

Last (family) name _____

Relationship to applicant _____

School attended _____

Start date (month/year) _____

End date (month/year) _____

Degree awarded _____

Relative 2

First (given) name _____

Middle name/initial _____

Last (family) name _____

Relationship to applicant _____

School attended _____

Start date (month/year) _____

End date (month/year) _____

Degree awarded _____

3. Parent/Guardian - 1

_____ Deceased

First (given) name _____

Middle name/initial _____

Last (family) name _____

Occupation _____

Highest level of education _____

Country _____

Street address--line 1 _____

Street address--line 2 _____

Street address--line 3 _____

City _____

State/province _____

Zip/postal code _____

Family continued

4. Parent/Guardian - 2

____ Deceased

First (given) name _____

Middle name/initial _____

Last (family) name _____

Occupation _____

Highest level of education _____

Country _____

Street address--line 1 _____

Street address--line 2 _____

Street address--line 3 _____

City _____

State/province _____

Zip/postal code _____

Employment

List all employment including internships..

Employer _____

Position _____

Hours per week _____

Start date _____

End date _____

Country _____

State/Province _____

City _____

Employment type (ex. Full time) _____

Reason for leaving _____

Employer _____

Position _____

Hours per week _____

Start date _____

End date _____

Country _____

State/Province _____

City _____

Employment type (ex. Full time) _____

Reason for leaving _____

Pace University School of Law
JD Application
Page 14 of 15

Employment continued

Employer _____

Position _____ Country _____

Hours per week _____ State/Province _____

Start date _____ City _____

End date _____ Employment type (ex. Full time) _____

Reason for leaving _____

Employer _____

Position _____ Country _____

Hours per week _____ State/Province _____

Start date _____ City _____

End date _____ Employment type (ex. Full time) _____

Reason for leaving _____

Total number of months full time work experience.

_____

List your extracurricular, community, or other activities in the order of their importance to you. Give a brief description of your involvement, including any special responsibilities or leadership positions held.

_____
_____
_____
_____
_____

Ethnic Status

Ethnic Status (Optional):

____ American Indian/Alaskan Native

____ Other

____ Asian/Pacific Islander-Chinese

____ Asian/Pacific Islander-Indian

____ Asian/Pacific Islander-Japanese

____ Asian/Pacific Islander-Korean

____ Asian/Pacific Islander-Other

____ Black - Caribbean/West Indian

____ Black/African American

____ Caucasian/White

____ Chicano/Mexican American

____ Hispanic/Latino

____ Hispanic/Latino - Central/South American

____ Hispanic/Latino - Cuban

____ Hispanic/Latino-Mexican

____ Hispanic/Latino-Puerto Rican

____ Multi-racial

____ Asian/Pacific Islander

Certification Statement

Please be sure that all of the Instructions to Applicants have been followed. An application will be considered only after it has been completed in full and the Office of Admissions has received all required documents. By submitting this application electronically, I understand that if I am admitted to the Law School and register as a student, the School will retain this application and all supporting materials and may make them available to state bar character committees, and I consent to such disclosure. I certify that the information provided by me in this application is true and complete. From time of application through enrollment, I shall promptly advise the Law School Office of Admissions in writing of any change in any of the facts indicated in this application. I understand that matriculation and attendance at any other law school (from time of application through enrollment) would render any offer of admission from Pace Law School void. I understand that falsification of this application and supporting materials will be grounds for its denial, or if I am accepted, for dismissal from the Law School. I further agree and authorize Pace Law School to publish, for public relations purposes, any photographs in which I appear. I understand that my admission to Pace Law School is a privilege and not a right and I agree that my admission, if granted, my registration and continuance on the rolls and graduation are subject to all policies, rules, regulations, and procedures set forth in the current bulletins, catalogs, online, and other publications and notices of Pace University and as they may be amended and further subject to the right of the authorities of Pace Law School to require my withdrawal for scholastic, disciplinary or other reasons, under circumstances deemed sufficient by them. Signature of Applicant:

_____

Date:

_____

Most law schools utilize LSAC to handle letters of recommendation. You simply have to arrange for your letters to be submitted through the Credential Assembly Service (CAS) that serves all member schools. The service is included in your LSDAS registration subscription. Your letters will be copied and sent to law schools along with your LSDAS report, or as received. To use this service, follow the directions for submitting letters outlined in the LSAT/CAS Registration and Information Book. Be sure to fill out and give each letter writer a letter of recommendation form from the LSAT/CAS Registration and Information Book.

Although the convenience of LSAC for disseminating letters of recommendation is attractive, and most students use this service, many times a personalized letter is better than a generic one. You may have a contact who has special ties to a law school where you are applying, either to the school generally, or to the dean or a faculty member. If this is the case, a personalized letter on your behalf discussing your interest in this particular school may be worth the extra effort. You may direct personal letters sent on your behalf to the CAS.

Occasionally, a student will get the idea that if one letter is good, then one hundred letters must be one hundred times better. Nothing could be further from the truth. A file containing a large number of letters of recommendation is likely to trigger the MEGO (My Eyes Glaze Over) phenomenon among admissions committee members and staff. It is much better to have a small number of really glowing personal recommendations than a sheaf of letters that bury the good recommendations in a sea of verbiage. Make sure that you know what your recommendations will say. An otherwise good application could easily be destroyed by an offhand negative comment. This seems to be so fundamental that it does not bear repeating, but anyone who has served on a law school Admissions Committee can recount applicants whose letters of reference did nothing to help their applications.

DEADLINES, DEADLINES, DEADLINES

All law schools specify deadlines for submission of the application materials to their institution. However, you should begin to explore your options in your junior year of college. This allows you enough time to narrow your choices, gather the appropriate information, and be prepared to submit timely applications in the fall of your senior year. Even if you later decide to work for a period of time after graduation, you keep your choices open by starting early.

First, determine when you are going to take the LSAT. (See the schedule of LSAT offerings for 2012–13; the dates for 2013–14 will be similar but not identical.) Registration materials are available through Law Services online, and at most law school admissions offices. Almost all ABA-approved law schools require the use of the Credential Assembly Service (CAS), and, therefore, upon registration for the exam, you should register simultaneously for the service. This service analyzes your transcript (you must have one sent to Law Services from each undergraduate institution you have attended) and submits a report of your undergraduate record along with your LSAT score and an unofficial copy of your transcript to the law schools you have indicated. You can add schools to this list later if you choose. Complete your CAS reports as early as possible. Most law schools will not treat your application as complete and act upon it unless all the required elements have been submitted. You can call law schools where you have applied to determine whether your application is complete, but do not reduce your chances of admission by ignoring something that can be easily fixed.

Send the transcript to LSAC once all your junior year courses have been completed. Typically, upward grade trends occur after the first year of college. Some law schools may even require fall grades in your senior year if a significant trend is noted.

The registration date for the LSAT should be made individually by each applicant. Since test preparation is essential, you should allow adequate time to properly prepare for the test. There are many commercial preparation courses, various books such as Barron's *LSAT,* as well as preparation materials through Law Services. (See also Chapters 12 and 13 of this Guide.)

You should be prepared the first time you sit for the exam; never enter the exam with the thought of it being a dry run. If you want to practice under exam conditions, you can take the GRE, MCAT, or other professional school exam, or purchase old tests from LSAC. You must understand that the content of these exams differs from discipline to discipline, and that none will replicate the LSAT; however, the format of the tests is often very similar. If you want to "practice" a real test, take the GRE or other professional school admission test, remember that you may be able to help your test-taking skills generally, but that each test measures different ability and knowledge.

LATE APPLICATIONS

When it comes to law school applications, time is of the essence. Not only should you know the application deadlines for all schools to which you apply (they are not all the same), but you should also understand that the earlier your application is completed the sooner it can be acted upon by admissions committees. Some schools send out all their acceptance letters at the same time, so as long as you meet the school's deadline, your application will be considered. Many, if not most, schools operate a rolling admissions process. This means that when an application is complete, it will be reviewed by the admissions director, admissions committee, or both. Typically, applications are placed into three groups: "admit," "hold," and "deny." The "admit" and "deny" candidates are notified right away, while the "hold" candidates are put in a ranked queue from which candidates are selected as seats become available. This queue will become the wait list from which applicants are taken when accepted students withdraw; but earlier in the year, it will provide the names of the students selected for admission. If your application is not complete, it will not be considered, and you will not be considered for open seats in the law school's entering class. Even if your application is not complete, you should submit as much information as you can as soon as you can.

THE WAITING PERIOD

When all the appropriate materials are filed with the admissions office, you begin a waiting period. The decision-making process takes time.

Once an application is received, the office of admissions opens a file on you, requests the CAS report, and, when all materials are received, reviews your application. The process may be held up if, for example, you have left blank questions on the application that were not marked "optional," or do not file a fee with the application, or do not sign the application form.

When you are notified that the file is complete and ready for review by the admissions committee, the process may take anywhere from two weeks to two months. Patience is essential; however, if you have not heard anything from a law school, do not hesitate to contact that school. You may be missing vital information, or your correspondence may have been delayed by the mail.

Every school employs a slightly different approach to making admissions decisions and notifying applicants of their acceptance. Many schools employ automatic acceptance and rejection categories for very high or low LSAT scores and GPAs. Most applicants fall somewhere in the middle, and their applications are reviewed more carefully by the admissions committee. Some schools may send out all acceptance letters at one time ("batch" admissions), while others notify applicants as decisions are made ("rolling" admissions). Although the notification process may begin prior to January 1 of the academic year preceding admission, most applicants will hear from law schools between February and April. Later decisions may occur for students who are included on a waiting list, from which they are drawn if other accepted students decide not to matriculate at the school. Waiting list decisions may be made as late as August.

A few schools offer conditional summer programs for students with marginal credentials. Typically, the final decision for these applicants is made on the basis of their performance in the summer courses. Although the experience of attending such programs is good preparation for law school itself, ABA standards do not permit schools to give law school credit for preadmission work.

The admissions office at the schools to which you apply will be able to explain the idiosyncrasies of their procedures, and keep you advised on the progress of your application. Don't call them every day, however, because excessive phone calls actually slow down the admissions process. Use common sense in deciding whether to call for assistance and information.

HELICOPTER PARENTS

In the era of helicopter parents, where well-meaning but sometimes misguided parents try to do everything they can to help their offspring achieve success, parental involvement in the law school admission process can become a problem. As an applicant for a graduate-level educational program, it is critical that you exercise a degree of independence, starting with the admissions process. You will be on you own once you start law school, so getting into law school should be your own effort as well. If your parents have been too involved in your educational and life decisions in the past, now is a good time to break from the past and establish your own professional identity. The Educational Rights and Privacy Act provides that educational information such as your application, academic records, and student files are under the control of adult children (and almost all law school applicants are over twenty-one), and may not be released to parents without the student's consent. Yet, law school admissions officers report that they are contacted frequently by parents of applicants, either seeking to obtain information or to complete some or all of their children's applications.

THE FINAL DECISION

Once the admissions committee reaches a final decision, you must begin your decision-making process. There are basically four scenarios you might find yourself facing: (1) you have multiple offers of admission; (2) you have one offer; (3) you are on one or more waiting lists; or (4) you have no offers. The second scenario is simple, and the fourth represents a challenge in terms of deciding what to do next. The first and third situations raise the specter of having to make choices from competing offers. The first scenario, albeit the most enviable one, of having to choose among more than one offer, can be maddening. The third scenario

can be frustrating when you are wait-listed for the school you really want to attend, but you have offers from one or more schools that are not your first choice. When faced with such a dilemma, you will simply have to make the best choice you can within the time frame involved. Most schools will require a deposit no earlier than April but as early as two weeks after your offer of admission is made.

Cost is always an issue, and you should recognize the need to submit the required financial aid forms in a timely manner. The submission of financial aid forms (Free Application for Federal Student Aid) does not have an impact on the admission decision. The filing of the appropriate forms should be completed at the time of application to the individual schools. If all the appropriate financial aid materials have been submitted, a law school should be able to provide you with a financial aid package at the time of acceptance, allowing you to make an educated decision. (See Chapter 8 of this Guide for more information on financial aid.)

by Gary A. Munneke, Professor of Law (see page 4), Angela D'Agostino, Assistant Dean for Students, and Cathy Alexander, former Director of Admissions, Pace University School of Law, White Plains, NY.

2012–2013 LSAT Dates and Registration Deadlines

Published Test Centers
(United States, Canada, and the Caribbean)

National Test Dates

National Test Dates	Regular Registration Online, by Mail, by Telephone (receipt deadline)	Late Registration by Mail (receipt deadline)	Late Registration Online, by Telephone (receipt deadline)
Monday, June 11, 2012	May 8, 2012	May 15, 2012	May 18, 2012
Saturday, October 6, 2012 / Wednesday, October 10, 2012[1]	September 4, 2012	September 13, 2012	September 14, 2012
Saturday, December 1, 2012 / Monday, December 3, 2012[1]	October 24, 2012	November 5, 2012	November 9, 2012
Saturday, February 9, 2013 / Monday, February 11, 2013[1]	January 8, 2013	January 15, 2013	January 18, 2013

Other LSAT Options

National Test Dates

National Test Dates	Test Center Change by Mail, Phone, Fax, Online (receipt deadline)	Nonpublished Test Centers—United States, Canada, and the Caribbean (receipt deadline)	LSAT Registration Refunds partial only (receipt deadline)
Monday, June 11, 2012	May 18, 2012 (mail, phone, fax) / May 20, 2012 (online)	May 4, 2012	May 18, 2012
Saturday, October 6, 2012 / Wednesday, October 10, 2012[1]	September 14, 2012 (mail, phone, fax) / September 16, 2012 (online)	August 31, 2012	September 14, 2012
Saturday, December 1, 2012 / Monday, December 3, 2012[1]	November 9, 2012 (mail, phone, fax) / November 11, 2012 (online)	October 26, 2012	November 9, 2012
Saturday, February 9, 2013 / Monday, February 11, 2013[1]	January 18, 2013 (mail, phone, fax) / January 20, 2013 (online)	January 4, 2013	January 18, 2013

LSAT Score Release Dates

National Test Dates

National Test Dates	Score by E-mail (For online account holders only. No additional charge.)	Score Report Mailed (Additional charges may apply.)
Monday, June 11, 2012	July 6, 2012	July 14, 2012
Saturday, October 6, 2012 / Wednesday, October 10, 2012[1]	October 31, 2012	November 8, 2012
Saturday, December 1, 2012 / Monday, December 3, 2012[1]	January 4, 2013	January 12, 2013
Saturday, February 9, 2013 / Monday, February 11, 2013[1]	March 6, 2013	March 10, 2013

(All score release dates are approximate.)

- **For Telephone Services: 215.968.1001** (for hours)
- **For Online Services: www.LSAC.org**
  Registration closes midnight ET on deadline date.

1 This test is for Saturday Sabbath observers only. For details, please see Saturday Sabbath Observers. This test is nondisclosed.

Test dates and times vary for some centers. Check your LSAT Admission Ticket to confirm the correct test date and time.

Scores by e-mail will take several hours from the beginning time to reach all test takers.

Please allow 5–7 days from this date for receipt of your score report.

Note *Walk-in registration on the day of the test is not permitted at any test center for any test administration.*

Registrants whose test registrations are received by mail during the late registration period and that are not accompanied by the late registration fee will be billed the fee, and a hold will be placed on their accounts.

Not every LSAT is *disclosed*. For a complete schedule of disclosed and nondisclosed LSAT administrations, please see Your Score Report and Test Disclosure. For all other info, including dates and info for test centers outside the United States, Canada, and the Carribean, contact *www.lsac.org*.

CHAPTER 6

What Are Your Chances of Law School Admission?

A PROFILE OF RECENT FIRST-YEAR LAW STUDENTS

The table in this section provides basic admissions statistics for the law schools that have been approved by the American Bar Association. All these schools offer the J.D. degree. The information has been compiled from the most recent available information received from schools. If you compare your own GPA and your LSAT score and percentile with those of students recently admitted, and if you note the number of students who applied and the number who were accepted, you will be able to get an idea of your chances of admission to any given law school.

Remember that your credentials may place you at the top of the applicant pool at one school, and at the bottom of the pool at another. Finding schools that will at least consider you is essential. If both your LSAT and GPA fall below the median for a school, your chances of being admitted are typically slim. Often applicants with lower LSATs have higher GPAs to offset their test scores, and vice versa. A school may be able to tell you whether there are realistic limits below which you will not be admitted. For example, a school may say that for the previous year it offered admission only to applicants who scored above 155 on the LSAT. If you have a 153, the likelihood of your being admitted to such a school would be nil. Conversely, if your scores are on the high side of a school's applicant pool, you are likely to be a strong candidate for that school (see the discussion on pages 19–21 for more information on this question). In any event, it is important for you to do your homework to get a sense of where you stand.

A blank cell on the chart means that information was not available.

The point has been made previously that timing is important. The earlier you take the LSAT, submit transcripts and other information to the LSDAS, and complete individual law school applications, the better your chances in the process. Since law schools make their decisions only on completed applications, if you are not in the pool, you are not in the game. Since many schools use a rolling admissions process—accepting candidates as soon as they decide to admit them, rather than sending out all offers of admission in a batch—the sooner you are in front of the admissions committee, the better. Even a negative decision can be helpful because a denial at one school might trigger your application at another.

LAW SCHOOL	ACADEMIC STATISTICS				ADMISSION STATISTICS		
	Median LSAT Percentile of Enrolled	Median LSAT Score of Enrolled	Lowest LSAT Percentile of Accepted	Median GPA (4.0 scale) of Enrolled	Total Applicants	Applicants Accepted	Applicants Enrolled
Albany Law School 80 New Scotland Avenue Albany, NY 12208 518-445-2326 Fax: 518-445-2369 *admissions@albanylaw.edu*	63	153		3.31	2153	1113	235
American University (Washington College of Law) 4801 Massachusetts Avenue, N.W. Washington, DC 20016-8186 202-274-4101 Fax: 202-274-4107 *wcladmit@wcl.american.edu*	85	162	47	3.44	7521	2075	475
Appalachian School of Law P.O. Box 2825 Grundy, VA 24614 276-935-4349 Fax: 276-935-8496 *npruitt@asl.edu*	40	149	32	3.08	1630	630	
Arizona State University (Sandra Day O'Connor College of Law) 1100 South McAllister Avenue, Box 877906 Tempe, AZ 85287-7906 480-965-1474 Fax: 480-727-7930 *chitra.damania@asu.edu*	85	162	27	3.62	2334	664	168
Atlanta's John Marshall Law School 1422 W. Peachtree St., NW Atlanta, GA 30309 404-872-3593 Fax: 404-873-3802 *admissions@johnmarshall.edu*		151	25	2.97	1789	712	211
Ave Maria School of Law 1025 Commons Circle Naples, Fl 34119 734-827-8063 Fax: 734-622-0123 *info@avemarialaw.edu*	46	151	16	3.15	1543	786	127
Barry University (School of Law) 6441 East Colonial Drive Orlando, FL 32807 321-206-5600 Fax: 321-206-5662 *acruz@mail.barry.edu*		149		2.95	2324	1347	273
Baylor University (School of Law) One Bear Place, #97288 Waco, TX 76798-7288 254-710-1911 Fax: 254-710-2316 *becky_beck@baylor.edu*	81	160	71	3.62	3436	1146	186
Boston College (Law School) 885 Centre Street Newton, MA 02459 617-552-4351 Fax: 617-552-2917 *bclawadm@bc.edu*	92	165		3.66	5685	1366	268
Boston University (School of Law) 765 Commonwealth Avenue Boston, MA 02215 617-353-3100 Fax: 617-353-0578 *bulawadm@bu.edu*	94	167	60	3.72	7073	1396	242

LAW SCHOOL	ACADEMIC STATISTICS				ADMISSION STATISTICS		
	Median LSAT Percentile of Enrolled	Median LSAT Score of Enrolled	Lowest LSAT Percentile of Accepted	Median GPA (4.0 scale) of Enrolled	Total Applicants	Applicants Accepted	Applicants Enrolled
Brigham Young University (J. Reuben Clark Law School) 342 JRCB Brigham Young University Provo, UT 84602 801-422-4277 Fax: 801-422-0389 kucharg@law.byu.edu	88	163	26	3.74	755	207	145
Brooklyn Law School 250 Joralemon Street Brooklyn, NY 11201 718-780-7906 Fax: 718-780-0395 admitq@brooklaw.edu	88	163		3.38	6017	1734	390
California Western School of Law 225 Cedar Street San Diego, CA 92101-3046 619-525-1401 Fax: 619-615-1401 admissions@cwsl.edu	50	153	25	3.28	2922	1348	340
Campbell University (Norman Adrian Wiggins School of Law) 225 Hillsborough Street, Suite 401 Releigh, NC 24603 919-865-5988 Fax: 919-865-5886	71	156		3.37	1525	460	161
Capital University (Law School) 303 East Broad Street Columbus, OH 43215-3200 614-236-6500 Fax: 614-236-6972 admissions@law.capital.edu	45	151	15	3.2	1055	682	211
Case Western Reserve University (School of Law) 11075 East Boulevard Cleveland, OH 44106 216-368-3600 Fax: 216-368-1042 lawadmissions@case.edu		158		3.48	1651	768	192
Catholic University of America (Columbus School of Law) Cardinal Station Washington, DC 20064 202-319-5151 Fax: 202-319-6285 admissions@law.edu		158		3.33	3299	1078	268
Chapman University (School of Law) One University Drive Orange, CA 92866 714-628-2500 Fax: 714-628-2501 metten@chapman.edu	74	158	26	3.55	2822	970	160
Charleston School of Law P.O. Box 535 Charleston, SC 29402 843-377-2143 Fax: 843-329-0491 jbenfield@charlestonlaw.org	52	152	13	3.13	2054	1018	224
Charlotte School of Law 2145 Suttle Avenue Charlotte, NC 28208 704-971-8542 Fax: 704-971-8599 admissions@charlottelaw.edu	50	151	140	3.11	2120	1163	249

LAW SCHOOL	ACADEMIC STATISTICS				ADMISSION STATISTICS		
	Median LSAT Percentile of Enrolled	Median LSAT Score of Enrolled	Lowest LSAT Percentile of Accepted	Median GPA (4.0 scale) of Enrolled	Total Applicants	Applicants Accepted	Applicants Enrolled
City University of New York (CUNY School of Law) 65-21 Main Street Flushing, NY 11367-1300 718-340-4210 Fax: 718-340-4435 mail.law.cuny.edu	64	155	44	3.29	1883	563	171
Cleveland State University (Cleveland-Marshall College of Law) 2121 Euclid Avenue LB138 Cleveland, OH 44115-2214 216-687-2304 Fax: 216-687-6881 christophe.lcak@law.csuohio.edu	60	154	13	3.28	1609	615	169
College of William & Mary (William & Mary Law School) P.O. Box 8795 Williamsburg, VA 23187-8795 757-221-3785 Fax: 757-221-3261 lawadm@wm.edu	92	165	33	3.73	5939	1306	217
Columbia University (School of Law) 435 West 116th Street New York, NY 10027 212-854-2670 Fax: 212-854-1109 admissions@law.columbia.edu	99	171	50	3.67	8020	1143	378
Cornell University (Law School) Myron Taylor Hall Ithaca, NY 14853-4901 607-255-5141 Fax: 607-255-7193 lawadmit@postoffice.law.cornell.edu	96	168		3.66	5556		204
Creighton University (School of Law) 2500 California Plaza Omaha, NE 68178 402-280-2586 Fax: 402-280-3161 lawadmit@creighton.edu	52	152	23	3.19	1232	705	135
De Paul University (College of Law) 25 East Jackson Boulevard Chicago, IL 60604 312-362-6831 Fax: 312-362-5280 lawinfo@depaul.edu	75	158		3.42	4817	2000	298
Drake University (Law School) 2507 University Avenue Des Moines, IA 50311 515-271-2782 Fax: 515-271-1990 lawadmit@drake.edu		156		3.4	1000	555	142
Drexel University (Earle Mack School of Law) 3320 Market Street Philadelphia, PA 15282 215-895 1LAW Fax: 215-571-4769 ypayton770@aol.com		159	25	3.42	2908	1038	149

LAW SCHOOL	ACADEMIC STATISTICS				ADMISSION STATISTICS		
	Median LSAT Percentile of Enrolled	Median LSAT Score of Enrolled	Lowest LSAT Percentile of Accepted	Median GPA (4.0 scale) of Enrolled	Total Applicants	Applicants Accepted	Applicants Enrolled
Duke University **(School of Law)** Science Drive and Towerview Road, Box 90362 Durham, NC 27708-0362 919-613-7020 Fax: 919-613-7257 *nash@law.duke.edu*		170		3.72	6102		211
Duquesne University **(School of Law)** 900 Locust Street, Hanley Hall Pittsburgh, PA 15282 412-396-6296 Fax: 412-396-1073 *campion@duq.edu*	55	153		3.35			192
Elon University **(School of Law)** 201 North Greene Street Greensboro, NC 27401 336-279-9200 Fax: 336-279-8199 *law@elon.edu*		153		3.2	854	400	130
Emory University **(School of Law)** Gambrell Hall, 1301 Clifton Road, N.E. Atlanta, GA 30322 404-727-6801 Fax: 404-727-2477 *erosenz@law.emory.edu*		166		3.57	4588	1149	248
Faulkner University **(Thomas Goode Jones School of Law)** 5345 Atlanta Highway Montgomery, AL 36109 334-386-7210 Fax: 334-386-7223 *law@faulkner.edu*	40	149		3.08	747	405	150
Florida Agricultural and Mechanical University **(Florida A & M University College of Law)** 201 Beggs Avenue Orlando, FL 32801 407-254-3268 *famulaw.admissions@famu.edu*		148		3.1	1891	715	281
Florida Coastal **(School of Law)** 8787 Baypine Rd. Jacksonville, FL 32256 904-680-7710 Fax: 904-680-7776 *admissions@fcsl.edu*	50	151	25	3.17	4663	1725	566
Florida International University **(College of Law)** FIU College of Law, RDB 1055 Miami, FL 33199 (305) 348-8006 Fax: (305) 348-2965 *miroa@fiu.edu*		154		3.4	2443	632	250
Florida State University **(College of Law)** 425 West Jefferson Street Tallahassee, FL 32306-1601 850-644-3787 Fax: 850-644-7284 *admissions@law.fsu.edu*	81	160		3.47	2650		200

LAW SCHOOL	ACADEMIC STATISTICS				ADMISSION STATISTICS		
	Median LSAT Percentile of Enrolled	Median LSAT Score of Enrolled	Lowest LSAT Percentile of Accepted	Median GPA (4.0 scale) of Enrolled	Total Applicants	Applicants Accepted	Applicants Enrolled
Fordham University (School of Law) 140 West 62nd Street New York, NY 10023 212-636-6810 Fax: 212-636-7984 *lawadmissions@law.fordham.edu*	92	165	62	3.53	7551	1999	479
George Mason University (School of Law) 3301 Fairfax Drive Arlington, VA 22201 703-993-8010 Fax: 703-993-8088 *aprice1@gmu.edu*	90	164	41	3.72	5354	1071	186
George Washington University (Law School) 2000 H Street, N.W. Washington, DC 20052 202-994-7230 Fax: 202-994-3597 *jd@law.gwu.edu*		167		3.82	8652	2355	474
Georgetown University (Law Center) 600 New Jersey Avenue, N.W. Washington, DC 20001 202-662-9010 Fax: 202-662-9439 *admis@law.georgetown.edu*	97	170	56	3.71	10062	2681	579
Georgia State University (College of Law) P.O. Box 4037 Atlanta, GA 30302-4037 404-413-9200 Fax: 404-413-9203 *cjgeorge@gsu.edu*	80	160	43	3.48	2731	433	223
Golden Gate University (School of Law) 536 Mission Street San Francisco, CA 94105-2968 415-442-6630 *lawadmit@ggu.edu*	52	152	12	3.05	2269	1357	229
Gonzaga University (School of Law) Box 3528 Spokane, WA 99220-3528 509-313-5532 Fax: 509-313-3697 *admissions@lawschool.gonzaga.edu*		155		3.33	1389	739	176
Hamline University (School of Law) 1536 Hewitt Avenue St. Paul, MN 55104-1284 651-523-2461 Fax: 651-523-3064 *lawadm@gw.hamline.edu*	56	153	18	3.36	1286	745	205
Harvard University (Harvard Law School) Cambridge, MA 02138 617-495-3179 *jdadmiss@law.harvard.edu*	75	176	25		6364	842	559
Hofstra University (Maurice A. Deane School of Law) 121 Hofstra University Hempstead, NY 11549 516-463-5916 Fax: 516-463-6264 *lawadmissions@hofstra.edu*	77	159	8	3.32	4566	1956	370

LAW SCHOOL	ACADEMIC STATISTICS				ADMISSION STATISTICS		
	Median LSAT Percentile of Enrolled	Median LSAT Score of Enrolled	Lowest LSAT Percentile of Accepted	Median GPA (4.0 scale) of Enrolled	Total Applicants	Applicants Accepted	Applicants Enrolled
Howard University 2900 Van Ness Street, N.W. Washington, DC 20008 202-806-8008 Fax: 202-806-8162 admissions@law.howard.edu	50	152		3.2	1225	372	140
Illinois Institute of Technology (Chicago-Kent College of Law) 565 West Adams Street Chicago, IL 60661 312-906-5020 Fax: 312-906-5274 admit@kentlaw.edu	80	160		3.52	3719	1441	308
Indiana University (Maurer School of Law) 211 South Indiana Avenue Bloomington, IN 47405-7001 812-855-4765 Fax: 812-855-0555 Lawadmis@indiana.edu	93	166	11	3.75	2751	925	242
Indiana University-Purdue University at Indianapolis (Robert H. McKinney School of Law) 530 West New York Street Indianapolis, IN 46202-3225 317-274-2459 Fax: 317-278-4780 khmiller@iupui.edu	67	156	14	3.44	1640	805	314
Inter American University of Puerto Rico (School of Law) P.O. Box 70351 San Juan, PR 00936-8351 787-751-1912, ext. 2013, 2526	64	139		3.28	945	393	246
John Marshall Law School 315 South Plymouth Court Chicago, IL 60604 312-987-1406 Fax: 312-427-5136 admission@jmls.edu		153		3.32	3513	1731	373
Lewis and Clark College (Lewis and Clark Law School) 10015 Southwest Terwilliger Boulevard Portland, OR 97219 503-768-6613 Fax: 503-768-6793 lawadmss@lclark.edu	83	161	30	3.49	2907	1143	226
Liberty University (School of Law) 1971 University Blvd. Lynchburg, VA 24502 434-592-5300 Fax: 434-592-0202 law@liberty.edu		150		3.27	414	200	99
Louisiana State University (Paul M. Hebert Law Center) 202 Law Center, 1 East Campus Drive Baton Rouge, LA 70803 225-578-8646 Fax: 225-578-8647 lynell.cadray@law.lsu.edu	72	157	25	3.44	1407	422	235
Loyola Marymount University (Loyola Law School Los Angeles) 919 Albany Street Los Angeles, CA 90015 213-736-1074 Fax: 213-736-6523 admissions@lls.edu		161		3.55	6781	1611	391

LAW SCHOOL	ACADEMIC STATISTICS				ADMISSION STATISTICS		
	Median LSAT Percentile of Enrolled	Median LSAT Score of Enrolled	Lowest LSAT Percentile of Accepted	Median GPA (4.0 scale) of Enrolled	Total Applicants	Applicants Accepted	Applicants Enrolled
Loyola University Chicago (School of Law) 25 East Pearson Street Chicago, IL 60611 312-915-7170 Fax: 312-915-7906 law-admissions@luc.edu	80	160		3.37	5040	1696	274
Loyola University of New Orleans (College of Law) 7214 St. Charles Avenue, P.O. Box 901 New Orleans, LA 70118 504-861-5575 Fax: 504-861-5772 ladmit@loyno.edu	56	153	15	3.22	1794	1071	242
Marquette University (Law School) Office of Admissions, P.O. Box 1881 Milwaukee, WI 53201-1881 414-288-6767 Fax: 414-288-0676 law.admission@marquette.edu	70	157	30	3.35	2029	924	213
Massachusetts School of Law 500 Federal Street Andover, MA 01810 978-681-0800 Fax: 978-681-6330 pcolby@mslaw.edu			3.25	400		294	248
Mercer University (Walter F. George School of Law) 1021 Georgia Avenue Macon, GA 31207 478-301-2605 Fax: 478-301-2989 Sutton_me@law.mercer.edu		155		3.4	1459	634	149
Michigan State University (College of Law) 368 Law College Bldg. East Lansing, MI 48824-1300 517-432-0222 Fax: 517-432-0098	50	157	15	3.54	3732	1185	393
Mississippi College (School of Law) 151 East Griffith Street Jackson, MS 39201 601-925-7152 pevans@mc.edu	40	149		3.19	1717	990	214
New England Law / Boston 154 Stuart Street Boston, MA 02116 617-422-7210 Fax: 617-422-7201 admit@admin.nesl.edu	48	151	30	3.15	2934	2105	385
New York Law School 185 West Broadway New York, NY 10013-2960 212-431-2888 Fax: 212-966-1522 admissions@nyls.edu	60	154		3.22	5997	2604	488
New York University (School of Law) 161 Avenue of the Americas, 5th Floor New York, NY 10013 212-998-6060 Fax: 212-995-4527 law.moreinfo@nyu.edu		172		37.1	7280	1759	450

LAW SCHOOL	ACADEMIC STATISTICS				ADMISSION STATISTICS		
	Median LSAT Percentile of Enrolled	Median LSAT Score of Enrolled	Lowest LSAT Percentile of Accepted	Median GPA (4.0 scale) of Enrolled	Total Applicants	Applicants Accepted	Applicants Enrolled
North Carolina Central University (School of Law) 640 Nelson Street Durham, NC 27707 919-530-6333 Fax: 919-530-6339 sbrownb@nccu.edu		148	145	3.2	2406	445	166
Northeastern University (School of Law) 400 Huntington Avenue Boston, MA 02115 617-373-2395 Fax: 617-373-8865 c.taubman@neu.edu	86	162	26	3.48	3674	1349	218
Northern Illinois University (College of Law) Swen Parson Hall, Room 151 DeKalb, IL 60115-2890 815-753-8595 Fax: 815-753-5680 lawadm@niu.edu	52	152	20	3.23	1058	475	103
Northern Kentucky University (Salmon P. Chase College of Law) Nunn Hall Highland Heights, KY 41099 859-572-5490 Fax: 859-572-6081 brayg@nku.edu	60	154	23	3.35	891	463	180
Northwestern University (School of Law) 375 East Chicago Avenue Chicago, IL 60611 312-503-8465 Fax: 312-503-0178 admissions@law.northwestern.edu	97	170	21	3.8	4548	864	264
Nova Southeastern University (Shepard Broad Law Center) 3305 College Avenue Fort Lauderdale, FL 33314-7721 954-262-6117 Fax: 954-262-3844 admission@nsu.law.nova.edu	44	150	11	3.22	2298	931	354
Ohio Northern University (Claude W. Pettit College of Law) 525 South Main Street Ada, OH 45810 419-772-2211 Fax: 419-772-3042	60	154	18	3.36	1227	502	112
Ohio State University (Michael E. Moritz College of Law) 55 West 12th Avenue, John Deaver Drinko Hall Columbus, OH 43210-1391 614-292-8810 Fax: 614-292-1383 lawadmit@osu.edu	88	163		3.63	2308	831	211
Oklahoma City University (School of Law) 2501 North Blackwelder Avenue Oklahoma City, OK 73106-1493 405-208-5354 Fax: 405-208-5814 lawadmit@okcu.edu	44	150	15	3.2	1334	721	224

LAW SCHOOL	ACADEMIC STATISTICS				ADMISSION STATISTICS		
	Median LSAT Percentile of Enrolled	Median LSAT Score of Enrolled	Lowest LSAT Percentile of Accepted	Median GPA (4.0 scale) of Enrolled	Total Applicants	Applicants Accepted	Applicants Enrolled
Pace University (School of Law) 78 North Broadway White Plains, NY 10603 914-422-4210 Fax: 914-989-8714 calexander@law.pace.edu	67	156	23	3.43	2735	1101	212
Pennsylvania State University (Dickinson School of Law) Lewis Katz Building University Park, PA 16802-1910 814-867-1251 Fax: 717-241-3503 dsladmit@psu.edu	77	159	44	3.55			
Pepperdine University (School of Law) 24255 Pacific Coast Highway Malibu, CA 90263 310-506-4631 Fax: 310-506-7668	77	158		3.3	3450	909	273
Phoenix School of Law One North Central Avenue Phoenix, AZ 85004 (602) 682-6800		148		3.09	2299	1677	526
Pontifical Catholic University of Puerto Rico (School of Law) 2250 Avenida las Americas suite 543 Ponce, PR 00717-9997 787-841-2000, ext. 1836 Fax: 787-840-4620	13			2.9			
Quinnipiac University (School of Law) 275 Mt. Carmel Avenue Hamden, CT 06518-1908 203-582-3400 Fax: 203-582-3339 ladm@quinnipiac.edu	67	156	30	3.33	2037	959	123
Regent University (School of Law) 1000 Regent University Drive Virginia Beach, VA 23464-9800 757-352-4584 Fax: 757-352-4139 lawschool@regent.edu	56	153	30	3.28	1312	445	154
Roger Williams University (School of Law) Ten Metacom Avenue Bristol, RI 02809-5171 401-254-4555 Fax: 401-254-4516 admissions@rwu.edu		151		3.3	1388	923	194
Rutgers University/Camden (School of Law) Fifth and Penn Streets Camden, NJ 08102 856-225-6102 Fax: 856-225-6537 admissions@camlaw.rutgers.edu	83	160	45	3.32	1163	649	282
Rutgers University/Newark (School of Law) Center for Law and Justice, 123 Washington St. Newark, NJ 07102 973-353-5557/5554 Fax: 973-353-3459 lawinfo@andromeda.rutgers.edu	75	158		3.33	3519	930	263

LAW SCHOOL	ACADEMIC STATISTICS				ADMISSION STATISTICS		
	Median LSAT Percentile of Enrolled	Median LSAT Score of Enrolled	Lowest LSAT Percentile of Accepted	Median GPA (4.0 scale) of Enrolled	Total Applicants	Applicants Accepted	Applicants Enrolled
Saint John's University (School of Law) 8000 Utopia Parkway Queens, NY 11439 718-990-6474 Fax: 718-990-2526 lawinfo@stjohns.edu		160		3.49	4057	1639	293
Saint Louis University (School of Law) 3700 Lindell Boulevard St. Louis, MO 63108 314-977-2800 Fax: 314-977-1464 admissions@law.slu.edu	60	154	18	3.39	1840	1068	295
Saint Mary's University (School of Law) One Camino Santa Maria San Antonio, TX 78228-8601 210-436-3523 Fax: 210-431-4202 wwilson@stmarytx.edu	60	154	18	3.08	1635	724	263
Saint Thomas University (School of Law) 16401 NW 37th Avenue Miami Gardens, FL 33054 305-623-2310 fkhan@stu.edu	44	150	13	3.08	2040	938	253
Samford University (Cumberland School of Law) 800 Lakeshore Drive Birmingham, AL 35229 205-726-2702 Fax: 205-726-2057 law.admissions@samford.edu	56	155		3.29	1405	588	152
Santa Clara University (School of Law) 500 El Camino Real Santa Clara, CA 95053 408-554-4800 Fax: 408-554-7897 lawadmissions@scu.edu	80	160	52	3.24	3689	1388	287
Seattle University (School of Law) 901 12th Avenue, Sullivan Hall, P.O. Box 222000 Seattle, WA 98122-4340 206-398-4200 Fax: 206-398-4058 lawadmis@seattleu.edu	71	157	25	3.32	2226	1031	322
Seton Hall University (School of Law) One Newark Center Newark, NJ 07102-5210 973-642-8747 Fax: 973-642-8876 admitme@shu.edu	78	159	44	3.5	3439	1664	266
South Texas College of Law 1303 San Jacinto Street Houston, TX 77002-7006 713-646-1810 Fax: 713-646-2906 admissions@stcl.edu		154		3.24	2307	1021	424
Southern Illinois University (School of Law) Lesar Law Building, Mail Code 6804 Carbondale, IL 62901 618-453-8858 Fax: 618-453-8921 lawadmit@siu.edu	56	153	26	3.3	699	353	120

LAW SCHOOL	ACADEMIC STATISTICS				ADMISSION STATISTICS		
	Median LSAT Percentile of Enrolled	Median LSAT Score of Enrolled	Lowest LSAT Percentile of Accepted	Median GPA (4.0 scale) of Enrolled	Total Applicants	Applicants Accepted	Applicants Enrolled
Southern Methodist University (Dedman School of Law) Office of Admissions, P.O. Box 750110 Dallas, TX 75275-0110 214-768-2550 Fax: 214-768-2549 *lawadmit@smu.edu*	91	164		3.76	2790	604	254
Southern New England School of Law 333 Faunce Corner Road North Dartmouth, MA 02747 508-998-9400 Fax: 508-998-9561 *cvidal@snesl.edu*		142	133	76	201	174	73
Southern University and A & M College (Law Center) Post Office Box 9294 Baton Rouge, LA 70813-9294 225-771-5340 Fax: 225-771-2121 *vwilkerson@sulc.edu*		146		2.8	1002	249	177
Southwestern University (Law School) 3050 Wilshire Boulevard Los Angeles, CA 90010-1106 213-738-6717 Fax: 213-383-1688 *admissions@swlaw.edu*	3	154		3.29	3355	1140	352
Stanford University (Stanford Law School) Crown Quadrangle, 559 Nathan Abbott Way Stanford, CA 94305-8610 650-723-4985 Fax: 650-723-0838 *admissions@law.stanford.edu*		170		3.88	4248	379	180
State University of New York (SUNY Buffalo Law School) 309 O'Brian Hall Buffalo, NY 14260 716-645-2907 Fax: 716-645-6676 *lwiley@buffalo.edu*	71	157	26	3.57	2104	689	208
Stetson University (Stetson University College of Law) 1401 61st Street South Gulfport, FL 33707 727-562-7802 Fax: 727-343-0136 *zuppo@law.stetson.edu*		155		3.36	3217	1210	344
Suffolk University (Law School) 120 Tremont Street Boston, MA 02108-4977 617-573-8144 Fax: 617-523-1367	64	155		3.26	2934	2038	538
Syracuse University (College of Law) Office of Admissions and Financial Aid, Suite 340 Syracuse, NY 13244-1030 315-443-1962 Fax: 315-443-9568	60	154		3.29	2069		223
Temple University (James E. Beasley School of Law) 1719 North Broad Street Philadelphia, PA 19122 215-204-5949 Fax: 215-204-1185 *lawadmis@temple.edu*	84	161	20	3.35	5243	1544	323

LAW SCHOOL	ACADEMIC STATISTICS				ADMISSION STATISTICS		
	Median LSAT Percentile of Enrolled	Median LSAT Score of Enrolled	Lowest LSAT Percentile of Accepted	Median GPA (4.0 scale) of Enrolled	Total Applicants	Applicants Accepted	Applicants Enrolled
Texas Southern University (Thurgood Marshall School of Law) 3100 Cleburne Avenue Houston, TX 77004 713-313-7114 Fax: 713-313-1049 cgardner@tmslaw.tsu.edu		147		2.91	2135	710	219
Texas Tech University (School of Law) 1802 Hartford Avenue Lubbock, TX 79409 806-742-3990, ext. 273 Fax: 806-742-4617 donna.williams@ttu.edu	64	155	20	3.49	1420	661	236
Texas Wesleyan University (School of Law) 1515 Commerce Street Fort Worth, TX 76102 817-212-4040 Fax: 817-212-4141 lawadmissions@law.txwes.edu	55	153	23	3.22	1915	764	236
Thomas Jefferson School of Law 1155 Island Avenue San Diego, CA 92101 619-297-9700 Fax: 619-294-4713 info@tjsl.edu		151	20	3	2697	1478	440
Thomas M. Cooley Law School 300 South Capitol Avenue Lansing, MI 48901 517-371-5140 Fax: 517-334-5718 admissions@cooley.edu		146		3.02	4032	3230	1161
Touro College (Jacob D. Fuchsberg Law Center) 225 Eastview Drive Central Islip, NY 11722 631-761-7010 Fax: 631-761-7019 gjustice@tourolaw.edu		149	15	3.04	2075	711	286
Tulane University (Law School) Weinmann Hall, 6329 Freret Street New Orleans, LA 70118 504-865-5930 Fax: 504-865-6710 admissions@law.tulane.edu		161	25	3.55	2800	1000	262
University of Akron (School of Law) 302 Buchtel Common Akron, OH 44325-2901 330-972-7331 Fax: 330-258-2343 lthorpe@uakron.edu	56	153	21	3.35	1647	883	175
University of Alabama (School of Law) Box 870382 Tuscaloosa, AL 35487-0382 205-348-5440 Fax: 205-348-3917 admissions@law.ua.edu	92	165		3.83	1872	473	160
University of Arizona (James E. Rogers College of Law) 120 E. Speedway, P.O. Box 210176 Tucson, AZ 85721-0176 520-621-3477 Fax: 520-621-9140 admissions@law.arizona.edu	89	162		3.5	2589	455	153

LAW SCHOOL	ACADEMIC STATISTICS				ADMISSION STATISTICS		
	Median LSAT Percentile of Enrolled	Median LSAT Score of Enrolled	Lowest LSAT Percentile of Accepted	Median GPA (4.0 scale) of Enrolled	Total Applicants	Applicants Accepted	Applicants Enrolled
University of Arkansas (School of Law) Robert A. Leflar Law Center, Waterman Hall Fayetteville, AR 72701 479-575-3102 Fax: 479-575-3937 jkmiller@uark.edu	67	156		3.47	1309	412	136
University of Arkansas at Little Rock (UALR William H. Bowen School of Law) 1201 McMath Avenue Little Rock, AR 72202-5142 501-324-9903 Fax: 501-324-9909 lawadm@ualr.edu	60	154	26	3.31	1529	475	145
University of Baltimore (School of Law) 1420 North Charles Street Baltimore, MD 21201-5779 410-837-4459 Fax: 410-837-4450 lwadmiss@ubmail.ubalt.edu; jzavrotny@ubalt.edu	61	153	23	3.23	2515	1102	384
University of California (Hastings College of the Law) 200 McAllister Street San Francisco, CA 94102 415-565-4623 Fax: 415-581-8946 admiss@uchastings.edu	86	162	23	3.6	5167	1791	414
University of California at Berkeley (School of Law) 215 Boalt Hall Berkeley, CA 94720 510-642-2274 Fax: 510-643-6222 adissions@law.berkeley.edu		167	48	3.79	7253	921	254
University of California at Davis (School of Law) Martin Luther King, Jr. Hall - 400 Mrak Hall Drive Davis, CA 95616-5201 530-752-6477 admissions@lawucdavis.edu	88	163	52	3.52	3320	1026	213
University of California at Los Angeles (UCLA School of Law) P.O. Box 951445 Los Angeles, CA 90095-1445 310-825-2080 Fax: 310-206-7227 admissions@law.ucla.edu	96	168	56	3.78	7328	1471	321
University of Chicago (Law School) 1111 East 60th Street Chicago, IL 60637 773-702-9484 Fax: 773-834-0942 admissions@law.uchicago.edu	98	171		3.87	4783	837	191
University of Cincinnati (College of Law) P.O. Box 210040 Cincinnati, OH 45221-0040 513-556-6805 Fax: 513-556-2391 admissions@law.uc.edu	80	160	33	3.57	1572	737	119

LAW SCHOOL	ACADEMIC STATISTICS				ADMISSION STATISTICS		
	Median LSAT Percentile of Enrolled	Median LSAT Score of Enrolled	Lowest LSAT Percentile of Accepted	Median GPA (4.0 scale) of Enrolled	Total Applicants	Applicants Accepted	Applicants Enrolled
University of Colorado **(Law School)** Campus Box 403, Wolf Law Building Boulder, CO 80309-0403 303-492-7203 Fax: 303-492-2542	90	164	48	3.64	3175	956	163
University of Connecticut **(School of Law)** 55 Elizabeth Street Hartford, CT 06105 860-570-5159 Fax: 860-570-5153 admissions@law.uconn.edu	78	159		3.45	2751	811	181
University of Dayton **(School of Law)** 300 College Park Dayton, OH 45469-2760 937-229-3555 Fax: 937-229-4194 lawinfo@notes.udayton.edu	40	149	13	3.1	1751	1214	177
University of Denver **(Sturm College of Law)** 2255 East Evans Avenue Denver, CO 80208 303-871-6135 Fax: 303-871-6992 admissions@law.du.edu	78	159	23	3.49	2425	986	297
University of Detroit Mercy **(School of Law)** 651 East Jefferson Avenue Detroit, MI 48226 313-596-0264 Fax: 313-596-0280 udmlawao@udmercy.edu	52	152	15	3.16	1461	626	223
University of Florida **(Fredric G. Levin College of Law)** 141 Bruton-Geer Hall, P.O. Box 117622 Gainesville, FL 32611-7622 352-273-0890 Fax: 352-392-4087 madorno@law.ufl.edu		162		3.64	3201	875	295
University of Georgia **(School of Law)** Hirsch Hall, 225 Herty Drive Athens, GA 30602-6012 706-542-7060 Fax: 706-542-5556 ugajd@uga.edu	90	165	40	3.6	3186	814	225
University of Hawaii at Manoa **(William S. Richardson School of Law)** 2515 Dole Street Honolulu, HI 96822 808-956-7966 Fax: 808-956-3813 lawadm@hawaii.edu	67	156	13	3.36	1309	257	116
University of Houston **(Law Center)** 100 Law Center Houston, TX 77204-6060 713-743-2280 Fax: 713-743-2194 lawadmissions@uh.edu	83	161	27	3.43	3357	903	252
University of Idaho **(College of Law)** P.O. Box 442321 Moscow, ID 83844-2321 208-885-2300 Fax: 208-885-5709 jfinney@uidaho.edu	61	154	15	3.25	665	372	130

LAW SCHOOL	ACADEMIC STATISTICS				ADMISSION STATISTICS		
	Median LSAT Percentile of Enrolled	Median LSAT Score of Enrolled	Lowest LSAT Percentile of Accepted	Median GPA (4.0 scale) of Enrolled	Total Applicants	Applicants Accepted	Applicants Enrolled
University of Illinois (College of Law) 504 East Pennsylvania Avenue Champaign, IL 61820 217-244-6415 Fax: 217-244-1478 admissions@law.uiuc.edu	96	166	25	3.6	2520	761	173
University of Iowa (College of Law) 320 Melrose Avenue Iowa City, IA 52242 319-335-9095 Fax: 319-335-9646 law-admissions@uiowa.edu	82	161		3.64	1872	729	180
University of Kansas (School of Law) 205 Green Hall, 1535 West 15th Street Lawrence, KS 66045 785-864-4378 Fax: 785-864-5054 admitlaw@ku.edu	71	157	18	3.51	819	401	134
University of Kentucky (College of Law) 209 Law Building Lexington, KY 40506-0048 606-257-7938 Fax: (859) 323-1061 lawadmissions@email.uky.edu		159	30	3.57	1114	456	130
University of La Verne (College of Law) 320 East D Street Ontario, CA 91764 909-460-2001 Fax: 909-460-2082 lawadm@ulv.edu	49	151	33	3.3	1007	429	109
University of Louisville (Louis D. Brandeis School of Law) University of Louisville Belknap Campus-Wilson W. Wyatt Hall Louisville, KY 40292 502-852-6364 Fax: 502-852-8971 brandon.hamilton@louisville.edu		156	16	3.42	1495	466	132
University of Maine (School of Law) 246 Deering Avenue Portland, ME 04102 207-780-4341 Fax: 207-780-4239 mainelaw@usm.maine.edu	64	155		3.36	988	474	91
University of Maryland (Francis King Cary School of Law) 500 West Baltimore Street Baltimore, MD 21201 410-706-3492 Fax: 410-706-1793 admissions@law.umaryland.edu	84	160	20	3.59	3747	598	290
University of Memphis (Cecil C. Humphreys School of Law) 1 North Front Street Memphis, TN 38103-2189 901-678-5403 Fax: 901-678-0741 lawadmissions@.memphis.edu	64	155	8	3.42	861	302	144

LAW SCHOOL	ACADEMIC STATISTICS				ADMISSION STATISTICS		
	Median LSAT Percentile of Enrolled	Median LSAT Score of Enrolled	Lowest LSAT Percentile of Accepted	Median GPA (4.0 scale) of Enrolled	Total Applicants	Applicants Accepted	Applicants Enrolled
University of Miami (School of Law) P.O. Box 248087, 1311 Miller Drive Coral Gables, FL 33124-8087 305-284-2523 Fax: 305-284-4400 *admissions@law.miami.edu*	74	158	23	3.38	4729	2195	447
University of Michigan (Law School) 625 South State Street Ann Arbor, MI 48109-1215 734-764-0537 Fax: 734-647-3218 *law.jd.admissions@umich.edu*	96	169		3.76	5424	1162	359
University of Minnesota (Law School) 229 19th Avenue South Minneapolis, MN 55455 612-625-3487 Fax: 612-626-1874 *jdadmissions@umn.edu*	94	167		3.8	3546	879	246
University of Mississippi (L.Q.C. Lamar Hall) P.O. Box 1848 Lamar Law Center University, MS 38677 662-915-6910 Fax: 662-915-1289 *bvinson@olemiss.edu*	64	155	15	3.59	1572	482	173
University of Missouri (School of Law) 103 Hulston Hall Columbia, MO 65211 573-882-6042 Fax: 573-882-9625 *heckm@missouri.edu*	75	158		3.48	851	348	133
University of Missouri-Kansas City (School of Law) 500 East 52nd Street Kansas City, MO 64110-2499 816-235-1644 Fax: 816-235-5276 *brooks@umkc.edu*	64	155	36	3.35	892	357	149
University of Montana (School of Law) Missoula, MT 59812 406-243-2698 Fax: 406-243-2576 *heidi.fanslow@umontana.edu*	60	155	5	3.44	429	196	85
University of Nebraska-Lincoln (College of Law) P.O. Box 830902 Lincoln, NE 68583-0902 402-472-2161 Fax: 402-472-5185 *lawadm@unl.edu*	70	157	33	3.51	825	400	130
University of Nevada, Las Vegas (William S. Boyd School of Law) 4505 Maryland Parkway, Box 451003 Las Vegas, NV 89154-1003 702-895-2440 Fax: 702-895-2414 *request@law.unlv.edu*		158		3.48	1737	384	158
University of New Hampshire School of Law 2 White Street Concord, NH 03301 603-228-9217 Fax: 603-229-0485 *admissions@law.unh.edu*	63	155	18	3.25	1247	627	146

LAW SCHOOL	ACADEMIC STATISTICS				ADMISSION STATISTICS		
	Median LSAT Percentile of Enrolled	Median LSAT Score of Enrolled	Lowest LSAT Percentile of Accepted	Median GPA (4.0 scale) of Enrolled	Total Applicants	Applicants Accepted	Applicants Enrolled
University of New Mexico (School of Law) MSC11-6070, 1 University of New Mexico Albuquerque, NM 87131-0001 505-277-0958 Fax: 505-277-9958 *witherington@law.unm.edu*		157		3.33	942	237	113
University of North Carolina at Chapel Hill (School of Law) Campus Box 3380, Van Hecke-Wettach Hall Chapel Hill, NC 27599-3380 919-962-5109 Fax: 919-843-7939 *law_admission@unc.edu*	88	163	30	3.51	2576	462	248
University of North Dakota (School of Law) Box 9003 Grand Forks, ND 58202 701-777-2104 Fax: 701-777-2217 *linda.kohoutek@thor.law.und.nodak.edu*		151		3.57	382	153	69
University of Notre Dame (Notre Dame Law School) P.O. Box 780 Notre Dame, IN 46556-0780 574-631-6626 Fax: 574-631-5474 *lawadmit@nd.edu*		166		3.64	3059	640	183
University of Oklahoma (College of Law) Andrew M. Coats Hall, 300 Timberdell Road Norman, OK 73019 405-325-4728 Fax: 405-325-0502 *rlucas@ou.edu*	74	158		3.48	1105	347	153
University of Oregon (School of Law, William W. Knight Law Center) 1515 Agate Street Eugene, OR 97403-1221 541-346-3846 Fax: 541-346-3984 *admissions@law.uoregon.edu*		159		3.34	2093	888	182
University of Pennsylvania (Law School) 3501 Sansom Street Philadelphia, PA 19104-6204 215-898-7400 Fax: 215-898-9606 *admissions@law.upenn.edu*	98	170		3.86	4952	863	266
University of Pittsburgh (School of Law) 3900 Forbes Avenue Pittsburgh, PA 15260 412-648-1413 Fax: 412-648-1318 *Mccall@law.pitt.edu*	78	159	23	3.45	2379	869	230
University of Puerto Rico (School of Law) P.O. Box 23349, UPR Station Rio Piedras, PR 00931-3349 787-999-9551 Fax: 787-999-9564 *arosario-lebron@law.upr.edu*	27	146	2	3.59	422	215	201

LAW SCHOOL	ACADEMIC STATISTICS				ADMISSION STATISTICS		
	Median LSAT Percentile of Enrolled	Median LSAT Score of Enrolled	Lowest LSAT Percentile of Accepted	Median GPA (4.0 scale) of Enrolled	Total Applicants	Applicants Accepted	Applicants Enrolled
University of Richmond (School of Law) 28 Westhampton Way Richmond, VA 23173 804-289-8189 Fax: 804-287-6516 *lawadmissions@richmond.edu*	86	162	48	3.5	2371	563	154
University of Saint Thomas (School of Law) 1000 LaSalle Ave. Minneapolis, MN 55403 651-962-4895 Fax: 651-962-4876 *lawschool@stthomas.edu*	67	156	11	3.44	1283	711	171
University of San Diego (School of Law) 5998 Alcala Park San Diego, CA 92110 619-260-4528 Fax: 619-260-2218 *jdinfo@sandiego.edu*	84	161		3.28	4694		359
University of San Francisco (School of Law) 2130 Fulton Street San Francisco, CA 94117-1080 415-422-6586 Fax: 415-422-5442 *lawadmissions@usfca.edu*	70	157	13	3.4	4215	1603	246
University of South Carolina (School of Law) 701 South Main Street Columbia, SC 29208 803-777-6605 Fax: 803-777-7751 *usclaw@law.sc.edu*		158		3.35	1986	725	213
University of South Dakota (School of Law) 414 East Clark Street Vermillion, SD 57069-2390 605-677-5443 Fax: 605-677-5417 *law.school@usd.edu*	44	150	4	3.27	400	236	88
University of Southern California (Gould School of Law) Los Angeles, CA 90089-0071 213-740-2523 *admissions@law.usc.edu*	96	167	52	3.69	5987	1528	199
University of Tennessee (College of Law) 1505 W. Cumberland Avenue Knoxville, TN 37996-1810 865-974-4131 Fax: 865-974-1572 *lawadmit@utk.edu*	80	160	11	3.53	1277	435	160
University of Texas at Austin (School of Law) 727 East Dean Keeton Street Austin, TX 78705 512-232-1200 Fax: 512-471-2765 *admissions@law.utexas.edu*	94	167	36	3.69	4759	1311	370
University of the District of Columbia (David A. Clarke School of Law) 4200 Connecticut Avenue, N.W. Washington, DC 20008 202-274-7341 Fax: 202-274-5583 *vcanty@udc.edu; lawadmission@udc.edu*	53	152	23	3	1601	336	123

LAW SCHOOL	ACADEMIC STATISTICS				ADMISSION STATISTICS		
	Median LSAT Percentile of Enrolled	Median LSAT Score of Enrolled	Lowest LSAT Percentile of Accepted	Median GPA (4.0 scale) of Enrolled	Total Applicants	Applicants Accepted	Applicants Enrolled
University of the Pacific **(McGeorge School of Law)** 3200 Fifth Avenue Sacramento, CA 95817 916-739-7105 Fax: 916-739-7301 *mcgeorge@pacific.edu*	75	158	44	3.4	3042	1293	330
University of Toledo **(College of Law)** 2801 West Bancroft Street, MS 507 Toledo, OH 43606-3390 419-530-4131 Fax: 419-530-4345 *law.utoledo.edu*		153		3.33	1440	626	137
University of Tulsa **(College of Law)** 3120 East Fourth Place Tulsa, OK 74104-2499 918-631-2406 Fax: 918-631-3630 *april-fox@utulsa.edu*	64	155	41	3.32	1515	582	107
University of Utah **(S. J. Quinney College of Law)** 332 South 1400, East Room 101 Salt Lake City, UT 84112 801-581-7479 Fax: 801-581-6897 *aguilarr@law.utah.edu*	83	161	21	3.54	1230	378	114
University of Virginia **(School of Law)** 580 Massie Road Charlottesville, VA 22903-1738 434-924-7351 Fax: 434-982-2128 *lawadmit@virginia.edu*	97	170	40	3.86	7379	688	357
University of Washington **(School of Law)** Box 353020 Seattle, WA 98195-3020 206-543-4078 Fax: 206-543-5671 *lawadm@u.washington.edu*	90	164	49	3.67	2656	586	182
University of West Los Angeles **(School of Law)** 9920 S. LaCienega Blvd. #404 Inglewood CA 90301-2902 301-342-5210 Fax: 310-342-5295 *tsmith@uwla.edu*	31	150	8	3.07	217	118	104
University of Wisconsin **(Law School)** 975 Bascom Mall Madison, WI 53706 608-262-5914 Fax: 608-263-3191 *admissions@law.wisc.edu*	88	163		3.67	2870	741	242
University of Wyoming **(College of Law)** Dept. 3035, 1000 East University Avenue Laramie, WY 82071 307-766-6416 Fax: 307-766-6417 *dburke@uwyo.edu*	56	153	15	3.38	540	242	69

LAW SCHOOL	ACADEMIC STATISTICS				ADMISSION STATISTICS		
	Median LSAT Percentile of Enrolled	Median LSAT Score of Enrolled	Lowest LSAT Percentile of Accepted	Median GPA (4.0 scale) of Enrolled	Total Applicants	Applicants Accepted	Applicants Enrolled
Valparaiso University (School of Law) Wesemann Hall, 656 S. Greenwich Street Valparaiso, IN 46383-6493 219-465-7821 Fax: 219-465-7808 *law.admissions@valpo.edu*		151		3.47	3248	810	214
Vanderbilt University (Law School) 131 21st Avenue South Nashville, TN 37203 615-322-6452 Fax: 615-322-1531 *admissions@law.vanderbilt.edu*	97	169		3.73	3987	1193	194
Vermont Law School P.O. Box 96, Chelsea Street South Royalton, VT 05068-0096 802-831-1239 Fax: 802-831-1174 *admiss@vermontlaw.edu*	64	154		3.26	1020	704	151
Villanova University (School of Law) 299 North Spring Mill Road Villanova, PA 19085 610-519-7010 Fax: 610-519-6291 *admissions@law.villanova.edu*	80	160	44	3.57	3014	1475	218
Wake Forest University (School of Law) P.O. Box 7206 Winston-Salem, NC 27109 336-758-5437 Fax: 336-758-4632 *admissions@law.wfu.edu*	93	163	40	3.6	2633	948	185
Washburn University (School of Law) 1700 SW College Avenue Topeka, KS 66621 785-670-1185 Fax: 785-670-1120 *admissions@washburnlaw.edu*		155	25	3.19	888	352	124
Washington and Lee University (School of Law) Lewis Hall Lexington, VA 24450 540-458-8503 Fax: 540-458-8586 *lawadm@wlu.edu*	90	164	44	3.65	3972	964	121
Washington University in St. Louis (School of Law) Box 1120, One Brookings Drive St. Louis, MO 63130 314-935-4525 Fax: 314-935-8778 *admiss@wulaw.wustl.edu*		168		3.66	3847	979	243
Wayne State University (Law School) 471 West Palmer Street Detroit, MI 48202 313-577-3937 Fax: 313-993-8129 *omjackson@wayne.edu*	70	157	18	3.39	1123	517	181

LAW SCHOOL	ACADEMIC STATISTICS				ADMISSION STATISTICS		
	Median LSAT Percentile of Enrolled	Median LSAT Score of Enrolled	Lowest LSAT Percentile of Accepted	Median GPA (4.0 scale) of Enrolled	Total Applicants	Applicants Accepted	Applicants Enrolled
West Virginia University (College of Law) P.O. Box 6130 Morgantown, WV 26506 304-293-5304 Fax: 304-293-6891 wvulaw.Admissions@mail.wvu.edu	60	154	33	3.41	1107	506	141
Western New England University (School of Law) 1215 Wilbraham Road Springfield, MA 01119 413-782-1406 Fax: 413-796-2067 admissions@law.wnec.edu	56	153	33	3.2	1170	593	106
Western State University (College of Law) 1111 North State College Blvd Fullerton, CA 92831 714-459-1101 Fax: 714-441-1748 adm@wsulaw.edu		151		3.09	1882	1068	237
Whittier College (Whittier Law School) 3333 Harbor Blvd. Costa Mesa, CA 92626 714-444-4141, ext. 121 Fax: 714-444-0250 info@law.whittier.edu	52	152	15	2.95	2245	1247	275
Widener University (Widener University School of Law) 4601 Concord Pike, P.O. Box 7474 Wilmington, DE 19803-0474 302-477-2162 Fax: 302-477-2224 law.admissions@law.widener.edu	52	152	14	3.12	2039	918	313
Widener University (Widener University School of Law) 3800 Vartan Way, P.O. Box 69381 Harrisburg, PA 17106-9381 717-541-3903 Fax: 717-541-3999 law.admissions@law.widener.edu	44	150	15	3.2	908	624	183
Willamette University (College of Law) 245 Winter Street S.E. Salem, OR 97301 503-370-6282 Fax: 503-370-6087 law-admission@willamette.edu	64	155		3.15	1092	538	141
William Mitchell College of Law 875 Summit Avenue St. Paul, MN 55105-3076 651-290-6343 Fax: 651-290-6414 admissions@wmitchell.edu	62	155	11	3.39	1536	935	309
Yale University (Yale Law School) P.O. Box 208329 New Haven, CT 06520-8215 203-432-4995 admissions.law@yale.edu	99	173	80	3.9	3173	252	205
Yeshiva University (Benjamin N. Cardozo School of Law) 55 Fifth Avenue New York, NY 10003 212-790-0274 Fax: 212-790-0482 lawinfo@yu.edu	90	162		3.6	4915	1499	379

CHAPTER 7

Which Law School?

The decision as to which law school to attend can be even more complicated than the decision whether to attend law school. Beware of law school admissions and recruitment people. They want you—actually they want your seat deposit. Most of them are personable, well-informed, and genuine. They are, however, selling a product: their school. The best defense against the hard sell is comparison shopping. Listen to a number of different pitches before you make a choice. Check out the various claims and promises relying on your own independent investigation rather than on stock promotional materials. *Barron's Guide to Law Schools* is particularly suited to help you accomplish this objective (see Part III of this Guide for more information).

Beware of family, friends, and prelaw advisors, who push you to attend a particular law school. Utilize impartial advice, particularly guidance from professional counselors and advisors, in making your decision. Their experience and knowledge can be invaluable. But remember! Your prelaw advisor may like a certain school because she graduated from it. Your career counselor may have been particularly impressed by the speech he heard at an open house for a certain law school. Your lawyer friend may or may not be privy to accurate information. Sometimes, opinions masked by objectivity are far from objective. And most important of all, remember that no single school is right for everyone.

Beware of letting your procrastination make decisions for you. There are many critical dates in the law school admission process. Don't be foreclosed from applying to schools, seeking financial aid, or pursuing any alternative because you didn't do it in time. If you want to make the best choice, you should seek to maximize your options, and the best way to maximize your options is to stay on top of the process. Start early. Develop a tickler file to remind you in advance about critical dates. Most calendar programs for personal computers allow you to save important dates. Set aside sufficient time to meet deadlines and accomplish your objectives. Remember that the easiest decision is not always the best one.

Barron's Guide to Law Schools contains chapters on the LSAT (Chapters 12 and 13), the job outlook for graduates, including starting salaries (Chapter 10), financial aid (Chapter 8), and profiles of law schools themselves (Chapters 15 and 16).

The checklist on page 66 may help you to clarify your objectives and focus your research efforts as you think about law school. It lists the primary questions you should address as you evaluate law schools. If you can determine what choices are best for you, you not only will increase your chances of being accepted, but also improve the likelihood that law school will be a rewarding experience.

GEOGRAPHY

Geographical considerations inevitably come into play. A majority of law school graduates accept positions in the region where they went to law school. Those who do not stay in the same geographic area tend to return to the region where they grew up or where they have family. This is true not only for so-called local and regional law schools, but for national law schools as well. It is easier to find a job if you are physically located in the area where your job search occurs. Thus, if you know where you want to settle after graduation, you may want to consider limiting your applications to law schools in that geographic area.

Although most law school graduates settle in the largest metropolitan areas, both law schools and legal employment are found in a variety of settings. You may want to consider, as an alternative to pursuing a legal education at a school in a big city, attending school or working in a smaller city or town, a suburban area within a larger metropolitan population, or a rural area. You may have business, political, or personal ties to a community that would make it advantageous to target that place for postgraduate

CHECKLIST ON CHOOSING A LAW SCHOOL

Where geographically do you want to go to law school?
Family considerations
- ☐ Desire to be close to parents, relatives
- ☐ Sick or special needs relatives for whom you have responsibilities
- ☐ Contacts that will help you as a practicing lawyer
- ☐ Work in a family business
- ☐ Financial considerations (such as needing to live at home)
- ☐ Family ties to a particular law school

Personal considerations
- ☐ Significant other lives in area
- ☐ Significant other works in area
- ☐ Friends or social activities
- ☐ Support groups (church, social clubs, business relationships)
- ☐ Health care
- ☐ Contacts that will help you as a practicing lawyer

Current job
- ☐ Future job prospects
- ☐ Knowledge of local business and legal community
- ☐ Work experience
- ☐ Employment opportunities

Community setting
- ☐ Urban
- ☐ Suburban
- ☐ Rural
- ☐ Ethnic or religious community

Regional preferences
- ☐ Northeast
- ☐ Midwest
- ☐ Southeast
- ☐ Southwest
- ☐ West Coast
- ☐ Mountains

What areas of law practice interest you?
- ☐ Representing individuals with ordinary legal problems
- ☐ Representing corporations in national and international business transactions
- ☐ Representing government entities in carrying out the law
- ☐ Representing people of limited means
- ☐ Engaging in law reform and other public interest activities

What programs does the law school you are considering offer?
- ☐ General legal curriculum
- ☐ Curriculum built around the law of a particular state
- ☐ Specialized course offerings in particular fields of law
- ☐ Access to part time and summer jobs
- ☐ Internship and externship opportunities
- ☐ Clinical programs designed to prepare you to practice law
- ☐ Sponsorship of and access to extracurricular cultural or legal activities

What kind of law school can you afford?
- ☐ State or private institution
- ☐ Evening (part time) or day (full time) program
- ☐ Availability of financial aid, scholarships

Cost of living in the community where the law school is located
- ☐ Housing in the community
- ☐ Campus housing
- ☐ Transportation
- ☐ Food and entertainment

What sort of atmosphere do you want in your law school?
Size of student body
- ☐ Large (1,000+ students)
- ☐ Medium (600–1,000 students)
- ☐ Small (fewer than 600 students)

Competitiveness of students
- ☐ Cutthroat atmosphere
- ☐ Cooperative atmosphere

Physical plant
- ☐ General appearance
- ☐ Classrooms
- ☐ Faculty and administrative offices
- ☐ Student space
- ☐ Technology support
- ☐ Parking and access to transportation

Library resources
- ☐ Available volumes
- ☐ Professional support
- ☐ Study space

Student services
- ☐ General attitude of students toward the institution
- ☐ Student government (Student Bar Association)
- ☐ Law reviews
- ☐ Moot court and other competitions
- ☐ Active student organizations
- ☐ Academic support
- ☐ Personal and crisis counseling

Educational approach
- ☐ Like *The Paper Chase*
- ☐ Indifferent to students
- ☐ Positive atmosphere for students
- ☐ Intellectually stimulating
- ☐ Focus on bar preparation

University community
- ☐ Part of a large university
- ☐ Part of a small university or liberal arts college
- ☐ Part of an urban university
- ☐ Law school is/is not situated on main university campus
- ☐ Independent law school not connected to university

Special Programs, concentration
- ☐ Areas of practice represented by curricular concentrations
- ☐ Graduate law programs
- ☐ Special centers and research projects

Which schools will accept you?
- ☐ LSAT Scores
- ☐ Undergraduate GPA
- ☐ Special considerations (such as ethnicity)
- ☐ Work, education, life experiences
- ☐ Other factors that make you unique
- ☐ Recommendations
- ☐ Opportunity for personal interview
- ☐ Timing of your application
- ☐ Availability of pre-law school preparatory program

employment. You or your family may have ties to a university or law school that would lead you to go to school there.

COURSE CONCENTRATION

You may want to give thought to what substantive areas of practice interest you. Although many entering law students do not have a clue about what areas of law they wish to pursue, sometime during the tenure of their legal education, they will have to make those choices. Other law students know before they begin law school that they are interested in a particular type of practice, and may choose a law school because of its curricular concentration in that field. Although the first year curriculum and many core upper-level electives are common in most law schools, different law schools will have different upper-level course offerings and concentrations. You should look carefully at law school web sites and catalogs, and talk to school representatives about these differences as part of the decision-making process. In addition, discuss law schools with alumni, or lawyers who may be in a position to compare different schools in a state or metropolitan area with more than one law school.

COST

What kind of school can you afford? State law schools are usually less expensive for residents than for nonresidents, or than private schools. Among private schools, tuition may differ considerably depending on the prestige of the institution and other considerations. Schools also differ considerably as to the amount of financial aid and scholarship funds that are available to incoming students. You may be able to get substantial financial assistance from a school that is less competitive academically than you could expect from a more prestigious institution. Additionally, schools with part-time or evening programs provide an opportunity for students to attend law school while continuing to work full time.

INSTITUTIONAL CULTURE

You should look carefully for information about the school's institutional culture. Although it is hard to discern sometimes, every school has a unique personality. Its geographic location and student body demographic makeup will affect the school's atmosphere. The background of the faculty members will, too. Do most of them have experience practicing law? Or did most come directly into teaching from postgraduate appellate clerkships? What is the size of the student body, the faculty, and average classes? In some ways, a larger law school may seem more vibrant and diverse, while a smaller law school will feel more intimate and supportive. Look at the competitiveness of the institution. Do you want to see how you fare in the most highly charged competitive environment? Do you want to be a big fish in a little pond? Will you be happy just to get accepted? Take a look at the physical plant, the library, and other resources available to the law school. Consider what benefits accrue to the law school from affiliation with its parent university. Think about the history of the university and the law school, and how the institutional roots have molded the law school culture today. Ask about the educational philosophy of the institution, whether it is highly theoretical, or practical and skills-oriented. Find out whether the curriculum focuses on the law of a particular jurisdiction, or is concentrated in some other way.

STUDENT LIFE

Observe whether current students are satisfied with services, such as financial aid and career services. Consider the availability of cocurricular and extracurricular groups, such as law review, moot court, law school student government, and other student organizations.

LIKELIHOOD OF ADMISSION

Finally, look at which law schools will accept you. If your LSAT and GPA are both very strong, you will have significantly more opportunities than people with less impressive credentials. If either your LSAT or GPA is less stellar, the number of law schools interested in you will inevitably drop. You may need to demonstrate your aptitude through other activities and experiences. If your LSAT and GPA are both low, you may find it challenging to find a single law school that will accept you (see pages 18–22). A few law schools offer programs that permit applicants to compete for slots during the summer prior to admission.

Some law schools may be located in a geographic area that does not draw as many applications as more populous ones. Some states accredit law schools not approved by the

American Bar Association (ABA). Graduates of non-ABA-approved schools usually can only take the bar in the state in which the school is accredited. These schools usually have fewer and less competitive applications, and for some people this may be the only way to go to law school. Before committing to a law school not approved by the ABA you should look carefully at all the factors described in the last paragraph (see also Chapter 16).

U.S. NEWS AND OTHER RANKINGS

Each year *U.S. News and World Report* produces a ranking of law schools that is relied on extensively by many law school applicants and their advisors. The rankings, based on both statistical data and surveys of lawyers, judges and legal educators, have a tendency to imbue a degree of certainty into the process of evaluating law schools that does not exist in reality. Other similar surveys, reported by different publications, fall into the same trap. They all presume that a single set of measurable criteria will work for all applicants. This is simply not the case.

The American Bar Association has circulated a statement warning students against the uncritical use of law school rankings (see box below). This position is supported by the Law School Admissions Council and most law school deans and admissions officers.

Rating of Law Schools

No rating of law schools beyond the simple statement of their accreditation status is attempted or advocated by the American Bar Association. Qualities that make one kind of school good for one student may not be as important to another. The American Bar Association and its Section of Legal Education and Admissions to the Bar have issued disclaimers of any law school rating system. Prospective law students should consider a variety of factors in making their choice among approved schools.

If you look at a ranking system such as *U.S. News,* do so with a skeptical eye. Remember that reputations in legal education are established over decades. Recognize that different schools are "best" for different people. And accept the fact that all ABA-approved law schools go through the same rigorous accreditation process. The process involves both quality standards and regular inspection of ABA-approved institutions. Thus, qualitative differences among law school educational programs are negligible, although the credentials of students who attend different schools may vary according to the relative prestige of those schools.

Rather than looking at a rough-tiered ranking of schools that means very little in terms of the quality of legal education you will receive, it makes more sense to rank specific factors that do have a relationship to the quality of education, to the experience that individual students will encounter in different schools, and to the potential to achieve the career choice most suited to the individual.

The following list includes a number of factors you can use to compare law schools. The information relevant to these factors is easily accessible in the school profiles included in this Guide, beginning on page 219. Some of the factors may require you to search law school web sites or consult other information sources. You might even call law schools with specific questions. The key, however, is to collect the same data from all the schools you are considering.

You may want to develop tables or charts comparing the schools on your list to see how well they do in the areas that are important to you. Remember: this list is just a guide; you may find some of the factors less germane to your personal evaluation of schools, and you may also think of other comparisons that are not included in the list. The message, however, is that you should rank schools on specific criteria that will have meaning to your choice of law school to attend, and ultimately to your success in the legal profession. You might be surprised what you learn.

- Student qualifications for enrolled students
  - LSAT
    - Median
    - Highest and lowest quartiles
  - Undergraduate GPA
    - Median
    - Highest and lowest quartiles
- Average age of students
  - Full-time students
  - Part-time students
- Diversity percentages
  - African Americans
  - Latinos
  - Asian Americans
  - Native Americans
  - GLBT students
  - Other significant religious, ethnic, political groups
  - Women

- ○ Foreign lawyers/law students
- Cost of tuition
- Location
  - ○ Urban
  - ○ Suburban
  - ○ Rural
  - ○ State Capital
  - ○ Cost of Living
- Availability of part-time enrollment option
- Financial aid
  - ○ Percentage of students on full academic scholarship
  - ○ Percentage of students on partial academic scholarship
  - ○ Percentage of students on full need-based scholarship
  - ○ Percentage of students on partial need-based scholarship
  - ○ Percentage of students with college work study, co-op, or other work-based financial aid
  - ○ Percentage of students with student loans
  - ○ Average loan indebtedness for students at graduation
- Organization of curriculum
  - ○ Law school religious or political affiliation
  - ○ First year courses
    - ■ Number of hours required
    - ■ Number of courses required
    - ■ Grading system/mandatory curve
  - ○ Legal research/writing program
    - ■ Full-time, adjunct, or student teachers
    - ■ Upper-level writing opportunities (seminars, drafting courses)
  - ○ Availability of clinical programs
    - ■ Practice areas
    - ■ Number of students served
  - ○ Professional skills courses
  - ○ Specialized programs
    - ■ Substantive concentrations
    - ■ Certificate programs
    - ■ Joint degree programs
    - ■ LLM programs
    - ■ Internships (Local, Abroad)
    - ■ Externships
  - ○ Availability of independent research opportunities with faculty members
  - ○ Availability of opportunities to serve as a faculty research assistant
- Library
  - ○ Number of library volumes
  - ○ Number of study spaces in the library
- Commitment to innovative technology?
  - ○ IT support
  - ○ Laptop requirement
  - ○ Wired or wireless classrooms
  - ○ Connectivity or computers in the library

- Class size
  - ○ First year class
    - ■ Average number of students in first year sections
    - ■ Number of small enrollment classes
  - ○ Graduates
  - ○ Attrition
- Faculty
  - ○ Student-to-faculty ratio
  - ○ Credentials
  - ○ Expertise in specialized fields
  - ○ Scholarship
  - ○ Community and bar activities
  - ○ Accessibility to students
  - ○ Percentage of tenured faculty
  - ○ Percentage of diversity faculty
- Career patterns
  - ○ Percentage of employed graduates
  - ○ Percentage of graduates practicing law
    - ■ Large Firms
    - ■ Small Firms
    - ■ Corporate Legal
    - ■ Government
    - ■ Judicial clerkships
    - ■ Legal services, public interest
    - ■ Nonlegal jobs
  - ○ Student employment
    - ■ Summer after first year
    - ■ Summer after second year
    - ■ Part-time legal employment
    - ■ Full-time employment for part-time students
    - ■ Nonlegal employment
  - ○ Geographic distribution of graduates
- Bar passage
  - ○ Percentage compared to state average where most graduates take the exam
  - ○ First time percentage
  - ○ Ultimate percentage (graduates who eventually pass a bar exam)
- Campus
  - ○ Part of larger university campus or standalone
  - ○ Transportation
  - ○ Parking
  - ○ Housing
  - ○ Safety, security
- Student activities
  - ○ Law reviews
  - ○ Moot court programs
  - ○ Student government
  - ○ Political, religious, ethnic, public interest organizations
- Services
  - ○ Career Services
    - ■ Career counseling
    - ■ Career library and resources
    - ■ Career programs
    - ■ Campus interviews (Number of firms, Cities represented)

- Job listings and contacts with firms not coming to campus
- Part-time job listings
- Assistance for alumni
- Government employment
- Public interest employment
- Health insurance and services
- Counseling services
- Child care
- Recreational facilities
- Students with disabilities

All of these factors are quantifiable, and as such permit you to compare schools to each other. Thus, if you are considering ten schools, you only have to look at the comparative data for those schools, but rather than saying that one school is in Tier 2 while another is in Tier 3, you can actually rank the schools based on factors that are important to you. This approach may be a little more labor intensive, but it is much more likely to produce an outcome that is tailored to your needs, priorities, and expectations.

CHAPTER 8

Is Financial Aid Available?

Unless you are independently wealthy, you are probably having some concerns about financing your legal education. The important thing to keep in mind is that funds are available to help you. The bulk of the assistance for law school students takes the form of student loans. There is very little money available for outright grants. Most law school students and their families are willing to take on a heavy debt load as an investment in the future.

There are certain concepts relative to financial aid that all applicants should know. All programs that are federally funded or sponsored have very strict requirements as to eligibility. Law school financial aid offices process the loan applications in accordance with these rules and regulations. They have very little leeway except in the awarding of institutional funds.

Federal Methodology (FM) Federal Methodology is the federally mandated method of determining financial need.

Merit Based Merit-based aid does not require a showing of need.

Base Year Base year is the prior calendar year and is used to calculate need under FM.

Independent Student Law school students are deemed to be independent due to their professional student status.

Budget The budget is set by the financial aid office each year. FM allows only *required* student expenses. These expenses are: tuition, fees, books, living expenses including room and board, transportation costs, an allowance for personal expenses, and miscellaneous expenses. Required student expenses will not cover, in most cases, car payments, credit card monthly payments, alimony, or mortgage payments.

Financial Need Financial need is the difference between expected family contribution and the total cost of attendance.

Packaging Policy Packaging policy is set by each law school and delineates the priorities for awarding financial aid.

CAMPUS-BASED PROGRAMS

Certain financial aid programs are referred to as campus-based. First in this category of aid would be scholarships and grants funded entirely by the law school. At most law schools the amount of money available for this form of aid is small. Since the money comes from the institution, the institution sets the requirements for receiving the aid. In most cases these awards will require a showing of need. Occasionally, a law school will have some merit-based aid.

Carl D. Perkins Loans are another form of campus-based aid. Each year the institution receives an allocation from the federal government for this program. It is basically a loan program administered by the institution in that the institution lends the money to the student and the institution is responsible for collecting the loans from the recipients. Perkins loans carry the lowest interest rate and at most schools are reserved for the neediest students. There is a cumulative limit of $40,000 on all Perkins loans, both graduate and undergraduate.

Another type of campus-based aid is the Federal Work Study (FWS) program. Again, the institution receives a yearly allocation from the federal government to fund this program. FWS is a need-based program and may be reserved for the neediest students. The financial aid award will indicate that the law student is eligible to receive a certain amount of money under the FWS program. This money can be earned either by working on campus or off campus. On-campus jobs take the form of working in the library or other law school offices or as research assistants for faculty members. Off-campus jobs can only be with nonprofit or governmental entities. Some examples would be work at a public defender's office, as a law clerk for a judge, or for a state or federal agency. FWS funds do not have to be repaid.

FEDERAL LOAN PROGRAMS

Other federal loan programs are available through the U.S. Department of Education. These loans were formally administered under the auspices of banks, credit unions, savings and loan associations, and other private lenders. The Stafford Student Loan is a relatively low-interest federal loan available to law school students. Law school students can borrow a maximum of $20,500 per academic year under this program but may not exceed $138,500 in total Stafford loans for law school. Federal Graduate Plus loans are now available as well, offering easy credit approval and eligibility for loan forgiveness based on public service employment.

OTHER LOAN PROGRAMS

Other loan programs are available to law school students but do not receive federal interest subsidies. These loan programs do not require demonstration of financial need and carry the highest interest rates. An applicant may also have to show a good credit rating or creditworthiness.

There are other private loan programs available. Your financial aid office will have information on these programs. The availability of loan programs changes periodically, so applicants should always check for the latest programs and terms.

OUTSIDE FUNDING

Various foundations and business and professional organizations offer assistance in financing your education. Some programs are geared for minority and disadvantaged students such as the Council on Legal Education Opportunity, the Earl Warren Legal Training Program, the ABA Legal Opportunity Scholarship, and the Mexican American Legal Defense Education Fund. The financial aid office can give you complete information on these other programs. As funds for most of these programs are limited, you should apply early.

Another source of outside funding comes from various state and county bar associations that award scholarships. The amounts and requirements will vary, but this possibility should not be overlooked.

Some states also offer grants to needy graduate students. Contact your local state guarantee agency to explore this option. Your financial aid office (both graduate and undergraduate) can supply you with their names and addresses.

Money is available to finance your legal education. But at what cost? The interest rate increases as you move from the Perkins loan (lowest interest) to the Stafford and the private loans. Borrowing decisions should be carefully made as these loans ultimately have to be repaid.

APPLICATION PROCESS

All law schools require that the financial information necessary to determine financial need be submitted to a national processing center. Most schools use the Free Application for Federal Student Aid (FAFSA). See *http://www. fafsa.ed.gov/.*

The FAFSA should be filed online as early as possible, and in any event prior to the FAFSA Priority Deadline, which was February 15 in 2012. Processing time for the FAFSA is approximately four to six weeks. Read the forms carefully and answer all required parts. After the FAFSA has been analyzed, a report will be sent to the schools you have designated.

When the law school financial aid office receives your report generated by the FAFSA, it will review your file in accordance with its packaging policy. This means that the expected student contribution will be subtracted from the school budget to arrive at financial need.

Some schools' packaging policies will require that the first level of need be met by the Stafford loan. If there is any remaining need, you may be eligible for Perkins loan funds and Federal Work Study. After the financial aid office determines your level of eligibility for aid, you will receive notification. This may be four to six weeks or longer after the receipt of the FAFSA report.

The loan applications must be completed, signed, and returned to the lender. If a credit report is required, it is done at this time. If the lender/guarantee agency approves your loan, the check will be disbursed. The approval process can take up to six weeks. For most loans the interest starts to accrue when the check is disbursed. In most cases the check will be made co-payable to the student and the law school. When the check arrives, you will be asked to endorse it, and then the school will endorse it and credit it to your account. If the amount credited is more than is owed, the school will process a refund check for you.

DEFERMENT

It is possible to defer repayment on student loans you received as an undergraduate as long as you are a full-time student. You should request deferment forms from your lender. Take these forms to the registrar at your law school. Federal regulations require that you be a matriculated student so these forms will not be signed and sent to your lender until after the semester starts.

It is important to file deferment forms and to know if they have to be filed annually with your lender. If you are not granted a deferment, don't make payments on your undergraduate loans, and are declared in default, you run the risk of being denied loans for your legal education.

REPAYMENT AND CONSOLIDATION

While the money is available to finance your legal education, ultimately it must be repaid. You will have to start making payments six to nine months after graduation. There are several different ways to repay a Federal Direct Loan.

A Standard Repayment Plan has a fixed monthly repayment amount for a fixed period of time, usually 10 years.

An Extended Repayment Plan has a lower fixed monthly payment amount, and loan repayment can be extended beyond the usual 10 years.

A Graduated Repayment Plan usually begins with lower monthly payments, and payment amounts increase at specified times. Payments may be for the usual 10-year period, or they may be extended beyond 10 years.

An Income-contingent Repayment Plan for Direct Stafford loans sets annual repayment amounts based on the borrower's income after leaving school. The loan is repaid over an extended period of time, not to exceed 25 years.

College Cost Reduction and Access Act was enacted in September 2007, creating a new loan forgiveness option for borrowers who hold public service jobs. To qualify for the public service loan forgiveness, a borrower must:

- Make 120 qualifying monthly payments on an elegibile Federal Direct Loan on or after October 1, 2007.
- Be employed in a public service job as defined in the CCRAA during the time he or she makes the qualifying monthly payments.
- Be employed in a public service job as defined in the CCRAA at the time the Secretary of Education forgives the loan.
- Make qualifying payments under one (or a combination of) the following:
  - Income contingent repayment plan
  - Income-based repayment plan
  - Standard repayment play with a 10-year repayment period
  - One of the other Direct Loan repayment plans under which the borrower paid a monthly amount that is not less than what the borrower would pay under a 10-year repayment plan.

To find out more information, please visit *http://www.nasfaa.org/PDFs/2007/FAQPublic.pdf.*

by Angela D'Agostino and Cathy Alexander, adapted from the original article by Christine A. Koterba, Director of Financial Aid, Widener University School of Law.

CHAPTER 9

What Should I Expect in Law School?

THE LAW SCHOOL CALENDAR

No two people are the same. A key to your success in law school will be your ability to channel the skills you already have into a new educational program, while building new skills that will serve you in the future as a lawyer. It may help you to understand what is happening during the first year of law school by looking at the law school calendar. Although every law school is slightly different from all the others, in many respects they are all much the same. Virtually every law school in the United States models its curriculum, particularly in the first year, after the socratic system promulgated at Harvard Law School in the 1870s. Although legal education has evolved in the past century, the general comment in this chapter will be substantially descriptive of your law school.

Orientation

Law school starts with orientation. Orientation is designed to introduce you to the law school community (and some would say to lull you into a false sense of security about the upcoming ten months). The first step is check-in. Check-in is run by the Admissions Office, and you will be greeted by the smiling countenance of the admissions officer who recruited you or dealt with you during the admissions process. The Admissions Office will want to make sure that you have paid your tuition, that your financial aid is in order, and that your registration is complete. Depending on how check-in is organized, you may or may not have to wait in a long line. If the line is long, it generally portends three to four years of the same thing.

After checking in, and grabbing a cup of hot coffee, you will proceed to an auditorium where you will be subjected to a series of speeches you will not remember. You will hear from the dean, some associate deans, assistant deans,

the financial aid officer, placement director, student bar president, law review editor, moot court board chair, head of security, and other administrators and students too numerous to name. They will all tell you how glad they are to see you, how talented you all are, and how their doors will always be open. You will never see most of them again. While most schools have abandoned the tactic, a few of them may still use the old "Look to the right of you; look to the left of you; one of you won't be here next August." The truth is, 90–95 percent of those who enter law school eventually will graduate.

After this convocation, you may be given a tour of the facilities, including the law library, by engaging upperclass students just dying to tell you what law school is "really like." You also may be solicited by various student organizations; they will all be around and still anxious for your membership after the first year.

ORIENTATION CHECKLIST

___Admissions
   ___College transcripts (if needed)
   ___Identification
___Financial aid (if applicable)
___Registrar—class schedule
___Bursar—bring checkbook if not prepaid
___Course assignments
___Bookstore
___Parking Sticker
___Locker
___ID photo
___Law school tour
___Find out who is "The Dean"
___Nearby food
___Library carrel (if available)

One of your first lessons in law school will be to separate the wheat from the chaff. Find out where the assignments are posted. Find out how you can sign up for a locker. Learn to recognize The Dean by sight. (There are many deans, but only one Dean.)

At many schools, class assignments for the first day are posted prior to orientation. An assignment sheet for each class will also tell you what books to buy for the course so you can go to the law school bookstore and pick up your books before the crowds arrive. Don't wait until school has started to obtain your books and start reading.

First Classes

Unlike classes in undergraduate school, the first classes in law school are generally real classes. The professor may simply walk in and call on a student for the first case. She may give a short speech on what will be expected of you in her course before turning to the cases. Or she may provide a background lecture for most of the first hour. It is likely that the professor will not simply say, "Hello, I'm Professor Jones. Your assignment for Tuesday will be to read the first 30 pages in the book. I'll see you Tuesday." During the first class, the professor may present certain special rules such as the maximum number of class cuts you are allowed, the number of times you may be unprepared before being dropped from the course, what the final exam will be like, what her office hours will be, what outside materials (hornbooks, treatises, etc.) you should read. Such information is important to know.

Such works as *One L* and *The Paper Chase* probably have instilled a sense of fear in the minds of many beginning law students. In reality, not all law professors are as intimidating as Professor Kingsfield, although the terror and alienation described there are very accurate.

You will find yourself in a lecture hall with roughly one hundred more or less equally frightened souls. Your sense of anonymity and privacy will be invaded by the seemingly all-knowing professor armed with a seating chart and an uncanny ability to identify the least prepared student in the class to discuss the case at hand.

During the first week of classes, you will learn the ground rules. Let there be no doubt about it: This is the lions versus the Christians, and regardless of your religious affiliation, you and your classmates are the Christians.

Also, during the first week, you will be introduced to the subject matter to be covered in each course, the professor's unique philosophy of legal education, a new language called legalese, and those ponderous, pictureless tomes called casebooks.

You will also begin to get acquainted with your fellow law students. You may meet a few individuals whom you come to know as real people. Most of your classmates will fall into one of two groups: the nameless faces who fill the classroom and the ones who, by virtue of having been called on or volunteered to speak in class, are identified by name (as in "Mr. Simon, who sits in the first row in Torts"). Custom dictates that you use last names to identify students (as in "Ms. Miller" or "Mr. Musser") and you refer to the teacher as "Professor" or "Dean" as appropriate.

You may encounter some upperclass students who offer with a certain patronizing smugness to teach you the tricks of the trade. A healthy sense of skepticism about the value or motives of such advice is a good sign that you will eventually become a successful lawyer.

Routine

After the first week of classes, you will begin to establish a pattern in each course, and a timetable for your entire life. The reading will average between 10 and 30 pages per night, per class. You may find that the progress in some of the classes is painfully slow, with the professor covering only a portion of the assigned reading each time. Some classes may move along at an almost military clip of three to four cases per class, no matter what. During the first few weeks, you will find yourself spending an inordinate amount of time briefing cases, attempting to fathom the classroom discussion, and wondering secretly if someone in the admissions office hadn't screwed up by sending you an acceptance letter. You will wonder with increasing frequency whether you screwed up in deciding to come to law school. During this phase of school, you may wonder why everyone else in the class but you seems to know what is going on.

When I was in law school, there was a guy named Holtzman, and although Holtzman was only three or four years older than most of the rest of us, it seemed that in every class he had some personal experience relating to the case. If the case involved shoes, he had been in the shoe business; if the case involved clothes, he had been in the clothing business; if the case involved doctors, he had been in the medical business.

Other students will amaze you with their seeming ability to converse freely with the professor in legalese, whereas you find yourself stuck at the *Bonjour Jean* stage. But you will derive hope from the fact that some students' comments will seem totally inane to you, reassuring you that you must be smarter than *someone* in the class. And you will find a wicked satisfaction in seeing a handful of students whose hands are always in the air given their comeuppance by the professor. In every class, there will be at least one individual who, no matter how bloodied by the fray, will keep coming back for more. A pack psychology will come to dominate the class and seek to drive out the weak or the deviant. By mid-semester, the fear of embarrassment in front of the class will inhibit all but the most fearless souls from making rash statements. This mentality is typified by graffito on a bathroom stall at one law school: "After the sixth week of class, if you don't know who the class jerk is, it's you."

These pressures to conform may dissuade some students from ever participating in class discussions unless specifically required to do so by the professor. By laughing at a fellow student, you help to create an environment where one day others may laugh at you.

As the semester wears on, the professor comes to be viewed not so much as a god, but as a common enemy. You learn that the classroom routine is a game the teacher always wins. You learn that the stupidest answers have some value, and you begin to recognize that even the most articulate students really don't know much more than you do. When you come to this realization, you will have reached another milestone in your law school journey.

The Wall

Somewhere between the tenth and twelfth week of classes you will hit the wall. It is during this period that some students actually drop out of school; virtually every student at least contemplates that possibility. By this time in the semester, your work is piling up, final exams are just around the corner, and you still don't have a clue what you need to know. At this point, when your psychological and physical resources are drained, you will wonder if you can possibly survive for two and a half or three and a half more years. It is critical when you hit the wall to press on. It may help during this period to talk to a sympathetic professor, mentor, or counselor. Family and loved ones, who up until now have been totally supportive, will seem to become part of the problem. Prelaw school friends may find that you have changed, and you may find yourself increasingly irritated that they never see the issue.

Panic

By about the thirteenth week of the semester, you will have no time to worry about such self-indulgent psychological concerns, because finals will be upon you. Some professors, in what is variously perceived as a last minute attempt to catch up with the syllabus or a final effort to break your backs, will increase the reading assignments to two or three times what they were at the beginning of the semester. A full-scale panic attack may threaten to debilitate you before the first test. Somehow, you will survive.

First Semester Finals

At last, final examinations will arrive. As a rule, law school exams average one hour of exam for each credit hour of class. The amount of material you will have to study will be immense. Whole parts of some courses may be incomprehensible when you go back to review them. When you walk out of these exams, your head will feel as if Evander Holyfield had used it as a punching bag. You will have no idea how well you did, but if you thought the test was easy, you probably missed something really big.

Semester Break

Semester break is the time when you regroup. Immediately after your last exam, your impulse will be to engage in the most hedonistic activity possible. Many will actually succumb to this impulse. Next, you will sleep for two days. Then, you will engage in mindless activity such as watching soap operas or football games, reading trashy novels, attending holiday parties, or vegging out with your family. If you are an evening student, you may not have the luxury of all of this R & R. However, to the extent possible, you should try to get away from both school and work for a while.

Toward the end of semester break, you will begin to think about law school again. You may do some reading for class. You may reflect about how you will avoid making the same mistakes you did the first semester. You will rush madly to clear up loose ends in your personal life, in order to give yourself time to devote your full attention to law school.

Renewed Hope

The second semester is better in some ways, and worse in others. It is better in that you know the ropes. You have a better picture of what to expect. You have a clearer idea of what it will take to succeed. On the other hand, the workload will pick up even more. The professors will take off at the same pace they ended the previous semester. In addition, at many schools a required moot court problem will swallow the bulk of your free time.

The January Blues

During January (and sometimes February or March) first semester grades will be posted. The wait for grades may be agonizing. The actual knowledge of your grades may be worse. Most students are disappointed in some or all of their marks. You learn how fast the track really is. Unfortunately, many students do not handle this experience well. They go into a depression from which they do not escape until after the bar exam. Although there is no grade for it, your grade point average may depend on your ability to bounce back psychologically and to learn from this experience.

Falling Behind

In all but the warmest climates, the arrival of spring will bring the last great temptation of the school year. When the flowers begin to bloom and warm winds touch the land, sitting in a law school classroom will not be your first choice of activities. Spring break may help but chances are good that you will fall behind in your reading and studying. If you are not careful, you could find yourself in the proverbial hot water.

The Mad Rush

As March dissolves into April, you will once again find yourself staring at final exams. If you have been diligent, you will simply experience anxiety about finishing the year on a high note; if you find yourself hopelessly behind your schedule, you will be working feverishly to catch up. The last two weeks of school will pass quickly, and your first year will be almost over.

Finals Again

Final exams in the spring will probably not seem as daunting. The experience will be the same as in the fall, but this time you will be more prepared for it mentally. The amount of work you cover in these exams will be more prodigious than in the fall. But the skills you have developed during the course of the year will make the load seem more manageable. This time, when finals are over, you will just go home, have dinner with friends, and go on about your business.

Over a period of 36 weeks, more or less, you will have been transformed from an ordinary person into a budding lawyer. Whether you want it or not, like it or not, or need it or not, you will never be the same again. The process is in some ways like marine boot camp, taking apart whatever you were before you arrived and rebuilding it into a new person. Whatever other criticisms of law school one might make, it certainly cannot be said that the program does not work.

LAW SCHOOL COURSES

The curricula at most American law schools are comparable. In fact, the first year law school curriculum has not changed appreciably in the past one hundred years. At the same time, there are minor variations in course offerings from school to school, reflecting differences in educational philosophy and institutional tradition.

Most law school courses are offered as 2-, 3-, or 4-semester-hour courses. Full-time first year students take five or six courses for a total of 15–16 credit hours; part-time students generally take one or two fewer courses and 10–11 hours. At some schools, grades are based on an entire year's work for 4- to 6-hour courses. You will study some, if not all, of the following courses during the first year of law school. Some schools will defer certain courses until the second year or not require them at all.

Torts

The word tort comes from an old French term meaning wrong. Torts as a law school subject area refers to a series of legal actions and remedies against wrongdoers for injuries sustained. Torts fall into three broad groups: *intentional torts* where an actor intends conduct that causes injury to another; *negligence torts* where an actor owing a duty to act with reasonable care toward another breaches that duty and causes injury resulting in damages; and *strict liability torts* where an actor causes injury to another without fault or intent but is held liable for policy reasons. You will study a number of distinct tort actions, including assault, battery, false imprisonment, and intentional infliction of emotional distress; negligence actions; misrepresentation; defamation; products liability; and privacy.

Property

The Property course deals with the rights associated with the ownership of property. In the beginning of the course you will probably discuss the origins of property rights in Anglo-American law. You will study such tantalizing questions as who owns the rights to the meteorite: the farmer in whose field it fell or the guy walking down the road who saw it fall? Some of us are still trying to figure that one out. A small portion of the course is devoted to the law of personal property, but the bulk of the year will involve issues relating to real property, or land. In the first semester, you will devote considerable time to basic concepts such as estates in land, transferability of land, and title. Some time during the year you will learn about future interests, those medieval devices for controlling the ownership of land beyond the life of the owner. In the second semester, you will deal with more modern concepts such as easements, zoning, and land use planning.

Contracts

Contracts involves the study of the body of law governing the making and breaking of agreements. You will learn what it takes to create a binding contract with another party. You will spend considerable time discussing what happens when one of the parties breaks its promises, or breaches the contract. You will learn about liquidated damages, specific performance, express and implied warranties, and unilateral contracts. Much of the course will deal with the development of contracts in the commercial setting, including the "battle of forms" and substitution of statutory law in the form of the Uniform Commercial Code for the common law in many situations.

Civil Procedure

Civil Procedure refers to the rules by which the civil courts operate. Most Civ Pro instructors utilize the Federal Rules of Civil Procedure in teaching their courses. Some of the course may touch upon historical material, such as the evolution of the English forms of action into the rules of procedure of today. Most of your time will be spent looking at such concepts as jurisdiction (including subject matter, personal, and diversity), standing, discovery, pleading, appeal, summary judgments, and numerous other provisions of the Rules. A substantial part of the course will address the Erie problem. The case of *Erie Railroad v. Tompkins* held that the federal courts, while applying federal procedural rules, must apply the substantive common law of the state. The ripples from this seemingly simple rule have extended far beyond the original case and have engrossed generations of judges, law professors, legal writers, and students (perhaps *engrossed* is too strong a word for the student response).

Constitutional Law

Many law schools require Constitutional Law during the first year. As the name suggests, Con Law deals with the enforcement of rights and duties established under the United States Constitution. Because there are so many constitutional issues, no two professors will emphasize exactly the same topics. You will look at some fundamental problems such as jurisdiction and standing, separation of powers, the commerce clause, and the privileges and immunities clause. You will deal with cases arising under the first, fifth, and fourteenth amendments as well as others. Perhaps most importantly, you will study the decision-making process in the United States Supreme Court from Chief Justice Marshall's power grab of judicial review in *Marbury v. Madison* to Chief Justice Rehnquist's reshaping the direction of the court in the 1980s.

Criminal Law

Criminal Law is the law of crimes. For a good portion of this course, you will grapple with concepts such as intent, *mens rea,* and lesser included offenses. You will learn the basic elements of crimes you have known about all your life, and a few you have never heard of before. You will study such issues as the right to trial by jury, double jeopardy, the state's burden of proof, and conspiracy.

Professional Responsibility

Although most law schools offer Professional Responsibility during the last year of law school, some require it during the second year, and a few the first. Professional Responsibility deals with the ethical obligations of the lawyer in representing clients. A few of the subjects you will cover in this course are: lawyer/client confidentiality, conflicts of interest, legal fees, advertising and solicitation of business, fitness to practice law, lawyer discipline, and candor to the tribunal. In a broader sense, however, professional responsibility addresses the role of the legal profession in society. What is a lawyer anyway? Are there limits on his or her conduct?

Is law a business, a profession, or both? What is the role of the Bar Association? Can one be a good lawyer and a good person at the same time?

Legal Writing

At every law school, there is a course known by a variety of names, but with a general aim of teaching you how to conduct legal research, draft legal briefs and memoranda, prepare and make oral arguments, and gain an understanding of a legal system. These courses are often much maligned by first-year students, but revered by lawyers who come to know the value of the skills they learned in that course. Legal Writing frequently requires a time commitment out of proportion with the amount of credit received. An important consideration during the course of the school year will be your ability to allocate time to Legal Writing in accordance with its relative importance and credit weight, and not to set aside work in other classes for research, writing, and advocacy projects.

THE PROFESSORS

Law students develop a special relationship with their first year teachers. It is not uncommon to experience a love/hate relationship with these professors. Later in law school you will wonder how you placed some of these individuals on such high pedestals. During the first semester of law school they will be like gods—not necessarily in their perfection of appearance, but in their seeming knowledge and omnipotence.

Many of those who become law teachers attained their positions by having done very well academically in law school. Additionally, many of them enter the profession after having served as judicial clerks for the United States Supreme Court or other prestigious tribunals. Increasingly, today, law teachers have some experience in the practice of law. They come from large law firms, corporations, and government agencies. All of them have made an affirmative decision to pursue a career in education, rather than one in a traditional area of law practice. Professors who worked in large law firms or possess more than a few years of experience probably have taken a considerable cut in pay to enter the teaching field. Although law professors as a group have a higher median income than the average of all lawyers, they probably could make more money doing something else.

THE STUDENTS

Classmates

Your classmates can be allies as well as foes during your struggle to master the first year of law school. They can help you to cope in a number of different ways. First, they can help you with assignments. If you happen to miss a class, you need to find someone whose notes you can review. If your own notes have gaps, you may be able to fill them with the help of someone else. If reading assignments or case citations are unclear, you should identify one or more people to call. Even though law school is a competitive environment, most students are willing to help out in this way, as long as their generosity is not abused.

You may study with one of more other students from time to time. Informal small group discussions are common even among students who do not organize formal study groups. In law school, a great amount of learning takes place outside the classroom, and to the extent that your out-of-class conversations are discussions begun during class, the learning process will continue.

If you have ever been to the zoo, you may recall watching a pride of lions or other large cats. The young ones will tussle and play endlessly. Sometimes Mom or Dad will play too, letting the kittens attack and snarl and slap. You know that the older cat can send the kittens flying with a flick of the paw, but they play along until they get bored. You know that the kittens are learning skills they will need as adults in the wild, and the big cats are helping in the process. You also know that the kittens learn from their mock battles with each other just as they do from Mom and Dad. In law school, the professors take on the role of the big cats, and you as kittens should learn from them. However, you should remember that you learn from the rest of the litter as well.

Your classmates can provide an outlet from the pressures of law school. Whether it involves coffee in the morning, eating lunch or dinner, exercising or working out, or partying, you need to socialize from time to time. Those of you who are married to people unconnected with the legal profession, and those who have jobs in nonlegal settings may find it less difficult to break away from law school psychologically. On the other hand, it may be more difficult to find the time to get to know your classmates socially. If you don't want your families and coworkers to despise you because you talk about law all the time, you should try to make some time to get to know your fellow law students in a social setting.

There is an insidious downside to developing relationships with your classmates. Several caveats are in order. Law school is very competitive. Some students will help no one. Some students will promise help, but fail to deliver. Some will take far more than they give. Always remember that the admissions committee did not pick the first year class on the basis of integrity. Although you will meet some of the most honest and honorable people you could hope to know, you may also encounter others who would stoop to any depth to get ahead, and use any means to reach a desired end. Most of you will conclude that you are unwilling to lie, cheat, and steal in order to succeed in law school. Do not be so naive as to believe that everyone feels the same. Beware of the snakes in the grass, and pick your friends carefully.

Your classmates can exert considerable pressure not to succeed. A collective striving for mediocrity may seem to be the norm. Those who study too much, talk too often in class, or don't get into the law school social scene may be branded as outsiders. You have had to deal with similar peer pressure since grade school. The point here is that the pressure to conform does not end in law school. You may have seen the gopher game at the boardwalk or midway. In this game, the gopher pops his head out of one of the number of round holes while the player, wielding a mallet, tries to knock him back into the hole again. If you imagine that the class is the midway player ready to knock down any gopher who has the audacity to stick his head up above the crowd, you get the picture.

One way the group may push you toward mediocrity is by encouraging you to socialize. Although occasional social activity is beneficial, too much can be the kiss of death. When study sessions deteriorate into bull sessions like you had when you were a freshman in college, when quick lunches extend into afternoon shopping trips, when an occasional class party becomes an evening ritual, then you will know you have exceeded the bounds of moderation.

Some semblance of self-discipline in the area of time management is absolutely essential. You must decide how much time you are willing to devote to personal and social activities, and live with that decision.

Socializing with other students can take on a more serious note: emotional involvement through love and dependency. Guess what? Law students fall in love. They fall in love with each other and with nonlaw students. It would be futile to say: "Don't fall in love." However, if you do, you will find yourself in turmoil. When you fall in love, your lover tends to become (at least during early stages of infatuation) all-important in your life. Unfortunately, so does law school. Justice Holmes once remarked that the law is a jealous mistress. This conflict appears in the play *Phantom of the Opera.* Christine, the heroine, is torn between her physical relationship with the Vicomte de Chegny and her passion to excel in her career represented by her relationship with the Phantom. It is interesting to note that the author of the book, Gaston Leroux, was himself a lawyer and may have understood the conflict in terms of the law.

A second dangerous emotional involvement is to buy into someone else's problems to the detriment of your own studies. Law students are not immune from the vagaries of life. Some of your friends will have serious problems while they are in school. The stress of law school may compound their anxiety. Some may turn to you to serve as an emotional crutch. In fact, some students are like magnets for those with problems. Lest your friend's difficulties drag you down, the best thing you can do is to get them to go to someone who can really help.

Upperclass Students

When you arrive at law school, you will find a place already populated by students who have gone before you. These upperclass students will be ready and willing to regale you with tales of their own experiences in the first year, to give you the inside scoop on all the profs, and to share the definitive answers on what you need to do to get ahead. Some of them will want you to join their organizations, come to their parties, or buy their old books. They may seem like the smug but grizzled veterans joined in the field by some new recruits in the standard war movie: "Don't worry, kid; I'll show you what you need to do to get out of this place alive." Of course, in the movies, the guy who says that always seems to get killed.

The lesson to learn is to take everything you hear with a grain of salt. You will find out information that is useful. Every law school has a grapevine, and the news, if not always accurate, is at least entertaining. Some of your sources may prove better than others. So use what you can and discard the rest.

Consider the motivation of the upperclass student who offers advice. Is this someone who just likes being a big shot? Someone who needs reaffirmation for his or her own decisions in law school (even if those choices have produced a record of mediocrity)? Someone who would like to ask you out? (Yes, this goes on in law school like everywhere else!) Someone who wants to sell you something (bar reviews, books, bar association memberships)? You do not have to shun all these people, just remember that they want something in return for their information. (In the words of Hannibal Lecter from *The Silence of the Lambs,* "Quid pro quo, Clarice.")

While casual advice should be approached with skepticism, it might be valuable to look for an upperclass mentor. Such a person might well be someone who has similar interests, career aspirations, problems, or background. For example, a first year student with young children at home might encounter an upperclass student who has gone through the same experience and survived. A mentor might be someone you happen to meet and become friendly with during the course of the year. Some schools even offer programs that assign upperclass mentors to first year students. However it occurs that a true mentoring relationship develops, take advantage of it.

A mentor can help to guide you through the law school maze, talk to you when you are down, share your joy when you are flush with success, and set an example for you to follow. Mentoring relationships are built upon a foundation of common interest, molded by walls of trust, and covered by a protective roof of the experience of the mentor for the student. Mentoring relationships are common in the legal profession, not only in law school but in practice as well. To the extent that you find a good mentor, you will discover that the law school experience is a more palatable one.

THE LAW SCHOOL CULTURE

Rules and Procedures

Law school culture is unique, created in part by the intense experience of those involved, and in part by the insular setting of the law school itself. Because most law students did not attend undergraduate school at the university where they attend law school, they tend to have limited interaction with the university community generally. The law school on many campuses is set apart on the edge of campus or on a separate campus altogether. Some law schools are not connected with an undergraduate university at all. There are advantages and disadvantages to attending an independent law school. Such a school can devote all its resources to the law students, but may lack the rich culture of a university setting.

There may be other differences about the physical location or layout of the law building(s) that make the law school environment unique. Does the law school share its campus with undergrads or graduate students? Does the law school share space with other departments? Are law school facilities located in one building or several? The presence or absence of a nonlegal academic community affects not only the type and extent of extracurricular programs and activities, but also the sense of the law school as an insular institution.

In one sense, every law school is different, but in another sense, every law school is the same. Regardless of the idiosyncrasies of different law schools, the process of legal education is similar everywhere.

In this environment, a distinct law school culture has evolved. Law schools have their own student government (the Student Bar Association or SBA), activities, social events, intramurals, and newspapers. Some law schools even have their own yearbooks. At many law schools, the students put on an annual comedy show, generally making fun of the faculty in a singular effort to even the score for a year's worth of abuse.

Within the law school culture, there are several common elements worth noting: First, rules and procedures take on a distinctly legal flavor. Announcements and information may be posted by the registrar, the Dean's Office, or teachers. You will be deemed to know what is in these notices by virtue of the doctrine of constructive notice. The upshot of this concept is that you have to watch out for announcements that pertain to you. The first example of constructive notice during your law school tenure will be the posting of class assignments on a wall or bulletin board prior to the beginning of classes. You will find very little hand-holding by law school teachers and administrators. Students who graduated from small intimate colleges may find this somewhat of a shock.

A second concept that permeates the rules and procedures is the notion of due process. Lawyers, more than those who are not trained in the law, tend to be aware of individual rights to hearings, representation, confrontation of accusers, and appeal. Most law schools operate under some code of conduct for dealing with academic dishonesty, as well as a code of academic standards to cover issues involving academic performance. Both sets of rules tend to focus heavily on due process and protection of the individual.

Another aspect of the law school culture is that it is a small world. The largest law school in the country has around 2,000 students; at most law schools the enrollment is no more than several hundred. The small size of the student body, combined with the nature of the educational process, means that students know much more about each other, law school affairs, and their professors than they did in all but the smallest undergraduate schools. Unlike your high school or college acquaintances, you will tend to maintain contact with many of your law school classmates throughout your career. At every law school there is a student grapevine, laden with information about everything from what courses to take, which firms to interview, to who is sleeping with whom. The old adage, "Believe a tenth of what you hear and half of what you see," is apropos.

Socializing and Breaks

You will find an abundance of opportunities for escape from law school studies in the form of parties and school-sponsored social events. During the year, there will be several receptions, mixers, and even a dance or two sponsored by the SBA. Many student organizations offer periodic social events for their members. And informal groups of students organize their own parties as a break from the grind of law school or meet at a local bar for drinks after class.

In fact, if you are interested, you can find a party almost every night. Unfortunately, partying leads you down a certain path of self-destruction in law school. Everyone needs an occasional break from study; however, the occasional break can easily become a regular habit. The party scene can become an escape from law school pressures generally, and may shift your values away from learning.

If you were a party animal in college, it may be difficult to break out of old patterns. Unfortunately, most of us cannot get by with the same antics we did in undergraduate school. In law school one all-nighter will not save a semester of neglect.

Law school provides abundant breaks between and during semesters. You will probably have two weeks or more between the end of first semester exams and the start of spring semester classes. Most schools provide a spring break midway through the second semester. And, of course, summers are open.

Students usually use breaks during the year either to get away for a vacation or to get ahead in their work. Sometimes you may not have a choice. If you decide to vacation, leave your guilt at home. If you take your books with you, plan and make time to study. If you have no time to study, do not make a pretense of it by surrounding yourself with symbols of law school while doing nothing to further your cause.

Summer vacation is another matter. Here are 12 to 14 weeks that you can utilize in a variety of different ways. How you choose to spend your summer vacation will have an impact, one way or the other, on your legal education.

A large percentage of law students work for legal employers during the summer. Although it is harder for them to find positions, many first year students take this option, even if they have to work for free. For some students, it is necessary to work in high paying nonlegal jobs in order to earn enough to come back to school the next year.

Many students go to summer school, at their institution or abroad. You may find, however, that you are so burned out that you simply want to relax. And some students do just that after the first year. If you want to travel, this might be the time to do it, before you take your first job.

Competition

A final note about the law school culture is that it is competitive. Entrance to law school was competitive; law school itself is competitive; and law practice by its nature is competitive. Your relationships with other students will be colored by competition. Ironically, many students try to deny the competitive nature of the process. They will say to each other that grades don't matter. They will ostracize fellow students who appear too competitive. They may deny to other students that they study as much as they do. On the other hand, competitiveness can go too far. In all likelihood, before you graduate from law school, you will hear about at least one cheating incident at your school. You will see other examples, such as library books being misshelved by unscrupulous students. If you should be tempted, it's not worth it. In the 1988 presidential campaign, a law school indiscretion may have cost one candidate the nomination for the presidency of the United States.

CHAPTER 10

What Are the Career Opportunities in Law?

Although it may seem quite early to begin to think about employment after law school, many prelaw students ask themselves whether they will find employment after investing thousands of dollars in a legal education. The simple answer is that most law students find employment when they graduate. Traditionally, this number has been about 90% about nine months after graduation, based on surveys conducted by NALP since the early 1970s. Some years were slightly better and other years worse than this benchmark, but it was a reliable measure of graduates' chances of employment. The surveys did not indicate how many law school graduates found employment after a year or eighteen months, or how many settled for a job that was not their choice, or how many accepted nonlegal or temporary jobs waiting for the right opportunity to come along. As the job market for lawyers collapsed after 2008, the overall employment rate for the Class of 2011 dropped to 85.6%. Only 65.4% accepted positions that required a law degree, and less than half went to work for law firms, according to NALP. No one kept statistics before the 1970s, so no one knows what it was like during the Great Depression of the 1930s, but 2011 was certainly one of the worst years ever. The simple truth remains, however, that over the past 3–5 years, most law school graduates found work, if not always in law, at least in areas where their legal training is useful, a record that far surpasses almost all other professions.

Students understand that the choice of law schools has an impact on the career choices they ultimately make. The school's reputation, geographic location, substantive curriculum, and many other factors go into determining what opportunities are most likely to be available to its graduates. For instance, law schools in the Washington, DC area typically have more graduates go to work for the federal government than law schools in other areas. Law schools with specialty programs may have a disproportionate number of graduates pursue careers in the specialty field.

First year law students are often surprised to discover that after spending considerable time and energy making a career choice to go to law school, they are now called upon to make additional career choices about what to do with their law degree. Law is practiced in many different ways and many different settings. Some legally trained individuals never practice law at all, but use their legal training in a variety of other fields.

A career counselor at your law school will be able to help you make decisions about your legal career. Although career services for law students may vary from school to school, most law schools employ full-time professionals who possess either a counseling or law degree (or both) to work with law students in developing career plans. Law professors may be able to help, not only with advising, but also with information about contacts and recommendations. The chart beginning on page 85 provides an overview of the career services of the law schools included in this guide. For a more extensive discussion of the career opportunities for law graduates and the career planning process, see Gary A. Munneke and Ellen Wayne, *The Legal Career Guide: From Law Student to Lawyer*, American Bar Association (2008). You cannot begin too early to start reflecting on career issues.

WORK DURING LAW SCHOOL

Many law students work in legal or law-related jobs while they are in law school. Still others will work in nonlegal jobs that lead them to legal jobs in the area of business where they were working, or into a totally alternative career. Many law students work in law firms, corporate law departments, or government law offices. These positions may be full-time or part-time, and they may be summer jobs, work during the school year, or permanent positions.

Many larger firms, government agencies, and corporate legal departments offer summer internship or clerkship programs as part of a formal recruiting process. These positions tend to be highly competitive, and hiring for them may be heavily influenced by academic performance in law school and the prestige of the law school attended. Many of the organizations that sponsor these summer programs use them as a tool to help make permanent hiring decisions. It is worth noting, however, that these organizations represent only a small percentage of the legal job market.

Even in law firms and other employers that do not regularly recruit on campus for summer clerks or permanent associates, it is common for students who work in these organizations during law school to accept positions there when they graduate. If they do not ultimately stay with the organization where they have worked, the experience they gain is still very likely to impress other employers with whom they apply. This kind of hands-on training is an excellent counterbalance to the more esoteric experience of law school.

Types of Employment

Law school graduates accept jobs in a variety of settings. The largest numbers go to work in private law firms. These firms provide legal services to clients for profit. The owners of the firms may be individual lawyers, practitioners, organizations of several hundred partners, or anything in between. In addition to the partners/owners, law firms also employ salaried junior lawyers or associates. Some of these associates may eventually become partners in the firm; some may remain as permanent associates or staff attorneys; and some may leave the firm to find other employment or start their own practices. Most attorneys practice in small firms of no more than 2–10 attorneys. The percentage of lawyers in private practice has decreased from around 80 percent in 1950 to around 65 percent today. It is important to remember that only 35 percent of all lawyers do not engage in the private practice of law.

Between 2008–2011, as the U.S. economy deteriorated, law firms faced economic challenges as well. Although some practice areas like bankruptcy and collections grew, other areas of practice, including corporate law declined. As clients faced uncertain times, there was less legal work to go around and fewer resources available to pay lawyers for their services. The popular legal press was filled with stories of law firms that closed their doors, of reduced partner compensation, of cuts in associate salaries, and the rescinding of job offers already made. Some

firms even gave newly-hired lawyers a sabbatical at reduced pay because there just was not enough work to keep them busy. The downturn drama has leveled off a bit over the past year but economic challenges remain.

Clearly, job opportunities for law school graduates over the past few years have not been as good as they had been in prior years. The legal job market has always been very resilient, and as the economy recovers, work for lawyers will expand, and job opportunities will increase. A law degree is a very versatile education, which means that law graduates can and do find work in a variety of different settings (See Gary A. Munneke, William D. Henslee, and Ellen Wayne, *Nonlegal Careers for Lawyers*, American Bar Association, 2007). Historically, as the legal job market constricts, law graduates and lawyers consider and are able to use their legal skills in organizations outside the practice of law, and this recession is no exception.

Many lawyers go into other lines of work outside the practice of law altogether, having never gone into law, or having left the practice at some time during their careers. Some of these people may simply want a law degree to supplement other qualifications they have. Others may become enticed by personal dreams or business deals along the way. Some, unfortunately, discover after going to law school and practicing law that they are not happy with the career choices they have made and leave the practice of law for greener pastures. The ranks of these legal expatriates are filled with entrepreneurs, athletes, writers, correspondents, inventors, entertainers, restaurateurs, and even a prominent wine critic. A list of well-known personalities who are also lawyers would surprise most people.

The National Association for Law Placement keeps and reports on employment statistics for American law schools (See http://www.nalp.org). An annual employment and salary survey is taken of each graduating class about nine months after graduation; because many legal employers do not make hiring decisions until after bar exam results are released and graduates are licensed to practice, the reporting delay produces a more accurate picture than a survey at the time of graduation. Nevertheless, the classes of 2008 through 2010 reflect the national economic downturn.

The breakdown for private practice shows that 50.9 percent of the law school graduates in 2010 entered private practice, down from a high of 64.3 percent some fifteen years earlier. A very small percentage of law students actually open

(*go to page 111*)

THE JOB OUTLOOK

SCHOOL	CAREER SERVICES — Facilities: Law Placement Office	University Placement Office	Services: Employment Counseling	Job Openings Information	Solo Practice Advice	Resume Preparation	Interview Counseling	Employment Planning	Job Interviews Arrangement	Law, Corporate, and Government Contact	Alumni Contacts	Part-Time/Summer Employment	Internships	Alumni Placement	PLACEMENT RECORD — Placement Within 6 to 9 Months	Private Practice 2-10 Attorneys	Private Practice 11-25 Attorneys	Private Practice 26-50 Attorneys	Private Practice 51-100 Attorneys	Judicial Clerkships	Government	Business/Industry	Public Interest	Military	Academic	Other	Average Starting Salary
Albany Law School 80 New Scotland Avenue, Albany, NY 12208, 518-445-2326, Fax: 518-445-2369, admissions@albanylaw.edu	•		•	•	•	•	•	•	•	•	•	•	•	•	91%	24	8	5		9	4	23	5			20	$32,500-$175,000
American University (Washington College of Law) 4801 Massachusetts Avenue, N.W., Washington, DC 20016-8186, 202-274-4101, Fax: 202-274-4107, wcladmit@wcl.american.edu	•		•	•		•	•	•	•	•	•	•	•	•	84%	11	4	2	2	12	21	18	13	3	1	15	$42,250-$160,000
Appalachian School of Law P.O. Box 2825, Grundy, VA 24614, 276-935-4349, Fax: 276-935-8496, nprult@asl.edu	•		•	•	•	•	•	•	•	•	•	•	•	•	64%	34	3			8	19	12	7			5	$26,000-$68,000
Arizona State University (Sandra Day O'Connor College of Law) 1100 S. McAllister Ave. - Box 877906, Tempe, AZ 85287-7906, 480-965-1474, Fax: 480-727-7930, chitra.demania@asu.edu			•	•	•	•	•	•	•	•	•	•	•	•	98%	31	6	2	3	7	13	14	8	1	4		$50,000-$125,000
Atlanta's John Marshall Law School 1422 W. Peachtree St., NW, Atlanta, GA 30309, 404-872-3593, Fax: 404-873-3802, admissions@johnmarshall.edu		•	•	•		•	•	•	•	•	•	•	•	•	94%	70					11	13	3		3		
Ave Maria School of Law 3475 Plymouth Road, Ann Arbor, MI 48105, 734-827-8063, Fax: 734-622-0123, info@avemarialaw.edu	•		•	•	•	•	•	•	•	•	•	•	•	•	74%	19	8	2	5	17	14	24	3		2	6	$46,300-$60,000
Barry University (School of Law) 6441 East Colonial Drive, Orlando, FL 32807, 321-206-5600, Fax: 321-206-5662, acruz@mail.barry.edu	•		•	•	•	•	•	•	•	•	•	•	•	•						1	15	16	7		3	58	

SCHOOL	AVERAGE STARTING SALARY	PLACEMENT RECORD — Percentage Breakdown of Type of Employer — OTHER	ACADEMIC	MILITARY	PUBLIC INTEREST	BUSINESS/INDUSTRY	GOVERNMENT	JUDICIAL CLERKSHIPS	PRIVATE PRACTICE 51-100 ATTORNEYS	PRIVATE PRACTICE 26-50 ATTORNEYS	PRIVATE PRACTICE 11-25 ATTORNEYS	PRIVATE PRACTICE 2-10 ATTORNEYS	PLACEMENT WITHIN 6 TO 9 MONTHS	CAREER SERVICES — Services — ALUMNI PLACEMENT	INTERNSHIPS	PART-TIME/SUMMER EMPLOYMENT	ALUMNI CONTACTS	LAW, CORPORATE, AND GOVERNMENT CONTACT	JOB INTERVIEWS ARRANGEMENT	EMPLOYMENT PLANNING	INTERVIEW COUNSELING	RESUME PREPARATION	SOLO PRACTICE ADVICE	JOB OPENINGS INFORMATION	EMPLOYMENT COUNSELING	Facilities — UNIVERSITY PLACEMENT OFFICE	LAW PLACEMENT OFFICE
Baylor University (School of Law) One Bear Place #97288, Waco, TX 76798-7288 254-710-1911 Fax: 254-710-2316 becky_beck@baylor.edu	$51,000-$93,122	17	2	1	1	10	12	10	3	8	11	25	98%	•	•	•	•	•	•	•	•	•	•	•	•	•	•
Boston College (Law School) 885 Centre Street, Newton, MA 02459 617-552-4351 Fax: 617-552-2917 bclawadm@bc.edu	$20,000-$160,000	38	6	2	6	9	11	15		2	2	10	91%	•	•	•	•	•	•	•	•	•	•	•	•		•
Boston University (School of Law) 765 Commonwealth Avenue, Boston, MA 02215 617-353-3100 Fax: 617-353-0578 bulawadm@bu.edu	$40,000-$175,000	58	14		5	8	8	8	1	2	2	8	87%	•	•	•	•	•	•	•	•	•	•	•	•		•
Brigham Young University (J. Reuben Clark Law School) 342 JRCB Brigham Young University, Provo, UT 84602 801-422-4277 Fax: 801-422-0389 kucharg@law.byu.edu	$30,000-$175,000	17	4	4	4	14	9	14	2	6	6	21	96%	•	•	•	•	•	•	•	•	•	•	•	•		•
Brooklyn Law School 250 Joralemon Street, Brooklyn, NY 11201 718-780-7906 Fax: 718-780-0395 admitq@brooklaw.edu	$31,200-$160,000	3	1	1	7	18	19	7	5	3	3	17	88%	•	•	•	•	•	•	•	•	•	•	•			•
California Western School of Law 225 Cedar Street, San Diego, CA 92101-3046 619-525-1401 Fax: 619-615-1401 admissions@cwsl.edu	$50,000-$200,000	7	1	2	7	13	12	5	3	6	3	41	91%	•	•	•	•	•	•	•	•	•	•	•	•		•
Campbell University (Norman Adrian Wiggins School of Law) 225 Hillsborough Street, Suite 401, Raleigh, NC 24603 919-865-5988 Fax: 919-865-5886	$54,500-$63,500				5	9	12	5	14	8	9	59	94%	•	•	•	•	•	•	•	•	•	•	•	•		•

School		Salary Range
Capital University (Law School) 303 East Broad Street Columbus, OH 43215-3200 614-236-6500 Fax: 614-236-6972 admissions@law.capital.edu	34 · 9 · 3 · 3 · 3 · 14 · 21 · 3 · 2 · 3 · 6 · 85% · (•)	$36,838–$73,884
Case Western Reserve University (School of Law) 11075 East Boulevard Cleveland, OH 44106 216-368-3600 Fax: 216-368-1042 lawadmissions@case.edu	17 · 5 · 4 · 1 · 5 · 17 · 23 · 12 · 3 · 1 · 92% · (•)	$42,000–$112,500
Catholic University of America (Columbus School of Law) Cardinal Station Washington, DC 20064 202-319-5151 Fax: 202-319-6285 admissions@law.edu	42 · 12 · 27 · 13 · 2 · 2 · 93% · (•)	$28,000–$135,000
Chapman University (School of Law) One University Drive Orange, CA 92866 714-628-2500 Fax: 714-628-2501 metten@chapman.edu	30 · 7 · 5 · 1 · 2 · 1 · 13 · 2 · 1 · 14 · 10 · 97% · (•)	$24,960–$160,000
Charleston School of Law P.O. Box 535 Charleston, SC 29402 843-377-2143 Fax: 843-329-0491 jbenfield@charlestonlaw.org	12 · 12 · 11 · 4 · 1 · 6 · 83% · (•)	$47,671–$57,240
Charlotte School of Law 2145 Suttle Avenue Charlotte, NC 28208 704-971-8542 Fax: 704-971-8599 admissions@charlottelaw.edu	(•)	
City University of New York (CUNY School of Law) 65-21 Main Street Flushing, NY 11367-1300 718-340-4210 Fax: 718-340-4435 mail.law.cuny.edu	9 · 4 · 1 · 11 · 10 · 10 · 41 · 6 · 13 · 81% · (•)	$43,000–$63,700
Cleveland State University (Cleveland-Marshall College of Law) 2121 Euclid Avenue LB138 Cleveland, OH 44115-2214 216-687-2304 Fax: 216-687-6881 christophe.cak@lawcsuohio.edu	23 · 5 · 2 · 15 · 28 · 3 · 1 · 18 · 89% · (•)	$60,000–$120,000
College of William & Mary (William & Mary Law School) P.O. Box 8795 Williamsburg, VA 23187-8795 757-221-3785 Fax: 757-221-3261 lawadm@wm.edu	13 · 4 · 3 · 2 · 21 · 16 · 9 · 5 · 6 · 2 · 19 · 91% · (•)	$30,000–$160,000

Placement Record

School	Average Starting Salary	Other	Academic	Military	Public Interest	Business/Industry	Government	Judicial Clerkships	Private Practice 51–100 Attorneys	Private Practice 26–50 Attorneys	Private Practice 11–25 Attorneys	Private Practice 2–10 Attorneys	Placement Within 6 to 9 Months
Columbia University (School of Law)	$35,000–$175,000	77			3	2	4	14					99%
Cornell University (Law School)	$46,000–$165,000	73			3	2	1	14	5	2	2	39	99%
Creighton University (School of Law)	$36,000–$110,000	11		2	4	12	9	8	4	5	6	22	87%
De Paul University (College of Law)	$20,000–$160,000	26	5		5	19	15	2	5	7	10	30	84%
Drake University (Law School)	$24,000–$130,000		1	1	2	23	15	4	2	1	11		95%
Drexel University (Earle Mack School of Law)	$70,360		4	4	7	21	4	10	25				83%
Duke University (School of Law)	$42,000–$135,000												95%

Career Services

School	Alumni Placement	Internships	Part-Time/Summer Employment	Alumni Contacts	Law, Corporate, and Government Contact	Job Interviews Arrangement	Employment Planning	Interview Counseling	Resume Preparation	Solo Practice Advice	Job Openings Information	Employment Counseling	University Placement Office	Law Placement Office
Columbia University (School of Law)	•	•	•	•	•	•	•	•	•		•	•		•
Cornell University (Law School)	•	•	•	•	•	•	•	•	•	•	•	•		•
Creighton University (School of Law)	•	•	•	•	•	•	•	•	•	•	•	•		•
De Paul University (College of Law)	•	•	•	•	•	•	•	•	•	•	•	•	•	•
Drake University (Law School)	•	•	•	•	•	•	•	•	•	•	•	•		•
Drexel University (Earle Mack School of Law)														
Duke University (School of Law)	•	•	•	•	•	•	•	•	•	•	•	•		•

School Contact Information

Columbia University (School of Law)
435 West 116th Street
New York, NY 10027
212-854-2670
Fax: 212-854-1109
admissions@law.columbia.edu

Cornell University (Law School)
Myron Taylor Hall
Ithaca, NY 14853-4901
607-255-5141
Fax: 607-255-7193
lawadmit@postoffice.law.cornell.edu

Creighton University (School of Law)
2500 California Plaza
Omaha, NE 68178
402-280-2586
Fax: 402-280-3161
lawadmit@creighton.edu

De Paul University (College of Law)
25 East Jackson Boulevard
Chicago, IL 60604
312-362-6831
lawinfo@depaul.edu

Drake University (Law School)
2507 University Avenue
Des Moines, IA 50311
515-271-2782
Fax: 515-271-1990
lawadmit@drake.edu

Drexel University (Earle Mack School of Law)
3320 Market Street
Philadelphia, PA 15282
215-895 1LAW
Fax: 215-571-4769
ypayton.770@aol.com

Duke University (School of Law)
Science Drive and Towerview Road,
Box 90362
Durham, NC 27708-0362
919-613-7020
Fax: 919-613-7257
nash@law.duke.edu

School	Salary Range													%
Duquesne University (School of Law) 900 Locust Street, Hanley Hall Pittsburgh, PA 15282 412-396-6296 Fax: 412-396-1073 campion@duq.edu	$24,000–$130,000	54	3		4	19	9	8						93%
Elon University (School of Law) 201 North Greene Street Greensboro, NC 27401 336-279-9200 Fax: 336-279-8199 law@elon.edu	$47,500–$72,500	19	1		3	21	8	5	1	1	4	37		92%
Emory University (School of Law) Gambrell Hall, 1301 Clifton Road, N.E. Atlanta, GA 30322 404-727-6801 Fax: 404-727-2477 erosenz@law.emory.edu	$52,000–$145,000	52			2	11	9	9	2	6	4	9		95%
Faulkner University (Thomas Goode Jones School of Law) 5345 Atlanta Highway Montgomery, AL 36109 334-386-7210 Fax: 334-386-7223 law@faulkner.edu														
Florida Agricultural and Mechanical University (Florida A & M University College of Law) 201 Beggs Avenue Orlando, FL 32801 407-254-3268 famulaw.admissions@famu.edu	$36,000–$61,250	24	6	4	6	20	17		1	1	1	19		63%
Florida Coastal (School of Law) 8787 Baypine Rd. Jacksonville, FL 32256 904-680-7776 Fax: 904-680-7710 admissions@fcsl.edu	$35,000–$80,000					18	18					63		90%
Florida International University (College of Law) FIU College of Law, RDB 1055 Miami, FL 33199 (305) 348-8006 Fax: (305) 348-2965 mirpa@fiu.edu	$42,000–$110,000				8 14			1	9	6	3	52		86%
Florida State University (College of Law) 425 W. Jefferson St. Tallahassee, FL 32306-1601 850-644-3787 Fax: 850-644-7284 admissions@law.fsu.edu	$31,800–$160,000	9	1	3	9	10	23	2	4	5	5	26		98%
Fordham University (School of Law) 140 West 62nd Street New York, NY 10023 212-636-6810 Fax: 212-636-7984 lawadmissions@law.fordham.edu														

School	George Mason University (School of Law)	George Washington University (Law School)	Georgetown University (Law Center)	Georgia State University (College of Law)	Golden Gate University (School of Law)	Gonzaga University (School of Law)	Hamline University (School of Law)
AVERAGE STARTING SALARY	$35,000–$170,000	$84,000–$145,000	$50,000–$160,000	$38,000–$160,000	$35,000–$100,000	$62,000–$70,000	$36,500–$240,000

PLACEMENT RECORD — Percentage Breakdown of Type of Employer

Type of Employer	George Mason	George Washington	Georgetown	Georgia State	Golden Gate	Gonzaga	Hamline
OTHER	14	35		17	6	16	5
ACADEMIC	7	6	3	4	14	2	1
MILITARY	2	1	2	2	2	3	1
PUBLIC INTEREST	4	4	14	6	4	7	7
BUSINESS/INDUSTRY	20	14	5	18	21	18	27
GOVERNMENT	19	20	17	8	17	6	8
JUDICIAL CLERKSHIPS	9	9	9	4	1	15	15
PRIVATE PRACTICE 51-100 ATTORNEYS		2	2	2	2	1	5
PRIVATE PRACTICE 26-50 ATTORNEYS	1	2	1	3	2	1	1
PRIVATE PRACTICE 11-25 ATTORNEYS	4	1	1	8	3	6	2
PRIVATE PRACTICE 2-10 ATTORNEYS	20	6	2	23	30	24	28
PLACEMENT WITHIN 6 TO 9 MONTHS	97%	95%	98%	93%	77%	90%	93%

CAREER SERVICES

Services

Service	George Mason	George Washington	Georgetown	Georgia State	Golden Gate	Gonzaga	Hamline
ALUMNI PLACEMENT	•	•	•	•	•	•	•
INTERNSHIPS	•	•	•	•	•	•	•
PART-TIME/SUMMER EMPLOYMENT	•	•	•	•	•	•	•
ALUMNI CONTACTS	•	•	•	•	•	•	•
LAW, CORPORATE, AND GOVERNMENT CONTACT	•	•	•	•	•	•	•
JOB INTERVIEWS ARRANGEMENT	•	•	•	•	•	•	•
EMPLOYMENT PLANNING	•	•	•	•	•	•	•
INTERVIEW COUNSELING	•	•	•	•	•	•	•
RESUME PREPARATION	•	•	•	•	•	•	•
SOLO PRACTICE ADVICE	•	•	•	•	•	•	•
JOB OPENINGS INFORMATION	•	•	•	•	•	•	•
EMPLOYMENT COUNSELING	•	•	•	•	•	•	•

Facilities

Facility	George Mason	George Washington	Georgetown	Georgia State	Golden Gate	Gonzaga	Hamline
UNIVERSITY PLACEMENT OFFICE							
LAW PLACEMENT OFFICE	•	•	•	•	•	•	•

School contact information

George Mason University (School of Law)
3301 Fairfax Drive
Arlington, VA 22201
703-993-8010
Fax: 703-993-8088
aprice1@gmu.edu

George Washington University (Law School)
2000 H Street, N.W.
Washington, DC 20052
202-994-7230
Fax: 202-994-3597
jd@law.gwu.edu

Georgetown University (Law Center)
600 New Jersey Avenue, N.W.
Washington, DC 20001
202-662-9010
Fax: 202-662-9439
admis@law.georgetown.edu

Georgia State University (College of Law)
P.O. Box 4037
Atlanta, GA 30302-4037
404-413-9200
Fax: 404-413-9203
cjgeorge@gsu.edu

Golden Gate University (School of Law)
536 Mission Street
San Francisco, CA 94105-2968
415-442-6630
lawadmit@ggu.edu

Gonzaga University (School of Law)
Box 3528
Spokane, WA 99220-3528
509-313-5532
Fax: 509-313-3697
admissions@lawschool.gonzaga.edu

Hamline University (School of Law)
1536 Hewitt Avenue
St. Paul, MN 55104-1284
651-523-2461
Fax: 651-523-3064
lawadm@gw.hamline.edu

School (Contact)												%	Salary
Harvard University (Harvard Law School) Cambridge, MA 02138 617-495-3179 jdadmiss@law.harvard.edu	64	1		8	3	4	22					99%	
Hofstra University (Maurice A. Deane School of Law) 121 Hofstra University Hempstead, NY 11549 516-463-5916 Fax: 516-463-6264 lawadmissions@hofstra.edu		9		5	23	10	2	2	2	6	27	91%	$50,000–$100,000
Howard University 2900 Van Ness Street, N.W. Washington, DC 20008 202-806-8008 Fax: 202-806-8162 admissions@law.howard.edu	19	1		3	19	30	16	3	3	1	5	94%	$30,000–$150,000
Illinois Institute of Technology (Chicago-Kent College of Law) 565 West Adams Street Chicago, IL 60661 312-906-5020 Fax: 312-906-5274 admit@kentlaw.edu		7		5	21	10	3	3	4	7	26	91%	$17,500–$160,000
Indiana University (Maurer School of Law) 211 S. Indiana Avenue Bloomington, IN 47405-7001 812-855-4765 Fax: 812-855-0555 Lawadmis@indiana.edu	1	7	4	8	15	13	8		4	3	18	91%	$27,000–$160,000
Indiana University-Purdue University at Indianapolis (Robert H. McKinney School of Law) 530 West New York Street Indianapolis, IN 46202-3225 317-274-2459 Fax: 317-278-4780 khmiller@iupui.edu	49	1	1	6	21	17	5	7	7		14	91%	$40,000–$160,000
Inter American University of Puerto Rico (School of Law) P.O. Box 70351 San Juan PR 00936-8351 787-751-1912, ext. 2013, 2526	3		1	21	23	2	2	2	7	10	29	86%	$28,000–$68,000
John Marshall Law School 315 South Plymouth Court Chicago, IL 60604 312-987-1406 Fax: 312-427-5136 admission@jmls.edu	5	1	2	23	17	2	3	3	7	24		90%	$27,000–$160,000
Lewis and Clark College (Lewis and Clark Law School) 10015 Southwest Terwilliger Boulevard Portland, OR 97219 503-768-6613 Fax: 503-768-6793 lawadmss@clark.edu	9	9		6	16	15	14		4	5	24	90%	$48,340

PLACEMENT RECORD

School	Average Starting Salary	Other	Academic	Military	Public Interest	Business/Industry	Government	Judicial Clerkships	Private Practice 51–100 Attorneys	Private Practice 26–50 Attorneys	Private Practice 11–25 Attorneys	Private Practice 2–10 Attorneys	Placement Within 6 to 9 Months
Liberty University (School of Law)	$30,000–$66,000	8	5	3	5	11	11	8	3	5	11	30	78%
Louisiana State University (Paul M. Hebert Law Center)	$27,500–$160,000				1	3	9	21	6	11	16	26	92%
Loyola Marymount University (Loyola Law School Los Angeles)	$60,000–$125,000												97%
Loyola University Chicago (School of Law)	$20,800–$177,000		3	1	6	22	11	7	4	1	5	25	90%
Loyola University of New Orleans (College of Law)	$39,200–$160,000	11	1		4	14	11	9	4	6	12	28	
Marquette University (Law School)	$35,000–$125,000		1		5	21	10	3	2	4	7	34	89%
Massachusetts School of Law													

CAREER SERVICES

School	Alumni Placement	Internships	Part-Time/Summer Employment	Alumni Contacts	Law, Corporate, and Government Contact	Job Interviews Arrangement	Employment Planning	Interview Counseling	Resume Preparation	Solo Practice Advice	Job Openings Information	Employment Counseling	University Placement Office	Law Placement Office
Liberty University (School of Law)	•	•	•	•	•	•	•	•	•	•	•	•		•
Louisiana State University (Paul M. Hebert Law Center)	•	•	•	•	•	•	•	•	•	•	•	•		•
Loyola Marymount University (Loyola Law School Los Angeles)	•	•	•	•	•	•	•	•	•	•	•	•		•
Loyola University Chicago (School of Law)	•	•	•	•	•	•	•	•	•	•	•	•	•	•
Loyola University of New Orleans (College of Law)	•	•	•	•	•	•	•	•	•	•	•	•		•
Marquette University (Law School)	•	•	•	•	•	•	•	•	•	•	•	•		•
Massachusetts School of Law		•		•				•		•		•		

School Addresses

Liberty University (School of Law)
1971 University Blvd.
Lynchburg, VA 24502
434-592-5300
Fax: 434-592-0202
law@liberty.edu

Louisiana State University (Paul M. Hebert Law Center)
202 Law Center, 1 East Campus Drive
Baton Rouge, LA 70803
225-578-8646
Fax: 225-578-8647
lynell.cadray@law.lsu.edu

Loyola Marymount University (Loyola Law School Los Angeles)
919 Albany Street
Los Angeles, CA 90015
213-736-1074
Fax: 213-736-6523
admissions@lls.edu

Loyola University Chicago (School of Law)
25 East Pearson Street
Chicago, IL 60611
312-915-7170
Fax: 312-915-7906
law-admissions@luc.edu

Loyola University of New Orleans (College of Law)
7214 St. Charles Avenue, P.O. Box 901
New Orleans, LA 70118
504-861-5575
Fax: 504-861-5772
ladmit@loyno.edu

Marquette University (Law School)
Office of Admissions, P.O. Box 1881
Milwaukee WI 53201-1881
414-288-6767
Fax: 414-288-0676
law.admission@marquette.edu

Massachusetts School of Law
500 Federal Street
Andover, MA 01810
978-681-0800
Fax: 978-681-6630
pcolby@mslaw.edu

School	Salary Range														%
Mercer University (Walter F. George School of Law) 1021 Georgia Avenue Macon, GA 31207 478-301-2605 Fax: 478-301-2989 Sutton_me@law.mercer.edu	$30,000–$155,000	15		2	7	5	12	12	3	3	3	9	3	31	85%
Michigan State University (College of Law) 230 Law College Bldg. East Lansing, MI 48824-1300 517-432-0222 Fax: 517-432-0098	$20,800–$135,000	11	10	1	8	21	8	7	2	1	4	2		26	92%
Mississippi College (School of Law) 151 E. Griffith Street Jackson, MS 39201 601-925-7152 pevans@mc.edu	$50,000–$77,500	12	1		2	10	17	12	5	4	2	2		34	87%
New England Law / Boston 154 Stuart Street Boston, MA 02116 617-422-7210 Fax: 617-422-7201 admit@admin.nesl.edu	$30,000–$135,000		3	2	4	29	10	2	2	2	5			29	84%
New York Law School 185 West Broadway New York, NY 10013-2960 212-431-2888 Fax: 212-966-1522 admissions@nyls.edu	$35,000–$160,000	4	2	2	4	27	16	3	2	3	3			25	89%
New York University (School of Law) 161 Avenue of the Americas, 5th Floor New York, NY 10013 212-998-6060 Fax: 212-995-4527 law.moreinfo@nyu.edu	$60,000–$160,000		1		14	3	7	13	1	1	1			2	98%
North Carolina Central University (School of Law) 640 Nelson Street Durham, NC 27707 919-530-6333 Fax: 919-530-6339 sbrownb@nccu.edu	$40,000–$60,000	9	1	2	8	18	22	4	2	3	2			22	88%
Northeastern University (School of Law) 400 Huntington Avenue Boston, MA 02115 617-373-2395 Fax: 617-373-8865 c.taubman@neu.edu	$37,500–$160,000	10	8		21	15	11	7	2	3	3			20	94%
Northern Illinois University (College of Law) Swen Parson Hall, Room 151 DeKalb, IL 60115-2890 815-753-8595 Fax: 815-753-5680 lawadm@niu.edu	$41,500–$59,250	5	5	3	9	21	17	3	3	1	4			28	85%

PLACEMENT RECORD / CAREER SERVICES

SCHOOL	AVERAGE STARTING SALARY	OTHER	ACADEMIC	MILITARY	PUBLIC INTEREST	BUSINESS/INDUSTRY	GOVERNMENT	JUDICIAL CLERKSHIPS	PRIVATE PRACTICE 51-100 ATTORNEYS	PRIVATE PRACTICE 26-50 ATTORNEYS	PRIVATE PRACTICE 11-25 ATTORNEYS	PRIVATE PRACTICE 2-10 ATTORNEYS	PLACEMENT WITHIN 6 TO 9 MONTHS
Northern Kentucky University (Salmon P. Chase College of Law)	$26,000–$105,000		5	1	5	22	5	8	2	2	8	30	88%
Northwestern University (School of Law)	$45,000–$160,000	6	1		5	10	2	11	62				
Nova Southeastern University (Shepard Broad Law Center)	$28,800–$250,000	6	2		6	18	8	1	4	5	12	38	81%
Ohio Northern University (Claude W. Pettit College of Law)	$33,000–$145,000	4	2	1	3	14	19	3	2	42	2	41	94%
Ohio State University (Michael E. Moritz College of Law)	$53,250–$115,000		7		4	20	21	6	42	42	42	42	
Oklahoma City University (School of Law)	$22,000–$120,000	19	3	2	6	14	13		2	2	22	15	83%
Pace University (School of Law)	$38,480–$160,000	2	15		6	20	10	5	4	1	4	24	79%

CAREER SERVICES

SCHOOL	ALUMNI PLACEMENT	INTERNSHIPS	PART-TIME/SUMMER EMPLOYMENT	ALUMNI CONTACTS	LAW, CORPORATE, AND GOVERNMENT CONTACT	JOB INTERVIEWS ARRANGEMENT	EMPLOYMENT PLANNING	INTERVIEW COUNSELING	RESUME PREPARATION	SOLO PRACTICE ADVICE	JOB OPENINGS INFORMATION	EMPLOYMENT COUNSELING	UNIVERSITY PLACEMENT OFFICE	LAW PLACEMENT OFFICE
Northern Kentucky University	•	•	•	•	•	•	•	•	•	•	•	•		•
Northwestern University	•	•	•	•	•	•	•	•	•	•	•	•		•
Nova Southeastern University	•	•	•	•	•	•	•	•	•	•	•			•
Ohio Northern University	•	•	•	•	•	•	•	•	•	•	•	•		•
Ohio State University	•	•	•	•	•	•	•	•	•	•	•	•		•
Oklahoma City University	•	•	•	•	•	•	•	•	•	•	•	•	•	•
Pace University	•	•	•	•	•	•	•	•	•	•	•	•	•	•

School contact information:

Northern Kentucky University (Salmon P. Chase College of Law)
Louie B. Nunn Hall
Highland Heights, KY 41099
859-572-5490
Fax: 859-572-6081
brayg@nku.edu

Northwestern University (School of Law)
375 East Chicago Avenue
Chicago, IL 60611
312-503-8465
Fax: 312-503-0178
admissions@law.northwestern.edu

Nova Southeastern University (Shepard Broad Law Center)
3305 College Avenue
Fort Lauderdale, FL 33314-7721
954-262-6117
Fax: 954-262-3844
admission@nsu.law.nova.edu

Ohio Northern University (Claude W. Pettit College of Law)
525 South Main Street
Ada, OH 45810
419-772-2211
Fax: 419-772-3042

Ohio State University (Michael E. Moritz College of Law)
55 West 12th Avenue, John Deaver Drinko Hall
Columbus, OH 43210-1391
614-292-8810
lawadmit@osu.edu

Oklahoma City University (School of Law)
2501 North Blackwelder Avenue
Oklahoma City, OK 73106-1493
405-208-5354
Fax: 405-208-5814
lawadmit@okcu.edu

Pace University (School of Law)
78 North Broadway
White Plains, NY 10603
914-422-4210
Fax: 914-989-8714
calexander@law.pace.edu

School													%	Salary Range
Pennsylvania State University (Dickinson School of Law) Lewis Katz Building University Park, PA 16802-1910 814-867-1251 Fax: 717-241-3503 *dsladmit@psu.edu*	14	4	1	4	23	12	19		3		19		84%	$40,500–$104,000
Pepperdine University (School of Law) 24255 Pacific Coast Highway Malibu, CA 90263 310-506-4631 Fax: 310-506-7668	50	50											95%	
Phoenix School of Law 4041 N. Central Ave. Suite 100 Phoenix, AZ 85012-3330 (602) 682-6800														
Pontifical Catholic University of Puerto Rico (School of Law) 2250 Avenida las Americas suite 543 Ponce, PR 00717-9997 787-841-2000, ext. 1836 Fax: 787-840-4620														$14,000–$24,000
Quinnipiac University (School of Law) 275 Mt. Carmel Avenue Hamden, CT 06518-1908 Fax: 203-582-3339 *ladm@quinnipiac.edu*		2		9	17	24	9		2	4	21		90%	$20,000–$220,000
Regent University (School of Law) 1000 Regent University Drive Virginia Beach, VA 23464-9800 757-352-4584 Fax: 757-352-4139 *lawschool@regent.edu*	27	3	1	2	11	20	8		1	4	21		87%	$42,500–$55,000
Roger Williams University (School of Law) Ten Metacom Avenue Bristol, RI 02809-5171 401-254-4555 Fax: 401-254-4516 *admissions@rwu.edu*	20	2	2	9	15	8	163		10	3	24		83%	$26,000–$116,000
Rutgers University/Camden (School of Law) Fifth and Penn Streets Camden, NJ 08102 856-225-6102 Fax: 856-225-6537 *admissions@camlaw.rutgers.edu*		2	2	4	14	10	30	13	10	6	11		92%	$45,000–$110,000
Rutgers University/Newark (School of Law) Center for Law and Justice, 123 Washington St. Newark, NJ 07102 973-353-5557/5554 Fax: 973-353-3459 *lawinfo@andromeda.rutgers.edu*		2	2	3	13	5	28	11	11	11	11		98%	$35,000–$192,000

School	LAW PLACEMENT OFFICE	UNIVERSITY PLACEMENT OFFICE	EMPLOYMENT COUNSELING	JOB OPENINGS INFORMATION	SOLO PRACTICE ADVICE	RESUME PREPARATION	INTERVIEW COUNSELING	EMPLOYMENT PLANNING	JOB INTERVIEWS ARRANGEMENT	LAW, CORPORATE, AND GOVERNMENT CONTACT	ALUMNI CONTACTS	PART-TIME/SUMMER EMPLOYMENT	INTERNSHIPS	ALUMNI PLACEMENT	PLACEMENT WITHIN 6 TO 9 MONTHS	PP 2-10 ATTORNEYS	PP 11-25 ATTORNEYS	PP 26-50 ATTORNEYS	PP 51-100 ATTORNEYS	JUDICIAL CLERKSHIPS	GOVERNMENT	BUSINESS/INDUSTRY	PUBLIC INTEREST	MILITARY	ACADEMIC	OTHER	AVERAGE STARTING SALARY
Saint John's University (School of Law) 8000 Utopia Parkway, Queens, NY 11439, 718-990-6474, Fax: 718-990-2526, lawinfo@stjohns.edu	●		●	●	●	●	●	●	●	●	●	●	●	●	92%	24	4	3	5	3	15	18	3		7		
Saint Louis University (School of Law) 3700 Lindell Boulevard, St. Louis, MO 63108, 314-977-2800, Fax: 314-977-1464, admissions@law.slu.edu	●		●	●	●	●	●	●	●	●	●	●	●	●	88%	23	9	1	3	5	14	19	8	2	2	14	$48,750-$60,000
Saint Mary's University (School of Law) One Camino Santa Maria, San Antonio, TX 78228-8601, 210-436-3523, Fax: 210-431-4202, wwilson@stmarytx.edu	●		●	●	●	●	●	●	●	●	●	●	●	●	89%	58	2	2		4	14	11	5	2	5		$30,000-$120,000
Saint Thomas University (School of Law) 16401 NW 37th Avenue, Miami Gardens, FL 33054, 305-623-2310, fkhan@stu.edu	●		●	●	●	●	●	●	●	●	●	●	●	●	74%	51	14	1	3	2	8	11	6		1	10	$41,000-$60,000
Samford University (Cumberland School of Law) 800 Lakeshore Drive, Birmingham, AL 35229, 205-726-2702, Fax: 205-726-2057, law.admissions@samford.edu	●		●	●	●	●	●	●	●	●	●	●	●	●	90%	22	7	4	7	7	6	16	6	1	1		$23,000-$110,000
Santa Clara University (School of Law) 500 El Camino Real, Santa Clara, CA 95053, 408-554-4800, Fax: 408-554-7897, lawadmissions@scu.edu	●		●	●	●	●	●	●	●	●	●	●	●	●	78%	9	2		2	1	9	15	5		5	34	$67,000-$107,995

School contact information

School	Address / Phone / Fax / Email
Seattle University (School of Law)	901 12th Avenue, Sullivan Hall, P.O. Box 222000, Seattle, WA 98122-4340 — 206-398-4200 — Fax: 206-398-4058 — lawadmis@seattleu.edu
Seton Hall University (School of Law)	One Newark Center, Newark, NJ 07102-5210 — 973-642-8747 — Fax: 973-642-8876 — admitme@shu.edu
South Texas College of Law	1303 San Jacinto Street, Houston, TX 77002-7006 — 713-646-1810 — Fax: 713-646-2906 — admissions@stcl.edu
Southern Illinois University (School of Law)	Lesar Law Building, Mail Code 6804, Carbondale, IL 62901 — 618-453-8858 — Fax: 618-453-8921 — lawadmit@siu.edu
Southern Methodist University (Dedman School of Law)	Office of Admissions, P.O. Box 750110, Dallas, TX 75275-0110 — 214-768-2550 — Fax: 214-768-2549 — lawadmit@smu.edu
Southern New England School of Law	333 Faunce Corner Road, North Dartmouth, MA 02747 — 508-998-9400 — Fax: 508-998-9561 — cvidal@snesl.edu
Southern University and A & M College (Law Center)	Post Office Box 9294, Baton Rouge, LA 70813-9294 — 225-771-5340 — Fax: 225-771-2121 — vwilkerson@sulc.edu
Southwestern University (Law School)	3050 Wilshire Boulevard, Los Angeles, CA 90010-1106 — 213-738-6717 — Fax: 213-383-1688 — admissions@swlaw.edu
Stanford University (Stanford Law School)	Crown Quadrangle, 559 Nathan Abbott Way, Stanford, CA 94305-8610 — 650-723-4985 — Fax: 650-723-0838 — admissions@law.stanford.edu

Data columns

School	%	1	2	3	4	5	6	7	8	9	10	11	Salary Range
Seattle University	90%	31	2	5	4	5	11	21	9		3		$43,500–$110,000
Seton Hall University	86%	15	2	4		36	5	12	2		2	12	$42,200–$160,000
South Texas College of Law	85%	31	7	4	3	2	11	21	3			18	$55,000–$100,000
Southern Illinois University	84%	32	10	3		5	20	15	1		2	11	$40,000–$58,000
Southern Methodist University	99%	29	8	12	7	4	6	16	1	1	2	18	$62,400–$160,000
Southern New England School of Law											5		
Southern University and A & M College	26%	24	2	3	5	21	10	6	2				
Southwestern University	97%	26	8	7	10	5	14	15	4		1	10	$52,000–$140,000
Stanford University	99%					32	4	2	3		2	57	

Feature indicators (•)

School	R1	R2	R3	R4	R5	R6	R7	R8	R9	R10	R11	R12	R13	R14
Seattle University	•	•	•	•	•	•	•	•	•	•	•	•	•	•
Seton Hall University	•	•	•	•	•	•	•	•	•	•	•	•	•	•
South Texas College of Law	•	•	•	•	•	•	•	•	•	•	•	•	•	•
Southern Illinois University	•	•	•	•	•	•	•	•	•	•	•	•	•	•
Southern Methodist University	•	•	•	•	•	•	•	•	•	•	•	•	•	•
Southern New England School of Law				•				•	•		•			•
Southern University and A & M College	•	•		•	•	•	•	•	•	•	•		•	•
Southwestern University	•	•	•	•	•	•	•	•	•	•	•	•	•	•
Stanford University	•	•	•	•	•	•	•	•	•	•	•	•	•	•

PLACEMENT RECORD — Percentage Breakdown of Type of Employer

School	Average Starting Salary	Placement within 6 to 9 Months	Private Practice 2-10 Attorneys	Private Practice 11-25 Attorneys	Private Practice 26-50 Attorneys	Private Practice 51-100 Attorneys	Judicial Clerkships	Government	Business/Industry	Public Interest	Military	Academic	Other
State University of New York (SUNY Buffalo Law School)	$25,000–$160,000	96%	26	8	5	5	2	13	14	7	3	4	
Stetson University (Stetson University College of Law)	$42,000–$110,000	85%	18	12	7	4	5	21	13	7	2	1	
Suffolk University (Law School)		84%	27	6	2	2	3	13	24	3	1	6	
Syracuse University (College of Law)	$36,700–$113,000	90%	20	6	5	6	15	13	16	4	2	3	10
Temple University (James E. Beasley School of Law)	$30,000–$160,000	93%	13	8	4	4	9	14	17	7		2	4
Texas Southern University (Thurgood Marshall School of Law)	$55,000	83%	60		3		3	9	21	4		4	
Texas Tech University (School of Law)	$25,000–$160,000	92%	29	8	3	5	6	15	18	3	2	2	9

CAREER SERVICES

Services (all schools, except where noted): Alumni Placement •; Internships •; Part-Time/Summer Employment •; Alumni Contacts •; Law, Corporate, and Government Contact •; Job Interviews Arrangement •; Employment Planning •; Interview Counseling •; Resume Preparation •; Solo Practice Advice •; Job Openings Information •; Employment Counseling •.

Facilities: University Placement Office — State University of New York (SUNY Buffalo) •. Law Placement Office — all schools •.

School contact information

State University of New York (SUNY Buffalo Law School)
309 O'Brian Hall
Buffalo, NY 14260
716-645-2907
Fax: 716-645-6676
lwiley@buffalo.edu

Stetson University (Stetson University College of Law)
1401 61st Street South
Gulfport, Fl 33707
727-562-7802
Fax: 727-343-0136
zuppo@law.stetson.edu

Suffolk University (Law School)
120 Tremont Street
Boston, MA 02108-4977
617-573-8144
Fax: 617-523-1367

Syracuse University (College of Law)
Office of Admissions and Financial Aid,
Suite 340
Syracuse, NY 13244-1030
315-443-1962
Fax: 315-443-9568

Temple University (James E. Beasley School of Law)
1719 North Broad Street
Philadelphia, PA 19122
215-204-1185
Fax: 215-204-5949
lawadmis@temple.edu

Texas Southern University (Thurgood Marshall School of Law)
3100 Cleburne Avenue
Houston, TX 77004
713-313-7114
Fax: 713-313-1049
cgardner@tmslaw.tsu.edu

Texas Tech University (School of Law)
1802 Hartford Avenue
Lubbock, TX 79409
806-742-3990, ext. 273
Fax: 806-742-4617
donna.williams@ttu.edu

School	Salary Range												%
Texas Wesleyan University (School of Law) 1515 Commerce Street Fort Worth, TX 76102 817-212-4040 Fax: 817-212-4141 *lawadmissions@law.txwes.edu*	$47,800–$75,000		2		3	26	14	1	7	3	5	32	79%
Thomas Jefferson School of Law 1155 Island Avenue San Diego, CA 92101 619-297-9700 Fax: 619-294-4713 *info@tjsl.edu*	$17,000–$140,000		5		1	19	10	2	1	2	5	45	85%
Thomas M. Cooley Law School 300 South Capitol Avenue Lansing, MI 48901 517-371-5140 Fax: 517-334-5718 *admissions@cooley.edu*			3		4	18	13	4		1	4	28	
Touro College (Jacob D. Fuchsberg Law Center) 225 Eastview Drive Central Islip, NY 11722 631-761-7010 Fax: 631-761-7019 *gjustice@tourolaw.edu*	$40,000–$63,000	2	3		5	23	21	2	2	5	6	31	78%
Tulane University (Law School) Weinmann Hall, 6329 Freret Street New Orleans, LA 70118 504-865-5930 Fax: 504-865-6710 *admissions@law.tulane.edu*	$35,000–$140,000	59	1		6	5	9	10		2		21	85%
University of Akron (School of Law) 302 Buchtel Common Akron, OH 44325-2901 330-972-7331 Fax: 330-258-2343 *lthorpe@uakron.edu*	$55,980–$130,000	10	5		6	25	17	6	3	2	5	25	92%
University of Alabama (School of Law) Box 870382 Tuscaloosa AL 35487-0382 205-348-5440 Fax: 205-348-3917 *admissions@law.ua.edu*	$50,000–$100,000		2		4	13	9	14	8	3	3	25	96%
University of Arizona (James E. Rogers College of Law) 120 E. Speedway, P.O. Box 210176 Tucson, AZ 85721-0176 520-621-3477 Fax: 520-621-9140 *admissions@law.arizona.edu*	$43,326–$79,622	5	1	2	5	10	17	22	15	12	8	3	94%
University of Arkansas (School of Law) Robert A. Leflar Law Center, Waterman Hall Fayetteville, AR 72701 479-575-3102 Fax: 479-575-3937 *jkmiller@uark.edu*		11	2		4	21	12	6	5	4	5	30	95%

Law Schools — Placement Record and Career Services

Career Services — Services (all of the following are marked ● for all six schools): Employment Counseling, Job Openings Information, Solo Practice Advice, Resume Preparation, Interview Counseling, Employment Planning, Job Interviews Arrangement, Law, Corporate, and Government Contact, Alumni Contacts, Part-Time/Summer Employment, Internships, Alumni Placement.

Facilities

School	Law Placement Office	University Placement Office
University of Arkansas at Little Rock (UALR William H. Bowen School of Law)	●	
University of Baltimore (School of Law)	●	
University of California (Hastings College of the Law)	●	
University of California at Berkeley (School of Law)	●	●
University of California at Davis (School of Law)	●	
University of California at Los Angeles (UCLA School of Law)	●	

Placement Record (Percentage Breakdown of Type of Employer)

School	Placement within 6 to 9 months	Private Practice 2–10 attorneys	Private Practice 11–25 attorneys	Private Practice 26–50 attorneys	Private Practice 51–100 attorneys	Judicial Clerkships	Government	Business/Industry	Public Interest	Military	Academic	Other	Average Starting Salary
University of Arkansas at Little Rock	91%	19	16		2	6	23	22	1		5	13	$39,000–$65,000
University of Baltimore	94%	18	3	3	2	23	13	18	5	1	3	10	$27,500–$145,000
University of California (Hastings)	94%	14	6	4	4	4	8	9	4		2	45	$26,000–$150,000
University of California at Berkeley	96%					10	8	1	13		3		$22,000–$235,000
University of California at Davis	98%	15	10	3	5	11	7	8	13		1	25	$30,000–$125,000
University of California at Los Angeles (UCLA)	94%	11	3	2	3	8	10	9	9	1	6	39	$25,000–$160,000

School Contact Information

University of Arkansas at Little Rock (UALR William H. Bowen School of Law)
1201 McMath Avenue
Little Rock, AR 72202-5142
501-324-9903
Fax: 501-324-9909
lawadm@ualr.edu

University of Baltimore (School of Law)
1420 North Charles Street
Baltimore, MD 21201-5779
410-837-4450
Fax: 410-837-4459
lwadmiss@ubmail.ubalt.edu;
jzavrotny@ubalt.edu

University of California (Hastings College of the Law)
200 McAllister Street
San Francisco, CA 94102
415-565-4623
Fax: 415-581-8946
admiss@uchastings.edu

University of California at Berkeley (School of Law)
215 Boalt Hall
Berkeley, CA 94720
510-642-2274
Fax: 510-643-6222
adissions@law.berkeley.edu

University of California at Davis (School of Law)
Martin Luther King, Jr. Hall -
400 Mrak Hall Drive
Davis, CA 95616-5201
530-752-6477
admissions@lawucdavis.edu

University of California at Los Angeles (UCLA School of Law)
P.O. Box 951445
Los Angeles, CA 90095-1445
310-825-2080
Fax: 310-206-7227
admissions@law.ucla.edu

School / Contact	C1	C2	C3	C4	C5	C6	C7	C8	C9	C10	C11	%	Salary
University of Chicago (Law School) 1111 East 60th Street, Chicago, IL 60637 · 773-702-9484 · Fax: 773-834-0942 · admissions@law.uchicago.edu	61	2		5	4	3	14	3	1	3	3	98%	$60,000–$160,000
University of Cincinnati (College of Law) P.O. Box 210040, Cincinnati, OH 45221-0040 · 513-556-6805 · Fax: 513-556-2391 · admissions@law.uc.edu		17	5	7	17	16	9	5	4	5	10	91%	
University of Colorado (Law School) Campus Box 403, Wolf Law Building, Boulder, CO 80309-0403 · 303-492-7203 · Fax: 303-492-2542	14	2		3	15	15	18	2	5	10	14	83%	$49,594–$86,359
University of Connecticut (School of Law) 55 Elizabeth Street, Hartford, CT 06105 · 860-570-5153 · Fax: 860-570-5159	6	3	1	5	20	13	10	4	4	6	16	86%	$15,000–$160,000
University of Dayton (School of Law) 300 College Park, Dayton, OH 45469-2760 · 937-229-3555 · Fax: 937-229-4194 · lawinfo@notes.udayton.edu	6	3	2	1	21	12	6	3	4	3	36	86%	$19,700–$135,000
University of Denver (Sturm College of Law) 2255 East Evans Avenue, Denver, CO 80208 · 303-871-6135 · Fax: 303-871-6992 · admissions@law.du.edu	3	4		7	19	22	9	1	4	4	20	91%	$25,000–$160,000
University of Detroit Mercy (School of Law) 651 East Jefferson Avenue, Detroit, MI 48226 · 313-596-0264 · Fax: 313-596-0280 · udmlawao@udmercy.edu	17	3		5	25	12	6	3	1	10	16	75%	$53,891
University of Florida (Fredric G. Levin College of Law) 141 Bruton-Geer Hall, P.O. Box 117622, Gainesville, FL 32611-7622 · 352-273-0890 · Fax: 352-392-4087 · madomo@law.ufl.edu	17	7		6	14	15	6	4	5	8	18	85%	$55,000–$92,500
University of Georgia (School of Law) Hirsch Hall, 225 Herty Drive, Athens, GA 30602-6012 · 706-542-7060 · Fax: 706-542-5556 · ugajd@uga.edu		1		2	8	18	14	4	3	7	25	96%	$53,285–$130,000

	University of Hawaii at Manoa (William S. Richardson School of Law)	University of Houston (Law Center)	University of Idaho (College of Law)	University of Illinois (College of Law)	University of Iowa (College of Law)	University of Kansas (School of Law)
CAREER SERVICES — FACILITIES						
Law Placement Office	•	•		•	•	•
University Placement Office			•			
SERVICES						
Employment Counseling	•	•	•	•	•	•
Job Openings Information	•	•	•	•	•	•
Solo Practice Advice	•	•	•	•	•	•
Resume Preparation	•	•	•	•	•	•
Interview Counseling	•	•	•	•	•	•
Employment Planning	•	•	•	•	•	•
Job Interviews Arrangement	•	•	•	•	•	•
Law, Corporate, and Government Contact	•	•	•	•	•	•
Alumni Contacts	•	•	•	•	•	•
Part-Time/Summer Employment	•	•	•	•	•	•
Internships	•	•	•	•	•	•
Alumni Placement	•	•	•	•	•	•
PLACEMENT RECORD						
Placement within 6 to 9 Months	80%	92%	75%	98%	90%	89%
Percentage Breakdown of Type of Employer						
Private Practice 2–10 Attorneys	12	18	22	10	20	24
Private Practice 11–25 Attorneys	2	11	4	7	5	11
Private Practice 26–50 Attorneys	8	5	1	1	3	3
Private Practice 51–100 Attorneys	5	3		3	3	3
Judicial Clerkships	27	4	22	6	7	2
Government	12	9	14	9	11	18
Business/Industry	2	23	17	12	21	11
Public Interest	15	4	4	1	3	8
Military	9	1		2	2	
Academic	2	2	4	3	1	2
Other	5	15	5	35		17
Average Starting Salary	$42,000–$70,000	$28,750–$160,000	$33,000–$160,000			$24,000–$160,000

School addresses:

University of Hawaii at Manoa (William S. Richardson School of Law)
2515 Dole Street
Honolulu, HI 96822
808-956-7966
Fax: 808-956-3813
lawadm@hawaii.edu

University of Houston (Law Center)
100 Law Center
Houston, TX 77204-6060
713-743-2280
Fax: 713-743-2194
lawadmissions@uh.edu

University of Idaho (College of Law)
P.O. Box 442321
Moscow, ID 83844-2321
208-885-2300
Fax: 208-885-5709
ffinney@uidaho.edu

University of Illinois (College of Law)
504 East Pennsylvania Avenue
Champaign, IL 61820
217-244-6415
Fax: 217-244-1478
admissions@law.uiuc.edu

University of Iowa (College of Law)
320 Melrose Avenue
Iowa City, IA 52242
319-335-9095
Fax: 319-335-9646
law-admissions@uiowa.edu

University of Kansas (School of Law)
205 Green Hall, 1535 West 15th Street
Lawrence, KS 66045
785-864-4378
Fax: 785-864-5054
admitlaw@ku.edu

School	Salary range													%
University of Kentucky (College of Law) — 209 Law Building, Lexington, KY 40506-0048; 606-257-7938; Fax: (859) 323-1061; lawadmissions@email.uky.edu	$42,000–$90,000	1		1	5	11	9	27	11	3	5	27	95%
University of La Verne (College of Law) — 320 East D Street, Ontario, CA 91764; 909-460-2001; Fax: 909-460-2082; lawadm@ulv.edu						14			14	14	5	38	
University of Louisville (Louis D. Brandeis School of Law) — University of Louisville Belknap Campus-Wilson W. Wyatt Hall, Louisville, KY 40292; 502-852-6364; Fax: 502-852-8971; brandon.hamilton@louisville.edu	$37,000–$103,000	3	3			15	17	5	9	9	15	28	95%
University of Maine (School of Law) — 246 Deering Avenue, Portland, ME 04102; 207-780-4341; Fax: 207-780-4239; mainelaw@usm.maine.edu	$47,000–$73	10	1		6	26	9	12	2	3	2	30	80%
University of Maryland (Francis King Carey School of Law) — 500 West Baltimore Street, Baltimore, MD 21201; 410-706-1793; Fax: 410-706-3492; admissions@law.umaryland.edu	$61,498–$150,000	19	5	2	5	10	13	25	2	4	3	12	98%
University of Memphis (Cecil C. Humphreys School of Law) — 1 North Front Street, Memphis, TN 38103-2189; 901-678-5403; Fax: 901-678-0741; lawadmissions@memphis.edu	$32,000–$125,000	6	6		3	6	13	11	3	1	13	29	86%
University of Miami (School of Law) — P.O. Box 248087, 1311 Miller Drive, Coral Gables, FL 33124-8087; 305-284-2523; Fax: 305-284-4400; admissions@law.miami.edu	$30,000–$160,000		2	2	11	11	11	6	6	5	22	28	84%
University of Michigan (Law School) — 625 South State Street, Ann Arbor, MI 48109-1215; 734-764-0537; Fax: 734-647-3218; law.jd.admissions@umich.edu	$39,000–$180,000	1	1	2	9	5	7	11	2	1	2	2	99%
University of Minnesota (Law School) — 229 19th Avenue South, Minneapolis, MN 55455; 612-625-3487; Fax: 612-626-1874; jdadmissions@umn.edu		57	1		11	16	11	15	1	2	3	14	98%

Placement Record — Percentage Breakdown of Type of Employer

School	Average Starting Salary	Other	Academic	Military	Public Interest	Business/Industry	Government	Judicial Clerkships	Private Practice 51–100 Attorneys	Private Practice 26–50 Attorneys	Private Practice 11–25 Attorneys	Private Practice 2–10 Attorneys	Placement Within 6 to 9 Months
University of Mississippi (L.Q.C. Lamar Hall)	$28,000–$100,000		2	2	4	6	10	18	8	7	5	28	93%
University of Missouri (School of Law)	$12,000–$120,000	17	3		7	19	15	5	1	3	8	22	82%
University of Missouri-Kansas City (School of Law)	$30,000–$110,000	22	2			15	11	12	3	3	8	25	73%
University of Montana (School of Law)	$47,369	11		1	8	5	11	21				29	88%
University of Nebraska-Lincoln (College of Law)	$32,000–$150,000	5	3	1	2	16	16	7	3	3	6	38	90%
University of Nevada, Las Vegas (William S. Boyd School of Law)	$56,000–$87,500	16	2	2	4	12	8	16	3	3	6	31	94%
University of New Hampshire School of Law	$50,000–$135,000	8	1		4	17	9	6	13	2	6	31	75%

Career Services (• = offered)

School	Alumni Placement	Internships	Part-Time/Summer Employment	Alumni Contacts	Law, Corporate, and Government Contact	Job Interviews Arrangement	Employment Planning	Interview Counseling	Resume Preparation	Solo Practice Advice	Job Openings Information	Employment Counseling	University Placement Office	Law Placement Office
University of Mississippi	•	•	•	•	•	•	•	•	•		•	•		•
University of Missouri	•	•	•	•	•	•	•	•	•	•	•	•	•	•
University of Missouri-Kansas City	•	•	•	•	•	•	•	•	•	•	•	•		
University of Montana	•	•	•	•	•	•	•	•	•	•	•	•		
University of Nebraska-Lincoln	•	•	•	•	•	•	•	•	•	•	•	•		
University of Nevada, Las Vegas	•	•	•	•	•	•	•	•	•	•	•			
University of New Hampshire	•	•	•	•	•	•	•	•	•	•	•	•		

School Contact Information

University of Mississippi (L.Q.C. Lamar Hall)
P.O. Box 1848 Lamar Law Center
University, MS 38677
662-915-6910
Fax: 662-915-1289
bvinson@olemiss.edu

University of Missouri (School of Law)
103 Hulston Hall
Columbia, MO 65211
573-882-6042
Fax: 573-882-9625
heckm@missouri.edu

University of Missouri-Kansas City (School of Law)
500 East 52nd Street
Kansas City, MO 64110-2499
816-235-1644
Fax: 816-235-5276
brooks@umkc.edu

University of Montana (School of Law)
Missoula, MT 59812
406-243-2698
Fax: 406-243-2576
heidi.fanslow@umontana.edu

University of Nebraska-Lincoln (College of Law)
P.O. Box 830902
Lincoln, NE 68583-0902
402-472-2161
Fax: 402-472-5185
lawadm@unl.edu

University of Nevada, Las Vegas (William S. Boyd School of Law)
4505 Maryland Parkway, Box 451003
Las Vegas, NV 89154-1003
702-895-2440
Fax: 702-895-2414
request@law.unlv.edu

University of New Hampshire School of Law
2 White Street
Concord, NH 03301
603-228-9217
Fax: 603-229-0485
admissions@law.unh.edu

School	Features	%												Salary Range
University of New Mexico (School of Law) MSC11-6070, 1 University of New Mexico Albuquerque, NM 87131-0001 505-277-0958 Fax: 505-277-0958 *witherington@law.unm.edu*	••••••••••••	91%	33	4	6	1	14	19	2	10		5	1	$24,000–$130,000
University of North Carolina at Chapel Hill (School of Law) Campus Box 3380, Van Hecke-Wettach Hall Chapel Hill, NC 27599-3380 919-962-5109 Fax: 919-843-7939 *law_admission@unc.edu*	••••••••••••	92%	22	1	3	3	15	12	14	11		2	17	$38,400–$160,000
University of North Dakota (School of Law) Box 9003 Grand Forks, ND 58202 701-777-2104 Fax: 701-777-2217 *linda.kohoutek@thor.law.und.nodak.edu*	••••••••••••	91%	34	7	2	9	15	14	7	8	3		1	$24,000–$90,000
University of Notre Dame (Notre Dame Law School) P.O. Box 780 Notre Dame, IN 46556-0780 574-631-6626 Fax: 574-631-5474 *lawadmit@nd.edu*	••••••••••••													
University of Oklahoma (College of Law) Andrew M. Coats Hall, 300 Timberdell Road Norman, OK 73019 405-325-4728 Fax: 405-325-0502 *rlucas@ou.edu*	••••••••••••	100%	30	9	1	3	5	14	19	3			16	$20,000–$160,000
University of Oregon (School of Law, William W. Knight Law Center) 1515 Agate Street Eugene, OR 97403-1221 541-346-3846 Fax: 541-346-3984 *admissions@law.uoregon.edu*	••••••••••••	90%					14	16	11	11	1	4	45	$24,000–$120,000
University of Pennsylvania (Law School) 3501 Sansom Street Philadelphia, PA 19104-6204 215-898-7400 Fax: 215-898-9606 *admissions@law.upenn.edu*	••••••••••••	98%	2	1	2	2	19	4	11	5		1	61	$48,450–$152,000
University of Pittsburgh (School of Law) 3900 Forbes Avenue Pittsburgh, PA 15260 412-648-1413 Fax: 412-648-1318 *Mccall@law.pitt.edu*	••••••••••••	82%	38	6	10	3	8	11	20	4	1	2	40	$42,000–$160,000
University of Puerto Rico (School of Law) P.O. Box 23349, UPR Station Rio Piedras, PR 00931-3349 787-999-9551 Fax: 787-999-9564 *arosario-lebron@law.upr.edu*	••••••••••••	81%	15	3	22		18	17	20			5		$24,000–$50,999

PLACEMENT RECORD

School	Average Starting Salary	Other	Academic	Military	Public Interest	Business/Industry	Government	Judicial Clerkships	Private Practice 51-100 Attorneys	Private Practice 26-50 Attorneys	Private Practice 11-25 Attorneys	Private Practice 2-10 Attorneys	Placement within 6 to 9 Months
University of Richmond (School of Law)	$40,000–$165,000	5			2	36	9	21	1	4	7	15	89%
University of Saint Thomas (School of Law)			2	2	6	21	11	11	2	4	5	22	88%
University of San Diego (School of Law)	$35,000–$160,000	4	2	1	5	17	13	2	11	10	14	28	97%
University of San Francisco (School of Law)	$38,000–$135,000	21			14	12	12	4	8	6	8	32	92%
University of South Carolina (School of Law)	$30,000–$160,000	9	2	2	3	105	17	25	1	2	6	21	89%
University of South Dakota (School of Law)	$45,306–$56,411	9	5		7	7	7	27		2	7	29	78%
University of Southern California (Gould School of Law)	$60,000–$160,000	37	4		5	10	11	7	5	2	3	14	92%

Percentage Breakdown of Type of Employer

CAREER SERVICES

School	Alumni Placement	Internships	Part-Time/Summer Employment	Alumni Contacts	Law, Corporate, and Government Contact	Job Interviews Arrangement	Employment Planning	Interview Counseling	Resume Preparation	Solo Practice Advice	Job Openings Information	Employment Counseling	University Placement Office	Law Placement Office
University of Richmond	•	•	•	•	•	•	•	•	•	•	•	•	•	•
University of Saint Thomas	•	•	•	•	•	•	•	•	•	•	•	•		•
University of San Diego	•	•	•	•	•	•	•	•	•	•	•	•		•
University of San Francisco	•	•	•	•	•	•	•	•	•	•	•	•		•
University of South Carolina	•	•	•	•	•	•	•	•	•	•	•	•		•
University of South Dakota	•	•	•	•	•	•	•	•	•	•	•	•	•	•
University of Southern California	•	•	•	•	•	•	•	•	•	•	•	•		•

Facilities: University Placement Office, Law Placement Office

School contact information

University of Richmond (School of Law)
28 Westhampton Way
Richmond, VA 23173
804-289-8189
Fax: 804-287-6516
lawadmissions@richmond.edu

University of Saint Thomas (School of Law)
1000 LaSalle Ave.
Minneapolis, MN 55403
651-962-4895
Fax: 651-962-4876
lawschool@stthomas.edu

University of San Diego (School of Law)
5998 Alcala Park
San Diego, CA 92110
619-260-4528
Fax: 619-260-2218
jdinfo@sandiego.edu

University of San Francisco (School of Law)
2130 Fulton Street
San Francisco, CA 94117-1080
415-422-6586
Fax: 415-422-5442
lawadmissions@usfca.edu

University of South Carolina (School of Law)
701 South Main Street
Columbia, SC 29208
803-777-6605
Fax: 803-777-7751
usclaw@law.sc.edu

University of South Dakota (School of Law)
414 East Clark Street
Vermillion, SD 57069-2390
605-677-5443
Fax: 605-677-5417
law.school@usd.edu

University of Southern California (Gould School of Law)
Los Angeles, CA 90089-0071
213-740-2523
admissions@law.usc.edu

School (address / contact)	%																Salary range
University of Tennessee (College of Law) 1505 W. Cumberland Avenue Knoxville, TN 37996-1810 865-974-4131 Fax: 865-974-1572 *lawadmit@utk.edu*	81%	27	4	6	16	11	13	12	4	3	4							$37,000–$145,000
University of Texas at Austin (School of Law) 727 East Dean Keeton Street Austin, TX 78705 512-232-1200 Fax: 512-471-2765 *admissions@law.utexas.edu*	99%	11	7	4	3	13	10	9	5	1	1	36						$47,000–$134,100
University of the District of Columbia (David A. Clarke School of Law) 4200 Connecticut Avenue, N.W. Washington, DC 20008 202-274-7341 Fax: 202-274-5583 *vcanty@udc.edu; lawadmission@udc.edu*	85%	29			3	10	21	17	14	1	5	4						$37,000–$66,000
University of the Pacific (McGeorge School of Law) 3200 Fifth Avenue Sacramento, CA 95817 916-739-7105 Fax: 916-739-7301 *mcgeorge@pacific.edu*	98%	50				2	25	8	9		3	1						$25,000–$135,000
University of Toledo (College of Law) 2801 West Bancroft Street, MS 507 Toledo, OH 43606-3390 419-530-4131 Fax: 419-530-4345 *law.utoledo.edu*	90%	19	3	1	1	6	11	24	8	1	5	21						$24,000–$105,000
University of Tulsa (College of Law) 3120 East Fourth Place Tulsa, OK 74104-2499 918-631-2406 Fax: 918-631-3630 *april-fox@utulsa.edu*	92%	31	6	3	1	1	16	21	6	1	4	11						$42,000–$83,000
University of Utah (S.J. Quinney College of Law) 332 South 1400, East Room 101 Salt Lake City, UT 84112 801-581-7479 Fax: 801-581-6897 *aguilarr@law.utah.edu*	91%	30	4	8	4	12	10	10	4	4	3	6						$40,000–$133,000
University of Virginia (School of Law) 580 Massie Road Charlottesville, VA 22903-1738 434-924-7351 Fax: 434-982-2128 *lawadmit@virginia.edu*	98%	6	1		2	14	14	3	7		1	53						$25,455–$180,000
University of Washington (School of Law) Box 353020 Seattle, WA 98195-3020 206-543-4078 Fax: 206-543-5671 *lawadmit@u.washington.edu*	96%	18	2	5	16	14	14	15	7	3	1	3						$48,150–$119,298

PLACEMENT RECORD — Percentage Breakdown of Type of Employer

School	Average Starting Salary	Other	Academic	Military	Public Interest	Business/Industry	Government	Judicial Clerkships	Private Practice 51–100 Attorneys	Private Practice 26–50 Attorneys	Private Practice 11–25 Attorneys	Private Practice 2–10 Attorneys	Placement Within 6 to 9 Months
University of West Los Angeles (School of Law)	$50,000–$90,000	25			13	13					13	38	
University of Wisconsin (Law School)		21	3	2	9	10	22	5	2	2	3	21	96%
University of Wyoming (College of Law)	$36,000–$120,000	4		2	8	11	11	4	4	2	9	48	79%
Valparaiso University (School of Law)	$35,000–$140,000	56	1		4	14	16	7					88%
Vanderbilt University (Law School)	$50,000–$160,000	34		2	8	6	14	18	4	3	5	5	96%
Vermont Law School	$30,000–$160,000	6	1	1	15	19	15	15	5	4	6	15	96%
Villanova University (School of Law)	$30,000–$160,000	19	3		4	15	8	15	5	5	6	20	80%

CAREER SERVICES

School	Alumni Placement	Internships	Part-Time/Summer Employment	Alumni Contacts	Law, Corporate, and Government Contact	Job Interviews Arrangement	Employment Planning	Interview Counseling	Resume Preparation	Solo Practice Advice	Job Openings Information	Employment Counseling	University Placement Office	Law Placement Office
University of West Los Angeles (School of Law)	●	●	●		●	●		●		●	●	●	●	
University of Wisconsin (Law School)	●	●	●	●	●	●	●	●	●	●	●	●		●
University of Wyoming (College of Law)	●	●	●	●	●	●	●	●	●	●	●	●	●	●
Valparaiso University (School of Law)	●	●	●	●	●	●	●	●	●	●	●	●		●
Vanderbilt University (Law School)	●	●	●	●	●	●	●	●	●	●	●			●
Vermont Law School	●	●	●	●	●	●	●	●	●	●	●	●		●
Villanova University (School of Law)	●	●	●	●	●	●	●	●	●	●	●	●		●

School Contact Information

University of West Los Angeles (School of Law)
Dept. 3035, 1000 East University Avenue
9920 S. LaCienega Blvd. #404
Inglewood CA 90301-2902
310-342-5210
Fax: 310-342-5295
tsmith@uwla.edu

University of Wisconsin (Law School)
975 Bascom Mall
Madison, WI 53706
608-262-5914
Fax 608-263-3191
admissions@law.wisc.edu

University of Wyoming (College of Law)
Dept. 3035, 1000 East University Avenue
Laramie, WY 82071
307-766-6416
Fax: 307-766-6417
dburke@uwyo.edu

Valparaiso University (School of Law)
Wesemann Hall, 656 S. Greenwich Street
Valparaiso, IN 46383-6493
219-465-7821
Fax: 219-465-7808
law.admissions@valpo.edu

Vanderbilt University (Law School)
131 21st Avenue South
Nashville, TN 37203
615-322-6452
Fax: 615-322-1531
admissions@law.vanderbilt.edu

Vermont Law School
P.O. Box 96, Chelsea Street
South Royalton, VT 05068-0096
802-831-1239
Fax: 802-831-1174
admiss@vermontlaw.edu

Villanova University (School of Law)
299 North Spring Mill Road
Villanova, PA 19085
610-519-7010
Fax: 610-519-6291
admissions@law.villanova.edu

School (Contact Information)	Salary Range												Grad %
Wake Forest University (School of Law) — P.O. Box 7206, Winston-Salem, NC 27109; 336-758-5437; Fax: 336-758-4632; admissions@law.wfu.edu	$73,000–$145,000	3	2		12	11	8	12	14	7	9	28	96%
Washburn University (School of Law) — 1700 SW College Avenue, Topeka, KS 66621; 785-670-1185; Fax: 785-670-1120; admissions@washburnlaw.edu	$30,000–$115,000		2	3	11	10	19	6		2	4	28	92%
Washington and Lee University (School of Law) — Lewis Hall, Lexington, VA 24450; 540-458-8503; Fax: 540-458-8586; lawadm@wlu.edu	$26,000–$160,000	14	9		9	7	21	21	5	2	2	12	94%
Washington University in St. Louis (School of Law) — Box 1120, One Brookings Drive, St. Louis, MO 63130; 314-935-4525; Fax: 314-935-8778; admiss@wulaw.wustl.edu		24	4		6	12	17	8	5	4	4	9	
Wayne State University (Law School) — 471 West Palmer Street, Detroit, MI 48202; 313-577-3937; Fax: 313-993-8129; emjackson@wayne.edu	$42,500–$105,000	18			5	18	9	5	3	17	14	24	86%
West Virginia University (College of Law) — P.O. Box 6130, Morgantown, WV 26506; 304-293-5304; Fax: 304-293-6891; wvulaw.Admissions@mail.wvu.edu	$145,000	12		2	4	24	10	21	3	16	5	25	92%
Western New England University (School of Law) — 1215 Wilbraham Road, Springfield, MA 01119; 413-782-1406; Fax: 413-796-2067; admissions@law.wnec.edu	$26,000–$103,000	5	3		6	26	16	7	16	2	1	20	82%
Western State University (College of Law) — 1111 North State College Blvd, Fullerton, CA 92831; 714-459-1101; Fax: 714-441-1748; adm@wsulaw.edu	$29,000–$160,000	1	4		2	9	7		4	3	9	58	74%
Whittier College (Whittier Law School) — 3333 Harbor Blvd, Costa Mesa, CA 92626; 714-444-4141, ext. 121; Fax: 714-444-0250; info@law.whittier.edu	$27,000–$120,000	4	6		6	31	5	1	6	6	1	40	84%

Feature columns (marked with • where present; each school shows • across all feature rows):

School	Features (●)
Wake Forest University	● ● ● ● ● ● ● ● ● ● ● ●
Washburn University	● ● ● ● ● ● ● ● ● ● ● ●
Washington and Lee University	● ● ● ● ● ● ● ● ● ● ● ●
Washington University in St. Louis	● ● ● ● ● ● ● ● ● ● ● ●
Wayne State University	● ● ● ● ● ● ● ● ● ● ● ● ●
West Virginia University	● ● ● ● ● ● ● ● ● ● ● ●
Western New England University	● ● ● ● ● ● ● ● ● ● ● ●
Western State University	● ● ● ● ● ● ● ● ● ● ● ●
Whittier College	● ● ● ● ● ● ● ● ● ● ● ●

	Widener University (Widener University School of Law)	Widener University (Widener University School of Law)	Willamette University (College of Law)	William Mitchell College of Law	Yale University (Yale Law School)	Yeshiva University (Benjamin N. Cardozo School of Law)
FACILITIES						
Law Placement Office	•	•	•	•	•	•
University Placement Office						
CAREER SERVICES — SERVICES						
Employment Counseling	•	•	•	•	•	•
Job Openings Information	•	•	•	•	•	•
Solo Practice Advice	•	•	•	•	•	
Resume Preparation	•	•	•	•		•
Interview Counseling	•	•	•	•	•	•
Employment Planning	•	•	•	•	•	•
Job Interviews Arrangement	•	•	•	•	•	•
Law, Corporate, and Government Contact	•	•	•	•	•	•
Alumni Contacts	•	•	•	•	•	•
Part-time/Summer Employment	•	•	•	•	•	•
Internships	•	•	•	•	•	•
Alumni Placement	•	•	•	•	•	•
PLACEMENT RECORD						
Placement Within 6 to 9 Months	88%	97%	87%	97%		93%
Private Practice 2-10 Attorneys	19	30	56	25		32
Private Practice 11-25 Attorneys	12	3	3	9		8
Private Practice 26-50 Attorneys	3	3	1	3		7
Private Practice 51-100 Attorneys	4		3	9		5
Judicial Clerkships	16	14	4	10		6
Government	9	21	8	6		14
Business/Industry	23	17	16	24		19
Public Interest	3	6	4	3		12
Military	1	1				1
Academic	2	2		1		1
Other	8	3	5			5
Average Starting Salary	$32,000–$150,000	$35,000–$135,000	$16,000–$120,000	$20,000–$200,000		$50,000–$160,000

School contact information

Widener University (Widener University School of Law)
4601 Concord Pike, P.O. Box 7474
Wilmington, DE 19803-0474
302-477-2162
Fax: 302-477-2224
law.admissions@law.widener.edu

Widener University (Widener University School of Law)
3800 Vartan Way, P.O. Box 69381
Harrisburg, PA 17106-9381
717-541-3903
Fax: 717-541-3999
law.admissions@law.widener.edu

Willamette University (College of Law)
245 Winter Street S.E.
Salem, OR 97301
503-370-6282
Fax: 503-370-6087
law-admission@willamette.edu

William Mitchell College of Law
875 Summit Avenue
St. Paul, MN 55105-3076
651-290-6343
Fax: 651-290-6414
admissions@wmitchell.edu

Yale University (Yale Law School)
P.O. Box 208329
New Haven, CT 06520-8215
203-432-4995
admissions.law@yale.edu

Yeshiva University (Benjamin N. Cardozo School of Law)
55 Fifth Avenue
New York, NY 10003
212-790-0274
Fax: 212-790-0482
lawinfo@yu.edu

their own law offices, a practice euphemistically referred to as "hanging out a shingle." More law graduates go to work in law offices of fewer than 10 lawyers than accept positions in large offices. The judicial cohort is made up of judicial clerks rather than judges and courts administrators for obvious reasons. The largest area of government practice for recent graduates is work in a prosecutor's office. Another area, often listed as a separate category, is the military, which recruits lawyers for the judge advocate general corps for the service branches, as well as individuals who have completed law school before fulfilling other military obligations. Very few law school graduates go into teaching, particularly law school teaching, directly out of law school, but an appreciable number pursue advanced degrees both in law and other fields. Very few graduates go straight into corporate legal deparments, known as "in-house" lawyers.

As you contemplate law school and subsequent career paths, you can take comfort in knowing that your chances of finding employment are good but challenging. While employment statistics may be collected at nine months following graduation, it can take up to a year for many law school graduates to find full-time legal employment. Of the class of 2010 whose employment status was known, 87.6 percent were employed, down from 90.7 percent three years earlier. Of those employed, 73.5 percent were in full-time positions for which a JD was required, but reported that they did not need a law degree to do the work they were handling. The remainder were unemployed or enrolled in advanced degree programs at the time of the NALP survey, approximately nine months after graduation. These numbers have remained fairly consistent over the period of thirty-five years during which NALP has surveyed law school graduates, though there has been an unsurprising decline consistent with the downturn in the economy. Not surprisingly, the employment picture is slightly better in years when the general economy is strong and slightly worse in years with recession. The NALP survey does support the observation that the legal job market is fairly stable and predictable. Competition for the most prestigious and desirable jobs can be fierce, although most people who want jobs as lawyers will eventually get them.

Employment in the Profession as a Whole

According to NALP, law graduates go into positions in the percentages not too different from the makeup of the legal profession as a whole. Based upon a 2010 lawyer population of more than 1.2 million lawyers, there are between 650,000 and 700,000 private practitioners in the United States. Roughly 40 percent (more than 250,000) of these lawyers work as solo practitioners. The next largest group of lawyers practice in small firms of two to five lawyers, followed by lawyers in firms of over one hundred lawyers, and the rest work in medium-sized firms of six to ninety-nine lawyers.

The most dramatic change in the makeup of law firms since 1980 has been the growth of large law firms. Before 1980, only a handful of law firms employed more than one hundred lawyers, but by 2010, hundreds of firms included several hundred lawyers, and the largest firms were over 3,000 lawyers. The percentage of private practitioners who work in large firms has grown over the course of the last two decades from less than 5 percent to over 20 percent of the practicing bar. Although the recession has produced some retrenchment among larger firms, the overall trend in this segment of the market during the last three decades has been growth. In addition, there are large law firms outside the United States even larger than the largest domestic firms. In a globalized economy, U.S. and foreign firms are often competing for the same business.

It is worth noting that the largest law firm in the United States is small compared to business entities in many other fields. There is no big five of law firms like there is in accounting, and there is no legal equivalent of Microsoft or Exxon Mobil.

Most lawyers will engage in the private practice of law at some point during their careers, but if six out of ten lawyers work in private practice, the remaining four are employed in a variety of different endeavors. Corporations (including both in-house counsel and other corporate positions), and government service in federal, state, and local agencies represent the largest of these groups. Government service also includes work as prosecutors and public defenders in the criminal justice system, judicial administration, and law enforcement.

Other lawyers work for political action or public interest organizations, serve in legislatures as representatives, or aides, and participate in political parties, campaigns, non-government organizations (NGOs), and other related activities. Such lawyers may draft legislation, organize campaigns, direct public policy initiatives, or exercise other forms of public service.

Geographic Locations

Lawyers work almost everywhere. More lawyers are concentrated in the largest population centers because of the high volume of legal and commercial activity that occurs in those areas. Lawyers are also concentrated in the seats of government, from Washington, DC, to state capitals, to county seats throughout the United States. Even in rural areas, lawyers can be found with offices close to the clients they serve. An increasing number of U.S. lawyers work outside the boundaries of the United States. With the increasing internationalization of business, lawyers have become a new kind of export.

The NALP employment statistics of law school graduates parallel the demographic patterns for lawyers as a whole. More legal jobs are found in the largest cities, but law graduates are dispersed to a wide variety of smaller places throughout the country as well. There is some evidence that location is linked to first employment, suggesting that people either choose their law school because of the geographic area or become attached to the area while they are in law school.

Another factor influencing where lawyers practice is the bar exam administered by each state. The bar exam represents a hurdle to entry into the practice of law because for most legal positions, it is necessary to pass the bar exam and then become licensed (or "admitted to practice") in the state where the lawyer will be working prior to beginning to serve clients. The majority of law graduates take only one bar exam, and are thus limited to the jurisdiction where they become licensed. A smaller number of graduates take the bar exam in two states, often states in close geographical proximity with overlapping economies, such as New York and New Jersey. Because of scheduling practicalities, it is almost impossible to sit for more than two bar exams at once, and as a result, very few lawyers are initially licensed in more than one or two states.

If graduates find employment in a jurisdiction where they do not pass the bar exam, they will lose those jobs (though most employers will give them a second chance). If they take the exam before they have a job, they will be limited in their job search to positions where they become licensed. Applicants to law school should be aware of these jurisdictional requirements and investigate the possibilities as appropriate.

Salaries

Lawyers' salaries are reported by various bar associations and consultant surveys, as well as by the U.S. Bureau of Labor Statistics and NALP. All of these surveys seem to show that there is a wide range of income among lawyers. NALP data show that there is bimodal curve for salary distribution, with clusters at either end of the spectrum. Some lawyers, particularly in the rural areas, may not have enough business to sustain a full-time practice. Lawyers in certain metropolitan areas with high lawyer populations may find competition for clients to be intense. Some of these lawyers may discover that even after years of practice they do not make a good living practicing law. On the other end of the spectrum are lawyers whose income is in the seven figure range.

Different surveys show discrepancies in reported results that may reflect more on their sampling techniques than actual differences, but most seem to point to an average income for all lawyers of between $100,000 and $150,000. These figures include not only law firm partners, but also semi-retired senior lawyers and employed lawyers.

The range of salaries for recent law school graduates is from as high as $160,000 in some large firms to as low as $30,000 in some rural areas, with a median of $63,000. Some evidence suggests that the highest salaries and perhaps the medium-range salaries have declined and may not return to their pre-recession levels, but the lowest salaries remain fairly stable.

Diversity

Before 1960, the legal profession was overwhelmingly Caucasian and male. Since that time, law schools have systematically recruited women and minority applicants. The percentage of law students from diverse ethnic, racial, and cultural backgrounds increased substantially, although not as much as critics have suggested they should. In an increasingly diverse society, larger numbers of diverse lawyers are needed to serve the needs of these populations. With respect to women, the numbers have swelled to over 50% at many law schools, and as these women graduate and enter the ranks of practitioners, the gender gap in the profession as a whole narrows. Some evidence points to a "glass ceiling" in the legal profession, suggesting that even if women are initially hired in equal numbers as men, there are fewer women at the top ranks of the firms where they work. Certainly, many women have assumed partnership and leadership roles in law firms, but gains have been slow enough that women's legal groups keep a close eye on progress.

CHAPTER 11

What Trends Are Affecting the Practice of Law?

Like other businesses and professions, the practice of law has changed dramatically in recent years. A revolution in technology has swept the business world. Computers have altered the way law is practiced in countless ways, including how lawyers relate to their clients. Technology has even altered the dynamics of how lawyers relate to each other in organizations.

During the first half of the twentieth century, most lawyers practiced alone. Since World War II, however, more and more lawyers have gone to work in ever-larger law firms. In these firms, partners hired junior lawyers—associates—to assist them in the delivery of legal services. The development of these large law firms paralleled the growth of corporations, which fueled an increase in the need for legal services, and for large firms.

During the same period of time the demographics of the U.S. population were also changing. More and more people were living in large cities or metropolitan areas. Waves of immigrants were producing an increasingly diverse society. Global conflict and worldwide interdependency became the norm. As a new world order emerged, the number of lawyers in the United States grew dramatically. As legal problems multiplied, so did the competition among service providers. Many lawyers were particularly ill-prepared for the dramatic changes in the practice of law that occurred during the twentieth century. Evolution is a good word to use to describe these developments, because they produced a kind of economic Darwinism, in which the fittest adapt and survive, and the less competitive individuals and forms of practice become extinct.

As someone who is thinking about going to law school, you should understand that this evolution is continuing and is likely to continue for the foreseeable future. You should recognize that the changes that have transformed other segments of business and industry have had an impact on the practice of law as well. You should know that some people will succeed in these times and some will not. Law, far from being a refuge from a competitive workplace, is subject to risks like most other fields of endeavor.

What you can do to improve the likelihood that you will be successful in this environment is seek to understand the changes that have occurred and that are likely to take place in the future. Of course, it is impossible to predict the future, but sensitivity to trends and insightful analysis of events can help you to adapt. Several areas are worth watching:

GLOBALIZATION

Electronic communication, air transportation, and global migration have produced a world that is inevitably interconnected. It is possible to know the local news almost anywhere in the world. The distribution of products and services transcends international boundaries, producing at the same time tremendous variety in the marketplace and increased homogeneity in availability. English has increasingly become the default language of world commerce. Stock markets in Asia, wars in Africa, and mergers in Europe all have an impact on business in America. Lawyers increasingly will be called upon to represent clients who have interests outside the United States, or who come from outside the United States and need a lawyer's assistance here. Lawyers themselves will face competition from foreign law firms, and even from organizations that provide law-related services, which would be viewed as unauthorized practice of law in the United States. Even lawyers who represent American companies and individuals exclusively are likely to have dealings with foreign companies, individuals, and governments because their clients have dealings with foreigners and non-U.S. entities.

TECHNOLOGY

The information revolution has transformed the way law is practiced. Today, most lawyers have a computer on their desktop and a BlackBerry or iPhone at their hip, with access to the Internet, legal databases, and software applications. Technology allows lawyers and law firms to practice more efficiently. These new resources also place additional demands on practitioners, particularly older lawyers, who grew up in an era when the most advanced technology needed to practice law was a fax machine. Technological advancements force lawyers to find new ways to ply their services, and to communicate with clients who are increasingly wired and connected themselves. As legal information and forms become increasingly available on the Internet and other electronic formats, the role of the lawyer shifts to one of information provider, interpreter, and advisor.

Over the course of the last two decades, computers and other technology have transformed the practice of law, as has been the case with other forms of business. Lawyers today regularly utilize a variety of technologies to communicate with clients and other parties, to file documents with the courts, to conduct research using the Internet, to prepare documents for clients, to support litigation, and to manage cases and files. Increasingly, law firms provide sophisticated web sites, some with interactive service delivery and client portals. Some firms are experimenting with outsourcing work to other countries where it can be performed more economically. Virtually all law firms recognize that technological change will continue to impact the practice of law in the near future.

DEMOGRAPHICS

The study of demographics—where people live and work—is important to any consideration of the marketplace for legal services because they determine where and what kinds of legal services are needed to serve the population. Over time, the population changes, which has an impact on the need for legal services. This section highlights the demographic changes that are likely to affect the way you practice law if you become a lawyer.

- One demographic trend that seems to be gaining momentum with the young professionals is the re-urbanization of inner cities abandoned by flight to the suburbs a half century before. In almost every major city, and many smaller ones, the number of people who both live and work in the city center is on the rise. In many cities, older buildings that were used for a variety of purposes have been renovated and refurbished as residences. At the same time, developers have begun new high-rise construction of both moderate and luxury housing. The evidence points to young professionals seeking the vibrant and diverse cultural life that cities can offer, and eschewing the hour-each-way commute their parents endured.

- A second demographic trend that has had a significant impact on lawyers is the entrance of large numbers of women into the workforce. Before the 1960s, only a handful of women entered the legal profession, and law firms were often an exclusively male domain. Over the past three decades, the legal profession has experienced a dramatic increase in the number of women lawyers. Today, at least half of all students at any given law school are women, and the percentage of women in the profession continues to increase. This change not only produces more opportunities for women in the practice of law, but it also puts pressure on law firms and other organizations that employ lawyers to assure that these opportunities are meaningful ones.

- More women lawyers have produced more two-career families where both spouses either choose to work or have to work in order to sustain a desired lifestyle. When one or both of the people in such a family is a lawyer, there can be a variety of interesting problems, from conflicts of interest between the two lawyers' firms, to employment in different cities, to questions about allocating responsibility for child care and housework.

- Since divorce hits one out of two American families, single parents are often forced to raise children without a partner. The problem of single parenting impacts not only the lawyers but also the support staff in law firms. The upheaval can be disruptive to organizations that are trying to provide quality legal services to clients. For law firms, most of which are very small organizations compared to nonlegal businesses, it can be difficult to accommodate the needs of employees in our complex society.

- Baby Boomers who went to law school between 1965 and 1985 will be retiring over the next two decades. This will produce an array of opportunities in politics, senior management in organizations, and other leadership roles in society. Preliminary research suggests that the Boomers will live longer, remain more active, and require more services than past generations of retirees. This observation is not so much about what will happen to the aging Boomer, but about the legal and other impacts that this will produce for the next generation of lawyers.

• A final demographic shift involves recent waves of migration into the United States. The issue of migration from Mexico, Central and South America has become a political football, but these are not the only new arrivals. The number of Asians, both from the Far East (China/Japan/Korea) and from the Indian subcontinent (India/Pakistan/Bangladesh) continues to rise. Immigrants from Africa, the Middle East, the former Soviet Bloc countries, and the Caribbean all continue to make America, if not a melting pot, at least an alphabet soup. Immigrants have a variety of legal needs, but often come from cultures where suspicion of government, lawyers, and the legal system makes them reticent to seek legal assistance. Immigrants often face language and social barriers in their adopted home as well. One thing is clear: the legal work serving these populations will continue to grow commensurate with the growth of the immigrant population.

LIFESTYLES

Many young lawyers must face fundamental lifestyle issues, enhanced in part by the great variety of choices available to them:

• How many hours a week do you and your spouse/partner want to put into the practice of law? Forty? Sixty? Eighty? One hundred? Lawyers at the higher end of the salary scale generally work very long hours.

• Do you want to have children or not?

• If so, when?

• Who will stay at home with young children and for how long?

• What kind of childcare and early education will children receive?

• What kind of geographical setting is most compatible with your interests, hobbies, and professional needs?

• The beach? The mountains? The big city? A rural county seat?

• Where do you see yourself in ten or twenty years as your practice matures?

• And family? Do you want the people you grew up with to be close at hand, or will you be satisfied to see them once or twice a year?

• Is the type of law that you hope to practice likely to be available in the geographic locale where you would like to live?

The answers to these questions are intimately wrapped up in the life choices you will be required to make in the coming years. One negative aspect of the practice of law is that the hours can be long and the work demanding. And state-based licensing means that lawyers are not as geographically mobile as other professionals. In the past, young lawyers were often forced to make sacrifices to meet the workloads imposed by their employers. It remains to be seen whether today's neophyte lawyers will press for reforms, and whether, if they do, law firms will respond. It is certain, however, that these lifestyle issues are not going away any time soon.

CHANGE

One common thread that cuts through all the trends described above is change. The world is changing in unprecedented ways, and will continue to change throughout the professional lives of those students entering law school in the coming years. The changes that we are experiencing are profound; they are transforming. Futurist Tom Peters says that we may be in the midst of the biggest revolution in the way people live since we came in off the savannahs to live in permanent villages—a 10,000-year sea change. Other observers might not go this far, but virtually everyone who has thought about the future believes that we are in the midst of something really big.

It should come as no surprise that the legal profession is undergoing dramatic change in the way legal services are delivered. Just as the industrial base of America has shifted to Third World countries, and the medical profession has endured the rise of managed care, lawyers face an increasingly competitive environment and pressures to deliver better services more economically. Although the number of law school graduates continues to climb, more and more lawyers either opt, or are forced, to work in settings outside of private practice (i.e., law firms). An increasing number of graduates accept positions in corporations, government service, private associations, accounting or professional services firms, banks, group legal services, private associations, and a variety of other organizations. Other lawyers start out in law firms, but move to some other type of organization, often one that has been a client of the firm. Some lawyers may abandon the law completely, but the vast majority of them continue to utilize their legal skills and "practice law" in a new environment.

Someone contemplating a career in law should appreciate the fact that the opportunities for lawyers are changing as the world around them changes. All this change creates tremendous challenges and risks, but it also generates unusual opportunities. It will be important for you to stay attuned to how society and the practice of law continue to evolve in order to maximize your opportunities and achieve your goals in the coming years.

These are not simple questions, and there are no easy answers. But both lawyers and applicants to law school will have to face these issues at some time or other. It makes sense to think now about how lifestyle questions will affect the career choices that you make as a lawyer, and try to make decisions that are consistent with your long-term personal needs.

SUBSTANTIVE PRACTICE AREAS

People often ask what are the growing practice areas in the law? There is probably no consensus answer to this question, and many pundits have attempted to predict substantive trends in the law—many with great imprecision. Understanding the risks inherent in such predictions, this author will offer insights into a number of practice areas that are likely to experience growth in the coming decade:

- **Health law.** In the United States there have been dramatic changes in the way health care services are delivered. The availability of medical treatment, risks associated with scientific advancement, and issues involving death and dying all present health care issues. Decisions about treatment are no longer limited to the patient and provider, but often involve a hospital and/or other corporate employer, and an insurance company or HMO. With a population that is graying demographically, health care issues can be expected to increase during the early part of the twenty-first century.

- **Elder law.** In addition to health care, older citizens have a variety of other issues that they must confront, from increased leisure associated with retirement to legal issues like estate planning, to a variety of other unique problems. An increasing number of lawyers are defining their practice in terms of these clients under the heading of Elder Law. The number of Americans age 55 and older continues to grow.

- **Business law.** Lawyers work for businesses of all sizes, as well as individuals. Businesses of all sizes require legal support on a regular basis, from formation to dissolution; companies and other entities require guidance in planning how to address legal problems in a highly regulated environment; they need lawyers to represent them when they have disputes with other organizations or individuals; and executives need lawyers to advise them as to how to handle internal legal problems. Entity lawyers may work in law firms (outside counsel), inside the organization (inhouse counsel), or within a nonlegal division of the entity. As the number of companies has grown, and the legal challenges of the business world have become more complex, the legal needs of business clients have expanded. Much of the growth of the legal profession in the last half of the 20th century could be attributed to business law, and despite some slowdown in this arena, business law is projected to continue to drive growth in the legal profession.

- **Transnational business.** The growing international interdependence of countries, particularly in the delivery of goods and services, will continue to produce a high level of complex legal work. Lawyers from this country and others around the world will be involved in solving the legal problems that these commercial transactions create. From the European community to the Pacific Rim, from the former Eastern bloc to Central and South America, American lawyers will find opportunities in all these areas.

- **Intellectual property law.** The growth in certain specialized businesses, particularly in the health care and computer technology industries, will require lawyers who have technological or scientific backgrounds to assist clients in protecting the new technologies they develop. While patent law and copyright law are not new, continued innovations, particularly those triggered by the

Internet, and growing technological sophistication, have created an increase in demand for lawyers to help clients secure patents and to help clients protect their intellectual property.

- **Environmental law.** Global warming and other environmental issues are protracted; resources are limited. It is inevitable that a world population of six billion will have to confront issues like global warming, extinction of animal species, resource allocation, and sustainable development. Lawyers involved in this process are likely to have their hands full for the foreseeable future.

- **Bankruptcy.** Both individuals and companies face financial challenges, which frequently lead to restructuring, refinancing, or in worst cases bankruptcy. Lawyers working with clients in this area often provide "workout" services extending for years after the financial crisis.

- **Communications and technology.** The Internet, satellite communications, cable, and other legal problems associated with computers and electronic technology will continue to evolve in the near future. Many of the concepts of common law from copyright to theft must be redefined in the electronic environment.

- **Leisure law.** Sports and entertainment law, travel law, and related subject areas will experience a period of growth in the coming years, as people have more and more free time. Even those who work long hours will be seeking leisure opportunities during their vacation periods. Many workers will be retiring earlier and looking for leisure activities to fill their time. Although this is a fairly small field of practice today, it is likely to grow in the coming decades.

- **Preventive law.** Estate planning, business planning, tax planning, and other areas where lawyers can advise individuals and businesses on how to avoid legal problems, rather than trying to help once things have fallen apart, will experience considerable growth. This will be not only because lawyers will be seeking these markets, but also because a more sophisticated client base will seek to have this kind of legal help more readily available.

- **Mediation and other forms of alternative dispute resolution.** More and more legal cases will be resolved without going to court, through mediation and alternative dispute resolution processes. Lawyers will be involved in these practice areas as well, because their legal skills of negotiation, persuasion, analysis, and organization will work well to help clients solve problems in a variety of different ways.

- **Employment law.** The proliferation of state and federal law governing the workplace has created a growing practice in employment law. Practice settings in private firms range from small and large law firms devoted exclusively to this area of practice to more general practice firms in which fewer than all of the lawyers specialize in this area. With the growth in business generally, and with large corporate mergers, there will continue to be a need for lawyers to advise clients on employee matters, such as ERISA and pension benefits, to train clients and their employees on prevention (e.g., harassment training) and to litigate or mediate employee complaints and claims arising under the many laws in this area.

Although the areas of practice described above represent fields where growth can be inferred from a variety of factual indicia, many other specialized or "boutique" practice areas will blossom in the coming years. Because virtually every form of human endeavor has legal implications, it follows that very little in life can be conducted outside the law. This means that there is a substantive practice area for almost anything you can imagine, and if you can imagine it, you can bet that somewhere there is a lawyer practicing in that field. Lawyers today are increasingly becoming specialists, who concentrate their practice in a narrow field of expertise. The general practitioner is a dying breed in law, just as in medicine. And as in medicine, the more complex society becomes, the more specialties emerge.

CONCLUSION

For someone about to enter law school, it should be clear that choosing to become a lawyer is just the beginning of a long path of career choices. Not only will law school graduates have to choose from a variety of practice settings, they will have to decide among an almost infinite array of substantive fields within the law. On top of all this, they will have to be astute enough to understand that the underpinnings of their decisions will be undergoing continual change.

The element of change will be a factor in every facet of life, whether you decide to attend law school or not, but if you do elect to go to law school, do not imagine that you will be immune from the forces that are transforming the rest of the world. If you remember that society and the practice of law are both changing, and continually reflect upon how these changes will affect you, you will improve your chances of achieving success professionally and personally.

Adapted from Gary A. Munneke, *Careers in Law,* VGM Professional Careers Series, 1992, pages 9–12, 15–17. Reprinted by permission.

PART II

Taking the LSAT

CHAPTER 12

The LSAT and the Admissions Process

The Law School Admission Test (LSAT) is required for all law school applicants. Although law school admissions committees consider a variety of criteria, there is little doubt that the LSAT plays a significant role in the selection process.

Preparation for the LSAT is the rule rather than the exception. This section is an introduction to the LSAT preparation process.

ANSWERS TO SOME COMMONLY ASKED QUESTIONS

What does the LSAT measure?

The LSAT is designed to measure a range of mental abilities related to the study of law; therefore, it is used by most law schools to evaluate their applicants.

Will any special knowledge of the law raise my score on the LSAT?

The LSAT is designed so that candidates from a particular academic background are given no advantage. The questions measure reading comprehension, logical reasoning, and analytical reasoning, drawing from a variety of verbal and analytical material.

Does a high score on the LSAT predict success in law school or in the practice of law?

Success on the LSAT demonstrates your ability to read with understanding and to reason clearly under pressure; surely these strengths are important to both the study and the practice of law, as is the ability to write well, measured by the LSAT Writing Sample. To say that success on the LSAT *predicts* success in law school may overstate the case, however, because success in law school also involves skills that are not measured by the LSAT.

When is the LSAT administered?

The regular administration of the test occurs nationwide four times each year, around the beginning of the fall, winter, spring, and summer seasons. Except for the summer month, the test is usually administered on a Saturday morning from 8:30 A.M. to about 1:00 P.M. For the past few years, the *summer exam* has been given on a Monday afternoon. Dates are announced annually by the Law School Admission Council (LSAC) in Newtown, PA.

What if I cannot take the test on a Saturday?

Some special arrangements are possible: Check the Law School Admission Services (LSAS) General Information Booklet in your registration packet. Those who must take the exam at a time when the regular administration occurs on Saturday, but who cannot participate on Saturday for religious reasons, may arrange for a special Monday administration.

How early should I register?

Regular registration closes about one month before the exam date. Late registration is available up to three weeks prior to the exam date. There is an additional fee for late registration.

Is walk-in registration available?

For security reasons, walk-in registration is no longer permitted. Be sure to read very carefully the General Information Booklet section on "registering to take the LSAT."

What is the LSDAS?

The LSDAS (Law School Data Assembly Service) compiles a report about each subscribing applicant. The report contains LSAT results, a summary of the applicant's academic work, and copies of college transcripts. A report is sent to each law school that the applicant designates. Thus, if you register for the LSDAS, you will not need to mail a separate transcript to each of your prospective law schools. REMINDER: You should review information regarding the Candidate Referral Service in your *LSAT & LSDAS Information Book*.

How is the LSAT used?

Your LSAT score is one common denominator by which a law school compares you to other applicants. Other factors also determine your acceptance to law school: a law school may consider your personal qualities, grade-point average, extracurricular achievements, and letters of recommendation. Requirements for admission vary widely from school to school, so you are wise to contact the law school of your choice for specific information.

How do I obtain registration forms and registration information?

The registration form covering both the LSAT and the LSDAS is available in the LSAT & LSDAS REGISTRATION/INFORMATION BOOK. Copies of the packet are available at the admissions offices of most law schools and the testing offices at most undergraduate universities and colleges. You may also obtain the book and more information by writing to Law Services, Box 2000, 662 Penn Street, Newtown, PA 18940-0998; by Internet using *www.LSAC.org*; by fax at (215) 968-1119; by e-mail at *Lsacinfor@LSAC.org* or by telephone at (215) 968-1001.

What is the structure of the LSAT?

The LSAT contains five 35-minute multiple-choice sections followed by a 35-minute Writing Sample. The Writing Sample does not count as part of your LSAT score. The common question types that do count toward your score are Logical Reasoning (two sections), Analytical Reasoning (one section), and Reading Comprehension (one section). In addition to these four sections, one experimental or pretest section will appear. This experimental or pretest section, which will probably be a repeat of one of the common question types, will not count in your score.

How is the LSAT scored?

The score for the objective portion of the test ranges from 120 to 180, and there is no penalty for wrong answers. The Writing Sample is unscored, but copies are sent to the law schools of your choice for evaluation.

What about question structure and value?

All LSAT questions, apart from the Writing Sample, are multiple-choice with five choices. All questions within a section are of equal value, regardless of difficulty.

Should I guess?

There is no penalty for guessing on the LSAT. Therefore, before you move on to the next question, at least take a guess. You should fill in guess answers for those you have left blank or did not get to, before time is called for that section. If you can eliminate one or more choices as incorrect, your chances for a correct guess increase.

How often can I take the LSAT?

You may take the LSAT more than once if you wish. But keep in mind that any report sent to you or to law schools will contain scores for any exams taken over the past few years, along with an average score for those exams. The law school receiving your scores will decide which score is the best estimate of your ability; many law schools rely on the average score as a figure. Normally, you may not take the test more than three times in a two-year period.

Is it at all possible to cancel my LSAT score?

You may cancel your score only within nine calendar days after taking the test.

How early should I arrive at the test center, and what should I bring?

Arrive at the test center 20 to 30 minutes before the time designated on your admission ticket. Bring three or four sharpened No. 2

pencils, an eraser, and a noiseless watch (no alarm, calculator, or beeping), as well as your LSAT Admission Ticket and proper identification as described in the LSAT & LSDAS Registration/Information Booklet.

Can I prepare for the LSAT?

Yes. Reading skills and test-taking strategies should be the focus of your preparation for the test as a whole. Success on the more specialized analytical sections of the test depends on your thorough familiarity with the types of problems you are likely to encounter and the reasoning process involved. For maximum preparation, work through this book and practice the strategies and techniques outlined in each section.

BASIC FORMAT OF THE LSAT AND SCORING

THE *ORDER* OF THE FOLLOWING MULTIPLE-CHOICE SECTIONS *WILL* VARY. The Experimental Section is not necessarily the last section.

	Section	Number of Questions	Minutes
I.	Logical Reasoning	24-26	35
II.	Analytical Reasoning	22-24 (4 sets)	35
III.	Reading Comprehension	26-28 (4 passages)	35
IV.	Logical Reasoning	24-26	35
V.	Experimental Section	varies	35
	Writing Sample	1 essay	35
TOTALS		118-132 questions (only 96-104 count toward your score)	210 minutes or 3 hours 30 minutes

NOTE: For your convenience, this Barron's text labels each section of this Model Test (e.g., Reading Comprehension, Logical Reasoning, etc.). In contrast, sections of the actual LSAT exam are not usually labeled.

The LSAT is scored on a 120 to 180 scale.

The following simple chart will give you a very general approximation of the LSAT scoring system. It shows the approximate percentage of right answers necessary on the LSAT to be in a certain score range.

Approximate % of right answers	Approximate Score Range
Between 75% and 100%	160-180
Between 50% and 75%	145-159
Between 25% and 50%	130-144
Between 0% and 25%	120-129

Note that this chart is meant to give you an *approximate* score range.

A Closer Look at the Timing—What It Really Means

Although the LSAT is comprised of five 35-minute multiple-choice sections and a 35-minute unscored essay, it is important to understand the timing breakdown and what it means. The test is actually broken down as follows:

105 min. {	Section I 35 minutes
	Section II 35 minutes
	Section III 35 minutes
	Short break—usually 10-15 minutes
70 min. {	Section IV 35 minutes
	Section V 35 minutes
	Very, very short break—usually 1 or 2 minutes
35 min. {	Writing Sample (Essay)—35 minutes

Notice that you are given three multiple-choice sections with no breaks in between. When they say "stop" at the end of 35 minutes they will immediately say something like, "Turn to the next section, make sure that you are in the right section, ready, begin." So, in essence, you are working three sections back to back to back. This means that when you practice you should be sure to practice testing for 1 hour and 45 minutes without a break.

After the short break, when you may get up, get a drink, and go to the restroom, you are back for two more back-to-back multiple-choice sections.

For the final 35-minute writing sample you will be given scratch paper to do your pre-writing or outlining.

Keep in mind that there will be some time taken before the exam and after the exam for clerical-type paperwork—distributing and picking up paperwork, filling out test forms, and so on.

Important Reminders

- At least half of your test will contain Logical Reasoning questions; prepare accordingly. Make sure that you are good at Logical Reasoning!
- The experimental or pretest section will usually repeat other sections and can appear in different places on the exam. At the time of the exam, you will not know which section is experimental. Take the test as if all of the sections count.
- Scoring will be from 120-180. This is the score, and the percentile rank that goes with it is what the law schools look at and are referring to in their discussions.
- All questions in a section are of equal value, so do not get stuck on any one question. The scores are determined by totaling all of your right answers on the test and then scaling.
- Answer all the easy questions first; then come back and answer the tougher questions. Don't be afraid to skip a question, but always at least take a guess.
- There is NO PENALTY for guessing, so at least take a guess before you move to the next question.

- The 35-minute Writing Sample will not be scored, but copies will be forwarded to the law schools to which you apply. Scratch paper will be provided for the Writing Sample only.
- Keep in mind that regardless of the format of your exam, two sections of Logical Reasoning, one section of Analytical Reasoning, and one section of Reading Comprehension always count toward your score.

SOME WORDS TO THE WISE

Ask a Few Questions

Before you actually start your study plan there are four basic questions that you should ask the law schools to which you are applying:

1. Considering my GPA and other qualifications, what score do you think I need to get into your law school?
2. When do you need to get my score reports? Or, When should I take the test to meet your deadlines?
3. What do you do if I take the LSAT more than once? Remember that when the law school receives your score report it will see a score for each time you've taken the test *and* an average of the scores. It is up to the law schools and their governing bodies as to what score(s) they will consider. Try to do your best on the first try and take the LSAT only once, if possible.
4. What do you do with my Writing Sample? Is it used as a tiebreaker? Do you score it yourself? Is it just another piece of the process?

Knowing the answers to most of these questions before you start your study will help you understand what is expected and will help you get mentally ready for the task ahead.

Excerpted from *Barron's LSAT,* by Jerry Bobrow, Ph.D., rev. by Bernard V. Zandy, Barron's Educational Series, Inc., 2009.

CHAPTER 13

A Model LSAT

This chapter contains a full-length Model Test. It is geared to the format of the LSAT and it is complete with answers and explanations. It is equivalent to the LSAT in question structure, number of questions, level of difficulty, and time allotments. (The questions used are not taken directly from the LSAT, as those questions are copyrighted and may not be reproduced.)

The Model Test should be taken under strict test conditions. The test ends with a 35-minute Writing Sample, which is not scored.

Section	Description	Number of Questions	Time Allowed
I	Logical Reasoning	26	35 minutes
II	Reading Comprehension	28	35 minutes
III	Analytical Reasoning	23	35 minutes
IV	Logical Reasoning	26	35 minutes
V	Reading Comprehension	28	35 minutes
	Writing Sample		35 minutes
TOTALS:		131	3 hours 30 minutes

Now please turn to the next page, remove your answer sheets, and begin the Model Test.

1   1   1   1   1

SECTION I
TIME — 35 MINUTES
26 QUESTIONS

Directions: In this section you will be given brief statements or passages and will be required to evaluate the reasoning involved. In some instances, more than one choice will appear to be a possible answer. You are to choose the *best* answer. Use common sense and reasonableness in making your selection; then mark the proper space on the answer sheet.

Questions 1–2

Professor: Probability is a curiously unstable concept. Semantically speaking, it is an assumption, a pure artifice, a concept that may or may not be true, but nevertheless facilitates a logical process. It is not a hypothesis because, by its very nature, it cannot be proved. Suppose we flip a coin that has a distinguishable head and tail. In our ignorance of the coming result we say that the coin has one chance in two of falling heads up, or that the probability of a head turning up is one-to-two. Here it must be understood that the one-to-two is not "true" but is merely a species of the genus probability.

1. The professor assumes that

   (A) nothing about our coin influences its fall in favor of either side or that all influences are counterbalanced by equal and opposite influences
   (B) probability can be dealt with or without the use of logic
   (C) an assumption must be plausible
   (D) the probability of the coin's landing on an edge is counterbalanced by the probability of its not landing on an edge
   (E) probability can be precisely calculated

2. The last sentence implies that

   (A) probability is not absolute
   (B) one-to-two is merely a guess
   (C) one-to-two is a worthless ratio
   (D) truth is not important
   (E) genus is a category of species

3. Self-confidence is a big factor in success. The person who thinks he can, will master most of the things he attempts. The person who thinks he can't, may not try.

   The author of these statements would agree that

   (A) nothing is impossible
   (B) no task is too large
   (C) success relies on effort
   (D) self-confidence is of utmost importance
   (E) trying is half the battle

GO ON TO THE NEXT PAGE ➤

4. People who risk riding on roller coasters are more likely to take risks in other areas of their lives than those who avoid roller coasters. So roller coaster riders are more likely than others to be successful in situations in which taking risks can result in benefit to them.

If the above comments are true, they most strongly support which one of the following statements?

(A) No roller coaster riders avoid taking risks in other areas of their lives, but some may take more risks than others.
(B) Risk taking in life decisions is important not only because of the possible financial gain but because of the psychological benefits produced.
(C) Some people who are not roller coaster riders may take more risks in other areas of their lives than do roller coaster riders.
(D) Mountain climbing is riskier than riding on roller coasters, so people who climb mountains will be more successful in other areas of their lives than are roller coaster riders.
(E) Risk taking in one type of activity indicates a likelihood of risk taking in other types of activities.

5. *Anthropologist:* For many years, anthropologists believed that the longevity of the men of the island of Zobu was the result of their active lives and their eating only fish from the lagoon and fruits and vegetables grown on the island. However, recent studies of the inhabitants of nearby Luku, where the way of life and diet are virtually identical with Zobu's, have revealed that the men there rarely survive beyond early middle age.

If the information in this paragraph is correct, it best supports which one of the following?

(A) There are important differences in the lagoons of the two islands of which scientists are unaware.
(B) The inhabitants of Luku and Zobu probably have many ancestors in common.
(C) The longevity of the natives of Zobu is not due simply to their diet and way of life.
(D) Some, though not all, of the residents of Luku live as long as some of the residents of Zobu.
(E) Since longevity depends on so many different factors, it is useless to compare longevity in one area with that in another.

1   **1**   **1**   **1**   **1**

<u>Questions 6–7</u>

Because college-educated men and women as a group earn more than those without college educations, and because in Eastern Europe and Latin America, 105 women are enrolled in colleges for every 100 men, the total earnings of college women in these areas should be equal to, if not greater than, the earnings of college men. But college women in Eastern Europe and in Latin America earn only 65 percent of what college men in these countries earn.

6. Which one of the following, if true, is most useful in explaining this discrepancy?

(A) The earning power of both men and women rises sharply in accord with their level of education.

(B) In some countries of Western Europe, the earning power of college-educated women is higher than that of men in Eastern Europe and Latin America.

(C) In Eastern Europe, more men than women who enter college fail to complete their educations.

(D) The largest percentage of women in Eastern European and Latin American universities study to become teachers; the largest percentage of men study engineering.

(E) In Eastern Europe and Latin America, about 60 percent of the total workforce is college educated.

7. Which one of the following is a faulty assumption based on the statistics of the passage?

(A) The passage assumes that all of the college women enter the workforce.

(B) The passage assumes conditions in Eastern Europe and in Latin America are the same.

(C) The passage assumes that men and women should be paid equally.

(D) The passage assumes that college-educated women outnumber women who have not attended college in Eastern Europe and Latin America.

(E) The passage assumes that all college-educated workers will be paid more than workers who do not have college educations.

GO ON TO THE NEXT PAGE ➤

8. *Economist:* When consumers are in a buying mood, and the cost of money is low, a shrewd retailer with a popular product will reduce prices of items that are selling slowly and will make up for any loss by raising prices on the product or products that are popular.

In which one of the following situations are these recommendations observed?

(A) At Easter, John's Markets offered one dozen eggs at half their usual price and hams and turkeys at a 40 percent discount, but because of heavy rains, they raised the price of many green vegetables.

(B) This Christmas, Arrow Clothiers is offering six-month interest-free charge accounts to any customers who purchase $50 or more of merchandise from their stock of discontinued summer wear and the fashionable new op-art neck wear.

(C) Since interest rates have reached a yearly low, the price of tax-free bonds is near an all-time high. Discount Brokerage has launched a campaign to sell off all of its holding in precious metals mutual funds that are now at their lowest price in years.

(D) Angus Jewelry is offering special savings for customers who make purchases in May. With graduations coming soon, they are offering engraved gold Swiss watches, as well as lower prices on heart-shaped jewelry items that were featured on Valentine's Day.

(E) Travel agents in Orlando are capitalizing on the lowered air-fares to lure tourists by offering special rates on hotel accommodations and discounted admission tickets to two of the large theme parks in the area.

9. While some cities impose tough, clear restrictions on demolitions of older buildings, our city has no protection for cultural landmarks. Designation as a landmark by the Cultural Heritage Commission can delay a demolition for only one year. This delay can be avoided easily by an owner's demonstrating an economic hardship. Developers who simply ignore designations and tear down buildings receive only small fines. Therefore, ...

Which one of the following best completes the passage above?

(A) the number of buildings protected by Cultural Heritage Commission designation must be increased

(B) developers must be encouraged to help preserve our older buildings

(C) the designation as landmark must be changed to delay demolition for more than one year

(D) developers who ignore designations to protect buildings must be subject to higher fines

(E) if our older buildings are to be saved, we need clearer and more rigorously enforced laws

10. Michael claimed that the large dent in the fender of the company-owned vehicle he had borrowed was caused by the careless act of another motorist, who backed into the car when it was parked in a public garage. Yet Michael's own car has several similar dents in its fenders, all of which he acknowledges as having been caused by his own careless driving. Therefore, Michael's contention that the dent in the formerly undented company-owned vehicle was caused by the careless act of another person is NOT true.

The reasoning in this argument is vulnerable because it

(A) fails to recognize that Michael could be lying about the dents in his own vehicle
(B) fails to recognize that the motorist who backed into him simply did not see him
(C) fails to acknowledge that many such accidents occur in parking garages
(D) presumes, without justification, that because Michael has caused similar dents to his own car, he caused the dent in the company car
(E) fails to take into consideration that Michael was recently named Employee of the Month

Questions 11–12

Sixty percent of the American people, according to the latest polls, now believe that inflation is the nation's most important problem. This problem of inflation is closely related to rising prices. The inflation rate has been 10 percent or more most of this year. Undoubtedly, our gluttonous appetite for high-priced foreign oil has been a major factor. We have been shipping billions of dollars overseas, more than foreigners can spend or invest here. Dollars are selling cheaply and this has forced the value of the dollar down. Government programs now being inaugurated to slow this trend are at best weak, but deserve our support, as they appear to be the best our government can produce. Hopefully, they won't fail as they have in the past.

11. The author of this passage implies that

(A) inflation cannot be stopped or slowed, because of a weak government
(B) the fear of inflation is not only unwarranted, but also detrimental
(C) 40 percent of non-Americans believe inflation is not the most important problem
(D) foreign oil is the sole reason for the sudden increase in inflation
(E) the present programs will probably not slow inflation

12. Which one of the following contradicts something in the preceding passage?

(A) Foreign oil is actually underpriced.
(B) The inflation rate has not risen for most of this year.
(C) Overseas investors are few and far between.
(D) Our government is trying a new approach to end inflation.
(E) The weakness of the programs stems from lack of support.

GO ON TO THE NEXT PAGE ➤

1   1   1   1   1

13. Sales of new homes in Arizona fell almost 20 percent in the month of February, compared to last year. Analysts attribute the decline to several factors. Record rainfalls kept both builders and buyers indoors for most of the month. The rise in the interest rates have brought mortgage rates to a ten-month high. Both the sales of new homes and housing starts have reached new lows. With every indication that mortgage rates will remain high for the rest of the year, Arizona home-builders foresee a very grim year ahead.

Which one of the following would add support to the conclusion of this passage?

(A) Last year's sales increased in the second half of the year, despite some increase in interest rates.
(B) Last year's sales were accelerated by good weather in January and February.
(C) Widespread advertising and incentives to attract buyers this February were ineffective.
(D) Rain in Arizona usually ends late in February.
(E) Home sales and building starts throughout the country are about the same this year as last year.

14. No one reads *Weight-Off* magazine unless he or she is fat. Everyone reads *Weight-Off* magazine unless he or she eats chocolate.

Which one of the following is inconsistent with the above?

(A) No one is fat and only some people eat chocolate.
(B) Some people are fat and no one eats chocolate.
(C) Everyone is fat.
(D) No one is fat and no one reads *Weight-Off*.
(E) No one who is fat eats chocolate.

15. *Jerry:* Every meal my wife cooks is fantastic.

Dave: I disagree. Most of my wife's meals are fantastic, too.

Dave's response shows that he understood Jerry to mean that

(A) Dave's wife does not cook fantastic meals
(B) only Jerry's wife cooks fantastic meals
(C) every one of Jerry's wife's meals is fantastic
(D) not every one of Jerry's wife's meals is fantastic
(E) no one cooks fantastic meals all the time

Questions 16–17

Commentators and politicians are given to enlisting the rest of America as allies, sprinkling such phrases as "Americans believe" or "Americans will simply not put up with" into their pronouncements on whatever issue currently claims their attentions. They cite polls showing 60 or 80 or 90 percent support for their views. There may (or may not) have been such polls, but even if the polls are real, their finer points will not be reported because they usually contradict the speaker's point. The alleged 80 percent support for a balanced budget amendment, for example, plummets to less than 30 percent if the pollster so much as mentions an entitlement program like social security. People do have opinions, but they are rarely so specific or so unequivocal as your news broadcaster or your senator would lead you to believe.

16. The argument of this passage would be less convincing if it could be shown that

   (A) In a recent poll, 80 percent of the Americans responding supported a balanced budget amendment.
   (B) Most polls used by television commentators are conducted by telephone calls lasting less than 35 seconds.
   (C) Far more Americans are indifferent to or badly informed about current affairs than are well informed.
   (D) The polls' predictions of who will be elected president have been correct about every presidential election since Truman defeated Dewey.
   (E) Many polls are based on samples that do not accurately represent the demographics of an area.

17. The argument of this passage proceeds by using all of the following EXCEPT:

   (A) supporting a general point with a specific example
   (B) questioning the honesty of politicians and commentators
   (C) reinterpreting evidence presented as supporting a position being rejected
   (D) pointing out inherent inconsistencies in the claims of the politicians and commentators
   (E) exposing the limitations of arguments based on statistics

18. The most often heard complaint about flights on Scorpio Airlines is that there is insufficient room in the cabin of the plane to accommodate all of the passengers' carry-on baggage. The number of passengers who carry on all of their luggage rather than checking it at the ticket counter has increased so much that on more than half of the flights on Scorpio Airlines passengers have difficulty finding space for their bags in the cabin of the plane. The company is considering ways to alleviate this problem.

All of the following are plausible ways of dealing with the problem EXCEPT:

   (A) reducing the allowable size of carry-on luggage
   (B) charging passengers who carry on more than one bag a fee
   (C) increasing the fares of flights on lightly traveled routes
   (D) reducing the seating capacity of the cabins to provide more space for luggage
   (E) offering a price reduction to ticket buyers who check their bags

19. X: "We discover new knowledge by the syllogistic process when we say, for example, 'All men are mortal; Socrates is a man; therefore Socrates is mortal.'"

Y: "Yes, but the fact is that if all men are mortal we cannot tell whether Socrates is a man until we have determined his mortality—in other words, until we find him dead. Of course, it's a great convenience to assume that Socrates is a man because he looks like one, but that's just a deduction. If we examine its formulation—'Objects that resemble men in most respects are men; Socrates resembles men in most respects; therefore Socrates is a man'—it's obvious that if he is a man, he resembles men in *all* necessary respects. So it's obvious we're right back where we started."

X: "Yes, we must know all the characteristics of men, and that Socrates has all of them, before we can be sure."

Which one of the following best expresses X's concluding observation?

(A) In deductive thinking we are simply reminding ourselves of the implications of our generalizations.
(B) It is often too convenient to arrive at conclusions simply by deduction instead of induction.
(C) Socrates' mortality is not the issue; the issue is critical thinking.
(D) Socrates' characteristics do not necessarily define his mortality.
(E) The key to the syllogistic process is using theoretical, rather than practical, issues of logic.

20. It takes a good telescope to see the moons of Neptune. I can't see the moons of Neptune with my telescope. Therefore, I do not have a good telescope.

Which one of the following most closely parallels the logic of this statement?

(A) It takes two to tango. You are doing the tango. Therefore, you have a partner.
(B) If you have a surfboard, you can surf. You do not have a surfboard. Therefore, you cannot surf.
(C) You need gin and vermouth to make a martini. You do not have any gin. Therefore, you cannot make a martini.
(D) If you know the area of a circle, you can find its circumference. You cannot figure out the circumference. Therefore, you do not know the area.
(E) You can write a letter to your friend with a pencil. You do not have a pencil. Therefore, you cannot write the letter.

GO ON TO THE NEXT PAGE ➤

Questions 21–22

Over 90 percent of our waking life depends on habits which for the most part we are unconscious of, from brushing our teeth in the morning to the time and manner in which we go to sleep at night. Habits are tools which serve the important function of relieving the conscious mind for more important activities. Habits are stored patterns of behavior which are found to serve the needs of the individual who has them and are formed from what once was conscious behavior which over years of repetition can become an automatic behavior pattern of the unconscious mind.

21. It can be inferred that the author bases his beliefs on

    (A) the testimony of a controlled group of students
    (B) biblical passages referring to the unconscious state
    (C) an intense psychological research
    (D) extensive psychological research
    (E) recent findings of clinical psychologists

22. The last sentence implies that

    (A) all repetitious patterns become unconscious behavior
    (B) conscious behavior eventually becomes habit
    (C) the unconscious mind causes repetitive behavior
    (D) automatic behavior patterns of the conscious mind are not possible
    (E) habits can be good or bad

Questions 23–24

It should be emphasized that only one person in a thousand who is bitten by a disease-carrying mosquito develops symptoms that require hospitalization, according to Dr. Reeves. But it is a potentially serious disease that requires close collaboration by citizens and local government to prevent it from reaching epidemic proportions.

Citizens should fill or drain puddles where mosquitoes breed. They should repair leaking swamp coolers and be sure swimming pools have a good circulating system. Make sure drain gutters aren't clogged and holding rainwater. Keep barrels and other water-storage containers tightly covered. Use good window screens.

23. Which one of the following statements, if true, would most strengthen the advice given in the second paragraph above?

    (A) Leaking swamp coolers are the primary cause of mosquito infestation.
    (B) It is possible to completely eliminate mosquitoes from a neighborhood.
    (C) No one can completely protect herself from being bitten by a mosquito.
    (D) Tightly covered water containers do not ensure the purity of the water in all cases.
    (E) Window screens seldom need to be replaced.

24. What additional information would strengthen the clarity of the second sentence above?

    (A) The names of some local governments that have fought against disease.
    (B) The name of the disease under discussion.
    (C) The names of those bitten by disease-carrying mosquitoes.
    (D) The full name of Dr. Reeves.
    (E) A description of the symptoms that a bitten person might develop.

25. That which is rare is always more valuable than that which is abundant. And so we are continually frustrated in our attempts to teach young people how to use time wisely; they have too much of it to appreciate its value.

Which one of the following statements, if true, would most weaken the argument above?

(A) Appreciation is not the same as obedience.

(B) Teaching something as abstract as the appreciation of time is difficult.

(C) Currency that is based on rare metals is more valuable than currency that is not.

(D) Many young people possess an intuitive knowledge of what time is, a knowledge they lose around middle age.

(E) The leisure time of people aged 18–24 has decreased significantly over the last 10 years.

26. Many theorists now believe that people cannot learn to write if they are constantly worrying about whether their prose is correct or not. When a would-be writer worries about correctness, his ability to be fluent is frozen.

With which one of the following statements would the author of the above passage probably agree?

(A) Writing theorists are probably wrong.

(B) Writing prose is different from writing poetry.

(C) Literacy is a function of relaxation.

(D) Fear blocks action.

(E) Most good writers are careless.

STOP

IF YOU FINISH BEFORE TIME IS CALLED, YOU MAY CHECK YOUR WORK ON THIS SECTION ONLY.
DO NOT WORK ON ANY OTHER SECTION IN THE TEST.

SECTION II
Time — 35 minutes
28 Questions

Directions: Read the passages and answer the questions following each passage by blackening the appropriate space on the answer sheet. You may refer back to the passages when answering the questions. Answer all questions on the basis of what is stated or implied.

The Sixth Amendment's right to the "assistance of counsel" has been the subject of considerable litigation
line in twentieth-century American courts.
(5) The emphasis has traditionally centered on the degree to which a criminal defendant can demand the assistance of counsel in various courts and at different hierarchical stages of the criminal
(10) proceeding. Although past courts have alluded to the idea that a defendant has a converse right to proceed without counsel, the issue had not been squarely addressed by the United States Supreme
(15) Court until late in its 1974–75 term. At that time, the Court held that within the Sixth Amendment rests an implied right of self-representation.

As early as 1964, Justice Hugo Black
(20) wrote that "the Sixth Amendment withholds from federal courts, in all criminal proceedings, the power and authority to deprive an accused of his life or liberty unless he has or waives
(25) the assistance of counsel." However, recognizing that the Sixth Amendment does not require representation by counsel, it is quite another thing to say that the defendant has a constitutional
(30) right to reject professional assistance and proceed on his own. Notwithstanding such a logical and legal fallacy, the Court has, by way of opinion, spoken of a Sixth Amendment "correlative right"
(35) to dispense with a lawyer's help. Many lower federal courts have seized upon this and supported their holdings on it, in whole or in part.

The basic motivation behind this
(40) proffered right of self-representation is that "respect for individual autonomy requires that (the defendant) be allowed to go to jail under his own banner if he so desires" and that he should not be
(45) forced to accept counsel in whom he has no confidence. Courts have ruled that neither due process nor progressive standards of criminal justice require that the defendant be represented at trial
(50) by counsel. The Supreme Court, in its 1975 decision, held that a defendant in a state criminal trial has a constitutional right to waive counsel and carry on his own case *in propria persona*. In raising
(55) this obscure privilege to a constitutional level, the Court stated that, so long as the defendant is made aware of the dangers and disadvantages of self-representation, his lack of technical
(60) legal knowledge will not deprive him of the right to defend himself personally.

The Court conceded that the long line of right to counsel cases have alluded
(65) to the idea that the assistance of counsel is a prerequisite to the realization of a fair trial. However, the Court noted that the presence of counsel is of minor significance when a stubborn,
(70) self-reliant defendant prohibits the lawyer from employing his knowledge and skills. This line of reasoning is concluded with the observation that "the defendant and not his lawyer or the state,
(75) will bear the personal consequences of a conviction." The logical extension of this premise brings the Court to its decision that, recognizing the traditional American respect for the individual,
(80) the defendant "must be free personally to decide whether in his particular case counsel is to his advantage."

GO ON TO THE NEXT PAGE ➤

1. According to the passage, the chief purpose of the Sixth Amendment is to

   (A) assure a defendant the assistance of counsel in capital cases
   (B) assure a defendant the assistance of counsel in civil cases
   (C) assure a defendant the assistance of counsel in criminal cases
   (D) allow a defendant to represent himself in a criminal trial
   (E) allow a defendant to represent himself in a civil trial

2. The "logical and legal fallacy" referred to in line 32 is probably

   (A) the ability to waive a right does not automatically give rise to a replacement of that right
   (B) the right to reject implies a correlative right to refuse to reject
   (C) the right to dispense with a lawyer's help
   (D) the right to legal assistance
   (E) the defendant who chooses to go to jail is free to do so

3. From the passage, the phrase *"in propria persona"* in line 54 means

   (A) in his own person
   (B) by an appropriate person
   (C) in place of another person
   (D) improperly
   (E) by using a stand-in

4. In allowing a defendant to refuse counsel, the Supreme Court may have reasoned all of the following EXCEPT:

   (A) A defendant who objected to a court-appointed attorney would prevent the lawyer from defending him effectively.
   (B) The assistance of counsel is necessary to the realization of a fair trial.
   (C) In the event of an unfavorable verdict, the defendant will suffer the consequences.
   (D) American tradition recognizes the individual's freedom to make decisions that will affect him.
   (E) It is possible that a defendant might defend himself more effectively than a court-appointed lawyer.

5. A defendant who is acting as counsel in his own defense must be

   (A) given additional legal assistance
   (B) allowed to give up his own defense if he chooses to do so before the trial has concluded
   (C) warned of the disadvantages of self-representation
   (D) assisted by the judge in areas where the defendant's lack of knowledge of technical legal terms is deficient
   (E) tried before a jury

6. All of the following are objections that might be raised to self-representation EXCEPT:

   (A) By accepting the right to self-representation, a defendant must waive his right to assistance of counsel.
   (B) A defendant determined to convict himself can do so more easily.
   (C) If the right to self-representation is not asserted before the trial begins, it is lost.
   (D) Self-representation has a tradition in American law that dates back to the colonial period.
   (E) A self-representation defendant may be unruly or disruptive.

African art could have been observed and collected by Europeans no earlier than the second half of the fifteenth century. Before that time Europe knew of Africa only through the writing of classical authors such as Pliny and Herodotus and the reports of a few Arabic travelers. Unfortunately, until the latter years of the nineteenth century Europe was little interested in the arts of Africa except as curiosities and souvenirs of exotic peoples. Indeed, with the growth of the slave trade, colonial exploitation, and Christian missionizing the arts were presented as evidence of the low state of heathen savagery of the African, justifying both exploitation and missionary zeal. Even with the early growth of the discipline of anthropology the assumption was that Africa was a continent of savages, low on the scale of evolutionary development, and that these savages, because they were "preliterate," could, by definition, have no history and no government worth notice.

In recent years the development of critical studies of oral traditions, of accounts by Islamic travelers of the great Sudanese kingdoms, of the descriptions of the coast by early European travelers, and—above all—of the concept of cultural relativism, has led to a far more realistic assessment of the African, his culture, history, and arts.

Cultural relativism is, in essence, the attitude whereby cultures other than one's own are viewed in *their* terms and on *their* merits. As an alternative to the prejudgment of missionaries and colonials it allows us to view the cultures and arts of the African without the necessity of judging his beliefs and actions against a Judeo-Christian moralistic base, or his art against a Greco-Renaissance yardstick.

Curiously, the "discovery" and enthusiasm for African art early in this century was not based on an objective, scientific assessment but rather resulted from an excess of romantic rebellion at the end of the last century against the Classical and Naturalist roots of western art. Unfortunately this uncritical adulation swept aside many rational concerns to focus upon African sculpture as if it were the product of a romantic, rebellious, *fin de siècle,* European movement. Obviously, African art is neither anti-classical nor anti-naturalistic: to be either it would have had to have had its roots in Classicism or in Naturalism, both European in origin. Nor was the concept of rebellion a part of the heritage of art in sub-Saharan Africa; rather, as we shall see, it was an art conservative in impulse and stable in concept.

We may admire these sculptures from a purely twentieth-century aesthetic, but if we so limit our admiration we will most certainly fail to understand them in the context of their appearance as documents of African thought and action.

In sharp contrast to the arts of the recent past in the Western world, by far the greatest part, in fact nearly all of the art of the history of the world, including traditional Africa, was positive in its orientation; that is, it conformed in style and meaning to the expectations—the norms—of its patrons and audience. Those norms were shared by nearly all members of the society; thus, the arts were conservative and conformist. However, it must be stressed that they were not merely passive reflections, for they contributed actively to the sense of well-being of the parent culture. Indeed, the perishable nature of wood—the dominant medium for sculpture—ensured that each generation reaffirmed its faith by re-creating its arts.

GO ON TO THE NEXT PAGE ➤

7. According to the passage, before the latter part of the nineteenth century, Europeans viewed African art as

(A) simple and direct
(B) odd but beautifully crafted
(C) savage and of little value
(D) ugly and of grotesque proportions
(E) warlike and lacking in beauty

8. According to the passage, which one of the following contributed to the initial dismissal of African art by Europeans?

(A) Europeans valued color and sophisticated techniques, both of which were absent in African arts.
(B) It was easier to justify exploitation of Africans if their art was dismissed as heathen.
(C) Europeans were made uncomfortable by the Africans' tendency to depict coarse acts and vulgar positions.
(D) It was important to reject African art because it was dangerous to a stable European society.
(E) It was believed that an influx of African art could seriously disrupt the market for European art.

9. According to the passage, all of the following contributed to a change in the European view of African art EXCEPT:

(A) the writings of Pliny
(B) cultural relativism
(C) Islamic travel accounts
(D) descriptions by early European travelers
(E) studies of oral traditions

10. Which one of the following most accurately represents the concept of cultural relativism as defined in the passage?

(A) The words "good" and "bad" are irrelevant when judging between works of art.
(B) One cannot enjoy a work of art without a complete understanding of the culture from which it came.
(C) The best art will always be art that is positive in its orientation.
(D) If an artist goes outside his own tradition in creating a work of art, that work of art will be inferior.
(E) To determine the success of a work of art, it should be judged against the values of its own culture.

11. According to the passage, the early twentieth-century European view of African art was inadequate because it

(A) was based on a limited number of objects available to the Western world
(B) was a result of a romantic rebellion against traditions in Western art
(C) did not take into account the importance of oral traditions
(D) was dependent on classical rather than naturalistic standards
(E) was dictated by the judgments of Christian missionaries

GO ON TO THE NEXT PAGE ➤

2 **2** **2** **2** **2**

12. Which one of the following best describes the author's point about the relationship between twentieth-century Western art and African art?

(A) African art and twentieth-century Western art both have their roots in a desire to escape tradition and rediscover man's primitive state.

(B) The techniques used in African sculpture are remarkably similar to the techniques used in twentieth-century Western sculpture.

(C) It isn't possible to enjoy African art if we judge it by twentieth-century European aesthetic standards.

(D) Compared to twentieth-century Western art, African art is conservative and conformist, in that it is in keeping with the expectations of its society.

(E) Because it was produced by artists unschooled in technique, African art does not display the sophistication and ingenuity of twentieth-century Western art.

13. According to the author, the use of wood in African art is especially significant because

(A) it is a simpler, more available medium than marble

(B) unlike the hardness of stone, its relative softness allows intricate carvings representing African beliefs

(C) it represents a rebellion from the media used in Western sculpture and a return to African roots

(D) it is unique to primitive cultures uncorrupted by the Western world.

(E) its impermanence ensures that each generation creates new art reaffirming the beliefs of the culture

14. In this passage, one of the principal methods the author uses to develop his subject is

(A) discussion and explanation of reactions to African art in the Western world

(B) examination and analysis of several specific African works of art

(C) criticism and refutation of Western traditions such as Classicism and Naturalism

(D) description and explanation of African religious and social beliefs

(E) discussion and analysis of the aesthetic principles at the foundation of African art

GO ON TO THE NEXT PAGE ➤

In the competitive model—the
economy of many sellers each with a
small share of the total market—the
line restraint on the private exercise of
(5) economic power was provided by other
firms on the same side of the market.
It was the eagerness of competitors
to sell, not the complaints of buyers,
that saved the latter from spoliation.
(10) It was assumed, no doubt accurately,
that the nineteenth-century textile
manufacturer who overcharged for his
product would promptly lose his market
to another manufacturer who did not.
(15) If all manufacturers found themselves
in a position where they could exploit a
strong demand, and mark up their prices
accordingly, there would soon be an
inflow of new competitors. The resulting
(20) increase in supply would bring prices
and profits back to normal.

As with the seller who was tempted
to use his economic power against the
customer, so with the buyer who was
(25) tempted to use it against his labor or
suppliers. The man who paid less than
the prevailing wage would lose his labor
force to those who paid the worker
his full (marginal) contribution to the
(30) earnings of the firm. In all cases the
incentive to socially desirable behavior
was provided by the competitor. It was
to the same side of the market—the
restraint of sellers by other sellers and of
(35) buyers by other buyers, in other words to
competition—that economists came to
look for the self-regulatory mechanisms
of the economy.

They also came to look to competition
(40) exclusively and in formal theory still do.
The notion that there might be another
regulatory mechanism in the economy

had been almost completely excluded
from economic thought. Thus, with the
(45) widespread disappearance of competition
in its classical form and its replacement
by the small group of firms if not in
overt, at least in conventional or tacit,
collusion, it was easy to suppose that
(50) since competition had disappeared, all
effective restraint on private power had
disappeared. Indeed, this conclusion was
all but inevitable if no search was made
for other restraints, and so complete was
(55) the preoccupation with competition that
none was made.

In fact, new restraints on private
power did appear to replace competition.
They were nurtured by the same process
(60) of concentration which impaired
or destroyed competition. But they
appeared not on the same side of the
market but on the opposite side, not
with competitors but with customers or
(65) suppliers. It will be convenient to have
a name for this counterpart of competition and I shall call it countervailing
power.

To begin with a broad and somewhat
(70) too dogmatically stated proposition,
private economic power is held in check
by the countervailing power of those
who are subject to it. The first begets
the second. The long trend toward
(75) concentration of industrial enterprise in
the hands of a relatively few firms has
brought into existence not only strong
sellers, as economists have supposed,
but also strong buyers, a fact they have
(80) failed to see. The two develop together,
not in precise step, but in such manner
that there can be no doubt that the one is
in response to the other.

2   **2**   **2**   **2**   **2**

15. Which one of the following would be the best title for this passage?

    (A) Capitalism and the Competitive Model
    (B) Competition and the Concept of "Countervailing Power"
    (C) Problems in American Capitalism
    (D) The Importance of Economic Regulatory Mechanisms
    (E) The Failure of the Classic Competition Model

16. In the classic competition model, when competitive manufacturers marked up prices because of strong demand, a return to normal was provided by

    (A) new manufacturers entering the market
    (B) refusal to buy on the part of customers
    (C) governmental intervention in the form of regulation
    (D) repositioning of the labor force
    (E) failure of weaker manufacturers

17. In the classic competition model, the incentive for manufacturers to behave in a socially desirable way toward workers was provided by

    (A) competition for the labor supply
    (B) competition for the customer
    (C) imbalance between supply and demand
    (D) self-regulation among competitors
    (E) humanistic economic theory

18. According to the author, which one of the following statements is true?

    (A) The classic model of competition was inadequate because it ignored the role of labor and rewarded individual greed.
    (B) The classic model of competition provided self-regulation prior to, but not after, the Industrial Revolution.
    (C) The classic model of competition was undermined by the "restraint of sellers by other sellers and of buyers by other buyers."
    (D) The classic model of competition was replaced by concentration of industrial enterprise and collusion among manufacturers.
    (E) The classic model of competition was destroyed by the growth of "countervailing power."

19. Examples of "countervailing power" in the regulation of the economic power of manufacturers could include all of the following EXCEPT:

    (A) organized customer boycotts
    (B) cooperative buying organizations
    (C) large retail chains
    (D) retailers developing their own sources of supply
    (E) organizations that network manufacturers

GO ON TO THE NEXT PAGE ➤

20. According to the author, a weakness of economic thought has been

    (A) a preoccupation with competition
    (B) a failure to recognize the need for reasonable government regulation
    (C) a belief in the "trickle-down" theory
    (D) a failure to recognize concentration of industrial enterprise
    (E) a bias toward unregulated capitalism

21. Which one of the following best describes the structure of this passage?

    (A) The first three paragraphs describe the strengths of economic competition and the fourth and fifth paragraphs describe its weaknesses.
    (B) The first paragraph presents the historical perspective on competition, the second and third present examples of its effect on the economy, and the fourth and fifth paragraphs set forth the idea of "countervailing power."
    (C) The first two paragraphs describe how competition is thought to work, the third paragraph provides a transition, and the fourth and fifth paragraphs describe "countervailing power."
    (D) The first three paragraphs describe the classic model of competition, while the fourth and fifth paragraphs describe "countervailing power."
    (E) The first three paragraphs present a view of competition in opposition to the author's, while the fourth and fifth paragraphs present the author's view.

Passage A

Antoine-Laurent Lavoisier (1743–1794) can justly be called the father of modern chemistry, not because of earth-
(5) shaking discoveries or experiments but because he introduced a new approach to the understanding of chemical reactions. Some of his conclusions were later called into question or improved upon, but his relentless pursuit of knowledge
(10) and logical reasoning led to hundreds of experiments, all of which challenged the preconceived scientific notions of his day.

Lavoisier at twenty-five was elected
(15) to France's Academy of Sciences, in large part because of his work in geology, not chemistry. In 1775, he was appointed to the Royal Gunpowder and Saltpeter Administration, and
(20) in his laboratory he produced better gunpowder, in part by focusing on the purity of its ingredients and improved methods of granulating the powder.

An important aspect of Lavoisier's
(25) work was his determination of the weights of reagents and products, including gaseous components, involved in chemical reactions. He believed that matter, identified by weight, would
(30) always be conserved through these reactions. Lavoisier's methods led to, among other things, his definitive proof that water was made up of oxygen and hydrogen.

(35) His methods also led him to challenge the phlogistic theory of combustion, which initially had been proposed by the German alchemist Johann Joachim Becher in the late 1600s and which
(40) was still widely accepted well into the eighteenth century. According to that theory, something called "phlogiston," named by Georg Ernst Stahl, existed in all materials and was released
(45) during combustion, the resulting ash being the remaining material, but "dephlogisticated." Since phlogiston wasn't—according to its proponents—a material substance, it was unweighable
(50) and without color or odor. Also according to the theory, acids produced by combustion were elementary substances, not the products of a chemical reaction. Lavoisier, through
(55) his experiments, came to recognize that

a chemical reaction with oxygen, not a vague principle called phlogiston, caused combustion.

(60) At first, Lavoisier referred to oxygen as "air in its purest form," but he later called it oxygen, from the Greek words *oxus*, meaning sharp, acidic, and *ginomai*, meaning to become or cause to be. He believed that oxygen caused the

(65) acids produced by combustion. Later, however, Sir Humphry Davy, Louis Joseph Gay-Lussac, and Louis-Jacques Thenard showed in their experiments with hydrochloric acid, chlorine, and

(70) hydrocyanic acid that acid could be produced without oxygen.

But Lavoisier, even though some of his ideas were later proved wrong, succeeded in turning away from

(75) alchemy and the theory of phlogiston. In the words of Justus von Liebig, Lavoisier's immortal glory "consists in this—that he infused into the body of the science a new spirit."

Passage B

(80) Among the definitions of *theory* is "the analysis of a set of facts in their relation to one another." That definition doesn't take us very far, however, because almost any set of facts can be

(85) analyzed in a dozen or more ways. In science, theories are set forth and later discarded, or modified, all the time.

For example, in the seventeenth century, heat was erroneously explained

(90) through theories of combustion. Johann Joachim Becher and Georg Ernst Stahl introduced the theory that phlogiston, present in all matter, was released during combustion. It was thought to be the

(95) source of heat. Phlogiston couldn't be weighed and, in fact, wasn't considered a material at all but rather a principle. Such notable scientists as Joseph Priestley (1733–1804), who conducted extensive

(100) research on the nature and property of gases, interpreted his results in terms of phlogiston. Priestley's experiments isolated and characterized eight gases, including oxygen, which he described as

(105) "dephlogisticated air."

Antoine Lavoisier, a French scientist who rightly explained combustion in terms of oxygen and not the principle of phlogiston, introduced another

(110) theory of heat. In his *Reflexions sur le*

phlogistique (1783), he argued that the phlogiston theory was inconsistent with his experimental results. Ironically, however, Lavoisier proposed a

(115) substance called *caloric* (which he considered an "element"—one of 33 substances that couldn't be broken down into simpler entities) as the source of heat. Like phlogiston, caloric couldn't

(120) be weighed, and Lavoisier called it "a subtle fluid." The quantity of caloric, according to Lavoisier, was constant throughout the universe and flowed from warmer to colder bodies.

(125) Not surprisingly, observable facts could be explained by the caloric theory. For instance, a hot bowl of soup cools at room temperature. Why? Because caloric slowly flows from regions

(130) dense with it (the hot soup) to regions less dense with it (the cooler air in the room). Another example is that air expands when heated. According to the caloric theory, this would be because

(135) caloric is absorbed by air molecules, thereby increasing the volume of the air.

Ultimately, the caloric theory as posited by Lavoisier was discarded. The calorists' principle of the conservation

(140) of heat was replaced by a principle of conservation of energy.

Modern thermodynamics defines heat not as a result of a "subtle fluid" but as a result of the kinetic energy of molecules.

22. Which of the following characterizes the main difference between Passage A and Passage B?

(A) Passage A praises Antoine Lavoisier, whereas Passage B discredits him.

(B) The focus in Passage A is on a scientist's work, while the focus in Passage B is on a particular theory.

(C) Passage A explains the phlogiston theory, whereas Passage B does not.

(D) In Passage A, the emphasis is on chemical reactions, while in Passage B the emphasis is on the scientific method.

(E) The author of Passage A is objective toward science, while the author of Passage B is skeptical.

GO ON TO THE NEXT PAGE ➤

23. The author of Passage B uses the term "ironically" in line 113 to

(A) emphasize how fallible scientists can be in interpreting their own results and the results of their predecessors
(B) undermine Lavoisier's designation as the "father of modern chemistry"
(C) note that while Lavoisier proved that phlogiston didn't exist, he introduced another nonexistent substance
(D) suggest the absurdity of scientific debates
(E) lighten the tone of the passage as a whole

24. According to Passage A, among Lavoisier's accomplishments was

(A) proving the chemical composition of water
(B) explaining the cause of heat
(C) changing the composition of gunpowder
(D) identifying caloric as a fluid
(E) isolating and characterizing eight gases

25. Which of the following best illustrates that facts can be explained by more than one theory (paragraph 1 of Passage B)?

(A) Hydrochloric acid cannot be produced without oxygen.
(B) The agent of combustion is weightless and odorless.
(C) Boiling water will cool at room temperature.
(D) Combustion results in ash made up of "dephlogisticated" material.
(E) Acids produced by combustion are elementary substances.

26. The author of Passage B would most likely agree with which of the following statements?

(A) Alchemy contributed nothing to science.
(B) Joseph Priestley was not as important as Antoine Lavoisier in the study of gases.
(C) Thermodynamics is an inexact science.
(D) A theory is a possible, but not necessarily the only, explanation of facts.
(E) The scientific method is seriously flawed and cannot be counted on to prove a fact.

27. According to information in Passage A and Passage B, Lavoisier believed that

(A) matter was not destroyed during a chemical reaction
(B) the acids produced during combustion were elementary substances
(C) molecular movement was responsible for the production of heat
(D) matter was converted to energy in chemical reactions
(E) a fluid called "caloric" caused combustion

28. In Passage B, Joseph Priestley is used as an example of

(A) a scientist who relied heavily on alchemy
(B) the importance of an open exchange of ideas between scientists
(C) a scientist who made a major discovery, as distinguished from Lavoisier
(D) a precursor to Lavoisier's experiments with gases
(E) the persistence of the phlogistic theory well into the eighteenth century

STOP

IF YOU FINISH BEFORE TIME IS CALLED, YOU MAY CHECK YOUR WORK ON THIS SECTION ONLY.
DO NOT WORK ON ANY OTHER SECTION IN THE TEST.

3 **3** **3** **3** **3**

SECTION III
TIME — 35 MINUTES
23 QUESTIONS

Directions: In this section you will be given groups of questions based on different sets of conditions. Drawing a simple diagram may be helpful in answering some of the questions. You are to choose the best answer and mark the corresponding space on your answer sheet.

Questions 1–6

There are five flagpoles lined up next to each other in a straight row in front of a school. Each flagpole flies one flag (red, white, or blue) and one pennant (green, white, or blue). The following are conditions that affect the placement of flags and pennants on the poles:
   On a given flagpole, the pennant and the flag cannot be the same color.
   Two adjacent flagpoles cannot fly the same color flags.
   Two adjacent flagpoles cannot fly the same color pennants.
   No more than two of any color flag or pennant may fly at one time.

1. If the 2nd and 5th pennants are blue, the 2nd and 5th flags are red, and the 3rd flag is white, then which one of the following must be true?

   (A) Two of the flags are white.
   (B) Two of the pennants are white.
   (C) The 4th pennant is green.
   (D) If the 1st pennant is green, then the 1st flag is blue.
   (E) If the 1st flag is white, then the 1st pennant is green.

2. If the 1st flag is red and the 2nd pennant is blue, then which one of the following is NOT necessarily true?

   (A) The 2nd flag is white.
   (B) If the 5th flag is red, then the 3rd flag is blue.
   (C) If the 4th pennant is green, then the 1st pennant is white.
   (D) If the 1st and 5th flags are the same color, then the 3rd flag is blue.
   (E) If the 4th pennant is green and the 5th pennant is white, then the 1st and 3rd pennants are different colors.

3. If the 1st and 3rd flags are white and the 2nd and 4th pennants are blue, then which one of the following is false?

   (A) The 4th flag is red.
   (B) The 1st pennant is green.
   (C) The 3rd pennant is not red.
   (D) The 5th pennant is green.
   (E) There is one blue flag.

GO ON TO THE NEXT PAGE ➤

3   **3**   **3**   **3**   **3**

4. If the 1st and 4th flags are blue, and the 3rd pennant is white, then which one of the following must be true?

   (A) If the 1st pennant is green, then the 5th pennant is white.
   (B) If the 5th pennant is white, then the 1st pennant is green.
   (C) The 2nd flag is red.
   (D) The 5th flag is red.
   (E) The 1st pennant is green.

5. If the 2nd flag is red and the 3rd flag is white, and the 4th pennant is blue, then which one of the following must be true?

   (A) If the 5th flag is white, then two of the pennants are blue.
   (B) If the 1st flag is white, then the 2nd flag is white.
   (C) If the 1st pennant is blue, then the 5th pennant is green.
   (D) If the 1st pennant is green, then the 5th flag is not blue.
   (E) If the 1st and 5th flags are the same color, then the 1st and 5th pennants are not the same color.

6. If the 1st flag and the 2nd pennant are the same color, the 2nd flag and the 3rd pennant are the same color, the 3rd flag and the 4th pennant are the same color, and the 4th flag and the 5th pennant are the same color, then which one of the following must be true?

   (A) The 1st pennant is white.
   (B) The 2nd flag is not white.
   (C) The 5th flag is red.
   (D) The 3rd pennant is blue.
   (E) The 4th flag is white.

Questions 7–13

In the Norfolk Library returned book section there are ten books standing next to each other on a shelf. There are two math books, two science books, three English books, and three poetry books. The books are arranged as follows:
   There is a math book on one end and an English book on the other end.
   The two math books are never next to each other.
   The two science books are always next to each other.
   The three English books are always next to each other.

7. If the 8th book is a math book, then which one of the following must be true?

   (A) The 5th book is a science book.
   (B) The 7th book is an English book.
   (C) The 6th book is not a poetry book.
   (D) The 4th book is next to an English book.
   (E) The 9th book is a science book.

8. If the 9th book is an English book and the 5th and 6th books are poetry books, then which one of the following must be true?

   (A) There is a math book next to a poetry book.
   (B) The 2nd book is a science book.
   (C) The 3 poetry books are all next to one another.
   (D) The 7th book is a math book.
   (E) The 4th book is not a poetry book.

GO ON TO THE NEXT PAGE ➤

3   **3**   **3**   **3**   **3**

9. If the 1st book is a math book and the 7th book is a science book, then which one of the following could be false?

   (A) Both math books are next to poetry books.
   (B) All three poetry books are next to each other.
   (C) The 2nd book is a poetry book.
   (D) The 10th book is an English book.
   (E) The 6th book is a science book.

10. If the 4th book is a math book and the 5th book is a science book, then which one of the following must be true?

   (A) An English book is next to a science book.
   (B) If the 7th book is a poetry book, then the 3rd book is an English book.
   (C) If the 8th book is an English book, then the 2nd book is a poetry book.
   (D) If the 10th book is a math book, then a poetry book is next to an English book.
   (E) The three poetry books are next to each other.

11. If no two poetry books are next to each other, then which one of the following must be true?

   (A) A science book is next to a math book.
   (B) The 7th book is a poetry book.
   (C) The 8th book is an English book.
   (D) An English book is next to a science book.
   (E) A poetry book is next to an English book.

12. If a science book is next to an English book, but not next to a poetry book, then which one of the following must be true?

   (A) The 7th book is a poetry book.
   (B) The 3rd book is an English book or a math book.
   (C) The 5th or the 6th book is a math book.
   (D) The three poetry books are not next to each other.
   (E) The 7th or the 10th book is a math book.

13. If the 7th and 8th books are poetry books, how many different arrangements are there for the ten books?

   (A) one
   (B) two
   (C) three
   (D) four
   (E) five

GO ON TO THE NEXT PAGE ➤

3 **3** **3** **3** **3**

Questions 14–18

State College offers the following courses for first-year students: languages (French, German, Italian), sciences (biology, chemistry, physics), and mathematics (algebra, statistics, trigonometry). Each student must enroll in exactly five of the courses, subject to the following conditions:

Not more than two math classes may be taken.
If physics is taken, then algebra cannot be taken.
If algebra is taken, then Italian must be taken.
Chemistry may be taken only if both trigonometry and French are taken.
If both German and biology are taken, then statistics cannot be taken.
Exactly one language must be taken.

14. Which one of the following could be a list of the five courses taken by a first-year student at State College?

(A) algebra, trigonometry, French, Italian, physics
(B) statistics, trigonometry, Italian, biology, physics
(C) algebra, statistics, French, Italian, chemistry
(D) algebra, statistics, trigonometry, French, chemistry
(E) statistics, trigonometry, German, biology, physics

15. If a first-year student at State College takes statistics, which one of the following pairs of courses may also be taken?

(A) Italian, chemistry
(B) algebra, German
(C) German, chemistry
(D) algebra, French
(E) chemistry, physics

16. Which one of the following could be a list of three of the courses taken by a first-year student at State College?

(A) algebra, French, biology
(B) algebra, Italian, physics
(C) statistics, German, chemistry
(D) statistics, chemistry, physics
(E) trigonometry, German, chemistry

17. Other than the language course, which one of the following could be a list of the courses taken by a first-year student at State College?

(A) algebra, statistics, biology, chemistry
(B) algebra, biology, chemistry, physics
(C) algebra, statistics, trigonometry, physics
(D) trigonometry, biology, chemistry, physics
(E) statistics, biology, chemistry, physics

18. If a first-year student at State College takes Italian, which one of the following pairs of courses must also be taken?

(A) German, biology
(B) biology, physics
(C) statistics, chemistry
(D) biology, chemistry
(E) algebra, French

GO ON TO THE NEXT PAGE ➤

3   **3**   **3**   **3**   **3**

Questions 19–23

Seven track and field coaches, A, B, C, D, E, F, and G, are each assigned to coach exactly one of four activities—sprints, distance, jumpers, and throwers. Coaching assignments are made subject to the following conditions:

Each sport is coached by one or two of the seven coaches.
B coaches jumpers.
Neither E nor F is a distance coach.
If C coaches sprints, F and G coach throwers.
If D coaches distance or throwers, A and G do not coach either distance or throwers.

19. If C and E coach sprints, which one of the following must be true?

(A) Distance has two coaches.
(B) G coaches jumping.
(C) A coaches jumping or throwing.
(D) D coaches jumping.
(E) Jumping has one coach.

20. If G coaches jumping and A coaches distance, which one of the following must be true?

(A) D coaches sprints.
(B) F coaches throwing.
(C) E coaches sprints.
(D) C coaches distance.
(E) F coaches sprints.

21. If D coaches throwing, which one of the following CANNOT be true?

(A) G coaches sprints.
(B) A coaches jumping.
(C) E coaches sprints.
(D) F coaches throwing.
(E) C coaches jumping.

22. If G is the only throwing coach, which one of the following could be true?

(A) D coaches distance.
(B) If F coaches sprints, D coaches sprints.
(C) A coaches jumping.
(D) If F coaches jumping, D coaches jumping.
(E) C and D coach the same sport.

23. If A does not coach sprints and D coaches distance, which one of the following CANNOT be true?

(A) C coaches distance.
(B) E coaches throwing.
(C) G coaches jumping.
(D) F coaches sprints.
(E) E coaches sprints.

STOP

4   4   4   4   4

SECTION IV
TIME — 35 MINUTES
26 QUESTIONS

<u>Directions:</u> In this section you will be given brief statements or passages and will be required to evaluate the reasoning involved. In some instances, more than one choice will appear to be a possible answer. You are to choose the *best* answer. Use common sense and reasonableness in making your selection; then mark the proper space on the answer sheet.

<u>Questions 1–2</u>

The spate of bills in the legislature dealing with utility regulation shows that our lawmakers recognize a good political issue when they see one. Among the least worthy is a proposal to establish a new "Consumers Utility Board" to fight proposed increases in gas and electric rates.

It is hardly a novel idea that consumers need representation when rates are set for utilities which operate as monopolies in their communities. That's exactly why we have a state Public Utilities Commission.

Supporters of the proposed consumer board point out that utility companies have the benefit of lawyers and accountants on their payrolls to argue the case for rate increases before the PUC. That's true. Well, the PUC has the benefit of a $40 million annual budget and a staff of 900—all paid at taxpayer expense—to find fault with these rate proposals if there is fault to be found.

1. Which one of the following is the best example to offer in support of this argument against a Consumers Utility Board?

   (A) the percentage of taxpayer dollars supporting the PUC
   (B) the number of lawyers working for the Consumers Utility Board
   (C) the number of concerned consumers
   (D) a PUC readjustment of rates downward
   (E) the voting record of lawmakers supporting the board

2. Which one of the following would most seriously weaken the above argument?

   (A) Private firms are taking an increasing share of the energy business.
   (B) Water rates are also increasing.
   (C) The PUC budget will be cut slightly, along with other state agencies.
   (D) Half of the PUC lawyers and accountants are also retained by utilities.
   (E) More tax money goes to education than to the PUC.

GO ON TO THE NEXT PAGE ➤

3. Most of those who enjoy music play a musical instrument; therefore, if Maria enjoys music, she probably plays a musical instrument.

Which one of the following most closely parallels the reasoning in the statement above?

(A) The majority of those who voted for Smith in the last election oppose abortion; therefore, if the residents of University City all voted for Smith, they probably oppose abortion.

(B) If you appreciate portrait painting you are probably a painter yourself; therefore, your own experience is probably the cause of your appreciation.

(C) Most of those who join the army are male; therefore, if Jones did not join the army, Jones is probably female.

(D) Over 50 percent of the high-school students polled admitted hating homework; therefore, a majority of high-school students do not like homework.

(E) If most workers drive to work, and Sam drives to work, then Sam must be a worker.

4. *Mayor:* There must be no official or unofficial meeting of two or more members of the City Council that is not open to the public or a matter of public record. Though certain subjects can only be discussed in private, the danger of elected officials pursuing a private agenda, rather than what most benefits the public, is a serious concern in an age when politicians are too often willing to promote their private interests behind closed doors.

On which one of the following grounds is this argument especially subject to criticism?

(A) It treats popular opinion as if it were conclusive evidence.

(B) It misleadingly generalizes from the actions of a few to the actions of an entire group.

(C) It concedes the point that effectively undermines its argument.

(D) It uses an ambiguous term without making clear which meaning of the term applies here.

(E) It reaches a conclusion based on limited evidence chosen only because that evidence supports the argument.

GO ON TO THE NEXT PAGE ➤

4   4   4   4   4

5. "Good personnel relations of an organization depend upon mutual confidence, trust, and goodwill. The basis of confidence is understanding. Most troubles start with people who do not understand each other. When the organization's intentions or motives are misunderstood, or when reasons for actions, practices, or policies are misconstrued, complete cooperation from individuals is not forthcoming. If management expects full cooperation from employees, it has a responsibility of sharing with them the information which is the foundation of proper understanding, confidence, and trust. Personnel management has long since outgrown the days when it was the vogue to 'treat them rough and tell them nothing.' Up-to-date personnel management provides all possible information about the activities, aims, and purposes of the organization. It seems altogether creditable that a desire should exist among employees for such information which the best-intentioned executive might think would not interest them and which the worst-intentioned would think was none of their business."

The above paragraph implies that one of the causes of the difficulty that an organization might have with its personnel relations is that its employees

(A) have not expressed interest in the activities, aims, and purposes of the organization
(B) do not believe in the good faith of the organization
(C) have not been able to give full cooperation to the organization
(D) do not recommend improvements in the practices and policies of the organization
(E) can afford little time to establish good relations with their organization

6. Of all psychiatric disorders, depression is the most common; yet, research on its causes and cures is still far from complete. As a matter of fact, very few facilities offer assistance to those suffering from this disorder.

The author would probably agree that

(A) depression needs further study
(B) further research will make possible further assistance to those suffering from depression
(C) most facilities are staffed by psychiatrists whose specialty is not depression
(D) those suffering from depression need to know its causes and cures
(E) depression and ignorance go hand in hand

7. *Editorial:* The politicians who wish to see the schools run like businesses will have some trouble establishing a standard of accountability. In the business world, profits provide a clear standard, measurable in numbers. But in public education, standards are culturally derived, and differ very widely among age, ethnic, and political groups. We can evaluate a school's record keeping or its facilities, but there is no way to use the standards of quality control that are used to judge the profitability of a business and apply them to the academic performance of students throughout a public school system.

To which one of the following is the writer of this passage objecting?

(A) the assumption that a school and a business are analogous
(B) the belief that profitability is a universal standard
(C) the assumption that schools, like businesses, can show a financial profit
(D) the belief that school vouchers are undemocratic
(E) the assumption that record keeping and facilities are adequate gauges of business success

GO ON TO THE NEXT PAGE ➤

4   4   4   4   4

8. *Ivan:* What the Church says is true because the Church is an authority.
Mike: What grounds do you have for holding that the Church is a genuine authority?
Ivan: The authority of the Church is implied in the Bible.
Mike: And why do you hold that the Bible is true?
Ivan: Because the Church holds that it is true.

Which one of the following is the best description of the reasoning involved in the argument presented in the foregoing dialogue?

(A) deductive
(B) inductive
(C) vague
(D) pointed
(E) circular

9. *Mary:* All Italians are great lovers.
Kathy: That is not so. I have met some Spaniards who were magnificent lovers.

Kathy's reply to Mary indicates that she has misunderstood Mary's remark to mean that

(A) every great lover is an Italian
(B) Italians are best at the art of love
(C) Spaniards are inferior to Italians
(D) Italians are more likely to be great lovers than are Spaniards
(E) there is a relationship between nationality and love

Questions 10–11

Mr. Dimple: Mrs. Wilson's qualifications are ideal for the position. She is intelligent, forceful, determined, and trustworthy. I suggest we hire her immediately.

10. Which one of the following, if true, would most weaken Mr. Dimple's statement?

(A) Mrs. Wilson is not interested in being hired.
(B) There are two other applicants whose qualifications are identical to Mrs. Wilson's.
(C) Mrs. Wilson is currently working for a rival company.
(D) Mr. Dimple is not speaking directly to the hiring committee.
(E) Mrs. Wilson is older than many of the other applicants.

11. Which one of the following, if true, offers the strongest support of Mr. Dimple's statement?

(A) All the members of the hiring committee have agreed that intelligence, trustworthiness, determination, and forcefulness are important qualifications for the job.
(B) Mr. Dimple holds exclusive responsibility for hiring new employees.
(C) Mr. Dimple has known Mrs. Wilson longer than he has known any of the other applicants.
(D) Mrs. Wilson is a member of Mr. Dimple's family.
(E) Mrs. Dimple is intelligent, forceful, determined, and trustworthy.

GO ON TO THE NEXT PAGE ➤

12. All of the candidates for the spring track team must have participated in fall cross-country and winter track. Some runners, however, find cross-country tedious, and refuse to run in the fall. Thus, some winter track runners who would like to be members of the spring track teams are not permitted to try out.

In which one of the following is the reasoning most like that of this passage?

(A) Mice become aggressive if confined in close quarters for an extended period of time, or if they are deprived of protein-rich foods. Therefore, highly aggressive mice have been closely confined and denied high-protein foods.

(B) Roses grown in full sun are less susceptible to mildew than roses grown in partial shade. Roses grown in partial shade are also more susceptible to black spot. Thus, roses should be grown in full sun.

(C) To qualify for the June primary, a candidate for office must reside in the district for six months and gather 500 signatures of district residents who support the candidate. Thus, a longtime district resident would not qualify for the June primary if she gathered only 300 signatures.

(D) A convenience store sells three chocolate bars for a dollar, and a large soft drink for 50 cents. A competitor sells four chocolate bars for a dollar, and a medium-size soft drink for 50 cents. Therefore, neither of the two stores offers more for the same price.

(E) The City Council has passed an ordinance that allows cyclists to use the city bike paths only if they are over 12 years old and are wearing bicycle helmets. Thus, parents with children under 12 will be unable to cycle with their families on the city bike paths unless they wear helmets.

13. When a dental hygienist cleans your teeth, you may not see much evidence that she is supervised by a dentist. Hygienists often work pretty much on their own, even though they are employed by dentists. Then why can't hygienists practice independently, perhaps saving patients a lot of money in the process? The patients would not have to pay the steep profit that many dentists make on the hygienists' labors.

Which one of the following statements weakens the argument above?

(A) Some patients might get their teeth cleaned more often if it costs less.

(B) Some dentists do not employ dental hygienists.

(C) Hygienists must be certified by state examinations.

(D) A dentist should be on hand to inspect a hygienist's work to make sure the patient has no problems that the hygienist is unable to detect.

(E) In some states, there are more female hygienists than male.

14. There are those of us who, determined to be happy, are discouraged repeatedly by social and economic forces that cause us nothing but trouble. And there are those of us who are blessed with health and wealth and still grumble and complain about almost everything.

To which one of the following points can the author be leading?

(A) Happiness is both a state of mind and a state of affairs.

(B) Both personal and public conditions can make happiness difficult to attain.

(C) Happiness may be influenced by economic forces and by health considerations.

(D) No one can be truly happy.

(E) Exterior forces and personal views determine happiness.

GO ON TO THE NEXT PAGE ➤

4   4   4   4   4

15. "Keep true, never be ashamed of doing right; decide on what you think is right and stick to it."—*George Eliot*

    If one were to follow Eliot's advice, one

    (A) would never change one's mind
    (B) would do what is right
    (C) might never know what is right
    (D) would never be tempted to do wrong
    (E) would not discriminate between right and wrong

16. To paraphrase Oliver Wendell Holmes, taxes keep us civilized. Just look around you, at well-paved superhighways, air-conditioned schools, and modernized prisons, and you cannot help but agree with Holmes.

    Which one of the following is the strongest criticism of the statement above?

    (A) The author never actually met Holmes.
    (B) The author does not acknowledge those of us who do not live near highways, schools, and prisons.
    (C) The author does not assure us that he has been in a modernized prison.
    (D) The author does not offer a biographical sketch of Holmes.
    (E) The author does not define "civilized."

Questions 17–18

Information that is published is part of the public record. But information that a reporter collects, and sources that he contacts, must be protected in order for our free press to function free of fear.

17. The above argument is most severely weakened by which one of the following statements?

    (A) Public information is usually reliable.
    (B) Undocumented evidence may bc used to convict an innocent person.
    (C) Members of the press act ethically in most cases.
    (D) The sources that a reporter contacts are usually willing to divulge their identity.
    (E) Our press has never been altogether free.

18. Which one of the following statements is consistent with the argument above?

    (A) Privileged information has long been an important and necessary aspect of investigative reporting.
    (B) Not all the information a reporter collects becomes part of the public record.
    (C) Tape-recorded information is not always reliable.
    (D) The victim of a crime must be protected at all costs.
    (E) The perpetrator of a crime must be protected at all costs.

Questions 19–21

A federal court ruling that San Diego County can't sue the government for the cost of medical care of illegal aliens is based upon a legal technicality that ducks the larger moral question. But the U.S. Supreme Court's refusal to review this decision has closed the last avenue of legal appeal.

The medical expenses of indigent citizens or legally resident aliens are covered by state and federal assistance programs. The question of who is to pay when an undocumented alien falls ill remains unresolved, however, leaving California counties to bear this unfair and growing burden.

19. The author implies that

    (A) the U.S. Supreme Court has refused to review the federal court ruling
    (B) the burden of medical expenses for aliens is growing
    (C) the larger moral question involves no legal technicalities
    (D) San Diego should find another avenue of appeal
    (E) the federal government is dodging the moral issue

20. Which one of the following arguments, if true, would most seriously weaken the argument above?

    (A) There are many cases of undocumented aliens being denied medical aid at state hospitals.
    (B) A private philanthropic organization has funded medical aid programs that have so far provided adequate assistance to illegal aliens nationwide.
    (C) Illegal aliens do not wish federal or state aid, because those accepting aid risk detection of their illegal status and deportation.
    (D) Undocumented aliens stay in California only a short time before moving east.
    (E) Judges on the Supreme Court have pledged privately to assist illegal aliens with a favorable ruling once immigration laws are strengthened.

21. Which one of the following changes in the above passage could strengthen the author's argument?

    (A) adding interviews with illegal aliens
    (B) a description of the stages that led to a rejection by the Supreme Court
    (C) a clarification with numbers of the rate at which the burden of medical expenses is growing
    (D) the naming of those state and federal assistance programs that aid indigent citizens
    (E) the naming of those California counties that do not participate in medical aid to illegal aliens

22. *Historian:* History is strewn with the wreckage of experiments in communal living, often organized around farms and inspired by religious or philosophical ideals. To the more noble failures can now be added Mao Tse-tung's notorious Chinese communes. The current rulers of China, still undoing the mistakes of the late Chairman, are quietly allowing their agricultural communes to . . . .

    Which one of the following is the most logical completion of the passage above?

    (A) evolve
    (B) increase
    (C) recycle
    (D) disintegrate
    (E) organize

23. *Sal:* Herb is my financial planner.
    Keith: I'm sure he's good; he's my cousin.

    Which one of the following facts is Keith ignoring in his response?

    (A) Financial planning is a professional, not a personal, matter.
    (B) Sal is probably flattering Keith.
    (C) Professional competence is not necessarily a family trait.
    (D) "Good" is a term with many meanings.
    (E) Sal's financial planner is no one's cousin.

4   4   4   4   4

24. Many very effective prescription drugs are available to patients on a "one time only" basis. Suspicious of drug abuse, physicians will not renew a prescription for a medicine that has worked effectively for a patient. This practice denies a patient her right to health.

Which one of the following is a basic assumption made by the author?

(A) A new type of medicine is likely to be more expensive.
(B) Physicians are not concerned with a patient's health.
(C) Most of the patients who need prescription renewals are female.
(D) Most physicians prescribe inadequate amounts of medicine.
(E) Patients are liable to suffer the same ailment repeatedly.

Questions 25–26

Forty years ago, hardly anybody thought about going to court to sue somebody. A person could bump a pedestrian with his Chrysler Airflow, and the victim would say something like "No harm done" and walk away. Ipso facto. No filing of codicils, taking of depositions, or polling the jury. Attorneys need not apply.

25. Which one of the following sentences most logically continues the above passage?

(A) The Chrysler Airflow is no longer the harmless machine it used to be.
(B) Fortunately, this is still the case.
(C) Unfortunately, times have changed.
(D) New legislation affecting the necessity for codicils is a sign of the times.
(E) But now, as we know, law schools are full of eager young people.

26. Which one of the following details, if true, would most strengthen the above statement?

(A) There were fewer courthouses then than now.
(B) The marked increase in pedestrian accidents is a relatively recent occurrence.
(C) Most citizens of 40 years ago were not familiar with their legal rights.
(D) The number of lawsuits filed during World War II was extremely low.
(E) Most young attorneys were in the armed forces 40 years ago.

STOP

IF YOU FINISH BEFORE TIME IS CALLED, YOU MAY CHECK YOUR WORK ON THIS SECTION ONLY.
DO NOT WORK ON ANY OTHER SECTION IN THE TEST.

5 **5** **5** **5** **5**

SECTION V
TIME — 35 MINUTES
28 QUESTIONS

<u>Directions:</u> Read the passages and answer the questions following each passage by blackening the appropriate space on the answer sheet. You may refer back to the passages when answering the questions. Answer all questions on the basis of what is stated or implied.

In the negotiation of tax treaties, developing nations, as a group, share two objectives somewhat at odds with those of developed-nation treaty
(5) partners. One such goal, attracting foreign investment, is in the broader context of foreign policy objectives. In the narrower realm of tax policy a common developing-country objective
(10) is to maximize the public capture of revenues from foreign investment activities.

Unfortunately for potential Third World treaty partners, this latter goal can
(15) conflict directly with the desires of both First World governments and individual investors. The preference of First World authorities for restricted source-based taxation is due to considerations
(20) of administrative feasibility. Such restrictions, though formally reciprocal, only produce equitable revenue effects when investment flows between treaty partners are relatively equal. However,
(25) when investment flows primarily in one direction, as it generally does from industrial to developing countries, the seemingly reciprocal source-based restrictions produce revenue sacrifices
(30) primarily by the state receiving most of the foreign investment and producing most of the income—namely, the developing country partner. The benefit is captured either by the taxpayer in the
(35) form of reduced excess credits, or by the treasury of the residence (First World) state as the taxpayer's domestically creditable foreign tax liabilities decrease.

The potential public revenue gain
(40) to the residence state further bolsters the industrial nations' preference for restrictions on source-based taxation—at the direct expense of the treaty partner's revenue goals.
(45) The facilitation of foreign investment by tax treaties, whereas potentially serving the tax-policy goal of maximizing public revenue, also (or even instead) may serve broader
(50) economic objectives of developing countries. Foreign investments may be seen as essential sources of technical and managerial knowledge, capital, jobs, and foreign exchange. As such, the
(55) significance of foreign investments as an immediate source of public revenue could pale next to their longer-term "ripple effect" on development. In the negotiation of tax treaties, then, a
(60) developing country might be expected to ignore revenue goals and accept substantial limitations on source-based taxation, at least insofar as such limitations could be expected to
(65) encourage investment.

Frequently, however, Third World nations take a considerably more aggressive approach, seeking treaty terms that, in effect, provide subsidies to
(70) private investors at the expense of First World treaty partners. The United States traditionally has followed a strict policy of "capital export neutrality," providing no tax incentives for investment in the
(75) Third World through either the Internal Revenue Code or tax treaty provisions.

GO ON TO THE NEXT PAGE ➤

1. Normally, a developing country will negotiate a tax treaty for the purpose of

   (A) attracting foreign workers
   (B) decreasing tax revenues
   (C) attracting international investment and reducing tax revenues
   (D) attracting foreign investment and increasing tax revenues
   (E) decreasing dependence on special interest local investors

2. We can infer that a reciprocal source-based taxation treaty between a First World and a developing nation will produce

   (A) greater revenues for the First World nation
   (B) greater revenues for the developing nation
   (C) equal revenues for each country
   (D) no revenues for either country
   (E) losses to the economy of the First World nation

3. In negotiated treaties with developing countries, a First World country is likely to prefer

   (A) unrestricted source-based taxation
   (B) reciprocal restricted source-based taxation
   (C) nonreciprocal source-based taxation
   (D) equal investment flow between the partners
   (E) limited investment flow between the partners

4. In a treaty with a developing country that generates an excess of foreign tax credits, all of the following are likely EXCEPT:

   (A) the treaty will require some reduction of at-source taxation
   (B) the treaty will discourage private investors
   (C) the treaty will not produce what is perceived as the optimal revenue-producing balance
   (D) the treaty will require some expansion of at-source taxation
   (E) the excess of tax credits will be larger if the source country reserves more taxing jurisdiction

5. According to the passage, all of the following are potential advantages of foreign investment to developing countries EXCEPT:

   (A) increased managerial expertise
   (B) increased capital
   (C) increased availability of new materials
   (D) increased foreign exchange
   (E) increased employment

6. A developing country that did not insist upon immediate higher public revenues might be expected to

   (A) deter foreign investment
   (B) increase foreign investment
   (C) avoid the "ripple effect"
   (D) decrease employment
   (E) decrease the availability of raw materials

5   **5**

The following paired passages discuss twentieth-century Mexican artists' interpretations of the pre-Columbian world.

Passage A

The pre-Columbian past is everywhere evident in Mexico. Material remains are abundant. Indigenous
line peoples comprise a great majority of
(5) the population. Twentieth-century artists have been cognizant of this past, with [Diego] Rivera at the forefront of those who champion it and José Clemente Orozco equally forceful in
(10) denouncing it. But, regardless of their attitudes toward this past, Mexican artists have not been able to ignore it. All muralists used various aspects of the pre-Columbian world in their
(15) mural programs. Rivera presented it as an ideal world in his National Palace murals, and the conquest as a heroic struggle against all odds. David Alfaro Siqueiros developed a thematic program
(20) in his murals at Chillán, Chile, and in Mexico City, in which Cuauhtemoc personifies the successful fight against the oppressor, symbolized by the centaur—half man, half beast. To
(25) Orozco, this world was inhabited by inhospitable gods, who appear to have more in common with the vengeful god in the Judaic tradition than with the pre-Columbian world. He, of course,
(30) overwhelms the opposition with a massive satyrical [sic] brush, as he on occasion did in his murals. In fact, it is when this part of his personality was allowed to go unchecked that we have
(35) caricature rather than painting.

At any rate, whatever the attitudes toward their pre-Columbian past— *negative* or *positive*—all used a European pictorial language. Even the
(40) techniques are European. The muralists' use of fresco and the thematic and formal programs fit into a European . . . tradition that was initiated in Florence during the fifteenth century by Masaccio
(45) and others. The content is Mexican, the expression is Mexican, the language is European.

Passage B

It must be kept in mind that Mexico was a colonized nation from the
(50) sixteenth to the nineteenth centuries and, despite the 1810 War of Independence that freed Mexico politically from Spain, the colonized mentality of the ruling classes maintained a position of
(55) imitation vis-à-vis European culture and a contempt for indigenous culture.

In Mexico, as in Latin America generally, nationalism has been one of the greatest forces impelling change.
(60) It has been deeply entwined with a necessary sense of dignity, pride, and affirmation. To counter engendered feelings of inferiority, intellectuals have reconstructed the past, and in so doing
(65) have created a mythology of ancient utopias. The Mexican painter who epitomized this tendency was Diego Rivera who, within a framework of Marxism, dialectically compared the
(70) positive and negative forces operating in a historical period, with an emphasis on the positive. In his vast epic of Mexican history on the staircase of the Palacio Nacional, Mexico City, he created a
(75) golden age, where Quetzalcoatl is the prophet. Cultural reaffirmation alone, however, is not the full substance of Rivera's mural. Mexico's Indian population also composed the largest and
(80) most exploited class of the country, the rural base on which the entire economic structure rested. To revitalize this class, to set before it, in a mural, not only its ancient tradition idealized but also its
(85) power to reconstruct the present and control the future, was to continue the work that the military phase of the revolution had started. This is the true significance of Rivera's murals, which
(90) rest on a twin construct of nationalism and indigenism.

Nationalism and indigenism were also elements in the work of both Siqueiros and Orozco, but serving
(95) different purposes. Siqueiros's 1944 mural *Cuauhtémoc Against the Myth* used the Aztec emperor as a symbol of the possibility of a struggle against seemingly overwhelming forces. On

GO ON TO THE NEXT PAGE ➤

(100) the surface, Orozco disdained the use of nationalism, partly because of his scorn for romanticized visions of Indian life "fit to flatter the tourist" and partly because of a middle-class snobbery
(105) directed at "hateful and degenerate types of the lower classes" that caused him to eschew the painting of "Indian sandals and dirty clothes." Nevertheless, his treatment of the positive aspects
(110) of the human condition often present Quetzalcoatl and the revolutionary heroes Hidalgo and Zapata in heroic and grandiose terms.

7. Which one of the following is the best description of the subject of both passages?

   (A) The reaction to colonialism by twentieth-century Mexican muralists
   (B) The techniques dominating the work of Mexican muralists
   (C) Pre-Columbian mysticism in the works of the muralists
   (D) The differences among the three main Mexican muralists
   (E) Pre-Columbian influence on three Mexican muralists

8. From information in both Passage A and Passage B, which one of the following can be inferred?

   (A) Diego Rivera most successfully captured pre-Columbian history in his murals.
   (B) The three major muralists rejected European painting techniques.
   (C) Of the three major muralists, Orozco's attitude toward the pre-Columbian past was the most ambivalent.
   (D) Siqueiros primarily produced murals depicting life during the period of colonialism.
   (E) Only Rivera used his art for political purposes.

9. Which one of the following statements illustrates a contrast between Passage A and Passage B?

   (A) Passage A mentions the technique used by the muralists, whereas Passage B does not.
   (B) Passage B praises the work of Rivera, Orozco, and Siqueiros, whereas Passage A is neutral toward Siqueiros.
   (C) Passage A places the works of the muralists in historical context, whereas Passage B places them in a sociopolitical context.
   (D) Passage B describes the public's reaction to the works of the muralists, whereas Passage A does not.
   (E) Passage A identifies Rivera as the most important of the Mexican muralists, whereas Passage B makes no judgment.

10. According to Passage A and Passage B, all of the following characterize Orozco EXCEPT:

    (A) his tendency to use caricature in his works
    (B) his portrayal of the gods as unfriendly
    (C) his snobbery toward the lower-class Indian population
    (D) his romanticized picture of the indigenous population
    (E) his use of satire

11. The term "cultural reaffirmation" (line 76) in Passage B refers to which one of the following?

    (A) The use of indigenous art and culture in the muralists' works
    (B) Antagonism toward European domination of art
    (C) The public's interest in and acceptance of pre-Columbian art
    (D) The insistence on a nationalistic spirit in modern Mexican art
    (E) Attempts by the muralists to glorify the accomplishments of pre-Columbian artists

GO ON TO THE NEXT PAGE ➤

5   **5**

12. According to Passage B, Diego Rivera's primary political intention in his mural of Mexican history was to

(A) show his feelings about Karl Marx
(B) depict the heroic battles of the revolution
(C) energize the Indian population and direct it to the future
(D) create an artistic language for modern Mexico
(E) preserve pre-Columbian symbolism and mythology

13. According to both passages, all of the following are mentioned or implied as characterizing the Mexican muralists EXCEPT:

(A) the use of Mexican subject matter
(B) disdain for European art
(C) recognition of the indigenous population
(D) appreciation for pre-Columbian works of art
(E) reference to Mexican heroes

War and change—political and economic foremost, but social and cultural not far behind—have been
line linked in America from the beginning.
(5) War was the necessary factor in the birth of the new American republic, as it has been in the birth of every political state known to us in history. War, chiefly the Civil War, in U.S.
(10) history has been a vital force in the rise of industrial capitalism, in the change of America from a predominantly agrarian and pastoral country to one chiefly manufacturing in nature. War,
(15) in focusing the mind of a country, stimulates inventions, discoveries, and fresh adaptations. Despite its manifest illth*, war, by the simple fact of the intellectual and social changes it
(20) instigates, yields results which are tonics to advancement.
  By all odds, the most important war in U.S. history, the war that released the greatest number and diversity of changes
(25) in American life, was the Great War, the war that began in Europe in August 1914 and engulfed the United States in April 1917. Great changes in America were immediate.
(30)   In large measure these changes reflected a release from the sense of isolation, insularity, and exceptionalism that had suffused so much of the American mind during the nineteenth
(35) century. The early Puritans had seen their new land as a "city upon a hill" with the eyes of the world on it. It was not proper for the New World to go to the Old for its edification; what
(40) was proper was for the Old World, grown feeble and hidebound, to come to America for inspiration. A great deal of that state of mind entered into what Tocqueville called the "American
(45) Religion," a religion compounded of Puritanism and ecstatic nationalism.

*illth = ill effects (word coined by the author earlier in the full selection)

GO ON TO THE NEXT PAGE ➤

5   **5**

What we think of today as modernity—in manners and morals as well as ideas and mechanical things—
(50) came into full-blown existence in Europe in the final part of the nineteenth century, its centers such cities as London, Paris, and Vienna. In contrast America was a "closed" society, one
(55) steeped in conventionality and also in a struggle for identity. This was how many Europeans saw America and it was emphatically how certain somewhat more sophisticated Americans
(60) saw themselves. The grand tour was a veritable obligation of better-off, ambitious, and educated Americans— the tour being, of course, of Europe.

Possibly the passage of American
(65) values, ideas, and styles from "closed" to "open," from the isolated to the cosmopolitan society, would have taken place, albeit more slowly, had there been no transatlantic war of 1914–1918. We
(70) can't be sure. What we do know is that the war, and America's entrance into it, gave dynamic impact to the processes of secularization, individualization, and other kinds of social-psychological
(75) change which so drastically changed this country from the America of the turn of the century to the America of the 1920s.

14. In the passage the author makes all of the following points about war EXCEPT:

(A) war increases the pace of changes that might occur anyway
(B) war stimulates new inventions and discoveries
(C) war causes social and intellectual changes
(D) war in a capitalistic society is inevitable
(E) war sometimes stimulates a closed society toward greater openness

15. If true, which of the following best illustrates the author's point about the effects of war on American society?

(A) During World War II, the Germans developed a variety of lethal nerve gas to use in the field.
(B) The development of radioactive isotopes used in treating cancer grew out of research to build the atomic bomb used in World War II.
(C) The American influenza epidemic of 1919 in all likelihood was a result of the return of infected soldiers from the battlefields of World War I.
(D) After the Civil War and the abolition of slavery in the South, racial intolerance across America grew in bitterness.
(E) A significant drain on America's material resources was a result of relaxed immigration policies occurring after World War II.

16. According to the author, World War I was the most important war in U.S. history because it

(A) ended the notion of a war to end all wars
(B) resulted in a weakened Germany that in turn led to Hitler's appeal
(C) changed America from a dominantly agrarian country to a manufacturing country
(D) led to more changes and a wider diversity of changes than any other American war
(E) made Americans more aware of advances made in European centers such as London, Paris, and Vienna

GO ON TO THE NEXT PAGE ➤

17. The main purpose of paragraph 3 is to

   (A) characterize the American mind in the nineteenth century
   (B) define Tocqueville's concept of American religion
   (C) indicate the main cause of America's entrance into World War I
   (D) contrast Civil War America with World War I America
   (E) indicate the areas of America's strength at the start of World War I

18. According to the author, which one of the following contributed to America's insularity before World War I?

   (A) The inability of all but the most wealthy, educated Americans to travel abroad
   (B) The nationalistic view that the New World (America) shouldn't turn to the Old World (Europe) for ideas
   (C) The emphasis on agrarian pursuits as opposed to belief in industry and technology
   (D) The puritanical idea that traveling widely in the world exposed one to sin and corruption
   (E) The superiority of the New World (America) to a feeble, decadent Old World (Europe)

19. Which one of the following best describes the main subject of this passage?

   (A) a comparison of wars in America
   (B) the benefits of war to society
   (C) the importance of World War I to changes in America
   (D) the contrast between the New World (America) and the Old World (Europe)
   (E) secularization and individualization in American society

20. The relationship of paragraph 1 to the rest of the passage is best described by which one of the following?

   (A) It presents a popular view that is proved inadequate by the rest of the passage.
   (B) It introduces a philosophical question that is then answered in the rest of the passage.
   (C) It outlines the contents of each of the other four paragraphs in the passage.
   (D) It sets up the first of four examples developed in the rest of the passage.
   (E) It presents a general idea that introduces the specific topic developed in the rest of the passage.

21. According to information in the passage, all of the following inferences can be made EXCEPT:

   (A) Well-to-do nineteenth-century American parents would be more likely to send their son to Europe than to California.
   (B) European "ecstatic nationalism" would be greater after World War I than before it.
   (C) Religious influence in the daily workings of American society would be less evident in 1920 than 1900.
   (D) A census in America 20 years after the Civil War would indicate more manufacturing operations than before the war.
   (E) In the nineteenth century, avant garde movements in art and literature would be more likely to originate in Europe than in the United States.

GO ON TO THE NEXT PAGE ➤

The theory of natural selection cites the fact that every organism produces more gametes and/or organisms than can possibly survive. If every gamete
(5) produced by a given species united in fertilization and developed into offspring, the world would become so overcrowded in a short period of time that there would be no room for
(10) successive generations. This does not happen. There is a balance that is maintained in the reproduction of all species and therefore natural populations remain fairly stable, unless
(15) upset by a change in conditions. In the struggle for existence, some organisms die and the more hardy survive.

The differences that exist between organisms of the same species, making
(20) one more fit to survive than another, can be explained in terms of variations. Variations exist in every species and in every trait in members of a species. Therefore some organisms can compete
(25) more successfully than others for the available food or space in which to grow, or they can elude their enemies better. These variations are said to add survival value to an organism.
(30) Survival value traits are passed on to the offspring by those individuals that live long enough to reproduce. As time goes on, these special adaptations for survival are perpetuated and new species evolve
(35) from a common ancestral species. The environment is the selecting agent in natural selection because it determines which variations are satisfactory for survival and which are not.
(40) The major weakness in Darwin's theory of natural selection is that he did not explain the source, or genetic basis, for variations. He did not distinguish between variations that are hereditary
(45) and those that are nonhereditary, making the assumption that all variations that have survival value are passed on to the progeny. Like Jean Baptiste Lamarck, Darwin believed
(50) in the inheritance of even acquired characteristics.

Hugo De Vries (1845–1935), a Dutch botanist, explained variations in terms of mutations. His study of 50,000 plants belonging to the evening primrose
(55) species enabled him to identify changes in the plants that were passed on from parent to offspring. In 1901 De Vries offered his mutation theory to explain
(60) organic evolution. Today, we know that mutations are changes in genes that can come about spontaneously or can be induced by some mutagenic agent. Spontaneous mutation rates are very
(65) low, and mutations alone do not affect major changes in the frequencies of alleles, which are alternative forms of genes that occupy a given place on a chromosone.
(70) An important cause of variation within species is genetic recombination that results from sexual reproduction. The genes of two individuals are sorted out and recombined into a new
(75) combination, producing new traits—and thus variation.

Gene flow is also responsible for the development of variations. It is the movement of new genes into a
(80) population. Gene flow often acts against the effects of natural selection. Genetic drift is a change in a gene pool that takes place in a population as a result of chance. If a mutation occurs in a
(85) gene of one person, and that person does not reproduce, the gene is lost to the population. Sometimes a small population breaks off from a larger one. Within that population is a mutant gene,
(90) and because the mating within the small population is very close, the frequencies of the mutant gene will increase. In the Amish population, for example, where there is little or no outbreeding,
(95) an increase in the homozygosity of the genes in the gene pool is evinced in the high frequencies of genetic dwarfism and polydactyly (six fingers). The isolated smaller population has a
(100) different gene frequency than the larger population from which it came. This is known as the "founder principle."

GO ON TO THE NEXT PAGE ➤

Genetic drift and the random mutations that increase or decrease as the result (105) of genetic drift are known as non-Darwinian evolution.

Another cause of variation is speciation, or the forming of new species from a species already in (110) existence. This can happen when a population becomes geographically divided and part of the original species continues life in a new habitat. The separated populations cannot interbreed. (115) Over evolutionary time, different environments present different selective pressures, and the change in gene pools will eventually produce new species.

22. The passage supports which one of the following statements?

(A) Spontaneous mutations cause the most significant evolutionary changes.
(B) Darwin's theory of evolution depends on rejecting the idea that acquired characteristics can be inherited.
(C) Variations among individual members of a species occur only when new genes move into an established population of that species.
(D) It is possible for a survival value trait to be eliminated from a species.
(E) New species are generally the result of genetic recombination.

23. Which one of the following, if true, would support the idea that acquired characteristics can be inherited?

(A) A spontaneous mutation causes some members of a rodent population to develop webbed feet. This segment of the population becomes isolated and is unable to breed with the original group. An exceptionally high frequency of webbed feet occurs in the successive generations of the isolated segment.
(B) A gene from a virus is experimentally transmitted to a fruit fly, making it vulnerable to carbon dioxide poison. This vulnerability is then passed on to the fruit fly's offspring.
(C) Antelopes raised in captivity are released into the wild. They run significantly more slowly than the wild antelope. After a year, the released antelopes' speed equals that of the wild antelopes.
(D) A population of long-haired dogs is shaved and bred with a population of hairless dogs. Their offspring include more hairless than long-haired pups.
(E) Fourteen different species of finches live on the Galapagos Islands. It is determined that all descended from a single species of finch found on mainland Peru.

5 **5** **5** **5**

24. The passage provides explanations for each of the following EXCEPT:

    (A) genetic drift
    (B) the founder principle
    (C) survival value
    (D) speciation
    (E) homozygosity

25. Random mutations are known as non-Darwinian evolution because they

    (A) are not necessarily related to the survival value of an organism
    (B) are more infrequent than spontaneous mutations
    (C) tend to refute Darwin's theories about the formation of species
    (D) occur only in small populations that have been isolated
    (E) were first described by Hugo De Vries, not Charles Darwin

26. The founder principle

    (A) accounts for genetic dwarfism
    (B) supports the importance of "weeding out" non-adaptive organisms
    (C) explains the concept of homozygosity
    (D) relates to gene frequencies in isolated populations
    (E) refutes Darwin's theory of natural selection

27. Based on the passage, which one of the following can be inferred about Charles Darwin?

    (A) Darwin did not believe the theory of genetic inheritance.
    (B) Darwin did not believe that genetic theories were relevant to evolution.
    (C) Darwin's work was more concerned with the survival value of traits than with the mechanics of how they were inherited.
    (D) Darwin's theories did not include a recognition that variation within members of a species was crucial to evolution.
    (E) Darwin was more interested in traits that were acquired and passed on than he was in genetically inherited traits.

28. In the passage, the author's primary concern is to

    (A) address briefly the history of evolutionary theory
    (B) provide a brief overview of the concept of variation
    (C) expose the weakness inherent in Darwin's evolutionary theory
    (D) differentiate between genetic and evolutionary theories
    (E) describe one of the ways in which nonadaptive traits can be inherited

STOP

IF YOU FINISH BEFORE TIME IS CALLED, YOU MAY CHECK YOUR WORK ON THIS SECTION ONLY.
DO NOT WORK ON ANY OTHER SECTION IN THE TEST.

Writing Sample

<u>Directions:</u> You have 35 minutes to write an essay in response to a given topic. Take a few minutes to plan your work before you begin writing. DO NOT WRITE ON A TOPIC OF YOUR OWN CHOICE. ESSAYS THAT DO NOT ADDRESS THE GIVEN TOPIC ARE UNACCEPTABLE.

The quality of your writing is more important than the length of your response or the content. Pay attention to organization, appropriate diction, and correct usage. You will not be expected to display any specialized knowledge in your response, nor will you be expected to write a "perfect" essay; law schools understand that you are writing under a time constraint, and will allow for the minor lapses in writing ability that might occur under this circumstance.

Only the lined area on your response sheets will be reproduced for the law schools, so do not write outside this space. Make sure your handwriting is legible.

Scratch Paper
Do not write your essay in this space

Sample Topic

Read the following descriptions of Thomas and Peters, candidates for the position of head coach of the Ventura Vultures professional football team. *Then, in the space provided, write an argument for appointing one candidate over the other.* Use the information in this description and assume that the two general policies below equally guide the Vultures' decision on the appointment:

- The head coach should possess the ability to work with players and coaching staff toward achieving a championship season.
- The head coach should successfully manage the behind-the-scenes activities of recruiting, analyzing scouting reports, and handling the media and fans in order to enhance the public relations and image of the team.

THOMAS has been General Manager of the Vultures for the past ten years. A physical education major with a master's in psychology, he knows the player personnel as well as anyone, including the coaching staff. His on-target assessment of player skills and weaknesses has been instrumental in building a more balanced team over the past decade through his skillful trading and recruitment of college athletes. As the chief managing officer, he has also enhanced the team's image by his careful press relationship and understated approach when negotiations with star players reached an impasse. He rarely alienates players, coaches, press, or fans with his even-handed (though sometimes unemotional) attitude, and the Vultures' owners feel fortunate that they were able to entice him away from his high-school coaching position, which he left 10 years ago. He has never played either pro or college ball.

PETERS is presently a wide receiver and defensive end for the Vultures. A one-time star, Peters has played both offense and defense for the Vultures since their inception in the league 14 years ago, a remarkable feat equaled by few in the game. He was elected captain of the team the past five years because of his charisma, although he occasionally angers management and fellow players with his strong comments about his philosophy of the game. His only experience in the front office was leading a player charity benefit for the Vultures, which raised more than $2,000,000 for abused Ventura County children. Although a high school dropout, Peters is a self-made man who firmly believes the key to life is having a strong educational background, even though he sometimes feels uncomfortable around college-educated athletes. The Vulture owners believe Peters may provide the emotional charge the team needs at its helm to win its first championship.

Scratch Paper
Do not write your essay in this space

Answer Key

Section I: Logical Reasoning

1. A	6. D	11. E	16. D	21. D	26. D
2. A	7. A	12. D	17. D	22. B	
3. D	8. B	13. C	18. C	23. B	
4. E	9. E	14. A	19. A	24. B	
5. C	10. D	15. B	20. D	25. E	

Section II: Reading Comprehension

1. C	6. D	11. B	16. A	21. C	26. D
2. A	7. C	12. D	17. A	22. B	27. A
3. A	8. B	13. E	18. D	23. C	28. E
4. B	9. A	14. A	19. E	24. A	
5. C	10. E	15. B	20. A	25. C	

Section III: Analytical Reasoning

1. E	5. A	9. B	13. B	17. D	21. E
2. C	6. C	10. C	14. B	18. B	22. B
3. D	7. D	11. E	15. E	19. D	23. C
4. B	8. A	12. C	16. D	20. A	

Section IV: Logical Reasoning

1. D	6. B	11. A	16. E	21. C	26. D
2. D	7. A	12. C	17. B	22. D	
3. A	8. E	13. D	18. A	23. C	
4. C	9. A	14. D	19. E	24. E	
5. B	10. B	15. B	20. B	25. C	

Section V: Reading Comprehension

1. D	6. B	11. A	16. D	21. B	26. D
2. A	7. E	12. C	17. A	22. D	27. C
3. B	8. C	13. B	18. B	23. B	28. B
4. D	9. A	14. D	19. C	24. E	
5. C	10. D	15. B	20. E	25. A	

MODEL TEST ANALYSIS

Doing model exams and understanding the explanations afterward are, of course, important in acquainting you with typical LSAT question types and successful approaches to the questions. However, another benefit of carefully analyzing these model tests is to understand the kinds of errors you are making and thus work to minimize them. For instance, if a very high percentage of your incorrect answers is due to "careless error" or "misread problem," then perhaps you are working much too fast and should slow your pace accordingly. If your incorrect answers are due primarily to "lack of knowledge," then a careful rereading and reworking of the appropriate question-type chapter may be in order. Or, if you find that you aren't completing a large number of questions because of lack of time, you may need to either increase your speed or learn to use the "one-check, two-check" technique more effectively.

This kind of analysis of the model tests will enable you to identify your particular weaknesses and thus remedy them.

Model Test Analysis

Section	Total Number of Questions	Number Correct	Number Incorrect	Number Unanswered*
I. Logical Reasoning	26			
II. Reading Comprehension	28			
III. Analytical Reasoning	23			
IV. Logical Reasoning	26			
V. Reading Comprehension	28			
Writing Sample				
TOTALS:	131			

*At this stage in your preparation, you should not be leaving any blank answer spaces. At least fill in a guess, as there is no penalty for a wrong answer.

NOTE: Refer to page 123 for instructions on obtaining your approximate score range.

Reasons for Incorrect Answers

You may wish to evaluate the explanations before completing this chart.

Section	Total Number Incorrect	Lack of Knowledge	Misread Problem	Careless Error	Unanswered or Wrong Guess
I. Logical Reasoning					
II. Reading Comprehension					
III. Analytical Reasoning					
IV. Logical Reasoning					
V. Reading Comprehension					
TOTALS:					

Explanation of Answers

Section I

1. **A** The author must assume that "nothing about our coin influences its fall in favor of either side or that all influences are counterbalanced by equal and opposite influences"; otherwise "our ignorance of the coming result" is untrue. Also, he mentions that the chances are one out of two that the coin will fall heads up; this could not be correct if the coin had been weighted or tampered with.

2. **A** (A) is implied by the author's statement that one-to-two is not "true." (B), (C), (D), and (E) are not implied and would not follow from the passage.

3. **D** The author is actually pointing out that self-confidence is of most importance. (C) and (E) focus on behavior, while the author is focusing on mental attitude.

4. **E** Only choice (E) is supported by these comments. The comments suggest that riding on roller coasters is taking a risk and that this risk translates to a proclivity to taking other risks in life. The passage doesn't suggest, however, that *no* roller coaster riders avoid taking risks elswhere (A), nor does it have any bearing on the importance of taking risks (B). Choice (C) is a difficult one to eliminate because the passage certainly doesn't rule out this possibility (the passage says "than other," not "than *all* others")—but it doesn't directly support it, either. The comments have nothing to do with varying levels or types of risk taking (D).

5. **C** If the diet and way of life of the men of the two islands are alike, but the life expectancies are very different, the cause of the difference is probably something other than diet and the way of life. Some of the other answers are reasonable inferences, but they do not follow so clearly from the paragraph as (C).

6. **D** None of the other four choices offer information that explains the discrepancy. If the women in college are preparing for a profession that pays less (teaching) than the profession the men will enter (engineering), the discrepancy is explained.

7. **A** To conclude that the women should earn as much as or more than the men, the passage must assume that all of the men and all of the women, or at least an equal number, enter the workforce. It also assumes that all of them, or at least an equal number, graduate from college, though the passage says only "are enrolled."

8. **B** The six-month interest-free charge is the money at a low cost; the stock of discontinued summer wear is the slow selling product, and the fashionable new neck wear is the popular product. None of the other choices covers all three conditions.

9. **E** Though all of the choices are plausible, (E) deals with all three of the problems mentioned in the paragraph. Each of the other choices deals only with one.

10. **D** Although Michael may be lying, there is no factual evidence to that effect. Michael is truthful and readily admits to the previous dents to his own vehicle (A). (B) and (C) reinforce Michael's contention that the dents were caused by someone else. Even (E) reflects positively on Michael's character, though it is not mentioned in the original set of conditions.

11. **E** The author states that the present programs are at best weak and hopefully won't fail as they have in the past.

12. **D** The statement that "Hopefully, they won't fail as they have in the past" tells us that our government is not trying a new approach to end inflation. (A) is close, but the passage states that foreign oil is "high-priced," not "overpriced." "High-priced" tells us the relative cost, not the actual comparative value.

13. **C** The conclusion is the prediction of a grim year for home-builders. Choices (A), (B), (D), and (E) do not point to continued bad sales, but (C), revealing that sales fell even with advertising and incentives, supports the prediction of a bad year ahead.

14. **A** Three possibilities exist:
(a) You read *Weight-Off* magazine, are fat, and do not eat chocolate.
(b) You are fat, eat chocolate, but do not read *Weight-Off* magazine.
(c) You eat chocolate, are not fat, and do not read *Weight-Off* magazine.

Thus, (A) is inconsistent by (a) and (b). (B) is not inconsistent if (b) and (c) are void of people. (C) is not inconsistent if (c) is void of people. (D) and (E) are not inconsistent by (c) and (a).

15. **B** Dave felt that Jerry implied that no one except Jerry's wife cooks fantastic meals.

16. **D** Only (D) offers an instance of success in the polls. (A) simply repeats a point of the passage without including the qualification that comes later. Choices (B), (C), and (E) would support rather than undermine the viewpoint of the passage.

17. **D** The passage does not point out inherent inconsistencies. It does support a point with a specific example (the two figures on the balanced budget poll), question the honesty of politicians (the phrase "or may not"), reinterprets the 80 percent support figure, and shows how statistics can be used to mislead.

18. **C** Decreasing the fares on lightly traveled routes might attract some passengers away from the overcrowded, more popular flights, but increasing the fares would not help to solve the luggage problem. The four other suggestions are plausible ways of dealing with the lack of space.

19. **A** X's new realization is expressed in his final sentence: "We must know all the characteristics of men, and that Socrates has all of them, before we can be sure." The "characteristics of men" are what is implied by the generalization "man," in "Socrates is a man." Therefore, deductive thinking is simply reminding ourselves of the particular specifics implied by generalizations.

20. **D** Symbolically, A is necessary to have B (a good telescope to see moons of Neptune). You do not have B (can't see moons with my telescope). Therefore, you cannot have A (a good telescope). (D) is the only choice that follows this line of reasoning. Symbolically, A is necessary to have B (knowing area of circle to find circumference). You do not have B (can't figure out circumference). Therefore, you cannot have A (area of circle).

21. **D** Extensive psychological research would most likely give the information that the author discusses. (E) limits the research to clinical psychologists and to recent findings.

22. **B** "Conscious behavior eventually becomes habit" is indirectly stated in the last sentence. (A) is a close answer, but that absolute word "all" is inconsistent with the words "can become" in the last sentence. This does not imply that they *must* become unconscious behavior.

23. **B** The given advice would be strengthened by the assurance that such measures are effective. Each of the other choices either weakens the advice, or addresses only a portion of the paragraph.

24. **B** The disease under discussion is termed "it," and thus its identity is unclear. The other choices either are not applicable to the second sentence or refer to terms that require no further definition.

25. **E** (E) weakens the argument that young people have abundant time. The other choices are only tangentially relevant to the argument.

26. **D** The passage says that worrying about writing unfortunately keeps one from writing at all; (D) summarizes this viewpoint. (B) and (C) are irrelevant notions; (A) contradicts the author's implied support for writing theorists; and (E) is an unreasonable, unsupported conclusion.

Section II

Passage 1

1. **C** The chief purpose of the Sixth Amendment was to ensure the assistance of counsel in criminal cases. The guarantee to the right of self-representation was not the chief purpose of the amendment although the amendment has been used to support it.

2. **A** The phrase refers to the end of the second paragraph. The author regards the waiving of the right to counsel as a choice, which should not be seen as a guarantee of the right of self-representation.

3. **A** The phrase "*in propria persona*" means "in his own person," "by himself," or "by herself."

4. **B** If the Court had believed a fair trial was impossible without the assistance of counsel, it would not have allowed self-representation.

5. **C** The passage emphasizes the importance of warning a defendant of the risks of self-representation.

6. **D** Though true, the tradition of self-representation is not a valid objection to the practice. In fact, it might be cited as an argument in favor of self-representing defendants.

Passage 2

7. **C** The passage states that African arts were curiosities and were presented as evidence of the "low state of heathen savagery of the African." The implication of lines 18–25 is that the arts, like the government and history, were not worth notice. (D) and (E) are incorrect; nothing is implied concerning the proportions or the subjects of African art. (A) and (B) both suggest a positive reaction to the art; this reaction is not supported by the passage.

8. **B** See lines 12–18. (C), whether true or not, is not supported by the passage. (D) is incorrect; Africa wasn't a threat to European society. In fact, Africans were exploited or made objects of missionary zeal. (A) and (E) are clearly irrelevant or incorrect.

9. **A** The writings of Pliny are cited as one of the early sources of knowledge about Africa—not one of the factors contributing to a change in the European view. See lines 26–34 for support of (B), (C), (D), and (E).

10. **E** Lines 35–38 make it clear that cultural relativism refers to viewing a culture in its own terms and on its own merits rather than judging it by the standards of one's own culture. (E) most clearly defines this point of view in relation to art. (A) is incorrect; the passage does not suggest that value judgments about works of art cannot be made, as long as the works are judged against the values of their own culture. (B) and (C) are irrelevant to the idea of cultural relativism. (D) is also irrelevant, and its judgment is not supported by any statements in the passage.

11. **B** See lines 46–53. The author states that when the attitude toward African art did change, it changed as a result of an "excess of romantic rebellion" against Classicism and Naturalism, not as a result of an objective assessment. No point is made in the passage about the availability of African art (A). (C) is unclear, and (D) is clearly inaccurate. The judgments of missionaries (E) were irrelevant to the twentieth-century European assessment of African art.

12. **D** See lines 75–85. One of the author's main points is that African art was very much in tune with its audience, unlike modern European art, which represented a rebellion against European traditions. (A) is the opposite of the point the author makes about African art. (B) and (E) are irrelevant and not supported by information in the passage. (C) is incorrect because although the author says we cannot have full understanding of African art if we judge it by twentieth-century Western aesthetic standards, we can still "admire" the works in a limited way. See lines 68–74.

13. **E** See lines 89–93. The author states that the works of art, while conservative and conformist, were not "passive reflections" of the culture; the perishable nature of wood ensured that every generation reaffirmed its faith. No comparison between wood and stone is made (with the exception of the implied comparison of impermanence and permanence). Therefore, (A) and (B) are incorrect. Also, no point is made about Western art or the Western world (C), (D).

14. **A** Throughout the passage the author talks about European or Western reactions to African art, from the earliest knowledge of Africa in Europe until the twentieth-century reassessment of African art. No specific works are analyzed (B), nor is any information included about African religious and social beliefs (D) or African aesthetic principles (E).

Passage 3

15. **B** (B) is the best choice because the passage first describes the classic model of competition and then introduces what the author refers to as the concept of "countervailing power." Although the ideas in (D) and (E) are both present in the passage, these titles are too restrictive. (A) is incomplete, and (C) is clearly wrong, in that the passage doesn't specifically address "American capitalism."

16. **A** (A) is directly from the passage (lines 17–21). Although (B) and (C) might occur, these are not part of the classic competition model described by the author. (E) would certainly not provide a return to normal prices; although it might offer a change in *supply*, it would not alter *demand*. Answer (D) is simply unclear.

17. **A** (A) is the best choice. See lines 26–32. (D) and (E) are clearly wrong. (C) is unclear. The second-best answer is (B), since the behavior of manufacturers is ultimately related to competition for the customer. However, (A) is the more specific answer provided by the passage.

18. **D** (D) is the best choice. See lines 44–52. (A) is incorrect because the classic model of competition does *not* ignore the role of labor (lines 26–30). Also, although the author might agree that greed undermined the classic model, this is not an issue addressed in the passage. (B) is incorrect because the author does not relate change in self-regulation of competition to any particular event, nor does he place it in a specific time frame. (C) is clearly the opposite of the point made in the passage. The restraint of "sellers by other sellers and buyers by other buyers" is part of the classic model of competition. (E) is incorrect because, according to the author, "countervailing power" did not destroy competition but grew as a result of a change in the classic model, i.e., the reduction of the number of competitors and resulting concentration of power among a small group of firms.

19. **E** Organizations that network manufacturers would not provide a customer- or supplier-generated restraint on them, which is the way the author defines "countervailing power." All of the other choices are possible wielders of "countervailing power."

20. **A** In lines 32–44 and lines 52–56, the author makes it clear that economists have almost exclusively focused on the classic model of competition in considering restraints on manufacturers. (B) is incorrect because the author does not discuss government regulation or the lack of it as part of economic theory. Similarly, (C) is incorrect; the "trickle-down" theory (i.e., that what is good for those at the top will ultimately benefit those at the bottom) is also not mentioned in the passage. (D) is contradicted in the passage; according to the author, economists did recognize the trend toward concentration (lines 44–52, 73–80). Finally, although the author might agree with (E), the passage suggests that economists have been preoccupied with the classic model of competition (including its built-in restraints) rather than biased toward "unregulated" capitalism. The preoccupation with the classic models led them to ignore other types of restraint in the economy.

21. **C** The passage sets up the classic model of competition in paragraphs 1 and 2. Paragraph 3 is a shift in the discussion to the idea that there might be a restraining mechanism exclusive of the competitive model that economists haven't recognized. Paragraphs 4 and 5 describe this restraining mechanism. The second-best answer is (D); however, paragraph 3 does provide a transition, which makes (C) the better choice.

Passage 4

22. **B** Although Passage B includes Lavoisier, its focus is on the caloric theory of heat, while Passage A covers other aspects of the scientist, not just one theory. Passage B, while showing how Lavoisier's theory of heat was later disproved, does not "discredit" him (A). (E) is also inaccurate; while showing how theories can be supplanted by new theories, the author's tone toward science is not skeptical.

23. **C** The use of the term follows the statement that Lavoisier disproved the theory of phlogiston, a nonexistent substance (or "flammability principle"). It is ironic that he then posits another substance, caloric, that cannot be weighed or measured.

24. **A** In lines 31–34, the passage states that Lavoisier's methods led to his proof that oxygen and hydrogen made up water, and therefore (A) is the best answer. Lavoisier's caloric theory was incorrect in explaining heat (B) and (D), and it was Priestley (mentioned in Passage B), not Lavoisier, who isolated eight gases (E). Although Passage A says that Lavoisier produced better gunpowder, there is no indication that he changed its composition (C).

25. **C** (C) is the best example of the author's point in the first paragraph. In lines 127–136, two specific examples are given of how observable facts can be explained by Lavoisier's caloric theory, a theory that was later proved wrong. None of the other choices are observable facts explained by the caloric theory.

26. **D** The best answer is (D), a point the author makes in the first paragraph. The passage doesn't imply either that alchemy "contributed nothing to science" (A) or that thermodynamics is an inexact science (C). Although (E) may seem like a possible answer, the author doesn't criticize the scientific method but merely suggests that theories can be disproved or modified in time.

27. **A** (A) is the best answer (lines 28–31). Although Lavoisier did believe in a fluid called caloric, he thought it caused heat, not combustion (E). (B) was part of the phlogiston theory, not Lavoisier's theory, and (C) and (D) are related to theories after Lavoisier.

28. **E** Passage B refers to Priestley as an important eighteenth century scientist who firmly believed in the phlogiston theory, making (E) the best answer.

Section III

Answers 1–6

UPPER-case letters denote colors given in the problem, and lower-case letters denote deduced colors.

1. **E**

1	2	3	4	5	
b/w	R	W	b	R	(flag)
w/g	B	g	w	B	(pennant)

The 3rd pennant cannot be blue or white, so therefore it is green. The 4th flag cannot be white or red, so it must be blue. The 4th pennant cannot be green or blue, so it must be white. The 1st flag cannot be red, so it is either blue or white. The 1st pennant cannot be blue, so it must be green or white.

2. **C**

1	2	3	4	5	
R	w	r/b			(flag)
g/w	B	g/w			(pennant)

(A) is clearly true. If the 5th flag is red, then the 3rd flag cannot be, since the 1st flag is red and we can have only two of any one color. Thus, (B) is true. If the 4th pennant is green, then the 3rd pennant must be white. But that does not determine the color of the 1st pennant. Thus, (C) is not necessarily true. (D) is the same as (A) and is also true. If the 4th pennant is green, this implies that the 3rd pennant must be white. If the 5th pennant is white, then the 1st pennant cannot be. Therefore, (E) is true.

3. **D** Here is what you start with:

	1	2	3	4	5
Flag	W		W		
Pennant		B		B	

The 2nd and 4th flags cannot be white because they are adjacent to white flags and they cannot be blue because they would be the same colors as the pennants on the same flagpoles. Therefore, they must be red (A).

	1	2	3	4	5
Flag	W	R	W	R	
Pennant		B		B	

For the same reasons, the 1st and 3rd pennants cannot be white or blue, so they must be green (B) and (C).

	1	2	3	4	5
Flag	W	R	W	R	
Pennant	G	B	G	B	

Since no more than two flags or pennants of the same color can be flying at the same time, the 5th flagpole must have a blue flag and a white pennant (E). The 5th pennant could not be green because there are already two green pennants flying (D). (D) is therefore false.

	1	2	3	4	5
Flag	W	R	W	R	B
Pennant	G	B	G	B	W

4. **B**

1	2	3	4	5	
B	w	r	B		(flag)
	W	g			(pennant)

Statement (B) is true since the 1st pennant cannot be blue or white. Statement (A) is false since the 5th pennant could be blue or white. Statement (C) is false since it is white. Statements (D) and (E) are false since they could be white.

5. **A**

1	2	3	4	5	
	R	W	r		(flag)
		g	B		(pennant)

If the 5th flag is white, then the 5th pennant must be green. Thus, the 1st and 2nd pennants cannot be green and cannot be the same color, so one of them is blue. Therefore, (A) is true. All the other statements are false.

6. C

1	2	3	4	5	
W	B	W	B	r	(flag)
g	W	B	W	B	(pennant)

1	2	3	4	5	
B	W	B	W	r	(flag)
g	B	W	B	W	(pennant)

Since blue and white are the two common colors between flags and pennants, the above are the only two arrangements possible. In both cases, the 5th flag is red and the 1st pennant is green.

Answers 7–13

7. D

1	2	3	4	5	6	7	8	9	10
E	E	E					M		M

If the 8th book is a math book, then the three English books must be in positions 1, 2, and 3, since they cannot be in positions 8, 9, and 10. Thus, the other math book is in position 10. The 4th book must be next to the English book in position 3.

8. A

1	2	3	4	5	6	7	8	9	10
M			P	P			E	E	E

If the 9th book is an English book, then so are the 8th and 10th books. Thus there is a math book in position 1. The science books must be in positions 2 and 3 *or* 3 and 4. This leaves only positions 4 and 7 for the other math book. Thus (A) is always true. (C) could be true, but does not have to be true. The 3rd poetry book could be in position 2.

9. B

1	2	3	4	5	6	7	8	9	10
M					S	S	E	E	E

If the 1st book is a math book, then the 8th, 9th, and 10th books must be the English books. If the 7th book is a science book, so must be the 6th book. This means that the other math book must be either the 3rd, the 4th, or the 5th book. The remainder of the books are poetry books, including the 2nd book.

10. C

1	2	3	4	5	6	7	8	9	10
M	P	P	M	S	S	P	E	E	

or

1	2	3	4	5	6	7	8	9	10
E	E	E	M	S	S	P	P	P	M

If the 4th book is a math book and the 5th book is a science book, then the 6th book is also a science book. This leaves two possible arrangements for the remaining books, as shown above. Statement (C) is the only correct one.

11. E

1	2	3	4	5	6	7	8	9	10
E	E	P						P	M

or

M	P						P	E	E

The poetry books must be in positions 4 and 9 *or* 2 and 7, depending on whether the math book is in position 1 or 10. See diagrams above. For example, let us assume that the math book is the 10th book. In order for no two poetry books to be next to each other, the 4th and 9th books must be poetry books, with the 3rd poetry book in either position 6 or 7, depending on the positions of the science books. The same argument holds if the 1st book is a math book.

12. C

1	2	3	4	5	6	7	8	9	10
E	E	E	S	M	P	P		P	M

and

M	P	P	P	M	S	S	E	E	

These are the two possible arrangements. We see that (A) is false, (B) could be false, (D) is false, and (E) could be false. Only (C) is always true.

13. B

1	2	3	4	5	6	7	8	9	10
E	E	E	M	S	S	P	P		P	M

and

E	E	E	S	S	M	P	P		P	M

These are the only two possible combinations; thus, (B) is the correct answer.

Answers 14–18

The initial conditions can be summarized as follows:

Total = 5
Languages   F, G, I
Sciences   B, C, P
Math   A, S, T
Math ≤ 2
PA̶
A → I
C → (only if T and F)
(G and B) → S̶
Languages = 1

14. B (A) and (C) are incorrect since only one language may be taken. (D) is incorrect because if algebra is taken, Italian must be taken. And (E) is incorrect because statistics cannot be taken if both German and biology are taken.

15. **E** Chemistry may be taken only if French is taken. If French is taken, then Italian cannot be taken, since only one language may be taken. (A) is incorrect. If algebra is taken, Italian must be taken, and thus German cannot be taken, making (B) the wrong choice. Chemistry may be taken only if French is taken, and therefore German cannot be taken, so (C) won't work. If algebra is taken, Italian must be taken and thus French cannot be taken, making (D) incorrect.

16. **D** If algebra is taken, Italian must be taken. If Italian is taken, then French cannot be taken, so (A) is the wrong choice. (B) is also the wrong choice since physics cannot be taken with algebra. And (C) and (E) won't work because if chemistry is taken, French must also be taken, and therefore German cannot be taken.

17. **D** Neither (A), (B), nor (E) will work because if chemistry is taken, trigonometry must be taken. (C) is incorrect since a maximum of two math classes may be taken, and if physics is taken, algebra cannot be taken.

18. **B** Both (A) and (E) won't work because a second language may not be taken. And (C) and (D) won't work because if chemistry is taken, French must be taken, and that would be a second language. Since Italian is taken, French is not, thus chemistry is not taken either. One math class must be eliminated, since all three cannot be taken. This leaves both biology and physics that must be taken.

Answers 19–23

From the information given, you could have constructed the following display:

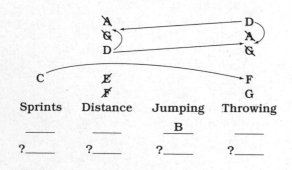

Sprints	Distance	Jumping	Throwing
		B	
?____	?____	?____	?____

19. **D** If C and E are both sprint coaches, then from the original conditions, F and G coach throwers. Since G coaches throwers, D cannot coach distance, so D must coach jumping.

Sprints	Distance	Jumping	Throwing
C		B	F
? E	?____	? D	? G

20. **A** If G coaches jumping and A coaches distance we have:

Sprints	Distance	Jumping	Throwing
	A	B	
?____	?____	? G	?____

If D coaches distance or throwing, A must coach sprints or jumping. Since A coaches distance, D cannot coach distance or throwing. This means D must coach sprints. The other choices are possible, but not necessarily true.

Sprints	Distance	Jumping	Throwing
D	A	B	
?____	?____	? G	?____

21. **E** If D coaches throwing, A and G cannot coach distance or throwing. This leaves only C to be the distance coach. So C CANNOT coach jumping.

Sprints	Distance	Jumping	Throwing
	C	B	D
?____	?____	?____	?____
		A̶	A̶
		G̶	G̶

(Above row: E̶ / F̶ notation appears over the columns.)

22. **B** If G is the only throwing coach, we have the following:

E̶
F̶

Sprints	Distance	Jumping	Throwing
____	____	B	G
?____	?____	?____	?__X

If D coaches distance or throwers, G must coach sprints or jumping. Since G coaches throwing, D does not coach distance or throwers. Thus, A and C must coach distance giving the following arrangement:

E̶
F̶

Sprints	Distance	Jumping	Throwing
____	A	B	G
?____	?__C	?____	?__X
	D̶		D̶

Choice (A) is incorrect since D doesn't coach distance.
Choice (C) is incorrect since A coaches distance.
Choice (D) is incorrect since, if F coaches jumping, D and E must coach sprints.
Choice (E) is incorrect since C and D coach different sports.

23. **C** If D coaches distance, A and G do not coach distance or throwing.

E̶
F̶

Sprints	Distance	Jumping	Throwing
A̶	D	B	____
?____	?____	?____	?____
	A̶		A̶
	G̶		G̶

Since A does not coach sprints, then A must coach jumping. So A and B coach jumping; therefore, G CANNOT coach jumping.

E̶
F̶

Sprints	Distance	Jumping	Throwing
A̶	D	B	____
?____	?____	?__A	?____
	A̶		A̶
	G̶		G̶

Section IV

1. **D** This choice provides the most direct evidence of the effectiveness of the PUC consumer action. Each of the other choices is only tangentially related to the argument.

2. **D** This choice most seriously weakens the author's contention that the PUC acts in the public interest. (C) is a weaker choice, especially because "slightly" softens the statement.

3. **A** This choice parallels both the reasoning and the structure of the original. The original reasoning may be summarized as follows: most $X \rightarrow Y$; therefore $X \rightarrow Y$ (probably).

4. **C** By conceding that certain subjects can only be discussed in private, the argument self-destructs. Several of the other choices are tempting, but none is as much to the point as choice (C).

5. **B** Since good personnel relations of an organization, according to the passage, rely upon "mutual confidence, trust and goodwill," one of the causes of personnel difficulties would most certainly be the employees' not believing in the good faith of the organization.

6. **B** In the second sentence, the author implies that the lack of facilities is related to the lack of research mentioned in the first sentence. In any case, the passage reveals the author's concern with both research and assistance, and therefore agrees more fully with (B) than with (A), which mentions research only.

7. **A** The "But" that begins the third sentence marks a contrast between the business world and the schools. The writer's point is that they are not alike and therefore cannot be run using the same standards of judgment.

8. **E** The correct answer is "circular." The argument that what the Church says is true is ultimately based upon this same assertion.

9. **A** Kathy believes Mary to have meant that only Italians are great lovers. Therefore, Kathy takes issue with this and points out in her reply that there are non-Italians who are great lovers. (A), if replaced for Mary's statement, would make Kathy's reply a reasonable one.

10. **B** Only (B) addresses Dimple's assumption that Mrs. Wilson is the only applicant whose qualifications are ideal. Other choices are irrelevant to the argument, although some may be relevant to the implied situation.

11. **A** Only (A) addresses the substance of Dimple's argument.

12. **C** The passage offers a pattern in which failure to meet one of two specific requirements results in a failure to qualify for something. In (C), the fall and winter track seasons become the residence requirement and the collecting of signatures. Failure to complete both leads to disqualification (for the spring team, for the June primary).

13. **D** The author of the argument avoids the issue of quality. The statement that stresses the incompleteness of the pro-hygienist position weakens it. (B) and (E) are irrelevant.

14. **D** The passage describes two types of obstacles to happiness: exterior forces and personal attitude. Both these factors are mentioned in (A), (B), (C), and (E). (D) requires the assumption that the two categories discussed by the author are the only categories.

15. **B** (A) may be eliminated because changing one's mind need not involve issues of right and wrong (in the moral sense that Eliot implies). (C) and (E) may be eliminated because they refute the underlying assumption of Eliot's words, that one can tell what is right. The passage does not address the issue of temptation (D).

16. **E** Without an implied or explicit definition of "civilized," the relevance of the examples is vague, at best. (A) and (D) are irrelevant considerations, and (B) and (C), although possibly relevant, do not address the most apparent weakness of the passage.

17. **B** (A) and (C) strengthen the argument. Although (D) and (E) partially weaken certain aspects of the argument, only (B) introduces a situation which suggests that freedom of the press may have harmful consequences.

18. **A** (B) and (C) are irrelevant to the argument. (D) and (E) contradict the implied assertion that a free press must be protected at all costs. Only (A) offers a statement both favorable to the concept of a free press and directly relevant to the subject discussed: the use of privileged information.

19. **E** By stating that "a legal technicality . . . ducks the . . . moral question," the author is implying that the federal government, which benefits from the technicality, is associated with dodging the issue. (A) and (B) restate explicit information; (C) is implausible; and (D) contradicts information in the passage.

20. **B** Private medical aid would render the author's argument unnecessary. (C), a choice worth considering, is not the best one because the author's focus is less on the aliens' needs than on the monetary burden borne by the counties.

21. **C** By documenting the rate at which the medical expense burden grows, the author could strengthen the argument that the situation he describes is indeed a burden.

22. **D** The passage talks about communes as failures. Therefore, the most logical completion must be a negative term consistent with failure. The only negative choice is (D).

23. **C** By linking Herb's ability with his "cousinhood," Herb is assuming that the latter determines the former; therefore, he is ignoring (C). (B) is irrelevant. (A) is too vague to be the best answer. (D) is inapplicable, because Keith uses "good" in a context that makes its meaning clear. Finally, (E) refers to contradictory information.

24. **E** In order to argue for the value of renewable prescriptions, the author must first assume that more medicine may be necessary, or, in other words, that the patient may suffer a relapse. Without the possibility of relapse, a call for more medicine that has already effected a cure ("worked effectively") is illogical.

25. **C** The passage consistently implies a difference between the past and the present, and (C) makes this contrast explicit. (B) contradicts the implication of the passage, while (A) and (D) narrow the focus unnecessarily, and (E) is irrelevant.

26. **D** This fact would strengthen the merely impressionistic evidence that lawsuits were less prevalent 40 years ago. It is the only choice dealing directly with the implied subject of the passage—lawsuits.

Section V

Passage 1

1. **D** According to the first paragraph, a developing country hopes to attract foreign investment and increase its revenues from taxation ("maximize the public capture of revenues").

2. **A** Unless the investment flow is equal in each direction, the First World nation from which the greater revenue is likely to come is more likely to benefit.

3. **B** According to the second paragraph, reciprocal source-based taxation produces revenue sacrifices by the state receiving most of the foreign investment, that is, the developing country.

4. **D** Excess foreign tax credits are a disincentive to private investors. If the at-source taxation is reduced, there will be fewer excess foreign credits.

5. **C** The passage makes no reference to the availability of raw materials. The four other options are cited.

6. **B** A country that reduced its revenue expectations would be expected to increase foreign investment.

Passage 2

7. **E** Both passages show how the pre-Columbian past affected Mexico's most prominent muralists. Answers (A) through (D), although perhaps true, are too narrow to define the subject of the passages.

8. **C** According to Passage A, Orozco denounced the pre-Columbian past (see lines 8–10, 24–29) and according to Passage B, he treated "the positive aspects of the human condition" in the person of Quetzalcoatl (lines 108–113). This suggests ambivalence. Although Passage B states that Rivera "epitomized" the creation of a mythology of ancient Mexico, it does not imply that he "most successfully" captured history in his murals (A). (B) and (D) are simply inaccurate. (E), which may seem a good answer, is not implied; although Passage B makes it clear that Rivera did use his art for political purposes (e.g., "within a Marxist framework" to inspire the indigenous population to "reconstruct the present and control the future"), it does not imply that the other muralists did not have political purposes.

9. **A** Passage A, in the last paragraph, states that the muralists' "pictorial language" and techniques—for example, the use of fresco—fit into the European tradition. Passage B makes no references to techniques. (B) through (E) are inaccurate.

10. **D** Orozco scorned romanticized visions of Indian life (lines 103–104). (A) through (E) are all mentioned in either Passage A or Passage B (and sometimes both). Note the word *except* in the question.

11. **A** To counter the "colonized mentality" of Mexico, the muralists reaffirmed their national heritage by turning to pre-Columbian history and art. This does not indicate, however, that they were antagonistic to Europe's role in art history (B), nor does it indicate the public's reaction (C). (D) and (E), which may seem possible answers, are not as accurate as (A). "Insistence" on a nationalistic spirit (D) is not mentioned, nor do the muralists "glorify" pre-Columbian artists, although they may glorify pre-Columbian deeds.

12. **C** See lines 82–88. Although (A), (B), (D), and (E) may be interests of Rivera, the passage makes it clear that revitalizing the Indian population was one of his primary "political" intentions.

13. **B** Neither passage indicates that the muralists disdained European art; in fact, Passage A states that the muralists used traditional European techniques. Both passages include or imply (A), (C), (D), and (E).

Passage 3

14. **D** The author says that war and change have been inevitably linked in America, and that war has been a vital force in the rise of capitalism, but he does not say that war is inevitable. All of the other answers are supported by the passage: (A)—lines 64–77; (B)—lines 14–17; (C)—lines 18–20; (E)—lines 64–69.

15. **B** See lines 13–17. Radioactive isotopes used in treating cancer are an example of a positive advance caused by preparations for war. On the other hand, lethal nerve gases (A), in addition to being a German and not an American development, did not lead to positive peacetime uses. (C), (D), and (E), while possibly effects of wars that have changed America, did not "yield results which are tonics to advancement."

16. **D** See lines 23–28. (C) is incorrect; the author states that this is a result of the Civil War. (E) is a statement supported by the passage, but is not the primary reason for World War I's importance. (A) and (B) are not supported by information in the passage.

17. **A** In this paragraph the author paints a picture of, and indicates some of the reasons for, the "isolation, insularity, and exceptionalism" of America before World War I. The paragraph does define "American Religion" (B), but this is too limited an answer to describe the paragraph's main point. (C) and (E) are not covered in this paragraph. There is no contrast drawn between Civil War America and World War I America (D).

18. **B** See lines 35–46. (A) is incorrect; the grand tour is cited as an example that sophisticated Americans saw a trip to Europe as necessary to overcome insularity and complete an education. No social comment is made about its availability only to the rich. (D) is also incorrect; Puritanism is cited in paragraph four, but not in the context indicated in this answer, i.e., the sin and corruption of the world. (E) might seem correct at first, but the passage does not state that America was in fact superior to Europe; it comments on the view that Americans had of their country. (C) is irrelevant; this point is not made in relation to America's insularity.

19. **C** After the first paragraph introduces the idea of war as a force of change, the passage is devoted to the importance of World War I in changing American society. (B) is incorrect; paragraph one concerns some of the benefits of war, but this is not the main topic of the passage; it is an underlying idea. (A) is also incorrect; the passage mentions the Civil War briefly but is mostly concerned with World War I. (D) and (E) are points touched on in the passage, but neither is the main subject.

20. **E** War as a force for change (the topic of paragraph one) is a general idea that introduces the passage's main subject of World War I. It is not a "popular view" that is refuted in the passage (A), nor does the passage ask a question (B). The first paragraph doesn't outline the contents of the passage (C), nor does it set up the first of four examples (D).

21. **B** "Ecstatic nationalism" is part of what Tocqueville called "American Religion." It would not increase in Europe after World War I. (A) can be inferred because Europe was seen as a necessity in a young man's education. (California would have been considered the Wild West.) The inference in (C) is supported by lines 70–77; (D), by lines 9–14; (E), by lines 47–56.

Passage 4

22. **D** In lines 81–87, the passage describes genetic drift, a change in the gene pool that occurs by chance. If an organism with a survival trait gene doesn't reproduce, the gene is lost. (A) is incorrect; the passage does not indicate which mutations are most "significant." (B) is contrary to fact; see lines 48–51. (C) is contradicted by several examples in the passage of the ways variations occur, and genetic recombination (E) is not cited as the cause of the formation of new species.

23. **B** The vulnerability to carbon dioxide was a trait from a gene that was transmitted to the fruit fly by an outside agent; it is therefore an acquired characteristic. That the fruit fly's offspring exhibit the same vulnerability supports the theory that acquired characteristics can be inherited. In (A), the webbed feet are not an acquired characteristic but a result of mutation and were perpetuated by inbreeding. (C) has no relevance to the question of inheritance, and in (D), the shaving of the dogs has nothing to do with the number of hairless offspring; genetic inheritance (dominant and recessive genes) account for that. (E) does not address the issue of how characteristics were transmitted.

24. **E** (A), (B), (C), and (D) are all explained (however briefly) in the passage. Although (E) is mentioned in line 95, it is not defined or explained.

25. **A** By definition, random mutations occur by chance and are therefore not necessarily related to any survival trait. Darwin's theory states that natural selection accounts for the perpetuation of traits. (B) is incorrect; although spontaneous mutations are said to be infrequent, the frequency of random mutations is not addressed. That random mutations occur doesn't refute or replace Darwin's evolutionary concept; it is simply another possibility for explaining the inheritance of certain traits (C). Both (D) and (E) are factually incorrect.

26. **D** The founder principle (lines 101–102) is that a smaller, isolated population has a gene frequency different from the larger population from which it came. (A) is incorrect because although the passage states that more genetic dwarfism occurs in the Amish population as a result of the founder principle, it does not state that the founder principle explains all genetic dwarfism. The principle doesn't refute the theory of natural selection (E), nor does it explain homozygosity (C), although the term is related. (B) is incorrect; nothing intrinsic in the principle supports the importance of "weeding out" non-adaptative organisms.

27. **C** Darwin was more concerned with why certain traits were passed on (survival of the fittest) than with the mechanics of inheritance. (A) and (B) are incorrect; the passage doesn't imply that Darwin had any opinion about genetics. (In fact, the concept of the gene was developed after Darwin's work.) (D) is incorrect because Darwin recognized that variation among members of a species was central to the idea of natural selection. Although the passage states that he believed acquired characteristics could be inherited, it does not imply that he felt acquired traits were more important than hereditary ones (E).

28. **B** Most of the passage deals briefly with how variation occurs, not with the history of a theory (A) or the differences between genetic and evolutionary theories (D). (C) may seem to be a good answer because the author mentions that Darwin's failure to address the source of variations is "a major weakness." "Expose," however, is too strong a word; the passage is focused not on Darwin's weakness but rather on brief explanations of variation. (E) is a minor, not the primary, concern of the passage.

ANALYZING YOUR LSAT SCORE: A BROAD RANGE SCORE APPROXIMATOR

The chart that follows is designed to give you a *general approximation* of the number of questions you need to get right to fall into a general score range and percentile rank on your LSAT. It should help you see if you are in the "ballpark" of the score you need. This range approximator is *not* designed to give you an exact score or to predict your LSAT score. The actual LSAT will have questions that are similar to the ones encountered in this book, but some questions may be either easier or more difficult. The variance in difficulty levels and testing conditions can affect your score range.

Obtaining Your Approximate Score Range

Although the LSAT uses a very precise formula to convert raw scores to scaled scores, for the purpose of this broad range approximation simply total the number of questions you answered correctly. Next, divide the total number of correct answers by the total number of questions on the sample test. This will give you the percent correct. Now look at the following chart to see the approximate percent you need to get right to get into your score range. Remember, on the actual test one of the sections is experimental and, therefore, doesn't count toward your score.

On the actual LSAT, the percent of correct answers to get certain scores will vary slightly from test to test, depending on the number of problems and level of difficulty of that particular exam.

An average score is approximately 151.

If you are not in the range that you wish to achieve, check the approximate percent of correct answers that you need to achieve that range. Carefully analyze the types of errors you are making and continue practicing and analyzing. Remember, in trying to approximate a score range, you must take the complete sample test under strict time and test conditions.

Approximate Scaled Score Range	Approx. % of Correct Answers Necessary	Approx. Score Percentile for Test-takers (Est. % below)
171–180	95 and up	99–99.9%
161–170	80–94%	88–98%
151–160	65–79%	53–85%
141–150	45–64%	17–48%
131–140	30–44%	3–15%
121–130	20–29%	0–2%

PART III

Profiles of Law Schools

CHAPTER 14

Overview of ABA-Approved Law Schools

At the time this book was researched, there were more than 200 law schools approved by the American Bar Association (including the U.S. Army Judge Advocate General's School, which is not profiled here). The ABA is the largest organization of lawyers in the world, and its members come from every state in the United States. Because the ABA is a voluntary bar association, its members are not required to join in order to practice law, although nearly 40 percent of all American lawyers are currently members.

The power to grant individuals a license to practice law resides in the highest court of each state; thus, every jurisdiction administers its own bar examination, character and fitness inquiry, and licensing procedures for admission to the bar. The states also administer the disciplinary process for sanctioning lawyers who violate ethics rules of professional conduct. Because each state adopts its own rules establishing who is eligible to take the bar examination, some states require all candidates to be graduates of ABA-approved law schools, while others do not (see Chapter 16 for a discussion of non-ABA-approved law schools).

Authority to approve the right of educational institutions to grant degrees has been delegated by Congress to the U.S. Department of Education, which in turn delegates the responsibility for approving degree programs to designated accrediting agencies. In the case of law schools, the agency that has been given this power is the American Bar Association. Within the ABA, accreditation matters are handled by the Accreditation Committee of the Section of Legal Education and Admissions to the Bar with the support of a Consultant on Legal Education. The standards of approval themselves are promulgated by the ABA's governing body, the House of Delegates, upon recommendation of the Section of Legal Education. The Accreditation Committee is charged with the inspection and evaluation of law schools and law school programs, not only when a school or program is started, but also periodically during the life of the institution. The purpose of the accreditation process is to assure that every law school in the United States meets a common set of quality standards, and that every degree awarded confers the same benefit on recipients as comparable degrees at other ABA-approved law schools.

The imprimatur of the ABA carries great weight with state bar admission authorities, and every state allows graduates of any ABA law school to sit for the bar exam. From an applicant's standpoint, graduating from an ABA-approved law school is like a stamp of approval, a ticket to seek admission to practice law anywhere in the country. From the point of view of a law student, ABA approval is a guarantee that certain basic educational requirements have been met, and that the education they receive will be comparable to the education at any other ABA-approved law school. Additional information on the accreditation process and law schools generally may be obtained by writing the ABA Section of Legal Education and Admissions to the Bar, 750 North Lake Shore Drive, Chicago, IL 60611 (*www.abanet.org/le*).

This does not mean that law schools are all the same. As this guide demonstrates, law schools come in many shapes and sizes. Some are more difficult to get into than others. Some offer special programs that set them apart from other schools. Some serve special audiences that others do not. Some are rated more highly than others. Neither the ABA nor this guide attempts to rank law schools. The ABA certifies that approved schools meet minimum standards, but encourages them to seek to exceed those standards. Barron's *Guide to Law Schools* provides a wealth of information to help applicants make the difficult decision about which law school is best for them. Implicit in this approach is the notion that different schools are right for different people, and that no single school is best for everyone.

The ranking of law schools by some publications may provide interesting reading, and may reflect the relative prestige of law schools as filtered through the eyes of the publication's editors, but the uncritical use of such rankings without looking at the facts and figures behind them can distort the process of selecting a law school. The real question should be: What are the top ten schools for you personally? The question is not: What are the top ten schools for some faceless editor at some magazine or publishing house?

The following table provides information about the tuition, programs, and academic community at schools that have been approved by the American Bar Association. This is designed to provide a quick overview of the schools, and should be used in conjunction with the detailed profiles of the individual schools that can be found in Chapter 15.

Most of the information on these charts should be self-explanatory. If you are uncertain about the significance of any item, consult the profile of the school for additional information or explanation.

In several sections of the table, a check (✔) indicates "yes" and a blank indicates "no." For example, under Calendar, the possibilities are Fall, Winter, Spring, and Summer. At any given school, you can begin your law studies only at those times indicated by a check.

Since most law schools operate on a semester basis, information about credits and required courses is given in terms of semester hours. If a school operates on the quarter system, the abbreviation *qh* is added.

Similarly, tuition is generally given for a full year. When part-time tuition is given per credit, this refers to semester courses unless the abbreviation *qh* is used.

Where a category does not apply to a school or when information was not available, the cell is left blank.

INSTITUTION	APPLICATIONS Fee	Deadline	Deadline Financial Aid	TUITION In State Full Time (Part Time)	Out of State Full Time (Part Time)	CALENDAR Fall	Winter	Spring	Summer	PROGRAMS Day	Evening	Credits for JD	Required Credits for Courses	Transferable Summer Courses	Joint Degree	Graduate Law Degree	ENROLLED Full Time (Part Time)	Average Age First Year	STUDENT BODY % Women	% Minority	Attrition Rate %	FACULTY Full Time (Part Time)	LIBRARY Volumes	Microforms
Albany Law School 80 New Scotland Avenue Albany, NY 12208 518-445-2326 Fax: 518-445-2369 admissions@albanylaw.edu	$60	Feb 15	rolling	$41,570 ($31,180)	$41,570 ($31,180)	4				4		87	42	4	4	4	672 (24)	24	45	27	1	55 (52)	292,140	429,883
American University (Washington College of Law) 4801 Massachusetts Avenue, N.W. Washington, DC 20016-8186 202-274-4101 Fax: 202-274-4107 wcladmit@wcl.american.edu	$70	March 1	March 1	$44,234 ($31,122)	$44,234 ($31,122)	4				4	4	86	32	4	4	4	1238 (261)	24	57	35	5	102 (142)	664,783	109,220
Appalachian School of Law P.O. Box 2825 Grundy, VA 24614 276-935-4349 Fax: 276-935-8496 npruitt@asl.edu	$60	June 1	July 1	$29,500	$26,500	4				4		90	69				340	26	35	6	3	20 (4)	128,552	104,163
Arizona State University (Sandra Day O'Connor College of Law) 1100 South McAllister Avenue, Box 877906 Tempe, AZ 85287-7906 480-965-1474 Fax: 480-727-7930 chitra.damania@asu.edu	$60	Feb 1	rolling	$23,959	$38,083	4				4	4	88	39	4	4	4	602	26	40	23	8	62 (68)	291,925	146,471
Atlanta's John Marshall Law School 1422 W. Peachtree St., WW Atlanta, GA 30309 404-872-3593 Fax: 404-873-3802 admissions@johnmarshall.edu	$50	open	open	$15,360 ($9,216)	$15,360 ($9,216)	4				4	4	88	63		4		345 (195)	24	51	32	8	35 (21)	96,000	711,151
Ave Maria School of Law 1025 Commons Circle Naples, FL 34119 734-827-8063 Fax: 734-622-0123 info@avemarialaw.edu	$50	April 1	June 1	$35,948	$35,948	4				4	4	90	60	4			331 (1)	25	35	17	4	28 (10)	117,104	5,319
Barry University (School of Law) 6441 East Colonial Drive Orlando, FL 32807 321-206-5600 Fax: 321-206-5662 acruz@mail.barry.edu		May 1	June	$33,630 ($25,180)	$33,630 ($25,180)	4				4	4	90	53 to 55	4			528 (180)	27	47	26	9	66 (30)	200,000	92,839
Baylor University (School of Law) One Bear Place, #97288 Waco, TX 76798-7288 254-710-1911 Fax: 254-710-2316 becky_beck@baylor.edu	$40	March 1	Feb 15	$36,750	$36,750	4		4	4	4		126	78	4	4	4	465	23	47	20	4	27 (29)	241,927	127,451

INSTITUTION	APPLICATIONS Fee	Deadline	Deadline Financial Aid	TUITION In State Full Time (Part Time)	Out of State Full Time (Part Time)	CALENDAR Fall	Winter	Spring	Summer	PROGRAMS Day	Evening	Credits for JD	Required Credits for Courses	Transferable Summer Courses	Joint Degree	Graduate Law Degree	ENROLLED Full Time (Part Time)	Average Age First Year	STUDENT BODY % Women	% Minority	Attrition Rate %	FACULTY Full Time (Part Time)	LIBRARY Volumes	Microforms
Boston College (Law School) 885 Centre Street Newton, MA 02459 617-552-4351 Fax: 617-552-2917 bclawadm@bc.edu	$75	March 1	March 15	$41,590	$41,590	4				4		85	36		4	4	784	24	46	22	1	65 (39)	486,339	236,194
Boston University (School of Law) 765 Commonwealth Avenue Boston, MA 02215 617-353-3100 Fax: 617-353-0578 bulawadm@bu.edu	$75	March 1	March 1	$41,780	$41,780	4				4		84	33		4	4	807	24	50	23	4	56 (19)	674,482	328,501
Brigham Young University (J. Reuben Clark Law School) 342 JRCB Brigham Young University Provo, UT 84602 801-422-4277 Fax: 801-422-0389 kucharg@law.byu.edu	$50	March 1	June 1	$10,600	$21,200	4				4		90	36		4	4	450	26	38	15	2	35 (48)	474,191	107,632
Brooklyn Law School 250 Joralemon Street Brooklyn, NY 11201 718-780-7906 Fax: 718-780-0395 admitq@brooklaw.edu		April 1		$48,090 ($36,068)	$48,090 ($36,068)	4		4		4	4	86	31	4	4	4	1224 (174)	24	45	24	4	73 (133)	589,975	321,053
California Western School of Law 225 Cedar Street San Diego, CA 92101-3046 619-525-1401 Fax: 619-615-1401 admissions@cwsl.edu	$55	April 1	April 1	$42,600 ($27,000)	$42,600 ($29,920)	4				4	4	89	43	4	4	4	791 (101)	27	55	28	18	52 (87)	345,342	161,909
Campbell University (Norman Adrian Wiggins School of Law) 225 Hillsborough Street, Suite 401 Raleigh, NC 24603 919-865-5988 Fax: 919-865-5886	$50	April 1	open	$16,700		4				4		90	67		4	4	402	26	50	11	9	25 (40)	106,265	87,368
Capital University (Law School) 303 East Broad Street Columbus, OH 43215-3200 614-236-6500 Fax: 614-236-6972 admissions@law.capital.edu	$40	May 1	May 1	$32,833 ($21,613)	$32,833 ($21,613)	4				4	4	89	46	4	4	4	456 (177)	28	44	12	9	40 (25)	263,655	64,791
Case Western Reserve University (School of Law) 11075 East Boulevard Cleveland, OH 44106 216-368-3600 Fax: 216-368-1042 lawadmissions@case.edu	$40	April 1	May 1	$42,450 ($769/hr)	$42,450 ($1,769/hr)	4				4	4	88	39	4	4	4	600 (5)	25	43	18	3	49 (54)	307,071	104,733

School	App Fee	Deadline 1	Deadline 2		Tuition (resident)	Tuition (non-resident)																		
Catholic University of America (Columbus School of Law) Cardinal Station Washington, DC 20064 202-319-5151 Fax: 202-319-6235 *admissions@law.edu*	$65	March 12	July 15	4	$21,540 ($555/hr)	$37,850 ($555/hr)	4			4	84	33	4	4	4	588 (318)	26	51	18	10	91 (87)	203,232	199,613
Chapman University (School of Law) One University Drive Orange, CA 92866 714-628-2500 Fax: 714-628-2501 *metten@chapman.edu*	$75	April 15	March 2	4	$41,460 ($30,476)	$33,000 ($30,476)	4			4	88	51-52	4	4	4	506	25	48	22	10	52	312,059	212,416
Charleston School of Law P.O. Box 535 Charleston, SC 29402 843-377-2143 Fax: 843-329-0491 *jbenfield@charlestonlaw.org*	$50	March 1	April 1	4	$36,674 ($29,466)	$36,674 ($29,466)	4			4	88	61	4			517 (191)	25	46	11	5	35 (40)	29,628	
Charlotte School of Law 2145 Suttle Avenue Charlotte, NC 28208 704-971-8542 Fax: 704-971-8599 *admissions@charlottelaw.edu*	$50	open		4	$35,344 ($28,279)	$35,344 ($28,278)	4	4		4	90	60	4			380 (101)	28	50	11	10	22 (27)	196,308	99,339
City University of New York (CUNY School of Law) 65-21 Main Street Flushing, NY 11367-1330 718-340-4210 Fax: 718-340-4435 *mail.law.cuny.edu*	$60	March 15	May 1	4	$11,420	$18,980	4			4	91	60	4			478	27	59	41	1	49 (10)	300,552	1,086,660
Cleveland State University (Cleveland-Marshall College of Law) 2121 Euclid Avenue LB138 Cleveland, OH 44115-2214 216-687-2304 Fax: 216-687-6881 *christophe.lcak@law.csuohio.edu*	$50	May 1	May 1	4	$19,864 ($15,280)	$27,204 ($20,926)	4			4	90	41	4	4	4	425 (132)	26	43	16	17	44 (37)	299,131	235,284
College of William & Mary (William & Mary Law School) P.O. Box 8795 Williamsburg, VA 23187-8795 757-221-3785 Fax: 757-221-3261 *lawadm@wm.edu*	$50	March 1	Feb 15	4	$26,200	$36,200	4			4	86	34	4	4	4	637	24	50	20	1	35 (72)	421,000	953,000
Columbia University (School of Law) 435 West 116th Street New York, NY 10027 212-854-2670 Fax: 212-854-1109 *admissions@law.columbia.edu*				4	$51,080	$40,000	4			4	83	35	4	4	4	1260	24	45	30		98 (69)	1,092,534	235,424
Cornell University (Law School) Myron Taylor Hall Ithaca, NY 14853-4901 607-255-5141 Fax: 607-255-7193 *lawadmit@postoffice.law.cornell.edu*	$80	Feb 1	March 15	4	$53,150	$53,150	4			4	84	36	4	4	4	612	23	48	37		52 (64)	676,000	5,500

INSTITUTION	APPLICATIONS Fee	Deadline	Deadline Financial Aid	TUITION In State Full Time (Part Time)	Out of State Full Time (Part Time)	CALENDAR Fall	Winter	Spring	Summer	PROGRAMS Day	Evening	Credits for JD	Required Credits for Courses	Transferable Summer Courses	Joint Degree	Graduate Law Degree	ENROLLED STUDENT BODY Full Time (Part Time)	Average Age First Year	% Women	% Minority	Attrition Rate %	FACULTY Full Time (Part Time)	LIBRARY Volumes	Microforms
Creighton University (School of Law) 2500 California Plaza, Omaha, NE 68178, 402-280-2586, Fax: 402-280-3161, lawadmit@creighton.edu	$50	May 1	March 1	$31,054 ($1,000/hr)	$31,054 ($1,000/hr)	4				4		94	55	4	4		431 (11)	24	37	12	5	31 (36)	386,876	183,068
De Paul University (College of Law) 25 East Jackson Boulevard, Chicago, IL 60604, 312-362-6831, Fax: 312-362-5280, lawinfo@depaul.edu	$60	March 1	March 1	$41,240 ($26,800)	$41,240 ($26,800)	4			4	4	4	86	40	4	4	4	328 (238)	24	47	22	4	54 (60)	218,184	192,926
Drake University (Law School) 2507 University Avenue, Des Moines, IA 50311, 515-271-2782, Fax: 515-271-1990, lawadmit@drake.edu	$50	April 1	March 1	$33,900 ($1,165/hr)	$33,900 ($1,165/hr)	4			4	4	4	90	41	4	4	4	434 (13)	25	47	11	8	37 (34)	344,752	123,027
Drexel University (Earle Mack School of Law) 3320 Market Street, Philadelphia, PA 19282, 215-895 1LAW, Fax: 215-571-4769		open		$34,450	$34,450	4			4	4		84	32		4		440	25	45	21		65 (31)	48,148	
Duke University (School of Law) Science Drive and Towerview Road, Box 90362, Durham, NC 27708-0362, 919-613-7020, Fax: 919-613-7257, nash@law.duke.edu	$70	February 15	March 15	$48,800	$48,800	4			4	4	4	86	56	4	4	4		25	41	23		57 (68)	680,479	78,554
Duquesne University (School of Law) 900 Locust Street, Hanley Hall, Pittsburgh, PA 15282, 412-396-6296, Fax: 412-396-1073, campion@duq.edu	$60	April 1	May 31	$33,064 ($25,410)	$33,064 ($25,410)	4				4	4	90	49	4	4	4	445 (194)	22	42	4	2	25 (49)	306,385	75,219
Elon University (School of Law) 201 North Greene Street, Greensboro, NC 27401, 336-279-9200, Fax: 336-279-8199, law@elon.edu	$50	June 30		$34,550	$34,550	4				4	4						365	23	45	15	8	22 (18)	188,726	131,313
Emory University (School of Law) Gambrell Hall, 1301 Clifton Road, N.E., Atlanta, GA 30322, 404-727-6801, Fax: 404-727-2477, erosenz@law.emory.edu	$70	March 1	April 1	$44,600	$44,600	4				4	4	90	47	4	4	4	715	23	48	31	2	64 (42)	308,364	107,514

Overview of ABA-Approved Law Schools 195

School / Contact	App. Fee	Deadline 1	Deadline 2	Tuition – Resident (full-time (part-time))	Tuition – Nonresident (full-time (part-time))			%	%		Enrollment								
Faulkner University (Thomas Goode Jones School of Law), 5345 Atlanta Highway, Montgomery, AL 36109, 334-386-7210, Fax: 334-386-7223, law@faulkner.edu	$30	June 15		$30,500	$30,500	4	4	90	51	4	323 (18)		38	11			29		
Florida Agricultural and Mechanical University (Florida A & M University College of Law), 201 Beggs Avenue, Orlando, FL 32801, 407-254-3268, famulaw.admissions@famu.edu	$33	May 31	March 1	$11,774 ($8,634)	$32,069 ($22,759)	4	4	90	48-49	4	509 (192)	25	48	53	71	3	46 (20)	391,247	252,042
Florida Coastal (School of Law), 8787 Baypine Rd., Jacksonville, FL 32256, 904-680-7710, Fax: 904-680-7776, admissions@fcsl.edu	$50	open	Feb 1	$27,570 ($22,060)	$27,570 ($22,060)	4	4	87	56	4	1231 (164)	27	48	18		8	62 (45)	223,820	469,002
Florida International University (College of Law), FIU College of Law, RDB 1055, Miami, FL 33199, (305) 348-8006, Fax: (305) 348-2965, miroa@fiu.edu	$20	May 1	April 1	$12,471 ($9,353)	$26,255 ($19,692)	4	4	90	31	4	300 (330)	26	48	54		5	32 (21)	213,410	123,491
Florida State University (College of Law), 425 West Jefferson Street, Tallahassee, FL 32306-1601, 850-644-3787, Fax: 850-644-7284, admissions@law.fsu.edu	$30	April 1	May 15	$18,303	$18,303	4	4	88	36	4	763	23	41	17		3	59 (29)	525,173	1,065,200
Fordham University (School of Law), 140 West 62nd Street, New York, NY 10023, 212-636-6810, Fax: 212-636-7984, lawadmissions@law.fordham.edu	$70	March 1	March 1	$47,360 ($35,520)	$47,360 ($35,520)	4	4	83	41	4	1244 (252)	25	47	25		1	88 (179)	379,621	254,317
George Mason University (School of Law), 3301 Fairfax Drive, Arlington, VA 22201, 703-993-8010, Fax: 703-993-8088, aprice1@gmu.edu	$35	April 1	June 1	$21,035 ($17,969)	$35,427 ($29,101)	4	4	89	40	4	510 (210)	25	43	15		1	38 (98)	253,097	219,802
George Washington University (Law School), 2000 H Street, N.W., Washington, DC 20052, 202-994-7230, Fax: 202-994-3597, jd@law.gwu.edu	$80	March 1	March 1	$45,750 ($32,170)	$45,750 ($32,170)	4	4	84	34	4	1430 (323)		43				100 (288)	663,521	274,704
Georgetown University (Law Center), 600 New Jersey Avenue, N.W., Washington, DC 20001, 202-662-9010, Fax: 202-662-9439, admis@law.georgetown.edu	$85	March 1	March 1	$46,865 ($33,500)	$46,865 ($33,500)	4	4	85	33	4	2216 (446)	26	47	47		17	151 (109)	551,414	595,414

INSTITUTION	APPLICATIONS Fee	Deadline	Deadline Financial Aid	TUITION In State Full Time (Part Time)	Out of State Full Time (Part Time)	CALENDAR Fall	Winter	Spring	Summer	PROGRAMS Day	Evening	Credits for JD	Required Credits for Courses	Transferable Summer Courses	Joint Degree	Graduate Law Degree	ENROLLED STUDENT BODY Full Time (Part Time)	Average Age First Year	% Women	% Minority	Attrition Rate %	FACULTY Full Time (Part Time)	LIBRARY Volumes	Microforms
Georgia State University (College of Law) P.O. Box 4037 Atlanta, GA 30302-4037 404-413-9200 Fax: 404-413-9203 cjgeorge@gsu.edu	$50	March 15	April 1	$12,528 ($11,484)	$32,592 ($29,876)	4				4	4	90	43	4	4		477 (201)	27	45	21	11	107 (71)	141,748	190,423
Golden Gate University (School of Law) 536 Mission Street San Francisco, CA 94105-2968 415-442-6630 lawadmit@ggu.edu	$60	April 1	rolling	$40,200 ($30,820)	$40,200 ($30,820)	4				4	4	88	57	4	4	4	570 (118)	27	54	34	12	39 (128)	392,711	247,778
Gonzaga University (School of Law) Box 3528 Spokane, WA 99220-3528 509-313-5532 Fax: 509-313-3697 admissions@lawschool.gonzaga.edu	$50	April 15	Feb 1	$33,960	$33,960	4				4	4	90	49	4	4	4	506	26	43	11	10	32 (27)	168,533	141,730
Hamline University (School of Law) 1536 Hewitt Avenue St. Paul, MN 55104-1284 651-523-2461 Fax: 651-523-3064 lawadm@gw.hamline.edu	$35	April 1	open	$34,485 ($24,970)	$34,485 ($24,970)	4				4	4	88	36	4	4	4	482 (135)	27	55	12	14	43 (83)	461,277	134,104
Harvard University (Harvard Law School) Cambridge, MA 02138 617-495-3179 jdadmiss@law.harvard.edu				$47,600		4				4		82	30	4	4	4	1679	24	48	37	1	102 (150)	2,000,000	1,973,552
Hofstra University (Maurice A. Deane School of Law) 121 Hofstra University Hempstead, NY 11549 516-463-5916 Fax: 516-463-6264 lawadmissions@hofstra.edu		April 15	April 1	$45,600 ($34,125)	$45,600 ($34,125)	4				4	4	87	42	4	4	4	1004 (70)	24	46	31	4	56 (78)	590,184	1,996,702
Howard University 2900 Van Ness Street, N.W. Washington, DC 20008 202-806-8008 Fax: 202-806-8162 admissions@law.howard.edu	$60		April 1	$27,960				4		4	4	88		4	4	4	420	25	60	94	5	33 (23)	428,494	54,000
Illinois Institute of Technology (Chicago-Kent College of Law) 565 West Adams Street Chicago, IL 60661 312-906-5020 Fax: 312-906-5274 admit@kentlaw.edu		March 1	March 1	$41,670 ($30,558)	$41,670 ($30,558)	4				4	4	87	42	4	4	4	780 (164)	25	45	23	12	73 (154)	56,182	152,812

School																						
Indiana University (Maurer School of Law) 211 South Indiana Avenue Bloomington, IN 47405-7001 812-855-4765 Fax: 812-855-0555 Lawadmis@indiana.edu	$50	open	March 10	$27,040	$44,512	4				4	88	31	4	4	689	24	37	17	1	56 (32)	452,110	1,712,348
Indiana University-Purdue University at Indianapolis (Robert H. McKinney School of Law) 530 West New York Street Indianapolis, IN 46202-3225 317-274-2459 Fax: 317-278-4780 khmiller@iupui.edu	$50	March 1	March 1	$21,517 ($15,969)	$43,015 ($31,915)	4				4	90	35	4	4	638 (324)	26	45	16	1	57 (86)	584,622	67,910
Inter American University of Puerto Rico (School of Law) P.O. Box 70351 San Juan, PR 00936-8351 787-751-1912, ext. 2013, 2526	$63	March 31	Aug 13	$13,710 ($10,511)	$13,710 ($10,511)	4				4	92	62	4	4	476 (414)	28	55	1	8	30 (5)	203,150	283,018
John Marshall Law School 315 South Plymouth Court Chicago, IL 60604 312-987-1406 Fax: 312-427-5136 admission@jmls.edu		March 1	April 1	$39,894 ($27,524)	$39,894 ($27,524)	4	4			4	90	48	4	4	1139 (407)	25	46	16	9	72 (133)	413,520	158,935
Lewis and Clark College (Lewis and Clark Law School) 10015 Southwest Terwilliger Boulevard Portland, OR 97219 503-768-6613 Fax: 503-768-6793 lawadmss@clark.edu	$50	March 1	March 1	$36,362 ($27,270)	$36,362 ($27,270)	4				4	90	28-35	4	4	493 (245)	28	52	23	4	67 (43)	209,973	316,739
Liberty University (School of Law) 1971 University Blvd. Lynchburg, VA 24502 434-592-5300 Fax: 434-592-0202 law@liberty.edu	$50			$29,088	$29,088	4				4	90	66	4	4	279	26	36	14		25 (14)	103,436	167,484
Louisiana State University (Paul M. Hebert Law Center) 202 Law Center, 1 East Campus Drive Baton Rouge, LA 70803 225-578-8646 Fax: 225-578-8647 lynell.cadray@law.lsu.edu	$50	March 1	April 1	$8,737 ($16,900)	$8,737	4					94	70		4	598	24	45	10	2	38 (50)	848,000	2,153,035
Loyola Marymount University (Loyola Law School Los Angeles) 919 Albany Street Los Angeles, CA 90015 213-736-1074 Fax: 213-736-6523 admissions@lls.edu				$42,490 ($28,410)	$42,490 ($28,410)	4				4	87	41	4	4	1021 (258)	23	50			79 (63)	620,274	275,309
Loyola University Chicago (School of Law) 25 East Pearson Street Chicago, IL 60611 312-915-7170 Fax: 312-915-7906 law-admissions@luc.edu		March 1	March 1	$38,780 ($29,110)	$38,870 ($29,110)	4				4	86	34	4	4	731 (138)	24	51	23	1	48 (129)	399,955	220,927

INSTITUTION	APPLICATIONS Fee	APPLICATIONS Deadline	APPLICATIONS Financial Aid Deadline	TUITION In State Full Time (Part Time)	TUITION Out of State Full Time (Part Time)	CALENDAR Fall	CALENDAR Winter	CALENDAR Spring	CALENDAR Summer	PROGRAMS Day	PROGRAMS Evening	PROGRAMS Credits for JD	PROGRAMS Required Credits for Courses	PROGRAMS Transferable Summer Courses	PROGRAMS Joint Degree	PROGRAMS Graduate Law Degree	ENROLLED STUDENT BODY Full Time (Part Time)	ENROLLED STUDENT BODY Average Age First Year	ENROLLED STUDENT BODY % Women	ENROLLED STUDENT BODY % Minority	ENROLLED STUDENT BODY Attrition Rate %	FACULTY Full Time (Part Time)	LIBRARY Volumes	LIBRARY Microforms
Loyola University of New Orleans (College of Law) 7214 St. Charles Avenue, P.O. Box 901 New Orleans, LA 70118 504-861-5575 Fax: 504-861-5772 ladmit@loyno.edu	$40	March 1	June 1	$37,230 ($24,820)	$37,230 ($24,820)	4				4	4	90	53	4	4	4	689 (131)	25	50	28	3	57 (25)	236,088	1,340,908
Marquette University (Law School) Office of Admissions, P.O. Box 1881 Milwaukee WI 53201-1881 414-288-6767 Fax: 414-288-0676 law.admission@marquette.edu	$50	April 1	March 1	$37,570 ($37,612)	$37,570 ($37,612)	4				4	4	90	38	4	4	4	587 (146)	25	44	19	7	48 (76)	390,869	168,520
Massachusetts School of Law 500 Federal Street Andover, MA 01810 978-681-0800 Fax: 978-681-6330 pcolby@mslaw.edu	$40	July 30	July 15	$14,990 ($11,992)	$14,990 ($11,992)							90	45				350 (350)	32	50	25	25	16 (80)		
Mercer University (Walter F. George School of Law) 1021 Georgia Avenue Macon, GA 31207 478-301-2605 Fax: 478-301-2989 Sutton_me@law.mercer.edu	$50	March 15	April 1	$36,560	$36,560	4				4	4	91	52	4	4	4	451	25	44	18	4	31 (48)	202,187	153,356
Michigan State University (College of Law) 368 Law College Bldg. East Lansing, MI 48824-1300 517-432-0222 Fax: 517-432-0098	$60	April 30	Feb 1	$34,452	$34,452	4				4	4	88	32	4	4	4	769 (199)	23	48	23	3	51 (48)	188,397	168,785
Mississippi College (School of Law) 151 East Griffith Street Jackson, MS 39201 601-925-7152 pevans@mc.edu		June 1		$29,150	$29,150	4				4		90	36	4	4	4	557 (19)	26	41	9	7	18 (65)	386,256	252,061
New England Law / Boston 154 Stuart Street Boston, MA 02116 617-422-7210 Fax: 617-422-7201 admit@admin.nesl.edu	$65	March 15	April 5	$40,904 ($30,680)	$40,904 ($30,680)	4				4	4	86	42	4		4	820 (322)	24	56	11	14	35 (68)	325,715	900,082
New York Law School 185 West Broadway New York, NY 10013-2960 212-431-2888 Fax: 212-966-1522 admissions@nyls.edu		April 1	April 15	$46,200 ($35,600)	$46,200 ($35,600)	4				4	4	86	40	4	4	4	1365 (400)	25	52	26	15	103 (118)	534,789	175,305

School	Fee	Deadline 1	Deadline 2	Tuition (res.)	Tuition (nonres.)			%			Applicants							
New York University (School of Law), 161 Avenue of the Americas, 5th Floor, New York, NY 10013, 212-998-6060, Fax: 212-995-4527, law.moreinfo@nyu.edu	$75	Feb 15	April 15	$48,950	$48,950	4	4	83	38 to 42	4	1464	24	41	25		141 (72)	1,102,008	146,900
North Carolina Central University (School of Law), 640 Nelson Street, Durham, NC 27707, 919-530-6333, Fax: 919-530-6339, sbrownb@nccu.edu	$40	March 31	June 30	$5,916 ($7,708)	$18,654 ($7,708)	4	4	88	55	4	437 (95)	26	59	55	22	31 (25)	416,852	1,149,510
Northeastern University (School of Law), 400 Huntington Avenue, Boston, MA 02115, 617-373-2395, Fax: 617-373-8865, c.taubman@neu.edu	$75	March 1	Feb 15	$42,180	$42,180	4	4	87	37	4	656	25	58	34	1	36 (45)	339,258	211,145
Northern Illinois University (College of Law), Swen Parson Hall, Room 151, DeKalb, IL 60115-2890, 815-753-8595, Fax: 815-753-5680, lawadm@niu.edu	$50	April 1	March 1	$18,688	$33,311	4	4	90	43	4	314 (4)	26	44	20	3	26 (8)	169,278	543,897
Northern Kentucky University (Salmon P. Chase College of Law), Nunn Hall, Highland Heights, KY 41099, 859-572-5490, Fax: 859-572-6081, brayg@nku.edu	$40	July 1	March 1	$15,054 ($11,580)	$32,812 ($25,240)	4	4	90	48	4	355 (218)	25	39	7	4	23 (25)	340,894	173,918
Northwestern University (School of Law), 375 East Chicago Avenue, Chicago, IL 60611, 312-503-8465, Fax: 312-503-0178, admissions@law.northwestern.edu	$100	Feb 15	Feb 1	$51,620	$51,620	4	4	83	29	4	801	26	47	37	1	71 (88)	603,543	1,085,231
Nova Southeastern University (Shepard Broad Law Center), 3305 College Avenue, Fort Lauderdale, FL 33314-7721, 954-262-6117, Fax: 954-262-3844, admission@nsu.law.nova.edu	$53	April 1	April 15	$32,750 ($24,560)	$32,750 ($24,560)	4	4	90	57	4	855 (195)	26	52	33	30	61 (118)	338,431	770,677
Ohio Northern University (Claude W. Pettit College of Law), 525 South Main Street, Ada, OH 45810, 419-772-2211, Fax: 419-772-3042		open	open	$30,270	$30,270	4	4	90	47	4	311	25	41	6	3	18 (15)	256,137	180,425
Ohio State University (Michael E. Moritz College of Law), 55 West 12th Avenue, John Deaver Drinko Hall, Columbus, OH 43210-1391, 614-292-8810, Fax: 614-292-1383, lawadmit@osu.edu	$60	March 15	Feb 15	$26,328	$41,278	4	4	88	37	4	693	23	43	20	1	54 (52)	431,911	1,413,566

INSTITUTION	APPLICATIONS Fee	Deadline	Financial Aid Deadline	TUITION In State Full Time (Part Time)	Out of State Full Time (Part Time)	CALENDAR Fall	Winter	Spring	Summer	PROGRAMS Day	Evening	Credits for JD	Required Credits for Courses	Transferable Summer Courses	Joint Degree	Graduate Law Degree	ENROLLED STUDENT BODY Full Time (Part Time)	Average Age First Year	% Women	% Minority	Attrition Rate %	FACULTY Full Time (Part Time)	LIBRARY Volumes	Microforms
Oklahoma City University (School of Law) 2501 North Blackwelder Avenue Oklahoma City, OK 73106-1493 405-208-5354 Fax: 405-208-5814 lawadmit@okcu.edu	$50	Aug 1	March 1	$34,715 ($25,130)	$34,715 ($25,130)	4				4	4	90	60	4	4		533 (90)	27	41	16	12	40 (56)	322,061	147,684
Pace University (School of Law) 78 North Broadway White Plains, NY 10603 914-422-4210 Fax: 914-989-8714 calexander@law.pace.edu	$65	March 1	Feb 15	$40,730 ($30,550)	$40,730 ($30,550)	4		4		4	4	88	37	4	4	4	644 (132)	24	57	20	15	44 (137)	406,732	62,322
Pennsylvania State University (Dickinson School of Law) Lewis Katz Building University Park, PA 16802-1910 814-867-1251 Fax: 717-241-3503 dsladmit@psu.edu	$60	March 31		$37,704	$37,704	4				4	4	88	40	4	4	4	596	24	44	14	2	71 (17)	638,086	1,605,054
Pepperdine University (School of Law) 24255 Pacific Coast Highway Malibu, CA 90263 310-506-4631 Fax: 310-506-7668			April 1	$42,780	$42,780	4		4		4	4	88	57	4	4	4	680	23	51	17	5	30	342,450	87,000
Phoenix School of Law One North Central Avenue Phoenix, AZ 85004 (602) 682-6800	$50			$37,760 ($30,540)		4				4	4	87	67	4			697 (272)	28	47	29		32 (29)		
Pontifical Catholic University of Puerto Rico (School of Law) 2250 Avenida las Americas suite 543 Ponce, PR 00717-9997 787-841-2000, ext. 1836 Fax: 787-840-4620		n/av	Check			4		4		4	4	94	82		4	4	220 (220)	24	50		11	14 (18)	135,000	15,000
Quinnipiac University (School of Law) 275 Mt. Carmel Avenue Hamden, CT 06518-1908 203-582-3400 Fax: 203-582-3339 ladm@quinnipiac.edu	$65	March 1	April 15	$44,270 ($31,000)	$44,270 ($31,000)	4				4	4	86	45	4	4	4	356 (82)	24	48	14	8	29 (34)	198,435	260,581
Regent University (School of Law) 1000 Regent University Drive Virginia Beach, VA 23464-9800 757-352-4584 Fax: 757-352-4139 lawschool@regent.edu	$50	June 1	June 1	$31,800 ($23,320)	$31,800 ($23,320)	4				4		90	73	4	4	4	422 (22)	25	49	15		29 (24)	131,049	1,001,511

School	App Fee	Deadline	Deadline	Tuition	Tuition															
Roger Williams University (School of Law) Ten Metacom Avenue Bristol RI 02809-5171 401-254-4555 Fax: 401-254-4516 *admissions@rwu.edu*	$60	March 15	Feb 15	$38,850	$38,850	4		4	4	90	48	4	4	555	25	50	14	12	37 (35)	312,281	1,088,017
Rutgers University/Camden (School of Law) Fifth and Penn Streets Camden, NJ 08102 856-225-6102 Fax: 856-225-6537 *admissions@camlaw.rutgers.edu*	$65	April 1	March 15	$22,746 ($18,960)	$34,478 ($28,740)	4		4	4	84	32	4	4	647 (218)	25	43	15	1	70 (55)	527,581	157,238
Rutgers University/Newark (School of Law) Center for Law and Justice, 123 Washington St. Newark, NJ 07102 973-353-5557/5554 Fax: 973-353-3459 *lawinfo@andromeda.rutgers.edu*		March 15	March 1	$25,407 ($12,730)	($18,814)	4		4	4	84	34 to 35	4	4	558 (260)	27	43	38	2	55 (31)	353,600	163,600
Saint John's University (School of Law) 8000 Utopia Parkway Queens, NY 11439 718-990-6474 Fax: 718-990-2526 *lawinfo@stjohns.edu*	$60	April 1	March 1	$46,450 ($34,840)	$46,450 ($34,840)	4		4	4	86	58	4	4	787 (148)	23	43	26		53 (70)	394,720	196,497
Saint Louis University (School of Law) 3700 Lindell Boulevard St. Louis, MO 63108 314-977-2800 Fax: 314-977-1464 *admissions@law.slu.edu*	$55	March 1	March 1	$35,730 ($26,070)	$35,730 ($26,070)	4		4	4	91	37-39	4	4	777 (133)	25	46	15	5	68 (57)	670,787	266,344
Saint Mary's University (School of Law) One Camino Santa Maria San Antonio, TX 78228-8601 210-436-3523 Fax: 210-431-4202 *wwilson@stmarytx.edu*	$55	March 1	March 31	$288,000 ($17,280)	$28,800 ($17,280)	4		4	4	90	46	4	4	665 (207)	25	43	35	16	38 (53)	635,241	415,495
Saint Thomas University (School of Law) 16401, NW 37th Avenue Miami Gardens, FL 33054 305-623-2310 *fkhan@stu.edu*	$60	May 1	May 31	$34,618	$34,618	4		4	4	90	58	4	4	720	25	51	49	7	45 (47)	211,493	1,270,722
Samford University (Cumberland School of Law) 800 Lakeshore Drive Birmingham, AL 35229 205-726-2702 Fax: 205-726-2057 *law.admissions@samford.edu*	$50	Feb 28	March 1	$34,528	$34,528	4		4	4	90	47	4	4	489	24	42	14	6	22 (34)	203,605	125,975
Santa Clara University (School of Law) 500 El Camino Real Santa Clara, CA 95053 408-554-4800 Fax: 408-554-7897 *lawadmissions@scu.edu*	$75	Feb 1	Feb 1	$41,790 ($29,254)	$41,790 ($29,254)	4		4	4	86	42	4	4	738 (229)	25	47	37	7	64 (43)	398,115	1,182,040

INSTITUTION	Fee	Deadline	Financial Aid Deadline	Tuition In State Full Time (Part Time)	Tuition Out of State Full Time (Part Time)	Fall	Winter	Spring	Summer	Day	Evening	Credits for JD	Required Credits for Courses	Transferable Summer Courses	Joint Degree	Graduate Law Degree	Enrolled Full Time (Part Time)	Average Age First Year	% Women	% Minority	Attrition Rate %	Faculty Full Time (Part Time)	Volumes	Microforms
Seattle University (School of Law) 901 12th Avenue, Sullivan Hall, P.O. Box 222000, Seattle, WA 98122-4340, 206-398-4200, Fax: 206-398-4058, lawadmis@seattleu.edu	$60	March 1	March 1	$39,210 ($28,754)	$39,210 ($28,754)	4			4	4	4	90	44	4	4		886 (196)	28	51	27	2	63 (43)	394,151	224,303
Seton Hall University (School of Law) One Newark Center, Newark, NJ 07102-5210, 973-642-8747, Fax: 973-642-8876, admitme@shu.edu	$65	April 1	April 1	$46,000 ($34,500)	$46,000 ($34,500)	4				4	4	88	44	4	4	4	770 (450)	25	41	18	2	75 (96)	443,681	498,403
South Texas College of Law 1303 San Jacinto Street, Houston, TX 77002-7006, 713-646-1810, Fax: 713-646-2906, admissions@stcl.edu	$55	Feb 15	May 1	$26,850 ($18,100)	$26,850 ($18,100)	4				4	4	90	46	4	4	4	996 (271)	26	46	31	4	55 (41)	237,970	295,556
Southern Illinois University (School of Law) Lesar Law Building, Mail Code 6804, Carbondale, IL 62901, 618-453-8858, Fax: 618-453-8921, lawadmit@siu.edu	$50	April 1	April 1	$12,750	$32,910	4		4		4	4	90	49	4	4	4	373 (3)	25	38	7	6	35 (8)	443,551	206,555
Southern Methodist University (Dedman School of Law) Office of Admissions, P.O. Box 750110, Dallas, TX 75275-0110, 214-768-2550, Fax: 214-768-2549, lawadmit@smu.edu	$75	Feb 15	June 1	$37,616 ($28,208)	$37,616 ($28,208)	4				4	4	87	37	4	4	4	572 (330)	25	47	23	3	47 (30)	637,217	140,625
Southern New England School of Law 333 Faunce Corner Road, North Dartmouth, MA 02747, 508-998-9400, Fax: 508-998-9561, cvidal@snesl.edu	$50	June 30	May 27	$21,800 ($735/hr)	$21,800 ($735/hr)							90	71-73		4		125 (111)	31	57	34		10 (20)	130,000	
Southern University and A & M College (Law Center) Post Office Box 9294, Baton Rouge, LA 70813-9294, 225-771-5340, Fax: 225-771-2121, wwilkerson@sulc.edu			April 15	$7,000	$13,000	4				4		96	75	4	4		413 (20)	27	48	69	10	28 (24)	453,396	206,603
Southwestern University (Law School) 3050 Wilshire Boulevard, Los Angeles, CA 90010-1106, 213-738-6717, Fax: 213-383-1688, admissions@swlaw.edu	$60	April 1	June 1	$42,000 ($28,000)	$42,000 ($28,000)	4				4	4	87	52	4	4	4	698 (274)	27	51	35	8	58 (33)	483,433	63,061

School	Fee	Deadline	Deadline	Tuition	Tuition														
Stanford University (Stanford Law School) Crown Quadrangle 559 Nathan Abbott Way Stanford, CA 94305-8610 650-723-4985 Fax: 650-723-0838 admissions@law.stanford.edu	$100	Feb 1	March 15	$44,880	$44,880	4	4	111	29	4	4	571	25	43	37		55	441,671	287,048
State University of New York (SUNY Buffalo Law School) 309 O'Brian Hall Buffalo, NY 14260 716-645-2907 Fax: 716-645-6676 lwiley@buffalo.edu	$75	March 15	March 1	$19,020	$32,020	4	4	90	40	4	4	663	25	47	15	1	57 (116)	299,106	295,016
Stetson University (Stetson University College of Law) 1401 61st Street South Gulfport, FL 33707 727-562-7802 Fax: 727-343-0136 zuppo@law.stetson.edu	$55	April 15	open	$35,146 ($24,282)	$35,146 ($24,282)	4	4	88	38	4	4	876 (208)	24	53	23	3	54 (54)	420,000	53,670
Suffolk University (Law School) 120 Tremont Street Boston, MA 02108-4977 617-573-8144 Fax: 617-523-1367	$60	March 1	March 1	$42,540 ($31,904)	$42,540 ($31,904)	4	4	84	43	4	4	1101 (580)	25	47	19	7	92 (138)	150,312	205,385
Syracuse University (College of Law) Office of Admissions and Financial Aid, Suite 340 Syracuse, NY 13244-1030 315-443-1962 Fax: 315-443-9563	$70	April 1	Feb 15	$44,000	$44,000	4	4	87	40	4	4	659 (7)	24	45	19		59 (54)	218,058	255,018
Temple University (James E. Beasley School of Law) 1719 North Broad Street Philadelphia, PA 19122 215-204-5949 Fax: 215-204-1185 lawadmis@temple.edu			n/app	$16,000 ($12,000)	$26,000 ($20,000)	4	4	87	40	4	4	1060	26	48	24	3	59 (212)	573,568	179,200
Texas Southern University (Thurgood Marshall School of Law) 3100 Cleburne Avenue Houston, TX 77004 713-313-7114 Fax: 713-313-1049 cgardner@tmslaw.tsu.edu	$55	April 1	April 1	$16,262	$21,212	4	4	90	70	4	4	632	27	46	80	35	34 (19)	251,722	62,907
Texas Tech University (School of Law) 1802 Hartford Avenue Lubbock, TX 79409 806-742-3990, ext 273 Fax: 806-742-4617 donna.williams@ttu.edu	$50	Feb 1	Feb 1	$17,724	$26,214	4	4	90	55	4	4	697	24	43	26	2	32 (10)	346,438	696,939
Texas Wesleyan University (School of Law) 1515 Commerce Street Fort Worth, TX 76102 817-212-4040 Fax: 817-212-4141 lawadmissions@law.txwes.edu	$55	March 31	March 31	$28,000 ($19,600)	$28,000 ($19,600)	4	4	90	51	4	4	431 (299)	27	46	22	12	34 (22)	285,196	769,301

INSTITUTION	Fee	Deadline	Deadline Financial Aid	Tuition In State Full Time (Part Time)	Tuition Out of State Full Time (Part Time)	Fall	Winter	Spring	Summer	Day	Evening	Credits for JD	Required Credits for Courses	Transferable Summer Courses	Joint Degree	Graduate Law Degree	Enrolled Full Time (Part Time)	Average Age First Year	% Women	% Minority	Attrition Rate %	Faculty Full Time (Part Time)	Volumes	Microforms
Thomas Jefferson School of Law 1155 Island Avenue San Diego, CA 92101 619-297-9700 Fax: 619-294-4713 info@tjsl.edu	$50	open	Feb 15	$41,000 ($30,000)	$41,000 ($30,000)	4	4	4	4	4	4	88	55	4	4	4	823 (330)	26	44	14		43 (41)	103,536	130,878
Thomas M. Cooley Law School 300 South Capitol Avenue Lansing, MI 48901 517-371-5140 Fax: 517-334-5718 admissions@cooley.edu	$25	Sept 1	Sept 1	$34,300 ($22,050)	$34,300 ($22,050)	4		4	4	4	4	90	63	4	4	4	781 (2364)	27	49	28	16	131 (286)	694,885	1,898,794
Touro College (Jacob D. Fuchsberg Law Center) 225 Eastview Drive Central Islip, NY 11722 631-761-7010 Fax: 631-761-7019 gjustice@tourolaw.edu		rolling	April 15	$21,405 ($15,960)		4				4	4	87	51 to 52	4	4	4	725	26	45	23	5	31 (41)	429,683	225,964
Tulane University (Law School) Weinmann Hall, 6329 Freret Street New Orleans, LA 70118 504-865-5930 Fax: 504-865-6710 admissions@law.tulane.edu	$60	March 15		$40,040	$40,040	4				4	4	88	32	4	4	4	775	24	48	15	5	42 (75)	408,756	263,252
University of Akron (School of Law) 302 Buchtel Common Akron, OH 44325-2901 330-972-7331 Fax: 330-258-2343 lthorpe@uakron.edu		March 1	May 1	$18,977 ($15,181)	$31,532 ($25,224)	4				4	4	88	44	4	4	4	318 (218)	26	43	14	13	37 (38)	259,519	377,025
University of Alabama (School of Law) Box 870382 Tuscaloosa, AL 35487-0382 205-348-5440 Fax: 205-348-3917 admissions@law.ua.edu	$40			$18,030	$30,950	4				4	4	90	36	4	4	4	509	25	41	14	2	38 (36)	464,870	157,256
University of Arizona (James E. Rogers College of Law) 120 E. Speedway, P.O. Box 210176 Tucson, AZ 85721-0176 520-621-3477 Fax: 520-621-9140 admissions@law.arizona.edu			March 1	$26,089		4				4		85	39	4	4	4	480	25	50	29	1	30 (55)	410,000	426,000

School	Col 1	Col 2	Col 3	Col 4	Col 5	Col 6	Col 7	Col 8	Col 9	Col 10	Col 11	Col 12	Col 13	Col 14	Tuition (a)	Tuition (b)	Deadline 1	Deadline 2	Fee
University of Arkansas (School of Law) Robert A. Leflar Law Center, Waterman Hall, Fayetteville, AR 72701, 479-575-3102, Fax: 479-575-3937, jkmiller@uark.edu	836,887	331,103	39 (34)		18	42	23	401	4	4	4	43	90		4	$23,160	$10,565	March 1	April 1	
University of Arkansas at Little Rock (UALR William H. Bowen School of Law) 1201 McMath Avenue, Little Rock, AR 72202-5142, 501-324-9903, Fax: 501-324-9909, lawadm@ualr.edu	593,296	320,407	27 (81)	1	15	44	26	325 (152)	4	4	4	45	90	4	4	$24,772	$12,177	March 1	April 15	
University of Baltimore (School of Law) 1420 North Charles Street, Baltimore, MD 21201-5779, 410-837-4459, Fax: 410-837-4450, lwadmiss@ubmail.ubalt.edu; jzavrotny@ubalt.edu	193,533	365,150	48 (92)	7	13	52	26	657 (425)	4	4	4	41	90	4	4	$18,015 ($16,908)	$11,964 ($11,892)	March 1		
University of California (Hastings College of the Law) 200 McAllister Street, San Francisco, CA 94102, 415-565-4623, Fax: 415-581-8946, admiss@uchastings.edu	71,568	707,264	60 (117)	2	38	54	25	1289	4	4	4	34	86	4	4	$49,336	$40,836	March 1	March 1	
University of California at Berkeley (School of Law) 215 Boalt Hall, Berkeley, CA 94720, 510-642-2274, Fax: 510-643-6222, admissions@law.berkeley.edu	188,598	875,000	152 (38)	1	32	55	25	898	4	4		32	85	4	4	$54,372	$50,164	March 2	February 1	$75
University of California at Davis (School of Law) Martin Luther King, Jr. Hall - 400 Mrak Hall Drive, Davis, CA 95616-5201, 530-752-6477, admissions@lawucdavis.edu	768,833	302,516	49 (14)	5	37	53	24	606	4	4	4	33	88	4	4	$45,474	$34,528	March 2	Feb 1	
University of California at Los Angeles (UCLA School of Law) P.O. Box 951445, Los Angeles, CA 90095-1445, 310-825-2080, Fax: 310-206-7227, admissions@law.ucla.edu	20,343	689,513	111 (63)	2	29	47	25	987	4	4		35	87	4	4	$54,767	$44,922	March 2	Feb 1	$75
University of Chicago (Law School) 1111 East 60th Street, Chicago, IL 60637, 773-702-9484, Fax: 773-834-0942, admissions@law.uchicago.edu	11,712	672,456	70 (31)	1	28	45	24	634	4	4	4	40	105	4	4	$47,502	$47,502	March 1	Feb 1	$75
University of Cincinnati (College of Law) P.O. Box 210040, Cincinnati, OH 45221-0040, 513-556-6805, Fax: 513-556-2391, admissions@law.uc.edu	781,570	437,356	28	1	16	41	25	409	4	4	4	36	90	4	4	$38,720	$22,204	March 1	March 1	$35

Institution	Fee	Deadline	Financial Aid Deadline	Tuition In State Full Time (Part Time)	Tuition Out of State Full Time (Part Time)	Fall	Winter	Spring	Summer	Day	Evening	Credits for JD	Required Credits for Courses	Transferable Summer Courses	Joint Degree	Graduate Law Degree	Enrolled Full Time (Part Time)	Average Age First Year	% Women	% Minority	Attrition Rate %	Faculty Full Time (Part Time)	Volumes	Microforms
University of Colorado (Law School) Campus Box 403, Wolf Law Building Boulder, CO 80309-0403 303-492-7203 Fax: 303-492-2542	$65	March 15	April 1	$29,214	$35,622	4				4		89	38	4	4	4	540	25	48	22	1	50 (31)	888,178	1,653,416
University of Connecticut (School of Law) 55 Elizabeth Street Hartford, CT 06105 860-570-5159 Fax: 860-570-5153 admissions@law.uconn.edu	$60	March 15	March 15	$21,240 ($14,800)	$44,736 ($31,220)	4				4	4	86	36	4	4	4	490 (207)	25	44	20	1	59 (75)	545,754	222,856
University of Dayton (School of Law) 300 College Park Dayton, OH 45469-2760 937-229-3555 Fax: 937-229-4194 lawinfo@notes.udayton.edu	$50	May 1	March 1	$33,678 ($33,678)	$33,678	4				4	4	90	79	4	4	4	497	25	41	12	1	25 (21)	195,218	689,730
University of Denver (Sturm College of Law) 2255 East Evans Avenue Denver, CO 80208 303-871-6135 admissions@law.du.edu	$45	June 1	open	$37,830 ($27,742)	$37,830 ($27,742)	4				4	4	90	40	4	4	4	769 (177)	26	49	17	5	74 (57)	241,077	178,930
University of Detroit Mercy (School of Law) 651 East Jefferson Avenue Detroit, MI 48226 313-596-0264 Fax: 313-596-0280 udmlawao@udmercy.edu	$50	April 15	April 1	$36,050 ($28,856)	$36,050 ($28,856)	4				4	4	90	51	4	4	4	556 (120)	26	46	16	13	52 (39)	392,744	197,510
University of Florida (Fredric G. Levin College of Law) 141 Bruton-Geer Hall, P.O. Box 117622 Gainesville, FL 32611-7622 352-273-0890 Fax: 352-392-4087 madorno@law.ufl.edu	$30	March 15	April 15	$18,710	$38,074	4				4	4	88	34	4	4	4	1044	23	45	25	2	73 (61)	643,282	318,270
University of Georgia (School of Law) Hirsch Hall, 225 Herty Drive Athens, GA 30602-6012 706-542-7060 Fax: 706-542-5556 ugajd@uga.edu	$50	March 1	July 1	$17,624	$34,732	4				4		88	36	4	4	4	691	24	43	20	2	46 (22)	390,000	504,653
University of Hawaii at Manoa (William S. Richardson School of Law) 2515 Dole Street Honolulu, HI 96822 808-956-7966 Fax: 808-956-3813 lawadm@hawaii.edu	$75	Feb 1	March 1	$16,728 ($12,546)	$31,872 ($23,904)	4				4	4	89	42	4	4	4	290 (75)	28	56	71	5	30 (26)	119,827	1,167,923

School	Fee	Deadline 1	Deadline 2	Tuition (res)	Tuition (nonres)																	
University of Houston (Law Center) 100 Law Center, Houston, TX 77204-6060; 713-743-2280; Fax: 713-743-2194; lawadmissions@uh.edu	$70	Feb 15	April 1	$11,733 ($7,822)	$17,071 ($11,380)	4			4	4	90	38	4	4	676 (154)	25	43	34	2	61 (146)	554,954	1,665,443
University of Idaho (College of Law) P.O. Box 442321, Moscow, ID 83844-2321; 208-885-2300; Fax: 208-885-5709; jfinney@uidaho.edu	$50	Feb 15	Feb 15	$14,040	$26,560	4			4	4	90	39	4	4	358	27	40	13	3	25 (33)	254,602	103,774
University of Illinois (College of Law) 504 East Pennsylvania Avenue, Champaign, IL 61820; 217-244-6415; Fax: 217-244-1478; admissions@law.uiuc.edu		March 15		$23,000	$33,000	4			4	4	90	33	4	4	587	24	40	26	2	40 (46)	615,739	928,746
University of Iowa (College of Law) 320 Melrose Avenue, Iowa City, IA 52242; 319-335-9095; Fax: 319-335-9646; law-admissions@uiowa.edu	$60	March 1	open	$24,682	$44,390	4			4	4	84	33	4	4	556	24	42	17	2	48 (12)	857,946	454,237
University of Kansas (School of Law) 205 Green Hall, 1535 West 15th Street, Lawrence, KS 66045; 785-864-4378; Fax: 785-864-5054; admitlaw@ku.edu	$55	May 1	Feb 15	$15,602	$27,790	4	4		4	4	90	37 to 38	4	4	463 (16)	25	39	15	2	35 (19)	360,139	101,732
University of Kentucky (College of Law) 209 Law Building, Lexington, KY 40506-0048; 606-257-7938; Fax: (859) 323-1061; lawadmissions@email.uky.edu	$50	March 1	March 15	$17,300	$30,710	4			4	4	90	34	4	4	415	23	43	15	3	24 (19)	346,201	254,293
University of La Verne (College of Law) 320 East D Street, Ontario, CA 91764; 909-460-2001; Fax: 909-460-2082; lawadm@ulv.edu	$60	July 1	May 15	$31,590 ($23,690)	$31,590	4			4	4	88	60	4	4	205 (105)	26	42	31	22	19 (12)	97,233	208,841
University of Louisville (Louis D. Brandeis School of Law) University of Louisville Belknap Campus-Wilson W. Wyatt Hall, Louisville, KY 40292; 502-852-6364; Fax: 502-852-8971; brandon.hamilton@louisville.edu	$50	March 15	June 1	$16,716	$32,128	4			4	4	90	44	4	4	363 (26)	26	45	8	5	34 (9)	417,747	190,390
University of Maine (School of Law) 246 Deering Avenue, Portland, ME 04102; 207-780-4341; Fax: 207-780-4239; mainelaw@usm.maine.edu		March 1	Feb 15	$22,986	$33,906	4			4	4	90	41	4	4	273 (14)	27	48	10	3	16 (13)	302,287	138,833

INSTITUTION	Fee	Deadline	Deadline Financial Aid	In State Full Time (Part Time)	Out of State Full Time (Part Time)	Fall	Winter	Spring	Summer	Day	Evening	Credits for JD	Required Credits for Courses	Transferable Summer Courses	Joint Degree	Graduate Law Degree	Full Time (Part Time)	Average Age First Year	% Women	% Minority	Attrition Rate %	Full Time (Part Time)	Volumes	Microforms
University of Maryland (Francis King Carey School of Law) 500 West Baltimore Street Baltimore, MD 21201 410-706-3492 Fax: 410-706-1793 admissions@law.umaryland.edu		March 1	March 1	$23,744 ($17,782)	$35,022 ($26,250)	4				4	4	85	34 to 35	4	4	4	678 (153)	25	55	35	1	56 (99)	353,820	141,718
University of Memphis (Cecil C. Humphreys School of Law) 1 North Front Street Memphis, TN 38103-2189 901-678-5403 Fax: 901-678-0741 lawadmissions@memphis.edu	$25	March 1	April 1	$13,942 ($12,464)	$35,814 ($33,000)	4				4		90	61	4	4	4	394 (27)	25	41	14	11	24 (42)	274,162	107,229
University of Miami (School of Law) P.O. Box 248087, 1311 Miller Drive Coral Gables, FL 33124-8087 305-284-2523 Fax: 305-284-4400 admissions@law.miami.edu	$60	Feb 4	March 1	$38,918	$38,918	4				4	4	88	72	4	4	4	1348 (135)	24	42	28	2	82 (107)	438,790	203,197
University of Michigan (Law School) 625 South State Street Ann Arbor, MI 48109-1215 734-764-0537 Fax: 734-647-3218 law.jd.admissions@umich.edu	$75	Feb 15	rolling	$46,586	$49,496	4			4	4	4	82	32	4	4	4	1149	24	46	21		94 (36)	1,026,712	1,722,515
University of Minnesota (Law School) 229 19th Avenue South Minneapolis, MN 55455 612-625-3487 Fax: 612-626-1874 jdadmissions@umn.edu	$75	April 1	April 1	$34,817	$43,385	4				4		88	33	4	4	4	752	25	44	19	6	66 (204)	1,084,527	383,310
University of Mississippi (L.Q.C. Lamar Hall) P.O. Box 1848 Lamar Law Center University, MS 38677 662-915-6910 Fax: 662-915-1289 bvinson@olemiss.edu		March 1		$11,293	$13,398	4			4	4	4	90	36 to 37	4	4	4	517	23	44	14	2	26 (16)	336,487	172,860
University of Missouri (School of Law) 103 Hulston Hall Columbia, MO 65211 573-882-6042 Fax: 573-882-9625 heckm@missouri.edu	$60	March 1	March 1	$16,644		4				4		89	45	4	4	4	425 (6)	25	38	15	11	28 (20)	421,208	112,921
University of Missouri-Kansas City (School of Law) 500 East 52nd Street Kansas City, MO 64110-2499 816-235-1644 Fax: 816-235-5276 brooks@umkc.edu	$60		March 1	$15,438 ($9,263)	$30,480 ($18,288)	4				4	4	91	51-54	4	4	4	438 (28)	26	36	11	10	48 (47)	230,215	125,573

School	App. Fee																					
University of Montana (School of Law) Missoula, MT 59812 406-243-2698 Fax: 406-243-2576 heidi.fanslow@umontana.edu	$60	March 15	Feb 15	$11,025	$26,908	4				4	90	58	4	4	253	28	41	7		22 (16)	135,535	35,109
University of Nebraska-Lincoln (College of Law) P.O. Box 830902 Lincoln, NE 68583-0902 402-472-2161 Fax: 402-472-5185 lawadm@unl.edu	$50	March 1	May 1	$10,788	$26,862				4	4	93	45	4	4	374	24	40	6	6	37 (28)	254,068	179,623
University of Nevada, Las Vegas (William S. Boyd School of Law) 4505 Maryland Parkway, Box 451003 Las Vegas, NV 89154-1003 702-895-2440 Fax: 702-895-2414 request@law.unlv.edu	$50	March 15	Feb 1	$18,000 ($643/hr)	$30,000 ($1,071/hr)	4			4	4	89	41	4	4	370 (118)	27	47	29		52 (23)	330,808	198,454
University of New Hampshire School of Law 2 White Street Concord, NH 03301 603-228-9217 Fax: 603-229-0485 admissions@law.unh.edu	$55	April 1	open	$39,900	$39,900	4			4	4	85	39	4	4	392 (2)	27	39	19	8	21 (27)	313,143	652,164
University of New Mexico (School of Law) MSC11-6070, 1 University of New Mexico Albuquerque, NM 87131-0001 505-277-0958 Fax: 505-277-9958 witherington@law.unm.edu	$50	Feb 15	March 1	$13,292	$31,421	4			4	4	86	45	4	4	362	28	51	45		34 (82)	403,430	155,256
University of North Carolina at Chapel Hill (School of Law) Campus Box 3380, Van Hecke-Wettach Hall Chapel Hill, NC 27599-3380 919-962-5109 Fax: 919-843-7939 law_admission@unc.edu	$75	March 1	March 1	$19,012	$34,120	4			4	4	86	31	4	4	772	23	51	28	3	43 (40)	540,098	42,241
University of North Dakota (School of Law) Box 9003 Grand Forks, ND 58202 701-777-2104 Fax: 701-777-2217 linda.kohoutek@thor.law.und.nodak.edu			Check	$14,400	$14,400	4			4	4	90	34	4	4	205	26	52	11	6	11 (16)	251,320	129,554
University of Notre Dame (Notre Dame Law School) P.O. Box 780 Notre Dame, IN 46556-0780 574-631-6626 Fax: 574-631-5474 lawadmit@nd.edu	$65	Feb 28	Feb 15	$42,870	$42,870	4			4	4	90	34	4	4	563	24	41	30	1	61 (47)	356,733	315,657
University of Oklahoma (College of Law) Andrew M. Coats Hall, 300 Timberdell Road Norman, OK 73019 405-325-4728 Fax: 405-325-0502 rlucas@ou.edu	$50	March 15	March 1	$19,051	$29,476	4			4	4	90	41	4	4	537	25	45	20	2	33 (15)	373,066	81,235

Institution	Fee	Deadline	Financial Aid Deadline	Tuition In State FT (PT)	Tuition Out of State FT (PT)	Fall	Winter	Spring	Summer	Day	Evening	Credits for JD	Required Credits for Courses	Transferable Summer Courses	Joint Degree	Graduate Law Degree	Enrolled FT (PT)	Avg Age First Year	% Women	% Minority	Attrition Rate %	Faculty FT (PT)	Volumes	Microforms
University of Oregon (School of Law, William W. Knight Law Center) 1515 Agate Street, Eugene, OR 97403-1221, 541-346-3846, Fax: 541-346-3984, admissions@law.uoregon.edu	$50	March 1	March 1	$26,146	$32,590	4				4	4	85	36	4	4	4	544	26	45	18	1	33 (51)	205,324	185,420
University of Pennsylvania (Law School) 3501 Sansom Street, Philadelphia, PA 19104-6204, 215-898-7400, Fax: 215-898-9606, admissions@law.upenn.edu	$80	March 1	March 1	$47,600	$47,600	4				4	4	89	24	4	4	4	805	24	47	31	1	83 (87)	1,134,376	240,852
University of Pittsburgh (School of Law) 3900 Forbes Avenue, Pittsburgh, PA 15260, 412-648-1413, Fax: 412-648-1318, Mccall@law.pitt.edu	$55	March 1	March 1	$27,892	$34,666	4				4	4	88	34	4	4	4	704	24	42	16	1	53 (108)	470,958	204,232
University of Puerto Rico (School of Law) P.O. Box 23349, UPR Station, Rio Piedras, PR 00931-3349, 787-999-9551, Fax: 787-999-9564, arosario-lebron@law.upr.edu	$20	Feb 15	May 1	$3,960	$3,960	4				4	4	92	46	4	4	4	523 (185)	24	52		5	29 (48)	283,745	172,059
University of Richmond (School of Law) 28 Westhampton Way, Richmond, VA 23173, 804-289-8189, Fax: 804-287-6516, lawadmissions@richmond.edu	$50	March 15	Feb 25	$35,430	$35,430				4	4		86	38	4	4	4	452 (5)	24	46	17	1	46 (80)	425,122	204,393
University of Saint Thomas (School of Law) 1000 LaSalle Ave., Minneapolis, MN 55403, 651-962-4895, Fax: 651-962-4876, lawschool@stthomas.edu		July 1	July 1	$34,599	$34,599	4				4	4	88	46	4	4	4	481 (2)	25	43	14	3	33 (64)	218,238	889,735
University of San Diego (School of Law) 5998 Alcala Park, San Diego, CA 92110, 619-260-4528, Fax: 619-260-2218, jdinfo@sandiego.edu	$50	Feb 1	March 2	$43,600 ($31,440)	$43,600 ($31,440)	4				4	4	85	35	4	4	4	824 (325)	24	44	29	2	56 (39)	529,802	226,282
University of San Francisco (School of Law) 2130 Fulton Street, San Francisco, CA 94117-1080, 415-422-6586, Fax: 415-422-5442, lawadmissions@usfca.edu	$60	Feb 1	Feb 15	$40,464 ($30,345)	$40,464 ($30,345)	4				4	4	84	48	4	4	4	601 (130)	27	55	39	10	36 (76)	148,872	190,326

School / Contact	App Fee	Deadline 1	Deadline 2	Tuition (Res.)	Tuition (Nonres.)	C6	C7	C8	C9	C10	C11	C12	Enroll.	C14	C15	C16	C17	Faculty	Volumes	Titles
University of South Carolina (School of Law) 701 South Main Street Columbia, SC 29208 803-777-6605 Fax: 803-777-7751 usclaw@law.sc.edu	$60	March 1	March 1	$21,026	$42,072	4			90	46	4	4	665	24	41	15	3	35 (18)	562,559	
University of South Dakota (School of Law) 414 East Clark Street Vermillion, SD 57069-2390 605-677-5443 Fax: 605-677-5417 law.school@usd.edu	$35	March 1		$6,304 ($4,202)	$18,270 ($12,180)	4			90	46	4	4	236 (1)	26	44	8	3	13	213,077	46,922
University of Southern California (Gould School of Law) Los Angeles, CA 90089-0071 213-740-2523 admissions@law.usc.edu	$70	Feb 1	March 1	$48,832	$48,832	4	4	4	88	35	4	4	648	23	49	38	1	45 (56)	459,058	92,809
University of Tennessee (College of Law) 1505 W. Cumberland Avenue Knoxville, TN 37996-1810 865-974-4131 Fax: 865-974-1572 lawadmit@utk.edu	$15	Feb 15	March 1	$14,044	$32,488	4	4	4	89	38	4	4	486 (1)	23	44	25	2	29 (36)	597,882	54,365
University of Texas at Austin (School of Law) 727 East Dean Keeton Street Austin, TX 78705 512-232-1200 Fax: 512-471-2765 admissions@law.utexas.edu	$70	Feb 1	March 31	$32,010	$47,532	4	4	4	86	38	4	4	1212	24	46	28	1	82 (62)	1,029,976	1,219,852
University of the District of Columbia (David A. Clarke School of Law) 4200 Connecticut Avenue, N.W. Washington, DC 20008 202-274-7341 Fax: 202-274-5583 vcanty@udc.edu; lawadmission@udc.edu	$35	March 15	March 31	$8,850	$17,700	4	4	4	90	75	4	4	266 (27)	28	60	50	5	20 (17)	257,000	114,989
University of the Pacific (McGeorge School of Law) 3200 Fifth Avenue Sacramento, CA 95817 916-739-7105 Fax: 916-739-7301 mcgeorge@pacific.edu	$50	May 1	open	$38,556 ($25,632)	$38,556 ($25,632)	4	4	4	88	59	4	4	660 (377)	25	50	28	14	55 (57)	509,762	294,936
University of Toledo (College of Law) 2801 West Bancroft Street, MS 507 Toledo, OH 43606-3390 419-530-4131 Fax: 419-530-4345 law.utoledo.edu		Aug 1	July 1	$19,118 ($14,338)	$30,222 ($22,667)	4	4	4	89	42	4	4	357 (80)	26	40	10	11	31	360,833	137,340
University of Tulsa (College of Law) 3120 East Fourth Place Tulsa, OK 74104-2499 918-631-2406 Fax: 918-631-3630 april-fox@utulsa.edu	$30	July 31	open	$31,836	$31,836	4	4	4	88	48-51	4	4	329 (50)	26	40	21	2	28 (39)	425,711	1,070,722
University of Utah (S.J. Quinney College of Law) 332 South 1400, East Room 101 Salt Lake City, UT 84112 801-581-7479 Fax: 801-581-6897 aguilar@law.utah.edu	$60	Feb 15	April 1	$20,760	$39,410	4	4	4	88	40	4	4	398	26	42	11	1	45 (37)	255,657	630,657

INSTITUTION	APP Fee	App Deadline	Financial Aid Deadline	Tuition In State Full Time (Part Time)	Tuition Out of State Full Time (Part Time)	Fall	Winter	Spring	Summer	Day	Evening	Credits for JD	Required Credits for Courses	Transferable Summer Courses	Joint Degree	Graduate Law Degree	Enrolled Full Time (Part Time)	Average Age First Year	% Women	% Minority	Attrition Rate %	Faculty Full Time (Part Time)	Library Volumes	Library Microforms
University of Virginia (School of Law) 580 Massie Road, Charlottesville, VA 22903-1738, 434-924-7351, Fax: 434-982-2128, lawadmit@virginia.edu	$80	March 1	Feb 17	$44,600	$49,600	4				4		86 quarters	29		4	4	1093	24	45	26	1	85 (100)	873,981	278,125
University of Washington (School of Law) Box 353020, Seattle, WA 98195-3020, 206-543-4078, Fax: 206-543-5671, lawadm@u.washington.edu	$60	Feb 15	Feb 28	$25,780	$39,850	4				4		135	49	4		4	545	26	46	21	2	51 (125)	663,540	200,955
University of West Los Angeles (School of Law) 9920 S. LaCienega Blvd. #404, Inglewood CA 90301-2902, 310-342-5210, Fax: 310-342-5295, tsmith@uwla.edu	$55	open	Aug 4	$22,680						4		85	69	4		4	33 (226)		51	30	10	4 (37)	27,500	15,000
University of Wisconsin (Law School) 975 Bascom Mall, Madison, WI 53706, 608-262-5914, Fax: 608-263-3191, admissions@law.wisc.edu	$56	March 1	March 1	$19,684	$38,811	4				4	4	90	40	4	4	4	748 (44)	24	44	21		57 (70)	467,966	174,057
University of Wyoming (College of Law) Dept. 3035, 1000 East University Avenue, Laramie, WY 82071, 307-766-6416, Fax: 307-766-6417, dburke@uwyo.edu	$50	March 1	March 1	$12,090	$24,420	4				4		89	38	4	4		226	25	47	14	4	17 (19)	145,916	154,014
Valparaiso University (School of Law) Wesemann Hall, 656 S. Greenwich Street, Valparaiso, IN 46383-6493, 219-465-7821, Fax: 219-465-7808, law.admissions@valpo.edu	$60	June 1	March 1	$37,240		4				4	4	90	57	4	4	4	486 (56)	25	46	18	15	37 (40)	332,337	936,822
Vanderbilt University (Law School) 131 21st Avenue South, Nashville, TN 37203, 615-322-6452, Fax: 615-322-1531, admissions@law.vanderbilt.edu	$50	March 15	Feb 15	$45,750	$45,750	4				4		88	38	4	4	4	586	23	46	19		47 (71)	491,027	757,763
Vermont Law School P.O. Box 96, Chelsea Street, South Royalton, VT 05068-0096, 802-831-1239, Fax: 802-831-1174, admiss@vermontlaw.edu	$60	March 1	March 1	$39,995 ($43,468)	$39,995 ($43,468)	4				4		87	52	4	4	4	566	26	50	10	8	59 (14)	255,118	123,387

School	App. Fee	Deadline	Deadline	Tuition (full-time)	Tuition (part-time)										
Villanova University (Villanova University School of Law) 299 North Spring Mill Road Villanova, PA 19085 610-519-7010 Fax: 610-519-6291 admissions@law.villanova.edu	$75	April 1	March 1	$37,390	$37,390	4	88	43	4	725	23	46	18	1	52 (65)	358,613	1,177,420
Wake Forest University (School of Law) P.O. Box 7206 Winston-Salem, NC 27109 336-758-5437 Fax: 336-758-4632 admissions@law.wfu.edu	$60	March 15	May 1	$37,940		4	89	41	4	523	24	42	21	3	48 (17)	423,007	1,416,489
Washburn University (School of Law) 1700 SW College Avenue Topeka, KS 66621 785-670-1185 Fax: 785-670-1120 admissions@washburnlaw.edu	$40	April 1	June 1	$17,220	$26,880	4	90	44	4	413	26	38	14	4	33 (51)	406,398	183,232
Washington and Lee University (School of Law) Lewis Hall Lexington, VA 24450 540-458-8503 Fax: 540-458-8586 lawadm@wlu.edu		March 1	Feb 15	$41,947	$41,947	4	85	45	4	395	23	46	14	2	38 (25)	472,707	1,274,234
Washington University in St. Louis (School of Law) Box 1120, One Brookings Drive St. Louis, MO 63130 314-935-4525 Fax: 314-935-8778 admiss@wulaw.wustl.edu	$70	March 1	March 1	$45,350	$45,350	4	86	37	4	847	23	40	26	3	67 (77)	705,730	1,481,896
Wayne State University (Law School) 471 West Palmer Street Detroit, MI 48202 313-577-3937 Fax: 313-993-8129 emjackson@wayne.edu	$50	March 15	June 30	$24,572 ($13,105)	$27,002 ($14,401)	4	86	35	4	452 (118)	25	42	18	3	47 (43)	630,196	225,401
West Virginia University (College of Law) P.O. Box 6130 Morgantown, WV 26506 304-293-5304 Fax: 304-293-6891 wvulaw.Admissions@mail.wvu.edu	$50	March 1	March 1	$16,420	$31,358	4	91	37	4	420 (7)	24	37	12	1	34 (25)	347,393	550,200
Western New England University (School of Law) 1215 Wilbraham Road Springfield, MA 01119 413-782-1406 Fax: 413-796-2067 admissions@law.wnec.edu	$50	March 15	rolling	$36,826 ($27,620)	$36,826 ($27,620)	4	88	46	4	319 (119)	25	53	11	9	38 (36)	375,070	235,661
Western State University (College of Law) 1111 North State College Blvd Fullerton, CA 92831 714-459-1101 Fax: 714-441-1748 adm@wsulaw.edu	$60	July 1	March 2	$36,994 ($24,740)	$36,994 ($24,740)	4	88	69	4	376 (135)	26	48	42		28 (19)	206,201	99,172

INSTITUTION	APPLICATIONS Fee	Deadline	Deadline Financial Aid	TUITION In State Full Time (Part Time)	Out of State Full Time (Part Time)	CALENDAR Fall	Winter	Spring	Summer	PROGRAMS Day	Evening	Credits for JD	Required Creits for Courses	Transferable Summer Courses	Joint Degree	Graduate Law Degree	ENROLLED Full Time (Part Time)	STUDENT BODY Average Age First Year	% Women	% Minority	Attrition Rate %	FACULTY Full Time (Part Time)	LIBRARY Volumes	Microforms
Whittier College (Whittier Law School) 3333 Harbor Blvd. Costa Mesa, CA 92626 714-444-4141, ext. 121 Fax: 714-444-0250 info@law.whittier.edu	$60	August 1	May 1	$39,140 ($26,110)	$39,140 ($26,110)	4				4	4	87	53	4		4	570 (136)	27	48	52	31	36 (30)	682,290	141,361
Widener University (Widener University School of Law) 4601 Concord Pike, P.O. Box 7474 Wilmington, DE 19803-0474 302-477-2162 Fax: 302-477-2224 law.admissions@law.widener.edu	$60	May 15	open	$36,360 ($26,664)	$36,360 ($26,664)	4				4	4	88	57	4	4	4	641 (339)	24	44	16	28	62 (44)	236,011	374,833
Widener University (Widener University School of Law) 3800 Vartan Way, P.O. Box 69381 Harrisburg, PA 17106-9381 717-541-3903 Fax: 717-541-3999 law.admissions@law.widener.edu	$60	May 15	open	$33,540 ($24,920)	$33,540 ($24,620)	4				4	4	88	66	4	4	4	358 (103)	23	48	10	13	30 (30)	258,433	332,319
Willamette University (College of Law) 245 Winter Street S.E. Salem, OR 97301 503-370-6282 Fax: 503-370-6087 law-admission@willamette.edu	$50	March 1	March 1	$29,600 ($32,460)	$29,600 ($32,460)	4				4	4	90	40	4	4	4	412 (2)	25	39	18	4	31 (29)	300,000	156,872
William Mitchell College of Law 875 Summit Avenue St. Paul, MN 55105-3076 651-290-6343 Fax: 651-290-6414 admissions@wmitchell.edu		May 1	March 15	$32,340 ($23,400)	$32,340 ($23,400)	4				4	4	86	46		4	4	686 (318)	24	49	13	8	36 (229)	355,102	155,379
Yale University (Yale Law School) P.O. Box 208329 New Haven, CT 06520-8215 203-432-4995 admissions.law@yale.edu	$75	Feb 15	March 15	$50,275	$50,275	4		4		4		83	21		4	4	629	24	49	32		65 (54)	1,294,682	321,732
Yeshiva University (Benjamin N. Cardozo School of Law) 55 Fifth Avenue New York, NY 10003 212-790-0274 Fax: 212-790-0482 lawinfo@yu.edu	$75	April 1	April 15	$4,788	$47,800	4				4		84	55		4	4	1038 (102)	24	52	22	7	58 (107)	579,289	1,338,310

Regional Maps Locating Many ABA-Approved Law Schools

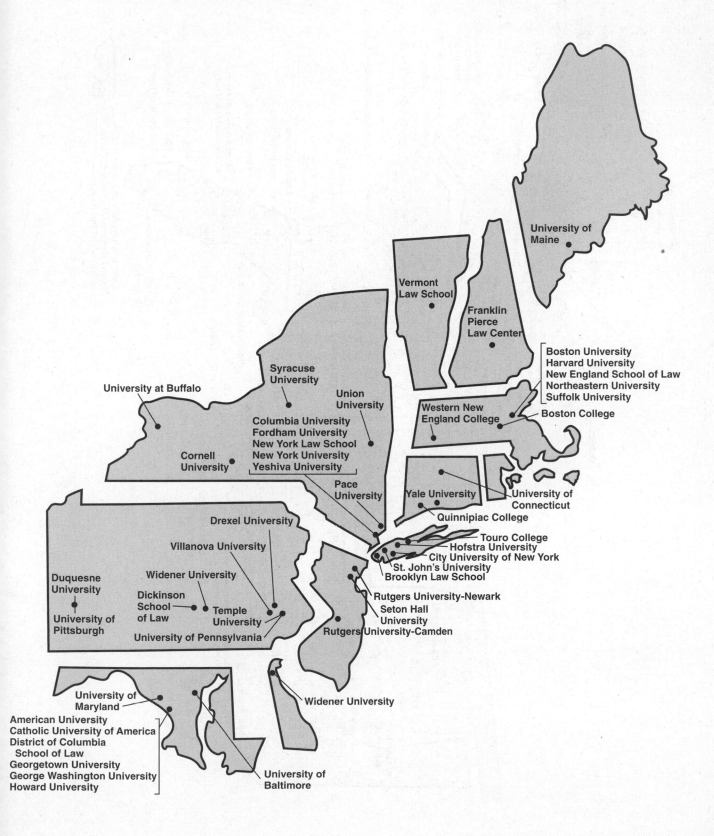

University of Maine

Vermont Law School

Franklin Pierce Law Center

Syracuse University

University at Buffalo

Union University

Boston University
Harvard University
New England School of Law
Northeastern University
Suffolk University

Boston College

Western New England College

Columbia University
Fordham University
New York Law School
New York University
Yeshiva University

Cornell University

Pace University

Yale University

University of Connecticut

Quinnipiac College

Drexel University

Touro College
Hofstra University
City University of New York
St. John's University
Brooklyn Law School

Villanova University

Duquesne University

University of Pittsburgh

Widener University

Dickinson School of Law

Temple University

University of Pennsylvania

Rutgers University-Newark

Seton Hall University

Rutgers University-Camden

University of Maryland

Widener University

American University
Catholic University of America
District of Columbia
 School of Law
Georgetown University
George Washington University
Howard University

University of Baltimore

CHAPTER 15

Profiles of ABA-Approved Law Schools

The school profiles included in Barron's *Guide to Law Schools* comprise a listing of law schools that are fully or provisionally approved by the American Bar Association and grant the J.D. degree. (One ABA-approved law school, the Judge Advocate General's School, located in Charlottesville, Virginia, and associated with the U.S. Army, is not included in our listings because it offers post-J.D. programs only.) The schools are arranged in alphabetical order by the name of the institution to which they are attached or, for independent law schools, by the name of the school. Also included for your convenience is a listing of the law schools by state.

So that you may use the profiles to best advantage, an explanation of the entries follows.

THE HEADING

The first-page heading of each profile presents the official name of the parent college or university (if any) and of the law school and the law school mailing address. The page two heading of each entry contains phone and fax numbers, followed by e-mail and web addresses; names and phone numbers of admissions and financial aid contacts; and a map showing the location within the respective state of each school.

THE CAPSULE

The capsule of each profile provides basic information about the law school. Wherever *n/av* is used in the capsule, it means the information was not available. Wherever *none* or *n/app* is used in the capsule, it means the category was not applicable to the law school.

Application filing dates and fees lead off the capsule.

Accrediting agencies, and **degrees granted** fill out this section of the capsule.

Accreditation Every school profiled is fully or provisionally approved by the American Bar Association. This means that the law school has met the educational standards set by the ABA regarding faculty, curricula, facilities, and other matters to qualify its graduates for admission to the Bar. In addition, membership in the Association of American Law Schools (AALS) is also indicated. Schools are not eligible for AALS membership until they have graduated three classes and have been in operation for five years. AALS membership is complementary to, but *not* competitive with, ABA approval.

Degrees Granted Law schools today offer the J.D. (Juris Doctor) degree, rather than the traditional LL.B. This recognizes the fact that virtually all law schools now require a B.A. for admission and that the curriculum of the law school represents graduate-level work. Law schools offering post-law school graduate work leading to such degrees as the LL.M. (Master of Laws), M.C.L. (Master of Comparative Law), and J.S.D. (Doctor of the Science of Law) degrees are noted.

These data are followed by **enrollment** figures for men, women, and minorities, and out-of-state students in the first-year class. Actual figures and percentages are both given.

This section also includes the number of applicants, accepted candidates, and enrolled first-year students.

The current **class profile** includes LSAT scoring and passing-the-bar information.

Finally, **tuition and fees** are graphically displayed for both in- and out-of-state applicants, showing comparisons with average nationwide figures. It is important to remember that tuition costs generally change at least yearly, and that changes can be substantial. Students are therefore urged to contact individual law schools for the most current tuition figures.

Also shown in this section is the percentage of current law students receiving **financial aid.**

Admissions The **admissions** section leads off the law school's descriptive passages, where some of the capsule information is reinforced.

The subsection *Requirements* includes whether a bachelor's degree is an absolute necessity and lists the factors considered in the admissions decision, such as LSAT percentile, GPA, and any nonacademic requirements. Virtually all of the law schools require the LSAT and a bachelor's degree, although some schools admit students without a bachelor's degree in exceptional cases. Very few schools require specific undergraduate courses or degrees or an admissions interview. Although not actual requirements, there are some qualities that schools seek in their applicants, such as preferred LSAT percentiles and GPAs. Where available, these preferred qualities also are given.

The subsection *Procedure* lists the application deadlines for various sessions, when the LSAT should be taken, the application fee, and when students are notified of the admissions decision. If a school makes admissions decisions on a rolling basis, it decides on each application as soon as possible after the file is complete and does not specify a notification deadline. As a general rule, it is best to submit applications as early as possible. Many schools require a tuition deposit to hold a place in the class. In some cases the deposit is refundable; in some, it is partially refundable; and in some, it is nonrefundable. Most schools participate in the Law School Data Assembly Service (LSDAS); if the school uses this application service, it is noted in this section.

The subsection *Special* describes admissions programs and includes information on special recruiting procedures and considerations for minority and disadvantaged students; whether the school's requirements for out-of-state students differ and whether transfer students are admitted. Although requirements for transfer with advanced standing differ from school to school, in general the applicant must have been in good standing at the school he or she is transferring from and must have completed a minimum of one year of law school study. Preadmissions courses offered by the school are also described.

Costs As noted in the explanation for the capsule, costs change from year to year; therefore, students are urged to contact the individual law schools for the most current figures. This section gives costs for tuition, additional fees, room and board, and books and supplies.

Financial Aid This section describes the availability of financial aid. It includes the percentage of students who receive aid; the types and sources of aid available, such as scholarships, grants, loans, part-time jobs, and assistantships; and the criteria for aid awards. The size of the average scholarship or grant is noted. Information on aid application deadlines and notification dates is also provided.

THE GENERAL DESCRIPTION

About the Law School This paragraph indicates, in general, whether the law school is part of a university or college, when it was founded, whether it is public or private, and its religious affiliation, if any. The school's educational philosophy, primary goals, and major characteristics are noted. Because law school programs often make use of law-related institutions, such as courts, jails, and public defenders' offices, the school's proximity to such institutions is noted. There is also information on the law school's facilities: the campus (its size, the type of area in which it is located, and its proximity to a large city); whether housing is available on campus; and whether the housing office helps students find off-campus accommodations. This section also describes the percentage of the campus accessible to physically disabled persons.

Calendar This section describes whether courses are offered for full-time and/or part-time students and whether they are offered during the day and/or evening. It also describes the minimum and maximum lengths of time allowed for completion of the program, when new students may enter the program, the availability of summer sessions, and the availability of transferable summer credits.

Programs Entries list the degrees granted, including graduate law degrees and joint degrees.

The subsection *Required* describes the number of credits needed for the J.D. and the minimum grade point average that must be maintained. The specific mandatory course requirements are listed, as well as any additional requirements for graduation. At some law schools required courses make up a major portion of the curriculum, whereas at others there are fewer required courses, allowing more room for electives. The majority of schools have a fairly even mix of mandatory and elective courses, although in most cases first-year courses are prescribed. Many law schools permit students to take a limited number of relevant graduate courses offered by other schools or departments of the institution.

Special programs are described in the subsection *Electives*. Clinical training programs offer a wide range of activities allied with, but separate from, traditional classroom studies. They cover such areas as working with legal aid societies and antipoverty groups; doing research for consumer-protection agencies; working with public defender programs or as interns in federal, district, or county attorneys' offices; and engaging in a multitude of legal or quasilegal activities. Some law schools offer a variety of programs and special activities, which allow all students to participate in some way. Other law schools have narrow or limited programs, or limit the number of students who may participate. Some schools have special or unusual seminars; some have programs involving study abroad; and some allow students to pursue independent study, usually under the supervision of a member of the law school faculty. Some schools also have tutorial or remedial programs. The most widely taken electives are listed here.

The subsection *Graduation Requirements* describes the minimum grade point average a student must maintain, whether or not there is an upper-division writing requirement, and what other requirements must be fulfilled.

Organizations Virtually all law schools have student-edited law reviews; some law schools publish more than one law review and some publish other types of legal journals and newspapers as well. Students selected to work on these publications gain valuable research, writing, and editing experience. Most schools also have moot court programs and engage in intramural and interschool competitions. Other campus activities and organizations, such as special interest or academic clubs and sororities and fraternities, are also listed in this section.

Library This section lists the resources of the law library, such as the total number of hardcopy volumes, the number of microform volume equivalents, the number of serial publications, and special collections or depositories. Computerized legal-research databases, such as LEXIS and WESTLAW, are noted, as well as the ratio of library volumes to faculty and to students, and the ratio of seats in the library to students. Recent improvements to the library are also described.

Faculty The number of full-time and part-time faculty members is given here. The percentage of full-time faculty members with a graduate law degree is noted. The ratio of full-time students to full-time faculty in an average class and in a clinic are noted here. In addition to regular classroom lectures, those law schools that have a regular program of inviting legal scholars, attorneys, and other notable speakers to campus to lecture on law-related topics are indicated. If the school has a chapter of the Order of the Coif, a national law school honor society, this is also noted here; the number of faculty who are members as well as the number of recent graduates who became members are sometimes given. Only students who are in the top 10 percent of their class are eligible for membership.

Students This paragraph gives an idea of the mix of backgrounds at a school. It includes, where available, data on the geographic distribution of the student body and on how many students enter directly from undergraduate school, have a graduate degree, or have full-time work experience. The average age of entering students is given, as is the age range. The attrition rate and reasons for discontinuing law study are noted.

The **Placement** sidebar is the final section offered for each school entry. Displayed here is information concerning the number of J.D.s awarded the previous academic year, followed by a listing of the placement services and special features available to students. Statistics relating to job interviews and job placement (and average starting salaries) follow. Finally, a breakdown of placement history is presented.

INDEX BY STATE OF ABA-APPROVED LAW SCHOOLS

ALABAMA
Faulkner University
Samford University
University of Alabama

ARIZONA
Arizona State University
Phoenix School of Law
University of Arizona

ARKANSAS
University of Arkansas
University of Arkansas at Little Rock

CALIFORNIA
American College of Law
California School of Law
California Western School of Law
Chapman University
Golden Gate University
Lincoln Law School
Loyola Marymount University
Pepperdine University
Santa Clara University
Southwestern University
Stanford University
Thomas Jefferson School of Law
Trinity International University School of Law
University of California
University of California at Berkeley
University of California at Davis
University of California at Los Angeles
University of La Verne
University of San Diego
University of San Francisco
University of Southern California
University of the Pacific
University of West Los Angeles
Western State University
Whittier College

COLORADO
University of Colorado
University of Denver

CONNECTICUT
Quinnipiac University
University of Connecticut
Yale University

DELAWARE
Widener University

DISTRICT OF COLUMBIA
American University
Catholic University of America
George Washington University
Georgetown University
Howard University
University of the District of Columbia

FLORIDA
Ave Maria School of Law
Barry University
Florida Agricultural and Mechanical University
Florida Coastal
Florida International University
Florida State University
Nova Southeastern University
Saint Thomas University
Stetson University
University of Florida
University of Miami

GEORGIA
Atlanta's John Marshall Law School
Emory University

Georgia State University
Mercer University
University of Georgia

HAWAII
University of Hawaii at Manoa

IDAHO
University of Idaho

ILLINOIS
De Paul University
Illinois Institute of Technology
John Marshall Law School
Loyola University Chicago
Northern Illinois University
Northwestern University
Southern Illinois University
University of Chicago
University of Illinois

INDIANA
Indiana University
Indiana University-Purdue University at Indianapolis
University of Notre Dame
Valparaiso University

IOWA
Drake University
University of Iowa

KANSAS
University of Kansas
Washburn University

KENTUCKY
Northern Kentucky University
University of Kentucky
University of Louisville

LOUISIANA
Louisiana State University
Loyola University of New Orleans
Southern University and A & M College
Tulane University

MAINE
University of Maine

MARYLAND
University of Baltimore
University of Maryland

MASSACHUSETTS
Boston College
Boston University
Harvard University
Massachusetts School of Law
New England School of Law
Northeastern University
Southern New England School of Law
Suffolk University
Western New England College

MICHIGAN
Michigan State University
Thomas M. Cooley Law School
University of Detroit Mercy
University of Michigan
Wayne State University

MINNESOTA
Hamline University
University of Minnesota
University of Saint Thomas
William Mitchell College of Law

MISSISSIPPI
Mississippi College
University of Mississippi

MISSOURI
Saint Louis University
University of Missouri-Columbia
University of Missouri-Kansas City
Washington University in St. Louis

MONTANA
University of Montana

NEBRASKA
Creighton University
University of Nebraska-Lincoln

NEVADA
University of Nevada, Las Vegas

NEW HAMPSHIRE
Franklin Pierce Law Center

NEW JERSEY
Rutgers University/Camden
Rutgers University/Newark
Seton Hall University

NEW MEXICO
University of New Mexico

NEW YORK
Albany Law School
Brooklyn Law School
City University of New York
Columbia University
Cornell University
Fordham University
Hofstra University
New York Law School
New York University
Pace University
Saint John's University
State University of New York
Syracuse University
Touro College
Yeshiva University

NORTH CAROLINA
Campbell University
Charlotte School of Law
Duke University
Elon University
North Carolina Central University
University of North Carolina at Chapel Hill
Wake Forest University

NORTH DAKOTA
University of North Dakota

OHIO
Capital University
Case Western Reserve University
Cleveland State University
Ohio Northern University
Ohio State University
University of Akron
University of Cincinnati
University of Dayton
University of Toledo

OKLAHOMA
Oklahoma City University
University of Oklahoma
University of Tulsa

OREGON
Lewis and Clark College
University of Oregon
Willamette University

PENNSYLVANIA
Drexel University
Duquesne University
Pennsylvania State University
Temple University
University of Pennsylvania
University of Pittsburgh
Villanova University
Widener University

PUERTO RICO
Inter American University of Puerto Rico
Pontifical Catholic University of Puerto Rico
University of Puerto Rico

RHODE ISLAND
Roger Williams University

SOUTH CAROLINA
Charleston School of Law
University of South Carolina

SOUTH DAKOTA
University of South Dakota

TENNESSEE
University of Memphis
University of Tennessee
Vanderbilt University

TEXAS
Baylor University
Saint Mary's University
South Texas College of Law
Southern Methodist University
Texas Southern University
Texas Tech University
Texas Wesleyan University
University of Houston
University of Texas at Austin

UTAH
Brigham Young University
University of Utah

VERMONT
Vermont Law School

VIRGINIA
Appalachian School of Law
College of William & Mary
George Mason University
Liberty University
Regent University
University of Richmond
University of Virginia
Washington and Lee University

WASHINGTON
Gonzaga University
Seattle University
University of Washington

WEST VIRGINIA
West Virginia University

WISCONSIN
Marquette University
University of Wisconsin

WYOMING
University of Wyoming

80 New Scotland Avenue
Albany, NY 12208

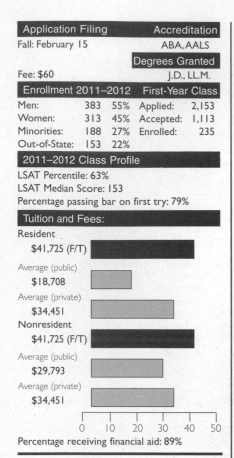

Application Filing	Accreditation
Fall: February 15	ABA, AALS

	Degrees Granted
Fee: $60	J.D., LL.M.

Enrollment 2011–2012   First-Year Class

Men:	383	55%	Applied:	2,153
Women:	313	45%	Accepted:	1,113
Minorities:	188	27%	Enrolled:	235
Out-of-State:	153	22%		

2011–2012 Class Profile

LSAT Percentile: 63%
LSAT Median Score: 153
Percentage passing bar on first try: 79%

Tuition and Fees:

Resident
$41,725 (F/T)

Average (public)
$18,708

Average (private)
$34,451

Nonresident
$41,725 (F/T)

Average (public)
$29,793

Average (private)
$34,451

0 10 20 30 40 50

Percentage receiving financial aid: 89%

ADMISSIONS

In the fall of 2011 first-year class, 2153 applied, 1113 were accepted, and 235 enrolled. Four transfers enrolled. The median LSAT percentile of the most recent first-year class was 63; the median GPA was 3.3 on a scale of 4.0.

Requirements

Applicants must have a bachelor's degree and take the LSAT. The most important admission factors include academic achievement, LSAT results, and general background. No specific undergraduate courses are required. Candidates are not interviewed.

Procedure

The application deadline for fall entry is February 15. Applicants should submit an application form, LSAT results, transcripts, a personal statement, the TOEFL (if applicable), a nonrefundable application fee of $60, and 2 letters of recommendation. Notification of the admissions decision is on a rolling basis. The law school uses the LSAC.

Special

The law school recruits minority and disadvantaged students through current minority students who assist the Admissions Office by recruiting at colleges and universities with large minority populations, by offering tuition scholarships and grants that are awarded to more than half of the accepted minority applicants, and by increased outreach by minority alumni. Requirements are different for out-of-state students. Transfer students must have one year of credit, must have attended an ABA-approved law school, and must submit a personal statement.

Costs

Tuition and fees for the 2011–2012 academic year are $41,570 for all full-time students. Tuition for part-time students is $31,180 for in-state students and $31,180 out-of-state. Books and supplies run $1,100.

Financial Aid

About 89% of current law students receive some form of aid. The average annual amount of aid from all sources combined, including scholarships, loans, and work contracts, is $51,647; maximum, $59,720. Awards are based on need and merit, along with diversity. The required financial statement is the FAFSA. The aid application deadline for fall entry is rolling. Special funds for minority or disadvantaged students include diversity scholarships and full or partial tuition waivers. First-year students are notified about their financial aid application at time of acceptance.

About the Law School

Albany Law School was established in 1851 and is independent. The 6-acre campus is in an urban area 150 miles north of New York City. The primary mission of the law school is to provide students with a quality education in accordance with ethical principles and professional standards. The curriculum is traditional, yet innovative, and stresses legal knowledge, professional skills, thought habits, and contemporary techniques and technologies. Students have access to federal, state, county, city, and local agencies, courts, correctional facilities, law firms, and legal aid organizations in the Albany area. Facilities of special interest to law students are the New York State Legislature, State House, and all government agencies. Inexpensive off-campus housing is readily available as well as privately owned dorm-style housing adjacent to campus. About 98% of the law school facilities are accessible to the physically disabled.

Calendar

The law school operates on a traditional semester basis. Courses for full-time students are offered days only, and must be completed within 3 years. For part-time students, courses are offered days only, and must be completed within 4 years. New full- and part-time students are admitted in the fall. There is a 7-week summer session. Transferable summer courses are offered.

Programs

In addition to the J.D., the law school offers the LL.M. The following joint degrees may be earned: J.D./M.B.A. (Juris Doctor/Master of Business Administration), J.D./M.P.A. (Juris Doctor/Master of Public Administation), J.D./M.R.P. (Juris Doctor/Master of Regional Planning), and J.D./M.S. (Juris Doctor/Master of Science in bioethics).

Required

To earn the J.D., candidates must complete 87 total credits, of which 42 are for required courses. They must maintain a minimum GPA of 1.7 in the required courses. The following first-year courses are required of all students: Constitutional Law I and II, Contracts I and II, Criminal Law, Evidence, Introduction to Civil Procedure, Introduction to Lawyering, Legal Methods, Property I and II, and Torts. Required upper-level courses consist of an upper-class writing requirement and The Legal Professional /Professional Responsibility seminar. The required orientation program for first-year students is a weeklong program that includes a "Legal Methods" class, social activities, and administrative activities.

Phone: 518-445-2326
Fax: 518-445-2369
E-mail: *admissions@albanylaw.edu*
Web: *www.albanylaw.edu*

Contact
Nadia Castriota, Assistant Dean for Admissions, 518-445-2326 for general inquiries; Andrea Wedler, Director of Financial Aid, 518-445-2357 for financial aid information.

Electives

The school offers concentrations in corporate law, criminal law, environmental law, family law, intellectual property law, internationl law, labor law, litigation, securities law, tax law, commercial law, constitutional law, civil procedure, health law, estate law, government administration and regulation, court administration, and perspectives on law and legal systems. In addition, a clinical program enables upper-level students to obtain practical experience in a public law office. A classroom component is available; students may earn 12 credits, 2 to 6 each semester. Clinics include the Civil Rights and Disabilities Law Project, Health Law Project, Litigation Project, Domestic Violence Project, Securities Arbitration Project, and Low-Income Taxpayer's Project. Seminars, worth 2 or 3 credits each semester, and research assistantships are open to upper-level students. Internships in government agencies are offered through the Government Law Center, and externships in public law offices are arranged through the Placement Clinic. Annual special lecture series include the Justice Jackson and the Edward L. Sobota Memorial Lecture Series. Summer study abroad may be arranged through other ABA-accredited law schools for upper-level students. Albany Law School offers the Nairobi International Institute in partnership with Widener University School of Law, the International Human Rights Internship Program, and the University of Paris Exchange Program. Tutorial programs include the Lewis A. Swyer Academic Success Program, which provides small-group and individual instruction in legal reasoning, case analysis and synthesis, writing, and study skills. Entering students who have been out of the academic environment for several years, those whose academic backgrounds differ substantially, and those with language, physical, or emotional handicaps are eligible. In addition to an extensive Diversity Scholarship program, a number of programs are sponsored by faculty, alumni, and student organizations for those students with unusual backgrounds, including those minorities who historically have been underrepresented in the legal profession. Several societies offer lectures, symposia, and other events, including the International Law Society and Environmental Law Society. The most widely taken electives are Business Organizations, Evidence, and New York Practice.

Graduation Requirements

In order to graduate, candidates must have a GPA of 2.0, and must have completed the upper-division writing requirement.

Organizations
Students edit the *Albany Law Review, Albany Law Journal of Science and Technology*, the *Albany Government Law Review*, the student newspaper *The Issue*, and the yearbook *The Verdict*. Intraschool moot court competitions include the Domenick L. Gabrielli Appellate Advocacy Competition, the Karen C. McGovern Senior Prize Trials, and the Donna Jo Morse Client Counseling Competition. Other interschool competitions include ABA Client Counseling, ABA Negotiations, and ABA National Appellate Advocacy competitions. Law student organizations, local chapters of national associations, and campus clubs include the Environmental Law Society, International Law Society, Intellectual Property Law Society, Phi Alpha Delta, Student Lawyers Guild, Amnesty International, Black Law Students Association, Latino Law Students Association, and Asian Pacific American Law Students Association.

Library
The law library contains 292,140 hardcopy volumes and 429,883 microform volume equivalents, and subscribes to 1,691 serial publications. Such online databases and networks as CALI, CIS Universe, DIALOG, LEXIS, Mathew Bender, OCLC First Search, WESTLAW, Wilsonline Indexes, New York Legislature Retrieval System, Court of Appeals online information service, and PACER are available to law students for research. Special library collections include a U.S. government documents depository, New York State documents research depository, and a New York Court of Appeals oral argument videotape repository. The ratio of library volumes to faculty is 5,963 to 1 and to students is 379 to 1. The ratio of seats in the library to students is 1 to 6.

Faculty
The law school has 55 full-time and 52 part-time faculty members, of whom 40 are women. About 25% of full-time faculty have a graduate law degree in addition to

Placement	
J.D.s awarded:	239

Services available through: a separate law school placement center.

Services: on-campus interviews with law firms, government agencies, public interest organizations, and businesses; off-campus interview programs in selected cities; job fairs and employer information sessions; career education programs; workshops; and panel discussions.

Special features: the law school graduate employment rate has exceeded the national average for more than a quarter of a century.

Full-time job interviews:	78 employers
Placement within 9 months:	91% of class
Average starting salary:	$32,500 to $175,000

Areas of placement:

Private practice 2–10 attorneys	24%
Private practice 11–23 attorneys	8%
Private practice 26–50 attorneys	5%
Private practice 101+ attorneys	20%
Business/industry	23%
Judicial clerkships	9%
Public interest	5%
Government	4%

the J.D. The ratio of full-time students to full-time faculty in an average class is 13 to 1; in a clinic, 8 to 1. The law school has a regular program of bringing visiting professors and other distinguished lecturers and visitors to campus.

Students
About 45% of the student body are women; 27%, minorities; 2%, African American; 5%, Asian American; 2%, Hispanic; and 1%, Native American. The majority of students come from New York (78%). The average age of entering students is 24; age range is 20 to 47. About 49% of students enter directly from undergraduate school, and 49% have worked full-time prior to entering law school. About 1% drop out after the first year for academic or personal reasons; 99% remain to receive a law degree.

AMERICAN UNIVERSITY
Washington College of Law

4801 Massachusetts Avenue, N.W.
Washington, DC 20016-8186

Application Filing	Accreditation
Fall: March 1	ABA, AALS

Degrees Granted
Fee: $70	J.D., LL.M., S.J.D.

Enrollment 2011–2012   First-Year Class

Men:	668	45%	Applied:	7,521
Women:	831	57%	Accepted:	2,075
Minorities:	525	35%	Enrolled:	475
Out-of-State:	n/av			

2011–2012 Class Profile
LSAT Percentile: 85%
LSAT Median Score: 162
Percentage passing bar on first try: 80%

Tuition and Fees:

Resident
$45,096 (F/T)

Average (public)
$18,708

Average (private)
$34,451

Nonresident
$45,096 (F/T)

Average (public)
$29,793

Average (private)
$34,451

0   10   20   30   40   50

Percentage receiving financial aid: 86%

ADMISSIONS
In the fall of 2011 first-year class, 7521 applied, 2075 were accepted, and 475 enrolled. Fifty-eight transfers enrolled. The median LSAT percentile of the most recent first-year class was 85; the median GPA was 3.4 on a scale of 4.0. The lowest LSAT percentile accepted was 47; the highest was 98.

Requirements
Applicants must have a bachelor's degree and take the LSAT. The most important admission factors include academic achievement, GPA, and LSAT results. No specific undergraduate courses are required. Candidates are not interviewed.

Procedure
The application deadline for fall entry is March 1. Applicants must submit their application form, LSAT results, transcripts, a personal statement, a nonrefundable application fee of $70, and a letter of recommendation. Notification of the admissions decision begins in late November. The law school uses the LSAC.

Special
The law school recruits minority and disadvantaged students in collaboration with the Office of Admissions and Office of Diversity Services. Every effort is made to attend recruiting events that are targeted to enroll the most diverse class possible. Requirements are different for out-of-state students. Transfer students must have one year of credit, attended an ABA-approved law school, a personal statement, and academic achievement.

Costs
Tuition and fees for the 2011–2012 academic year are $44,234 for all full-time students. Tuition for part-time students is $31,122 for in-state students and $31,122 out-of-state. On-campus room and board costs about $15,102 annually; books and supplies run $1,500.

Financial Aid
About 86% of current law students receive some form of aid. The average annual amount of aid from all sources combined, including scholarships, loans, and work contracts, is $56,131; maximum, $96,171. Awards are based on need and merit combined. Required financial statements are the FAFSA and Need Access Application. The aid application deadline for fall entry is March 1. Special funds for minority or disadvantaged students include need-based grants and donor-sponsored scholarships. First-year students are notified about their financial aid application within 2 weeks of acceptance, provided application is made by the filing deadline.

About the Law School
American University Washington College of Law was established in 1896 and is a private institution. The campus is in an urban area in Washington, D.C., 3 miles from downtown. The primary mission of the law school is to provide an individualized, high-quality legal education by engaging the community, the nation, and the world through a vision that integrates theory and practice, doctrine and experiential learning, and skills and values, all in a diverse and demanding environment. Students have access to federal, state, county, city, and local agencies, courts, correctional facilities, law firms, and legal aid organizations in the Washington area, including the U.S. Congress, U.S. Supreme Court, Library of Congress, IMF, World Bank, and other NGO's Facilities. Of special interest to law students is more than 1000 approved extern sites at federal agencies, courts, trade associations, and public interest organizations. Housing for students is easily found in many apartment buildings and private homes, which are located nearby. All law school facilities are accessible to the physically disabled.

Calendar
The law school operates on a traditional semester basis. Courses for full-time students are offered both day and evening, and must be completed within 5 years. For part-time students, courses are offered both day and evening, and must be completed within 6 years. New full- and part-time students are admitted in the fall. There is a 9-week summer session. Transferable summer courses are offered.

Programs
In addition to the J.D., the law school offers the LL.M. and S.J.D. Students may take relevant courses in other programs and apply credit toward the J.D.; a maximum of 6 credits may be applied. The following joint degrees may be earned: J.D./M.A. (Juris Doctor/Master of Arts in International Affairs), J.D./M.B.A. (Juris Doctor/Master of Business Administration), J.D./M.P.A. (Juris Doctor/Master of Public Administration), J.D./M.P.P. (Juris Doctor/Master of Public Policy), J.D./M.S. (Juris Doctor/Master of Science in Law, Justice, and Society), LL.M./LL.M. (Master of Law in International Legal Studies/Master of Law in Law and Government), LL.M./LL.M. (Master of Law in Law and Government/Master of Law in Trial Advocacy), LL.M./M.B.A. (Master of Law/Master of Business Administration), LL.M./M.P.A. (Master of Law/Master of Public Administration), and LL.M./M.P.P. (Master of Law/Master of Public Policy).

Required
To earn the J.D., candidates must complete 86 total credits, of which 32 are for required courses. They must maintain a minimum GPA of 2.0 in the required courses. The following first-year courses

Phone: 202-274-4101
Fax: 202-274-4107
E-mail: wcladmit@wcl.american.edu
Web: www.wcl.american.edu

Contact

Admissions Office, 202-274-4101 for general inquiries; Financial Aid Office, 202-274-4040 for financial aid information.

DISTRICT OF COLUMBIA

are required of all students: Contracts, Criminal Law, Legal Rhetoric I and II, Property, Torts, Civil Procedure, and Constitutional Law. Required upper-level courses consist of Criminal Procedure I and Legal Ethics. The required orientation program for first-year students is 3 days and includes registration, dean's and faculty welcome, academic orientation, technology and financial aid sessions, a reception, and Student Bar Association social activities.

Electives

The Washington College of Law offers concentrations in corporate law, criminal law, environmental law, family law, intellectual property law, internation law, juvenile law, labor law, litigation, securities law, tax law, torts and insurance, human rights law, arbitration, international, environment, and administrative law. In addition, clinical experiences offered to students include: the Civil Practice Clinic, International Human Rights Law Clinic, and Community and Economic Development Clinic. Internships are also available, under faculty supervision, with government agencies, international organizations, and non-profit entities. The Independent Study Program permits directed research under faculty supervision. The Field Component Program offers field work with the Securities and Exchange Commission, the Commodities Futures Trading Commission, the State Department, and the National Association of Securities Dealers. Special lectures include an extensive series of conferences and speaker series that deal with topics of contemporary interest. Student organizations sponsor lectures and panel discussions on a wide range of topics. Study abroad consists of summer programs in Chile (study involving legal structures in Latin America), Istanbul, London/Paris/Geneva (international business, human rights, and environmental law); a semester exchange: Paris-X Nanterre, France; Hong Kong Exchange; Canada, Mexico, Netherlands, Belgium, Finland, Germany, Australia, Spain; and dual degree programs in Spain and Canada. There is a Peer Counseling Program. An academic support program is available for all students, but remedial programs are not provided. The Office of Diversity Services offers minority programs and advisory services. The most widely taken electives are Evidence, Business Associations, and Administrative Law.

Graduation Requirements

In order to graduate, candidates must have a GPA of 2.0, completed the upper-division writing requirement, and a lawyering skills requirement.

Organizations

Students edit the *American University Law Review, Administrative Law Review*, (ABA Section Publication), *American University International Law Review, American University Journal of Gender, Social Policy and the Law, American Jurist, Business Law Brief, Criminal Law Brief, Human Rights Brief, Modern American*, and *Sustainable Development Law and Policy*. Three moot court competitions are Alvina Reckman Myers First-Year Moot Court Competition, the Inter-American Moot Court Competition, and the Burton D. Wechsler First Amendment Moot Court Competition. Students participate in approximately 12 competitions, including the Jean Pictet Competition, and the VIS Moot International Arbitration Team. Law student organizations, local chapters of national associations, and campus organizations include Equal Justice Foundation, Law and Government Society, Women's Law Association, American Constitution Society, Black Law Students Association, Hispanic Law Students Association, Lambda Law Society, Federalist Society, and Phi Delta Phi.

Library

The law library contains 664,783 hardcopy volumes, 109,220 microform volume equivalents, and subscribes to 5,594 serial publications. Online databases and networks include CALI, CIS Universe, DIALOG, Dow-Jones, Infotrac, Legal-Trac, LEXIS, Mathew Bender, OCLC First Search, RLIN, WESTLAW, and Wilsonline Indexes. HeinOnline, Access UN, UN Human Rights, UN Treaty, BNA, CCH, and MOML are also available to law students for research. Special library collections include European Community and U.S. government depositories, as well as the Baxter Collection in International Law, Cicchino Collection, Goodman Collection of Rare Books, Iran-Contra Affair, Judicial Documents Collection, the National Bank Rev. Collection, and Neal Miller Legal Fiction. The ratio of library volumes to faculty is 6,647 to 1 and to students is 379 to 1. The ratio of seats in the library to students is 1 to 3.

Placement

J.D.s awarded:	459

Services available through: a separate law school placement center.

Services: mock interview programs, access to alumni mentors and regional recruitment programs in Boston, Los Angeles, and New York.

Special features: 7 full-time career counselors all with JDs. Several counselors have specific areas of focus including international, judicial, public interest, government, and alumni counseling.

Full-time job interviews:	39 employers
Summer job interviews:	93 employers
Placement by graduation:	69% of class
Placement within 9 months:	84% of class
Average starting salary:	$42,250 to $160,000

Areas of placement:

Private practice 2–10 attorneys	11%
Private practice 11–23 attorneys	4%
Private practice 26–50 attorneys	2%
Private practice 51–100 attorneys	2%
Government	21%
Business/industry	18%
Public interest	13%
Judicial clerkships	12%
Academic	1%

Faculty

The law school has 102 full-time and 142 part-time faculty members, of whom 94 are women. According to AAUP standards for Category I institutions, faculty salaries are above average. About 24% of full-time faculty have a graduate law degree in addition to the J.D.; about 23% of part-time faculty have one. The ratio of full-time students to full-time faculty in an average class is 11 to 1; in a clinic, 8 to 1. The law school has a regular program of bringing visiting professors and other distinguished lecturers and visitors to campus. There is a chapter of the Order of the Coif; 454 graduates are members.

Students

About 57% of the student body are women; 35%, minorities; 9%, African American; 8%, Asian American; 15%, Hispanic; and 1%, Native American. The majority of students come from the Midwest (12%). The average age of entering students is 24; age range is 20 to 52. About 5% drop out after the first year for academic or personal reasons; 95% remain to receive a law degree.

P.O. Box 2825
Grundy, VA 24614

Application Filing	Accreditation
Fall: June 1	ABA
	Degrees Granted
Fee: $60	J.D.

Enrollment 2011–2012		First-Year Class	
Men:	220 65%	Applied:	1,630
Women:	120 35%	Accepted:	630
Minorities:	20 6%	Enrolled:	0
Out-of-State:	252 74%		

2011–2012 Class Profile
LSAT Percentile: 40%
LSAT Median Score: 149
Percentage passing bar on first try: 73%

Tuition and Fees:

Resident
$30,025 (F/T)

Average (public)
$18,708

Average (private)
$34,451

Nonresident
$27,025 (F/T)

Average (public)
$29,793

Average (private)
$34,451

0   10   20   30   40   50

Percentage receiving financial aid: 95%

ADMISSIONS

In the fall of 2011 first-year class, 1630 applied, 630 were accepted, and enrolled. Seven transfer students enrolled. The median LSAT percentile of the most recent first-year class was 40; the median GPA was 3.1 on a scale of 4.0. The lowest LSAT percentile accepted was 32; the highest was 55.

Requirements
Applicants must have a bachelor's degree and take the LSAT. Minimum acceptable GPA is 2.0 on a scale of 4.0. The most important admission factors include GPA, LSAT results, and academic achievement. No specific undergraduate courses are required and candidates are not interviewed.

Procedure
The application deadline for fall entry is June 1. Applicants should submit an application form, LSAT results, transcripts, personal statement, nonrefundable application fee of $60, and 2 letters of recommendation. Notification of the admissions decision is after December 31. The law school uses the LSAC.

Special
The law school recruits minority and disadvantaged students by attending events at schools with minority student populations; distributing targeted literature; and through its mentoring program. Requirements are different for out-of-state students. Transfer students must submit a personal statement and 2.0 GPA at an ABA-approved or state-approved law school.

Costs

Tuition and fees for the 2011–2012 academic year are $29,500 for full-time in-state students and $26,500 for out-of-state students. Books and supplies run $1,500.

Financial Aid

About 95% of current law students receive some form of aid. The average annual amount of aid from all sources combined, including scholarships, loans, and work contracts, is $31,171; maximum, $41,090. Awards are based on need and merit combined. Required financial statements are the FAFSA, and Students applying for need-based aid are required to complete a need assessment application to determine eligibility. The aid application deadline for fall entry is July 1. First-year students are notified about their financial aid application at time of acceptance.

About the Law School

Appalachian School of Law was established in 1997 and is a private institution. The 3-acre campus is located in a small town in downtown Grundy, Virginia. The mission of the law school is to train lawyers to be community leaders. Students have access to federal, state, county, city, and local agencies, courts, correctional facilities, law firms, and legal aid organizations in the Grundy area. There is an adequate supply of rental properties for students off campus. All law school facilities are accessible to the physically disabled.

Calendar

The law school operates on a traditional semester basis. Courses for full-time students are offered days only and must be completed within 5 years. There is no part-time program. New full-time students are admitted in the fall. There is no summer session. Transferable summer courses are not offered.

Programs

Required
To earn the J.D., candidates must complete 90 total credits, of which 69 are for required courses. They must maintain a minimum GPA of 2.0 in the required courses. The following first-year courses are required of all students: Civil Procedure I and II, Contracts I and II, Criminal Law, Introduction to Law, Legal Process I and II, Property I and II, and Torts. Required upper-level courses consist of 2 practicum courses, a seminar, Business Associations, Constitutional Law I and II, Criminal Procedure, Dispute Resolution, Estates and Trusts, Evidence, Externship, Family Law, Payment Systems, Professional Responsibility, and Secured Transactions. The required orientation program for first-year students is 1-week, covering skills needed to be a successful law student, core issues of professionalism, and an introduction to Central Appalachia. A substantive component of the Torts course is also included.

Electives
Offers concentrate on ADR/Lawyers as a Problem Solver. In addition, all students take a 2-credit seminar in their third year. The seminars include Cyberlaw, Environmental Law, and the First Amendment. Students also participate in a 3-credit internship during the summer after their first year. Judicial Chambers, prosecutors' and public defenders' offices, and legal aid organizations are typical placements. An Academic Success Program is open to all first-year students. The most widely taken electives are Remedies, Advanced Torts, and Conflict of Laws.

Graduation Requirements
In order to graduate, candidates must have a GPA of 2.0 and complete the upper-division writing requirement.

Phone: 276-935-4349
800-895-7411
Fax: 276-935-8496
E-mail: *npruitt@asl.edu*
Web: *www.asl.edu*

Contact
Nancy Pruitt, Director of Student Services, 800-895-7411 for general inquiries; Hannah Sawyers, Financial Aid Officer, 800-895-7411 for financial aid information.

VIRGINIA

Organizations
The primary law review is the *Appalachian Journal of Law*. Students also edit the *Appalachian National Resources Law Journal*. There is a National Appellate Advocacy Competition, Wechsler National Criminal Law Competition, Gabrielli National Family Law Competition, ATLA Student Trial Advocacy Competition, ABA Client Counseling Competition, and ABA Negotiation Competition. Law student organizations, local chapters of national organizations, and campus organizations include the Black Law Students Association, Federalist Society, Equal Justice Works, Phi Alpha Delta, ATLA, Phi Delta Phi, Democratic Society, Republican Law Students Association, and Appalachian Women in Law.

Library
The law library contains 128,552 hardcopy volumes and 104,163 microform volume equivalents, and subscribes to 917 serial publications. Online databases and networks include CALI, CIS Universe, DIALOG, Dow-Jones, Infotrac, Legal-Trac, LEXIS, Mathew Bender, OCLC First Search, WESTLAW, CCH, BNA, and HeinOnline, which are available to law students for research. Special library collections include Appalachian Collection, government document depository, and 4th Circuit briefs. The ratio of library volumes to faculty is 6,428 to 1 and to students is 378 to 1.

Faculty
The law school has 20 full-time and 4 part-time faculty members, of whom 10 are women. About 33% of full-time faculty have a graduate law degree in addition to the J.D. The ratio of full-time students to full-time faculty in an average class is 21 to 1. The law school has a regular program of bringing visiting professors and other distinguished lecturers and visitors to campus.

Students
About 35% of the student body are women; 6%, minorities; 1%, African American; 1%, Asian American; and 3%, Hispanic. The majority of students come from Virginia (26%). The average age of entering students is 26; age range is 21 to 55. About 46% of students enter directly from undergraduate school.

Placement

J.D.s awarded:	108

Services available through: a separate law school placement center.

Special features: online job board, subscriptions to job databases, bimonthly career services newsletter, and job search counseling.

Full-time job interviews:	6 employers
Summer job interviews:	5 employers
Placement by graduation:	41% of class
Placement within 9 months:	64% of class
Average starting salary:	$26,000 to $68,000

Areas of placement:

Solo Practice	5%
Private practice 2–10 attorneys	34%
Private practice 11–23 attorneys	3%
Government	19%
Business/industry	12%
Judicial clerkships	8%
Public interest	7%
Military	3%

ARIZONA STATE UNIVERSITY

Sandra Day O'Connor College of Law

1100 South McAllister Avenue
Box 877906
Tempe, AZ 85287-7906

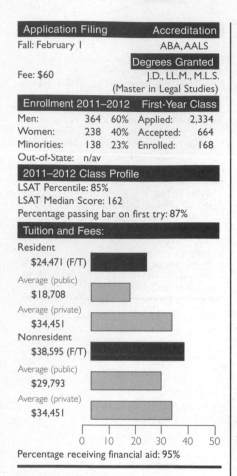

Application Filing	Accreditation
Fall: February 1	ABA, AALS

	Degrees Granted
Fee: $60	J.D., LL.M., M.L.S.
	(Master in Legal Studies)

Enrollment 2011–2012		First-Year Class	
Men:	364 60%	Applied:	2,334
Women:	238 40%	Accepted:	664
Minorities:	138 23%	Enrolled:	168
Out-of-State:	n/av		

2011–2012 Class Profile
LSAT Percentile: 85%
LSAT Median Score: 162
Percentage passing bar on first try: 87%

Tuition and Fees:

Resident
$24,471 (F/T)

Average (public)
$18,708

Average (private)
$34,451

Nonresident
$38,595 (F/T)

Average (public)
$29,793

Average (private)
$34,451

0   10   20   30   40   50

Percentage receiving financial aid: 95%

ADMISSIONS

In the fall of 2011 first-year class, 2334 applied, 664 were accepted, and 168 enrolled. The median LSAT percentile of the most recent first-year class was 85; the median GPA was 3.6 on a scale of 4.3. The lowest LSAT percentile accepted was 27; the highest was 99.

Requirements
Applicants must have a bachelor's degree and take the LSAT. No specific undergraduate courses are required. Candidates are not interviewed.

Procedure
The application deadline for fall entry is February 1. Applicants should submit an application form, LSAT results, transcripts, a personal statement, TOEFL results (if applicable), a nonrefundable application fee of $60, a résumé no longer than 3 typed pages, and statements explaining affirmative answers to the conduct questions.

Notification of the admissions decision is November through May on a rolling basis. The law school uses the LSAC.

Special
The law school recruits minority and disadvantaged students by means of e-mail and mail invitations, personal contact, the involvement of current students and alumni, affordable tuition rates, and scholarship programs. Requirements are different for out-of-state students. Transfer students must have one year of credit, must have attended an ABA-approved law school, and must have a personal statement.

Costs

Tuition and fees for the 2011–2012 academic year are $23,959 for full-time in-state students and $38,083 for out-of-state students. On-campus room and board costs about $12,124 annually; books and supplies run $1,850.

Financial Aid

About 95% of current law students receive some form of aid. The average annual amount of aid from all sources combined, including scholarships, loans, and work contracts, is $37,027; maximum, $87,942. Awards are based on need and merit combined. The required financial statement is the FAFSA. The aid application deadline for fall entry is rolling. Special funds for minority or disadvantaged students exist. First-year students are notified about their financial aid application throughout spring and summer.

About the Law School

Arizona State University Sandra Day O'Connor College of Law was established in 1967 and is a public institution. The 700-acre campus is in an urban area in downtown Tempe, part of the Phoenix Metroplex. The primary mission of the law school is pioneering a new model for twenty-first century legal education, one that reinvents the modern law school as not just an institution that trains lawyers, but as a multifaceted legal studies center that engages in developing solutions to the world's global challenges and that seeks to educate a broad cross-section of contemporary society. Students have access to federal, state, county, city, and local agencies,

courts, correctional facilities, law firms, and legal aid organizations in the Tempe area. More than 150 externships are available. Facilities of special interest to law students abound in Phoenix, the fifth largest city in the U.S. and the largest state capital. It is home to the Chief Judge of the 9th Circuit Court of Appeals, a federal courthouse, the Arizona Supreme Court, Arizona Court of Appeals, and the Arizona legislature. Housing for students is available on campus and designated specifically for graduate students. Housing is found off campus. All law school facilities are accessible to the physically disabled.

Calendar

The law school operates on a traditional semester basis. Courses for full-time and part-time students are offered both day and evening, and must be completed within 84 months. New full-time students are admitted in the fall. There is a 5-week summer session. Transferable summer courses are offered.

Programs

In addition to the J.D., the law school offers the LL.M. and M.L.S. (Master in Legal Studies). Students may take relevant courses in other programs and apply credit toward the J.D.; a maximum of 6 credits may be applied. The following joint degrees may be earned: J.D./M.D. (Juris Doctor/Doctor of Medicine with Mayo Medical School), J.D./M.B.A. (Juris Doctor/Master of Business Administration), J.D./M.S.W. (Juris Doctor/Master of Social Work), J.D./Ph.D. (Juris Doctor/Ph.D. in justice and social inquiry), and J.D/Ph.D. (Juris Doctor/Ph.D. in Psychology).

Required
To earn the J.D., candidates must complete 88 total credits, of which 39 are for required courses. The following first-year courses are required of all students: Civil Procedure, Constitutional Law I, Contracts, Criminal Law, Law and the Regulatory State course, Legal Advocacy, Legal Method and Writing, Property, and Torts. Required upper-level courses consist of Criminal Procedure or Constitutional Law II and Professional Responsibility. The required orientation program for first-year students lasts several days and introduces students to legal professionalism and to the practicalities of legal study.

Phone: 480-965-1474
Fax: 480-727-7930
E-mail: chitra.damania@asu.edu
Web: www.law.asu.edu

Contact
Chitra Damania, Director of Admissions, 480-965-1474 for general inquiries; Joseph Lindsay, Director of Financial Aid, 480-965-1474 for financial aid information.

ARIZONA

Placement

J.D.s awarded:	174

Services available through: a separate law school placement center.
Services: on campus and out-of-state job fairs.
Special features: personal individualized service for students and graduates.

Full-time job interviews:	21 employers
Summer job interviews:	53 employers
Placement by graduation:	87% of class
Placement within 9 months:	98% of class
Average starting salary:	$50,000 to $125,000

Areas of placement:
Private practice 2–10 attorneys	31%
Private practice 11–23 attorneys	6%
Private practice 26–50 attorneys	2%
Private practice 51–100 attorneys	3%
Public interest	8%
Judicial clerkships	7%
Academic	4%
Business/industry	14%
Government	13%
Military	1%

66% have worked full-time prior to entering law school. About 3% drop out after the first year for academic or personal reasons; 97% remain to receive a law degree.

Electives

The Sandra Day O'Connor College of Law offers concentrations in environmental law, intellectual property law, internationl law, tax law, as well as certificates in Indian law, intellectual property, environmental law, and health law. In addition, current offerings include a Criminal Practice Clinic, a Civil Justice Clinic, and a Technology Ventures Clinic, each worth 6 credits. Third-year students are given preference for clinics and seminars; 25 to 30 seminars per semester are offered (worth 2 or 3 credit hours). Externships and field work allow upper-level students to gain up to 12 credits while working in one of the more than 150 organized externships. A number of research opportunities are also available for students. The college sponsors numerous annual lecture series and several major symposia yearly. Study abroad is possible through a semester exchange program with Universidad Torcuato Di Tella, Buenos Aires, University of Victoria, British Columbia, National University, Singapore, Université René Descartes, Paris, France, and Bocconi University School of Law, Milan, Italy. There is an Academic Success Program available. A number of Phoenix firms offer minority legal writing programs. The most widely taken electives are Evidence, Business Associations, and Trusts and Estates.

Graduation Requirements

In order to graduate, candidates must have a GPA of 2.0, must have completed the upper-division writing requirement, and must complete 88 credit hours, including the required courses, the graduation writing requirement, the flexible writing requirement, and the practical skills requirement.

Organizations

Students edit the *Arizona State Law Journal*. Students also assist faculty in editing *Jurimetrics: The Journal of Law, Science, and Technology*. Students also publish their own newspaper: *Res Ipsa Loquitur*. Students are urged to participate in the ABA Dispute Resolution Section's "Representation in Mediation" Competition, the Jessup International Moot Court Competition, and a Client Counseling Competition. Other competitions include the Judge Tang Essay Competition, the Oplinger Closing Argument Competition, the Jenckes Competition, and numerous

other writing competitions. Student organizations include Government and Public Interest Law, Law and Science Student Association, and Corporate Ad Business Law Student Association. Local chapters of national associations include the American Bar Association Law Student Division, John P. Morris Black Law Students Association, and Native American Law Student Association. Other organizations affiliated campuswide include Phi Alpha Delta, the ASU Graduate and Professional Association, and the Chicano/Latino Law Student Association.

Library

The law library contains 291,925 hardcopy volumes and 146,471 microform volume equivalents, and subscribes to 38,981 serial publications. Such online databases and networks as CALI, CIS Universe, Infotrac, Legal-Trac, LEXIS, OCLC First Search, WESTLAW, Wilsonline Indexes, and Academic Universe are available to law students for research. Special library collections include Anglo-American case reports and statutes and special collections of Indian law, Mexican law, law and technology, and English legal history. The ratio of library volumes to faculty is 4,708 to 1 and to students is 484 to 1. The ratio of seats in the library to students is 1 to 1.

Faculty

The law school has 62 full-time and 68 part-time faculty members, of whom 41 are women. According to AAUP standards for Category I institutions, faculty salaries are average. About 13% of full-time faculty have a graduate law degree in addition to the J.D. The ratio of full-time students to full-time faculty in an average class is 10 to 1; in a clinic, 6 to 1. The law school has a regular program of bringing visiting professors and other distinguished lecturers and visitors to campus. There is a chapter of the Order of the Coif; 28 faculty are members.

Students

About 40% of the student body are women; 23%, minorities; 2%, African American; 3%, Asian American; 11%, Hispanic; 5%, Native American; and 3%, 2 or more races. The average age of entering students is 26; age range is 20 to 47. About 36% of students enter directly from undergraduate school, 10% have a graduate degree, and

1422 W. Peachtree St., NW
Atlanta, GA 30309

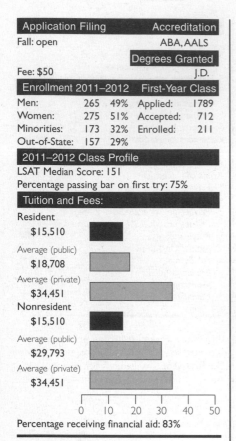

Application Filing			Accreditation	
Fall: open			ABA, AALS	
			Degrees Granted	
Fee: $50				J.D.

Enrollment 2011–2012		First-Year Class		
Men:	265	49%	Applied:	1789
Women:	275	51%	Accepted:	712
Minorities:	173	32%	Enrolled:	211
Out-of-State:	157	29%		

2011–2012 Class Profile
LSAT Median Score: 151
Percentage passing bar on first try: 75%

Tuition and Fees:

Resident
$15,510

Average (public)
$18,708

Average (private)
$34,451

Nonresident
$15,510

Average (public)
$29,793

Average (private)
$34,451

Percentage receiving financial aid: 83%

ADMISSIONS

In the fall 2011 first-year class, 1789 applied, 712 were accepted, and 211 enrolled. Fourteen transfers enrolled. The median GPA of the most recent first-year class was 2.97. The lowest LSAT percentile accepted was 25; the highest was 75.

Requirements

Applicants must have a bachelor's degree and take the LSAT. Minimum acceptable GPA is 2.0 on a scale of 4.0. The most important admission factors include LSAT results, GPA, and general background. No specific undergraduate courses are required. Candidates are not interviewed.

Procedure

The application deadline for fall entry is open. Applicants should submit an application form, LSAT results, transcripts, a personal statement, a nonrefundable application fee of $50, 2 letters of recommendation, TOEFL (if applicable), and a resume. Notification of the admissions

decision is on a rolling basis. The latest acceptable LSAT test date for fall entry is June. The law school uses the LSAC.

Special

The law school recruits minority and disadvantaged students through college visits, advertisements, and referrals. Requirements are not different for out-of-state students. Transfer students must have one year of credit, must have attended an ABA-approved law school, and must be in good academic standing at the school from which they are transferring.

Costs

Tuition and fees for the 2011–2012 academic year are $15,510 for all full-time students. Tuition for part-time students is $9366 per year. Books and supplies run $1200.

Financial Aid

About 83% of current law students receive some form of aid. The average annual amount of aid from all sources combined, including scholarships, loans, and work contracts, is $30,000; maximum, $51,720. Awards are based on need. The required financial statement is the FAFSA. The aid application deadline for fall entry is open. First-year students are notified about their financial aid application at time of enrollment.

About the Law School

Atlanta's John Marshall Law School was established in 1933 and is a private institution. The campus is in midtown Atlanta. The primary mission of the law school is to prepare competent and professional lawyers who possess a strong social conscience, continually demonstrate high ethical standards, and are committed to the improvement of the legal system and society. Students have access to federal, state, county, city, and local agencies, courts, correctional facilities, law firms, and legal aid organizations in the Atlanta area. Facilities of special interest to law students include more new classrooms, new trial and appellate courtrooms, and a café serving breakfast, lunch, and dinner. There is unlimited access to wireless Internet, online legal databases, and state of the art technology in multiple classrooms allowing for interactive learning

experiences. Housing for students is available in the local Atlanta rental market. All law school facilities are accessible to the physically disabled.

Calendar

The law school operates on a traditional semester basis. Courses for full-time students are offered both day and evening, and must be completed within 4 years. For part-time students, courses are offered both day and evening, and must be completed within 5 years. New full- and part-time students are admitted in the fall. There is a 7-week summer session. Transferable summer courses are offered.

Programs

Students may take relevant courses in other programs and apply credit toward the J.D.; a maximum of 30 credits may be applied.

Required

To earn the J.D., candidates must complete 88 total credits, of which 63 are for required courses. They must maintain a minimum GPA of 2.0 in the required courses. The following first-year courses are required of all students: Civil Procedure I and II, Contracts I and II, Legal Research, Writing, and Analysis I and I, Real Property I and II, and Torts I and II. Required upper-level courses consist of Business Organizations, Constitutional Law I and II, Criminal Law, Criminal Procedure, Evidence, Legal Drafting, Legal Research, Writing, and Analysis III, Professional Responsibility, Remedies, and Sales and Secured Transactions. Students are not required to take clinical courses but the law school does offer the opportunity to obtain clinical hours through its pro bono and externship programs. The required orientation program for first-year students is a comprehensive 4-day program.

Electives

The Atlanta's John Marshall Law School offers concentrations in corporate law, criminal law, entertainment law, environmental law, family law, intellectual property law, international law, juvenile law, labor law, litigation, securities law, sports law, tax law, torts and insurance, and public law. In addition, seminars are available

Phone: 404-872-3593
Fax: 404-873-3802
E-mail: *admissions@johnmarshall.edu*
Web: *www.johnmarshall.edu*

Contact
Shannon Keef, Director, 404-872-3593 for general inquiries; James Smith, Director of Financial Aid, 404-872-3593 for financial aid information.

GEORGIA

for students with advanced standing in such areas as privacy law, death penalty, and forensic evidence, for 2 credits each. There are numerous internship opportunities offered in various areas of law. The Directed Research Program for 2 credits involves comprehensive individual research projects under the supervision of a faculty member, resulting in a scholarly paper. An Externship Program worth 2 to 4 credits is available. Students are placed in a public law office and work under the supervision of a licensed attorney, certified under the third-year practice act of the Georgia Supreme Court. The Fred Gray Social Justice Seminar and the Annual Bobby Lee Cook Practical Legal Symposium draw some of Georgia's top attorneys as featured presenters. Study abroad, including a Micronesian Externship Program, for 2 to 3 credits is available to all students in good standing. Academic support is available to all students. The most widely taken electives are Georgia Practice and Procedure, Environmental Law, and Sports and Entertainment Law.

Graduation Requirements
In order to graduate, candidates must have a GPA of 2.0 and must have completed the upper-division writing requirement.

Organizations
The primary law review is *Atlanta's JMLS Law Review*. Students edit the student newspaper *SBA Newsletter*. Other publications include *Dean's Weekly Announcements*. Moot court competitions include the Frederick Douglass Moot Court Competition, NACD Trial Competition Team, and ABA Appellate Advocacy Team. Other competitions include the American Trial Lawyers Association Competition Team, ABA Client Interviewing and Counseling Competition, and National Moot Court Competition. Law student organizations, local chapters of national associations, and campus organizations include the Sports and Entertainment Law Society, Intellectual Property Club, Health Law Society, American Trial Lawyers Association,

Sigma Delta Kappa-Alpha Chi Chapter, Phi Alpha Delta-Hollowell Chapter, Georgia Association of Women Lawyers, Student Bar Associaton, and Black Law Students Association.

Library
The law library contains 96,000 hard-copy volumes and 711,151 microform volume equivalents, and subscribes to 402 serial publications. Such online databases and networks as CALI, Infotrac, Legal-Trac, LEXIS, Mathew Bender, NEXIS, OCLC First Search, WESTLAW, HeinOnline, BNA.LOM, Pacer, LLMC.COM, CCH New Business and Finance ProQuest, SSLN, JSTOR, and Lexis Congressional are available to law students for research. The ratio of library volumes to faculty is 2743 to 1 and to students is 178 to 1. The ratio of seats in the library to students is 1 to 3.

Faculty
The law school has 35 full-time and 21 part-time faculty members, of whom 28 are women. About 1% of full-time faculty have a graduate law degree in addition to the J.D.; about 2% of part-time faculty have one. The ratio of full-time students to full-time faculty in an average class is 13 to 1. The law school has a regular program of bringing visiting professors and other distinguished lecturers and visitors to campus.

Students
About 51% of the student body are women; 32%, minorities; 19%, African American; 3%, Asian American; and 3%, Hispanic. The majority of students come from Georgia (71%). The average age of entering students is 24; age range is 21 to 55. About 60% of students enter directly from undergraduate school, 20% have a graduate degree, and 40% have worked full-time prior to entering law school. About 8% drop out after the first year for academic or personal reasons; 74% remain to receive a law degree.

Placement
J.D.s awarded:	106
Services available through: the university placement center.	
Special features: on-campus interviews, resume forwarding, and 1000+ job postings a year.	
Placement by graduation:	97% of class
Placement within 9 months:	94% of class
Average starting salary:	$60,069
Areas of placement:	
Private practice 2–10 attorneys	64%
Judicial Clerkships	5%
Government	10%
Business/Industry	15%
Public Interest	4%
Academic	2%

AVE MARIA SCHOOL OF LAW

1025 Commons Circle
Naples, FL 34119

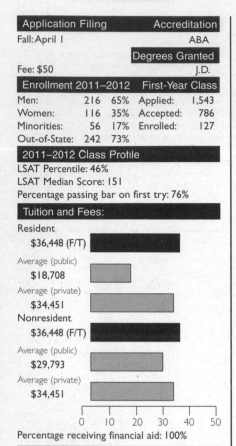

Application Filing		Accreditation
Fall: April 1		ABA
		Degrees Granted
Fee: $50		J.D.

Enrollment 2011–2012		First-Year Class	
Men:	216 65%	Applied:	1,543
Women:	116 35%	Accepted:	786
Minorities:	56 17%	Enrolled:	127
Out-of-State:	242 73%		

2011–2012 Class Profile
LSAT Percentile: 46%
LSAT Median Score: 151
Percentage passing bar on first try: 76%

Tuition and Fees:

Resident
$36,448 (F/T)

Average (public)
$18,708

Average (private)
$34,451

Nonresident
$36,448 (F/T)

Average (public)
$29,793

Average (private)
$34,451

0 10 20 30 40 50

Percentage receiving financial aid: 100%

ADMISSIONS

In the fall of 2011 first-year class, 1543 applied, 786 were accepted, and 127 enrolled. The median LSAT percentile of the most recent first-year class was 46; the median GPA was 3.2 on a scale of 4.0. The lowest LSAT percentile accepted was 16; the highest was 98.

Requirements
Applicants must have a bachelor's degree and take the LSAT. The most important admission factors include academic achievement, a letter of recommendation, and character or personality. No specific undergraduate courses are required. Candidates are not interviewed.

Procedure
The application deadline for fall entry is April 1. Applicants should submit an application form, LSAT results, transcripts, personal statement, TOEFL score (if applicable), nonrefundable application fee of $50, and 2 letters of recommendation.

Notification of the admissions decision is on a rolling basis. The law school uses the LSAC.

Special
The law school recruits minority and disadvantaged students through visits to historically Black colleges and universities, mailings to minority students, participation in events sponsored by minority organizations, attendance at minority student conferences, and hosting an annual program for high school students entitled "A Pathway to Law." Requirements are different for out-of-state students. Transfer students must have one year of credits, have a minimum GPA of 3, attended an ABA-approved law school, personal statement, transcripts, and a letter of good standing from an ABA-approved law school.

Costs

Tuition and fees for the 2011–2012 academic year are $35,948 for all full-time students. Books and supplies run $900.

Financial Aid

About 100% of current law students receive some form of aid. The average annual amount of aid from all sources combined, including scholarships, loans, and work contracts, is $44,775; maximum, $51,990. Awards are based on need and merit combined. Required financial statement is the FAFSA. The aid application deadline for fall entry is June 1. First-year students are notified about their financial aid application at time of acceptance.

About the Law School

Ave Maria School of Law was established in 1999 and is a private institution. The campus is located in a suburban area. The primary mission of the law school is to educate lawyers with the finest professional skills, characterized by the harmony of faith and reason, and the Catholic intellectual tradition. Students have access to federal, state, county, city, and local agencies, courts, correctional facilities, law firms, and legal aid organizations in the Naples area.

Calendar

The law school operates on a traditional semester basis. Courses for full-time students are offered both day and evening

and must be completed within 5 years. There is no part-time program. New full-time students are admitted in the fall. There is no summer session. Transferable summer courses are not offered.

Programs

Students may take relevant courses in other programs and apply credit toward the J.D.; a maximum of 8 credits may be applied.

Required
To earn the J.D., candidates must complete 90 total credits, of which 60 are for required courses. They must maintain a minimum GPA of 1.0 in the required courses. The following first-year courses are required of all students: Civil Procedure I and II, Contracts I and II, Criminal Law, Moral Foundations of the Law I and II, Property I and II, Research, Writing, Advocacy I and II, and Torts I and II. Required upper-level courses consist of Business Organizations, Constitutional Law, Criminal Procedure, Evidence, Federal Taxation, Jurisprudence, Law Ethics, Public Policy, Professional Responsibility, Research, Writing, and Advocacy III. The required orientation program for first-year students is a week long and includes programs to develop effective study strategies, meetings with faculty and administrators, and exposure to perspectives on legal study and practice.

Electives
Clinics include the Women's Immigrant Rights Clinic, Asylum Clinic, Patent Law Clinic, and Advanced Clinic. Completion of first-year courses is required. Seminars include First Amendment, Bioethics, and National Security Law. Upper-level students are eligible to enroll in several 2-credit seminars, which are generally limited to a maximum of 16 students. The Externship Program allows students to complement their classroom experience with work experience in a variety of legal settings, including working for a state or federal judge, assisting at a local prosecutor's office, or working for a government agency. Externships are available to upper-level students with a minimum GPA of 2.7. Under the supervision of a faculty member, students may pursue directed research. Students may participate in the

Phone: 239-687-5300
E-mail: info@avemarialaw.edu
Web: www.avemarialaw.edu

Contact

Maria Montagnini, Administrative Assistant, 734-827-8063 for general inquiries; JoAnn Maseman, Director of Financial Aid, 734-827-8051 for financial aid information.

Volunteer Tax Assistance Program. The distinguished Speaker Series brings a number of local and national guest speakers to reflect on their roles in the profession. The Ave Maria Lecture is an annual address from a nationally-recognized public figure. Students are permitted to enroll in summer study abroad programs with advance permission. The Academic Support Program offers activities and services throughout the year designed to help students perform to the best of their abilities. It is staffed by a full-time attorney. While the Academic Support Program offers services to all students, one-on-one programs are designed for at-risk students to provide targeted assistance. The law school has recently hosted annual meetings of the Society of Catholic School Scientists and University Faculty for life. The most widely taken electives are Trial Advocacy, Employment Law, and Trusts and Estates.

Graduation Requirements

In order to graduate, candidates must have a GPA of 2.0, complete the upper-division writing requirement, and minimum of 6 full-time semesters, and the recommendation of faculty.

Organizations

The primary law review is the *Ave Maria Law Review*. Internal moot court competitions include the St. Thomas More Moot Court Competition (first-year students), the Ave Maria Intramural Appellate Competition, and the Ave Maria Intramural Trial Competition. The law school participates in several competitions annually, including the ABA National Client Counseling Competition, and the Herbert Wechsler Criminal Law Moot Court Competition. Law student organizations, local chapters of national associations, and campus organizations include Business Law Society, Women Lawyers Association, Minority Law Students Association, Delta Theta Phi, Phi Alpha Delta, Federalist Society, Law Partners, Lex Vitae Society, and Intellectual Property Group.

Library

The law library contains 117,104 hardcopy volumes and 5,319 microform volume equivalents, and subscribes to 1,027 serial publications. Online databases and networks include CALI, CIS Universe, Infotrac, Legal-Trac, LEXIS, Mathew Bender, OCLC First Search, WESTLAW, and Wilsonline Indexes. In addition, 40 total online databases, digital congressional, and U.S. Supreme Court are also available to law students for research. Special library collections include Canon Law and Bioethics. The ratio of library volumes to faculty is 4,182 to 1 and to students is 353 to 1. The ratio of seats in the library to students is 1 to 1.

Faculty

The law school has 28 full-time and 10 part-time faculty members, of whom 13 are women. About 29% of full-time faculty have a graduate law degree in addition to the J.D. The ratio of full-time students to full-time faculty in an average class is 28 to 1; in a clinic, 10 to 1. The law school has a regular program of bringing visiting professors and other distinguished lecturers and visitors to campus.

Students

About 35% of the student body are women; 17%, minorities; 2%, African American; 7%, Asian American; 7%, Hispanic; and 1%, Native American. The majority of students come from Florida (27%). The average age of entering students is 25; age range is 21 to 43. About 49% of students enter directly from undergraduate school, 5% have a graduate degree, and 50% have worked full-time prior to entering law school. About 4% drop out after the first year for academic or personal reasons; 84% remain to receive a law degree.

Placement

J.D.s awarded:	123
Services available through: a separate law school placement center.	
Services: educational programs on careers.	
Special features: Mock Interview Program for first-year students and Lawyer-Mentor Program.	
Full-time job interviews:	8 employers
Summer job interviews:	10 employers
Placement by graduation:	35% of class
Placement within 9 months:	74% of class
Average starting salary:	$46,300 to $60,000
Areas of placement:	
Private practice 2–10 attorneys	19%
Private practice 11–23 attorneys	8%
Private practice 26–50 attorneys	2%
Private practice 51–100 attorneys	5%
Business/industry	24%
Judicial clerkships	17%
Government	14%
501+ attorneys 3%,	
Solo practitioners 3%	6%
Public interest	3%
Academic	2%

BARRY UNIVERSITY

School of Law

6441 East Colonial Drive
Orlando, FL 32807

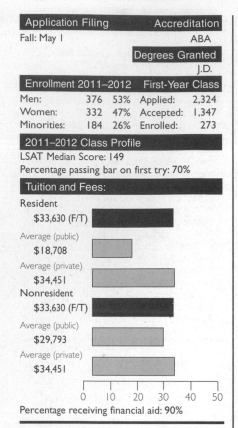

ADMISSIONS

In the fall of 2011 first-year class, 2324 applied, 1347 were accepted, and 273 enrolled. The median GPA of the most recent first-year class was 2.96.

Requirements

Applicants must have a bachelor's degree and take the LSAT. No specific undergraduate courses are required. Candidates are not interviewed.

Procedure

The application deadline for fall entry is May 1. Applicants should submit an application form, LSAT results, transcripts, personal statement, and 2 (supplemental) letters of recommendation. Notification of the admissions decision is on a rolling basis. The law school uses the LSAC.

Special

The law school recruits minority and disadvantaged students through the Early Start Program, a 4-week summer program held prior to orientation. Requirements are different for out-of-state students. Transfer students must have one year of credits, have a minimum GPA of 2.5, attended an ABA-approved law school, and a personal statement.

Costs

Tuition and fees for the 2011–2012 academic year are $33,630 for all full-time students. Tuition for part-time students is $25,180 for in-state students and $25,180 out-of-state.

Financial Aid

About 90% of current law students receive some form of aid. Required financial statement is the FAFSA. The aid application deadline for fall entry is June. First-year students are notified about their financial aid application after a seat deposit is received (commitment to enroll).

About the Law School

Barry University School of Law was established in 1999 and is a private institution. The 20-acre campus is located in an urban area 15 minutes from downtown Orlando. The primary mission of the law school is to provide a learning environment that challenges students to accept intellectual, personal, ethical, spiritual, and social responsibilities. Students have access to federal, state, county, city, and local agencies, courts, correctional facilities, law firms, and legal aid organizations in the Orlando area. Facilities of special interest to law students include a 2-story law center building, a moot court building, an administration building, law library, and a new legal advocacy center. Housing for students is plentiful off campus. All law school facilities are accessible to the physically disabled.

Calendar

The law school operates on a traditional semester basis. Courses for full-time students are offered both day and evening and must be completed within 6 semesters. For part-time students, courses are offered evenings only and must be completed within 8 semesters. New full- and part-time students are admitted in the fall. There is a summer session. Transferable summer courses are offered.

Programs

Required

To earn the J.D., candidates must complete 90 total credits, of which 53 to 55 are for required courses. They must maintain a minimum GPA of 1.8 in the required courses. The following first-year courses are required of all students: Civil Procedure, Constitutional Law, Contracts, Criminal Law, Legal Methods, Legal Research and Writing I and II, Property, and Torts. Required upper-level courses consist of Business Organizations, Commercial Course, Evidence, Federal Taxation, Perspectives Course, and Professional Responsibility. The required orientation program for first-year students is 3 days including instruction on legal briefing, a mock class, and professional responsibility.

Electives

The School of Law offers concentrations in environmental law, family law, and litigation. In addition, Clinics include the Children and Families Clinic, Immigration Clinic, and Earth Justice Clinic. Various internships are available. Externships include Mediation, Public Defender's Office, Judicial, State Attorney's Office, and Business. Study abroad in Spain is available (joint program with St. Thomas Law).

Graduation Requirements

In order to graduate, candidates must have a GPA of 2.0 and complete the upper-division writing requirement.

Organizations

Students edit *Barry University Law Review*, the student newspaper *The Advocate*, and *Moot Points*. Law student organizations, local chapters of national associations, and campus organizations include Moot Court Board, St. Thomas More Society, Trial Advocacy Team, Phi Alpha Delta, Delta Theta Phi, Christian Legal Society, Hispanic American Association, James C. Collier Black Law Students Association, Environmental Law Society, Real Estate Committee, and Asian American Law Student Association.

Phone: 321-206-5600
866-JD-BARRY
Fax: 321-206-5662
E-mail: acruz@mail.barry.edu
Web: http://barry.edu/law

Contact

Sheri Lagomarsino, Associate Dean, 321-206-5600 for general inquiries; Connie Allman, Director of Financial Aid, 321-206-5621 or 866-JD-BARRY for financial aid information.

Library

The law library contains 200,000 hardcopy volumes and 92,839 microform volume equivalents, and subscribes to 1,600 serial publications. Online databases and networks include CALI, Legal-Trac, LEXIS, OCLC First Search, and WESTLAW, which are available to law students for research. The ratio of library volumes to faculty is 7,143 to 1 and to students is 280 to 1. The ratio of seats in the library to students is 1 to 2.

Faculty

The law school has 66 full-time and 30 part-time faculty members, of whom 33 are women. According to AAUP standards for Category IIA institutions, faculty salaries are average. About 9% of full-time faculty have a graduate law degree in addition to the J.D. The ratio of full-time students to full-time faculty in an average class is 16 to 1.

Students

About 47% of the student body are women; 26%, minorities; 7%, African American; 6%, Asian American; 12%, Hispanic; and 1%, Native American. The average age of entering students is 27; age range is 20 to 55. About 9% drop out after the first year for academic or personal reasons; 91% remain to receive a law degree.

Placement	
J.D.s awarded:	175
Services available through: a separate law school placement center.	
Areas of placement:	
Private practice 2–100 attorneys	58%
Business/industry	16%
Government	15%
Public interest	7%
Academic	3%
Judicial clerkships	1%

BAYLOR UNIVERSITY
School of Law

One Bear Place, #97288
Waco, TX 76798-7288

Application Filing
Fall: March 1
Spring: November 1
Fee: $40

Accreditation
ABA, AALS

Degrees Granted
J.D.

Enrollment 2011–2012 — First-Year Class

Men:	246	53%	Applied:	3,436
Women:	219	47%	Accepted:	1,146
Minorities:	93	20%	Enrolled:	186
Out-of-State:	121	26%		

2011–2012 Class Profile
LSAT Percentile: 81%
LSAT Median Score: 160
Percentage passing bar on first try: 93%

Tuition and Fees:

Resident
$38,408 (F/T)
Average (public) $18,708
Average (private) $34,451

Nonresident
$38,408 (F/T)
Average (public) $29,793
Average (private) $34,451

0   10   20   30   40   50

Percentage receiving financial aid: 91%

ADMISSIONS
In the fall of 2011 first-year class, 3436 applied, 1146 were accepted, and 186 enrolled. One transfer student enrolled. The median LSAT percentile of the most recent first-year class was 81; the median GPA was 3.6 on a scale of 4.0. The lowest LSAT percentile accepted was 71; the highest was 87.

Requirements
Applicants must have a bachelor's degree and take the LSAT. The most important admission factors include LSAT results, GPA, and general background. No specific undergraduate courses are required and candidates are not interviewed.

Procedure
The application deadline for fall entry is March 1. Applicants should submit an application form, LSAT results, transcripts, a personal statement, LSAC, a nonrefundable application fee of $40, 2 letters of recommendation, and a personal

statement. Notification of the admissions decision is 4 to 6 weeks after the application deadline. The law school uses the LSAC.

Special
The law school recruits minority and disadvantaged students the same as non-minority students. A member of the Law School faculty serves as the Minority Law Student Adviser. Requirements are different for out-of-state students. Transfer students must have one year of credit, have a minimum GPA of 3, have attended an ABA-approved law school, a personal statement, to be competitive with the applicant pool, and the applicants should be in the top 5 to 10% of their class at a comparable law school.

Costs
Tuition and fees for the 2011–2012 academic year are $36,750 for all full-time students. On-campus room and board costs about $9,708 annually; books and supplies run $2,007.

Financial Aid
About 91% of current law students receive some form of aid. The average annual amount of aid from all sources combined, including scholarships, loans, and work contracts, is $38,234; maximum, $56,884. Awards are based on need and merit combined. Required financial statement is the FAFSA. The aid application deadline for fall entry is February 15. Special funds for minority or disadvantaged students include a limited number of scholarships ranging from one-third to full tuition for students who have overcome educational and/or emotional disadvantages or other personal hardship experiences. First-year students are notified about their financial aid application before enrollment.

About the Law School
Baylor University School of Law was established in 1849 and is a private institution. The 432-acre campus is in an urban area 92 miles south of Dallas. The primary mission of the law school is to train students in all facets of the law including theoretical analysis, practical application, legal writing and advocacy, negotiation, and counseling skills to equip them to practice effectively in any area of the law.

Students have access to federal, state, county, city, and local agencies, courts, correctional facilities, law firms, and legal aid organizations in the Waco area. Facilities of special interest to law students include a $33 million, state-of-the-art 128,000 square foot facility. Housing for students consists of private and university rental housing, including numerous rooms and condominiums near the Baylor campus and other properties throughout the city of Waco. All law school facilities are accessible to the physically disabled.

Calendar
The law school operates on a quarter basis. Courses for full-time students are offered days only and must be completed within 5 years. For part-time students, courses are offered days only and must be completed within 5 years. New full-time students are admitted in the fall, spring, and summer. There is an 11-week summer session. Transferable summer courses are offered.

Programs
Students may take relevant courses in other programs and apply credit toward the J.D.; a maximum of 12 credits may be applied. The following joint degrees may be earned: J.D./M.B.A. (Juris Doctor/Master of Business Administration), J.D/M.P.P.A. (Juris Doctor/Master of Public Policy Administration), and J.D./M.Tax (Juris Doctor/Master of Taxation).

Required
To earn the J.D., candidates must complete 126 total credits, of which 78 are for required courses. They must maintain a minimum GPA of 2.0 in the required courses. The following first-year courses are required of all students: Appellate Advocacy and Procedure, Civil Procedure, Contracts I and II, Criminal Law, Criminal Procedure, Introduction to Law and Lawyering, Legal Analysis, Research, and Communication I, II, and III, Legislative, Administrative Process and Procedure, Property I and II, and Torts I and II. Required upper-level courses consist of Basic Tax and Accounting for Lawyers, Business Organization I, Constitutional Law, Practice Court I, Practice Court II, Practice Court III, Professional Responsibility, and Trusts and Estates Remedies. All students must take clinical courses.

Phone: 254-710-1911
800-BAYLOR
Fax: 254-710-2316
E-mail: becky_beck@baylor.edu
Web: law.baylor.edu

Contact

Becky L. Beck, Assistant Dean of Admissions, 254-710-2529 for general inquiries; Office of Financial Aid, Baylor University, 254-710-2611 for financial aid information.

TEXAS

The required orientation program for first-year students is a 3-day program that covers introduction to the legal profession and life as a law student.

Electives

The School of Law offers concentrations in criminal law, international law, litigation, business transactions, administrative law, estate planning, and business litigation. In addition, the 2-quarter Practice Court Program is required in the third year and includes rigorous hands-on training. Students are required to complete at least 4 mini trials and 1 large trial along with several other exercises. There are real-life client opportunities for pro bono divorce cases and other client opportunities for penalty cases. A Supreme Court seminar is available. Internships are available in the District Attorney's Office, U.S. Attorney's Office, U.S. District Court, U.S. Bankruptcy Court, Texas Attorney General's Office-Child Support Division, Legal Services Office, the Texas Supreme Court, and Court of Criminal Appeals. Independent studies are available for second- and third-year students under faculty supervision. Field work opportunities are available in a number of offices such as General Counsel for Texas Life Insurance Co. Special lecture series include the Frank Wilson Memorial, W.R. White Memorial, R. Matt Dawson Lecture Series, and the John William Minton and Florence Dean Minton Endowed Law School Lecture Series. Students may study in Guadalajara, Mexico during a 2-week program in August. A faculty-conducted tutorial program is available for students placed on academic probation as well as for other interested students. There is a designated faculty Minority Student Adviser and a Diversity in Law Students Association. There is an Environmental Law program once a year and various speakers throughout the year. The most widely taken electives are Client Counseling, Alternative Dispute Resolution, Advanced Criminal Procedure, Administration of Estates, Appellate Procedure, Trusts and Estates II, and Secured Transactions.

Graduation Requirements

In order to graduate, candidates must have a GPA of 2.0 and completed the upper-division writing requirement.

Organizations

The primary law review is the *Baylor Law Review*. Moot court competitions include the Dawson and Sodd Fall Moot Court and the Strasburger and Price Spring Moot Court. Intrascholastic competitions are the Naman, Howell, Smith and Lee Client Counseling Competition, and the Bob Wortham Mock Trial Tournament of Champions. Interscholastic competitions include the National Trial, National Moot Court, National Appellate Advocacy, Texas Young Lawyers Moot Court, National Negotiations, and National Client Counseling. Organizations include Women's Legal Society, American Constitution Society, Civil Rights Society, Baylor University Student Bar Association, Diversity in Law Association, Civil Rights Society, R.E.B Baylor Chapter of Phi Alpha, James P. Alexander Senate of Delta Theta Phi, and the Hemphill Inn Chapter of Phi Delta Phi.

Library

The law library contains 241,927 hardcopy volumes and 127,451 microform volume equivalents, and subscribes to 2,212 serial publications. Online databases and networks include CALI, DIALOG, Legal-Trac, LEXIS, OCLC First Search, RLIN, WESTLAW, and NEXIS, which are available to law students for research. Special library collections include the Frank M. Wilson Rare Book Room Collection, which contains first editions and rare printings of legal writings, novels, and research titles relating to law. The ratio of library volumes to faculty is 8,960 to 1 and to students is 520 to 1. The ratio of seats in the library to students is 1 to 2.

Faculty

The law school has 27 full-time and 29 part-time faculty members, of whom 11 are women. According to AAUP standards for Category I institutions, faculty salaries are below average. About 25% of full-time faculty have a graduate law degree in addition to the J.D.; about 3% of part-time faculty have one. The ratio of full-time students to full-time faculty in an average class is 25 to 1; in a clinic, 2 to 1. The law school has a regular program of bringing visiting professors and other distinguished lecturers and visitors to campus.

Placement

J.D.s awarded:	130

Services available through: a separate law school placement center, the university placement center, and reciprocity may be requested from other law schools.

Services: resource library; use of telephone/fax/typewriter for job search purposes.

Special features: the Direct Contact Program, Resume Collection Program, job search skills programs, mock interviews, guest speaker panel discussions, and participation in various job fairs in Texas as well as out of state.

Full-time job interviews:	17 employers
Summer job interviews:	47 employers
Placement within 9 months:	98% of class
Average starting salary:	$51,000 to $93,122

Areas of placement:

Private practice 2–10 attorneys	25%
Private practice 11–23 attorneys	11%
Private practice 26–50 attorneys	8%
Private practice 51–100 attorneys	3%
Private practice 100+ attorneys	17%
Government	12%
Judicial clerkships	10%
Business/industry	10%
Academic	2%
Public interest	1%
Military	1%

Students

About 47% of the student body are women; 20%, minorities; 2%, African American; 9%, Asian American; 9%, Hispanic; and 1%, Native American. The majority of students come from Texas (74%). The average age of entering students is 23; age range is 18 to 46. About 76% of students enter directly from undergraduate school, 3% have a graduate degree, and 21% have worked full-time prior to entering law school. About 4% drop out after the first year for academic or personal reasons; 96% remain to receive a law degree.

BOSTON COLLEGE

Law School

885 Centre Street
Newton, MA 02459

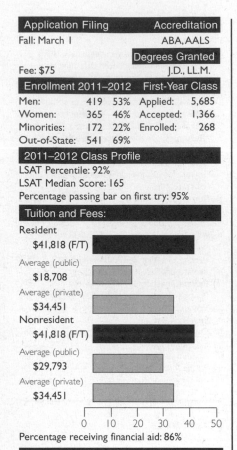

Application Filing	Accreditation
Fall: March 1	ABA, AALS

	Degrees Granted
Fee: $75	J.D., LL.M.

Enrollment 2011–2012		First-Year Class	
Men:	419 53%	Applied:	5,685
Women:	365 46%	Accepted:	1,366
Minorities:	172 22%	Enrolled:	268
Out-of-State:	541 69%		

2011–2012 Class Profile
LSAT Percentile: 92%
LSAT Median Score: 165
Percentage passing bar on first try: 95%

Tuition and Fees:

Resident
$41,818 (F/T)

Average (public)
$18,708

Average (private)
$34,451

Nonresident
$41,818 (F/T)

Average (public)
$29,793

Average (private)
$34,451

0 10 20 30 40 50

Percentage receiving financial aid: 86%

ADMISSIONS

In the fall of 2011 first-year class, 5685 applied, 1366 were accepted, and 268 enrolled. Fifteen transfers enrolled. The median LSAT percentile of the most recent first-year class was 92; the median GPA was 3.7 on a scale of 4.0.

Requirements

Applicants must have a bachelor's degree and take the LSAT. Minimum acceptable GPA is 2.0 on a scale of 4.0. The most important admission factors include academic achievement, character or personality, and undergraduate curriculum. No specific undergraduate courses are required. Candidates are not interviewed.

Procedure

The application deadline for fall entry is March 1. Applicants should submit an application form, LSAT results, transcripts, a personal statement, a nonrefundable application fee of $75, 2 letters of recommendation, and the LSAC report.

Notification of the admissions decision is on a rolling basis. The law school uses the LSAC.

Special

The law school recruits minority and disadvantaged students through a program of active outreach by the Admissions Committee and minority student organizations. Requirements are different for out-of-state students. Transfer students must have one year of credit, attended an ABA-approved law school, and a personal statement. Applicants are considered on a space-available basis.

Costs

Tuition and fees for the 2011–2012 academic year are $41,590 for all full-time students. Books and supplies run $1,300.

Financial Aid

About 86% of current law students receive some form of aid. The average annual amount of aid from all sources combined, including scholarships, loans, and work contracts, is $47,750; maximum, $60,908. Awards are based on need and merit combined. Required financial statements are the FAFSA and the Need Access online application. The aid application deadline for fall entry is March 15. Special funds for minority or disadvantaged students include additional tuition remission.

About the Law School

Boston College Law School was established in 1929 and is a private institution. The 40-acre campus is located in a suburban area 6 miles west of downtown Boston. The primary mission of the law school is to provide a quality legal education in the Jesuit, Catholic tradition to a highly qualified and diverse group of men and women to prepare them to serve their communities and serve as leaders in the profession. Students have access to federal, state, county, city, and local agencies, courts, correctional facilities, law firms, and legal aid organizations in the Newton area. Facilities of special interest to law students include a $16 million library, a $13 million classroom building with state-of-the-art audiovisual and computing capabilities, and a Career Resources Center. Housing for students is extensive, including ample rental housing in Newton

and the surrounding communities. All law school facilities are accessible to the physically disabled.

Calendar

The law school operates on a traditional semester basis. Courses for full-time students are offered days only and must be completed within 4 years. There is no part time program. New full-time students are admitted in the fall. There is no summer session. Transferable summer courses are not offered.

Programs

In addition to the J.D., the law school offers the LL.M. Students may take relevant courses in other programs and apply credit toward the J.D.; a maximum of 12 credits may be applied. The following joint degrees may be earned: J.D./M.A. (Juris Doctor/Master of Arts in Education), J.D./M.A.P. (Juris Doctor/Master of Arts in Philosophy), J.D./M.B.A. (Juris Doctor/Master of Business Administration), J.D./M.Ed. (Juris Doctor/Master of Education), and J.D./M.S.W. (Juris Doctor/Master of Social Work).

Required

To earn the J.D., candidates must complete 85 total credits, of which 36 are for required courses. They must maintain a minimum GPA of 2.0 in the required courses. The following first-year courses are required of all students: Civil Procedure, Constitutional Law, Contracts, Criminal Law, Legal Research and Writing, Property, and Torts. Required upper-level courses consist of class meeting ABA upper level writing, class meeting lawyering skill, class meeting perspective on law and justice, Constitutional Law II, and Professional Responsibility. The required orientation program for first-year students is a day followed by 2 sessions on subsequent days. Orientation covers introduction to the law school, perspectives on differences, and legal ethics orientation.

Electives

The Law School offers concentrations in corporate law, criminal law, environmental law, family law, intellectual property law, internationl law, juvenile law, litigation, securities law, tax law, torts and insurance, and clinical programs. In addition,

Phone: 617-552-4351
Fax: 617-552-2917
E-mail: bclawadm@bc.edu
Web: www.bc.edu/lawschool

Contact

Rita C. Jones, Assistant Dean Admissions and Financial Aid, 617-552-4351 for general inquiries and/or financial aid information.

MASSACHUSETTS

clinics include the Civil Litigation Clinic, Women and the Law Clinic, the Criminal Justice Clinic, Housing Clinic, and Community Enterprise Clinic, each worth 7 credits. Internships include the Semester in Practice and the Attorney General's Program. Special lecture series include the Legal History Roundtable, Criminal Law Roundtable, and faculty workshops. A London program is offered to second- and third-year students for 13 credits. The International Criminal Tribunals (ICT) offers a unique opportunity to work onsite at the criminal tribunal established by the UN Security Council. Tutorial programs are available to students who require them. Programming for minority students is sponsored by student groups. Minority students are actively recruited. The most widely taken electives are Taxation, Corporations, and Evidence.

Graduation Requirements

In order to graduate, candidates must have a GPA of 2.0 and completed the upper-division writing requirement.

Organizations

Students edit the *Boston College Law Review, Boston College Environmental Affairs Law Review, Boston College International and Comparative Law Review, Boston College Third World Law Journal, Uniform Commercial Code Reporter Digest*, and the online newsletter, *The Counselor*. Moot court competitions include the Wendell F. Grimes Moot Court, Jessup International Moot Court, and National Moot Court competitions. Other competitions include the Mock Trial, Negotiations, Client Counseling, Administrative Law Moot Court, Braxton Craven Moot Court, Bankruptcy Moot Court, European Union Law Moot Court, Frederick Douglass Moot Court, Saul Lefkowitz, Trademark Moot Court, and Immigration Law Moort Court. Law student organizations include International Law Society, Public Interest Law Foundation, and Environmental Law Society. Local chapters of national associations include the ABA-Law Student Division, National Lawyers Guild, and Phi Alpha Delta. Campus clubs and other organizations include the Black Law Students Association, Lambda,

Latino Law Students Association, Asian Pacific American Law Students Association, South Asian Law Student Association, and Jewish Law Student Association.

Library

The law library contains 486,339 hardcopy volumes and 236,194 microform volume equivalents, and subscribes to 2,549 serial publications. Online databases and networks include CALI, CIS Universe, DIALOG, Infotrac, Legal-Trac, LEXIS, Mathew Bender, OCLC First Search, RLIN, WESTLAW, and Wilsonline Indexes. Access UN, HeinOnline, CCH Internet, Research Network, Congressional Quarterly, Environment and Safety Library, Bloomberg Law, are among the others available to law students for research. Special library collections include the Daniel R. Coquillette Rare Book collection and the U.S. Government Documents Depository. The ratio of library volumes to faculty is 7,369 to 1 and to students is 607 to 1. The ratio of seats in the library to students is 1 to 1.

Faculty

The law school has 65 full-time and 39 part-time faculty members, of whom 37 are women. About 54% of full-time faculty have a graduate law degree in addition to the J.D. The ratio of full-time students to full-time faculty in an average class is 13 to 1; in a clinic, 6 to 1. The law school has a regular program of bringing visiting professors and other distinguished lecturers and visitors to campus. There is a chapter of the Order of the Coif.

Students

About 46% of the student body are women; 22%, minorities; 4%, African American; 10%, Asian American; 7%, Hispanic; and 2%, Foreign National. The majority of students come from Massachusetts (31%). The average age of entering students is 24; age range is 21 to 40. About 40% of students enter directly from undergraduate school, 9% have a graduate degree, and 60% have worked full-time prior to entering law school. About 1% drop out after the first year for academic or personal reasons; 99% remain to receive a law degree.

Placement

J.D.s awarded:	265

Services available through: a separate law school placement center.

Special features: Mandatory IL meeting with assigned Career Service counselors, dedicated public service counselor, over 80 skills workshops and career panels and programs offered yearly, on-campus and off-campus recruitment programs in 8 national cities, and two government/public interest consortium programs.

Full-time job interviews:	81 employers
Summer job interviews:	240 employers
Placement by graduation:	76% of class
Placement within 9 months:	91% of class
Average starting salary:	$20,000 to $160,000

Areas of placement:

Private practice 2–10 attorneys	10%
Private practice 11–23 attorneys	2%
Private practice 26–50 attorneys	2%
Over 101 attorneys	38%
Judicial clerkships	15%
Government	11%
Business/industry	9%
Public interest	6%
Academic	6%
Military	2%

BOSTON UNIVERSITY

School of Law

765 Commonwealth Avenue
Boston, MA 02215

Application Filing	Accreditation
Fall: March 1	ABA, AALS

	Degrees Granted
Fee: $75	J.D., LL.M.

Enrollment 2011–2012		First-Year Class	
Men:	401 50%	Applied:	7,073
Women:	406 50%	Accepted:	1,396
Minorities:	186 23%	Enrolled:	242
Out-of-State:	525 65%		

2011–2012 Class Profile
LSAT Percentile: 94%
LSAT Median Score: 167
Percentage passing bar on first try: 92%

Tuition and Fees:

Resident
$42,654 (F/T)

Average (public)
$18,708

Average (private)
$34,451

Nonresident
$42,654 (F/T)

Average (public)
$29,793

Average (private)
$34,451

0   10   20   30   40   50
Percentage receiving financial aid: 89%

ADMISSIONS

In the fall of 2011 first-year class, 7073 applied, 1396 were accepted, and 242 enrolled. Forty-six transfers enrolled. The median LSAT percentile of the most recent first-year class was 94; the median GPA was 3.7 on a scale of 4.3. The lowest LSAT percentile accepted was 60; the highest was 99.

Requirements
Applicants must have a bachelor's degree and take the LSAT. No specific undergraduate courses are required. Candidates are not interviewed.

Procedure
The application deadline for fall entry is March 1. Applicants should submit an application form, LSAT results, transcripts, TOEFL (for international students only), a nonrefundable application fee of $75, 2 letters of recommendation, and a resume. Notification of the admissions decision is on a rolling basis. The law school uses the LSAC.

Special
The law school recruits minority and disadvantaged students by means of the Candidate Referral Service, LSAC forums, active minority groups on campus, alumni contacts, and the recruiting efforts of the Associate Director of Academic and Multicultural Affairs. Requirements are different for out-of-state students. Transfer students must have one year of credits, have attended an ABA-approved law school, and must submit a transfer application.

Costs

Tuition and fees for the 2011–2012 academic year are $41,780 for all full-time students. On-campus room and board costs about $12,070 annually; books and supplies run $1,374.

Financial Aid

About 89% of current law students receive some form of aid. The average annual amount of aid from all sources combined, including scholarships, loans, and work contracts, is $50,572; maximum, $60,332. Awards are based on need and merit, along with public interest. Required financial statements are the FAFSA and need access. The aid application deadline for fall entry is March 1. Special funds for minority or disadvantaged students include Martin Luther King Jr., Whitney Young, Norbert Simmons, and Barbara Jordan fellowships and scholarships. First-year students are notified about their financial aid application at time of acceptance.

About the Law School

Boston University School of Law was established in 1872 and is a private institution. The 132-acre campus is in an urban area in Boston. The primary mission of the law school is to prepare a diverse body of students for the ethical practice of law around the globe at the highest levels of quality and integrity and serve the public interest. Students have access to federal, state, county, city, and local agencies, courts, correctional facilities, law firms, and legal aid organizations in the Boston area. Facilities of special interest to law students include the University's Fitness and Recreation Center, the Tsai Performance Center, rowing and sailing programs on the Charles River. Additional amenities of Boston are the Boston Symphony, opera, theater, and sports. Rental apartment housing units are

available within walking distance of the school, in addition to suburban accommodations easily reached by mass transportation lines. Graduate student apartments are available on campus. About 98% of the law school facilities are accessible to the physically disabled.

Calendar

The law school operates on a traditional semester basis. Courses for full-time students are offered days only and must be completed within 3 years. For part-time students, courses are offered and LL.M. graduate studies are offered part-time both day and evening. New full- and part-time students are admitted in the fall. There is no summer session. Transferable summer courses are not offered.

Programs

In addition to the J.D., the law school offers the LL.M. Students may take relevant courses in other programs and apply credit toward the J.D.; a maximum of 16 credits may be applied. The following joint degrees may be earned: J.D./LL.M. (Banking and Financial Law), J.D./M.S. (Communications), J.D./M.B.A. (Health Sector Management), J.D./LL.M. (Intellectual Property), J.D./M.A. (International Relations), J.D./M.B.A. (Management), J.D./M.A. (Philosophy), J.D./M.A. (Preservation Studies), J.D./M.P.H. (Public Health), and J.D./LL.M. (Tax).

Required
To earn the J.D., candidates must complete 84 total credits, of which 33 are for required courses. They must maintain a minimum GPA of 2.0 in the required courses. The following first-year courses are required of all students: Civil Procedure, Constitutional Law, Contracts, Criminal Law, Legal Writing and Research, Property, and Torts. Required upper-level courses consist of Professional Responsibility. All students choose from voluntary clinical and externship program offerings that include: Civil Litigation, Criminal Law, Legislative Policy and Drafting, Africa i-Parliaments and Legislative Counsel Clinics. The required orientation program for first-year students is a program including building tours, panel discussions, faculty talks, and social events.

Electives
The School of Law offers concentrations in corporate law, internationl law, litigation,

MASSACHUSETTS

health law, and business organizations and finance law. In addition, clinics for upper-level students include 3–8 credits in Legislative Services, Criminal Trial Advocacy, and Civil Litigation Clinic. Credit varies from 3 to 8 hours. More than 70 seminars for varying credit are open to upper-level students. Semester-inpractice options include a human rights externship in Geneva, government lawyering in Washington, D.C., a death penalty externship at the Southern Center for Human Rights in Atlanta, and an independent proposal externship outside of Boston. A variety of other externships, geared toward individual student interest, is offered for various credits. Independent Study with a faculty member (supervised research and writing) is offered to upper-level students for 1 to 3 credits. Special lecture series include the Distinguished Speaker Series, Shapiro Lecture, Legal History Lectures, Intellectual Property Speaker Series, Law and Economics seminar, Faculty Workshops, and Faculty Brown Bag lunch talks. The school offers 13 overseas study programs in Lyon, Beijing, Geneva, Hamburg, Madrid, Singapore, Paris, Oxford, Tel Aviv, Leiden, Buenos Aires, Florence, and Hong Kong. The Students Affair Office coordinates a Voluntary Academic Support Program for first-year students whose first-semester grades indicate that they need assistance. The program is offered in the second semester of the first year for no credit. The classes focus on outlining and exam-taking skills. The law school has an individualized academic support program for second- and third-year students. In addition, the Student Affairs Office, together with minority student organizations, sponsors an orientation program for incoming minority students. Minority law student organizations include APALSA (Asian-Pacific American students); BLSA (Black students); LALSA (Latin American students); SALSA (South Asian American students), and OUTLAW (gay, lesbian, and transgender students). A Student Organization Activities Fair, sponsored by the Student Bar Association, introduces students to school organizations and groups. A formal lecture series and other lectures arranged by faculty student organizations, or through a research center, are given regularly by well-known outside speakers throughout the academic year. The most widely taken electives are Corporations, Evidence, Federal Income Taxation.

Contact

Alissa Leonard, Assistant Dean, Admissions and Financial Aid, 617-353-3100 for general inquiries and financial aid information.

Graduation Requirements

In order to graduate, candidates must have a GPA of 2.3, have completed the upper-division writing requirement, and have researched and written a major paper on a topic of their choice. The paper is faculty supervised and evaluated.

Organizations

Students edit the *Boston University Law Review, American Journal of Law and Medicine, Annual Review of Banking Law, Boston University International Law Journal, Public Interest Law Journal,* and *Journal of Science and Technology Law.* All first-year students participate in the intramural J. Newton Esdaile Moot Court program during the spring semester. Second-year students may participate in the Edward C. Stone Appellate Moot Court Competition in the fall; the top advocates from the Stone Competition advance to the Homer Albers Prize Moot Court Competition during the spring semester of their second year. Teams of third-year students are sent to national intramural competitions such as National Moot Court, National Appellate Advocacy and Craven Constitutional Law. Students may participate in the Association of Trial Lawyers of America National Student Trial Advocacy Competition and the ABA Negotiation and Client Counseling competitions. The law school supports more than 30 student organizations, including Student Bar Association; Women's Law Association; and Corporate Law Society. Other organizations include the Arts Law Association; Civil Liberties Association; and Communications, Entertainment, and Sports Law Association. There are local chapters of Federalist Society, Phi Alpha Delta, and Phi Delta Phi.

Library

The law library contains 674,482 hardcopy volumes and 328,501 microform volume equivalents, and subscribes to 3,396 serial publications. Online databases and networks include CALI, CIS Universe, DIALOG, Dow-Jones, Infotrac, Legal-Trac, LEXIS, OCLC First Search, WESTLAW, and Wilsonline Indexes. The law school has access to more than 100 electronic databases, which are available to law students for research. Special library archives include intellectual property, banking and financial law, health law, human rights, tax law, and international law collections. The ratio of library volumes to faculty is 12,490 to 1 and

Placement

J.D.s awarded:	273

Services available through: a separate law school placement center.

Services: extensive off-campus interview programs in 8 cities and numerous specialty job fairs; job search strategy and interview workshops; numerous presentations on areas of practice and law-related careers featuring alumni.

Special features: Staff includes 7 attorneys, 4 administrators, and part-time attorney advisers.

Full-time job interviews:	19 employers
Summer job interviews:	64 employers
Placement by graduation:	82% of class
Placement within 9 months:	87% of class
Average starting salary:	$40,000 to $175,000

Areas of placement:

Private practice 2–10 attorneys	8%
Private practice 11–23 attorneys	2%
Private practice 26–50 attorneys	2%
Private practice 51–100 attorneys	1%
Academic	14%
Judicial clerkships	8%
Government	8%
Business/industry	8%
Public interest	5%

to students is 844 to 1. The ratio of seats in the library to students is 1 to 1.

Faculty

The law school has 56 full-time and 19 part-time faculty members, of whom 53 are women. According to AAUP standards for Category I institutions, faculty salaries are above average. About 19% of full-time faculty have a graduate law degree in addition to the J.D.; about 13% of part-time faculty have one. The ratio of full-time students to full-time faculty in an average class is 37 to 1; in a clinic, 11 to 1. The law school has a regular program of bringing visiting professors and other distinguished lecturers and visitors to campus.

Students

About 50% of the student body are women; 23%, minorities; 5%, African American; 12%, Asian American; and 6%, Hispanic. The majority of students come from Massachusetts (35%). The average age of entering students is 24; age range is 21 to 44. About 15% of students have a graduate degree. About 4% drop out after the first year for academic or personal reasons; 95% remain to receive a law degree.

Phone: 617-353-3100
Fax: 617-353-0578
E-mail: bulawadm@bu.edu
Web: www.bu.edu/LAW

J. Reuben Clark Law School

342 JRCB Brigham Young University
Provo, UT 84602

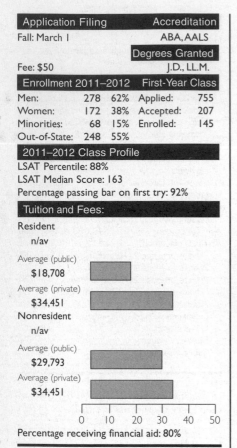

Application Filing	Accreditation
Fall: March 1	ABA, AALS
	Degrees Granted
Fee: $50	J.D., LL.M.

Enrollment 2011–2012		First-Year Class	
Men:	278 62%	Applied:	755
Women:	172 38%	Accepted:	207
Minorities:	68 15%	Enrolled:	145
Out-of-State:	248 55%		

2011–2012 Class Profile
LSAT Percentile: 88%
LSAT Median Score: 163
Percentage passing bar on first try: 92%

Tuition and Fees:

Resident
n/av

Average (public)
$18,708

Average (private)
$34,451

Nonresident
n/av

Average (public)
$29,793

Average (private)
$34,451

Percentage receiving financial aid: 80%

ADMISSIONS

In the fall of 2011 first-year class, 755 applied, 207 were accepted, and 145 enrolled. Three transfers enrolled. The median LSAT percentile of the most recent first-year class was 88; the median GPA was 3.7 on a scale of 4.0. The lowest LSAT percentile accepted was 26; the highest was 99.

Requirements
Applicants must have a bachelor's degree and take the LSAT. The most important admission factors include LSAT results and GPA. No specific undergraduate courses are required. Candidates are not interviewed.

Procedure
The application deadline for fall entry is March 1. Applicants should submit an application form, LSAT results, transcripts, a personal statement, a nonrefundable application fee of $50, 2 letters of recommendation, ecclesiastical endorsement, and Dean's Certification. Notification of the admissions decision is no later than April 15. The law school uses the LSAC.

Special
The law school recruits minority and disadvantaged students by direct mail, law forums, visiting undergraduate institutions, and personal contact from students, alumni, and friends of the law school. The school works closely with the Minority Law Students Association in recruiting minority students. Requirements are different for out-of-state students. Transfer students must have one year of credit, must have attended an ABA-approved law school, must submit a personal statement, and must be in the top third of the class in their prior school.

Costs

Tuition and fees for the 2011–2012 academic year are $10,600 for full-time in-state students and $21,200 for out-of-state students. On-campus room and board costs about $10,972 annually; books and supplies run $1,656.

Financial Aid

About 80% of current law students receive some form of aid. The average annual amount of aid from all sources combined, including scholarships, loans, and work contracts, is $10,000; maximum, $17,000. Awards are based on need and merit combined. Required financial statements are the CSS Profile and the FAFSA. The aid application deadline for fall entry is June 1. Special funds for minority or disadvantaged students are available. First-year students are notified about their financial aid application at time of acceptance.

About the Law School

Brigham Young University J. Reuben Clark Law School was established in 1973 and is a private institution. The 544-acre campus is in a suburban area 45 miles south of Salt Lake City. The primary mission of the law school is to affirm the strength brought to the law by a student's personal religious conviction. The school encourages public service and professional excellence, and the promotion of fairness and virtue founded upon the rule of law. Students have access to federal, state, county, city, and local agencies, courts, correctional facilities, law firms, and legal aid organizations in the Provo area. The International Center for Law and Religion Studies affords opportunities for international involvement with issues of global importance. Housing for students is available within easy access of the school. All law school facilities are accessible to the physically disabled.

Calendar

The law school operates on a traditional semester basis. Courses are offered days only, and must be completed within 3 years. New students are admitted in the fall. There is no summer session. Transferable summer courses are not offered.

Programs

In addition to the J.D., the law school offers the LL.M. Students may take relevant courses in other programs and apply credit toward the J.D.; a maximum of 9 credits may be applied. The following joint degrees may be earned: J.D./M.Acc. (Juris Doctor/ Master of Accountancy), J.D./M.B.A. (Juris Doctor/Master of Business Administration), J.D./M.Ed. (Juris Doctor/Master of Education), J.D./M.P.A. (Juris Doctor/Master of Public Administration), and J.D./M.P.P. (Juris Doctor/Master of Public Policy).

Required
To earn the J.D., candidates must complete 90 total credits, of which 36 are for required courses. They must maintain a minimum GPA of 2.7 in the required courses. The following first-year courses are required of all students: Civil Procedure, Contracts, Criminal Law, Introduction to Advocacy, Legal Research and Writing, Legislation & Regulation, Property, Structures of the Constitution, and Torts. Required upper-level courses consist of a substantial paper, Advanced Legal Research, and Professional Responsibility. The required orientation program for first-year students is a 3-day program that includes an introduction to the study of law and legal research.

Electives
The law school has LawHelp seminars worth up to 15 credits in which second- and third-year students provide legal services to clients under the direction of an attorney. Each first-year student

Phone: 801-422-4277

Fax: 801-422-0389

E-mail: *kucharg@law.byu.edu*

Web: *www.law.byu.edu*

Contact

Admissions Director, 801-422-4277 for general inquiries; Paul Conrad, Financial Aid Officer, 801-422-2698 for financial aid information.

has 1 class taught in seminar/small section form; 41 seminars are available for second-and third-year students. Students are allowed up to 15 credit hours for judicial, prosecutorial, government, private law firm, and public interest internships; 2 credit hours for research programs; and 15 for field work. The Career Services Office offers a weekly lecture series course, which features guest speakers from practice area specialties. Student organizations sponsor speakers on topics ranging from practical lawyering skills to jurisprudential theory. Students interested in study-abroad programs sponsored by other law schools may transfer credit. Each first year course has a weekly tutorial. Additionally, the Academic Success Program includes study skills workshops and individual tutors. The most widely taken electives are Constitutional Law, Secured Transactions, and Wills and Estates.

Graduation Requirements

In order to graduate, candidates must have a GPA of 2.7 and must have completed the upper-division writing requirement.

Organizations

Students edit the *Brigham Young University Law Review*, *BYU Journal of Public Law*, and *BYU Education and Law Journal*. The *Clark Memorandum* is a semiannual Law Society and alumni magazine. *Amicus Briefs* is constantly updated online. The school sends teams to the Jessup International Moot Court Competition and 5 other competitions annually. Other competitions include the John Welch Award for Outstanding Writing, the A.H. Christensen Advocacy Award, the Woody Deem Trial Advocacy Competition, BYU Research and Writing Award, and Le Boeuf Bankruptcy Scholar Award. Law student organizations include Minority Law Students Association, Women's Law Forum, and Government and Politics Legal Society. Local chapters of national associations include Public Interest Law Foundation (NAPIL), Federalist Society, and Phi Delta Phi. Campus clubs and other organizations include the Student Intellectual Property Association (SIP-LA), International and Comparative Law Society, and Sports and Entertainment Law Society (SPENT).

Library

The law library contains 474,191 hardcopy volumes and 107,632 microform volume equivalents, and subscribes to 4,447 serial publications. Such online databases and networks as CALI, DIALOG, Dow-Jones, Infotrac, Legal-Trac, LEXIS, OCLC First Search, WESTLAW, Wilsonline Indexes, HeinOnline, BNA, CCH, RIA, Making of Modern Law: Legal Treatises, Making of Modern Law: U.S. Supreme Court Records and Briefs, LLMC-Digital, LexisNexis Congressional Universe, Tax Notes, GLIN, Pratt's Banking Law Library, Index to Foreign Legal Periodicals, Constitutions of the Countries of the World, International Law in Domestic Courts, and Foreign Law Guide are available to law students for research. Special library collections include U.S. government documents and Utah State documents depositories, American Indian Law Collection, and Canadian and U.K. collections. The ratio of library volumes to faculty is 11,028 to 1 and to students is 1,063 to 1. The ratio of seats in the library to students is 1 to 1.

Faculty

The law school has 35 full-time and 48 part-time faculty members, of whom 26 are women. About 2% of full-time faculty have a graduate law degree in addition to the J.D. The ratio of full-time students to full-time faculty in an average class is 17 to 1. The law school has a regular program of bringing visiting professors and other distinguished lecturers and visitors to campus. There is a chapter of the Order of the Coif; 27 faculty and 493 graduates are members.

Students

About 38% of the student body are women; 15%, minorities; 1%, African American; 3%, Asian American; 7%, Hispanic; and 1%, Native American. The average age of entering students is 26; age range is 20 to 50. About 2% drop out after the first year for academic or personal reasons; 98% remain to receive a law degree.

Placement

J.D.s awarded:	151

Services available through: a separate law school placement center.

Services: weekly lecture series course that features attorneys speaking on different areas of practice, resume review service, workshops, and seminars.

Special features: networking groups, a professional development skills training course, satellite interviewing programs, attorney mock interviewing programs, video interviews, a judicial clerkship handbook, a job hunt handbook, a legal career planning handbook, and alumni receptions.

Full-time job interviews:	13 employers
Summer job interviews:	44 employers
Placement by graduation:	69% of class
Placement within 9 months:	96% of class
Average starting salary:	$30,000 to $175,000

Areas of placement:

Private practice 2–10 attorneys	21%
Private practice 11–23 attorneys	6%
Private practice 26–50 attorneys	6%
Private practice 51–100 attorneys	2%
Judicial clerkships	14%
Business/industry	14%
Government	9%
Public interest	4%
Military	4%
Academic	4%

BROOKLYN LAW SCHOOL

250 Joralemon Street
Brooklyn, NY 11201

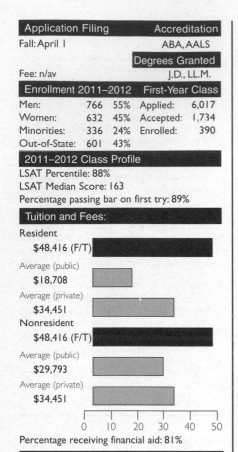

Application Filing	Accreditation
Fall: April 1	ABA, AALS
	Degrees Granted
Fee: n/av	J.D., LL.M.

Enrollment 2011–2012			First-Year Class	
Men:	766	55%	Applied:	6,017
Women:	632	45%	Accepted:	1,734
Minorities:	336	24%	Enrolled:	390
Out-of-State:	601	43%		

2011–2012 Class Profile
LSAT Percentile: 88%
LSAT Median Score: 163
Percentage passing bar on first try: 89%

Tuition and Fees:

Resident
$48,416 (F/T)

Average (public)
$18,708

Average (private)
$34,451

Nonresident
$48,416 (F/T)

Average (public)
$29,793

Average (private)
$34,451

0   10   20   30   40   50

Percentage receiving financial aid: 81%

ADMISSIONS
In the fall of 2011 first-year class, 6017 applied, 1734 were accepted, and 390 enrolled. Thirty-three transfers enrolled. The median LSAT percentile of the most recent first-year class was 88; the median GPA was 3.4 on a scale of 4.0.

Requirements
Applicants must have a bachelor's degree and take the LSAT. The most important admission factors include college attended, GPA, and LSAT results. No specific undergraduate courses are required. Candidates are not interviewed.

Procedure
The application deadline for fall entry is April 1. Applicants should submit an application form, LSAT results, transcripts, a personal statement, 2 letters of recommendation, transcripts, and the Dean's Certification Form. Notification of the admissions decision is on a rolling basis beginning January. The law school uses the LSAC.

Special
The law school recruits minority and disadvantaged students by means of recruitment visits to historically Black colleges and universities; various minority law career days and professional school forums sponsored by colleges and/or national minority student organizations; assistance from school chapters of Asian, Black, and Latin American Law Student Associations in recruitment efforts; the LSAC Candidate Referral Service (CRS); and a series of orientation programs for prospective students hosted at the law school. Requirements are different for out-of-state students. Transfer students must have a minimum GPA of 3, must have attended an ABA-approved law school, must submit a personal statement, and must have a letter of good standing from the dean of the current school.

Costs
Tuition and fees for the 2011–2012 academic year are $48,090 for all full-time students. Tuition for part-time students is $36,068 for in-state students and $36,068 out-of-state. On-campus room and board costs about $17,765 annually; books and supplies run $1,400.

Financial Aid
About 81% of current law students receive some form of aid. The average annual amount of aid from all sources combined, including scholarships, loans, and work contracts, is $47,091; maximum, $72,784. Awards are based on need and merit. Required financial statements are the FAFSA, Need Access Form, and the IRS Form 1040 for the applicant as well as parents. Also required are the school's financial assistance application forms. No application is required for merit-based awards. Special funds for minority or disadvantaged students include the Geraldo Rivera Scholarship; MLK, Jr. Scholarship; Judith Bregman Scholarship; William Randolph Hearst Scholarship; Edgardo Lopez Scholarship; James McClendon Jr. Scholarship; Lark-Barranco Scholarship; and the Opportunity Grant. First-year students are notified about their financial aid application at time of acceptance.

About the Law School
Brooklyn Law School was established in 1901 and is independent. The 1-acre campus is in an urban area in New York City. The primary mission of the law school is to train practicing attorneys as well as to help

students develop the intellectual capacity required to succeed whether they choose to practice law or pursue an alternative career with a legal background. Students have access to federal, state, county, city, and local agencies, courts, correctional facilities, law firms, and legal aid organizations in the Brooklyn area. Nearby are the U.S. district court, appellate court, state supreme and family courts, city civil and criminal courts, U.S. attorney's office, and Legal Aid Society. Facilities of special interest to law students include a technologically advanced library and fully wired classrooms with more than 2,400 student-accessible wired network connections, and wireless network connections in academic and residential buildings. Housing for students guaranteed for first-year students and is available for over 500 students in 10 residence halls located in the Brooklyn Heights Historic District. All law school facilities are accessible to the physically disabled.

Calendar
The law school operates on a traditional semester basis. Courses for full-time students are offered both day and evening, and must be completed within 4 years. For part-time students, courses are offered evenings only, and must be completed within 5 years. New full- and part-time students are admitted in the fall. There is a 7-week summer session. Transferable summer courses are offered.

Programs
In addition to the J.D., the law school offers the LL.M. Students may take relevant courses in other programs and apply credit toward the J.D.; a maximum of 9 credits may be applied. The following joint degrees may be earned: J.D./M.A. (Juris Doctor/Master of Arts in Law and Political Science), J.D./M.B.A. (Juris Doctor/Master of Business Administration), J.D./M.S. (Juris Doctor/Master of Science in Library and Information Science), and J.D./M.S. (Juris Doctor/Master of Urban Planning).

Required
To earn the J.D., candidates must complete 86 total credits, of which 31 are for required courses. They must maintain a minimum GPA of 2.3 in the required courses. The following first-year courses are required of all students: Civil Procedure, Constitutional Law, Contracts, Criminal Law, Legal Process, Legal Writing, Property, and

Phone: 718-780-7906
Fax: 718-780-0395
E-mail: *admitq@brooklaw.edu*
Web: *brooklaw.edu*

Contact
Dean of Admissions and Financial Aid, 718-780-7906 for general inquiries; Nancy Zahzam, Financial Aid Director, 718-780-7915 (nancy.zahzam@brooklaw.edu) for financial aid information.

NEW YORK

Torts. Required upper-level courses consist of a skills course and an upper-class writing requirement. The required orientation program for first-year students is held a week before classes begin. Students receive faculty and student advisers, start the Introduction to the Study of Law course and the First-Year Legal Writing Program, and participate in workshops.

Electives
The Brooklyn Law School offers concentrations in corporate law, criminal law, entertainment law, family law, intellectual property law, internationl law, juvenile law, labor law, litigation, media law, securities law, sports law, tax law, torts and insurance, international business, public interest, and human rights. In addition, any student who has completed the first year of study may take clinics in bankruptcy, community development, and criminal practice. Seminars range from 1 to 2 credits. All students who have completed their first year of study may enroll in internships with judges, criminal justice agencies, and a wide range of organizations in areas such as environmental law, children's rights, business regulation, and intellectual property. Up to 3 credits may be earned by any upper-level student who, under the supervision of a faculty member, researches and writes a paper of publishable quality. The Media and Society Lecture Series brings journalists from around the country to address current issues involving the media. The Abraham L. Pomerantz Lectures focus on corporate or securities law topics and related professional responsibility issues. Summer study sponsored by the law school in Bologna, Italy, and Beijing, China, is available. There are exchange programs with Buceris University in Hamburg, Germany, University of Essex in England, and in Argentina, Hong Kong, Ireland, and Israel. Upper-level students may also pursue study abroad through other law schools if they demonstrate, in writing, special need and obtain the written approval of the Associate Dean for Academic Affairs. First-year students may take advantage of year-long support services offered through the Academic Success Program. A summer Legal Process course and various tutorial programs specifically target affirmative action students. Special interest groups include the Edward V. Sparer Public Interest Fellowship Program; the Center for the Study of International Business Law Fellowship Program; the Center for Law, Language, and Cognition; Center for Health, Science, and Public

Policy; and the International Human Rights Fellowship. The most widely taken electives are Corporations, Evidence, and Criminal Procedure.

Graduation Requirements
In order to graduate, candidates must have a GPA of 2.3, must have completed the upper-division writing requirement, and must pass the Legal Profession and skills courses.

Organizations
Students edit the *Brooklyn Law Review*, *Brooklyn Journal of International Law*, *Journal of Law and Public Policy*, *Brooklyn Journal of Corporate, Financial and Commercial Law*, and *The Docket*. Moot court teams annually compete in 15 to 18 tournaments including the ABA's National Moot Court Competition, Phillip C. Jessup International Law Moot Competition, and the National First Amendment Competition co-sponsored by Vanderbilt University and the Freedom Forum. Other competitions include the Texas Young Lawyer's Association National Trial Competition, College of Trial Lawyers, the Dominick L. Gabriella Family Law Competition, and the Ruby R. Vale Interschool Corporate Moot Court Competition. Law student organizations include the Association of Trial Lawyers of America, National Lawyers Guild, and Legal Association of Women. Local Chapters of national associations include the Brooklyn Law Students for the Public Interest, BLS Students Against Domestic Violence, and Entertainment, Arts and Sports Law Society. Other campus organizations include the Student Bar Association, and Asian, Black, and Latin American Law Student associations.

Library
The law library contains 589,975 hard-copy volumes and 321,053 microform volume equivalents, and subscribes to 1,401 serial publications. Such online databases and networks as CALI, CIS Universe, DIALOG, Legal-Trac, LEXIS, OCLC First Search, WESTLAW, Wilsonline Indexes, CCH Tax Service, IntelliConncct (CCH Health and HR), CIS Statistical Universe, IndexMaster, HeinOnline, LawPro, UN Access, UN Treaty, JSTOR, BNA All, RIA Checkpoint, Isino Law, NatLaw and Justis, LEXIS NEXIS Serials, LEXIS NEXIS Congressional, Bloomberg, Making of Modern Law, InterAm Database, Juta Law, Kluwer Arbitration, Lawtel, Law 360, Oxford Reports (Intel Law), and Project MUSE

Placement

J.D.s awarded:	454

Services available through: a separate law school placement center.
Services: online job listings and specialized public interest counseling through the law school's Office of Public Service Program.
Special features: a network of 18,000 alumni, assigning every first-year student to career counselors during the first semester, and a large professional and support staff.

Full-time job interviews:	25 employers
Summer job interviews:	60 employers
Placement by graduation:	78% of class
Placement within 9 months:	88% of class
Average starting salary:	$31,200 to $160,000

Areas of placement:

Private practice 2–10 attorneys	17%
Private practice 11–23 attorneys	3%
Private practice 26–50 attorneys	3%
Private practice 51–100 attorneys	5%
Government	19%
Business/industry	18%
Judicial clerkships	7%
Public interest	7%
Private practice 100+ attorneys	3%
Military	1%
Academic	1%

are available to law students for research. Brooklyn Law School Library is a selective U.S. government depository. Also, the library has an extensive international law collection, which it developed by participating in the New York Joint International Law Program library consortium. The ratio of seats in the library to students is 1 to 2.

Faculty
The law school has 73 full-time and 133 part-time faculty members, of whom 71 are women. About 10% of full-time faculty have a graduate law degree in addition to the J.D. The ratio of full-time students to full-time faculty in an average clinic is 7 to 1. The law school has a regular program of bringing visiting professors and other distinguished lecturers and visitors to campus.

Students
About 45% of the student body are women; 24%, minorities; 9%, African American; 12%, Asian American; and 6%, Hispanic. The majority of students come from New York (57%). The average age of entering students is 24; age range is 21 to 42. About 28% of students enter directly from undergraduate school, and 6% have a graduate degree. About 4% drop out after the first year for academic or personal reasons; 96% remain to receive a law degree.

CALIFORNIA WESTERN SCHOOL OF LAW

225 Cedar Street
San Diego, CA 92101-3046

Application Filing
Fall: April 1
Spring: November 1
Fee: $55

Accreditation
ABA, AALS

Degrees Granted
J.D., LL.M., M.C.L.

Enrollment 2011–2012 · First-Year Class

Men:	401	45%	Applied:	2,922
Women:	491	55%	Accepted:	1,348
Minorities:	250	28%	Enrolled:	340
Out-of-State:	285	32%		

2011–2012 Class Profile
LSAT Percentile: 50%
LSAT Median Score: 153
Percentage passing bar on first try: 84%

Tuition and Fees:

Resident
$42,700 (F/T)

Average (public)
$18,708

Average (private)
$34,451

Nonresident
$42,700 (F/T)

Average (public)
$29,793

Average (private)
$34,451

0 10 20 30 40 50

Percentage receiving financial aid: 92%

ADMISSIONS
In the fall of 2011 first-year class, 2922 applied, 1348 were accepted, and 340 enrolled. Six transfer students enrolled. The median LSAT percentile of the most recent first-year class was 50; the median GPA was 3.3 on a scale of 4.0. The lowest LSAT percentile accepted was 25; the highest was 75.

Requirements
Applicants must have a bachelor's degree and take the LSAT. The most important admission factors include LSAT results, GPA, and writing ability. No specific undergraduate courses are required. Candidates are not interviewed.

Procedure
The application deadline for fall entry is April 1. Applicants should submit an application form, LSAT results, transcripts, personal statement, nonrefundable application fee of $55, 2 letters of recommendation, and a resume. Notification of the admissions

decision is on a rolling basis. The law school uses the LSAC.

Special
The law school recruits minority and disadvantaged students through a combined effort with the Office of Admissions and the Office of Diversity Services, which coordinates the diversity recruitment program and maintains working relationships with law firms, alumni, professional and community organizations, and college administrators who provide valuable resources for minority students. Requirements are different for out-of-state students. Transfer students must have one year of credits, attended an ABA-approved law school, a personal statement, submit an official transcript, and 2 letters of recommendation, preferably from a law school dean or professors.

Costs
Tuition and fees for the 2011–2012 academic year are $42,600 for all full-time students. Tuition for part-time students is $27,000 for in-state students and $29,920 out-of-state. Books and supplies run $1,867.

Financial Aid
About 92% of current law students receive some form of aid. The average annual amount of aid from all sources combined, including scholarships, loans, and work contracts, is $48,499; maximum, $60,498. Awards are based on need and merit combined. Required financial statements are the FAFSA and California Western School of Law financial aid application. The aid application deadline for fall entry is April 1. Special funds for minority or disadvantaged students include scholarships. First-year students are notified about their financial aid application at time of acceptance.

About the Law School
California Western School of Law was established in 1924 and is a private institution. The campus is in an urban area in San Diego. The primary mission of the law school is to educate lawyers who will be creative problem solvers, and who will contribute to improving the lives of their clients and the quality of justice in society. Students have access to federal, state, county, city, and local agencies, courts, correctional facilities, law firms, and legal aid

organizations in the San Diego area. The San Diego Law Library is within walking distance. Facilities of special interest to law students are within walking distance and include courts, law firms, city, state, and federal agencies, and county law library. Housing for students is off campus. The school has a housing coordinator to assist students with finding housing. Most students live within 5 to 10 minutes of school. About 95% of the law school facilities are accessible to the physically disabled.

Calendar
The law school operates on a trimester basis. Courses for full-time students are offered days only and must be completed within 5 years. For part-time students, courses are offered days only and must be completed within 6 years. New full- and part-time students are admitted in the fall and spring. There is a 15-week summer session. Transferable summer courses are offered.

Programs
In addition to the J.D., the law school offers the LL.M. and M.C.L. Students may take relevant courses in other programs and apply credit toward the J.D.; a maximum of 12 credits may be applied. The following joint degrees may be earned: J.D./M.B.A. (Juris Doctor/Master of Business Administration), J.D./M.S.W. (Juris Doctor/Master of Social Work), and J.D./Ph.D. (Juris Doctor/Ph.D. in Political Science or History).

Required
To earn the J.D., candidates must complete 89 total credits, of which 43 are for required courses. They must maintain a minimum GPA of 74.0 in the required courses. The following first-year courses are required of all students: Civil Procedure I and II, Contracts I and II, Criminal Law, Legal Skills I and II, Property I and II, and Torts I. Required upper-level courses consist of Constitutional Law I, Criminal Procedure, Evidence, Legal Skills III, Professional Responsibility, and Torts II. First-year students must also attend a 1-day general orientation.

Electives
The law school offers concentrations in corporate law, criminal law, entertainment

Phone: 619-525-1401
800-255-4252
Fax: 619-615-1401
E-mail: *admissions@cwsl.edu*
Web: *www.californiawestern.edu*

Contact

Admissions Office, 619-525-1401 for general inquiries; William Kahler, Director of Financial Aid, 619-525-7060 for financial aid information.

CALIFORNIA

law, environmental law, family law, intellectual property law, internationl law, juvenile law, labor law, litigation, media law, sports law, telecommunication law, and biotechnology law. In addition, there is a wide variety of specialized seminar courses open to upper-level students. The school has an internship program open to upper-level students; students may take up to 10 credit hours and will receive 1 credit hour for a weekly seminar. Students may assist faculty as research assistants. Special lecture series include the Faculty Speakers Series, the Scholar in Residence Series, and the S. Houston Lay International Law and Relations Series. Students may participate in a study-abroad program and transfer up to 8 credit hours of work from consortium schools. California Western sponsors study-abroad programs in New Zealand, Malta, England (London), and Ireland (Galway). Tutorial programs include Introduction to Legal Skills, the Enrichment Program, and the Bar Prep Program. The Office of Diversity Services coordinates a mentor program for students with local minority lawyers, and sponsors tutorials. The school sponsors more than 30 student organizations that cover a wide range of interests and topics. The most widely taken electives are Alternative Dispute Resolution, Constitutional Law II, and Business Organizations.

Graduation Requirements

In order to graduate, candidates must have a GPA of 74.0, must have completed the upper-division writing requirement, and must have taken a practicum course.

Organizations

Students edit the *California Western Law Review*, the *California Western International Law Journal*, the *Environmental Law Newsletter*, and the student newspaper *Commentary*. Moot court competitions include the National Appellate Advocacy, Roger J. Traynor Moot Court, and Phillip C. Jessup International Law. Law student organizations include Public Interest Law Foundation, Phi Alpha Delta, and Student Bar Association. Local chapters of national associations include La Raza Law Students Association, Women's Law Caucus, and Black Law Students Association. Other campus organizations include Entertainment Sports Law Society, International Law Society, and Family Law Society.

Library

The law library contains 345,342 hard-copy volumes and 161,909 microform volume equivalents, and subscribes to 5,006 serial publications. Such online databases and networks as CALI, CIS Universe, DIA-LOG, Legal-Trac, LEXIS, Mathew Bender, OCLC First Search, WESTLAW, Wilsonline Indexes, Lexis Nexis Congressional, JSTOR, and Live Edgar are available to law students for research. Special library collections include collections on problem solving, constitutional and human rights law, military law, and international law. California Western is a partial California Depository Library. The ratio of library volumes to faculty is 6,641 to 1 and to students is 358 to 1. The ratio of seats in the library to students is 1 to 2.

Faculty

The law school has 52 full-time and 87 part-time faculty members, of whom 62 are women. About 25% of full-time faculty have a graduate law degree in addition to the J.D.; about 10% of part-time faculty have one. The ratio of full-time students to full-time faculty in an average class is 18 to 1; in a clinic, 1 to 1. The law school has a regular program of bringing visiting professors and other distinguished lecturers and visitors to campus.

Students

About 55% of the student body are women; 28%, minorities; 3%, African American; 14%, Asian American; 10%, Hispanic; 1%, Native American. The majority of students come from California (68%). The average age of entering students is 27; age range is 20 to 59. About 4% of students have a graduate degree. About 18% drop out after the first year for academic or personal reasons; 72% remain to receive a law degree.

Placement

J.D.s awarded:	247

Services available through: a separate law school placement center.

Services: nonlegal career alternatives, judicial clerkships, and decision-making counseling.

Special features: intensive individual planning and counseling, Alumni Career Advisor/mentor program, minority career development program, government legal careers job fair, public interest job fair, 5 career counselors on staff, a Pro Bono Program, and practice area/career option panels.

Full-time job interviews:	10 employers
Summer job interviews:	40 employers
Placement by graduation:	47% of class
Placement within 9 months:	91% of class
Average starting salary:	$50,000 to $200,000

Areas of placement:

Private practice 2–10 attorneys	41%
Private practice 11–23 attorneys	3%
Private practice 26–50 attorneys	6%
Private practice 51–100 attorneys	3%
Private practice 100+ attorneys	7%
Business/industry	13%
Government	12%
Public interest	7%
Judicial clerkships	5%
Military	2%
Academic	1%

CAMPBELL UNIVERSITY

Norman Adrian Wiggins School of Law

225 Hillsborough Street, Suite 401
Raleigh, NC 24603

Application Filing		Accreditation
Fall: April 1		ABA
		Degrees Granted
Fee: $50		J.D.

Enrollment 2011–2012			First-Year Class	
Men:	202	50%	Applied:	1,525
Women:	200	50%	Accepted:	460
Minorities:	44	11%	Enrolled:	161
Out-of-State:	80	20%		

2011–2012 Class Profile
LSAT Percentile: 71%
LSAT Median Score: 156
Percentage passing bar on first try: 95%

Tuition and Fees:

Resident
$16,955 (F/T)

Average (public)
$18,708

Average (private)
$34,451

Nonresident
n/av

Average (public)
$29,793

Average (private)
$34,451

Percentage receiving financial aid: 94%

ADMISSIONS

In the fall of 2011 first-year class, 1525 applied, 460 were accepted, and 161 enrolled. Four transfers enrolled. The median LSAT percentile of the most recent first-year class was 71; the median GPA was 3.4 on a scale of 4.0.

Requirements

Applicants must have a bachelor's degree and take the LSAT. The most important admission factors include LSAT results, GPA, and personal interview. No specific undergraduate courses are required. Candidates are interviewed.

Procedure

The application deadline for fall entry is April 1. Applicants should submit an application form, LSAT results, transcripts, a personal statement, a nonrefundable application fee of $50, and 2 letters of recommendation. Notification of the admissions decision is on a rolling basis. The law school uses the LSAC.

Special

The law school recruits minority and disadvantaged students by visiting minority organizations and hosting minority organizations and events. Requirements are different for out-of-state students. Transfer students must have one year of credit, must have attended an ABA-approved law school, and must submit a personal statement.

Costs

Tuition and fees for the 2011–2012 academic year are $16,700 for full-time in-state students. Books and supplies run $2,000.

Financial Aid

About 94% of current law students receive some form of aid. The average annual amount of aid from all sources combined, including scholarships, loans, and work contracts, is $48,866; maximum, $55,980. Awards are based on need and merit combined. The required financial statement is the FAFSA. The aid application deadline for fall entry is open. First-year students are notified about their financial aid application at time of acceptance.

About the Law School

Campbell University Norman Adrian Wiggins School of Law was established in 1976 and is a private institution. The campus is in an urban area located in downtown Raleigh. The primary mission of the law school is to build futures, shape careers, and combine theory and practice to provide a solid foundation for the practice of law, while instilling ethical and professional responsibility. Students have access to federal, state, county, city, and local agencies, courts, correctional facilities, law firms, and legal aid organizations in the Raleigh area. Facilities of special interest to law students include a students commons with a coffee shop on the second floor of the law school. All law school facilities are accessible to the physically disabled.

Calendar

The law school operates on a traditional semester basis. Courses are offered days only, and must be completed within 5 years. New students are admitted in the fall. There is a 7-week summer session. Transferable summer courses are not offered.

Programs

The following joint degrees may be earned: J.D./M.B.A. (Juris Doctor/Master of Business Administration), J.D./M.P.A. (Juris Doctor/Master of Public Administration in conjunction), and J.D./M.T.W.M. (Juris Doctor/Master in Trust and Wealth Management).

Required

To earn the J.D., candidates must complete 90 total credits, of which 67 are for required courses. They must maintain a minimum GPA of 75.0 in the required courses. The following first-year courses are required of all students: Advocacy, Civil Procedure I, Constitutional Courts, Criminal Law, Legal Research and Writing, Practical Skills and Values, Professional Responsibility Lecture Series, Property I and II, and Torts I and II. Required upper-level courses consist of Business Organizations, Commercial Law I and II, Constitutional Law I, Criminal Procedure, Evidence, Income Taxation, Jurisprudence, Perspectives on Professionalism and Leadership or Perspectives, Professional Responsibility and Ethics, Trial Advocacy, and Wills and Trusts. The required orientation program for first-year students is typically 3 days, and is focused on an introduction to the study of law.

Electives

The Norman Adrian Wiggins School of Law offers concentrations in litigation and business law. In addition, clinics include Trial Advocacy, a required "simulated" clinic offering 7 credit hours over 2 semesters, an Elder Law Clinic worth 8 credit hours, and Juvenile Justice Mediation worth 3 credit hours. Seminars include Environmental Law, Insurance Law, and Intellectual Property. Public-service internships are available to second- and third-year students for a maximum of 4 hours credit. Externships are available. The Professionalism Lecture Series is required of all first-year students. Special interest group programs include Campbell Law Innocence Project. The law school has an Academic Success Program to assist students. The most widely taken electives are Family Law, Remedies, and Workers' Compensation.

Graduation Requirements

In order to graduate, candidates must have a GPA of 75.0.

Phone: 919-865-5988
334-4111, ext. 4650
Fax: 919-865-5886
Web: law.campbell.edu

Contact

Admissions, 910-865-5988 for general inquiries; Samatha Collinash, Assistant Director, 919-865-5990 for financial aid information.

NORTH CAROLINA

Organizations

Students edit the *Campbell Law Review* and the *Campbell Law Observer*. Moot Court competitions entered by students are the ABA National Appellate Advocacy, National Moot Court, John Marshall National Moot Court, and the International Arbitration Competition. Other competitions are the National Trial, American Trial Lawyers Association, National Student Trial Advocacy, ABA Client Counseling and Negotiation Competition, and the NITA Tournament of Champions Trial Competition. Law student organizations, local chapters of national associations, and campus organizations include the Student Bar Association, ABA-Law Student Division, Black Law Students Association, Delta Theta Phi-Bryan Senate and Phi Alpha Delta fraternities, the Christian Legal Society, Academy of Trial Lawyers, and Women in Law.

Library

The law library contains 106,265 hardcopy volumes and 87,368 microform volume equivalents, and subscribes to 2,588 serial publications. Such online databases and networks as CALI, CIS Universe, Dow-Jones, Infotrac, Legal-Trac, LEXIS, Mathew Bender, OCLC First Search, WESTLAW, Wilsonline Indexes, Current Index to Legal Periodicals, Full Text and Retrospective, Making of Modern Law, Legal Treatises, Making of Modern Law: Historic Trials, Making of Modern Law: Supreme Court, BNA Premier, English

Collection Online Law Module, Audio Case Files, RIA Checkpoint, LMC Digital, Religion Case Law Reporter, Legal Forms, Index Master, Historical Statistics of the United States, Oxford International Encyclopedia of Legal History, and HeinOnline are available to law students for research. Special library collections include Trial Advocacy, Ethics and Jurisprudence, Public Interest Law, church-state, and Federal Taxation collections. The ratio of library volumes to faculty is 4,251 to 1 and to students is 264 to 1. The ratio of seats in the library to students is 1 to 2.

Faculty

The law school has 25 full-time and 40 part-time faculty members, of whom 14 are women. About 20% of full-time faculty have a graduate law degree in addition to the J.D.; about 2% of part-time faculty have one. The ratio of full-time students to full-time faculty in an average class is 17 to 1; in a clinic, 8 to 1.

Students

About 50% of the student body are women; 11%, minorities; 4%, African American; 2%, Asian American; 2%, Hispanic; and 1%, Native American. The majority of students come from North Carolina (80%). The average age of entering students is 26; age range is 22 to 58. About 9% drop out after the first year for academic or personal reasons; 91% remain to receive a law degree.

Placement

J.D.s awarded:	109

Services available through: a separate law school placement center.

Services: in- and out-of-state job fairs.

Special features: targeted mailings sent to regions of North Carolina, press releases issued on student activities, alumni assistance in specific areas of job search, a separate placement resource center and library, and a North Carolina job fair.

Full-time job interviews:	16 employers
Summer job interviews:	28 employers
Placement by graduation:	67% of class
Placement within 9 months:	94% of class
Average starting salary:	$54,500 to $63,500
Areas of placement:	
Private practice 2–10 attorneys	59%
Private practice 11–23 attorneys	9%
Private practice 26–50 attorneys	8%
Private practice 51–100 attorneys	14%
Government	12%
Business/industry	9%
Judicial clerkships	5%
Public interest	5%

CAPITAL UNIVERSITY
Law School

303 East Broad Street
Columbus, OH 43215-3200

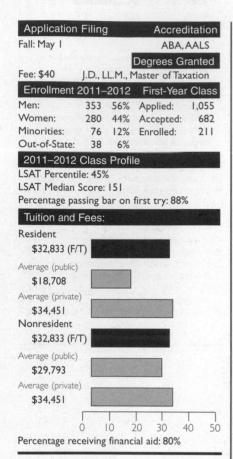
ADMISSIONS

In the fall of 2011 first-year class, 1055 applied, 682 were accepted, and 211 enrolled. Ten transfers enrolled. The median LSAT percentile of the most recent first-year class was 45; the median GPA was 3.2 on a scale of 4.0. The lowest LSAT percentile accepted was 15; the highest was 92.

Requirements

Applicants must have a bachelor's degree and take the LSAT. Minimum acceptable GPA is 2.0 on a scale of 4.0. The most important admission factors include letters of recommendation, LSAT results, and academic achievement. No specific undergraduate courses are required. Candidates are not interviewed.

Procedure

The application deadline for fall entry is May 1. Applicants should submit an application form, LSAT results, transcripts, a nonrefundable application fee of $40,

2 letters of recommendation, an essay or personal statement, and a $100 tuition deposit for accepted students; a second $100 seat deposit is due by June 13. Notification of the admissions decision is on a rolling basis. The law school uses the LSAC.

Special

The law school recruits minority and disadvantaged students by means of targeted mailings, use of minority students, faculty, and alumni in the recruitment process, and financial assistance programs. Requirements are different for out-of-state students. Transfer students must have one year of credit and must have attended an ABA-approved law school.

Costs

Books and supplies run $1,500.

Financial Aid

About 80% of current law students receive some form of aid. The average annual amount of aid from all sources combined, including scholarships, loans, and work contracts, is $41,574; maximum, $48,179. Awards are based on need and merit combined. The required financial statement is the FAFSA. The aid application deadline for fall entry is May 1. Special funds for minority or disadvantaged students include teaching and research assistantships, grants and scholarships, work-study awards, low-interest student loans, and endowed scholarships. First-year students are notified about their financial aid application at time of acceptance.

About the Law School

Capital University Law School was established in 1903 and is a private institution. The campus is in an urban area in the Discovery District of downtown Columbus. Capital University Law School offers dedicated students the intellectual, ethical, and practical foundation to become successful lawyers and leaders. Students have access to federal, state, county, city, and local agencies, courts, correctional facilities, law firms, and legal aid organizations in the Columbus area. The law school is located in downtown Columbus, near the state capital; therefore, students have access to the state legislature and committees, the governor's office, and the

state supreme court. Housing for students is available off campus; the university helps students find suitable housing. All law school facilities are accessible to the physically disabled.

Calendar

The law school operates on a traditional semester basis. Courses for full-time students are offered both day and evening, and must be completed within 7 years. For part-time students, courses are offered both day and evening, and must be completed within 7 years. New full- and part-time students are admitted in the fall. There are 10- and 5-week summer sessions. Transferable summer courses are offered.

Programs

In addition to the J.D., the law school offers the LL.M. and Master of Taxation. Students may take relevant courses in other programs and apply credit toward the J.D.; a maximum of 9 credits may be applied. The following joint degrees may be earned: J.D./LL.M. (Juris Doctor/Master of Laws in Taxation), J.D./M.B.A. (Juris Doctor/Master of Business Administration), J.D./M.S.A. (Juris Doctor/Master of Sports Administration), J.D./M.S.N. (Juris Doctor/Master of Science in Nursing), and J.D./M.T.S. (Juris Doctor/Master of Theological Studies).

Required

To earn the J.D., candidates must complete 89 total credits, of which 46 are for required courses. They must maintain a minimum GPA of 2.0 in the required courses. The following first-year courses are required of all students: Civil Procedure I, Constitutional Law I, Contracts I and II, Criminal Law, Legal Writing I and II, Property I and II, and Torts I and II. Required upper-level courses consist of a perspective course, a writing or research requirement, Civil Procedure II, Constitutional Law II, Evidence, Federal Personal Income Tax, Legal Drafting, and Professional Responsibility. The required orientation program for first-year students is a four-day program geared toward preparing students for the study of law. It includes a mock classroom discussion, ethics panels, reading and briefing exercises, and meetings with faculty, staff, and upper-class students.

Phone: 614-236-6500
Fax: 614-236-6972
E-mail: admissions@law.capital.edu
Web: law.capital.edu

Contact

Assistant Dean of Admission and Financial Aid, 614-236-6310 for general inquiries.

OHIO

Electives

The Law School offers concentrations in environmental law, family law, labor law, governmental affairs, labor and employment, publicly held companies, small business entities, alternative dispute resolution, and litigation and criminal law. Clinics in general, civil, and criminal litigation are available to students who have qualified as legal interns. Several seminars are offered each year in a variety of subjects. Externships are available through the local, state, and federal courts, and through several government agencies and nonprofit organizations. Students may serve as research assistants for law professors or enroll in independent studies. All students must satisfy an upper-class scholarship requirement. Field work may be done through the externship programs, as well as the clinics. Special lecture series include the Sullivan Lectures, Wells Conference, and faculty symposia. All students are welcome to participate in the 1L Academic Success Protocol conducted during the first year of instruction in which students are extensively trained in effective exam taking and legal problem-solving skills. A second-year, one-credit legal analysis course is available to 2L students. One-on-one academic coaching is available to all students at any time. The law school's office of multicultural affairs offers programs for minority students. Special interest group programs include the National Center for Adoption Law and Policy, Center for Dispute Resolution, graduate tax and business law programs, and Tobacco Public Policy Center. The most widely taken electives are Business Associations I and II, Payment Systems, and Secured Transactions.

Graduation Requirements

In order to graduate, candidates must have a GPA of 2.0, and must have completed the upper-division writing and other requirements.

Organizations

Students edit *The Capital University Law Review* and the *Adoption Law News Summary*. Moot court competitions include National Moot Court, Sports Law, and Labor Law competitions. Other competitions include Negotiation, First Year Moot Court, Environmental Law, Frederick Douglass Competition, Jessup International Competition, Tax Law Competition, and Mock Trial. Student organizations include the ABA-Law Student Division, Black Law Students Association, and the Intellectual Property Law Society. There are local chapters of the Federalist Society, Christian Legal Society, and Phi Alpha Delta. Other law student organizations include Corporate and Business Law Society, Environmental Law Society, and Sports and Entertainment Law.

Library

The law library contains 263,655 hard-copy volumes and 64,791 microform volume equivalents, and subscribes to 510 serial publications. Such online databases and networks as CALI, CIS Universe, LEXIS, OCLC First Search, WESTLAW, HeinOnline, OCLC First Search, BNA, and CCH are available to law students for research. Special library collections include American Law of Taxation. The ratio of library volumes to faculty is 7,323 to 1 and to students is 479 to 1. The ratio of seats in the library to students is 1 to 1.

Faculty

The law school has 40 full-time and 25 part-time faculty members, of whom 22 are women. According to AAUP standards for Category IIA institutions, faculty salaries are above average. About 23% of full-time faculty have a graduate law degree in addition to the J.D. The ratio of full-time students to full-time faculty in an average class is 15 to 1; in a clinic, 8 to 1. The law school has a regular program of bringing visiting professors and other distinguished lecturers and visitors to campus.

Students

About 44% of the student body are women; 12%, minorities; 7%, African American; 2%, Asian American; and 2%, Hispanic. The majority of students come from Ohio (94%). The average age of entering students is 28; age range is 20 to 63. About 34% of students enter directly from undergraduate school, and 6% have a graduate degree. About 9% drop out after the first year for academic or personal reasons; 91% remain to receive a law degree.

Application Filing	Accreditation
Fall: April 1	ABA, AALS

	Degrees Granted
Fee: $40	J.D., LL.M., LL.M. in U.S. and Global Legal Studies, International Business

Enrollment 2011–2012   First-Year Class

Men:	343	57%	Applied:	1,651
Women:	262	43%	Accepted:	768
Minorities:	109	18%	Enrolled:	192
Out-of-State:	399	66%		

2011–2012 Class Profile

LSAT Median Score: 158
Percentage passing bar on first try: 90%

Tuition and Fees:

Resident
$42,564 (F/T)

Average (public)
$18,708

Average (private)
$34,451

Nonresident
$42,564 (F/T)

Average (public)
$29,793

Average (private)
$34,451

0 10 20 30 40 50

Percentage receiving financial aid: 85%

ADMISSIONS

In the fall of 2011 first-year class, 1651 applied, 768 were accepted, and 192 enrolled. Twenty-three transfers enrolled. The median GPA of the most recent first-year class was 3.5.

Requirements

Applicants must have a bachelor's degree and take the LSAT. The most important admission factors include academic achievement, LSAT results, and GPA. No specific undergraduate courses are required. Candidates are interviewed.

Procedure

The application deadline for fall entry is April 1. Applicants should submit an application form, LSAT results, transcripts, a nonrefundable application fee of $40, a personal statement, a resume, and an LSAC report. Notification of the admissions decision is between January 1 and May 1.

Special

The law school recruits minority and disadvantaged students by means of attendance at law school fairs likely to be attended by minority and disadvantaged students, financial assistance, and participation in the Midwest Minority Recruitment Fair. Requirements are different for out-of-state students. Transfer students must have one year of credit, must have attended an ABA-approved law school, and must have performed well at the school from which they are transferring.

Costs

Tuition and fees for the 2011–2012 academic year are $42,450 for all full-time students. Books and supplies run $1,576.

Financial Aid

About 85% of current law students receive some form of aid. The average annual amount of aid from all sources combined, including scholarships, loans, and work contracts, is $42,300; maximum, $62,631. Awards are based on merit. Required financial statements are the FAFSA and either copies of the student's previous year's federal tax return or a student's statement of income (if the student was not required to file a tax return) if selected for verification by FAFSA. The aid application deadline for fall entry is May 1. Special funds for minority or disadvantaged students include leadership grants, which may be offered to candidates with outstanding academic credentials whose interesting backgrounds will enhance the quality of the student body. First-year students are notified about their financial aid application approximately 4 weeks after the aid application is complete and the student has been admitted.

About the Law School

Case Western Reserve University School of Law was established in 1892 and is a private institution. The 128-acre campus is in an urban area 4 miles east of downtown Cleveland. The mission of Case Western Reserve University School of Law is to provide a theoretical and practical legal education for the future leaders of our region, our nation, and the world, to advance knowledge and understanding of the law both within the scholarly community and the larger world, and to promote the role of lawyers as social engineers in

pursuit of a good society and social justice. Students have access to federal, state, county, city, and local agencies, courts, correctional facilities, law firms, and legal aid organizations in the Cleveland area. Cleveland is home to many of the nation's top law firms and Fortune 500 companies. Facilities of special interest to law students include the state-of-the-art computer laboratory and the moot court room, along with a legal clinic that operates as a law firm within the law school setting. Affordable housing is available nearby. All law school facilities are accessible to the physically disabled.

Calendar

The law school operates on a traditional semester basis. Courses are offered both day and evening, and must be completed within 3 years. New students are admitted in the fall. There is a 6-week summer session. Transferable summer courses are offered.

Programs

In addition to the J.D., the law school offers the LL.M. and the LL.M. in U.S. and Global Legal Studies and International Business. Students may take relevant courses in other programs and apply credit toward the J.D.; a maximum of 9 credits may be applied. The following joint degrees may be earned: J.D./C.N.M. (Juris Doctor/Certificate of Nonprofit Management), J.D./M.A. (Juris Doctor/Master of Art History and Museum Studies), J.D./M.A. (Juris Doctor/Master of Arts in Legal History), J.D./M.A. (Juris Doctor/Master of Bioethics), J.D./M.B.A (Juris Doctor/Master of Business Administration), J.D./M.D. (Juris Doctor/Doctor of Medicine), J.D./M.P.H. (Juris Doctor/Master of Public Health), J.D./M.P.S. (Juris Doctor/Master of Political Science), J.D./M.S. (Juris Doctor/Master of Science in Biochemistry), and J.D./M.S.S.A. (Juris Doctor/Master of Science in Social Work).

Required

To earn the J.D., candidates must complete 88 total credits, of which 39 are for required courses. They must maintain a minimum GPA of 2.3 in the required courses. The following first-year courses are required of all students: a perspectives course, CASE ARC: Core I and II, Civil Procedure, Constitutional Law,

Phone: 216-368-3600
800-756-0036
Fax: 216-368-1042
E-mail: lawadmissions@case.edu
Web: law.case.edu

Contact

Tonya Phillips, Director of Financial Aid, 216-368-3602 for financial aid information.

OHIO

Contracts, Criminal Law, Property, and Torts. Required upper-level courses consist of a substantial research paper, CASE ARC: CORE III and SRC, and Professional Responsibility. More than 50 clinical course positions are available to third-year students. The required orientation program for first-year students is an intensive week-long orientation that includes 17 hours of instruction in the innovative CASE ARC Integrated Lawyering Skills Program.

Electives

The School of Law offers concentrations in corporate law, criminal law, intellectual property law, internationl law, litigation, health law, law technology, public law, law arts, and national security law. Clinical courses provide students with the opportunity to sit first chair and represent clients in a variety of cases. A wide variety of seminars is limited to 12 students, and range from Copyright in the Digital Millennium to Wrongful Convictions. Judicial externships with federal, district, and circuit court judges are available to selected students for 3 credits. Supervised research with faculty is worth 2 credit hours, and is offered to second- and third-year students. Field work is also available for credit through the Coast Guard Defense Lab. Special lecture series include the Klatsky Seminar in Human Rights and the Distinguished Intellectual Property Lecture. A study-abroad program is available in Russia, Canada, Mexico, and Australia. An academic assistance program offers tutorial assistance to first- and second-year students, primarily on exam technique and general writing skills. The most widely taken electives are Evidence, Business Associations, Criminal Procedure, and Wills and Trusts.

Graduation Requirements

In order to graduate, candidates must have a GPA of 2.3, must have completed the upper-division writing requirement, and must have completed the CASE ARC Integrated Lawyering Skills Program and Professional Responsibility.

Organizations

Students edit the *Case Western Reserve Law Review, Health Matrix: The Journal of Law-Medicine, Journal of International Law, Canada-United States Law Journal,*

The Internet Law Journal, and the newspaper *The Docket.* Students compete in the local Dean Dunmore Moot Court competition; the National Moot Court, held regionally and in New York; Niagara, Canada-U.S. relations; and the local Jessup competition sponsored by the International Law Society. Other competitions include the Jonathan M. Ault Mock Trial in Houston. Law student organizations, local chapters of national associations, and campus organizations include Big Buddies, the Student Intellectual Property Law Association, the Student International Law Association, the Student Health Law Association, Phi Delta Phi, Women's Law Association, and J. Reuben Clark Law Society.

Library

The law library contains 307,071 hardcopy volumes and 104,733 microform volume equivalents, and subscribes to 968 serial publications. Such online databases and networks as CALI, CIS Universe, Infotrac, Legal-Trac, LEXIS, Mathew Bender, OCLC First Search, WESTLAW, Wilsonline Indexes, Academic Universe, HeinOnline, JSTOR, NetLibrary, and BNA are available to law students for research. Special library collections include a U.S. government documents depository and a Canadian government documents depository. The ratio of library volumes to faculty is 5,483 to 1 and to students is 437 to 1. The ratio of seats in the library to students is 1 to 2.

Faculty

The law school has 49 full-time and 54 part-time faculty members, of whom 31 are women. According to AAUP standards for Category I institutions, faculty salaries are above average. The ratio of full-time students to full-time faculty in an average class is 13 to 1; in a clinic, 8 to 1. The law school has a regular program of bringing visiting professors and other distinguished lecturers and visitors to campus. There is a chapter of the Order of the Coif.

Students

About 43% of the student body are women; 18%, minorities; 5%, African American; 9%, Asian American; and 3%, Hispanic. The average age of entering students is 25; age range is 21 to 49. About 32%

Placement

J.D.s awarded:	203

Services available through: a separate law school placement center.

Services: videoconference interviews and mock interviews.

Special features: national relationships that create opportunities and connect Case law students with prospective employers. Recently, the fall and spring interview programs included on-campus interviews and off-campus interview trips to Washington, D.C., Chicago, New York City, Southern California, and New England.

Placement by graduation:	52% of class
Placement within 9 months:	92% of class
Average starting salary:	$42,000 to $112,500

Areas of placement:

Private practice 2–10 attorneys	17%
Private practice 11–23 attorneys	5%
Private practice 26–50 attorneys	4%
Private practice 51–100 attorneys	1%
Business/industry	23%
Government	17%
Public interest	12%
Judicial clerkships	5%
Military	3%
Academic	1%

of students enter directly from undergraduate school, and 16% have a graduate degree. About 3% drop out after the first year for academic or personal reasons; 96% remain to receive a law degree.

CATHOLIC UNIVERSITY OF AMERICA

Columbus School of Law

Cardinal Station
Washington, DC 20064

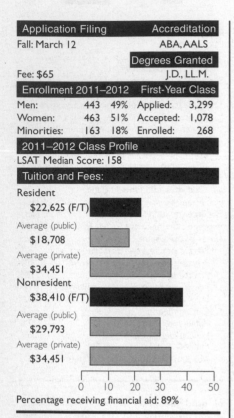

Application Filing		Accreditation
Fall: March 12		ABA, AALS
		Degrees Granted
Fee: $65		J.D., LL.M.

Enrollment 2011–2012			First-Year Class	
Men:	443	49%	Applied:	3,299
Women:	463	51%	Accepted:	1,078
Minorities:	163	18%	Enrolled:	268

2011–2012 Class Profile
LSAT Median Score: 158

Tuition and Fees:

Resident
$22,625 (F/T)

Average (public)
$18,708

Average (private)
$34,451

Nonresident
$38,410 (F/T)

Average (public)
$29,793

Average (private)
$34,451

0 10 20 30 40 50

Percentage receiving financial aid: 89%

ADMISSIONS

In the fall of 2012 first-year class, 3299 applied, 1078 were accepted, and 268 enrolled. Nine transfers enrolled. The median GPA of the most recent first-year class was 3.3.

Requirements

Applicants must have a bachelor's degree and take the LSAT. The most important admission factors include LSAT results, GPA, and letter of recommendation. No specific undergraduate courses are required. Candidates are not interviewed.

Procedure

The application deadline for fall entry is March 12. Applicants should submit an application form, LSAT results, transcripts, a nonrefundable application fee of $65, and 2 letters of recommendation. Notification of the admissions decision is on a rolling basis. The law school uses the LSAC.

Special

The law school recruits minority and disadvantaged students by visiting colleges and geographical areas with large minority populations. Minority applicants are encouraged to write brief background statements as part of the admissions process. Special consideration is given to applicants who plan to attend the Council on Legal Education Opportunity (CLEO) program and to Pre Law Summer Institute (PLSI) for Native American Students. Requirements are different for out-of-state students. Transfer students must have one year of credit, have attended an ABA-approved law school, be in good standing, and be competitive in class rank.

Costs

Tuition and fees for the 2012–2013 academic year are $21,540 for full-time in-state students and $37,850 for out-of-state students. Books and supplies run $1,500.

Financial Aid

About 89% of current law students receive some form of aid. The average annual amount of aid from all sources combined, including scholarships, loans, and work contracts, is $44,676; maximum, $64,170. Awards are based on need and merit, along with community service in conjunction with other considerations. Required financial statement is the FAFSA. The aid application deadline for fall entry is July 15. Special funds for minority or disadvantaged students include scholarships that are merit based. First-year students are notified about their financial aid application at time of acceptance.

About the Law School

Catholic University of America Columbus School of Law was established in 1898 and is a private institution. The 154-acre campus is in an urban area in a non-commercial area, accessible by public. The primary mission of the law school is to provide a small, diverse student body with a quality legal education and to prepare students for the ethical practice of law. Students have access to federal, state, county, city, and local agencies, courts, correctional facilities, law firms, and legal aid organizations in the Washington area. The Library of Congress and the U.S.

Supreme Court are nearby. Facilities of special interest to law students consist of a new law school facility, completed in 1994, that houses all components of the school. Law students also have access to the university's athletic complex, including a pool, Nautilus equipment, sauna, tennis courts, and a track. Housing for students is available in a variety of apartments and private rooms that are within easy traveling distance. All law school facilities are accessible to the physically disabled.

Calendar

The law school operates on a traditional semester basis. Courses for full-time students are offered days only and must be completed within 5 years. For part-time students, courses are offered evenings only and must be completed within 6 years. New full- and part-time students are admitted in the fall. There is a 7- to 8-week summer session. Transferable summer courses are offered.

Programs

In addition to the J.D., the law school offers the LL.M. Students may take relevant courses in other programs and apply credit toward the J.D. The following joint degrees may be earned: J.D./J.C.L. (Juris Doctor/Licentiate of Canon Law), J.D./M.A. (Juris Doctor/Master of Arts in Politics, Philosophy, or History), J.D./M.L.S. (Juris Doctor/Master of Library Science), and J.D./M.S.W. (Juris Doctor/Master of Social Work).

Required

To earn the J.D., candidates must complete 84 total credits, of which 33 are for required courses. They must maintain a minimum GPA of 2.1 in the required courses. The following first-year courses are required of all students: Civil Procedure, Constitutional Law, Contracts, Criminal Law, Lawyering Skills, Property, Social Justice and the Law, and Torts. Required upper-level courses consist of Professional Responsibility. The required orientation program for first-year students occurs during the first week and consists of the beginning of the Lawyering Skills course, a general introduction to the law library and the law school, study skills, and social activities.

Phone: 202-319-5151
Fax: 202-319-6285
E-mail: admissions@law.edu
Web: www.law.edu

Contact

David Schrock, Financial Aid Director, 202-319-5143 for financial aid information.

DISTRICT OF COLUMBIA

Electives

The Columbus School of Law offers concentrations in corporate law, criminal law, entertainment law, environmental law, family law, intellectual property law, internationl law, juvenile law, labor law, litigation, maritime law, media law, securities law, sports law, tax law, torts and insurance, communications law, securities and corporate law, public policy, law and religion, and jurisprudence. In addition, The law school has 4 one-semester and 2 year-long clinics offering from 6 to 12 credits including General Practice, Families & the Law, and Advocacy for the Elderly. Seminars are also open only to upper-level students. Students from the law school participate in nearly 200 externship placements annually in all organizations, and law firms of all sizes and specialties. Students may serve as research assistants to law faculty members. Field work opportunities are available through the general externship program as well as the Immigration and Human Rights Clinic and seminars such as the Public Policy Practicum and the Education Law Practicum. Special lecture series are the Pope John XXIII Lectures, the Brendan F. Brown Distinguished Lectures and Scholars-in-Residence, and the Mirror of Justice Lectures. The International Business and Trade Summer Law Program is a 6-week summer program that takes place at the historic Jagiellonian University in Krakow, Poland and is open to students who have completed their first year of law school and are in good standing. Student groups and individual faculty members conduct informal tutorial sessions. A Writing Consultant is available for individualized legal writing assistance. The most widely taken electives are Evidence, Corporations, and Family Law.

Graduation Requirements

In order to graduate, candidates must have a GPA of 2.2, and have completed the upper-division writing requirement.

Organizations

Student-edited publications include *The Catholic University of America Law Review*. Other law reviews include the *Journal of Contemporary Health Law and Policy, and CommLaw Conspectus.* Moot Court teams compete in the Sutherland Cup Competition, National Telecommunications Law Competition and Jessup Cup International Law Competition. Other competitions include the Securities Law Competition, and the Trials Competition. Student organizations include the Students for Public Interest Law, Advocates for Life, and Communications Law Students. Law student organizations include the student divisions of the ABA, the American Society of International Law, and Black Law Students Organization. Local chapters of national associations include Thurgood Marshall American Inn of Court and Pope John Paul II Guild of Catholic Lawyers.

Library

The law library contains 203,232 hardcopy volumes and 199,613 microform volume equivalents, and subscribes to 5,276 serial publications. Such online databases and networks as CALI, CIS Universe, Infotrac, Legal-Trac, LEXIS, OCLC First Search, WESTLAW, and Wilsonline Indexes are available to law students for research. Special library collections include a partial U.S. government depository that can be accessed through hard copy, CD-ROMs, and the Internet. The collection also includes large concentrations in Congressional documents, international law, law and religion, military law, telecommunications law, and UN documents. The collection also includes large concentrations in Congressional documents, international law, law and religion, military law, telecommunications law, and UN documents. The ratio of library volumes to faculty is 3,332 to 1 and to students is 214 to 1. The ratio of seats in the library to students is 1 to 2.

Faculty

The law school has 91 full-time and 87 part-time faculty members, of whom 54 are women. According to AAUP standards for Category 1 institutions, faculty salaries are average. The ratio of full-time students to full-time faculty in an average class is 15 to 1. The law school has a regular program of bringing visiting professors and other distinguished lecturers and visitors to campus.

Placement

J.D.s awarded:	245

Services available through: a separate law school placement center.

Special features: individual and group consultations, on-campus interviewing, consortium interviewing conferences, resume collection service, workshops on planning and executing a job search, writing resumes and cover letters, developing interviewing skills, building legal credentials, understanding specific legal markets, and a broad range of programming and networking opportunities.

Full-time job interviews:	75 employers
Placement within 9 months:	93% of class
Average starting salary:	$28,000 to $135,000

Areas of placement:

Private practice 2–10 attorneys	42%
Government	27%
Business/industry	13%
Judicial clerkships	12%
Public interest	2%
Academic	2%

Students

About 51% of the student body are women; 18%, minorities; 5%, African American; 10%, Asian American; and 3%, Hispanic. The average age of entering students is 26; age range is 21 to 46. About 10% drop out after the first year for academic or personal reasons.

One University Drive
Orange, CA 92866

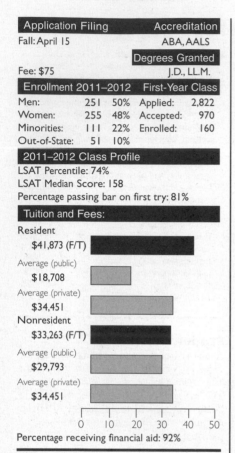

Application Filing			Accreditation
Fall: April 15			ABA, AALS
			Degrees Granted
Fee: $75			J.D., LL.M.

Enrollment 2011–2012			First-Year Class	
Men:	251	50%	Applied:	2,822
Women:	255	48%	Accepted:	970
Minorities:	111	22%	Enrolled:	160
Out-of-State:	51	10%		

2011–2012 Class Profile
LSAT Percentile: 74%
LSAT Median Score: 158
Percentage passing bar on first try: 81%

Tuition and Fees:

Resident
$41,873 (F/T)

Average (public)
$18,708

Average (private)
$34,451

Nonresident
$33,263 (F/T)

Average (public)
$29,793

Average (private)
$34,451

0 10 20 30 40 50

Percentage receiving financial aid: 92%

ADMISSIONS

In the fall of 2011 first-year class, 2822 applied, 970 were accepted, and 160 enrolled. Nine transfers enrolled. The median LSAT percentile of the most recent first-year class was 74; the median GPA was 3.5 on a scale of 4.0. The lowest LSAT percentile accepted was 26; the highest was 99.

Requirements

Applicants must have a bachelor's degree and take the LSAT. Minimum acceptable GPA is 2.0 on a scale of 4.0. The most important admission factors include undergraduate curriculum, writing ability, and academic achievement. No specific undergraduate courses are required. Candidates are not interviewed.

Procedure

The application deadline for fall entry is April 15. Applicants should submit an application form, transcripts, a personal statement, TOEFL (where indicated), a nonrefundable application fee of $75, 2 letters of recommendation, resume, and CAS report (which includes LSAT, transcripts, and letters of recommendation). Notification of the admissions decision is usually within 6 to 8 weeks. The law school uses the LSAC.

Special

The law school recruits minority and disadvantaged students by recruiting at colleges and universities that have a high percentage of minority and disadvantaged students, by advertising in and supporting publications reaching the various ethnic and disadvantaged communities, and by hosting and attending special events. Requirements are different for out-of-state students. Transfer students must have one year of credit, a personal statement, 2 letters of recommendation (one from a law professor), an official law transcript, a letter of good standing, and an updated CAS Report.

Costs

Tuition and fees for the 2011–2012 academic year are $41,460 for full-time in-state students and $33,000 for out-of-state students. On-campus room and board costs about $14,580 annually; books and supplies run $1,680.

Financial Aid

About 92% of current law students receive some form of aid. The average annual amount of aid from all sources combined, including scholarships, loans, and work contracts, is $55,515; maximum, $70,959. Awards are based on need and merit. The required financial statement is the FAFSA. The aid application deadline for fall entry is March 2. Students receive an offer of aid after an offer of admissions is made provided the application is complete.

About the Law School

Chapman University School of Law was established in 1995 and is a private institution. The 52-acre campus is in a suburban area in Orange, California. The primary mission of the law school is to provide personalized education in a challenging academic environment that stimulates intellectual inquiry, embraces diverse ideas and viewpoints, and fosters competent, ethical lawyering. Students have access to federal, state, county, city, and local agencies, courts, correctional facilities, law firms, and legal aid organizations in the Orange area. Facilities of special interest to law students include a state-of-the-art law building, with drop ports throughout, digital document cameras, touch screen computers at podiums, electronic courtrooms, assisted-listening devices, and a law library. Limited university-owned housing is available for law school students. Various apartment complexes are within proximity of the law school. All law school facilities are accessible to the physically disabled.

Calendar

The law school operates on a traditional semester basis. Courses for full-time students are offered both day and evening, and must be completed within 5 years. For part-time students, courses are offered days only and must be completed within 6 years. New full- and part-time students are admitted in the fall. There is a 7-week summer session. Transferable summer courses are offered.

Programs

In addition to the J.D., the law school offers the LL.M. Students may take relevant courses in other programs and apply credit toward the J.D.; a maximum of 8 credits may be applied. The following joint degrees may be earned: J.D./M.B.A. (Juris Doctor/Master of Business Administration) and J.D./M.F.A. (Juris Doctor/Master of Fine Arts in Film and Television).

Required

To earn the J.D., candidates must complete 88 total credits, of which 51–52 are for required courses. They must maintain a minimum GPA of 2.0 in the required courses. The following first-year courses are required of all students: Civil Procedure I and II, Contracts I and II, Criminal Law, Legal Research and Writing I and II, Property I and II, and Torts I and II. Required upper-level courses consist of a writing requirement, Constitutional Law I and II, Corporations, Evidence, Federal Income Tax, Lawyering Skills, and Professional Responsibility. The required orientation program for first-year students lasts approximately 3 days and includes an introduction to the process of legal education and analysis, professionalism oath, legal education in practice, as well as informal social events and information sessions on navigating through the law school experience.

Phone: 714-628-2500
877-Chaplaw
Fax: 714-628-2501
E-mail: *metten@chapman.edu*
Web: *chapman.edu/law*

Contact

Monica Martinez, Admissions Coordinator, 714-628-2525 for general inquiries; Kathleen Clark, Director of Financial Aid, 714-628-2510 (*lawfinaid@chapman.edu*) for financial aid information.

CALIFORNIA

Electives

The School of Law offers concentrations in corporate law, entertainment law, environmental law, internationl law, litigation, tax law, land use/real estate, and advocacy and dispute resolution. In addition, a U.S. Tax Court Clinic, Ninth Circuit Appellate Advocacy Clinic, Constitutional Jurisprudence Clinic, Family Violence Clinic, Mediation Clinic, Entertainment Law Clinic, Tax Appeals Clinic, and Elder Law Clinic are available for students for varying academic credit. A variety of seminar-type courses for upperclassmen are offered, ranging from 2 to 4 credits. Various externship opportunities, including judicial externships, are available to students in good standing; credits vary with a maximum of 10. Special lecture series include the Distinguished Jurist in Residence Program, Chapman Dialogues, International Law Lecture Series, and Entertainment Law Lecture Series, and they are open to all students for no credit. There is a study-abroad program in England and Australia. The Academic Achievement Program offers lectures and workshops, individualized tutoring for students, and referrals to university or outside programs or support services designed to meet identified special student needs. Remedial programs include additional legal writing and research programs. Minority programs include Diversity Week. The most widely taken electives are Externships, Wills and Trusts, and Criminial Police Practice.

Graduation Requirements

In order to graduate, candidates must have a GPA of 2.0, must have completed the upper-division writing requirement, and must have satisfied ABA residency requirements.

Organizations

Students edit the *The Chapman Law Review, Nexus: A Journal of Opinion, Criminal Justice Journal*, and the student newspaper, *The Chapman Law Courier*. Moot Court competitions include ABA National Appellate Advocacy Competition, Traynor Moot Court, and Thomas Tang Moot Court Competition. Other competitions include American Trial Lawyers Association Competition, Vis International Arbitration Competition, International Arbitration Competition, ABA Client Counseling Competition, National Environmental Law Moot Court Competition, National Moot Court Competition, and Luke Charles Moore Invitational Moot Court Competition. Student organizations include the Student Bar Association, International Law Society, Minority Law Students Association, Land Resources Society, Tax Law Society, and Entertainment and Sports Law Society. Law student organizations inclue the Phi Alpha Delta and National Lawyers Guild.

Library

The law library contains 312,059 hardcopy volumes and 212,416 microform volume equivalents, and subscribes to 236 serial publications. Such online databases and networks as CALI, LEXIS, OCLC First Search, WESTLAW, Wilsonline Indexes, BNA Online, and HeinOnline Libraries, and Checkpoint (RIA) are available to law students for research. The library maintains special collections to support the career services department of the law school. The ratio of library volumes to faculty is 9,000 to 1 and to students is 520 to 1. The ratio of seats in the library to students is 1 to 2.

Faculty

The law school has 52 full-time faculty members, of whom 23 are women. According to AAUP standards for Category IIA institutions, faculty salaries are well above average. About 11% of full-time faculty have a graduate law degree in addition to the J.D. The ratio of full-time students to full-time faculty in an average class is 10 to 1. The law school has a regular program of bringing visiting professors and other distinguished lecturers and visitors to campus.

Students

About 48% of the student body are women; 22%, minorities; 1%, African American; 14%, Asian American; 7%, Hispanic; and 1%, Native American. The majority of students come from California (90%). The average age of entering students is 25; age range is 20 to 50. About 47% of students enter directly from undergraduate school, and 6% have a graduate degree. About 10% drop out after the first year for academic or personal reasons; 82% remain to receive a law degree.

Placement

J.D.s awarded:	177

Services available through: a separate law school placement center.

Services: information sessions, panels, law firm nights, mock interviews, a mentor and e-mentor program, off-site recruiting events, cover letter review, web-based mock interviewing, and assistance for postgraduate and judicial clerkships.

Special features: provide specialized counseling for L.L.M. students.

Full-time job interviews:	24 employers
Summer job interviews:	29 employers
Placement by graduation:	86% of class
Placement within 9 months:	97% of class
Average starting salary:	$24,960 to $160,000

Areas of placement:

Private practice 2–10 attorneys	30%
Private practice 11–23 attorneys	7%
Private practice 26–50 attorneys	5%
Private practice 51–100 attorneys	1%
Academic	14%
Business/industry	13%
Private practice 100+ attorneys	10%
Judicial clerkships	2%
Public interest	2%
Government	1%
Military	1%

P.O. Box 535
Charleston, SC 29402

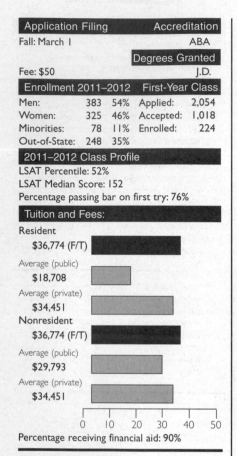

Application Filing	Accreditation
Fall: March 1	ABA

Degrees Granted	
Fee: $50	J.D.

Enrollment 2011–2012		First-Year Class	
Men:	383 54%	Applied:	2,054
Women:	325 46%	Accepted:	1,018
Minorities:	78 11%	Enrolled:	224
Out-of-State:	248 35%		

2011–2012 Class Profile
LSAT Percentile: 52%
LSAT Median Score: 152
Percentage passing bar on first try: 76%

Tuition and Fees:

Resident
$36,774 (F/T)

Average (public)
$18,708

Average (private)
$34,451

Nonresident
$36,774 (F/T)

Average (public)
$29,793

Average (private)
$34,451

0   10   20   30   40   50

Percentage receiving financial aid: 90%

ADMISSIONS

In the fall of 2011 first-year class, 2054 applied, 1018 were accepted, and 224 enrolled. Five transfers enrolled. The median LSAT percentile of the most recent first-year class was 52; the median GPA was 3.1 on a scale of 4.0. The lowest LSAT percentile accepted was 13; the highest was 97.

Requirements

Applicants must have a bachelor's degree and take the LSAT. The most important admission factors include LSAT results, GPA, and general background. No specific undergraduate courses are required. Candidates are interviewed.

Procedure

The application deadline for fall entry is March 1. Applicants should submit an application form, LSAT results, transcripts, a personal statement, a nonrefundable application fee of $50, 2 letters of recommendation, Dean's Certification,

and a resume. Notification of the admissions decision is December-August. The law school uses the LSAC.

Special

The law school recruits minority and disadvantaged students through visits to minority colleges and universities, a minority recruitment day, and CRS/CAS. Requirements are different for out-of-state students. Transfer students must have one year of credit, must have attended an ABA-approved law school, and must submit a personal statement.

Costs

Tuition and fees for the 2011–2012 academic year are $36,674 for all full-time students. Tuition for part-time students is $29,466 for in-state students and $29,466 out-of-state. Books and supplies run $1,250.

Financial Aid

About 90% of current law students receive some form of aid. The average annual amount of aid from all sources combined, including scholarships, loans, and work contracts, is $44,979; maximum, $56,024. Awards are based on need and merit combined. Required financial statements are the FAFSA and School Specific Scholarship Application. The aid application deadline for fall entry is April 1. Special funds for minority or disadvantaged students are available. First-year students are notified about their financial aid application after acceptance and prior to enrollment.

About the Law School

Charleston School of Law was established in 2003 and is a private institution. The campus is in historic Charleston. The primary mission of the law school is to teach the practice of law as a profession serving the public. Students have access to federal, state, county, city, and local agencies, courts, correctional facilities, law firms, and legal aid organizations in the Charleston area. Housing for students is not available on campus; numerous options are available in the area. All law school facilities are accessible to the physically disabled.

Calendar

The law school operates on a traditional semester basis. Courses for full-time students are offered both day and evening, and must be completed within 84 months. For part-time students, courses are offered both day and evening, and must be completed within 84 months. New full- and part-time students are admitted in the fall. There are 2- and 8-week summer sessions. Transferable summer courses are offered.

Programs

Required

To earn the J.D., candidates must complete 88 total credits, of which 61 are for required courses. They must maintain a minimum GPA of 2.0 in the required courses. The following first-year courses are required of all students: Civil Procedure I and II, Contracts I and II, Legal Research, Analysis, and Writing I and II, Property I and II, and Torts I and II. Required upper-level courses consist of a skills course, Advanced Writing Requirement, Business Associations, Commercial Law, Constitutional Law I and II, Criminal Law, Criminal Procedure, Evidence, Professional Respsonsibility, Secured Transactions, and Wills, Trusts, and Estates. 2 credit hours of a skills course is required for graduation The required orientation program for first-year students lasts 4 days.

Electives

After the first year, students may complete an externship with more than 100 options from public defender, to solicitor, to various judges. Damages, Mass Torts, Information Privacy Law, and Advanced Appellate Advocacy seminars are offered. Internships are available through the public defender, solicitor, and Heirs Property Project. Research positions with faculty members and tutorial programs include the Academic Success Program. Special lecture series consist of a professionalism series (3 of 6 required per semester). A cooperative study-abroad program with Stetson University is available. Minority programs are offered through the Office of Student Diversity and Mentoring. The most widely taken electives are Trial Advocacy, Equity, and Law Office Management.

Phone: 843-377-2143
Fax: 843-329-0491
E-mail: jbenfield@charlestonlaw.org
Web: charlestonlaw.edu

Contact

Associate Dean, 843-377-2143 for general inquiries; Julia Cunningham, Associate Director of Financial Aid, 843-377-1102 for financial aid information.

SOUTH CAROLINA

Graduation Requirements

In order to graduate, candidates must have a GPA of 2.0, must have completed the upper-division writing requirement, and must have completed other requirements, including 30 hours of documented pro bono work.

Organizations

Students edit the *Charleston Law Review, Federal Courts Law Review, MALABU (Maritime Law Bulletin)*, and RESOLVED: Journal of Alternative Dispute Resolution. Law student organizations, local chapters of national associations, and campus organizations include BLSA, Women in Law, Environmental Law Society, International Law Society, Criminal Law Society, Children's Advocacy and Family Law Society, James L. Petirsu Inn of Court, and Sir Francis Drake Admiralty Inn of Court.

Library

The law library contains 29,628 hardcopy volumes and subscribes to 479 serial publications. Such online databases and networks as CALI, CIS Universe, Legal-Trac, LEXIS, Mathew Bender, OCLC First Search, WESTLAW, Wilsonline Indexes, and many others are available to law students for research. Special library collections include an extensive digital collection. The ratio of library volumes to faculty is 741 to 1 and to students is 42 to 1. The ratio of seats in the library to students is 1 to 2.

Faculty

The law school has 35 full-time and 40 part-time faculty members, of whom 34 are women. The ratio of full-time students to full-time faculty in an average class is 60 to 1. The law school has a regular program of bringing visiting professors and other distinguished lecturers and visitors to campus.

Students

About 46% of the student body are women; 11%, minorities; 7%, African American; 1%, Asian American; and 2%, Hispanic. The majority of students come from South Carolina (65%). The average age of entering students is 25; age range is 21 to 46. About 65% of students enter directly from undergraduate school, 6% have a graduate degree, and 35% have worked full-time prior to entering law school. About 5% drop out after the first year for academic or personal reasons; 95% remain to receive a law degree.

Placement

J.D.s awarded:	163

Services available through: a separate law school placement center.

Special features: a Director of Public Service and Pro Bono who administers the Pro Bono Program through the Department of Career Services.

Full-time job interviews:	5 employers
Summer job interviews:	12 employers
Placement within 9 months:	83% of class
Average starting salary:	$47,671 to $57,240

Areas of placement:

Private practice	6%
Judicial clerkships	12%
Government	12%
Business/industry	11%
Public interest	4%
Academic	1%

CHARLOTTE SCHOOL OF LAW

2145 Suttle Avenue
Charlotte, NC 28208

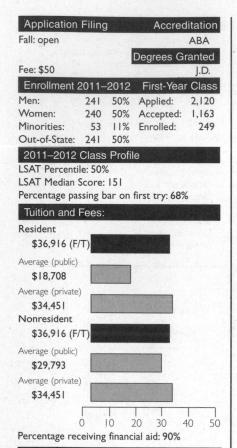

Application Filing
Fall: open

Fee: $50

Accreditation
ABA

Degrees Granted
J.D.

Enrollment 2011–2012 | First-Year Class

Men:	241	50%	Applied:	2,120
Women:	240	50%	Accepted:	1,163
Minorities:	53	11%	Enrolled:	249
Out-of-State:	241	50%		

2011–2012 Class Profile
LSAT Percentile: 50%
LSAT Median Score: 151
Percentage passing bar on first try: 68%

Tuition and Fees:

Resident
$36,916 (F/T)

Average (public)
$18,708

Average (private)
$34,451

Nonresident
$36,916 (F/T)

Average (public)
$29,793

Average (private)
$34,451

0   10   20   30   40   50

Percentage receiving financial aid: 90%

ADMISSIONS

In the fall of 2011 first-year class, 2120 applied, 1163 were accepted, and 249 enrolled. Five transfers enrolled. The median LSAT percentile of the most recent first-year class was 50; the median GPA was 3.1 on a scale of 4.6. The lowest LSAT percentile accepted was 140; the highest was 168.

Requirements
Applicants must have a bachelor's degree.

Procedure
The application deadline for fall entry is open. Applicants should submit an application form, LSAT results, transcripts, a personal statement, and an application fee of $50. Notification of the admissions decision is rolling. The law school uses the LSAC.

Special
Requirements are different for out-of-state students. Transfer students must have attended an ABA-approved law school, must submit a personal statement, and must be currently enrolled in law school.

Costs

Tuition and fees for the 2011–2012 academic year are $35,344 for all full-time students. Tuition for part-time students is $28,279 for in-state students and $28,279 out-of-state. Books and supplies run $1,925.

Financial Aid

About 90% of current law students receive some form of aid. The average annual amount of aid from all sources combined, including scholarships, loans, and work contracts, is $12,725; maximum, $56,485. Awards are based on merit. Required financial statement is the FAFSA. First-year students are notified about their financial aid application at time of acceptance.

About the Law School

Charlotte School of Law was established in 2006 and is independent. The primary mission of the law school is to ensure students are equipped with practical skills that will allow them to thrive in a professional setting, to motivate and energize the student community in evey aspect of the law school experience, and to place a strong emphasis on serving the underserved through community service and pro bono work. Students have access to federal, state, county, city, and local agencies, courts, correctional facilities, law firms, and legal aid organizations in the Charlotte area. Facilities of special interest to law students include a 4-story modern building. All law school facilities are accessible to the physically disabled.

Calendar

The law school operates on a traditional semester basis. Courses for full-time students are offered both day and evening, and must be completed within 5 years. For part-time students, courses are offered both day and evening, and must be completed within 7 years. New full- and part-time students are admitted in the fall and spring. There is a 5-week summer session. Transferable summer courses are offered.

Programs

Required
To earn the J.D., candidates must complete 90 total credits, of which 60 are for required courses. They must maintain a minimum GPA of 2.0 in the required courses. The following first-year courses are required of all students: Civil Procedure I and II, Contracts I and II, Lawyering Process I and II, Passport to Effective Practice, Property I and II, and Torts I and II. Required upper-level courses consist of a skills course, an advanced writing course, Business Associations, Commercial Law, Constitutional Law I and II, Criminal Procedure, Evidence, Professional Responsibility, and Wills and Trusts. The required orientation program for first-year students is 3 to 4 days.

Electives
Clinics include Business Law Clinic (3 credits), Parent Representation Clinic (3 credits), and Wrongful Conviction Clinic (2 credits). Seminars include Art Law Clinic (2 credits), Business Drafting Seminar (2–3 credits), and White Collar Crime Seminar (2–3 credits). Internships and externships are available. The law school offers externship fieldwork for 2 to 4 credits. This upper-level elective provides an opportunity for students to learn "in role." As part of the students services program, the law school provides students with academic support services through the Charlotte Law Program for Academic Success. Charlotte Law has several student organizations to support students of color such as the Latin American Law Society.

Graduation Requirements
In order to graduate, candidates must have a GPA of 2.0, and must have completed the upper-division writing requirement and 20 hours of pro bono and community service work.

Organizations

Students edit the *Charlotte Law Review* and the student newspaper, *The Docket*. Moot Court Competitions include the Jessup International Law Competition, Gibbons Criminal Law Competition, Saul Lefkowitch Intellectual Property Moot Court Competition, and the Frederick Douglass Moot Court Competition. Other

Phone: 704-971-8542
Fax: 704-971-8599
E-mail: admissions@charlottelaw.edu
Web: charlottelaw.edu

Contact

Carrie Mansfield, 704-971-8542 for general inquiries; Laren Mack, Financial Aid Director, 704-971-8546 for financial aid information.

NORTH CAROLINA

competitions include American Association of Justice (AAJ), Student Trial Advocacy Competition, and National Trial Competition in Atlanta, Georgia. Law student organizations, local chapters of national associations, and campus clubs and organizations include Women in Law, International Law Society, Environmental Law Society, Federalist Society, Delta Theta Phi, Phi Alpha Delta, Phi Delta Phi, Public Interest Law Society, Charlotte Law Cares, and Real Estate Society.

Library

The law library contains 196,308 hard-copy volumes and 99,339 microform volume equivalents, and subscribes to 13,473 serial publications. Such online databases and networks as CALI, Legal-Trac, LEXIS, Mathew Bender, OCLC First Search, WESTLAW, eLibrary, HeinOnline, JSTOR, Loislaw, LexisNexis Congressional, LLMC Digital, Making of Modern Law, Oxford Scholarship Online, ProQuest, Supreme Court Database, U.S. Supreme Court Records and Briefs, BNA, and CCH are available to law students for research. The ratio of library volumes to faculty is 8,923 to 1 and to students is 408 to 1. The ratio of seats in the library to students is 1 to 2.

Faculty

The law school has 22 full-time and 27 part-time faculty members, of whom 25 are women. About 18% of part-time faculty have a graduate law degree in addition to the J.D. The ratio of full-time students to full-time faculty in an average class is 45 to 1; in a clinic, 6 to 1. The law school has a regular program of bringing visiting professors and other distinguished lecturers and visitors to campus.

Students

About 50% of the student body are women; 11%, minorities; 6%, African American; 1%, Asian American; 4%, Hispanic; and 1%, Native American. The average age of entering students is 28; age range is 20 to 55. About 10% drop out after the first year for academic or personal reasons; 90% remain to receive a law degree.

Placement

J.D.s awarded:	64

Services available through: a separate law school placement center.

CITY UNIVERSITY OF NEW YORK

CUNY School of Law

65-21 Main Street
Flushing, NY 11367-1300

Application Filing	Accreditation
Fall: March 15	ABA

	Degrees Granted
Fee: $60	J.D.

Enrollment 2011–2012   First-Year Class

Men:	180	38%	Applied:	1,883
Women:	300	59%	Accepted:	563
Minorities:	197	41%	Enrolled:	171
Out-of-State:	173	36%		

2011–2012 Class Profile
LSAT Percentile: 64%
LSAT Median Score: 155
Percentage passing bar on first try: 73%

Tuition and Fees:

Resident
$13,132 (F/T)

Average (public)
$18,708

Average (private)
$34,451

Nonresident
$20,692 (F/T)

Average (public)
$29,793

Average (private)
$34,451

0   10   20   30   40   50

Percentage receiving financial aid: 83%

ADMISSIONS
In the fall of 2011 first-year class, 1883 applied, 563 were accepted, and 171 enrolled. Three transfers enrolled. The median LSAT percentile of the most recent first-year class was 64; the median GPA was 3.3 on a scale of 4.0. The lowest LSAT percentile accepted was 44; the highest was 97.

Requirements
Applicants must have a bachelor's degree and take the LSAT. The most important admission factors include academic achievement and letters of recommendation. No specific undergraduate courses are required. Candidates are not interviewed.

Procedure
The application deadline for fall entry is March 15. Applicants should submit an application form, LSAT results, transcripts, a personal statement, LSAC report, a nonrefundable application fee of $60, 2 letters of recommendation, and a personal statement. Notification of

the admissions decision is beginning in January.

Special
The law school recruits minority and disadvantaged students through programs similar to those used by most other law schools. Requirements are different for out-of-state students. Transfer students must have one year of credit, must have attended an ABA-approved law school, must submit a personal statement, and must have demonstrated a commitment to public interest/public service.

Costs
Tuition and fees for the 2011–2012 academic year are $11,420 for full-time in-state students and $18,980 for out-of-state students.

Financial Aid
About 83% of current law students receive some form of aid. The average annual amount of aid from all sources combined, including scholarships, loans, and work contracts, is $34,460; maximum, $49,129. Awards are based on need and merit combined. The required financial statement is the FAFSA. The aid application deadline for fall entry is May 1. Special funds for minority or disadvantaged students include the Professional Opportunity Scholarship, CLEO, Puerto Rican Bar Association, and various other scholarships. First-year students are notified about their financial aid application on a rolling basis.

About the Law School
City University of New York CUNY School of Law was established in 1983 and is a public institution. The campus is in an urban area in the New York City borough of Queens. The primary mission of the law school is to train lawyers to serve the underprivileged and disempowered and to make a difference in their communities. Students have access to federal, state, county, city, and local agencies, courts, correctional facilities, law firms, and legal aid organizations in the Flushing area. There are several notable in-house clinical programs. Facilities of special interest to law students include a state-of-the-art building in Long Island City, New York. Housing for students is

available off campus. About 99% of the law school facilities are accessible to the physically disabled.

Calendar
The law school operates on a traditional semester basis. Courses are offered both day and evening. New students are admitted in the fall. There is an 8-week summer session. Transferable summer courses are offered.

Programs
Students may take relevant courses in other programs and apply credit toward the J.D.; a maximum of 6 credits may be applied.

Required
To earn the J.D., candidates must complete 91 total credits, of which 60 are for required courses. They must maintain a minimum GPA of 2.5 in the required courses. The following first-year courses are required of all students: Civil Procedure I, Contracts I and II, Criminal Law: Torts, Law and Family Relations, Lawyering Seminar I and II, and Liberty, Equality, and Due Process. Required upper-level courses consist of a clinic or concentration, Constitutional Structures and the Law, Core Doctrine, Evidence, Lawyering Seminar III, Property, and Public Institutions. All students must take clinical courses. The required orientation program for first-year students is a 1-week academic, skills, and social program, including court visits.

Electives
The CUNY School of Law offers concentrations in family law, litigation, health, mediation, domestic violence, elder law, immigration law, women's rights, refugee rights, civil rights, and community economic development. In addition, all students must enroll in a clinic (12 to 16 credits) or a concentration (12 credit internship). Current clinic offerings include Immigrant and Refugee Rights, Elder Law, Battered Women's Rights, Defender, International Women's Human Rights, Mediation, and Community Economic Development. All third-year students at CUNY law represent clients under the supervision of attorneys at one of the largest law firms in Queens (Main

Phone: 718-340-4210
Fax: 718-340-4435
E-mail: quon@mail.law.cuny.edu
Web: www.law.cuny.edu

Contact
Helena Quon, Director of Admissions, 718-340-4210 for general inquiries; Angela Joseph, Director of Financial Aid, 718-340-4292 for financial aid information.

NEW YORK

Street Legal Services, Inc. situated on the law school campus). Each first-year student takes 2 4-credit lawyering seminars. Limited to 24 students, these seminars imbed lawyering skills such as legal analysis, legal research, legal writing, interviewing, counseling, and negotiating in doctrine taught in first-year courses. Second-year students choose a lawyering seminar in an area of interest. Recent lawyering seminar offerings include Trial Advocacy, Civil Pre-Trial Process, Mediation, Criminal Defense, Juvenile Rights, Nonprofit Representation, Economic Justice, Community Economic Development, and Writing from a Judicial Perspective. Internships are available in connection with the concentration program in placements related to specially-designed courses. Current areas are civil rights/discrimination and health law. Students spend 2 full days in the field and 8 hours in class. Field work is connected to concentrations and to a 3-credit summary school course. Special lecture series are sponsored by various student organizations. A professional skills center and a writing center are available to support students. Special offerings are also available to second- and third-semester students who are experiencing difficulty. The most widely taken electives are NY Practice, Criminal Procedure, and Business Associations.

Graduation Requirements
In order to graduate, candidates must have a GPA of 2.5, and must have completed the upper-division writing requirement and a clinic/concentration.

Organizations
Students edit the *New York City Law Review*, and participate in the annual Moot Court Competition, Phillip C. Jessup International Law Moot Court Competition, and the John J. Gibbons Criminal Procedure Competition. They also participate in the Immigration Law Moot Court Competition, the annual Domenick L. Gabrielli National Family Moot Court Competition, and the annual Nassau Academy of Law Moot Court Competition. Student Organizations, local chapters of national associations, and campus

organizations include the Labor Coalition for Workers' Rights and Economic Justice, Domestic Violence Coalition, Mississippi Project, National Lawyers Guild, American Civil Liberties Union, Black Law Students Association, Public Interest Law Organization, International Law Organization, and Outlaw.

Library
The law library contains 300,552 hardcopy volumes and 1,086,660 microform volume equivalents, and subscribes to 19,000 serial publications. Such online databases and networks as CALI, Infotrac, LEXIS, Mathew Bender, OCLC First Search, WESTLAW, CIAO, Earthscape, LLMC Digital, HeinOnline, Gale Virtual Reference Library, Global Jurist, Index to Foreign Legal Periodicals, BNA, ProQuest Congressional, IStar, EBSCO Host, Bloomberg Law, and eBrary are available to law students for research. The school is a member of the New York Joint International Law Program Consortium. The ratio of library volumes to faculty is 5,094 to 1 and to students is 683 to 1. The ratio of seats in the library to students is 1 to 1.

Faculty
The law school has 49 full-time and 10 part-time faculty members, of whom 39 are women. About 49% of full-time faculty have a graduate law degree in addition to the J.D.; about 10% of part-time faculty have one. The ratio of full-time students to full-time faculty in an average class is 10 to 1; in a clinic, 8 to 1. The law school has a regular program of bringing visiting professors and other distinguished lecturers and visitors to campus.

Students
About 59% of the student body are women; 41%, minorities; 9%, African American; 12%, Asian American; and 17%, Hispanic. The majority of students come from New York (64%). The average age of entering students is 27; age range is 20 to 44. About 11% of students have a graduate degree. About 1% drop out after the first year for academic or personal reasons; 99% remain to receive a law degree.

CLEVELAND STATE UNIVERSITY

Cleveland-Marshall College of Law

2121 Euclid Avenue LB138
Cleveland, OH 44115-2214

Application Filing	Accreditation
Fall: May 1	ABA, AALS

Degrees Granted
J.D., LL.M.

Enrollment 2011–2012   First-Year Class

Men:	318	57%	Applied:	1,609
Women:	239	43%	Accepted:	615
Minorities:	89	16%	Enrolled:	169
Out-of-State:	111	20%		

2011–2012 Class Profile

LSAT Percentile: 60%
LSAT Median Score: 154
Percentage passing bar on first try: 83%

Tuition and Fees:

Resident
$19,864 (F/T)

Average (public)
$18,708

Average (private)
$34,451

Nonresident
$27,204 (F/T)

Average (public)
$29,793

Average (private)
$34,451

0 10 20 30 40 50

Percentage receiving financial aid: 87%

ADMISSIONS

In the fall of 2011 first-year class, 1609 applied, 615 were accepted, and 169 enrolled. Twenty transfers enrolled. The median LSAT percentile of the most recent first-year class was 60; the median GPA was 3.3 on a scale of 4.0. The lowest LSAT percentile accepted was 13; the highest was 97.

Requirements
Applicants must have a bachelor's degree and take the LSAT. Minimum acceptable GPA is 2.0 on a scale of 4.0. The most important admission factors include academic achievement, LSAT results, and general background. No specific undergraduate courses are required. Candidates are not interviewed.

Procedure
The application deadline for fall entry is May 1. Applicants should submit an application form, LSAT results, transcripts, a personal statement, TOEFL (if applicable), 2 letters of recommendation,

and a personal statement. Notification of the admissions decision is on a rolling basis beginning in December. The law school uses the LSAC.

Special
The law school recruits minority and disadvantaged students by means of the Legal Career Opportunities Program (LCOP), a special admissions program for applicants whose background and experience deserve special consideration. The Admissions Committee invites applicants whose test scores or undergraduate grade point averages are not strong but whose skills, accomplishments, and other qualifications merit consideration. The Admissions Committee seeks to admit candidates who have encountered adversity but have a record of accomplishment, either academic or professional. LCOP begins in the early part of June and continues through mid-July; students earn 2 or 3 semester credits, depending on the summer course that is offered, and credit is applied to the J.D. degree. Requirements are different for out-of-state students. Transfer students must have a minimum GPA of 3, must have attended an ABA-approved law school, and must submit a personal statement.

Costs

On-campus room and board costs about $13,000 annually.

Financial Aid

About 87% of current law students receive some form of aid. The average annual amount of aid from all sources combined, including scholarships, loans, and work contracts, is $18,076; maximum, $36,152. Awards are based on need and merit combined. Required financial statements are the FAFSA and Law Aid Application. The aid application deadline for fall entry is May 1. Special funds for minority or disadvantaged students are available. Students who complete the admissions and financial aid materials are considered for these funds. First-year students are notified about their financial aid application at time of acceptance.

About the Law School

Cleveland State University Cleveland-Marshall College of Law was established in 1897 and is a public institution. The

85-acre campus is in an urban area in downtown Cleveland. The primary mission of the law school is to foster a more just society through legal education, service, and scholarship, and to enable a diverse population of students to become accomplished, ethical citizen-lawyers who will make significant contributions to the region, the nation, and the world. Students have access to federal, state, county, city, and local agencies, courts, correctional facilities, law firms, and legal aid organizations in the Cleveland area. Facilities of special interest to law students are the intramural competitions, student health services, library, university and law recreation center, Cleveland Public Library, physical education facilities, University Circle Cultural Arts Center, Playhouse Square, student counseling services, professional sports team, museums, and the Rock 'N' Roll Hall of Fame and Museum. Housing for students is available on campus, in the city, and in nearby suburbs, many within a 15- to 20-minute commuting distance. All law school facilities are accessible to the physically disabled.

Calendar

The law school operates on a traditional semester basis. Courses for full-time students are offered days only in the first year; afterward, in the day and evening, and they must be completed within 6 years. For part-time students, courses are offered both day and evening, and must be completed within 6 years. New full- and part-time students are admitted in the fall. There is an 8-week summer session. Transferable summer courses are offered.

Programs

In addition to the J.D., the law school offers the LL.M. Students may take relevant courses in other programs and apply credit toward the J.D.; a maximum of 8 credits may be applied. The following joint degrees may be earned: J.D./M.A.E.S. (Juris Doctor/Master of Environmental Studies), J.D./M.B.A. (Juris Doctor/Master of Business Administration), J.D./M.P.A. (Juris Doctor/Master of Public Administration), J.D/M.S.E.S. (Juris Doctor/Master of Environmental Science), and J.D./M.U.P.D.D. (Juris Doctor/Master of Urban Planning, and Design and Development).

Phone: 216-687-2304
866-687-2304
Fax: 216-687-6881
E-mail: *christopher.lucak@law.csuohio.edu*
Web: *www.law.csuohio.edu*

Contact

Christopher Lucak, Assistant Dean for Admissions, 216-687-2304 for general inquiries and financial aid information.

OHIO

Required

To earn the J.D., candidates must complete 90 total credits, of which 41 are for required courses. They must maintain a minimum GPA of 2.0 in the required courses. The following first-year courses are required of all students: Civil Procedure, Contracts, Criminal Law, Legal Writing, Legislation and Regulation, Property, and Torts. Required upper-level courses consist of Constitutional Law, Evidence, and Legal Profession. Students must take a skills course, which includes clinical courses. The required orientation program for first-year students is 4 days and includes social activities, legal writing and substantive classes, library tours, peer adviser meetings, and technology setup.

Electives

The Cleveland-Marshall College of Law offers concentrations in corporate law, criminal law, internationl law, labor law, litigation, and civil litigation and dispute resolution. There is also a health law certificate. The Employment Law Clinic offers from 6 to 10 credits, the Urban Development Law Clinic offers from 2 to 10 credits, the Fair Housing Clinic offers from 2 to 8 credits, and the Environmental Law Clinic offers 2 to 4 credits. Upper-level students may take seminars and up to 3 hours of independent research; seminar papers fulfill the upper-level writing requirement. A judicial externship is worth 6 credits; students work 24 hours a week in a federal or state appellate court. A U.S. attorney externship is worth 4 credits; students are placed in a civil or criminal U.S. attorney's office. There are independent/public service externships worth 4 to 6 hours. Special lecture series include the Cleveland-Marshall Lecture Series, the Criminal Law Forums, and Labor and Employment Lecture Series. Students may participate in study-abroad programs run by ABA/AALS-approved law schools. Cleveland-Marshall also sponsors an ABA/AALS summer program in St. Petersburg, Russia. First-year students admitted to the Legal Career Opportunities Program are offered a course in legal process. An Academic Excellence program is offered. Cleveland-Marshall has a Manager of Student Affairs who oversees minority programs. A variety of special interest group programs are available. The most widely taken electives are Advocacy, Business, and Employment Law.

Graduation Requirements

In order to graduate, candidates must have a GPA of 2.0, must have completed the upper-division writing requirement, and must have filled other upper-level requirements.

Organizations

Students edit the *Cleveland State Law Review*, the *Journal of Law and Health*, and the newspaper *The Gavel*. The college sends teams to various competitions throughout the United States including the National Appellate Advocacy, International Environmental Law, and National Criminal Procedure competitions. Other competitions include the Jessup International Law, Entertainment and Communication Law, National Animal Advocacy, Information Technology and Privacy Law, and Evidence competitions. Law student organizations, local chapters of national associations, and campus organizations include Entertainment and Sports Law Association, Federalist Society, Student Public Interest Law Organization, ABA-Law Student Division, Delta Theta Phi, Black Law Students Association, Criminal Law Society, and the Association for Environmental Law and Sustainability.

Library

The law library contains 299,131 hardcopy volumes and 235,284 microform volume equivalents, and subscribes to 1,652 serial publications. Such online databases and networks as CALI, CIS Universe, LEXIS, WESTLAW, Wilsonline Indexes, the Internet, SCHOLAR, OhioLINK, HeinOnline, LLMC Online, Gongwer, EPIC, and OCLC are available to law students for research. Special library collections include federal government documents. The ratio of library volumes to faculty is 12,536 to 1 and to students is 843 to 1. The ratio of seats in the library to students is 1 to 1.

Faculty

The law school has 44 full-time and 37 part-time faculty members, of whom 34 are women. According to AAUP standards for Category I institutions, faculty salaries are below average. About 20% of full-time faculty have a graduate law degree in addition to the J.D. The ratio of full-time students to full-time faculty in an average class is 25 to 1; in a clinic, 4 to 1. The law

Placement

J.D.s awarded:	178

Services available through: a separate law school placement center.

Services: practice interviews, matching students with local attorneys for interest interviews, and career-related workshops.

Special features: there is individualized counseling, skills and cover letter development, references and resources, and job postings containing more than 1000 employment opportunities annually.

Full-time job interviews:	14 employers
Summer job interviews:	31 employers
Placement by graduation:	54% of class
Placement within 9 months:	89% of class
Average starting salary:	$60,000 to $120,000

Areas of placement:

Private practice 2–10 attorneys	23%
Private practice 11–23 attorneys	4%
Private practice 26–50 attorneys	1%
Private practice 51–100 attorneys	2%
Business/industry	28%
Solo practice	18%
Government	15%
Judicial clerkships	5%
Public interest	3%
Academic	1%

school has a regular program of bringing visiting professors and other distinguished lecturers and visitors to campus.

Students

About 43% of the student body are women; 16%, minorities; 10%, African American; 3%, Asian American; and 3%, Hispanic. The majority of students come from Ohio (80%). The average age of entering students is 26; age range is 20 to 44. About 35% of students enter directly from undergraduate school, and 8% have a graduate degree. About 17% drop out after the first year for academic or personal reasons; 83% remain to receive a law degree.

William & Mary Law School

P.O. Box 8795
Williamsburg, VA 23187-8795

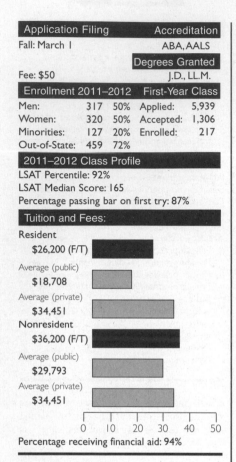

Application Filing	Accreditation
Fall: March 1	ABA, AALS
	Degrees Granted
Fee: $50	J.D., LL.M.

Enrollment 2011–2012			First-Year Class	
Men:	317	50%	Applied:	5,939
Women:	320	50%	Accepted:	1,306
Minorities:	127	20%	Enrolled:	217
Out-of-State:	459	72%		

2011–2012 Class Profile
LSAT Percentile: 92%
LSAT Median Score: 165
Percentage passing bar on first try: 87%

Tuition and Fees:

Resident
$26,200 (F/T)

Average (public)
$18,708

Average (private)
$34,451

Nonresident
$36,200 (F/T)

Average (public)
$29,793

Average (private)
$34,451

0   10   20   30   40   50

Percentage receiving financial aid: 94%

ADMISSIONS
In the fall of 2011 first-year class, 5939 applied, 1306 were accepted, and 217 enrolled. Eleven transfer students enrolled. The median LSAT percentile of the most recent first-year class was 92; the median GPA was 3.7 on a scale of 4.0. The lowest LSAT percentile accepted was 33; the highest was 99.

Requirements
Applicants must have a bachelor's degree and take the LSAT. Minimum acceptable GPA is 2.0 on a scale of 4.0. No specific undergraduate courses are required. Candidates are interviewed.

Procedure
The application deadline for fall entry is March 1. Applicants should submit an application form, LSAT results, transcripts, personal statement, nonrefundable application fee of $50, 2 letters of recommendation, and LSAC evaluation. Notification of the admissions decision is November through April. The law school uses the LSAC.

Special
The law school recruits minority and disadvantaged students on- and off-campus recruitment, brochures, grant proposals, LSAC Candidate Referral Services, BLSA Programs, DiscoverLaw.org, and financial aid. Requirements are different for out-of-state students. Transfer students must have one year of credits, attended an ABA-approved law school, personal statement, and have 26 law credit hours.

Costs
On-campus room and board costs about $14,400 annually; books and supplies run $1,400.

Financial Aid
About 94% of current law students receive some form of aid. The average annual amount of aid from all sources combined, including scholarships, loans, and work contracts, is $36,486; maximum, $57,750. Awards are based on need and merit combined. Required financial statement is the FAFSA. The aid application deadline for fall entry is February 15. Special funds for minority or disadvantaged students are available. Diversity is a factor in awarding scholarships. First-year students are notified about their financial aid application from November through April.

About the Law School
College of William & Mary William & Mary Law School was established in 1779 and is a public institution. The 1200-acre campus is located in a small town 45 miles west of Norfolk, 45 miles east of Richmond. The primary mission of the law school is to provide students with a superior legal education in a close-knit collegial environment, and to offer the opportunity to confront the demands of constructive citizenship and leadership. Students have access to federal, state, county, city, and local agencies, courts, correctional facilities, law firms, and legal aid organizations in the Williamsburg area. The National Center for State Courts and Colonial Williamsburg are nearby. Facilities of special interest to law students are The Center for Legal and Court Technology, the world center for courtroom technology research, housed within the McGlothlin Courtroom, the world's most technologically advanced courtroom. The project has an extensive student staff, trains all second-year students in hands-on courtroom technology use, and supports the law school activities and courses, such as the legal technology seminar and technology augmented trial advocacy. The law school is a wireless facility allowing access to online Internet services throughout the building and adjacent patios and lawns. Housing for students is available on-campus in graduate apartments located next to the law school building. Commercial apartments, townhouses, and other area housing are available as well. Williamsburg is "family friendly" with many neighborhoods and services for those students with children. All law school facilities are accessible to the physically disabled.

Calendar
The law school operates on a traditional semester basis. Courses for full-time students are offered days only and must be completed within 3 years (expanded to allow for leaves of absence). There is no part-time program. New full-time students are admitted in the fall. There is a 4-week summer session. Transferable summer courses are offered.

Programs
In addition to the J.D., the law school offers the LL.M. Students may take relevant courses in other programs and apply credit toward the J.D.; a maximum of 6 credits may be applied. The following joint degrees may be earned: J.D./M.A. (Juris Doctor/ Master of Arts in American Studies), J.D./ M.B.A. (Juris Doctor/Master of Business Administration), and J.D./M.P.P. (Juris Doctor/Master of Public Policy).

Required
To earn the J.D., candidates must complete 86 total credits, of which 34 are for required courses. They must maintain a minimum GPA of 1.8 in the required courses. The following first-year courses are required of all students: Civil Procedure, Constitutional Law, Criminal Law, Legal Skills, Property, and Torts. Required upper-level courses consist of Legal Skills and Professional Responsibility. The required orientation program for first-year students is a 1-week program designed to introduce legal analysis, legal vocabulary, legal teaching methods, legal writing, and the law firm structure of the Legal Skills Program.

Phone: 757-221-3785
Fax: 757-221-3261
E-mail: lawadm@wm.edu
Web: www.law.wm.edu

Contact

Faye F. Shealy, Associate Dean, 757-221-3785 for general inquiries; Ed Irish, Director of Student Financial Aid, 757-221-2420 for financial aid information.

VIRGINIA

Electives

Clinics combine a classroom component with supervised work in an office setting and include domestic violence, children's advocacy, veterans benefits, and federal tax practice. Seminars are open to both second- and third-year students (size limited to 15 to 25 students) and include civil rights, corporate drafting, and legal technology. Internships include Attorney General Practice, Virginia Court of Appeals, Criminal Litigation, Non-Profit Organizations, and Private Practice/In-House Counsel. Research programs include independent research, advanced research, and directed reading. They are open to second- and third-year students and must be completed with a supervising professor. Field work is offered through an externship program open to second- and third-year students. Externships require a minimum of 40 hours of work, a synopsis of work done, a journal, and an evaluation by the supervising attorney or judge. Placements may be made with a judge, nonprofit organization, private practice, or government agency. Special lectures include the Institute of Bill of Rights Law, Cutler Lectures, and George Wythe Lectures. Study abroad is available in the summer in Madrid, Spain and open to any second- or third-year student who applies from an ABA accredited law school. In addition, semester abroad exchange programs are available to second- and third-year students in China, Japan, New Zealand, Spain, Austria, and Luxemborg. Tutorial programs are available to any first-year student. Minority programs are arranged by minority student organizations. Special interest group programs are arranged by individual student organizations. The most widely taken electives are criminal procedure, evidence, and corporations.

Graduation Requirements

In order to graduate, candidates must have a GPA of 2.0 and complete the upper-division writing requirement.

Organizations

Students edit the *William and Mary Law Review, William & Mary Bill of Rights Journal, William and Mary Journal of Women in the Law, William and Mary Environmental Law and Policy Review*, and *William and Mary Business Law Review*. Ten teams compete each year at competitions such as the National

Tournament, ABA Tournament, and Vanderbilt University First Amendment Invitational Tournament. Each year the school sponsors the National Trial Team competitions and the Bushrod T. Washington Moot Court Tournament, which is open to first-year students. The William B. Spong, Jr. Invitational Moot Court Tournament attracts 24 teams from throughout the nation annually. The Alternative Dispute Resolution team hosts an ABA competition every 3 to 5 years. Law student organizations, local chapters of national associations, and campus organizations include the Sports and Entertainment Law Society, International Law Society, and Military Law Society, Lesbian and Gay Student Association, Black Law Students Association, Phi Alpha Delta, Christian Legal Society, Public Service Fund, and George Wythe Society.

Library

The law library contains 421,000 hardcopy volumes and 953,000 microform volume equivalents, and subscribes to 4,200 serial publications. Online databases and networks include CALI, Dow-Jones, Legal-Trac, LEXIS, Mathew Bender, OCLC First Search, WESTLAW, First Search, VIVA, LexisNexis Academic Factiva, ProQuest Congressional, Factiva, and EbscoHost, which are available to law students for research. Special library collections include Thomas Jefferson, and George Wythe law collections, environmental law, Roman law, constitutional law, jurisprudence, and intellectual property. The ratio of library volumes to faculty is 12,030 to 1 and to students is 650 to 1. The ratio of seats in the library to students is 1 to 1.

Faculty

The law school has 35 full-time and 72 part-time faculty members, of whom 32 are women. According to AAUP standards for Category 1 institutions, faculty salaries are average. About 11% of full-time faculty have a graduate law degree in addition to the J.D.; about 6% of part-time faculty have one. The ratio of full-time students to full-time faculty in an average class is 34 to 1; in a clinic, 6 to 1. The law school has a regular program of bringing visiting professors and other distinguished lecturers and visitors to campus. There is a chapter of the Order of the Coif; 12 faculty and 595 graduates are members.

Placement

J.D.s awarded:	204

Services available through: a separate law school placement center and students have access to the University's other career services offices.

Services: in person and online mock interviews, video conference and Skype interviews, summer public service fellowships, post-graduate public service fellowships, off-campus interview programs, loan repayment assistance, judicial clerkships, and externships for academic credit.

Special features: The career services staff includes advisors who have significant professional experience. The emphasis is on individualized career planning for students with extensive programs and resources designed to help them make informed career choices.

Full-time job interviews:	22 employers
Summer job interviews:	77 employers
Placement by graduation:	78% of class
Placement within 9 months:	91% of class
Average starting salary:	$30,000 to $160,000

Areas of placement:

Private practice 2–10 attorneys	13%
Private practice 11–23 attorneys	4%
Private practice 26–50 attorneys	3%
Private practice 51–100 attorneys	2%
Judicial clerkships	21%
Government	16%
Business/industry	9%
Military	6%
Public interest	5%
Academic	2%

Students

About 50% of the student body are women; 20%, minorities; 11%, African American; 4%, Asian American; 2%, Hispanic; and 14%, Unknown. The majority of students come from Virginia (28%). The average age of entering students is 24; age range is 18 to 36. About 60% of students enter directly from undergraduate school, 8% have a graduate degree, and 40% have worked full-time prior to entering law school. About 1% drop out after the first year for academic or personal reasons; 99% remain to receive a law degree.

School of Law

435 West 116th Street
New York, NY 10027

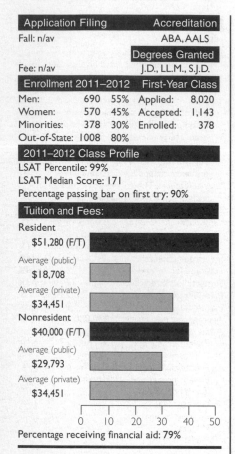

Application Filing		Accreditation
Fall: n/av		ABA, AALS
		Degrees Granted
Fee: n/av		J.D., LL.M., S.J.D.

Enrollment 2011–2012			First-Year Class	
Men:	690	55%	Applied:	8,020
Women:	570	45%	Accepted:	1,143
Minorities:	378	30%	Enrolled:	378
Out-of-State:	1008	80%		

2011–2012 Class Profile
LSAT Percentile: 99%
LSAT Median Score: 171
Percentage passing bar on first try: 90%

Tuition and Fees:

Resident
$51,280 (F/T)

Average (public)
$18,708

Average (private)
$34,451

Nonresident
$40,000 (F/T)

Average (public)
$29,793

Average (private)
$34,451

0   10   20   30   40   50

Percentage receiving financial aid: 79%

ADMISSIONS

In the fall of 2011 first-year class, 8020 applied, 1143 were accepted, and 378 enrolled. Forty-eight transfers enrolled. The median LSAT percentile of the most recent first-year class was 99; the median GPA was 3.7 on a scale of 4.0. The lowest LSAT percentile accepted was 50; the highest was 99.

Requirements
Applicants must have a bachelor's degree and take the LSAT. No specific undergraduate courses are required. Candidates are not interviewed.

Procedure
Applicants should submit an application form, LSAT results, transcripts, and 2 letters of recommendation. Notification of the admissions decision is December through April. The law school uses the LSAC.

Special
The law school recruits minority and disadvantaged students through outreach efforts, counseling initiatives, and national database searches with invitations to apply. Requirements are different for out-of-state students. Transfer students must have one year of credit, must have attended an ABA-approved law school, and must have completed the first year with distinction at an ABA-approved law school or at an accredited Canadian law school.

Costs

Tuition and fees for the 2011–2012 academic year are $51,080 for full-time in-state students. On-campus room and board costs about $16,950 annually; books and supplies run $950.

Financial Aid

About 79% of current law students receive some form of aid. The average annual amount of aid from all sources combined, including scholarships, loans, and work contracts, is $47,000; maximum, $65,000. Awards are based on need. Required financial statements are the FAFSA and Need Access application. First-year students are notified about their financial aid application at time of acceptance.

About the Law School

Columbia University School of Law was established in 1858 and is a private institution. The 36-acre campus is in an urban area of the Morningside Heights section of northwest Manhattan. The primary mission of the law school is to serve as one of the world's leading centers of research and scholarship regarding law and its role in society. Students have access to federal, state, county, city, and local agencies, courts, correctional facilities, law firms, and legal aid organizations in the New York area. The city of New York offers students a broad range of opportunities. Facilities of special interest to law students are the law school's main building, William C. Warren hall, home to Morningside Heights Legal Services and the Center for Public Interest Law. Housing for students includes on-campus apartments, available to both single students and couples; the Off-Campus Housing Office (OCHA) helps students find housing. All admitted first-year students who apply for housing by May 1 are guaranteed some type of university housing for all 3 years of the J.D. program. About 98% of the law school facilities are accessible to the physically disabled.

Calendar

The law school operates on a traditional semester basis. Courses are offered days only. New students are admitted in the fall. There is no summer session. Transferable summer courses are not offered.

Programs

In addition to the J.D., the law school offers the LL.M. and S.J.D. Students may take relevant courses in other programs and apply credit toward the J.D.; a maximum of 10 credits may be applied. The following joint degrees may be earned: J.D./M.F.A. (Juris Doctor/Master of Arts in Theater Arts), J.D./M.B.A. (Juris Doctor/Master of Business Administration), J.D./M.I.A. (Juris Doctor/Master of International Affairs), J.D./M.P.A. (Juris Doctor/Master of Public Administration), J.D./M.P.H. (Juris Doctor/Master of Public Health), J.D./M.P.H. (Juris Doctor/Master of Science in journalism or urban planning), J.D./M.Phil. (Juris Doctor/Master of Arts or Doctor of Philosophy), and J.D./M.S. (Juris Doctor/Master of Social Work).

Required
To earn the J.D., candidates must complete 83 total credits, of which 35 are for required courses. The following first-year courses are required of all students: Civil Procedure, Constitutional Law, Contracts, Criminal Law, Critical Legal Thought, Foundation of the Regulatory State, Foundation Year Moot Court, Law and Contemporary Society, Law and Economics, Law and Social Science, Lawyering Across Multiple Legal Orders, Legal Methods and Legal Writing and Research, Legislation, Property, The Rule of Law: Perspectives on Legal Thought, and Torts. Required upper-level courses consist of a minimum of writing credits earned, a pro bono service requirement, and Profession of Law (focusing on professional ethics). Clinics are electives. The required orientation program for first-year students lasts 2 days and starts before the Legal Methods course begins. Topics covered include student services, law school and university administrative matters, computer training, and financial aid information. Several social events for students and faculty take place on campus and around New York City.

Electives
The School of Law offers concentrations in corporate law, criminal law, entertainment

Phone: 212-854-2670
Fax: 212-854-1109
E-mail: *admissions@law.columbia.edu*
Web: *www.law.columbia.edu*

Contact

Admissions Office, 212-854-2674 for general inquiries; Assistant Dean of Registration, 212-854-6522 for financial aid information.

NEW YORK

law, environmental law, family law, internationl law, labor law, litigation, media law, securities law, sports law, tax law, torts and insurance, constitutional law, human rights law, labor law, history and philosophy of law, health care and the law, and education law. In addition, clinics such as child advocacy, law and the arts, environmental law, human rights, lawyering in the digital age, mediation, nonprofit organizations/small business, and prisoners and families offer client-based experiences to upper-class students for 5 to 7 points. 130 seminars are offered annually in such areas as Constitutional Law, Corporate Law, and Human Rights for 2 points (generally). Admission to a seminar is by lottery. Additional training through internships is available through arrangements with city agencies and consumer advocacy groups; clerkships with criminal, appellate, and federal court judges; and the pro bono service requirement. Research may be done as part of the legal writing requirement. Credit may be earned in journal work, independent, or supervised research. Law school lectures regularly bring leading figures from business, politics, entertainment, and areas of the law and judiciary to Columbia. Columbia established a Dean's Breakfast Series in which distinguished alumni from the law school come and meet informally with small groups of students. There is a 4-year double degree program with the University of Paris, giving students a J.D. and Maitrise en Droit; a 3-year J.D./D.E.S.S. with the Institut d'Etudes Politique Sciences, a 4-year program with the University of London, giving students a J.D. and LL.B., a 3-year program with the University of London where students receive a Columbia J.D. and University of London LL.M., and a 3-year program with the Institute for Law and Finance (Johann Wolfgang Goethe University, Frankfurt) where students receive a Columbia J.D. and Institute for Law LL.M. Moreover, there are semester abroad programs in Argentina, France, Germany, Hungary, Israel, Italy, Japan, the Netherlands, Singapore, South Africa, and Switzerland. Students may also elect to initiate a study abroad program in additional countries. The most widely taken electives are Corporations, Federal Income Taxation, and Evidence.

Graduation Requirements

In order to graduate, candidates must have completed the upper-division writing requirement and satisfied degree requirements (including pro bono service) and a course in professional responsibility and ethics in the third year.

Organizations

Students edit the *Columbia Law Review, Columbia Journal of Environmental Law, Columbia Human Rights Law Review, Columbia Journal of Law and Social Problems, Columbia Journal of Transactional Law, Columbia Journal of Asian Law, American Review of International Arbitration, Columbia-VLA Journal of Law and the Arts, Columbia Business Law Review, Columbia Journal of Gender and the Law, Parker School Journal of East European Law, Columbia Journal of European Law, Columbia Science and Technology Law Review,* and *National Black Law Journal.* Students also edit the newspaper *Columbia Law School News* and the yearbook *Pegasus.* The Moot Court Committee sponsors the Harlan Fiske Stone Honor Competition and the Jerome Michael Jury Trials. Students also participate in the Jessup International Moot Court Competition. Other competitions include the Frederick Douglass National Competition and Native American Law Students Moot Court Competition. Law student organizations, local chapters of national associations, and campus organizations include Columbia Law School Women's Association, American Civil Liberties Union, Columbia Workers' Rights Coalition, Society for Chinese Law, Civil Rights Society, Environmental Law Society, Columbia Society of International Law, American Civil Liberties Union, Federalist Society, and National Lawyers Guild.

Library

The law library contains 1,092,534 hardcopy volumes and 235,424 microform volume equivalents, and subscribes to 6,472 serial publications. Such online databases and networks as CALI, CIS Universe, DIALOG, Infotrac, Legal-Trac, LEXIS, Mathew Bender, OCLC First Search, RLIN, WESTLAW, Wilsonline Indexes, Jutastat, CCH, PLC Global, UN ODS, TIARA TREATIES, BNA, China Law and Practice, Constitutions of the World (Oceana), Foreign Law Guide, HeinOnline, Indexmaster, Inter-Am Database, Arbitration Online, LLMC digital, Making of Modern Law, PACER, BNA International/Intellectual Property, and others are available to law students for research. Special library collections include a notable collection on foreign law,

Placement

Services available through: a separate law school placement center.

Services: extensive judicial clerkship counseling and international internship opportunities.

Special features: resource library, web-based alumni jobs newsletter, career adviser program, a public interest program, extensive web-based student job listings and resource database, and one of the largest on-campus recruiting programs in the country.

Full-time job interviews:	750 employers
Summer job interviews:	750 employers
Placement by graduation:	99% of class
Placement within 9 months:	99% of class
Average starting salary:	$35,000 to $175,000

Areas of placement:

Private practice 100+ attorneys	77%
Judicial clerkships	14%
Government	4%
Public interest	3%
Business/industry	2%

Roman law, and a large rare book collection of more than 30,000 volumes, the Perlin/Rosenberg Papers, as well as papers from the Nuremberg Trials and the South African Treason Trials, and a gift of the papers of Telford Taylor, who was the main U.S. prosecutor at the Nuremberg Trials. The ratio of library volumes to faculty is 11,148 to 1 and to students is 880 to 1. The ratio of seats in the library to students is 1 to 4.

Faculty

The law school has 98 full-time and 69 part-time faculty members, of whom 51 are women. According to AAUP standards for Category I institutions, faculty salaries are well above average. About 15% of full-time faculty have a graduate law degree in addition to the J.D.; about 10% of part-time faculty have one. The ratio of full-time students to full-time faculty in an average class is 13 to 1; in a clinic, 8 to 1. The law school has a regular program of bringing visiting professors and other distinguished lecturers and visitors to campus.

Students

About 45% of the student body are women; 30%, minorities; 10%, African American; 18%, Asian American; and 7%, Hispanic. The average age of entering students is 24. About 33% of students enter directly from undergraduate school, and 11% have a graduate degree.

Law School

Myron Taylor Hall
Ithaca, NY 14853-4901

Application Filing		Accreditation	
Fall: February 1		ABA, AALS	
		Degrees Granted	
Fee: $80		J.D., LL.M., S.J.D.	
Enrollment 2011–2012		First-Year Class	
Men:	315 51%	Applied:	5,556
Women:	297 48%	Enrolled:	204
Minorities:	226 37%		
Out-of-State:	435 71%		

2011–2012 Class Profile
LSAT Percentile: 96%
LSAT Median Score: 168

Tuition and Fees:

Resident
$53,150 (F/T)

Average (public)
$18,708

Average (private)
$34,451

Nonresident
$53,150 (F/T)

Average (public)
$29,793

Average (private)
$34,451

0   10   20   30   40   50

Percentage receiving financial aid: 80%

ADMISSIONS
In the fall of 2011 first-year class, 5556 applied and 204 enrolled. Ten transfers enrolled. The median LSAT percentile of the most recent first-year class was 96; the median GPA was 3.7 on a scale of 4.0.

Requirements
Applicants must have a bachelor's degree and take the LSAT. No specific undergraduate courses are required. Candidates are not interviewed.

Procedure
The application deadline for fall entry is February 1. Applicants should submit an application form, LSAT results, a nonrefundable application fee of $80, 2 letters of recommendation, and a personal statement. Transcripts must be sent via the LSAC. Notification of the admissions decision is mid to late December.

Special
The law school recruits minority and disadvantaged students by aggressively encouraging them to apply. In addition, a student's minority or disadvantaged status is considered to be a positive part of the application; offers of financial aid are also made. Requirements are different for out-of-state students. Transfer students must have one year of credit, must have attended an ABA-approved law school, and must be in the top 10% of the class.

Costs
On-campus room and board costs about $11,250 annually; books and supplies run $1,100.

Financial Aid
About 80% of current law students receive some form of aid. The average annual amount of aid from all sources combined, including scholarships, loans, and work contracts, is $43,000; maximum, $72,380. Awards are based on need and merit combined. Required financial statements are the FAFSA and Need Access. The aid application deadline for fall entry is March 15. Special funds for minority or disadvantaged students include need-based enhanced grants. First-year students are notified about their financial aid application at time of acceptance.

About the Law School
Cornell University Law School was established in 1888 and is a private institution. The 745-acre campus is in a small town 250 miles northwest of New York City. The primary mission of the law school is to teach law within the context of humanity. Students have access to federal, state, county, city, and local agencies, courts, correctional facilities, law firms, and legal aid organizations in the Ithaca area. A full range of opportunities consistent with a small city is available to students. Facilities of special interest to law students are the Legal Aid Clinic, Berger International Legal Studies Program, and the Legal Information Institute. Housing for students is ample both on and off campus. About 90% of the law school facilities are accessible to the physically disabled.

Calendar
The law school operates on a traditional semester basis. Courses are offered days only and must be completed within 3 years. New students are admitted in the fall. There is a 6-week summer session. Transferable summer courses are offered.

Programs
In addition to the J.D., the law school offers the LL.M. and S.J.D. Students may take relevant courses in other programs and apply credit toward the J.D.; a maximum of 12 credits may be applied. The following joint degrees may be earned: J.D./D.M.A. (Juris Doctor/Doctor of Musical Arts), J.D./D.V.M. (Juris Doctor/Doctor of Veterinary Medicine), J.D./M.A. (Juris Doctor/Master of Arts), J.D./M.Arch. (Juris Doctor/Master of Architecture), J.D./M.B.A. (Juris Doctor/Master of Business Administration), J.D./M.D. (Juris Doctor/Doctor of Medicine), J.D./M.Eng. (Juris Doctor/Master of Engineering), J.D./M.F.A. (Juris Doctor/Master of Fine Arts), J.D./M.F.S. (Juris Doctor/Master of Food Science), J.D./M.H.A. (Juris Doctor/Master of Health Administration), J.D./M.M.H. (Juris Doctor/Master of Hospitality Management), J.D./M.I.L.R. (Juris Doctor/Master of Industrial and Labor Relations), J.D./M.L.A. (Juris Doctor/Master of Landscape Architecture), J.D./M.P.A. (Juris Doctor/Master of Public Administration), J.D./M.P.S. (Juris Doctor/Master of Professional Studies), J.D./M.R.P. (Juris Doctor/Master of Regional Planning), J.D./M.S. (Juris Doctor/Master of Science), J.D./M.A.T. (Juris Doctor/Master of Teaching), and J.D./Ph.D. (Juris Doctor/Doctor of Philosophy).

Required
To earn the J.D., candidates must complete 84 total credits, of which 36 are for required courses. They must maintain a minimum GPA of 2.3 in the required courses. The following first-year courses are required of all students: Civil Procedure, Constitutional Law, Contracts, Criminal Law, Lawyering, Property, and Torts. Required upper-level courses consist of a writing requirement (2 writing courses) and a professional responsibility course. The required orientation program for first-year students is a 2-day introduction to the school.

NEW YORK

Phone: 607-255-5141
Fax: 607-255-7193
E-mail: lawadmit@lawschool.cornell.edu
Web: lawschool.cornell.edu

Contact

Financial Aid Office, 607-255-6292 for financial aid information.

Placement

J.D.s awarded:	200

Services available through: a separate law school placement center.

Services: off-campus job fairs in major U.S. cities.

Special features: the Public Interest Low Income Protection Plan for loan forgiveness and moderate payback plans program is for students who intend to work in the public or nonprofit sector. Public Interest Foundation and work-study grants are available for summer public interest work.

Placement by graduation:	95% of class
Placement within 9 months:	99% of class
Average starting salary:	$46,000 to $165,000

Areas of placement:

Private practice 11–23 attorneys	2%
Private practice 26–50 attorneys	2%
Private practice 51–100 attorneys	5%
Private practice 100+ attorneys	73%
Judicial clerkships	14%
Public interest	3%
Government	1%

Electives

The Law School offers concentrations in advocacy, business law and regulation, general practice, and public law. In addition, clinics, worth 4 to 6 credits, include the Legal Aid Clinic, Innocence Clinic, and LGBT Clinic. Multiple seminars in the upper-division are open to a maximum of 16 students per semester. Internships include the judicial externship, neighborhood legal services, criminal justice, and legislative. Full-term externships are worth 12 credits at approved sites. Special lecture series are the Berger International Lecture Series, the Berger Program in International Law, Clarke Lectures (part of Clarke program in East Asian Law and Culture), and Cyrus Mehri Lecture Series in public interest with 14 partner schools. A minority orientation program and a diversity weekend for admitted applicants are held. The most widely taken electives are Corporations, Evidence, and Federal Income Taxation.

Graduation Requirements

In order to graduate, candidates must have a GPA of 2.3, and must have completed the upper-division writing requirement, first-year lawyering program, and professional responsibility course.

Organizations

Students edit the *Cornell Law Review*, *Cornell Journal of Law and Public Policy*, *Cornell International Law Journal*, *LII Bulletin-NY*, *LII Bulletin-Patent*, the student newspaper *Tower*, and the *Cornell Law Forum*. A variety of moot court competitions, such as the Cuccia Cup, Jessup, and Niagara CISG, are held, mostly at the school. Law student organizations include the Herbert W. Briggs Society of International Law, Cornell Law Students Association, and Environment Law Association. There are local chapters of National Lawyers Guild, Phi Delta Phi, and Order of the Coif.

Library

The law library contains 676,000 hardcopy volumes and 5,500 microform volume equivalents, and subscribes to 6,387 serial publications. Such online databases and networks as CALI, CIS Universe, DIALOG, Dow-Jones, Infotrac, Legal-Trac, LEXIS, Mathew Bender, OCLC First Search, RLIN, WESTLAW, and Wilsonline Indexes are available to law students for research. Special library collections include international and foreign law collections, a U.S. government documents depository, the Bennett Collection of Statutory Materials, Donovan Nuremberg Trials Collection, and rare books. The ratio of library volumes to faculty is 12,641 to 1 and to students is 1,077 to 1. The ratio of seats in the library to students is 1 to 1.

Faculty

The law school has 52 full-time and 64 part-time faculty members, of whom 30 are women. About 30% of full-time faculty have a graduate law degree in addition to the J.D.; about 1% of part-time faculty have one. The ratio of full-time students to full-time faculty in an average class is 10 to 1; in a clinic, 8 to 1. The law school has a regular program of bringing visiting professors and other distinguished lecturers and visitors to campus. There is a chapter of the Order of the Coif; 30 faculty and 18 graduates are members.

Students

About 48% of the student body are women; 37%, minorities; 7%, African American; 14%, Asian American; 14%, Hispanic; and 2%, Native American. The average age of entering students is 23; age range is 21 to 48. About 33% of students enter directly from undergraduate school, 10% have a graduate degree, and 70% have worked full-time prior to entering law school.

CREIGHTON UNIVERSITY

School of Law

2500 California Plaza
Omaha, NE 68178

Application Filing		Accreditation
Fall: May 1		ABA, AALS
		Degrees Granted
Fee: $50		J.D.

Enrollment 2011–2012			First-Year Class	
Men:	277	63%	Applied:	1,232
Women:	165	37%	Accepted:	705
Minorities:	53	12%	Enrolled:	135
Out-of-State:	287	65%		

2011–2012 Class Profile
LSAT Percentile: 52%
LSAT Median Score: 152
Percentage passing bar on first try: 84%

Tuition and Fees:

Resident
$32,464 (F/T)

Average (public)
$18,708

Average (private)
$34,451

Nonresident
$32,464 (F/T)

Average (public)
$29,793

Average (private)
$34,451

Percentage receiving financial aid: 89%

ADMISSIONS

In the fall of 2011 first-year class, 1232 applied, 705 were accepted, and 135 enrolled. Four transfers enrolled. The median LSAT percentile of the most recent first-year class was 52; the median GPA was 3.2 on a scale of 4.3. The lowest LSAT percentile accepted was 23; the highest was 99.

Requirements
Applicants must have a bachelor's degree and take the LSAT. The most important admission factors include LSAT results, GPA, and general background. No specific undergraduate courses are required. Candidates are not interviewed.

Procedure
The application deadline for fall entry is May 1. Applicants should submit an application form, LSAT results, transcripts, a personal statement, a nonrefundable application fee of $50, 2 letters of recommendation, and a resume. Notification of the admissions decision is on a rolling basis. The law school uses the LSAC.

Special
The law school recruits minority and disadvantaged students by means of a substantial Diversity Scholarship Program, attending law and graduate fairs, participating in LSAC'S Discover Law.org program, providing application fee waivers, and providing an opportunity to contact current students. Requirements are different for out-of-state students. Transfer students must have one year of credit, must have attended an ABA-approved law school, and must submit a personal statement.

Costs

Tuition and fees for the 2011–2012 academic year are $31,054 for all full-time students. On-campus room and board costs about $14,400 annually; books and supplies run $1,155.

Financial Aid

About 89% of current law students receive some form of aid. The average annual amount of aid from all sources combined, including scholarships, loans, and work contracts, is $43,938; maximum, $52,050. Awards are based on need and merit. The required financial statement is the FAFSA. The aid application deadline for fall entry is March 1. Special funds for minority or disadvantaged students include a substantial scholarship program known as the Ryan Diversity Scholarship. First-year students are notified about their financial aid application at time of acceptance.

About the Law School

Creighton University School of Law was established in 1904 and is a private institution. The 129-acre campus is in an urban area near downtown Omaha. The primary mission of the law school is to train lawyers to practice in every jurisdiction in the United States and to prepare men and women to render morally responsible services in all phases of the administration of justice. Students have access to federal, state, county, city, and local agencies, courts, correctional facilities, law firms, and legal aid organizations in the Omaha area. The state's capital and legislature are 45 minutes away by car. Facilities of special interest to law students include the Ahmanson Law Center, which houses all functions of the law school under one roof. The law

school is adjacent to the Harper Student Center, which houses the financial aid office, a bookstore, and other student services resources. Housing for students is available in a university-owned high-rise apartment complex located 2 blocks from the law school, available for use by professional students and families. Additional privately owned apartment complexes are located within walking distance. About 99% of the law school facilities are accessible to the physically disabled.

Calendar

The law school operates on a traditional semester basis. Courses for full-time students are offered both day and evening, and must be completed within 3 years. For part-time students, courses are offered both day and evening, and must be completed within 6 years. New full- and part-time students are admitted in the fall. There is a 6-week summer session. Transferable summer courses are offered.

Programs

Students may take relevant courses in other programs and apply credit toward the J.D. The following joint degrees may be earned: J.D./M.A. (Juris Doctor/Master of Arts in International Relations), J.D./M.B.A. (Juris Doctor/Master of Business Administration), J.D./M.S. (Juris Doctor/Master of Science in Government Organization and Leadership), J.D./M.S. (Juris Doctor/Master of Science in Information Tech Management), and J.D./M.S. (Juris Doctor/Master of Science in Negotiation and Dispute Resolution).

Required
To earn the J.D., candidates must complete 94 total credits, of which 55 are for required courses. They must maintain a minimum GPA of 2.0 in the required courses. The following first-year courses are required of all students: Civil Procedure I and II, Constitutional Law I and II, Contracts I and II, Legal Research and Writing I and II, Property I and II, and Torts I and II. Required upper-level courses consist of Business Associations, Criminal Procedure, Evidence, Legal Research and Writing III, Professional Responsibility, Secured Transactions in Personal Property, and Trusts and Estates I. The required orientation program for first-year students is a 2-day

Phone: 402-280-2586
800-282-5835
Fax: 402-280-3161
E-mail: *lawadmit@creighton.edu*
Web: *www.creighton.edu/law*

Contact

Andrea D. Bashara, Assistant Dean, 402-280-2586 for general inquiries; Paula Kohles, Associate Director, 402-280-2731 for financial aid information.

NEBRASKA

program that includes an introduction to the Socratic method, preparing for the first day of class, a financial aid presentation, a technology orientation, and mentor group introductions.

Electives

The School of Law offers concentrations in corporate law, criminal law, internationl law, and litigation. In addition, clinics include the Milton R. Abrahams Legal Clinic and the Community Economic Development Clinic, which are worth 2 to 4 credits and are open to third-year students who have completed all required courses. Seminars, worth 2 and 3 credits, include Comparative Criminal Procedure, International Human Rights Law, and Mediation Seminar. Internships are offered to eligible upper-level students in many different city, county, and federal offices and legal aid offices. Participants serve as law clerks to the various attorneys and judges, for 3 nonclassroom hours. Students may select research topics and write papers for credit under the guidance of a faculty member. Special lecture series include the annual TePoel Lecture Series, Lane Foundation Lectures, and the Koley Lectures. The law school has an exchange program with Universidad Pontificia Comillas in Madrid, Spain. Students may earn up to 12 hours of law school credit through the exchange program. The Black Law Students Association and Latino Law Students Association offer tutorial programs to members. The law school has a Director of Academic Excellence to assist students in developing their skills for academic success. Tutors are available for first-year courses. A Legal Writing Center is available to assist students in developing their writing skills. The most widely taken electives are Marriage and Divorce, Federal Income Taxation, and Criminal Law.

Graduation Requirements

In order to graduate, candidates must have a GPA of 2.0 and must have completed the upper-division writing requirement.

Organizations

Students edit the *Creighton Law Review*. Moot Court opportunities include the second-year intramural ABA regional, national, and international tournaments as well as invitational tournaments. Other competitions include the Negotiation Competition, Client Counseling, ABA National Criminal Justice Trial Advocacy Competition, Jessup International Moot Court Competition, and essay competitions. Student organizations include J. Reuben Clark, Fellowship of Christian Law Students, and American Constitution Society for Law and Policy. There are local chapters of Phi Alpha Delta, Phi Delta Phi, and the American Bar Association Law Student Division. Other student organizations include the Public Interest Law Forum, Women's Law Student Association, and International Law Society.

Library

The law library contains 386,876 hardcopy volumes and 183,068 microform volume equivalents, and subscribes to 1,575 serial publications. Such online databases and networks as CALI, CIS Universe, Infotrac, Legal-Trac, LEXIS, Mathew Bender, OCLC First Search, WESTLAW, Wilsonline Indexes, HeinOnline, Academic Universe, Making of Modern Law, RIA Checkpoint, ILP and ILP Retro, Intelliconnect, LLMC Digital, and Proquest Legislative Insight are available to law students for research. Special library collections include a selective U.S. government depository consisting of a complete Congressional Information Service Legislative History service from 1970 to the present, Nebraska Appellate and Supreme Court briefs, and a rare book collection containing approximately 750 British and American legal texts from the 15th through the 19th centuries. The ratio of library volumes to faculty is 13,817 to 1 and to students is 863 to 1. The ratio of seats in the library to students is 1 to 4.

Faculty

The law school has 31 full-time and 36 part-time faculty members, of whom 21 are women. According to AAUP standards for Category IIA institutions, faculty salaries are above average. About 42% of full-time faculty have a graduate law degree in addition to the J.D. The ratio of full-time students to full-time faculty in an average class is 17 to 1; in a clinic, 6 to 1. The law school has a regular program of bringing visiting professors and other distinguished lecturers and visitors to campus.

Placement

J.D.s awarded:	154
Services available through: a separate law school placement center.	
Special features: web page (job postings are password protected).	
Full-time job interviews:	18 employers
Summer job interviews:	18 employers
Placement by graduation:	53% of class
Placement within 9 months:	87% of class
Average starting salary:	$36,000 to $110,000
Areas of placement:	
Private practice 2–10 attorneys	39%
Private practice 11–23 attorneys	6%
Private practice 26–50 attorneys	5%
Private practice 51–100 attorneys	4%
Private practice 101+ attorneys	11%
Business/industry	12%
Government	9%
Judicial clerkships	8%
Public interest	4%
Military	2%

Students

About 37% of the student body are women; 12%, minorities; 3%, African American; 5%, Asian American; and 4%, Hispanic. The majority of students come from Nebraska (35%). The average age of entering students is 24; age range is 21 to 46. About 46% of students enter directly from undergraduate school, and 7% have a graduate degree. About 5% drop out after the first year for academic or personal reasons; 91% remain to receive a law degree.

DE PAUL UNIVERSITY
College of Law

25 East Jackson Boulevard
Chicago, IL 60604

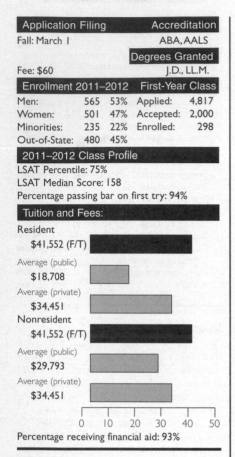

Application Filing	Accreditation
Fall: March 1	ABA, AALS

	Degrees Granted
Fee: $60	J.D., LL.M.

Enrollment 2011–2012		First-Year Class	
Men:	565 53%	Applied:	4,817
Women:	501 47%	Accepted:	2,000
Minorities:	235 22%	Enrolled:	298
Out-of-State:	480 45%		

2011–2012 Class Profile
LSAT Percentile: 75%
LSAT Median Score: 158
Percentage passing bar on first try: 94%

Tuition and Fees:

Resident
$41,552 (F/T)

Average (public)
$18,708

Average (private)
$34,451

Nonresident
$41,552 (F/T)

Average (public)
$29,793

Average (private)
$34,451

0 10 20 30 40 50

Percentage receiving financial aid: 93%

ADMISSIONS
In the fall of 2011 first-year class, 4817 applied, 2000 were accepted, and 298 enrolled. Thirty-four transfers enrolled. The median LSAT percentile of the most recent first-year class was 75; the median GPA was 3.4 on a scale of 4.0.

Requirements
Applicants must have a bachelor's degree and take the LSAT. No specific undergraduate courses are required. Candidates are not interviewed.

Procedure
The application deadline for fall entry is March 1. Applicants should submit an application form, LSAT results, transcripts, a personal statement, a nonrefundable application fee of $60, and a letter of recommendation. Accepted students must pay a $600 deposit, which can be paid in two $300 installments. Notification of the admissions decision is on a rolling basis. The law school uses the LSAC.

Special
The law school recruits minority and disadvantaged students by attending recruitment programs at historically black colleges and other universities with a substantial number of minority students. The College of Law also recruits minority students through direct mail and a number of on-campus programs. In addition, scholarships are awarded to minority students. Requirements are different for out-of-state students. Transfer students must have one year of credit, must have a minimum GPA of 2, must have attended an ABA-approved law school, and must submit a personal statement, CAS report, law school transcripts, and letter of good standing.

Costs
Tuition and fees for the 2011–2012 academic year are $41,240 for all full-time students. Tuition for part-time students is $26,800 for in-state students and $26,800 out-of-state. On-campus room and board costs about $13,130 annually; books and supplies run $1,480.

Financial Aid
About 93% of current law students receive some form of aid. The average annual amount of aid from all sources combined, including scholarships, loans, and work contracts, is $47,890; maximum, $75,812. Awards are based on need and merit combined. The required financial statement is the FAFSA. The aid application deadline for fall entry is March 1. Scholarship awards are available to students who contribute to diversity and have financial need. All students are eligible for consideration. First-year students are notified about their financial aid application after March 1.

About the Law School
De Paul University College of Law was established in 1898 and is a private institution. The campus is in an urban area in downtown Chicago. The primary mission of the law school is to train and educate men and women who will ethically and competently represent the legal profession in local and international settings and in private practice, business, or government. Students have access to federal, state, county, city, and local agencies, courts, correctional facilities, law firms, and legal aid organizations in the Chicago area. Extensive clinical and externship opportunities are available. The College of Law has newly renovated amphitheater-style video-equipped classrooms, a state-of-the-art moot court room, a legal clinic, new student housing, and a law library. There is an 18-story downtown Chicago residence available to law students. The Office of Admission also assists students in locating off-campus apartments. About half of the student body is from out of state. All law school facilities are accessible to the physically disabled.

Calendar
The law school operates on a traditional semester basis. Courses for full-time students are offered both day and evening, and must be completed within 5 years. For part-time students, courses are offered both day and evening, and must be completed within 5 years. New full- and part-time students are admitted in the fall. There is a 7-week summer session. Transferable summer courses are offered.

Programs
In addition to the J.D., the law school offers the LL.M. Students may take relevant courses in other programs and apply credit toward the J.D.; a maximum of 10 credit hours may be applied. The following joint degrees may be earned: J.D./M.A. (Juris Doctor/Master of Arts in International Studies), J.D./M.B.A. (Juris Doctor/Master of Business Administration), J.D./M.S. (Juris Doctor/Master of Computer Science), and J.D./M.S. (Juris Doctor/Master of Science).

Required
To earn the J.D., candidates must complete 86 total credits, of which 40 are for required courses. They must maintain a minimum GPA of 2.0 in the required courses. The following first-year courses are required of all students: Civil Procedure, Constitutional Process I, Contracts, Criminal Law, Legal Analysis, Property, Research and Communication I and II, and Torts. Required upper-level courses consist of Legal Analysis, Legal Profession, Professional Skills, Research and Communication III, and Upper-Level Writing Course. First year students attend a mandatory 2-day program for full-time students and a 3-evening program for part-time students.

Phone: 312-362-6831
800-428-7453
Fax: 312-362-5280
E-mail: *lawinfo@depaul.edu*
Web: *law.depaul.edu*

Contact
Priscilla Miller, Associate Director, 312-362-6831 for general inquiries; Office of Financial Aid, 312-362-8091 for financial aid information.

ILLINOIS

Electives

The College of Law offers concentrations in corporate law, criminal law, entertainment law, family law, intellectual property law, internationl, juvenile law, labor law, litigation, media law, securities law, sports law, tax law, torts and insurance, health law, information technology, arts and museum law, international human rights law, and public interest law. In addition, upper-level students may enroll in legal clinics, such as Technology and Intellectual Property, Criminal Appeals, Death Penalty, Immigration and Asylum Law, and Family and Child Law. Each clinic is worth 3 hours of credit. Seminars are 3-credit hour courses taken during the last year of legal studies. The College of Law also offers numerous internships. Students work with a government agency (such as the State Attorney's Office, the Public Defender's Office, or the judiciary) or other non-profit and for-profit organizations. Students may undertake an independent study project in which they develop an in-depth, publishable research paper under the guidance of a professor. Courses with a field work component are offered in Commercial Law, Criminal Justice, Environmental Law, Family Law, Judicial, Intellectual Property, Labor Law, Tax Law, Health Law, International Human Rights, and Mediation, as well as a legal clinic. An annual Visiting Scholar program is offered. Students may study abroad in an exchange program in conjunction with University College in Dublin, Ireland, as well as summer programs offered in Beijing, China; Chiapas, Mexico; San Jose, Costa Rica; Sydney, Australia; Buenos Aires; Amsterdam, Netherlands; and Prague, Czech Republic. An extensive Academic Support Program under the supervision of a full-time education specialist is offered. A wide range of services and activities for students-of-color are provided by DePaul's Black, Latino, and Asian student associations. An Assistant Dean for Community Affairs and Outreach is on the staff of the law school. Special interest programs include the Women's Law Caucus, Public Interest Law Association, Human Rights Bar Association, Environmental Law Society, Labor Law Society, International Law Society, and Gay and Lesbian Society. The College also sponsors the following institutes: Health Law Institute; Center for Intellectual Property and Information Technology; Schiller, DuCanto & Fleck Family Law Center; International Human Rights Law Institute; Center for Justice in

Capital Cases; International Aviation Law Institute; and the Center for Law and Science. The most widely taken electives are Litigation Strategies, Alternate Dispute Resolution, and Corporate Law.

Graduation Requirements

In order to graduate, candidates must have a GPA of 2.0, and must have completed the upper-division writing requirement and a required seminar.

Organizations
Students edit the *De Paul Law Review, Health Care Law Journal, Business & Commercial Law Journal, Intellectual Property Law Digest, Journal of Art, Technology and Intellectual Property Law, Journal of Sports Law and Contemporary Problems*, and the *Journal of Social Justice*. Students participate in an annual international moot court competition. The Moot Court Society enters national and international competitions. Negotiations, Client Counseling, and Jessup International Moot Court competitions are held annually. Law student organizations, local chapters of national associations, and campus clubs and organizations include the Women's Law Caucus, Student Bar Association, Phi Alpha Delta, Phi Delta Phi, Decalogue Society, Federalist Society for Law & Public Policy Studies, International Law Society, and Justinian Society of Lawyers.

Library
The law library contains 218,184 hardcopy volumes and 192,926 microform volume equivalents, and subscribes to 6,180 serial publications. Such online databases and networks as CALI, CIS Universe, Infotrac, Legal-Trac, LEXIS, OCLC First Search, WESTLAW, Wilsonline Indexes, BNA-ALL, Making of Modern Law, and CCH Tax are available to law students for research. Special library collections include an official U.S. government depository, and tax law, health law, and human rights law collections. The ratio of library volumes to faculty is 2,693 to 1 and to students is 204 to 1. The ratio of seats in the library to students is 1 to 2.

Faculty
The law school has 54 full-time and 60 part-time faculty members, of whom 41

Placement

J.D.s awarded:	329

Services available through: a separate law school placement center and the university placement center.

Services: career and advisory programs are available, as well as an Alumni Job Newsletter, in-office copier, and Network, Internet, LEXIS, and WESTLAW capabilities.

Special features: the De Paul College of Law Alumni Board is very active in career planning and placement programs, and supports a proactive approach to students and alumni career development. Westlaw and Yahoo groups are also used to inform students of job opportunities. The office offers online, document, and digital libraries, as well as an online event calendar.

Full-time job interviews:	10 employers
Summer job interviews:	20 employers
Placement by graduation:	76% of class
Placement within 9 months:	84% of class
Average starting salary:	$20,000 to $160,000
Areas of placement:	
Private practice 2–10 attorneys	22%
Private practice 11–23 attorneys	10%
Private practice 26–50 attorneys	7%
Private practice 51–100 attorneys	5%
Private practice 100+ attorneys	26%
Business/industry	19%
Government	15%
Public interest	5%
Academic	5%
Judicial clerkships	2%

are women. According to AAUP standards for Category I institutions, faculty salaries are average. The ratio of full-time students to full-time faculty in an average class is 13 to 1; in a clinic, 8 to 1. The law school has a regular program of bringing visiting professors and other distinguished lecturers and visitors to campus. There is a chapter of the Order of the Coif; 50 faculty are members.

Students
About 47% of the student body are women; 22%, minorities; 6%, African American; 6%, Asian American; 9%, Hispanic; and 1%, Native American. The majority of students come from Illinois (55%). The average age of entering students is 24; age range is 20 to 46. About 41% of students enter directly from undergraduate school, and 7% have a graduate degree. About 4% drop out after the first year for academic or personal reasons; 96% remain to receive a law degree.

DRAKE UNIVERSITY
Law School

2507 University Avenue
Des Moines, IA 50311

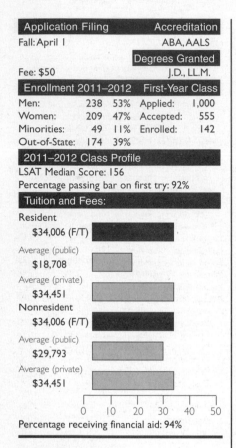

Application Filing	Accreditation
Fall: April 1	ABA, AALS

Degrees Granted	
Fee: $50	J.D., LL.M.

Enrollment 2011–2012			First-Year Class	
Men:	238	53%	Applied:	1,000
Women:	209	47%	Accepted:	555
Minorities:	49	11%	Enrolled:	142
Out-of-State:	174	39%		

2011–2012 Class Profile
LSAT Median Score: 156
Percentage passing bar on first try: 92%

Tuition and Fees:

Resident
$34,006 (F/T)

Average (public)
$18,708

Average (private)
$34,451

Nonresident
$34,006 (F/T)

Average (public)
$29,793

Average (private)
$34,451

0   10   20   30   40   50

Percentage receiving financial aid: 94%

ADMISSIONS

In the fall of 2011 first-year class, 1000 applied, 555 were accepted, and 142 enrolled. One transfer enrolled. The median GPA of the most recent first-year class was 3.4.

Requirements
Applicants must have a bachelor's degree and take the LSAT. The most important admission factors include LSAT results, GPA, and undergraduate curriculum. No specific undergraduate courses are required and candidates are not interviewed.

Procedure
The application deadline for fall entry is April 1. Applicants should submit an application form, LSAT results, transcripts, TOEFL (if applicable), a nonrefundable application fee of $50, 2 letters of recommendation, and a personal statement. Notification of the admissions decision is within 4 to 6 weeks after the file is complete. Notification begins in late January. The law school uses the LSAC.

Special
The law school recruits minority and disadvantaged students by means of targeted efforts at nationally identified feeder schools for students of color, the use of the Candidate Referral Service (CRS), and an on-campus recruitment event. Requirements are different for out-of-state students. Transfer students must have one year of credit, must have attended an ABA-approved law school, and must rank in the upper half of their current law school class and have certification of good academic standing and eligibility to re-enroll at that school.

Costs

Tuition and fees for the 2011–2012 academic year are $33,900 for all full-time students. On-campus room and board costs about $16,400 annually; books and supplies run $1,500.

Financial Aid

About 94% of current law students receive some form of aid. The maximum annual amount of aid from all sources combined, including scholarships, loans, and work contracts, is $52,535. Awards are based on need and merit. The required financial statement is the FAFSA. The aid application deadline for fall entry is March 1. Special funds for minority or disadvantaged students are available. First-year students are notified about their financial aid application some time after admission and before a seat deposit is required.

About the Law School

Drake University Law School was established in 1865 and is a private institution. The 120-acre campus is located in an urban area 5 miles northwest of downtown Des Moines. The primary mission of the law school is to provide law students with the opportunities to benefit from hands-on learning experiences and to gain the skills needed to be successful in the legal profession in whatever career path they choose in any geographic location. Students have access to federal, state, county, city, and local agencies, courts, correctional facilities, law firms, and legal aid organizations in the Des Moines area. Facilities of special interest to law students are the Constitutional Law Center; Agricultural Law Center; Neal and Bea Smith Legal Clinic and Legislative

Practice Center; Joan and Lyle Middleton Center for Children's Rights; and the Intellectual Property Law Center. Housing for students consists of university-owned and privately-owned apartments located within walking distance of the campus. Housing is also available in city suburbs just 15 minutes from campus. About 99% of the law school facilities are accessible to the physically disabled.

Calendar

The law school operates on a traditional semester basis. Courses for full-time students are offered days only, and must be completed within 6 years. For part-time students, courses are offered days only, and must be completed within 6 years. New full- and part-time students are admitted in the fall and summer. There is a 7-week summer session. Transferable summer courses are offered.

Programs

In addition to the J.D., the law school offers the LL.M. Students may take relevant courses in other programs and apply credit toward the J.D.; a maximum of 6 credits may be applied. The following joint degrees may be earned: J.D./M.A. (Juris Doctor/Master of Arts in Political Science), J.D./M.B.A. (Juris Doctor/Master of Business Administration), J.D./M.H.A. (Juris Doctor/Master of Health Administration), J.D./M.S. (Juris Doctor/Master of Science in Agricultural Economics), J.D./M.P.A. (Juris Doctor/Master of Public Administration), J.D./M.P.H. (Juris Doctor/Master of Public Health), J.D./M.S.W. (Juris Doctor/Master of Social Work), and J.D./Pharm.D. (Juris Doctor/Doctor of Pharmacy).

Required
To earn the J.D., candidates must complete 90 total credits, of which 41 are for required courses. They must maintain a minimum GPA of 2.0 in the required courses. The following first-year courses are required of all students: Appelate Practice, Civil Procedure I and II, Constitutional Law I, Contracts I and II, Criminal Law, Legal Research, Writing, Property, and Torts. Required upper-level courses consist of Advanced Writing Seminar, Constitutional Law II, Evidence, Legal Ethics and Professional Responsibility, and Professional Skills Course. All

IOWA

Phone: 515-271-2782
800-44-DRAKE, ext. 2782
Fax: 515-271-1990
E-mail: lawadmit@drake.edu
Web: www.law.drake.edu

Contact

Andrew English, Associate Director of Admission and Financial Aid, 515-271-2782; 800-44-DRAKE, ext. 2782 for general inquiries; Kara Blanchard, Director of Admission and Financial Aid, 515-271-2782; 800-44-DRAKE, ext. 2782 for financial aid information.

students who have completed 45 hours of class may take the clinical courses as electives. The required orientation program for first-year students is 3 days and includes a formal welcome, registration instructions, law school tour, fee payment session, small group meetings, computer training, sessions on professionalism, and the noncredit Introduction to Law course.

Electives

The Law School offers concentrations in corporate law, criminal law, environmental law, family law, intellectual property law, internationl law, juvenile law, labor law, litigation, securities law, tax law, torts and insurance, agricultural law, constitutional law, and public interest law. In addition, the law school's clinical programs include the General Civil Practice Clinic, Criminal Defense Clinic, Elder Law Clinic, and the Middleton Children's Rights Clinic. Generally, students must have completed 45 hours of classroom credit prior to enrolling; however, prerequisites vary. To enroll in seminars, students must have completed 30 hours with a 2.0 GPA. Generally, 1 to 3 hours of credit may be granted for a seminar course. Internships are available in administrative law, the legislature, the judiciary, insurance, environmental law, securities, probate, health law, and others. Credit varies from 1 to 4 credit hours and prerequisites vary. Independent research may be undertaken for 1 to 3 credit hours and is graded on a credit/no credit basis. Special lecture series include the Constitutional Law Resource Center Speaker Series, the Dwight D. Opperman Lecture in Constitutional Law, and the Intellectual Property Law Center Symposia. Drake offers a 4-week summer abroad program in Nantes, France worth up to 6 credits; credit may also be accepted from programs offered by other law schools. The Academic Support Program is offered to all students. In addition, the Legal Writing Tutorial Services are led by an English professor and are offered to all students, while second- and third-year students offer tutorial services to first-year students and to upper-level students in Evidence. Special interest group programs include the Summer Institute in Constitutional Law and the Summer Institute in Agricultural Law. The most widely taken electives are Trial Advocacy, Client Representation and Litigation, and Advanced Client Representation and Litigation.

Graduation Requirements

In order to graduate, candidates must have a GPA of 2.0, must have completed the upper-division writing requirement, must have completed 6 semesters for residence credit and 90 hours for academic credit, and must have satisfied the advanced writing requirement through either independent study or course work.

Organizations

Students edit the *Drake Law Review* and the *Drake Journal of Agricultural Law*. Moot court teams are sent to the C. Edwin Moore Appellate Advocacy, National Moot Court, and National Appellate Advocacy competitions. Other competitions include the National Mock Trial Competition, Client Counseling Competition, Negotiations Competition, and Environmental Moot Court. Law student organizations, local chapters of national associations, and campus organizations include the Student Bar Association, Drake Law Women, International Law Society, Student Bar Association, Delta Theta Phi Law Fraternity, American Bar Association-Student Division, Order of Barristers, and American Association for Justice.

Library

The law library contains 344,752 hardcopy volumes and 123,027 microform volume equivalents, and subscribes to 3,342 serial publications. Online databases and networks include CALI, CIS Universe, Legal-Trac, LEXIS, OCLC First Search, WESTLAW, RIA Checkpoint, BNA Premier, CCH Intelliconnect, HeinOnline, Index to Legal Periodicals, Making of Modern Law, and Rise of American Law, which are available to law students for research. Special library collections include a government depository; agricultural, tax, computer, and constitutional law collections; Neal Smith Congressional Archives; and National Bar Association Archives. The ratio of library volumes to faculty is 9,318 to 1 and to students is 771 to 1. The ratio of seats in the library to students is 1 to 1.

Faculty

The law school has 37 full-time and 34 part-time faculty members, of whom 29 are women. According to AAUP standards for Category 11A institutions, faculty salaries are above average. About 35% of full-

Placement

J.D.s awarded:	141

Services available through: a separate law school placement center.
Services: workshops, panel speakers, mentors, networking opportunities, mock interviews, and job fairs.
Special features: a nationwide network of alumni in specific geographic and practice areas has been developed to assist students with employment opportunities.

Full-time job interviews:	12 employers
Summer job interviews:	13 employers
Placement within 9 months:	95% of class
Average starting salary:	$24,000 to $130,000

Areas of placement:

Private practice 2–10 attorneys	30%
Private practice 11–23 attorneys	11%
Private practice 26–50 attorneys	1%
Private practice 51–100 attorneys	2%
Judicial clerkships	4%
Business/industry	23%
Public interest	2%
Government	15%
Military	1%
Academic	1%

time faculty have a graduate law degree in addition to the J.D. The ratio of full-time students to full-time faculty in an average class is 14 to 1; in a clinic, 7 to 1. The law school has a regular program of bringing visiting professors and other distinguished lecturers and visitors to campus. There is a chapter of the Order of the Coif; 17 faculty and 647 graduates are members.

Students

About 47% of the student body are women; 11%, minorities; 4%, African American; 2%, Asian American; and 5%, Hispanic. The majority of students come from Iowa (61%). The average age of entering students is 25; age range is 19 to 53. About 39% of students enter directly from undergraduate school, and 8% have a graduate degree. About 8% drop out after the first year for academic or personal reasons; 92% remain to receive a law degree.

Earle Mack School of Law

3320 Market Street
Philadelphia, PA 15282

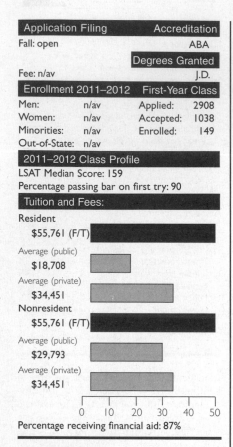

Application Filing	Accreditation
Fall: open	ABA
	Degrees Granted
Fee: n/av	J.D.

Enrollment 2011–2012	First-Year Class	
Men:	n/av	Applied: 2908
Women:	n/av	Accepted: 1038
Minorities:	n/av	Enrolled: 149
Out-of-State:	n/av	

2011–2012 Class Profile
LSAT Median Score: 159
Percentage passing bar on first try: 90

Tuition and Fees:

Resident
$55,761 (F/T)

Average (public)
$18,708

Average (private)
$34,451

Nonresident
$55,761 (F/T)

Average (public)
$29,793

Average (private)
$34,451

0 10 20 30 40 50

Percentage receiving financial aid: 87%

ADMISSIONS

In the fall of 2011 first-year class, 2908 applied, 1038 were accepted, and 149 enrolled. Nine transfers enrolled. The median GPA of the most recent first-year class was 3.4. The lowest LSAT percentile accepted was 25; the highest was 75.

Requirements
Applicants must take the LSAT. No specific undergraduate courses are required. Candidates are not interviewed.

Procedure
The application deadline for fall entry is open. Applicants should submit an application form, LSAT results, at least 2 letters of recommendation, and LSAC registration materials. Notification of the admissions decision is on a rolling basis.

Special
The law school recruits minority and disadvantaged students through affiliation agreements with minority, ethnic, and religious bar associations. Students also are encouraged to attend bar association events and events encouraging diversity in the profession. The Philadelphia Trial Lawyers Association has initiated a mentoring program that pairs trial lawyers with students of color. Requirements are different for out-of-state students. Transfer students must have attended an ABA-approved law school.

Costs

On-campus room and board costs about $21,311 annually.

Financial Aid

About 87% of current law students receive some form of aid. The maximum annual amount of aid from all sources combined, including scholarships, loans, and work contracts, is $32,000. Awards are based on need and merit combined. The required financial statement is the FAFSA. Special funds for minority or disadvantaged students are available. First-year students are notified about their financial aid application December 1.

About the Law School

Drexel University Earle Mack School of Law was established in 2006 and is a private institution in Philadelphia. The primary mission of the law school is to provide knowledge of the law, training in practical skills, and commitment to professionalism.

Calendar

The law school operates on a trimester basis. Courses are offered both day and evening. New students are admitted in the fall and summer. Transferable summer courses are not offered.

Programs

The following joint degrees may be earned: J.D./Ph.D. (Juris Doctor/Doctor in Psychology).

Required
The following first-year courses are required of all students: Interviewing, Counseling, and Negotiation, Introduction to Law, Legal Methods, and Research. Required upper-level courses consist of Drafting Appealate Advocacy, Drafting Litigation, Drafting Perspective, and Employment Discrimination. The optional orientation program for first-year students is 4 days.

Electives
The Earle Mack School of Law offers concentrations in health law, business law, and entrepreneurship law. Clinics include the Civil Litigation Field Clinic, Criminal Litigation Field Clinic, and Public Health and Environmental Law Field Clinic. There is an Academic Skills Program that is available to all students.

Library

The law library contains 48,148 hardcopy volumes. Such online databases and networks as CALI, LEXIS, WESTLAW, American Legal Institute (ALI) Library, Bloomberg BNA, CCH IntelliConnect, Constitutions of the Countries of the World and Constitutions of the United States: National and State, CQ Judicial Staff Directory, CQ Political Reference Suite, CQ Supreme Court Collection, The Economist Historical Archive, Eighteenth Century Collections Online-Law (1700–1799), Expanded Academic, FDsys, Foreign Law Guide, Gale Virtual Reference Library (GVRL) Law EBooks, GovSearch, HeinOnline, Index to Foreign Legal Periodicals, Index to Legal Periodicals Full Text, Index to Legal Periodicals Retrospective, IndexMaster, JSTOR, LawInfoChina.com, Law Library Microform Consortium (LLMC) Digital, Leadership, Library on the Internet, The Legal Intelligencer, Legal Scholarship Network (LSN), LegalTrac, LexisNexis Academic, LexisNexis Congressional, LexisNexis Statistical, Making of Modern Law: Trials, 1600–1926, Making of Modern Law: US and UK Legal Treatises 1800–1926, Making of the Modern World: The Goldsmiths-Kress

Phone: 215-895 ILAW
Fax: 215-571-4769
E-mail: tiffany.e.partlowe@drexel.edu
Web: earlemacklaw.drexel.edu

Contact

Associate Director of Law School Admissions, 215-571-4752 for general inquiries; Mary deRivera, Assistant Director of Financial Aid, 215-895-1044 for financial aid information.

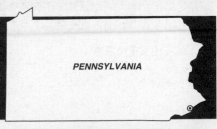

PENNSYLVANIA

Library of Economic Literature, Manupatra, NCCUSL, National Moot Court Competition, NCJRS Abstracts Database, NY Times (1980–present), NY Times (Historical, 1851–2003), Palawlibrary.com, Pennsylvania Law Weekly, Proceedings of the Old Bailey, ProQuest Congressional, ProQuest Research Library, RIA Checkpoint Tax Research System, Social Science Research Network (SSRN), Tax Analysts Web Services, THOMAS, United Nations Documentation Center, United Nations Treaty Collection, U.S. Congressional Documents Library, and U.S. Supreme Court Records and Briefs are available to law students for research.

Faculty

The law school has 65 full-time and 31 part-time faculty members. According to AAUP standards for Category 1 institutions, faculty salaries are above average. The ratio of full-time students to full-time faculty in an average class is 16 to 1.

Students

About 45% of the student body are women; and 21%, minorities. The average age of entering students is 25; age range is 21 to 48.

Placement	
J.D.s awarded:	n/av
Services available through:	
Full-time job interviews:	n/av
Summer job interviews:	n/av
Placement by graduation:	n/av
Placement within 9 months:	n/av
Average starting salary:	n/av
Areas of placement:	n/av

DUKE UNIVERSITY

School of Law

Science Drive and Towerview Road,
Box 90362
Durham, NC 27708-0362

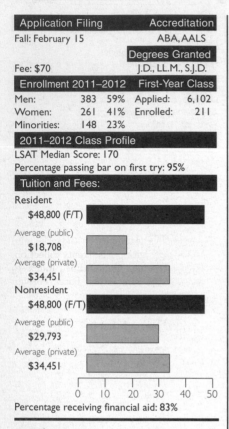

Application Filing	Accreditation
Fall: February 15	ABA, AALS

	Degrees Granted
Fee: $70	J.D., LL.M., S.J.D.

Enrollment 2011–2012		First-Year Class	
Men:	383 59%	Applied:	6,102
Women:	261 41%	Enrolled:	211
Minorities:	148 23%		

2011–2012 Class Profile
LSAT Median Score: 170
Percentage passing bar on first try: 95%

Tuition and Fees:

Resident
$48,800 (F/T)

Average (public)
$18,708

Average (private)
$34,451

Nonresident
$48,800 (F/T)

Average (public)
$29,793

Average (private)
$34,451

Percentage receiving financial aid: 83%

ADMISSIONS
In the fall of 2011 first-year class, 6102 applied and 211 enrolled. Seven transfers enrolled. The median GPA of the most recent first-year class was 3.7.

Requirements
Applicants must have a bachelor's degree and take the LSAT. No specific undergraduate courses are required. Candidates are not interviewed.

Procedure
The application deadline for fall entry is February 15. Applicants should submit an application form, LSAT results, transcripts, a personal statement, a non-refundable application fee of $70, and 2 academic letters of recommendation. Notification of the admissions decision is on a rolling basis. The law school uses the LSAC.

Special
The law school recruits minority and disadvantaged students through minority student organizations, faculty, and alumni and by encouraging participation in the Admitted Students Weekend and/or other visits to the law school. Requirements are different for out-of-state students. Transfer students must have one year of credit, must have attended an ABA-approved law school, must submit a personal statement, and must be eligible to re-enroll and otherwise be in good standing at the current law school.

Financial Aid
About 83% of current law students receive some form of aid. Awards are based on need and merit combined. The required financial statement is the FAFSA. The aid application deadline for fall entry is March 15. Special funds for minority or disadvantaged students consist of need-based scholarships. First-year students are notified about their financial aid application shortly after acceptance.

About the Law School
Duke University School of Law was established in 1930 and is a private institution. The campus is in an urban area in Durham. The primary mission of the law school is to prepare students for service as lawyers and leaders in the legal profession and society by providing a rigorous education; a collaborative, supportive, and diverse learning enviroment; and scholarship, research, and programs that serve our community and address the challenges we face in our profession and our society. Students have access to federal, state, county, city, and local agencies, courts, correctional facilities, law firms, and legal aid organizations in the Durham area. The school is an integral part of Duke University, so students have access to all the resources of a major research university. Duke Law School is located in a single building equipped with state-of-the-art teaching spaces, collaborative work and study spaces, a recently renovated library, and physical proximity to other graduate schools on the Duke University campus. Housing for students on campus is limited, but there are ample rental units in the surrounding area. All law school facilities are accessible to the physically disabled.

Calendar
The law school operates on a traditional semester basis. Courses are offered days only, and must be completed within 3 years. New students are admitted in the fall and summer. There is a 9-week summer session. Transferable summer courses are not offered.

Programs
In addition to the J.D., the law school offers the LL.M. and S.J.D. Students may take relevant courses in other programs and apply credit toward the J.D.; a maximum of 3 credits may be applied. The following joint degrees may be earned: J.D./LL.M. (Juris Doctor/Master of Laws in Comparative and International Law), J.D./M.A. (Juris Doctor/Master of Arts), J.D./M.B.A. (Juris Doctor/Master of Business Administration), J.D./M.D. (Juris Doctor/Doctor of Medicine), J.D./M.E.M. (Juris Doctor/Master of Environmental Management), J.D./M.P.P. (Juris Doctor/Master of Public Policy), J.D./M.S. (Juris Doctor/Master of Science in Mechanical Engineering or Electrical Engineering), J.D./M.T.S. (Juris Doctor/Master of Theological Studies), and J.D./Ph.D. (Juris Doctor/Doctor of Philosophy in Political Science).

Required
To earn the J.D., candidates must complete 84 total credits, of which 32 are for required courses. They must maintain a minimum GPA of 2.1 in the required courses. The following first-year courses are required of all students: Civil Procedure, Constitutional Law, Contracts, Criminal Law, Legal Research and Writing, Property, and Torts. Required upper-level courses consist of Ethics/Professional Responsibility. All clinical courses are electives. The required orientation program for first-year students occurs the week before the start of classes, introducing students to the school's BluePrint to Lead (Lawyer Education and Development) and culminating in a public service outing with upper-level students, faculty, and administration.

Electives
The Duke University School of Law offers concentrations in intellectual property, international law, national security law, enviromental studies, and business law. For students interested in structuring

Phone: 919-613-7020
Fax: 919-613-7257
E-mail: admissions@law.duke.edu
Web: http://admissions.law.duke.edu

Contact

William J. Hoye, Associate Dean for Admissions, 919-613-7020 for general inquiries; John Ahlers, Director of Financial Aid, 919-613-7025 for financial aid information.

NORTH CAROLINA

study in a particular field, the law school offers individual academic advising on course work and progression study. There are six in-house legal clinics. The Guantanamo Defense Clinic assists the Chief Defense Counsel for Guantanamo detainees with trial preparation. In the AIDS Legal Assistance Project, students help clients with HIV/AIDS prepare wills, apply for government benefits, and handle other issues. The Children's Education Law Clinic represents low-income children in special education, school discipline, and disability benefits cases. The Community Enterprise Law Clinic help students develop transactional skills in a community development law setting. The Low-Income Tax Payer Clinic helps clients in disputes with the IRS. In Wrongful Convictions, students investigate prisoners' claims of actual innocence and, in Animal Law, students investigate issues of animal cruelty and pursue animal-protection law reform advocacy. In each clinic, students provide between 75 and 100 hours of client work. Clinics are open to all upper-class students. Seminars are offered in Bioethics, Corporate Reorganization, Entertainment Law, National Security Law, and many others. An international externship program in which students earn credit for law placements at agencies such as the U.S. Trade Representative Office and the State Department exist. 3L students can develop a "capstone" project that integrates advanced knowledge in a particular subject with a hands-on practice component. Some capstone projects are extensions of successful clinic experiences; others include writing an appellate brief or preparing congressional testimony with a faculty member, or working with a law reform commission. Students may take up to 3 semester hours of independent research toward their J.D. degree. Rules vary for J.D./LL.M. and LL.M. students. All independent research taken for credit is completed in cooperation with faculty. The Pro Bono Project connects volunteer law students with attorneys in nonprofit and governmental organizations as well as with attorneys engaged in private pro bono practice. Lecture series include the Duke Law Journal Lecture, Intellectual Property "Hot Topics" Conference, Great Lives in the Law, Brainerd Currie Memorial Lecture, the Kip and Meredith Frye Lecture in Intellectual Property, Herbert L. Bernstein Memorial Lecture in International and Comparative Law, and the Rabbi Seymour Siegel Lecture in Medical-Legal Ethics. Study abroad is possible through the Summer Institutes in Transnational Law in Geneva or Hong Kong. This program is required of incoming J.D./LL.M. students, and is also open to J.D. students. Students may accrue up to 6 hours of academic credit. Remediation is provided when needed. Charting Courses is an annual event designed to foster interactive dialogue among Duke Law School's African-American students, alumni, faculty, and administrators. All minorities are welcome to attend. Duke Law School has over 50 student organizations, with the majority having special interest programming. The most widely taken electives are Business Associations, Evidence, and Intellectual Property.

Graduation Requirements

In order to graduate, candidates must have a GPA of 2.1, and must have completed the upper-division writing requirement and Ethics/Professional Responsibility.

Organizations

Students edit the *Duke Law Journal, Law and Contemporary Problems, Alaska Law Review, Duke Journal of Comparative and International Law, Duke Environmental Law and Policy Forum, Duke Journal of Gender Law and Policy, Duke Law and Technology Review, Duke Journal of Constitutional Law and Public Policy, Duke Law Magazine,* and *The Duke Law Daily.* Moot court competitions include the Jessup International Law Moot Court, National Moot Court, and ABA National Appellate Practice Advocacy Competition. The Moot Court Board Organizes and conducts the annual Hardt Cup competition for first-year students and the Dean's Cup for second- and third-year students. There are more than 50 student organizations including The Community Roundable, the Duke Student Bar Association, and the Duke Blueprint to LEAD (Lawyer Education and Development).

Library

The law library contains 680,479 hardcopy volumes and 78,554 microform volume equivalents, and subscribes to 7,852 serial publications. Such online databases and networks as CALI, CIS Universe, Infotrac, Legal-Trac, LEXIS, Mathew Bender, OCLC First Search, WESTLAW,

Placement

J.D.s awarded:	213
Services available through: a separate law school placement center.	
Services: alumni network, and on-campus interviewing by employers, judges, and government agencies.	
Special features: the Career Center works with each student to identify goals and plan a career that meets those goals.	
Full-time job interviews:	250 employers
Summer job interviews:	n/av
Placement by graduation:	95% of class
Placement within 9 months:	95% of class
Average starting salary:	$42,000 to $135,000

Wilsonline Indexes, CCH Business and Tax, LLMC Digital, U.N. treaty collection, RIA Checkpoint, HeinOnline, Index to Foreign Legal Periodicals, Pacer, Foreign Law Guide, Current Index to Legal Periodicals, and others are available to law students for research. The ratio of seats in the library to students is 1 to 1.

Faculty

The law school has 57 full-time and 68 part-time faculty members, of whom 41 are women. According to AAUP standards for Category 1 institutions, faculty salaries are well above average. About 18% of full-time faculty have a graduate law degree in addition to the J.D.; about 1% of part-time faculty have one. The ratio of full-time students to full-time faculty in an average class is 10 to 1; in a clinic, 11 to 1. The law school has a regular program of bringing visiting professors and other distinguished lecturers and visitors to campus. There is a chapter of the Order of the Coif.

Students

About 41% of the student body are women; 23%, minorities; 7%, African American; 11%, Asian American; and 5%, Hispanic. The average age of entering students is 25; age range is 20 to 38. About 35% of students enter directly from undergraduate school, and 10% have a graduate degree.

DUQUESNE UNIVERSITY

School of Law

900 Locust Street, Hanley Hall
Pittsburgh, PA 15282

Application Filing	Accreditation
Fall: April 1	ABA, AALS

Degrees Granted	
Fee: $60	J.D., LL.M. for foreign lawyers

Enrollment 2011–2012			First-Year Class	
Men:	361	56%	Applied:	n/av
Women:	278	42%	Accepted:	n/av
Minorities:	26	4%	Enrolled:	192
Out-of-State:	492	77%		

2011–2012 Class Profile
LSAT Percentile: 55%
LSAT Median Score: 153
Percentage passing bar on first try: 82%

Tuition and Fees:

Resident
$33,752 (F/T)

Average (public)
$18,708

Average (private)
$34,451

Nonresident
$33,752 (F/T)

Average (public)
$29,793

Average (private)
$34,451

0   10   20   30   40   50

Percentage receiving financial aid: 80%

ADMISSIONS

In the fall of 2011 first-year class, 192 enrolled. The median LSAT percentile of the most recent first-year class was 55; the median GPA was 3.3 on a scale of 4.0.

Requirements

Applicants must have a bachelor's degree and take the LSAT. The most important admission factors include academic achievement, LSAT results, and life experience. No specific undergraduate courses are required and candidates are not interviewed.

Procedure

The application deadline for fall entry is April 1. Applicants should submit an application form, LSAT results, transcripts, TOEFL (for foreign students), a nonrefundable application fee of $60, and 2 letters of recommendation. Notification of the admissions decision is on a rolling basis. The law school uses the LSAC.

Special

The law school recruits minority and disadvantaged students by means of Candidate Referral Service minority search, law fairs, contact with minority coordinators, and assistance with scholarships and grants. Requirements are different for out-of-state students. Transfer students must have one year of credit, have attended an ABA-approved law school, and admission depends on space availability.

Costs

Tuition and fees for the 2011–2012 academic year are $33,064 for all full-time students. Tuition for part-time students is $25,410 for in-state students and $25,410 out-of-state. On-campus room and board costs about $10,510 annually; books and supplies run $1,500.

Financial Aid

About 80% of current law students receive some form of aid. Awards are based on need and merit, along with minority status. Required financial statements are the FFS, the CSS Profile, and the FAFSA. The aid application deadline for fall entry is May 31. Special funds for minority or disadvantaged students consist of scholarships and grants. First-year students are notified about their financial aid application at time of acceptance.

About the Law School

Duquesne University School of Law was established in 1911 and is a private institution. The 47-acre campus is located in an urban area in Pittsburgh. The primary mission of the law school is to educate students in the fundamental principles of law, to assist students in forming sound judgment, and to develop facility in legal research and writing. Students have access to federal, state, county, city, and local agencies, courts, correctional facilities, law firms, and legal aid organizations in the Pittsburgh area. Varied clinical programs supervised by the school allow students to gain practical experience. Facilities of special interest to law students District Attorney's Office Clinical Program, the Department of Environmental Resources Clinical Program, in-house Economic and Community Development Clinic, Neighborhood Legal Services Clinic, and Civil and Family Justice. Housing for students is available off campus. All

law school facilities are accessible to the physically disabled.

Calendar

The law school operates on a traditional semester basis. Courses for full-time students are offered both day and evening and must be completed within 4 years. For part-time students, courses are offered both day and evening and must be completed within 5 years. New full- and part-time students are admitted in the fall. There is a 5-week summer session. Transferable summer courses are offered.

Programs

In addition to the J.D., the law school offers the LL.M. for foreign lawyers. The following joint degrees may be earned: J.D./M.A.H.E. (Juris Doctor/Master of Arts in Health Care Ethics), J.D./M.B.A. (Juris Doctor/Master of Business Administration), J.D./M. Div. (Juris Doctor/Master of Divinity in conjunction with Pittsburgh), and J.D./M.S.E.S.M. (Juris Doctor/Master of Science in Environmental Science and Math).

Required

To earn the J.D., candidates must complete 86 total credits, of which 56 are for required courses. They must maintain a minimum GPA of 3.0 in the required courses. The following first-year courses are required of all students: Civil Procedure I, Contracts, Criminal Law and Procedure (second year for evening students), Legal Process and Procedure, Legal Research and Writing, Property (second year for evening students), and Torts. Required upper-level courses consist of Basic Federal Income Taxation, Commercial Transactions I and II, Constitutional Law, Corporations, Evidence, and Professional Responsibility. The required orientation program for first-year students consists of 1 week of sessions on requirements in the first year. The students meet with student mentors.

Electives

The School of Law offers concentrations in corporate law, criminal law, environmental law, family law, intellectual property law, international law, labor law, litigation, securities law, tax law, torts and insurance, and health care. Clinics, for all upper-division classes, include the U.S.

Phone: 412-396-6296
Fax: 412-396-1073
E-mail: *campion@duq.edu*
Web: *law.duq.edu*

Contact
Jospeh P. Campion Jr., Director of Admissions, 412-396-6296 for general inquiries; Richard Esposito, Financial Aid Director, 412-396-6607 for financial aid information.

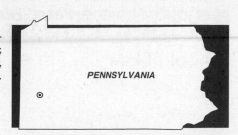

PENNSYLVANIA

Attorney's Program, District Attorney's Program, and Pennsylvania Department of Environmental Resources Program. Also open to upper-division students are internships and seminars. Seminar topics include labor arbitration, collective bargaining, and trial tactics. Upper-division students are eligible to serve as faculty research assistants. Special lectures are given by the guest speakers who visit the school throughout the year. Law students may request permission to participate in study-abroad programs offered by other ABA-approved law schools. There are summer study-abroad programs in China, Ireland, and Vatican City. The Black Law Students Association sponsors a tutoring program. Special interest programs are offered by the Public Interest Law Association, Health Care Law Association, Law Review, *Juris* magazine, Black Law Students Association, Corporate Law Society, and Women's Law Association.

Graduation Requirements
In order to graduate, candidates must have a GPA of 3.0 and complete the upper-division writing requirement.

Organizations
Students edit the *Duquesne Law Review; Juris*, a newsmagazine; and the *Duquesne Business Law Journal*. Moot courts include a trial moot court, an appellate moot court, a corporate moot court, and a tax moot court. Law student organizations, local chapters of national associations, and campus organizations include the Environmental Law Association, the Intellectual Property & Technological Law Society, Health Care Law Association, Phi Alpha Delta, Association of Trial Lawyers of America, and ABA – Law Student Division, and Criminal Law Association.

Library
The law library contains 306,385 hardcopy volumes and 75,219 microform vol-

ume equivalents, and subscribes to 173 serial publications. Online databases and networks include CALI, CIS Universe, Infotrac, Legal-Trac, LEXIS, Mathew Bender, OCLC First Search, WESTLAW, and Innovative Millennium, which are available to law students for research. The library entered into a unique public/ private agreement to manage the Allegment County Law Library as part of its special collections. Students have full access to this library, in addition to the U.S. government documents depository, and extensive Pennsylvania legal research collection. The ratio of library volumes to faculty is 8,856 to 1 and to students is 329 to 1. The ratio of seats in the library to students is 1 to 2.

Faculty
The law school has 25 full-time and 49 part-time faculty members, of whom 24 are women. According to AAUP standards for Category I institutions, faculty salaries are below average. About 32% of full-time faculty have a graduate law degree in addition to the J.D.; about 10% of part-time faculty have one. The ratio of full-time students to full-time faculty in an average class is 20 to 1. The law school has a regular program of bringing visiting professors and other distinguished lecturers and visitors to campus.

Students
About 42% of the student body are women; 4%, minoritics; 15%, African American; 17%, Asian American; 6%, Hispanic; and 3%, Native American. The majority of students come from Pennsylvania (23%). The average age of entering students is 22; age range is 20 to 48. About 25% of students have worked full-time prior to entering law school. About 2% drop out after the first year for academic or personal reasons; 95% remain to receive a law degree.

Placement
J.D.s awarded:	206

Services available through: a separate law school placement center and a full-time Career Services Office for law students.

Special features: individual counseling for students, videotaped mock interviews, and focus groups for nontraditional students, networking opportunities, alumni/student mentor program.

Full-time job interviews:	13 employers
Summer job interviews:	26 employers
Placement by graduation:	37% of class
Placement within 9 months:	93% of class
Average starting salary:	$24,000 to $130,000

Areas of placement:
Private practice 100+ attorneys	54%
Business/industry	19%
Government	9%
Judicial clerkships	8%
Public interest	4%
Academic	3%

ELON UNIVERSITY

School of Law

201 North Greene Street
Greensboro, NC 27401

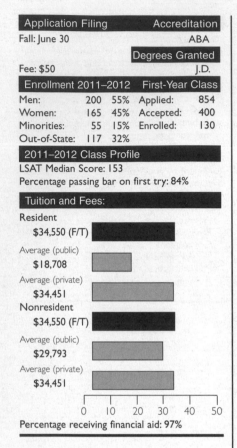

Application Filing	Accreditation
Fall: June 30	ABA

	Degrees Granted
Fee: $50	J.D.

Enrollment 2011–2012		First-Year Class	
Men:	200 55%	Applied:	854
Women:	165 45%	Accepted:	400
Minorities:	55 15%	Enrolled:	130
Out-of-State:	117 32%		

2011–2012 Class Profile
LSAT Median Score: 153
Percentage passing bar on first try: 84%

Tuition and Fees:

Resident
$34,550 (F/T)

Average (public)
$18,708

Average (private)
$34,451

Nonresident
$34,550 (F/T)

Average (public)
$29,793

Average (private)
$34,451

Percentage receiving financial aid: 97%

ADMISSIONS

In the fall of 2011 first-year class, 854 applied, 400 were accepted, and 130 enrolled. Three transfers enrolled. The median GPA of the most recent first-year class was 3.2.

Requirements

Applicants must have a bachelor's degree and take the LSAT. The most important admission factors include general background, GPA, and LSAT results. No specific undergraduate courses are required. Candidates are not interviewed.

Procedure

The application deadline for fall entry is June 30. Applicants should submit an application form, LSAT results, transcripts, a personal statement, a nonrefundable application fee of $50, 2 letters of recommendation, and a resume. Notification of the admissions decision is by December 31. The law school uses the LSAC.

Special

The law school recruits minority and disadvantaged students through Diversity Day and the MLK program at the law school, attendance at recruiter events hosted by and for minority applicants, and scholarships to aid diverse students. Requirements are different for out-of-state students. Transfer students must have one year of credit, must have attended an ABA-approved law school, and must submit a personal statement.

Costs

Tuition and fees for the 2011–2012 academic year are $34,550 for all full-time students. Books and supplies run $1,600.

Financial Aid

About 97% of current law students receive some form of aid. The average annual amount of aid from all sources combined, including scholarships, loans, and work contracts, is $46,963. Awards are based on need and merit combined. The required financial statement is the FAFSA. Special funds for minority or disadvantaged students are available. First-year students are notified about their financial aid application at time of acceptance.

About the Law School

Elon University School of Law was established in 2005 and is a private institution. The campus is in an urban area of Greensboro. Elon Law prepares students to be exceptional lawyers through a rigorous core curriculum, including a leadership program that equips students to address regional, national, and global challenges, in an environment that emphasizes innovative teaching and an array of field-based experiences. Students have access to federal, state, county, city, and local agencies, courts, correctional facilities, law firms, and legal aid organizations in the Greensboro area. Greensboro is the hub of the judicial system in central NC. Courts located within blocks of the law school include the U.S. District Court and U.S. Bankruptcy Court for the middle district of NC. In addition, several branches of the North Carolina General Court of Justice, including the Superior, District, Drug Treatment, Mental Health, and Small Claims courts, are a short walk from the law school. The North Carolina Business

Court is housed inside the law school. Several law firms and municipal offices are located within blocks of the law school as well. Greensboro is also home to 7 colleges and universities and 50,000 undergraduate and post-graduate students. Housing for students is available off-campus. All law school facilities are accessible to the physically disabled.

Calendar

The law school operates on a modified semester (4-1-4) basis. Courses are offered both day and evening, and must be completed within 84 months. New students are admitted in the fall. There is a 6-week summer session. Transferable summer courses are not offered.

Programs

Required

To earn the J.D., candidates must complete 90 total credits, of which 49 are for required courses. They must maintain a minimum GPA of 2.0 in the required courses. The following first-year courses are required of all students: Civil Procedure I and II, Contracts I and II, Criminal Law, Lawyering, Leadership, and Professionalism, Legal Method and Communication I and II, Property I and II, and Torts I and II. Required upper-level courses consist of Business Associations, Constitutional Law I and II, Criminal Procedure, Evidence, Leadership and Public Law, and Professional Responsibility. The required orientation program for first-year students is a 1-week program that introduces students to the study of law, the legal profession, as well as the services available to them. Throughout the week, L2 and L3 students are available to help with the transition to law school.

Electives

The School of Law offers concentrations in corporate law, litigation, public interest law, and general practice. In addition, second- and third-year students may take clinics such as the Juvenile Clinic, Humanitarian Immigration Law Clinic, and Wills Clinic for 3 credit hours each. Available seminars include Negotiation, Interviewing and Counseling, and Separation of Powers, also for 3 credit hours each. Field work includes Legal Aid. There is the Joseph M. Bryan Distinguished

Phone: 336-279-9200
1-888 ELON LAW
Fax: 336-279-8199
E-mail: law@elon.edu
Web: law.elon.edu

Contact

Lynette Lorensetti, Associate Director, 336-278-7640 for financial aid information.

NORTH CAROLINA

Leadership Lecture Series and the tutorial prpogram, L.E.T.S. Study. The most widely taken electives are First Amendent, Wills and Trusts, and Remedies.

Graduation Requirements

In order to graduate, candidates must have a GPA of 2.0 and must have completed the upper-division writing requirement.

Organizations

Students edit the *Elon Law Review*. Moot court competitions include William C. Vis International Commercial Arbitration Moot, ABA National Appellate Advocacy Competition, J. Braxton Craven Moot Court Competition, and National Moot Court Competition. Law students organizations, local chapters of national associations, and campus organizations include Family Law Society, Black Law Students Association, Delta Theta Phi, Phi Alpha Delta, Federalist Society, Intercarsity Christian Fellowship, Public Interest Law Society, and Innocence Project.

Library

The law library contains 188,726 hardcopy volumes and 131,313 microform volume equivalents, and subscribes to 210 serial publications. Such online databases and networks as CALI, CIS Universe, Infotrac, Legal-Trac, LEXIS, OCLC First Search, WESTLAW, Wilsonline Indexes, DARTS, FLG, CCH, BNA, and Leadership Library on the Internet are available to law students for research. The ratio of library volumes to faculty is 8,578 to 1 and to students is 518 to 1. The ratio of seats in the library to students is 1 to 1.

Faculty

The law school has 22 full-time and 18 part-time faculty members, of whom 14 are women. According to AAUP standards for Category IIA institutions, faculty salaries are above average. About 29% of full-time faculty have a graduate law degree in addition to the J.D. The ratio of full-time students to full-time faculty in an average class is 18 to 1; in a clinic, 10 to 1. The law school has a regular program of bringing visiting professors and other distinguished lecturers and visitors to campus.

Students

About 45% of the student body are women; 15%, minorities; 9%, African American; 2%, Asian American; 1%, Hispanic; and 1%, Hawaiian/Pacific Islander. The majority of students come from North Carolina (68%). The average age of entering students is 23. About 8% drop out after the first year for academic or personal reasons; 92% remain to receive a law degree.

Placement	
J.D.s awarded:	99
Full-time job interviews:	3 employers
Summer job interviews:	6 employers
Placement by graduation:	29% of class
Placement within 9 months:	92% of class
Average starting salary:	$47,500 to $72,500
Areas of placement:	
Private practice 2–10 attorneys	37%
Private practice 11–23 attorneys	4%
Private practice 26–50 attorneys	1%
Private practice 51–100 attorneys	1%
Solo practice	19%
Business/industry	21%
Government	8%
Judicial clerkships	5%
Public interest	3%
Academic	1%

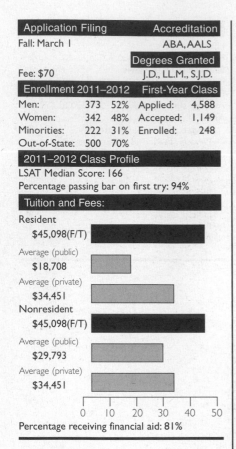

Application Filing	Accreditation
Fall: March 1	ABA, AALS

	Degrees Granted
Fee: $70	J.D., LL.M., S.J.D.

Enrollment 2011–2012		First-Year Class	
Men:	373 52%	Applied:	4,588
Women:	342 48%	Accepted:	1,149
Minorities:	222 31%	Enrolled:	248
Out-of-State:	500 70%		

2011–2012 Class Profile
LSAT Median Score: 166
Percentage passing bar on first try: 94%

Tuition and Fees:

Resident
$45,098(F/T)

Average (public)
$18,708

Average (private)
$34,451

Nonresident
$45,098(F/T)

Average (public)
$29,793

Average (private)
$34,451

0   10   20   30   40   50

Percentage receiving financial aid: 81%

ADMISSIONS

In the fall of 2011 first-year class, 4588 applied, 1149 were accepted, and 248 enrolled. Twenty-two transfer students enrolled. The median GPA of the most recent first-year class was 3.57.

Requirements

Applicants must have a bachelor's degree and take the LSAT. The most important admission factors include LSAT results, GPA, and academic achievement. No specific undergraduate courses are required and candidates are not interviewed.

Procedure

The application deadline for fall entry is March 1. Applicants should submit an application form, LSAT results, transcripts, personal statement, TOEFL (for foreign applicants), nonrefundable application fee of $70, 2 letters of recommendation, résumé, and a list of extracurricular activities. Notification of the admissions decision is from January to May. The law school uses the LSAC.

Special

The law school recruits minority and disadvantaged students by visiting historically black colleges, attending college law fairs in the fall, sending mailings to minority students, and hosting several special on-site visits throughout the year. Requirements are different for out-of-state students. Transfer students must have one year of credits, attend an ABA-approved law school, personal statement, and rank in the top 50% of their class (top 20% to 25% is preferred).

Costs

Tuition and fees for the 2011–2012 academic year are $44,600 for all full-time students. On-campus room and board costs about $16,516 annually; books and supplies run $2,000.

Financial Aid

About 81% of current law students receive some form of aid. The average annual amount of aid from all sources combined, including scholarships, loans, and work contracts, is $41,748. Awards are based on need and merit. Loans are either need or non-need, depending on the loan. Required financial statement is the FAFSA. The aid application deadline for fall entry is April 1. There are scholarships or special funds available for minority or disadvantaged students based on merit and need. First-year students are notified about their financial aid application some time shortly after students are accepted, but before a tuition deposit is required.

About the Law School

Emory University School of Law was established in 1916 and is a private institution. The 600-acre campus is located in an urban area 7 miles northeast of Atlanta. The primary mission of the law school is to provide integrative, international, interdisciplinary legal study, and scholarly excellence to a diverse community. The school educates leaders in society based on a common quest for knowledge, pursuit of public service, and advocacy for justice. Students have access to federal, state, county, city, and local agencies, courts, correctional facilities, law firms, and legal aid organizations in the Atlanta area. Students have access to national and regional businesses. Facilities of special interest to law students are the

more than 45 clinics with federal agencies, judges, public interest offices, and businesses. Housing for students is available from the University and private parties. There are also many options outside the university, including apartments, condos and rental homes. All law school facilities are accessible to the physically disabled.

Calendar

The law school operates on a traditional semester basis. Courses for full-time students are offered both day and evening and must be completed within 6 years. There is no part-time program. New full-time students are admitted in the fall. There is no summer session. Transferable summer courses are not offered.

Programs

In addition to the J.D., the law school offers the LL.M. and S.J.D. Students may take relevant courses in other programs and apply credit toward the J.D.; a maximum of 6 credits may be applied. The following joint degrees may be earned: J.D./Ph.D. (Juris Doctor/Doctor of Philosophy in Religion), J.D./M.A. (Juris Doctor/Master of Arts in Judaic Studies), J.D./M.B.A. (Juris Doctor/Master of Business Administration), J.D./M.Div. (Juris Doctor/Master of Divinity), J.D./M.P.H. (Juris Doctor/Master of Public Health), J.D./M.T.S. (Juris Doctor/Master of Theological Studies), and J.D./REES (Juris Doctor/Russian East European Studies Certificate).

Required

To earn the J.D., candidates must complete 90 total credits, of which 47 are for required courses. They must maintain a minimum GPA of 2.3 in the required courses. The following first-year courses are required of all students: Appellate Advocacy, Civil Procedure I and II, Constitutional Law, Contracts, Criminal Law, Legal Methods, Legal Writing, Property, Research, and Torts. Required upper-level courses consist of a writing requirement, Business Associations, Evidence, Legal Profession, and Trial Techniques. The required orientation program for first-year students is a 2-day period prior to registration and 1 day of optional activities that introduce students to the university and the law school communities. Students also attend a small section class during orientation.

Phone: 404-727-6801
Fax: 404-727-2477
E-mail: erosenz@law.emory.edu
Web: www.law.emory.edu

Contact

Ethan Rosenzweig, Assistant Dean of Admission, 404-727-6857 for general inquiries; Brenda Hill, Associate Director of Financial Aid, 404-727-6039 for financial aid information.

GEORGIA

Placement

J.D.s awarded:	221

Services available through: a separate law school placement center.

Special features: personal advising and programming designed to assist students, specific advising in public interest law by the Associate Director of Career Services, and off-campus job fairs in New York, Washington, D.C., Chicago, Dallas, and Los Angeles, among others.

Placement by graduation:	97% of class
Placement within 9 months:	95% of class
Average starting salary:	$52,000 to $145,000

Areas of placement:

Private practice 2–10 attorneys	9%
Private practice 11–25 attorneys	4%
Private practice 26–50 attorneys	6%
Private practice 51–100 attorneys	2%
50% private practice 101 + attorneys; 2% unknown	52%
Business/industry	11%
Judicial clerkships	9%
Government	9%
Public interest	2%

Electives

The School of Law offers concentrations in corporate law, environmental law, intellectual property law, internationl law, litigation, tax law, law and religion, child advocacy, and feminist jurisprudence and legal theory. Clinics are generally available to second- and third-year students, as are Seminars. During the summer, most students have paid internships with firms, businesses, government offices, or public interest agencies. A small number of students may be offered research assistantships. Field placements are open to second- and third-year students for academic credit with more than 50 local businesses and federal and state courts and agencies. Students may take advantage of ABA accredited law school study abroad programs. Tutorials are offered to all students by professors on an individual basis. Academic assistance is made available to any student by request. Special consideration is given to minority students in the admissions process; and the diversity office offers programs and initiatives to build community and prepare students for success in diverse legal communities. The most widely taken electives are Criminal Procedure, Individual Tax, and Family Law.

Graduation Requirements

In order to graduate, candidates must have a GPA of 2.3 and complete the upper-division writing requirement.

Organizations

Student-edited publications are the *Emory Law Journal, Emory International Law Review*, and *Emory Bankruptcy Journal*. Annually, moot court teams participate in internal competitions, the Georgia Intra-State Moot Court, the National First Amendment Moot Court, and the Jessup International Law Moot Court competitions. Other competitions include the Frederick Douglass Moot Court Competition, the Negotiation Competition, and the National Hispanic Bar Association Moot Court Competition. Law student organizations include the Alternative Dispute Resolutions Society, the Emory Public

Interest Committee, and the Health Law Society. There are also local chapters of national associations, including the Association of Trial Lawyers of America, the Federalist Society for Law and Public Policy, and Phi Alpha Delta. Campus clubs and other organizations include Legal Association of Women Students, Black Law Students Association, and Emory Gay and Lesbian Advocates.

Library

The law library contains 308,364 hardcopy volumes and 107,514 microform volume equivalents, and subscribes to 3,867 serial publications. Online databases and networks include CALI, CIS Universe, DIALOG, Dow-Jones, Infotrac, Legal-Trac, LEXIS, Mathew Bender, OCLC First Search, RLIN, WESTL , and Wilsonline Indexes, which are available to law students for research. Special library collections include a European Union depository and a federal depository. The ratio of library volumes to faculty is 4,818 to 1 and to students is 431 to 1. The ratio of seats in the library to students is 1 to 1.

Faculty

The law school has 64 full-time and 42 part-time faculty members, of whom 39 are women. The ratio of full-time students to full-time faculty in an average class is 11 to 1; in a clinic, 2 to 1. The law school has a regular program of bringing visiting professors and other distinguished lecturers and visitors to campus. There is a chapter of the Order of the Coif.

Students

About 48% of the student body are women; 31%, minorities; 10%, African American; 13%, Asian American; 12%, Hispanic; and 5% Foreign. The majority of students come from Georgia (30%). The average age of entering students is 23; age range is 20 to 50. About 45% of students enter directly from undergraduate school. About 2% drop out after the first year for academic or personal reasons; 98% remain to receive a law degree.

Thomas Goode Jones School of Law

5345 Atlanta Highway
Montgomery, AL 36109

Application Filing	Accreditation
Fall: June 15	ABA, AALS
	Degrees Granted
Fee: $30	J.D.

Enrollment 2011–2012			First-Year Class	
Men:	213	62%	Applied:	747
Women:	128	38%	Accepted:	405
Minorities:	38	11%	Enrolled:	150

2011–2012 Class Profile
LSAT Percentile: 40%
LSAT Median Score: 149
Percentage passing bar on first try: 89%

Tuition and Fees:

Resident
$30,870 (F/T)

Average (public)
$18,708

Average (private)
$34,451

Nonresident
$30,870 (F/T)

Average (public)
$29,793

Average (private)
$34,451

0   10   20   30   40   50

ADMISSIONS
In the fall of 2011 first-year class, 747 applied, 405 were accepted, and 150 enrolled. One transfer enrolled. The median LSAT percentile of the most recent first-year class was 40; the median GPA was 3.1 on a scale of 4.0.

Requirements
Applicants must have a bachelor's degree and take the LSAT. No specific undergraduate courses are required. Candidates are not interviewed.

Procedure
The application deadline for fall entry is June 15. Applicants should submit an application form, LSAT results, transcripts, a personal statement, and a nonrefundable application fee of $30. The law school uses the LSAC.

Special
Requirements are different for out-of-state students. Transfer students must have attended an ABA-approved law school, must submit a personal statement, and must be in good standing.

Costs
Tuition and fees for the 2011–2012 academic year are $30,500 for all full-time students. Books and supplies run $3,000.

Financial Aid
The required financial statement is the FAFSA.

About the Law School
Faulkner University Thomas Goode Jones School of Law was established in 1928 and is a private institution. The campus is in an urban area. Students have access to federal, state, county, city, and local agencies, courts, correctional facilities, law firms, and legal aid organizations in the Montgomery area. Housing for students is not available on campus. All law school facilities are accessible to the physically disabled.

Calendar
The law school operates on a traditional semester basis. Courses for full-time students are offered days only. New students are admitted in the fall. There is an 8-week summer session. Transferable summer courses are offered.

Programs

Required
To earn the J.D., candidates must complete 90 total credits, of which 51 are for required courses. The following first-year courses are required of all students: Civil Procedure, Contracts, Criminal Law, Legal Research and Writing, Property, and Torts. Required upper-level courses consist of Business Associations, Constitutional Law, Evidence, Practice Skills, Professional Responsibility, and Remedies. The required orientation program for first-year students is a 4-day introduction to analytical reasoning, legal research and writing, the court system, and professionalism.

Electives
The Thomas Goode Jones School of Law offers concentrations in corporate law, criminal law, entertainment law, environmental law, family law, intellectual property law, international law, juvenile law, labor law, litigation, securities law, sports law, tax law, torts and insurance, and alternative dispute resolution. Students may participate in the Elder Law Clinic, Family Violence Clinic, and the Mediation Clinic.

Graduation Requirements
In order to graduate, candidates must have a GPA of 2.0 and must have completed the upper-division writing requirement and practical skills or oral advocacy course.

Organizations
Students edit the *Faulkner Law Review*. Students participate in the National Moot Court Competition, ABA National Appellate Competition, National Health Law Moot Court Competition, and Buffalo/Niagara National Mock Trial Competition. Other competitions include National Trial Competition, Thurgood Marshall Mock Trial Competition, ABA Employment Law National Mock Trial Competition, William Daniel National Criminal Law Mock Trial Competition, AAJ National Trial Competition, and ABA Representation in Mediation Competition. Law student organizations, local chapters of national associations, and campus clubs and organizations include the Christian Legal Society, Women's Students Association, Federalist Society, American Constitution Society, American Association for Justice, Black Law Students Association, Phi Alpha Delta, Animal Law Society, Board of Advocates, and Jones Law Republicans.

Phone: 334-386-7210
800-879-9816
Fax: 334-386-7223
E-mail: law@faulkner.edu
Web: www.faulkner.edu/law

Contact

Andrew R. Matthews, Assistant Dean for Student Services, 334-386-7210 for general inquiries; William G. Jackson, Director of Financial Aid, 334-386-7195 for financial aid information.

ALABAMA

Faculty

The law school has 29 full-time faculty members, of whom 10 are women. About 15% of full-time faculty have a graduate law degree in addition to the J.D. The ratio of full-time students to full-time faculty in an average class is 40 to 1; in a clinic, 12 to 1. The law school has a regular program of bringing visiting professors and other distinguished lecturers and visitors to campus. There is a chapter of the Order of the Coif; 1 faculty is a member.

Students

About 38% of the student body are women; 13%, minorities; 7%, African American; 2%, Asian American; 2%, Hispanic; and 2%, Native American.

Placement

J.D.s awarded:	65

Services available through: a separate law school placement center.

FLORIDA AGRICULTURAL AND MECHANICAL UNIVERSITY

Florida A & M University College of Law

201 Beggs Avenue
Orlando, FL 32801

Application Filing	Accreditation
Fall: May 31	ABA
	Degrees Granted
Fee: $33	J.D.

Enrollment 2011–2012			First-Year Class	
Men:	326	47%	Applied:	1,891
Women:	375	53%	Accepted:	715
Minorities:	498	71%	Enrolled:	281
Out-of-State:	77	11%		

2011–2012 Class Profile

LSAT Median Score: 148
Percentage passing bar on first try: 66%

Tuition and Fees:

Resident
$11,903 (F/T)

Average (public)
$18,708

Average (private)
$34,451

Nonresident
$32,198 (F/T)

Average (public)
$29,793

Average (private)
$34,451

Percentage receiving financial aid: 86%

ADMISSIONS

In the fall of 2011 first-year class, 1891 applied, 715 were accepted, and 281 enrolled. The median GPA of the most recent first-year class was 3.1.

Requirements

Applicants must have a bachelor's degree and take the LSAT. The most important admission factors include academic achievement, LSAT results, and writing ability. No specific undergraduate courses are required and candidates are not interviewed.

Procedure

The application deadline for fall entry is May 31. Applicants should submit an application form, LSAT results, transcripts, $33 application fee, 2 letters of recommendation, and a personal statement. Notification of the admissions decision is on a rolling basis. The law school uses the LSAC.

Special

Requirements are different for out-of-state students. Transfer students must have attended an ABA-approved law school. A maximum of 30 credit hours may be given for work at another ABA-approved Law School with a minimum GPA of 3.0.

Costs

Tuition and fees for the 2011–2012 academic year are $11,774 for full-time in-state students and $32,069 for out-of-state students. Tuition for part-time students is $8,634 for in-state students and $22,759 out-of-state. Books and supplies run $1,000.

Financial Aid

About 86% of current law students receive some form of aid. The average annual amount of aid from all sources combined, including scholarships, loans, and work contracts, is $29,508; maximum, $56,000. Awards are based on need and merit combined. Required financial statement is the FAFSA. The aid application deadline for fall entry is March 1. There are special funds available for minority or disadvantaged students. A grant is also available for black students in the day program based on merit that has the possibility of renewal each year. First-year students are notified about their financial aid application at time of acceptance.

About the Law School

Florida Agricultural and Mechanical University College of Law was established in 2000 and is a public institution. The campus is located in an urban area of Orlando. The primary mission of the law school is to increase access to the legal system for underrepresented persons and to provide access to educational training and opportunities for students seeking to serve the needs of traditionally underserved people and communities. Students have access to federal, state, county, city, and local agencies, courts, correctional facilities, law firms, and legal aid organizations in the Orlando area. Facilities of special interest to law students include a state-of-the-art moot court room. All law school facilities are accessible to the physically disabled.

Calendar

The law school operates on a traditional semester basis. Courses for full-time students are offered both day and evening and must be completed within 5 years. For part-time students, courses are offered both day and evening and must be completed within 6 years. New full- and part-time students are admitted in the fall. There is a 10-week summer session. Transferable summer courses are not offered.

Programs

Required

To earn the J.D., candidates must complete 90 total credits, of which 48–49 are for required courses. They must maintain a minimum GPA of 2.0 in the required courses. The following first-year courses are required of all students: Civil Procedure I and II, Constitutional Law I, Contracts I and II, Legal Methods I and II, Property I and II, and Torts I and II. Required upper-level courses consist of Business Organizations, Clinical or Pro Bono Program, Constitutional Law II, Criminal Law, Evidence, Mission-related courses, and Professional Responsibility. All students must take clinical courses. The required orientation program for first-year students includes a 1 week program designed to facilitate student's entry to law schools. Case briefing, study skills, sample classes, debt and time management, and professionalism are all covered.

Electives

The Florida A & M University College of Law offers concentrations in international law. In addition, all upper-division students are eligible to participate in clinics. Some clinics have prerequisites such as Evidence or Trial Practice. Clinics include Community Economic Development, Homelessness and Legal Advocacy, Guardian or Trial Practice, Evidence, and Trial Practice. All upper-division students are eligible to participate in internship programs. The Academic Success and Bar Preparation Program provides tutorial assistance to students.

Phone: 407-254-3268
E-mail: *famulaw.admissions@famu.edu*
Web: *law.famu.edu*

Contact
Office of Admissions, 407-254-3286 for general inquiries; Kareman Campbell, 407-254-4016 for financial aid information.

FLORIDA

Graduation Requirements
In order to graduate, candidates must have a GPA of 2.0, complete the upper-division writing requirement, and mission-related courses.

Organizations
Students edit the *Florida A&M University College–Law Review* and the newspaper, *The FAMU Lawyer*. Other publications include *The Record*. Moot court competitions include the American Bar Association (ABA) Moot Court Competition, Frederick Douglass Moot Court Competition, and Saul Lefkowitz Moot Court Competition. Other competitions include the BMI Cardozo Entertainment Communications Law Moot Court Competition, and Thurgood Marshall Mock Trial Competition. Law student organizations include the Student Bar Association, Black Law Students Association, and Women's Law Caucus. Local chapters of national associations include the Phi Alpha Delta Law Fraternity, International Hispanic American Law Students Association, and Federalist Law Society. Campus clubs and other organizations include the Criminal Law Association, Christian Legal Society, and Enterntainment, Arts and Sports Law Society.

Library
The law library contains 391,247 hardcopy volumes and 252,042 microform volume equivalents, and subscribes to 2,072 serial publications. Online databases and networks include CALI, CIS Universe, Infotrac, Legal-Trac, LEXIS, OCLC First Search, WESTLAW, and Wilsonline Indexes. Others are CCH Business and Tax, RIA, HeinOnline, and BNA, which are available to law students for research. Special library collections include Virgil Hawkins Collection, and International Law Collection. The ratio of library volumes to faculty is 8,020 to 1 and to students is 602 to 1. The ratio of seats in the library to students is 1 to 1.

Faculty
The law school has 46 full-time and 20 part-time faculty members, of whom 29 are women. According to AAUP standards for Category IIA institutions, faculty salaries are above average. About 13% of full-time faculty have a graduate law degree in addition to the J.D.; about 15% of part-time faculty have one. The ratio of full-time students to full-time faculty in an average class is 19 to 1. The law school has a regular program of bringing visiting professors and other distinguished lecturers and visitors to campus.

Students
About 53% of the student body are women; 71%, minorities; 55%, African American; 3%, Asian American; 11%, Hispanic; 1%, Native American; and 1%, other. The majority of students come from Florida (89%). The average age of entering students is 25; age range is 19 to 57. About 14% of students enter directly from undergraduate school, and 15% have a graduate degree. About 3% drop out after the first year for academic or personal reasons; 97% remain to receive a law degree.

Placement

J.D.s awarded:	164

Services available through: a separate law school placement center.
Services: Individual one-to-one mentoring pairing a law student with a practitioner in his/her area of interest.
Special features: Speaker's Series (special guest speakers).

Placement within 9 months of graduation:	63% of class
Average starting salary:	$36,000 to $61,250

Areas of placement:

Private practice 2–10 attorneys	19%
Private practice 11–25 attorneys	1%
Private practice 26–50 attorneys	1%
Private practice 51–100 attorneys	1%
Business/industry	20%
Government	17%
Public interest	6%
Academic	6%
Military	4%

FLORIDA COASTAL

School of Law

8787 Baypine Rd.
Jacksonville, FL 32256

Application Filing			Accreditation
Fall: open			ABA
Spring: open			**Degrees Granted**
Fee: $50			J.D.

Enrollment 2011–2012		First-Year Class	
Men:	728 52%	Applied:	4,663
Women:	667 48%	Accepted:	1,725
Minorities:	251 18%	Enrolled:	566
Out-of-State:	837 60%		

2011–2012 Class Profile
LSAT Percentile: 50%
LSAT Median Score: 151
Percentage passing bar on first try: 84%

Tuition and Fees:

Resident
$28,870 (F/T)

Average (public)
$18,708

Average (private)
$34,451

Nonresident
$28,870 (F/T)

Average (public)
$29,793

Average (private)
$34,451

0   10   20   30   40   50

Percentage receiving financial aid: 85%

ADMISSIONS

In the fall of 2011 first-year class, 4663 applied, 1725 were accepted, and 566 enrolled. Thirty-five transfers enrolled. The median LSAT percentile of the most recent first-year class was 50; the median GPA was 3.2 on a scale of 4.0. The lowest LSAT percentile accepted was 25; the highest was 95.

Requirements

Applicants must have a bachelor's degree and take the LSAT. Minimum acceptable GPA is 2.0 on a scale of 4.0. The most important admission factors include LSAT results, GPA, and life experience. No specific undergraduate courses are required and candidates are not interviewed.

Procedure

The application deadline for fall entry is open. Applicants should submit an application form, LSAT results, a nonrefundable application fee of $50, and 2 letters of recommendation. Notification of the admissions decision is on a rolling basis. The law school uses the LSAC.

Special

The law school recruits minority and disadvantaged students through law forums, career fairs, and scholarships. Requirements are different for out-of-state students. Transfer students must have a minimum GPA of 2 and have attended an ABA-approved law school.

Costs

Tuition and fees for the 2011–2012 academic year are $27,570 for all full-time students. Tuition for part-time students is $22,060 for in-state students and $22,060 out-of-state. Books and supplies run $1,200.

Financial Aid

About 85% of current law students receive some form of aid. The average annual amount of aid from all sources combined, including scholarships, loans, and work contracts, is $18,500; maximum, $27,750. Awards are based on need and merit combined. Required financial statements are the FAFSA and Institutional application. First-year students are notified about their financial aid application at time of acceptance.

About the Law School

Florida Coastal School of Law was established in 1996 and is an independent institution. The 5-acre campus is in a suburban area near downtown Jacksonville and the beach. The primary mission of the law school is to distinguish itself as a forward-moving, globally interactive, and culturally diverse institution dedicated to having a positive impact on its students, the community, the legal profession, and the justice system. Students have access to federal, state, county, city, and local agencies, courts, correctional facilities, law firms, and legal aid organizations in the Jacksonville area. Facilities of special interest to law students include the Information Resources and Technology Division; the Center for Strategic Governance and Information Initiatives, and an on-campus teen court. Housing for students includes a large variety of close and affordable off-campus apartments and homes. All law school facilities are accessible to the physically disabled.

Calendar

The law school operates on a traditional semester basis. Courses for full-time students are offered both day and evening and must be completed within 5 years. For part-time students, courses are offered both day and evening and must be completed within 6 years. New full- and part-time students are admitted in the fall and spring. There is an 8-week summer session. Transferable summer courses are offered.

Programs

Students may take relevant courses in other programs and apply credit toward the J.D.; a maximum of 6 credits may be applied.

Required

To earn the J.D., candidates must complete 87 total credits, of which 56 are for required courses. They must maintain a minimum GPA of 2.0 in the required courses. The following first-year courses are required of all students: Civil Procedure I and II, Contracts I and II, Criminal Law, Lawyering Process I and II, Property I and II, and Torts I and II. Required upper-level courses consist of an advanced writing requirement, Business Associations, Constitutional Law I and II, Criminal Procedure, Evidence, Family Law, Professional Responsibility, and Sales. All students must take clinical courses. The required orientation program for first-year students is 2 1/2 days and includes interactions with faculty, staff, and students; the role of the lawyer and professionalism; the responsibilities of the future lawyer and student ethics; Academic Success programs; and a reception.

Electives

The School of Law offers concentrations in corporate law, criminal law, entertainment law, environmental law, family law, international law, juvenile law, labor law, litigation, maritime law, media law, securities law, sports law, tax law, and intellectual property and public interest law. In addition, third-year clinics include Criminal, Civil, Municipal, Domestic Violence, and Caribbean Law Clinic. Seminars, available to upper-division students only, include Environmental Law, Sports Law, Appellate Advocacy, and Maritime Law. Other

Phone: 904-680-7710
877-210-2591
Fax: 904-680-7776
E-mail: *admissions@fcsl.edu*
Web: *www.fcsl.edu*

Contact

Office of Admissions, 904-680-7710 for financial aid information.

FLORIDA

seminars may be offered periodically depending upon the interest of students and faculty. Internships are available with federal and state court judges. Students must have completed Professional Responsibility, Evidence, and Constitutional Law. Advanced Legal Research is open to upper-division students, and Independent study with a full-time faculty member is also available. The School of Law invites practitioners, judges, and other public figures to speak on a variety of topics, including legal practice, legal education, and jurisprudence. An Academic Success program is aimed at serving three groups of students: (1) incoming students considered at risk because of low LSAT scores or low GPA; (2) or students who are re-entering school after a long absence; and (3) current students who are at risk or on academic probation. The program consists of workshops on a variety of topics, including case briefing, study aids, and exam-taking. In addition, the School of Law has tutors for all first-year classes. Students may also meet with the program director to deal with individual problem issues. The most widely taken electives are Remedies, Trusts and Estates, and Florida Practice and Procedure.

Graduation Requirements
In order to graduate, candidates must have a GPA of 2.0 and complete the upper-division writing requirement.

Organizations

Students edit the *Florida Coastal School of Law Review* and the newspaper, *Coastal Tidings*. Moot court competitions include the Robert Orseck Memorial Moot Court and the E. Earl Zehemer Memorial Moot Court. Law student organizations include the Student Bar Association, Black Law Students Association, and CAPIL. There is a local chapter of ABA-Law Students Division, Phi Alpha Delta, and Law and Technology Society. Other organizations include the Environmental and Land Use Club, Hispanic American Law Students Association, and Sports Law Association.

Library

The law library contains 223,820 hardcopy volumes and 469,002 microform volume equivalents, and subscribes to 3,125 serial publications. Online databases and networks include CALI, CIS Universe, Infotrac, Legal-Trac, LEXIS, Mathew Bender, OCLC First Search, and WESTLAW. CCH Internet Tax, HR and Business Networks, UN Treaty Collection, and HeinOnline also are available to law students for research. The ratio of library volumes to faculty is 3,610 to 1 and to students is 210 to 1. The ratio of seats in the library to students is 1 to 8.

Faculty

The law school has 62 full-time and 45 part-time faculty members, of whom 50 are women. About 13% of full-time faculty have a graduate law degree in addition to the J.D.; about 7% of part-time faculty have one. The ratio of full-time students to full-time faculty in an average class is 18 to 1; in a clinic, 12 to 1. The law school has a regular program of bringing visiting professors and other distinguished lecturers and visitors to campus.

Students

About 48% of the student body are women; 18%, minorities; 11%, African American; 3%, Asian American; 3%, Hispanic; and 1%, Native American. The majority of students come from Florida (40%). The average age of entering students is 27; age range is 21 to 68. About 50% of students enter directly from undergraduate school, 20% have a graduate degree, and 50% have worked full-time prior to entering law school. About 8% drop out after the first year for academic or personal reasons; 92% remain to receive a law degree.

Placement

J.D.s awarded:	82

Services available through: a separate law school placement center.
Services: job opportunity list service and job fairs.
Special features: extensive programming on a variety of career development topics including practice areas, work environments, alternative careers, and transition from school to the work force.

Full-time job interviews:	6 employers
Summer job interviews:	5 employers
Placement by graduation:	40% of class
Placement within 9 months:	90% of class
Average starting salary:	$35,000 to $80,000
Areas of placement:	
Private practice 2-10 attorneys	63%
Government	18%
Business/industry	18%

FLORIDA INTERNATIONAL UNIVERSITY

College of Law

FIU College of Law, RDB 1055
Miami, FL 33199

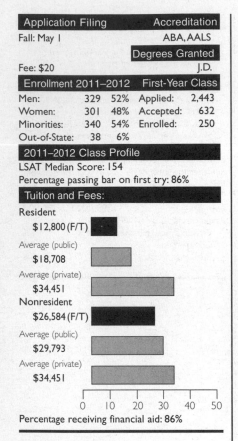

Application Filing		Accreditation	
Fall: May 1		ABA, AALS	
		Degrees Granted	
Fee: $20			J.D.

Enrollment 2011–2012		First-Year Class	
Men:	329 52%	Applied:	2,443
Women:	301 48%	Accepted:	632
Minorities:	340 54%	Enrolled:	250
Out-of-State:	38 6%		

2011–2012 Class Profile
LSAT Median Score: 154
Percentage passing bar on first try: 86%

Tuition and Fees:

Resident
$12,800 (F/T)

Average (public)
$18,708

Average (private)
$34,451

Nonresident
$26,584 (F/T)

Average (public)
$29,793

Average (private)
$34,451

Percentage receiving financial aid: 86%

ADMISSIONS
In the fall of 2011 first-year class, 2443 applied, 632 were accepted, and 250 enrolled. Seven transfers enrolled. The median GPA of the most recent first-year class was 3.40.

Requirements
Applicants must have a bachelor's degree and take the LSAT. Minimum acceptable GPA is 2.0 on a scale of 4.0. The most important admission factors include GPA, LSAT results, and writing ability. No specific undergraduate courses are required. Candidates are not interviewed.

Procedure
The application deadline for fall entry is May 1. Applicants should submit an application form, LSAT results, transcripts, a personal statement, a nonrefundable application fee of $20, and 3 letters of recommendation. Notification of the admissions decision is on a rolling basis. The law school uses the LSAC.

Special
The law school recruits minority and disadvantaged students by participation and sponsorship of pipeline initiatives, minority targeted events, application fee waiver programs, and direct mailing campaigns. Requirements are different for out-of-state students. Transfer students must have one year of credit, have attended an ABA-approved law school, and a personal statement.

Costs
Tuition and fees for the 2011–2012 academic year are $12,471 for full-time in-state students and $26,255 for out-of-state students. Tuition for part-time students is $9,353 for in-state students and $19,692 out-of-state. On-campus room and board costs about $10,680 annually; books and supplies run $2,652.

Financial Aid
About 86% of current law students receive some form of aid. The average annual amount of aid from all sources combined, including scholarships, loans, and work contracts, is $34,239; maximum, $50,496. Awards are based on need and merit combined. Required financial statement is the FAFSA. The aid application deadline for fall entry is February 1. First-year students are notified about their financial aid application at time of acceptance.

About the Law School
Florida International University College of Law was established in 2000 and is a public institution. The 584-acre campus is in an urban area of Miami Dade County, Florida. The primary mission of the law school is to serve the citizens of the State of Florida, particularly south Florida, by providing access to the legal profession through a high quality educational program. Students have access to federal, state, county, city, and local agencies, courts, correctional facilities, law firms, and legal aid organizations in the Miami area. Housing for students is in wing of residence hall. All law school facilities are accessible to the physically disabled.

Calendar
The law school operates on a traditional semester basis. Courses for full-time students are offered both day and evening and must be completed within 7 years. For part-time students, courses are offered both day and evening and must be completed within 7 years. New full- and part-time students are admitted in the fall. There is a 12-week summer session. Transferable summer courses are offered.

Programs
Students may take relevant courses in other programs and apply credit toward the J.D.; a maximum of 6 credits may be applied. The following joint degrees may be earned: J.D./M.B.A. (Juris Doctor/Master of Business Administration), J.D./M.S.C.J. (Juris Doctor/Master of Criminal Justice), J.D./M.S.E. (Juris Doctor/Master of Environmental Studies), J.D./M.I.B. (Juris Doctor/Master of International Business), J.D./M.A.L.A.C.S. (Juris Doctor/Master of Latin American and Caribbean Studies), J.D./M.P.Psych. (Juris Doctor/Master of Psychology), J.D./M.P.A. (Juris Doctor/Master of Public Administration), and J.D./M.S.W. (Juris Doctor/Master of Social Work).

Required
To earn the J.D., candidates must complete 90 total credits, of which 31 are for required courses. They must maintain a minimum GPA of 2.0 in the required courses. The following first-year courses are required of all students: Civil Procedure, Constitutional Law, Contracts, Criminal Law, Introduction to International and Comparative Law, Legal Skills and Values I and II, Property, and Torts. Required upper-level courses consist of International and Comparative Law, Legal Skills and Values III, Professional Responsibility, and Two litigation and alternative dispute resolution courses. The required orientation program for first-year students is 3 days including coaching by legal writing instructors on writing briefs and preparing for class in a series of mock classes.

Contact
Alma O. Miro', Director of Admissions and Finance, 305-348-8006 for general inquiries; Alma O. Miro', Director of Admissions and Finance, 305-348-8006 for financial aid information.

FLORIDA

Electives
In addition, clinics, open to second- and third-year students, include Community Development Clinic, Criminal Law Clinic, Immigration and Human Rights Clinic, and Juvenile Justice Judicial Clinic. All second-, third-, and fourth-year students are eligible to enroll in a seminar. Seminars include Critical Race Theory, Constitutional Theory, and Islamic Law 2 credits each. Internships may be done under the supervision of a professor, most done in international or foreign settings. Research programs include the Legal Skills and Values program. All students are required to complete 30 hours of community service with a pro bono organization. Special lecture series include the Faculty Colloquia Series. Study abroad is available in Sevilla, Spain. The College of Law has a comprehensive tutorial and academic support program, which is headed by the Assistant Dean of the Academic Support Program. The most widely taken electives are Evidence, Business Organizations, Sales.

Graduation Requirements
In order to graduate, candidates must have a GPA of 2.0 and complete the upper-division writing requirement as part of a seminar.

Organizations
The primary law review is the *Florida International University College of Law, Law Review*. Moot court competitions include the Wechler First Amendment Moot Court Competition, Orseck Memorial Moot Court Competition, and the National Moot Court Competition. Other competitions include the ABA Negotiations Competition, Bedell Trial Advocacy Competition, and ATLA Trial Competition. Law student organizations include the Black Law Students Association, Student Bar Association, and Hispanic Law Students Association. Local chapters of national associations include Phi Alpha Delta, Federalist Society, American Inns of Court, and Student Government Association.

Library
The law library contains 213,410 hardcopy volumes and 123,491 microform volume equivalents, and subscribes to 1,500 serial publications. Online databases and networks include CALI, CIS Universe, Infotrac, Legal-Trac, LEXIS, Mathew Bender, OCLC First Search, RLIN, WESTLAW, and Wilsonline Indexes, which are available to law students for research. Special library collections include Focus on Cuba, Latin America, and Caribbean legal materials; Focus on international and comparative law; national security and human rights. The ratio of library volumes to faculty is 6,669 to 1 and to students is 339 to 1. The ratio of seats in the library to students is 1 to 2.

Faculty
The law school has 32 full-time and 21 part-time faculty members, of whom 26 are women. According to AAUP standards for Category I institutions, faculty salaries are average. About 45% of full-time faculty have a graduate law degree in addition to the J.D. The ratio of full-time students to full-time faculty in an average class is 40 to 1; in a clinic, 8 to 1. The law school has a regular program of bringing visiting professors and other distinguished lecturers and visitors to campus.

Students
About 48% of the student body are women; 54%, minorities; 9%, African American; 2%, Asian American; 43%, Hispanic; 1%, Native American; and 45%, other. The majority of students come from Florida (94%). The average age of entering students is 26; age range is 19 to 58. About 5% drop out after the first year for academic or personal reasons; 83% remain to receive a law degree.

Placement	
J.D.s awarded:	118
Services available through: a separate law school placement center	
Special features: Public Service Fellows Program, mock interviews, workshop series, and one-on-one counseling	
Full-time job interviews:	12 employers
Summer job interviews:	19 employers
Placement by graduation:	21% of class
Placement within 9 months:	86% of class
Average starting salary:	$42,000 to $110,000
Areas of placement:	
Private practice 2-10 attorneys	52%
Private practice 11-25 attorneys	3%
Private practice 26-50 attorneys	6%
Private practice 51-100 attorneys	9%
Public interest	14%
Business/industry	8%
Judicial clerkships	1%

FLORIDA STATE UNIVERSITY
College of Law

425 West Jefferson Street
Tallahassee, FL 32306-1601

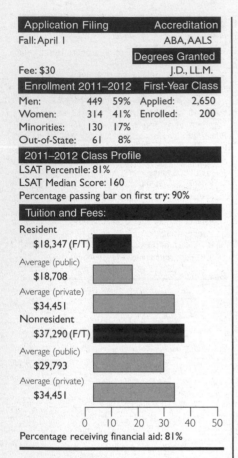

Application Filing		Accreditation
Fall: April 1		ABA, AALS
		Degrees Granted
Fee: $30		J.D., LL.M.

Enrollment 2011–2012		First-Year Class	
Men:	449 59%	Applied:	2,650
Women:	314 41%	Enrolled:	200
Minorities:	130 17%		
Out-of-State:	61 8%		

2011–2012 Class Profile
LSAT Percentile: 81%
LSAT Median Score: 160
Percentage passing bar on first try: 90%

Tuition and Fees:

Resident
$18,347 (F/T)

Average (public)
$18,708

Average (private)
$34,451

Nonresident
$37,290 (F/T)

Average (public)
$29,793

Average (private)
$34,451

0   10   20   30   40   50

Percentage receiving financial aid: 81%

ADMISSIONS
In the fall of 2011 first-year class, 2650 applied and 200 enrolled. Twenty-seven transfers enrolled. The median LSAT percentile of the most recent first-year class was 81; the median GPA was 3.5 on a scale of 4.0.

Requirements
Applicants must have a bachelor's degree and take the LSAT. The most important admission factors include GPA, LSAT results, and academic achievement. No specific undergraduate courses are required and candidates are not interviewed.

Procedure
The application deadline for fall entry is April 1. Applicants should submit an application form, LSAT results, transcripts, a personal statement, a nonrefundable application fee of $30, 2 letters of recommendation, and resume. Notification of the admissions decision is on a rolling basis. The law school uses the LSAC.

Special
The law school recruits minority and disadvantaged students through the LSAC, by sponsoring special programs throughout the year, by recruiting at colleges and universities, and through electronic outreach. Requirements are different for out-of-state students. Transfer students must have one year of credit, a personal statement, and be in the top third of their class.

Costs
Tuition and fees for the 2011–2012 academic year are $18,303 for all full-time students. On-campus room and board costs about $9,000 annually; books and supplies run $1,000.

Financial Aid
About 81% of current law students receive some form of aid. The average annual amount of aid from all sources combined, including scholarships, loans, and work contracts, is $22,750; maximum, $48,250. Awards are based on need and merit. Approximately 35% of the entering class received a scholarship for the first year. Awards range from $1,000 to $15,000. Required financial statement is the FAFSA. The aid application deadline for fall entry is April 1. Special funds for minority or disadvantaged students include diversity enhancement scholarships. First-year students are notified about their financial aid application at time of acceptance.

About the Law School
Florida State University College of Law was established in 1966 and is a public institution. The 1620-acre campus is in a suburban area in Tallahassee, the state capital. The primary mission of the law school is to ensure, through a multidisciplinary teaching approach, that students are prepared for a rapidly changing legal profession and can successfully compete anywhere. Students have access to federal, state, county, city, and local agencies, courts, correctional facilities, law firms, and legal aid organizations in the Tallahassee area. Facilities of special interest to law students: the College of Law is located 1 block from the Florida Supreme Court building and within 5 blocks of federal, state, district, county, and bankruptcy courts, the State

Legislature, and the State and Supreme Court law libraries. Housing for students: Dorms for single students and apartments for both single and married students are available. A housing office helps students find off-campus accommodations. All law school facilities are accessible to the physically disabled.

Calendar
The law school operates on a traditional semester basis. Courses for full-time students are offered both day and evening and must be completed within 3 years. New students are admitted in the fall. There is a 7-week summer session. Transferable summer courses are offered.

Programs
In addition to the J.D., the law school offers the LL.M. Students may take relevant courses in other programs and apply credit toward the J.D.; a maximum of 6 credits may be applied. The following joint degrees may be earned: J.D./M.B.A. (Juris Doctor/Master of Business Administration), J.D./M.P.A. (Juris Doctor/Master of Public Administration), J.D./M.S. (Juris Doctor/Master of Science in Economics or International Affairs), J.D./M.S.L.I.W. (Juris Doctor/Master of Science in Library Information Studies), J.D./M.S.P. (Juris Doctor/Master of Science in Urban and Regional Planning), and J.D./M.S.W. (Juris Doctor/Master of Social Work).

Required
To earn the J.D., candidates must complete 88 total credits, of which 36 are for required courses. They must maintain a minimum GPA of 69.0 in the required courses. The following first-year courses are required of all students: Civil Procedure, Constitutional Law I, Contracts I and II, Criminal Law, Legal Writing and Research I and II, Property I and II, and Torts. Required upper-level courses consist of a skills training course, a writing requirement course, Constitutional Law II, and Professional Responsibility. All students must complete 20 hours of civil pro bono work. The required orientation program for first-year students is a 2-day program that includes an introduction to legal education, research and writing, and ethics/professionalism.

Phone: 850-644-3787
Fax: 850-644-7284
E-mail: admissions@law.fsu.edu
Web: www.law.fsu.edu

Contact

Director of Admissions and Records, 850-644-3787 for general inquiries; Gail Rogers, 850-644-5716 for financial aid information.

FLORIDA

Electives

The College of Law offers concentrations in corporate law, criminal law, environmental law, international law, litigation, tax law, business law, and economics. In addition, The college offers more than 60 externship placements, either full- or part-time, including judicial clerkships, administrative agency placements, and many civil and criminal lawyering programs. A variety of specialized seminars are offered, such as business reorganization, cyberlaw, and energy law. The college offers an in-house legal clinic, and the Public Interest Law Center, which represents children, persons with disabilities, and victims of domestic violence. Twenty hours of pro bono service in the field is required for graduation. Special lecture series include the Mason Ladd Memorial Lectures, Distinguished Lectures in Environmental Law, and numerous Faculty Enrichment Speakers. Study abroad is available during the summer terms at Oxford University in England and through exchange programs with Griffith University in Brisbane, Australia and Erasmus University in Rotterdam, the Netherlands. There is a summer program for minority undergraduate students. The most widely taken electives are Evidence, Business Associations, and Transfers.

Graduation Requirements

In order to graduate, candidates must have a GPA of 69.0, complete the upper-division writing requirement, 20 hours of pro bono work, 6 semester residency requirement, and the skills training requirement.

Organizations

The primary law review is the *Florida State University Law Review*. Other law journals include the *Journal of Land Use and Environmental Law*, begun in 1983 and the state's first and only student publication in environmental and land law use. Students also edit the *Journal of Transnational Law and Policy*. The *Florida State University Business Review* is a joint effort between law and business students. The college's moot court team participates in many regional and national competitions each year, including the Florida Bar Robert Orseck Moot Court

Competition, Juvenile Law National Moot Court Competition, and the John Gibbons National Constitutional Criminal Law Moot Court Competition. The mock trial team takes part in 2 state-wide competitions as well as regional and national competitions each year. Law school organizations include the Student Bar Association, Black Students Association and the LAWtinos. Local chapters of national associations include the Women's Law Symposium dispute resolution society and OUTlaw. Law school organizations include Phi Alpha Delta; Christian Legal Society; and Entertainment, Art, and Sports Law Society.

Library

The law library contains 525,173 hardcopy volumes and 1,065,200 microform volume equivalents, and subscribes to 3,580 serial publications. Online databases and networks include CALI, CIS Universe, Dow-Jones, Infotrac, Legal-Trac, LEXIS, Mathew Bender, OCLC First Search, WESTLAW, Wilsonline Indexes, and more than 500 other databases, which are available to law students for research. Special library collections include rare English, American, and Floridian legal materials, including a first edition of Blackstone's Commentaries, and videotapes of oral arguments before the Florida Supreme Court of cases since 1985. The ratio of library volumes to faculty is 8,901 to 1 and to students is 688 to 1. The ratio of seats in the library to students is 1 to 2.

Faculty

The law school has 59 full-time and 29 part-time faculty members, of whom 40 are women. According to AAUP standards for Category I institutions, faculty salaries are below average. About 7% of full-time faculty have a graduate law degree in addition to the J.D. The ratio of full-time students to full-time faculty in an average class is 14 to 1; in a clinic, 12 to 1. The law school has a regular program of bringing visiting professors and other distinguished lecturers and visitors to campus. There is a chapter of the Order of the Coif; 39 faculty and 554 graduates are members.

Placement

J.D.s awarded:	233

Services available through: a separate law school placement center and the university placement center.

Services: various workshops/lectures on specific placement topics such as Internet job hunting, judicial clerkships, and job searches beyond OCI and practice area panels.

Special features: job postings available online for students and alumni along with a "Mach Speed Mock Interview" event.

Full-time job interviews:	24 employers
Summer job interviews:	50 employers
Placement by graduation:	76% of class
Placement within 9 months:	98% of class
Average starting salary:	$31,800 to $160,000

Areas of placement:

Private practice 2–10 attorneys	26%
Private practice 11–25 attorneys	5%
Private practice 26–50 attorneys	5%
Private practice 51–100 attorneys	4%
Private practice 101–500 attorneys	9%
Government	23%
Business/industry	10%
Public interest	9%
Military	3%
Judicial clerkships	2%
Academic	1%

Students

About 41% of the student body are women; 17%, minorities; 8%, African American; 2%, Asian American; 6%, Hispanic; and 1%, Puerto Rican. The majority of students come from Florida (92%). The average age of entering students is 23; age range is 20 to 45. About 43% of students enter directly from undergraduate school. About 3% drop out after the first year for academic or personal reasons; 97% remain to receive a law degree.

FORDHAM UNIVERSITY
School of Law

140 West 62nd Street
New York, NY 10023

Application Filing		Accreditation
Fall: March 1		ABA, AALS
		Degrees Granted
Fee: $70		J.D., LL.M., S.J.D.

Enrollment 2011–2012		First-Year Class	
Men:	796 53%	Applied:	7,551
Women:	700 47%	Accepted:	1,999
Minorities:	374 25%	Enrolled:	479
Out-of-State:	688 46%		

2011–2012 Class Profile
LSAT Percentile: 92%
LSAT Median Score: 165
Percentage passing bar on first try: 90%

Tuition and Fees:

Resident
$47,986 (F/T)

Average (public)
$18,708

Average (private)
$34,451

Nonresident
$47,986 (F/T)

Average (public)
$29,793

Average (private)
$34,451

0   10   20   30   40   50

Percentage receiving financial aid: 78%

ADMISSIONS
In the fall of 2011 first-year class, 7551 applied, 1999 were accepted, and 479 enrolled. Seventeen transfers enrolled. The median LSAT percentile of the most recent first-year class was 92; the median GPA was 3.5 on a scale of 4.0. The lowest LSAT percentile accepted was 62; the highest was 99.

Requirements
Applicants must have a bachelor's degree and take the LSAT. No specific undergraduate courses are required. Candidates are not interviewed.

Procedure
The application deadline for fall entry is March 1. Applicants should submit an application form, LSAT results, transcripts, a personal statement, TOEFL (if applicable), and a nonrefundable application fee of $70. Notification of the admissions decision is 6 to 8 weeks after application is completed. The law school uses the LSAC.

Special
The law school recruits minority and disadvantaged students by means of attendance at forums and law fairs, LSAC Candidate Referral Service, alumni assistance, and current minority students contacting accepted minority applicants. Requirements are different for out-of-state students. Transfer students must have one year of credit, must have a minimum GPA of 3, must have attended an ABA-approved law school, must submit a personal statement, must fulfill a 2-year residency requirement at Fordham, and must submit a letter of good standing and a statement of intent.

Costs
Tuition and fees for the 2011–2012 academic year are $47,360 for all full-time students. Tuition for part-time students is $35,520 for in-state students and $35,520 out-of-state.

Financial Aid
About 78% of current law students receive some form of aid. The average annual amount of aid from all sources combined, including scholarships, loans, and work contracts, is $45,359; maximum, $73,573. Awards are based on need and merit combined. The required financial statement is the FAFSA. The aid application deadline for fall entry is May 15. Special funds for minority or disadvantaged students include funds contributed by benefactors of the school. Also, some funds are specifically allocated to assist these groups. First-year students are notified about their financial aid application at time of acceptance.

About the Law School
Fordham University School of Law was established in 1905 and is a private institution. The 8-acre campus is in an urban area in the Lincoln Center area of New York City. Fordham University School of Law is committed to providing a complete legal education that integrates legal theory, practice, and ethics. Through teaching, scholarship, and training, the school seeks to provide a broad foundation in legal analysis and doctrine, to offer insights into how law affects and can improve social life, and to develop in students the skills and values necessary for thinking critically about how lawyers can best contribute

to their community. Students have access to federal, state, county, city, and local agencies, courts, correctional facilities, law firms, and legal aid organizations in the New York area. Lincoln Center, with its many cultural attractions, is nearby. Facilities of special interest to law students include the law school and attached buildings, which include an amphitheater, a moot court room, conference rooms, cafeteria, and library with private study rooms. Housing for students is available in a 250-bed, 20-story university residence hall connected to the law school, or within the immediate neighborhood or greater metropolitan area. All law school facilities are accessible to the physically disabled.

Calendar
The law school operates on a traditional semester basis. Courses for full-time students are offered primarily during the day and must be completed within 3 years. For part-time students, courses are offered primarily in the evening, and must be completed within 4 years. New full- and part-time students are admitted in the fall. There is a 9-week summer session. Transferable summer courses are offered.

Programs
In addition to the J.D., the law school offers the L.L.M. and S.J.D. Students may take relevant courses in other programs and apply credit toward the J.D.; a maximum of 13 credits may be applied. The following joint degrees may be earned: J.D./M.A. (Juris Doctor/Master of Arts in International Political Economy), J.D./M.B.A. (Juris Doctor/Master of Business Administration), and J.D./M.S.W. (Juris Doctor/Master of Social Work).

Required
To earn the J.D., candidates must complete 83 total credits, of which 41 are for required courses. They must maintain a minimum GPA of 2.0 in the required courses. The following first-year courses are required of all students: Civil Procedure, Contracts, Criminal Justice, Legal Process, Legal Writing and Research, Legislation and Regulation, Property, and Torts. Required upper-level courses consist of Constitutional Law, Corporations and Partnerships, and Professional Responsibility. The professional skills requirement may be satisfied by courses including clinics, advanced

Contact

Kathryn Espiritu, Director of Admissions, 212-636-6810 for general inquiries; Stephen G. Brown, Assistant Dean of Enrollment Services, 212-636-7178 for financial aid information.

NEW YORK

legal writing, and more. The required orientation program for first-year students is usually held for 5–6 days, and covers registration and basic technical skills.

Electives

The School of Law offers concentrations in corporate law, criminal law, entertainment law, environmental law, family law, intellectual property law, international law, juvenile law, labor law, litigation, maritime law, media law, securities law, sports law, tax law, torts and insurance, European Community law, trial advocacy, public interest law, and professional responsibility. In addition, clinics, which are open to upper-class students who have satisfied prerequisites, include Criminal Defense, Immigration Law, and Community Economic Development. Seminars, usually worth 2 or 3 credits, are also open to upper-class students; a selection of recent offerings includes Advanced Copyright Law, Civil Rights, and Environmental Law. After the first year, students may participate in a broad range of actual practice settings in federal and state courts, administrative agencies, prosecutors' and defenders' offices, and nonprofit agencies for 2 credits. Research is done through the Stein Institute of Law and Ethics Research Fellowships and the Crowley International Human Rights Program. Field work may be undertaken in the Crowley International Human Rights Program and in the noncredit pro bono program, where students assist in preparing cases under the direction of attorneys from the Legal Aid Society and various public agencies and nonprofit organizations through Fordham's Public Interest Center. Special lecture series include John F. Sonnett Lectures by distinguished judges and litigators; Stein Lectures in ethics and professional responsibility; Noreen E. McNamara Lectures by outstanding women in the profession; and Robert L. Levine Lectures by distinguished legal scholars. Students may study abroad for up to 1 year for up to 24 credits in approved subjects. The law school operates a summer program in Dublin, Belfast, and South Korea. The noncredit Academic Enrichment Program provides training in briefing cases, study strategies, and exam-taking techniques. The school contributes to the CLEO program. The Student Bar Association funds several student-run minority organizations. Public service programs include a nonle-

gal community service project; advocacy projects for battered women, low-income tenants, and unemployed individuals; and student-funded fellowships for summer work at public interest organizations. The most widely taken electives are Criminal Procedure, Evidence, and International Business Transactions.

Graduation Requirements

In order to graduate, candidates must have a GPA of 2.0, and must have completed the upper-division writing requirement, professional skills requirement, and professional responsibilities requirement.

Organizations

Students edit the *Fordham Law Review, Fordham Urban Law Journal, Fordham International Law Journal, Fordham Environmental Law Journal, Fordham Entertainment, Mass Media, and Intellectual Property Journal,* and *Fordham Journal of Corporate and Financial Law*. Moot court competitions include the intramural William Hughes Mulligan and the I. Maurice Wormser and the interschool Irving R. Kaufman Securities Law competitions. Teams also compete at the National Moot Court, Jessup International Law, Craven Constitutional Law, Cardozo Entertainment Law, National Trial Advocacy, National Tax, and National Products Liability competitions. There are approximately 40 student-run organizations at the law school, including the Student Bar Association, Fordham Law Women, and Stein Scholars. There are local chapters of the Federalist Society, National Lawyers Guild, BLSA, LALSA, APALSA and Phi Alpha Delta. Campus clubs include Habitat for Humanity, Equal Justice Works, and the Sports Law Association.

Library

The law library contains 379,621 hardcopy volumes and 254,317 microform volume equivalents, and subscribes to 4,401 serial publications. Such online databases and networks as CALI, CIS Universe, DIALOG, Dow-Jones, Infotrac, Legal-Trac, LEXIS, OCLC First Search, RLIN, WESTLAW, and Wilsonline Indexes are available to law students for research. The law school is home to a number of special collections and repositories. The ratio of library volumes to faculty is 4,314 to 1 and

Placement

J.D.s awarded:	428

Services available through: a separate law school placement center.

Services: self-assessment seminars, mock interviews, and networking/job prospecting workshops.

Special features: the school designs its own programs to ensure that students have opportunities to interact with alumni and employers.

to students is 231 to 1. The ratio of seats in the library to students is 1 to 3.

Faculty

The law school has 88 full-time and 179 part-time faculty members, of whom 106 are women. According to AAUP standards for Category I institutions, faculty salaries are above average. About 45% of full-time faculty have a graduate law degree in addition to the J.D.; about 8% of part-time faculty have one. The ratio of full-time students to full-time faculty in an average class is 45 to 1. The law school has a regular program of bringing visiting professors and other distinguished lecturers and visitors to campus. There is a chapter of the Order of the Coif.

Students

About 47% of the student body are women; 25%, minorities; 4%, African American; 10%, Asian American; and 10%, Hispanic. The majority of students come from New York (54%). The average age of entering students is 25; age range is 20 to 69. About 31% of students enter directly from undergraduate school, 9% have a graduate degree, and 60% have worked full-time prior to entering law school. About 1% drop out after the first year for academic or personal reasons; 99% remain to receive a law degree.

GEORGE MASON UNIVERSITY

School of Law

3301 Fairfax Drive
Arlington, VA 22201

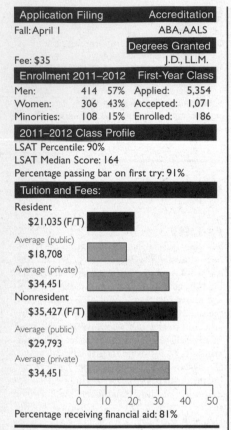

Application Filing	Accreditation
Fall: April 1	ABA, AALS

	Degrees Granted
Fee: $35	J.D., LL.M.

Enrollment 2011–2012		First-Year Class	
Men:	414 57%	Applied:	5,354
Women:	306 43%	Accepted:	1,071
Minorities:	108 15%	Enrolled:	186

2011–2012 Class Profile
LSAT Percentile: 90%
LSAT Median Score: 164
Percentage passing bar on first try: 91%

Tuition and Fees:

Resident
$21,035 (F/T)

Average (public)
$18,708

Average (private)
$34,451

Nonresident
$35,427 (F/T)

Average (public)
$29,793

Average (private)
$34,451

0   10   20   30   40   50

Percentage receiving financial aid: 81%

ADMISSIONS

In the fall of 2011 first-year class, 5354 applied, 1071 were accepted, and 186 enrolled. Five transfer students enrolled. The median LSAT percentile of the most recent first-year class was 90; the median GPA was 3.7 on a scale of 4.0. The lowest LSAT percentile accepted was 41; the highest was 99.

Requirements

Applicants must have a bachelor's degree and take the LSAT. The most important admission factors include LSAT results, class rank, and GPA. No specific undergraduate courses are required and candidates are not interviewed.

Procedure

The application deadline for fall entry is April 1. Applicants should submit an application form, LSAT results, transcripts, nonrefundable application fee of $35, 2 letters of recommendation, and a 500-word personal statement. Notification

of the admissions decision is December through April. The law school uses the LSAC.

Special

The law school recruits minority and disadvantaged students through the Law Services' Candidate Referral Service, Law School Forums, regional law fairs, and CLEO. Requirements are different for out-of-state students. Transfer students must have one year of credits, a minimum GPA of 3, attended an ABA-approved law school, and a personal statement.

Financial Aid

About 81% of current law students receive some form of aid. The average annual amount of aid from all sources combined, including scholarships, loans, and work contracts, is $33,502. Awards are based on merit. Required financial statement is the FAFSA. The aid application deadline for fall entry is March 1. First-year students are notified about their financial aid application between the time of acceptance and the first day of school.

About the Law School

George Mason University School of Law was established in 1979 and is a public institution. The 1-acre campus is located in a suburban area 2 miles south of Washington, D.C. The mission of the law school is to provide superior legal education programs leading to the first professional degree in law, and the Juris Doctor. The school stresses the case method. Students have access to federal, state, county, city, and local agencies, courts, correctional facilities, law firms, and legal aid organizations in the Arlington area. Housing for students is not available on the metro campus. All law school facilities are accessible to the physically disabled.

Calendar

The law school operates on a traditional semester basis. Courses for full-time students are offered during the day only in the first year; day and night thereafter, and must be completed within 3-5 years. For part-time students, courses are offered during the evening only in the first year; day and night thereafter, and must be completed within 4–5 years. New full- and part-time students are admitted

in the fall. There is an 8-week summer session. Transferable summer courses are offered.

Programs

In addition to the J.D., the law school offers the LL.M. The following joint degrees may be earned: J.D./M.P.P. (Juris Doctor/Master of Public Policy).

Required

To earn the J.D., candidates must complete 89 total credits, of which 40 are for required courses. They must maintain a minimum GPA of 2.3 in the required courses. The following first-year courses are required of all students: Civil Procedure, Constitutional Law: The Founding, Contracts I and II, Criminal Law, Economic Foundations of Legal Studies, Legal Research, Writing and Analysis I and II, Property, and Torts. Required upper-level courses consist of a minimum of 2 upper-level courses that require substantial papers, Appellate Writing and Legal Drafting, Constitutional Law I: Structure of Government, and Professional Responsibility. The required orientation program for first-year students is presented during the first week of school. The program lasts 2 days and consists of presentations by the administration, legal writing classes, and small group meetings with faculty alumni, and student advisers.

Electives

The School of Law offers concentrations in corporate law, criminal law, intellectual property law, international law, litigation, securities law, tax law, patent law, regulatory law, technology law, legal and economic theory, personal law, international business law, homeland and national security law, communications law, and technology law. Clinics are limited to upper-level students. Seminars, taken in the second, third, or fourth year, consist of a minimum of 2 upper-level courses in which substantial papers are required or there is a satisfaction of track thesis requirement. Internships are limited to upper-level students. The Law and Economics Center administers a series of interdisciplinary symposia, lectures, and conferences devoted to current topics in law and economics. The National Center for Technology and Law also hosts conferences and programs. There is a University

Phone: 703-993-8010
Fax: 703-993-8088
E-mail: uprice1@gmu.edu
Web: www.law.gmu.edu

Contact
Alison H. Price, Associate Dean and Director of Admissions, 703-993-8264 for general inquiries; Heidi Granger, Office of Financial Aid, 703-993-2353 for financial aid information.

VIRGINIA

of Hamburg (Germany) exchange program in Law and Economics. Tutorial programs consist of Fundamental Skills Saturday sessions, and day long spring session for students in academic jeopardy. Minority programs include the L. Douglas Wilder Seminar Series. Special interest groups include GLBT forums and panels and J. Reuben Clark Law Society Conference sponsorship. The most widely taken electives are Evidence, Administrative Law, and Business Associations.

Graduation Requirements
In order to graduate, candidates must have a GPA of 2.3 and complete the upper-division writing requirement.

Organizations
Students edit the *George Mason University Law Review, Civil Rights Law Journal, Journal of International Commercial Law, Journal of Law, Economics and Policy,* and the newspaper *The Docket*. The school sponsors several in-house competitions each year, and sends teams to numerous national and regional competitions. Other competitions include the Law and Economics Competition, Trial Advocacy Association Competition, and the Mediation Advocacy Competition. Law student organizations include the Business Law Society, National Security Law Society, and the Intellectual Property Law Society. Local chapters of national associations include the Student Bar Association, Association for Public Interest Law, and the Black Law Students Association. Campus clubs and other organizations include local chapters of the ABA-Law Student Division, Phi Delta Phi (Lewis Powell Inn), and Phi Alpha Delta (George Mason Chapter).

Library
The law library contains 253,097 hardcopy volumes and 219,802 microform volume equivalents. Online databases and networks include CALI, CIS Universe, DIALOG, Dow-Jones, LEXIS, OCLC First Search, WESTLAW, and Wilsonline Indexes. ALADIN, VIVA, TWEN, BNA, Index to Legal Periodicals, Law Library Microform Consortium Digital, HeinOnline, RIA Checkpoint, LEXIS NEXIS Congressional Research Digital Collection, Making of Modern Law, and Westlaw Business are other resources available to law students for research. Special library collections include business, economic theory and history, ethics and philosophy, banking, patent law, and law and economics. The school is also a participant in the Federal Government Documents Depository. The ratio of library volumes to faculty is 6,660 to 1 and to students is 352 to 1.

Faculty
The law school has 38 full-time and 98 part-time faculty members, of whom 36 are women. According to AAUP standards for Category I institutions, faculty salaries are average. About 42% of full-time faculty have a graduate law degree in addition to the J.D.; about 9% of part-time faculty have one. The law school has a regular program of bringing visiting professors and other distinguished lecturers and visitors to campus.

Students
About 43% of the student body are women; 15%, minorities; 1%, African American; 9%, Asian American; 3%, Hispanic; and 1%, Native American. The average age of entering students is 25. About 15% of students have a graduate degree. About 1% drop out after the first year for academic or personal reasons; 95% remain to receive a law degree.

Placement

J.D.s awarded:	170
Services available through: a separate law school placement center.	
Services: mock interview program, career advisory network, job fairs.	
Special features: required first-year counseling sessions; open door office hours; combined career counseling, academic advisor, and alumni services office.	
Full-time job interviews:	17 employers
Summer job interviews:	49 employers
Placement by graduation:	90% of class
Placement within 9 months:	97% of class
Average starting salary:	$35,000 to $170,000
Areas of placement:	
Private practice 2–10 attorneys	20%
Private practice 11–25 attorneys	4%
Private practice 26–50 attorneys	1%
Private practice 100 + attorneys	14%
Business/industry	20%
Government	19%
Judicial clerkships	9%
Academic	7%
Public interest	4%
Military	2%

Law School

2000 H Street, N.W.
Washington, DC 20052

Application Filing	Accreditation
Fall: March 1	ABA, AALS

	Degrees Granted
Fee: $80	J.D., LL.M., S.J.D.

Enrollment 2011–2012		First-Year Class	
Men:	956 55%	Applied:	8,652
Women:	797 43%	Accepted:	2,355
Minorities:	n/av n/av	Enrolled:	474

2011–2012 Class Profile
LSAT Median Score: 167
Percentage passing bar on first try: 93%

Tuition and Fees:

Resident
$45,750 (F/T)

Average (public)
$18,708

Average (private)
$34,451

Nonresident
$45,750 (F/T)

Average (public)
$29,793

Average (private)
$34,451

0   10   20   30   40   50

Percentage receiving financial aid: 80%

ADMISSIONS

In the fall of 2011 first-year class, 8652 applied, 2355 were accepted, and 474 enrolled. The median GPA of the most recent first-year class was 3.82.

Requirements

Applicants must have a bachelor's degree and take the LSAT. The most important admission factors include academic achievement, LSAT results, and writing ability. No specific undergraduate courses are required. Candidates are interviewed.

Procedure

The application deadline for fall entry is March 1. Applicants should submit an application form, LSAT results, transcripts, nonrefundable application fee of $80, and two letters of recommendation (recommended, but not required). Notification of the admissions decision is as soon as a decision is made. The law school uses the LSAC.

Special

The law school recruits minority and disadvantaged students by participating in law forums throughout the country and visiting schools with large minority populations. In addition, each admitted applicant is contacted by a currently enrolled student. Requirements are different for out-of-state students. Transfer students must have one year of credit, have attended an ABA-approved law school. Admissions decisions are based on the applicant's law school record and the amount of space available.

Costs

On-campus room and board costs about $18,500 annually; books and supplies run $1,550.

Financial Aid

About 80% of current law students receive some form of aid. The average annual amount of aid from all sources combined, including scholarships, loans, and work contracts, is $53,074; maximum, $76,400. Awards are based on need and merit combined. Required financial statements are the FAFSA and The GW Law Financial Aid Application. The aid application deadline for fall entry is June 1. First-year students are notified about their financial aid application at time of acceptance.

About the Law School

George Washington University Law School was established in 1865 and is a private institution. The campus is located in an urban area in downtown Washington, D.C. The primary mission of the law school is to offer students the opportunity to study and observe lawmaking at its source, by combining a wide variety of courses in public law with the traditional fields of law. Students have access to federal, state, county, city, and local agencies, courts, correctional facilities, law firms, and legal aid organizations in the Washington area. Extensive clinical opportunities exist in the nation's capital. Housing for students consists of a limited number of spaces available on campus in efficiency, 1- and 2-bedroom apartments.

Calendar

The law school operates on a traditional semester basis. Courses for full-time students are offered both day and evening and must be completed within 3 years. For part-time students, courses are offered both day and evening and must be completed within 4 years. New full- and part-time students are admitted in the fall. There is a 7-week summer session. Transferable summer courses are offered.

Programs

In addition to the J.D., the law school offers the LL.M. and S.J.D. Students may take relevant courses in other programs and apply credit toward the J.D.; a maximum of 6 credits may be applied. The following joint degrees may be earned: J.D./M.A. (Juris Doctor/Master of Arts in various disciplines), J.D./M.B.A. (Juris Doctor/Master of Business Administration), J.D./M.P.A. (Juris Doctor/Master of Public Administration), J.D./M.P.H. (Juris Doctor/Master of Public Health), J.D./M.P.P. (Juris Doctor/Master of Public Policy), LL.M/M.A. (Master of Laws/Master of Art in various disciplines), and LL.M./M.P.H. (Master of Laws/Master of Public Health).

Required

To earn the J.D., candidates must complete 84 total credits, of which 34 are for required courses. They must maintain a minimum GPA of 1.7 in the required courses. The following first-year courses are required of all students: Civil Procedure I and II, Constitutional Law I, Contracts I and II, Criminal Law, Introduction to Advocacy, Legal Research and Writing, Property, and Torts. Required upper-level courses consist of Professional Responsibility and Ethics. The required orientation program for first-year students is a 3-day program that includes registration.

Electives

The Law School offers concentrations in corporate law, criminal law, environmental law, family law, intellectual property law, international law, labor law, litigation, securities law, tax law, torts and insurance, government contracts, intellectual property, and constitutional law. Clinics include

Phone: 202-994-7230
Fax: 202-994-3597
E-mail: jd@law.gwu.edu
Web: www.law.gwu.edu

Contact
Law Financial Aid Office, 202-994-6592 for financial aid information.

DISTRICT OF COLUMBIA

the Small Business Community Economic Development, Family Justice Litigation, and Immigration, all open to upper-level students. The Federal Sentencing Seminar, Sexuality and the Law Seminar, and Law in Cyberspace, are all open to second- or third-year students. Internships are available to second- and third-year students. Students arrange independent projects with state or federal public interest organizations. Through the Enrichment Program, speakers are brought to the law school for lectures and informal seminars that are open to all students. The law school offers 2 summer study abroad programs: An international human rights program is offered with Oxford University and an intellectual property program is offered with the Munich I.P. Law Center. Third-year students serving as Resource Fellows assist other students who are in academic difficulty. The Writing Center serves as a resource for all students. Minority programs are sponsored by groups such as the Black Law Students Association, Hispanic Law Students Association, and Asian/Pacific American Law Students Association and East Asian Law Society. Special interest groups include the Law Association for Women, Christian Law Society, Law Students for the Arts, International Law Society, Student Animal Defense Fund, Lambda Law and politically-oriented groups. The most widely taken electives are Federal Income Taxation, Evidence, and Corporations.

Graduation Requirements
In order to graduate, candidates must have a GPA of 1.7, complete the upper-division writing requirement, and complete the required curriculum, as well as completion of a skills course, such as on negotiation or trial advocacy, or a clinic.

Organizations
Students edit the *The George Washington Law Review*, *The George Washington International Law Journal*, and the newspaper *Nota Bene*. The *American Intellectual Property Law Association Quarterly Journal*, a publication of the AIPLA, is housed at the law school. The Moot Court Board sponsors the Van Vleck Appellate Moot Court competition, the Jessup Cup Competition in international law, and the Giles S. Rich in patent law. Teams participate in other moot court competitions around the country. In-house alternative

dispute resolution competitions are held in negotiations and client counseling. Law student organizations, local chapters of national associations, and campus clubs and organizations include the Equal Justice Foundation, Evening Law Student Association, International Law Society, the Student Bar Association, Legal Support Group, Black Law Students Association, Environmental Law Society, Phi Alpha Delta, Phi Delta Phi, and the Federalist Society.

Library
The law library contains 663,521 hard-copy volumes and 274,704 microform volume equivalents, and subscribes to 4,425 serial publications. Online databases and networks include CALI, CIS Universe, DIALOG, Legal-Trac, LEXIS, Mathew Bender, OCLC First Search, WESTLAW, and Wilsonline Indexes. The school also subscribes to additional online databases, which are available to law students for research. Special library collections include unique materials in the areas of environmental law, intellectual property law, international law, government procurement law, legal history, and French law. The ratio of library volumes to faculty is 8,294 to 1 and to students is 390 to 1. The ratio of seats in the library to students is 1 to 3.

Faculty
The law school has 100 full-time and 288 part-time faculty members, of whom 128 are women. The ratio of full-time students to full-time faculty in an average class is 15 to 1; in a clinic, 8 to 1. The law school has a regular program of bringing visiting professors and other distinguished lecturers and visitors to campus. There is a chapter of the Order of the Coif.

Students
About 43% of the student body are women; 5%, African American; 10%, Asian American; 7%, Hispanic; and 10%, students who did not report ethnicity on application.

Placement	
J.D.s awarded:	506
Services available through: a separate law school placement center	
Special features: online job listings, and an evening student counselor	
Full-time job interviews:	400 employers
Placement by graduation:	93% of class
Placement within 9 months:	95% of class
Average starting salary:	$84,000 to $145,000
Areas of placement:	
Private practice 2–10 attorneys	6%
Private practice 11–25 attorneys	1%
Private practice 26–50 attorneys	2%
Private practice 51–100 attorneys	2%
Government	20%
Business/industry	14%
Judicial clerkships	9%
Academic	6%
Public interest	4%
Military	1%

GEORGETOWN UNIVERSITY
Law Center

600 New Jersey Avenue, N.W.
Washington, DC 20001

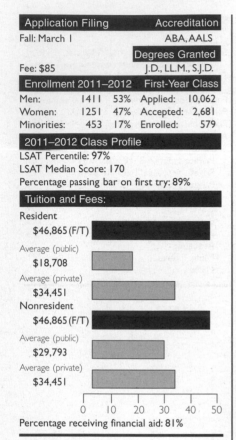

Application Filing	Accreditation
Fall: March 1	ABA, AALS
	Degrees Granted
Fee: $85	J.D., LL.M., S.J.D.

Enrollment 2011–2012		First-Year Class	
Men:	1411 53%	Applied:	10,062
Women:	1251 47%	Accepted:	2,681
Minorities:	453 17%	Enrolled:	579

2011–2012 Class Profile
LSAT Percentile: 97%
LSAT Median Score: 170
Percentage passing bar on first try: 89%

Tuition and Fees:

Resident
$46,865 (F/T)

Average (public)
$18,708

Average (private)
$34,451

Nonresident
$46,865 (F/T)

Average (public)
$29,793

Average (private)
$34,451

0 10 20 30 40 50

Percentage receiving financial aid: 81%

ADMISSIONS
In the fall of 2011 first-year class, 10062 applied, 2681 were accepted, and 579 enrolled. Seventy-one transfer students enrolled. The median LSAT percentile of the most recent first-year class was 97; the median GPA was 3.7 on a scale of 4.0. The lowest LSAT percentile accepted was 56; the highest was 99.

Requirements
Applicants must have a bachelor's degree and take the LSAT. The most important admission factors include academic achievement, LSAT results, and life experience. No specific undergraduate courses are required. Candidates are interviewed.

Procedure
The application deadline for fall entry is March 1. Applicants should submit an application form, LSAT results, transcripts, personal statement, nonrefundable application fee of $85, letter of recommendation, transcripts (must be received through the LSAC); and a resume. Notification of the admissions decision is approximately 6 to 12 weeks. The law school uses the LSAC.

Special
The law school recruits minority and disadvantaged students by means of an outreach program that encourages qualified minority and disadvantaged students to apply. Requirements are different for out-of-state students. Transfer students must have one year of credits, attended an ABA-approved law school, and a personal statement.

Costs
On-campus room and board costs about $22,560 annually; books and supplies run $1,075.

Financial Aid
About 81% of current law students receive some form of aid. The average annual amount of aid from all sources combined, including scholarships, loans, and work contracts, is $52,145; maximum, $66,000. Awards are based on need and merit combined. Required financial statements are the CSS Profile, the FAFSA, and Need Access Application. The aid application deadline for fall entry is March 1. First-year students are notified about their financial aid application after acceptance and completion of financial aid requirements. Awards are given on a rolling basis.

About the Law School
Georgetown University Law Center was established in 1870 and is a private institution. The 7-acre campus is located in an urban area in Washington, D.C. Georgetown Law has a strong tradition of public service and is dedicated to the principle that law is but a means, justice is the end. Students have access to federal, state, county, city, and local agencies, courts, correctional facilities, law firms, and legal aid organizations in the Washington area. Other resources include the U.S. Supreme Court, federal courts, the U.S. Congress, and major federal departments and agencies, many of which are within walking distance. On-campus housing is available in the Gewirz Student Center, which offers furnished apartment units. Law students are supported through a variety of other housing programs. All law school facilities are accessible to the physically disabled.

Calendar
The law school operates on a traditional semester basis. Courses for full-time students are offered both day and evening and must be completed within 5 years. There is no part-time program. New students are admitted in the fall. There is a 7-week summer session. Transferable summer courses are offered.

Programs
In addition to the J.D., the law school offers the LL.M. and S.J.D. Students may take relevant courses in other programs and apply credit toward the J.D.; a maximum of 6 credits may be applied. The following joint degrees may be earned: J.D./Govt. (Juris Doctor/Doctor in Government), J.D./M.A.A.S. (Juris Doctor/Master of Arts in Arab studies), J.D./M.A.G.E.S. (Juris Doctor/Master of Arts in German and European studies), J.D./M.A.R.E.E.S. (Juris Doctor/Master of Arts in Russian and East European Studies), J.D./M.A.S.S.P. (Juris Doctor/Master of Arts in Security Studies), J.D./M.A.L.A.S (Juris Doctor/Master of Arts Latin American studies), J.D./M.B.A. (Juris Doctor/Master of Business Administration), J.D./M.S.F.S. (Juris Doctor/Master of Foreign Science), J.D./LL.M (Juris Doctor/Master of Laws in Taxation), J.D./M.P.H. (Juris Doctor/Master of Public Health), J.D./M.P.P. (Juris Doctor/Master of Public Policy), and J.D./Phil. (Juris Doctor/Master or Doctor of Philosophy).

Required
To earn the J.D., candidates must complete 85 total credits, of which 33 are for required courses. They must maintain a minimum GPA of 1.7 in the required courses. The following first-year courses are required of all students: Civil Procedure, Constitutional Law I, Contracts, Criminal Justice, Democracy and Coercion, Elective (1), Government Processes, Law in Context, Legal Justice Seminar, Legal Practice: Writing and Analysis, Legal Process and Society, Legal Research and Writing, Property, Property in Time, and Torts. Required upper-level courses consist of Legal Writing seminar or supervised research and writing project and Professional Responsibility. The required orientation program for first-year students is a 4-day program encompassing social, cultural, and legal events throughout the week on and off campus. Typically,

Phone: 202-662-9010
Fax: 202-662-9439
E-mail: udmis@law.georgetown.edu
Web: www.law.georgetown.edu

Contact
Charles Pruett, Assistant Dean, 202-662-9210 for financial aid information.

orientation includes a review of academic services and student activities, an introduction to first-year course work by faculty members, a series of talks by the faculty on legal topics as well as faculty-guided tours of historical and legal sites in Washington, D.C. and an address by the University president and Law Center dean.

Electives
The Law Center offers concentrations in corporate law, criminal law, entertainment law, environmental law, family law, intellectual property law, international law, juvenile law, labor law, litigation, maritime law, securities law, tax law, torts and insurance, commercial law, constitutional law and government, and administrative law and government. In addition, The Law Center offers 14 in-house clinical courses. Clinics include appellate advocacy, criminal defense, and civil rights. More than 250 seminars are offered on such topics as environmental law, intellectual property law, and international law. Many students pursue externships with government agencies, judges, and other organizations. The Law Center also offers a unique international internship program through which students can intern abroad with law firms, nongovernmental organizations, and corporate in-house legal departments. Supervised research projects may be undertaken under the guidance of a faculty member. Some courses involve field work. Several special lecture series held each academic year bring prominent legal scholars, judges, lawyers, and business executives to the Law Center. The Law Center offers a summer law program in London with distinguished professors from Europe and the U.S., as well as the opportunity to study abroad for a semester at prestigious institutions in Europe, Asia, and India. The tutorial program is open to all students; however, it is primarily designed for first-year students. Each of the first-year sections is assigned an upper-class tutor who meets with students on a weekly basis. A writing center is open to all students. These programs are not remedial. They do, however, provide academic support. A diversity clerkship program is offered by the Center Services Office, and other educational programs are sponsored by the Career Services Office and minority students groups. The most widely taken electives are Constitutional Law II, Corporations, and Evidence.

Graduation Requirements
In order to graduate, candidates must have a GPA of 2.0, complete the upper-division writing requirement, and Professional Responsibility course.

Organizations
Student-edited publications include the *Georgetown Law Journal, American Criminal Law Review, Georgetown Journal of Gender and the Law, Georgetown Immigration Law Journal, Georgetown International Environmental Law Review, Georgetown Journal of Legal Ethics, The Tax Lawyer, Georgetown Journal of Law and Public Policy, Georgetown Journal on Poverty Law and Policy, Georgetown Journal of International Law, Georgetown Journal of Law,* and *Modern Critical Race Perspective,* and the newspaper, *Georgetown Law Weekly.* Other publications include *The Bright Line.* Georgetown competes in more than a dozen moot court competitions, including the Philip C. Jessup International Law Moot Court Competition, the ABA National Appellate Advocacy Competition, and the European Tax College Moot Court Competition. Georgetown also fields teams in more than a dozen mock trial and alternative dispute resolution competitions, including the American Association for Justice's Student Trial Advocacy Competition, the Texas Young Lawyer's Association National Trial Competition, and the Vis International *Commercial Arbitration* Moot. There are 75 student organizations.

Library
The law library contains 551,414 hardcopy volumes and 595,414 microform volume equivalents, and subscribes to 13,547 serial publications. Online databases and networks include CALI, CIS Universe, DIALOG, Legal-Trac, LEXIS, Mathew Bender, OCLC First Search, WESTLAW, Wilsonline Indexes, OCLC, and FirstSearch, which are available to law students for research. Special library collections include rare books as well as international law and tax collections. The ratio of library volumes to faculty is 4,409 to 1 and to students is 430 to 1. The ratio of seats in the library to students is 1 to 2.

Faculty
The law school has 151 full-time and 109 part-time faculty members, of whom 83

Placement

J.D.s awarded:	647

Services available through: a separate law school placement center, online services, and Office of Public Interest and Community Service.

Services: public interest organizations, small firm job fairs, regional job fairs in cities nationwide, and a large international internship program.

Special features: Offers the largest on-campus recruitment program in the country; multiple programs for students interested in domestic, international, traditional private practice, and public interest settings; extensive resource database for students. In addition, the Law Center's Office of Public Interest and Community Service (OPICS) provides specialty career advising to students and alumni interested in pursuing legal careers in public interest or the government. OCS and OPICS conduct individual and group counseling, skills workshops, job fairs, and other programs related to private and public interest employment and pro bono service.

Full-time job interviews:	280 employers
Summer job interviews:	700 employers
Placement by graduation:	98% of class
Placement within 9 months:	98% of class
Average starting salary:	$50,000 to $160,000

Areas of placement:

Private practice 2–10 attorneys	2%
Private practice 11–25 attorneys	1%
Private practice 26–50 attorneys	1%
Private practice 51–100 attorneys	2%
Government	17%
Public interest	14%
Judicial clerkships	9%
Business/industry	5%
Academic	3%
Military	2%

are women. The ratio of full-time students to full-time faculty in an average clinic is 7 to 1. The law school has a regular program of bringing visiting professors and other distinguished lecturers and visitors to campus. There is a chapter of the Order of the Coif; 67 graduates are members.

Students
About 47% of the student body are women; 21%, minorities; 9%, African American; 6%, Asian American; 7%, Hispanic; and 2%, foreign nationals. The average age of entering students is 26; age range is 18 to 60. About 26% of students enter directly from undergraduate school, 3% have a graduate degree, and 67% have worked full-time prior to entering law school.

College of Law

P.O. Box 4037
Atlanta, GA 30302-4037

Application Filing	Accreditation
Fall: March 15	ABA, AALS

Degrees Granted
Fee: $50	J.D.

Enrollment 2011–2012		First-Year Class	
Men:	370 55%	Applied:	2,731
Women:	308 45%	Accepted:	433
Minorities:	142 21%	Enrolled:	223
Out-of-State:	88 13%		

2011–2012 Class Profile
LSAT Percentile: 80%
LSAT Median Score: 160
Percentage passing bar on first try: 93%

Tuition and Fees:

Resident
$14,770 (F/T)

Average (public)
$18,708

Average (private)
$34,451

Nonresident
$39,834 (F/T)

Average (public)
$29,793

Average (private)
$34,451

0 10 20 30 40 50

Percentage receiving financial aid: 67%

ADMISSIONS

In the fall of 2011 first-year class, 2731 applied, 433 were accepted, and 223 enrolled. Twelve transfer students enrolled. The median LSAT percentile of the most recent first-year class was 80; the median GPA was 3.5 on a scale of 4.0. The lowest LSAT percentile accepted was 43; the highest was 97.

Requirements
Applicants must have a bachelor's degree and take the LSAT. The most important admission factors include academic achievement, LSAT results, and GPA. No specific undergraduate courses are required, and candidates are not interviewed.

Procedure
The application deadline for fall entry is March 15. Applicants should submit an application form, LSAT results, transcripts, a personal statement, LSAC report, TOEFL (for applicants whose native language is not English), nonrefundable application fee of $50, and 2 letters of recommendation. Notification of the admissions decision begins in January. The law school uses the LSAC.

Special
The law school recruits minority and disadvantaged students by means of visiting other colleges and universities during graduate and professional program days, speaking to pre-law clubs and classes, and recruiting at schools with large minority student populations. The law school also visits high schools and co-sponsors a law camp for those students in the summer. Requirements are different for out-of-state students. Transfer students must have one year of credits, attended an ABA-approved law school, personal statement, letter from the dean of the student's previous law school stating that the student is in good standing and is eligible to return to the school, and stating the student's class ranking.

Costs

Tuition and fees for the 2011–2012 academic year are $12,528 for full-time in-state students and $32,592 for out-of-state students. Tuition for part-time students is $11,484 for in-state students and $29,876 out-of-state. On-campus room and board costs about $10,986 annually; books and supplies run $ 750.

Financial Aid

About 67% of current law students receive some form of aid. The average annual amount of aid from all sources combined, including scholarships, loans, and work contracts, is $17,415; maximum, $30,000. There are loans available that are need- and non-need-based. Required financial statement is the FAFSA. The aid application deadline for fall entry is April 1. Scholarships and special funds are available for minority or disadvantaged students. First-year students are notified about their financial aid application at time of acceptance.

About the Law School

Georgia State University College of Law was established in 1982 and is a public institution. The 34-acre campus is located in an urban area in the city of Atlanta. The primary mission of the law school is to provide both part- and full-time programs that are designed for students wishing to gain a knowledge of the law, of legal institutions, and of legal processes. The college is equally committed to part- and full-time legal studies. Students have access to federal, state, county, city, and local agencies, courts, correctional facilities, law firms, and legal aid organizations in the Atlanta area. A variety of institutions and law-related agencies are located in the metropolitan Atlanta area. Facilities of special interest to law students include the Richard B. Russell Federal Building; Federal Reserve Bank; state capitol building; state legislature; federal, state and local court systems; and offices of the U.S. attorney, state attorney general, and county and city District Attorneys. Housing for students is on a first-come, first-serve, basis in the University Lofts, which accommodates 2000 students in modern apartments. All law school facilities are accessible to the physically disabled.

Calendar

The law school operates on a traditional semester basis. Courses for full-time students are offered both day and evening and must be completed within 6 years. For part-time students, courses are offered both day and evening and must be completed within 6 years. New full- and part-time students are admitted in the fall. There is a 7-week summer session. Transferable summer courses are offered.

Programs

Students may take relevant courses in other programs and apply credit toward the J.D.; a maximum of 14 semester hours credits may be applied. The following joint degrees may be earned: J.D./M.A. (Juris Doctor/Master of Arts in Philosophy), J.D./ M.B.A. (Juris Doctor/Master of Business Administration), J.D./M.B.A. (Juris Doctor/Master of Business Administration/ Master of Health Administration), J.D./ M.C.R.P. (Juris Doctor/Master of City and Regional Planning), J.D./M.S.H.A. (Juris Doctor/Master of Health Administration), and J.D./M.P.A. (Juris Doctor/Master of Public Administration).

Required
To earn the J.D., candidates must complete 90 total credits, of which 43 are for required courses. They must maintain a minimum GPA of 2.2 in the required courses. The following first-year courses

GEORGIA

Phone: 404-413-9200
Fax: 404-413-9203
E-mail: cjgeorge@gsu.edu
Web: www.law.gsu.edu

Contact

Director of Admissions, 404-413-9004 for general inquiries; Louis Scott, Director of Financial Aid, 404-413-2137 for financial aid information.

are required of all students: Civil Procedure I and II, Contracts I and II, Criminal Law, Legal Bibliography, Property I and II, Research Writing and Advocacy I and II, and Torts I and II. Required upper-level courses consist of Constitutional Law, Evidence, Litigation, and Professional Responsibility. The required orientation program for first-year students occurs the week before classes begin in August. It is designed to familiarize students with some of the first-year required courses, college personnel, facilities, and procedures.

Electives

The College of Law offers concentrations in corporate law, criminal law, environmental law, family law, international law, labor law, litigation, sports law, tax law, torts and insurance, and health law. In addition, second- and third-year students may enroll in the Tax Clinic and the Center for Law, and Health and Society's Health Law Partnership (HeLP) Clinic. Students in the Tax Clinic assist individual clients in preparing their cases for presentation before the Small Claims Division of the U.S. Tax Court and the Administrative Appeals Office of the Internal Revenue Service. Students in the HeLP Clinic have opportunities to work on cases related to children's health and welfare. Seminars are offered to students who have completed the prerequisites. Internships include working for local district attorneys, solicitors, and defenders; clerking for county, state, and federal judges; and placement in a variety of other governmental or public interest organizations. Independent research may be selected by third-year students upon approval by a faculty adviser and the administration. Field work includes pro bono work. Special lecture series include the Henry J. Miller Distinguished Lecture Series. The College of Law offers 2 study-abroad programs. Law students can participate in the Summer Academy for International Commercial Arbitration conducted in Europe, which includes visits to arbitral institutions in Vienna, Budapest, Prague, and Venice. Law and graduate students may also participate in "The Urban Environment: Law, Policy and Culture-The Rio Experience." The administration offers an academic enrichment program for students who need or desire additional help in required courses. Minority and special interest programs are usually sponsored by student organizations and/or faculty

members. The most widely taken electives are Basic Tax; Wills, Trusts, and Estates; and Criminal Procedure.

Graduation Requirements

In order to graduate, candidates must have a GPA of 2.2 and complete the upper-division writing requirement.

Organizations

The primary law review is the *Georgia State University Law Review*. Students edit *The Docket*, *The Black Letter Law*, and *The Federalist*. The Moot Court Society competes 7 or 8 times a year. Other competitions include the National Moot Court Competition, sponsored by the Association of the Bar of New York City; National Appellate Advocacy Competition, sponsored by the ABA; William W. Daniel Mock Trial Invitational; and Lone Star Classic Mock Trial Competition. Student organizations include the Student Trial Lawyers Association, Intellectual Property Law Society, and Hispanic Students Bar Association. Local chapters of national associations include the Association of Women Law Students, Black Law Students Association, Environmental Law Society, and Student Health Lawyers Association. Other groups include Delta Theta Phi, Phi Alpha Delta, and Phi Delta Phi law fraternities.

Library

The law library contains 141,748 hardcopy volumes and 190,423 microform volume equivalents, and subscribes to 1,212 serial publications. Online databases and networks include CALI, CIS Universe, Legal-Trac, LEXIS, OCLC First Search, WESTLAW, and Wilsonline Indexes. HeinOnline, Galileo, BNA, Making of Modern Law, Juris, and Oxford are also available to law students for research. Special library collections include Georgia Law, Health Law, as well as a large electronic database. The ratio of library volumes to faculty is 1,162 to 1 and to students is 209 to 1. The ratio of seats in the library to students is 1 to 2.

Faculty

The law school has 107 full-time and 71 faculty members, of whom 56 are women. According to AAUP standards for Category I institutions, faculty salaries are below

Placement

J.D.s awarded:	186

Services available through: a separate law school placement center.

Services: programming and counseling on career options for lawyers, and participating in national and regional job fairs.

Special features: state-of-the-art Internet-based job listings service for students and alumni, personalized, one-on-one job search planning sessions for first-year, second-year, and third-year students in addition to alumni transitioning into other practice areas and legal-related or alternative careers.

Full-time job interviews:	17 employers
Summer job interviews:	60 employers
Placement within 9 months of graduation:	93% of class
Average starting salary:	$38,000 to $160,000

Areas of placement:

Private practice 2–10 attorneys	23%
Private practice 11–25 attorneys	8%
Private practice 26–50 attorneys	3%
Private practice 51–100 attorneys	2%
Private practice over 100 attorneys	17%
Business/industry	18%
Government	8%
Public interest	6%
Judicial clerkships	4%
Academic	4%
Military	2%

average. About 30% of full-time faculty have a graduate law degree in addition to the J.D.; about 10% of part-time faculty have one. The ratio of full-time students to full-time faculty in an average class is 10 to 1; in a clinic, 11 to 1. The law school has a regular program of bringing visiting professors and other distinguished lecturers and visitors to campus.

Students

About 45% of the student body are women; 21%, minorities; 7%, African American; 5%, Asian American; 1%, Hispanic; and 7%, students may select multiracial as an ethnic classification. The majority of students come from Georgia (87%). The average age of entering students is 27; age range is 21 to 55. About 55% of students enter directly from undergraduate school, 10% have a graduate degree, and 30% have worked full-time prior to entering law school. About 11% drop out after the first year for academic or personal reasons; 89% remain to receive a law degree.

536 Mission Street
San Francisco, CA 94105-2968

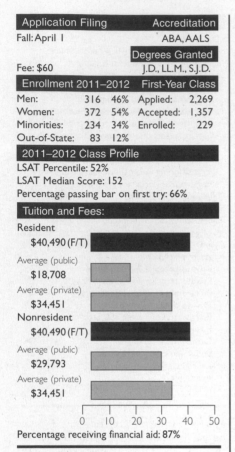

Application Filing	Accreditation
Fall: April 1	ABA, AALS
	Degrees Granted
Fee: $60	J.D., LL.M., S.J.D.

Enrollment 2011–2012			First-Year Class	
Men:	316	46%	Applied:	2,269
Women:	372	54%	Accepted:	1,357
Minorities:	234	34%	Enrolled:	229
Out-of-State:	83	12%		

2011–2012 Class Profile
LSAT Percentile: 52%
LSAT Median Score: 152
Percentage passing bar on first try: 66%

Tuition and Fees:

Resident
$40,490 (F/T)

Average (public)
$18,708

Average (private)
$34,451

Nonresident
$40,490 (F/T)

Average (public)
$29,793

Average (private)
$34,451

0 10 20 30 40 50

Percentage receiving financial aid: 87%

ADMISSIONS
In the fall of 2011 first-year class, 2269 applied, 1357 were accepted, and 229 enrolled. Four transfers enrolled. The median LSAT percentile of the most recent first-year class was 52; the median GPA was 3.0 on a scale of 4.0. The lowest LSAT percentile accepted was 12; the highest was 92.

Requirements
Applicants must have a bachelor's degree and take the LSAT. The most important admission factors include academic achievement, LSAT results, and life experience. No specific undergraduate courses are required. Candidates are not interviewed.

Procedure
The application deadline for fall entry is April 1. Applicants should submit an application form, LSAT results, transcripts, a personal statement, TOEFL results (for non-English speakers), a nonrefundable application fee of $60, 2 letters of recommendation, and a resume. Notification of the admissions decision is 6 to 8 weeks after the application. The law school uses the LSAC.

Special
The law school recruits minority and disadvantaged students by targeting recruiting to underrepresented communities, supporting the CLEO program and the law school's diversity scholarship program, and participating in LSAC-sponsored minority programs. Requirements are different for out-of-state students. Transfer students must have one year of credit, must have attended an ABA-approved law school, must have a personal statement, and must submit their prior law school transcript.

Costs
Tuition and fees for the 2011–2012 academic year are $40,200 for all full-time students. Tuition for part-time students is $30,820 for in-state students and $30,820 out-of-state. On-campus room and board costs about $14,850 annually; books and supplies run $1,400.

Financial Aid
About 87% of current law students receive some form of aid. The average annual amount of aid from all sources combined, including scholarships, loans, and work contracts, is $54,000; maximum, $66,349. Awards are based on need and merit combined. Required financial statements are the FAFSA and institutional form. The aid application deadline for fall entry is rolling. Special funds for minority or disadvantaged students include a scholarship fund reserved for minority students or those from disadvantaged backgrounds. First-year students are notified about their financial aid application at time of acceptance.

About the Law School
Golden Gate University School of Law was established in 1901 and is a private institution. The campus is in an urban area in the legal and financial district in downtown San Francisco. The primary mission of the law school is to provide students with the intellectual and moral foundation that will enable them to become ethical, competent, and socially responsible professionals in a complex and interrelated legal world. Students have access to federal, state, county, city, and local agencies, courts, correctional facilities, law firms, and legal aid organizations in the San Francisco area. Many internships, externships, and other clinical programs take advantage of government offices, courts, and law firms in the city. Housing for students is not available on campus, but the housing office helps students find accommodations off campus. All law school facilities are accessible to the physically disabled.

Calendar
The law school operates on a traditional semester basis. Courses for full-time students are offered both day and evening, and must be completed within 3 years (84 months maximum). For part-time students, courses are offered evenings only and must be completed within 4 years (84 months maximum). New full- and part-time students are admitted in the fall. There is a 7-week summer session. Transferable summer courses are offered.

Programs
In addition to the J.D., the law school offers the LL.M. and S.J.D. The following joint degrees may be earned: J.D./Ph.D. (Juris Doctor/Doctor of Philosophy in Clinical Psychology) and J.D./M.B.A. (Juris Doctor/Master of Business Administration).

Required
To earn the J.D., candidates must complete 88 total credits, of which 57 are for required courses. They must maintain a minimum GPA of 2.2 in the required courses. The following first-year courses are required of all students: Civil Procedure I and II, Contracts I and II, Criminal Law, Lawyering Elective, Property, Torts, and Writing Research I and II. Required upper-level courses consist of Appellate Advocacy, Constitutional Law I and II, Criminal Procedure I, Evidence, and Professional Responsibility. Students are encouraged to enroll in any of the many clinics. The required orientation program for first-year students is a 4-day program held before classes begin.

Phone: 415-442-6630
800-GGU-4YOU
E-mail: lawadmit@ggu.edu
Web: www.ggu.edu/law

Contact

Admissions Office, 415-442-6630 for general inquiries; Director of Financial Aid, 415-442-6635 for financial aid information.

Electives

The School of Law offers concentrations in corporate law, criminal law, environmental law, family law, intellectual property law, international law, juvenile law, labor law, litigation, tax law, real estate law, and public interest law. In addition, the school offers 2 on-site clinics and 10 field placement clinics. Clinics include Environmental Law and Justice, Women's Employment Rights, Civil Practice, and Public Interest/Government. Seminars are worth 2 credits, and prerequisites vary. Topics include Asian Pacific Trade, Social Justice, Domestic Violence, and Settlement of Litigation Disputes. Full- and part-time internships with law firms, government agencies, and judges are offered. There is also an Honors Lawyering Program through which students spend 2 semesters working as legal apprentices. Students may pursue independent research under the direction of faculty members. Courses are offered in Advanced Legal Research, Solving Legal Problems, and Tax Research. Special lecture series are offered annually. Summer study abroad is possible in Paris, France. An Academic Success Program develops skills and legal analysis and exam writing. Elective and required courses are offered in legal analysis, legal methods, and legal reasoning; special problems courses are offered in substantive areas of law. There is a diversity scholarship program, specialized course offerings, and certificates of specialization. The most widely taken electives are Tax, Remedies, and Intellectual Property.

Graduation Requirements

In order to graduate, candidates must have a GPA of 2.2 and must have completed the upper-division writing requirement.

Organizations

Students edit the *Golden Gate University Law Review, Annual Survey of International and Comparative Law,* and *Environmental Law Journal.* Teams attend various national and international contests, including the Jessup International Moot Court Competition, Environmental Law Moot Court, and Intellectual Property Moot Court. Other competitions attended are the National Mock Trial Competition, Association of Trial Lawyers of America Competition, and the ABA's Criminal Justice Trial Competition. Law student organizations, local chapters of national associations, and campus clubs and organizations include Student Bar Association, Queer Law Student Association, Asian Pacific American Law Student Association, Latino American Law Student Association, Black Law Students Association, National Lawyers Guild, Phi Delta Phi, Federalist Society, Public Interest Law Foundation, Environmental Law Society, and International Law Society.

Library

The law library contains 392,711 hardcopy volumes and 247,778 microform volume equivalents, and subscribes to 3,626 serial publications. Such online databases and networks as CALI, Infotrac, Legal-Trac, LEXIS, WESTLAW, ProQuests Legislative Insight, HeinOnline, Intelliconnect, and CEB Onlaw are available to law students for research. Special library collections include a depository for both California and federal documents, digital commons, and the Jesse Carter Collection. Its collections emphasize taxation, real estate, land use, and individual rights. The ratio of library volumes to faculty is 10,070 to 1 and to students is 688 to 1. The ratio of seats in the library to students is 1 to 1.

Faculty

The law school has 39 full-time and 128 part-time faculty members, of whom 74 are women. About 10% of full-time faculty have a graduate law degree in addition to the J.D.; about 7% of part-time faculty have one. The ratio of full-time students to full-time faculty in an average class is 15 to 1; in a clinic, 6 to 1. The law school has a regular program of bringing visiting professors and other distinguished lecturers and visitors to campus.

Students

About 54% of the student body are women; 34%, minorities; 18%, Asian American; 1%, Hispanic; and 12%, other. The majority of students come from California (88%). The average age of entering students is 27; age range is 20 to 60. About 40% of students have worked full-time prior to entering law school. About 12% drop out after the first year for academic or personal reasons; 76% remain to receive a law degree.

Placement

J.D.s awarded:	192

Services available through: a separate law school placement center.

Services: encourage private firms and public agencies to list job opportunities and solicit on-campus interviews.

Special features: Law Career Services provides individualized attention from four career advisors who are former attorneys. Close collaboration with the school's externships, clinics, and Honors Lawyering Program helps students to integrate practical experience into the curriculum.

Full-time job interviews:	10 employers
Summer job interviews:	16 employers
Placement within 9 months of graduation:	77% of class
Average starting salary:	$35,000 to $100,000

Areas of placement:

Private practice 2–10 attorneys	30%
Private practice 11–25 attorneys	3%
Private practice 26–50 attorneys	2%
Private practice 51–100 attorneys	2%
Business/industry	21%
Government	17%
Academic	14%
Public interest	4%
Judicial clerkships	1%

GONZAGA UNIVERSITY

School of Law

Box 3528
Spokane, WA 99220-3528

Application Filing	Accreditation
Fall: April 15	ABA, AALS

	Degrees Granted
Fee: $50	J.D.

Enrollment 2011–2012			First-Year Class	
Men:	288	57%	Applied:	1,389
Women:	218	43%	Accepted:	739
Minorities:	56	11%	Enrolled:	176

2011–2012 Class Profile
LSAT Median Score: 155
Percentage passing bar on first try: 77%

Tuition and Fees:

Resident
$34,105 (F/T)

Average (public)
$18,708

Average (private)
$34,451

Nonresident
$34,105 (F/T)

Average (public)
$29,793

Average (private)
$34,451

0   10   20   30   40   50

Percentage receiving financial aid: 96%

ADMISSIONS
In the fall of 2011 first-year class, 1389 applied, 739 were accepted, and 176 enrolled. Seven transfers enrolled. The median GPA of the most recent first-year class was 3.3.

Requirements
Applicants must have a bachelor's degree and take the LSAT. The most important admission factors include academic achievement, letter of recommendation, and general background. No specific undergraduate courses are required and candidates are not interviewed.

Procedure
The application deadline for fall entry is April 15. Applicants should submit an application form, LSAT results, transcripts, TOEFL (for international applicants), nonrefundable application fee of $50, 2 letters of recommendation, a resume, LSAC report, and personal statement. Notification of the admissions decision is after January 1. The law school uses the LSAC.

Special
The law school recruits minority and disadvantaged students by means of targeted mailings, online chat rooms, law school forums and fairs, alumni referrals, pre-law advisors, open houses, and campus visits. A recent law school graduate was hired full-time to focus on minority recruiting. Requirements are different for out-of-state students. Transfer students must have one year of credit, and attended an ABA-approved law school. Transfer students are accepted on a space available basis, and must be in good standing and eligible to return to their previous law school.

Costs
Tuition and fees for the 2011–2012 academic year are $33,960 for all full-time students. Books and supplies run $1,000.

Financial Aid
About 96% of current law students receive some form of aid. The average annual amount of aid from all sources combined, including scholarships, loans, and work contracts, is $45,230; maximum, $47,162. Awards are based on need and merit combined. Required financial statement is the FAFSA. The aid application deadline for fall entry is February 1. Special funds for minority or disadvantaged students include scholarships. First-year students are notified about their financial aid application within 1 month of acceptance if FAFSA is complete.

About the Law School
Gonzaga University School of Law was established in 1912 and is a private institution. The 94-acre campus is located in an urban area 1 mile from downtown Spokane. The mission of the law school is to preserve and develop a humanistic, Catholic, and Jesuit legal education. Students have access to federal, state, county, city, and local agencies, courts, correctional facilities, law firms, and legal aid organizations in the Spokane area. Facilities of special interest to law students include the Chastek Law Library, the Foley Library Center, computer labs, the Rudolf fitness center, and the McCarthy Arena. Students have university housing and private apartments, often within a 10-block radius of the law school. About 90% of the law

school facilities are accessible to the physically disabled.

Calendar
The law school operates on a traditional semester basis. Courses for full-time students are offered both day and evening. Not all classes are available in the evening. Courses must be completed within 5 years. There is no part-time program. New full-time students are admitted in the fall. There is a 10-week summer session. Transferable summer courses are offered.

Programs
Students may take relevant courses in other programs and apply credit toward the J.D.; a maximum of 6 credits may be applied. The following joint degrees may be earned: J.D./M.S.W. (Juris Doctor/ Master of Social Work), J.D./M.Acc. (Juris Doctor/Master of Accounting), and J.D./M.B.A. (Juris Doctor/Master of Business Administration).

Required
To earn the J.D., candidates must complete 90 total credits, of which 49 are for required courses. They must maintain a minimum GPA of 2.2 in the required courses. The following first-year courses are required of all students: Civil Procedure, Contracts, Criminal Law, Legal Research and Writing I and II, Litigation Skills and Professional Lab, Perspectives on the Law, Property, Torts, and Transactional Skills and Professionalism Lab. Required upper-level courses consist of a public service requirement, experiential learning requirement, Constitutional Law (civil liberties), Constitutional Law (government structure), Evidence, Legal Writing and Research III and IV, and Professional Responsibility. All students must take clinical courses. The required orientation program for first-year students consists of 3 days of introduction to the legal system, introduction to the law, and information regarding Gonzaga.

Electives
Upper-level students must participate in either in-house or outplacement clinics. Various upper-level seminars are offered, including those on International Human Rights, Ethical Problems in the

Phone: 509-313-5532
800-793-1710
Fax: 509-313-3697
E-mail: *admissions@lawschool.gonzaga.edu*
Web: *http://www.law.gonzaga.edu*

Contact
Susan Lee, Director of Admissions, 509-313-5532 or 800-793-1710 for general inquiries; Joan Henning, Coordinator of Financial Services, 509-313-3859 for financial aid information.

WASHINGTON

Representation of Children, and Employment Discrimination. Internships are available when 60 credits have been completed. Directed research programs must be supervised by a faculty member. Special lecture series include the William O. Douglass Lecture, Paul and Lita Luvera Lecture, International Law Symposium, and Quackenbush Lecture. There is a summer law program in Florence, Italy, and China. The Academic Resource Program provides tutorial assistance to participating first-year students. The Student Bar Association sponsors group tutorials for all first-year courses. Minority programs are sponsored by the Multicultural Law Caucus, Black Law Students Association, Hispanic Law Caucus, Sexual Orientation Diversity Alliance. Indian Law Caucus, and Asian Pacific Islander Law Caucus. Special interest group programs include the Public Interest Law Project, Street Law, Property Law Interest Group, and Criminal Defense Law Caucus. The most widely taken electives are Criminal Procedure, Wills and Trusts, and Business Associations.

Graduation Requirements
In order to graduate, candidates must have a GPA of 2.2, complete the upper-division writing requirement, and 90 credit hours and 30 hours of public service.

Organizations
Students edit the *Gonzaga Law Review, Gonzaga Journal of International Law,* a journal specializing in international law, business, political, and socioeconomic issues and the student newspaper, *The Advocate.* Moot court competitions include the National Appellate Advocacy, Jessup Cup, and National Moot Court. Teams also take part in the Negotiation, National Trial, Client Counseling, Tax, Saul Lefkowitz, and Giles Rich Patent competitions. Law student organizations, local chapters of national associations, and campus organizations include the Women's Law Caucus, International Law Society, Multicultural Law Caucus, Student Bar Association, Gonzaga Public Interest Law Project, Environmental Law Caucus, Phi Alpha Delta, and Alpha Sigma Nu, ACLU, and National Native American Law Students Association.

Library
The law library contains 168,533 hardcopy volumes and 141,730 microform volume equivalents, and subscribes to 2,173 serial publications. Online databases and networks include CALI, CIS Universe, Legal-Trac, LEXIS, OCLC First Search, WESTLAW, Wilsonline Indexes, as well as other online databases, which are available to law students for research. Special library collections include ABA Archives; American Indian Selected Publications; Canon Law Materials; Federal Legislative Histories; Hein's American Law Institution Publications; Hein's Legal Thesis and Dissertations; Karol Llewellyn Papers; Scrapbooks of the Honorable Richard Guy; selected Nineteenth Century treatises; Washington Supreme Court and Court of Appeal briefs; Federal Depository Library. The ratio of library volumes to faculty is 5,437 to 1 and to students is 334 to 1. The ratio of seats in the library to students is 1 to 1.

Faculty
The law school has 32 full-time and 27 part-time faculty members, of whom 23 are women. The ratio of full-time students to full-time faculty in an average class is 15 to 1; in a clinic, 6 to 1.

Students
About 43% of the student body are women; 11%, minorities; 1%, Asian American; 2%, Hispanic; 1%, Native American; and 3%, Unknown. The average age of entering students is 26; age range is 20 to 58. About 10% drop out after the first year for academic or personal reasons; 90% remain to receive a law degree.

Placement

J.D.s awarded:	160

Services available through: a separate law school placement center.
Services: on-campus interviews, workshops, Resource Library, Spring Career Fest, consortium, and Public Interest Career Fest.
Special features: counseling on employment and mock interviews, cover letter and resume review, presentations and workshops on areas of practice, and graduate/alumni networking events in other cities.

Full-time job interviews:	10 employers
Summer job interviews:	28 employers
Placement within 9 months of graduation:	90% of class
Average starting salary:	$62,000 to $70,000

Areas of placement:

Private practice 2–10 attorneys	24%
Private practice 11–25 attorneys	6%
Private practice 26–50 attorneys	1%
Private practice 51–100 attorneys	1%
Private practice-size unknown	16%
Business/industry	18%
Judicial clerkships	15%
Public interest	7%
Government	6%
Military	3%
Academic	2%

HAMLINE UNIVERSITY
School of Law

1536 Hewitt Avenue
St. Paul, MN 55104-1284

Application Filing	Accreditation
Fall: April 1	ABA, AALS

Degrees Granted	
Fee: $35	J.D., LL.M.

Enrollment 2011–2012		First-Year Class	
Men:	281 46%	Applied:	1,286
Women:	336 55%	Accepted:	745
Minorities:	74 12%	Enrolled:	205
Out-of-State:	62 10%		

2011–2012 Class Profile
LSAT Percentile: 56%
LSAT Median Score: 153
Percentage passing bar on first try: 85%

Tuition and Fees:

Resident
$34,555 (F/T)

Average (public)
$18,708

Average (private)
$34,451

Nonresident
$34,555 (F/T)

Average (public)
$29,793

Average (private)
$34,451

0   10   20   30   40   50

Percentage receiving financial aid: 96%

ADMISSIONS
In the fall of 2011 first-year class, 1286 applied, 745 were accepted, and 205 enrolled. Three transfers enrolled. The median LSAT percentile of the most recent first-year class was 56; the median GPA was 3.4 on a scale of 4.0. The lowest LSAT percentile accepted was 18; the highest was 99.

Requirements
Applicants must have a bachelor's degree and take the LSAT. No specific undergraduate courses are required. Candidates are not interviewed.

Procedure
The application deadline for fall entry is April 1. Applicants should submit an application form, LSAT results, transcripts, a personal statement, a non-refundable application fee of $35, and 2 letters of recommendation. Notification of the admissions decision is 2 to 6 weeks after the file is completed. The law school uses the LSAC.

Special
The law school recruits minority and disadvantaged students through strategic recruitment, diversity scholarships, and an admissions recruitment program geared specifically for minority students. The school also participates in CLEO. Requirements are different for out-of-state students. Transfer students must have one year of credit, must have attended an ABA-approved law school, must submit a personal statement, and must submit a letter of good standing and a transcript from the previous institution.

Costs
Tuition and fees for the 2011–2012 academic year are $34,485 for all full-time students. Tuition for part-time students is $24,970 for in-state students and $24,970 out-of-state. On-campus room and board costs about $10,551 annually; books and supplies run $2,000.

Financial Aid
About 96% of current law students receive some form of aid. The average annual amount of aid from all sources combined, including scholarships, loans, and work contracts, is $45,782; maximum, $55,239. Awards are based on need and merit combined. The required financial statement is the FAFSA. The aid application deadline for fall entry is open. Special funds for minority or disadvantaged students include the equivalent of 9 full-tuition scholarships. First-year students are notified about their financial aid application at time of acceptance.

About the Law School
Hamline University School of Law was established in 1972 and is a private institution. The 50-acre campus is in an urban area located between St. Paul and Minneapolis. The primary mission of the law school is to educate students to apply legal knowledge with disciplined imagination, a global perspective, and creative conflict resolution skills. Students have access to federal, state, county, city, and local agencies, courts, correctional facilities, law firms, and legal aid organizations in the St. Paul area. The state capital is minutes away from the campus. Facilities of special interest to law students include an expanded Law Center. The library addition provides increased study

space and the entire building has wireless Internet access. The law building is in the middle of campus with easy access to dining, athletic, and extracurricular facilities. Housing for students is readily available, both on and off campus. On campus, there is apartment-style housing, as well as dorm space. All law school facilities are accessible to the physically disabled.

Calendar
The law school operates on a traditional semester basis. Courses for full-time students are offered both day and evenings, and must be completed within 7 years. For part-time students, courses are offered on weekends, and must be completed within 7 years. New full- and part-time students are admitted in the fall. There is an 8-week summer session. Transferable summer courses are offered.

Programs
In addition to the J.D., the law school offers the LL.M. Students may take relevant courses in other programs and apply credit toward the J.D.; a maximum of 12 credits may be applied. The following joint degrees may be earned: J.D./M.A.P.A. (Juris Doctor/ Master of Arts in Public Administration), J.D./M.A.N.M. (Juris Doctor/Master of Arts in Nonprofit Management), J.D./M.A.O.L. (Juris Doctor/ Master of Arts in Organizational Leadership), J.D./M.B.A. (Juris Doctor/Master of Business Administration), and J.D./M.F.A. (Juris Doctor/Master of Fine Arts in Creative Writing).

Required
To earn the J.D., candidates must complete 88 total credits, of which 36 are for required courses. They must maintain a minimum GPA of 2.0 in the required courses. The following first-year courses are required of all students: Civil Procedure I and II, Constitutional Law I, Contracts I and II, Criminal Law, International Law, Legal Research and Writing I and II, Practice Problem Solving & Professionalism, Property, and Torts I. Required upper-level courses consist of a seminar course, a skills course, Legal Research & Writing III, and Professional Responsibility. Students must take a skills course, and clinics are one way to meet requirement. The required orientation program for first-year students is 2 days, and

Phone: 651-523-2461
800-388-3688
Fax: 651-523-3064
E-mail: *lawadm@gw.hamline.edu*
Web: *web.hamline.edu/law*

consists of an introduction to the school, campus, and legal studies and professional responsibility.

Electives
The School of Law offers concentrations in corporate law, criminal law, international law, juvenile law, labor law, litigation, alternative dispute resolution, commercial law, government and regulatory affairs, health law, intellectual property, and social justice. In addition, 3- or 4-credit clinics provide upper-level students with practical experience in such areas as child advocacy, immigration law, public interest law, unemployment compensation law, alternative dispute resolution, trial practice, and education law. In seminars, 15 upper-level students per semester engage in an in-depth study of a selected topic for 3 credits. Internships for 3 to 12 credits offer upper-level students the opportunity to work with expert practitioners in various types of legal practice. Upper-level students may be research assistants for professors. Credit is given only if research assistance is structured as an independent study. Special lectures are open to the school community and to the public. Credit is not given. Opportunities for study abroad consist of summer programs at the University of Bergen (Norway), Queen Mary University of London (England), Central European University (Budapest, Hungary), and January term programs at Hebrew University (Jerusalem) and Puerto Rico. The Academic Success Program, which includes help with legal writing and substantive review of courses, is offered to students who need remedial assistance. Offerings include special scholarship programs and student organizations for minority students coordinated by the Assistant Dean for Student and Multicultural Affairs. A variety of student organizations exists to fit every interest. The most widely taken electives are Corporations, Evidence, and Criminal Procedure.

Graduation Requirements
In order to graduate, candidates must have a GPA of 2.0, must have completed the upper-division writing requirement,

Contact
Office of Admissions, 651-523-2461 or 800-388-3688 for general inquiries; Lynette Wahl, Associate Director of Financial Aid, 651-523-2280 for financial aid information.

and must have taken Professional Responsibility, a seminar, and a skills course.

Organizations
Students edit the *Hamline Law Review*, the *Hamline Journal of Public Law and Policy*, and the *Journal of Law and Religion*. There are many moot court competitions, including National Moot Court, Frederick Douglass, and Rich Intellectual Property Competition. Other competitions include Client Counseling and Negotiation. Law student organizations, local chapters of national organizations, and campus organizations include the Student Bar Association, Women's Legal Caucus, Multicultural Law Students Association, Delta Theta Phi, Phi Alpha Delta, ABA-Law School Division, Minnesota Justice Foundation, International Society, and Center for International Students.

Library
The law library contains 461,277 hardcopy volumes and 134,104 microform volume equivalents, and subscribes to 902 serial publications. Such online databases and networks as CALI, CIS Universe, DIALOG, Infotrac, Legal-Trac, LEXIS, OCLC First Search, WESTLAW, and Wilsonline Indexes, are available to law students for research. Special library collections include a U.S. government selective depository collection, Law & Popular Culture, and the David Coben Slavery Collection. The ratio of library volumes to faculty is 3,661 to 1 and to students is 748 to 1. The ratio of seats in the library to students is 1 to 2.

Faculty
The law school has 43 full-time and 83 part-time faculty members, of whom 57 are women. According to AAUP standards for Category 11A institutions, faculty salaries are above average. About 42% of full-time faculty have a graduate law degree in addition to the J.D. The ratio of full-time students to full-time faculty in an average class is 28 to 1; in a clinic, 6 to 1. The law school has a regular program of bringing visiting professors and other distinguished lecturers and visitors to campus.

MINNESOTA

Placement

J.D.s awarded:	177

Services available through: a separate law school placement center.
Special features: HU Slink Mentor Program, comprehensive IL orientation, and 1:1 3L transition interviews.

Full-time job interviews:	31 employers
Summer job interviews:	43 employers
Placement within 9 months of graduation:	93% of class
Average starting salary:	$36,500 to $240,000

Areas of placement:

Private practice 2–10 attorneys	28%
Private practice 11–25 attorneys	2%
Private practice 26–50 attorneys	1%
Private practice 51–100 attorneys	5%
Business/industry	27%
Judicial clerkships	15%
Government	8%
Public interest	7%
Private practice solo	5%
Military	1%
Academic	1%

Students
About 55% of the student body are women; 12%, minorities; 3%, African American; 4%, Asian American; 4%, Hispanic; and 1%, Native American. The majority of students come from Minnesota (90%). The average age of entering students is 27; age range is 21 to 63. About 11% of students have a graduate degree. About 14% drop out after the first year for academic or personal reasons; 86% remain to receive a law degree.

Harvard Law School

Cambridge, MA 02138

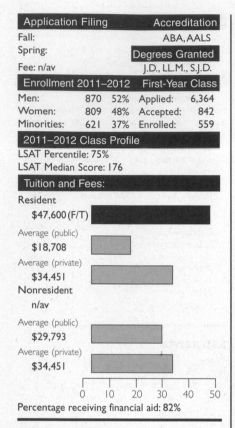

Application Filing		Accreditation	
Fall:		ABA, AALS	
Spring:		**Degrees Granted**	
Fee: n/av		J.D., LL.M., S.J.D.	
Enrollment 2011–2012		**First-Year Class**	
Men:	870 52%	Applied:	6,364
Women:	809 48%	Accepted:	842
Minorities:	621 37%	Enrolled:	559
2011–2012 Class Profile			
LSAT Percentile: 75%			
LSAT Median Score: 176			

Tuition and Fees:

Resident
$47,600 (F/T)

Average (public)
$18,708

Average (private)
$34,451

Nonresident
n/av

Average (public)
$29,793

Average (private)
$34,451

0   10   20   30   40   50

Percentage receiving financial aid: 82%

ADMISSIONS

In the fall of 2011 first-year class, 6364 applied, 842 were accepted, and 559 enrolled. Thirty transfers enrolled.

Requirements

Applicants must have a bachelor's degree and take the LSAT. No specific undergraduate courses are required. Candidates are not interviewed.

Procedure

Applicants should submit an application form, LSAT results, transcripts, and 2 letters of recommendation, and students are urged to visit the school. A personal statement and a college certification form are required as well. Accepted students must make a deposit of $500. Notification of the admissions decision is on a rolling basis. The law school uses the LSAC.

Special

The law school recruits minority and disadvantaged students by encouraging all who would like to study law at Harvard

to apply. Requirements are different for out-of-state students. Transfer students must have one year of credit, must have attended an ABA-approved law school, and must have outstanding records in college and in the first year of law school.

Costs

On-campus room and board costs about $19,050 annually; books and supplies run $1,175.

Financial Aid

About 82% of current law students receive some form of aid. The average annual amount of aid from all sources combined, including scholarships, loans, and work contracts, is $53,706. Awards are based on need. Required financial statements are the CSS Profile, the FAFSA, and Need Access. First-year students are notified about their financial aid application some time after admission.

About the Law School

Harvard University Harvard Law School was established in 1817 and is a private institution. The campus is in an urban area of Cambridge. The primary mission of the law school is to stress an understanding of the principles of law and a mastery of such skills as oral advocacy, research, and legal writing, and to educate lawyers to be capable of addressing legal problems in a changing society. Students have access to federal, state, county, city, and local agencies, courts, correctional facilities, law firms, and legal aid organizations in the Cambridge area. Facilities of special interest to law students include 20 buildings for classrooms, dormitories, student activities, libraries, Wasserstein Hall, and Caspersen Student Center, Clinical Wing (WCC). Housing for students consists of law school dormitories, Harvard-affiliated housing, and off-campus housing. There is housing for single and married students. All law school facilities are accessible to the physically disabled.

Calendar

The law school operates on a traditional semester basis. Courses are offered days only, and must be completed within 3 years. New students are admitted in the fall. There is no summer session. Transferable summer courses are not offered.

Programs

In addition to the J.D., the law school offers the LL.M. and S.J.D. Students may take relevant courses in other programs and apply credit toward the J.D.; a maximum of 10 credits through cross credits may be applied. The following joint degrees may be earned: J.D./M.A. (Juris Doctor/Master of Arts), J.D./M.A.L.D. (Juris Doctor/Master of Arts in Law and Diplomacy with Tufts), J.D./M.B.A. (Juris Doctor/Master of Business Administration), J.D./LL.M. (Juris Doctor/Master of Laws with University of Cambridge, England), J.D./M.P.A. (Juris Doctor/Master of Public Administration), J.D./M.P.H (Juris Doctor/Master of Public Health), J.D./M.P.P. (Juris Doctor/Master of Public Policy), and J.D./Ph.D. (Juris Doctor/ Doctor of Philosophy).

Required

To earn the J.D., candidates must complete 82 total credits, of which 30 are for required courses. The following first-year courses are required of all students: an elective, Civil Procedure, Contracts, Criminal Law, Lawyering, Property, and Torts. Required upper-level courses consist of a professional responsibility requirement and a written work requirement. The required orientation program for first-year students lasts 2 days and is comprehensive.

Electives

The Law School has no formal program of offering concentrations in particular specialties. However, because the curriculum is so extensive, it allows for many different paths of study. Students are encouraged to discuss their plans with faculty members involved in relevant areas of study and are encouraged to take courses in a number of different fields, as well as in other parts of the university. The school offers a broad array of clinical opportunities to students. The Criminal Justice Institute is Harvard Law School's curriculum-based clinical program in criminal law. The Harvard Defenders is a student-operated organization dedicated to providing quality legal representation to people with low income in criminal show-cause hearings and welfare fraud. The Harvard Legal Aid Bureau is a student-run legal services office dedicated to providing legal assistance to low-income people and to

Phone: 617-495-3179
E-mail: *jdadmiss@law.harvard.edu*
Web: *law.harvard.edu*

Contact
Admissions Office, 617-495-3179.

MASSACHUSETTS

creating a clinical education environment in which its members learn from legal practice. The Harvard Mediation Program (HMP) works to resolve disputes both in and out of the courts in the Boston area. Students can participate also in a wide variety of externships for credit, including the Harvard Immigration and Refugee Clinic, Office of Attorney General, U.S. and District Attorneys offices as well as numerous government agencies and nonprofit organizations. More than 30 courses offer clinical field work experience and 2 others include simulated exercises. There are 75 seminars, including those on affirmative action, the federal budgetary process, and corporate theory. Internships are available for credit. Research programs may be conducted with Berkman Center for Internet & Society; Charles Hamilton Houston Institute for Race and Justice; Child Advocacy Program; East Asian Legal Studies Program; Environmental Law Program; Foundations of Private Law; Harvard Initiative on Law and Philosophy; HLS-Brookings Project on Law and Security; Project on Disability; Human Rights Program; Institute for Global Law and Policy; Islamic Legal Studies Program; John M. Olin Center: Law, Economics and Business; Labor and Worklife Program; Petrie Flow Center for Health Law Policy, Biotechnology and Bioethics; Program on Corporate Governance; Program on International Financial Systems; Program on Negotiation; Program on Legal Profession; Project on Law and Mind Sciences; and the Tax Law Program. Field work is available in business, civil and criminal, mediation, and environmental law. A number of courses provide students with field work in local courts and government agencies, and others provide instruction in aspects of legal practice through simulated casework and a problem-oriented approach. Special lecture series include the BSA Speaker Series, the DSAC Brown-Bag Lunch Discussion Series, East Asian Legal Studies Speaker Program, HLS Forum, Human Rights Program Speaker Series, and Introduction to the World of Law. The Saturday School, in an effort to increase dialogue between faculty and students, offers a series of informal lectures by individuals from diverse backgrounds and careers such as law professors, judges, former prison inmates, writers, artists, government and law enforcement officials, and health care providers. Law students

may propose a 1 semester course of study at a foreign institution. The most widely taken electives are Constitutional Law, Taxation, and Corporations.

Graduation Requirements
In order to graduate, candidates must have completed the upper-division writing requirement.

Organizations
Students edit the *Harvard Law Review, Blackletter Law Journal, Civil Rights-Civil Liberties Law Review, Human Rights Journal, Journal of Law and Public Policy, Journal of Law and Technology, Journal on Legislation, Journal of Law & Gender, International Law Journal, Environmental Law Review, Latino Law Review, Negotiation Law Review,* the student newspaper, the *Harvard Law Record,* and a yearbook. Moot court opportunities include the Ames Competition, which offers moot court competitions for first-year and upper-class students. The school also participates in interschool contests, including the Willston Legislative Drafting Competition and the Jessup International Law Moot Court Competition. Students may choose to participate in more than 90 student organizations and 17 publications.

Library
The law library contains 2,000,000 hardcopy volumes and 1,973,552 microform volume equivalents, and subscribes to 15,303 serial publications. Such online databases and networks as CALI, DIALOG, LEXIS, WESTLAW, Harvard Online Library Information System (HOLLIS), HeinOnline, CCH Research Network, Compustat, Index Master, LawMemo.com, LawTRIO, Lawyers Weekly USA, LLMC Digital, Mass. Social Law Library, Pike & Fischer, Quicklaw, and TRACfed are available to law students for research. Special library collections include a comprehensive collection of Anglo-American reports and treatises, and a special collection on international law as well as rare books and a 30,000-item art collection. The ratio of seats in the library to students is 1 to 2.

Faculty
The law school has 102 full-time and 150 part-time faculty members. According

Placement
Services available through: a separate law school placement center and separate Office of Public Interest Advising.
Services: on-campus interviews for first, second-, and third-year students.

Full-time job interviews:	800 employers
Placement by graduation:	96% of class
Placement within 9 months:	99% of class
Areas of placement:	
Private Practice	64%
Judicial clerkships	22%
Public interest	8%
Government	4%
Business/industry	3%
Academic	1%

to AAUP standards for Category I institutions, faculty salaries are well above average. The law school has a regular program of bringing visiting professors and other distinguished lecturers and visitors to campus.

Students
About 48% of the student body are women; 37% are minorities. The average age of entering students is 24; age range is 20 to 37. About 24% of students enter directly from undergraduate school, and 13% have a graduate degree. About 1% drop out after the first year for academic or personal reasons; 99% remain to receive a law degree.

Maurice A. Deane School of Law

121 Hofstra University
Hempstead, NY 11549

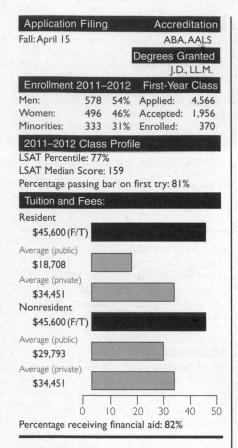

Application Filing	Accreditation
Fall: April 15	ABA, AALS

Degrees Granted
J.D., LL.M.

Enrollment 2011–2012			First-Year Class	
Men:	578	54%	Applied:	4,566
Women:	496	46%	Accepted:	1,956
Minorities:	333	31%	Enrolled:	370

2011–2012 Class Profile
LSAT Percentile: 77%
LSAT Median Score: 159
Percentage passing bar on first try: 81%

Tuition and Fees:

Resident
$45,600 (F/T)

Average (public)
$18,708

Average (private)
$34,451

Nonresident
$45,600 (F/T)

Average (public)
$29,793

Average (private)
$34,451

0 10 20 30 40 50

Percentage receiving financial aid: 82%

ADMISSIONS

In the fall of 2011 first-year class, 4566 applied, 1956 were accepted, and 370 enrolled. Twenty-six transfer students enrolled. The median LSAT percentile of the most recent first-year class was 77; the median GPA was 3.3 on a scale of 4.0. The lowest LSAT percentile accepted was 8; the highest was 99.

Requirements

Applicants must have a bachelor's degree and take the LSAT. The most important admission factors include general background, LSAT results, and academic achievement. No specific undergraduate courses are required and candidates are not interviewed.

Procedure

The application deadline for fall entry is April 15. Applicants should submit an application form, LSAT results, transcripts, and a personal statement. Notification of the admissions decision is on a rolling basis. The law school uses the LSAC.

Special

The law school recruits minority and disadvantaged students By means of student, faculty, graduate, and administrator visits to a diverse range of institutions to increase the number of law students from traditionally excluded groups. Scholarships are also available. Requirements are different for out-of-state students. Transfer students must have one year of credits, attended an ABA-approved law school, and a personal statement.

Costs

On-campus room and board costs about $16,946 annually; books and supplies run $1,400.

Financial Aid

About 82% of current law students receive some form of aid. The average annual amount of aid from all sources combined, including scholarships, loans, and work contracts, is $45,000; maximum, $69,000. Awards are based on need and merit combined. Required financial statements are the FAFSA and Need Access application. The aid application deadline for fall entry is April 1. First-year students are notified about their financial aid application at time of acceptance.

About the Law School

Hofstra University Maurice A. Deane School of Law was established in 1970 and is a private institution. The 240-acre campus is located in a suburban area 25 miles east of New York City. The mission of the law school is to prepare students for success in the practice of law by combining rigorous intellectual discussion with hands-on training in the skills required to excel in today's competitive legal environment. Students have access to federal, state, county, city, and local agencies, courts, correctional facilities, law firms, and legal aid organizations in the Hempstead area. Facilities of special interest to law students include the university library center, athletic facilities, cultural programs, and social events. Housing for students on and near campus in suite and apartment style residence halls. Many law students also rent houses or apartments within a short commuting distance from the university. All law school facilities are accessible to the physically disabled.

Calendar

The law school operates on a traditional semester basis. Courses for full-time students are offered days only and must be completed within 3 years. For part-time students, courses are offered days only and must be completed within 4 years. New full- and part-time students are admitted in the fall. There is a 7-week summer session. Transferable summer courses are offered.

Programs

In addition to the J.D., the law school offers the LL.M. Students may take relevant courses in other programs and apply credit toward the J.D.; a maximum of 9 credits may be applied. The following joint degrees may be earned: J.D./M.B.A. (Juris Doctor/ Master of Business Administration).

Required

To earn the J.D., candidates must complete 87 total credits, of which 42 are for required courses. The following first-year courses are required of all students: Civil Procedure I and II, Contracts I and II, Criminal Law, Introduction to Administrative Law, Legal Analysis, Writing & Research I and II, Property, Torts, and Transnational Law. Required upper-level courses consist of Constitutional Law I and II, Professional Responsibility course, Upper-class writing requirements I and II, and Upper-class skills requirement. The required orientation program for first-year students is a 3-day program that includes legal method classes taught by faculty members, general lectures, panels concerning student services, and social activities. "Continuing orientation" is available throughout the year.

Electives

The Maurice A. Deane School of Law offers concentrations in corporate law, criminal law, environmental law, family law, intellectual property law, international law, juvenile law, labor law, litigation, securities law, tax law, constitutional law, and health law. In addition, students may enroll in the Housing Rights, Criminal Justice, Child Advocacy, Mediation, Not-For-Profit Organizations, Securities Arbitration, or Political Asylum clinics. Upper-class students may choose from a large number of 2- to 3-credit seminars. First-year students take 1 required substantive course in a small section of 25 to 30 students. Students may enroll in the Externship Program, and

Phone: 516-463-5916
Fax: 516-463-6264
E-mail: *lawadmissions@hofstra.edu*
Web: *law.hofstra.edu*

Contact

John Chambers, Associate Dean for Enrollment Management, 516-463-5916 for general inquiries; Gerard Anderson, Director of Financial Aid, 516-463-5929 for financial aid information.

NEW YORK

work for judges or in nonprofit or government agencies, dealing with civil and criminal matters. Faculty-supervised independent study is also available. The law school offers special problems seminars, in which 3 to 5 students work closely with a professor in a tutorial setting on a topic of current interest. In addition, the law school offers an extensive Pro Bono Student Volunteer Program, in which more than 400 students have donated their efforts to assist attorneys and other agencies with cases. Through the Unemployment Action Center, students provide assistance to unemployed persons seeking benefits. A Visiting Scholar Program brings to the law school a distinguised scholar for a visit of 3 to 4 days; the visiting scholar teaches classes, gives a lecture, and meets informally with students and faculty. Annually scheduled lectures involve experts in bankruptcy law, family law, legal ethics, and health law, as well as features by distinguished jurists, scholars, and practitioners. The law school offers summer programs in Nice, France, in cooperation with the University of Nice Law School in Sydney, Australia in cooperation with the University of New South Wales Faculty of Law, and in Sorrento, Italy in conjunction with Naples University. A winter study abroad in Curacao is also available. Hofstra law students may also participate in a seminar abroad with any other E.A.C.L.E. institution. An exchange program with Soochow University (China) will also be available shortly. Students must meet with the Assistant Dean for Student Affairs with any request for student tutorial support services. Incoming students may be selected by the tutorial committee to participate in a voluntary enhancement program taught by faculty. The Director of Multicultural Student Affairs is responsible for minority student affairs, minority recruitment and admissions, the coordination of the law school's Enhancement Program and the coordination of the Dwight L. Greene Scholarship Program. Specific initiatives to support the students of color include: an Open House for minority applicants, Law Day for admitted students of color, a Minority Student Orientation Program for incoming students, a first-year reception, mentoring programs, and other programs throughout the year. Chapters of BALSA, LALSA, and APALSA are very active at the law school. The most widely taken electives are Business Organizations; Criminal Procedure; and Wills, Trusts and Estates.

Graduation Requirements

In order to graduate, candidates must have a GPA of 2.2, complete the upper-division writing requirement, as well as complete 2 upper-level writing requirements.

Organizations

Students edit the *Hofstra Law Review, Hofstra Labor and Employment Law Journal, Family Court Review, Journal of International Business and Law*, and the law school student newspaper, *Conscience*. Teams compete annually in the following national competitions; the National Moot Court Competition, the Robert F. Wagner, Jr. Labor & Employment Law Competition, the Conrad L. Duberstein Competition, and the Phillip Jessup International Law Competition. Students also participate in the Nassau County Bar Association's Long Island Moot Court Competition sponsored by the Nassau Academy of Law and also intramural competitions sponsored by the Hofstra Law School Moot Court Association. Law student organizations include the Corporate Law Society, Hofstra Law Women, and The International Law Society. There are local chapters of Asian-Pacific American Law Students Association, Black American Law Students Association, Latino American Law Students Association, and Phi Alpha Delta. Hofstra University supports more than 100 student cultural, media, sports, creative, service, and politically and socially active clubs.

Library

The law library contains 590,184 hardcopy volumes and 1,996,702 microform volume equivalents, and subscribes to 730 serial publications. Online databases and networks include CALI, CIS Universe, Infotrac, Legal-Trac, LEXIS, and WESTLAW. In addition, Wilsonline Indexes, Child Law Practice, AccessUN, ADRworld, CIAO, CILP, Legal Trac, LLMC, NLRB, RIA, Smart CLIP, Bloomberg BNA Core package, Tax & Accounting, CCH Health & Human Resources, and Kluwer Arbitration are other resources available to law students for research. Special library collections include Records and briefs of U.S. Supreme Court cases (1832 to the present) and of the New York Court of Appeals and Appellate Division; federal depository materials; and all U.N. documents (1976 to the present) on microfiche. Additional microfiche holdings are the ABA archival collection (1878 to

Placement

J.D.s awarded:	297

Services available through: a separate law school placement center

Special features: One-on-one videotaped interview skills training programs, resume and cover letter review, computerized employer databases, and professional success and leadership development programs.

Full-time job interviews:	16 employers
Summer job interviews:	21 employers
Placement within 9 months of graduation:	91% of class
Average starting salary:	$50,000 to $100,000

Areas of placement:

Private practice 2–10 attorneys	27%
Private practice 11–25 attorneys	6%
Private practice 26–50 attorneys	2%
Private practice 51–100 attorneys	2%
Business/industry	23%
Government	10%
Academic	9%
Public interest	5%
Judicial clerkships	2%

the present) and the archival collection of the American Law Institute. The ratio of library volumes to faculty is 10,593 to 1 and to students is 562 to 1. The ratio of seats in the library to students is 1 to 3.

Faculty

The law school has 56 full-time and 78 part-time faculty members, of whom 36 are women. According to AAUP standards for Category I institutions, faculty salaries are above average. About 25% of full-time faculty have a graduate law degree in addition to the J.D.; about 7% of part-time faculty have one. The ratio of full-time students to full-time faculty in an average class is 15 to 1; in a clinic, 8 to 1. The law school has a regular program of bringing visiting professors and other distinguished lecturers and visitors to campus.

Students

About 46% of the student body are women; 31%, minorities; 9%, African American; 11%, Asian American; 6%, Hispanic; and 3%, other. The average age of entering students is 24; age range is 19 to 70. About 46% of students enter directly from undergraduate school, 6% have a graduate degree, and 54% have worked full-time prior to entering law school. About 4% drop out after the first year for academic or personal reasons; 96% remain to receive a law degree.

2900 Van Ness Street, N.W.
Washington, DC 20008

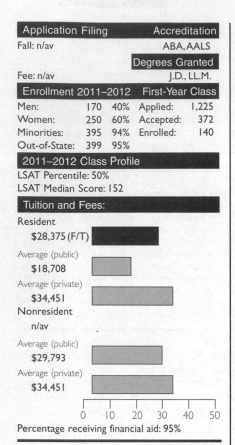

Application Filing		Accreditation
Fall: n/av		ABA, AALS
		Degrees Granted
Fee: n/av		J.D., LL.M.

Enrollment 2011–2012			First-Year Class	
Men:	170	40%	Applied:	1,225
Women:	250	60%	Accepted:	372
Minorities:	395	94%	Enrolled:	140
Out-of-State:	399	95%		

2011–2012 Class Profile
LSAT Percentile: 50%
LSAT Median Score: 152

Tuition and Fees:

Resident
$28,375 (F/T)

Average (public)
$18,708

Average (private)
$34,451

Nonresident
n/av

Average (public)
$29,793

Average (private)
$34,451

0   10   20   30   40   50

Percentage receiving financial aid: 95%

ADMISSIONS

In the fall of 2011 first-year class, 1225 applied, 372 were accepted, and 140 enrolled. Ten transfer students enrolled. The median LSAT percentile of the most recent first-year class was 50; the median GPA was 3.2 on a scale of 4.0.

Requirements

Applicants must have a bachelor's degree and take the LSAT. Minimum acceptable LSAT percentile is 35 and minimum acceptable GPA is 3.0 on a scale of 4.0. The most important admission factors include general background, GPA, and LSAT results. No specific undergraduate courses are required and candidates are not interviewed.

Procedure

Applicants should submit an application form, LSAT results, transcripts, 2 letters of recommendation, a personal statement and the Dean's survey. Notification of the admissions decision is on a rolling basis. The law school uses the LSAC.

Special

Requirements are different for out-of-state students. Transfer students must have one year of credits, have a minimum GPA of 3, attended an ABA-approved law school, and be ranked in the upper one-quarter to one-third of their class.

Costs

Tuition and fees for the 2011–2012 academic year are $27,960 for full-time in-state students. On-campus room and board costs about $12,891 annually; books and supplies run $1,351.

Financial Aid

About 95% of current law students receive some form of aid. The average annual amount of aid from all sources combined, including scholarships, loans, and work contracts, is $18,000; maximum, $36,000. Awards are based on merit. Required financial statement is the FAFSA. The aid application deadline for fall entry is April 1. First-year students are notified about their financial aid application at time of acceptance.

About the Law School

Howard University was established in 1869 and is a private institution. The 22-acre campus is located in an urban area in northwest Washington DC. The mission of Howard University school of law includes the provision of quality education for any student, with emphasis on the educational opportunities for those students from traditionaly underserved communities. Students have access to federal, state, county, city, and local agencies, courts, correctional facilities, law firms, and legal aid organizations in the Washington area. Students have access to the Washington Consortium of Law Libraries, which offers use of all law libraries in the D.C. metropolitan area. Facilities of special interest to law students include the superior moot court room. Housing for students is limited on campus; most students live off campus. All law school facilities are accessible to the physically disabled.

Calendar

The law school operates on a traditional semester basis. Courses for full-time students are offered both day and evening

and must be completed within 5 Years. For part-time students, courses are offered both day and evening. New full-time students are admitted in the fall and spring. There is no summer session. Transferable summer courses are offered.

Programs

In addition to the J.D., the law school offers the LL.M. Students may take relevant courses in other programs and apply credit toward the J.D.; a maximum of 30 credits may be applied. The following joint degrees may be earned: J.D./M.B.A. (Juris Doctor/Master of Business Administration).

Required

To earn the J.D., candidates must complete 88 total credits. They must maintain a minimum GPA of 72.0 in the required courses. The following first-year courses are required of all students: Civil Procedure, Constitutional Law I, Contracts, Criminal Law, Legal Method, Legal Research and Writing, Property, and Torts I and II. Required upper-level courses consist of Constitutional Law II, Evidence, Legal Writing II, Legal Writing III, Professional Responsibility, and Skills. The required orientation program for first-year students is two weeks long, and includes an introduction to legal methods.

Electives

A wide range of clinics are available to third-year students. Second and third-year students may take seminars. Internships are available to third-year students, and they may also participate in research. All students may attend tutorials, and special lectures for no credit. After the first year of study, students may undertake a study-abroad program. ABA-approved courses are offered at HUSL/University of Western Capetown, South Africa. The most widely taken electives are Federal Tax; Wills, Trusts, and Estates; and Administrative Law.

Graduation Requirements

In order to graduate, candidates must complete the upper-division writing requirement.

Phone: 202-806-8009
Fax: 202-806-8162
E-mail: admissions@law.howard.edu
Web: www.law.howard.edu

Contact

Reginald McGahee, Assistant Dean of Admissions, 202-806-8009 for general inquiries; Norman James, Financial Aid Officer, 202-806-8005 for financial aid information.

DISTRICT OF COLUMBIA

Organizations

Students edit the *Howard Law Journal* and the newspaper, *The Barrister*. Other law reviews include the Social Justice Law Review. Moot court competitions include ABA National Appellate Advocacy-Northeast Regional, Frederick Douglass National, and Huver I. Brown. Law student organizations, local chapters of national association, and campus clubs and organizations include ABA, Phi Alpha Delta, NBLSA, Student Bar Association, Entertaiment Law Association, International Law Society, Black Law Students Association, and Public Interest Law Society.

Library

The law library contains 428,494 hard-copy volumes and 54,000 microform volume equivalents, and subscribes to 1,643 serial publications. Online databases and networks include CALI, DIALOG, Legal-Trac, LEXIS, Mathew Bender, WESTLAW, and Internet, which are available to law students for research. Special library collections include Fats Waller Litigation Files and a civil rights collection. The ratio of library volumes to faculty is 12,985 to 1 and to students is 1,033 to 1. The ratio of seats in the library to students is 1 to 3.

Faculty

The law school has 33 full-time and 23 part-time faculty members, of whom 19 are women. According to AAUP standards for Category 1 institutions, faculty salaries are average. About 10% of full-time faculty have a graduate law degree in addition to the J.D.; about 4% of part-time faculty have one. The ratio of full-time students to full-time faculty in an average class is 17 to 1; in a clinic, 8 to 1. The law school has a regular program of bringing visiting professors and other distinguished lecturers and visitors to campus.

Students

About 60% of the student body are women; 94%, minorities; 87%, African American; 4%, Asian American; 4%, Hispanic; and 5%, Caucasian. The majority of students come from District of Columbia (5%). The average age of entering students is 25; age range is 21 to 48. About 80% of students enter directly from undergraduate school, 7% have a graduate degree, and 20% have worked full-time prior to entering law school. About 5% drop out after the first year for academic or personal reasons; 94% remain to receive a law degree.

Placement

Services available through: a separate law school placement center.

Special features: Summer Clerkship Program (for the summer following a student's first year) and workshops and seminars featuring Howard Law alumni and other practitioners regarding legal career settings, practice specialities, and employment trends; first-year summer clerkship program (through partnerships with major law firms and corporations; summer associate training program; workshops and seminars on job search skills, legal careers settings and practice specialties and employment trends.

Full-time job interviews:	109 employers
Summer job interviews:	169 employers
Placement by graduation:	80% of class
Placement within 9 months:	94% of class
Average starting salary:	$30,000 to $150,000

Areas of placement:

Private practice 2–10 attorneys	5%
Private practice 11–25 attorneys	1%
Private practice 26–50 attorneys	3%
Private practice 51–100 attorneys	3%
Government	30%
Business/industry	19%
Judicial clerkships	16%
Public interest	3%
Academic	1%

ILLINOIS INSTITUTE OF TECHNOLOGY

Chicago-Kent College of Law

565 West Adams Street
Chicago, IL 60661

Application Filing		Accreditation	
Fall: March 1		ABA, AALS	
		Degrees Granted	
		J.D., LL.M.	

Enrollment 2011–2012		First-Year Class	
Men:	521 55%	Applied:	3,719
Women:	423 45%	Accepted:	1,441
Minorities:	217 23%	Enrolled:	308
Out-of-State:	406 43%		

2011–2012 Class Profile
LSAT Percentile: 80%
LSAT Median Score: 160
Percentage passing bar on first try: 97%

Tuition and Fees:

Resident
$42,633 (F/T)

Average (public)
$18,708

Average (private)
$34,451

Nonresident
$42,633 (F/T)

Average (public)
$29,793

Average (private)
$34,451

Percentage receiving financial aid: 92%

ADMISSIONS

In the fall of 2011 first-year class, 3719 applied, 1441 were accepted, and 308 enrolled. Thirty-nine transfers enrolled. The median LSAT percentile of the most recent first-year class was 80; the median GPA was 3.5 on a scale of 4.0.

Requirements

Applicants must have a bachelor's degree and take the LSAT. No specific undergraduate courses are required. Candidates are not interviewed.

Procedure

The application deadline for fall entry is March 1. Applicants should submit an application form, LSAT results, transcripts, a personal statement, and one letter of recommendation. Admitted applicants must submit a nonrefundable seat deposit, payable in 2 installments in April and June. Notification of the admissions decision is on a rolling basis. The law school uses the LSAC.

Special

The law school recruits minority and disadvantaged students through minority student law days, direct mail, and events sponsored by minority law student groups. Chicago-Kent also hosts the PreLaw Undergraduate Scholars program ("PLUS"), a rigorous four-week summer program that is designed to provide undergraduate students with a "taste" of the law school experience. The program is primarily directed at undergraduate students from disadvantaged groups that are underrepresented in the legal profession. Requirements are different for out-of-state students. Transfer students must have one year of credit, must have attended an ABA-approved law school, and must submit a personal statement, a letter of good standing from the dean of their law school, and a letter of recommendation from a law professor.

Costs

Tuition and fees for the 2011–2012 academic year are $41,670 for all full-time students. Tuition for part-time students is $30,558 for in-state students and $30,558 out-of-state. On-campus room and board costs about $15,030 annually; books and supplies run $1,400.

Financial Aid

About 92% of current law students receive some form of aid. The average annual amount of aid from all sources combined, including scholarships, loans, and work contracts, is $46,550; maximum, $68,676. Awards are based on need and merit combined. The required financial statement is the FAFSA. The aid application deadline for fall entry is March 1. Special funds for minority or disadvantaged students are available. First-year students are notified about their financial aid application at time of acceptance.

About the Law School

Illinois Institute of Technology Chicago-Kent College of Law was established in 1888 and is a private institution. The campus is in an urban area in downtown Chicago. The primary mission of the law school is to provide students with a solid grounding in legal theory and ethics, along with innovative approaches to teaching and skills training. Students have access to federal, state, county, city, and local agencies, courts, correctional facilities, law firms, and legal aid organizations in the Chicago area. The college is located in the Loop, Chicago's central business district, providing access to federal, state, county, and city agencies, courts, and law firms. Facilities of special interest to law students include a state-of-the-art building that houses the law school and the university's Stuart School of Business. The building features a three-story atrium, five-level library, technologically advanced courtroom, auditorium, computer labs, student lounges, and cafeteria. It also houses a sophisticated computer network with both wireless and hard-wired network connections, which allow students to access network resources from almost anywhere in the building. Housing for students is available in nearby urban and suburban neighborhoods and on-campus housing is available on the university's main campus. A free shuttle runs between the campuses. All law school facilities are accessible to the physically disabled.

Calendar

The law school operates on a traditional semester basis. Courses for full-time students are offered both day and evening, and must be completed within 6 years. For part-time students, courses are offered both day and evening, and must be completed within 7 years. New full- and part-time students are admitted in the fall. There is an 8-week summer session. Transferable summer courses are offered.

Programs

In addition to the J.D., the law school offers the LL.M. Students may take relevant courses in other programs and apply credit toward the J.D.; a maximum of 12 credits may be applied. The following joint degrees may be earned: J.D./LL.M (Juris Doctor/Master of Laws in Taxation or Financial Services), J.D./M.B.A. (Juris Doctor/Master of Business Administration), J.D./M.E.M. (Juris Doctor/Master of Science in Environmental Management), J.D./M.P.A. (Juris Doctor/Master of Public Administration), J.D./M.P.H. (Juris Doctor/Master of Public Health), and J.D./M.S. (Juris Doctor/Master of Science in Financial Markets and Trading).

Required

To earn the J.D., candidates must complete 87 total credits, of which 42 are for required courses. They must maintain a minimum GPA of 2.3 in the required courses. The following first-year courses are required of all students: Civil Procedure, Contracts, Criminal Law, Legal Writing I and II, Legislative Process, Property, and Torts. Required upper-level courses consist of Constitutional Law, Legal Writing III and IV, Professional

Contact

Assistant Dean for Admissions, 312-906-5020 for general inquiries; Ada Chin, Director of Financial Aid, 312-906-5180 for financial aid information.

ILLINOIS

Responsibility, and seminar. The required orientation program for first-year students is a 3-day program combining introductory programs, library tours, computer training, legal research and writing, and small sessions with current students and faculty.

Electives

The Chicago-Kent College of Law offers concentrations in corporate law, criminal law, environmental law, intellectual property law, international law, labor law, and litigation. The law school offers certificate programs in eight areas: Environmental and Energy Law, Intellectual Property Law, International and Comparative Law, Labor and Employment Law, Litigation and Alternative Dispute Resolution, Public Interest Law, Criminal Litigation, and Business Law. In addition, students may take clinical work in areas, including criminal, civil, employment discrimination, and others through the Chicago-Kent-Law Offices for 3–4 credits. One seminar of 2 hours credit is required of all students. Recently offered seminars include Bioethics and the Law, Race-Conscious Remedies, and Current Energy Issues. An Advanced Externship Program places students with public agencies and teaching attorneys in areas such as environmental, bankruptcy, and international law. A Judicial Externship program places students in clerkships with federal judges. Students can take individual research for 1 credit per semester, working under the supervision of a professor. Special lecture series include the Morris Lecture in International and Comparative Law, the Piper Lecture in Labor Law, and the Green Lecture in Law and Technology. Study abroad is possible through programs in England, Germany, Denmark, France, Norway, China, Mexico, New Zealand, and Switzerland. The college accepts credits from most ABA-accredited law school study-abroad programs. The Academic Support Program is offered to students based on factors including LSAT score, undergraduate and graduate GPA, undergraduate course of study, years out of school, native language, and disabilities. The Office of Student Professional Development assists in the recruitment of minority students and students from historically disadvantaged backgrounds through visits to high schools and colleges, collaboration with college counselors and pre-law advisers, and community outreach. A certificate program for J.D. students in environmental and energy law includes a series of electives in land use and energy and environmental law, as well as interdisciplinary classes in the economic analysis of environmental problems.

There are similar certificate programs in other areas. The most widely taken electives are Evidence, Commercial Law Survey, and Business Organizations.

Graduation Requirements

In order to graduate, candidates must have a GPA of 2.3 and must have completed the upper-division writing requirement.

Organizations

Students edit the *Chicago-Kent Law Review*, which is published 3 times a year. *The Journal of Intellectual Property*, The *Employee Rights and Employment Policy Journal*, *The Journal of International and Comparative Law*, and the *Seventh Circuit Review*. The student newspaper is *The Commentator*. The Moot Court Honor Society, which enters its members in more than 10 intercollegiate competitions annually, sponsors the Ilana Diamond Rovner Appellate Advocacy Competition. First-year students compete in the Charles Evans Hughes Moot Court Competition. The College of Law's student organizations, local chapters of national associations, and campus organizations include the Environmental Law Society, International Law Society, the Intellectual Property Law Society, the Society of Women in Law, Asian Pacific American Law Society, Black and Hispanic-Latino Law Students associations, Phi-Alpha Delta, and National Lawyers Guild.

Library

The law library contains 56,182 hard-copy volumes and 152,812 microform volume equivalents, and subscribes to 332 serial publications. Such online databases and networks as CALI, CIS Universe, DIALOG, Dow-Jones, Infotrac, Legal-Trac, LEXIS, OCLC First Search, RLIN, WESTLAW, Wilsonline Indexes, Internet, EPIC, ProQuest, Illinet, Lexis Congressional, Fastcase, Law360, and Bloomberg are available to law students for research. Special library collections include a depository of federal documents, a special collection on law and the aging, as well as international organization documents (UN, EU, GATT, among others). The ratio of library volumes to faculty is 2,476 to 1 and to students is 596 to 1. The ratio of seats in the library to students is 1 to 2.

Faculty

The law school has 73 full-time and 154 part-time faculty members, of whom 67 are women. According to AAUP standards for Category 1 institutions, faculty salaries

Placement

J.D.s awarded:	336

Services available through: a separate law school placement center.

Special features: six full-time staff members, including 5 career counselors and an administrative assistant. One career counselor serves as a designated public interest career strategist. There is a resource center with reference materials, 6 computers for online/Internet research, and 2 laser printers for resume printing. One set of career resources is housed in the law school's library, enabling students to check out resources for home use. A job-posting system is password protected online. The office sponsors a fall on-campus interview program and participation in various job fairs including: 4 minority job fairs, 2 public interest career conferences, the Patent Law Interview Program, and the International Student Interview Program (ISIP) for foreign lawyers pursuing an LL.M. degree.

Full-time job interviews:	18 employers
Summer job interviews:	51 employers
Placement by graduation:	68% of class
Placement within 9 months:	91% of class
Average starting salary:	$17,500 to $160,000

Areas of placement:

Private practice 2–10 attorneys	26%
Private practice 11–25 attorneys	7%
Private practice 26–50 attorneys	4%
Private practice 51–100 attorneys	3%
Academic	7%
Public interest	5%
Judicial clerkships	3%
Business/industry	21%
Government	10%

are above average. About 12% of full-time faculty have a graduate law degree in addition to the J.D.; about 8% of part-time faculty have one. The ratio of full-time students to full-time faculty in an average class is 12 to 1; in a clinic, 10 to 1. The law school has a regular program of bringing visiting professors and other distinguished lecturers and visitors to campus. There is a chapter of the Order of the Coif; 63 faculty and 653 graduates are members.

Students

About 45% of the student body are women; 23%, minorities; 4%, African American; 8%, Asian American; and 10%, Hispanic. The majority of students come from Illinois (57%). The average age of entering students is 25; age range is 21 to 53. About 40% of students enter directly from undergraduate school, 8% have a graduate degree, and 60% have worked full-time prior to entering law school. About 12% drop out after the first year for academic or personal reasons; 88% remain to receive a law degree.

211 South Indiana Avenue
Bloomington, IN 47405-7001

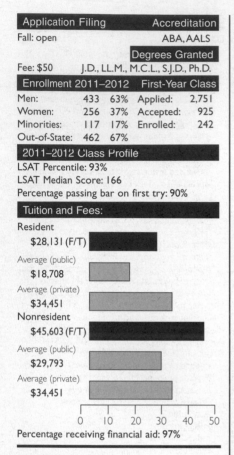

Application Filing		Accreditation
Fall: open		ABA, AALS
		Degrees Granted
Fee: $50		J.D., LL.M., M.C.L., S.J.D., Ph.D.

Enrollment 2011–2012		First-Year Class	
Men:	433 63%	Applied:	2,751
Women:	256 37%	Accepted:	925
Minorities:	117 17%	Enrolled:	242
Out-of-State:	462 67%		

2011–2012 Class Profile
LSAT Percentile: 93%
LSAT Median Score: 166
Percentage passing bar on first try: 90%

Tuition and Fees:

Resident
$28,131 (F/T)

Average (public)
$18,708

Average (private)
$34,451

Nonresident
$45,603 (F/T)

Average (public)
$29,793

Average (private)
$34,451

0   10   20   30   40   50

Percentage receiving financial aid: 97%

ADMISSIONS
In the fall of 2011 first-year class, 2751 applied, 925 were accepted, and 242 enrolled. The median LSAT percentile of the most recent first-year class was 93; the median GPA was 3.8 on a scale of 4.0. The lowest LSAT percentile accepted was 11; the highest was 99.

Requirements
Applicants must have a bachelor's degree and take the LSAT. The most important admission factors include LSAT results, GPA, and academic achievement. No specific undergraduate courses are required. Candidates are not interviewed.

Procedure
The application deadline for fall entry is open. Applicants should submit an application form, LSAT results, transcripts, a personal statement, a nonrefundable application fee of $50, 2 letters of recommendation, a residence form included in the application packet (required of all applicants regardless of residence), and a resume (required). Notification of the admissions decision is December until class is filled. The law school uses the LSAC.

Special
The law school recruits minority and disadvantaged students by participating in law fairs and private visits at historic minority colleges and universities, as well as in major urban areas. The school also participates in activities of minority-focused organizations such as the National Society of Black Engineers. The school hosts an annual Minority Law Day as part of the Law School Admission council's "Discover Law" initiative. Requirements are different for out-of-state students. Transfer students must have one year of credits, attended an ABA-approved law school, a personal statement, have a superior law school record, credentials comparable to the class in which they wish to transfer (in terms of LSAT score and GPA), and provide reasons for the transfer. Space availability is also a factor in the acceptance decision.

Costs
Tuition and fees for the 2011–2012 academic year are $27,040 for full-time in-state students and $44,512 for out-of-state students. On-campus room and board costs about $13,396 annually; books and supplies run $1,800.

Financial Aid
About 97% of current law students receive some form of aid. The average annual amount of aid from all sources combined, including scholarships, loans, and work contracts, is $46,599; maximum, $66,484. Awards are based on need and merit, and varies by type of award. Required financial statement is the FAFSA. The aid application deadline for fall entry is March 10. Special funds for minority or disadvantaged students include Education Opportunity Fellowships, which reduces nonresident tuition to the resident level, and outside private donor scholarships for disadvantaged students. The law school participates in the Indiana Conference for Legal Education Opportunity, which provides scholarships and other programs for minority or disadvantaged students. First-year students are notified about their financial aid application at time of acceptance.

About the Law School
Indiana University Maurer School of Law was established in 1842 and is a public institution. The 1931-acre campus is located in an urban area 50 miles southwest of Indianapolis. The primary mission of the law school is to provide its graduates with a rich combination of legal reasoning and practical lawyering skills in a collegial and supportive culture characterized by constant open interaction between students and faculty. Students have access to federal, state, county, city, and local agencies, courts, correctional facilities, law firms, and legal aid organizations in the Bloomington area. Facilities of special interest to law students include clinics housed in a separate off-campus building, which allows students to meet and serve their clients in a typical law firm environment. The School of Law is 100% wireless, allowing students to access the Internet and conduct legal research everywhere. Housing for students includes excellent on-campus housing, as well as a variety of affordable private housing units in the neighborhood adjacent to the law school. All law school facilities are accessible to the physically disabled.

Calendar
The law school operates on a traditional semester basis. Courses are taught in the evening and must be completed within 3 years. For part-time students, courses are offered. There is no part-time program. New full-time students are admitted in the fall and summer. There is a 5-week summer session. Transferable summer courses are offered.

Programs
In addition to the J.D., the law school offers the LL.M., M.C.L., S.J.D., and Ph.D. Students may take relevant courses in other programs and apply credit toward the J.D.; a maximum of 6 credits may be applied. The following joint degrees may be earned: J.D./LL.B (Juris Doctor/Bachelor of Laws), J.D./M.A. (Juris Doctor/Master of Arts in East Asian Studies), J.D./M.A. (Juris Doctor/Master of Arts in Journalism), J.D./M.A. or M.S. (Juris Doctor/Master of Arts in Science in Telecommunications), J.D./M.B.A. (Juris Doctor/Master of Business Administration), J.D./M.B.A.A. (Juris Doctor/Master of Business Administration in Accounting), J.D./M.P.A. (Juris Doctor/Master of Professional Arts in Public Affairs), J.D./M.P.A. (Juris Doctor/Master of Professional Accountancy), J.D./M.S. (Juris Doctor/Master of Science in Biotechnology), J.D./M.S.E.S. (Juris Doctor/Master of Science in Environmental Science), and J.D./M.S. (Juris Doctor/Master of Science in Library Information Science).

Phone: 812-855-4765
Fax: 812-855-0555
E-mail: Lawadmis@indiana.edu
Web: www.law.indiana.edu

Contact
Frank Motley, Assistant Dean for Admissions, 812-855-4765 for general inquiries; Paul Leopold, Director of Financial Aid, 812-855-7746 for financial aid information.

INDIANA

Required
To earn the J.D., candidates must complete 88 total credits, of which 31 are for required courses. They must maintain a minimum GPA of 2.3 in the required courses. The following first-year courses are required of all students: Civil Procedure, Constitutional Law, Contracts, Criminal Law, Legal Research and Writing I and II, Property, The Legal Profession, and Torts. Required upper-level courses consist of at least 1 course in which writing is used as a means of instruction. All students must take clinical courses. The required program for first-year students is a 2-day orientation program immediately preceding the beginning of classes. At this time, Law School policies and procedures, academic regulations, course requirements, and special services (career planning, educational assistance) are discussed.

Electives
The Indiana University Maurer School of Law offers concentrations in corporate law, criminal law, entertainment law, environmental law, family law, intellectual property law, international law, juvenile law, labor law, litigation, maritime law, media law, securities law, sports law, tax law, torts and insurance, communications law, Internet law, and cybersecurity. In addition, second- and third-year students may enroll (with varying credits given) in any of the clinics offered including the Elmore Entrepreneurship Law Clinic, the Conservation Law Clinic, and the Community Legal Services Clinic. Ten to 14 seminars are offered each semester for second and third-year students. Recent seminar offerings include Counterinsurgency and the Law, Voting Rights, and Biotechnological Innovation and the Law. Internships are available during all 3 years of law study with a variety of public agencies, nonprofit organizations, faculty members and public interest groups. Students may study abroad in Poland, Germany, France, Spain, China, Hong Kong, New Zealand, and England. Students selected as Steward Fellows spend a summer working in private industry, law firms, or nongovernmental organizations in India and Brazil. Summer law study programs are offered in London, Oxford, Paris, Dublin, Florence, Barcelona, and Moscow. There is no formal remedial program, but there is a voluntary Academic Enhancement Program with group instruction and one-on-one instruction available. The Law School participates in the Indiana Conference for Legal Education Opportunity. Minority students find support and enrichment of the law school experience from the Black Law Students Association, the Latino Law Students Association, and the Asian Pacific Islander Law Students Association. The most widely taken electives are Business Law, Intellectual Property, and Trial Practice/Litigation.

Graduation Requirements
In order to graduate, candidates must have a GPA of 2.3, have completed the upper-division writing requirement, and must be in residence in an approved law school for 6 semesters of full-time study.

Organizations
Students edit the Indiana Law Journal, Indiana Journal of Law and Social Equality, Indiana Journal of Global Legal Studies, IP Theory. Students participate in the Sherman Minton Moot Court Competition, Jessup International Moot Court Competition, and Telecommunications Moot Court Competition. Other competitions include the Trial Practice Competition and Negotiations Competition. Student organizations include the Intellectual Property Association, International Law Society, and the Public Interest Law Foundation.

Library
The law library contains 452,110 hardcopy volumes and 1,712,348 microform volume equivalents, and subscribes to 11,740 serial publications. Online databases and networks include CALI, CIS Universe, Dow-Jones, Infotrac, LegalTrac, LEXIS, Mathew Bender, OCLC First Search, WESTLAW, and Wilsonline Indexes. HeinOnline, BNA Library, CCH Library, Making of Modern Law, U.S. Supreme Court Records and Briefs (1832–1978), Thomas, RIA Checkpoint, CQ.Com, Communications, Energy, Securities Mosaic, and JUSTIS are also available to law students for research. Special library collections include a depository for records and briefs of the U.S. Supreme Court, Indiana Court of Appeals, and Indiana Supreme Court. Additionally, the library is also a selective depository for U.S. government publications as well as rare books and archives. The ratio of library volumes to faculty is 9,774 to 1 and to students is 725 to 1. The ratio of seats in the library to students is 1 to 1.

Faculty
The law school has 56 full-time and 32 part-time faculty members, of whom 28 are women. According to AAUP standards

Placement
J.D.s awarded:	197

Services available through: a separate law school placement center.

Services: job fairs and career planning seminars, videotaped mock interview program, judicial clerkship series, workshops covering all aspects of job searches and speed interview workshops. The course on the legal profession introduces students to career options and guides discovery of their strengths and interests.

Special features: office staffed by experienced career services specialists; extensive resource collection and handout series on career options and job search strategies; an alumni career network; weekly career seminars; an employer visitation program; and 1-on-1 counseling sessions.

Full-time job interviews:	15 employers
Summer job interviews:	50 employers
Placement by graduation:	82% of class
Placement within 9 months:	91% of class
Average starting salary:	$27,000 to $160,000

Areas of placement:
Private practice 2–10 attorneys	18%
Private practice 11–25 attorneys	3%
Private practice 26–50 attorneys	4%
Private practice 101-500 + attorneys	1%
Business/industry	15%
Government	13%
Judicial clerkships	8%
Public interest	8%
Academic	7%
Military	4%

for Category I institutions, faculty salaries are average. About 31% of full-time faculty have a graduate law degree in addition to the J.D. The ratio of full-time students to full-time faculty in an average class is 10 to 1; in a clinic, 5 to 1. The law school has a regular program of bringing visiting professors and other distinguished lecturers and visitors to campus. There is a chapter of the Order of the Coif; 32 faculty are members.

Students
About 37% of the student body are women; 21%, minorities; 6%, African American; 5%, Asian American; 5%, Hispanic; and 5%, other. The average age of entering students is 24; age range is 21 to 49. About 43% of students enter directly from undergraduate school, 9% have a graduate degree, and 49% have worked full-time prior to entering law school. About 1% drop out after the first year for academic or personal reasons; 99% remain to receive a law degree.

INDIANA UNIVERSITY-PURDUE UNIVERSITY AT INDIANAPOLIS

Robert H. McKinney School of Law

530 West New York Street
Indianapolis, IN 46202-3225

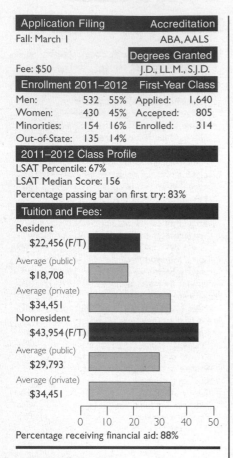

Application Filing	Accreditation
Fall: March 1	ABA, AALS

	Degrees Granted
Fee: $50	J.D., LL.M., S.J.D.

Enrollment 2011–2012		First-Year Class	
Men:	532 55%	Applied:	1,640
Women:	430 45%	Accepted:	805
Minorities:	154 16%	Enrolled:	314
Out-of-State:	135 14%		

2011–2012 Class Profile
LSAT Percentile: 67%
LSAT Median Score: 156
Percentage passing bar on first try: 83%

Tuition and Fees:

Resident
$22,456 (F/T)

Average (public)
$18,708

Average (private)
$34,451

Nonresident
$43,954 (F/T)

Average (public)
$29,793

Average (private)
$34,451

0 10 20 30 40 50

Percentage receiving financial aid: 88%

ADMISSIONS
In the fall of 2011 first-year class, 1640 applied, 805 were accepted, and 314 enrolled. Seventeen transfers enrolled. The median LSAT percentile of the most recent first-year class was 67; the median GPA was 3.4 on a scale of 4.0. The lowest LSAT percentile accepted was 14; the highest was 99.

Requirements
Applicants must have a bachelor's degree and take the LSAT. The most important admission factors include undergraduate curriculum, LSAT results, and academic achievement. No specific undergraduate courses are required. Candidates are not interviewed.

Procedure
The application deadline for fall entry is March 1. Applicants should submit an application form, LSAT results, transcripts, a personal statement, a nonrefundable application fee of $50, and 2 letters of recommendation. Notification of the admissions decision is on a rolling basis. The law school uses the LSAC.

Special
The law school recruits minority and disadvantaged students by means of Minority Law Day, visits to historically black colleges and universities, visits to areas and universities with high Latino populations, CLEO, ICLEO, and LSAC candidate referral search. Requirements are different for out-of-state students. Transfer students must have one year of credits, attended an ABA-approved law school, and a personal statement. Acceptance also depends on space availability.

Costs
Tuition and fees for the 2011–2012 academic year are $21,517 for full-time in-state students and $43,015 for out-of-state students. Tuition for part-time students is $15,969 for in-state students and $31,915 out-of-state. On-campus room and board costs about $14,460 annually; books and supplies run $1,100.

Financial Aid
About 88% of current law students receive some form of aid. The average annual amount of aid from all sources combined, including scholarships, loans, and work contracts, is $32,047. Awards are based on need and merit. If awards are from a private donor, requirements differ. The required financial statement is the FAFSA. The aid application deadline for fall entry is March 1. Special funds for minority or disadvantaged students consist of awards from private donors as well as Indiana CLEO for underrepresented groups in the legal field. First-year students are notified about their financial aid application at time of acceptance.

About the Law School
Indiana University-Purdue University at Indianapolis Robert H. McKinney School of Law was established in 1895 and is a public institution. The campus is located in an urban area in Indianapolis. The primary mission of the law school is to provide a legal education that will equip graduates with highly refined analytical and problem-solving skills, compassion, and ethics. Students have access to federal, state, county, city, and local agencies, courts, correctional facilities, law firms, and legal aid organizations in the Indianapolis area. Facilities of special interest to law students include the Indiana Supreme Court and the NCAA. Housing for students is available for single students in university-owned housing. Most of the students live in off-campus apartments. All law school facilities are accessible to the physically disabled.

Calendar
The law school operates on a traditional semester basis. Courses for full-time students are offered days only and must be completed within 7 years. For part-time students, courses are offered evenings only and must be completed within 7 years. New full- and part-time students are admitted in the fall. There is an 8-week summer session. Transferable summer courses are offered.

Programs
In addition to the J.D., the law school offers the LL.M. and S.J.D. The following joint degrees may be earned: J.D./M.D. (Juris Doctor/Doctor of Medicine), J.D./M. Phil. (Juris Doctor/Master of Arts in Philosophy), J.D./M.B.A. (Juris Doctor/Master of Business Administration), J.D./M.H.A. (Juris Doctor/Master of Health Administration), J.D./M.L.S. (Juris Doctor/Master of Library Science), J.D./M.P.A. (Juris Doctor/Master of Public Affairs), J.D./M.P.H. (Juris Doctor/Master of Public Health), and J.D./M.S.W. (Juris Doctor/Master of Social Work).

Required
To earn the J.D., candidates must complete 90 total credits, of which 35 are for required courses. They must maintain a minimum GPA of 2.3 in the required courses. The following first-year courses are required of all students: Civil Procedure I and II, Contracts I and II, Constitutional Law, Criminal Law, Legal Writing I and II, Property, and Torts. Required upper-level courses consist of Legal Research and Professional Responsibility. The required orientation program for first-year students is 2 days in the fall, and covers case briefing, outlining, library use, and basic computer use.

Phone: 317-274-2459
Fax: 317-278-4780
E-mail: *khmiller@iupui.edu*
Web: *indylaw.indiana.edu*

Contact
Karen Miller, Assistant Director for Admissions, 317-274-2459 for general inquiries; Leandra Ross, Assistant Director of Student Financial Aid Services, 317-274-4162 for financial aid information.

INDIANA

Electives

The Robert H. McKinney School of Law offers concentrations in corporate law, criminal law, environmental law, intellectual property law, internationl law, labor law, litigation, tax law, health law, international human rights, and state and local government law. In addition, halfway through their studies, students may take clinics in Civil Practice, Disability, Criminal Defense, Appellate Practice, Wrongful Conviction, and Immigration Law. Clients are represented by students under the supervision of faculty members. Seminars are available for 2 credits in areas such as evidence, international law, health law, and American legal history. Externships for students are offered in banking; commercial; environmental; immigration; corporate; criminal defense; international, federal, state, and local government law; with federal and state courts and agencies; public defender; and prosecution. Credit varies from none to 2 hours. Research opportunities are available through the Center for Law and Health, as well as the law journals. A special lecture series is active at the law school with various speakers and topics of interest. Summer study abroad is available in China, and the Croatia program. Tutorial programs are offered through the Dean's Tutorial Society, led by students and led by a faculty member. A Diversity Law Day is held for prospective students. Indiana CLEO is available for underrepresented groups in the legal profession. The most widely taken electives are International Law, Health Law, and Advocacy Skills.

Graduation Requirements

In order to graduate, candidates must have a GPA of 2.3 and have completed the upper-division writing requirement.

Organizations

Students edit the *Indiana Law Review, Indiana International and Comparative Law Review*, and the *Indiana Health Law Review*. Moot court teams are sent annually to the ABA-National Appellate Advocacy Competition, the Privacy Competition in Chicago, and the Philip C. Jessup International Law Competition. Teams also compete in the Client Counseling and Law and European Law competitions. Law student organizations,

local chapters of national associations, and campus organizations include the Equal Justice Works, LAMBDA Law Society, Sports and Entertainment Law Society, International Law Society, Black Law Students Association, and Phi Alpha Delta.

Library

The law library contains 584,622 hardcopy volumes and 67,910 microform volume equivalents, and subscribes to 6,542 serial publications. Online databases and networks include CALI, CIS Universe, DIALOG, Dow-Jones, Infotrac, LegalTrac, LEXIS, Mathew Bender, OCLC First Search, WESTLAW, and Wilsonline Indexes. HeinOnline, CCH Intelliconnect, BNA, LLMC, RIA Checkpoint, Making of Modern Law, Oxford Scholarship Online, Walters Kluwer Law, and CILP are also available to law students for research. Special library collections include United States government and United Nations publications. The ratio of library volumes to faculty is 12,180 to 1 and to students is 726 to 1. The ratio of seats in the library to students is 1 to 1.

Faculty

The law school has 57 full-time and 86 part-time faculty members, of whom 53 are women. According to AAUP standards for Category IIA institutions, faculty salaries are above average. About 29% of part-time faculty have a graduate law degrees in addition to the J.D. The ratio of full-time students to full-time faculty in an average class is 10 to 1; in a clinic, 8 to 1. The law school has a regular program of bringing visiting professors and other distinguished lecturers and visitors to campus.

Students

About 45% of the student body are women; 16%, minorities; 7%, African American; 6%, Asian American; and 1%, Native American. The majority of students come from Indiana (86%). The average age of entering students is 26; age range is 21 to 43. About 36% of students enter directly from undergraduate school, 9% have a graduate degree, and 64% have worked full-time prior to entering law school. About 1% drop out after the first year for academic or personal reasons; 99% remain to receive a law degree.

Placement

J.D.s awarded:	251

Services available through: a separate law school placement center.

Services: mock interviews, a 24-hour resume service, on-campus interviews, video interviews/conference.

Special features: panel discussions on alternative and nontraditional careers, the "A day in the life" series highlighting the judiciary, corporate law, clerkships, and public interest careers, among others; mock interviews; "Surving and Thriving" programs.

Placement within 9 months of graduation:	91% of class
Average starting salary:	$40,000 to $160,000

Areas of placement:

Law firms 1-500+ lawyers	49%
Business/industry	21%
Government	17%
Public interest	6%
Judicial clerkships	5%
Military	1%
Academic	1%

INTER AMERICAN UNIVERSITY OF PUERTO RICO

School of Law

P.O. Box 70351
San Juan, PR 00936-8351

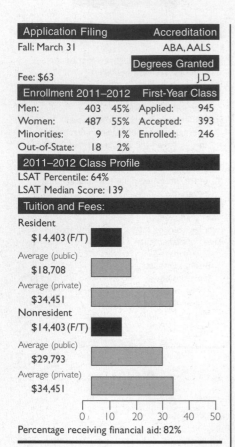

Application Filing			Accreditation	
Fall: March 31			ABA, AALS	
			Degrees Granted	
Fee: $63			J.D.	
Enrollment 2011–2012			**First-Year Class**	
Men:	403	45%	Applied:	945
Women:	487	55%	Accepted:	393
Minorities:	9	1%	Enrolled:	246
Out-of-State:	18	2%		

2011–2012 Class Profile
LSAT Percentile: 64%
LSAT Median Score: 139

Tuition and Fees:

Resident
$14,403 (F/T)

Average (public)
$18,708

Average (private)
$34,451

Nonresident
$14,403 (F/T)

Average (public)
$29,793

Average (private)
$34,451

0 10 20 30 40 50

Percentage receiving financial aid: 82%

ADMISSIONS

In the fall of 2011 first-year class, 945 applied, 393 were accepted, and 246 enrolled. Thirty-one transfers enrolled. The median LSAT percentile of the most recent first-year class was 64; the median GPA was 3.3 on a scale of 4.0.

Requirements

Applicants must have a bachelor's degree and take the LSAT. Minimum acceptable GPA is 2.5 on a scale of 4.0. The most important admission factors include GPA and LSAT results. No specific undergraduate courses are required. Candidates are not interviewed.

Procedure

The application deadline for fall entry is March 31. Applicants should submit an application form, LSAT results, transcripts, EXADEP scores, and a nonrefundable application fee of $63. Applicants must also be fluent in Spanish. Accepted students must pay a $125 seat deposit. Notification of the admissions decision is by May 20. The law school uses the LSAC.

Special

Requirements are different for out-of-state students in that they are required to submit evidence of their authorization to study in Puerto Rico, as well as the documents required by the Immigration and Naturalization Office of the U.S. Department of Justice. Transfer students must have a minimum GPA of 3 and must have attended an ABA-approved law school.

Costs

Tuition and fees for the 2011–2012 academic year are $13,710 for all full-time students. Tuition for part-time students is $10,511 for in-state students and $10,511 out-of-state.

Financial Aid

About 82% of current law students receive some form of aid. The average annual amount of aid from all sources combined, including scholarships, loans, and work contracts, is $9,727; maximum, $33,150. Awards are based on need and merit. The required financial statement is the FAFSA. The aid application deadline for fall entry is August 13. First-year students are notified about their financial aid application at time of acceptance.

About the Law School

Inter-American University of Puerto Rico School of Law was established in 1961 and is a private institution. The 7-acre campus is in an urban area in metropolitan San Juan. The primary mission of the law school is to train professionals competent for public and private practice through a broad background in history and development of the law, particularly how it affects contemporary Puerto Rican legal issues and institutions, and also to promote legal research and continued legal education of its alumni and others in the legal profession. Students have access to federal, state, county, city, and local agencies, courts, correctional facilities, law firms, and legal aid organizations in the San Juan area. The school's location grants students access to additional resources such as the University of Puerto Rico Law School, the Puerto Rico Bar Association, and Federal District Court. Facilities of special interest to law students are the moot courtroom and law library. Housing for students is available in the neighborhood for those students who reside outside

the metropolitan area. The school does not provide housing facilities. All law school facilities are accessible to the physically disabled.

Calendar

The law school operates on a traditional semester basis. Courses for full-time students are offered both day and evening, and must be completed within 3 to 6 years. For part-time students, courses are offered both day and evening, and must be completed within 4 to 8 years. New full- and part-time students are admitted in the fall. There are 4- and 5-week summer sessions. Transferable summer courses are not offered.

Programs

The following joint degrees may be earned: J.D./M.B.A. (Juris Doctor/Master of Business Administration).

Required

To earn the J.D., candidates must complete 92 total credits, of which 62 are for required courses. They must maintain a minimum GPA of 2.0 in the required courses. The following first-year courses are required of all students: Civil Procedure-Successions, Constitutional Law I, Criminal Law, Criminal Procedure, Family Law, Introduction to Law, Property Law, Research Analysis and Writing, and Torts. Required upper-level courses consist of Administrative Law, Constitutional Law II, Criminal Procedure, Ethics of the Legal Profession, Evidence, General Theory Obligations and Contracts, History of Puerto Rican Law, Litigation: Theory, Doctrine, and Practice, and Mortgage Law. All students must take clinical courses. The required orientation program for first-year students is a summer introductory course and a program during the week preceding the fall semester.

Electives

The School of Law offers concentrations in corporate law, criminal law, environmental law, family law, intellectual property law, international law, labor law, litigation, tax law, and torts and insurance. The Legal Aid Clinic involves students in offering legal advice, handling cases before courts and administrative agencies, and drafting legal documents for 4 credits.

Phone: 787-751-1912, ext. 2013, 2526
Web: www.inter.edu

Contact

Dean of Students, 787-751-1912, ext. 2011 for general inquiries; Ricardo Crespo, Director of Financial Aid, 787-751-1912, ext. 2014 for financial aid information.

PUERTO RICO

Seminars provide in-depth study in various areas of law and are worth 3 credits each. Tutorial programs for 2 credits are available in courts and government agencies. The most widely taken electives are Labor Law, Employment Law, and Commercial Law.

Graduation Requirements

In order to graduate, candidates must have a GPA of 2.0 and must have completed the upper-division writing requirement.

Organizations

The primary law review is the *Revista Juridica de la Universidad Interamerica de Puerto Rico*, which is edited by students, professors, and scholars. Other law reviews include *CLAVE*. The student newspaper is the *Student Council Bulletin*. Other publications include *AD REM*. Moot court competitions include the Animal Law Moot Court. Student council members serve on law school committees. There are local chapters of the ABA-Law Student Division, National Law Students Association, Phi Alpha Delta-Luis Munoz Morales chapter, and the National Hispanic Bar Association-Law Student Division.

Library

The law library contains 203,150 hard-copy volumes and 283,018 microform volume equivalents, and subscribes to 904 serial publications. Such online databases and networks as CALI, Infotrac, Legal-Trac, LEXIS, OCLC First Search, RLIN, WESTLAW, Internet, LIBIS (the university's library), MICROJURIS (Puerto Rican Law Data Base), JTS (Jurisprudence of Supreme Court), HeinOnline, and Lex Juris are available to law students for research. The library has 3 private collections of civil law books, including rare books. The ratio of library volumes to faculty is 8,796 to 1 and to students is 244 to 1. The ratio of seats in the library to students is 1 to 2.

Faculty

The law school has 30 full-time and 5 part-time faculty members, of whom 31 are women. About 84% of full-time faculty have a graduate law degree in addition to the J.D.; about 34% of part-time faculty have one. The ratio of full-time students to full-time faculty in an average class is 13 to 1; in a clinic, 4 to 1. The law school has a regular program of bringing visiting professors and other distinguished lecturers and visitors to campus.

Students

About 55% of the student body are women; and 1%, minorities. The majority of students come from Puerto Rico (98%). The average age of entering students is 28; age range is 21 to 57. About 87% of students enter directly from undergraduate school, and 13% have a graduate degree. About 8% drop out after the first year for academic or personal reasons; 92% remain to receive a law degree.

Placement

J.D.s awarded:	132

Services available through: the university placement center and Office of the Dean of Students-Career Placement Office.
Special features: international law internships.

Full-time job interviews:	20 employers
Summer job interviews:	18 employers
Placement by graduation:	14% of class
Placement within 9 months:	86% of class
Average starting salary:	$28,000 to $68,000

Areas of placement:

Private practice 2–10 attorneys	14%
Private practice 11–25 attorneys	10%
Private practice 26–50 attorneys	7%
Private practice 51–100 attorneys	7%
Government	23%
Business/industry	21%
Academic	3%
Judicial clerkships	2%
Public interest	1%

315 South Plymouth Court
Chicago, IL 60604

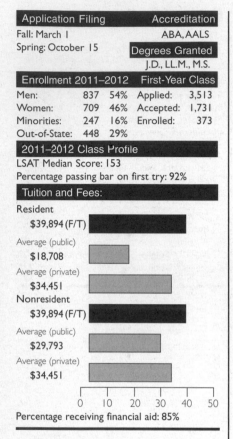

Application Filing		Accreditation	
Fall: March 1		ABA, AALS	
Spring: October 15		**Degrees Granted**	
		J.D., LL.M., M.S.	

Enrollment 2011–2012		First-Year Class	
Men:	837 54%	Applied:	3,513
Women:	709 46%	Accepted:	1,731
Minorities:	247 16%	Enrolled:	373
Out-of-State:	448 29%		

2011–2012 Class Profile
LSAT Median Score: 153
Percentage passing bar on first try: 92%

Tuition and Fees:

Resident
$39,894 (F/T)

Average (public)
$18,708

Average (private)
$34,451

Nonresident
$39,894 (F/T)

Average (public)
$29,793

Average (private)
$34,451

0 10 20 30 40 50

Percentage receiving financial aid: 85%

ADMISSIONS

In the fall of 2011 first-year class, 3513 applied, 1731 were accepted, and 373 enrolled. Twenty-six transfers enrolled. The median GPA of the most recent first-year class was 3.3.

Requirements

Applicants must have a bachelor's degree and take the LSAT. The most important admission factors include life experience, LSAT results, and academic achievement. No specific undergraduate courses are required. Candidates are not interviewed.

Procedure

The application deadline for fall entry is March 1. Applicants should submit an application form, LSAT results, transcripts, TOEFL results (if applicable), and LSAC report. Notification of the admissions decision is 2 to 5 weeks after their file is complete. The law school uses the LSAC.

Special

The law school recruits minority and disadvantaged students through special mailings and outreach to minority institutions and diversity mock trial competitions. Requirements are different for out-of-state students. Transfer students must have a minimum GPA of 2.75 and must have attended an ABA-approved law school.

Costs

Books and supplies run $2,340.

Financial Aid

About 85% of current law students receive some form of aid. The maximum annual amount of aid from all sources combined, including scholarships, loans, and work contracts, is $60,120. Awards are based on need and merit combined. The required financial statement is the FAFSA. The aid application deadline for fall entry is April 1. First-year students are notified about their financial aid application at time of acceptance.

About the Law School

John Marshall Law School was established in 1899 and is independent. The campus is in an urban area in Chicago. The primary mission of the law school is to provide students with an intellectually challenging foundation in legal principles and a rigorous background in lawyering skills. Students have access to federal, state, county, city, and local agencies, courts, correctional facilities, law firms, and legal aid organizations in the Chicago area. Housing for students is readily available and assistance is provided through the admissions office. All law school facilities are accessible to the physically disabled.

Calendar

The law school operates on a traditional semester basis. Courses for full-time students are offered both day and evening, and must be completed within 7 years. For part-time students, courses are offered days, evenings, and Saturdays, and must be completed within 7 years. New full- and part-time students are admitted in the fall and spring. There is an 8-week summer session. Transferable summer courses are offered.

Programs

In addition to the J.D., the law school offers the LL.M. and M.S. Students may take relevant courses in other programs and apply credit toward the J.D.; a maximum of 6 credits may be applied. The following joint degrees may be earned: J.D./M.B.A. (Juris Doctor/Master of Business Administration) and J.D./M.P.A. (Juris Doctor/Master of Public Administration).

Required

To earn the J.D., candidates must complete 90 total credits, of which 48 are for required courses. They must maintain a minimum GPA of 2.3 in the required courses. The following first-year courses are required of all students: Civil Procedure I, Constitutional Law I, Contracts I and II, Criminal Law, Lawyering Skills I and II, Property, and Torts. Required upper-level courses consist of Civil Procedure II, Constitutional Law II, Evidence, Lawyering Skills Drafting, Moot Court-Herzog, Professional Responsibility, and Trial Advocacy. All students must take clinical courses. The required orientation program for first-year students is 3 days for day students and 4 evenings for evening students entering with the August class, and 4 evenings for day and evening students entering with the January class. The program consists of both academic and administrative presentations.

Electives

The John Marshall Law School offers concentrations in corporate law, intellectual property law, international law, tax law, advocacy and dispute resolution, business law, estate planning, general practice, informatics, intellectual property law, real estate law, information technology law, public interest law, health law, alternative dispute resolution, trial advocacy, elder law, and sustainability. In addition, clinics are open to students with at least 53 hours and prior approval. Clinics offer from 2 to 4 credits per semester and are with the Chicago Corporation Counsel, Fair Housing, Legal Aid Bureau, Illinois Attorney General, intellectual property law, judicial and legislative clerkships, Legal Aid Bureau, Public Defender, State's Attorney of Cook County, Travelers and Immigrants Aid, the U.S. Attorney, Northern District of Illinois and John Marshall's Deteraus Legal Support Center and Clinic.

Phone: 312-987-1406
800-537-4280
Fax: 312-427-5136
E-mail: admission@jmls.edu
Web: www.jmls.edu

Contact
Admission and Student Affairs, 312-987-1406 for general inquiries; Yara Santana, Director, 312-427-2737, ext. 510 for financial aid information.

ILLINOIS

Seminars are worth 2 to 3 credits, and are in the areas of banking, business planning, computers, constitutional law, counseling and negotiating, estate planning, information technology, rights of prisoners, scientific evidence, international criminal law, taxation, and trial advocacy. Research programs, worth 1 to 2 credits, are open to students who have at least 59 hours. A scholarly paper must be produced from research supervised by a faculty member. There is an ABA-approved Intellectual Property Law Summer Program in Beijing. Special interest groups are the Center for Information Technology and Privacy Law, Center for Intellectual Property Law, Fair Housing Legal Support Center, Center for Advocacy and Dispute Resolution, Center for Real Estate Law, Center for Tax Law and Employee Benefits, and Center for International Law. The most widely taken electives are Corporations, Estates and Trusts, and Commercial Law.

Graduation Requirements
In order to graduate, candidates must have a GPA of 2.3, must have completed the upper-division writing requirement, and must have completed 4 semesters of lawyering skills.

Organizations
Student-edited publications are *The John Marshall Law Review*, the *Journal of Computer and Information Law*, the *Review of Intellectual Property Law*, and the student newspaper *Decisive Utterance*. Teams are sent annually to more than 20 interscholastic moot court and trial competitions. The John Marshall Law School hosts the annual International Moot Court Competition in Information Technology and Privacy Law and the annual National Criminial Justice Trial Advocacy Competition with the American Bar Association. Law student organizations, local chapters of national associations, and campus organizations include Phi Alpha Delta, Phi Delta Phi, Delta Theta Phi, Student Bar Association, Illinois State Bar Association-Law Student Division, ABA-Law Student Division. Asian and Pacific Island Law Students Association, Black Law Students Association, and Latino Law Students Association.

Library
The law library contains 413,520 hardcopy volumes and 158,935 microform volume equivalents, and subscribes to 6,647 serial publications. Such online databases and networks as CALI, LEXIS, OCLC First Search, WESTLAW, Wilsonline Indexes, HeinOnline, BNA-All, JSTOR, ILCLE, Smartbook, Kluwer International, and Ebscohost are available to law students for research. Special library collections include a U.S. government documents depository, Chinese language intellectual property law collection, animal rights law collection, academic success collection, career success collection, and popular reading collection. The ratio of library volumes to faculty is 5,169 to 1 and to students is 252 to 1. The ratio of seats in the library to students is 1 to 2.

Faculty
The law school has 72 full-time and 133 part-time faculty members, of whom 63 are women. About 25% of full-time faculty have a graduate law degree in addition to the J.D.

Students
About 46% of the student body are women; 16%, minorities; 8%, African American; 6%, Asian American; 8%, Hispanic; and 1%, Native American. The majority of students come from Illinois (71%). The average age of entering students is 25; age range is 21 to 53. About 33% of students enter directly from undergraduate school, 14% have a graduate degree, and 40% have worked full-time prior to entering law school. About 9% drop out after the first year for academic or personal reasons; 80% remain to receive a law degree.

Placement

J.D.s awarded:	403

Services available through: a separate law school placement center and career services office.

Special features: mentor program and mandatory career services training for first-year students in November followed by required one-on-one counseling sessions with an assigned counselor.

Full-time job interviews:	9 employers
Summer job interviews:	15 employers
Placement within 9 months of graduation:	90% of class
Average starting salary:	$27,000 to $160,000

Areas of placement:

Private practice 2–10 attorneys	29%
Private practice 11–25 attorneys	7%
Private practice 26–50 attorneys	3%
Private practice 51–100 attorneys	2%
Business/industry	23%
Government	17%
Academic	5%
Judicial clerkships	2%
Public interest	2%
Military	1%

LEWIS AND CLARK COLLEGE

Lewis and Clark Law School

10015 Southwest Terwilliger
Boulevard
Portland, OR 97219

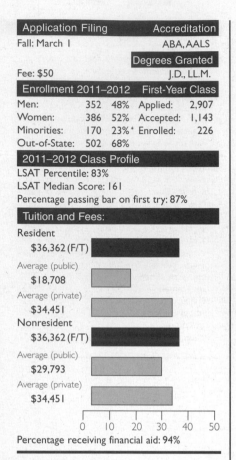

Application Filing	Accreditation
Fall: March 1	ABA, AALS

Degrees Granted
Fee: $50	J.D., LL.M.

Enrollment 2011–2012		First-Year Class	
Men:	352 48%	Applied:	2,907
Women:	386 52%	Accepted:	1,143
Minorities:	170 23%	Enrolled:	226
Out-of-State:	502 68%		

2011–2012 Class Profile
LSAT Percentile: 83%
LSAT Median Score: 161
Percentage passing bar on first try: 87%

Tuition and Fees:

Resident
$36,362 (F/T)

Average (public)
$18,708

Average (private)
$34,451

Nonresident
$36,362 (F/T)

Average (public)
$29,793

Average (private)
$34,451

0   10   20   30   40   50

Percentage receiving financial aid: 94%

ADMISSIONS

In the fall of 2011 first-year class, 2907 applied, 1143 were accepted, and 226 enrolled. Fifty-one transfer students enrolled. The median LSAT percentile of the most recent first-year class was 83; the median GPA was 3.5 on a scale of 4.0. The lowest LSAT percentile accepted was 30; the highest was 99.

Requirements
Applicants must have a bachelor's degree and take the LSAT. The most important admission factors include LSAT results, GPA, and writing ability. No specific undergraduate courses are required and candidates are not interviewed.

Procedure
The application deadline for fall entry is March 1. Applicants should submit an application form, LSAT results, transcripts, personal statement, nonrefundable application fee of $50, 2 letters of recommendation, an essay, resumé, LSAC report of undergraduate work, and

optional statements on extracurricular activities or special circumstances. Notification of the admissions decision is on a rolling basis. The law school uses the LSAC.

Special
The law school recruits minority and disadvantaged students by having law school representatives visit undergraduate institutions with significant ethnic enrollment; by inviting prelaw advisers from undergraduate schools with large ethnic minority populations to visit the campus; by partnering with the Oregon State Bar to attract and retain ethnic minority students in Oregon; and by contacting ethnic minority candidates who take the LSAT. Requirements are different for out-of-state students. Transfer students must have one year of credit, have attended an ABA-approved law school, a personal statement, achieved strong academic standing at the school from which the student is transferring, and present a compelling reason for wishing to transfer to Lewis and Clark.

Costs
Books and supplies run $1,600.

Financial Aid
About 94% of current law students receive some form of aid. The average annual amount of aid from all sources combined, including scholarships, loans, and work contracts, is $38,106; maximum, $75,812. Awards are based on need and merit combined. Required financial statement is the FAFSA. The aid application deadline for fall entry is March 1. Special funds for minority or disadvantaged students consist of scholarship funds from the college, Oregon State Bar funds, and a special Native American Scholarship. First-year students are notified about their financial aid application at time of acceptance.

About the Law School
Lewis and Clark College Lewis and Clark Law School was established in 1884 and is a private institution. The 31-acre campus is located in a suburban area within Portland. The primary mission of the law school is to train and educate students about the law and about being ethical, well-rounded professionals. The school

also strives to advance the knowledge, skills, and professionalism of legal practitioners. Students have access to federal, state, county, city, and local agencies, courts, correctional facilities, law firms, and legal aid organizations in the Portland area. The American Inns of Court; clinical internship seminars; externships, and the Oregon student appearance rule, which allows students to appear in court, are available to students. Facilities of special interest to law students include a 640-acre wilderness park bordering the campus and the undergraduate school, which has indoor and outdoor pools, a gymnasium, and tennis and racquetball courts. Housing for students consists of a wide variety of off-campus apartments and houses that students share at reasonable rents. Campus-owned houses are also available for law students to rent. All law school facilities are accessible to the physically disabled.

Calendar
The law school operates on a traditional semester basis. Courses for full-time students are offered both day and evening and must be completed within 7 years. For part-time students, courses are offered both day and evening and must be completed within 7 years. New full- and part-time students are admitted in the fall. There is a 2–5-week summer session. Transferable summer courses are not offered.

Programs
In addition to the J.D., the law school offers the LL.M. The following joint degrees may be earned: J.D./L.L.M. (Juris Doctor/Master of Laws).

Required
To earn the J.D., candidates must complete 90 total credits, of which 28–35 are for required courses. They must maintain a minimum GPA of 1.7 in the required courses. The following first-year courses are required of all students: Civil Procedure I and II, Constitutional Law I, Contracts, Criminal Procedure I (full-time students), Legal Analysis and Writing I and II, Legal Elements, Property (full-time students), and Torts. Required upper-level courses consist of Constitutional Law II, Criminal Law (part-time students), Professionalism, Property (part-time students),

Contact

Diana Meyer, Assistant Director of Financial Services, 503-768-7090 for financial aid information.

OREGON

and Seminar. The required orientation program for first-year students is a 1-day program consisting of student registration and introduction to school and student life.

Electives

The Lewis and Clark Law School offers concentrations in corporate law, criminal law, environmental law, family law, intellectual property law, international law, juvenile law, labor law, litigation, securities law, tax law, torts and insurance, employment law, animal law, and public interest law. In addition, the law school operates a clinic in downtown Portland. The clinic serves indigent clients and performs civil work in the areas of consumer, landlord-tenant, employment law, and tax law, and is available to all upper-division students. Students interested in environmental law may participate in the Pacific Environmental Advocacy Center, the International Environmental Law Project, and clinical internship seminars. Seminars are available in a variety of subjects, limited to 20 students and usually require a paper. Each upper-division student must take 1 seminar to graduate. A 3-hour seminar is offered in conjunction with a 10-hour per week placement in areas including criminal law, natural resources, and intellectual property. The school also offers full semester or summer externships, which require a substantial paper in addition to working full time in an approved placement with significant faculty supervision. Students may work as research assistants to faculty members, write for law reviews, and perform independent research projects for credit with faculty. Special lecture series include the Higgins Visit and the distinguished visitors series. There are also faculty colloquia and speakers invited by various student groups. The school has partnerships with the summer abroad program at the University of San Diego and with the China program at the University of Missouri-Kansas City. Students participate in study abroad with any ABA law schools and apply these credits at Lewis and Clark. An academic support program that focuses on study skills and group support is available to students. The school actively recruits ethnic minority candidates and actively participates and hosts diversity pipline programs. Students may participate in a wide variety of student organizations including, but not limited to, the Business Law Society, Environmental Law Caucus,

Minority Law Student Association, and the Student Animal Legal Defense Fund, and the Public Interest Law Project. The most widely taken electives are Business/Corporate Law, Environmental, and Intellectual Property.

Graduation Requirements

In order to graduate, candidates must have a GPA of 2.0, and complete the upper-division writing requirement.

Organizations

The school has three law reviews. The primary law review is *Environmental Law Review*. Moot court competitions consist of a negotiation competition, environmental law, Moot court and tax law. A writing competition for the best paper in the area of international law is sponsored by the law firm of Ragen, Davis, and Wright. Law student organizations include Intellectual Property Society Public Interest Project, and Minority Law Student Association. Student Bar Association, other campus organizations include Outlaw, Students Advocating Business Environmental Responsibility, and local chapters of national associations include Student Animal Legal Defense Fund, and National Lawyers Guild.

Library

The law library contains 209,973 hard-copy volumes and 316,739 microform volume equivalents, and subscribes to 1,430 serial publications. Online databases and networks include CALI, CIS Universe, Legal-Trac, LEXIS, OCLC First Search, WESTLAW, UN Treaty Collections, HeinOnline, JSTOR, OED Online, BNA Online and Making of Modern Law, RIA, and LLMC Digital, which are available to law students for research. Special library collections include the Milton Pearl Environmental Law Collection, the Samuel Johnson Public Land Law papers, the crime victims collection, and the legal history collection. The ratio of library volumes to faculty is 4,014 to 1 and to students is 423 to 1. The ratio of seats in the library to students is 1 to 2.

Faculty

The law school has 67 full-time and 43 part-time faculty members, of whom 48 are women. According to AAUP standards

Placement

J.D.s awarded:	211

Services available through: a separate law school placement center.

Services: extensive resource library, 2 mentor programs, practice mock interview programs, monthly jobs newsletter, a comprehensive web site with postings and resources, on-campus interview program, and public interest/pro bono honors program.

Special features: Regular information panels given by alumni and other Portland practitioners, a public-interest career information fair, breakfast with judges, clerking opportunities available throughout the year; pro bono honors program, an alumni network around the country, law firm receptions for first-year students, mandatory first year classes, a comprehensive handbook, and individual counseling.

Full-time job interviews:	6 employers
Summer job interviews:	24 employers
Placement within 9 months of graduation:	90% of class
Average starting salary:	n/av

Areas of placement:

Private practice 2–10 attorneys	24%
Private practice 11–25 attorneys	5%
Private practice 26–50 attorneys	4%
Business/industry	16%
Government	15%
Judicial clerkships	14%
Academic	9%
Public interest	6%

for Category IIB institutions, faculty salaries are above average. About 10% of full-time faculty have a graduate law degree in addition to the J.D. The ratio of full-time students to full-time faculty in an average class is 25 to 1; in a clinic, 7 to 1. The law school has a regular program of bringing visiting professors and other distinguished lecturers and visitors to campus.

Students

About 52% of the student body are women; 23%, minorities; 3%, African American; 8%, Asian American; 8%, Hispanic; 3%, Native American; and 2%, Unknown. The majority of students come from Oregon (32%). The average age of entering students is 28; age range is 20 to 57. About 4% drop out after the first year for academic or personal reasons; 89% remain to receive a law degree.

LIBERTY UNIVERSITY

School of Law

1971 University Blvd.
Lynchburg, VA 24502

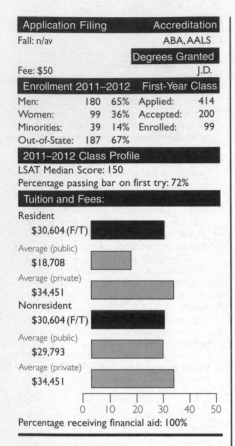

Application Filing		Accreditation
Fall: n/av		ABA, AALS
		Degrees Granted
Fee: $50		J.D.

Enrollment 2011–2012			First-Year Class	
Men:	180	65%	Applied:	414
Women:	99	36%	Accepted:	200
Minorities:	39	14%	Enrolled:	99
Out-of-State:	187	67%		

2011–2012 Class Profile
LSAT Median Score: 150
Percentage passing bar on first try: 72%

Tuition and Fees:

Resident
$30,604 (F/T)

Average (public)
$18,708

Average (private)
$34,451

Nonresident
$30,604 (F/T)

Average (public)
$29,793

Average (private)
$34,451

0 10 20 30 40 50

Percentage receiving financial aid: 100%

ADMISSIONS

In the fall of 2011 first-year class, 414 applied, 200 were accepted, and 99 enrolled. Two transfer students enrolled. The median GPA of the most recent first-year class was 3.23.

Requirements

Applicants must have a bachelor's degree and take the LSAT. The most important admission factors are a letter of recommendation and LSAT results. No specific undergraduate courses are required. Candidates are interviewed.

Procedure

Applicants should submit an application form, LSAT results, transcripts, personal statement, nonrefundable application fee of $50, and 2 letters of recommendation. Notification of the admissions decision is shortly after submission of complete application. The law school uses the LSAC.

Special

The law school recruits minority and disadvantaged students through campus visits, advertising, special events, and CLEO membership. Requirements are different for out-of-state students. Transfer students must have one year of credits, a minimum GPA of 2, personal statement, and a letter from previous law school.

Costs

Tuition and fees for the 2011–2012 academic year are $29,088 for all full-time students. Books and supplies run $1,800.

Financial Aid

About 100% of current law students receive some form of aid. The average annual amount of aid from all sources combined, including scholarships, loans, and work contracts, is $36,672; maximum, $48,066. Awards are based on need and merit, along with subsidized loans that are need-based. Required financial statement is the FAFSA. Special funds for minority or disadvantaged students include one minority scholarship category. First-year students are notified about their financial aid application during application process.

About the Law School

Liberty University School of Law was established in 2004 and is a private institution. The 6500-acre campus is located in an urban area near Central Virginia in the Blue Ridge Mountains. The mission of the law school is to equip future leaders in law with a superior legal education in fidelity to the Christian faith expressed through the Holy Scriptures. Students have access to federal, state, county, city, and local agencies, courts, correctional facilities, law firms, and legal aid organizations in the Lynchburg area. The law school has a partnership with Liberty Counsel, a public interest law firm with an office in Lynchburg. Facilities of special interest to law students include a 330-seat ceremonial courtroom with a 9-seat bench, which is an exact replica of the U.S. Supreme Court bench; wireless access throughout law school; proximity of law library to classrooms; and a massive fitness center. Housing for students consists of affordable off-campus apartments and homes. About 98% of the law school facilities are accessible to the physically disabled.

Calendar

The law school operates on a traditional semester basis. Courses for full-time students are offered both day and evening and must be completed within 7 years. There is no part-time program. New full-time students are admitted in the fall. There is a 2–3-week summer session. Transferable summer courses are offered.

Programs

The following joint degrees may be earned: J.D./Ed.D. (Juris Doctor/Doctor of Education), J.D./M.A. (Juris Doctor/Master of Arts in History), J.D./M.A. (Juris Doctor/Master of Arts in Human Services), J.D./M.A.P.P. (Juris Doctor/Master of Arts in Public Policy), J.D./M.B.A. (Juris Doctor/Master of Business Administration), J.D./M.Div. (Juris Doctor/Master of Divinity), and J.D./M.Ed. (Juris Doctor/Master of Education).

Required

To earn the J.D., candidates must complete 90 total credits, of which 66 are for required courses. They must maintain a minimum GPA of 2.0 in the required courses. The following first-year courses are required of all students: Civil Procedure I and II, Contracts I and II, Foundations of Law I and II, Lawyering Skills I and II, and Torts I and II. Required upper-level courses consist of Business Associations, Constitutional Law I and II, Criminal Law, Criminal Procedure, Evidence, Lawyering Skills III and IV, Lawyering Skills V and VI, Professional Responsibility, Taxation of Individuals, Wills, Trusts, and Estates. The required orientation program for first-year students is 4½ days of case briefing, other academic preparation, and student activities.

Electives

The law school offers clinical experience in the Constitutional Law Clinic. The school offers seminars in First Amendment Law, Juvenile Law, and School Law. Non-paid, non-credit internships in government and nonprofit organizations are also available to students. Fieldwork includes a Criminal Law Externship and a Judicial Clerk Externship. The law school hosts a Speakers Forum bringing in members of the bench and bar as well as hosting a broad range of special lectures. Tutorial and

Phone: 434-592-5300
Fax: 434-592-5400
E-mail: law@liberty.edu
Web: law.liberty.edu

Contact
Office of Admissions and Financial Aid, (434) 592-5300 for general inquiries; Coordinator of Financial Aid, (434) 592-5431 for financial aid information.

remedial programs include the Academic Support Program. Special interest groups include the Alternative Dispute Resolution (ADR) Board and the Moot Court Board. The most widely taken electives are Administrative Law and Business Planning.

Graduation Requirements
In order to graduate, candidates must have a GPA of 2.0 and complete the upper-division writing requirement.

Organizations
Students edit the *Liberty University Law Review*. Students participate in the Thurgood A. Marshall Memorial Moot Court Competition, Regent National Constitutional Law Moot Court Competition, and the ABA Appellate Advocacy Competition. Other competitions include the Robert R. Merhige National Environmental Negotiation Competition, ABA Client Counseling Competition, and the ABA Negotiation Competition. Law student organizations include the Moot Court Board, and the ADR Board. Local chapters of national associations include the Student Bar Association, Federalist Society, and the Christian Legal Society. Other campus organizations include the International Law Society.

Library
The law library contains 103,436 hardcopy volumes and 167,484 microform volume equivalents, and subscribes to 1,207 serial publications, Online databases and networks include CALI, CIS Universe, Infotrac, Legal-Trac, LEXIS, OCLC First Search, WESTLAW, Wilsonline Indexes, BNA, CCH, CILP, LSN, LLMC, RIA, HeinOnline, and others, which are available to law students for research. The ratio of library volumes to faculty is 7,670 to 1 and to students is 1,110 to 1. The ratio of seats in the library to students is 1 to 1.

Faculty
The law school has 25 full-time and 14 part-time faculty members, of whom 11 are women. About 16% of full-time faculty have a graduate law degree in addition to the J.D.; about 1% of part-time faculty have one. The ratio of full-time students to full-time faculty in an average class is 13 to 1. The law school has a regular program of bringing visiting professors and other distinguished lecturers and visitors to campus.

Students
About 36% of the student body are women; 14%, minorities; 5%, African American; 3%, Asian American; 4%, Hispanic; 1%, Native American. The average age of entering students is 26; age range is 20 to 57. About 13% of students have a graduate degree.

Placement

J.D.s awarded:	90
Services available through: a separate law school placement center.	
Services: organized events to inform students and prepare them professionally.	
Full-time job interviews:	3 employers
Summer job interviews:	3 employers
Placement by graduation:	42% of class
Placement within 9 months:	78% of class
Average starting salary:	$30,000 to $66,000
Areas of placement:	
Private practice 2–10 attorneys	30%
Private practice 11–25 attorneys	11%
Private practice 26–50 attorneys	5%
Private practice 51–100 attorneys	3%
Government	11%
Business/industry	11%
Judicial clerkships	8%
Public interest	5%
Academic	5%
Military	3%

Paul M. Hebert Law Center

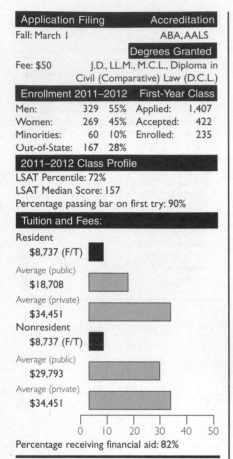

Application Filing	Accreditation
Fall: March 1	ABA, AALS

Degrees Granted	
Fee: $50	J.D., LL.M., M.C.L., Diploma in Civil (Comparative) Law (D.C.L.)

Enrollment 2011–2012   First-Year Class

Men:	329	55%	Applied:	1,407
Women:	269	45%	Accepted:	422
Minorities:	60	10%	Enrolled:	235
Out-of-State:	167	28%		

2011–2012 Class Profile

LSAT Percentile: 72%
LSAT Median Score: 157
Percentage passing bar on first try: 90%

Tuition and Fees:

Resident
$8,737 (F/T)

Average (public)
$18,708

Average (private)
$34,451

Nonresident
$8,737 (F/T)

Average (public)
$29,793

Average (private)
$34,451

Percentage receiving financial aid: 82%

ADMISSIONS

In the fall of 2011 first-year class, 1407 applied, 422 were accepted, and 235 enrolled. Three transfer students enrolled. The median LSAT percentile of the most recent first-year class was 72; the median GPA was 3.4 on a scale of 4.0. The lowest LSAT percentile accepted was 25; the highest was 98.

Requirements

Applicants must have a bachelor's degree and take the LSAT. The most important admission factors include academic achievement, LSAT results, and letter of recommendation. No specific undergraduate courses are required, and candidates are not interviewed.

Procedure

The application deadline for fall entry is March 1. Applicants should submit an application form, LSAT results, transcripts, personal statement, nonrefundable application fee of $50, 2 letters of recommendation, and a $500 seat deposit credited toward tuition. Notification of the admissions decision is on a rolling basis. The law school uses the LSAC.

Special

The law school recruits minority and disadvantaged students by means of an active recruiting program that identifies students through test scores and information received through the Law Services Candidate Referral Program. Requirements are different for out-of-state students. Transfer students must have one year of credit, attended an ABA-approved law school, personal statement, reasons for transferring, and provide information on their overall first-year academic performance.

Costs

On-campus room and board costs about $11,081 annually; books and supplies run $1,700.

Financial Aid

About 82% of current law students receive some form of aid. Awards are based on need and merit combined. Required financial statements are the FFS and the FAFSA. The aid application deadline for fall entry is April 1. First-year students are notified about their financial aid application shortly after applying.

About the Law School

Louisiana State University Paul M. Hebert Law Center was established in 1906 and is a public institution. The campus is located in an urban area in Baton Rouge. The primary mission of the law school is to produce highly competent and ethical lawyers capable of serving the cause of justice in private practice, in public service, and in commerce and industry, both in Louisiana and elsewhere; to support and assist the continuing professional endeavors of our alumni; and to be of service to all members of the legal profession of this state. Students have access to federal, state, county, city, and local agencies, courts, correctional facilities, law firms, and legal aid organizations in the Baton Rouge area. Legislative and executive branches of state government are also accessible to students. Housing for students is available in residence halls, as well as rooms and apartments in privately owned facilities and university facilities. All law school facilities are accessible to the physically disabled.

Calendar

The law school operates on a traditional semester basis. Courses for full-time students are offered days only and must be completed within 4 years. There is no part-time program. New full-time students are admitted in the fall. There is a 7-week summer session. Transferable summer courses are offered.

Programs

In addition to the J.D., the law school offers the LL.M., M.C.L., and Diploma in Civil (Comparative) Law (D.C.L.). Students may take relevant courses in other programs and apply credit toward the J.D.; a maximum of 12 hours credits may be applied. The following joint degrees may be earned: J.D./D.C.L. (Juris Doctor/Diploma in Civil Law), J.D./M.B.A. (Juris Doctor/Master of Business Administration), J.D./M.M.C. (Juris Doctor/Master of Mass Communications), and J.D./M.P.A. (Juris Doctor/Master of Public Administration).

Required

To earn the J.D., candidates must complete 94 total credits, of which 70 are for required courses. They must maintain a minimum GPA of 2.0 in the required courses. The following first-year courses are required of all students: Administration of Criminal Justice I, Basic Civil Procedure, Civil Law Property, Contracts, Constitutional Law I, Criminal Law, Legal Research and Writing I and II, Legal Traditions and Systems, Obligations, and Torts. Required upper-level courses consist of Evidence, Legal Profession, and Trial Advocacy. The required orientation program for first-year students is a day and a half and includes tours and a student activities expo. It also provides some 2 hours with students, about 1 hour with faculty, and a 2-hour Professionalism Program sponsored by the Louisiana State Bar Association.

Electives

The Paul M. Hebert Law Center offers concentrations in corporate law, criminal law, environmental law, family law, international

Phone: 225-578-8646
Fax: 225-578-8647
E-mail: *lynell.cadray@law.lsu.edu*
Web: *lwww.law.lsu.edu*

Contact
Mary Parker, Executive Director, 225-578-3103 for financial aid information.

LOUISIANA

law, juvenile law, labor law, litigation, maritime law, media law, securities law, tax law, and torts and insurance. In addition, third-year students may take clinical courses in preparing for trials and oral arguments. With faculty approval, students may conduct supervised independent research. Special lecture series are the Edward Douglass White Lectures, the James J. Bailey Lectures, and the John H. Tucker, Jr. Lectures. Students may study for 6 weeks during the summer in France. Freshman tutorial programs are available. There are externships whereby 5 students may be selected to work under the supervision of any agency and the instructor in certain courses.

Graduation Requirements
In order to graduate, candidates must have a GPA of 2.0, complete the upper-division writing requirement, and take a seminar, which requires students to submit a paper.

Organizations

Students edit the *Louisiana Law Review* and the newspaper *Civilian*. Moot court competitions include the Tullis Moot Court at the Law Center and at the regional and national Jessup Moot Court and National Moot Court competitions. Teams also participate in the F. Lee Bailey, Frederick Douglass, and Entertainment Law moot courts, and the American Trial Lawyers and Louisiana State Bar Association, Young Lawyers Division, Mock Trial competitions. Law student organizations, local chapters of national associations, and campus organizations include the Student Bar Association, and the Moot Court Board, the Public Interest Law Society, the LSU Law ACLU, Phi Alpha Delta, Phi Delta Phi, the Tax Club, the Black Law Students Association, and the Legal Association of Women.

Library

The law library contains 848,000 hardcopy volumes and 2,153,035 microform volume equivalents, and subscribes to 8,221 serial publications. Online databases and networks include CALI, CIS Universe, DIALOG, Dow-Jones, LEXIS, OCLC First Search, WESTLAW, and Wilsonline Indexes. OCLC, ONLINE public access catalog, the Internet, HeinOnline, LLMC Digital, JSTOR, and BNA are also available to law students for research. Special library collections include a digital library, a U.S. government document depository, a depository for Louisiana Supreme Court and Court of Appeals briefs and records, and international, comparative, and foreign law collections, which include Roman Law, and Judge Paul M. Hebert Nuremberg War Crimes Trial Archive. The ratio of library volumes to faculty is 22,316 to 1 and to students is 1,418 to 1. The ratio of seats in the library to students is 1 to 1.

Faculty

The law school has 38 full-time and 50 part-time faculty members, of whom 21 are women. About 27% of full-time faculty have a graduate law degree in addition to the J.D.; about 8% of part-time faculty have one. The ratio of full-time students to full-time faculty in an average class is 16 to 1; in a clinic, 10 to 1. The law school has a regular program of bringing visiting professors and other distinguished lecturers and visitors to campus. There is a chapter of the Order of the Coif.

Students

About 45% of the student body are women; 10%, minorities; 8%, African American; 1%, Asian American; and 1%, Hispanic. The majority of students come from Louisiana (72%). The average age of entering students is 24; age range is 21 to 52. About 80% of students enter directly from undergraduate school, 10% have a graduate degree, and 20% have worked full-time prior to entering law school. About 2% drop out after the first year for academic or personal reasons; 98% remain to receive a law degree.

Placement

Services available through: a separate law school placement center and Law Center Career Services
Services: participation in 20 U.S.-wide job fairs and a judicial clerkship preparation course
Special features: resume quick check, mock interviews for students, individual counseling, guest speakers, special programs, a career services library, and a judicial clerkship preparation course

Full-time job interviews:	38 employers
Summer job interviews:	78 employers
Placement within 9 months of graduation:	92% of class
Average starting salary:	$27,500 to $160,000

Areas of placement:

Private practice 2–10 attorneys	26%
Private practice 11–25 attorneys	16%
Private practice 26–50 attorneys	11%
Private practice 51–100 attorneys	6%
Government	9%
Business/industry	3%
Judicial clerkships	21%
Public interest	1%

Loyola Law School Los Angeles

919 Albany Street
Los Angeles, CA 90015

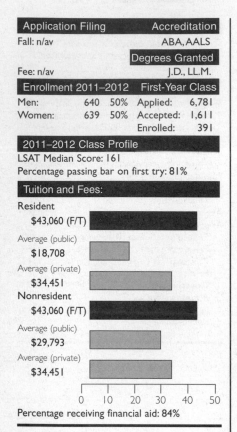

Application Filing	Accreditation
Fall: n/av	ABA, AALS
	Degrees Granted
Fee: n/av	J.D., LL.M.

Enrollment 2011–2012		First-Year Class	
Men:	640 50%	Applied:	6,781
Women:	639 50%	Accepted:	1,611
		Enrolled:	391

2011–2012 Class Profile
LSAT Median Score: 161
Percentage passing bar on first try: 81%

Tuition and Fees:

Resident
$43,060 (F/T)

Average (public)
$18,708

Average (private)
$34,451

Nonresident
$43,060 (F/T)

Average (public)
$29,793

Average (private)
$34,451

Percentage receiving financial aid: 84%

ADMISSIONS

In the fall of 2011 first-year class, 6781 applied, 1611 were accepted, and 391 enrolled. The median GPA of the most recent first-year class was 3.5.

Requirements
Applicants must have a bachelor's degree and take the LSAT. The most important admission factors include academic achievement, LSAT results, and general background. No specific undergraduate courses are required. Candidates are not interviewed.

Procedure
Applicants should submit an application form, LSAT results, transcripts, a personal statement, TOEFL results (where applicable), and a letter of recommendation. Notification of the admissions decision is December through June. The law school uses the LSAC.

Special
The law school recruits minority and disadvantaged students with programs such as Open House, campus visits by faculty, and financial support for outstanding minority applicants. Additionally, there is a Summer Institute program for students who need additional preparation prior to law school. Requirements are different for out-of-state students. Transfer students must have one year of credit, must have attended an ABA-approved law school, must have a personal statement, and must have above average grades at the prior law school.

Costs

Tuition and fees for the 2011–2012 academic year are $42,490 for all full-time students. Tuition for part-time students is $28,410 for in-state students and $28,410 out-of-state. On-campus room and board costs about $16,190 annually; books and supplies run $1,050.

Financial Aid

About 84% of current law students receive some form of aid. Awards are based on need and merit combined. The required financial statement is the FAFSA. First-year students are notified about their financial aid application at time of acceptance.

About the Law School

Loyola Marymount University Loyola Law School Los Angeles was established in 1920 and is a private institution. The 3-acre campus is in an urban area a little west of downtown Los Angeles. The primary mission of the law school is to educate men and women who will be leaders of both the legal profession and society, demonstrating in their practice of law and public service the highest standards of personal integrity, professional ethics, and a deep concern for social justice in the Jesuit Marymount tradition. Students have access to federal, state, county, city, and local agencies, courts, correctional facilities, law firms, and legal aid organizations in the Los Angeles area. Housing for students is not available on campus, but there is a housing referral service. All law school facilities are accessible to the physically disabled.

Calendar

The law school operates on a traditional semester basis. Courses for full-time students are offered both day and evening and must be completed within 5 years. For part-time students, courses are offered both day and evening and must be completed within 5 years. New full- and part-time students are admitted in the fall. There is a 7½-week summer session. Transferable summer courses are offered.

Programs

In addition to the J.D., the law school offers the LL.M. Students may take relevant courses in other programs and apply credit toward the J.D.; a maximum of 6 credits may be applied. The following joint degrees may be earned: J.D./LL.M. (Juris Doctor/Doctor of Taxes) and J.D./M.B.A. (Juris Doctor/Master of Business Administration).

Required
To earn the J.D., candidates must complete 87 total credits, of which 41 are for required courses. They must maintain a minimum GPA of 2.1 in the required courses. The following first-year courses are required of all students: Civil Procedure, Constitutional Law I, Contracts, Criminal Law, Legal Research and Writing, Property, and Torts. Required upper-level courses consist of Constitutional Law II, Ethical Lawyering, Evidence, and the upper division writing requirement. The required orientation program for first-year students is 2 to 3 days.

Electives
The Loyola Law School Los Angeles offers concentrations in corporate law, criminal law, entertainment law, environmental law, family law, intellectual property law, international law, juvenile law, labor law, litigation, media law, securities law, sports law, tax law, and torts and insurance. In addition, clinics are open to advanced students in good academic standing for a maximum of 14 credits. Seminars and research programs are open to advanced students; these students are also eligible for internships, field work, and study-abroad programs. Seminars are generally worth 2 units each. The law school offers

Phone: 213-736-1074
Fax: 213-736-6523
E-mail: admissions@lls.edu
Web: www.lls.edu

Contact

Dean for Enrollment Management, 213-736-1140 for financial aid information.

CALIFORNIA

4 study abroad programs: Costa Rica, Bologna, Italy, Beijing, China, and Cyprus. Tutorials are available to students with academic need.

Graduation Requirements

In order to graduate, candidates must have a GPA of 2.0, must have completed the upper-division writing requirement, and must have 58 resident credits in addition to 40 hours of community service work.

Organizations

The primary student-edited law reviews are *Loyola of Los Angeles Law Review*, *Loyola of Los Angeles International and Comparative Law Review,,* and *Loyola of Los Angeles Entertainment Law Review*, as well as the campus electronic newsletter In Brief. Annual moot court competitions include the Jessup International Moot Court, National Civil Trial Competition, and ABA competition. Other competitions include the Byrne Trial Advocacy Competition, which includes on- and off-campus competitions in the fall and spring, the Black Law Students Association (BLSA) Moot Court Competition, the Hispanic National Association Moot Court Competition, and VIS Arbitration Moot Court. Law student organizations include the Women's Law Association, Asian Pacific American Law Student's Association (APALSA), and Business Law Association. Local chapters of national associations include Phi Alpha Delta, National Lawyers Guild, and Public Interest Law Association. Other campus organizations include the Entertainment and Sports Law Society, Criminal Law Society, and St. Thomas More Honor Society.

Library

The law library contains 620,274 hard-copy volumes and 275,309 microform volume equivalents, and subscribes to 7,019 serial publications. Such online databases and networks as CALI, CIS Universe, Infotrac, Legal-Trac, LEXIS, Mathew Bender, OCLC First Search, RLIN, WESTLAW, Wilsonline Indexes, Congressional Masterfile I and II, Congressional Universe, State Net, and ORION are available to law students for research. Special library collections include federal and state depositories and foreign collections of selected European, Latin American, and Pacific Rim countries. A complete U.S. legislative history from 1970 to the present includes all available records and briefs of the U.S. Supreme Court.

Faculty

The law school has 79 full-time and 63 part-time faculty members, of whom 55 are women. The ratio of full-time students to full-time faculty in an average class is 16 to 1. The law school has a regular program of bringing visiting professors and other distinguished lecturers and visitors to campus. There is a chapter of the Order of the Coif.

Students

About 50% of the student body are women. The average age of entering students is 23.

Placement

J.D.s awarded:	403

Services available through: a separate law school placement center.

Services: information on practice areas, computer-assisted job search, and on-campus interview programs.

Special features: numerous workshops and panel discussions, an extensive resource library, special programs for students interested in pursuing government or public interest careers, and programs promoting issues of diversity and minority recruitment and hiring.

Placement within 9 months of graduation:	97% of class
Average starting salary:	$60,000 to $125,000

School of Law

25 East Pearson Street
Chicago IL, 60611

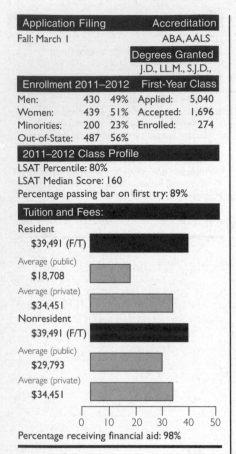

Application Filing	Accreditation
Fall: March 1	ABA, AALS

Degrees Granted
J.D., LL.M., S.J.D.,

Enrollment 2011–2012		First-Year Class	
Men:	430 49%	Applied:	5,040
Women:	439 51%	Accepted:	1,696
Minorities:	200 23%	Enrolled:	274
Out-of-State:	487 56%		

2011–2012 Class Profile
LSAT Percentile: 80%
LSAT Median Score: 160
Percentage passing bar on first try: 89%

Tuition and Fees:

Resident
$39,491 (F/T)

Average (public)
$18,708

Average (private)
$34,451

Nonresident
$39,491 (F/T)

Average (public)
$29,793

Average (private)
$34,451

0 10 20 30 40 50

Percentage receiving financial aid: 98%

ADMISSIONS

In the fall of 2011 first-year class, 5040 applied, 1696 were accepted, and 274 enrolled. Twenty-six transfers enrolled. The median LSAT percentile of the most recent first-year class was 80; the median GPA was 3.4 on a scale of 4.0.

Requirements
Applicants must have a bachelor's degree and take the LSAT. The most important admission factors include academic achievement, GPA, and LSAT results. No specific undergraduate courses are required. Candidates are not interviewed.

Procedure
The application deadline for fall entry is March 1. Applicants should submit an application form, LSAT results, transcripts, a personal statement, and 2 academic letters of recommendation. Notification of the admissions decision is after February 15. The law school uses the LSAC.

Special
The law school recruits minority and disadvantaged students through national law forums and university-sponsored law days. Requirements are different for out-of-state students. Transfer students must have one year of credit, must have a minimum GPA of 3, must have attended an ABA-approved law school, must submit a personal statement, and must be in the top 25% of their class.

Costs

Tuition and fees for the 2011–2012 academic year are $38,780 for full-time in-state students and $38,870 for out-of-state students. Tuition for part-time students is $29,110 for in-state students and $29,110 out-of-state. On-campus room and board costs about $11,150 annually; books and supplies run $1,200.

Financial Aid

About 98% of current law students receive some form of aid. The average annual amount of aid from all sources combined, including scholarships, loans, and work contracts, is $28,837; maximum, $52,380. Awards are based on need and merit combined. The required financial statement is the FAFSA. The aid application deadline for fall entry is March 1. Special funds for minority or disadvantaged students include a variety of merit-based scholarships. First-year students are notified about their financial aid application mid-March.

About the Law School

Loyola University Chicago School of Law was established in 1908 and is a private institution. The campus is in an urban area in Chicago. Loyola University Chicago School of Law is a student-focused law center inspired by the Jesuit tradition of academic excellence, intellectual openness, and service to others. Our mission is to educate diverse, talented students to be responsible leaders in a rapidly changing, interdependent world, to prepare graduates who will be ethical advocates for justice and the rule of law, and to contribute to a deeper understanding of law and legal institutions through a commitment to research, scholarship, and public service. Students have access to federal, state, county, city, and local agencies, courts, correctional facilities, law firms, and legal

aid organizations in the Chicago area. Loyola's expanding and recently renovated facilities enjoy a prime location in the heart of Chicago. Its Water Tower Campus offers student housing, a book store, coffee shops, and a cafeteria. Recent renovations to law school buildings have added ceremonial courtrooms and offices. Housing for students is available in a residence hall across from the law school, in apartments within walking distance of the law school, and in various Chicago neighborhoods. All law school facilities are accessible to the physically disabled.

Calendar

The law school operates on a traditional semester basis. Courses for full-time students are offered both day and evening, and must be completed within 84 months. For part-time students, courses are offered both day and evening, and must be completed within 84 months. New full- and part-time students are admitted in the fall. There is a 10-week summer session. Transferable summer courses are offered.

Programs

In addition to the J.D., the law school offers the LL.M., S.J.D., Master of Jurisprudence, and Doctorate of Law. Students may take relevant courses in other programs and apply credit toward the J.D.; a maximum of 9 credits may be applied. The following joint degrees may be earned: J.D./M.A. (Juris Doctor/Master of Arts in Comparative Law and Education and in Political Science), J.D./M.B.A. (Juris Doctor/ Master of Business Administration), and J.D./M.S.W. (Juris Doctor/ Master of Social Work).

Required
To earn the J.D., candidates must complete 86 total credits, of which 34 are for required courses. They must maintain a minimum GPA of 2.0 in the required courses. The following first-year courses are required of all students: Civil Procedure, Constitutional Law, Contracts, Criminal Law, Legal Research, Legal Writing I and II, Perspective Elective, Property, and Torts. Required upper-level courses consist of Advocacy, Experiential Learning, Professional Responsibility, and Skills. The required orientation program for first-year students is 3 half-days.

Phone: 312-915-7170
800-545-5744
Fax: 312-915-7906
E-mail: *law-admissions@luc.edu*
Web: *www.luc.edu/law*

Contact

Law Admission and Financial Assistance, 312-915-7170 for general inquiries; Farah Dalal, 312-915-7170 for financial aid information.

ILLINOIS

Electives

The School of Law offers concentrations in corporate law, criminal law, family law, intellectual property law, international law, juvenile law, labor law, litigation, tax law, advocacy law, child and family law, health law, international law and practice, public interest law, and tax law. In addition, clinical legal experience is gained through the Loyola University Community Law Center, the Federal Tax Clinic, the Child Law Clinic, and the Business Law Clinic. Seminars, of which there are a variety, are offered for 2 to 3 credit hours to all students after the first year. Second- and third-year law students receive 3 hours credit for teaching a course called Street Law in Chicago-area high schools. Externships are available every semester; supervised experience is offered in judicial, criminal, corporate, health law, child law, and government for 2 or 3 credit hours. Individualized research projects, under the supervision of a faculty member, are available every semester for 1 or 2 hours credit. Special lecture series include the Philip H. Corboy Lecture, the Wing-Tat Lee Lecture on international and comparative law, the Christopher T. Hurley Lecture, and the Law and Literature Lecture. Study-abroad programs include the Rome Program and the Beijing Program. Rome and Beijing are each 4–5-week summer programs offering 4 or 5 elective courses for 2 credits each. There is a 2-week London Advocacy Program and a Chile immersion program. Tutors are assigned to each first-year course section. Loyola's Academic Enhancement Program is conducted during the spring semester. The voluntary program provides extensive tutoring and faculty mentors to students who fall within the lower 20% of the first-year class. Minority programs include the Dean's Diversity Committee and the minority membership program. The Child Advocacy Program utilizes interdisciplinary instruction and field experience to train students to become child advocates. The Public Interest Law Program provides law students with opportunities to explore public interest law through the legal clinic. The most widely taken electives are Evidence, Business Organization, and Federal Income Taxation.

Graduation Requirements

In order to graduate, candidates must have a GPA of 2.0.

Organizations

Student-edited publications include the *Loyola Law Journal, Loyola Consumer Law Review, Annals of Health Law, Public Interest Law Reporter, Children's Legal Rights Journal,* and the *International Law Review.* Moot Court competitions include the National Moot Court, Jessup Competition, and Wagner (labor law). Other competitions include the National Mock Trial Competition and the Client Counseling Competition and Negotiations Competition, both sponsored by the ABA. Loyola also participates annually in the Intraschool Moot Court Competition, Chicago Bar, Illinois Bar, Niagara, Sutherland Rich (intellectual property), National Juvenile Law, National Health Law, ABA, Hispanic Bar, Frederick Douglass, Willem Vis, and Thomas Tang competitions. Law student organizations and local chapters of national associations include Phi Alpha Delta, Decalogue Society, Health Law Society, Child Law Society, and National Lawyers Guild. There are more than 30 active student organizations which provide the law community with a broad range of legal topics and interests. Other campus organizations include Black Law Students Association, American Society of International Law, and Latin American Law Students Association.

Library

The law library contains 399,955 hardcopy volumes and 220,927 microform volume equivalents, and subscribes to 1,254 serial publications. Such online databases and networks as CALI, CIS Universe, Infotrac, Legal-Trac, LEXIS, OCLC First Search, WESTLAW, Wilsonline Indexes, CCH, BNA, HeinOnline, Pegasus, WorldCat, LLMC-Digital, CIAO, Constitutions of the U.S. (National and State), and SmartBooks are available to law students for research. Special library collections include a G.P.O. depository, an Illinois depository, and a collection on medical jurisprudence, as well as the papers of Chief Justice Mary Ann McMorrow. The ratio of library volumes to faculty is 8,333 to 1 and to students is 485 to 1. The ratio of seats in the library to students is 1 to 2.

Faculty

The law school has 48 full-time and 129 part-time faculty members, of whom 77 are women. According to AAUP standards

Placement

J.D.s awarded:	249

Services available through: a separate law school placement center.

Services: job listings web sites available to students and alumni.

Special features: mock interviews, minority job fairs, the Patent Law Interview Program, the Midwest Public Interest Law Career Conference, 3 computer terminals and printer for resume and cover letter production and career research, the Public Service Law Network Worldwide Internet database, job listings web sites, and reciprocity with all accredited law schools.

Full-time job interviews:	9 employers
Summer job interviews:	24 employers
Placement by graduation:	67% of class
Placement within 9 months:	90% of class
Average starting salary:	$20,800 to $177,000

Areas of placement:

Private practice 2–10 attorneys	25%
Private practice 11–25 attorneys	5%
Private practice 26–50 attorneys	1%
Private practice 51–100 attorneys	4%
Business/industry	22%
Government	11%
Judicial clerkships	7%
Public interest	6%
Academic	3%
Military	1%

for Category I institutions, faculty salaries are average. About 5% of full-time faculty have a graduate law degree in addition to the J.D. The ratio of full-time students to full-time faculty in an average class is 14 to 1; in a clinic, 10 to 1. The law school has a regular program of bringing visiting professors and other distinguished lecturers and visitors to campus.

Students

About 51% of the student body are women; 23%, minorities; 9%, African American; 5%, Asian American; and 7%, Hispanic. Many students come from Illinois (44%). The average age of entering students is 24; age range is 21 to 59. About 33% of students enter directly from undergraduate school, 10% have a graduate degree, and 66% have worked full-time prior to entering law school. About 1% drop out after the first year for academic or personal reasons; 97% remain to receive a law degree.

College of Law

7214 St. Charles Avenue, P.O. Box 901
New Orleans, LA 70118

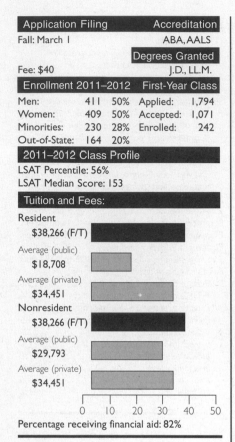

Application Filing	Accreditation
Fall: March 1	ABA, AALS
	Degrees Granted
Fee: $40	J.D., LL.M.

Enrollment 2011–2012		First-Year Class	
Men:	411 50%	Applied:	1,794
Women:	409 50%	Accepted:	1,071
Minorities:	230 28%	Enrolled:	242
Out-of-State:	164 20%		

2011–2012 Class Profile
LSAT Percentile: 56%
LSAT Median Score: 153

Tuition and Fees:

Resident
$38,266 (F/T)

Average (public)
$18,708

Average (private)
$34,451

Nonresident
$38,266 (F/T)

Average (public)
$29,793

Average (private)
$34,451

0   10   20   30   40   50

Percentage receiving financial aid: 82%

ADMISSIONS

In the fall of 2011 first-year class, 1794 applied, 1071 were accepted, and 242 enrolled. Four transfers enrolled. The median LSAT percentile of the most recent first-year class was 56; the median GPA was 3.2 on a scale of 4.0. The lowest LSAT percentile accepted was 15; the highest was 97.

Requirements
Applicants must take the LSAT. Minimum acceptable GPA is 2.0 on a scale of 4.0. The most important admission factors include LSAT results, GPA, and academic achievement. No specific undergraduate courses are required and candidates are not interviewed.

Procedure
The application deadline for fall entry is March 1. Applicants should submit an application form, LSAT results, transcripts, personal statement, nonrefundable application fee of $40, letters of recommendation (3 are recommended).

Notification of the admissions decision is 4 to 6 weeks after the file is complete. The law school uses the LSAC.

Special
The law school recruits minority and disadvantaged students through alumni involvement, recruitment at institutions with traditionally minority-dominated enrollment, the use of CLEO, and the purchase of names and addresses of minority prospects from LSAC. Requirements are different for out-of-state students. Transfer students must have one year of credits, attended an ABA-approved law school, personal statement, and entering LSAT and undergraduate GPA eligible for acceptance at Loyola and above average law school GPA.

Costs

Tuition and fees for the 2011–2012 academic year are $37,230 for all full-time students. Tuition for part-time students is $24,820 for in-state students and $24,820 out-of-state. On-campus room and board costs about $13,000 annually; books and supplies run $1,550.

Financial Aid

About 82% of current law students receive some form of aid. The average annual amount of aid from all sources combined, including scholarships, loans, and work contracts, is $35,000; maximum, $60,357. Awards are based on need and merit combined. Required financial statement is the FAFSA. The aid application deadline for fall entry is June 1. Special funds for minority or disadvantaged students consist of grants based on merit alone. First-year students are notified about their financial aid application at time of acceptance.

About the Law School

Loyola University of New Orleans College of Law was established in 1914 and is a private institution. The 4-acre campus is located in an urban area. The primary mission of the law school is to educate future members of the bar to be skilled advocates and sensitive counselors-at-law committed to ethical standards in pursuit of human dignity for all. Students have access to federal, state, county, city, and local agencies, courts, correctional

facilities, law firms, and legal aid organizations in the New Orleans area. Facilities of special interest to law students include the U.S. Court of Appeals for the Fifth Circuit, the Supreme Court of the State of Louisiana, the U.S. Court for the Eastern District of Louisiana, and the Louisiana Legislature. Housing for students is available in a residence hall located across the street from the law school building; there is no married student housing on campus. All law school facilities are accessible to the physically disabled.

Calendar

The law school operates on a traditional semester basis. Courses for full-time students are offered and required courses, day only; electives, day and evening and must be completed within 5 years. For part-time students, courses are offered (and required courses), evening only; electives, (day and evening) and must be completed within 5 years. New full- and part-time students are admitted in the fall. There is an 8-week summer session. Transferable summer courses are offered.

Programs

In addition to the J.D., the law school offers the LL.M. The following joint degrees may be earned: J.D./M.B.A. (Juris Doctor/Master of Business Administration), J.D./M.P.A. (Juris Doctor/Master of Public Administration), and J.D./M.U.R.P. (Juris Doctor/Master of Urban and Regional Planning).

Required
To earn the J.D., candidates must complete 90 total credits, of which 53 are for required courses. They must maintain a minimum GPA of 2.0 in the required courses. The following first-year courses are required of all students: Civil Law Property I or Common Law Property I, Civil Law Property II or Common Law Property II, Civil Procedure I and II, Criminal Law, Legal Profession, Legal Research and Writing, Moot Court, and Torts I and II. Required upper-level courses consist of Business Organizations, Constitutional Criminal Procedure, Constitutional Law I, Donations or Civil Law of Persons or Security Rights or Property, Evidence, Law and Poverty, Louisiana Donations and Trusts, Sales and Leases (Civil Law Division), and

Phone: 504-861-5575
Fax: 504-861-5772
E-mail: ladmit@loyno.edu
Web: law.loyno.edu

Contact
K. Michele Allison-Davis, Assistant Dean of Admissions, 504-861-5575 for general inquiries; Nadine Lauret, Assistant Director of Financial Aid, 504-861-5551 for financial aid information.

LOUISIANA

Successions or Trusts and Estates. Loyola has a mandatory skills curriculum; courses that students must take for 8 skills points are drawn from the following categories: office practice, trial practice, appellate practice, and pro bono practice. The required orientation program for first-year students is held for 8 days prior to the beginning of classes. Students attend a 13-hour Legal Methods course designed to provide the fundamentals of briefing cases, classroom interaction, outlining for exams and other essentials needed to begin law school confidently. Students also complete requirements for registration, receive welcoming remarks from university officials, meet professors, and meet with upper-level students.

Electives
The College of Law offers concentrations in corporate law, criminal law, environmental law, family law, international law, litigation, maritime law, tax law, civil law, common law, and public interest law. In addition, there are several clinics for third-year students. At the Loyola Law Clinic, students participate in a clinical setting, working on both civil and criminal cases, as well as mediation. Seminars are offered as part of the regular curriculum. Second- and third-year law students in the upper third of their class may participate in externship programs. Students devote at least 12 hours a week to various assignments. Independent research projects may be undertaken under the supervision of a professor. A Street Law course is available. Loyola offers several lecture series that promote the legal profession. There are study-abroad programs in Cuernavaca, Mexico; Brazil or Costa Rica; Moscow and St. Petersburg, Russia; Budapest, Hungary; and Vienna, Austria. All programs are open to second- and third-year students. Second- and third-year students may serve as Teacher Assistants (T.A.) in the Legal Research and Writing and Moot Court programs. The Academic Success Program is maintained for students who need assistance with organizing and preparing for classes and exams. Diversity grants based on merit are available, for entering first-year students. The most widely taken electives are Mediation, Family Law, and Negotiable Instruments.

Graduation Requirements
In order to graduate, candidates must have a GPA of 2.0, complete the upper-division writing requirement, have fulfilled the Perspective requirement 1 of 3 possible courses that give a philosophical and historical perspective on law.

Organizations
Students edit the Loyola Law Review, Loyola Journal of Public Interest Law, Maritime Law Journal, Loyola Law and Technology Annual, and the newspaper, The Code. Moot court competitions include the National Moot Court Competition, Stetson International Environment Moot Court Competition, and National Mardi Gras Invitational Competition. Other competitions include the William C. Vis International Commercial Arbitration Competition, Frederick Douglass Moot Court Competition (participation by the Black Law Students Association), the Thomas Tang Competition (participation by the Asian Pacific American Law Student Association), Pepperdine Entertainment Law Competition, Jerome Prince Memorial Evidence Competition, First Amendment Competition, and St. John's Duberstein Bankruptcy Competition. Law student organizations, local chapters of national associations, and campus organizations include the Student Bar Association, Black Law Students Association, Hispanic-American Law Students Association, Delta Theta Phi, Phi Delta Phi, National Lawyers Guild, Communications Law Society, JD/MBA Society, and Loyola Environmental Law Society.

Library
The law library contains 236,088 hardcopy volumes and 1,340,908 microform volume equivalents, and subscribes to 3,050 serial publications. Online databases and networks include CALI, CIS Universe, DIALOG, Infotrac, Legal-Trac, LEXIS, OCLC First Search, WESTLAW, and Wilsonline Indexes, which are available to law students for research. Special library collections include French, Quebec, and Scottish law; U.S. government documents and Louisiana state documents; and WTO depository. The ratio of library volumes to faculty is 8,097 to 1 and to students is 459 to 1. The ratio of seats in the library to students is 1 to 2.

Placement
J.D.s awarded:	238

Services available through: a separate law school placement center and the university placement center.
Services: coordination of speakers for various employment opportunities, a student news and job information monthly newsletter, and a resume bank.

Full-time job interviews:	49 employers
Average starting salary:	$39,200 to $160,000

Areas of placement:
Private practice 2–10 attorneys	28%
Private practice 11–25 attorneys	12%
Private practice 26–50 attorneys	6%
Private practice 51–100 attorneys	4%
Business/industry	14%
Government	11%
Judicial clerkships	9%
Public interest	4%
Academic	1%

Faculty
The law school has 57 full-time and 25 part-time faculty members, of whom 30 are women. According to AAUP standards for Category IIA institutions, faculty salaries are above average. About 20% of full-time faculty have a graduate law degree in addition to the J.D. The ratio of full-time students to full-time faculty in an average class is 16 to 1; in a clinic, 10 to 1. The law school has a regular program of bringing visiting professors and other distinguished lecturers and visitors to campus.

Students
About 50% of the student body are women; 28%, minorities; 12%, African American; 4%, Asian American; 10%, Hispanic; and 1%, Native American. The majority of students come from Louisiana (80%). The average age of entering students is 25; age range is 21 to 48. About 3% drop out after the first year for academic or personal reasons; 97% remain to receive a law degree.

Law School

Office of Admissions,
P.O. Box 1881
Milwaukee, WI 53201-1881

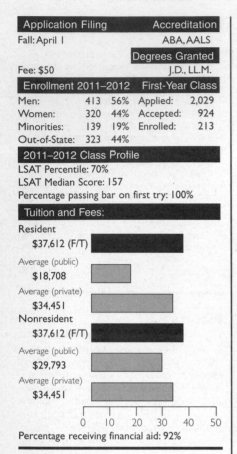

Application Filing		Accreditation	
Fall: April 1		ABA, AALS	
		Degrees Granted	
Fee: $50		J.D., LL.M.	

Enrollment 2011–2012			First-Year Class	
Men:	413	56%	Applied:	2,029
Women:	320	44%	Accepted:	924
Minorities:	139	19%	Enrolled:	213
Out-of-State:	323	44%		

2011–2012 Class Profile

LSAT Percentile: 70%
LSAT Median Score: 157
Percentage passing bar on first try: 100%

Tuition and Fees:

Resident
$37,612 (F/T)

Average (public)
$18,708

Average (private)
$34,451

Nonresident
$37,612 (F/T)

Average (public)
$29,793

Average (private)
$34,451

Percentage receiving financial aid: 92%

ADMISSIONS

In the fall of 2011 first-year class, 2029 applied, 924 were accepted, and 213 enrolled. Thirteen transfers enrolled. The median LSAT percentile of the most recent first-year class was 70; the median GPA was 3.3 on a scale of 4.0. The lowest LSAT percentile accepted was 30; the highest was 95.

Requirements
Applicants must have a bachelor's degree and take the LSAT. No specific undergraduate courses are required. Candidates are not interviewed.

Procedure
The application deadline for fall entry is April 1. Applicants should submit an application form, LSAT results, transcripts, a personal statement, the TOEFL (if applicable), a nonrefundable application fee of $50, and a letter of recommendation. Accepted students must pay a nonrefundable $450 first tuition deposit

and a $450 second tuition deposit; both are applied to the first-semester tuition. Notification of the admissions decision is on a rolling basis. The law school uses the LSAC.

Special
The law school recruits minority and disadvantaged students through CRS, contacts with current students and alumni of color, targeted recruitment, and visits to law forums and college campuses with significant minority representation. Requirements are different for out-of-state students. Transfer students must have one year of credit, must have attended an ABA-approved law school, must submit a personal statement, and must complete 56 credits at Marquette.

Costs

Tuition and fees for the 2011–2012 academic year are $37,570 for all full-time students. On-campus room and board costs about $12,950 annually; books and supplies run $1,200.

Financial Aid

About 92% of current law students receive some form of aid. The average annual amount of aid from all sources combined, including scholarships, loans, and work contracts, is $41,783; maximum, $74,842. Awards are based on need and merit combined. The required financial statement is the FAFSA. The aid application deadline for fall entry is March 1. Special funds for minority or disadvantaged students include targeted scholarships. First-year students are notified about their financial aid application after acceptance but prior to enrollment if financial aid forms were filed in a timely fashion.

About the Law School

Marquette University Law School was established in 1892 and is a private institution. The 90-acre campus is in an urban area adjacent to downtown Milwaukee. The primary mission of the law school is to offer a balanced curriculum noted for its comprehensive teaching of both the theory and practice of law and to instill in students a sense of professional responsibility. Marquette graduates are admitted to the Wisconsin bar without taking the bar exam. Students have access to federal,

state, county, city, and local agencies, courts, correctional facilities, law firms, and legal aid organizations in the Milwaukee area. The municipal courthouse is located 2 blocks away. The federal courthouse is approximately one-half mile away. Housing for students consists of campus area apartments. The Office of Residence Life assists students with off-campus accommodations. All law school facilities are accessible to the physically disabled.

Calendar

The law school operates on a traditional semester basis. Courses for full-time students are offered both day and evening, and must be completed within 4 years. For part-time students, courses are offered both day and evening, and must be completed within 6 years. New full- and part-time students are admitted in the fall. There are two 5-week summer sessions. Transferable summer courses are offered.

Programs

In addition to the J.D., the law school offers the LL.M. Students may take relevant courses in other programs and apply credit toward the J.D.; a maximum of 6 credits may be applied. The following joint degrees may be earned: J.D./M.A. (Juris Doctor/Master of Arts) and J.D./M.B.A. (Juris Doctor/Master of Business Administration).

Required
To earn the J.D., candidates must complete 90 total credits, of which 38 are for required courses. They must maintain a minimum GPA of 2.0 in the required courses. The following first-year courses are required of all students: Civil Procedure, Constitutional Law, Contracts, Criminal Law, Legal Analysis, Writing, and Research I and II, Property, and Torts. Required upper-level courses consist of a perspectives course, a process elective, a public law elective, a seminar, a workshop course, Advanced Legal Research, Evidence, The Law Governing Lawyers, and Trusts and Estates. While not required, typically over 80% of graduates have taken at least one clinical course. The required orientation program for first-year students lasts two full days prior to the start of the semester and includes all aspects of law school. Students meet with professors and upper-class students in small groups.

Phone: 414-288-6767
Fax: 414-288-0676
E-mail: law.admission@marquette.edu
Web: http://law.marquette.edu

Contact

Office of Student Financial Aid, 414-288-4000 for financial aid information.

WISCONSIN

Electives

The law school offers concentrations in corporate law, criminal law, environmental law, family law, intellectual property law, international law, juvenile law, labor law, litigation, sports law, tax law, torts and insurance, dispute resolution, water law, estate planning, health care law, and real estate law. Clinical training is available through the Prosecutor Clinic, Defender Clinic, Unemployment Compensation Clinic, and Small Claims Mediation Clinic. Seminars provide students with an opportunity to work intensely under faculty supervision. Internships are available in both appellate and trial courts, including the Wisconsin Supreme Court, the U.S. Court of Appeals for the Seventh Circuit, and the Milwaukee County Circuit courts. Research programs provide students with an appreciation of the relationship of law to other disciplines and an understanding of the process through which legal doctrine is formed as well as comparisons of the American legal system with other legal systems. Supervised field-work programs provide students with the opportunity to intern with a variety of governmental and public service agencies. There is an Academic Support Program for first-year students. The school actively recruits minority students. The most widely taken electives are skills courses, upper-level electives in specific doctrinal areas, and clinical courses.

Graduation Requirements

In order to graduate, candidates must have a GPA of 2.0, must have completed the upper-division writing requirement, and must have completed a minimum 56 credits at Marquette Law School.

Organizations

Students edit the *Marquette Law Review, Marquette Sports Law Review, Marquette Intellectual Property Law Review, Marquette Elder's Advisor*, and the *Federation of Insurance and Corporate Counsel Quarterly*. Moot court competitions include the Jenkins Moot Court, sports law, and alternative dispute resolution competitions. National competitions include the National Moot Court, Philip C. Jessup International, Giles Rich Intellectual Property, and Sports Law Moot Court. Law student organizations, local chapters of national associations, and campus organizations include the Student Bar Association, Health Law Society, Environmental Law Society, Public Interest Law Society, Sports Law Society, Black Law Students Association, Delta Theta Phi, Phi Alpha Delta, and Phi Delta Phi.

Library

The law library contains 390,869 hardcopy volumes and 168,520 microform volume equivalents, and subscribes to 522 serial publications. Such online databases and networks as CALI, Legal-Trac, LEXIS, WESTLAW, BNA, HeinOnline, Proquest Congressional, Lexis-Nexis Academic Universe, MOML, Proquest CCH Intelliconnect, Fast Case, JSTOR, Max-Planck, NewsBank, SBRNet, Shepard's, and Tax Analysis are available to law students for research. Special library collections include a federal depository. The ratio of seats in the library to students is 1 to 1.

Faculty

The law school has 48 full-time and 76 part-time faculty members, of whom 53 are women. According to AAUP standards for Category I institutions, faculty salaries are average. About 4% of full-time faculty have a graduate law degree in addition to the J.D. The ratio of full-time students to full-time faculty in an average class is 16 to 1. The law school has a regular program of bringing visiting professors and other distinguished lecturers and visitors to campus.

Students

About 44% of the student body are women; 19%, minorities; 6%, African American; 4%, Asian American; 7%, Hispanic; and 1%, Native American. The majority of students come from Wisconsin (56%). The average age of entering students is 25; age range is 19 to 53. About 47% of students enter directly from undergraduate school, and 5% have a graduate degree. About 7% drop out after the first year for academic or personal reasons; 93% remain to receive a law degree.

Placement

J.D.s awarded:	230
Services available through: a separate law school placement center.	
Services: mock interviews.	
Special features: personal counseling with students and access to a computer and a laser printer in the office to prepare resumes and cover letters.	
Full-time job interviews:	13 employers
Summer job interviews:	32 employers
Placement by graduation:	52% of class
Placement within 9 months:	89% of class
Average starting salary:	$35,000 to $125,000
Areas of placement:	
Private practice 2–10 attorneys	34%
Private practice 11–25 attorneys	7%
Private practice 26–50 attorneys	4%
Private practice 51–100 attorneys	2%
Business/industry	21%
Government	10%
Public interest	5%
Judicial clerkships	3%
Academic	1%

500 Federal Street
Andover, MA 01810

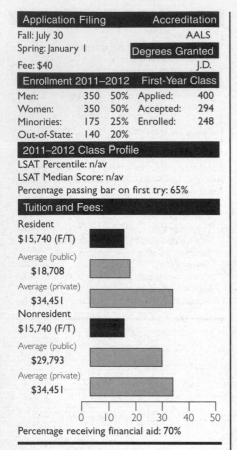

Application Filing		Accreditation
Fall: July 30		AALS
Spring: January 1		**Degrees Granted**
Fee: $40		J.D.

Enrollment 2011–2012		First-Year Class	
Men:	350 50%	Applied:	400
Women:	350 50%	Accepted:	294
Minorities:	175 25%	Enrolled:	248
Out-of-State:	140 20%		

2011–2012 Class Profile
LSAT Percentile: n/av
LSAT Median Score: n/av
Percentage passing bar on first try: 65%

Tuition and Fees:

Resident
$15,740 (F/T)

Average (public)
$18,708

Average (private)
$34,451

Nonresident
$15,740 (F/T)

Average (public)
$29,793

Average (private)
$34,451

0   10   20   30   40   50

Percentage receiving financial aid: 70%

ADMISSIONS

In the fall of 2011 first-year class, 400 applied, 294 were accepted, and 248 enrolled. Eight transfers enrolled. The median GPA of the most recent first-year class was 3.25.

Requirements
Applicants must have a bachelor's degree. No specific undergraduate courses are required. Candidates are not interviewed.

Procedure
The application deadline for fall entry is July 30. Applicants should submit an application form, transcripts, a personal statement, MSLAT, a nonrefundable application fee of $40, 3 letters of recommendation, and a personal interview. Notification of the admissions decision is weekly. The law school uses the LSAC.

Special
The law school recruits minority and disadvantaged students from traditional minority colleges. Requirements are different for out-of-state students. Transfer students must have a minimum GPA of 3 and a personal statement.

Costs

Tuition and fees for the 2011–2012 academic year are $14,990 for all full-time students. Tuition for part-time students is $11,992 for in-state students and $11,992 out-of-state.

Financial Aid

About 70% of current law students receive some form of aid. Required financial statement is the FAFSA. The aid application deadline for fall entry is July 15. First-year students are notified about their financial aid application at time of acceptance.

About the Law School

Massachusetts School of Law was established in 1988 and is a private institution. The campus is located in a rural area of Andover, MA. The primary mission of the law school is to provide a high-quality, practical education so students can become successful lawyers in the private sector. Students have access to federal, state, county, city, and local agencies, courts, correctional facilities, law firms, and legal aid organizations in the Andover area. Facilities for law students include an extensive law library and computer laboratory. There is no housing available for students. All law school facilities are accessible to the physically disabled.

Calendar

The law school operates on a traditional semester basis. Courses for full-time students are offered both day and evening and must be completed within 4 years. For part-time students, courses are offered both day and evening and must be completed within 5 years. New full- and part-time students are admitted in the fall and spring. There are 2 4-week summer sessions. Transferable summer courses are not offered.

Programs

Required
To earn the J.D., candidates must complete 90 total credits, of which 45 are for required courses. They must maintain a minimum GPA of 2.0 in the required courses. The following first-year courses are required of all students: Civil Procedure, Contract Law, Contracts, Criminal Law, Criminal Procedure, Property, Torts, and Writing for Lawyers. Required upper-level courses consist of Business Associations, Constitutional Law, Evidence, Motions, Research Writing I and II, UCC Articles 2, 3, 4, and 9. The required orientation program for first-year students is 1 week.

Electives
The law school offers concentrations in corporate law, criminal law, family law, juvenile law, labor law, litigation, tax law, torts, and insurance. The most widely taken electives are family law, case preparation, and wills and trusts.

Graduation Requirements
In order to graduate, candidates must have a GPA of 2.0.

Phone: 978-681-0800
Fax: 978-681-6330
E-mail: *mslaw@mslaw.edu*
Web: *www.mslaw.edu*

Contact
Director of Admission. 978-681-0800 for general inquiries; Director of Financial Aid, 978-681-0800 for financial aid information

MASSACHUSETTS

Library
Online databases and networks the school subscribes to include CALI, Legal-Trac, LEXIS, Mathew Bender, and WEST-LAW, which are available to law students for research. Special library collections include MCLE and Mass Practice.

Faculty
The law school has 16 full-time and 80 part-time faculty members, of whom 45 are women. The ratio of full-time students to full-time faculty in an average class is 15 to 1; in a clinic, 8 to 1. The law school has a regular program of bringing visiting professors and other distinguished lecturers and visitors to campus.

Students
About 50% of the student body are women; and 25%, minorities. The majority of students come from Massachusetts (80%). The average age of entering students is 32; age range is 22 to 65. About 35% of students enter directly from undergraduate school, 25% have a graduate degree, and 65% have worked full-time prior to entering law school. About 25% drop out after the first year for academic or personal reasons; 75% remain to receive a law degree.

Placement
J.D.s awarded:	125
Special features: Seminars and CLE's	

MERCER UNIVERSITY

Walter F. George School of Law

1021 Georgia Avenue
Macon, GA 31207

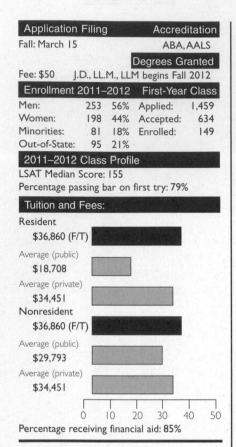

Application Filing		Accreditation	
Fall: March 15		ABA, AALS	

Degrees Granted			
Fee: $50	J.D., LL.M., LLM begins Fall 2012		

Enrollment 2011–2012		First-Year Class	
Men:	253 56%	Applied:	1,459
Women:	198 44%	Accepted:	634
Minorities:	81 18%	Enrolled:	149
Out-of-State:	95 21%		

2011–2012 Class Profile

LSAT Median Score: 155
Percentage passing bar on first try: 79%

Tuition and Fees:

Resident
$36,860 (F/T)

Average (public)
$18,708

Average (private)
$34,451

Nonresident
$36,860 (F/T)

Average (public)
$29,793

Average (private)
$34,451

Percentage receiving financial aid: 85%

ADMISSIONS

In the fall of 2011 first-year class, 1459 applied, 634 were accepted, and 149 enrolled. Eight transfer students enrolled. The median GPA of the most recent first-year class was 3.41.

Requirements

Applicants must have a bachelor's degree and take the LSAT. The most important admission factors include LSAT results, GPA, and writing ability. No specific undergraduate courses are required. Candidates are not interviewed.

Procedure

The application deadline for fall entry is March 15. Applicants should submit an application form, LSAT results, transcripts, personal statement, nonrefundable application fee of $50, 2 letters of recommendation, personal statement to be used as a writing sample. Notification of the admissions decision is on a rolling basis. The law school uses the LSAC.

Special

The law school recruits minority and disadvantaged students by visiting colleges that are traditionally minority schools and by using the Candidate Referral Service of Law Services to identify potential minority students. The law school also hosts events on campus. Requirements are different for out-of-state students. Transfer students must have one year of credits, attended an ABA-approved law school, personal statement, be in top 50% of their class, submit a letter of good standing from their dean, have 2 letters of recommendation from their professors, subscribe to LSAC, and submit a current transcript of all law schools attended to Mercer.

Costs

Tuition and fees for the 2011–2012 academic year are $36,560 for all full-time students. On-campus room and board costs about $16,632 annually; books and supplies run $1,482.

Financial Aid

About 85% of current law students receive some form of aid. The average annual amount of aid from all sources combined, including scholarships, loans, and work contracts, is $50,894; maximum, $54,974. Students are awarded merit scholarships and need- and non-need based loans. Required financial statements are the FAFSA and institutional application. The aid application deadline for fall entry is April 1. Special funds for minority or disadvantaged students include the National CLEO Program. First-year students are notified about their financial aid application at the time of application to law school.

About the Law School

Mercer University Walter F. George School of Law was established in 1873 and is a private institution. The 130-acre campus is located in an urban area 80 miles south of Atlanta. The primary mission of the law school is to produce genuinely good lawyers, in an ethical and pragmatic sense, who are well-equipped to begin their careers in the practice of law. Students have access to federal, state, county, city, and local agencies, courts, correctional facilities, law firms, and legal aid organizations in the Macon area. Facilities of special interest to law students include a 4-story reproduction of Independence Hall that sits atop Coleman Hill about a mile from the Main Mercer University campus. Each first year law student receives a laptop computer. Mercer has excellent programs in legal research and writing, ethics and professionalism, and law and public service. Housing for students consists of privately owned and university owned apartments available within walking distance of the school, as well as multiple apartment complexes throughout the city. All law school facilities are accessible to the physically disabled.

Calendar

The law school operates on a traditional semester basis. Courses for full-time students are offered both day and evening and summer school offers evening classes and must be completed within 3 years. For part-time students, courses are offered both day and evening and summer school offers evening classes and must be completed within 7 years. New full- and part-time students are admitted in the fall. There is a 7-week summer session. Transferable summer courses are offered.

Programs

In addition to the J.D., the law school offers the LL.M. and LLM begins Fall 2012. Students may take relevant courses in other programs and apply credit toward the J.D.; a maximum of 12 hours for J.D./M.B.A. degree credits may be applied. The following joint degrees may be earned: J.D./M.B.A. (Juris Doctor/Master of Business Administration).

Required

To earn the J.D., candidates must complete 91 total credits, of which 52 are for required courses. The following first-year courses are required of all students: American Constitutional System, Contracts I and II, Criminal Law, Introduction to Law Study, Introduction to Legal Research, Jurisdiction and Judgments, Legal Profession, Legal Writing I, Property, and Torts. Required upper-level courses consist of Advanced Writing Requirement, Advanced Skills Course, Civil Lawsuits, Evidence, Introduction to Alternative Dispute Resolution, Introduction to Counseling, Law of Lawyering, Legal Writing II, and Statutory Law and Analysis. All

Phone: 478-301-2605
800-637-2378
Fax: 478-301-2989
E-mail: *Sutton_me@law.mercer.edu*
Web: *www.Law.Mercer.edu*

Contact

Marilyn E. Sutton, Assistant Dean of Admissions and Financial Aid, 478-301-2605 for general inquiries; Leah Aiken, Director of Admissions and Financial Aid, 478-301-5902 for financial aid information.

GEORGIA

students must take Introduction to Counseling and Introduction to Dispute Resolution courses. Each student also must elect at least 1 course from a list of advanced skills courses that use simulations of law practice situations. Mercer Law School has a three-day orientation program that includes meeting senior administrators and faculty, discussion of the honor code and other information important to new students. First-year students also participate in small group sessions that focus on cultural competency and global law practice. All first-year students receive a laptop and participate in technology and library orientation. Also during the first week, students visit the Federal and Superior Courthouses and hear from the judges in those courts. In addition, students participate in the professionalism orientation organized by the State Bar of Georgia. Students begin in a large plenary session, and then meet in small groups with local attorneys and judges to discuss hypothetical ethical scenarios and other interesting considerations that might potentially come up in law practice.

Electives

The Walter F. George School of Law offers concentrations in corporate law, criminal law, environmental law, family law, intellectual property law, international law, labor law, litigation, media law, securities law, tax law, torts and insurance, legal writing, research and drafting certificate program, and law and public service program. In addition, clinics include the Public Defender Criminal Defense Clinic, worth 3 credits; the Habeaus Project for second- and third-year students, worth 4 credits. Each student must elect at least 1 seminar in the third year or 2 credit hours. Approximately 15 seminars are offered each year on a range of subjects from legal ethics to mass media. Supervised internships of 2 to 4 credit hours may be arranged under the Public Interest Practicum Program. Judicial Field Placement, a 3 to 4 credit course for second-year students, places students with federal and state court judges to serve as clerks. There is a weekly classroom component as well. Mercer offers numerous lecture series including the John James lecture, Law Review Symposium, and Ethics and Professionalism symposium. Study abroad programs are available in conjunction with Stetson University Law School. An academic tutorial program offers one-on-one mentoring to any

student in academic difficulty. Minority programs include Mercer's BLSA organization, which conducts minority orientation prior to the first year. Various minority groups on campus visit HBC schools during the year and work with BLSA and minority student organizations. Mercer Pro Bono Clinic and Public Interest Foundation provide volunteer services for local legal aid organizations. The most widely taken electives are Business Associations, Criminal Procedure, and Trial Practice.

Graduation Requirements

In order to graduate, candidates must have a GPA of 76.0 and complete the upper-division writing requirement.

Organizations

Students edit the *Mercer Law Review*, and the *Journal of Southern Legal History*. National moot court competitions held annually are the National Moot Court, Gabrielli National Family Law, and Gibbons National Criminal Procedure. Other competitions include the Georgia Intrastate, Vale National Corporate Law, National Negotiation, National Client Counseling, National Civil Rights, and Frederick Douglass competitions. Law student organizations include the Association of Women Law Students, Student Bar Association, and Project Equality. There are local chapters of Phi Alpha Delta, Phi Delta Phi, and Black Law Student Association. Other campus organizations include Environmental Law Society, International Law Society, and Legal Aid Volunteer Association.

Library

The law library contains 202,187 hardcopy volumes and 153,356 microform volume equivalents, and subscribes to 2,130 serial publications. Online databases and networks include CALI, CIS Universe, Legal-Trac, LEXIS, OCLC First Search, WESTLAW, and Wilsonline Indexes. Additional databases include Galileo, CQ Researcher, LLMC digital, HeinOnline, JSTOR, CCH, KIA, and BNA, which are available to law students for research. Special library collections include Georgia legal research materials, federal depository library, and Southern legal history. The ratio of library volumes to faculty is 10,957 to 1 and to students is 791 to 1. The ratio of seats in the library to students is 1 to 1.

Placement

J.D.s awarded:	131

Services available through: a separate law school placement center.

Special features: videotaped practice interviews and critiques, job fairs and consortia, and seminars and educational panels on types of practice and interviewing.

Full-time job interviews:	3 employers
Summer job interviews:	18 employers
Placement by graduation:	41% of class
Placement within 9 months:	85% of class
Average starting salary:	$30,000 to $155,000

Areas of placement:

Private practice 2–10 attorneys	31%
Private practice 11–25 attorneys	9%
Private practice 26–50 attorneys	3%
Private practice 51–100 attorneys	3%
Judicial clerkships	12%
Government	12%
Public interest	7%
Business/industry	5%
Military	2%

Faculty

The law school has 31 full-time and 48 part-time faculty members, of whom 25 are women. According to AAUP standards for Category IIA institutions, faculty salaries are average. About 23% of full-time faculty have a graduate law degree in addition to the J.D.; about 18% of part-time faculty have one. The ratio of full-time students to full-time faculty in an average class is 13 to 1. The law school has a regular program of bringing visiting professors and other distinguished lecturers and visitors to campus.

Students

About 43% of the student body are women; 18%, minorities; 9%, African American; 6%, Asian American; 1%, Hispanic; 1%, Native American; and 1%, Chicano/Mexican, Puerto Rican. The majority of students come from the South (90%). The average age of entering students is 23; age range is 19 to 37. About 4% drop out after the first year for academic or personal reasons; 96% remain to receive a law degree.

MICHIGAN STATE UNIVERSITY

College of Law

368 Law College Bldg.
East Lansing, MI 48824-1300

Application Filing		Accreditation	
Fall: April 30		ABA, AALS	
		Degrees Granted	
Fee: $60		J.D., LL.M.	

Enrollment 2011–2012		First-Year Class	
Men:	505 52%	Applied:	3,732
Women:	463 48%	Accepted:	1,185
Minorities:	223 23%	Enrolled:	393
Out-of-State:	513 53%		

2011–2012 Class Profile
LSAT Percentile: 50%
LSAT Median Score: 157
Percentage passing bar on first try: 87%

Tuition and Fees:

Resident
$34,783 (F/T)

Average (public)
$18,708

Average (private)
$34,451

Nonresident
$34,783 (F/T)

Average (public)
$29,793

Average (private)
$34,451

0   10   20   30   40   50

Percentage receiving financial aid: 88%

ADMISSIONS

In the fall of 2011 first-year class, 3732 applied, 1185 were accepted, and 393 enrolled. Forty-four transfer students enrolled. The median LSAT percentile of the most recent first-year class was 50; the median GPA was 3.5 on a scale of 4.0. The lowest LSAT percentile accepted was 15; the highest was 93.

Requirements
Applicants must have a bachelor's degree and take the LSAT. Minimum acceptable GPA is 2.0 on a scale of 4.0. The most important admission factors include GPA, LSAT results, and academic achievement. No specific undergraduate courses are required. Candidates are not interviewed.

Procedure
The application deadline for fall entry is April 30. Applicants should submit an application form, LSAT results, transcripts, a nonrefundable application fee of $60, 2 required letters of recommendation,

and a resume. Notification of the admissions decision is on a rolling basis. The law school uses the LSAC.

Special
The law school recruits minority and disadvantaged students through attendance at law fairs on the campuses of universities that have a highly diversified population and contact via the LSAC candidate referral service. Requirements are different for out-of-state students. Transfer students must have one year of credits, a minimum GPA of 3.0, attended an ABA-approved law school, be in good academic standing, and be eligible to return to the law school they currently attend.

Costs

Tuition and fees for the 2011–2012 academic year are $34,452 for all full-time students. On-campus room and board costs about $9,548 annually; books and supplies run $1,415.

Financial Aid

About 88% of current law students receive some form of aid. The average annual amount of aid from all sources combined, including scholarships, loans, and work contracts, is $40,200; maximum, $50,220. Awards are based on need and merit combined. Required financial statements are the FAFSA and internal application for need-based awards. The aid application deadline for fall entry is February 1. There are also special funds for minority or disadvantaged students, as well as trustee scholarships (but these are not race exclusive). First-year students are notified about their financial aid application at time of acceptance.

About the Law School

Michigan State University College of Law was established in 1891 and is a private institution. The campus is located in a suburban area just outside the state capital. The primary mission of the law school is to provide a rigorous educational program which prepares a diverse community of students to be national and international leaders. Students have access to federal, state, county, city, and local agencies, courts, correctional facilities, law firms, and legal aid organizations in the East Lansing area. Through

the externship programs, a number of local courts are used officially as training forums for students. Facilities of special interest to students include the law library, classrooms, offices for faculty, administrators, and student organizations, study and lounge facilities, the Moot Court, the computer laboratory, and the Career Services Office. The building supports wireless technology. Housing for students is available both on and off campus. On-campus housing includes both residence halls and apartments. All law school facilities are accessible to the physically disabled.

Calendar

The law school operates on a traditional semester basis. Courses for full-time students are offered both day and evening and must be completed within 7 years. For part-time students, courses are offered both day and evening and also must be completed within 7 years. New full- and part-time students are admitted in the fall. There is an 8-week summer session. Transferable summer courses are offered.

Programs

In addition to the J.D., the law school offers the LL.M. Students may take relevant courses in other programs and apply credit toward the J.D.; a maximum of 6 credits may be applied. The following joint degrees may be earned: J.D./M.A. (Juris Doctor/Master of Arts), J.D./M.B.A. (Juris Doctor/Master of Business Administration), J.D./M.L.R.H.R. (Juris Doctor/Master of Labor Relations and Human Resources), J.D./M.P.A. (Juris Doctor/Master of Public Administration), and J.D./M.S. (Juris Doctor/Master of Science).

Required
To earn the J.D., candidates must complete 88 total credits, of which 32 are for required courses. They must maintain a minimum GPA of 2.0 in the required courses. The following first-year courses are required of all students: Advocacy, Civil Procedure I, Constitutional Law I, Contract Negotiation, Contracts, Criminal Law, Lawyers & Ethics, Property, Regulatory State, Research, Writing and Analysis, and Torts I. Required upper-level courses consist of Professional Responsibility. The required orientation program

Phone: 517-432-0222
844-9352
Fax: 517-432-0098
E-mail: roboskie@law.msu.edu
Web: www.law.msu.edu

Contact
Admission and Financial Aid, 517-432-0222 for general inquiries; John Garcia 517-432-6810, for financial aid information.

MICHIGAN

for first-year students consists of 4 days of intensive study in the foundations of law. Students are taught research skills, use of library techniques, how to brief a case, and how to write an exam. Day 5 is devoted to community service.

Electives
The College of Law offers concentrations in corporate law, criminal law, environmental law, family law, international law, litigation, media law, tax law, health law; certificate in law and social work, indigenous law, public law and regulation; and criminal law. In addition, clinics include the Rental House Clinic, Tax Clinic, Small Business and Nonprofit Clinic, and the Chance at Childhood Clinic. Many seminars in specialized areas are offered each year, allowing students to explore areas of interest in depth with expert faculty members. The MSU Law Career Services assists students in identifying, preparing for, and applying for internships, including judicial clerkships. In addition to the *MSU Law Review*, there are 6 additional student-run publications. Students may also enroll in directed studies and apply for positions as research assistants. Various externship programs are available, including a federal externship in Washington, D.C. and a Summer International Externship Program in Canada. There are student-faculty, and alumni-sponsored lecture series featuring experts on current matters of law. The Law College offers a cooperative study program with the University of Ottawa and a joint J.D./LL.B. program. Through the Canadian summer program, students participate in the Houses of Parliament in Ottawa and Montreal. The Law College also sponsors a summer abroad program in Guadalajara, Mexico and law students participate in other ABA-approved programs. The Law College houses the Office of Diversity Services. There are also a variety of student organizations that focus on issues and services for minority students. The most widely taken electives are Business Enterprises, Decendents Estates & Trusts, and Criminal Procedure.

Graduation Requirements
In order to graduate, candidates must have a GPA of 2.0 and have completed the upper-division writing and Professional Skills course requirement.

Organizations
Students edit the *Michigan State Law Review, Michigan State Journal of International Law, Michigan State Journal of Medicine and Law, Michigan State Entertainment and Sports Law Journal, Michigan State Journal of Gender and Law, Michigan State Journal of Business and Securities Law*, and the student newspaper, *Res Ipsa Loquitor*. A Moot Court offers intramural competitions. The Law College participates in regional, national, and international moot court competitions, including the Cathy Bennett National Trial Competition, Jessup International Moot Court Competition, and Pepperdine Entertainment Law Competition. The Law College hosts the National Trial Advocacy Competition, which attracts 18 competing school teams each fall. Law student organizations include Women's Law Caucus, Jewish Legal Society, and Christian Legal Society. Local chapters of national associations include ABA-Student Division, Amnesty International, and Phi Alpha Delta. Campus clubs and other organizations include the Association of Trial Lawyers, Military Law Society, and Public Interest Society.

Library
The law library contains 188,397 hardcopy volumes and 168,785 microform volume equivalents, and subscribes to 20,933 serial publications. Online databases and networks include CALI, CIS Universe, Infotrac, Legal-Trac, LEXIS, OCLC First Search, WESTLAW, Wilsonline Indexes, and BNA-ALL, which are available to law students for research. There are special library collections on international, labor, and taxation, as well as a Government Printing Office depository; and law practice materials. The ratio of library volumes to faculty is 3,694 to 1 and to students is 194 to 1. The ratio of seats in the library to students is 1 to 3.

Faculty
The law school has 51 full-time and 48 part-time faculty members, of whom 38 are women. According to AAUP standards for Category I institutions, faculty salaries are above average. The ratio of full-time students to full-time faculty in an average class is 14 to 1; in a clinic, 11 to 1. The law school has a regular program of bringing visiting professors and other distinguished lecturers and visitors to campus.

Placement

J.D.s awarded:	276
Services available through: a separate law school placement center	
Special features: Symplicity, Online job listing service	
Full-time job interviews:	11 employers
Summer job interviews:	27 employers
Placement within 9 months of graduation:	92% of class
Average starting salary:	$20,800 to $135,000
Areas of placement:	
Private practice 2–10 attorneys	26%
Private practice 11–25 attorneys	4%
Private practice 26–50 attorneys	1%
Private practice 51–100 attorneys	2%
Business/industry	21%
Academic	10%
Government	8%
Public interest	8%
Judicial clerkships	7%
Military	1%

Students
About 48% of the student body are women; 23%, minorities; 8%, African American; 7%, Asian American; 4%, Hispanic; 2%, Native American; and 2%, Multicultural. The majority of students come from Michigan (47%). The average age of entering students is 23; age range is 20 to 51. About 72% of students enter directly from undergraduate school, 5% have a graduate degree, and 18% have worked full-time prior to entering law school. About 3% drop out after the first year for academic or personal reasons; 94% remain to receive a law degree.

MISSISSIPPI COLLEGE

School of Law

151 East Griffith Street
Jackson, MS 39201

Application Filing	Accreditation
Fall: June 1	ABA, AALS

Degrees Granted
J.D., LL.M.

Enrollment 2011–2012		First-Year Class	
Men:	347 60%	Applied:	1,717
Women:	229 41%	Accepted:	990
Minorities:	52 9%	Enrolled:	214
Out-of-State:	334 58%		

2011–2012 Class Profile
LSAT Percentile: 40%
LSAT Median Score: 149
Percentage passing bar on first try: 75%

Tuition and Fees:

Resident
$29,150 (F/T)

Average (public)
$18,708

Average (private)
$34,451

Nonresident
$29,150 (F/T)

Average (public)
$29,793

Average (private)
$34,451

Percentage receiving financial aid: 84%

ADMISSIONS

In the fall of 2011 first-year class, 1717 applied, 990 were accepted, and 214 enrolled. The median LSAT percentile of the most recent first-year class was 40; the median GPA was 3.2 on a scale of 4.0.

Requirements
Applicants must have a bachelor's degree and take the LSAT. The most important admission factors include LSAT results, GPA, and academic achievement. No specific undergraduate courses are required. Candidates are not interviewed.

Procedure
The application deadline for fall entry is June 1. Applicants should submit an application form, LSAT results, transcripts, and a personal statement. Notification of the admissions decision is on a rolling basis. The law school uses the LSAC.

Special
The law school recruits minority and disadvantaged students by means of recruiting at historically black institutions. Scholarship and stipends are designated for tuition for minority students. Requirements are different for out-of-state students. Transfer students must have one year of credit, must have a minimum GPA of 2, must have attended an ABA-approved law school, and must submit a personal statement, an LSAC report, 2 letters of recommendation from their current law faculty, and a letter of good standing from their current law school dean.

Costs

Books and supplies run $1,200.

Financial Aid

About 84% of current law students receive some form of aid. The average annual amount of aid from all sources combined, including scholarships, loans, and work contracts, is $35,000; maximum, $50,375. Awards are based on need and merit combined. The required financial statement is the FAFSA. First-year students are notified about their financial aid application at time of acceptance.

About the Law School

Mississippi College School of Law was established in 1975 and is a private institution. The campus is in an urban area in Jackson. The primary mission of the law school is to impart to its students quality education within the context of a Christian institution and to instill in them the highest degree of professional proficiency and integrity. Students have access to federal, state, county, city, and local agencies, courts, correctional facilities, law firms, and legal aid organizations in the Jackson area. Housing for students is available off campus. Some on-campus housing at the Clinton campus may be available. All law school facilities are accessible to the physically disabled.

Calendar

The law school operates on a traditional semester basis. Courses for full-time students are offered days only, and must be completed within 3 years. For part-time students, courses are offered days only, and must be completed within 5

years. New full- and part-time students are admitted in the fall. There is a 9-week summer session. Transferable summer courses are offered.

Programs

In addition to the J.D., the law school offers the LL.M. The following joint degrees may be earned: J.D./M.B.A. (Juris Doctor/Master of Business Administration).

Required
To earn the J.D., candidates must complete 90 total credits, of which 36 are for required courses. They must maintain a minimum GPA of 2.0 in the required courses. The following first-year courses are required of all students: Civil Procedure I and II, Contracts I and II, Criminal Law, Legal Analysis, Legal Research and Legal Writing, Property, and Torts I and II. Required upper-level courses consist of a writing requirement, Appellate Advocacy, Constitutional Law, and Professional Responsibility and Ethics. The required orientation program for first-year students is a 3-day program that includes how to brief a case, an introduction to basic legal methods, and the development of the Anglo-American legal system.

Electives
The School of Law offers concentrations in corporate law, family law, litigation, and general and government-related areas. In addition, seminars are open to all upper-class students and are usually worth 2 credit hours. The externship program is a small, select program that provides closely supervised externships with legal/judicial offices and governmental agencies; 2 credit hours are generally given. Legal research and writing programs provide an opportunity to work directly with a faculty member on a topic of the student's choice for 2 credit hours. Field work is possible through the extern program, which is open to upper-class students. Placement is with government and nonprofit entities for 1 to 3 hours during a semester to provide hands-on training. A remedial writing workshop is offered to first-year students exhibiting need based upon a written submission; no credit is offered. A 3 credit-hour special interest program, Comparative Legal Systems: Civil Law and Common Law, is offered to students interested in Louisiana law. The most

Phone: 601-925-7152
800-738-1236
E-mail: pevans@mc.edu
Web: http:// law.mc.edu

Contact

Patricia H. Evans, Assistant Dean of Admissions, 601-925-7150 for general inquiries; Jackie Banes, 601-925-7110 for financial aid information.

widely taken electives are Trial Practice, Pretrial Practice, and Counseling and Negotiations.

Graduation Requirements

In order to graduate, candidates must have a GPA of 2.0 and must have completed the upper-division writing requirement.

Organizations

Students edit the *Mississippi College Law Review* and the student paper, *Legal Eye*. The moot court board conducts the appellate competitions. Law student organizations include the Law Student Association, Women's Student Bar Association, and Environmental Club. There are local chapters of Phi Alpha Delta and Phi Delta Phi.

Library

The law library contains 386,256 hardcopy volumes and 252,061 microform volume equivalents, and subscribes to 3,100 serial publications. Such online databases and networks as CALI, CIS Universe, DIALOG, LEXIS, Mathew Bender, WESTLAW, and Wilsonline Indexes are available to law students for research. Special library collections include a partial government printing office depository for U.S. government documents. The ratio of library volumes to faculty is 4,653 to 1 and to students is 670 to 1. The ratio of seats in the library to students is 1 to 1.

Faculty

The law school has 18 full-time and 65 part-time faculty members, of whom 41 are women. According to AAUP standards for Category IIA institutions, faculty salaries are below average. About 35% of full-time faculty have a graduate law degree in addition to the J.D. The ratio of full-time students to full-time faculty in an average class is 18 to 1; in a clinic, 18 to 1.

Students

About 41% of the student body are women; 9%, minorities; 7%, African American; 1%, Asian American; and 1%, Hispanic. The average age of entering students is 26; age range is 20 to 57. About 70% of students enter directly from undergraduate school, 10% have a graduate degree, and 20% have worked full-time prior to entering law school. About 7% drop out after the first year for academic or personal reasons; 93% remain to receive a law degree.

Placement

J.D.s awarded:	165
Services available through: a separate law school placement center.	
Services: work-study program.	
Placement by graduation:	40% of class
Placement within 9 months:	87% of class
Average starting salary:	$50,000 to $77,500
Areas of placement:	
Private practice 2–10 attorneys	34%
Private practice 11–25 attorneys	2%
Private practice 26–50 attorneys	4%
Private practice 51–100 attorneys	5%
Public interest	2%
Government	17%
Judicial clerkships	12%
Business/industry	10%
Academic	1%

154 Stuart Street
Boston, MA 02116

Application Filing		Accreditation
Fall: March 15		ABA, AALS
		Degrees Granted
Fee: $65		J.D., LL.M.

Enrollment 2011–2012			First-Year Class	
Men:	498	44%	Applied:	2,934
Women:	644	56%	Accepted:	2,105
Minorities:	126	11%	Enrolled:	385
Out-of-State:	662	58%		

2011–2012 Class Profile
LSAT Percentile: 48%
LSAT Median Score: 151
Percentage passing bar on first try: 92%

Tuition and Fees:

Resident
$40,984 (F/T)

Average (public)
$18,708

Average (private)
$34,451

Nonresident
$40,984 (F/T)

Average (public)
$29,793

Average (private)
$34,451

0 10 20 30 40 50

Percentage receiving financial aid: 92%

ADMISSIONS

In the fall of 2011 first-year class, 2934 applied, 2105 were accepted, and 385 enrolled. Two transfer students enrolled. The median LSAT percentile of the most recent first-year class was 48; the median GPA was 3.2 on a scale of 4.0. The lowest LSAT percentile accepted was 30; the highest was 92.

Requirements

Applicants must have a bachelor's degree and take the LSAT. Minimum acceptable GPA is 2.0 on a scale of 4.0. The most important admission factors include satisfactory GPA and LSAT results. No specific undergraduate courses are required, and candidates are not interviewed.

Procedure

The application deadline for fall entry is March 15. Applicants should submit an application form, LSAT results, transcripts, a personal statement, a nonrefundable application fee of $65, 2 letters of recommendation, a personal statement, and the CAS Report. Notification of the admissions decision is on a rolling basis. The law school uses the LSAC.

Special

The law school recruits minority and disadvantaged students through attendance at minority recruitment fairs, at institutions and cities with large minority populations. Recruitment is also done through participation in CLEO and CRS searches through LSAC; as well as connecting minority applicants with minority alumni and current students; and through scholarships. Requirements are different for out-of-state students. Transfer students must have one year of credits, a personal statement, a minimum average of C+, and a dean's letter of good standing.

Costs

Tuition and fees for the 2011–2012 academic year are $40,904 for all full-time students. Tuition for part-time students is $30,680 for in-state students and $30,680 out-of-state. Books and supplies run $1,250.

Financial Aid

About 92% of current law students receive some form of aid. The average annual amount of aid from all sources combined, including scholarships, loans, and work contracts, is $43,758; maximum, $62,184. Awards are based on need and merit combined. Required financial statements are the FAFSA, the institutional application, and federal tax returns. The aid application deadline for fall entry is April 5. Special funds for minority or disadvantaged students include the MacLean Grant for disadvantaged students and the Jacqueline Lloyd Grant and Charles Hamilton Houston Scholarship for minority students. First-year students are notified about their financial aid application at time of acceptance.

About the Law School

New England Law / Boston was established in 1908 and is an independent institution. The campus is located in an urban area in Boston. The primary mission of the law school is to prepare students to be successful lawyers and leaders in the public and private sector through integrated practical, theoretical, and ethical education in the highest caliber. Students have access to federal, state, county, city, and local agencies, as well as courts, correctional facilities, law firms, and legal aid organizations in the Boston area. Boston is the state capital and a center for state and regional legal activity and offers many opportunities for law students. The Clinical Law Office provides hands-on experience and assists low income clients, as well as overseeing other clinical courses and placements at agencies, such as the attorney general's office and Massachusetts Revenue Department. Four academic centers offer additional experimental learning opportunities. There is no housing available for students on campus. However, assistance is provided for finding housing and roommates. About 98% of the law school facilities are accessible to the physically disabled.

Calendar

The law school operates on a traditional semester basis. Courses for full-time students are offered both day and evening and must be completed within 5 years. For part-time students, courses are offered both day and evening and must be completed within 6 years. New full- and part-time students are admitted in the fall. There is an 8-week summer session. Transferable summer courses are offered.

Programs

In addition to the J.D., the law school offers the LL.M. Students may take relevant courses in other programs and apply credit toward the J.D.; a maximum of 6 credits may be applied.

Required

To earn the J.D., candidates must complete 86 total credits, of which 42 are for required courses. They must maintain a minimum GPA of 2.0 in the required courses. The following first-year courses are required of all students: Civil Procedure, Constitutional Law, Contracts, Criminal Law, Legal Research and Writing 1, Property, and Torts. Required upper-level courses consist of Criminal Procedure I, Evidence, Law and Ethics of Lawyering, and Legal Research and Writing II. The required orientation program for first-year students is a 2-day full-time, 3-day part-time program with panel discussions on legal issues and lectures on the legal process, how to brief a case, and the procedures of a civil case.

Phone: 617-422-7210
Fax: 617-422-7201
E-mail: admit@admin.nesl.edu
Web: www.nesl.edu

Contact
Michelle L'etoile, Director of Admissions, 617-422-7210 for general inquiries; Eric Krupski, Director of Financial Aid, 617-422-7298 for financial aid information.

MASSACHUSETTS

Electives
Concentrations include corporate law, criminal law, environmental law, family law, international law, litigation, and tax law. In addition, clinics are available to second- and third-year day division students and third- and fourth-year evening division students for 2 to 6 credits. All upper-class students may take electives for 2 to 3 credits. Final-year students may undertake research programs for a 2 credit maximum per year. New England Law / Boston, in cooperation with 3 other law schools, sponsors 6 summer abroad programs and 3 semester abroad programs. Students may spend a summer studying in Prague, Chile, Ireland, London, or Malta. Students may also spend a semester studying in the Netherlands, or at the University of Paris X in Nanterre. The school will accept credit for courses taken in any summer-abroad program approved by the American Bar Association. A tutorial program and the Academic Excellence program are offered. A noncredit remedial research and writing program is open to first-year students. Noncredit minority programs are open to all students. The most widely taken electives are Wills, Estates and Trusts, Business Organization and UCC: Sales.

Graduation Requirements
In order to graduate, candidates must have a GPA of 2.0 and completed the upper-division writing requirement, and 86 credits.

Organizations
Students edit *New England Law Review*, *New England Journal on Criminal and Civil Confinement*, and the student newspaper, *Due Process*. Other publications include the *New England Journal of International and Comparative Law*. Students participate in an annual in-house Honors Moot Court Competition and Trial Competition. Other competitions include the National Appellate Moot Court Competition, National Trial Competition, National Tax Moot Court, Jessup International Moot Court, Environmental Moot Court, Frederick Douglass Moot Court, and occasionally the ABA Appellate Advocacy Competition. Student organizations include the Student Bar Association, Public Interest Law Association, and Minority Students Association. There are local chapters of the ABA-Law Student Division, Phi Alpha Delta, and Phi Delta Phi.

Library
The law library contains 325,715 hardcopy volumes and 900,082 microform volume equivalents, and subscribes to 533 serial publications. Online databases and networks include CALI, CIS Universe, Legal-Trac, LEXIS, Mathew Bender, OCLC First Search, WESTLAW, and Wilsonline Indexes. JSTOR, BNA, Bloomberg Law; Academic Search Premier; CCH Intelliconnect; HeinOnline; Lawtel, LLMC Digital, and Oxford Scholarship Online are also available to law students for research. Special library collections include women and the law, Portia Law School archives, a Massachusetts continuing legal education depository, all standard legal research materials, such as court reports, statutes, treatises, restatements, and legal periodicals. The ratio of library volumes to faculty is 7,441 to 1 and to students is 319 to 1. The ratio of seats in the library to students is 1 to 2.

Faculty
The law school has 35 full-time and 68 part-time faculty members, of whom 39 are women. About 22% of full-time faculty have a graduate law degree in addition to the J.D.; about 23% of part-time faculty have one. The ratio of full-time students to full-time faculty in an average class is 23 to 1; in a clinic, 8 to 1. The law school has a regular program of bringing visiting professors and other distinguished lecturers and visitors to campus.

Students
About 56% of the student body are women; 11%, minorities; 2%, African American; 4%, Asian American; 2%, Hispanic; and 2%, two or more races. The majority of students come from Massachusetts (42%). The average age of entering students is 24; age range is 21 to 54. About 14% drop out after the first year for academic or personal reasons; 86% remain to receive a law degree.

Placement

J.D.s awarded:	309
Services available through: a separate law school placement center.	
Services: lists of law firm corporate and government contacts and computerized job search resources and assistance with judicial clerkships.	
Special features: required first-year career counseling provided to each student, job search resources, career workshops, alumni mentoring and networking.	
Full-time job interviews:	11 employers
Summer job interviews:	11 employers
Placement by graduation:	48% of class
Placement within 9 months:	84% of class
Average starting salary:	$30,000 to $135,000
Areas of placement:	
Private practice 2–10 attorneys	29%
Private practice 11–25 attorneys	5%
Private practice 26–50 attorneys	2%
Private practice 51–100 attorneys	2%
Business/industry	29%
Government	10%
Public interest	4%
Academic	3%
Judicial clerkships	2%
Military	2%

185 West Broadway
New York, NY 10013-2960

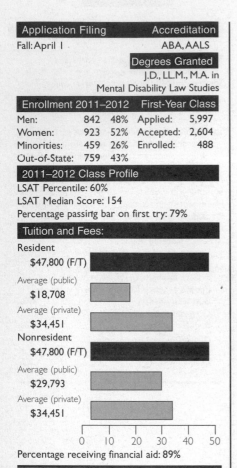

Application Filing	Accreditation
Fall: April 1	ABA, AALS

Degrees Granted
J.D., LL.M., M.A. in
Mental Disability Law Studies

Enrollment 2011–2012			First-Year Class	
Men:	842	48%	Applied:	5,997
Women:	923	52%	Accepted:	2,604
Minorities:	459	26%	Enrolled:	488
Out-of-State:	759	43%		

2011–2012 Class Profile
LSAT Percentile: 60%
LSAT Median Score: 154
Percentage passing bar on first try: 79%

Tuition and Fees:

Resident
$47,800 (F/T)

Average (public)
$18,708

Average (private)
$34,451

Nonresident
$47,800 (F/T)

Average (public)
$29,793

Average (private)
$34,451

0 10 20 30 40 50

Percentage receiving financial aid: 89%

ADMISSIONS

In the fall of 2011 first-year class, 5997 applied, 2604 were accepted, and 488 enrolled. Thirty-two transfers enrolled. The median LSAT percentile of the most recent first-year class was 60; the median GPA was 3.2 on a scale of 4.0.

Requirements

Applicants must have a bachelor's degree and take the LSAT. No specific undergraduate courses are required. Candidates are not interviewed.

Procedure

The application deadline for fall entry is April 1. Applicants should submit an application form, LSAT results, transcripts, a personal statement, and a letter of recommendation. Notification of the admissions decision is on a rolling basis. The law school uses the LSAC.

Special

The law school recruits minority and disadvantaged students through diversity recruitment efforts initiated by minority recruitment coordinators, including outreach to prelaw advisors at minority-serving institutions, partnerships with CLEO, PRLDEF/Latino Justice and other such organizations, and active participation in networks for minority professionals in legal education. Requirements are different for out-of-state students. Transfer students must have one year of credit, must have attended an ABA-approved law school, must submit a personal statement, and must have a bachelor's degree from a regionally accredited college or university.

Costs

Tuition and fees for the 2011–2012 academic year are $46,200 for all full-time students. Tuition for part-time students is $35,600 for in-state students and $35,600 out-of-state. On-campus room and board costs about $17,322 annually; books and supplies run $1,300.

Financial Aid

About 89% of current law students receive some form of aid. The average annual amount of aid from all sources combined, including scholarships, loans, and work contracts, is $53,165; maximum, $71,021. Awards are based on need. The required financial statement is the FAFSA. The aid application deadline for fall entry is April 15. Special funds for minority or disadvantaged students are available. First-year students are notified about their financial aid application contingent upon its completion.

About the Law School

New York Law School was established in 1891 and is independent. The campus is in an urban area in the historic TriBeCa district of New York City. The motto "Learn law, Take action" expresses the law school's commitment to teach students to use the skills and knowledge they acquire as lawyers to do something valuable for others. By fostering an internal culture that embraces innovation and creativity, the law school encourages students to develop the ability to adapt to new situations as they arise, to modify their behavior when change requires it, and to graduate with a commitment to a lifetime of learning. Through an extensive program

for professional development, with an emphasis on integrity and professionalism, the faculty and staff engage students in ongoing improvement of the legal profession. Students have access to federal, state, county, city, and local agencies, courts, correctional facilities, law firms, and legal aid organizations in the New York area. New York Law School is the home to ten academic centers. These hubs of specialized study enable invaluable exchange between students and expert practitioners. The Law School has its own residence hall located in the East Village in Manhattan. There are 99 beds in 2- and 3-bedroom apartments, some with terraces or balconies. Each apartment has a kitchen and full bathroom. All law school facilities are accessible to the physically disabled.

Calendar

The law school operates on a traditional semester basis. Courses for full-time students are offered both day and evening, and must be completed within 3 years. For part-time students, courses are offered both day and evening, and must be completed within 4 years. New full- and part-time students are admitted in the fall. There is an 8-week summer session. Transferable summer courses are offered.

Programs

In addition to the J.D., the law school offers the LL.M. and M.A. in Mental Disability Law Studies. Students may take relevant courses in other programs and apply credit toward the J.D.; a maximum of 10 credits may be applied. The following joint degrees may be earned: J.D./M.A. (Juris Doctor/Master in Forensic Psychology) and J.D./M.B.A. (Juris Doctor/Master of Business Administration).

Required

To earn the J.D., candidates must complete 86 total credits, of which 40 are for required courses. They must maintain a minimum GPA of 2.0 in the required courses. The following first-year courses are required of all students: Civil Procedure, Contracts, Criminal Law, Legislation and Regulation, Legal Practice I and II, Property, and Torts. Required upper-level courses consist of an advanced writing requirement, Constitutional Law, Evidence, and Professional Responsibility. There are seven clinics, several field place-

Phone: 212-431-2888
877-YES-NYLS
Fax: 212-966-1522
E-mail: admissions@nyls.edu
Web: www.nyls.edu

Contact

Susan Gross, Senior Director, 212-431-2888 or 877-YES-NYLS for general inquiries; Office of Admissions and Financial Aid, 212-431-2828 for financial aid information.

NEW YORK

ment courses, externships, workshops, and currently twelve project-based learning courses and simulation courses offered to New York Law School students. The required orientation program for first-year students is a week long, is integrated into the first week of classes, and designed to ease the anxieties of incoming students by having them meet informally with professors and fellow students at planned social events as well as introducing them to the rigors of law studies.

Electives

The school offers concentrations in corporate law, criminal law, entertainment law, environmental law, family law, intellectual property law, international law, labor law, litigation, media law, securities law, tax law, torts and insurance, business and commercial law, constitutional law, procedure and evidence, property and real estate, public interest law, administrative law and practice, and immigration law. In addition, clinics are available in Criminal Law, Mediation, Elder Law, Securities Arbitration, and Urban Law. Students gain additional legal practice experience through workshop courses. These courses link a seminar in a specialized body of law to field placements in offices and agencies practicing in that area of the law. Externships and judicial internships provide opportunities to do actual legal work, in private or public law offices or in judges' chambers, while being supervised by a practitioner at the placement site and meeting with a faculty member at the school. Special lecture series include the Stiefel Symposium, Fall Executive Speakers Series, New York City Law Breakfasts, Solomon Lecture, Professional Development Seminar, Faculty Lecture Series, Dean's Roundtable, Spotlight on Women, CV Starr Lecture, Otto Walter Lecture Series, and Faculty Presentation Day. Independent study programs are available. Students may participate in study-abroad programs offered by other law schools. The Academic Support Program consists of a condensed introductory course in legal methods in the summer followed by weekly tutorial meetings with second- and third-year teaching fellows through the first academic year. The admission/financial aid officers have responsibility for minority recruitment and enrollment initiatives in conjunction with the Office of Student Life, Asian American Law Students Association, Black Law Students Association, Latino Law Students Association, South Asian Law Students

Association, and Stonewall Law Students Association. Special interest group programs include Media Law Project, Domestic Violence Project, New York Law School Civil Liberties Union, Public Interest Coalition, and Trial Lawyers Association. The most widely taken electives are Corporations, Intellectual Property, and New York Practice.

Graduation Requirements

In order to graduate, candidates must have a GPA of 2.0 and must have completed the upper-division writing requirement.

Organizations

Students edit the *New York Law School Law Review* and the student newspaper *De Novo*. Students may participate in the Froessel Moot Court intramural competition. Students become members of the Moot Court Association by invitation and may represent the school in intramural competitions held at law schools nationwide. The Robert F. Wagner Labor Law Moot Court competition is hosted by the school each spring. Law student organizations include Business Law Society, International Law Society, Stonewall Law Students Association, Evening Students Association, Legal Association for Women, and Civil Liberties Union. There are local chapters of Phi Alpha Delta, Phi Delta Phi, and Amnesty International.

Library

The law library contains 534,789 hardcopy volumes and 175,305 microform volume equivalents, and subscribes to 5,680 serial publications. Such online databases and networks as CALI, CIS Universe, DIALOG, Legal-Trac, LEXIS, OCLC First Search, WESTLAW, Wilsonline Indexes, Law Schools Online, Index to UN documents, and others are available to law students for research. Special library collections include a U.S. government documents depository and the archival collection of Judge Roger J. Miner. The ratio of library volumes to faculty is 2,421 to 1 and to students is 303 to 1. The ratio of seats in the library to students is 1 to 4.

Faculty

The law school has 103 full-time and 118 part-time faculty members, of whom 87 are women. About 13% of full-time faculty

Placement

J.D.s awarded:	515

Services available through: a separate law school placement center.

Services: more than 200 law firms participate in recruitment programs.

Special features: more than 100 programs and skills-based workshops often in collaboration with student organizations and our alumni office. All 1L students participate in a Professional Development Seminar that begins during the first week of law school. During the seminar, students learn about different practice areas and settings and get hands on assistance with their job searches, resumes, cover letters, interview skills, and networking. Through our "Mentor Match Program" upper class students meet alumni mentors. Our online presence includes a job database, alumni network, and job search resources. In addition, we have a library collection of job search and career planning materials, information on law firms, corporations, government agencies, the judiciary, and public interest organizations.

Full-time job interviews:	7 employers
Summer job interviews:	25 employers
Placement within 9 months of graduation	89% of class
Average starting salary:	$35,000 to $160,000

Areas of placement:

Private practice 2–10 attorneys	25%
Private practice 11–25 attorneys	3%
Private practice 26–50 attorneys	3%
Private practice 51–100 attorneys	2%
Business/industry	27%
Government	16%
Public interest	4%
Judicial clerkships	3%
Academic	2%

have a graduate law degree in addition to the J.D. The ratio of full-time students to full-time faculty in an average class is 17 to 1; in a clinic, 20 to 1. The law school has a regular program of bringing visiting professors and other distinguished lecturers and visitors to campus.

Students

About 52% of the student body are women; 26%, minorities; 7%, African American; 4%, Asian American; and 13%, Hispanic. The majority of students come from New York (57%). The average age of entering students is 25; age range is 20 to 55. About 30% of students enter directly from undergraduate school, and 9% have a graduate degree. About 15% drop out after the first year for academic or personal reasons; 85% remain to receive a law degree.

School of Law

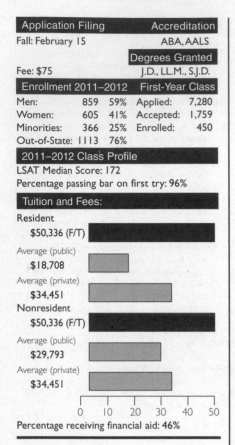

Application Filing	Accreditation
Fall: February 15	ABA, AALS

	Degrees Granted
Fee: $75	J.D., LL.M., S.J.D.

Enrollment 2011–2012		First-Year Class	
Men:	859 59%	Applied:	7,280
Women:	605 41%	Accepted:	1,759
Minorities:	366 25%	Enrolled:	450
Out-of-State:	1113 76%		

2011–2012 Class Profile
LSAT Median Score: 172
Percentage passing bar on first try: 96%

Tuition and Fees:

Resident
$50,336 (F/T)

Average (public)
$18,708

Average (private)
$34,451

Nonresident
$50,336 (F/T)

Average (public)
$29,793

Average (private)
$34,451

Percentage receiving financial aid: 46%

ADMISSIONS

In the fall of 2011 first-year class, 7280 applied, 1759 were accepted, and 450 enrolled. Fifty-six transfers enrolled. The median GPA of the most recent first-year class was 3.7.

Requirements
Applicants must have a bachelor's degree and take the LSAT. No specific undergraduate courses are required. Candidates are not interviewed.

Procedure
The application deadline for fall entry is February 15. Applicants should submit an application form, LSAT results, transcripts, a personal statement, a nonrefundable application fee of $75, and a letter of recommendation. Notification of the admissions decision is by late April. The law school uses the LSAC.

Special
The law school recruits minority and disadvantaged students. NYU seeks to enroll a student body from a broad spectrum of society, including members of groups underrepresented in the profession as well as persons who have experienced socioeconomic and/or educational disadvantage. Requirements are different for out-of-state students. Transfer students must have one year of credit, must have attended an ABA-approved law school, and must submit a personal statement, all college and law school transcripts, LSAT scores, a letter of recommendation from a law school professor, and a statement of good standing from a dean.

Costs

Tuition and fees for the 2011–2012 academic year are $48,950 for all full-time students. On-campus room and board costs about $21,252 annually; books and supplies run $1,400.

Financial Aid

About 46% of current law students receive some form of aid. The average annual amount of aid from all sources combined, including scholarships, loans, and work contracts, is $23,805; maximum, $48,950. Awards are based on need and merit combined. Required financial statements are the FAFSA and Need Access application. The aid application deadline for fall entry is April 15. First-year students are notified about their financial aid application at time of acceptance.

About the Law School

New York University School of Law was established in 1835 and is a private institution. The campus is in New York City. The primary mission of the law school is to produce men and women who are leaders of the bar, public and private, in a world that operates across national boundaries. Students have access to federal, state, county, city, and local agencies, courts, correctional facilities, law firms, and legal aid organizations in the New York area. Facilities of special interest to law students include Vanderbilt Hall, Furman Hall, Wolf Hall, and 22 Washington Square North. These buildings contain classrooms, faculty and administrative offices, the library, and are home to the law school's many centers and institutes.

D'Agostino and Mercer halls are student residences, with meeting rooms, student journal offices, and a conference center. Housing for students is available for virtually all first-year students who request it, including couples and families; 2 law school-owned apartment buildings are within 4 blocks of the campus. About 95% of the law school facilities are accessible to the physically disabled.

Calendar

The law school operates on a traditional semester basis. Courses are offered both day and evening, and must be completed within 6 semesters. New students are admitted in the fall. There is no summer session. Transferable summer courses are not offered.

Programs

In addition to the J.D., the law school offers the LL.M. and S.J.D. Students may take relevant courses in other programs and apply credit toward the J.D.; a maximum of 10 credits may be applied. The following joint degrees may be earned: J.D./LL.M. (Juris Doctor/Master of Laws in Taxation), J.D./J.D. (Juris Doctor/Juris Doctor with Melbourne Law School), J.D./M.A. (Juris Doctor/Master of Arts), J.D./M.B.A. (Juris Doctor/Master of Business Administration), J.D./M.P.A. (Juris Doctor/Master of Public Administration), J.D./M.P.A. (Juris Doctor/Master of Public Administration with Harvard University), J.D./M.P.A. (Juris Doctor/Master of Public Administration with Princeton), J.D./M.P.P. (Juris Doctor/Master of Public Policy with Harvard University), J.D./ M.S.W. (Juris Doctor/Master of Social Work), J.D./M.U.P. (Juris Doctor/Master of Urban Planning), and J.D./Ph.D. (Juris Doctor/Doctor of Philosophy).

Required
To earn the J.D., candidates must complete 83 total credits, of which 38 to 42 are for required courses. The following first-year courses are required of all students: an elective, Contracts, Criminal Law, Lawyering, Procedure, Property, The Administrative and Regulatory State, and Torts. Required upper-level courses consist of an upper-level writing requirement, Constitutional Law, and Professional Responsibility. Clinics and advocacy courses are electives. The required orientation

Phone: 212-998-6060
Fax: 212-995-4527
E-mail: *law.moreinfo@nyu.edu*
Web: *www.law.nyu.edu*

Contact

Joel Schoenecter, Director of Student Financial Service, 212-998-6050 for financial aid information.

NEW YORK

program for first-year students is a 6-day academic and social orientation period before the start of classes, followed by a series of optional weekly programs during the first term.

Electives

The School of Law offers concentrations in corporate law, criminal law, entertainment law, environmental law, family law, intellectual property law, international law, juvenile law, labor law, litigation, maritime law, media law, securities law, sports law, tax law, torts and insurance, global law, public interest law, real estate law, constitutional law, interdisciplinary law, and business administrative law. In addition, clinics provide simulated and actual trial experience; they include the Equal Justice and Capital Defender Clinic, Civil Rights Clinic, and International Human Rights Clinic. There are 29 clinics offered. Seminars are offered in areas such as constitutional law, corporate and commercial law, legal political and social philosophy, and international law. The law school provides guaranteed summer funding to all first- and second-year students who want to work in public interest and government positions. These summer internships are with public interest organizations worldwide. Additionally, Root-Tilden-Kern Scholars participate in a 10-week internship in public interest law. Students may also register for Directed Research, which requires a substantial paper that may fulfill part of the upper-level writing requirement. Research is also part of the law school's specialized programs and fellowships. Special lecture series include the Leadership in Public Interest Series, the National Center on Philanthropy, and the Law Specker Series. Study abroad is possible through a 1-semester exchange program with the Universities of Paris, Amsterdam, Copenhagen, and Cape Town, as well as universities in Belgium, Italy, Brazil, Canada, England, Germany, Japan, Australia, Argentina, and Singapore. Tutorial assistance is available through the Office of Student Affairs. The law school's 25 centers and institutes, as well as its over 60 student organizations, present programs throughout the year.

Graduation Requirements

In order to graduate, candidates must have completed the upper-division writing requirement and attend 6 semesters of classes on a full-time basis.

Organizations

Students edit the *New York University Law Review*, *Annual Survey of American Law*, *Journal of International Law and Politics*, *Environmental Law Journal*, *Review of Law and Social Change*, *Journal of Legislation and Public Policy*, *Journal of Law & Business*, *Journal of Law & Liberty*, the newspaper, *The Commentator*, and the *Moot Court Board Casebook*. Members of the Moot Court Board enter intraschool and nationwide competitions, as well as develop moot court cases for use in nationwide competition. The law school administers the Orison S. Marden Competition, and the Immigration Law Competition. There are more than 60 funded law student organizations on campus, including the Student Bar Association.

Library

The law library contains 1,102,008 hardcopy volumes and 146,900 microform volume equivalents, and subscribes to 4,880 serial publications. Such online databases and networks as CALI, CIS Universe, DIALOG, Dow-Jones, Legal-Trac, LEXIS, OCLC First Search, RLIN, WESTLAW, Wilsonline Indexes, CCH, and others are available to law students for research. Special library collections include the Anglo-American collection, which includes recognized strengths in tax, legal history, intellectual property, constitutional law, the law of democratic institutions, and public international law. The library is also a depository for U.S. government Documents and European Union documents. The ratio of library volumes to faculty is 7,816 to 1 and to students is 753 to 1. The ratio of seats in the library to students is 1 to 2.

Faculty

The law school has 141 full-time and 72 part-time faculty members, of whom 65 are women. About 17% of full-time faculty have a graduate law degree in addition to the J.D. The ratio of full-time students to full-time faculty in an average class is 9 to 1; in a clinic, 8 to 1. The law school has a regular program of bringing visiting professors and other distinguished lecturers and visitors to campus. There is a chapter of the Order of the Coif.

Placement

J.D.s awarded:	495

Services available through: a separate law school placement center.

Special features: Early Interview Week held each August, including employers nationwide; public interest/government and international job fairs; and mentoring programs and co-sponsorship of events, panels, and programs with student groups. Annual Career Fair in January, along with networking, interviewing, and resume development workshops throughout the year, are also available.

Placement by graduation:	97% of class
Placement within 9 months:	98% of class
Average starting salary:	$60,000 to $160,000

Areas of placement:

Private practice 2–10 attorneys	2%
Private practice 11–25 attorneys	1%
Private practice 51–100 attorneys	1%
Government	7%
Business/industry	3%
Public interest	14%
Judicial clerkships	13%
Academic	1%

Students

About 41% of the student body are women; 25%, minorities; 7%, African American; 11%, Asian American; and 7%, Hispanic. The average age of entering students is 24; age range is 20 to 37. About 33% of students enter directly from undergraduate school, 9% have a graduate degree, and 55% have worked full-time prior to entering law school.

NORTH CAROLINA CENTRAL UNIVERSITY

School of Law

640 Nelson Street
Durham, NC 27707

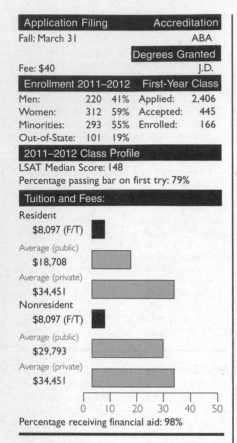

Application Filing		Accreditation
Fall: March 31		ABA

		Degrees Granted
Fee: $40		J.D.

Enrollment 2011–2012		First-Year Class	
Men:	220 41%	Applied:	2,406
Women:	312 59%	Accepted:	445
Minorities:	293 55%	Enrolled:	166
Out-of-State:	101 19%		

2011–2012 Class Profile
LSAT Median Score: 148
Percentage passing bar on first try: 79%

Tuition and Fees:

Resident
$8,097 (F/T)

Average (public)
$18,708

Average (private)
$34,451

Nonresident
$8,097 (F/T)

Average (public)
$29,793

Average (private)
$34,451

0   10   20   30   40   50

Percentage receiving financial aid: 98%

ADMISSIONS
In the fall of 2011 first-year class, 2406 applied, 445 were accepted, and 166 enrolled. The median GPA of the most recent first-year class was 3.2. The lowest LSAT percentile accepted was 145; the highest was 151.

Requirements
Applicants must have a bachelor's degree and take the LSAT. The most important admission factors include academic achievement, LSAT results, and general background. No specific undergraduate courses are required. Candidates are not interviewed.

Procedure
The application deadline for fall entry is March 31. Applicants should submit an application form, LSAT results, transcripts, a nonrefundable application fee of $40, and 2 letters of recommendation. Accepted students who intend to enroll must submit a non-refundable $100 seat deposit. Notification of the admissions decision is on a rolling basis. The law school uses the LSAC.

Special
The law school recruits minority and disadvantaged students by attending recruitment events, by posting diversity links on the school's web site, and by hosting a Performance-Based Admissions Program, which is designed to identify applicants who have the potential to succeed in law school but whose undergraduate transcripts and LSAT scores do not meet traditional standards. Requirements are different for out-of-state students. Transfer students must have a minimum GPA of 2, must have attended an ABA-approved law school, must have 1 year of residence at the School of Law, and must be in good standing with the previous law school.

Costs
Tuition and fees for the 2011–2012 academic year are $5,916 for full-time in-state students and $18,654 for out-of-state students. Tuition for part-time students is $7,708 for in-state students and $7,708 out-of-state. On-campus room and board costs about $9,457 annually; books and supplies run $2,100.

Financial Aid
About 98% of current law students receive some form of aid. The average annual amount of aid from all sources combined, including scholarships, loans, and work contracts, is $22,500; maximum, $44,706. Awards are based on need and merit combined. The required financial statement is the FAFSA. The aid application deadline for fall entry is June 30. Special funds for minority or disadvantaged students include Title III grants and scholarships. First-year students are notified about their financial aid application at time of acceptance.

About the Law School
North Carolina Central University School of Law was established in 1939 and is a public institution. The 135-acre campus is in an urban area 20 miles from Raleigh. The primary mission of the law school is to provide a challenging and broad-based educational program designed to stimulate intellectual inquiry, and foster in each student a sense of community service, professional responsibility, and personal integrity. The law school student body is diverse in terms of gender, ethnicity, economic, and experiential backgrounds. Students have access to federal, state, county, city, and local agencies, courts, correctional facilities, law firms, and legal aid organizations in the Durham area. Facilities of special interest to law students include a modern law library, computer laboratory, academic support programs, individual offices for student organizations, Wi-Fi access throughout the building, Smart-Board technology in each classroom, and access to the Virtual Justice Broadband Project: Technology Assisted Legal Instruction and Services (TALIAS). Some on-campus housing is available for single students, but married students must live off campus. About 95% of the law school facilities are accessible to the physically disabled.

Calendar
The law school operates on a traditional semester basis. Courses for full-time students are offered days only, and must be completed within 3 years. For part-time students, courses are offered evenings only, and must be completed within 4 years. New full- and part-time students are admitted in the fall. There is a 6-week summer session. Transferable summer courses are offered.

Programs
Students may take relevant courses in other programs and apply credit toward the J.D.; a maximum of 6 hours credits may be applied. The following joint degrees may be earned: J.D./M.B.A. (Juris Doctor/Master of Business Administration) and J.D./M.L.S. (Juris Doctor/Master of Library and Information Services).

Required
To earn the J.D., candidates must complete 88 total credits, of which 55 are for required courses. They must maintain a minimum GPA of 2.0 in the required courses. The following first-year courses are required of all students: Civil Procedure I and II, Contracts I and II, Criminal Law, Legal Reasoning and Analysis, Legal Research and Persuasion, Property I and II, and Torts I and II. Required upper-level courses consist of Advanced Legal Writing I and II (Senior Writing Evening Program), Business Associations (Corporations Evening

Phone: 919-530-6333
Fax: 919-530-6030
E-mail: sbrownb@nccu.edu
Web: law.nccu.edu

Contact

Sandra Brown Bechtold, Director of Enrollment, 919-530-5243 for general inquiries; Steve Douglas, Assistant Dean, Financial Aid, 919-530-6365 for financial aid information.

NORTH CAROLINA

Program), Constitutional Law I, Decedents' Estates, Evidence, Legal Letters (Day), N.C. Distinctions, Professional Responsibility, Sales and Secured Transactions, Senior Writing (Evening), and Taxation. Although not required, students are encouraged to enroll in the clinical program. There is a model law office that houses clinical facilities. The required orientation program for first-year students lasts 4 days and includes pre-enrollment seminars.

Electives

The School of Law offers concentrations in environmental law, intellectual property law, juvenile law, litigation, sports law, dispute resolution, biotechnology and pharmaceutical law, and civil rights and Constitutional law certificates. The Clinical Experience Program consists of preliminary courses in the pre-trial process, local rules, mock client interview, and practice with mock trials and oral arguments. For field placements, students work with in-house attorneys in various specialty areas or extern with government officials, legal services agencies, and attorneys in North Carolina. Clinics may be taken by third-year students who receive 2 to 4 credit hours for their work. The Pro Bono Clinic offers many opportunities for second- and third-year students to volunteer in local special interest agencies and organizations. The law school offers approximately 15 seminar classes where the attendance is capped at 20 students. The seminars require 3 writing assignments in such classes dealing with employment discrimination, critical race theory, and sexuality and the law. A number of internships with companies, judges, and practitioners are available. The law school is a member of an inter-institutional enrollment program that includes Duke University School of Law and University of North Carolina School of Law. The law school offers a General Externship Program for students to extern in specialty areas of the law. Placements must be approved by the Clinic Director and are available to second- and third-year students. There are also field components to the domestic violence, criminal, and civil clinics. The law school offers summer study in Costa Rica. An academic support program is available to students for assistance with specific academic needs, problems, and adjustment expectations. Tutorials in each first-year substantive course and selected upper-level courses are open to all interested students. In addition,

the law school offers a noncredit writing laboratory for 1 hour every week in the fall and spring semesters. There are active student organizations for the Innocence Project, Sports and Entertainment Law, Public Interest Law, Intellectual Property, and many other areas. The most widely taken electives are clinical programs, Criminal Procedure, and Trial Practice.

Graduation Requirements

In order to graduate, candidates must have a GPA of 2.0, must have completed the upper-division writing requirement, and must have satisfied oral, practical skills, and writing components of the program.

Organizations

Students edit *The North Carolina Central Law Review* and the *Review of Biotechnology and Pharmaceutical Law*. Moot court competitions include the J. Braxton Craven, Jr. Memorial Moot Court Competition; Saul Lefkowitz Moot Court Competition; and the Ernest B. Fullwood Moot Court Competition. Other competitions include the Trial Advocacy Competition, National Trial Competition, and the Association of Trial Lawyers of America (ATLA) Trial Competition. Law student organizations include the Student Bar Association, Black Law Students Association, and the Public Interest Law Association. There are local chapters of Phi Alpha Delta and Phi Delta Phi. Other organizations include Women's Caucus, Sports and Entertainment Law Association, and Outlaw Alliance.

Library

The law library contains 416,852 hardcopy volumes and 1,149,510 microform volume equivalents, and subscribes to 650 serial publications. Such online databases and networks as CALI, CIS Universe, Infotrac, Legal-Trac, LEXIS, OCLC First Search, WESTLAW, Wilsonline Indexes, BNA Premier, Fastcase, ProQuest Congressional, RIA Checkpoint, HeinOnline, Making of Modern Law including Trials and Supreme Court Records and Briefs, Foreign Law Guide, CCH Intellectual Property Library, and CCH Omnitax are available to law students for research. Special library collections include the Jack Greenberg Collection (items donated by the noted civil rights attorney), the personal papers and Supreme Court book collection of John D. Fassett (items donated

Placement

J.D.s awarded:	178

Services available through: a separate law school placement center.

Services: workshop sessions on various practice areas; mock interviews; and participation in job fairs.

Special features: placement programs that bring in recruiters from government, private firms, legal services, and corporations.

Full-time job interviews:	10 employers
Summer job interviews:	30 employers

Placement within 9 months
of graduation:	88% of class
Average starting salary:	$40,000 to $60,000

Areas of placement:
Private practice 2–10 attorneys	22%
Private practice 11–25 attorneys	2%
Private practice 26–50 attorneys	3%
Private practice 51–100 attorneys	1%
Solo practice	9%
Government	22%
Business/industry	18%
Public interest	8%
Judicial clerkships	4%
Military	2%
Academic	1%

by former Supreme Court Clerk and influential attorney), and the Floyd D. McKissick Collection (items purchased in the name of the noted NC attorney). The ratio of library volumes to faculty is 14,374 to 1 and to students is 758 to 1. The ratio of seats in the library to students is 1 to 2.

Faculty

The law school has 31 full-time and 25 part-time faculty members, of whom 34 are women. According to AAUP standards for Category IIA institutions, faculty salaries are above average. About 35% of full-time faculty have a graduate law degree in addition to the J.D. The ratio of full-time students to full-time faculty in an average class is 17 to 1; in a clinic, 10 to 1. The law school has a regular program of bringing visiting professors and other distinguished lecturers and visitors to campus.

Students

About 59% of the student body are women; 55%, minorities; 51%, African American; 2%, Asian American; 2%, Hispanic; and 1%, Native American. The majority of students come from North Carolina (81%). The average age of entering students is 26; age range is 16 to 42. About 22% drop out after the first year for academic or personal reasons; 76% remain to receive a law degree.

NORTHEASTERN UNIVERSITY
School of Law

400 Huntington Avenue
Boston, MA 02115

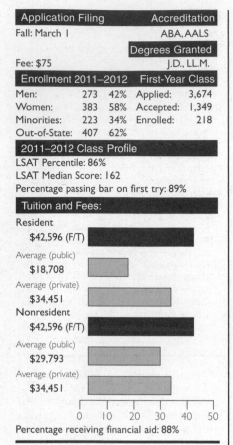

Application Filing	Accreditation
Fall: March 1	ABA, AALS
	Degrees Granted
Fee: $75	J.D., LL.M.

Enrollment 2011–2012		First-Year Class	
Men:	273 42%	Applied:	3,674
Women:	383 58%	Accepted:	1,349
Minorities:	223 34%	Enrolled:	218
Out-of-State:	407 62%		

2011–2012 Class Profile
LSAT Percentile: 86%
LSAT Median Score: 162
Percentage passing bar on first try: 89%

Tuition and Fees:

Resident
$42,596 (F/T)

Average (public)
$18,708

Average (private)
$34,451

Nonresident
$42,596 (F/T)

Average (public)
$29,793

Average (private)
$34,451

0 10 20 30 40 50

Percentage receiving financial aid: 88%

ADMISSIONS
In the fall of 2011 first-year class, 3674 applied, 1349 were accepted, and 218 enrolled. Twenty transfers enrolled. The median LSAT percentile of the most recent first-year class was 86; the median GPA was 3.5 on a scale of 4.0. The lowest LSAT percentile accepted was 26; the highest was 98.

Requirements
Applicants must have a bachelor's degree and take the LSAT. The most important admission factors include general background, LSAT results, and GPA of the student. No specific undergraduate courses are required and candidates are not interviewed.

Procedure
The application deadline for fall entry is March 1. Applicants should submit an application form, LSAT results, transcripts, a personal statement, TOEFL (if indicated), a nonrefundable application fee of $75, 2 letters of recommendation, and a resume. Notification of the admissions decision is on a modified rolling basis. The law school uses the LSAC.

Special
The law school recruits minority and disadvantaged students by visiting HBCUs, providing scholarships, participating in CLEO activities and connecting prospective students to current students and/or graduates. Requirements are different for out-of-state students. Transfer students must have one year of credits, attended an ABA-approved law school, a personal statement, 1 letter from the dean of their current law school attesting to their good standing and eligibility, and at least 1 recommendation from a first-year law professor.

Costs
Tuition and fees for the 2011–2012 academic year are $42,180 for all full-time students. On-campus room and board costs about $18,000 annually; books and supplies run $1,500.

Financial Aid
About 88% of current law students receive some form of aid. The average annual amount of aid from all sources combined, including scholarships, loans, and work contracts, is $50,597; maximum, $70,081. Awards are based on need and merit combined. Required financial statement is the FAFSA. The aid application deadline for fall entry is February 15. First-year students are notified about their financial aid application at time of acceptance.

About the Law School
Northeastern University School of Law was established in 1898 and is a private institution. The 67-acre campus is located in an urban area in Boston. The primary mission of the law school is to help law students see the practice of law as a way to realize their goals, to find meaning and purpose in life, and to be of service to others in ways that are intellectually satisfying and personally rewarding. Students have access to federal, state, county, city, and local agencies, courts, correctional facilities, law firms, and legal aid organizations in the Boston area. Northeastern Law School has 900 co-op employers

located throughout the world. Housing for students is available on campus. All law school facilities are accessible to the physically disabled.

Calendar
The law school operates on a first year - semester; upper level - quarter basis. Courses for full-time students are offered days only and must be completed within 7 years. There is no part-time program. New full-time students are admitted in the fall. There is a 12-week summer session. Transferable summer courses are offered.

Programs
In addition to the J.D., the law school offers the LL.M. Students may take relevant courses in other programs and apply credit toward the J.D.; a maximum of 12 credits may be applied. The following joint degrees may be earned: J.D./M.E.L.P. (Juris Doctor/Master in Environmental Law and Policy), J.D./M.A. (Juris Doctor/ Master of Arts in Sustainable International Development), J.D./M.B.A. (Juris Doctor/Master of Business Administration), J.D./M.P.H. (Juris Doctor/Master of Public Health), J.D./M.S. (Juris Doctor/Master of Science in Accounting), and J.D./M.S./ Ph.D. (Juris Doctor/Master of Science/ Doctor of Philosophy).

Required
To earn the J.D., candidates must complete 87 total credits, of which 37 are for required courses. The following first-year courses are required of all students: Civil Procedure, Constitutional Issues, Contracts, Criminal Justice, Legal Skills in Social context, Property, and Torts. Required upper-level courses include Professional Responsibility. Students are required to complete a course on practice, ethics, and professionalism before the mandatory four supervised legal internships under the school's program of cooperative legal education. In the second and third year of school, students alternate every three months between full-time class work and full-time co-op work. The school also offers traditional clinical courses as electives for upper-level students. The required orientation program for first-year students is 2 to 3 days and introduces students to the first-year curriculum, faculty, law school, and university services.

Phone: 617-373-2395
Fax: 617-373-8865
E-mail: c.taubman@neu.edu
Web: northeastern.edu.law

Contact

Assistant Dean and Director, 617-373-2395 for general inquiries; Linda Schoendorf, Director of Financial Aid, 617-373-4620 for financial aid information.

MASSACHUSETTS

Electives

The School of Law offers concentrations in corporate law, criminal law, environmental law, family law, intellectual property law, international law, labor law, litigation, tax law, public interest, advocacy, and human rights. Clinical courses for upper-level students include Certiorari Clinic/Criminal Appeals, Criminal Advocacy, Poverty Law and Practice, Public Health Legal Clinic, Domestic Rights, and Prisoners Rights. Global Aids Policy Seminar, International Human Rights Legal Research Seminar, and Transactional Drafting Seminar. Research assistant positions are available with individual professors. Students are required to complete 4 distinct cooperative legal education externship quarters during the second and third year of school, alternating every 3 months between full-time classes and full-time work. Special lecture series include the Northern Law Forum, Gordon Lecture and Givelber Distinguished Lecture Program. Study abroad is possible, as well as international co-op placements. There are many academic support programs, including the Legal Writing Workshop, Legal Analysis Workshop, and Analytical Skills Workshop. Upper-level courses include Advanced Legal Research, Legal Research and Writing, Academic Success Legal Analysis, and a 1 credit bar preparation course. Minority students may take advantage of the Analytical Skills Workshop. Special interest group programs include the Tobacco Products Liability Project, Prisoner's Assistance Project, Domestic Violence Institute, Human Rights and the Global Economy, and Public Health Advocacy Institute. The most widely taken electives are Evidence, Corporations, Federal Courts and the Federal System, and Trusts and Estates.

Graduation Requirements

In order to graduate, candidates must have completed the upper-division writing requirement, cooperative education, and a public interest requirement.

Organizations

Moot Court Competitions include the Frederick Douglass Moot Court Competition, ABA National Appellate Advocacy, and National Trial Moot Court. Law student organizations include Jewish Law Students, Legal Environmental Advocacy Forum (LEAP), and International Law Society. Local chapters of national associations include National Lawyers Guild, Queer Caucus, and Jewish Law Students Association. Other organizations include the Black Law Students Association, Asian Pacific Law Students Association, and Latino/Latina Law Students Association. Students edit the *Northeastern University Law Journal*, and the *Primary Law Review*.

Library

The law library contains 339,258 hardcopy volumes and 211,145 microform volume equivalents, and subscribes to 2,140 serial publications. Online databases and networks include CALI, CIS Universe, DIALOG, Infotrac, Legal-Trac, LEXIS, Mathew Bender, OCLC First Search, WESTLAW, Wilsonline Indexes, Social Law Library's online database, BNA core with Tax Management; CCH Business and Finance: CCH Health and Human Resources; HeinOnline; CIAO; Constitutions of the Countries of the World; Environment Law Reporter; Government Search; International Law in Domestic Courts; LLMC Digital; Treaties and International Agreements Online. There are also more than 300 additional databases and research networks through the university library that are available to law students for research. Special library collections include the Sara Ehrmann Collection on the death penalty and the Pappas Public Interest Law Collection. The ratio of library volumes to faculty is 9,424 to 1 and to students is 517 to 1.

Faculty

The law school has 36 full-time and 45 part-time faculty members, of whom 42 are women. According to AAUP standards for Category I institutions, faculty salaries are above average. About 8% of full-time faculty have a graduate law degree in addition to the J.D.; about 10% of part-time faculty have one. The ratio of full-time students to full-time faculty in an average class is 17 to 1; in a clinic, 6 to 1. The law school has a regular program of bringing visiting professors and other distinguished lecturers and visitors to campus.

Placement

J.D.s awarded:	190

Services available through: a separate law school placement center.

Services: a Career Resource Library, materials prepared by the Office of Career Services on career related topics, on-campus interview programs, and participation in numerous job fairs and informational programs.

Special features: The director of the office is an attorney and the associate director has a master's degree in management. Our Career Services office works in collaboration with the office of Cooperative Legal Education to provide career counseling as well as guarantee one year of practical legal experience (4, 3-month, full-time legal internships) prior to graduation. Approximately 40% of graduates obtain their first job from one of their internships.

Full-time job interviews:	10 employers
Summer job interviews:	21 employers
Placement within 9 months of graduation:	94% of class
Average starting salary:	$37,500 to $160,000

Areas of placement:

Private practice 2–10 attorneys	20%
Private practice 11–25 attorneys	3%
Private practice 26–50 attorneys	3%
Private practice 51–100 attorneys	2%
Private practice 100+ attorneys	10%
Public interest	21%
Business/industry	15%
Government	11%
Academic	8%
Judicial clerkships	7%

Students

About 58% of the student body are women; 34%, minorities; 10%, African American; 9%, Asian American; 11%, Hispanic; 1%, Native American; and 3%, two or more races. The majority of students come from Massachusetts (38%). The average age of entering students is 25; age range is 20 to 45. About 29% of students enter directly from undergraduate school, 11% have a graduate degree, and 71% have worked full-time prior to entering law school. About 1% drop out after the first year for academic or personal reasons; 99% remain to receive a law degree.

College of Law

Swen Parson Hall, Room 151
DeKalb, IL 60115-2890

Application Filing		Accreditation	
Fall: April 1		ABA, AALS	
		Degrees Granted	
Fee: $50		J.D.	

Enrollment 2011–2012		First-Year Class	
Men:	178 56%	Applied:	1,058
Women:	140 44%	Accepted:	475
Minorities:	64 20%	Enrolled:	103
Out-of-State:	54 17%		

2011–2012 Class Profile
LSAT Percentile: 52%
LSAT Median Score: 152
Percentage passing bar on first try: 87%

Tuition and Fees:

Resident
$18,688 (F/T)

Average (public)
$18,708

Average (private)
$34,451

Nonresident
$33,311 (F/T)

Average (public)
$29,793

Average (private)
$34,451

0 10 20 30 40 50

Percentage receiving financial aid: 95%

ADMISSIONS

In the fall of 2011 first-year class, 1058 applied, 475 were accepted, and 103 enrolled. The median LSAT percentile of the most recent first-year class was 52; the median GPA was 3.2 on a scale of 4.0. The lowest LSAT percentile accepted was 20; the highest was 86.

Requirements
Applicants must have a bachelor's degree and take the LSAT. The most important admission factors include academic achievement, LSAT results, and letter of recommendation. No specific undergraduate courses are required. Candidates are not interviewed.

Procedure
The application deadline for fall entry is April 1. Applicants should submit an application form, LSAT results, transcripts, a personal statement, a nonrefundable application fee of $50, 2 letters of recommendation, CAS report, and resume.

Notification of the admissions decision is on a rolling basis. The law school uses the LSAC.

Special
The law school recruits minority and disadvantaged students. BLSA, LLSA, ALSN, and the Women's Law Caucus work closely with the Admissions Office to increase the student body's diversity. Graduate assistants in the Office of Admissions participate in various recruiting events throughout the year, including the Annual Illinois Latino Law Forum. Requirements are different for out-of-state students. Transfer students must have one year of credit, must have attended an ABA-approved law school, and must submit a personal statement.

Costs

Books and supplies run $1,600.

Financial Aid

About 95% of current law students receive some form of aid. The average annual amount of aid from all sources combined, including scholarships, loans, and work contracts, is $29,342; maximum, $59,451. Awards are based on need and merit combined. Required financial statements are the FAFSA and in-house financial aid verification form. The aid application deadline for fall entry is March 1. Special funds for minority or disadvantaged students include scholarships for partial- or full-tuition waivers (some with stipends.) First-year students are notified about their financial aid application after acceptance.

About the Law School

Northern Illinois University College of Law was established in 1979 and is a public institution. The 755-acre campus is in a small town 65 miles west of Chicago. Our mission is to prepare students to become effective, creative, and ethical lawyers, ready to serve the legal needs of their communities. Students have access to federal, state, county, city, and local agencies, courts, correctional facilities, law firms, and legal aid organizations in the DeKalb area. Our facilities include a full service law library, adjacent to the main university library; a computer laboratory for law students; 2 courtrooms; and

7 smart classrooms equipped with updated technology. Available housing includes Neptune Hall, one block away from the law school, the first floor of which is designated and equipped for law students. There are also many affordable apartment options surrounding the campus. All law school facilities are accessible to the physically disabled.

Calendar

The law school operates on a traditional semester basis. Courses for full-time students are offered days only, and must be completed within 3 years. For part-time students, courses are offered days only, and must be completed within 7 years. New full- and part-time students are admitted in the fall. There is a 6-week summer session. Transferable summer courses are offered.

Programs

Students may take relevant courses in other programs and apply credit toward the J.D.; a maximum of 6 credits may be applied. The following joint degrees may be earned: J.D./M.B.A. (Juris Doctor/Master of Business Administration) and J.D./M.P.A. (Juris Doctor/Master of Public Administration).

Required
To earn the J.D., candidates must complete 90 total credits, of which 43 are for required courses. They must maintain a minimum GPA of 2.2 in the required courses. The following first-year courses are required of all students: Basic Legal Research I and II, Civil Procedure I and II, Constitutional Law I, Contract I and II, Criminal Law, Legal Writing and Advocacy I and II, Property, and Torts I. Required upper-level courses consist of a writing seminar, Constitutional Law II, Lawyering Skills, and Professional Responsibility. The required orientation program for first-year students is a week long, introducing the process of briefing cases, case synthesis, outlining, exam preparation, and ethics and professionalism.

Electives
The Zeke Giorgi Legal Clinic offers clinics in criminal defense, domestic abuse, elder law, and mediation. Clinics are 4 credit hours. All students must complete a 3-hour

Phone: 815-753-8595
892-3050
Fax. 815-753-5680
E-mail: *lawadm@niu.edu*
Web: *niu.edu/law*

Contact

Admissions Staff, 815-753-8595 for general inquiries.

ILLINOIS

seminar in their fourth or fifth semester. The College of Law offers a 6 credit hour study abroad program in Agen, France every summer. Seminars include Comparative Labor and Employment Law; Disability Law; and Women, Law, and the Global Economy. Externships are offered in the Judicial Externship Program, which places students with state and federal judges; civil and criminal externships are also available with state criminal prosecutors and public defenders, and appellate defender externships are available at the Illinois Appellate Defender Office. There is the annual Riley Lecture Series on Professionalism and the annual Law Review Symposium Series. The Academic Support Program is available for students who may need additional support during the first years of law school. Each minority group has a student organization. Speakers on a variety of topics are sponsored by the Women's Law Caucus, International Law Society, Federalist Society, BLSA, and LLSA. The most widely taken electives are Agency, Corporations, and Real Estate Transactions.

Graduation Requirements

In order to graduate, candidates must have a GPA of 2.2 and must have completed the upper-division writing requirement.

Organizations

The Northern Illinois University Law Review is a student-edited publication. Teams compete at the National Moot Court, Chicago Bar Association, and International Information Technology and Privacy Law competitions. Other competitions include the ABA Client Counseling, the ABA National Appellate Advocacy, and National Trial Advocacy, Negotiation, and Alternative Dispute Resolution. Student organizations include the International Law Society, Women's Law Caucus, and the Public Interest Law Society. There are local chapters of Phi Alpha Delta and Delta Theta Phi. Other organizations include BLSA, LLSA, and Moot Court Society.

Library

The law library contains 169,278 hardcopy volumes and 543,897 microform volume equivalents, and subscribes to 1,726 serial publications. Such online databases and networks as CALI, CIS Universe, Legal-Trac, LEXIS, OCLC First Search, WESTLAW, BNA, HeinOnline, Versus Law, CCH Intelliconnect, RIA, GovSearch, IICLE, and Making of Modern Law are available to law students for research. The law library is a Selective Federal Document Depository. The ratio of library volumes to faculty is 10,927 to 1 and to students is 532 to 1. The ratio of seats in the library to students is 1 to 1.

Faculty

The law school has 26 full-time and 8 part-time faculty members, of whom 14 are women. According to AAUP standards for Category I institutions, faculty salaries are well below average. About 8% of full-time faculty have a graduate law degree in addition to the J.D. The ratio of full-time students to full-time faculty in an average class is 34 to 1; in a clinic, 6 to 1. The law school has a regular program of bringing visiting professors and other distinguished lecturers and visitors to campus.

Students

About 44% of the student body are women; 20%, minorities; 8%, African American; 5%, Asian American; and 7%, Hispanic. The majority of students come from Illinois (83%). The average age of entering students is 26; age range is 21 to 50. About 41% of students enter directly from undergraduate school, 13% have a graduate degree, and 59% have worked full-time prior to entering law school. About 3% drop out after the first year for academic or personal reasons; 97% remain to receive a law degree.

Placement

J.D.s awarded:	92
Services available through:	a separate law school placement center and the university placement center.
Services:	participating in regional and national job fairs.
Special features:	individual career counseling for students and alumni about traditional and nontraditional jobs for law graduates.
Full-time job interviews:	8 employers
Summer job interviews:	10 employers
Placement within 9 months of graduation:	85% of class
Average starting salary:	$41,500 to $59,250
Areas of placement:	
Private practice 2–10 attorneys	28%
Private practice 11–25 attorneys	4%
Private practice 26–50 attorneys	1%
Private practice 51–100 attorneys	3%
Private practice 101–250 attorneys	5%
Business/industry	21%
Government	17%
Public interest	9%
Academic	5%
Judicial clerkships	3%
Military	3%

Salmon P. Chase College of Law

Nunn Hall
Highland Heights, KY 41099

Application Filing		Accreditation
Fall: July 1		ABA, AALS
		Degrees Granted
Fee: $40		J.D.

Enrollment 2011–2012			First-Year Class	
Men:	349	61%	Applied:	891
Women:	224	39%	Accepted:	463
Minorities:	40	7%	Enrolled:	180
Out-of-State:	241	42%		

2011–2012 Class Profile

LSAT Percentile: 60%
LSAT Median Score: 154
Percentage passing bar on first try: 81%

Tuition and Fees:

Resident
$15,124 (F/T)

Average (public)
$18,708

Average (private)
$34,451

Nonresident
$32,882 (F/T)

Average (public)
$29,793

Average (private)
$34,451

0 10 20 30 40 50

Percentage receiving financial aid: 87%

ADMISSIONS

In the fall of 2011 first-year class, 891 applied, 463 were accepted, and 180 enrolled. Four transfers enrolled. The median LSAT percentile of the most recent first-year class was 60; the median GPA was 3.3 on a scale of 4.0. The lowest LSAT percentile accepted was 23; the highest was 96.

Requirements
Applicants must have a bachelor's degree and take the LSAT. The most important admission factors include LSAT results, GPA, and writing ability. No specific undergraduate courses are required. Candidates are not interviewed.

Procedure
The application deadline for fall entry is July 1. Applicants should submit an application form, LSAT results, transcripts, a personal statement, a nonrefundable application fee of $40, 2 letters of recommendation, and answers to all applicable essay questions. A $150 acceptance deposit must be submitted after an offer has been made and a $300 registration deposit is required preceding enrollment. Notification of the admissions decision is on a rolling basis. The law school uses the LSAC.

Special
The law school recruits minority and disadvantaged students by participating in prelaw and career fairs geared toward diverse attendees; collaborating with the Black Law Students Association and the Latino Law Group; offering diversity scholarships; participating in programs sponsored by the Law School Admissions Council; and hosting Diversity Days on campus. Requirements are different for out-of-state students. Transfer students must have a minimum GPA of 3, must have attended an ABA-approved law school, must submit a personal statement, must be in good standing and eligible to continue study, and must provide an official transcript documenting acceptably high-quality performance.

Costs

Tuition and fees for the 2011–2012 academic year are $15,054 for full-time in-state students and $32,812 for out-of-state students. Tuition for part-time students is $11,580 for in-state students and $25,240 out-of-state. On-campus room and board costs about $9,330 annually; books and supplies run $1,000.

Financial Aid

About 87% of current law students receive some form of aid. The average annual amount of aid from all sources combined, including scholarships, loans, and work contracts, is $26,995; maximum, $49,688. Awards are based on need and merit. The required financial statement is the FAFSA. The aid application deadline for fall entry is March 1. Special funds for minority or disadvantaged students are available. First-year students are notified about their financial aid application at time of acceptance.

About the Law School

Northern Kentucky University Salmon P. Chase College of Law was established in 1893 and is a public institution. The 300-acre campus is in a suburban area seven miles southeast of Cincinnati. The primary mission of the law school is to provide an intellectually rigorous education in legal theory and professional skills and to instill the ideals of ethics, leadership, and public engagement. Students have access to federal, state, county, city, and local agencies, courts, correctional facilities, law firms, and legal aid organizations in the Highland Heights area. The school is located in a major metropolitan area that provides a wide variety of opportunities for law students. Housing is available on campus through NKU's Office of University Housing, and includes suites and apartments. There are also several private, off-campus apartment communities nearby. All law school facilities are accessible to the physically disabled.

Calendar

The law school operates on a traditional semester basis. Courses for full-time students are offered both day and evening, and must be completed within 3 years. For part-time students, courses are offered both day and evening, and must be completed within 4 years. New full- and part-time students are admitted in the fall. There are 2- and 8-week summer sessions. Transferable summer courses are offered.

Programs

Students may take relevant courses in other programs and apply credit toward the J.D.; a maximum of 12 credits may be applied. The following joint degrees may be earned: J.D./M.B.A. (Juris Doctor/Master of Business Administration), J.D./M.B.I. (Juris Doctor/Master of Business Informatics), and J.D./H.M.I. (Juris Doctor/Master of Health Informatics).

Required
To earn the J.D., candidates must complete 90 total credits, of which 48 are for required courses. They must maintain a minimum GPA of 2.0 in the required courses. The following first-year courses are required of all students: Basic Legal Skills I and II, Civil Procedure I and II, Contracts I and II, Legal Analysis and Problem Solving, Property I and II, and Torts I and II. Required upper-level courses consist of Constitutional Law I and II, Criminal Law, Criminal Procedure, Evidence, and Professional Responsibility. Students are not required to take a clinical course; however, the law school

Phone: 859-572-5490
888-465-7316
Fax: 859-572-6081
E-mail: *brayg@nku.edu*
Web: *http://chaselaw.nku.edu*

Contact

Gina Bray, Admissions Specialist, 859-572-5490 for general inquiries; Leah Stewart, Director, Student Financial Assistance, 859-572-6437 for financial aid information.

KENTUCKY

provides several opportunities for students to do so. The required orientation program for first-year students consists of Legal Analysis and Problem Solving (LAPS), which is a two-week one-credit required course that takes place before the fall semester begins. LAPS focuses on the skills needed of law students such as case briefing and participation in the Socratic method. Information about law school requirements is provided as well.

Electives

The Salmon P. Chase College of Law offers concentrations in labor law and tax law and certificate programs in advocacy, transactional law, and labor and employment law. Students may earn academic credit while working under the supervision of licensed practicing attorneys in specialized externship clinics such as the Kentucky Innocence Project, the Constitutional Litigation Clinic, and the Local Government Law Center. Externships are also available in the areas of intellectual property, criminal prosecution, criminal defense, labor law, children's law, and in government agencies and offices. The Chase Local Government Law Center clinical internship allows students to research and draft answers to questions from local governments, to participate in the drafting of model ordinances for cities and counties, and to be involved in the development and production of local government practice guides on matters ranging from criminal law to land use and zoning. Seminars include Business, Technology, and Regulation, Constitutional Law, and Criminal Law/Justice. An active supervised independent research program is offered. Public policy research opportunities are available through the in-house Local Government Law Center. The Law Review sponsors a national symposium twice each year. Chase's Student Success Initiatives program provides a wide range of workshops, one-on-one help with writing, and question-and-answer sessions provided by Chase faculty. The Student Success Initiative program also addresses remedial issues. Individual assistance is available from Chase's Office of Student Success Initiatives. Professional and social activities, as well as special tutorial assistance are available in conjunction with the Black Lawyers Association of Cincinnati (BLAC) and the Cincinnati Bar Association/BLAC Lawyers' Association

Roundtable. A variety of programs throughout the year are sponsored by the Chase Public Interest Group, Student Bar Association, International Law Society, and National Women's Law Caucus. The most widely taken electives are Modern Real Estate Transactions and Mediation Contract Drafting.

Graduation Requirements

In order to graduate, candidates must have a GPA of 2.0, must have completed the upper-division writing requirement, and must have performed fifty hours of pro bono service.

Organizations

The primary law review is the *Northern Kentucky Law Review*. Students participate in a variety of moot court competitions at numerous locations, including the Evan A. Evans Constitutional Law Moot Court Competition, August A. Rendigs, Jr., National Moot Court Competition, and the Robert F. Wagner National Labor and Employment Law Moot Court Competition. Other competitions include the National Trial Advocacy Competition, AAJ Student Trial Advocacy Competition, and the Jerome Prince Memorial Evidence Moot Court Competition. Law student organizations include the Chase Public Interest Group, Black Law Students Association, and the Chase IP Society. The International Law Students Association, Sports and Entertainment and Law Association, and the Chase Latino Law Association are among the campus student groups.

Library

The law library contains 340,894 hardcopy volumes and 173,918 microform volume equivalents, and subscribes to 2,432 serial publications. Such online databases and networks as CALI, CIS Universe, Infotrac, Legal-Trac, LEXIS, Mathew Bender, OCLC First Search, WESTLAW, Wilsonline Indexes, Kentucky Virtual Library, BNA-Online, CCH Online, HeinOnline, and Lexis Serial Set are available to law students for research. Special library collections include Kentucky Appellate Court Briefs and the Justice Donald C. Wintersheimer Digital Collection. The ratio of library volumes to faculty is 12,775 to 1 and to students is 612 to 1. The ratio of seats in the library to students is 1 to 3.

Placement

J.D.s awarded:	181

Services available through: a separate law school placement center.
Services: mock intervies and job fair assistance
Special features: workshops and job fairs, including participation in the Tri-State Diversity Recruitment Program, BLAC-CBA Roundtable Minority Clerkship Program, Equal Justice Works Career Fair, Loyola Patent Law Program, Indianapolis Bar Association Diversity Job Fair, Southeastern Intellectual Property Job Fair, and Tennessee Bar Association, Diversity Job Fair.

Full-time job interviews:	10 employers
Summer job interviews:	23 employers
Placement by graduation:	34% of class
Placement within 9 months:	88% of class
Average starting salary:	$26,000 to $105,000

Areas of placement:

Private practice 2–10 attorneys	30%
Private practice 11–25 attorneys	8%
Private practice 26–50 attorneys	2%
Private practice 51–100 attorneys	2%
Business/industry	22%
Judicial clerkships	8%
Government	5%
Public interest	5%
Academic	5%
Military	1%

Faculty

The law school has 23 full-time and 25 part-time faculty members, of whom 21 are women. According to AAUP standards for Category 11A institutions, faculty salaries are average. About 32% of full-time faculty have a graduate law degree in addition to the J.D.; about 4% of part-time faculty have one. The ratio of full-time students to full-time faculty in an average class is 40 to 1; in a clinic, 5 to 1. The law school has a regular program of bringing visiting professors and other distinguished lecturers and visitors to campus.

Students

About 39% of the student body are women; 7%, minorities; 3%, African American; 2%, Asian American; and 1%, Hispanic. The majority of students come from Kentucky (58%). The average age of entering students is 25; age range is 20 to 47. About 28% of students enter directly from undergraduate school, and 11% have a graduate degree. About 4% drop out after the first year for academic or personal reasons; 96% remain to receive a law degree.

NORTHWESTERN UNIVERSITY

School of Law

375 East Chicago Avenue
Chicago, IL 60611

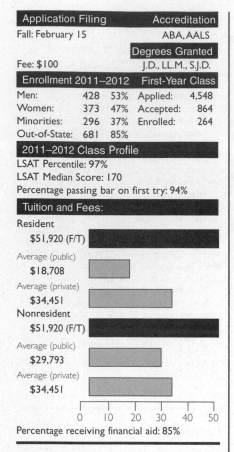

Application Filing	Accreditation
Fall: February 15	ABA, AALS

	Degrees Granted
Fee: $100	J.D., LL.M., S.J.D.

Enrollment 2011–2012		First-Year Class	
Men:	428 53%	Applied:	4,548
Women:	373 47%	Accepted:	864
Minorities:	296 37%	Enrolled:	264
Out-of-State:	681 85%		

2011–2012 Class Profile
LSAT Percentile: 97%
LSAT Median Score: 170
Percentage passing bar on first try: 94%

Tuition and Fees:

Resident
$51,920 (F/T)

Average (public)
$18,708

Average (private)
$34,451

Nonresident
$51,920 (F/T)

Average (public)
$29,793

Average (private)
$34,451

0   10   20   30   40   50

Percentage receiving financial aid: 85%

ADMISSIONS

In the fall of 2011 first-year class, 4548 applied, 864 were accepted, and 264 enrolled. Seventy-three transfers enrolled. The median LSAT percentile of the most recent first-year class was 97; the median GPA was 3.8 on a scale of 4.0. The lowest LSAT percentile accepted was 21; the highest was 100.

Requirements

Applicants must have a bachelor's degree and take the LSAT. The most important admission factors include academic achievement, life experience, and personal interview. No specific undergraduate courses are required. Candidates are interviewed.

Procedure

The application deadline for fall entry is February 15. Applicants should submit an application form, LSAT results, transcripts, a personal statement, a nonrefundable application fee of $100, a letter of recommendation, and a resume. Registra-

tion with LSAC is required. Interviews are strongly encouraged. Notification of the admissions decision is by April 30.

Special

The law school recruits minority and disadvantaged students through the efforts of the Director of Diversity Education and Outreach. Requirements are different for out-of-state students. Transfer students must have one year of credit, must have attended an ABA-approved law school, and must submit a personal statement.

Costs

Tuition and fees for the 2011–2012 academic year are $51,620 for all full-time students. On-campus room and board costs about $14,040 annually; books and supplies run $1,418.

Financial Aid

About 85% of current law students receive some form of aid. Awards are based on need and merit combined. Required financial statements are the FAFSA and Need Access Financial Aid Application Form. The aid application deadline for fall entry is February 1. First-year students are notified about their financial aid application before April 30 if all required documents are received by the Office of Admission and Financial Aid before the February 1 deadline.

About the Law School

Northwestern University School of Law was established in 1859 and is a private institution. The 20-acre campus is in an urban area in Chicago. The primary mission of the law school is to advance the understanding of law and legal institutions and to produce graduates who are prepared to lead and succeed in a rapidly changing world. Students have access to federal, state, county, city, and local agencies, courts, correctional facilities, law firms, and legal aid organizations in the Chicago area. The Arthur Rubloff Building, an addition to the school, houses the American Bar Foundation. Facilities of special interest to law students consist of 1 fully equipped, modern courtroom. The Bluhm Legal Clinic is housed in a modern and spacious facility and mirrors the setting of major urban law firms. About 90% of the law school facilities are accessible to the physically disabled.

Calendar

The law school operates on a traditional semester basis. Courses are offered both day and evening, and must be completed within 3 years. New students are admitted in the fall and summer. There is a 10-week summer session. Transferable summer courses are not offered.

Programs

In addition to the J.D., the law school offers the LL.M. and S.J.D. Students may take relevant courses in other programs and apply credit toward the J.D.; a maximum of 10 credits may be applied. The following joint degrees may be earned: J.D./D.E.S.S. (Juris Doctor/Doctor of Science), J.D./LL.M. (Juris Doctor/Master of Laws in Taxation and International Human Rights), J.D./M.B.A. (Juris Doctor/Master of Business Administration), and J.D./Ph.D. (Juris Doctor/Doctor of Philosophy).

Required

To earn the J.D., candidates must complete 83 total credits, of which 29 are for required courses. They must maintain a minimum GPA of 2.3 in the required courses. The following first-year courses are required of all students: Civil Procedure, Communication and Legal Reasoning, Constitutional Law, Contracts, Criminal Law, and Property. Required upper-level courses consist of a senior research project and Legal Ethics. The required orientation program for first-year students is 1 week before classes begin. First-year students register and receive class assignments, meet with their faculty advisers, tour the school, and attend team building and diversity workshops as well as social functions.

Electives

The School of Law offers concentrations in corporate law, environmental law, intellectual property law, international law, litigation, dispute resolution, and law and social policy. In addition, clinics are open to second- and third-year students. A sequence of simulation-based courses offered in the second year includes Clinical Trial Advocacy and Pre-Trial Litigation, as well as case-based instruction. Students also take clinically based Evidence, which presents the principles of evidence in the context of simulated cases. Course credits vary between 3 and 4 hours.

Phone: 312-503-8465
Fax: 312-503-0178
E-mail: admissions@law.northwestern.edu
Web: www.law.northwestern.edu

Contact
Johann Lee, Assistant Dean, 312-503-8465 for general inquiries and for financial aid information.

Students can represent clients through the Children and Family Justice Center, Entrepreneurship Law Center, Center for International Human Rights, Center on Wrongful Convictions, Investor Protection Center, MacArthur Justice Center, and the Appellate Advocacy Center. Seminars are offered in legal history, civil rights litigation, race relations, and other areas. Through the Owen L. Coon/James L. Rahl Senior Research Program, a third-year student may earn up to 14 credits for advanced research under the personal supervision of 1 or more faculty members. Completion of this project fulfills the graduation writing requirement. Directed reading and research, supervised by faculty members, is available to second-year students. Practicums consist of 10 to 12 hours per week of field work and a weekly 2-hour seminar. Practicums are available in the areas of corporate counsel, judicial, mediation, public interest, and criminal law. Annually, the Rosenthal Lecture Series brings preeminent figures in law and related fields to the school. The Pope and John Lecture on Professionalism deals with ethics and professional responsibility. The Howard J. Trienens Visiting Judicial Scholar Program brings leading jurists to the school to lecture on legal issues and to meet informally with students. The Brodsky Family Northwestern JD-MBA Lecture Series brings prominent figures in law and business. Study-abroad opportunities include Catholic University of Leuven, Belgium; Free University of Amsterdam, The Netherlands; Tel Aviv University, Israel; Universidad Torcuato Di Tella in Argentina; Bond University, Australia; University of the Andes in Chile; Bucerius Law School in Germany; National University of Singapore; University of Lucerne in Switzerland; and Instituto de Empresa in Spain. Tutorial programs are offered through the Dean of Students on an individual basis. The Director of Diversity Education and Outreach provides academic admission, placement counseling, and other supportive services. The most widely taken electives are Evidence, Business Association, and Estates and Trusts.

Graduation Requirements
In order to graduate, candidates must have a GPA of 2.3, and must have completed the upper-division writing requirement and Professional Skills and Perspective electives.

Organizations
Student-edited publications include the *Northwestern University Law Review, Journal of Criminal Law and Criminology, Northwestern Journal of International Law and Business, Northwestern Journal of Technology and Intellectual Property, Journal of International Human Rights, Journal of Social Policy*, and the newspaper, *The Pleader*. Annual moot court competitions are the Arlyn Miner First-Year Moot Court Program, Julius H. Miner Moot Court, Philip C. Jessup International Law Moot Court, and William C. Vis International Commercial Arbitration Moot Court. Other competitions are the John Paul Stevens Prize for academic excellence, Lowden-Wigmore Prizes for best student paper in international law, Arlyn Miner Book Award for the best brief by a first-year student, Harold D. Shapiro Prize for best student in an international economics relations class, the West Publishing Company Awards for scholastic achievement, and the Nathan Burkhan Memorial Competition for best paper on copyright law. Law student organizations, local chapters of national associations, and campus organizations include Order of the Coif; Amnesty International; Feminists for Social Change; National Lawyers Guild; The Federalist Society; ABA-Law Students Division; Diversity Coalition; SERV (Student Effort to Rejuvenate Volunteering); and Wigmore Follies, an annual student-run variety show.

Library
The law library contains 603,543 hardcopy volumes and 1,085,231 microform volume equivalents, and subscribes to 4,297 serial publications. Such online databases and networks as CIS Universe, Legal-Trac, LEXIS, OCLC First Search, WESTLAW, Wilsonline Indexes, CCH, RIA Checkpoint, Intelliconnect, and others are available to law students for research. Special library collections include domestic and international law and rare and special collections, including Supreme Court papers of Justice Arthur J. Goldberg. The ratio of library volumes to faculty is 6,858 to 1 and to students is 753 to 1. The ratio of seats in the library to students is 1 to 1.

Placement

J.D.s awarded:	273

Services available through: a separate law school placement center.
Services: arrangement of job fairs for off-campus interviews, online searchable resume database service, and alumni coaching program.

Full-time job interviews:	390 employers
Summer job interviews:	390 employers
Average starting salary:	$45,000 to $160,000

Areas of placement:

Private practice 51–100 attorneys	62%
Judicial clerkships	11%
Business/industry	10%
Public interest	5%
Government	2%
Academic	1%

Faculty
The law school has 71 full-time and 88 part-time faculty members, of whom 51 are women. According to AAUP standards for Category I institutions, faculty salaries are well above average. About 5% of full-time faculty have a graduate law degree in addition to the J.D. The ratio of full-time students to full-time faculty in an average class is 10 to 1; in a clinic, 7 to 1. The law school has a regular program of bringing visiting professors and other distinguished lecturers and visitors to campus. There is a chapter of the Order of the Coif; 40 faculty and 20 graduates are members.

Students
About 47% of the student body are women; 37%, minorities; 7%, African American; 18%, Asian American; 7%, Hispanic; and 1%, Native American. The average age of entering students is 26; age range is 19 to 41. About 5% of students enter directly from undergraduate school, 13% have a graduate degree, and 95% have worked full-time prior to entering law school. About 1% drop out after the first year for academic or personal reasons; 99% remain to receive a law degree.

Shepard Broad Law Center

3305 College Avenue
Fort Lauderdale, FL 33314-7721

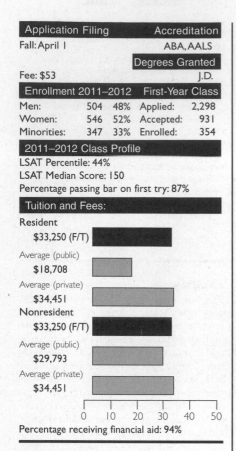

Application Filing			Accreditation
Fall: April 1			ABA, AALS

		Degrees Granted
Fee: $53		J.D.

Enrollment 2011–2012			First-Year Class	
Men:	504	48%	Applied:	2,298
Women:	546	52%	Accepted:	931
Minorities:	347	33%	Enrolled:	354

2011–2012 Class Profile
LSAT Percentile: 44%
LSAT Median Score: 150
Percentage passing bar on first try: 87%

Tuition and Fees:

Resident
$33,250 (F/T)

Average (public)
$18,708

Average (private)
$34,451

Nonresident
$33,250 (F/T)

Average (public)
$29,793

Average (private)
$34,451

0   10   20   30   40   50

Percentage receiving financial aid: 94%

ADMISSIONS

In the fall of 2011 first-year class, 2298 applied, 931 were accepted, and 354 enrolled. Eight transfers enrolled. The median LSAT percentile of the most recent first-year class was 44; the median GPA was 3.2 on a scale of 4.0. The lowest LSAT percentile accepted was 11; the highest was 97.

Requirements
Applicants must have a bachelor's degree and take the LSAT. The most important admission factors include undergraduate curriculum, academic achievement, and life experience. No specific undergraduate courses are required, and candidates are not interviewed.

Procedure
The application deadline for fall entry is April 1. Applicants should submit an application form, LSAT results, transcripts, a nonrefundable application fee of $53, and letters of recommendation

(2 are suggested). Notification of the admissions decision is on a rolling basis. The law school uses the LSAC.

Special
The law school recruits minority and disadvantaged students by means of on-campus minority programs, attendance at historically black college fairs, and participation in and maintenance of a good relationship with the CLEO program. Requirements are different for out-of-state students. Transfer students must have one year of credit, have attended an ABA-approved law school, have grades C or higher in required courses, and provide a letter of good standing from the current dean. Foreign attorneys are also admitted.

Costs

Tuition and fees for the 2011–2012 academic year are $32,750 for all full-time students. Tuition for part-time students is $24,560 for in-state students and $24,560 out-of-state. On-campus room and board costs about $14,938 annually; books and supplies run $2,356.

Financial Aid

About 94% of current law students receive some form of aid. The average annual amount of aid from all sources combined, including scholarships, loans, and work contracts, is $40,885. Awards are based on need and merit; loans are need-based. Most scholarships are merit-based; some are need-based. Required financial statements are the FAFSA. No statements are required for merit-based aid. The aid application deadline for fall entry is April 15. Special funds for minority or disadvantaged students include scholarship funds.

About the Law School

Nova Southeastern University Shepard Broad Law Center was established in 1974 and is a private institution. The 232-acre campus is in a suburban area 3 miles west of Fort Lauderdale, Florida. The primary mission of the law school is to ensure that students develop the knowledge, skills, and values that are at the heart of becoming trusted, highly adept professional lawyers who are respected for serving their clients, their communities, and justice. Students have access to federal, state, county, city, and local agencies, courts,

correctional facilities, law firms, and legal aid organizations in the Fort Lauderdale area. Facilities of special interest to law students include the law center's building, the Leo C. Goodwin Sr. Hall. All students can access computing facilities from anywhere in the building using wireless technology. Housing for students is in 4 university-owned apartment buildings; there are also numerous apartments available near the campus. All law school facilities are accessible to the physically disabled.

Calendar

The law school operates on a traditional semester basis. Courses for full-time students are offered both day and evening and must be completed within 5 years. For part-time students, courses are offered evenings only and some day classes are available and must be completed within 6 years. New full- and part-time students are admitted in the fall. There is an 8-week summer session. Transferable summer courses are offered.

Programs

Students may take relevant courses in other programs and apply credit toward the J.D.; a maximum of 4 (8 in joint-degree) credits may be applied. The following joint degrees may be earned: J.D./M.B.A. (Juris Doctor/Master of Business Administration), J.D./M.S. (Juris Doctor/Master of Science in Computer Science), J.D./M.S. (Juris Doctor/Master of Science in Conflict Analysis & Resolution), and J.D./M.U.R.P. (Juris Doctor/Masters of Urban and Regional Planning).

Required
To earn the J.D., candidates must complete 90 total credits, of which 57 are for required courses. They must maintain a minimum GPA of 2.0 in the required courses. The following first-year courses are required of all students: Civil Procedure, Constitutional Law I, Contracts, Criminal Law, Lawyering Skills and Values I and II, Legal Study Skills I and II, Property, and Torts. Required upper-level courses consist of Advanced Lawyering Skills and Values (2 semesters), Advanced Legal Analysis, an upper class writing requirement, Business Entities, Constitutional Law II, Criminal Procedure, Evidence, Family Law, Professional Responsibility,

Phone: 954-262-6117
800-986-6529
Fax: 954-262-3844
E-mail: admission@nsu.law.nova.edu
Web: www.nsulaw.nova.edu

Contact
Anneke Greenaway, Interim, Assistant Dean of Admissions, 954-262-6117 for general inquiries; Marsheila Bryant, Counselor, Financial Aid, 800-522-3243 for financial aid information.

and Wills and Trusts. The required orientation program for first-year students includes a week-long event that serves as an introduction to the law school experience before classes begin.

Electives
The Shepard Broad Law Center offers concentrations in corporate law, criminal law, environmental law, international law, litigation, tax law, torts and insurance, children and family, and health law. In addition, the clinics offer the opportunity for students who work with families and children, an environmental group, an international agency, a prosecutor or public defender, a corporation or business firm, a personal injury firm, or a mediation program. Upper-level students may take seminars for credits. As interns, students earn credits researching for a judge or serving as a Guardian ad Litem. The Career Development Office sponsors lecture series on various types of law practices. The Law Center offers a dual degree program with the University of Barcelona and similar opportunities in other countries. Tutorial programs consist of the Academic Resource Program and the Critical Skills Program. Special interest group programs are the Individuals with Disabilities Project and Guardian ad Litem. Both offer credit for working to protect the rights of the disabled and children. The most widely taken electives are Sales, Remedies, and Florida Constitutional Law.

Graduation Requirements
In order to graduate, candidates must have a GPA of 2.0, complete the upper-division writing requirement, and pass all required courses.

Organizations
Students edit the *Nova Law Review*, the *Journal of International and Comparative Law*, and the student newspaper *Broadly Speaking*. Intramural moot court competitions are held in the fall for upper-class students and in the winter for first-year students; Law Center frequently hosts a Round Robin Moot Court Competition. A team competes in the American Trial Lawyers Association trial competition as well as other moot court and trial competitions. Law student organizations

include the Business Law Students Association, Christian Legal Society, and Jewish Law Students Association. Local chapters of national associations include Hispanic Law Students Association, Black Law Students Association, and Asian/Pacific Islands Law Students Association. Campus organizations include the International Law Society, Entertainment and Sports Law Society, and the Student Bar Association.

Library
The law library contains 338,431 hardcopy volumes and 770,677 microform volume equivalents, and subscribes to 746 serial publications. Online databases and networks include CALI, CIS Universe, DIALOG, Dow-Jones, Infotrac, LegalTrac, LEXIS, Mathew Bender, OCLC First Search, WESTLAW, Wilsonline Indexes, which are available to law students for research. Special library collections include state, federal, and United Nations depositories and collections in tax, criminal law, international law, children/family, jurisprudence, admiralty, trial practice, and law and popular culture. The ratio of library volumes to faculty is 5,548 to 1 and to students is 322 to 1. The ratio of seats in the library to students is 1 to 2.

Faculty
The law school has 61 full-time and 118 part-time faculty members, of whom 70 are women. According to AAUP standards for Category 1 institutions, faculty salaries are average. About 28% of full-time faculty have a graduate law degree in addition to the J.D.; about 13% of part-time faculty have one. The ratio of full-time students to full-time faculty in an average class is 62 to 1; in a clinic, 20 to 1. The law school has a regular program of bringing visiting professors and other distinguished lecturers and visitors to campus.

Students
About 52% of the student body are women; 33%, minorities; 6%, African American; 5%, Asian American; and 22%, Hispanic. The average age of entering students is 26; age range is 21 to 67. About 30% drop out after the first year for academic or personal reasons; 70% remain to receive a law degree.

Placement
J.D.s awarded:	302

Services available through: a separate law school placement center.

Services: Southeastern Minority Job Fair, Southeastern Intellectual Property Job Fair, Public Interest Law Day, and Loyola (Chicago) Patent Law Interview Program.

Special features: online job posting system and a monthly alumni job bulletin.

Full-time job interviews:	22 employers
Summer job interviews:	22 employers
Placement within 9 months of graduation:	81% of class
Average starting salary:	$28,800 to $250,000

Areas of placement:
Private practice 2–10 attorneys	38%
Private practice 11–25 attorneys	12%
Private practice 26–50 attorneys	5%
Private practice 51–100 attorneys	4%
Business/industry	18%
Government	8%
Public interest	6%
Academic	2%
Judicial clerkships	1%

OHIO NORTHERN UNIVERSITY

Claude W. Pettit College of Law

525 South Main Street
Ada, OH 45810

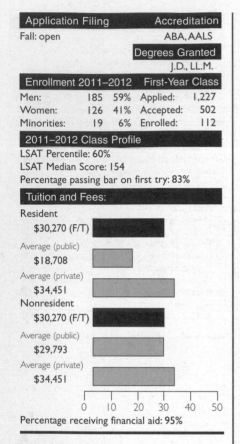

Application Filing	Accreditation
Fall: open	ABA, AALS

Degrees Granted
J.D., LL.M.

Enrollment 2011–2012		First-Year Class	
Men:	185 59%	Applied:	1,227
Women:	126 41%	Accepted:	502
Minorities:	19 6%	Enrolled:	112

2011–2012 Class Profile
LSAT Percentile: 60%
LSAT Median Score: 154
Percentage passing bar on first try: 83%

Tuition and Fees:

Resident
$30,270 (F/T)

Average (public)
$18,708

Average (private)
$34,451

Nonresident
$30,270 (F/T)

Average (public)
$29,793

Average (private)
$34,451

0   10   20   30   40   50

Percentage receiving financial aid: 95%

ADMISSIONS

In the fall of 2011 first-year class, 1227 applied, 502 were accepted, and 112 enrolled. Five transfers enrolled. The median LSAT percentile of the most recent first-year class was 60; the median GPA was 3.4 on a scale of 4.0. The lowest LSAT percentile accepted was 18; the highest was 94.

Requirements

Applicants must have a bachelor's degree and take the LSAT. Minimum acceptable GPA is 2.0 on a scale of 4.0. The most important admission factors include LSAT results, GPA, and college attended. No specific undergraduate courses are required. Candidates are interviewed.

Procedure

The application deadline for fall entry is open. Applicants should submit an application form, LSAT results, transcripts, and maximum of 3 letters of recommendation. Notification of the admissions decision is on a rolling basis. The law school uses the LSAC.

Special

The law school recruits minority and disadvantaged students underrepresented in the legal profession by visiting minority colleges and universities, hosting on-campus events, attending national minority recruitment events, and doing targeted communication. Requirements are different for out-of-state students. Transfer students must have attended an ABA-approved law school, must provide a letter of good standing, and must submit a transcript of law school work, undergraduate transcripts, and an LSAC report.

Costs

On-campus room and board costs about $7,604 annually; books and supplies run $1,000.

Financial Aid

About 95% of current law students receive some form of aid. The average annual amount of aid from all sources combined, including scholarships, loans, and work contracts, is $44,969. Awards are based on need and merit combined. Required financial statements are the FAFSA and the school's financial aid application. The aid application deadline for fall entry is open. Special funds for minority or disadvantaged students are available. First-year students are notified about their financial aid application at time of acceptance.

About the Law School

Ohio Northern University Claude W. Pettit College of Law was established in 1885 and is a private institution. The 280-acre campus is in a small town 80 miles northwest of Columbus. The primary mission of the law school is to educate and train students from diverse backgrounds to become responsible and successful practitioners capable of exemplary legal service in roles throughout society. Students have access to federal, state, county, city, and local agencies, courts, correctional facilities, law firms, and legal aid organizations in the Ada area. Facilities of special interest to law students include the Lima Legal Aid Office, ONU Legal Aid Clinic, and Legal Services of Northern Ohio. Housing for students is available on campus and reasonable off-campus housing is also available. All law school facilities are accessible to the physically disabled.

Calendar

The law school operates on a modified semester (4-1-4) basis. Courses are offered both day and evening, and must be completed within 5 years. New students are admitted in the fall and summer. There is an 8-week summer session. Transferable summer courses are offered.

Programs

In addition to the J.D., the law school offers the LL.M. The following joint degrees may be earned: J.D./M.P.P.A (Juris Doctor/Master of Public Policy in Accounting).

Required

To earn the J.D., candidates must complete 90 total credits, of which 47 are for required courses. They must maintain a minimum GPA of 2.0 in the required courses. The following first-year courses are required of all students: Civil Procedure I and II, Contracts I and II, Criminal Law, Legal Problem Solving and Analysis, Legal Research and Writing I and II, Property I and II, Public Law & The Legal Process, and Torts. Required upper-level courses consist of Analytical Methods for Lawyers, Business Organizations I, Constitutional Law I, Evidence, Federal Income Tax, and Legal Profession. Students must complete 10 hours of skills courses chosen from a wide range of options, including clinics. The required orientation program for first-year students comprises a 2-day introduction to university and law school procedures and the instructional approach followed by 4 special continuing orientation programs.

Electives

The Claude W. Pettit College of Law offers concentrations in corporate law, criminal law, international law, litigation, torts and insurance, bankruptcy and commercial law, real estate law, and public law and policy. Clinics include Legal Aid, Bankruptcy, and Transactional. Seminars are open to second- and third-year students, and include Women and the Law and Land Use Planning. There are civil and criminal internship programs. Students are required to do a major research project, worth 2 credits, as part of the seminar requirement. Field work includes judicial externships with state and federal courts, criminal externships, and governmental-legislative externships.

Phone: 419-772-2211
877-452-9668
Fax: 419-772-3042
Web: www.law.onu.edu

Contact
Director of Law Admissions, 419-772-2211 for general inquiries; Financial Aid Director, 419-772-2272 for financial aid information.

OHIO

The Annual Kormendy Lecture Series sponsors prominent national legal figures. Lecturers have included Justice Clarence Thomas. The college will give credit for ABA-approved law schools' study-abroad programs with prior approval. There is an Icelandic Study Exchange Program. The Academic Support Program includes student tutors for all required courses. Minority students benefit from the Black Law Students Association-sponsored study groups and the Academic Success Program. Special interest groups include International Law Society, Legal Association of Women, and Environmental Law Society. The most widely taken electives are Criminal Procedure, Decedents' Estates and Trusts, and Commercial Transactions.

Graduation Requirements
In order to graduate, candidates must have a GPA of 2.0 and must have completed the upper-division writing requirement.

Organizations
Students edit the *Ohio Northern University Law Review*. Teams compete in the Jessup International Law Competition, tax competitions, and ABA Nationals. Law student organizations include Sports Law Society, Street Law, and International Law Society. Local chapters of national associations include Environmental Law Society, Federalist Society, and Constitutional Law Society. Campus clubs include the Student Bar Association, Legal Association of Women, and Black Law Students Association.

Library
The law library contains 256,137 hardcopy volumes and 180,425 microform volume equivalents, and subscribes to 1,868 serial publications. Such online databases and networks as CALI, CIS Universe, Infotrac, Legal-Trac, LEXIS, Mathew Bender, OCLC First Search, WESTLAW, Wilsonline Indexes, HeinOnline, Caseworker, Foreign Law Guide, JSTOR, The Making of Modern Law, RIA Checkpoint, and PACER are available to law students for research. Special library collections include a federal government depository and the Celebrezze archives. The ratio of library volumes to faculty is 12,884 to 1 and to students is 1,214 to 1. The ratio of seats in the library to students is 1 to 1.

Faculty
The law school has 18 full-time and 15 part-time faculty members, of whom 10 are women. About 56% of full-time faculty have a graduate law degree in addition to the J.D. The ratio of full-time students to full-time faculty in an average class is 12 to 1; in a clinic, 6 to 1. The law school has a regular program of bringing visiting professors and other distinguished lecturers and visitors to campus.

Students
About 41% of the student body are women; 6%, minorities; 3%, African American; 1%, Asian American; 1%, Hispanic; and 1%, Native American. The average age of entering students is 25; age range is 21 to 47. About 44% of students enter directly from undergraduate school, and 6% have a graduate degree. About 3% drop out after the first year for academic or personal reasons; 86% remain to receive a law degree.

Placement

J.D.s awarded:	90
Services available through: a separate law school placement center.	
Services: fall and spring on-campus interviewing and resume collection program and fall mock interview program.	
Special features: an active membership in NALP and the Ohio Law Placement Consortium (OLPC), through which the college participates in a variety of joint recruiting projects throughout the year.	
Full-time job interviews:	6 employers
Summer job interviews:	45 employers
Placement within 9 months of graduation:	94% of class
Average starting salary:	$33,000 to $145,000
Areas of placement:	
Private practice 2–10 attorneys	41%
Private practice 11–25 attorneys	2%
Private practice 51–100 attorneys	2%
Private practice 101–501+ attorneys	4%
Government	19%
Business/industry	14%
Judicial clerkships	3%
Public interest	3%
Academic	2%
Military	1%

Michael E. Moritz College of Law

55 West 12th Avenue,
John Deaver Drinko Hall
Columbus, OH 43210-1391

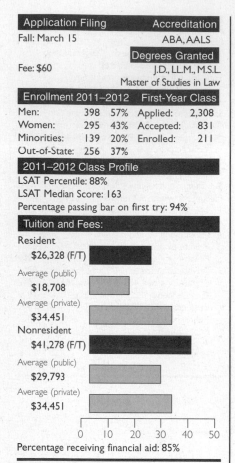

Application Filing		Accreditation	
Fall: March 15		ABA, AALS	
		Degrees Granted	
Fee: $60		J.D., LL.M., M.S.L.	
		Master of Studies in Law	

Enrollment 2011–2012			First-Year Class	
Men:	398	57%	Applied:	2,308
Women:	295	43%	Accepted:	831
Minorities:	139	20%	Enrolled:	211
Out-of-State:	256	37%		

2011–2012 Class Profile
LSAT Percentile: 88%
LSAT Median Score: 163
Percentage passing bar on first try: 94%

Tuition and Fees:

Resident
$26,328 (F/T)

Average (public)
$18,708

Average (private)
$34,451

Nonresident
$41,278 (F/T)

Average (public)
$29,793

Average (private)
$34,451

0 10 20 30 40 50

Percentage receiving financial aid: 85%

ADMISSIONS

In the fall of 2011 first-year class, 2308 applied, 831 were accepted, and 211 enrolled. Eleven transfers enrolled. The median LSAT percentile of the most recent first-year class was 88; the median GPA was 3.6 on a scale of 4.0.

Requirements

Applicants must have a bachelor's degree and take the LSAT. The most important admission factors include academic achievement, undergraduate curriculum, and life experience. No specific undergraduate courses are required. Candidates are not interviewed.

Procedure

The application deadline for fall entry is March 15. Applicants should submit an application form, LSAT results, transcripts, a personal statement, a nonrefundable application fee of $60, 2 letters of recommendation, and the Academic Records

Office Evaluation form. Notification of the admissions decision is on a rolling basis. The law school uses the LSAC.

Special

The law school recruits minority and disadvantaged students through participation in CLEO and as a part of the overall recruitment program. Requirements are different for out-of-state students. Transfer students must have one year of credit, must have attended an ABA-approved law school, and must submit a personal statement.

Costs

Books and supplies run $3,980.

Financial Aid

About 85% of current law students receive some form of aid. The average annual amount of aid from all sources combined, including scholarships, loans, and work contracts, is $44,686; maximum, $81,092. Awards are based on need and merit combined. The required financial statement is the FAFSA. The aid application deadline for fall entry is February 15. Special funds for minority or disadvantaged students are available. First-year students are notified about their financial aid application shortly after acceptance.

About the Law School

Ohio State University Michael E. Moritz College of Law was established in 1891 and is a public institution. The 3200-acre campus is in an urban area 2 miles north of downtown Columbus. The primary mission of the law school is the creation of outstanding lawyers, effective leaders, and principled citizens ready to make a difference. Students have access to federal, state, county, city, and local agencies, courts, correctional facilities, law firms, and legal aid organizations in the Columbus area. Facilities of special interest to law students include the state legislature and state supreme court. Housing for students is available in 3 campus dormitories reserved for graduate and professional students; there are plenty of off-campus housing facilities sufficient for all students. There is also an apartment complex adjacent to the law school. All law school facilities are accessible to the physically disabled.

Calendar

The law school operates on a traditional semester basis. Courses are offered days only, and must be completed within 5 years. New students are admitted in the fall. There is an 8-week summer session. Transferable summer courses are offered.

Programs

In addition to the J.D., the law school offers the LL.M. and M.S.L. (Master of Studies in Law). Students may take relevant courses in other programs and apply credit toward the J.D.; a maximum of 5 credits may be applied. The following joint degrees may be earned: J.D./M.A. (Juris Doctor/Master of Arts), J.D./M.B.A. (Juris Doctor/Master of Business Administration), and J.D./M.H.A. (Juris Doctor/Master of Health and Hospital Administration).

Required

To earn the J.D., candidates must complete 88 total credits, of which 37 are for required courses. They must maintain a minimum GPA of 2.0 in the required courses. The following first-year courses are required of all students: Civil Procedure I, Constitutional Law, Contracts, Criminal Law, Legal Analysis & Writing I and II, Legislation, Property, and Torts. Required upper-level courses consist of a legal profession course, a seminar course, an upper-level writing course, and Appellate Advocacy I. The required orientation program for first-year students is 3 days, and covers case briefing, professional responsibility, and college policies and offices. There are also 2 days of student-sponsored social activities.

Electives

The Michael E. Moritz College of Law offers concentrations in corporate law, criminal law, family law, intellectual property law, international law, juvenile law, labor law, litigation, media law, securities law, tax law, torts and insurance, alternative dispute resolution, and civil rights law. In addition, second- and third-year students may take clinics. Second-year students take simulation clinics such as pretrial litigation, negotiation, and client counseling. They may also participate in the legislation, special education, and mediation clinics. Third-year students may act as legal interns representing clients under faculty supervision in the Civil Law, Juvenile Law,

Phone: 614-292-8810
Fax: 614-292-1492
E-mail: lawadmit@osu.edu
Web: moritzlaw.osu.edu

Contact

Kathy S. Northern, Associate Dean, 614-292-8810 for general inquiries; Robert L. Solomon, Assistant Dean, 614-292-8807 for financial aid information.

OHIO

and Prosecutorial and Defense Practica. At least one seminar must be taken by second- or third-year students; seminars range from creative and Constitutional aspects of law to those devoted to a student's research in a specific legal area. Internships are available with certain federal and state judges and through the D.C. Summer Program. Research programs include opportunities for independent study. There are field work opportunities to work for the public and private sector, as well as opportunities to do volunteer work. Special lectures are supported by the Ohio State Law Forum, which invites distinguished academicians, jurists, and practitioners; speakers are also invited by faculty and student groups. Study abroad is possible through the Oxford Summer Program. Students can earn up to 6 credits during the summer. Study abroad at Oxford is also possible through the Spring Semester Program. A legal methods program, designed to help certain first-year students who may need more time and attention adapting to law school, is available. The Black Law Students Association, Caribbean Law Students Associations, Hispanic Law Students Association, Asian Law Students Association, and Middle Eastern Law Students Association sponsor various events and programs. There are approximately 50 special interest student organizations that include the Sports and Entertainment Law Society, Pro Bono Research Group, Public Interest Law Forum, Women's Law Caucus, Health Law Society, and J. Rueben Clark Society. The most widely taken electives are those that are directly bar-related (e.g., Evidence and Corporations), international law offerings, and alternative dispute resolution offerings.

Graduation Requirements

In order to graduate, candidates must have a GPA of 2.0, must have completed the upper-division writing requirement, and must have completed an ethics course.

Organizations

Students edit the *Ohio State Law Journal, Journal on Dispute Resolution, Ohio State Journal of Criminal Law, I/S: A Journal of Law and Policy for the Information Society, Entrepreneurial Business Law Journal,* and the student newspaper *Hearsay.* Other student organizations have newsletters, which they publish periodically. Appellate Practice is the first moot court experience

required of all students. The college has 17 separate moot court teams. There are also several National Trial Competition teams and 2 mediations teams. There are also intraschool moot court, negotiation, and trial competitions. Law student organizations and campus organizations include Law School Democrats, Law School Republicans, Military Law Association, Student Bar Association, Pro Bono Research Group, and the International Law Society. There are local chapters of legal fraternities, as well as a student section of the American Bar Association.

Library

The law library contains 431,911 hardcopy volumes and 1,413,566 microform volume equivalents, and subscribes to 8,984 serial publications. Such online databases and networks as CALI, CIS Universe, Dow-Jones, Legal-Trac, LEXIS, OCLC First Search, WESTLAW, Wilsonline Indexes, LCS, and OCLC are available to law students for research. Special library collections include a government depository, a large foreign law collection, and materials on dispute resolution. The ratio of library volumes to faculty is 8,638 to 1 and to students is 608 to 1. The ratio of seats in the library to students is 1 to 1.

Faculty

The law school has 54 full-time and 52 part-time faculty members, of whom 41 are women. The ratio of full-time students to full-time faculty in an average class is 14 to 1; in a clinic, 8 to 1. The law school has a regular program of bringing visiting professors and other distinguished lecturers and visitors to campus. There is a chapter of the Order of the Coif.

Students

About 43% of the student body are women; 20%, minorities; 7%, African American; 6%, Asian American; and 5%, Hispanic. The majority of students come from Ohio (63%). The average age of entering students is 23; age range is 20 to 47. About 50% of students enter directly from undergraduate school, 12% have a graduate degree, and 50% have worked full-time prior to entering law school. About 1% drop out after the first year for academic or personal reasons; 99% remain to receive a law degree.

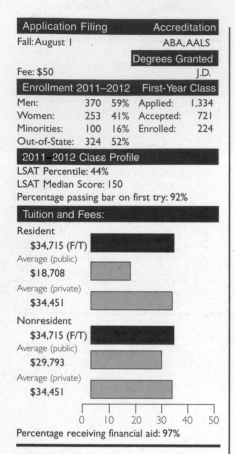

Application Filing		Accreditation
Fall: August 1		ABA, AALS

		Degrees Granted
Fee: $50		J.D.

Enrollment 2011–2012		First-Year Class	
Men:	370 59%	Applied:	1,334
Women:	253 41%	Accepted:	721
Minorities:	100 16%	Enrolled:	224
Out-of-State:	324 52%		

2011–2012 Class Profile
LSAT Percentile: 44%
LSAT Median Score: 150
Percentage passing bar on first try: 92%

Tuition and Fees:

Resident
$34,715 (F/T)

Average (public)
$18,708

Average (private)
$34,451

Nonresident
$34,715 (F/T)

Average (public)
$29,793

Average (private)
$34,451

0   10   20   30   40   50

Percentage receiving financial aid: 97%

ADMISSIONS

In the fall of 2011 first-year class, 1334 applied, 721 were accepted, and 224 enrolled. Three transfers enrolled. The median LSAT percentile of the most recent first-year class was 44; the median GPA was 3.2 on a scale of 4.0. The lowest LSAT percentile accepted was 15; the highest was 97.

Requirements
Applicants must have a bachelor's degree and take the LSAT. Minimum acceptable GPA is 2.0 on a scale of 4.0. The most important admission factors include undergraduate curriculum, GPA, and LSAT results. No specific undergraduate courses are required. Candidates are not interviewed.

Procedure
The application deadline for fall entry is August 1. Applicants should submit an application form, LSAT results, transcripts, a personal statement, a non-refundable application fee of $50, 2 letters of recommendation, a personal statement, and a resume. Notification of the admissions decision is as soon as a decision has been made. The law school uses the LSAC.

Special
The law school recruits minority and disadvantaged students through directed mailings and visits to campuses with high minority concentrations that are complemented by events at the law school co-hosted by minority student organizations throughout the academic year. Upon acceptance, minority and diversity candidates are contacted by students and alumni who answer questions and ease concerns about cost, prospects for success, and the job market. Requirements are different for out-of-state students. Transfer students must have attended an ABA-approved law school, must submit a personal statement, must complete their last 45 hours at the school, must be in good standing at their former law school, and must submit a letter from the dean along with official transcripts.

Costs

On-campus room and board costs about $8,400 annually; books and supplies run $1,800.

Financial Aid

About 97% of current law students receive some form of aid. The average annual amount of aid from all sources combined, including scholarships, loans, and work contracts, is $24,780; maximum, $45,609. Awards are based on need and merit. The required financial statement is the FAFSA. The aid application deadline for fall entry is March 1. First-year students are notified about their financial aid application approximately 1 to 2 weeks after their financial file is completed.

About the Law School

Oklahoma City University School of Law was established in 1907 and is a private institution. The 104-acre campus is in an urban area about 2 miles from the state capital building. The primary mission of the law school is to help students become responsible professionals through a rigorous program of instruction that focuses on students' intellectual and professional development and enables them to become leaders in law, business, government, and civic life, and to improve law and legal institutions through research and scholarship. Students have access to federal, state, county, city, and local agencies, courts, correctional facilities, law firms, and legal aid organizations in the Oklahoma City area. Oklahoma City, as the state capital, is a major center for law, business, health care, and government. Facilities of special interest to law students include the nearby state capital complex, which contains the Supreme Court, the Court of Criminal Appeals, the Court of Civil Appeals, the state legislature, and various state administrative and regulatory agencies. The law school is also near the U.S. District Court and numerous other federal and state entities, law firms, the Oklahoma Medical Center, and business institutions. Housing for students is in on-campus residence halls and an on-campus apartment complex. Many inexpensive private apartments are also available in the metro area. All law school facilities are accessible to the physically disabled.

Calendar

The law school operates on a traditional semester basis. Courses for full-time students are offered both day and evening, and must be completed within 4 years. For part-time students, courses are offered both day and evening, and must be completed within 5 years. New full- and part-time students are admitted in the fall. There is an 8-week summer session. Transferable summer courses are offered.

Programs

The following joint degrees may be earned: J.D./M.B.A. (Juris Doctor/Master of Business Administration).

Required
To earn the J.D., candidates must complete 90 total credits, of which 60 are for required courses. They must maintain a minimum GPA of 4.0 in the required courses. The following first-year courses are required of all students: Civil Procedure I and II, Contracts I and II, Criminal Law, Legal Analysis, Legal Research and Writing I and II, Property, and Torts. Required upper-level courses consist of Agency and Business Associations, Administrative Law, Constitutional Law I and II, Consumer Bankruptcy, Corporations, Criminal Procedure I, Evidence, Income Tax Law, Legal Profession, Sales and

Phone: 405-208-5354
866-529-6281
Fax: 405-208-5814
E-mail: lawadmit@okcu.edu
Web: www.okcu.edu/law

Contact

Jennifer Killman, Senior Counselor, 405-208-5419 for financial aid information.

Leases, Secured Transactions, and Wills, Trusts, and Estates. The required orientation program for first-year students is a 6-day program that includes a course on Legal Analysis for academic credit.

Electives

The School of Law offers concentrations in business law, health law, public law, and client representation in alternative dispute resolution. The law school offers an extensive externship program through which students earn academic credit while working under the guidance of attorneys and judges in numerous settings, including the United States District Court, federal and state courts, corporate legal departments, government agencies, and the criminal justice system. Approximately 6 seminars are offered each semester on advanced topics. Recent seminars include Bioethics, Current Developments in Corporate Law, and Tribal Law. Students who obtain a legal intern's license (authorized by the state of Oklahoma) and have a sponsoring attorney may appear alone in court on certain matters. With a supervising attorney present, they may handle any court proceeding. Students may conduct research through seminars, advanced research courses, supervised papers, or directed research projects. They may also assist faculty members as research assistants. An externship program is offered with live-client placements in many courts and governmental business offices in or near Oklahoma City. The Native American Legal Resource Center also offers clinical opportunities. The annual Quinlan Lecture Series presents a nationally preeminent legal scholar or jurist. The annual Brennan Lecture presents a national prominent scholar or jurist in the field of state constitutional law. The Center on State Constitutional Law and Government presents several prominent state and local public officials each year. OCU co-sponsors 4 summer international programs (4 credit hours each) in Tianjn, China; Granada, Spain; Freiburg, Germany; The Hague, the Netherlands; and Buenos Aires, Argentina. The academic achievement program includes individual tutoring by faculty and upper-class students, programming by the Director of Academic Achievement, and a bar exam preparation program. Students with writing difficulties may seek help from the University Writing Center. The law school's Native American Legal Resource Center works closely with Indian

tribes in the state of Oklahoma and administers numerous federal grants to assist tribes. There are numerous opportunities to engage in pro bono services. The most widely taken electives are Consumer Bankruptcy, Agency and Business Associations, and Administrative Law.

Graduation Requirements

In order to graduate, candidates must have a GPA of 2.0 and must have completed the upper-division writing requirement.

Organizations

The Oklahoma City University Law Review publishes 3 issues annually. The Student Bar Association publishes *The Verdict*, a bimonthly newsletter. Moot court competitions include the ABA National Appellate Moot Court Competition, the Jessup International Law Moot Court Competition, and the AAJ Trial Competition. Other competitions include the ACTL National Trial Competition, Frederick Douglass National Moot Court Competition, Native American Law Moot Court Competition, ACS National Appellate Moot Court Competition, and ABA National Mediation Moot Court Competition. Law student organizations include Black Law Students Association, Hispanic Law Students Association, and ABA-Law Student Division. Campus organizations include Sports and Entertainment Law Association, American Constitution Society, and Federalist Society.

Library

The law library contains 322,061 hard-copy volumes and 147,684 microform volume equivalents, and subscribes to 1,118 serial publications. Such online databases and networks as CALI, CIS Universe, Infotrac, Legal-Trac, LEXIS, OCLC First Search, WESTLAW, Wilsonline Indexes, Index Master, Legal-Trac, LLMC Digital, HeinOnline, JSTOR, Index to Legal Periodicals, Audio Case Files, Befress Legal Journal, CCH Internet Tax Research, Constitutions of the Countries of the World, eBrary, EBSCO, Foreign Law Guide, NewsBank, Oxford English Dictionary, RIA Checkpoint Academic Advantage, U.S. Congressional Serial Set (LexisNexis), WorldCat, A to Z List of Journals, and BNA databases are available to law students for research. Special library collections include the Native American collection with a concentration

Placement

J.D.s awarded:	145

Services available through: a separate law school placement center and the university placement center.

Special features: the Professional and Career Development Center is staffed by 4 full-time career services personnel who help students develop career goals and plans, locate resources including alumni mentors, and find employment.

Full-time job interviews:	4 employers
Summer job interviews:	12 employers
Placement within 9 months of graduation:	83% of class
Average starting salary:	$22,000 to $120,000

Areas of placement:

Private practice 2–10 attorneys	15%
Private practice 11–25 attorneys	22%
Private practice 26–50 attorneys	2%
Private practice 51–100 attorneys	2%
Solo practice	19%
Business/industry	14%
Government	13%
Public interest	6%
Academic	3%
Military	2%

on the Indian tribes of Oklahoma. The ratio of library volumes to faculty is 10,735 to 1 and to students is 517 to 1. The ratio of seats in the library to students is 1 to 2.

Faculty

The law school has 40 full-time and 56 part-time faculty members, of whom 41 are women. According to AAUP standards for Category 11A institutions, faculty salaries are below average. About 31% of full-time faculty have a graduate law degree in addition to the J.D. The ratio of full-time students to full-time faculty in an average class is 18 to 1; in a clinic, 8 to 1. The law school has a regular program of bringing visiting professors and other distinguished lecturers and visitors to campus.

Students

About 41% of the student body are women; 16%, minorities; 3%, African American; 3%, Asian American; 4%, Hispanic; 5%, Native American; and 8%, Mexican American. The average age of entering students is 27; age range is 21 to 53. About 64% of students enter directly from undergraduate school, and 8% have a graduate degree. About 12% drop out after the first year for academic or personal reasons; 88% remain to receive a law degree.

Application Filing

Fall: March 1	
Spring: November 15	
Fee: $65	

Accreditation

ABA, AALS

Degrees Granted

J.D., LL.M., S.J.D.

Enrollment 2011–2012   First-Year Class

Men:	332	43%	Applied:	2,735
Women:	444	57%	Accepted:	1,101
Minorities:	155	20%	Enrolled:	212
Out-of-State:	326	42%		

2011–2012 Class Profile

LSAT Percentile: 67%
LSAT Median Score: 156
Percentage passing bar on first try: 77%

Tuition and Fees:

Resident
$41,174 (F/T)

Average (public)
$18,708

Average (private)
$34,451

Nonresident
$41,174 (F/T)

Average (public)
$29,793

Average (private)
$34,451

0   10   20   30   40   50

Percentage receiving financial aid: 92%

ADMISSIONS

In the fall of 2011 first-year class, 2735 applied, 1101 were accepted, and 212 enrolled. Seven transfers enrolled. The median LSAT percentile of the most recent first-year class was 67; the median GPA was 3.4 on a scale of 4.0. The lowest LSAT percentile accepted was 23; the highest was 97.

Requirements

Applicants must have a bachelor's degree and take the LSAT. Minimum acceptable GPA is 2.0 on a scale of 4.0. The most important admission factors include LSAT results, GPA, and general background. No specific undergraduate courses are required. Candidates are not interviewed.

Procedure

The application deadline for fall entry is March 1. Applicants should submit an application form, LSAT results, transcripts, a personal statement, a nonrefundable application fee of $65, 2 letters of recommendation, and TOEFL results (if applicable). Notification of the admis-

sions decision is on a rolling basis. The law school uses the LSAC.

Special

The law school recruits minority and disadvantaged students by hosting a Law Day for minority students each year and visiting colleges and universities with significant populations of historically underrepresented students. Since 1999, Pace Law has cohosted the Puerto Rican Legal Defense and Education Fund Program. Requirements are different for out-of-state students. Transfer students must have one year of credit, must have attended an ABA-approved law school, must submit a personal statement, and must have a maximum of 30 transfer credits from state-approved law schools.

Costs

Tuition and fees for the 2011–2012 academic year are $40,730 for all full-time students. Tuition for part-time students is $30,550 for in-state students and $30,550 out-of-state. On-campus room and board costs about $13,440 annually; books and supplies run $1,800.

Financial Aid

About 92% of current law students receive some form of aid. The average annual amount of aid from all sources combined, including scholarships, loans, and work contracts, is $42,000; maximum, $63,056. Awards are based on need and merit combined. The required financial statement is the FAFSA. The aid application deadline for fall entry is February 15. Special funds for minority or disadvantaged students include diversity scholarship/grant funds for first-year students in an effort to provide financial assistance for those who are underrepresented in the legal community. First-year students are notified about their financial aid application from March 15 through August 30.

About the Law School

Pace University School of Law was established in 1976 and is a private institution. The 12-acre campus is in a suburban area in White Plains. Educating students in an open, collaborative, and caring environment to be competent ethical lawyers is the school's primary mission. Students have access to federal, state, county, city, and local agencies, courts, correctional facilities, law firms, and legal aid organizations in the White Plains area. Major state courts for

the New York State Ninth Judicial District, county and federal courts, county government, and the district attorney's office are within walking distance. Facilities of special interest to law students include the Judicial Institute of the State of New York, an innovative center for judicial education, which is housed in a state-of-the-art facility at Pace. The Women's Justice Center, Land Use Law Center, and Institute for International Commercial Law are other facilities of interest to students. Housing for students includes an on-campus residence hall providing single rooms. The university also assists students in locating off-campus accommodations close to campus. All law school facilities are accessible to the physically disabled.

Calendar

The law school operates on a traditional semester basis. Courses for full-time students are offered days only during the first year, and must be completed within 3 years. For part-time students, courses are offered both day and evening, and must be completed within 4 years. New full-time students are admitted in the fall and spring. New part-time students are admitted in the fall. There is a 7-week summer session. Transferable summer courses are offered.

Programs

In addition to the J.D., the law school offers the LL.M. and S.J.D. Students may take relevant courses in other programs and apply credit toward the J.D.; a maximum of 10 credits may be applied. The following joint degrees may be earned: J.D./M.A. (Juris Doctor/Master of Women's Studies with Sarah Lawrence College), J.D./M.B.A. (Juris Doctor/Master of Business Administration with Pace University Lubin School of Business), J.D./M.E.M. (Juris Doctor/Master of Environmental Management with Yale School of Forestry and Environmental Studies), J.D./M.P.A. (Juris Doctor/Master of Public Administration with Pace University Dyson College of Arts and Sciences), and J.D./M.S. (Juris Doctor/Master of Environmental Policy with Bard College Center for Environmental Policy).

Required

To earn the J.D., candidates must complete 88 total credits, of which 37 are for required courses. They must maintain a minimum GPA of 2.3 in the required courses. The following first-year courses are required of all students: Civil

Phone: 914-422-4210
Fax: 914-989-8714
E-mail: hgranison@law.pace.edu
Web: www.law.pace.edu

Contact
Henry C. Granison, Director, 914-422-4210 for general inquiries; Adriana Pace, Associate Director, Financial Aid, 914-422-4050 for financial aid information.

NEW YORK

Procedure I and II, Constitutional Law, Contracts, Criminal Law, First Year Legal Skills Program I and II, Property , and Torts. Required upper-level courses consist of Federal Income Tax, Professional Responsibility, and upper-level skills and writing requirements. The required orientation program for first-year students consists of a 3-day program prior to the beginning of fall semester classes, with a substantive law component that emphasizes briefing techniques and lectures.

Electives
The School of Law offers concentrations in corporate law, criminal law, environmental law, family law, intellectual property law, international law, juvenile law, labor law, litigation, securities law, tax law, torts and insurance, health law, and land use and real estate law. In addition, Pace offers 6 clinics, including criminal defense, post-conviction exoneration, environmental protection, representation of immigrants, disabled and elderly clients, and investors with complaints against stockbrokers. Clinics are generally 6 credits per semester. They are available to upper-level students who have taken prerequisite courses. Pace offers more than 30 seminars, including The Supreme Court and the Constitution, Feminist Legal Theory, and Comparative Environmental Law: Brazil and the U.S. (taught in Brazil). Externships include serving as clerks for federal, state, and family court judges; assisting in criminal prosecutions; working in federal and state environmental agencies in New York and Washington, D.C.; clerking in law firms with international law practices in New York and abroad; working in public interest organizations; and helping missions of small island states in the United Nations on matters involving global warming. Students serve as research assistants for professors, and in the Environmental Law Center, the Land Use Law Center, the Women's Justice Center, the Energy and Climate Center, and the Institute for International Commercial Law. All students take Legal Skills in their first year, may take upper-level Advanced Legal Research, and must complete an upper-level research and writing project. The school hosts 5 academic lectures each year: Dyson Lecture, Garrison and Kerlin Lecture in Environmental Law, Blank Lecture on Ethics, Hopkins Lecture, and Sloan Lecture on International Law. A semester at the University College of London's Faculty of Laws is available each spring for second- and third-year students as well as visiting students from other

ABA-accredited institutions. Tutorial programs include the Academic Success Program, the Dean's Scholar program, and a writing specialist. Minority programs include Legal Education Opportunity (LEO). Pace has active student organizations in various areas of law, including property, entertainment and sports, family, land use and real estate, and criminal law. The most widely taken electives are Family Law, Environmental Law, and International Law.

Graduation Requirements
In order to graduate, candidates must have a GPA of 2.3 and must have completed the upper-division writing requirement.

Organizations
Students edit the *Pace Law Review*, the *Pace Environmental Law Review*, the *Pace International Law Review*, the student newspaper *Hearsay*, and *Journal of Court Innovation*. The Moot Court Board sponsors the required competition for all first-year students and sends teams to national and international competitions, including the National Environmental Law Moot Court Competition, the Willem C. Vis International Commercial Arbitration Moot Court, the ABA Client Counseling Competition, the National Criminal Justice Trial Advocacy Competition, and the American Association for Justice Student Trial Advocacy Competition. Student organizations include the Student Bar Association, Women's Association of Law Students, and the Environmental Law Society. Phi Alpha Delta has a local chapter. Other organizations include International Law Society, Health Law Society, and Latino/Black Law Students organizations.

Library
The law library contains 406,732 hardcopy volumes and 62,322 microform volume equivalents, and subscribes to 1,583 serial publications. Such online databases and networks as CALI, Infotrac, LegalTrac, LEXIS, Mathew Bender, WESTLAW, Wilsonline Indexes, BNA, ProQuest Congressional WorldCat, JSTOR, HeinOnline, LLMC Digital, and Making of Modern Law are available to law students for research. Special library collections include a selective U.S. government depository, the David Sive and law school archives, and a collection on environmental law. The ratio of library volumes to faculty is 9,039 to 1 and to students is 596 to 1. The ratio of seats in the library to students is 1 to 1.

Placement
J.D.s awarded:	223

Services available through: a separate law school placement center and the university placement center.
Services: seminars and workshops, online job listings for students and alumni, webinars, databases and guides for judicial clerkships, and private and public sector employment and fellowship opportunities.
Special features: videotaped mock interviews, webinars, mentor programs, career newsletter, and topical guides.

Full-time job interviews:	8 employers
Summer job interviews:	7 employers
Placement within 9 months of graduation:	79% of class
Average starting salary:	$38,480 to $160,000

Areas of placement:
Private practice 2–10 attorneys	24%
Private practice 11–25 attorneys	4%
Private practice 26–50 attorneys	1%
Private practice 51–100 attorneys	4%
Private practice 501+ attorneys	2%
Business/industry	20%
Academic	15%
Government	10%
Public interest	6%
Judicial clerkships	5%

Faculty
The law school has 44 full-time and 137 part-time faculty members, of whom 70 are women. According to AAUP standards for Category I institutions, faculty salaries are above average. About 5% of full-time faculty have a graduate law degree in addition to the J.D.; about 2% of part-time faculty have one. The ratio of full-time students to full-time faculty in an average class is 16 to 1; in a clinic, 8 to 1. The law school has a regular program of bringing visiting professors and other distinguished lecturers and visitors to campus.

Students
About 57% of the student body are women; 20%, minorities; 4%, African American; 7%, Asian American; and 5%, Hispanic. The majority of students come from New York (58%). The average age of entering students is 24; age range is 22 to 60. About 37% of students enter directly from undergraduate school, 8% have a graduate degree, and 63% have worked full-time prior to entering law school. About 15% drop out after the first year for academic or personal reasons; 84% remain to receive a law degree.

Dickinson School of Law

Lewis Katz Building
University Park, PA 16802-1910

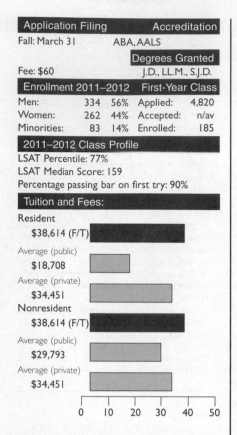

Application Filing	Accreditation
Fall: March 31	ABA, AALS

	Degrees Granted
Fee: $60	J.D., LL.M., S.J.D.

Enrollment 2011–2012		First-Year Class	
Men:	334 56%	Applied:	4,820
Women:	262 44%	Accepted:	n/av
Minorities:	83 14%	Enrolled:	185

2011–2012 Class Profile
LSAT Percentile: 77%
LSAT Median Score: 159
Percentage passing bar on first try: 90%

Tuition and Fees:

Resident
$38,614 (F/T)

Average (public)
$18,708

Average (private)
$34,451

Nonresident
$38,614 (F/T)

Average (public)
$29,793

Average (private)
$34,451

0 10 20 30 40 50

ADMISSIONS
In the Fall of 2011 first-year class, 4820 applied, were accepted, and 185 enrolled. Five transfer student enrolled. The median LSAT percentile of the most recent first-year class was 77; the median GPA was 3.5 on a scale of 4.0. The lowest LSAT percentile accepted was 44; the highest was 97.

Requirements
Applicants must have a bachelor's degree and take the LSAT. No specific undergraduate courses are required, and candidates are not interviewed.

Procedure
The application deadline for fall entry is March 31. Applicants should submit an application form, LSAT results, transcripts, personal statement, nonrefundable application fee of $60, 2 (preferably academic) letters of recommendation, and a record of work experience and two statements: a 2-page personal statement. Notification of the admissions decision is on a rolling basis. The law school uses the LSAC.

Special
The law school recruits minority and disadvantaged students by means of minority forums such as the LSAT Candidate Referral Service, recruitment outreach to historically black colleges and recruitment by current minority students and alumni. The Law School also offers a week-long, Explore Law program, which is targeted at Penn State undergraduate minorities entering their sophomore or junior years. Requirements are different for out-of-state students. Transfer students must have one year of credits, attend an ABA-approved law school, and a personal statement.

Costs
Tuition and fees for the 2011–2012 academic year are $37,704 for all full-time students. On-campus room and board costs about $11,412 annually; books and supplies run $1,456.

Financial Aid
About 92% of current law students receive some form of aid. The average annual amount of aid from all sources combined, including scholarships, loans, and work contracts, is $45,988; maximum, $61,670. Awards are based on need and merit combined. Required financial statements are the FAFSA and Penn State Law Financial Aid Application. First-year students are notified about their financial aid application at time of acceptance.

About the Law School
The Pennsylvania State University, Dickinson School of Law was established in 1834 and is a public institution. The 8566-acre campus is located in a small town 24 miles southwest of Harrisburg. The mission of The Dickinson School of Law is to improve "the lives of the people of Pennsylvania, the nation, and the world" through exemplary legal teaching, scholarship, and service. We believe that these activities are integrated, each supporting and reinforcing the others. Because law is the foundation of social order and prosperity, we recognize our unique responsibility and opportunity as a law faculty. We are committed to reaping the distinct advantages of residing in a major research institution, because we believe that legal education and scholarship are enhanced by knowledge of other fields of study and collaboration with faculty in other disciplines.

We are committed to educating a diverse student body, making the Penn State Law education as broadly accessible as is feasible. Our activities reflect our belief that human interaction is increasingly global; we strive to prepare students to contribute through law to a global society, and we contribute to the resolution of international problems through research and service. Students have access to federal, state, county, city, and local agencies, courts, correctional facilities, law firms, and legal aid organizations in the University Park area. The law school's curriculum includes a wide range of experimental learning opportunities, including a Washington, D.C. Semester Program for third year students wishing to spend their final semester of law school working for a federal agency or a non-profit organization in Washington, D.C. The law school also offers several international externship opportunities for students in both government agencies and non-governmental non-profit organizations, including the international Criminal Tribunal at The Hague. The University has new and renovated facilities for the law school in Carlisle and University Park. Both buildings offer state-of-the-art classrooms, libraries, courtrooms, and study spaces. Both are pervasively interconnected by a high-definition audiovisual telecommunications system that permits the seamless transmission and real-time exchange of courses, lectures, and programs between the law school's two buildings and with compatibly equipped buildings and institutions anywhere in the world, a capacity the law school regularly leverages. On campus graduate housing is available for both single students and students with families at the law school's University Park location. In addition, there is a wide-range of affordable off-campus housing (e.g., rental homes, duplexes, and apartments) in both University Park and Carlisle. The law school also provides a roommate matching service. About 98% of the law school facilities are accessible to the physically disabled.

Calendar
The law school operates on a traditional semester basis. Courses for full-time students are offered days only and must be completed within 4.5 years. There is no part-time program. New full-time students are admitted in the fall. There is no summer session. Transferable summer courses are not offered.

Phone: 814-867-1251
800-840-1122
Fax: 814-863-7274
E-mail: *admission@law.psu.edu*
Web: *www.law.psu.edu*

Contact
Barbara W. Guillaume, Director of Admissions, 717-240-5207 for general inquiries; Susan Bogart, Financial Aid Director, 814-853-0469 for financial aid information.

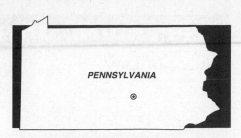

PENNSYLVANIA

Programs
In addition to the J.D., the law school offers the LL.M. and S.J.D. Students may take relevant courses in other programs and apply credit toward the J.D.; a maximum of 6 credits may be applied. Many joint degrees are available.

Required
To earn the J.D., candidates must complete 88 total credits, of which 40 are for required courses. They must maintain a minimum GPA of 2.0 in the required courses. The following first-year courses are required of all students: Civil Procedure, Constitutional Law, Contracts, Criminal Law, Criminal Procedure, Elements of Law, Legal Analysis, Research and Writing I and II, Property, and Torts. Required upper-level courses consist of Professional Responsibility, Professional Skills, and Seminar Course. Students are required to take a professional skills course, which may include enrollment in one of the law school's clinics. Clinical opportunities at the law school focus on child advocacy, immigrants' rights, appellate civil rights litigation, rural economic development, international sustainable development, disability law, elder and consumer protection law, and family law. The law school's student orientation is a one and one-half day program that is designed to introduce students to the law school, the University, and to the expectations of the legal profession. During this program, students receive focused guidance on academic preparation in the law school context. In addition, the program offers students the opportunity to meet their new classmates and professors.

Electives
Pennsylvania State University, Dickinson School of Law offers concentrations in corporate law, criminal law, entertainment law, environmental law, family law, intellectual property law, international law, juvenile law, labor law, litigation, maritime law, media law, securities law, sports law, tax law, torts and insurance, arbitration, mediation and dispute resolution; science and technology law; public interest law. The most widely taken electives are Corporations, Evidence, and Trusts and Estates.

Graduation Requirements
In order to graduate, candidates must have a GPA of 2.0 and complete the upper-division writing requirement.

Organizations
The primary law review is the *Penn State Law Review*. Other law reviews include the *Penn State International Review* the *Penn State Environmental Law Review*, and the World Arbitration and Mediation Review. *Res Ipsa Loquitur* is the student yearbook. The school generally fields as many as 10 teams in various interscholastic moot court competitions. The competitions include Jessup International, National Appellate, and National Trial. Other competitions include a securities law competition, an international commercial arbitration competition, and a labor law competition. Law student organizations, local chapters of national associations, and campus organizations include PILF, International Law Society, The Federalist Society, ABA-Law Student Division, Amnesty International, Toastmasters International, Women's Law Caucus, Minority Law Students Association, and Phi Alpha Delta.

Library
The law library contains 638,086 hardcopy volumes and 1,605,054 microform volume equivalents, and subscribes to 1,231 serial publications. Online databases and networks include CALI, CIS Universe, Dow-Jones, Infotrac, Legal-Trac, LEXIS, OCLC First Search, and WESTLAW. Other resources are HeinOnline, BNA-All, CCH, LLMC Digital, MOML, IFLP, ProQuest Congressional, and CQ Library; Eur-Lex; JSTOR; PACER; ProQuest Library; and OCLC WorldCAT, which are available to law students for research. Special library collections include a U.S. government depository, European Community and United Nations documents, and Pennsylvania briefs and records. The ratio of seats in the library to students is 1 to 2.

Placement

J.D.s awarded:	190
Services available through: a separate law school placement center.	
Services: digitally recorded practice interviews	
Special features: high-definition video conferencing equipment for students to interview remotely.	
Full-time job interviews:	40 employers
Summer job interviews:	50 employers
Placement by graduation:	42% of class
Placement within 9 months:	84% of class
Average starting salary:	$40,500 to $104,000
Areas of placement:	
Private practice 2–10 attorneys	19%
Private practice 11–25 attorneys	1%
Private practice 26–50 attorneys	3%
Private practice 101+ attorneys	14%
Business/industry	23%
Judicial clerkships	19%
Government	12%
Public interest	4%
Academic	4%
Military	1%

Faculty
The law school has 71 full-time and 17 part-time faculty members, of whom 39 are women. About 48% of full-time faculty have a graduate law degree in addition to the J.D.; about 29% of part-time faculty have one. The ratio of full-time students to full-time faculty in an average class is 9 to 1; in a clinic, 5 to 1. The law school has a regular program of bringing visiting professors and other distinguished lecturers and visitors to campus.

Students
About 44% of the student body are women; 14%, minorities; 6%, African American; 5%, Asian American; 1%, Hispanic; and 3%, non-US resident. The average age of entering students is 24; age range is 18 to 45. About 43% of students enter directly from undergraduate school, and 5% have a graduate degree. About 2% drop out after the first year for academic or personal reasons; 98% remain to receive a law degree.

PEPPERDINE UNIVERSITY

School of Law

24255 Pacific Coast Highway
Malibu, CA 90263

Application Filing	Accreditation
Fall: n/av	ABA, AALS

Degrees Granted
Fee: n/av   J.D., Master of Dispute Resolution

Enrollment 2011–2012		First-Year Class	
Men:	333 49%	Applied:	3,450
Women:	347 51%	Accepted:	909
Minorities:	116 17%	Enrolled:	273
Out-of-State:	306 45%		

2011–2012 Class Profile
LSAT Percentile: 77%
LSAT Median Score: 158
Percentage passing bar on first try: 70%

Tuition and Fees:

Resident
$42,780 (F/T)

Average (public)
$18,708

Average (private)
$34,451

Nonresident
$42,780 (F/T)

Average (public)
$29,793

Average (private)
$34,451

0   10   20   30   40   50

Percentage receiving financial aid: 87%

ADMISSIONS
In the fall of 2011 first-year class, 3450 applied, 909 were accepted, and 273 enrolled. Thirty transfers enrolled. The median LSAT percentile of the most recent first-year class was 77; the median GPA was 3.3 on a scale of 4.0.

Requirements
Applicants must have a bachelor's degree and take the LSAT. No specific undergraduate courses are required. Candidates are not interviewed.

Procedure
Applicants should submit an application form, 2 letters of recommendation, a resume, a personal statement, a response to the school of law's mission, and a seat deposit. Notification of the admissions decision is on a rolling basis. The law school uses the LSAC.

Special
The law school recruits minority and disadvantaged students by actively encouraging applications from ethnic minorities. Requirements are different for out-of-state students. Transfer students must have one year of credit, must have attended an ABA-approved law school, must submit an official law school transcript, must submit a letter from the dean indicating the student's eligibility to continue his or her studies and indicating the student's class rank, and must supply a photocopy of the current school's LSAC report. The student must rank in the top 30% of the first-year law class.

Costs
On-campus room and board costs about $17,306 annually; books and supplies run $980.

Financial Aid
About 87% of current law students receive some form of aid. The maximum annual amount of aid from all sources combined, including scholarships, loans, and work contracts, is $37,084. Awards are based on need and merit. The required financial statement is the FAFSA. The aid application deadline for fall entry is April 1. Special funds for minority or disadvantaged students consist of the Diversity Scholarship, based on academic and personal achievement. First-year students are notified about their financial aid application 2 weeks after acceptance notification.

About the Law School
Pepperdine University School of Law was established in 1969 and is a private institution. The 830-acre campus is in a small town 30 miles north of Los Angeles. The primary mission of the law school is to provide highly qualified students with a distinctive and solid legal education. The school maintains a Christian emphasis. Students have access to federal, state, county, city, and local agencies, courts, correctional facilities, law firms, and legal aid organizations in the Malibu area. Facilities of special interest to law students include the Odell McConnell Law Center, which overlooks the Pacific Ocean. This facility contains an auditorium-classroom, law library, classrooms, an atrium, an appellate courtroom, a trial courtroom, cafeteria, lounges, and student services offices. Housing for students is limited on campus; on-campus apartments house 4 students in each of the 36 apartments. All law school facilities are accessible to the physically disabled.

Calendar
The law school operates on a traditional semester basis. Courses for full-time students are offered days only. New students are admitted in the fall. There is a 7½-week summer session. Transferable summer courses are offered.

Programs
In addition to the J.D., the law school offers the Master of Dispute Resolution. The following joint degrees may be earned: J.D./M.B.A. (Juris Doctor/Master of Business Administration), J.D./M.D.R. (Juris Doctor/Master of Dispute Resolution), and J.D./M.P.P. (Juris Doctor/Master of Public Policy).

Required
To earn the J.D., candidates must complete 88 total credits, of which 57 are for required courses. They must maintain a minimum GPA of 72.0 in the required courses. The following first-year courses are required of all students: Civil Pleadings and Procedure I and II, Contracts I and II, Criminal Law, Criminal Procedure, Legal Research and Writing I and II, Real Property I and II, and Torts I and II. Required upper-level courses consist of Constitutional Law I and II, Corporations, Evidence, Federal Income Taxation, Legal Ethics, Remedies, and Wills and Trusts. The required orientation program for first-year students is a 4-day program that includes introductions to legal ethics, the socratic method, case briefing, note taking, outlining, and legal research and writing.

Electives
The School of Law offers concentrations in corporate law, criminal law, entertainment law, environmental law, family law, international law, labor law, tax law, tort law, property law, intellectual property law, advocacy and dispute resolution, public interest, technology and entrepreneurship, and constitutional law. In addition, clinical opportunities are available with the district attorney's offices of Los Angeles and Ventura counties, and with state and federal court judges in Los Angeles and Ventura counties. Also, smaller programs

Phone: 310-506-4631
Fax: 310-506-7668
Web: http://law.pepperdine.edu

Contact
Director of Financial Aid, 310-506-4633 for financial aid information.

offer training in corporate and securities law, tax law, juvenile law, domestic arbitration, labor law, consumer protection, trade regulation, and with various media industries. Second- and third-year students may study in the London Law Program during the fall and summer semesters. Courses are taught by British and American faculty. The most widely taken electives are the London Law Program, entertainment and sports law courses, and technology and entrepreneurship.

Graduation Requirements
In order to graduate, candidates must have a GPA of 72.0.

Organizations
Students edit the *Pepperdine Law Review, National Association of Administrative Law Journal*, and *Dispute Resolution Journal*. First-year students participate in an appellate advocacy experience. Upper-level students compete for places on teams that attend the National Moot Court and other competitions. Each spring there is the Dalsimer Moot Court intraschool competition. Law student organizations include the Student Bar Association, Asian Pacific American Law Students Association, and Black Law Students Association. There are local chapters of Delta Theta Phi, Phi Alpha Delta, and Phi Delta Phi.

Library
The law library contains 342,450 hardcopy volumes and 87,000 microform volume equivalents, and subscribes to 1,300 serial publications. Such online databases and networks as DIALOG, LEXIS, and WESTLAW are available to law students for research. The ratio of library volumes to faculty is 11,415 to 1 and to students is 504 to 1.

Faculty
The law school has 30 full-time faculty members, of whom 8 are women. The law school has a regular program of bringing visiting professors and other distinguished lecturers and visitors to campus.

Students
About 51% of the student body are women; 17%, minorities; 5%, African American; 6%, Asian American; 5%, Hispanic; and 1%, Native American. The majority of students come from California (55%). The average age of entering students is 23; age range is 20 to 55. About 6% of students have a graduate degree. About 5% drop out after the first year for academic or personal reasons.

Placement
Services available through: the School of Law Career Development Office.
Services: co-sponsors workshops on practice specialties.
Special features: seminars to assist students in preparing resumes and improving job search and interviewing skills, and counseling expertise in practice areas and alternative careers.

Full-time job interviews:	220 employers
Placement by graduation:	59% of class
Placement within 9 months:	95% of class

PHOENIX SCHOOL OF LAW

One North Central Avenue
Phoenix, AZ 85004

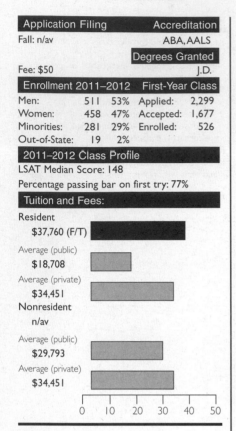

Application Filing		Accreditation	
Fall: n/av		ABA, AALS	
		Degrees Granted	
Fee: $50		J.D.	

Enrollment 2011–2012		First-Year Class	
Men:	511 53%	Applied:	2,299
Women:	458 47%	Accepted:	1,677
Minorities:	281 29%	Enrolled:	526
Out-of-State:	19 2%		

2011–2012 Class Profile
LSAT Median Score: 148
Percentage passing bar on first try: 77%

Tuition and Fees:

Resident
$37,760 (F/T)

Average (public)
$18,708

Average (private)
$34,451

Nonresident
n/av

Average (public)
$29,793

Average (private)
$34,451

0 10 20 30 40 50

ADMISSIONS
In the fall of 2011 first-year class, 2299 applied, 1677 were accepted, and 526 enrolled. Seven transfers enrolled. The median GPA of the most recent first-year class was 3.1.

Requirements
Applicants must have a bachelor's degree and take the LSAT. Minimum acceptable GPA is 2.0 on a scale of 4.0. The most important admission factors include academic achievement, writing ability, and life experience. No specific undergraduate courses are required. Candidates are not interviewed.

Procedure
Applicants should submit an application form, LSAT results, transcripts, a personal statement, a nonrefundable application fee of $50, 2 letters of recommendation, and copy of a resume and CAS report. Notification of the admissions decision is immediately after decision is made. The law school uses the LSAC.

Special
The law school recruits minority and disadvantaged students through minority bar associations, and at institutions with large minority populations. Requirements are different for out-of-state students. Transfer students must have attended an ABA-approved law school and must have a personal statement.

Costs
On-campus room and board costs about $12,316 annually; books and supplies run $9,849.

Financial Aid
First-year students are notified about their financial aid application at time of acceptance.

About the Law School
Phoenix School of Law was established in 2005 and is a private institution. The campus is in an urban area of downtown Phoenix. The primary mission of the law school is to train students for the practice of law, especially among underserved populations. Students have access to federal, state, county, city, and local agencies, courts, correctional facilities, law firms, and legal aid organizations in the Phoenix area. Facilities of special interest to law students include modern classroom technology.

Calendar
The law school operates on a traditional semester basis. Courses for full-time students are offered both day and evening and must be completed within 5 years. For part-time students, courses are offered both day and evening and must be completed within 6 years. New full- and part-time students are admitted in the fall and spring. There is a 7-week summer session. Transferable summer courses are offered.

Programs
Students may take relevant courses in other programs and apply credit toward the J.D.; a maximum of 6 credits may be applied.

Required
To earn the J.D., candidates must complete 87 total credits, of which 67 are for required courses. The following first-year courses are required of all students: Civil Procedure I and II, Contracts I and II, Criminal Law, Lawyering Process, Property I and II, and Torts I and II. Required upper-level courses consist of Business Associations, Commercial Law, Constitutional Law I and II, Criminal Procedure, Evidence, Family Law/Community Property, General Practice Skills, Professional Responsibility, Property II, and Trusts and Estates. The required orientation program for first-year students is 2 days.

Electives
Students may take clinics (worth 2–4 credit hours) and externships (worth 2–4 credit hours) as long as they have a 2.0 GPA. The most widely taken electives are Pre-Trial Practice, Trial Practice, and Intellectual Property.

Phone: (602) 682-6800
1-800-PHXLAW1
E-mail: nsegovia@phoenixlaw.edu
Web: phoenixlaw.edu

Contact

Communications Director, 602-682-6855 for general inquiries; Debbie Richards, Financial Aid Coordinator, 602-682-6842 for financial aid information.

ARIZONA

Placement

J.D.s awarded: 69
Services available through: a separate law school placement center.

Graduation Requirements

In order to graduate, candidates must have a GPA of 2.0 and must have completed the upper-division writing requirement, along with 30 pro bono hours.

Organizations

Students edit the *Phoenix Law Review* and the student newspaper *The Sidebar*. Moot court competitions for students include the ABA Moot Court Competition, National Moot Court Competition, and the John J. Gibbons Criminal Procedure Moot Court Competition. Other competitions include Judge Thomas Tang Competition and National Association of Women's Lawyers–Selma Moidel Smith Law Student Writing Competition. Law student organizations, local chapters of national associations, and campus organizations include Federalist Society, International Law Society, Intellectual Property Law Society, Phoenix Law Women's Association, Black Law Students Association, Public Interest Law Project, Alternative Dispute Resolution, Juggling Club, and Hispanic Law Students Association.

Library

Such online databases and networks as CALI, CIS Universe, Legal-Trac, LEXIS, Mathew Bender, OCLC First Search, WESTLAW, HeinOnline, CCH, BNA, and Pro Quest are available to law students for research.

Faculty

The law school has 32 full-time and 29 part-time faculty members, of whom 34 are women. The ratio of full-time students to full-time faculty in an average class is 21 to 1; in a clinic, 5 to 1. The law school has a regular program of bringing visiting professors and other distinguished lecturers and visitors to campus.

Students

About 47% of the student body are women; 29%, minorities; 7%, African American; 5%, Asian American; 14%, Hispanic; and 1%, Native American. The majority of students come from Arizona (98%). The average age of entering students is 28; age range is 23 to 55.

PONTIFICAL CATHOLIC UNIVERSITY OF PUERTO RICO

School of Law

2250 Avenida las Americas suite 543
Ponce, PR 00717-9997

ADMISSIONS

The median GPA was 2.9 on a scale of 4.0.

Requirements

Applicants must have a bachelor's degree and take the LSAT. Minimum acceptable GPA is 2.5 on a scale of 4.0. The most important admission factors include GPA, LSAT results, and general background. No specific undergraduate courses are required. Candidates are not interviewed.

Procedure

Applicants should submit an application form and transcripts. The law school uses the LSAC.

Special

Requirements are different for out-of-state students. Transfer students must have a minimum GPA of 2.

Financial Aid

About 52% of current law students receive some form of aid. The average annual amount of aid from all sources combined, including scholarships, loans, and work contracts, is $2,000. Awards are based on need and merit combined. Check with the school for current application deadlines.

About the Law School

Pontifical Catholic University of Puerto Rico School of Law was established in 1961 and is a private institution. The 92-acre campus is in an urban area 60 miles from San Juan. The primary mission of the law school is to develop lawyers with a thorough training in the law and a practical mastery of legal techniques within the context of Catholic teachings. Students have access to federal, state, county, city, and local agencies, courts, correctional facilities, law firms, and legal aid organizations in the Ponce area. Housing for students is available.

Calendar

The law school operates on a traditional semester basis. Courses for full-time students are offered both day and evening. For part-time students, courses are offered both day and evening. New full- and part-time students are admitted in the fall.

There is a summer session. Transferable summer courses are not offered.

Programs

In addition to the J.D., the law school offers the LL.M. Students may take relevant courses in other programs and apply credit toward the J.D. The following joint degrees may be earned: J.D./M.B.A. (Juris Doctor/Master of Business Administration).

Required

To earn the J.D., candidates must complete 94 total credits, of which 82 are for required courses. The following first-year courses are required of all students: Constitutional Law, Criminal Procedure, Family Law, Introduction to Law, Legal Bibliography and Writing, Logic and Redaction, Moral and Dogmatic Theory, Obligations, and Property Law. Required upper-level courses consist of Administrative Law, Advanced Logical Analysis, Appellate Practice, Civil Procedure I and II, Corporations, Evidence, Federal Jurisdiction, Legal Clinics, Legal Ethics, Mercantile Law, Mortgages, Negotiable Instruments, Notarial Law, Special Contracts, Special Logical Procedures, Successions and Donations, and Torts.

Electives

Clinical training is provided through the school's downtown Ponce Legal Aid Clinic for indigent clients and through judicial clerkships in superior and federal district courts and placements with district attorney's offices. The Center for Legal and Social Investigations allows for research under the supervision of a faculty director.

Phone: 787-841-2000, ext. 1836
Fax: 787-840-4620
Web: www.pucpr.edu

Contact

Associate Dean, 787-841-2000, ext. 341 for general inquiries; Director, 787-841-2000 for financial aid information.

PUERTO RICO

Organizations

The primary law review is the *Revista de Derecho Puertorriqueno*, which is edited by a student board. Law student organizations include the Law Student Division of the American Bar Association, National Law Students of Puerto Rico, and the Women's Rights Organization. Local chapters of national associations are Delta Theta Phi and Phi Alpha Delta.

Library

The law library contains 135,000 hardcopy volumes and 15,000 microform volume equivalents. Special library collections include deposits of U.S. government and United Nations documents.

Faculty

The law school has 14 full-time and 18 part-time faculty members. About 50% of full-time faculty have a graduate law degree in addition to the J.D. The ratio of full-time students to full-time faculty in an average class is 12 to 1.

Students

About 50% of the student body are women. The average age of entering students is 24; age range is 21 to 51. About 50% of students enter directly from undergraduate school. About 11% drop out after the first year for academic or personal reasons.

Placement	
Average starting salary:	$14,000 to $24,000
Areas of placement:	
Academic	50%

QUINNIPIAC UNIVERSITY

School of Law

275 Mt. Carmel Avenue
Hamden, CT 06518-1908

Application Filing	Accreditation
Fall: March 1	ABA, AALS
	Degrees Granted
Fee: $65	J.D., LL.M.

Enrollment 2011–2012		First-Year Class	
Men:	227 52%	Applied:	2,037
Women:	211 48%	Accepted:	959
Minorities:	61 14%	Enrolled:	123
Out-of-State:	180 41%		

2011–2012 Class Profile
LSAT Percentile: 67%
LSAT Median Score: 156
Percentage passing bar on first try: 81%

Tuition and Fees:

Resident
$45,050 (F/T)

Average (public)
$18,708

Average (private)
$34,451

Nonresident
$45,050 (F/T)

Average (public)
$29,793

Average (private)
$34,451

Percentage receiving financial aid: 93%

ADMISSIONS

In the Fall of 2011 first-year class, 2037 applied, 959 were accepted, and 123 enrolled. Four transfers enrolled. The median LSAT percentile of the most recent first-year class was 67; the median GPA was 3.3 on a scale of 4.0. The lowest LSAT percentile accepted was 30; the highest was 97.

Requirements
Applicants must have a bachelor's degree and take the LSAT. The most important admission factors include undergraduate curriculum and LSAT results. No specific undergraduate courses are required, and candidates are not interviewed.

Procedure
The application deadline for fall entry is March 1. Applicants should submit an application form, LSAT results, transcripts, personal statement, nonrefundable application fee of $65, 2 letters of recommendation, and a résumé. Notification of the admissions decision is on a rolling basis. The law school uses the LSAC.

Special
The law school recruits minority and disadvantaged students by means of student search, community outreach programs, the CLEO program, minority days on campus, and attendance at various minority programs, pipeline program with inner city high school. Requirements are different for out-of-state students. Transfer students must have one year of credits, attend an ABA-approved law school, personal statement, letter of good standing from the dean of the law school from which the student is transferring, and law school class rank.

Costs

Tuition and fees for the 2011–2012 academic year are $44,270 for all full-time students. Tuition for part-time students is $31,000 for in-state students and $31,000 out-of-state. Books and supplies run $1,200.

Financial Aid

About 93% of current law students receive some form of aid. The average annual amount of aid from all sources combined, including scholarships, loans, and work contracts, is $45,014; maximum, $72,179. Awards are based on need and merit combined. Required financial statement is the FAFSA. The aid application deadline for fall entry is April 15. Special funds for minority or disadvantaged students and distinguished scholar awards are available. First-year students are notified about their financial and aid application at time of acceptance.

About the Law School

Quinnipiac University School of Law was established in 1978 and is a private institution. The 500-acre campus is in a suburban area 90 miles north of New York City; 2 hours from Boston. The primary mission of the law school is to educate students, through theory in classrooms and practice in clinics and externships, to be prepared to practice law in any environment in the 21st century. Students have access to federal, state, county, city, and local agencies, courts, correctional facilities, law firms, and legal aid organizations in the Hamden area. Facilities of special interest to law students include the School of Law Library, Fitness Center, and Grand Courtroom. Housing for students is avail-

able off-campus in the area. The Office of Admissions assists students with housing opportunities. All law school facilities are accessible to the physically disabled.

Calendar

The law school operates on a traditional semester basis. Courses for full-time students are offered both day and evening and must be completed within 84 months. For part-time students, courses are offered both day and evening and must be completed within 84 months. New full- and part-time students are admitted in the fall. There is a 7-week summer session. Transferable summer courses are offered.

Programs

In addition to the J.D., the law school offers the LL.M. Students may take relevant courses in other programs and apply credit toward the J.D.; a maximum of nine credits may be applied. The following joint degrees may be earned: J.D./M.B.A. (Juris Doctor/Master of Business Administration).

Required
To earn the J.D., candidates must complete 86 total credits, of which 45 are for required courses. They must maintain a minimum GPA of 2.0 in the required courses. The following first-year courses are required of all students: Civil Procedure I and II, Constitutional Law, Contracts I and II, Criminal Law, Legal Skills I and II, Property, and Torts. Required upper-level courses consist of Administrative Law, Business Organizations, Commercial Law, Evidence, Federal Income Taxation, Lawyer's Professional Responsibility, and Trusts and Estates. The required orientation program for first-year students is a 2-day general introductory program to the school, the faculty, the administration, and the students.

Electives
The School of Law offers concentrations in criminal law, family law, intellectual property law, juvenile law, litigation, tax law, health law, and dispute resolution. In addition, students may participate in a Civil Clinic during the day or evening. There is also a Tax Law Clinic. Seminars are varied. Quinnipiac offers 9 externship programs in areas such as public interest, corporate counsel, judicial, legislative,

Phone: 203-582-3400
800-462-1944
Fax: 203-582-3339
E-mail: ladm@quinnipiac.edu
Web: www.law.quinnipiac.edu

Contact

Ed Wilkes, Executive Dean, Enrollment Services, 203-582-3400 for general inquiries; Odette Franceskino, Director of Financial Aid, 203-582-3405 for financial aid information.

CONNECTICUT

criminal justice, family and juvenile law, legal services, mediation, and field placement II. There are various research programs. Special lecture series include the Quinnipiac-Yale Dispute Resolution Lecture Series. There is an ABA - accredited summer program in Ireland with Trinity College (Dublin). An academic support program and writing program are available to students at the law school. A supplemental bar review class, offered free of charge to Quinnipiac graduates is offered. There is a special minority recruitment and information day at the law school. The Thurgood Marshall Awards reception in the evening recognizes individual achievement and service to the school and community. The most widely taken electives are Criminal Procedure, Tax, Trusts and Estates.

Graduation Requirements

In order to graduate, candidates must have a GPA of 2.0 and complete the upper-division writing requirement.

Organizations

Students edit the *Quinnipiac Law Review, Quinnipiac Probate Law Journal, Quinnipiac Health Law Journal,* and the student newspaper, *The Quinnipiac Legal Times.* Moot court competitions are the National Appellate Advocacy Competition, Albert Mugel Tax Moot Court Competition, and Domenick Gabrielli National Family Law Moot Court competition. The Mock Trial Society competes in American Association for Justice Student Trial Advocacy National Competition, Texas Young Lawyers Association Competition, and the American Bar Association Criminal Justice Division Mock Trial Competition. There are more than 30 student organizations on campus. These, including local chapters of national associations, and campus organizations are Tax Law Society, APALSA, Public Interest Law Project, Student Bar Association, Women's Law Society, the Black Students Association, Phi Alpha Delta, and Phi Delta Phi.

Library

The law library contains 198,435 hard-copy volumes and 260,581 microform volume equivalents, and subscribes to 1,139 serial publications. Online databases and networks include CALI, CIS Universe, Infotrac, Legal-Trac, LEXIS, Mathew Bender, OCLC First Search, and WESTLAW. Wilsonline Indexes, CILP, Constitution of Countries of the World, Criminal Justice periodicals, IFLP, LLMC-Digital, Qcat Online Catalog, RIA Checkpoint, Statistical Universe, Congressional Universe, HeinOnline, BNA, and more than 200 other databases are available to law students for research. Special library collections include a federal government depository library collection, a tax collection, a Connecticut collection, and a health law collection. The ratio of library volumes to faculty is 7,286 to 1 and to students is 1,048 to 1. The ratio of seats in the library to students is 1 to 1.

Faculty

The law school has 29 full-time and 34 part-time faculty members, of whom 20 are women. According to AAUP standards for Category IIA institutions, faculty salaries are well above average. About 26% of full-time faculty have a graduate law degree in addition to the J.D. The ratio of full-time students to full-time faculty in an average class is 13 to 1; in a clinic, 6 to 1. The law school has a regular program of bringing visiting professors and other distinguished lecturers and visitors to campus.

Students

About 48% of the student body are women; 14%, minorities; 2%, African American; 5%, Asian American; 5%, Hispanic; 1%, Native American; and 1%, two or more races. The majority of students come from Connecticut (59%). The average age of entering students is 24; age range is 21 to 46. About 45% of students enter directly from undergraduate school, 2% have a graduate degree, and 35% have worked full-time prior to entering law school. About 8% drop out after the first year for academic or personal reasons; 90% remain to receive a law degree.

Placement

J.D.s awarded:	134

Services available through: a separate law school placement center.

Services: counseling on cover letter preparation, mock interviews, educational and informational programs, and participation in national career fairs.

Special features: staff members with J.D. degrees counsel students and develop employment opportunities for students and graduates. There is also on Alumni Career Networking Event.

Full-time job interviews:	8 employers
Summer job interviews:	16 employers
Placement within 9 months of graduation:	90% of class
Average starting salary:	$20,000 to $220,000

Areas of placement:

Private practice 2–10 attorneys	21%
Private practice 11–25 attorneys	4%
Private practice 26–50 attorneys	2%
Government	24%
Business/industry	17%
Judicial clerkships	9%
Public interest	9%
Academic	2%

School of Law

1000 Regent University Drive
Virginia Beach, VA 23464-9800

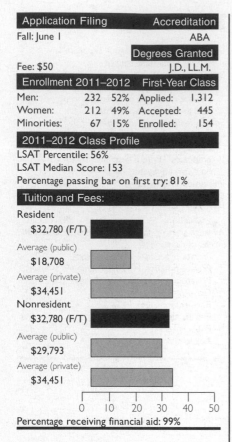

Application Filing	Accreditation
Fall: June 1	ABA

	Degrees Granted
Fee: $50	J.D., LL.M.

Enrollment 2011–2012		First-Year Class	
Men:	232 52%	Applied:	1,312
Women:	212 49%	Accepted:	445
Minorities:	67 15%	Enrolled:	154

2011–2012 Class Profile
LSAT Percentile: 56%
LSAT Median Score: 153
Percentage passing bar on first try: 81%

Tuition and Fees:

Resident
$32,780 (F/T)

Average (public)
$18,708

Average (private)
$34,451

Nonresident
$32,780 (F/T)

Average (public)
$29,793

Average (private)
$34,451

0   10   20   30   40   50

Percentage receiving financial aid: 99%

ADMISSIONS

In the Fall of 2011 first-year class, 1312 applied, 445 were accepted, and 154 enrolled. Six transfers enrolled. The median LSAT percentile of the most recent first-year class was 56; the median GPA was 3.3 on a scale of 4.0. The lowest LSAT percentile accepted was 30; the highest was 98.

Requirements

Applicants must have a bachelor's degree and take the LSAT. Minimum acceptable LSAT percentile is 30 and minimum acceptable GPA is 2.5 on a scale of 4.0. The most important admission factors include academic achievement, LSAT results, and GPA. No specific undergraduate courses are required, and candidates are not interviewed.

Procedure

The application deadline for fall entry is June 1. Applicants should submit an application form, LSAT results, transcripts, a personal statement, a nonrefundable application fee of $50, and 3 letters of recommendation. Notification of the admissions decision is on a rolling basis. The law school uses the LSAC.

Special

The law school recruits minority and disadvantaged students through recruitment travel, referrals, CRS mailings, and special scholarships. Requirements are different for out-of-state students. Transfer students must have one year of credit, have a minimum GPA of 2.5, have attended an ABA-approved law school, and a personal statement.

Costs

Tuition and fees for the 2011–2012 academic year are $31,800 for all full-time students. Tuition for part-time students is $23,320 for in-state students and $23,320 out-of-state. On-campus room and board costs about $10,170 annually; books and supplies run $1,500.

Financial Aid

About 99% of current law students receive some form of aid. The average annual amount of aid from all sources combined, including scholarships, loans, and work contracts, is $53,680; maximum, $56,722. Awards are based on need and merit, along with leadership and public interest awards. Required financial statement is the FAFSA. The aid application deadline for fall entry is June 1. Special funds for minority or disadvantaged students consist of law school grants and scholarships available to qualified students. First-year students are notified about their financial aid application.

About the Law School

Regent University School of Law was established in 1986 and is a private institution. The 80-acre campus is in a suburban area 7 miles southeast of Norfolk, Virginia. The primary mission of the law school is to train lawyers to participate effectively and professionally in the private and public sectors of this nation while affirming their understanding of the relationship between Christian principles and the practice of law. Students have access to federal, state, county, city, and local agencies, courts, correctional facilities, law firms, and legal aid organizations in the Virginia Beach area. Facilities of special interest to law students include a 134,000-square-foot law center equipped with the latest technology in audiovisual equipment, such as cameras for simultaneous broadcasting. There is also a 350-seat moot court/city council chamber. Housing for students consists of university-owned and operated apartments. All law school facilities are accessible to the physically disabled.

Calendar

The law school operates on a traditional semester basis. Courses for full-time students are offered days only and Required courses are offered during the day, but some electives are offered in the evening and must be completed within 5 years. For part-time students, courses are offered days only. Required courses are offered during the day, but some electives are offered in the evening. and must be completed within 6 years. New full- and part-time students are admitted in the fall. There is a 7-week summer session. Transferable summer courses are offered.

Programs

In addition to the J.D., the law school offers the LL.M. The following joint degrees may be earned: J.D./M.A. (Juris Doctor/Master of Arts in Communication, Counseling, Government, Journalism, Management & Organ), J.D./M.B.A. (Juris Doctor/Master of Business Administration), and J.D./M. Div. (Juris Doctor/Master of Divinity).

Required

To earn the J.D., candidates must complete 90 total credits, of which 73 are for required courses. They must maintain a minimum GPA of 2.0 in the required courses. The following first-year courses are required of all students: Christian Foundations of Law, Civil Procedure I and II, Contracts I and II, Legal Analysis Research and Writing I and II, Property I and II, and Torts I and II. Required upper-level courses consist of Business Associations, Constitutional Criminal Procedure, Constitutional Law I and II, Criminal Law, Evidence, Professional Responsibility, Professional Skills Practicum, and UCC I. Clinical courses are offered but not required. The required orientation program for first-year students is a 4-day program including a legal study skills workshop covering preparation for class, case briefing, outlining, and exam

Phone: 757-352-4584
877-267-5072
Fax: 757-352-4139
E-mail: *lawschool@regent.edu*
Web: *www.regent.edu/law/admissions*

Contact

Bonnie G. Creef, Director of Admissions and Financial Aid, 757-352-4584 for general inquiries; Julie Anjo, Assistant Director of Admissions and Financial Aid, 757-226-4584 for financial aid information.

VIRGINIA

preparation and taking; and a student affairs orientation covering law school policies and procedures and including a professionalism ceremony. The optional fifth day consists of a community service project.

Electives

The School of Law offers concentrations in corporate law, criminal law, family law, intellectual property law, international law, litigation, and tax law. The school lists courses in areas of a concentration as a curricular guide; students need not declare concentration to graduate. In addition, third-year students may participate in the Litigation Clinic. Second- or third-year students may take any seminar offered, including Race and the Law, Gender and the Law, and Elder Law. Internships are available as research assistants or law clerks for public interest law firms, local legal aid offices, prosecutors' and public defenders' offices, and the court system. Research programs include Advanced Legal Research and Writing, Academic Legal Scholarship, and Independent Studies. Practical experience may be gained through externships in an approved study program with a public interest or nonprofit firm, a judicial officer, or an attorney working in the federal or state government. A variety of distinguished guests come to campus each year to address the law school community. Study abroad includes a summer session in Strasbourg, France, which emphasizes international human rights and jurisprudence, and a summer session in Jerusalem and Haifa, Israel, which emphasizes biblical law, Qur'anic law, and the modern Israeli legal system. A mandatory summer academic success program is offered to select admits. The program is not for credit. The school also has student exchange relationships with educational institutions in Spain, China, and South Korea. The School of Law has an active Black Law Students Association (BLSA) and has hosted several BLSA events. The most widely taken electives are Family Law, UCC II, and Wills, Trusts & Estates.

Graduation Requirements

In order to graduate, candidates must have a GPA of 2.0, complete the upper-division writing requirement, an upper-division oral skills requirement, and a bar preparation course (for non-honors students).

Organizations

Students edit the *Regent Law Review, Regent Journal for International Law,* and *The Regent Journal of Law & Public Policy.* Moot court competitions for students include the Annual National Constitutional Law Moot Court Competition; Mid-Atlantic Regional Tournament of the American Collegiate Moot Court Competition; New York Regional Competition; William & Mary Spong Competition. Other competitions include ABA Negotiations Competition; ABA Mediation Competition; ABA Client Counseling Competition; Richmond Environmental Competition; Liberty Government Contracts Negotiations Competition. Trial advocacy boards include: ABA Labor & Employment Trial Advocacy Competition; Texas Young Lawyers National Trial Competition; Capitol City Challenge; Stetson Criminal Pre-Trial Competition; American Association of Justice Trial Advocacy Competition. Law student organizations, include The American Bar Association/Law Student Division, Black Law Students Association, Business Transactions Law Society, Christian Legal Society/Local Chapter, Federalist Society/Local Chapter, Hispanic Law Student Association, International Law Society, Intellectual Property and Entertainment Law Society, Regent Law Review, Law Wives, Moot Court Board, Alternative Dispute Resolution Board, Newman Club, Phi Alpha Delta/Local Chapter, Public Interest Legal Advocate of Regent University, Regent Journal of International Law, Regent Journal of Law and Public Policy, Regent Students for Life, Student Bar Association, Trial Advocacy Board, Virginia Bar Association/Law Student Division.

Library

The law library contains 131,049 hardcopy volumes and 1,001,511 microform volume equivalents, and subscribes to 529 serial publications. Online databases and networks include CALI, CIS Universe, DIALOG, Dow-Jones, Legal-Trac, LEXIS, OCLC First Search, and WESTLAW. Other resources are AccessUN, Arbitration Law Online, HeinOnline, Lawyers Weekly USA Online, Legal Scholarship Network (LSN), LLMC-Digital, Making of Modern Law, Legal Treatises 1800–1926, RIA Checkpoint, Virginia Lawyers Weekly Online, Virginia Supreme Court Records and Briefs, BE Press, JSTOR, Oxford Digital Reference Shelf, ProQuest, Rise of American Law, Versus Law, World Cat, Oxford University Press, and Cambridge

Placement	
J.D.s awarded:	119

Services available through: a separate law school placement center.

Special features: extensive career planning and professional development seminars, participation in career planning programs, panel discussions, and mock interviews, as well as one-to-one counseling of law students. Examples of fall programs include topics such as Interview Skills Workshop, Résumé Preparation, Focusing on a Litigation Career, and Solo Practice.

Full-time job interviews:	4 employers
Summer job interviews:	22 employers
Placement by graduation:	29% of class
Placement within 9 months:	87% of class
Average starting salary:	$42,500 to $55,000
Areas of placement:	
Private practice 2–10 attorneys	21%
Private practice 11–25 attorneys	4%
Private practice unknown	27%
Government	20%
Business/industry	11%
Judicial clerkships	8%
Academic	3%
Public interest	2%
Military	1%

University Press, which are available to law students for research. Special library collections include The Founders Collection, The John Brabner-Smith Library and Papers, The Ralph Johnson Bunche Library, The Mary Elizabeth Menefee Collection of Law & Film, The First Amendment & Civil Rights Collection, and Early American Political Sermons. The ratio of library volumes to faculty is 4,368 to 1 and to students is 295 to 1. The ratio of seats in the library to students is 1 to 1.

Faculty

The law school has 29 full-time and 24 part-time faculty members, of whom 13 are women. About 6% of full-time faculty have a graduate law degree in addition to the J.D.; about 8% of part-time faculty have one. The ratio of full-time students to full-time faculty in an average class is 22 to 1; in a clinic, 7 to 1. The law school has a regular program of bringing visiting professors and other distinguished lecturers and visitors to campus.

Students

About 49% of the student body are women; 15%, minorities; 4%, African American; 5%, Asian American; and 3%, Hispanic. The average age of entering students is 25; age range is 19 to 58.

School of Law

Ten Metacom Avenue
Bristol, RI 02809-5171

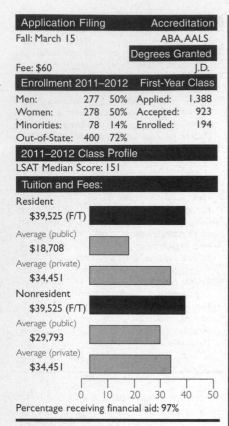

Application Filing		Accreditation	
Fall: March 15		ABA, AALS	
		Degrees Granted	
Fee: $60			J.D.
Enrollment 2011–2012		**First-Year Class**	
Men:	277 50%	Applied:	1,388
Women:	278 50%	Accepted:	923
Minorities:	78 14%	Enrolled:	194
Out-of-State:	400 72%		

2011–2012 Class Profile
LSAT Median Score: 151

Tuition and Fees:

Resident
$39,525 (F/T)

Average (public)
$18,708

Average (private)
$34,451

Nonresident
$39,525 (F/T)

Average (public)
$29,793

Average (private)
$34,451

0   10   20   30   40   50

Percentage receiving financial aid: 97%

ADMISSIONS

In the fall of 2011 first-year class, 1388 applied, 923 were accepted, and 194 enrolled. The median GPA of the most recent first-year class was 3.3.

Requirements

Applicants must have a bachelor's degree and take the LSAT. Minimum acceptable GPA is 2.0 on a scale of 4.0. The most important admission factors include LSAT results, GPA, and academic achievement. No specific undergraduate courses are required. Candidates are not interviewed.

Procedure

The application deadline for fall entry is March 15. Applicants should submit an application form, LSAT results, transcripts, a personal statement, the TOEFL (if applicable), a nonrefundable application fee of $60, a letter of recommendation, and a resume. Notification of the admissions decision is on a rolling basis. The law school uses the LSAC.

Special

The law school recruits minority and disadvantaged students by actively recruiting diverse students from local area colleges and universities and by actively supporting diverse students once admitted through student organizations, academic support, and other programs. The Office of Admissions works closely with the Office of Diversity and Outreach to increase diversity by actively recruiting at historically black colleges and universities and major law school admissions fairs. Requirements are different for out-of-state students. Transfer students must have a minimum GPA of 2, must have attended an ABA-approved law school, must submit a personal statement, and must have a letter of good standing from their prior law school.

Costs

Tuition and fees for the 2011–2012 academic year are $38,850 for all full-time students. On-campus room and board costs about $11,600 annually; books and supplies run $1,100.

Financial Aid

About 97% of current law students receive some form of aid. The average annual amount of aid from all sources combined, including scholarships, loans, and work contracts, is $47,991; maximum, $58,660. Awards are based on merit. Required financial statements are the FAFSA and institutional application. The aid application deadline for fall entry is February 15. First-year students are notified about their financial aid application once they are accepted and the necessary financial aid paperwork has been completed.

About the Law School

Roger Williams University School of Law was established in 1992 and is a private institution. The 140-acre campus is in the historic seacoast town of Bristol, 15 miles from Providence and Newport. The primary mission of the law school is to prepare students for the competent and ethical practice of law. Students have access to federal, state, county, city, and local agencies, courts, correctional facilities, law firms, and legal aid organizations in the Bristol area. There are also state library archives and libraries at Brown University, University of Rhode Island, Providence College, Rhode Island Historical Society, and Rhode Island archives. Facilities of special interest to law students include the Criminal Defense and Immigration clinics located in Providence, as well as the Mediation Clinic in Bristol. Nearby Bristol and Warren have numerous apartments available in private homes and apartment complexes. Housing is available in 1-bedroom apartments and townhouses 2 miles from campus. All law school facilities are accessible to the physically disabled.

Calendar

The law school operates on a traditional semester basis. Courses are offered both day and evening, and must be completed within 84 months. New students are admitted in the fall. There is a 7-week summer session. Transferable summer courses are offered.

Programs

Students may take relevant courses in other programs and apply credit toward the J.D.; a maximum of 9 to 15 credits may be applied. The following joint degrees may be earned: J.D./M.M.A. (Juris Doctor/Master of Marine Affairs), J.D./M.S. (Juris Doctor/Master of Science), and J.D./M.S.C.J. (Juris Doctor/Master of Science in Criminal Justice).

Required

To earn the J.D., candidates must complete 90 total credits, of which 48 are for required courses. They must maintain a minimum GPA of 2.0 in the required courses. The following first-year courses are required of all students: Civil Procedure I and II, Contracts I and II, Criminal Law, Legal Methods I and II, Property, and Torts I and II. Required upper-level courses consist of Constitutional Law I and II, Criminal Procedure: Investigation, Evidence, Legal Methods, and Professional Responsibility. The required orientation program for first-year students is held 3 days prior to the first day of classes and includes an introduction to the judicial system and the study of law, case briefing, exam-taking techniques, professionalism, student services introductions, and social events.

Electives

Third-year students may participate in the Criminal Defense Clinic, the Mediation

Phone: 401-254-4555
800-633-2727
Fax: 401-254-4516
E-mail: *admissions@rwu.edu*
Web: *http://law.rwu.edu*

Contact

Michael W. Donnelly-Boylen, Assistant Dean of Admissions, 800-633-2727 for general inquiries; Denise Rousseau, Assistant Director, Financial Aid, 401-254-4510 for financial aid information.

Clinic, or the Immigration Clinic, for 6 credits. Seminars, available to second- and third-year students span the breadth of the curriculum. They are worth 2 credits each. Special legal perspectives courses are worth 1 credit. Internships for third-year students consist of judicial and public interest clerkships worth 5 credits. There is faculty-supervised directed research for 1 or 2 credits. Students are required to perform 20 hours of public service prior to graduation. A special lecture series includes topics on marine affairs and public interest law. Study abroad is available through the London Summer Program. There are workshops on studying, case briefing, course outlining, and exam taking. The school has a rigorous Academic Support Program. The school's Office of Diversity and Outreach sponsors a variety of programs designed to address the needs of a diverse student body. The school has a wide range of special interest student groups. The most widely taken electives are Wills and Trusts, Business Organizations, and Family Law.

Graduation Requirements

In order to graduate, candidates must have a GPA of 2.0 and must have completed the upper-division writing requirement.

Organizations

Students edit the *Roger Williams University Law Review*. The primary internal competition is the Esther Clark Moot Court Competition. Students also participate in the National Moot Court Competition and the John R. Brown Admiralty Moot Court Competition. Other competitions include Mock Trial, Mediation, Negotiation, and Client Counseling. Law student organizations include the Maritime Law Society, Multicultural Law Students Association, and Sports and Entertainment Law Society. Local chapters of national associations include the American Trial Lawyers Association, ABA, and National Association of Public Interest Lawyers. Other campus organizations include Women's Law Caucus, LGBT Alliance, and the Federalist Society.

Library

The law library contains 312,281 hard-copy volumes and 1,088,017 microform volume equivalents, and subscribes to 2,949 serial publications. Such online databases and networks as CALI, CIS Universe, Legal-Trac, LEXIS, OCLC First Search, WESTLAW, Wilsonline Indexes, BNA, CCH Intelliconnect, Constitutions of the Countries of the World, Current Index to Legal Periodicals, CVN Law School, Foreign Law Guide, HeinOnline, Index to Foreign Legal Periodicals, International Courts of General Jurisdiction, International Law in Domestic Courts, JSTOR, Legal Information Reference Center, Making of Modern Law: Legal Treatises, Max Planck Encyclopedia of Public International Law, Morningstar Investment Research Center, Oxford Dictionaries Online, Oxford Reports on International Law, Oxford Scholarship Online, Project Muse, Small Business Reference Center, and Social Law Library's Massachusetts Administrative Law and Substantive Law databases are available to law students for research. Special library collections include Rhode Island Law, the State Justice Institute depository, Maritime Law, and Portuguese-American Comparative Law collections. The ratio of library volumes to faculty is 8,440 to 1 and to students is 562 to 1. The ratio of seats in the library to students is 1 to 1.

Faculty

The law school has 37 full-time and 35 part-time faculty members, of whom 28 are women. About 20% of full-time faculty have a graduate law degree in addition to the J.D.; about 11% of part-time faculty have one. The ratio of full-time students to full-time faculty in an average class is 40 to 1; in a clinic, 10 to 1. The law school has a regular program of bringing visiting professors and other distinguished lecturers and visitors to campus.

Students

About 50% of the student body are women; 14%, minorities; 3%, African American; 3%, Asian American; 7%, Hispanic; and 1%, Native American. The average age of entering students is 25; age range is 21 to 50. About 48% of students enter directly from undergraduate school, and 4% have a graduate degree. About 12% drop out after the first year for academic or personal reasons; 88% remain to receive a law degree.

Placement

J.D.s awarded:	145

Services available through: a separate law school placement center.

Special features: Legal Career Options Day, Rhode Island State Government Internship Program, extensive one-on-one counseling sessions, Mock Interview Program, coordinated programs with the Rhode Island Bar Association, online job database, and mentor programs.

Full-time job interviews:	8 employers
Summer job interviews:	11 employers
Placement within 9 months of graduation:	83% of class
Average starting salary:	$26,000 to $116,000

Areas of placement:

Private practice 2–10 attorneys	24%
Private practice 11–25 attorneys	3%
Private practice 26–50 attorneys	1%
Judicial clerkships	13%
Solo practice	20%
Business/industry	15%
Public interest	9%
Government	8%
Military	2%
Academic	2%

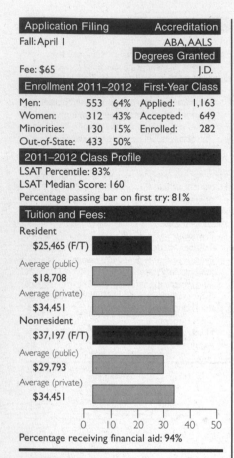

Application Filing	Accreditation
Fall: April 1	ABA, AALS
	Degrees Granted
Fee: $65	J.D.

Enrollment 2011–2012		First-Year Class	
Men:	553 64%	Applied:	1,163
Women:	312 43%	Accepted:	649
Minorities:	130 15%	Enrolled:	282
Out-of-State:	433 50%		

2011–2012 Class Profile
LSAT Percentile: 83%
LSAT Median Score: 160
Percentage passing bar on first try: 81%

Tuition and Fees:

Resident
$25,465 (F/T)

Average (public)
$18,708

Average (private)
$34,451

Nonresident
$37,197 (F/T)

Average (public)
$29,793

Average (private)
$34,451

0   10   20   30   40   50

Percentage receiving financial aid: 94%

ADMISSIONS
In the fall of 2011 first-year class, 1163 applied, 649 were accepted, and 282 enrolled. Thirty-six transfers enrolled. The median LSAT percentile of the most recent first-year class was 83; the median GPA was 3.3 on a scale of 4.0. The lowest LSAT percentile accepted was 45; the highest was 98.

Requirements
Applicants must have a bachelor's degree and take the LSAT. Minimum acceptable LSAT percentile is 45 and minimum acceptable GPA is 2.5 on a scale of 4.0. The most important admission factors include LSAT results, GPA, and general background. No specific undergraduate courses are required. Candidates are not interviewed.

Procedure
The application deadline for fall entry is April 1. Applicants should submit an application form, LSAT results, transcripts, a personal statement, a nonrefundable application fee of $65, and 2 letters of recommendation. Notification of the admissions decision is on a rolling basis. The law school uses the LSAC.

Special
The law school recruits minority and disadvantaged students by means of mail, student organizations, interviews, campus visits, and law forums. Requirements are different for out-of-state students. Transfer students must have one year of credit, must have attended an ABA-approved law school, and must submit a personal statement.

Costs
Tuition and fees for the 2011–2012 academic year are $22,746 for full-time in-state students and $34,478 for out-of-state students. Tuition for part-time students is $18,960 for in-state students and $28,740 out-of-state. On-campus room and board costs about $11,853 annually; books and supplies run $1,550.

Financial Aid
About 94% of current law students receive some form of aid. The average annual amount of aid from all sources combined, including scholarships, loans, and work contracts, is $28,767; maximum, $58,000. Awards are based on need and merit combined. The required financial statement is the FAFSA. The aid application deadline for fall entry is March 15. Special funds for minority or disadvantaged students include funds that are available from state, university, and school programs. First-year students are notified about their financial aid application at time of acceptance.

About the Law School
Rutgers University/Camden School of Law was established in 1926 and is a public institution. The 25-acre campus is in an urban area adjacent to the Center City district of Philadelphia. The primary mission of the law school is to provide a dynamic program of professional training, distinguished legal scholarship, and service to the bar and community. Students have access to federal, state, county, city, and local agencies, courts, correctional facilities, law firms, and legal aid organizations in the Camden area. Facilities of special interest to law students include computer laboratories, e-mail accounts, Internet connections, and online legal research. Housing for students is available in a 6-story apartment complex that houses 248 students in 62 graduate apartments. Off-campus housing on the Delaware River is also available. About 90% of the law school facilities are accessible to the physically disabled.

Calendar
The law school operates on a traditional semester basis. Courses for full-time students are offered both day and evening, and must be completed within 5 years. For part-time students, courses are offered both day and evening, and must be completed within 5 years. New full-time students are admitted in the fall. New part-time students are admitted in the fall and summer. There is a 7-week summer session. Transferable summer courses are offered.

Programs
Students may take relevant courses in other programs and apply credit toward the J.D.; a maximum of 6 credits may be applied. The following joint degrees may be earned: J.D./D.O. (Juris Doctor/Doctor of Osteopathic Medicine), J.D./M.B.A. (Juris Doctor/Master of Business Administration), J.D./M.D. (Juris Doctor/Doctor of Medicine), J.D./M.P.A. (Juris Doctor/Master of Public Administration), J.D./M.P.A.P. (Juris Doctor/Master of Public Affairs and Politics), and J.D./M.S.W. (Juris Doctor/Master of Social Work).

Required
To earn the J.D., candidates must complete 84 total credits, of which 32 are for required courses. They must maintain a minimum GPA of 2.0 in the required courses. The following first-year courses are required of all students: Civil Procedure, Constitutional Law, Contracts, Criminal Law, Legal Research and Writing, Moot Court I, Property, and Torts. Required upper-level courses consist of elective courses with writing components and Professional Responsibility. The required orientation program for first-year students is 2 days prior to the start of classes; there is a briefing on reading and analyzing cases, library usage, legal writing, professional responsibility, and general study techniques, as well as an introduction to computer usage and student organizations and social events.

Phone: 856-225-6102
800-466-7561
Fax: 856-225-6537
E-mail: admissions@camlaw.rutgers.edu
Web: www.camlaw.rutgers.edu

Contact

Maureen B. O'Boyle, Associate Director of Admissions, 856-225-6102 for general inquiries; Linda Taylor-Burch, 856-225-6039 for financial aid information.

Electives

The School of Law offers concentrations in corporate law, criminal law, environmental law, family law, international law, labor law, litigation, tax law, health law, and public interest law. In addition, clinics, which are worth 4 to 6 credits, include a Small Business Counseling Clinic, Child and Family Advocacy Clinic, Children's Justice Clinic, Domestic Violence Clinic, and a Civil Practice Clinic. The Pro Bono/Public Interest program enables students to represent clients, under the supervision of attorneys in domestic violence, children's SSI disability benefits, death penalty, immigration, and bankruptcy cases. As part of its Lawyering Program, the law school has many seminars covering a wide variety of areas of practice, including Business Ethics and Law, Citizenship, Civil Disobedience, Law, Politics, and Democracy, Patent Prosecution, Sex Discrimination, and Marshall Brennan Fellows. Each seminar is limited to 14 students, and credit available ranges from 2 to 3 course credits. The law school offers extensive opportunities for students to earn academic credit while working for various public and private nonprofit agencies and for state and federal judges. In addition to the work, students attend seminars relating to the work done in their placement. Rutgers has placed students in externships in virtually every federal and state agency in the New Jersey, Philadelphia, and Delaware area. Credit for externships can range from 3 to 6 credits. Third-year law students may take independent study for 1 to 2 credits under the supervision of a faculty member. Select students can also participate in several programs, including the Eagleton Fellowship Program, which give them an opportunity to work closely with the New Jersey state executive branch. These programs and fellowships often have a significant research component. The annual state Constitution Law Lecture and Corman Distinguished Lecture bring nationally known scholars and jurists to the law school. Students can study abroad through any ABA-approved program. Students have studied in France, Italy, Great Britain, Japan, and a variety of other countries. There are individual and group tutorials in the school's Academic Success Program, as well as workshops on study techniques and test taking and individual subject review for all students. The law school has several noncredit minority programs designed to provide a support system for minority students and increase the presence of minority students on campus. The most widely taken electives are Evidence, Commercial Law, and Business Organizations.

Graduation Requirements

In order to graduate, candidates must have a GPA of 2.0 and must have completed the upper-division writing requirement.

Organizations

Students edit the *Rutgers Law Journal, the Rutgers Journal of Law and Public Policy,* and the *Rutgers Journal of Law and Religion.* A highlight of the upper-level curriculum is the Judge James A. Hunter III Advanced Moot Court Program. Other moot court competitions include the National Moot Court Competition, Jessup International Moot Court Competition, the Gibbons National Criminal Procedure Moot Court Competition, Admiralty Moot Court Competition, National Black Law Students Association Frederick Douglass Competition, National Latino Law Students Association Moot Court Competition, and the Environmental Moot Court Competition. Law student organizations include the Student Bar Association, Association for Public Interest Law, and the Francis Deak International Law Society. There are local chapters and clubs of all major national law student organizations, including Phi Alpha Delta, Women's Law Caucus, Black Law Students Association, Hispanic Students Association, Student Bar Association, Latino Law Students Association, and Asian Pacific American Students Association.

Library

The law library contains 527,581 hardcopy volumes and 157,238 microform volume equivalents, and subscribes to 1,953 serial publications. Such online databases and networks as CALI, Dow-Jones, Legal-Trac, LEXIS, Mathew Bender, OCLC First Search, WESTLAW, and Wilsonline Indexes are available to law students for research. Special library collections include a historical collection of Soviet and Eastern European legal matters and a U.S. government depository library. The ratio of library volumes to faculty is 10,039 to 1 and to students is 631 to 1. The ratio of seats in the library to students is 1 to 2.

Faculty

The law school has 70 full-time and 55 part-time faculty members, of whom 47 are women. According to AAUP standards for

Placement

J.D.s awarded:	243

Services available through: a separate law school placement center and University Career Services Center for joint degree candidates.

Services: assistance with LEXIS, WESTLAW, and the Internet career searches, and fall and spring on-campus interview programs.

Special features: interview workshops, on-campus interview programs, career forums, resource library, participation in a consortium with the law schools of the University of Pennsylvania, Temple, and Villanova, full service Career Services Office with 3 full-time professional career services staff members in addition to 1 full-time pro bono coordinator and public interest adviser, videotaped mock interviews, individualized and small group career workshops, career panels, and several alumni and attorney mentoring programs.

Full-time job interviews:	150 employers
Summer job interviews:	150 employers
Placement by graduation:	75% of class
Placement within 9 months:	92% of class
Average starting salary:	$45,000 to $110,000

Areas of placement:

Private practice 2–10 attorneys	11%
Private practice 11–25 attorneys	6%
Private practice 26–50 attorneys	10%
Private practice 51–100 attorneys	13%
Judicial clerkships	30%
Business/industry	14%
Government	10%
Public interest	4%
Academic	2%

Category IIA institutions, faculty salaries are well above average. About 40% of full-time faculty have a graduate law degree in addition to the J.D.; about 20% of part-time faculty have one. The ratio of full-time students to full-time faculty in an average class is 10 to 1; in a clinic, 8 to 1. The law school has a regular program of bringing visiting professors and other distinguished lecturers and visitors to campus.

Students

About 43% of the student body are women; 15%, minorities; 4%, African American; 6%, Asian American; 5%, Hispanic; and 1%, Native American. The average age of entering students is 25; age range is 21 to 52. About 39% of students enter directly from undergraduate school, 97% have a graduate degree, and 34% have worked full-time prior to entering law school. About 1% drop out after the first year for academic or personal reasons; 99% remain to receive a law degree.

School of Law

Center for Law and Justice,
123 Washington St.
Newark, NJ 07102

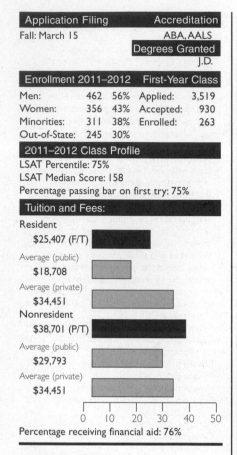

Application Filing	Accreditation
Fall: March 15	ABA, AALS

Degrees Granted
J.D.

Enrollment 2011–2012		First-Year Class	
Men:	462 56%	Applied:	3,519
Women:	356 43%	Accepted:	930
Minorities:	311 38%	Enrolled:	263
Out-of-State:	245 30%		

2011–2012 Class Profile
LSAT Percentile: 75%
LSAT Median Score: 158
Percentage passing bar on first try: 75%

Tuition and Fees:

Resident
    $25,407 (F/T)

Average (public)
    $18,708

Average (private)
    $34,451

Nonresident
    $38,701 (P/T)

Average (public)
    $29,793

Average (private)
    $34,451

Percentage receiving financial aid: 76%

ADMISSIONS

In the fall of 2011 first-year class, 3519 applied, 930 were accepted, and 263 enrolled. Twenty-five transfers enrolled. The median LSAT percentile of the most recent first-year class was 75; the median GPA was 3.3 on a scale of 4.0.

Requirements
Applicants must have a bachelor's degree and take the LSAT. The most important admission factors include academic achievement, LSAT results, and GPA. No specific undergraduate courses are required. Candidates are not interviewed.

Procedure
The application deadline for fall entry is March 15. Applicants should submit an application form, LSAT results, transcripts, a personal statement, and letters of recommendation. Notification of the admissions decision is on a rolling basis. The school uses LSAC.

Special
The law school recruits minority and disadvantaged students through participation in LSAC forums, participation in Puerto Rican Legal Defense Fund Law Day, visits to historically black colleges, black, Latino, and Asian law days, and contact with high school and college students. The Minority Student Program is open to disadvantaged students of all races. Requirements are different for out-of-state students. Transfer students must have one year of credit, must have a minimum GPA of 3, must have attended an ABA-approved law school, and must submit a personal statement and letter of good standing.

Costs

Tuition for part-time students is $12,730 for in-state students and $18,814 out-of-state. On-campus room and board costs about $13,000 annually; books and supplies run $1,300.

Financial Aid

About 76% of current law students receive some form of aid. Awards are based on need and merit. The required financial statement is the FAFSA. The aid application deadline for fall entry is March 1. Special funds for minority or disadvantaged students consist of the Ralph Bunche Fellowships, which provide tuition and a stipend; the C. Clyde Ferguson Scholarships, which provide full in-state tuition and housing for New Jersey residents; Marie Slocum Scholarship; Judge Herbert Tate, Sr. Scholarship; Judge John Dios Scholarship; and others. First-year students are notified about their financial aid application several weeks after an offer of admission.

About the Law School

Rutgers University/Newark School of Law was established in 1908 and is a public institution. The 11-acre campus is in an urban area in the city of Newark, 8 miles southwest of New York City. The primary mission of the law school is to prepare students for professional practice by offering high-quality education in all fields of law, as well as to preserve and expand knowledge as part of a national community of legal scholars, and to serve the public by working to achieve social justice through law. Students have access to federal, state, county, city, and local agencies, courts, correctional facilities, law firms, and legal aid organizations in the Newark area. Also nearby are the American Civil Liberties Union and public interest organizations. Facilities of special interest to law students are the federal courts and county and state court complexes, which are located in downtown Newark, the Newark Museum and Public Library, and the New Jersey Performing Arts Center, which is located just a few blocks away. The Center For Law and Justice is a technologically advanced building, and its courtroom is periodically used for hearing oral arguments by the state appellate court. Housing for students is available on campus. Most students live in nearby communities, however. All law school facilities are accessible to the physically disabled.

Calendar

The law school operates on a traditional semester basis. Courses for full-time students are offered both day and evening, and must be completed within 5 years. For part-time students, courses are offered both day and evening, and must be completed within 6 years. New full- and part-time students are admitted in the fall. There is a 7-week summer session. Transferable summer courses are offered.

Programs

Students may take relevant courses in other programs and apply credit toward the J.D.; a maximum of 12 credits may be applied. The following joint degrees may be earned: J.D./M.A. (Juris Doctor/Master of Arts in Criminal Justice or Political Science), J.D./M.B.A. (Juris Doctor/Master of Business Administration), J.D./M.C.R.P. (Juris Doctor/Master in City and Regional Planning), J.D./M.D. (Juris Doctor/Doctor of Medicine), J.D./M.S.W. (Juris Doctor/Master of Social Work), and J.D./Ph.D. (Juris Doctor/Doctor of Philosophy).

Required
To earn the J.D., candidates must complete 84 total credits, of which 34 to 35 are for required courses. They must maintain a minimum GPA of 1.7 in the required courses. The following first-year courses are required of all students: a required freshman elective, Civil Procedure, Constitutional Law, Contracts, Criminal Law, Legal Research and Writing I and II,

Phone: 973-353-5557/5554
Fax: 973-353-3459
E-mail: *lawinfo@andromeda.rutgers.edu*
Web: *http://law.newark.rutgers.edu*

Contact

Anita Walton, Assistant Dean for Admissions, 973-353-5557/5554 for general inquiries; Nicky Fornarotto, Coordinator for Financial Aid, 973-353-1702 for financial aid information.

Property, and Torts. Required upper-level courses consist of an upper-level writing requirement and Professional Responsibility. All students may elect to choose among extensive in-house clinical programming. The required orientation program for first-year students is 3 days and covers Professional Responsibility, registration, student services, health and safety issues, and an Introduction to Legal Research course, and provides opportunities to meet upper-class students and all student organization representatives.

Electives

The School of Law offers concentrations in corporate law, criminal law, entertainment law, environmental law, family law, international law, juvenile law, labor law, litigation, media law, securities law, sports law, tax law, torts and insurance, constitutional law, health law, and intellectual property. In addition, students can earn up to 8 credits per semester for clinics. Clinics are open only to upper-level students, and some require students to be in their final year. Clinics include Constitutional Rights, Women's Rights, Environmental Law, Urban Legal, Federal Tax, Special Education, Women and Aids, Domestic Violence, Child Advocacy Project, and Transactional Law/Community Development. Some 20 seminars are offered each semester for 2 credits each. They are open to all upper-level students and offer the opportunity to write a substantial legal paper that meets the writing requirement. Upper-level students with grades of B– or better may engage in internships with state or federal magistrates, justices, or judges for 3 credits; they are supported by a weekly in-house seminar. Externships are available with the Attorney General's office, the Security and Exchange Commission, and the National Labor Relations Board. An Intellectual Property Externship is also offered. Students may assist full-time faculty members in their research for 2 or 3 credits. Independent research may be undertaken by upper-level students for 2 or 3 credits with faculty permission. Special lecture series include Miller, Stoffer, and Weintraub lectureships, which are given annually. Students may enroll for up to 12 credits in an ABA/AALS sponsored semester-abroad program. Approximately 25 students engage in this study, from China to Greece and at the University of Leiden-Holland. First-year students are

tutored by upper-level students with good grades; tutors may earn 2 credits. The Minority Student Program is dependent on socioeconomic status, regardless of race. The school also has programs on behalf of women, minority groups, and gay and lesbian groups. The most widely taken electives are Evidence, Business Associations, and Copyright.

Graduation Requirements

In order to graduate, candidates must have a GPA of 2.0 and must have completed the upper-division writing requirement.

Organizations

Students edit the *Rutgers Law Review, Computer and Technology Law Journal, Women's Rights Law Reporter, Race and the Law Review, Bankruptcy Law Journal, Alternative Dispute Resolution Journal*, and *Rutgers Law Record*. Students compete in the Nathan Baker Mock Trial, David Cohn Moot Court, and the ABA Negotiations competitions. Students participate in approximately 25 to 30 writing competitions, among them the Nathan Burkan Copyright Competition. Law student organizations, local chapters of national associations, and campus organizations include Student Bar Association, Public Interest Law Foundation, Federalist Society, Student Lawyers Guild, Association of Black Law Students, Intellectual Property Law Society, Medicine and Health Law Society, Women's Law Forum, and International Law Students Society.

Library

The law library contains 353,600 hardcopy volumes and 163,600 microform volume equivalents, and subscribes to 3,120 serial publications. Such online databases and networks as DIALOG, LEXIS, RLIN, and WESTLAW are available to law students for research. Special library collections include depositories for U.S. and New Jersey documents. The ratio of library volumes to faculty is 6,429 to 1 and to students is 432 to 1. The ratio of seats in the library to students is 1 to 2.

Faculty

The law school has 55 full-time and 31 part-time faculty members, of whom 32 are women. About 6% of full-time faculty have a graduate law degree in addition to

Placement	
J.D.s awarded:	198

Services available through: a separate law school placement center.
Services: extensive on-campus interviewing program as well as co-sponsorship of off-campus job fairs, and career panels on specific practice areas, judicial clerkships, networking, and job search skills.
Special features: individual counseling, the alumni/ae job hotline, and videotaped mock interviews.

Full-time job interviews:	59 employers
Summer job interviews:	68 employers
Placement within 9 months of graduation:	98% of class
Average starting salary:	$35,000 to $192,000

Areas of placement:

Private practice 2–10 attorneys	11%
Private practice 11–25 attorneys	11%
Private practice 26–50 attorneys	11%
Private practice 51–100 attorneys	11%
Judicial clerkships	28%
Business/industry	13%
Government	5%
Public interest	3%
Military	2%
Academic	2%

the J.D. The ratio of full-time students to full-time faculty in an average class is 17 to 1; in a clinic, 8 to 1. There is a chapter of the Order of the Coif; 37 faculty and 186 graduates are members.

Students

About 43% of the student body are women; 38%, minorities; 13%, African American; 12%, Asian American; 10%, Hispanic; and 1%, Native American. The majority of students come from New Jersey (70%). The average age of entering students is 27; age range is 21 to 55. About 40% of students enter directly from undergraduate school, 23% have a graduate degree, and 34% have worked full-time prior to entering law school. About 2% drop out after the first year for academic or personal reasons; 97% remain to receive a law degree.

School of Law

8000 Utopia Parkway
Queens, NY 11439

Application Filing		Accreditation
Fall: April 1		ABA, AALS
		Degrees Granted
Fee: $60		J.D., LL.M.

Enrollment 2011–2012			First-Year Class	
Men:	536	57%	Applied:	4,057
Women:	399	43%	Accepted:	1,639
Minorities:	243	26%	Enrolled:	293

2011–2012 Class Profile
LSAT Median Score: 160
Percentage passing bar on first try: 88%

Tuition and Fees:

Resident
$46,450 (F/T)

Average (public)
$18,708

Average (private)
$34,451

Nonresident
$46,450 (F/T)

Average (public)
$29,793

Average (private)
$34,451

0   10   20   30   40   50

ADMISSIONS

In the fall of 2011 first-year class, 4057 applied, 1639 were accepted, and 293 enrolled. The median GPA of the most recent first-year class was 3.5.

Requirements

Applicants must have a bachelor's degree and take the LSAT. No specific undergraduate courses are required. Candidates are not interviewed.

Procedure

The application deadline for fall entry is April 1. Applicants should submit an application form, LSAT results, transcripts, a personal statement, a nonrefundable application fee of $60, and up to 3 letters of recommendation. Notification of the admissions decision is on a rolling basis. The law school uses the LSAC.

Special

The law school recruits minority and disadvantaged students through special visits to historically black colleges and universities, open houses, need-based and academic scholarships to improve diversity, and the Summer Institute Program. Requirements are different for out-of-state students. Transfer students must have one year of credit, must have attended an ABA-approved law school, and must submit a personal statement.

Costs

Tuition and fees for the 2011–2012 academic year are $46,450 for all full-time students. Tuition for part-time students is $34,840 for in-state students and $34,840 out-of-state. On-campus room and board costs about $17,700 annually; books and supplies run $1,400.

Financial Aid

Awards are based on need and merit combined. The required financial statement is the FAFSA. The aid application deadline for fall entry is March 1. Special funds for minority or disadvantaged students are available. First-year students are notified about their financial aid application at time of acceptance.

About the Law School

Saint John's University School of Law was established in 1925 and is a private institution. The 100-acre campus is in a suburban area in New York City (Queens county). The primary mission of the law school is to prepare students to enter the legal profession with excellent lawyering skills and a commitment to high principles of professionalism and community service. Students have access to federal, state, county, city, and local agencies, courts, correctional facilities, law firms, and legal aid organizations in the Queens area. There are a variety of programs at the law school, including clinics, externships, colloquia, and trial and appellate experiences. Facilities of special interest to law students include a renovated moot court room and adjoining classrooms, providing faculty and students with state-of-the-art learning spaces. There is state-of-the-art technology in all classrooms, including wireless capability throughout the law school. Housing for students is available at the university and assistance is provided in locating area housing. A roommate list is also available. All law school facilities are accessible to the physically disabled.

Calendar

The law school operates on a traditional semester basis. Courses for full-time students are offered both day and evening, and must be completed within 3 years. For part-time students, courses are offered both day and evening, and must be completed within 4 years. New full- and part-time students are admitted in the fall. There is an 8-week summer session. Transferable summer courses are offered.

Programs

In addition to the J.D., the law school offers the LL.M. Students may take relevant courses in other programs and apply credit toward the J.D.; a maximum of 3 credits may be applied. The following joint degrees may be earned: J.D./LL.M. (Juris Doctor/Master of Laws in Legal Studies), J.D./B.A. or B.S. (Juris Doctor/ Bachelor of Arts or Bachelor of Science), J.D./M.A. (Juris Doctor/Master of Arts in Government and Politics), and J.D./ M.B.A. (Juris Doctor/Master of Business Administration).

Required

To earn the J.D., candidates must complete 86 total credits, of which 58 are for required courses. They must maintain a minimum GPA of 2.0 in the required courses. The following first-year courses are required of all students: Civil Procedure, Constitutional Law, Contracts I and II, Criminal Law, Introduction to Law, Legal Analysis and Writing, Property, and Torts. Required upper-level courses consist of Professional Responsibility. The required orientation program for first-year students is held throughout a 2-week-long program in which students participate in sessions and take Introduction to Law.

Electives

The School of Law offers concentrations in corporate law, criminal law, entertainment law, environmental law, family law, intellectual property law, international law, juvenile law, labor law, litigation, maritime law, securities law, sports law, tax law, torts and insurance, and estate administration and real estate (property) law. In addition, clinics include the Elder Law Clinic, the Domestic Violence Clinic, and the Prosecution Clinic. Seminars include Civil Practice, Constitutional Rights, and

Phone: 718-990-6474
Fax: 718-990-2526
E mail: *lawinfo@stjohns.edu*
Web: *www.law.stjohns.edu*

Contact

Admissions Office, 718-990-6474 for general inquiries; Jorge Rodriguez, Assistant Vice President/Executive Director, 718-990-6403 for financial aid information.

NEW YORK

Race and the Law. Students also have the opportunity to be placed with administrative, city, state, and federal judges in the Judicial Externship. Research programs include the St. Thomas More Institute for Legal Research. Each year the school hosts guest speakers, Judge-in-Residence and Scholar-in-Residence programs, and various other symposia. Students may study at the law school's Rome, Italy campus and earn a minimum of 4 credits during the month-long program. Tutorial programs include academic support and the Writing Center. The law school hosts a conditional admit program called Summer Institute. The most widely taken electives are New York Practice, Criminal Procedure I, and Family Law.

Graduation Requirements

In order to graduate, candidates must have a GPA of 2.0, and must have completed the upper-division writing requirement and the advanced writing requirement, which is intended to ensure that all students have the opportunity after the first year to compose at least one scholarly article for which they must analyze, synthesize, organize, and present substantive material.

Organizations

The primary law review is the *St. John's Law Review*. Other law reviews include the *Journal of Civil Rights and Economic Development, Journal of Catholic Legal Studies, New York International Law Review, American Bankruptcy Institute Law Review*, and *N.Y. Litigator*. The student newspaper is *The Forum* and the yearbook is *Res Gestae*. Moot court competitions include John J. Gibbons National Criminal Procedure Moot Court, Sutherland Cup Moot Court, and Domenick L. Gabrielli National Moot Court competitions. The law school hosts the Conrad B. Duberstein Moot Court

Competition. Other competitions include the Intra-School, First Year Trial, Client Counseling, Criminal Law Institute, and Civil Trial Institute competitions. Law student organizations, local chapters of national associations, and campus organizations include Student Bar Association, Labor Relations and Employment Law Society, and Entertainment, Arts, and Sports Law Society. There are local chapters of Delta Theta Phi, Phi Alpha Delta, and Phi Delta Phi. Campus clubs and other organizations include The Corporate and Securities Law Society, Admiralty Law Society, and Family Law Society.

Library

The law library contains 394,720 hard-copy volumes and 196,497 microform volume equivalents. Such online databases and networks as CALI, CIS Universe, DIALOG, Infotrac, Legal-Trac, LEXIS, Mathew Bender, OCLC First Search, WESTLAW, and Wilsonline Indexes are available to law students for research. Special library collections include the Thomas More Collection and the Ronald H. Brown Collection Civil Rights Collection.

Faculty

The law school has 53 full-time and 70 part-time faculty members, of whom 48 are women. The ratio of full-time students to full-time faculty in an average class is 15 to 1. The law school has a regular program of bringing visiting professors and other distinguished lecturers and visitors to campus.

Students

About 43% of the student body are women; 26%, minorities; 5%, African American; and 8%, Asian American. The average age of entering students is 23; age range is 20 to 39.

Placement

Services available through: a separate law school placement center.

Services: Career Development posts all job listings and administers its fall and spring recruitment programs using an online web-based system.

Special features: technology is utilized extensively by Career Development to communicate with students. An internal web site contains internship and fellowship postings, and provides access to Career Development information such as handbooks and directories, announcements, a calendar of events, links to job searches, and links to other web sites.

Placement within 9 months of graduation:	92% of class
Areas of placement:	
Private practice 2–10 attorneys	24%
Private practice 11–25 attorneys	4%
Private practice 26–50 attorneys	3%
Private practice 51–100 attorneys	5%
Business/industry	18%
Government	15%
Academic	7%
Judicial clerkships	3%
Public interest	3%

SAINT LOUIS UNIVERSITY

School of Law

3700 Lindell Boulevard
St. Louis, MO 63108

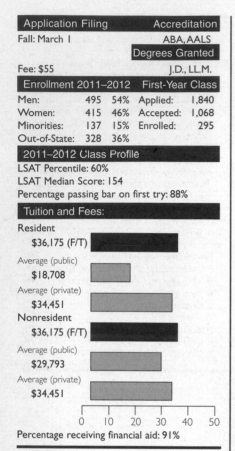

Application Filing	Accreditation
Fall: March 1	ABA, AALS
	Degrees Granted
Fee: $55	J.D., LL.M.

Enrollment 2011–2012			First-Year Class	
Men:	495	54%	Applied:	1,840
Women:	415	46%	Accepted:	1,068
Minorities:	137	15%	Enrolled:	295
Out-of-State:	328	36%		

2011–2012 Class Profile

LSAT Percentile: 60%
LSAT Median Score: 154
Percentage passing bar on first try: 88%

Tuition and Fees:

Resident
$36,175 (F/T)

Average (public)
$18,708

Average (private)
$34,451

Nonresident
$36,175 (F/T)

Average (public)
$29,793

Average (private)
$34,451

Percentage receiving financial aid: 91%

ADMISSIONS

In the fall of 2011 first-year class, 1840 applied, 1068 were accepted, and 295 enrolled. Thirteen transfers enrolled. The median LSAT percentile of the most recent first-year class was 60; the median GPA was 3.4 on a scale of 4.0. The lowest LSAT percentile accepted was 18; the highest was 95.

Requirements

Applicants must have a bachelor's degree and take the LSAT. The most important admission factors include LSAT results and GPA. No specific undergraduate courses are required. Candidates are not interviewed.

Procedure

The application deadline for fall entry is March 1. Applicants should submit an application form, LSAT results, transcripts, a personal statement, TOEFL (if applicable), a nonrefundable application fee of $55, and 2 letters of recommendation. Accepted students must pay a $250 nonrefundable deposit to reserve a place and a $350 final nonrefundable deposit to confirm attendance. Notification of the admissions decision is on a rolling basis. The law school uses the LSAC.

Special

The law school recruits minority and disadvantaged students through minority student associations, faculty and student outreach, the Minority Clerkship Program, and recruiting at colleges and universities throughout the United States. Requirements are different for out-of-state students. Transfer students must have one year of credit, must have attended an ABA-approved law school, and must submit a personal statement.

Costs

Tuition and fees for the 2011–2012 academic year are $35,730 for all full-time students. Tuition for part-time students is $26,070 for in-state students and $26,070 out-of-state. Books and supplies run $1,660.

Financial Aid

About 91% of current law students receive some form of aid. The average annual amount of aid from all sources combined, including scholarships, loans, and work contracts, is $44,297; maximum, $59,632. Awards are based on need and merit. The required financial statement is the FAFSA. The aid application deadline for fall entry is March 1. Special funds for minority or disadvantaged students are available. First-year students are notified about their financial aid application at time of acceptance.

About the Law School

Saint Louis University School of Law was established in 1843 and is a private institution. The 300-acre campus is in an urban area in midtown St. Louis. The primary mission of the law school is to advance the understanding and the development of law, and prepare students to achieve professional success and personal satisfaction through leadership and service to others. The School of Law is guided by the Jesuit tradition of academic excellence, freedom of inquiry, and respect for individual differences. Students have access to federal, state, county, city, and local agencies, courts, correctional facilities, law firms, and legal aid organizations in the St. Louis area. The school features the William H. Kniep Courtroom and the School of Law Clinical Building. Housing for students consists of off-campus housing, which is readily available and affordable. All law school facilities are accessible to the physically disabled.

Calendar

The law school operates on a traditional semester basis. Courses for full-time students are offered both day and evening, and must be completed within 3 years. For part-time students, courses are offered both day and evening, and must be completed within 5 years. New full- and part-time students are admitted in the fall. There is an 8-week summer session. Transferable summer courses are offered.

Programs

In addition to the J.D., the law school offers the LL.M. Students may take relevant courses in other programs and apply credit toward the J.D.; a maximum of 6 credits may be applied. The following joint degrees may be earned: J.D./M.A. (Juris Doctor/Master of Accounting), J.D./M.A. (Juris Doctor/Master of Arts in Public Administration), J.D./M.A. (Juris Doctor/Master of Arts in Public Health Policy), J.D./M.A. (Juris Doctor/Master of Arts in Sociology and Criminal Justice), J.D./M.A. (Juris Doctor/Master of Arts in Urban Affairs), J.D./M.B.A. (Juris Doctor/Master of Business Administration), J.D./M.H.A. (Juris Doctor/Master of Health Care Administration), J.D./M.P.H. (Juris Doctor/Master of Public Health), J.D./M.S.W. (Juris Doctor/Master of Social Work), and J.D./Ph.D. (Juris Doctor/Doctor in Health Care Ethics).

Required

To earn the J.D., candidates must complete 91 total credits, of which 37–39 are for required courses. They must maintain a minimum GPA of 2.0 in the required courses. The following first-year courses are required of all students: Civil Procedure I and II, Constitutional Law I, Contracts I and II, Criminal Law, Legal Research and Writing I and II, Property, and Torts. Required upper-level courses consist of a humanities course, a seminar, Legal Profession (Professional Ethics), and professional skills course. The required orientation program for

MISSOURI

first-year students is 3 days and includes a service project.

Electives

The School of Law offers concentrations in corporate law, criminal law, environmental law, intellectual property law, international-al law, labor law, litigation, tax law, health law, and urban development. In addition, clinical training includes the Civil Clinic, Judicial Process Clinic, and the Externship Program, all for 3 to 6 credits. An average of 18 seminars for 2 credits are offered each semester. Internships are available through clinical externship and judicial clerkship clinical programs. Law school students have opportunities for directed research with individual faculty members for 1 to 6 hours. Fieldwork consists of a Corporate Counsel Practitioner Program for 3 credits. Special lecture series include the Richard Childress Memorial Lecture Series, Adler-Rosecan Lecture, Center for Health Law Distinguished Speaker Series, First 100 Years of Women Speaker Series, and the James Millstone Lecture. Summer study abroad is available in Berlin, Germany; Cork, Ireland; Bern, Switzerland; Paris or Oleans, France; and Madrid, Spain. All students have open access to academic advising and support. Intensive programs for students struggling after 1 semester are offered. Minority programs consist of the Summer Institute and a Minority Clerkship Program. Special interest group programs include the William C. Wefel Center for Employment Law, Center for Health Law Studies, and Center for International Comparative Law. The most widely taken electives are Health Law, Employment Law/Business, and International Law.

Graduation Requirements

In order to graduate, candidates must have a GPA of 2.0.

Organizations

Students edit the *Saint Louis University Law Journal, Public Law Review*, and *Saint Louis University Journal of Health Law Policy*. Students may participate in the Jessup International Moot Court Program, National Health Law Moot Court Competition, and Intellectual Property Moot Court Competition.

Phone: 314-977-2800
800-SLU-FOR-U
Fax: 314-977-1464
E-mail: admissions@law.slu.edu
Web: www.law.slu.edu

Contact

Assistant Dean and Director of Admissions, 314-977-2800 for general inquiries; Jackie Koerner, Financial Aid Coordinator, 314-977-3369 for financial aid information.

Other competitions include the Client Counseling Competition. Law student organizations, local chapters of national associations, and campus organizations include Public Interest Law Group, Black Law Students Association, Latin American Law Students Association, Phi Alpha Delta, Delta Theta Phi, Phi Delta Phi, ABA-Student Division, and Public Interest Law Group.

Library

The law library contains 670,787 hardcopy volumes and 266,344 microform volume equivalents, and subscribes to 2,672 serial publications. Such online databases and networks as CALI, CIS Universe, DIALOG, Infotrac, LEXIS, OCLC First Search, WESTLAW, Wilsonline Indexes, BNA, CCH, HeinOnline, CIAO, JSTOR, and others are available to law students for research. Special library collections include the Leonor K. Sullivan Congressional Papers, the Leo C. Brown Arbitration Papers, the Irish Law Collection, the Jewish Law Collection, and the Polish Law Collection. The ratio of library volumes to faculty is 8,825 to 1 and to students is 760 to 1. The ratio of seats in the library to students is 1 to 2.

Faculty

The law school has 68 full-time and 57 part-time faculty members, of whom 57 are women. About 36% of full-time faculty have a graduate law degree in addition to the J.D. The ratio of full-time students to full-time faculty in an average class is 14 to 1; in a clinic, 7 to 1. The law school has a regular program of bringing visiting professors and other distinguished lecturers and visitors to campus.

Students

About 46% of the student body are women; 15%, minorities; 5%, African American; 4%, Asian American; 4%, Hispanic; and 2%, multicultural. The majority of students come from Missouri (64%). The average age of entering students is 25; age range is 20 to 52. About 95% of students enter directly from undergraduate school, and 5% have a graduate degree. About 5% drop out after the first year for academic or personal reasons; 88% remain to receive a law degree.

Placement

J.D.s awarded:	272

Services available through: a separate law school placement center.
Services: special programs on various areas of practice, such as health law, and international, corporate, government, public interest, and judicial clerkships.
Special features: an extensive career library with a computer search service.

Full-time job interviews:	60 employers
Summer job interviews:	45 employers
Placement by graduation:	59% of class
Placement within 9 months of graduation:	88% of class
Average starting salary:	$48,750 to $60,000

Areas of placement:

Private practice 2–10 attorneys	23%
Private practice 11–25 attorneys	9%
Private practice 26–50 attorneys	1%
Private practice 51–100 attorneys	3%
Private practice 100+ attorneys	14%
Business/industry	19%
Government	14%
Public interest	8%
Judicial clerkships	5%
Military	2%
Academic	2%

Saint Louis University   **401**

SAINT MARY'S UNIVERSITY

School of Law

One Camino Santa Maria
San Antonio, TX 78228-8601

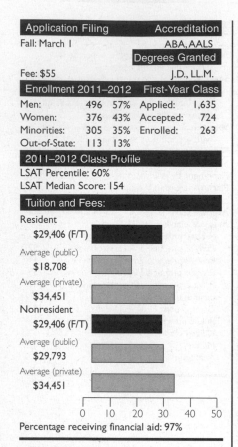

Application Filing		Accreditation
Fall: March 1		ABA, AALS
		Degrees Granted
Fee: $55		J.D., LL.M.

Enrollment 2011–2012			First-Year Class	
Men:	496	57%	Applied:	1,635
Women:	376	43%	Accepted:	724
Minorities:	305	35%	Enrolled:	263
Out-of-State:	113	13%		

2011–2012 Class Profile
LSAT Percentile: 60%
LSAT Median Score: 154

Tuition and Fees:

Resident
$29,406 (F/T)

Average (public)
$18,708

Average (private)
$34,451

Nonresident
$29,406 (F/T)

Average (public)
$29,793

Average (private)
$34,451

Percentage receiving financial aid: 97%

ADMISSIONS

In the fall of 2011 first-year class, 1635 applied, 724 were accepted, and 263 enrolled. Five transfer students enrolled. The median LSAT percentile of the most recent first-year class was 60; the median GPA was 3.1 on a scale of 4.0. The lowest LSAT percentile accepted was 18; the highest was 98.

Requirements
Applicants must have a bachelor's degree and take the LSAT. Minimum acceptable GPA is 2.0 on a scale of 4.0. The most important admission factors include character or personality, academic achievement, and LSAT results. No specific undergraduate courses are required, and candidates are not interviewed.

Procedure
The application deadline for fall entry is March 1. Applicants should submit an application form, a personal statement, a nonrefundable application fee of $55, and

letters of recommendation (up to five may be accepted). Notification of the admissions decision is beginning in November and ending in April. The law school uses the LSAC.

Special
The law school recruits minority and disadvantaged students through both the regular admissions selection process and the Summer Skills Enhancement Program. Requirements are different for out-of-state students. Transfer students must have one year of credits, a minimum GPA of 2.5, attended an ABA-approved law school, and a personal statement.

Costs

Tuition and fees for the 2011–2012 academic year are $28,800 for full-time in-state students and $28,800 for out-of-state students. Tuition for part-time students is $17,280 for in-state students and $17,280 out-of-state. On-campus room and board costs about $10,094 annually; books and supplies run $1,500.

Financial Aid

About 97% of current law students receive some form of aid. The average annual amount of aid from all sources combined, including scholarships, loans, and work contracts, is $33,642; maximum, $48,000. Awards are based on need. Required financial statement is the FAFSA. The aid application deadline for fall entry is March 31. Special funds for minority or disadvantaged students include funds based on need. First-year students are notified about their financial aid application at time of acceptance.

About the Law School

Saint Mary's University School of Law was established in 1948 and is a private institution. The 135-acre campus is located in a suburban area in San Antonio, Texas. The primary mission of the law school is to offer a solid curriculum of traditional legal studies, which teaches students the practical skills necessary to practice effective public service advocacy. Students have access to federal, state, county, city, and local agencies, courts, correctional facilities, law firms, and legal aid organizations in the San Antonio area. Housing is available on-campus in resident dormitory

facilities for single students only. Additional information and application forms may be obtained from the Director of Housing. All law school facilities are accessible to the physically disabled.

Calendar

The law school operates on a traditional semester basis. Courses for full-time students are offered both day and evening and must be completed within 5 years. For part-time students, courses are offered evenings only and must be completed within 7 years. New full- and part-time students are admitted in the fall. There is a 5 1/2-week summer session. Transferable summer courses are offered.

Programs

In addition to the J.D., the law school offers the LL.M. The following joint degrees may be earned: J.D./M.A. (Juris Doctor/Master of Arts in Accounting or Communication Arts), J.D./M.B.A. (Juris Doctor/Master of Business Administration), J.D./M.P.A. (Juris Doctor/Master of Public Administration in Justice Administration), and J.D./M.S. (Juris Doctor/Master of Science in Computer Science and Engineering).

Required
To earn the J.D., candidates must complete 90 total credits, of which 46 are for required courses. They must maintain a minimum GPA of 2.0 in the required courses. The following first-year courses are required of all students: Civil Procedure, Constitutional Law, Contracts I and II, Criminal Law, Legal Research and Writing II, Legal Writing I, Property I and II, and Torts I and II. Required upper-level courses consist of Business and Commercial Transactions, Civil and Criminal Litigation, Evidence, Persons and Property, Philosophy of Law and Lawyers, Practice Skills, Professional Responsibility, Public and International Law, and Texas Civil Procedure I. Although not required, law students are urged to participate in clinics for credit in the third year or as volunteers in the first and second years. The required orientation program for first-year students consists of a 1-day orientation session during which first-year law students receive an introduction to successful legal studies at St. Mary's.

Phone: 210-436-3523
866-639-5831
Fax: 210-431-4202
E-mail: wwilson@stmarytx.edu
Web: www.stmarytx.edu

Contact

William Wilson, Ph.D., 210-436-3523 for general inquiries; Director of Financial Assistance, 210-431-6743 for financial aid information.

TEXAS

Electives

The School of Law offers concentrations in corporate law, criminal law, environmental law, family law, international law, juvenile law, labor law, litigation, maritime law, securities law, tax law, and torts and insurance. In addition, Civil Justice Clinic, Criminal Justice Clinic, and Immigration and Human Rights Clinic are open to second- and third-year students. Limited to an enrollment of 12 students, seminars are opportunities for research and discussion on advanced or special issues. Past seminars have included Natural Resource Protection Law; Doing Business with Mexico; International Law; Mediation; Health Care Crisis; First Amendment/ Reporter Privilege; and International Arbitration. Two judicial internships in Austin, Texas are also offered. Students are required to do field work in the clinical programs. St. Mary's sponsors conferences and symposia on such diverse topics as United Nations Law and Legal Research, and Human Rights in the Americas. St. Mary's Center for Terrorism Law's Distinguished Speaker Series brings nationally recognized experts to present on various topics in the field of terrorism. St. Mary's Institute on World Legal Problems is conducted 5 weeks each summer, during the months of July and August at the University of Innsbruck, Austria. Beginning the second semester of the first year, students who scored poorly in their first-semester examinations are required to attend small-group tutorials. Each year, 20 students are accepted into the Law Skills Enhancement Program. The Minority Law Students Association, the Black Allied Law Students Association, and the Asian-Pacific American Law Students Association offer tutorials to first-year students who are members. Special-interest groups include the Society of Legal Entrepreneurs, Education Law Association, and Environmental Law Society. Several student groups, including the Women's Bar Association, and the Minority Law Students Association, have developed mentor relationships with local bar associations. The most widely taken electives are Wills and Estates, Trusts, and Business Associations.

Graduation Requirements

In order to graduate, candidates must have a GPA of 2.0 and completed the upper-division writing requirement.

Organizations

Students edit the *St. Mary's University School of Law Journal* and *The Scholar: St. Mary's Law Review on Minority Issues*. Moot court competitions include the Norvell Moot Court Competition, the Walker Moot Court, and the National ABA Regional Moot Court competition. Other competitions include the Shannon Thurmond Giltner Novice Mock Trial, National Mock Trial, and the ABA Client-Counseling. Law student organizations are the Student Bar Association, Family Law Association, and William Sessions American Inn of Court. Local chapters of national associations are Delta Theta Phi, Delta Alpha Delta, and Harlan Society. Campus clubs and other organizations include the Student Aggie Bar Association, the Longhorn Bar Association, and Hispanic Law Association.

Library

The law library contains 635,241 hardcopy volumes and 415,495 microform volume equivalents, and subscribes to 3,583 serial publications. Online databases and networks include CALI, CIS Universe, Infotrac, LEXIS, Mathew Bender, OCLC First Search, WESTLAW, and Wilsonline Indexes. IndexMaster, Access UN, CCH Legal Research Network, Checkpoint, CCH Tax Research Network, Foreign Law Guide, HeinOnline, Inter AM Legal Periodicals Index, Lexis Congressional Universe, LLMC Digital, LoisLaw, United Nations Treaty, and World Catalog are additional resources available to law students for research. Special library collections include Mexican legal materials, microtext of records and briefs of the United States Supreme Court, and legal documents from the United Nations and from American, British, Canadian, and international law. The library is also a depository for U.S. government documents. The ratio of library volumes to faculty is 17,646 to 1 and to students is 737 to 1. The ratio of seats in the library to students is 1 to 3.

Faculty

The law school has 38 full-time and 53 part-time faculty members, of whom 39 are women. About 23% of full-time faculty have a graduate law degree in addition to the J.D. The ratio of full-time students to full-time faculty in an average class is 22

Placement

J.D.s awarded:	248

Services available through: a separate law school placement center.

Services: individual strategy sessions, programming, networking opportunities.

Special features: The Office of Career Services arranges programming and career counseling throughout the year to assist students in career planning and job searches. The office also has a Student Resource Center, a job bank, and a resume bank. In addition, the office facilitates networking opportunities for its students with members of the bar and alumni.

Full-time job interviews:	25 employers
Summer job interviews:	25 employers
Placement within 9 months of graduation:	89% of class
Average starting salary:	$30,000 to $120,000

Areas of placement:

Private practice 2–10 attorneys	58%
Private practice 11–25 attorneys	2%
Private practice 26–50 attorneys	2%
Government	14%
Business/industry	11%
Public interest	5%
Academic	5%
Judicial clerkships	4%
Military	2%

to 1; in a clinic, 4 to 1. The law school has a regular program of bringing visiting professors and other distinguished lecturers and visitors to campus.

Students

About 43% of the student body are women; 35%, minorities; 4%, African American; 3%, Asian American; 27%, Hispanic; and 1%, Native American. The majority of students come from Texas (87%). The average age of entering students is 25; age range is 21 to 50. About 16% drop out after the first year for academic or personal reasons; 84% remain to receive a law degree.

SAINT THOMAS UNIVERSITY

School of Law

16401 NW 37th Avenue
Miami Gardens, FL 33054

Application Filing		Accreditation	
Fall: May 1		ABA, AALS	
		Degrees Granted	
Fee: $60	J.D., LL.M., S.J.D., BA/JD, JSD		

Enrollment 2011–2012		First-Year Class	
Men:	365 51%	Applied:	2,040
Women:	355 51%	Accepted:	938
Minorities:	353 49%	Enrolled:	253
Out-of-State:	115 16%		

2011–2012 Class Profile
LSAT Percentile: 44%
LSAT Median Score: 150
Percentage passing bar on first try: 85%

Tuition and Fees:

Resident
$34,618 (F/T)

Average (public)
$18,708

Average (private)
$34,451

Nonresident
$34,618 (F/T)

Average (public)
$29,793

Average (private)
$34,451

0   10   20   30   40   50
Percentage receiving financial aid: 93%

ADMISSIONS
In the fall of 2011 first-year class, 2040 applied, 938 were accepted, and 253 enrolled. Four transfers enrolled. The median LSAT percentile of the most recent first-year class was 44; the median GPA was 3.1 on a scale of 4.0. The lowest LSAT percentile accepted was 13; the highest was 83.

Requirements
Applicants must have a bachelor's degree and take the LSAT. Minimum acceptable GPA is 2.5 on a scale of 4.0. The most important admission factors include GPA, LSAT results, and undergraduate curriculum. No specific undergraduate courses are required, and candidates are not interviewed.

Procedure
The application deadline for fall entry is May 1. Applicants should submit an application form, LSAT results, transcripts, a personal statement, TOEFL (international applicants), a nonrefundable application fee of $60, and a letter of recommendation. Notification of the admissions decision is on a rolling basis. The law school uses the LSAC.

Special
The law school recruits minority and disadvantaged students through recruiting at various historically black and Hispanic colleges and universities, and direct mail to target population using Candidate Referral Service (CRS), Cleo member, Discover Law (LSAC), PRLDEF. Requirements are different for out-of-state students. Transfer students must have one year of credits, a minimum GPA of 2.65, attended an ABA-approved law school, a personal statement, letter of good standing, be in the top 50% of their class, provide law school transcripts.

Costs
On-campus room and board costs about $16,380 annually; books and supplies run $1,250.

Financial Aid
About 93% of current law students receive some form of aid. The average annual amount of aid from all sources combined, including scholarships, loans, and work contracts, is $46,203; maximum, $58,823. Awards are based on need and merit combined. Required financial statement is the FAFSA. The aid application deadline for fall entry is May 31. First-year students are notified about their financial aid application at time of acceptance.

About the Law School
Saint Thomas University School of Law was established in 1984 and is a private institution. The 140-acre campus is in a suburban area 15 miles northwest of downtown Miami. The primary mission of the law school is to provide a personalized, value-oriented legal education to a diverse student body, including those from groups traditionally underrepresented by and within the legal profession. Students have access to federal, state, county, city, and local agencies, courts, correctional facilities, law firms, and legal aid organizations in the Miami Gardens area. Housing for students include on-campus dormitories and a variety of off-campus housing, located within a few miles of the campus. All law school facilities are accessible to the physically disabled.

Calendar
The law school operates on a traditional semester basis. Courses for full-time students are offered both day and evening and must be completed within 5 years. There is no part-time program. New full-time students are admitted in the fall. There is a 7-week summer session. Transferable summer courses are offered.

Programs
In addition to the J.D., the law school offers the LL.M., S.J.D., BA/JD, and JSD. The following joint degrees may be earned: J.D./M.B.A. (Juris Doctor/Master of Business Administration in Accounting), J.D./M.B.A. (Juris Doctor/Master of Business Administration in Internation), J.D./M.B.A. (Juris Doctor/Master of Business Administration in Sports), J.D./M.S. (Juris Doctor/Master of Science in Marriage and Family), and J.D./M.S. (Juris Doctor/Master of Science in Sports Administration).

Required
To earn the J.D., candidates must complete 90 total credits, of which 58 are for required courses. They must maintain a minimum GPA of 2.0 in the required courses. The following first-year courses are required of all students: Advanced Legal Research and Writing, Civil Procedure I and II, Contracts I and II, Legal Analysis, Writing, and Research, Property I and II, and Torts I and II. Required upper-level courses consist of Appellate Advocacy, Art of Lawyering (dependent on grade at end of first year), Business Associations, Constitutional Law I and II, Criminal Law, Criminal Procedure I, Evidence, Professional Responsibility, Senior Writing Requirement, and Wills and Trusts. All students must take clinical courses. The required orientation program for first-year students is a 2-day program during which students register, are introduced to legal research and writing, learn how to brief a case, meet faculty, administration, and staff, and learn about student organizations.

Electives
The School of Law offers concentrations in environmental law, tax law, and Intercultural Human Rights. In addition, the

Phone: 305-623-2310
800-245-4569
E-mail: jbryant@stu.edu
Web: www.stu.edu/law

Contact

Jiovanna Bryant, Interim Director of Admissions, 305-623-2310 for general inquiries; Andy Marrero, Student & Financial Affairs Counselor, 305-474-2409 for financial aid information.

law school sponsors two in-house clinics: Immigration Clinic and Tax Clinic. The law school offers a wide range of seminars available to upper-class students, including Church-State Relation, Cyberlaw, Exploring Principles of Earth Jurisprudence, Environmental Law, Immigration Law, Health Law Policy, Land Use Planning, Rule of Law, Sixth Amendment in Modern Jurisprudence, and Women and the Law. The law school's Clinical Program includes internships in the Appellate Litigation, Bankruptcy Clinic, Civil Practice, Criminal Practice, Elder Law, Family Court, Florida Supreme Court, Judicial, and the Pax Romana United Nations Clinic. A lecture series every fall features presentations geared primarily to first-year students on effective note taking, time management and student strategies, stress management, the importance of writing well, and effective exam preparation. St. Thomas sponsors a month-long summer-abroad program in Spain. In addition, upper-class students may take an ABA-accredited summer-abroad program sponsored by law schools other than St. Thomas. Legal fraternities and other student organizations offer lecture series, mentoring programs, and other projects. The most widely taken electives are Family Law, White Collar Crime, and Law and Literature.

Graduation Requirements

In order to graduate, candidates must have a GPA of 2.0, complete the upper-division writing requirement, and complete 90 credit hours including required courses. Additional graduation requirements include completing 40 hours of pro bono work, pass a competency exam, satisfy the Senior Writing Requirement, and complete six credits of Professional Skills Courses.

Organizations

Students edit the *St. Thomas Law Review, Intercultural Human Rights Law Review* and the newspaper *Plead the Fifth*. Moot court competitions include the Phillip Jessup International Law Moot Court, National Entertainment Law Moot Court, and the National Labor Law Moot Court. Other competitions include the American Bar Association National Trial Tournament, the American Trial Lawyers Association National Trial Tournament, the National Trial Advocacy Competition, and the Frederick Douglass Trial Advocacy Competition. Student organizations include the Caribbean Association of Law Students, St. Thomas More Catholic Law Society, and Tax Law Society. Local chapters of national associations include the American Bar Association/Law Student Division (ABA/LSD), Asian Pacific American Law Student Association (APALSA), and Black Law Student Association (BLSA). Campus clubs and organizations include the Entertainment and Sports Law Society, Florida Association for Women Lawyers (FAWL), and Cuban American Bar Association (CABA), Law Student Division.

Library

The law library contains 211,493 hardcopy volumes and 1,270,722 microform volume equivalents, and subscribes to 2,920 serial publications. Online databases and networks include CALI, CIS Universe, DIALOG, Legal-Trac, LEXIS, Mathew Bender, OCLC First Search, WESTLAW, and Wilsonline Indexes. Bloomberg BNA Publications, CCH, EBSCO EBooks Collection, Eighteenth Century Collection Digital Archive: Law, Foreign Law Guide, HeinOnline, Index to Foreign Legal Periodicals, JSTOR, LLMC-Digital, Making of Modern Law: Primary Sources, 1620–1926, Max Planck Encyclopedia of Public International Law, Oceana Treaties and International Agreements Online, Oxford Bibliographies Online - International Relations, Oxford English Dictionary Online, Oxford Reprts on International Law, and PreQuest Congressional are also available to law students for research. The ratio of library volumes to faculty is 4,608 to 1 and to students is 272 to 1. The ratio of seats in the library to students is 1 to 1.

Faculty

The law school has 45 full-time and 47 part-time faculty members, of whom 32 are women. About 13% of full-time faculty have a graduate law degree in addition to the J.D.; about 3% of part-time faculty have one. The ratio of full-time students to full-time faculty in an average class is 16 to 1; in a clinic, 8 to 1. The law school has a regular program of bringing visiting professors and other distinguished lecturers and visitors to campus.

Placement

J.D.s awarded:	202

Services available through: a separate law school placement center.

Services: providing monthly newsletter for students, monthly job listings for alumni, and written guides on aspects of job search and career planning, conducting workshops and seminars, participating in southeastern job fairs, sponsoring guest speakers on areas of legal practice, judicial clerkships, and alternative careers, participating in minority opportunity programs and mentoring programs with alumni and the Florida Bar Association and the Broward and Dade County Bar Associations.

Special features: individualized attention for all students. The Office conducts mandatory individual meetings with first-year students, sets aside 4 hours daily for appointments with advanced and graduating students, and schedules exit interviews.

Full-time job interviews:	4 employers
Summer job interviews:	8 employers
Placement within 9 months of graduation:	74% of class
Average starting salary:	$41,000 to $60,000

Areas of placement:

Private practice 2–10 attorneys	51%
Private practice 11–25 attorneys	14%
Private practice 26–50 attorneys	1%
Private practice 51–100 attorneys	3%
Business/industry	11%
Government	8%
Public interest	6%
Judicial clerkships	2%
Academic	1%

Students

About 51% of the student body are women; 49%, minorities; 6%, African American; 3%, Asian American; 37%, Hispanic; 1%, Native American; and 4%, other. The majority of students come from Florida (84%). The average age of entering students is 25; age range is 20 to 54. About 63% of students enter directly from undergraduate school, 5% have a graduate degree, and 37% have worked full-time prior to entering law school. About 7% drop out after the first year for academic or personal reasons; 83% remain to receive a law degree.

Cumberland School of Law

800 Lakeshore Drive
Birmingham, AL 35229

Application Filing		Accreditation
Fall: February 28		ABA, AALS
		Degrees Granted
Fee: $50		J.D., M.C.L.

Enrollment 2011–2012   First-Year Class

Men:	284	58%	Applied:	1,405
Women:	205	42%	Accepted:	588
Minorities:	68	14%	Enrolled:	152
Out-of-State:	205	42%		

2011–2012 Class Profile

LSAT Percentile: 56%
LSAT Median Score: 155
Percentage passing bar on first try: 91%

Tuition and Fees:

Resident
$31,848 (F/T)

Average (public)
$18,708

Average (private)
$34,451

Nonresident
$31,848 (F/T)

Average (public)
$29,793

Average (private)
$34,451

0   10   20   30   40   50

Percentage receiving financial aid: 85%

ADMISSIONS

In the fall of 2011 first-year class, 1405 applied, 588 were accepted, and 152 enrolled. Sixteen transfers enrolled. The median LSAT percentile of the most recent first-year class was 56; the median GPA was 3.3 on a scale of 4.0.

Requirements
Applicants must have a bachelor's degree and take the LSAT. The most important admission factors include LSAT results, GPA, and academic achievement. No specific undergraduate courses are required. Candidates are not interviewed.

Procedure
The application deadline for fall entry is February 28. Applicants should submit an application form, a personal statement, a nonrefundable application fee of $50, 2 letters of recommendation, LSAT results, transcripts, and letters of recommendation must come from CAS. Notification of the admissions decision is on a rolling basis. The law school uses the LSAC.

Special
The law school recruits minority and disadvantaged students by means of recruiting at historically black colleges and universities. The Black Law Students Association is active in on-campus recruiting. Also, alumni actively assist with student recruitment. Requirements are different for out-of-state students. Transfer students must have one year of credit, must have a minimum GPA of 3, must have attended an ABA-approved law school, must have a personal statement, must have attended an AALS- and ABA-approved school, and must have a letter of good standing from the dean of the former law school.

Costs

Tuition and fees for the 2011–2012 academic year are $34,528 for all full-time students. Books and supplies run $2,000.

Financial Aid

About 85% of current law students receive some form of aid. The average annual amount of aid from all sources combined, including scholarships, loans, and work contracts, is $24,551; maximum, $55,529. Awards are based on need and merit combined. The required financial statement is the FAFSA. The aid application deadline for fall entry is March 1. Special funds for minority or disadvantaged students include full or partial tuition scholarships. First-year students are notified about their financial aid application at time of acceptance.

About the Law School

Samford University Cumberland School of Law was established in 1847 and is a private institution. The 300-acre campus is in a suburban area 6 miles from downtown Birmingham. The primary mission of the law school is to educate students to be responsible lawyers, trained to exercise their professional skills competently with sensitivity to the needs and concerns of their clients, and to act in strict accord with the highest ethical standards. Students have access to federal, state, county, city, and local agencies, courts, correctional facilities, law firms, and legal aid organizations in the Birmingham area. Facilities of special interest to law students include an $8.4 million, 61,000-square-foot free-standing library connected to the law

school building by a covered breezeway on the second floor, easily accessible to physically disabled students. Housing for students is available off campus in any number of nearby neighborhoods. Assistance in obtaining apartment rental information is provided by an apartment locator service. About 95% of the law school facilities are accessible to the physically disabled.

Calendar

The law school operates on a traditional semester basis. Courses for full-time students are offered days only and must be completed within 4 years. New full-time students are admitted in the fall. There is a 9-week summer session. Transferable summer courses are offered.

Programs

In addition to the J.D., the law school offers the M.C.L. Students may take relevant courses in other programs and apply credit toward the J.D.; a maximum of 12 credits may be applied. The following joint degrees may be earned: J.D./M.Acc. (Juris Doctor/Master of Accounting), J.D./M.A. (Juris Doctor/Master of Arts in Theological Studies), J.D./M.B.A. (Juris Doctor/Master of Business Administration), J.D./M. Div. (Juris Doctor/Master of Divinity), J.D./M.P.A. (Juris Doctor/Master of Public Administration), J.D./M.P.H. (Juris Doctor/Master of Public Health), J.D./M.S. (Juris Doctor/Master of Science in Bioethics), and J.D./M.S. (Juris Doctor/Master of Science in Environmental Management).

Required
To earn the J.D., candidates must complete 90 total credits, of which 47 are for required courses. They must maintain a minimum GPA of 2.0 in the required courses. The following first-year courses are required of all students: Civil Procedure I and II, Contracts I and II, Criminal Law, Evidence, Lawyering and Legal Reasoning I and II, Real Property, and Torts. Required upper-level courses consist of Business Organizations, Constitutional Law I and II, Payment Systems or Secured Transactions, Professional Responsibility, Wills, Trusts, and Estates. The required orientation program for first-year students is designed to introduce new students to the school, the faculty, and the curriculum. Entering students begin the required Lawyering and Legal Reasoning

Phone: 205-726-2702
800-888-7213
Fax: 205-726-2057
E-mail: law.admissions@samford.edu
Web: cumberland.samford.edu

Contact

Jennifer Y Simms, Assistant Dean, 800-888-7213 for general inquiries; Laine Smith, Director of Financial Aid, 800-888-7245 for financial aid information.

ALABAMA

course and receive instruction on the briefing of cases and demonstration of law school teaching methods. This 6-credit hour, 2-semester course provides students with intensive hands-on experience in practical lawyering skills.

Electives

The Cumberland School of Law offers concentrations in corporate law, criminal law, environmental law, family law, intellectual property law, international law, juvenile law, labor law, litigation, securities law, tax law, torts and insurance, and trial advocacy. In addition, The Center for Advocacy and Clinical Education offers upper-level students externships for 3 credit hours. Seminars are offered for 2 credit hours. Research programs are directed by individual professors and are aimed at upper-level students. Field work placement is available with government agencies, federal judges, litigation placements, and corporations. Special lecture series include the Cordell Hull Speakers Forum, the Ray Rushton Distinguished Lecturer Series, the Thurgood Marshall Speakers' Forum, the Faculty Colloquium, and the Work in Progress Program. Study-abroad programs include international and comparative law at Sidney Sussex College, Cambridge, England, and the Federal University of Ceasa, Fortaleza, Brazil. A writing laboratory is available for students who need additional coaching in this critical skill. The Black Law Students Association sponsors a tutorial program, a mentor program, a speakers forum, and special recognition events. Special interest group programs include Women in Law, Community Service Organization, Trial Advocacy Board, and Henry Upson Sims Moot Court Board. The most widely taken electives are Mediation, Basic Skills in Trial Advocacy, and Law Office Practice and Management.

Graduation Requirements

In order to graduate, candidates must have a GPA of 2.0 and must have completed the upper-division writing requirement and upper-level skills course.

Organizations

Students edit the *Cumberland Law Review*, the *American Journal of Trial Advocacy*, and the newspaper *Pro Confesso*. Moot court competitions include the Justice Janie Shores, Gordon T. Saad, and the Robert Donworth Freshman moot courts. Student organizations include the Association of Trial Lawyers of America, ABA-Student Division, and Federalist Society. Local chapters of national organizations include Phi Alpha Delta and Phi Delta Phi. Other organizations include the State Student Bar Associations of Alabama, Florida, Georgia, and other southern states.

Library

The law library contains 203,605 hard-copy volumes and 125,975 microform volume equivalents, and subscribes to 2,078 serial publications. Such online databases and networks as CALI, Legal-Trac, LEXIS, WESTLAW, and HeinOnline are available to law students for research. The library has special collections on Constitutional Law, Ethics, Legal History, and Trial Practice, and maintains an archival collection for the Cumberland School of Law. The ratio of library volumes to faculty is 5,885 to 1 and to students is 420 to 1. The ratio of seats in the library to students is 1 to 1.

Faculty

The law school has 22 full-time and 34 part-time faculty members, of whom 12 are women. According to AAUP standards for Category IIA institutions, faculty salaries are above average. About 22% of full-time faculty have a graduate law degree in addition to the J.D. The ratio of full-time students to full-time faculty in an average class is 18 to 1; in a clinic, 10 to 1. The law school has a regular program of bringing visiting professors and other distinguished lecturers and visitors to campus.

Students

About 42% of the student body are women; 14%, minorities; 4%, African American; 1%, Asian American; 1%, Hispanic; 1%, Native American; and 1%, foreign national. The majority of students come from Alabama (58%). The average age of entering students is 24; age range is 20 to 48. About 34% of students enter directly from undergraduate school, and 8% have a graduate degree. About 6% drop out after the first year for academic or personal reasons; 94% remain to receive a law degree.

Placement

J.D.s awarded:	140

Services available through: a separate law school placement center.

Services: national and regional law fairs.

Special features: numerous workshops and programs focused on interviewing, job search skills, and legal career specialties, in addition to a resource library for students. An office manages on-campus interviews and job postings through Symplicity to assist employers in meeting their hiring needs. The office staff also meet regularly with employers across the South to gather information on hiring trends and to market students and graduates.

Full-time job interviews:	6 employers
Summer job interviews:	38 employers
Placement by graduation:	54% of class
Placement within 9 months:	90% of class
Average starting salary:	$23,000 to $110,000

Areas of placement:

Private practice 2–10 attorneys	22%
Private practice 11–25 attorneys	7%
Private practice 26–50 attorneys	4%
Private practice 51–100 attorneys	7%
Business/industry	16%
Judicial clerkships	7%
Government	6%
Public interest	6%
Military	1%
Academic	1%

SANTA CLARA UNIVERSITY

School of Law

500 El Camino Real
Santa Clara, CA 95053

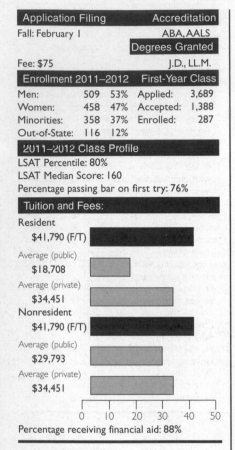

Application Filing	Accreditation
Fall: February 1	ABA, AALS

	Degrees Granted
Fee: $75	J.D., LL.M.

Enrollment 2011–2012   First-Year Class

Men:	509	53%	Applied:	3,689
Women:	458	47%	Accepted:	1,388
Minorities:	358	37%	Enrolled:	287
Out-of-State:	116	12%		

2011–2012 Class Profile
LSAT Percentile: 80%
LSAT Median Score: 160
Percentage passing bar on first try: 76%

Tuition and Fees:

Resident
$41,790 (F/T)

Average (public)
$18,708

Average (private)
$34,451

Nonresident
$41,790 (F/T)

Average (public)
$29,793

Average (private)
$34,451

0   10   20   30   40   50

Percentage receiving financial aid: 88%

ADMISSIONS

In the fall of 2011 first-year class, 3689 applied, 1388 were accepted, and 287 enrolled. Twenty-two transfers enrolled. The median LSAT percentile of the most recent first-year class was 80; the median GPA was 3.2 on a scale of 4.0. The lowest LSAT percentile accepted was 52; the highest was 99.

Requirements
Applicants must have a bachelor's degree and take the LSAT. The most important admission factors include LSAT results, undergraduate curriculum, and GPA. No specific undergraduate courses are required. Candidates are not interviewed.

Procedure
The application deadline for fall entry is February 1. Applicants should submit an application form, LSAT results, transcripts, a nonrefundable application fee of $75, and letters of recommendation (optional). Notification of the admissions decision is December through May. The law school uses the LSAC.

Special
The law school recruits minority and disadvantaged students by means of ethnic student organizations that advise the faculty admissions committee and by providing substantial financial assistance. Requirements are different for out-of-state students. Transfer students must have one year of credit, must have attended an ABA-approved law school, and must have a letter of good standing from their prior school.

Costs
On-campus room and board costs about $14,056 annually; books and supplies run $1,244.

Financial Aid
About 88% of current law students receive some form of aid. The average annual amount of aid from all sources combined, including scholarships, loans, and work contracts, is $44,242; maximum, $63,746. Awards are based on need and merit combined. The required financial statement is the FAFSA. The aid application deadline for fall entry is February 1. Special funds for minority or disadvantaged students consist of the Law Faculty Scholarship and the Diversity Scholarship. First-year students are notified about their financial aid application at the time of acceptance for scholarships; other aid decisions are made known upon completion of financial aid applications.

About the Law School
Santa Clara University School of Law was established in 1911 and is a private institution. The 104-acre campus is in a suburban area less than 1 mile west of San Jose and 45 miles south of San Francisco. The primary mission of the law school is wholly consistent with the Jesuit purpose in professional education: to train men and women of competence, conscience, and compassion. Students have access to federal, state, county, city, and local agencies, courts, correctional facilities, law firms, and legal aid organizations in the Santa Clara area. Santa Clara is in the heart of Silicon Valley. Students have access to all of the resources in the San Francisco Bay area, including state and federal courthouses and agencies. Externships are available in private industry and non-profits. Facilities of special interest to law students are Heafey Law Library, Bergin Hall faculty office building, Bannan Hall, which houses classrooms and the law student lounge, and Katherine and George Alexander Community Law Center, Loyal Hall, which houses the Law Career Center, Legal Research and Writing Faculty, Law Review, Northern California Innocence Project, Center for Public Interest and Social Justice, Center for Global Law and Policy, and High Tech Law Institute. Several university housing complexes are set aside for law students, and there is off-campus housing. About 97% of the law school facilities are accessible to the physically disabled.

Calendar
The law school operates on a traditional semester basis. Courses for full-time students are offered both day and evening, and must be completed within 5 years. For part-time students, courses are offered both day and evening, and must be completed within 5 years. New full- and part-time students are admitted in the fall. There is a 7–8-week summer session. Transferable summer courses are offered.

Programs
In addition to the J.D., the law school offers the LL.M. Students may take relevant courses in other programs and apply credit toward the J.D.; a maximum of 12 credits may be applied. The following joint degrees may be earned: J.D./M.B.A. (Juris Doctor/Master of Business Administration) and J.D./M.S.I.S. (Juris Doctor/Master of Science in Information Systems).

Required
To earn the J.D., candidates must complete 86 total credits, of which 42 are for required courses. They must maintain a minimum GPA of 2.3 in the required courses. The following first-year courses are required of all students: Constitutional Law I, Contracts, Criminal Law, Legal Research and Writing, Pleading and Civil Procedure, Property, and Torts. Required upper-level courses consist of Advocacy, Constitutional Law II, Evidence, and The Legal Profession. The required orientation program for first-year students lasts 3 days and introduces them to the study of law and the legal profession.

Phone: 408-554-5048
Fax: 408-554-7897
E-mail: lawadmissions@scu.edu
Web: http://law.scu.edu

Contact
Assistant Dean for Admission, 408-554-4800 for general inquiries; Financial Aid Counselor, 408-554-5048 for financial aid information.

Electives
The School of Law offers concentrations in corporate law, criminal law, environmental law, intellectual property law, international law, litigation, tax law, high-tech law, and public interest law. In addition, through the on-campus Law Clinic Office, upper-division students practice law under the supervision of faculty. Students participate in all phases of a case, from the initial client interview through trial, and may receive 3 to 6 credits. The focus of the Criminal Law Clinic is the Northern California Innocence Project. Fifteen to 20 seminars are offered each year in areas such as social justice and public interest law, sports law, drug abuse law, high-technology and intellectual property, and international law. Internships are in high-tech, civil practice, and the criminal justice system. Judicial externships are offered with the California Supreme Court and other state and federal courts. Faculty members engage students as research assistants for a variety of projects. During the academic year, students have access to the courts and legal community of the San Francisco Bay Area. The voluntary Pro Bono Project matches students and alumni for work on pro bono cases. The school hosts lectures on topics ranging from intellectual property issues to current events in international law. The Institute of International and Comparative Law sponsors summer law study-abroad programs in Strasbourg, France; Geneva, Switzerland; Oxford, England; Hong Kong; Singapore; Seoul, Korea; Tokyo, Japan; Munich, Germany; Istanbul, Turkey; Sydney, Australia; The Hague, Netherlands; San Jose, Costa Rica; Vienna, Austria; Bratislava, Slovakia; and Budapest, Hungary. The Academic Success Program offers personal and tutorial support to students identified through the admission process as needing academic support. Tutorial support emphasizes legal analysis and uses the writing of briefs, outlines, and exams to develop this skill. The Assistant Dean for Admissions and Financial Aid acts as a mentor to students of color. The minority alumni network actively supports current students. Students may earn a certificate in public interest law by taking 14 units, plus a unit of Public Interest Seminar, and completing a practicum. Certificates are also offered in international law and high-technology law with varying requirements. The most widely taken electives are Business Organizations and Remedies.

Graduation Requirements
In order to graduate, candidates must have a GPA of 2.3, must have completed the upper-division writing requirement, and must have completed 86 semester units and the required course of study.

Organizations
Students edit the *Santa Clara Law Review, Computer and High Technology Law Journal*, and the *Santa Clara Journal of International Law*. The student newspaper is *The Advocate*. Moot court competitions include the Jessup International Moot Court, Traynor Moot Court, and the Giles Rich Moot Court. Other competitions include ABA Client Counseling Competition, ABA National Trial Competition, and the Negotiation Competition. Student organizations, local chapters of national associations, and campus organizations include Intellectual Property Association, Public Interest Coalition, International Law Society, Phi Alpha Delta, Phi Delta Phi, Amnesty International, ACLU, Student Bar Association, BALSA, and Women in Law.

Library
The law library contains 398,115 hardcopy volumes and 1,182,040 microform volume equivalents, and subscribes to 4,417 serial publications. Such online databases and networks as CALI, CIS Universe, DIALOG, Dow-Jones, Infotrac, Legal-Trac, LEXIS, Mathew Bender, OCLC First Search, RLIN, WESTLAW, Wilsonline Indexes, Link+, Indexmaster, HeinOnline, CIAO, CCH Internet Research, JSTOR, UN Readex Bureau of National Affairs, BE Press, BNA's Core Package, Daily Journal Online, ILP, Oxford University Press, Vault, and Westpack are available to law students for research. Special library collections include the proceedings of the House Judiciary Committee on the Watergate Hearings. The ratio of library volumes to faculty is 8,203 to 1 and to students is 393 to 1. The ratio of seats in the library to students is 1 to 2.

Faculty
The law school has 64 full-time and 43 part-time faculty members, of whom 52 are women. According to AAUP standards for Category IIA institutions, faculty salaries are well above average. About 6% of full-time faculty have a graduate law

Placement

J.D.s awarded:	290

Services available through: a separate law school placement center and Law Career Services.
Special features: fall and spring on-campus interview programs, career-oriented workshops and events, a web site with current listings and job search tips, extensive resource library, and reciprocity with other Bay area and ABA-accredited law schools.

Full-time job interviews:	8 employers
Summer job interviews:	59 employers
Placement by graduation:	66% of class
Placement within 9 months:	78% of class
Average starting salary:	$67,000 to $107,995

Areas of placement:

Private practice 2–10 attorneys	9%
Private practice 11–25 attorneys	2%
Private practice 51–100 attorneys	2%
Business/industry	15%
Government	9%
Public interest	5%
Academic	5%
Judicial clerkships	1%

degree in addition to the J.D. The ratio of full-time students to full-time faculty in an average class is 12 to 1; in a clinic, 8 to 1. The law school has a regular program of bringing visiting professors and other distinguished lecturers and visitors to campus. There is a chapter of the Order of the Coif; 5 faculty and 240 graduates are members.

Students
About 47% of the student body are women; 37%, minorities; 2%, African American; 25%, Asian American; 9%, Hispanic; and 1%, Native American. The majority of students come from California (88%). The average age of entering students is 25; age range is 21 to 53. About 12% of students have a graduate degree. About 7% drop out after the first year for academic or personal reasons; 95% remain to receive a law degree.

SEATTLE UNIVERSITY
School of Law

901 12th Avenue, Sullivan Hall,
P.O. Box 222000
Seattle, WA 98122-4340

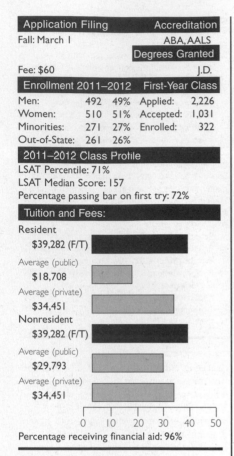

Application Filing	Accreditation
Fall: March 1	ABA, AALS

	Degrees Granted
Fee: $60	J.D.

Enrollment 2011–2012		First-Year Class	
Men:	492 49%	Applied:	2,226
Women:	510 51%	Accepted:	1,031
Minorities:	271 27%	Enrolled:	322
Out-of-State:	261 26%		

2011–2012 Class Profile
LSAT Percentile: 71%
LSAT Median Score: 157
Percentage passing bar on first try: 72%

Tuition and Fees:

Resident
$39,282 (F/T)

Average (public)
$18,708

Average (private)
$34,451

Nonresident
$39,282 (F/T)

Average (public)
$29,793

Average (private)
$34,451

Percentage receiving financial aid: 96%

ADMISSIONS
In the fall of 2011 first-year class, 2226 applied, 1031 were accepted, and 322 enrolled. Twenty-three transfer students enrolled. The median LSAT percentile of the most recent first-year class was 71; the median GPA was 3.3 on a scale of 4.0. The lowest LSAT percentile accepted was 25; the highest was 96.

Requirements
Applicants must have a bachelor's degree and take the LSAT. The most important admission factors include GPA, LSAT results, and personal interview. No specific undergraduate courses are required. Candidates are not interviewed.

Procedure
The application deadline for fall entry is March 1. Applicants should submit an application form, LSAT results, transcripts, personal statement, the TOEFL (for international students educated abroad), nonrefundable application fee

of $60, 2 letters of recommendation, and a resume. Notification of the admissions decision is January 1 to May 1. The law school uses the LSAC.

Special
The law school recruits minority and disadvantaged students through admission officer visits, minority community service organizations, minority prelaw and bar associations, candidate referral services, prelaw adviser mailings, and a fee waiver program. Requirements are different for out-of-state students. Transfer students must have one year of credits, attended an ABA-approved law school, personal statement, and be in good academic standing and in the top third of their class.

Costs
Tuition and fees for the 2011–2012 academic year are $39,210 for all full-time students. Tuition for part-time students is $28,754 for in-state students and $28,754 out-of-state. On-campus room and board costs about $11,556 annually; books and supplies run $1,172.

Financial Aid
About 96% of current law students receive some form of aid. The average annual amount of aid from all sources combined, including scholarships, loans, and work contracts, is $45,401; maximum, $62,840. Awards are based on need and merit combined. Required financial statement is the FAFSA. The aid application deadline for fall entry is March 1. Special funds for minority or disadvantaged students range from $3000 to (3) full-tuition awards and may be renewable, with conditions, for the full term of legal studies. First-year students are notified about their financial aid application within 3 weeks of the offer of admission.

About the Law School
Seattle University School of Law was established in 1972 and is a private institution. The 48-acre campus is located in an urban area on Seattle's First Hill. The mission of the law school is to educate outstanding lawyers who are leaders for a just and humane world. Students have access to federal, state, county, city, and local agencies, courts, correctional facilities, law firms, and legal aid organizations

in the Seattle area. They have access to Appellate Court, U.S. District Court, and Superior Court as well as the King County Youth Detention Center. Facilities of special interest to law students include Sullivan Hall, which contains classrooms and seminar spaces. The entire building is wired for the use of online legal research services such as Westlaw and other Internet uses. There is also an online electronic teaching laboratory. The law school is also wireless. All law school facilities are accessible to the physically disabled.

Calendar
The law school operates on a traditional semester basis. Courses for full-time students are offered both day and evening and must be completed within 7 years. For part-time students, courses are offered both day and evening and must be completed within 7 years. New full- and part-time students are admitted in the fall and summer. There is a 6- to 8-week summer session. Transferable summer courses are offered.

Programs
Students may take relevant courses in other programs and apply credit toward the J.D. a maximum of 4 credits may be applied. The following joint degrees may be earned: J.D./M.A.C.J. (Juris Doctor/Master of Arts in Criminal Justice), J.D./M.A.T.L. (Juris Doctor/Master of Arts in Transformation Leadership), J.D./M.B.A. (Juris Doctor/Master of Business Administration), J.D./M.I.B (Juris Doctor/Master of International Business), J.D./M.A.C. (Juris Doctor/Master of Professional Accounting), J.D./M.P.A. (Juris Doctor/Master of Public Health), J.D./M.S. (Juris Doctor/Master of Science in Finance), and J.D./M.S.A.L (Juris Doctor/Master of Sports Administration and Leadership).

Required
To earn the J.D., candidates must complete 90 total credits, of which 44 are for required courses. They must maintain a minimum GPA of 2.0 in the required courses. The following first-year courses are required of all students: Civil Procedure, Contracts, Criminal Law, Legal Writing, Property, and Torts. Required upper-level courses consist of a professional skills course, Constitutional Law, Legal Writing II, and Professional

Phone: 206-398-4200
800-471-1767
Fax: 206-398-4058
E-mail: *lawadmis@seattleu.edu*
Web: *www.law.seattleu.edu*

Contact

Carol Cochran, Assistant Dean for Admission, 206-398-4200 for general inquiries; Kathleen Koch, Assistant Dean for Student Financial Services, 206-398-4250 for financial aid information.

WASHINGTON

Responsibility. The required orientation program for first-year students consists of a 2-day series of workshops and, throughout the year, seminars on both academic and nonacademic issues.

Electives

The School of Law offers concentrations in corporate law, criminal law, environmental law, family law, intellectual property law, international law, labor law, litigation, tax law, health, commercial law, estate planning, inequality/poverty law, and real estate law. In addition, clinics include the Youth Advocacy Clinic, in which third-year students, supervised by faculty members, represent clients as youth or status offenders. Seminars are available in numerous limited-enrollment advanced classes, with subjects ranging from First Amendment to Tax Policy to Human Rights. Part-time externships are available for students in the judiciary and with several preapproved agencies and governmental organizations. Full-time judicial externships are also available. Research programs include work with faculty members conducting research in subjects such as involuntary commitment of the mentally ill and freedom of the press and the First Amendment; independent study on topics of student interest is also encouraged. More than 80% of students are employed in law-related field work positions each year with corporate firms, partnerships, federal, state, and local public agencies, and nonprofit associations. The Alumni/ae Lecture Series brings distinguished scholars, jurists, and practitioners to campus to comment on compelling legal issues. Students may participate in study-abroad programs sponsored by other ABA law schools. The school has study-abroad programs in Brazil, Ireland, and South Africa. The Academic Resource Center, staffed by a tenured professor and full-time J.D. alumna, offers tutorial services as well as group workshops and seminars. The Access Admission Program, designed for historically disadvantaged, physically challenged, and older applicants (limited to 30 students a year), is an intensive program integrating first-year classes with group instruction. Minority programs are conducted through the Black Law Students Association, Latino Law Student Society, and Asian/Pacific Islander Law Students Association. Special interest group programs include activities by the

Environmental Law Society, International Law Society, and Entertainment/Sports Law Society. The most widely taken electives are Administrative Law, Business Entities, and Intellectual Property.

Graduation Requirements

In order to graduate, candidates must have a GPA of 2.0 and complete the upper-division writing requirement.

Organizations

Students edit the *Seattle University Law Review,* the *Seattle Journal of Social Justice,* and the newspaper *The Prolific Reporter.* Moot court competitions include Jessup International Law, Pace Environmental Law, and Frederick Douglass. Other competitions include National Appellate Moot Court Competition, Association of Trial Lawyers of America, Client Counseling, and Negotiation. Law student organizations include the Student Bar Association, Public Interest Law Foundation, and Federalist Society. Other organizations include Amnesty International, Black Law Students Association, and Human Rights Network. There are local chapters of American Trial Lawyers Association, Phi Alpha Delta, and American Civil Liberties Union.

Library

The law library contains 394,151 hardcopy volumes and 224,303 microform volume equivalents, and subscribes to 2,172 serial publications. Online databases and networks include CALI, CIS Universe, DIALOG, Legal-Trac, LEXIS, OCLC First Search, WESTLAW. The library also subscribes to almost 40 e-resources, including database encyclopedias, e-books, and e-journals, which are available to law students for research. Special library collections include a U.S. government documents depository, Mc Naughton's Recreational Reading Collection; Walker Collection; Faculty Read Book Collection; Jerome McCristal Culp Jr. Collection of Race Gender and Seprals. The ratio of library volumes to faculty is 6,159 to 1 and to students is 393 to 1. The ratio of seats in the library to students is 1 to 2.

Faculty

The law school has 63 full-time and 43 part-time faculty members, of whom 42

Placement

J.D.s awarded:	314

Services available through: a separate law school placement center.
Services: comprehensive lists of judges, courts, and application requirements for judicial clerkships.
Special features: résumé and cover letter writing workshops; mock interviews; career panels highlighting various areas of law practice; brown bag sessions to review job hunting, application, and interviewing process; career counseling by all-attorney staff; daily job postings online; sessions offered both day and evenings to accommodate all students.

Full-time job interviews:	8 employers
Summer job interviews:	51 employers
Placement by graduation:	51% of class
Placement within 9 months:	90% of class
Average starting salary:	$43,500 to $110,000

Areas of placement:

Private practice 2–10 attorneys	31%
Private practice 11–25 attorneys	2%
Private practice 26–50 attorneys	5%
Business/industry	21%
Government	11%
Public interest	9%
Judicial clerkships	5%
Academic	3%

are women. About 21% of full-time faculty have a graduate law degree in addition to the J.D. The ratio of full-time students to full-time faculty in an average class is 12 to 1; in a clinic, 8 to 1. The law school has a regular program of bringing visiting professors and other distinguished lecturers and visitors to campus.

Students

About 51% of the student body are women; 27%, minorities; 3%, African American; 10%, Asian American; 6%, Hispanic; 1%, Native American; and 5%, Multi-cultural. The majority of students come from Washington (74%). The average age of entering students is 28; age range is 20 to 56. About 28% of students enter directly from undergraduate school, 12% have a graduate degree, and 85% have worked full-time prior to entering law school. About 2% drop out after the first year for academic or personal reasons; 90% remain to receive a law degree.

One Newark Center
Newark, NJ 07102-5210

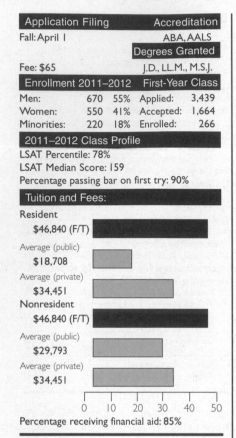

Application Filing		Accreditation
Fall: April 1		ABA, AALS
		Degrees Granted
Fee: $65		J.D., LL.M., M.S.J.

Enrollment 2011–2012			First-Year Class	
Men:	670	55%	Applied:	3,439
Women:	550	41%	Accepted:	1,664
Minorities:	220	18%	Enrolled:	266

2011–2012 Class Profile
LSAT Percentile: 78%
LSAT Median Score: 159
Percentage passing bar on first try: 90%

Tuition and Fees:

Resident
$46,840 (F/T)

Average (public)
$18,708

Average (private)
$34,451

Nonresident
$46,840 (F/T)

Average (public)
$29,793

Average (private)
$34,451

0 10 20 30 40 50

Percentage receiving financial aid: 85%

ADMISSIONS

In the fall of 2011 first-year class, 3439 applied, 1664 were accepted, and 266 enrolled. Sixteen transfers enrolled. The median LSAT percentile of the most recent first-year class was 78; the median GPA was 3.5 on a scale of 4.0. The lowest LSAT percentile accepted was 44; the highest was 99.

Requirements
Applicants must have a bachelor's degree and take the LSAT. The most important admission factors include academic achievement, LSAT results, and GPA. No specific undergraduate courses are required. Candidates are not interviewed.

Procedure
The application deadline for fall entry is April 1. Applicants should submit an application form, LSAT results, transcripts, a personal statement, the TOEFL (if applicable), a nonrefundable application fee of $65, and 2 letters of recommendation. Notification of the admissions

decision is on a rolling basis. The law school uses the LSAC.

Special
The law school recruits minority and disadvantaged students by reaching out to historically black colleges and minority bar associations to encourage applications from highly qualified students of color. The Legal Education Opportunities (LEO) Institute and the Dorothy Day Scholarship are intended to help in the recruitment of a diverse pool of students. Requirements are different for out-of-state students. Transfer students must have one year of credit, must have a minimum GPA of 3, must have attended an ABA-approved law school, and must submit a personal statement.

Costs

Tuition and fees for the 2011–2012 academic year are $46,000 for all full-time students. Tuition for part-time students is $34,500 for in-state students and $34,500 out-of-state. Books and supplies run $1,500.

Financial Aid

About 85% of current law students receive some form of aid. The average annual amount of aid from all sources combined, including scholarships, loans, and work contracts, is $33,500; maximum, $51,180. Awards are based on need and merit combined. The required financial statement is the FAFSA. The aid application deadline for fall entry is April 1. Special funds for minority or disadvantaged students are need-based. First-year students are notified about their financial aid application at the time of acceptance.

About the Law School

Seton Hall University School of Law was established in 1951 and is a private institution. The 2-acre campus is in an urban area in Newark. The primary mission of the law school is to provide an excellent legal education to students who are highly qualified for the study of law, to disseminate knowledge, and to provide an environment for research and writing. Students have access to federal, state, county, city, and local agencies, courts, correctional facilities, law firms, and legal aid organizations in the Newark area.

The law school's location is home to many firms, offering students opportunities as interns, clerks, and summer associates. Nearby are government offices and federal and county courthouses. Ample and affordable rental housing is available in the vicinity. All law school facilities are accessible to the physically disabled.

Calendar

The law school operates on a traditional semester basis. Courses for full-time students are offered both day and evening, and must be completed within 6 years. For part-time students, courses are offered both day and evening, and must be completed within 6 years. New full- and part-time students are admitted in the fall. There is an 8-week summer session. Transferable summer courses are offered.

Programs

In addition to the J.D., the law school offers the LL.M. and M.S.J. Students may take relevant courses in other programs and apply credit toward the J.D.; a maximum of 12 credits may be applied. The following joint degrees may be earned: B.S./J.D. (Bachelor of Science/Juris Doctor), M.D./M.S.J. (Doctor of Medicine/Master of Science in Jurisprudence), J.D./M.A.D.I.R. (Juris Doctor/Master of Arts in International Diplomacy), J.D./M.B.A. (Juris Doctor/Master of Business Administration), and J.D./M.D. (Juris Doctor/Doctor of Medicine).

Required
To earn the J.D., candidates must complete 88 total credits, of which 44 are for required courses. They must maintain a minimum GPA of 2.0 in the required courses. The following first-year courses are required of all students: Civil Procedure, Constitutional Law, Contracts, Criminal Law, Legal Research and Writing, Property, and Torts. Required upper-level courses consist of Appellate Advocacy, Business Associations, Evidence, Federal Income Taxation, Persuasion and Advocacy, and Professional Responsibility. Students may apply to the particular clinic they seek to join. The required orientation program for first-year students is a 2-day program commencing immediately before the start of classes with activities continuing into the first week of classes.

Phone: 973-642-8747
888-415-7271
Fax: 973-642-8876
E-mail: *admitme@shu.edu*
Web: *http://law.shu.edu*

Contact
Dean of Admissions and Financial Resource, 973-642-8747 or 888-415-7271 for general inquiries; Director of Financial Resource Management, 973-642-8744 for financial aid information.

Electives

The School of Law offers concentrations in intellectual property law and health law. In addition, the Center for Social Justice's for-credit clinical programs and pro bono program allow students to engage in a legal apprenticeship with an average of 15 hours per week performing legal duties, such as interviewing and counseling clients, conferring with adversaries, taking depositions, conducting research, and participating in trials. Students acquire the practical skills, knowledge, and experience that both train them and make them more attractive to prospective employers. Clincial programs include the Civil Litigation Clinic, Family Law Clinic, Immigration and Human Rights Clinic, Impact Litigation Clinic, and the Pro Bono Program. There is a minimum cumulative GPA of 2.6 with certain course prerequisites. Students are encouraged to enroll in at least 1 or 2 seminars or small group courses in subjects that interest them. The Advanced Writing Requirement is a required seminar course to meet graduation standards and is 2 to 3 credits per course. Elective seminars include drafting, simulation, and skills courses, offered for 2 to 4 credits each. Internships include judicial, not-for-profit organizations, and federal and state government. Research program opportunities, offered to second- and third-year students, include independent research, seminars, and the opportunity to serve as a faculty research assistant. The Center for Social Justice sponsors a pro bono program that places students in a variety of legal settings during all 3 years of law school. The law school sponsors innumerable programs. Recent speakers have included Janet Reno, Scott Turow, Akhil Amar, Cornell West, Arthur Miller, Randy Barnett, Erwin Chemerinsky, and Maya Angelou. There are summer study-abroad programs in Italy, Egypt, and Ireland. Academic support services are available to students in academic difficulty. Minority programs include the Partners in Excellence (PIE) Program, which seeks to attract a diverse pool of highly talented students who will enrich the academic life of the law school, and the Legal Education Opportunities (LEO) Institute, which is intended to provide educationally disadvantaged students the opportunity to demonstrate their ability to succeed in the study of law. The most widely taken electives are Criminal Procedure, Estates and Trusts, and Commercial Law Survey.

Graduation Requirements

In order to graduate, candidates must have a GPA of 2.0 and must have completed the upper-division writing requirement.

Organizations
Students edit the *Seton Hall Law Review, Journal of Sports and Entertainment Law, Seton Hall Legislative Journal, Seton Hall Circuit Review*, and the newspaper *Res Ipsa Loquitur*. Moot court competitions include National Moot Court Competition, National Appellate Advocacy, and Craven's Constitutional Law Moot Court Competition. Other competitions include Alternative Dispute Resolution and various writing competitions. Law student organizations, local chapters of national associations, and campus organizations include Jewish Law Society, Public Interest Network, Entertainment and Sports Law Society, St. Thomas More Society, Health Law Forum, Women's Law Forum, Black Law Students Association, Federalist Society, and American Constitution Society.

Library
The law library contains 443,681 hardcopy volumes and 498,403 microform volume equivalents, and subscribes to 7,485 serial publications. Such online databases and networks as LEXIS, WESTLAW, BNA, CCH, European Union Law Library, Legal Scholarship Network, LOISLAW, Tax Analysts, LLMC, RIACheckpoint, Environmental Law Reporter, Global Jurist, Indexmaster, HeinOnline, and New York Legal Publishing Corporation are available to law students for research. Special library collections include the Rodino Papers and depositories for federal and New Jersey State documents. The ratio of library volumes to faculty is 6,622 to 1 and to students is 364 to 1. The ratio of seats in the library to students is 1 to 2.

Faculty
The law school has 75 full-time and 96 part-time faculty members, of whom 63 are women. According to AAUP standards for Category I institutions, faculty salaries are average. About 25% of full-time faculty have a graduate law degree in addition to the J.D.; about 10% of part-time faculty have one. The ratio of full-time students to full-time faculty in an

J.D.s awarded:	320
Services available through: a separate law school placement center.	
Services: mentor programs, mock interviews, summer public interest fellowships, loan forgiveness program, and externship program.	
Special features: an evening placement counselor, public interest director, newsletters, online services, and clerkship counselor.	
Full-time job interviews:	100 employers
Summer job interviews:	100 employers
Placement by graduation:	79% of class
Placement within 9 months:	86% of class
Average starting salary:	$42,200 to $160,000
Areas of placement:	
Private practice 2–10 attorneys	15%
Private practice 11–25 attorneys	2%
Private practice 26–50 attorneys	4%
Private practice 51–100 attorneys	4%
Private practice 101+ attorneys	12%
Judicial clerkships	36%
Business/industry	12%
Government	5%
Public interest	2%
Academic	2%

average class is 15 to 1; in a clinic, 6 to 1. The law school has a regular program of bringing visiting professors and other distinguished lecturers and visitors to campus. There is a chapter of the Order of the Coif; 10 faculty are members.

Students
About 41% of the student body are women; 18%, minorities; 4%, African American; 8%, Asian American; and 5%, Hispanic. The average age of entering students is 25; age range is 21 to 47. About 33% of students enter directly from undergraduate school, 11% have a graduate degree, and 66% have worked full-time prior to entering law school. About 2% drop out after the first year for academic or personal reasons; 97% remain to receive a law degree.

1303 San Jacinto Street
Houston, TX 77002-7006

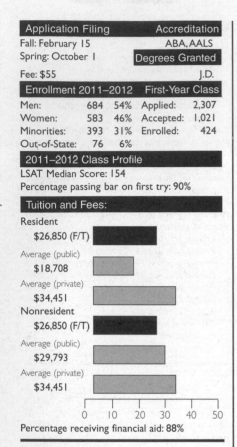

Application Filing	Accreditation
Fall: February 15	ABA, AALS
Spring: October 1	**Degrees Granted**
Fee: $55	J.D.

Enrollment 2011–2012			First-Year Class	
Men:	684	54%	Applied:	2,307
Women:	583	46%	Accepted:	1,021
Minorities:	393	31%	Enrolled:	424
Out-of-State:	76	6%		

2011–2012 Class Profile

LSAT Median Score: 154
Percentage passing bar on first try: 90%

Tuition and Fees:

Resident
$26,850 (F/T)

Average (public)
$18,708

Average (private)
$34,451

Nonresident
$26,850 (F/T)

Average (public)
$29,793

Average (private)
$34,451

Percentage receiving financial aid: 88%

ADMISSIONS

In the fall of 2011 first-year class, 2307 applied, 1021 were accepted, and 424 enrolled. Fourteen transfers enrolled. The median GPA of the most recent first-year class was 3.25.

Requirements

Applicants must have a bachelor's degree and take the LSAT. The most important admission factors include LSAT results, GPA, and life experience. No specific undergraduate courses are required. Candidates are not interviewed.

Procedure

The application deadline for fall entry is February 15. Applicants should submit an application form, personal statement, nonrefundable application fee of $55, 2 letters of recommendation, and a resume. Notification of the admissions decision is on a rolling basis. The law school uses the LSAC.

Special

The law school recruits minority and disadvantaged students by offering application fee waivers for those with documented need. South Texas considers ethnicity and disadvantaged backgrounds in the admissions process and offers scholarships to those who qualify. Requirements are different for out-of-state students. Transfer students must have one year of credit, attended an ABA approved law school, a personal statement, be ranked in the upper 10% of their current law school class, and be able to provide a letter of good standing.

Costs

Books and supplies run $2,150.

Financial Aid

About 88% of current law students receive some form of aid. The average annual amount of aid from all sources combined, including scholarships, loans, and work contracts, is $37,161; maximum, $48,000. Awards are based on need and merit combined. Required financial statement is the FAFSA. The aid application deadline for fall entry is May 1. Special funds for minority or disadvantaged students include institutional and external scholarship for minority students and students who have faced economic or other obstacles to pursuing a legal education. First-year students are notified about their financial aid application at the time of application.

About the Law School

South Texas College of Law was established in 1923 and is independent. The campus is in an urban area in downtown Houston. The primary mission of the law school is to provide a diverse body of students with the opportunity to obtain an exceptional legal education, preparing graduates to serve their communities and the profession with distinction. Facilities of special interest to law students include its 4 Centers of Excellence and its skills and clinical programs: Advocacy Program, the Frank Evans Center for Conflict Resolution, the Corporate Compliance Center, and the Transactional Practice Center. Housing for students is not available on campus. However, high-rise apartments are within walking distance of the campus. Apartment locators are available,

usually at no cost. All law school facilities are accessible to the physically disabled.

Calendar

The law school operates on a traditional semester basis. Courses for full-time students are offered both day and evening and must be completed within 7 years. For part-time students, courses are offered both day and evening and must be completed within 7 years. New full-time students are admitted in the fall and spring. New part-time students are admitted in the fall. There is an 8-week summer session. Transferable summer courses are offered.

Programs

The following joint degrees may be earned: J.D./M.B.A. (Juris Doctor/Master of Business Administration).

Required

To earn the J.D., candidates must complete 90 total credits, of which 46 are for required courses. They must maintain a minimum GPA of 2.2 in the required courses. The following first-year courses are required of all students: Civil Procedure, Constitutional Law, Contracts I and II, Criminal Law, Legal Research and Writing I and II, Property I, and Torts I and II. Required upper-level courses consist of 2 hours of professional skills, Evidence, Federal Income Tax, Professional Responsibility, Property II, and substantial research paper. The required orientation program for first-year students is 2 days and is generally scheduled the week prior to the beginning of classes. Students are introduced to the law and legal profession.

Electives

Electives concentrate on trial and appellate advocacy, alternative dispute resolution, and transactional law practice. In addition, upper-level students can earn credits in clinics including the Criminal Process Clinic, Judicial Process Clinic and the Public Interest Clinic. Seminars are also offered. Internships are normally offered during the fall, spring, and summer. Each year, the College hosts the Fred Parks Distinguished Lecture Series and the Turner Lecture Series in Professionalism. South Texas co-sponsors a

Phone: 713-646-1810
Fax: 713-646-2906
E-mail: *admissions@stcl.edu*
Web: *www.stcl.edu*

Contact
Alicia Cramer, Director of Admissions, 713-646-1810 for general inquiries; Carlos Clark, Director of Scholarships and Financial Aid, 713-646-1820 for financial aid information.

TEXAS

number of ABA-approved summer abroad programs, in addition to 2 cooperative semester abroad programs. South Texas also administers an academic assistance program that includes individual counseling and study skills seminars on the outlining process, as well as preparing for and taking exams. The most widely taken electives are Oil and Gas, Criminal Procedure, and Wills, Trusts, and Estates.

Graduation Requirements
In order to graduate, candidates must have a GPA of 2.0 and complete the upper-division writing requirement.

Organizations
Students edit the *South Texas Law Review, Corporate Counsel Review, Currents: International Trade Law Journal, Corporate Counsel Review,* and the newspaper, *Annotations.* Students enrolled in the Moot Court Competition course are selected to participate in numerous national moot court and mock trial competitions held annually. South Texas has more than 25 registered organizations in which students can participate. Students at South Texas have the opportunity to become members of numerous active student organizations representing a wide range of interests. There are local chapters of Phi Delta Phi, Phi Alpha Delta, and Delta Theta Phi.

Library
The law library contains 237,970 hardcopy volumes and 295,556 microform volume equivalents, and subscribes to 3,501

serial publications. Online databases and networks include CALI, CIS Universe, Infotrac, Legal-Trac, LEXIS, Mathew Bender, OCLC First Search, WESTLAW, and Wilsonline Indexes, which are available to law students for research. Special library collections include a U.S. government selective depository and a rare books collection, college archives, and various manuscript collections. The ratio of library volumes to faculty is 4,327 to 1 and to students is 197 to 1. The ratio of seats in the library to students is 1 to 2.

Faculty
The law school has 55 full-time and 41 faculty members, of whom 33 are women. About 22% of full-time faculty have a graduate law degree in addition to the J.D. The ratio of full-time students to full-time faculty in an average class is 23 to 1; in a clinic, 19 to 1. The law school has a regular program of bringing visiting professors and other distinguished lecturers and visitors to campus.

Students
About 46% of the student body are women; 31%, minorities; 4%, African American; 9%, Asian American; 15%, Hispanic; 1%, Native American; and 68%, Unknown. The majority of students come from Texas (94%). The average age of entering students is 26; age range is 21 to 53. About 36% of students enter directly from undergraduate school, and 6% have a graduate degree. About 4% drop out after the first year for academic or personal reasons.

Placement
J.D.s awarded:	399
Services available through: a separate law school placement center.	
Special features: seminars and speaker programs, skills training workshops, networking events, and coordination of campus interviews and recruitment.	
Full-time job interviews:	11 employers
Summer job interviews:	30 employers
Placement within 9 months of graduation:	85% of class
Average starting salary:	$55,000 to $100,000
Areas of placement:	
Private practice 2–10 attorneys	31%
Private practice 11–25 attorneys	7%
Private practice 26–50 attorneys	4%
Private practice 51–100 attorneys	3%
Business/industry	21%
Government	11%
Public interest	3%
Judicial clerkships	2%

SOUTHERN ILLINOIS UNIVERSITY

School of Law

Lesar Law Building, Mail Code 6804
Carbondale, IL 62901

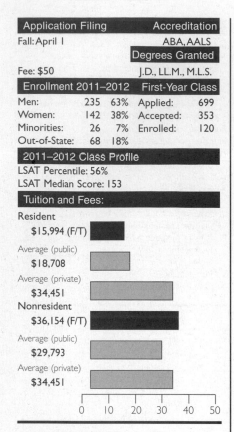

Application Filing	Accreditation
Fall: April 1	ABA, AALS
	Degrees Granted
Fee: $50	J.D., LL.M., M.L.S.

Enrollment 2011–2012		First-Year Class	
Men:	235 63%	Applied:	699
Women:	142 38%	Accepted:	353
Minorities:	26 7%	Enrolled:	120
Out-of-State:	68 18%		

2011–2012 Class Profile
LSAT Percentile: 56%
LSAT Median Score: 153

Tuition and Fees:

Resident
$15,994 (F/T)

Average (public)
$18,708

Average (private)
$34,451

Nonresident
$36,154 (F/T)

Average (public)
$29,793

Average (private)
$34,451

0   10   20   30   40   50

ADMISSIONS

In the fall of 2011 first-year class, 699 applied, 353 were accepted, and 120 enrolled. Eight transfers enrolled. The median LSAT percentile of the most recent first-year class was 56; the median GPA was 3.3 on a scale of 4.0. The lowest LSAT percentile accepted was 26; the highest was 92.

Requirements
Applicants must have a bachelor's degree and take the LSAT. The most important admission factors include LSAT results, GPA, and academic achievement. No specific undergraduate courses are required. Candidates are not interviewed.

Procedure
The application deadline for fall entry is April 1. Applicants should submit an application form, LSAT results, transcripts, a personal statement, a nonrefundable application fee of $50, 2 letters of recommendation, and the Admissions Committee Memorandum. Notification of the admissions decision is as early as possible. The law school uses the LSAC.

Special
The law school recruits minority and disadvantaged students by means of the Candidate Referral Service; special programs at the School of Law; networking; contacting institutions that serve underrepresented students; and engaging current law students and minority student organizations in recruiting efforts. Requirements are different for out-of-state students. Transfer students must have one year of credit, must have attended an ABA-approved law school, and must submit a personal statement. Applicants may be admitted if it appears likely that they will successfully complete the School of Law curriculum. Factors considered include the applicant's law school record, class rank, law school attended, LSAT, and GPA.

Costs

Tuition and fees for the 2011–2012 academic year are $12,750 for full-time in-state students and $32,910 for out-of-state students. On-campus room and board costs about $11,214 annually; books and supplies run $1,150.

Financial Aid

Awards are based on need and merit combined. The required financial statement is the FAFSA. The aid application deadline for fall entry is April 1. First-year students are notified about their financial aid application at time of acceptance.

About the Law School

Southern Illinois University School of Law was established in 1973 and is a public institution. The 3290-acre campus is in a small town 100 miles southeast of St. Louis, Missouri. The primary mission of the law school is to train lawyers who will be competent to practice law now and in the future, exhibit leadership, and adhere to the ethical standards of the legal profession. Students have access to federal, state, county, city, and local agencies, courts, correctional facilities, law firms, and legal aid organizations in the Carbondale area. Facilities of special interest to law students include 24-hour keypad access to the law building and library, a wireless network, and distance-learning capabilities allowing live correspondence with national and international legal

experts. The courtroom and classrooms are equipped with the latest technology. The library houses a vast collection of legal materials to meet the demanding research needs of the prospective lawyer. There is plenty of off-campus housing available within 10 minutes of the law school. All law school facilities are accessible to the physically disabled.

Calendar

The law school operates on a traditional semester basis. Courses are offered days only, and must be completed within 5 years. New students are admitted in the fall. There is an 8-week summer session. Transferable summer courses are offered.

Programs

In addition to the J.D., the law school offers the LL.M. and M.L.S. Students may take relevant courses in other programs and apply credit toward the J.D.; a maximum of 6 credits may be applied. The following joint degrees may be earned: J.D./M. Acct. (Juris Doctor/Master of Accounting), J.D./M.B.A. (Juris Doctor/Master of Business Administration), J.D./M.D. (Juris Doctor/Doctor of Medicine), J.D./M.P.A. (Juris Doctor/Master of Public Administration), J.D./M.S.ECE (Juris Doctor/Master of Science in Electrical Engineering), and J.D./M.S.Ed. (Juris Doctor/Master of Educational Administration), and J.D./M.S.W. (Juris Doctor/Master of Social Work).

Required
To earn the J.D., candidates must complete 90 total credits, of which 49 are for required courses. They must maintain a minimum GPA of 2.3 in the required courses. The following first-year courses are required of all students: Civil Procedure I, Contracts I and II, Criminal Law, Lawyering Skills I and II, Legislative and Administrative Process, Professionalism and the Law, Property I and II, and Torts. Required upper-level courses consist of a writing requirement, Civil Procedure II, Constitutional Law, Evidence, and Legal Profession. Students must choose from a menu of skills courses. The required orientation program for first-year students involves a 3-day program of presentations aimed at providing vital information to entering students.

Phone: 618-453-8858
800-739-9187
Fax: 618-453-8921
E-mail: *lawadmit@siu.edu*
Web: *www.lawsiu.edu*

Contact

Akami Marik, Director of Admissions, 618-453-8858 or 800-739-9187 for general inquiries; Terri Harfst, Director of Financial Aid, 618-453-4334 for financial aid information.

ILLINOIS

Electives

The School of Law offers concentrations in corporate law, criminal law, environmental law, family law, intellectual property law, international law, labor law, litigation, tax law, torts and insurance, health Law, public interest Law, and real estate law. In addition, 3 in-house clinics are offered to upper-level law students for up to 12 hours of credit: the elder law clinic, the domestic violence clinic, and the juvenile justice clinic. Senior seminars are available to students who have completed 31 semester hours. Students must fulfill the senior writing requirements upon graduation by taking the senior writing seminar Designated Elective course, journal credit, or Advanced Appelate Moot Court. Upper-level law students may enroll for up to 15 hours in externships; credit is earned by working in a public interest or legal services agency or for local prosecutors and public defenders, for judges, or for local and state agencies. Independent research and a writing credit is allowed under certain conditions. Each year the law school hosts the Lesar Lecture Series and the Dr. Arthur Grayson Distinguished Lecture (Law and Medicine). The law school cosponsors a summer study-abroad program in Ireland. All first-year students participate in the Academic Success Program, which includes structured study groups led by upper-class students. The school makes individual accommodations to the needs of its disabled students. The most widely taken electives are Criminal Procedure, Introduction to Commercial Law, and Corporations.

Graduation Requirements

In order to graduate, candidates must have a GPA of 2.3, must have completed the upper-division writing requirement, and must maintain a 2.3 GPA for courses taken during the third year of law school.

Organizations

Students edit the *Southern Illinois University Law Journal* and the *Journal of Legal Medicine*. The Moot Court Board sends teams to numerous competitions, including the ABA National Appellate Advocacy Competition, Criminal Procedure Moot Court Competition, Gibbons National Criminal Procedure Moot Court Competition, and National Asylum and Refugee Law Competition. Students also participate in National Trial Advocacy competitions. Law student organizations include the Black Law Students Association, Lesbian and Gay Law Students Association, and Women's Law Forum. Local chapters of national associations include Amnesty International, Federalist Society, and the ABA Law School Division. Campus organizations include the Environmental Law Society, International Law Society, and the Student Bar Association.

Library

The law library contains 443,551 hardcopy volumes and 206,555 microform volume equivalents, and subscribes to 1,707 serial publications. Such online databases and networks as CALI, CIS Universe, Infotrac, Legal-Trac, LEXIS, Mathew Bender, OCLC First Search, WESTLAW, Wilsonline Indexes, HeinOnline, Fastcase, News Bank Info Web, BNA Databases, CALI, Current Index to Legal Periodicals, Illinois Institute for Continuing Legal Education (IICLE) Smart Books, and others are available to law students for research. Special library collections include a federal government selective depository library and Illinois state comprehensive document depository. The ratio of library volumes to faculty is 10,315 to 1 and to students is 1,180 to 1. The ratio of seats in the library to students is 1 to 1.

Placement		
Services available through: a separate law school placement center.		
Full-time job interviews:		3 employers
Summer job interviews:		6 employers
Placement within 9 months of graduation:		84% of class
Average starting salary:	$40,000 to $58,000	
Areas of placement:		
Private practice 2–10 attorneys		32%
Private practice 11–25 attorneys		10%
Private practice 26–50 attorneys		3%
Private practice 50+ attorneys		11%
Government		20%
Business/industry		15%
Judicial clerkships		5%
Academic		2%
Public interest		1%

Faculty

The law school has 35 full-time and 8 part-time faculty members, of whom 23 are women. According to AAUP standards for Category I institutions, faculty salaries are well below average. About 18% of full-time faculty have a graduate law degree in addition to the J.D. The law school has a regular program of bringing visiting professors and other distinguished lecturers and visitors to campus.

Students

About 38% of the student body are women; 7%, minorities; 1%, African American; 3%, Asian American; 1%, Hispanic; and 1%, Native American. The majority of students come from Illinois (82%). The average age of entering students is 25; age range is 21 to 48. About 48% of students enter directly from undergraduate school, and 9% have a graduate degree. About 6% drop out after the first year for academic or personal reasons; 94% remain to receive a law degree.

Dedman School of Law

Office of Admissions, P.O. Box 750110
Dallas, TX 75275-0110

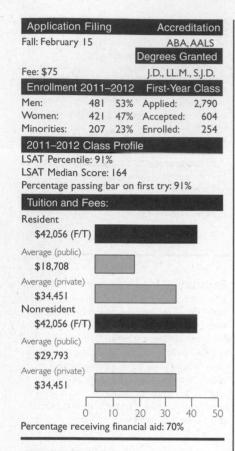

Application Filing	Accreditation
Fall: February 15	ABA, AALS
	Degrees Granted
Fee: $75	J.D., LL.M., S.J.D.

Enrollment 2011–2012			First-Year Class	
Men:	481	53%	Applied:	2,790
Women:	421	47%	Accepted:	604
Minorities:	207	23%	Enrolled:	254

2011–2012 Class Profile
LSAT Percentile: 91%
LSAT Median Score: 164
Percentage passing bar on first try: 91%

Tuition and Fees:

Resident
$42,056 (F/T)

Average (public)
$18,708

Average (private)
$34,451

Nonresident
$42,056 (F/T)

Average (public)
$29,793

Average (private)
$34,451

0   10   20   30   40   50

Percentage receiving financial aid: 70%

ADMISSIONS

In the fall of 2011 first-year class, 2790 applied, 604 were accepted, and 254 enrolled. Forty-one transfer students enrolled. The median LSAT percentile of the most recent first-year class was 91; the median GPA was 3.8 on a scale of 4.0.

Requirements

Applicants must have a bachelor's degree and take the LSAT. Minimum acceptable GPA is 2.0 on a scale of 4.0. No specific undergraduate courses are required and candidates are not interviewed.

Procedure

The application deadline for fall entry is February 15. Applicants should submit an application form, LSAT results, transcripts, a nonrefundable application fee of $75, 2 letters of recommendation, a resume, and optional statements. Notification of the admissions decision is on a rolling basis beginning in December. The law school uses the LSAC.

Special

The law school recruits minority and disadvantaged students by means of school visitations, special mailings, and a minority Pre-Law Symposium held every year in the spring. Requirements are different for out-of-state students. Transfer students must have one year of credit, attended an ABA-approved law school. Admission for transfers is highly competitive; the student must be in good standing at his/her previous law school.

Costs

Tuition and fees for the 2011–2012 academic year are $37,616 for all full-time students. Tuition for part-time students is $28,208 for in-state students and $28,208 out-of-state. On-campus room and board costs about $19,800 annually; books and supplies run $2,000.

Financial Aid

About 70% of current law students receive some form of aid. Awards are based on need and merit combined. Required financial statements are the FAFSA, and others, depending on the type of scholarship being sought. The aid application deadline for fall entry is June 1. Special funds for minority or disadvantaged students include scholarships, which are available on a need and merit basis and are designed to promote the diversity of the student body and the legal profession, and to assist those who have had fewer academic opportunities. First-year students are notified about their financial aid application at time of acceptance.

About the Law School

Southern Methodist University Dedman School of Law was established in 1925 and is a private institution. The 6-acre campus is located in a suburban area 5 miles north of downtown Dallas. The primary mission of the law school is to prepare students for the competent and ethical practice of law through a curriculum that combines training in the science and method of law, knowledge of the substance and procedure of law, understanding of the role of law in an international society, and practical experience in handling professional problems. Students have access to federal, state, county, city, and local agencies, courts, correctional facilities, law

firms, and legal aid organizations in the Dallas area. Facilities of special interest to law students include the Underwood Law Library, and Carr Collins Hall, Career Services, financial aid, a public service department, and a dining hall. All classrooms are equipped with multimedia presentation facilities and wireless access. Housing for students consists of both single- and married-student housing, available on campus on a first-come, first-served basis. All law school facilities are accessible to the physically disabled.

Calendar

The law school operates on a traditional semester basis. Courses for full-time students are offered both day and evening and must be completed within 5 years. For part-time students, courses are offered both day and evening and must be completed within 5 years. New full- and part-time students are admitted in the fall. There is a 7-week summer session. Transferable summer courses are not offered.

Programs

In addition to the J.D., the law school offers the LL.M. and S.J.D. Students may take relevant courses in other programs and apply credit toward the J.D.; a maximum of 6 credits may be applied. The following joint degrees may be earned: J.D./M.A. (Juris Doctor/Master of Arts in applied economics) and J.D./M.B.A. (Juris Doctor/Master of Business Administration).

Required

To earn the J.D., candidates must complete 87 total credits, of which 37 are for required courses. They must maintain a minimum GPA of 2.0 in the required courses. The following first-year courses are required of all students: Civil Procedure, Constitutional Law I, Contracts, Criminal Law, Legal Research, Writing, and Advocacy, Property, and Torts. Required upper-level courses consist of a general writing requirement, an edited writing seminar, Constitutional Law II, Professional Responsibility, and Professional Skills course. Clinical courses are available for students who have completed 44 hours and met certain prerequisites. The required orientation program for first-year students consists of a 2-day introduction to the study of law.

Phone: 214-768-2550
888-768-5291
Fax: 214-768-2549
E-mail: lawadmit@smu.edu
Web: law.smu.edu

Contact

Office of Admissions, 214-768-2550 for general inquiries; Stan Eddy, Financial Aid Counselor, 214-768-3348 for financial aid information.

TEXAS

Electives

The Dedman School of Law offers concentrations in corporate law, criminal law, environmental law, family law, intellectual property law, international law, litigation, securities law, and tax law. In addition, child advocacy, civil, consumer advocacy, criminal defense, criminal prosecution, small business, and federal taxpayers clinics are also offered. Clinics may be taken by students who have completed 44 hours, are in good academic standing, and have met certain course prerequisites. Seminars include such topics as Advanced Commercial Law, Antitrust, and Civil Rights. Directed Research is worth a maximum of 3 hours. Field work may be done through Directed Studies, and is worth 1 to 2 hours. A mandatory 30 hours of pro bono legal work is required for graduation. The special lecture series includes the Murrah Lecture and the Tate Lecture. A 6-week summer program at University College in Oxford, England is provided for students who wish to study abroad. In addition, students can participate in other approved study-abroad programs. The Academic Skills Assessment (ASAP) program is available by invitation only to first-year law students. The non-credit Student Mentoring program is also available for all first-year law students. Minority programs include Minority Law Day, the Diversity Clerkship Program, Southeastern Minority Job Fair, Sunbelt Minority Job Fair, the Black/Hispanic/Asian ABA Pacific American Law Students Associations, and Multicultural Orientation. Special interest group programs include the Board of Advocates, Student Bar Association, Association of Public Interest, Law and Association of Law and Politics.

Graduation Requirements

In order to graduate, candidates must have a GPA of 2.0, complete the upper-division writing requirement, and 30 hours of pro bono work.

Organizations

Students edit the *SMU Law Review, Journal of Air Law and Commerce, The International Lawyer, SMU Science* and *Technology Law Review*, and *Law and Business Review of the Americas*. Moot court competitions include the Jackson and Walker, Phillip C. Jessup International Moot Court, and Howie and Sweeney competitions. Other competitions include the ABA Client Counseling, ABA Negotiations, ABA Hispanic National Bar Association Moot Court, Thomas Tang Moot Court, and John Marshall II Moot Court. Local chapters of national associations include the BLSA, APALSA, HLSA, Criminal Law Association, and Corporate Law Association, Law student organizations include Student Bar Association, Board of Advocates, and Barristers. Other law student organizations include Federalist Law Society, OWLS, and Phi Alpha Delta.

Library

The law library contains 637,217 hardcopy volumes and 140,625 microform volume equivalents, and subscribes to 4,987 serial publications. Online databases and networks include CALI, CIS Universe, Infotrac, Legal-Trac, LEXIS, Mathew Bender, OCLC First Search, WEST-LAW, and Wilsonline Indexes. Others are HeinOnline, Lexis/Nexis Congressional, Oceana Online, Access UN, BNA, CCH, Foreign Law Guide, Inter Am, Law Into China, Lawtel Eu, Making of Modern Law, Oxford Scholarship online, and others, which are available to law students for research. Special library collections include a rare book room with 9000 volumes; papers and professional library of Sir Joseph Gold; Dallas (Texas) Independent School District Desegregation Litigation Papers; Steinberg collection of Jewish law. The ratio of library volumes to faculty is 13,558 to 1 and to students is 706 to 1. The ratio of seats in the library to students is 1 to 1.

Faculty

The law school has 47 full-time and 30 part-time faculty members, of whom 23 are women. According to AAUP standards for Category I institutions, faculty salaries are above average. About 40% of full-time faculty have a graduate law degree in addition to the J.D. The ratio of full-time students to full-time faculty in an average class is 15 to 1; in a clinic, 8 to 1. The law school has a regular program of bringing visiting professors and other distinguished lecturers and visitors to campus. There is a chapter of the Order of the Coif; 90 graduates are members.

Placement

J.D.s awarded:	283
Services available through: a separate law school placement center.	
Special features: 7 professionals on staff, including 5 SMU law graduates.	
Full-time job interviews:	25 employers
Summer job interviews:	100 employers
Placement by graduation:	72% of class
Placement within 9 months:	99% of class
Average starting salary:	$62,400 to $160,000
Areas of placement:	
Private practice 2–10 attorneys	29%
Private practice 11–25 attorneys	8%
Private practice 26–50 attorneys	12%
Private practice 51–100 attorneys	7%
Private practice 101–500+ attorneys	18%
Business/industry	16%
Government	6%
Judicial clerkships	4%
Academic	2%
Public interest	1%
Military	1%

Students

About 47% of the student body are women; 23%, minorities; 5%, African American; 7%, Asian American; 9%, Hispanic; 1%, Native American; and 1%, Unknown. The average age of entering students is 25; age range is 21 to 53. About 11% of students have a graduate degree. About 3% drop out after the first year for academic or personal reasons; 97% remain to receive a law degree.

School of Law

333 Faunce Corner Road
North Dartmouth, MA 02747

Application Filing		Accreditation
Fall: June 30		n/av
	Degrees Granted	
Fee: $50		J.D.

Enrollment 2011–2012		First-Year Class	
Men:	104 44%	Applied:	201
Women:	132 57%	Accepted:	174
Minorities:	80 34%	Enrolled:	73
Out-of-State:	219 93%		

2011–2012 Class Profile
LSAT Median Score: 142
Percentage passing bar on first try: 78%

Tuition and Fees:

Resident
$22,175 (F/T)

Average (public)
$18,708

Average (private)
$34,451

Nonresident
$22,175 (F/T)

Average (public)
$29,793

Average (private)
$34,451

0 10 20 30 40 50

Percentage receiving financial aid: 80%

ADMISSIONS
In the fall of 2011 first-year class, 201 applied, 174 were accepted, and 73 enrolled. Two transfers enrolled. The median GPA of the most recent first-year class was 76. The lowest LSAT percentile accepted was 133; the highest was 157.

Requirements
Applicants must have a bachelor's degree and take the LSAT. The most important admission factors include LSAT results, writing ability, general background, and letter of recommendation. No specific undergraduate courses are required and candidates are not interviewed.

Procedure
The application deadline for fall entry is June 30. Applicants should submit an application form, LSAT results, transcripts, a nonrefundable application fee of $50, 2 letters of recommendation, and a personal statement. Notification of the admissions decision is on a rolling basis. The law school uses the LSAC.

Special
Requirements are different for out-of-state students.

Costs
Tuition and fees for the 2011–2012 academic year are $21,800 for all full-time students. Books and supplies run $600.

Financial Aid
About 80% of current law students receive some form of aid. The maximum annual amount of aid from all sources combined, including scholarships, loans, and work contracts, is $34,800. Awards are based on need and merit combined. Required financial statement is the FAFSA. The aid application deadline for fall entry is May 27.

About the Law School
Southern New England School of Law was established in 1981 and is a private institution. The 8-acre campus is located in a suburban area. Students have access to federal, state, county, city, and local agencies, courts, correctional facilities, law firms, and legal aid organizations in the North Dartmouth area. Facilities of special interest to law students include a community development clinic. Housing for students consists of local area rentals. Some dorms at the University of Massachusetts-Dartmouth are also available. All law school facilities are accessible to the physically disabled.

Calendar
The law school operates on a traditional semester basis. Courses for full-time students are offered both day and evening and must be completed within 3 years. For part-time students, courses are offered both day and evening and must be completed within 6 years. New full- and part-time students are admitted in the fall. There is a 9-week summer session. Transferable summer courses are not offered.

Programs
The following joint degrees may be earned: J.D./M.P.P. (Joint Juris Doctor/Master in Public Policy).

Required
To earn the J.D., candidates must complete 90 total credits, of which 71–73 are for required courses. They must maintain a minimum GPA of 70.0 in the required courses. The following first-year courses are required of all students: Civil Procedure, Contracts, Criminal Law, Legal Skills I and II, Property, and Torts. Required upper-level courses consist of Legal Skills III and IV, Ethics, Business Organizations, Constitutional Law, Evidence, Trusts and Estates, Criminal Procedure, 1 code course, 1 upper level writing requirement, 2 practice courses, Bar Preparation, and Commercial Law. All students must take clinical courses. There is a required orientation program for first-year students.

Electives
Legal clinics are worth 6 credits. Internships include legal clerking and judicial clerkships. The study abroad program includes The Hague Criminal War Tribunal. The most widely taken electives are Federal Courts, Family Law, and Chapter 93A.

Graduation Requirements
In order to graduate, candidates must have a GPA of 70.0, must have completed the upper-division writing requirement, and must have satisfied all academic and financial conditions.

Organizations
Moot court competitions include Jessup, Intellectual Property, and National Moot Court. Law student organizations and local chapters of national associations include the Student Bar Association, Black Law Students Association, Legal Association of Women, and Delta Theta Phi.

Phone: 508-998-9400
800-213-0060
Fax: 508-998-9561
E-mail: cvidal@snesl.edu
Web: www.snesl.edu

Contact

Carol A. Vidal, Registrar, 508-998-9600 for general inquiries; Sandra Leger Silva, Director of Financial Aid, 508-998-9600, ext. 112 for financial aid information

MASSACHUSETTS

Library

The law library contains 130,000 hard-copy volumes, and such online databases and networks as CALI, LEXIS, and WESTLAW, which are available to law students for research.

Faculty

The law school has 10 full-time and 20 faculty members, of whom 12 are women. 100% of full-time faculty have a graduate law degree in addition to the J.D. The ratio of full-time students to full-time faculty in an average class is 19 to 1; in a clinic, 2 to 1. The law school has a regular program of bringing visiting professors and other distinguished lecturers and visitors to campus.

Students

About 57% of the student body are women; 34%, minorities; 15%, African American; 6%, Asian American; and 3%, Hispanic. The average age of entering students is 31; age range is 23 to 62. About 27% of students enter directly from undergraduate school.

Placement	
J.D.s awarded:	51

SOUTHERN UNIVERSITY AND A & M COLLEGE

Law Center

Post Office Box 9294
Baton Rouge, LA 70813-9294

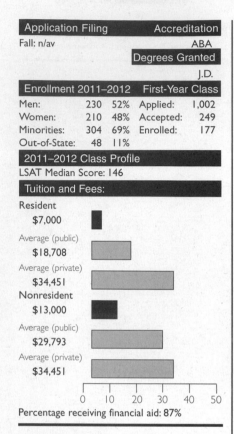

Application Filing	Accreditation
Fall: n/av	ABA

Degrees Granted
J.D.

Enrollment 2011–2012			First-Year Class	
Men:	230	52%	Applied:	1,002
Women:	210	48%	Accepted:	249
Minorities:	304	69%	Enrolled:	177
Out-of-State:	48	11%		

2011–2012 Class Profile
LSAT Median Score: 146

Tuition and Fees:

Resident
$7,000

Average (public)
$18,708

Average (private)
$34,451

Nonresident
$13,000

Average (public)
$29,793

Average (private)
$34,451

0 10 20 30 40 50

Percentage receiving financial aid: 87%

ADMISSIONS

In the fall 2011 first-year class, 1002 applied, 249 were accepted, and 177 enrolled. Figures in the above capsule and in this profile are approximate. One transfer enrolled. The median GPA of the most recent first-year class was 2.8.

Requirements

Applicants must have a bachelor's degree and take the LSAT. Minimum acceptable GPA is 2.0 on a scale of 4.0. The most important admission factors include LSAT results, GPA, and academic achievement. No specific undergraduate courses are required. Candidates are not interviewed.

Procedure

Applicants should submit an application form, LSAT results, transcripts, 2 letters of recommendation, and a personal statement. Notification of the admissions decision begins in February. The latest acceptable LSAT test date for fall entry is February. Check with the school for current application deadlines. The law school uses the LSAC.

Special

The law school recruits minority and disadvantaged students by participating in various programs at minority feeder schools. Requirements are not different for out-of-state students. Transfer students must have one year of credit, MUST have a minimum GPA of 2.5, MUST have attended an ABA-approved law school, and must spend at least 1 year at the law center if transferring from a Louisiana law school or 2 if transferring from others.

Costs

Tuition and fees for the 2011–2012 academic year are $7,000 for full-time in-state students and $13,000 for out-of-state students. Tuition for part-time students is $3,000 in-state and $8,000 out-of-state. On-campus room and board costs about $8,000 annually; books and supplies run $1,900.

Financial Aid

About 87% of current law students received some form of aid. The average annual amount of aid from all sources combined, including scholarships, loans, and work contracts, was $17,022; maximum, $21,622. Awards are based on need and merit. The required financial statement is the FAFSA. Check with the school for current application deadlines. First-year students are notified about their financial aid application at time of acceptance.

About the Law School

Southern University and A & M College Law Center was established in 1947 and is a public institution. The campus is in an urban area in Baton Rouge. The primary mission of the law school is to prepare students for the practice of law with specific emphasis upon minorities and the disadvantaged; the program of study is designed to give students a comprehensive knowledge of both the civil law and common law and knowledge of a lawyer's ethics and responsibility to society. Students have access to federal, state, county, city, and local agencies, courts, correctional facilities, law firms, and legal aid organizations in the Baton Rouge area. Housing for students is convenient and ample. About 90% of the law school facilities are accessible to the physically disabled.

Calendar

The law school operates on a traditional semester basis. Courses for full-time students are offered days only, and must be completed within 5 years. There is no part-time program. New students are admitted in the fall. There is a 6-week summer session. Transferable summer courses are offered.

Programs

The following joint degree may be earned: J.D./M.P.A. (Juris Doctor/Master of Public Administration).

Required

To earn the J.D., candidates must complete 96 total credits, of which 75 are for required courses. They must maintain a minimum GPA of 2.0 in the required courses. The following first-year courses are required of all students: Basic Civil Procedure, Civil Law Property, Constitutional Law I, Contracts, Criminal Law, Family Law, Legal Research, Legal Writing I and II, Obligations, and Torts I and II. Required upper-level courses consist of Advanced Legal Writing I and II, Agency and Partnership, Civil Procedure I and II, Commercial Papers, Conflict of Laws, Constitutional Law II, Corporations, Criminal Procedure, Evidence, Federal Jurisdiction and Procedure, Professional Responsibility, Sales and Leases, Security Devices, Successions and Donations, and Trial Advocacy. The required orientation program for first-year students is a 1- or 2-day program, with emphasis on analysis, reading comprehension, case briefing, and communication skills.

Electives

Administrative, Juvenile, Criminal, Elderly, Tax, and Domestic Law clinics are limited to third-year students who may earn 6 credit hours. Seminars are available in various subject areas for second- and third-year students. Individual student research projects are available for 1 credit hour under the supervision of a professor. Nationally recognized legal scholars are invited each semester to lecture on current issues. At least 3 lectures are scheduled during the school year. First-year students are required to participate in 1 monthly session and tutorial programs 2 times a week. The most widely taken electives are Civil

Phone: 225-771-5340
800-537-1135
Fax: 225-771-2121
E-mail: vwilkerson@sulc.edu
Web: www.sulc.edu

Contact

Jerome Harris, Director of Financial Aid, 225-771-2141 for financial aid information.

LOUISIANA

Rights, Law Office Practice, and Workers' Compensation.

Graduation Requirements

In order to graduate, candidates must have a GPA of 2.0 and must meet a residency requirement (6 semesters).

Organizations

Students edit the *Southern University Law Review* and the student newspaper, *The Public Defender*. Moot court competitions include the annual National Moot Court competition, the In-House Round Robin, and Thurgood Marshall competitions. Student organizations, local chapters of national associations, and campus organizations include Student Bar Association, Black Law Students Association, Student Trial Lawyers Association, Phi Alpha Delta, Delta Theta Phi, ABA-Law Student Division, Environmental Law Society, Women in Law, and Sports and Entertainment Legal Association.

Library

The law library contains 453,396 hardcopy volumes and 206,603 microform volume equivalents, and subscribes to 731 serial publications. Such online databases and networks as CALI, DIALOG, Legal-Trac, LEXIS, LOIS, NEXIS, OCLC First Search, and WESTLAW are available to law students for research. Special library collections include civil rights and civil law collections, state and federal depositories, and a South African Law Collection. The ratio of library volumes to faculty is 16,193 to 1 and to students is 1,098 to 1. The ratio of seats in the library to students is 1 to 65.

Faculty

The law school has 28 full-time and 24 part-time faculty members, of whom 19 are women. According to AAUP standards for Category IIA institutions, faculty salaries are well below average. About 20% of full-time faculty have a graduate law degree in addition to the J.D.; about 15% of part-time faculty have one. The ratio of full-time students to full-time faculty in an average class is 15 to 1; in a clinic, 12 to 1. The law school has a regular program of bringing visiting professors and other distinguished lecturers and visitors to campus.

Students

About 48% of the student body are women; 69%, minorities; 68%, African American, and 1% Asian American. The majority of students come from the South (96%). The average age of entering students is 27; age range is 22 to 54. About 60% of students enter directly from undergraduate school, 20% have a graduate degree, and 40% have worked full-time prior to entering law school. About 10% drop out after the first year for academic or personal reasons; 90% remain to receive a law degree.

Placement

Services available through: a separate law school placement center.
Special features: web site information on job opportunities and newsletters from other campuses.

Full-time job interviews:	7 employers
Summer job interviews:	17 employers
Placement by graduation:	74% of class
Placement within 9 months:	26% of class

Areas of placement:

Private practice 2–10 attorneys	24%
Private practice 11–25 attorneys	2%
Private practice 26–50 attorneys	3%
Private practice 51–100 attorneys	5%
Judicial clerkships	21%
Solo practice	8%
Government	10%
Business/industry	6%
Academic	5%
Public interest	2%

SOUTHWESTERN UNIVERSITY

Law School

3050 Wilshire Boulevard
Los Angeles, CA 90010-1106

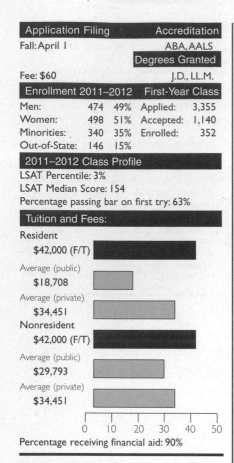

Application Filing	Accreditation
Fall: April 1	ABA, AALS

Degrees Granted
Fee: $60	J.D., LL.M.

Enrollment 2011–2012		First-Year Class	
Men:	474 49%	Applied:	3,355
Women:	498 51%	Accepted:	1,140
Minorities:	340 35%	Enrolled:	352
Out-of-State:	146 15%		

2011–2012 Class Profile
LSAT Percentile: 3%
LSAT Median Score: 154
Percentage passing bar on first try: 63%

Tuition and Fees:

Resident
$42,000 (F/T)

Average (public)
$18,708

Average (private)
$34,451

Nonresident
$42,000 (F/T)

Average (public)
$29,793

Average (private)
$34,451

0   10   20   30   40   50

Percentage receiving financial aid: 90%

ADMISSIONS

In the fall of 2011 first-year class, 3355 applied, 1140 were accepted, and 352 enrolled. Thirty-two transfers enrolled. The median LSAT percentile of the most recent first-year class was 3; the median GPA was 3.3 on a scale of 4.0.

Requirements
Applicants must have a bachelor's degree and take the LSAT. The most important admission factors include LSAT results and GPA. No specific undergraduate courses are required. Candidates are not interviewed.

Procedure
The application deadline for fall entry is April 1. Applicants should submit an application form, LSAT results, transcripts, a personal statement, a nonrefundable application fee of $60, and up to 3 letters of recommendation (strongly recommended). Notification of the admissions decision is on a rolling basis. The law school uses the LSAC.

Special
The law school recruits minority and disadvantaged students by means of participation by admissions staff in minority recruitment programs at undergraduate campuses around the country, a Law Day program held at the law school for minority junior college and university students, admissions receptions on campus, public service announcements in print and broadcast media, scholarship programs, and programs for prospective students sponsored by minority student organizations at the law school. Requirements are different for out-of-state students. Transfer students must have one year of credit, must have a minimum GPA of 2, must have attended an ABA-approved law school, must submit a personal statement, and must have a maximum of 43 transferable semester units; they must also submit a letter of good standing from that school's dean.

Financial Aid

About 90% of current law students receive some form of aid. The average annual amount of aid from all sources combined, including scholarships, loans, and work contracts, is $25,000; maximum, $45,000. Awards are based on need and merit combined. Required financial statements are the FAFSA and the school's financial aid application. The aid application deadline for fall entry is June 1. Special funds for minority or disadvantaged students consist of approximately a dozen different scholarship funds, the most significant of which is the John J. Schumacher Minority Leadership Scholarship Program for outstanding academic and leadership potential. First-year students are notified about their financial aid application within 2 weeks of acceptance.

About the Law School

Southwestern University Law School was established in 1911 and is a private institution. The 2-acre campus is in an urban area in Los Angeles. The primary mission of the law school is to produce, through full-time, part-time, traditional, and non-traditional Juris Doctorate and Master of Laws programs, highly skilled graduates who are capable of integrating theory and practice to meet the challenges of the twenty-first century. With a faculty committed to promoting the highest level of professionalism, Southwestern strives to create a vibrant and diverse academic community with a student-centered approach to legal education. Students have access to federal, state, county, city, and local agencies, courts, correctional facilities, law firms, and legal aid organizations in the Los Angeles area. Facilities

of special interest to law students include the renovated Bullocks Wilshire building, a historic landmark, which accommodates the law library and features state-of-the-art computer laboratories, tiered classrooms, study rooms, a fitness center, and the Julian C. Dixon Courtroom and Advocacy Center. Housing for students is not available on campus; however, apartments and homes are located nearby. About 99% of the law school facilities are accessible to the physically disabled.

Calendar

The law school operates on a traditional semester basis. Courses for full-time students are offered days only, with some evening electives available, and must be completed within 5 years. For part-time students, courses are offered both day and evening, and must be completed within 5 years. New full- and part-time students are admitted in the fall. There is an 8-week summer session. Transferable summer courses are offered.

Programs

In addition to the J.D., the law school offers the LL.M.

Required
To earn the J.D., candidates must complete 87 total credits, of which 52 are for required courses. They must maintain a minimum GPA of 2.0 in the required courses. The following first-year courses are required of all students: an elective option, Civil Procedure I and II, Contracts I and II, Criminal Law, Legal Analysis, Writing and Skills I and II, Property, and Torts. Required upper-level courses consist of a seminar that satisfies a writing requirement, Business Associations, Constitutional Law I and II, Evidence, and Legal Profession. Simulation training is part of required courses such as Legal Analysis, Writing, and Skills and electives such as Civil Pre-Trial Practice, Interviewing, Counseling and Negotiating, and Trial Advocacy. The required orientation program for first-year students is a week-long program featuring formal presentations by deans and faculty, a Legal Process course, a luncheon/dinner for students and faculty members, and panels with current students.

Electives
The Law School offers concentrations in corporate law, criminal law, entertainment law, environmental law, family law, intellectual property law, international law, juvenile law, labor law, litigation, media

Phone: 213-738-6717
Fax: 213-383-1688
E-mail: admissions@swlaw.edu
Web: www.swlaw.edu

Contact
Lisa Gear, Admissions Director, 213-738-6717 for general inquiries; Wayne Mahoney, Financial Aid Director, 213-738-6719 for financial aid information.

law, sports law, tax law, torts and insurance, technology, and innovation and commercialization. In addition, a Children's Rights Clinic, Immigration Rights Clinic, externships, and a simulated clinical experience are available through courses such as Legal Analysis, Writing, and Skills, Interviewing, Counseling and Negotiation, and Trial Advocacy. Credit varies per experience (2 to 10 units). Seminars offered for 2 units require in-depth research, analysis, and writing. Titles encompass many areas of the law, including intellectual property, international law, and private and public sector administrative issues. Practical experience may be gained through more than 100 part- and full-time externships available in the judiciary, public interest law firms, federal, state, and local government offices, and entertainment industry settings. Two to ten units per externship placement may be earned on a credit/no credit basis. A limited number of judicial externships in Mexican and Argentine courts are also available through the summer program in Guatajuato, Mexico and Buenos Aires, Argentina, as well as legal organizations through the summer program in Vancouver, Canada. Paid faculty research assistant positions are available. Special lecture series include the Law Review Distinguished Lecture Series, Faculty Speakers Committee Lecture Series, Career Development Panels, Public Interest Law Speakers, Treusch Public Service Lecture, "Conversations with" Entertainment Law Series, and a variety of speakers presented by student organizations. Study-abroad programs featuring international and comparative law courses taught by school faculty and other international legal experts are offered in Vancouver, Canada, Buenos Aires, Argentina, London, and Guatajuato, Mexico. Formal tutorial programs for first-year students and all students on academic probation are offered. Student organizations and faculty members sponsor research and exam-writing tutorials, and librarians conduct tutorials for new law clerks. The Academic Support Program is available for a selected number of entering students the summer prior to matriculation, and for interested students throughout the academic year. Southwestern has a Diversity Affairs Director to provide counseling and programming to students from admissions to graduation and beyond. Other programs offered for minority students include a Minority Career Development seminar, other panel presentations by minority attorneys and judges, and job search skills reviews sponsored by the Placement Office in conjunction with minority bar and law student associations. A number of ethnic/minority law student organizations each have their own

programming as well. A Diversity Day for prospective students provides information on admissions and financial aid processes, and the law school also hosts regional job fairs and alumni roundtables for BLSA, APALSA, LLSA, and LGBT organizations, among others. The most widely taken electives are Copyright, Trial Advocacy, and Wills and Trusts.

Graduation Requirements
In order to graduate, candidates must have a GPA of 2.0 and must have completed the upper-division writing requirement.

Organizations
Students edit the *Southwestern University Law Review*, the *Southwestern Journal of Law and Trade in the Americas*, a law journal devoted to the legal and economic issues of North, Central, and South America, the *Journal of International Media and Entertainment Law*, a joint publication with the ABA Forum on Communications Law, and the student newspaper, *The Commentator*. Moot court competitions include the National Telecommunications Moot Court Competition, Stetson International Environmental Law Moot Court Competition, and the Burton D. Wechsler First Amendment Moot Court Competition. A formal Trial Advocacy Honors Program fields several teams at competitions around the country. Teams also compete in the National Black Law Students Association's Frederick Douglass Moot Court, Interscholastic Client Counseling, and the Interscholastic Negotiation Competitions. Law student organizations, local chapters of national associations, and campus organizations include the Women's Law Association, Entertainment and Sports Law Society, International Law Society, Phi Alpha Delta Law Fraternity, American Association for Justice, National Lawyers Guild, OUTlaw, Media Law Forum, and Environmental Law Forum.

Library
The law library contains 483,433 hard-copy volumes and 63,061 microform volume equivalents, and subscribes to 4,663 serial publications. Such online databases and networks as CALI, LEXIS, WESTLAW, Wilsonline Indexes, HeinOnline, Index to Foreign Legal Periodicals, Index to Legal Periodicals, IndexMaster, Legal Scholarship Network, LLMC Digital, Marcive, Shepard's Online, Smart CILP, United Nations Treatises, and World Trade Law.net are available to law students for research. Special library collections include U.S. and California depositories,

Placement
J.D.s awarded:	258

Services available through: the school's placement center.
Services: videotaped mock interviews conducted by alumni practitioners.
Special features: career seminars, panel presentations on various areas of law practice, workshops on job search techniques and interview strategies, joint Career Day and interview programs with other law schools, a comprehensive career resource library, and on-campus interview programs in the fall and spring.

Placement by graduation:	85% of class
Placement within 9 months:	97% of class
Average starting salary:	$52,000 to $140,000

Areas of placement:
Private practice 2–10 attorneys	26%
Private practice 11–25 attorneys	8%
Private practice 26–50 attorneys	7%
Private practice 51–100 attorneys	10%
Business/industry	15%
Government	14%
Unknown	10%
Judicial clerkships	5%
Public interest	4%
Academic	1%

a trial practice collection, and extensive collections in taxation, constitutional law, and entertainment law. The ratio of library volumes to faculty is 8,335 to 1 and to students is 497 to 1. The ratio of seats in the library to students is 1 to 2.

Faculty
The law school has 58 full-time and 33 part-time faculty members, of whom 32 are women. About 20% of full-time faculty have a graduate law degree in addition to the J.D. The ratio of full-time students to full-time faculty in an average class is 16 to 1. The law school has a regular program of bringing visiting professors and other distinguished lecturers and visitors to campus.

Students
About 51% of the student body are women; 35%, minorities; 5% African American; 16%, Asian American; 12%, Hispanic; and 1%, Native American. The majority of students come from California (85%). The average age of entering students is 27; age range is 20 to 55. About 30% of students enter directly from undergraduate school, 12% have a graduate degree, and 35% have worked full-time prior to entering law school. About 8% drop out after the first year for academic or personal reasons; 80% remain to receive a law degree.

Stanford Law School

Crown Quadrangle,
559 Nathan Abbott Way
Stanford, CA 94305-8610

Application Filing		Accreditation
Fall: February 1		ABA, AALS
		Degrees Granted
Fee: $100		J.D., LL.M., S.J.D., M.L.S., J.S.M.

Enrollment 2011–2012		First-Year Class	
Men:	327 57%	Applied:	4,248
Women:	244 43%	Accepted:	379
Minorities:	211 37%	Enrolled:	180

2011–2012 Class Profile
LSAT Median Score: 170
Percentage passing bar on first try: 96%

Tuition and Fees:

Resident
$46,080 (F/T)

Average (public)
$18,708

Average (private)
$34,451

Nonresident
$46,080 (F/T)

Average (public)
$29,793

Average (private)
$34,451

0 10 20 30 40 50

Percentage receiving financial aid: 80%

ADMISSIONS
In the fall of 2011 first-year class, 4248 applied, 379 were accepted, and 180 enrolled. Fifteen transfers enrolled. The median GPA of the most recent first-year class was 3.9.

Requirements
Applicants must have a bachelor's degree and take the LSAT. No specific undergraduate courses are required. Candidates are not interviewed.

Procedure
The application deadline for fall entry is February 1. Applicants should submit an application form, LSAT results, transcripts, a personal statement, a nonrefundable application fee of $100, 2 letters of recommendation, and a statement of good standing from the undergraduate dean. Notification of the admissions decision is on a rolling basis. The law school uses the LSAC.

Special
The law school recruits minority and disadvantaged students by attending law forums and law days, and by making individual school visits. Requirements are different for out-of-state students. Transfer students must have one year of credit, must have attended an ABA-approved law school, and must submit a personal statement.

Costs
Tuition and fees for the 2011–2012 academic year are $44,880 for all full-time students. On-campus room and board costs about $17,955 annually; books and supplies run $1,863.

Financial Aid
About 80% of current law students receive some form of aid. The maximum annual amount of aid from all sources combined, including scholarships, loans, and work contracts, is $69,915. Awards are based on need. Required financial statements are the FAFSA and Need Access Form. The aid application deadline for fall entry is March 15. First-year students are notified about their financial aid application upon receipt of the Need Access and FAFSA analyses.

About the Law School
Stanford University Stanford Law School was established in 1893 and is a private institution. The 6109-acre campus is in a suburban area 35 miles south of San Francisco. The primary mission of the law school is to be a national and world leader in the education of lawyers and in the expansion of legal knowledge through research with the ultimate aim of improving the legal orders of the domestic and global communities. Students have access to federal, state, county, city, and local agencies, courts, correctional facilities, law firms, and legal aid organizations in the Stanford area. Housing for students is guaranteed to all new students who apply for housing by a specified date and are willing to live anywhere on campus. Law students are given priority for Munger Residence Hall. All law school facilities are accessible to the physically disabled.

Calendar
The law school operates on a trimester basis. Courses are offered days only, and must be completed within 10 trimesters.

New students are admitted in the fall. There is no summer session. Transferable summer courses are not offered.

Programs
In addition to the J.D., the law school offers the LL.M., S.J.D., M.L.S., and J.S.M. Students may take relevant courses in other programs and apply credit toward the J.D.; a maximum of 31 credits may be applied. The following joint degrees may be earned: J.D./M.A. (Juris Doctor/Master of Arts), J.D./M.A. (Juris Doctor/Master of Arts with Johns Hopkins University), J.D./M.B.A. (Juris Doctor/Master of Business Administration), J.D./M.P.H. (Juris Doctor/Master of Public Health with Princeton University), J.D./M.S. (Juris Doctor/Master of Science), and J.D./Ph.D. (Juris Doctor/Doctor of Philosophy).

Required
To earn the J.D., candidates must complete 111 total credits, of which 29 are for required courses. The following first-year courses are required of all students: Civil Procedure, Constitutional Law, Contracts, Criminal Law, Federal Litigation, Legal Research and Writing, Property, and Torts. The required orientation program for first-year students is a 2-day program that includes introductions to policies, programs, and resources.

Electives
The Stanford Law School offers concentrations in corporate law, criminal law, entertainment law, environmental law, family law, intellectual property law, international law, juvenile law, labor law, litigation, maritime law, media law, securities law, sports law, tax law, and torts and insurance. In addition, the law school offers courses with clinical components from 2 to 12 units of credit in a variety of areas. A variety of seminars, worth 2 to 3 units, is offered to upper-level students each year. Externships, from 4 to 12 units of credit, are offered to upper-level students each year, typically in the Bay area. The law school offers 3 types of directed research comprising from 1 to 13 units of credit. This is an opportunity for students beyond the first-year program in law to research problems in any field of law. A wide variety of lecture series are sponsored by both the law school and its student organizations. The law school also

Phone: 650-723-4985
Fax: 650-723-0838
E-mail: *admissions@law.stanford.edu*
Web: *law.stanford.edu*

Contact
Dewayne Barnes, Associate Director of Financial Aid, 650-723-9247 for financial aid information.

offers foreign study options with a number of schools. The most widely taken electives are Evidence, Corporations, and Tax.

Graduation Requirements
In order to graduate, candidates must have completed the upper-division writing requirement and at least 1 advanced course that contains 1 or more units of ethics instruction, as well as a course comprising substantial instruction in professional skills.

Organizations
The primary law review is the *Stanford Law Review*. Students also edit the *Environmental Law Journal, Stanford Journal of Law, Business and Finance, Stanford Journal of Civil Rights and Civil Liberties,* and *Stanford Technology Law Review*. The Kirkwood Moot Court Competition is held in February each year. Law student organizations include Stanford Law Students Association. Local chapters of national associations include American Constitution Society and Federalist Society.

Library
The law library contains 441,671 hardcopy volumes and 287,048 microform volume equivalents, and subscribes to 6,922 serial publications. Such online databases and networks as CALI, CIS Universe, DIALOG, Infotrac, Legal-Trac, LEXIS, OCLC First Search, RLIN, WESTLAW, Wilsonline Indexes, BNA (Premier Package), Bloomberg Law, CEB OnLAW, CourtLink, Current Index to Legal Periodicals, Eighteenth Century Collections Online, Environmental Law Reporter, Foreign Law Guide, Foreign Legal Periodicals, Goldstein on Copyright (CCH IntelliConnect), HeinOnline, Index to Legal Periodicals and Books, Justis International Law Reports and UK Statutes and Statutory Instruments with JustCite, Knowledge Mosaic, LawInfoChina, LLMC Digital, Leadership Library and Leadership Network, Legal Scholarship Network, LexisAdvance, Manupatra, Max Planck Encyclodpedia of Public International Law (MPEPIL - Online Edition), MoML (Making of Modern Law), MoML Trials 1600–1926, RIA Checkpoint, PACER, Supreme Court Records and Briefs, TRACFED, VLex, WestlawNext, and WorldTradeLaw.net are available to law students for research. Special library

collections include U.S. government documents and California state documents. The ratio of library volumes to faculty is 9,898 to 1 and to students is 900 to 1. The ratio of seats in the library to students is 1 to 1.

Faculty
The law school has 55 full-time faculty members, of whom 17 are women. According to AAUP standards for Category I institutions, faculty salaries are well above average. The ratio of students to faculty in an average class is 9 to 1. The law school has a regular program of bringing visiting professors and other distinguished lecturers and visitors to campus. There is a chapter of the Order of the Coif.

Students
About 43% of the student body are women; 37%, minorities; 7%, African American; 10%, Asian American; and 13%, Hispanic. The average age of entering students is 25; age range is 21 to 40. About 30% of students enter directly from undergraduate school, and 25% have a graduate degree.

Placement

J.D.s awarded:	176
Services available through: a separate law school placement center.	
Services: externships are coordinated through the Director of Public Interest Programs.	
Special features: counseling and advising students regarding job search, career decisions, and public service.	
Placement within 9 months of graduation:	99% of class
Areas of placement:	
Private Practice	57%
Judicial clerkships	32%
Government	4%
Public interest	3%
Business/industry	2%
Academic	2%

Application Filing	Accreditation
Fall: March 15	ABA, AALS
	Degrees Granted
Fee: $75	J.D., LL.M.
Enrollment 2011–2012	**First-Year Class**

Men:	352	53%	Applied:	2,104
Women:	311	47%	Accepted:	689
Minorities:	99	15%	Enrolled:	208
Out-of-State:	66	10%		

2011–2012 Class Profile
LSAT Percentile: 71%
LSAT Median Score: 157
Percentage passing bar on first try: 84%

Tuition and Fees:

Resident
$20,718 (F/T)

Average (public)
$18,708

Average (private)
$34,451

Nonresident
$20,718 (F/T)

Average (public)
$29,793

Average (private)
$34,451

0 10 20 30 40 50

Percentage receiving financial aid: 95%

ADMISSIONS

In the fall of 2011 first-year class, 2104 applied, 689 were accepted, and 208 enrolled. Forty-one transfers enrolled. The median LSAT percentile of the most recent first-year class was 71; the median GPA was 3.6 on a scale of 4.0. The lowest LSAT percentile accepted was 26; the highest was 99.

Requirements
Applicants must have a bachelor's degree and take the LSAT. Minimum acceptable LSAT percentile is 44 and minimum acceptable GPA is 2.0 on a scale of 4.0. The most important admission factors include writing ability, LSAT results, and academic achievement. No specific undergraduate courses are required. Candidates are not interviewed.

Procedure
The application deadline for fall entry is March 15. Applicants should submit an application form, LSAT results,

transcripts, a personal statement, TOEFL (if applicable), a nonrefundable application fee of $75, 2 letters of recommendation, and a resume. Notification of the admissions decision is as early as December. The law school uses the LSAC.

Special
The law school recruits minority and disadvantaged students through targeted recruitment efforts at colleges with significant minority student populations and participation in a tuition waiver program for EOP, HEOP, and SEEK students. Requirements are different for out-of-state students. Transfer students must have one year of credit, must have attended an ABA-approved law school, must submit a personal statement, and must submit a letter of reference from a law professor, a letter of good standing from the current law school, the first page of the CAS report, an official law school transcript, the law school application, and the $75 application fee.

Costs

Tuition and fees for the 2011–2012 academic year are $19,020 for full-time in-state students and $32,020 for out-of-state students. On-campus room and board costs about $12,304 annually; books and supplies run $1,161.

Financial Aid

About 95% of current law students receive some form of aid. The average annual amount of aid from all sources combined, including scholarships, loans, and work contracts, is $22,900; maximum, $29,020. Awards are based on need and merit combined. The required financial statement is the FAFSA. The aid application deadline for fall entry is March 1. Special funds for minority or disadvantaged students include graduate tuition waivers based on participation in an EOP, HEOP, or SEEK program while an undergraduate. First-year students are notified about their financial aid application at time of acceptance.

About the Law School

State University of New York SUNY Buffalo Law School was established in 1887 and is a public institution. The 154-acre campus is in a suburban area 3 miles

north of Buffalo in Amherst, New York. The primary mission of the law school is to provide an outstanding legal education through interdisciplinary teaching that emphasizes the role lawyers and the law play within the broader context of American society while providing practice-ready attorneys. Students have access to federal, state, county, city, and local agencies, courts, correctional facilities, law firms, and legal aid organizations in the Buffalo area. Facilities of special interest to law students include the nation's only fully functioning state court housed on a university campus. Housing for students is available in apartment-style on-campus housing, as well as ample graduate student housing. All law school facilities are accessible to the physically disabled.

Calendar

The law school operates on a 4-1-4 modified semester. Courses are offered both day and evening, and must be completed within 5 years. New students are admitted in the fall. There is a 7-week summer session. Transferable summer courses are offered.

Programs

In addition to the J.D., the law school offers the LL.M. Students may take relevant courses in other programs and apply credit toward the J.D.; a maximum of 9 credits may be applied. The following joint degrees may be earned: J.D./M.A. (Juris Doctor/Master of Applied Economics), J.D./M.B.A. (Juris Doctor/Master of Business Administration), J.D./M.L.S (Juris Doctor/Master of Library Science), J.D./M.P.H. (Juris Doctor/Master of Public Health), J.D./M.S.W. (Juris Doctor/Master of Social Work), J.D./M.U.P. (Juris Doctor/Master of Urban Planning), J.D./Ph.D. (Juris Doctor/Doctor of Philosophy), and J.D./Pharm.D. (Juris Doctor/Doctor of Pharmacy).

Required
To earn the J.D., candidates must complete 90 total credits, of which 40 are for required courses. The following first-year courses are required of all students: Civil Procedure, Constitutional Law, Contracts, Criminal law, Legal Analysis, Writing, and Research, Legal Profession and Ethics, Property, and Torts. Required upper-level courses consist of a seminar, a skills course, and Advanced Legal Analysis, Writing, and Research. The required orientation

Phone: 716-645-2907
Fax: 716-645-6676
E-mail: lwiley@buffalo.edu ·
Web: www.law.buffalo.edu

Contact

Lillie Wiley-Upshaw, Vice Dean, 716-645-2907 for general inquiries; Brezetta Stevenson, Financial Aid Coordinator, 716-645-7324 for financial aid information.

NEW YORK

program for first-year students lasts 1 week and includes an introduction to faculty, administrators, and student organizations as well as an introductory course on legal methods, reasoning, argument, legal institutions, ethics, and the profession.

Electives

The SUNY Buffalo Law School offers concentrations in corporate law, criminal law, environmental law, family law, intellectual property law, international law, labor law, litigation, tax law, technology and intellectual property. In addition, upper-division students may take clinical courses for 3 to 4 credit hours each semester for up to 4 semesters after the first year of law school. Topics include affordable housing; elder law; community economic development; securities law; mediation; environment and policy law; environment and development; and women, children and social justice. Upper-division students must take at least one 3-credit hour seminar. Numerous seminars are offered and students may enroll in multiple seminars. Externships are available in public interest, governmental, and international settings. Upper-division students may take individual research for 3 to 6 credit hours and may participate in any of several law school research centers. Field placements are associated with various courses, including child welfare, criminal law, legislative externships, and judicial clerkships. Special lecture series include the Mitchell Lecture and Baldy Center Lecture Series. There are summer internships abroad with leading human rights organizations through the Buffalo Human Rights Center. There is also a semester-long program entitled the University of Buffalo Law School's New York City Program in Finance and Law, which requires a student to live in New York City for one semester. Academic support is available for students in need with a full-time faculty member. Special interest group programs include the Buffalo Public Interest Law Program, Domestic Violence Task Force, and Prison Task Force. The most widely taken electives are Corporations, Evidence, and Federal Income Tax I.

Graduation Requirements

In order to graduate, candidates must have completed the upper-division writing requirement and 90 credit hours.

Organizations

Students edit the *Buffalo Law Review, Buffalo Human Rights Law Review, Buffalo Women's Law Journal, Buffalo Intellectual Property Law Journal, Buffalo Interest Law Journal*, and the newspaper, *The Opinion*. Other publications include the *New Criminal Law Review, Buffalo Human Rights Law Review*, and the *ABA Journal of Affordable Housing and Community Development Law*. Moot court competitions include the Desmond Intramural held in November, the Mugel National Tax Moot Court held in the spring, and the Herbert Wechsler National Criminal Moot Court. Other competitions include Jessup International Moot Court Competition, First Year Moot Court Competition, Buffalo-Niagara Invitational Mock Trial Tournament, and Frederick Douglass Moot Court. Law student organizations, local chapters of national associations, and campus organizations include the Asian American Law Students Association, Black Law Students Association, Latin American Law Students Association, Sports and Entertainment Law Society, Alternative Dispute Resolution Group, Buffalo Criminal Law Society, Association of Trial Lawyers of America, Phi Alpha Delta, and American Civil Liberties Union.

Library

The law library contains 299,106 hardcopy volumes and 295,016 microform volume equivalents, and subscribes to 6,627 serial publications. Such online databases and networks as CALI, CIS Universe, Dow-Jones, Infotrac, Legal-Trac, LEXIS, Mathew Bender, OCLC First Search, WESTLAW, Wilsonline Indexes, LRS (New York Legislation), and others are available to law students for research. Special library collections include a U.S. government document depository, the Morris L. Cohen rare book collection, the papers of John Lord O'Brian, the Berman Human Rights collection, and a substantial United Nations documents collection. The ratio of library volumes to faculty is 10,609 to 1 and to students is 792 to 1. The ratio of seats in the library to students is 1 to 1.

Faculty

The law school has 57 full-time and 116 part-time faculty members, of whom 62 are women. According to AAUP

Placement

J.D.s awarded:	244

Services available through: a separate law school placement center and the university placement center.

Services: alumni mentoring program, alumni career panels, and training and skills-building programs that provide networking opportunities.

Special features: an employment bulletin that is sent free to graduates, a unique 1L mentorship program, required individual career counseling for 1LS, and 3LS, robust programming, and podcast series.

Full-time job interviews:	18 employers
Summer job interviews:	27 employers
Placement by graduation:	67% of class
Placement within 9 months:	96% of class
Average starting salary:	$25,000 to $160,000

Areas of placement:

Private practice 2–10 attorneys	26%
Private practice 11–25 attorneys	8%
Private practice 26–50 attorneys	5%
Private practice 51–100 attorneys	5%
Business/industry	14%
Government	13%
Public interest	7%
Academic	4%
Military	3%
Judicial clerkships	2%

standards for Category I institutions, faculty salaries are above average. About 26% of full-time faculty have a graduate law degree in addition to the J.D.; about 4% of part-time faculty have one. The ratio of full-time students to full-time faculty in an average class is 12 to 1; in a clinic, 10 to 1. The law school has a regular program of bringing visiting professors and other distinguished lecturers and visitors to campus.

Students

About 47% of the student body are women; 15%, minorities; 4%, African American; 4%, Asian American; 3%, Hispanic; and 1%, Native American. The majority of students come from New York (90%). The average age of entering students is 25; age range is 20 to 57. About 44% of students enter directly from undergraduate school, 6% have a graduate degree, and 37% have worked full-time prior to entering law school. About 1% drop out after the first year for academic or personal reasons; 96% remain to receive a law degree.

Stetson University College of Law

1401 61st Street South
Gulfport, FL 33707

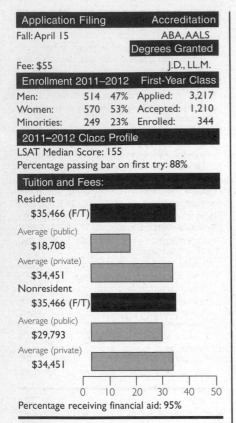

Application Filing	Accreditation
Fall: April 15	ABA, AALS
	Degrees Granted
Fee: $55	J.D., LL.M.

Enrollment 2011–2012		First-Year Class	
Men:	514 47%	Applied:	3,217
Women:	570 53%	Accepted:	1,210
Minorities:	249 23%	Enrolled:	344

2011–2012 Class Profile
LSAT Median Score: 155
Percentage passing bar on first try: 88%

Tuition and Fees:

Resident
$35,466 (F/T)

Average (public)
$18,708

Average (private)
$34,451

Nonresident
$35,466 (F/T)

Average (public)
$29,793

Average (private)
$34,451

Percentage receiving financial aid: 95%

ADMISSIONS

In the fall of 2011 first-year class, 3217 applied, 1210 were accepted, and 344 enrolled. Twelve transfers enrolled. The median GPA of the most recent first-year class was 3.4.

Requirements
Applicants must have a bachelor's degree and take the LSAT. No specific undergraduate courses are required. Candidates are not interviewed.

Procedure
The application deadline for fall entry is April 15. Applicants should submit an application form, LSAT results, transcripts, a personal statement, TOEFL (if applicable), a nonrefundable application fee of $55, 2 letters of recommendation, a personal statement, and a resume. Notification of the admissions decision is on a rolling basis. The law school uses the LSAC.

Special
The law school recruits minority and disadvantaged students by means of CRS mailings, CLEO, law school forums, college campus visits to minority-oriented schools, the Minority Youth Prelaw Conference, and diversity initiatives. Requirements are different for out-of-state students. Transfer students must have one year of credit, must have attended an ABA-approved law school, and must submit a personal statement and a complete official transcript, including their standing at their current law school.

Costs

Tuition and fees for the 2011–2012 academic year are $35,146 for all full-time students. Tuition for part-time students is $24,282 for in-state students and $24,282 out-of-state.

Financial Aid

About 95% of current law students receive some form of aid. The average annual amount of aid from all sources combined, including scholarships, loans, and work contracts, is $18,959; maximum, $40,146. Awards are based on need and merit combined. The required financial statement is the FAFSA. The aid application deadline for fall entry is open. Special funds for minority or disadvantaged students include Stetson diversity scholarships and matching CLEO scholarships. First-year students are notified about their financial aid application after the confirmation deposit is paid.

About the Law School

Stetson University College of Law was established in 1900 and is a private institution. The 21-acre campus is in a suburban area of Gulfport, Florida, with a satellite campus in downtown Tampa. Stetson University College of Law provides a dynamic and supportive scholarly community in which students learn, inside and outside of the classroom and by example, to become outstanding lawyers and leaders who serve the profession and society. Students have access to federal, state, county, city, and local agencies, courts, correctional facilities, law firms, and legal aid organizations in the Gulfport area. Facilities of special interest to law students include 7 courtrooms. Housing for students is available in residence halls, 2-bedroom apartments, and school-owned houses; also, housing options are available in the community. All law school facilities are accessible to the physically disabled.

Calendar

The law school operates on a traditional semester basis. Courses for full-time students are offered both day and evening, and must be completed within 3 years. For part-time students, courses are offered evenings only, and must be completed within 4 years. New full- and part-time students are admitted in the fall. There is an 8-week summer session. Transferable summer courses are offered.

Programs

In addition to the J.D., the law school offers the LL.M. The following joint degrees may be earned: J.D./M.B.A. (Juris Doctor/Master of Business Administration), J.D./M.D. (Juris Doctor/Doctor of Medicine), and J.D./M.P.H. (Juris Doctor/Master of Public Health).

Required
To earn the J.D., candidates must complete 88 total credits, of which 38 are for required courses. They must maintain a minimum GPA of 2.3 in the required courses. The following first-year courses are required of all students: Civil Procedure, Constitutional Law, Contracts I and II, Criminal Law, Real Property, Research and Writing I and II, and Torts. Required upper-level courses consist of a code requirement, a skills requirement, a writing requirement, an administrative law requirement, Evidence, and Professional Responsibility. The required orientation program for first-year students is a 3-day program that introduces the students to the three Cs of professionalism-character, competence, and commitment. The competence (or academic portion) is led by full-time faculty members. The orientation includes pro bono activities and character development activities.

Electives
The Stetson University College of Law offers concentrations in international law, litigation, advocacy, and elder law. In addition, clinic programs, available to third-year students, include the Civil Poverty Clinic, Elder Consumer Protection Clinic,

Phone: 727-562-7802
877-LAW STET
Fax: 727-343-0136
E-mail: zuppo@law.stetson.edu
Web: www.law.stetson.edu

Contact

Laura Zuppo, Executive Director of Admissions, 727-562-7802 for general inquiries and financial aid information.

Labor Law Clinic, Local Government Clinic, Prosecution Clinic, and Public Defender Clinic. Most clinics are for 5 credit hours. Many seminars for second- and third-year students are offered each year. Internships with federal and state court judges (trial, appellate, and supreme court) are available for upper-level students for 4 credit hours or 12 hours for supreme court. Practicum programs are available with state and federal agencies. There is a summer internship program in Washington D.C. Individual research projects may be arranged for 1 or 2 credit hours. An Inns of Court program, featuring a prominent speaker, is offered. Other programs are sponsored by faculty, student organizations, and the Office of Career Development. Second- and third-year students may participate in study-abroad programs offered through Stetson and other law schools. Stetson sponsors summer-abroad programs in Granada, Spain; Tianjin, China; Buenos Aires, Argentina; and The Hague, the Netherlands. There is also a winter intercession program in the Cayman Islands and a spring break travel-abroad program. Individual tutors are available for students. Stetson has a comprehensive Academic Success Program. Special interest group programs include an honors program for top students, Black Law Students Association, Student Bar Association, Ambassador program, HBA, AALSA, SALSA, and LAMBDA. The most widely taken electives are Trial Advocacy, Alternative Dispute Resolution, and Criminal Procedure.

Graduation Requirements

In order to graduate, candidates must have a GPA of 2.3, must have completed the upper-division writing requirement, and must have completed 60 hours of public service.

Organizations

Students edit the *Stetson Law Review*, the peer-edited journals *Journal of International Aging Law and Policy* and *Journal of Wildlife and Policy,* and the student newspaper *The Brief.* Annually, students compete in 16 to 18 competitions, including the National Moot Court, Willem C. Vis International Commercial Arbitration Moot, and the Jessup International Moot Court competitions. Other competitions include state, regional and national mock trial competitions; regional and national

client counseling competitions; regional and national mediation competitions; and regional and national negotiation competitions. Law student organizations, local chapters of national associations, and campus organizations include the Elder Law Society, Environmental Law Society, International Law Society, Phi Alpha Delta, Phi Delta Phi, Business Law Society, Student Bar Association, ABA-Law Student Division, and Black Law Students Association.

Library

The law library contains 420,000 hard-copy volumes and 53,670 microform volume equivalents, and subscribes to 2,607 serial publications. Such online databases and networks as CALI, CIS Universe, DIALOG, Infotrac, Legal-Trac, LEXIS, Mathew Bender, OCLC First Search, WESTLAW, BNA Antitrust and Trade Regulation Report, BNA Criminal Law Reporter, BNA Family Law Report, BNA Labor and Employment Law Library, the Annals of the American Academy of Political and Social Science, Value Line Research and Historial Reports, and the Journal of Sport and Social Issues are available to law students for research. Special library collections include a depository for selected U.S. government publications and a Nuremburg Trials historial archival collection. The ratio of library volumes to faculty is 8,077 to 1 and to students is 387 to 1. The ratio of seats in the library to students is 1 to 2.

Faculty

The law school has 54 full-time and 54 part-time faculty members, of whom 44 are women. About 35% of full-time faculty have a graduate law degree in addition to the J.D.; about 5% of part-time faculty have one. The ratio of full-time students to full-time faculty in an average class is 16 to 1; in a clinic, 10 to 1. The law school has a regular program of bringing visiting professors and other distinguished lecturers and visitors to campus.

Students

About 53% of the student body are women; 23%, minorities; 7%, African American; 3%, Asian American; 9%, Hispanic; and 1%, Native American. The average age of entering students is 24; age range is 19 to 55. About 3% drop out after the first year for academic or personal reasons; 97% remain to receive a law degree.

Placement

J.D.s awarded:	352
Services available through: a separate law school placement center.	
Services: on-campus interviewing programs in the fall and spring semesters.	
Special features: resource room for student use, including computers for job searches on LexisNexis and WESTLAW, a fax machine, and a laser printer for resume and cover letter production.	
Placement within 9 months of graduation:	85% of class
Average starting salary:	$42,000 to $110,000
Areas of placement:	
Private practice 2–10 attorneys	18%
Private practice 11–25 attorneys	12%
Private practice 26–50 attorneys	7%
Private practice 51–100 attorneys	4%
Government	21%
Business/industry	13%
Public interest	7%
Judicial clerkships	5%
Military	2%
Academic	1%

Application Filing	Accreditation
Fall: March 1	ABA, AALS
	Degrees Granted
Fee: $60	J.D., LL.M., S.J.D.

Enrollment 2011–2012		First-Year Class	
Men:	890 53%	Applied:	2,934
Women:	791 47%	Accepted:	2,038
Minorities:	319 19%	Enrolled:	538
Out-of-State:	639 38%		

2011–2012 Class Profile
LSAT Percentile: 64%
LSAT Median Score: 155
Percentage passing bar on first try: 87%

Tuition and Fees:

Resident
$42,660 (F/T)

Average (public)
$18,708

Average (private)
$34,451

Nonresident
$42,660 (F/T)

Average (public)
$29,793

Average (private)
$34,451

0   10   20   30   40   50

ADMISSIONS

In the fall of 2011 first-year class, 2934 applied, 2038 were accepted, and 538 enrolled. Sixteen transfers enrolled. The median LSAT percentile of the most recent first-year class was 64; the median GPA was 3.3 on a scale of 4.0.

Requirements
Applicants must have a bachelor's degree and take the LSAT. The most important admission factors include academic achievement, GPA, and LSAT results. No specific undergraduate courses are required. Candidates are interviewed.

Procedure
The application deadline for fall entry is March 1. Applicants should submit an application form, LSAT results, transcripts, a personal statement, TOEFL (if applicable), a nonrefundable application fee of $60, and a letter of recommendation. Accepted students must pay a $500 tuition deposit by April 15; a second deposit of $300 is due June 1. Notification of the admissions decision is on a rolling basis. The law school uses the LSAC.

Special
The law school recruits minority and disadvantaged students by means of an admissions committee, which gives consideration to students who have overcome economic and social disadvantages or have been subjected to discrimination of any form. Requirements are different for out-of-state students. Transfer students must have one year of credit, must have a minimum GPA of 3, must have attended an ABA-approved law school, must submit a personal statement, and must be in good academic standing. The application must be completed by early June. The dean of each previous law school must provide a letter of good standing and a final transcript.

Costs

Tuition and fees for the 2011–2012 academic year are $42,540 for all full-time students. Tuition for part-time students is $31,904 for in-state students and $31,904 out-of-state. Books and supplies run $1,000.

Financial Aid

The average annual amount of aid from all sources combined, including scholarships, loans, and work contracts, is $39,606; maximum, $61,452. Awards are based on need and merit combined. Required financial statements are the FAFSA, Need Access form, and a federal income tax return. The aid application deadline for fall entry is March 1. Special funds for minority or disadvantaged students are available through a number of financial assistance programs. First-year students are notified about their financial aid application on a rolling basis, beginning March 1st, for accepted students.

About the Law School

Suffolk University Law School was established in 1906 and is a private institution. The campus is in downtown Boston on the Freedom Trail. The primary mission of the law school is to give capable men and women the opportunity to study law regardless of background or circumstances. Now one of the largest law schools in the country, Suffolk University Law School has remained true to its mission to provide excellent education and training for a diverse student body. Students have access to federal, state, county, city, and local agencies, courts, correctional facilities, law firms, and legal aid organizations in the Boston area. Facilities of special interest to law students include the Center for International Legal Studies, Juvenile Justice Center, and Rappaport Center for Law and Public Services. Housing for students is not available on campus, but assistance for obtaining housing in the area is available. All law school facilities are accessible to the physically disabled.

Calendar

The law school operates on a traditional semester basis. Courses for full-time students are offered both day and evening, and must be completed within 3 years. For part-time students, courses are offered both day and evening, and must be completed within 4 years. New full- and part-time students are admitted in the fall. There is a 10-week summer session. Transferable summer courses are offered.

Programs

In addition to the J.D., the law school offers the LL.M. and S.J.D. Students may take relevant courses in other programs and apply credit toward the J.D.; a maximum of 12 credits may be applied. The following joint degrees may be earned: J.D./M.B.A. (Juris Doctor/Master of Business Administration), J.D./M.P.A. (Juris Doctor/Master of Public Administration), J.D./M.S.C.J. (Juris Doctor/Master of Criminal Justice), J.D./M.S.F. (Juris Doctor/Master of Science in Finance), and J.D./M.S.I.E. (Juris Doctor/Master of Science in International Economics).

Required
To earn the J.D., candidates must complete 84 total credits, of which 43 are for required courses. They must maintain a minimum GPA of 2.0 in the required courses. The following first-year courses are required of all students: Civil Procedure, Constitutional Law, Contracts, Criminal Law, Legal Practice Skills, Property, and Torts. Required upper-level courses consist of base menu courses, Professional Responsibility, and skills menu courses. Clinical courses are

Phone: 617-573-8144
Fax: 617-523-1367
Web: www.law.suffolk.edu

Contact

Gail Ellis, Dean of Admissions, 617-573-8144 for general inquiries; Jana Cox, Director of Financial Aid, 617-573-8147 for financial aid information.

MASSACHUSETTS

not required, but are strongly recommended. The required orientation program for first-year students includes an introduction to classmates, professors, and law school administrators in various receptions and programs. New students also meet with upper-class students and are trained on the school's computer systems. They participate in a program aimed at preparing them for what to expect during their first year of law school and are introduced to case briefing, outlining, and time management.

Electives

The law school offers concentrations in intellectual property law, international law, litigation, health and biomedical law, business law, and financial services. In addition, clinic programs include the Suffolk Defenders, Suffolk Prosecutors, and Battered Women's Clinic. Seminars are available in such areas as advanced evidence, family law practice, and jurisprudence. The Civil and Judicial Internship Program allows students to gain 2 to 5 credits per semester for supervised legal work performed for government or nonprofit agencies, private law firms and companies, and state and federal courts. Many students act as research assistants for individual faculty members. Work-study programs are available. The Donahue Lecture Series presents 3 to 4 national scholars who lecture on various topics in legal education. Students may participate in study-abroad programs. A summer study-abroad program is available at the University of Lund in Lund, Sweden. Tutorial programs are available through the Academic Support Program and the Peer Mentoring Program. There are multicultural groups such as the Asian Pacific American Law Students Association, Black Law Students Association, Hispanic Law Students Association, Native American Law Students Association, and South Asian Law Students Association. The most widely taken electives are Evidence, Family Law, and Corporations.

Graduation Requirements

In order to graduate, candidates must have a GPA of 2.0 and must have completed the upper-division writing requirement.

Organizations

The primary law review is the *Suffolk University Law Review*. Other law reviews include the *Suffolk Transnational Law Review; the Journal of High Technology*, an online publication; the *Journal of Health and Biomedical Law*; and the *Journal of Trial and Appellate Advocacy*. The student newspaper is the *Dicta*. Moot court competitions include the Justice Tom C. Clark Appellate Advocacy Competition, the Walter H. McLaughlin Appellate Advocacy Competition, 2nd Year Day/3rd Year Mock Trial Competition, 3rd Year Day/4th Year Evening Mock Trial Competition, Burton D. Wechsler First Amendment Moot Court Competition, and National Civil Trial Competition. Law student organizations include the International Law Society, Student Bar Association, Phi Alpha Delta, Phi Delta Phi, the National Lawyers Guild, National Women's Law Student Association, Shelter Legal Services, ISAIL, and SPILG.

Library

The law library contains 150,312 hardcopy volumes and 205,385 microform volume equivalents, and subscribes to 1,294 serial publications. Such online databases and networks as CALI, CIS Universe, Legal-Trac, LEXIS, OCLC First Search, WESTLAW, Wilsonline Indexes, HeinOnline, EBSCO Host, BNA, JSTOR, Social Law Library Databases, and others are available to law students for research. Special library collections include collections on lawyers and judges, famous trials, law and literature, environmental law, criminal law, intellectual property law, biomedical law, and trial practice materials. The ratio of library volumes to faculty is 1,634 to 1 and to students is 89 to 1. The ratio of seats in the library to students is 1 to 2.

Faculty

The law school has 92 full-time and 138 part-time faculty members, of whom 73 are women. According to AAUP standards for Category IIA institutions, faculty salaries are well above average. About 38% of full-time faculty have a graduate law degree in addition to the J.D.; about 20% of part-time faculty have one. The ratio of full-time students to full-time faculty in an average class is 17 to 1; in a clinic, 10 to 1. The law school has a regular program of bringing visiting professors and other distinguished lecturers and visitors to campus.

Placement

J.D.s awarded:	495

Services available through: a separate law school placement center.

Services: professional directories, notices of employment, judicial clerkship information, library facilities for employment information, and panel discussions.

Special features: the fall on-campus recruitment program, to which the Career Services Office invites law firms, corporations, legal services offices, and state and federal agencies to interview students for employment. The school is also a member of the Massachusetts Law School Consortium and the Northeast Law School Consortium, which sponsor other recruitment and career-related programs.

Full-time job interviews:	14 employers
Summer job interviews:	37 employers
Placement by graduation:	47% of class
Placement within 9 months:	84% of class
Areas of placement:	
Private practice 2–10 attorneys	27%
Private practice 11–25 attorneys	6%
Private practice 26–50 attorneys	2%
Private practice 51–100 attorneys	2%
Business/industry	24%
Government	13%
Academic	6%
Judicial clerkships	3%
Public interest	3%
Military	1%

Students

About 47% of the student body are women; 19%, minorities; 3%, African American; 9%, Asian American; and 6%, Hispanic. The majority of students come from Massachusetts (62%). The average age of entering students is 25; age range is 21 to 63. About 26% of students enter directly from undergraduate school, and 7% have a graduate degree. About 7% drop out after the first year for academic or personal reasons; 93% remain to receive a law degree.

College of Law

Office of Admissions and Financial Aid,
Suite 340
Syracuse, NY 13244-1030

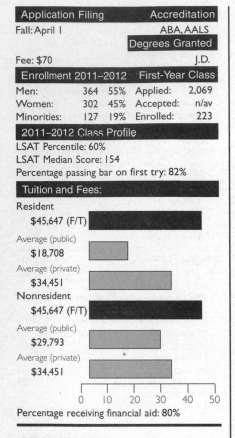

Application Filing	Accreditation
Fall: April 1	ABA, AALS
	Degrees Granted
Fee: $70	J.D.

Enrollment 2011–2012		First-Year Class	
Men:	364 55%	Applied:	2,069
Women:	302 45%	Accepted:	n/av
Minorities:	127 19%	Enrolled:	223

2011–2012 Class Profile
LSAT Percentile: 60%
LSAT Median Score: 154
Percentage passing bar on first try: 82%

Tuition and Fees:

Resident
$45,647 (F/T)

Average (public)
$18,708

Average (private)
$34,451

Nonresident
$45,647 (F/T)

Average (public)
$29,793

Average (private)
$34,451

0 10 20 30 40 50

Percentage receiving financial aid: 80%

ADMISSIONS

The median LSAT percentile of a recent first-year class was 60; the median GPA was 3.3 on a scale of 4.0.

Requirements

Applicants must have a bachelor's degree and take the LSAT. The most important admission factors include GPA, LSAT results, and academic achievement. No specific undergraduate courses are required. Candidates are not interviewed.

Procedure

The application deadline for fall entry is April 1. Applicants should submit an application form, LSAT results, transcripts, a personal statement, a nonrefundable application fee of $70, 2 letters of recommendation, and a resume. Notification of the admissions decision is on a rolling basis from January to March. The law school uses the LSAC.

Special

The law school recruits minority and disadvantaged students by means of an in-house Legal Education Opportunity Program, students of color law forums, the CLEO program, and by application review. Requirements are different for out-of-state students. Transfer students must have one year of credit, must have a minimum GPA of 3, must have attended an ABA-approved law school, and must submit a personal statement.

Costs

Tuition and fees for the 2011–2012 academic year are $44,000 for all full-time students. On-campus room and board costs about $11,270 annually; books and supplies run $1,250.

Financial Aid

About 80% of current law students receive some form of aid. Awards are based on need and merit combined. Required financial statements are the FAFSA, the College of Law application form, tax returns, and W2s. The aid application deadline for fall entry is February 15. Special funds for minority or disadvantaged students include need-based tuition grants. First-year students are notified about their financial aid application at time of acceptance.

About the Law School

Syracuse University College of Law was established in 1895 and is a private institution. The 200-acre campus is in an urban area 3 miles east of Syracuse. The primary mission of the law school is guided by the philosophy that the best way to educate lawyers to practice in today's world is to engage them in a process of interdisciplinary learning while teaching them to apply what they learn in the classroom to real legal issues, problems, and clients. Students have access to federal, state, county, city, and local agencies, courts, correctional facilities, law firms, and legal aid organizations in the Syracuse area. Housing for students is available both on and off campus. On-campus housing options include apartment complexes for law and graduate students. About 87% of the law school facilities are accessible to the physically disabled.

Calendar

The law school operates on a traditional semester basis. Courses for full-time students are offered days only, and must be completed within 5 years. For part-time students, courses are offered days only, and must be completed within 5 years. New full- and part-time students are admitted in the fall. There is a 7-week summer session. Transferable summer courses are offered.

Programs

Students may take relevant courses in other programs and apply credit toward the J.D.; a maximum of 6 credits may be applied. The following joint degrees may be earned: J.D./M.A. (Juris Doctor/ Master of Arts in International Relations), J.D./M.B.A. (Juris Doctor/Master of Business Administration), J.D./M.P.A. (Juris Doctor/Master of Public Administration), J.D./M.S. (Juris Doctor/Master of Science), and J.D./Ph.D. (Juris Doctor/Doctor of Philosophy).

Required

To earn the J.D., candidates must complete 87 total credits, of which 40 are for required courses. They must maintain a minimum GPA of 2.2 in the required courses. The following first-year courses are required of all students: Civil Procedure, Constitutional Law I, Contracts, Criminal Law, Legal Communication and Research, Legislation and Policy, Property, and Torts. Required upper-level courses consist of a third-semester research and writing course, a writing requirement, Constitutional Law II, and Professional Responsibility. The required orientation program for first-year students is a 5-day program that includes academic sessions, book discussions, alumni and students panels, professionalism programs, and social activities.

Electives

The College of Law offers concentrations in corporate law, environmental law, family law, intellectual property law, international law, labor law, litigation, tax law, technology commercialization law, law and economics, national security and counterterrorism law, indigenous law, and disability law. In addition, second- and third-year students may take clinics for 12 credits in Community Development

Phone: 315-443-1962
Fax: 315-443-9568
Web: www.law.syr.edu

Contact
Admissions Office, 315-443-1962 for general inquiries; Director of Financial Aid, 315-443-1963 for financial aid information.

NEW YORK

Law, Disabilities Rights, and Children's Rights and Family Law, and 6 credits in the Low Income Taxpayer Clinic, the Securities Arbitration/Consumer Law Clinic, and the Elder Law Clinic. Second- and third-year students may also earn 1 to 2 credits per semester for seminars. A study-abroad summer program is available in London. Tutorial programs are offered to first-year students. Minority programs include the Legal Education Opportunity Program.

Graduation Requirements
In order to graduate, candidates must have a GPA of 2.2 and must have completed the upper-division writing requirement.

Organizations
Law students edit the *Syracuse Law Review, Journal of International Law and Commerce, The Labor Lawyer, The Law & Technology Journal,* and *The Digest.* Annually, students compete in the Mackenzie Lewis Competition, Lionel O. Grossman Trial Competition, and Jessup Moot Court competition. Law student organizations include Black Law Students Association, Phi Alpha Delta, Asian Pacific American Law Students Association, Law Student Senate, Syracuse Public Interest Network, and Latin American Law Students Association.

Library
The law library contains 218,058 hardcopy volumes and 255,018 microform volume equivalents, and subscribes to 3,300 serial publications. Such online databases and networks as CALI, CIS Universe, DIALOG, Infotrac, Legal-Trac, LEXIS, OCLC First Search, WESTLAW, Wilsonline Indexes, BNA, HeinOnline, Heins Foreign and International Law Resources, Heins U.S. Congressional Documents, LexisNexis Congressional, LLMC Digital, U.S. Serial Set Digital Collection, and Index to Foreign Legal Periodicals are available to law students for research. Special library collections include ones on legal history, legal education, New York state law, tax law and policy, law of indigenous peoples, trial practice skills, and law technology and management. The law library is depository for U.S. Government documents. The ratio of library volumes to faculty is 3,696 to 1 and to

students is 327 to 1. The ratio of seats in the library to students is 1 to 2.

Faculty
The law school has 59 full-time and 54 part-time faculty members, of whom 34 are women. According to AAUP standards for Category I institutions, faculty salaries are average. About 25% of full-time faculty have a graduate law degree in addition to the J.D. The ratio of full-time students to full-time faculty in an average class is 21 to 1; in a clinic, 10 to 1. The law school has a regular program of bringing visiting professors and other distinguished lecturers and visitors to campus. There is a chapter of the Order of the Coif.

Students
About 45% of the student body are women; 19%, minorities; 4%, African American; 10%, Asian American; 3%, Hispanic; and 1%, Native American. The average age of entering students is 24; age range is 21 to 47. About 7% of students have a graduate degree.

Placement	
J.D.s awarded:	206

Services available through: a separate law school placement center.
Services: workshop on networking, career speaker series, and identifying clerkship opportunities.
Special features: individual counseling for law students.

Placement within 9 months of graduation:	90% of class
Average starting salary:	$36,700 to $113,000

Areas of placement:
Private practice 2–10 attorneys	20%
Private practice 11–25 attorneys	6%
Private practice 26–50 attorneys	5%
Private practice 51–100 attorneys	6%
Private practice firm 100+ attorneys	10%
Business/industry	16%
Judicial clerkships	15%
Government	13%
Public interest	4%
Academic	3%
Military	2%

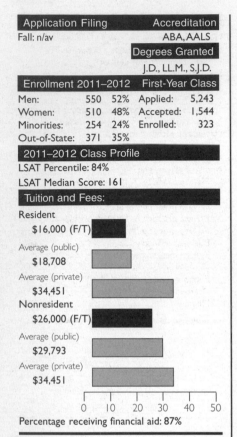

Application Filing		Accreditation
Fall: n/av		ABA, AALS
		Degrees Granted
		J.D., LL.M., S.J.D.

Enrollment 2011–2012			First-Year Class	
Men:	550	52%	Applied:	5,243
Women:	510	48%	Accepted:	1,544
Minorities:	254	24%	Enrolled:	323
Out-of-State:	371	35%		

2011–2012 Class Profile
LSAT Percentile: 84%
LSAT Median Score: 161

Tuition and Fees:

Resident
$16,000 (F/T)

Average (public)
$18,708

Average (private)
$34,451

Nonresident
$26,000 (F/T)

Average (public)
$29,793

Average (private)
$34,451

0 10 20 30 40 50

Percentage receiving financial aid: 87%

ADMISSIONS

In the fall of 2011 first-year class, 5243 applied, 1544 were accepted, and 323 enrolled. Eight transfer students enrolled. The median LSAT percentile of the most recent first-year class was 84; the median GPA was 3.3 on a scale of 4.0. The lowest LSAT percentile accepted was 20; the highest was 99.

Requirements
Applicants must have a bachelor's degree and take the LSAT. Minimum acceptable GPA is 2.3 on a scale of 4.0. No specific undergraduate courses are required, and candidates are not interviewed.

Procedure
Applicants should submit an application form, LSAT results, transcripts, TOEFL (when English is not a student's primary language), 3 letters of recommendation, and a personal statement. Notification of the admissions decision is on a rolling basis. The law school uses the LSAC.

Special
The law school recruits minority and disadvantaged students through visits to colleges and cities with large minority populations; faculty and student contact with minority applicants; special programs sponsored by minority student organizations in conjunction with the Law School Annual Open House; and the LSAC Candidate Referral Service. The Sp.A.C.E. program, the law school's discretionary admissions process, seeks to identify applicants whose GPA and LSAT scores may not fully represent their abilities and potential, including minority applicants and economically disadvantaged applicants. Requirements are different for out-of-state students. Transfer students must have one year of credits, attended an ABA-approved law school or an ABA/AALS member law school, and rank in the top 20% of their class after completion of 1 year. Availability of seats is also a factor in admission.

Costs

On-campus room and board costs about $10,262 annually; books and supplies run $1,500.

Financial Aid

About 87% of current law students receive some form of aid. The average annual amount of aid from all sources combined, including scholarships, loans, and work contracts, is $21,958; maximum, $43,382. Awards may be based on merit only, need only, or a combination of need and merit. Required financial statement is the FAFSA. Special funds for minority or disadvantaged students include a limited number of partial tuition scholarships that are awarded to students admitted through the Sp.A.C.E. program (the discretionary admissions process) who have outstanding performance records and demonstrated financial need. First-year students are notified about their financial aid application after admission, and when their financial aid forms are received and processed.

About the Law School

Temple University James E. Beasley School of Law was established in 1895 and is a public institution. The 87-acre campus is located in an urban area 2 miles north of downtown Philadelphia. The mission of the law school is a commitment to excellence in teaching, scholarship, and service. They

believe that legal education must provide practical and theoretical knowledge. The school seeks to maintain and strengthen its tradition of accessibility and diversity to pursue the goals of excellence in higher education and equal justice under the law. Students have access to federal, state, county, city, and local agencies, courts, correctional facilities, law firms, and legal aid organizations in the Philadelphia area. The Temple Legal Aid Office is housed in the law school's main building. Facilities of special interest to law students include Barrack Hall, with student services offices, classrooms, and student organization offices. The law school complex consists of Klein Hall with a large moot court room, 2 trial courtrooms; an 11-level open-stack law library with 2 multilevel reading rooms; wired and wireless network access throughout the library and law school buildings; 750 study carrels, table seats; and Shusterman Hall, a legal conference center. Housing for students on campus is apartment-style; many students choose off-campus housing. The Admissions Office maintains updated information on housing prospects and a list of students seeking roommates. All law school facilities are accessible to the physically disabled.

Calendar

The law school operates on a traditional semester basis. Courses for full-time students are offered days only and must be completed within 3 years. For part-time students, courses are offered both day and evening and must be completed within 4 years. New full- and part-time students are admitted in the fall. There is a 6- to 8-week summer session. Transferable summer courses are offered.

Programs

In addition to the J.D., the law school offers the LL.M. and S.J.D. Students may take relevant courses in other programs and apply credit toward the J.D.; a maximum of 12 credits may be applied. The following joint degrees may be earned: J.D./M.B.A. (Juris Doctor/ Master of Business Administration), J.D./LL.M. (Juris Doctor/Master of Laws in taxation), and J.D./LL.M. (Juris Doctor/Master of Laws in transnational law).

Required
To earn the J.D., candidates must complete 87 total credits, of which 40 are for required courses. They must maintain a minimum GPA of 2.0 in the required courses. The fol-

Phone: 215-204-5949
800-560-1428
Fax: 215-204-1185
E-mail: *lawadmis@temple.edu*
Web: *www.temple.edu/lawschool*

Contact

Admissions Staff, 215-204-8925 or 800-560-1428 for general inquiries; Financial Aid Office, 215-204-8943 or 800-560-1428 for financial aid information.

PENNSYLVANIA

lowing first-year courses are required of all students: Civil Procedure I, Constitutional Law, Contracts I and II, Criminal Law I, Legal Writing and Research, Legal Decision Making, Property, and Torts. Required upper-level courses consist of Professional Responsibility and 2 writing requirements. The school offers, but does not require, participation in an extensive selection of clinical opportunities. The required orientation program for first-year students consists of a 5-day program that provides an overview of academic requirements, faculty regulations, university and law school services, financial aid, general placement information, and social activities.

Electives

The James E. Beasley School of Law offers concentrations in corporate law, criminal law, environmental law, family law, international law, juvenile law, litigation, securities law, tax law, torts and insurance, trial advocacy, public interest law, technology law, intellectual property law, and constitutional and civil rights law. In addition, extensive clinics worth 3 or 4 credits per semester, are offered to third- and fourth-year students in the areas of civil litigation, criminal litigation, transactional work and mediation. There is an extensive number of writing seminar courses. All students are required to take 2 upper-level writing courses. Three writing seminars include Race & Ethnicity, Constitutional Law and Foreign Policy, and the Law of Electronic Commerce. Dean's Invitational Forums, Honorable Clifford Scott Green Lecture, Herbert H. Kolsby Lecture, Friel-Scanlan lecture, Institute for International and Comparative Law lecture series, and numerous other lectures offered by faculty members and guests of the law school. Summer sessions are available in Rome, Italy; Athens, Greece; and Tel Aviv, Israel. A full semester abroad is offered in Tokyo, Japan; Beijing, China; and Cork, Ireland. All these sessions are open to students after their first year. Students also have the option of designing an individualized study abroad program at law school throughout the world. Some faculty conduct guided research in a tutorial format. There is a faculty mentoring program for students who are having academic difficulty. Special interest group programs include the Public Interest Scholars Program, which provides a comprehensive plan of coursework, mentoring, and tuition support. The most widely taken electives are Evidence, Business Associations, and Taxation.

Graduation Requirements

In order to graduate, candidates must have a GPA of 2.0, complete the upper-division writing requirement, as well as Professional Responsibility.

Organizations

Students edit the *Temple Law Review, Temple International and Comparative Law Journal, Temple Environmental Law and Technology Journal, Temple Journal of Science, Technology, and Environmental Law,* and the newspaper *Class Action.* Moot court competitions include the I. Herman Stern and Samuel J. Polsky Moot Court competitions held annually at the school; students also attend other competitions throughout the country. Outside competitions include the Jessup International, ABA National Negotiation, National Invitational Tournament of Champions, National Trial Competition, National Association of Criminal Defense Lawyers, and American Trial Lawyers Association Competition. More than 30 different student organizations flourish at the law school. The Student Bar Association acts as the students' representative in the law school administration, and is the umbrella organization that oversees the many diverse student activities and organizations. There are local chapters of the Black Law Students Association, Moot Court, National Lawyers Guild.

Library

The law library contains 573,568 hardcopy volumes and 179,200 microform volume equivalents, and subscribes to 3,048 serial publications. Online databases and networks include CALI, CIS Universe, DIALOG, Dow-Jones, Infotrac, Legal-Trac, LEXIS, Mathew Bender, OCLC First Search, RLIN, and WESTLAW. Additional resources include Wilsonline Indexes, HeinOnline, PA Code Online, CCH Tax Online, EAHorney, Gale Yellowbooks, Berkeley Online Journals, BNA Online, and WestPac, which are available to law students for research. Special library collections include the Anglophonic collection, African collection, Rawle history collection, Ellsberg Watergate collection, Temple Trial collection, U.S. government depository and depository for briefs and records for Pennsylvania. The ratio of library volumes to faculty is 9,721 to 1 and to students is 549 to 1.

Placement

Services available through: a separate law school placement center.

Special features: programs on federal and state judicial clerkships; specific outreach to small and medium-size firms; access to workshops on resume writing, interviewing skills and networking; mock interview program; career panels; online career planning resources; and co-sponsorship of regional job fairs. Temple is a founder of the Philadelphia Area Minority Job Fair. Counseling on public interest and public service careers handled by the Career Planning Officer's Director for Public Interest Law Programs.

Full-time job interviews:	61 employers
Summer job interviews:	85 employers
Placement by graduation:	70% of class
Placement within 9 months:	93% of class
Average starting salary:	$30,000 to $160,000

Areas of placement:

Private practice 2–10 attorneys	13%
Private practice 11–25 attorneys	8%
Private practice 26–50 attorneys	4%
Private practice 51–100 attorneys	4%
Business/industry	17%
Government	14%
Judicial clerkships	9%
Public interest	7%
Academic	2%

Faculty

The law school has 59 full-time and 212 part-time faculty members, of whom 81 are women. According to AAUP standards for Category I institutions, faculty salaries are above average. About 29% of full-time faculty have a graduate law degree in addition to the J.D. The ratio of full-time students to full-time faculty in an average class is 17 to 1. The law school has a regular program of bringing visiting professors and other distinguished lecturers and visitors to campus.

Students

About 48% of the student body are women; 24%, minorities; 8%, African American; 11%, Asian American; 4%, Hispanic; and 4%, Native American. The majority of students come from Pennsylvania (65%). The average age of entering students is 26; age range is 19 to 52. About 26% of students enter directly from undergraduate school, 16% have a graduate degree, and 74% have worked full-time prior to entering law school. About 3% drop out after the first year for academic or personal reasons; 97% remain to receive a law degree.

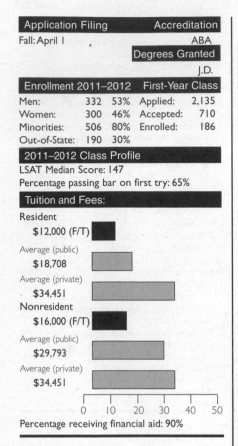

Application Filing	Accreditation
Fall: April 1	ABA

Degrees Granted
J.D.

Enrollment 2011–2012		First-Year Class	
Men:	332 53%	Applied:	2,135
Women:	300 46%	Accepted:	710
Minorities:	506 80%	Enrolled:	186
Out-of-State:	190 30%		

2011–2012 Class Profile
LSAT Median Score: 147
Percentage passing bar on first try: 65%

Tuition and Fees:

Resident
$12,000 (F/T)

Average (public)
$18,708

Average (private)
$34,451

Nonresident
$16,000 (F/T)

Average (public)
$29,793

Average (private)
$34,451

0   10   20   30   40   50
Percentage receiving financial aid: 90%

ADMISSIONS

In the fall of 2011 first-year class, 2135 applied, 710 were accepted, and 186 enrolled. One transfer student enrolled. The median GPA of the most recent first-year class was 2.92.

Requirements

Applicants must have a bachelor's degree and take the LSAT. The most important admission factors include LSAT results and GPA. No specific undergraduate courses are required, and candidates are not interviewed.

Procedure

The application deadline for fall entry is April 1. Applicants should submit an application form, LSAT results, a personal statement, and 2 letters of recommendation. Notification of the admissions decision is between February and May (majority). The law school uses the LSAC.

Special

The law school recruits minority and disadvantaged students through the Office of Admissions' Candidate Referral Service program and college campus visits. The majority of students are members of minority groups. Requirements are different for out-of-state students. Transfer students must have attended an ABA-approved law school, a personal statement, and have been academically successful at their first school of attendance.

Costs

On-campus room and board costs about $7,000 annually; books and supplies run $1,900.

Financial Aid

About 90% of current law students receive some form of aid. The average annual amount of aid from all sources combined, including scholarships, loans, and work contracts, is $20,500; maximum, $23,725. Awards are based on need and merit combined. Required financial statement is the FAFSA. The aid application deadline for fall entry is April 1. First-year students are notified about their financial aid application after the financial aid forms are processed and before enrollment if the application was submitted before the deadline.

About the Law School

Texas Southern University Thurgood Marshall School of Law was established in 1947 and is a public institution. The 6-acre campus is located in an urban area 7 miles south of downtown Houston. The primary mission of the law school is, to not only meet the needs of students in general, but of minority and disadvantaged students as well. Students have access to federal, state, county, city, and local agencies, courts, correctional facilities, law firms, and legal aid organizations in the Houston area. There are also adjunct faculty in certain areas of specialty and 2 writing-skills specialists. There is a strong clinical program and a very competitive moot court program. Facilities of special interest to law students include several computer rooms offering terminals for online legal research, as well as for offline student use. Housing for students consists of a privately managed campus apartment community, for which law students receive

priority consideration. All law school facilities are accessible to the physically disabled.

Calendar

The law school operates on a traditional semester basis. Courses for full-time students are offered days only and must be completed within 4 years. New full-time students are admitted in the fall. There is a 9-week summer session. Transferable summer courses are offered.

Programs

Students may take relevant courses in other programs and apply credit toward the J.D.; a maximum of 6 credits may be applied. The following joint degrees may be earned: J.D./M.B.A. (Juris Doctor/ Master of Business Administration) and J.D./M.P.A. (Juris Doctor/Master of Public Administration).

Required

To earn the J.D., candidates must complete 90 total credits, of which 70 are for required courses. They must maintain a minimum GPA of 2.0 in the required courses. The following first-year courses are required of all students: Civil Procedure, Criminal Law, Contracts I and II, Lawyering Process/Legal Writing I and II, Property I and II, and Torts I and II. Required upper-level courses consist of, Appellate Litigation, Basic Federal Income Taxation, Business Associations, Federal Jurisdiction and Procedure, a writing seminar, Constitution Law, Consumer Rights, Criminal Procedure, Trial Simulation, Evidence, Commercial Law, Professional Responsibility, Wills and Trusts, and Texas Practice. The required orientation program for first-year students consists of a 1-week introduction and lectures on skills.

Electives

The Thurgood Marshall School of Law offers concentrations in litigation and tax law. In addition, clinics include criminal law, administrative law, and civil law. Seminars include criminal trial practice, writing, and First Amendment. Internships are available through the clinics offered, including a judicial internship with federal and state judges. Research programs allow for independent research

Phone: 713-313-7114
Fax: 713-313-7297
E-mail: cgardner@tmslaw.tsu.edu
Web: www.tsulaw.edu

Contact

Carolyn Gardner, Admissions Officer, 713-313-7114 for general inquiries; Karen Percival, Financial Aid Counselor, 713-313-7243 for financial aid information.

TEXAS

and thesis research. A special lecture series, the Quodlibet, is a faculty- and student-sponsored program on current legal issues that is debated by faculty. Students may participate in study-abroad programs sponsored by other ABA-approved law schools. Each first-year section is assigned a student tutor who reviews substantive materials, discusses hypotheticals, and provides study help for each professor's class. The Legal Education Advancement Program (LEAP) is a 6-week summer program to develop oral and written legal analysis skills. Minority students are offered the third-year Mentor Program in which students are assigned alumni mentors through the bar examination. Academic counseling on course selection and personal goals is available. The most widely taken electives are Estate Planning, Legal Clinics, and Oil and Gas Law.

Graduation Requirements

In order to graduate, candidates must have a GPA of 2.0 and complete the upper-division writing requirement.

Organizations

The primary law review is the *Thurgood Marshall Law Review*. The student magazine is *The Solicitor*. The James M. Douglas Board of Advocates sponsors numerous moot court and mock trial programs. Law student organizations include the Student Bar Association, Black Law Students Association, and Chicano Law Students Association. There are local chapters of Asian Pacific American Law Students Association, Phi Alpha Delta, and Phi Delta Phi.

Library

The law library contains 251,722 hardcopy volumes and 62,907 microform volume equivalents, and subscribes to 465 serial publications. Online databases and networks include CALI, CIS Universe, Infotrac, Legal-Trac, LEXIS, Mathew Bender, OCLC First Search, WESTLAW, Legal-Trac, and 19th Century, which are available to law students for research. Special library collections include the Dominion Reports, federal government depositories, and civil rights. The ratio of library volumes to faculty is 7,403 to 1 and to students is 398 to 1. The ratio of seats in the library to students is 1 to 3.

Faculty

The law school has 34 full-time and 19 part-time faculty members, of whom 14 are women. About 39% of full-time faculty have a graduate law degree in addition to the J.D. The ratio of full-time students to full-time faculty in an average class is 60 to 1; in a clinic, 10 to 1.

Students

About 46% of the student body are women; 80%, minorities; 49%, African American; 7%, Asian American; 26%, Hispanic. The majority of students come from Texas (70%). The average age of entering students is 27; age range is 20 to 35. About 60% of students enter directly from undergraduate school, 10% have a graduate degree, and 40% have worked full-time prior to entering law school. About 35% drop out after the first year for academic or personal reasons; 65% remain to receive a law degree.

Placement

J.D.s awarded:	140

Services available through: a separate law school placement center.

Services: participation in numerous job fairs in and out of state.

Special features: Attorneys address students about legal career opportunities and participate in interview role-playing. Resumes are also individually critiqued. In addition, mock interview seminars are conducted, as well as workshops in preparation for summer legal internships.

Summer job interviews:	28 employers
Placement by graduation:	72% of class
Placement within 9 months:	72% of class
Average starting salary:	$47,000
Areas of placement:	
Private practice 2–10 attorneys	88%
Government	7%
Business/industry	4%
Public interest	2%

TEXAS TECH UNIVERSITY

School of Law

1802 Hartford Avenue
Lubbock, TX 79409

Application Filing	Accreditation
Fall: March 15	ABA, AALS
	Degrees Granted
Fee: $50	J.D.

Enrollment 2011–2012			First-Year Class	
Men:	371	58%	Applied:	1,855
Women:	266	42%	Accepted:	652
Minorities:	159	25%	Enrolled:	213
Out-of-State:	32	5%		

2011–2012 Class Profile
LSAT Percentile: 67%
LSAT Median Score: 156
Percentage passing bar on first try: 95%

Tuition and Fees:

Resident
$16,200 (F/T)

Average (public)
$18,708

Average (private)
$34,451

Nonresident
$23,610 (F/T)

Average (public)
$29,793

Average (private)
$34,451

0 10 20 30 40 50

Percentage receiving financial aid: 86%

ADMISSIONS

In the fall of 2011 first-year class, 1855 applied, 652 were accepted, and 213 enrolled. Ten transfers enrolled. The median LSAT percentile of the most recent first-year class was 67; the median GPA was 3.4 on a scale of 4.0. The lowest LSAT percentile accepted was 15; the highest was 95.

Requirements
Applicants must have a bachelor's degree and take the LSAT. The most important admission factors include LSAT results, GPA, and life experience. No specific undergraduate courses are required, and candidates are interviewed.

Procedure
The application deadline for fall entry is March 15. Applicants should submit an application form, LSAT results, transcripts, a personal statement, TOEFL (if necessary), a nonrefundable application fee of $50, 2 letters of recommendation,

and a résumé. Notification of the admissions decision begins in November. The law school uses the LSAC.

Special
The law school recruits minority and disadvantaged students and encourages campus visitation. Requirements are different for out-of-state students. Transfer students must have one year of credits, attended an ABA-approved law school, a personal statement, ranked in the upper 25% of their first-year class, and be in good standing.

Costs
Tuition and fees for the 2011–2012 academic year are $12,975 for full-time in-state students and $20,385 for out-of-state students. On-campus room and board costs about $8,110 annually; books and supplies run $1,000.

Financial Aid
About 86% of current law students receive some form of aid. The average annual amount of aid from all sources combined, including scholarships, loans, and work contracts, is $24,398; maximum, $37,121. Awards are based on need and merit combined. Required financial statement is the FAFSA. The aid application deadline for fall entry is April 15. Special funds for minority or disadvantaged students includes private scholarships. First-year students are notified about their financial aid application in March.

About the Law School
Texas Tech University School of Law was established in 1967 and is a public institution. The 1839-acre campus is located in an urban area of Lubbock. The primary mission of the law school is to educate and train individuals for the ethical practice of law, engage in productive, effective scholarship both within our academic community and within the larger academic community throughout our state and nation; and to render public service. Students have access to federal, state, county, city, and local agencies, courts, correctional facilities, law firms, and legal aid organizations in the Lubbock area. A medical school/teaching hospital is nearby. Housing for students is available on-campus, as well as numerous

rental properties close to the law school and throughout the city. All law school facilities are accessible to the physically disabled.

Calendar
The law school operates on a traditional semester basis. Courses for full-time students are offered days only and must be completed within 3 years. There is no part-time program. New full-time students are admitted in the fall. There is a 2–5 week summer session. Transferable summer courses are offered.

Programs
Students may take relevant courses in other programs and apply credit toward the J.D.; a maximum of 12 hours credits may be applied. The following joint degrees may be earned: J.D./M.S.E. (Juris Doctor/Master of Science in Engineering), J.D./M.S.H.T.S. (Juris Doctor/Master of Science in Horticulture), J.D./M.S.S.S. (Juris Doctor/Master of Science in Soil), J.D./M.D. (Juris Doctor/Doctor of Medicine), J.D./M.S.A.C. (Juris Doctor/Master of Accounting), J.D./M.B.A. (Juris Doctor/Master of Business Administration), J.D./M.P.A. (Juris Doctor/Master of Public Administration), J.D./M.S. (Juris Doctor/Master of Science in agriculture economics), J.D./M.S.B.T. (Juris Doctor/ Master of Science in biotechnology), J.D./ M.S.E.T. (Juris Doctor/Master of Science in environmental toxicology), and J.D./ M.S.P.F.P. (Juris Doctor/Master of Science in personal financial planning).

Required
To earn the J.D., candidates must complete 90 total credits, of which 55 are for required courses. They must maintain a minimum GPA of 2.0 in the required courses. The following first-year courses are required of all students: Civil Procedure, Constitutional Law, Contracts, Criminal Law, Legal Practice I and II, Property, and Torts. Required upper-level courses consist of Business Entities, Evidence, Commercial Law, Criminal Procedure, Income Taxation, Professional Responsibility, and Wills and Trusts. The required orientation program for first-year students is 3 1/2 days. The program introduces students to professionalism and to basic legal skills, ethics and analysis.

Phone: 806-742-3990, ext. 273
Fax: 806-742-4617
E-mail: *donna.williams@ttu.edu*
Web: *www.law.ttu.edu*

Contact

Admissions Assistant, 806-742-3990, ext. 273 for general inquiries; Marth Harrison, Senior Financial Aid Advisor, 806-742-3990, ext. 307 for financial aid information.

TEXAS

Electives

The School of Law offers concentrations in corporate law, criminal law, environmental law, intellectual property law, international law, litigation, securities law, and tax law. The School of Law also has programs in Business Law, Health Law, and Law and Science. In addition, third-year students may take clinics including Low Income Tax, Civil Litigation, and Criminal Justice. Second- and third-year students who have completed prerequisites may take seminar courses. A number of externships are available to second- and third-year students for credit. Independent research programs are available for advanced students and in conjunction with the 3 Centers of Excellence. There are various special lecture series, including the Sandra Day O'Connor Lecture Series. There is a Summer Law Institute in Guanajuato, Mexico, and an exchange program in Lyon, France, and Melbourne, Australia. There is an Academic Success Program available for students needing tutorial help. Student organizations regularly sponsor programs for their members and the larger community. There are more than 50 special interest student groups that sponsor programs. The most widely taken electives are Texas Pretrial Procedure, Texas Trial and Appellate, and Family Law.

Graduation Requirements

In order to graduate, candidates must have a GPA of 2.0 and complete the upper-division writing requirement.

Organizations

Students edit the *Texas Tech Law Review, Texas Tech Journal of Texas Administrative Law Journal, The Texas Bank Lawyer, Estate Planning and Community Property Journal* and *Texas Tech Lawyer Alumni Magazine.* Moot court competitions include the ABA National Appellate Advocacy Competition, National Moot Court Competition, and Philip C. Jessup International Law Moot Court Competition. Other competitions include the TYLA National Trial Competition, AAJ National Student Trial Advocacy Competition, and ABA Negotiation Competition. Law student organizations, local chapters of national associations, and campus organizations include Texas Tech Student Bar Association, Board

of Barristers, Student Public Interest Initiative, Women's Caucus, Black Law Students Association, Volunteer Law Students Association, Delta Theta Phi, Phi Alpha Delta, and Phi Delta Phi.

Library

The law library contains 331,191 hardcopy volumes and 675,175 microform volume equivalents, and subscribes to 3,194 serial publications. Online databases and networks include CALI, CIS Universe, LEXIS, Mathew Bender, OCLC First Search, WESTLAW, and Wilsonline Indexes. RIA Checkpoint, HeinOnline, BNA, Serial Set, UN Treaty Collection, LLMC, LSN, CCH Business, and CCH Legal Pro are others available to law students for research. Special library collections include a federal government documents depository. The ratio of library volumes to faculty is 5,401 to 1 and to students is 297 to 1. The ratio of seats in the library to students is 1 to 3.

Faculty

The law school has 38 full-time and 24 part-time faculty members, of whom 19 are women. According to AAUP standards for Category I institutions, faculty salaries are below average. About 49% of full-time faculty have a graduate law degree in addition to the J.D.; about 11% of part-time faculty have one. The ratio of full-time students to full-time faculty in an average class is 15 to 1; in a clinic, 11 to 1. The law school has a regular program of bringing visiting professors and other distinguished lecturers and visitors to campus. There is a chapter of the Order of the Coif; 17 faculty and 591 graduates are members.

Students

About 42% of the student body are women; 25%, minorities; 4%, African American; 4%, Asian American; 15%, Hispanic; and 1%, Native American. The majority of students come from Texas (95%). The average age of entering students is 24; age range is 21 to 49. About 5% drop out after the first year for academic or personal reasons; 89% remain to receive a law degree.

Placement

J.D.s awarded:	206

Services available through: a separate law school placement center.
Special features: participation in 4 off-campus recruitment programs in conjunction with various law schools.

Full-time job interviews:	5 employers
Summer job interviews:	56 employers
Placement by graduation:	40% of class
Placement within 9 months:	92% of class
Average starting salary:	$25,000 to $160,000

Areas of placement:

Private practice 2–10 attorneys	29%
Private practice 11–25 attorneys	15%
Private practice 26–50 attorneys	12%
Private practice 51–100 attorneys	2%
Government	17%
Business/industry	17%
Judicial clerkships	5%
Military	4%
Public interest	3%
Academic	1%

TEXAS WESLEYAN UNIVERSITY

School of Law

1515 Commerce Street
Fort Worth, TX 76102

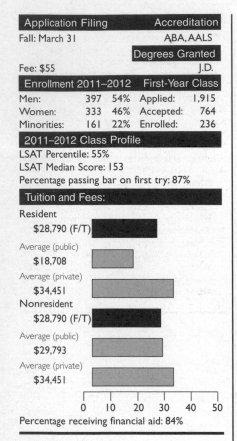

Application Filing	Accreditation
Fall: March 31	ABA, AALS

	Degrees Granted
Fee: $55	J.D.

Enrollment 2011–2012		First-Year Class	
Men:	397 54%	Applied:	1,915
Women:	333 46%	Accepted:	764
Minorities:	161 22%	Enrolled:	236

2011–2012 Class Profile
LSAT Percentile: 55%
LSAT Median Score: 153
Percentage passing bar on first try: 87%

Tuition and Fees:

Resident
$28,790 (F/T)

Average (public)
$18,708

Average (private)
$34,451

Nonresident
$28,790 (F/T)

Average (public)
$29,793

Average (private)
$34,451

Percentage receiving financial aid: 84%

ADMISSIONS

In the fall of 2011 first-year class, 1915 applied, 764 were accepted, and 236 enrolled. Eight transfer students enrolled. The median LSAT percentile of the most recent first-year class was 55; the median GPA was 3.2 on a scale of 4.3. The lowest LSAT percentile accepted was 23; the highest was 92.

Requirements

Applicants must have a bachelor's degree and take the LSAT. The most important admission factors include GPA, LSAT results, and writing ability. No specific undergraduate courses are required, and candidates are not interviewed.

Procedure

The application deadline for fall entry is March 31. Applicants should submit an application form, LSAT results, transcripts, personal statement, nonrefundable application fee of $55, 2 letters of recommendation, and a resume.

Notification of the admissions decision is on a rolling basis. The law school uses the LSAC.

Special

The law school recruits minority and disadvantaged students through personal meetings, on-campus events, LSAC forums, phone and e-mail contact, CLEO, PCSI, LSPI. Requirements are different for out-of-state students. Transfer students must have one year of credits, have a minimum GPA of 3, attended an ABA-approved law school, personal statement, letter of good standing from the home law school, application fee, professor's recommendation, and a letter of request to transfer. A maximum of 30 hours can be transferred (pass/fail credits transfer).

Costs

Tuition and fees for the 2011–2012 academic year are $28,000 for all full-time students. Tuition for part-time students is $19,600 for in-state students and $19,600 out-of-state. Books and supplies run $1,800.

Financial Aid

About 84% of current law students receive some form of aid. The average annual amount of aid from all sources combined, including scholarships, loans, and work contracts, is $22,847; maximum, $45,020. Awards are based on need and merit combined. Required financial statement is the FAFSA. Special funds for minority or disadvantaged students diversity scholarship awards. First-year students are notified about their financial aid application the time of acceptance or time of file completion, whichever is later.

About the Law School

Texas Wesleyan University School of Law was established in 1989 and is a private institution. The campus is in an urban area in downtown Fort Worth. The primary mission of the law school is to provide legal education to a diverse student body, recognizing the need for both knowledge and skills, as well as professionalism. Students have access to federal, state, county, city, and local agencies, courts, correctional facilities, law firms, and legal aid organizations in the Fort Worth area. Housing for students is at the main

campus (a 10-minute drive). There are a variety of apartment and home options for rent and purchase. All law school facilities are accessible to the physically disabled.

Calendar

The law school operates on a traditional semester basis. Courses for full-time students are offered days only and must be completed within 6 years. For part-time students, courses are offered both day and evening and must be completed within 6 years. New full- and part-time students are admitted in the fall. There is a 7-week summer session. Transferable summer courses are offered.

Programs

Required

To earn the J.D., candidates must complete 90 total credits, of which 51 are for required courses. They must maintain a minimum GPA of 2.3 in the required courses. The following first-year courses are required of all students: Civil Procedure, Constitutional Law, Contracts, Criminal Law, Legal Analysis, Legislation & Regulation, Property, Research, Writing I & II, and Torts. Required upper-level courses consist of Business Associations, Criminal Procedure, Evidence, Legal Analysis, Professional Responsibility, Research, Writing III, and Wills & Estates. All students must take clinical courses. The required orientation program for first-year students is a 1-day orientation that includes Introduction to Law class in Case Analysis, Case Briefing, Hierarchy of Authority, and Court Structure.

Electives

The School of Law offers concentrations in corporate law, criminal law, environmental law, family law, intellectual property law, international law, litigation, tax law, and real estate law. In addition, there is a Law Clinic, Family Mediation Clinic, and Mediation Clinic. Seminars, open to upper-level students, include Law and Elderly, Computers and Law, and Race and Racism. After completing 45 hours and maintaining a minimum GPA 2.33, a student can earn up to 6 hours working with a private attorney under the supervision of a faculty member. Directed Research programs and Directed Readings

Phone: 817-212-4040
800-733-9529
Fax: 817-212-4141
E-mail: *lawadmissions@law.txwes.edu*
Web: *www.law.txwes.edu*

Contact

Emily Finlow, Records Manager, 817-212-4040 for general inquiries; Doug Akins, Financial Aid Officer, 817-212-4090 for financial aid information.

TEXAS

are available. Special lecture series include the Eldon Mahon Lecture Series. An Academic Support Program provides assistance to students, including facilitated study groups and exam-taking workshops. Remedial programs include the Summer Enrichment Program. The most widely taken electives are Tax, Family Law, and Texas Procedure.

Graduation Requirements

In order to graduate, candidates must have a GPA of 2.3, complete the upper-division writing requirement, and 30 hours of pro bono legal services.

Organizations

Students edit the *Texas Wesleyan Law Review* and *The Rambler*. There are fall and spring intraschool moot court competitions, as well as the ABA/LSD National Moot Court, Texas Young Lawyers Moot Court, and Jessup International Moot Court competitions. Other competitions include the ABA/LSD National Negotiations competition. Law student organizations, local chapters of national associations, and campus organizations include Texas Aggie Wesleyan Legal Society, Intellectual Property Association, Wesleyan Innocence Project, Delta Theta Phi, Phi Delta Phi, Phi Alpha Delta, HLSA, BLSA, ABA/LSD, and Christian Legal Society.

Library

The law library contains 285,196 hardcopy volumes and 769,301 microform volume equivalents, and subscribes to 5,233 serial publications. Online databases and networks include CALI, CIS Universe, Legal-Trac, LEXIS, OCLC First Search, WESTLAW. BNA All, HeinOnline, Audio Casefiles, CCH Intelliconnect Network, Gammel's Laws of Texas-19th Century Texas Law Online, GPO monthly catalog, LLMC Digital, Making of Modern Law, RIA Checkpoint, Tax Analysts, Current Index to Legal Periodicals, Index to Legal Periodicals Retrospective, Index to Foreign Legal Periodicals, International Encyclopedia of Laws, Armed Conflict Database, JSTOR, and Sage Journals are also available to law students for research. Special library collections include the Chief Justice Joe Greenhill, Sr. Collection. The ratio of library volumes to faculty is 5,093 to 1 and to students is 391 to 1. The ratio of seats in the library to students is 1 to 2.

Faculty

The law school has 34 full-time and 22 part-time faculty members, of whom 25 are women. According to AAUP standards for Category IIA institutions, faculty salaries are above average. About 38% of full-time faculty have a graduate law degree in addition to the J.D. The ratio of full-time students to full-time faculty in an average class is 19 to 1; in a clinic, 8 to 1. The law school has a regular program of bringing visiting professors and other distinguished lecturers and visitors to campus.

Students

About 46% of the student body are women; 22%, minorities; 5%, African American; 5%, Asian American; 9%, Hispanic; and 2%, Unknown. The average age of entering students is 27; age range is 20 to 48. About 9% of students have a graduate degree. About 12% drop out after the first year for academic or personal reasons; 88% remain to receive a law degree.

Placement

J.D.s awarded:	227

Services available through: a separate law school placement center, Law School Career Services Office; counseling on joining local and state bar associations, networking, and professional development.

Special features: job fairs, career services library, job search workshop, career services handbook and packet given to students at orientation, alumni outreach, online job bank, on-campus interviews.

Full-time job interviews:	6 employers
Summer job interviews:	11 employers
Placement by graduation:	41% of class
Placement within 9 months:	79% of class

Areas of placement:

Private practice 2–10 attorneys	32%
Private practice 11–25 attorneys	5%
Private practice 26–50 attorneys	3%
Business/industry	26%
Government	14%
Public interest	3%
Academic	2%
Judicial clerkships	1%

THOMAS JEFFERSON SCHOOL OF LAW

1155 Island Avenue
San Diego, CA 92101

Application Filing	Accreditation
Fall: open	ABA, AALS
Spring: open	**Degrees Granted**
Fee: $50	J.D., LL.M., J.S.D. and J.S.M.

Enrollment 2011–2012		First-Year Class	
Men:	600 52%	Applied:	2,697
Women:	553 44%	Accepted:	1,478
Minorities:	161 14%	Enrolled:	440
Out-of-State:	657 57%		

2011–2012 Class Profile

LSAT Median Score: 151

Tuition and Fees:

Resident
$41,000 (F/T)

Average (public)
$18,708

Average (private)
$34,451

Nonresident
$41,000 (F/T)

Average (public)
$29,793

Average (private)
$34,451

Percentage receiving financial aid: 94%

ADMISSIONS

In the fall of 2011 first-year class, 2697 applied, 1478 were accepted, and 440 enrolled. Seven transfers enrolled. The median GPA of the most recent first-year class was 3. The lowest LSAT percentile accepted was 20; the highest was 90.

Requirements

Applicants must take the LSAT. Minimum acceptable GPA is 2.0 on a scale of 4.0. The most important admission factors include LSAT results, academic achievement, and life experience. No specific undergraduate courses are required. Candidates are not interviewed.

Procedure

The application deadline for fall entry is open. Applicants should submit an application form, LSAT results, transcripts, a personal statement, a nonrefundable application fee of $50, 2 letters of recommendation, a personal statement, and a resume. Notification of the admissions decision is rolling decisions. The law school uses the LSAC.

Special

The law school recruits minority and disadvantaged students through the LSAC and law school fairs and forums. Requirements are different for out-of-state students. Transfer students must submit a personal statement.

Costs

Books and supplies run $1,900.

Financial Aid

About 94% of current law students receive some form of aid. The average annual amount of aid from all sources combined, including scholarships, loans, and work contracts, is $46,135; maximum, $69,980. Awards are based on need and merit combined. Required financial statements are the FAFSA and an institutional application. The aid application deadline for fall entry is February 15. First-year students are notified about their financial aid application at the time an application for admission is received.

About the Law School

Thomas Jefferson School of Law was established in 1969 and is a private institution. The campus is in East Village in downtown San Diego. The primary mission of the law school is to provide an outstanding legal education for a nationally based student body in a collegiate and supportive environment with attention to newly emerging areas of law, particularly those related to technological development, globalization, and the quest for social justice. Students have access to federal, state, county, city, and local agencies, courts, correctional facilities, law firms, and legal aid organizations in the San Diego area. There are also county law libraries available. Housing for students is not available on campus. The Student Services Department can assist with various housing alternatives. All law school facilities are accessible to the physically disabled.

Calendar

The law school operates on a traditional semester basis. Courses for full-time students are offered both day and evening, and must be completed within 5 years. For part-time students, courses are offered both day and evening, and must be completed within 6 years. New full- and part-time students are admitted in the fall and spring. There is an 8-week summer session. Transferable summer courses are offered.

Programs

In addition to the J.D., the law school offers the LL.M., J.S.D., and J.S.M. Students may take relevant courses in other programs and apply credit toward the J.D.; a maximum of 8 credits may be applied. The following joint degrees may be earned: J.D./M.B.A. (Juris Doctor/Master of Business Administration).

Required

To earn the J.D., candidates must complete 88 total credits, of which 55 are for required courses. They must maintain a minimum GPA of 2.0 in the required courses. The following first-year courses are required of all students: Civil Procedure I and II, Contracts I and II, Criminal Law, Criminal Procedure, Legal Writing I, Property I, and Torts I and II. Required upper-level courses consist of Constitutional Law I and II, Corporations, Evidence, Legal Writing II, Professional Responsibility, Property II, and Remedies. The required orientation program for first-year students is 2 days.

Electives

The law school offers concentrations in corporate law, criminal law, entertainment law, environmental law, family law, intellectual property law, internationl law, litigation, media law, sports law, tax law, Constitutional and civil rights, government and administrative law, intellectual property, health law, public law, real property law, skills training, and clinical education. Students can earn a maximum of 5 units by working in various government agencies, state and federal courts, or legal aid clinics. Small seminars are offered in specialty areas and are open to all students. Topics vary. A judicial internship program places qualified students in state and federal courts. Research assistantships are available through individual instructors. Students can earn a maximum of 10 units while working in nonpaid positions at select governmnet agencies, corporations, law firms, and public-interest organizations. An Alumni Perspectives series annually features successful alumni who share their practice experience and

Phone: 619-297-9700
800-936-7529
Fax: 619-961-1300
E-mail: info@tjsl.edu
Web: www.tjsl.edu

Contact
Michelle Allison, Associate Director of Admissions, 619-297-9700, ext. 4222 for general inquiries; Marc Berman, Director of Financial Assistance, 619-297-9700, ext. 4271 for financial aid information.

CALIFORNIA

expertise with students. Native American Law Students Association, Iranian Jurisprudence Society, Christian Legal Society, Jewish Student Union, Women's Law Association, La Raza, Pan Asian Lawyers Student Association, and Black Law Students Association offer mentoring and networking programs for minority students.

Graduation Requirements
In order to graduate, candidates must have a GPA of 2.0 and must have completed the upper-division writing requirement.

Organizations
Students edit the *Thomas Jefferson Law Review*. Other publications include *The Thomas Jefferson School of Law News* and *The Jeffersonian*. Moot court competitions include the National Appellate Advocacy Competition, William Jessup Moot Court Competition, and Pepperdine Entertainment Law Moot Court Competition. Other competitions include A.T.L.A. Mock Trial, Young Texas Lawyers Association Mock Trial, San Diego Defense Lawyers, Intra-School National Mock Trial, and William Daniel Mock Trial Competition. Local chapters of national associations include International Law Society, Public Interest Law Foundation, and Environmental Law Society. Other campus organizations include Black Law Students Association, Pan Asian Law Students Association, and La Raza Law Students Association.

Library
The law library contains 103,536 hardcopy volumes and 130,878 microform volume equivalents, and subscribes to 2,629 serial publications. Such online databases and networks as CALI, CIS Universe, DIALOG, Infotrac, Legal-Trac, LEXIS, Mathew Bender, OCLC First Search, WESTLAW, and many others are available to law students for research. Special library collections include Thomas Jefferson's writings and books, videos, and other material about Thomas Jefferson, as well as intellectual law and California legal collections. The ratio of library volumes to faculty is 2,358 to 1 and to students is 158 to 1. The ratio of seats in the library to students is 1 to 2.

Faculty
The law school has 43 full-time and 41 part-time faculty members, of whom 31 are women. About 18% of full-time faculty have a graduate law degree in addition to the J.D. The ratio of full-time students to full-time faculty in an average class is 19 to 1. The law school has a regular program of bringing visiting professors and other distinguished lecturers and visitors to campus.

Students
About 44% of the student body are women; 35%, minorities; 6%, African American; 4%, Asian American; 14%, Hispanic; 1%, Native American; and 8%, Pacific Islander. The average age of entering students is 26; age range is 21 to 53.

Placement
Services available through: a separate law school placement center.
Services: lecture series and panel presentations; access to on-campus and regional job fairs; access to symplicity online job posting system, and numerous online job posting sites.
Special features: all counselors are attorneys, and have practical legal experience including law firms, judicial clerkship, public interest, and government.

Placement by graduation:	28% of class
Placement within 9 months:	85% of class
Average starting salary:	$47,800 to $75,000

Areas of placement:

Private practice 2–10 attorneys	45%
Private practice 11–25 attorneys	5%
Private practice 26–50 attorneys	2%
Private practice 51–100 attorneys	7%
Business/industry	19%
Government	10%
Academic	5%
Judicial clerkships	2%
Public interest	1%

300 South Capitol Avenue
Lansing, MI 48901

Application Filing	Accreditation
Fall: September 1	ABA

	Degrees Granted
Fee: $25	J.D., LL.M.

Enrollment 2011–2012		First-Year Class	
Men:	1927 51%	Applied:	4,032
Women:	1818 49%	Accepted:	3,230
Minorities:	1049 28%	Enrolled:	1,161

2011–2012 Class Profile
LSAT Median Score: 146
Percentage passing bar on first try: 71%

Tuition and Fees:

Resident
$34,340 (F/T)

Average (public)
$18,708

Average (private)
$34,451

Nonresident
$34,240 (F/T)

Average (public)
$29,793

Average (private)
$34,451

0   10   20   30   40   50

Percentage receiving financial aid: 96%

ADMISSIONS
In the fall of 2011 first-year class, 4032 applied, 3230 were accepted, and 1161 enrolled. Eleven transfers enrolled. The median GPA of the most recent first-year class was 3.2.

Requirements
Applicants must take the LSAT. The most important admission factors include character or personality, GPA, and LSAT results. No specific undergraduate courses are required, and candidates are not interviewed.

Procedure
The application deadline for fall entry is September 1. Applicants should submit an application form, LSAT results, transcripts, and a nonrefundable application fee of $25. Notification of the admissions decision is on a rolling basis. The law school uses the LSAC.

Special
The law school recruits minority and disadvantaged students through recruitment travel and by attending law forums and job fairs. Requirements are different for out-of-state students. Transfer students must have one year of credits, have a minimum GPA of 2.0, attended an ABA-approved law school. Students can transfer up to 30 credits for classes in which they have received a grade of C or better. They must be in good standing at their last school.

Costs
Tuition and fees for the 2011–2012 academic year are $34,300 for all full-time students. Tuition for part-time students is $22,050 for in-state students and $22,050 out-of-state. Books and supplies run $1,400.

Financial Aid
About 96% of current law students receive some form of aid. Awards are based on need and merit combined. Required financial statement is the FAFSA. The aid application deadline for fall entry is September 1. Special funds for minority or disadvantaged students are available. First-year students are notified about their financial aid application at time of acceptance.

About the Law School
Thomas M. Cooley Law School was established in 1972 and is a private institution. The campus is in a suburban area at 5 campuses throughout Michigan and Florida. The primary mission of the law school is to prepare graduates for entry into the legal profession. Students have access to federal, state, county, city, and local agencies, courts, correctional facilities, law firms, and legal aid organizations in the Lansing area. An extensive externship program provides access to national lawyers' networks. Facilities of special interest to law students include a legal research library and courtroom at each campus, as well as an Academic Resource Center. There is a variety of housing options available for students at each campus. All law school facilities are accessible to the physically disabled.

Calendar
The law school operates on a year-round basis. Courses for full-time students are offered day, evening, and weekends, and

must be completed within 5 years. For part-time students, courses are offered day, evening, and weekends, and must be completed within 6 years. New full- and part-time students are admitted in the fall, winter, and summer. There is a 15-week summer session. Transferable summer courses are offered.

Programs
In addition to the J.D., the law school offers the LL.M. Students may take relevant courses in other programs and apply credit toward the J.D.; a maximum of 6 credits may be applied. The following joint degrees may be earned: J.D./M.B.A. (Juris Doctor/Master of Business Administration), J.D./LL.M. (Juris Doctor/Master of Laws (various disciplines)), J.D./M.P.A. (Juris Doctor/Master of Public Affairs), and J.D./M.S.W. (Juris Doctor/Master of Social Work).

Required
To earn the J.D., candidates must complete 90 total credits, of which 63 are for required courses. They must maintain a minimum GPA of 2.0 in the required courses. The following first-year courses are required of all students: Civil Procedure I and II, Contracts Law I and II, Criminal Law, Criminal Procedure, Introduction to Law, Personal and Professional Responsibility, Property I and II, and Torts I and II. Required upper-level courses consist of Advanced Writing, Business Organizations, Constitutional Law I and II, Equity and Remedies, Evidence, Secured Transactions, Taxation, Wills, Trusts, and Estates. All students must take clinical courses. The required orientation program for first-year students is a 2-day orientation program prior to start of the first semester.

Electives
Concentrations are offered in environmental law, tax law, general practice, solo and small firm, administrative law, constitutional law, and civil rights. In-house clinics include the Sixty Plus Elder Law Clinic, Estate Planning Clinic, Public Defender Clinic, Innocence Project, and Domestic Violence Clinic. Practice seminars are conducted in alternate dispute resolution, appellate practice, and civil procedure. Research and Writing, Advanced Research and Writing, and

Phone: 517-371-5140
800-874-3511
Fax: 517-334-5718
E-mail: admissions@cooley.edu
Web: www.cooley.edu

Contact

Asst. Dean for Admissions, 517-371-5140 ext. 2244 for general inquiries.

MICHIGAN

Law Practice courses provide training in brief writing and oral argument conducted before sitting Circuit Court judges. Directed Studies allow independent research and writing projects. Cooley has an extensive third-year externship program, which places senior students in work settings for 1 or 2 terms throughout the United States. A special lecture series includes the Krinock Lecture and professionalism lectures. The winter term offers study abroad in Australia and New Zealand; the summer term offers Canadian courses in Toronto. Through the Student Tutorial Services, upper-class students help new students form study groups. Faculty members may offer special seminars on study techniques. In addition, the Academic Resource Center coordinates tutorials on exam skills and study techniques and offers individual counseling. The Academic Resource Center provides free assistance for any student requesting it, including Testing Seminars, practice exams, individual counseling, and study skills seminars. Minority programs include BALSA, APALSA, Hispanic Law Society, African Legal Scholars Association, Gay Rights Alliance and Native American Law Students Association. Bar preparation programs are available for all students, as well as the Professional Portfolio Program. The most widely taken electives are Law Practice, Trial Workshop, and Family Law.

Graduation Requirements

In order to graduate, candidates must have a GPA of 2.0, completed the upper-division writing requirement. In addition, a clinic, externship, or comparable practical experience is required.

Organizations

Students edit the *Cooley Law Review*, the *Thomas M. Cooley Journal of Practical and Clinical Law*, the newspaper the *Pillar*, and the *Benchmark*, a magazine published each trimester. The Law School competes in the Frederick Douglass Moot Court, Chicago Bar Association Moot Court, and State of Michigan Moot Court. Other competitions include Environmental Law Moot Court, Evans Competition, National Trial Competition, NACDL, Criminal Justice Trial Advocacy Competition, and Client Counseling Competition. Law student organizations, local chapters of national associations, and campus organizations include the Black Law Students Association, the Criminal Law Society, the ABA-Law Student Division, Phi Delta Phi, International Law Society, ATLA, and Sports Law Club.

Library

The law library contains 694,885 hardcopy volumes and 1,898,794 microform volume equivalents, and subscribes to 3,395 serial publications. Online databases and networks include CALI, CIS Universe, Infotrac, Legal-Trac, LEXIS, Mathew Bender, OCLC First Search, WESTLAW, and Wilsonline Indexes. The school also subscribes to other online databases, which are available to law students for research. Special library collections include a depository for U.S. government documents and special collections in Intellectual Property, Tax, and Ethics. The ratio of library volumes to faculty is 6,812 to 1 and to students is 263 to 1. The ratio of seats in the library to students is 1 to 1.

Faculty

The law school has 131 full-time and 286 part-time faculty members, of whom 149 are women. According to AAUP standards for Category IIA institutions, faculty salaries are well above average. About 11% of full-time faculty have a graduate law degree in addition to the J.D. The ratio of full-time students to full-time faculty in an average class is 22 to 1; in a clinic, 8 to 1. The law school has a regular program of bringing visiting professors and other distinguished lecturers and visitors to campus.

Students

About 49% of the student body are women; 28%, minorities; 15%, African American; 5%, Asian American; 5%, Hispanic; and 1%, Native American. The average age of entering students is 27; age range is 20 to 60. About 16% drop out after the first year for academic or personal reasons.

Placement

J.D.s awarded:	927

Services available through: a separate law school placement center.

Special features: The school has a full-service Career and Professional Development Office.

Full-time job interviews:	9 employers
Summer job interviews:	10 employers
Average starting salary:	$17,000 to $140,000

Areas of placement:

Private practice 2–10 attorneys	28%
Private practice 11–25 attorneys	4%
Private practice 26–50 attorneys	1%
Private practice 51–100 attorneys	1%
Business/industry	18%
Government	13%
Judicial clerkships	4%
Public interest	4%
Academic	3%

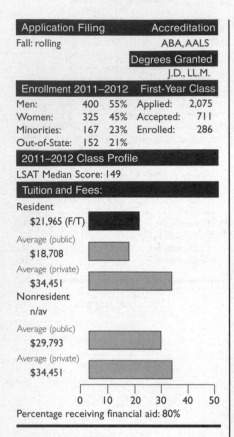

Application Filing	Accreditation
Fall: rolling	ABA, AALS

Degrees Granted
J.D., LL.M.

Enrollment 2011–2012		First-Year Class	
Men:	400 55%	Applied:	2,075
Women:	325 45%	Accepted:	711
Minorities:	167 23%	Enrolled:	286
Out-of-State:	152 21%		

2011–2012 Class Profile

LSAT Median Score: 149

Tuition and Fees:

Resident
$21,965 (F/T)

Average (public)
$18,708

Average (private)
$34,451

Nonresident
n/av

Average (public)
$29,793

Average (private)
$34,451

0   10   20   30   40   50

Percentage receiving financial aid: 80%

ADMISSIONS

In the fall of 2011 first-year class, 2075 applied, 711 were accepted, and 286 enrolled. Thirteen transfers enrolled. The median GPA of the most recent first-year class was 3.0. The lowest LSAT percentile accepted was 15; the highest was 88.

Requirements

Applicants must have a bachelor's degree and take the LSAT. The most important admission factors include academic achievement, LSAT results, and general background. No specific undergraduate courses are required. Candidates are not interviewed.

Procedure

The application deadline for fall entry is rolling. Applicants should submit an application form, LSAT results, transcripts, a personal statement, optional letters of recommendation, and a personal statement. Notification of the admissions decision is on a rolling basis. The law school uses the LSAC.

Special

The law school recruits minority and disadvantaged students by means of visits to historically black colleges, as well as colleges and universities with significant minority populations; the use of Law Services' Candidate Referral Service; Council on Legal Education Opportunity (CLEO); the Legal Education Access Program; and other forums. Requirements are different for out-of-state students. Transfer students must have one year of credit, must submit a personal statement, must be in good academic standing, and must submit a copy of the LSAC report, an official transcript, and a letter of good standing from the law school currently attended.

Costs

Tuition and fees for the 2011–2012 academic year are $21,405 for full-time in-state students. Tuition for part-time students is $15,960 for in-state students.

Financial Aid

About 80% of current law students receive some form of aid. The average annual amount of aid from all sources combined, including scholarships, loans, and work contracts, is $18,500; maximum, $45,111. Awards are based on need and merit combined. The required financial statement is the FAFSA. The aid application deadline for fall entry is April 15. Special funds for minority or disadvantaged students consist of the Touro Grant, awarded based on financial need; Perkins Loan and College Work Study, awarded based on need; and incentive awards, based on need and merit. First-year students are notified about their financial aid application after acceptance but before enrollment.

About the Law School

Touro College Jacob D. Fuchsberg Law Center was established in 1980 and is a private institution. The 11-acre campus is in a suburban area approximately 40 miles east of New York City. The primary mission of the law school is to produce graduates ready for real-world practice. The student experience is characterized by extensive faculty-student interaction, innovative student support systems, and a commitment to a lawyer's moral and ethical obligations. Students have access to federal, state, county, city, and local agencies, courts, correctional facilities,

law firms, and legal aid organizations in the Central Islip area. Facilities of special interest to law students include law firms, local and New York City attorneys' offices, and public interest agencies and firms. Housing for students is available on-campus and off-campus. The school's Housing Information Network and mailings identify available accommodations and students who wish to share housing. About 98% of the law school facilities are accessible to the physically disabled.

Calendar

The law school operates on a traditional semester basis. Courses for full-time students are offered days only, and must be completed within 6 years. For part-time students, courses are offered both day and evening, and must be completed within 6 years. New full- and part-time students are admitted in the fall. There is a 4- and 7-week summer session. Transferable summer courses are offered.

Programs

In addition to the J.D., the law school offers the LL.M. The following joint degrees may be earned: J.D./M.B.A. (Juris Doctor/Master of Business Administration), J.D./M.P.A. (Juris Doctor/Master of Public Administration in Health Care), and J.D./M.S.W. (Juris Doctor/Master of Social Work).

Required

To earn the J.D., candidates must complete 87 total credits, of which 51 to 52 are for required courses. They must maintain a minimum GPA of 2.0 in the required courses. The following first-year courses are required of all students: Civil Procedure I and II, Contracts I and II, Criminal Law I, Legal Methods I and II, Property I, and Torts I and II. Required upper-level courses consist of Advanced Writing Requirement, Business Organizations I, Constitutional Law I and II, Evidence, Perspective Requirement, Professional Responsibility, Property II, Public Interest Requirement, and Trusts and Estates. The required orientation program for first-year students is a 5-day program that deals mostly with legal methods and provides an introduction to law; case assignments are given in advance for students to read, brief, and discuss.

Contact
Assistant Dean of Administration, 631-421-2244, ext. 302 for general inquiries; Associate Director of Financial Aid, 631-421-2244, ext. 322 for financial aid information.

NEW YORK

Electives

The Jacob D. Fuchsberg Law Center offers concentrations in corporate law, criminal law, family law, international law, litigation, torts and insurance, public interest and civil rights, intellectual property, real estate law, health law, and immigration law. In addition, clinical offerings include Family Law (6 credits), Criminal Law (5 credits), and International Human Rights/Immigration Litigation (4 credits). Seminars are open to all students who have satisfied the prerequisites. Law and Medicine: Selected Topics in Law, Medicine, and Ethics; Patent Practice Seminar; and Selected Topics in Corporate Law are three examples. Internships are arranged through the Career Planning Office for positions during the semester and in the summer. Externships are also available in-house, at the Law Center's Domestic Violence Project and at the Housing Rights Project. Second- and third-year students may apply to be paid research assistants for a faculty member. Also, students may take Independent Research for 1 to 3 credits. Field work may be done through Career Planning externships, through the pro bono requirement, and through clinical offerings. Annually, the Law Center hosts the 3 lecture series: Distinguished Jurist in Residence; Distinguished Public Interest Lawyer in Residence; and the Bruce K. Gould Book Award. Any student in good academic standing may take up to 6 credits at an ABA-approved summer program. Such programs are evaluated on a case-by-case basis. The Office of Student Affairs arranges summer placements abroad in London, Paris, Lisbon, Brussels, Cork, Tel Aviv, Jerusalem, and Moscow. The Writing Resources Clinic provides writing specialists to assist students. The Professional Development Program, designed to help first-year students adapt to the rigors of law school, provides teaching assistants in most required courses, as well as TA mentors and TA tutors for writing skills. Minority students may take advantage of the Legal Education Access Program (LEAP), which offers an orientation program, a lecture series, discussion groups, mentor program, and individual counseling. Special interest groups include the Institute for Jewish Law and the Institute for Business Law and Technology. The most widely taken electives are New York Practice, Family Law, and Criminal Procedure.

Graduation Requirements

In order to graduate, candidates must have a GPA of 2.0, must have completed the upper-division writing requirement, and must have successfully completed all the required courses and additional requirements (Perspective Requirement, Public Interest Requirement, and Advanced Writing Requirement).

Organizations
Students edit the *Touro Law Review*, the newspaper *The Restatement*, and the yearbook *Res Ipsa*. Students compete in the Albany Law School Family Law Moot Court Competition, Benjamin N. Cardozo National Moot Court in Entertainment Law, and Brooklyn Law School's Jerome Prince Invitational Evidence Competition. Other competitions include the New York State Bar Association Legal Ethics Writing Competition, the Nathan Burkan Copyright Law, Association of Trial Lawyers of America, and ABA Negotiation and Counseling competitions. Law student organizations include the Student Bar Association, Delta Theta Phi International Law Fraternity, and Women's Bar Association. There are local chapters of ABA-Law Student Division, National Jewish Students Network, and American Civil Liberties Union. Other organizations include BLSA, Jewish Law Students Association, and PILOT (public interest student organization).

Library
The law library contains 429,683 hardcopy volumes and 225,964 microform volume equivalents, and subscribes to 1,400 serial publications. Such online databases and networks as CALI, Legal-Trac, LEXIS, OCLC First Search, WESTLAW, and full Internet access are available to law students for research. Special library collections include an official depository for selected U.S. government publications, a selective New York State depository, an extensive Judaica collection, and rare English, American, and foreign legal works. The ratio of library volumes to faculty is 13,860 to 1 and to students is 598 to 1. The ratio of seats in the library to students is 1 to 2.

Faculty
The law school has 31 full-time and 41 part-time faculty members, of whom 18 are women. About 33% of full-time faculty

Placement
Services available through: a separate law school placement center.
Services: employer panels, resource library, judicial clerkship screening committee, job prospectus, and alumni newsletter online daily.

Full-time job interviews:	14 employers
Summer job interviews:	9 employers
Placement by graduation:	57% of class
Placement within 9 months:	78% of class
Average starting salary:	$40,000 to $63,000

Areas of placement:

Private practice 2–10 attorneys	31%
Private practice 11–25 attorneys	6%
Private practice 26–50 attorneys	5%
Private practice 51–100 attorneys	2%
Business/industry	23%
Government	21%
Public interest	5%
Academic	3%
Judicial clerkships	2%

have a graduate law degree in addition to the J.D. The ratio of full-time students to full-time faculty in an average class is 35 to 1; in a clinic, 8 to 1. The law school has a regular program of bringing visiting professors and other distinguished lecturers and visitors to campus.

Students
About 45% of the student body are women; 23%, minorities; 11%, African American; 6%, Asian American; and 7%, Hispanic. The majority of students come from New York (79%). The average age of entering students is 26; age range is 20 to 63. About 60% of students enter directly from undergraduate school, 25% have a graduate degree, and 64% have worked full-time prior to entering law school. About 5% drop out after the first year for academic or personal reasons; 90% remain to receive a law degree.

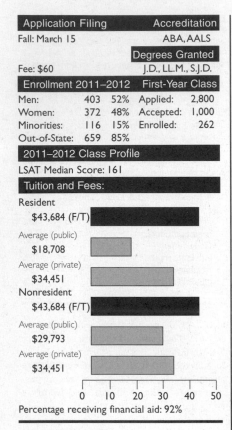

Application Filing	Accreditation
Fall: March 15	ABA, AALS

	Degrees Granted
Fee: $60	J.D., LL.M., S.J.D.

Enrollment 2011–2012 / First-Year Class

Men:	403	52%	Applied:	2,800
Women:	372	48%	Accepted:	1,000
Minorities:	116	15%	Enrolled:	262
Out-of-State:	659	85%		

2011–2012 Class Profile
LSAT Median Score: 161

Tuition and Fees:

Resident
$43,684 (F/T)

Average (public)
$18,708

Average (private)
$34,451

Nonresident
$43,684 (F/T)

Average (public)
$29,793

Average (private)
$34,451

Percentage receiving financial aid: 92%

ADMISSIONS
In the fall of 2011 first-year class, 2800 applied, 1000 were accepted, and 262 enrolled. Fifteen transfers enrolled. The median GPA of the most recent first-year class was 3.55. The lowest LSAT percentile accepted was 25; the highest was 99.

Requirements
Applicants must take the LSAT. The most important admission factors include LSAT results, GPA, and academic achievement. No specific undergraduate courses are required. Candidates are interviewed.

Procedure
The application deadline for fall entry is March 15. Applicants should submit an application form, LSAT results, transcripts, a personal statement, a nonrefundable application fee of $60, and up to 3 recommended letters of recommendation. Notification of the admissions decision is from December 15 through the summer. The law school uses the LSAC.

Special
The law school recruits minority and disadvantaged students by actively visiting undergraduate schools, using the CRS, and following up. Requirements are different for out-of-state students. Transfer students must have one year of credits, personal statement, and have a good law school record.

Costs
Tuition and fees for the 2011–2012 academic year are $40,040 for all full-time students. Books and supplies run $1,500.

Financial Aid
About 92% of current law students receive some form of aid. The average annual amount of aid from all sources combined, including scholarships, loans, and work contracts, is $50,000; maximum, $64,134. Awards are based on need and merit, along with loans are based on need, while scholarships are based on merit. Required financial statement is the FAFSA. Special funds for minority or disadvantaged students are available. First-year students are notified about their financial aid application in the spring.

About the Law School
Tulane University Law School was established in 1847 and is a private institution. The 110-acre campus is located in an urban area in uptown New Orleans. The primary mission of the law school is to provide the best possible professional training so that graduates will become effective and ethical lawyers with skills that qualify them to practice law anywhere in the United States or the world. Students have access to federal, state, county, city, and local agencies, courts, correctional facilities, law firms, and legal aid organizations in the New Orleans area. There are five levels of courts in New Orleans: state trial, appellate, and supreme; and federal trial and appellate. Facilities of special interest to law students are the Reily Recreation Center, Freeman School of Business, and numerous cultural opportunities throughout the city. Housing for students is available in neighborhood surrounding the campus. About 95% of the law school facilities are accessible to the physically disabled.

Calendar
The law school operates on a traditional semester basis. Courses for full-time students are offered days only and with a small number of elective courses offered during the evening and must be completed within 6 semesters, although limited leaves of absence are permitted. There is no part-time program. New full-time students are admitted in the fall. There is a 6-week summer session. Transferable summer courses are offered.

Programs
In addition to the J.D., the law school offers the LL.M. and S.J.D. The following joint degrees may be earned: J.D./M.Acc. (Juris Doctor/Master of Accounting), J.D./M.A. (Juris Doctor/Master of Arts in Latin American Studies), J.D./M.B.A. (Juris Doctor/Master of Business Administration), J.D./M.H.A. (Juris Doctor/Master of Health Administration), J.D./M.P.H. (Juris Doctor/Master of Public Health in community health sciences), J.D./M.P.H. (Juris Doctor/Master of Public Health in global environmental health sciences), J.D./M.S. (Juris Doctor/Master of Science in international development), and J.D./M.S.W. (Juris Doctor/Master of Social Work).

Required
To earn the J.D., candidates must complete 88 total credits, of which 32 are for required courses. They must maintain a minimum GPA of 2.0 in the required courses. The following first-year courses are required of all students: Civil Procedure, Constitutional Law, Contracts I, Contracts II or Oblications I, Criminal Law, Legal Research and Writing, Property (Civil or Common), and Torts. Required upper-level courses consist of 30 hours of community service and Legal Profession. The required orientation program for first-year students is 5 days of logistical and administrative information plus sessions on case briefing, career development, legal analysis, and LRW.

Electives
The Law School offers concentrations in environmental law, internationl law, maritime law, sports law, European legal studies, and civil law. In addition, 6 different clinics, including representation of actual clients, are available for third-year students for 8 credits. Second- and

Phone: 504-865-5930
Fax: 504-865-6710
E-mail: *admissions@law.tulane.edu*
Web: *www.law.tulane.edu*

Contact

Susan Krinsky, Associate Dean for Admission, 504-865-5930 for general inquiries; Georgia Whiddon, 504-865-5931 for financial aid information.

LOUISIANA

third-year students may earn 2 to 3 credits for seminars that are offered in various advanced legal areas and typically require an extensive research paper. Judicial and other externships, 1-year (2-semester) externship programs worth 4 credits, are offered to third-year students. Upper-level students may undertake directed research with individual faculty members for a maximum of 3 credits. Field work in some courses, particularly advanced environmental law, is offered. Many special lecture series are also offered each year. Students may earn 3 to 6 credits for the summer study-abroad program, offered in 6 countries and held for 2 to 4 weeks. In addition, some semester-long exchange programs are available with universities abroad. Selected first-year students may take the tutorial course, Legal Analysis, for 1 credit. Support and placement programs for minority students are sponsored by the school, including an assistant dean. Special interest group programs are provided by 40 student organizations. The most widely taken electives are Business Enterprises, Evidence, and Trusts and Estates.

Graduation Requirements

In order to graduate, candidates must have a GPA of 2.0, have completed the upper-division writing requirement, and have performed 30 hours of mandatory pro bono work.

Organizations

Students edit the *Tulane Law Review, Tulane Maritime Law Journal, Tulane Environmental Law Journal, Journal of Law and Sexuality, Tulane Journal of International and Comparative Law, Civil Law Forum, Sports Law Journal, Journal of Technology and Intellectual Property,* and the student newspaper *Dicta*. There are separate intraschool trial and appellate competitions for second- and third-year students, plus a variety of interschool competitions, including the Jessup International, Negotiations, and Trial competitions. Law student organizations, local chapters of national associations, and campus organizations include the Environmental Law Society, Public Interest Law Foundation, International Law Society, American Civil Liberties Union, Child Advocates, Tulane Law Women, Public Interest Law Foundation, BLSA, Federal Society, and American Constitution Society.

Library

The law library contains 408,756 hardcopy volumes and 263,252 microform volume equivalents, and subscribes to 1,118 serial publications Such online databases and networks as CALI, Infotrac, Legal-Trac, LEXIS, OCLC First Search, WESTLAW, Wilsonline Indexes, and the law school subscribes to many other databases and networks available to law students for research. Special library collections include canon law, European law, civil law, maritime law, Roman Law, and the Judge John Minor Wisdom Papers Collection, comparative law, Sherman Law & Literature. The ratio of library volumes to faculty is 10,220 to 1 and to students is 527 to 1. The ratio of seats in the library to students is 1 to 1.

Faculty

The law school has 42 full-time and 75 part-time faculty members, of whom 27 are women. According to AAUP standards for Category I institutions, faculty salaries are average. About 35% of full-time faculty have a graduate law degree in addition to the J.D.; about 24% of part-time faculty have one. The ratio of full-time students to full-time faculty in an average class is 35 to 1; in a clinic, 14 to 1. The law school has a regular program of bringing visiting professors and other distinguished lecturers and visitors to campus. There is a chapter of the Order of the Coif; 80 faculty are members.

Students

About 48% of the student body are women; 15%, minorities; 6%, African American; 1%, Asian American; 6%, Hispanic; 1%, Native American; and 1%, 2 or more ethnicities. The majority of students come from Louisiana (15%). The average age of entering students is 24; age range is 19 to 49. About 38% of students enter directly from undergraduate school, 8% have a graduate degree, and 81% have worked full-time prior to entering law school. About 5% drop out after the first year for academic or personal reasons; 92% remain to receive a law degree.

Placement

J.D.s awarded:	241

Services available through: a separate law school placement center.

Services: videotaped mock interviews, law firm tours and orientations, job fairs and placement consortia, and introduction to new cities.

Special features: career mini-course for first-year students.

Full-time job interviews:	100 employers
Summer job interviews:	100 employers
Placement by graduation:	50% of class
Placement within 9 months:	85% of class
Average starting salary:	$35,000 to $140,000

Areas of placement:

Private practice 2–501 attorneys	59%
Judicial clerkships	10%
Government	9%
Public interest	6%
Business/industry	5%
Academic	1%

UNIVERSITY OF AKRON

School of Law

302 Buchtel Common
Akron, OH 44325-2901

Application Filing	Accreditation
Fall: March I	ABA, AALS
	Degrees Granted
Fee: n/av	J.D., LL.M.

Enrollment 2011–2012			First-Year Class	
Men:	308	57%	Applied:	1,647
Women:	228	43%	Accepted:	883
Minorities:	75	14%	Enrolled:	175
Out-of-State:	123	23%		

2011–2012 Class Profile
LSAT Percentile: 56%
LSAT Median Score: 153
Percentage passing bar on first try: 92%

Tuition and Fees:

Resident
$21,873 (F/T)

Average (public)
$18,708

Average (private)
$34,451

Nonresident
$34,428 (F/T)

Average (public)
$29,793

Average (private)
$34,451

0   10   20   30   40   50

Percentage receiving financial aid: 86%

ADMISSIONS

In the fall of 2011 first-year class, 1647 applied, 883 were accepted, and 175 enrolled. Six transfers enrolled. The median LSAT percentile of the most recent first-year class was 56; the median GPA was 3.3 on a scale of 4.0. The lowest LSAT percentile accepted was 21; the highest was 95.

Requirements
Applicants must have a bachelor's degree and take the LSAT. Minimum acceptable GPA is 2.0 on a scale of 4.0. The most important admission factors include LSAT results, GPA, and general background. No specific undergraduate courses are required. Candidates are not interviewed.

Procedure
The application deadline for fall entry is March 1. Applicants should submit an application form, LSAT results, transcripts, a personal statement, TOEFL (if applicable), and 2 to 3 letters of recommendation. Notification of the admissions decision is 4 to 6 weeks after the application. The law school uses the LSAC.

Special
The law school recruits minority and disadvantaged students by means of publications, visiting colleges with a large percentage of minority students, sending mailings, holding recruitment days, participating in minority law fairs, granting scholarships, and advertising. In addition, minority law students and alumni contact minority admittees to welcome them. Requirements are different for out-of-state students. Transfer students must have one year of credit, must have a minimum GPA of 3, must have attended an ABA-approved law school, and must submit a personal statement.

Costs

Tuition and fees for the 2011–2012 academic year are $18,977 for full-time in-state students and $31,532 for out-of-state students. Tuition for part-time students is $15,181 for in-state students and $25,224 out-of-state. On-campus room and board costs about $11,134 annually; books and supplies run $900.

Financial Aid

About 86% of current law students receive some form of aid. Awards are based on need and merit combined. Required financial statements are the FAFSA and the Institutional Aid Application. The aid application deadline for fall entry is May 1. First-year students are notified about their financial aid application at time of acceptance.

About the Law School

University of Akron School of Law was established in 1921 and is a public institution. The 170-acre campus is in an urban area 40 miles south of Cleveland, Ohio. The primary mission of the law school is to prepare students to become outstanding members of the bench and bar. Students have access to federal, state, county, city, and local agencies, courts, correctional facilities, law firms, and legal aid organizations in the Akron area. There is the Akron Municipal Court, Summit County Court, Ninth District Court of Appeals, and Federal Court. Facilities of special interest to law students include the Intellectual Property Center and the Legal Clinic. Housing for students is available on campus in graduate housing; many off-campus affordable housing options are available within walking distance or a short drive. All law school facilities are accessible to the physically disabled.

Calendar

The law school operates on a traditional semester basis. Courses for full-time students are offered both day and evening, and must be completed within 6 years. For part-time students, courses are offered both day and evening, and must be completed within 6 years. New full- and part-time students are admitted in the fall. There are 5- and 10-week summer sessions. Transferable summer courses are offered.

Programs

In addition to the J.D., the law school offers the LL.M. Students may take relevant courses in other programs and apply credit toward the J.D.; a maximum of 6 graduate level credits may be applied. The following joint degrees may be earned: J.D./ L.L.M. (Juris Doctor/L.L.M. in Intellectual Property Law), J.D./M.A.P. (Juris Doctor/ Master of Applied Politics), J.D./M.B.A. (Juris Doctor/Master of Business Administration), J.D./M.P.A. (Juris Doctor/Master of Public Administration), and J.D./M.Tax. (Juris Doctor/Master of Taxation).

Required
To earn the J.D., candidates must complete 88 total credits, of which 44 are for required courses. They must maintain a minimum GPA of 2.0 in the required courses. The following first-year courses are required of all students: Civil Procedure I and II, Contracts I and II, Criminal Law, Introduction: Law and Legal Systems, Legal Analysis, Research, and Writing I and II, Property I and II, and Torts I and II. Required upper-level courses consist of Advanced Legal Research, a general writing requirement, Constitutional Law I and II, Evidence, Legal Drafting, and Professional Responsibility. The required orientation program for first-year students, Introduction to Law and Legal Systems, is a 1-week course held during the first week of classes.

Electives
The School of Law offers concentrations in corporate law, criminal law, intellectual property law, internationl law, labor law, litigation, tax law, and public interest law.

Phone: 330-972-7331
800-4-AKRON-U
Fax: 330-258-2343
E-mail: lthorpe@uakron.edu
Web: www.uakron.edu/law

Contact

Lauri S. Thorpe, Assistant Dean, 330-972-7331, 800-4-AKRON-U, 330-972-6367 for general inquiries; University Financial Aid Office, 330-972-7032 for financial aid information.

OHIO

In addition, the Trial Litigation and the Civil Litigation clinics allow third-year students to be certified legal interns to represent clients in court; in the clinical seminar, students with strong academic records may clerk for judges. There is also a clinic in Appellate Review. Clinic students may be placed in-house or externally for credit after their first year. Students with an intern certificate may represent clients in civil and misdemeanor cases in court. The SEED Clinic allows students to provide legal support to emerging businesses in the greater Akron area. Seminars include Feminist and Race Theory, International Investment, and Business Planning. Internships for academic credit (clinical seminars) are coordinated and monitored by the clinic staff. Public interest fellowships are coordinated by the Law Center Planning Office. Traditional employment opportunities are also coordinated through the Career Planning Office. All students must write a significant research paper in order to graduate. Individual studies and research may be taken under the guidance of a faculty member. Upper-division students may apply to become a research assistant for a law faculty member. Research may be in conjunction with a course. Field work is offered through the School of Law Legal Clinic for credit or the Career Planning and Placement Office or on a voluntary basis. Special lecture series are held during the fall and spring semesters in a wide variety of areas, with emphasis on intellectual property and Constitutional law. Study abroad is only available through another ABA-accredited law school's study-abroad program. With permission of the associate dean, students may assume visiting status at another ABA-accredited law school and transfer credits back to Akron. The Academic Success Program provides individual and group workshop programming, including tutoring. Student mentors also assist individuals or groups in specific courses and in building skills for success in law school and practice. No formal remedial programs are required. The Black Law Students Association (BLSA) sponsors outlining and exam-taking seminars, adopt-a-school, scholarships, an annual dinner/dance, regional job fairs, Frederick Douglass Moot Court Competition, and travel to regional and national BLSA events. The Asian Latino Law Students Association (ALLSA) coordinates various service projects for the community involving law student volunteers. The Gay-Straight Law Students Alliance coordinates co-curricular programming and community service projects. The

school participates in a minority clerkship program with the bar association, leading law firms, and judges. The most widely taken electives are Administration of Criminal Justice; Wills, Trusts and Estates; and Corporations.

Graduation Requirements

In order to graduate, candidates must have a GPA of 2.0 and must have completed the upper-division writing and other requirements.

Organizations

Students edit the *Akron Law Review*, *Akron Tax Journal*, *Akron Intellectual Property Journal*, and the online *Journal of Constitutional Law*. The moot court team attends the ABA/LSD-National Appellate Advocacy competition, National Moot Court competition, New York Bar National Moot Court Competition, and Jessup International Law Competition. A trial team attends competitions sponsored by Association of Trial Lawyers of America, National Institute for Trial Advocacy, the Academy of Trial Lawyers of Allegheny County, PA, and other associations. Law student organizations, local chapters of national associations, and campus organizations include the Intellectual Property and Technology Law Association, National Association of Criminal Defense Lawyers, Sports and Entertainment Law Society, International Law Society, Student Bar Association, Law Association for Women's Rights, Phi Alpha Delta, Phi Delta Phi, and Black Law Students Association.

Library

The law library contains 259,519 hardcopy volumes and 377,025 microform volume equivalents. Such online databases and networks as CALI, CIS Universe, Infotrac, Legal-Trac, LEXIS, Mathew Bender, OCLC First Search, WESTLAW, Wilsonline Indexes, 100 databases on Ohiolink, BNA Premier Plus, and LLMC Digital are available to law students for research. Special library collections include an intellectual property collection. The ratio of library volumes to faculty is 8,318 to 1 and to students is 562 to 1. The ratio of seats in the library to students is 1 to 2.

Faculty

The law school has 37 full-time and 38 part-time faculty members, of whom 26

Placement

J.D.s awarded:	116

Services available through: a separate law school placement center, the university placement center, and the College of Business Placement Center.

Services: judicial clerkship programs, mentor program, preparatory career planning workshops and seminars, mock interview program, on-campus interviews, and the government and public interest information fair.

Special features: individualized counseling and assistance to students with all phases of the job search, computerized job postings, participation in off-campus hiring programs for intellectual property and public interest law, participation in local as well as off-campus hiring programs for minority students, law clerk for hire database, and minority clerkship program.

Full-time job interviews:	10 employers
Summer job interviews:	18 employers
Placement by graduation:	56% of class
Placement within 9 months:	92% of class
Average starting salary:	$55,980 to $130,000

Areas of placement:

Private practice 2–10 attorneys	21%
Private practice 11–25 attorneys	5%
Private practice 26–50 attorneys	2%
Private practice 51–100 attorneys	3%
Business/industry	25%
Government	17%
Solo practioners	10%
Judicial clerkships	6%
Public interest	6%
Academic	5%

are women. According to AAUP standards for Category I institutions, faculty salaries are below average. About 19% of full-time faculty have a graduate law degree in addition to the J.D. The ratio of full-time students to full-time faculty in an average class is 14 to 1; in a clinic, 1 to 1. The law school has a regular program of bringing visiting professors and other distinguished lecturers and visitors to campus.

Students

About 43% of the student body are women; 14%, minorities; 6%, African American; 4%, Asian American; and 4%, Hispanic. The majority of students come from Ohio (77%). The average age of entering students is 26; age range is 21 to 59. About 58% of students enter directly from undergraduate school, and 9% have a graduate degree. About 13% drop out after the first year for academic or personal reasons; 87% remain to receive a law degree.

UNIVERSITY OF ALABAMA

School of Law

Box 870382
Tuscaloosa, AL 35487-0382

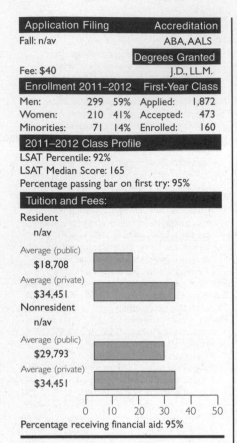

Application Filing
Fall: n/av

Accreditation
ABA, AALS

Degrees Granted
Fee: $40
J.D., LL.M.

Enrollment 2011–2012 **First-Year Class**

Men:	299	59%	Applied:	1,872
Women:	210	41%	Accepted:	473
Minorities:	71	14%	Enrolled:	160

2011–2012 Class Profile
LSAT Percentile: 92%
LSAT Median Score: 165
Percentage passing bar on first try: 95%

Tuition and Fees:

Resident
n/av

Average (public)
$18,708

Average (private)
$34,451

Nonresident
n/av

Average (public)
$29,793

Average (private)
$34,451

0   10   20   30   40   50

Percentage receiving financial aid: 95%

ADMISSIONS

In the fall of 2011 first-year class, 1872 applied, 473 were accepted, and 160 enrolled. Twenty Seven transfers enrolled. The median LSAT percentile of the most recent first-year class was 92; the median GPA was 3.8 on a scale of 4.0.

Requirements

Applicants must have a bachelor's degree and take the LSAT. The most important admission factors include LSAT results, GPA, and academic achievement. No specific undergraduate courses are required. Candidates are not interviewed.

Procedure

Applicants should submit an application form, LSAT results, transcripts, a personal statement, the TOEFL for the LL.M. International Program and International JD, a nonrefundable application fee of $40, a letter of recommendation, and supplemental information as required by the application questions. Notification of the admissions decision is on a rolling basis. The law school uses the LSAC.

Special

The law school recruits minority and disadvantaged students by means of recruiters visiting undergraduate institutions and mailings; participating annually in law forums; and involving students, alumni, and faculty in recruitment efforts. Requirements are different for out-of-state students in that residency is one of many factors considered by the admission committee. Transfer students must have one year of credit, must have attended an ABA-approved law school, and must submit a personal statement. Applicants should have a collegiate academic record and an LSAT score that would have qualified the student for entry-level admission to the school. They must be in good standing at the current law school, as evidenced by a letter from the dean of that school, must not be on any kind of probationary status, and must rank academically high at that school. It is rare for an applicant outside the top 25% of the class to be admitted.

Costs

Tuition and fees for the 2011–2012 academic year are $18,030 for full-time in-state students and $30,950 for out-of-state students. Books and supplies run $1,400.

Financial Aid

About 95% of current law students receive some form of aid. Awards are based on need and merit. The School of Law provides significant merit-based scholarship support to students. Applicants are considered automatically for scholarships. Applications for loans may consider financial information. The required financial statement is the FAFSA. First-year students are notified about their financial aid application at time of acceptance.

About the Law School

University of Alabama School of Law was established in 1872 and is a public institution. The 20-acre campus is in a small town 60 miles southwest of Birmingham. The primary mission of the law school is to prepare future lawyers for their critical role in society, as well as to become a dynamic part of the community. Students have access to federal, state, county, city, and local agencies, courts, correctional facilities, law firms, and legal aid organizations in the Tuscaloosa area. Facilities of special interest to law students include the moot court and trial advocacy rooms, student lounge, student study areas, and clinic program offices. Students may apply for limited housing available in residence halls and university-owned and operated apartments and efficiency units. The majority of the law students live off campus. All law school facilities are accessible to the physically disabled.

Calendar

The law school operates on a traditional semester basis. Courses for full-time students are offered days only and must be completed within 74 months. New full-time students are admitted in the fall. There is a 5-week summer session. Transferable summer courses are offered.

Programs

In addition to the J.D., the law school offers the LL.M. Students may take relevant courses in other programs and apply credit toward the J.D.; a maximum of 6 credits may be applied. The following joint degrees may be earned: J.D./Ph.D. (Juris Doctor/Doctor of Philosophy in Economics Dual Program (Dual enrollment)), J.D./M.B.A. (Juris Doctor/Master of Business Administration), J.D./LL.M. (Juris Doctor/Masters in Business Transactions (Dual enrollment)), J.D./M.C.E. (Juris Doctor/Masters in Civil Engineering (Dual enrollment)), and J.D./LL.M. (Juris Doctor/Masters in Taxation (Dual enrollment)).

Required

To earn the J.D., candidates must complete 90 total credits, of which 36 are for required courses. The following first-year courses are required of all students: Civil Procedure, Constitutional Law, Contracts, Criminal Law, Evidence, Legal Research, Legal Writing, Moot Court, Property, and Torts. Required upper-level courses consist of at least one seminar, The Legal Profession, and three credit hours of professional skills courses. The required orientation program for first-year students is a 2 1/2-day program geared toward making the transition into law school as smooth as possible.

Phone: 205-348-5440
Fax: 205-348-7945
E-mail: admissions@law.ua.edu
Web: www.law.ua.edu

Contact

Jami Gates, Assistant Director of Admissions, 205-348-5440 for general inquiries; Noah Funderburg, Associate Dean, 205-348-5680 for financial aid information.

ALABAMA

Electives

The School of Law offers concentrations in corporate law, criminal law, environmental law, internationl law, litigation, and tax law. In addition, clinics are offered for 3 to 4 credit hours. Students may take 2-credit hour internships in which a student clerks for a judge. Seminars are small groups of second- and third-year students. Instruction is on a more informal and advanced basis than in basic courses. A written paper is required. First-year students are required to carry out a closely supervised program in legal research and writing. They must also participate in a moot court program in appellate advocacy involving substantial library research. A course in advanced legal research is offered as a 2-hour elective for upper-level students. Four credit externships are available during the summer and academic year in a great variety of placements. Special lecture series include the Hugo L. Black Lecture, established in 1996 to honor the U.S. Supreme Court Justice Hugo L. Black, who was a 1906 graduate of the law school, and the Daniel J. Meador Lecture, established in 1994 to honor Professor Meador, a 1951 graduate. Study abroad is available through a program at the University of Fribourg and the Australian National University in Canberra, Australia. Students at Fribourg take 2 classes for 5 hours of credit. Several programs support a diversified student body. Special interest group programs include the Future Trial Lawyers Association, Dorbin Association(support group for women), Black Law Students Association, and the Alabama Public Interest Law Association to name a few. The most widely taken electives are Trial Advocacy, Criminal Procedure, and Business Organizations.

Graduation Requirements

In order to graduate, candidates must have a GPA of 2.3 and must have completed the upper-division writing requirement.

Organizations

Students edit the *Alabama Law Review, Law and Psychology Review, The Alabama Civil Rights & Civil Liberties Law Review, and The Journal of the Legal Profession*. The school participates annually in the National Moot Court, Phillip C. Jessup International Law Moot Court, and Frederick Douglass Moot Court competitions, and in competitions involving environmental law, labor law, bankruptcy law, intellectual property law, and tax law. The law school also participates in 4 to 5 trial advocacy competitions each year and in 3 to 5 additional moot court competitions. Law school organizations, local chapters of national associations, and campus organizations include Phi Alpha Delta, Phi Delta Phi, Delta Theta Phi, Bench and Bar Society, Environmental Law Society, American Civil Liberties Union, Amnesty International, the American Constitution Society, and the Black Law Students Association.

Library

The law library contains 464,870 hardcopy volumes and 157,256 microform volume equivalents. Such online databases and networks as CALI, DIALOG, Infotrac, Legal-Trac, LEXIS, OCLC First Search, WESTLAW, OCLC, HeinOnline, Making of Modern Law, LLMC Digital, and BNA Online are available to law students for research. Special library collections include several thousand photographs, the papers of former U.S. Senator Howell Heflin, of former Congressman Kenneth A. Roberts, of former director of the Federal Deposit Insurance Corporation George LeMaistre, and of former professors John C. Payne and Jay Murphy. In addition, the Bounds Law Library maintains a replica of U.S. Supreme Court Justice Hugo L. Black's Alexandria, VA library. It also includes all decisions of appellate-level state and federal courts, all state and federal codes, Alabama and federal rules and regulations, and the decisions of selected agencies and of principal courts of the Commonwealth nations. There are also extensive treatise holdings. The ratio of library volumes to faculty is 12,233 to 1 and to students is 913 to 1. The ratio of seats in the library to students is 1 to 1.

Faculty

The law school has 38 full-time and 36 part-time faculty members, of whom 18 are women. According to AAUP standards for Category I institutions, faculty salaries are average. About 33% of full-time faculty have a graduate law degree in addition to the J.D. The ratio of full-time students to full-time faculty in an average class is 10 to 1; in a clinic, 7 to 1. The law school has a regular program

Placement

J.D.s awarded:	166

Services available through: a separate law school placement center.

Special features: fall and spring on-campus interviewing and resume forwarding programs, participation in job fairs, seminars, various publications, telephone and message/mail delivery service, LEXIS and WESTLAW computers, programs on nontraditional legal careers, and other job possibilities.

Full-time job interviews:	n/av
Summer job interviews:	56 employers
Placement by graduation:	81% of class
Placement within 9 months:	96% of class
Average starting salary:	$50,000 to $100,000

Areas of placement:

Private practice 2–10 attorneys	25%
Private practice 11–25 attorneys	3%
Private practice 26–50 attorneys	3%
Private practice 51–100 attorneys	8%
Government	9%
Public interest	4%
Academic	2%
Judicial clerkships	14%
Business/industry	13%

of bringing visiting professors and other distinguished lecturers and visitors to campus. There is a chapter of the Order of the Coif; 17 faculty and 738 graduates are members.

Students

About 41% of the student body are women; 14%, minorities; 9%, African American; 1%, Asian American; 2%, Hispanic; and 1%, two or more races. The average age of entering students is 25. About 2% drop out after the first year for academic or personal reasons; 98% remain to receive a law degree.

UNIVERSITY OF ARIZONA

James E. Rogers College of Law

120 E. Speedway, P.O. Box 210176
Tucson, AZ 85721-0176

Application Filing	Accreditation
Fall: n/av	ABA, AALS

	Degrees Granted
	J.D., LL.M.

Enrollment 2011–2012		First-Year Class	
Men:	240 50%	Applied:	2,589
Women:	240 50%	Accepted:	455
Minorities:	139 29%	Enrolled:	153
Out-of-State:	144 30%		

2011–2012 Class Profile
LSAT Percentile: 89%
LSAT Median Score: 162

Tuition and Fees:

Resident
$26,089 (F/T)

Average (public)
$18,708

Average (private)
$34,451

Nonresident
n/av

Average (public)
$29,793

Average (private)
$34,451

Percentage receiving financial aid: 85%

ADMISSIONS

In the fall of 2011 first-year class, 2589 applied, 455 were accepted, and 153 enrolled. Eight transfers enrolled. The median LSAT percentile of the most recent first-year class was 89; the median GPA was 3.5 on a scale of 4.0.

Requirements

Applicants must have a bachelor's degree and take the LSAT. The most important admission factors include academic achievement and LSAT results. No specific undergraduate courses are required. Candidates are not interviewed.

Procedure

Applicants should submit an application form, LSAT results, transcripts, TOEFL for foreign applicants, 2 letters of recommendation, a CAS report, a personal statement, and a resume. Notification of the admissions decision is December through May. The law school uses the LSAC.

Special

The law school recruits minority and disadvantaged students through a strong recruitment and retention program. Ethnicity is one of many qualitative factors considered by the Admissions Committee. Requirements are different for out-of-state students in that admission is slightly more competitive for nonresident students. Generally 70% of enrollees are residents and 30% are nonresidents; however, more than 50% of admission offers go to non-residents. Transfer students must have one year of credit, must have attended an ABA-approved law school, and should be ranked in the top tenth to the top quarter of their class. Space in the class and nature of law school attended are always factors, as are undergraduate record, LSAT score, admissibility as a first-year applicant, personal statement, and letters of recommendation from law faculty with whom the applicant has studied.

Costs

On-campus room and board costs about $12,018 annually; books and supplies run $1,000.

Financial Aid

About 85% of current law students receive some form of aid. The average annual amount of aid from all sources combined, including scholarships, loans, and work contracts, is $10,000; maximum, $30,000. Awards are based on need and merit combined. The required financial statement is the FAFSA. The aid application deadline for fall entry is March 1. Special funds for minority or disadvantaged students are available. First-year students are notified about their financial aid application between acceptance and enrollment, generally between February and June.

About the Law School

University of Arizona James E. Rogers College of Law was established in 1925 and is a public institution. The 325-acre campus is in an urban area near downtown Tucson. The primary mission of the law school is to integrate the study of interdisciplinary issues with the traditional legal course of study in a small law school of approximately 480 students, with a rigorous yet collegial atmosphere. Students have access to federal, state, county, city, and local agencies, courts,

correctional facilities, law firms, and legal aid organizations in the Tucson area. In addition, Arizona is home to many Native American tribes, all with their own tribal governments and trial court systems. Facilities of special interest to law students include classrooms, a moot court room, seminar rooms, a student lounge, a library, a computer laboratory for students, and a fully equipped computerized courtroom. Housing for students includes plenty of affordable off-campus rental housing and a new graduate student apartment-type residence hall on campus. All law school facilities are accessible to the physically disabled.

Calendar

The law school operates on a traditional semester basis. Courses for full-time students are offered days only, and must be completed within 3 years. New full-time students are admitted in the fall. There is a 5-week summer session. Transferable summer courses are offered.

Programs

In addition to the J.D., the law school offers the LL.M. Students may take relevant courses in other programs and apply credit toward the J.D.; a maximum of 6 credits may be applied. The following joint degrees may be earned: J.D./Ph.D. (Juris Doctor/Doctor of Philosophy in Psychology), J.D./M.A. (Juris Doctor/Master of Arts in Economics), J.D./M.B.A. (Juris Doctor/Master of Business Administration), and J.D./M.P.A. (Juris Doctor/Master of Public Administration).

Required

To earn the J.D., candidates must complete 85 total credits, of which 39 are for required courses. They must maintain a minimum GPA of 2.0 in the required courses. The following first-year courses are required of all students: Civil Procedure, Constitutional Law, Contracts, Criminal Procedure, Legal Analysis, Writing and Research, Property, and Torts. Required upper-level courses consist of an advanced writing seminar, Evidence, and Professional Responsibility. Many clinical and trial advocacy opportunities are available, but none are required. The required orientation program for first-year students lasts 3 days and encompasses academic and cultural aspects of the law

Phone: 520-621-3477
Fax: 520-621-9140
E-mail: admissions@law.arizona.edu
Web: www.law.arizona.edu

Contact

Dan Nunez, Admissions Office, 520-621-3477 for general inquiries; Henrietta Stover, Assistant Dean, Financial Services, 520-626-8101, Kim Marlow for financial aid information.

ARIZONA

school experience; 3 follow-up sessions during the first semester of school are held on ethics, stress, exam taking, and various other matters.

Electives

The James E. Rogers College of Law offers concentrations in corporate law, criminal law, environmental law, family law, internationl law, litigation, securities law, tax law, torts and insurance, Indian law, and human rights. In addition, clinics include a Domestic Violence Clinic, Child Advocacy Clinic, Indigenous Peoples Law Clinic, Immigration Law Clinics (3 to 5 units per credit), and Prosecution and Defense Clinics. These clinics are open to second- and third-year students who have completed Evidence and Ethics (Professional Responsibility). The college has a diverse set of offerings for its advanced research and writing seminars, ranging from the Warren Court to a death penalty seminar. Also offered is a rich variety of small seminars and colloquia. Internships may be taken with the state legislature, with the offices of U.S. senators and the White House Drug Policy Office, and with the Navajo, Tohono O'odham, and Pascua Yacqui tribal governments. Students may take up to 6 units of independent study with faculty supervision. Students may hear special lectures through the Isaac Marks Memorial Lectures, Rosentiel Scholar-in-Residence Program, McCormick Society Lectures, and the Jeanne Kiewit Taylor Visiting Faculty Program. Study abroad is possible in Puerto Rico at the University of Puerto Rico Law School. The college accepts credit for participation in ABA-approved international programs sponsored by other schools. All first-year students may participate in tutorial programs. Special scholarship efforts, mentoring, tutorial assistance, and a weeklong "Bridge Program" are offered to all students. The most widely taken electives are Federal Income Tax, Corporations, and Employment Law.

Graduation Requirements

In order to graduate, candidates must have a GPA of 2.0 and must have completed the upper-division writing requirement, which entails writing a paper of "publishable quality."

Organizations

The primary law review is the *Arizona Law Review*. Students also edit *The Arizona Journal for International Law*, and *The Journal of Psychology, Public Policy and Law*. Other publications include *Environmental Law Newsletter*, and *The Bulletin*. Students may participate in a wide range of regional, national, and international moot court competitions. Other competitions include Richard Grand Damages, Grand Writing, and Jenkes competitions. Law student organizations, local chapters of national associations, and campus organizations include the Student Bar Association, Law Women's Association, Phi Alpha Delta, Phi Delta Phi, American Civil Liberties Union, ABA-Law Student Division, Black Law Students Association, LaRaza/Hispanic National Bar Association, Native American Law Student Association, and Asian American Law Student Association.

Library

The law library contains 410,000 hardcopy volumes and 426,000 microform volume equivalents, and subscribes to 3,650 serial publications. Such online databases and networks as CALI, DIALOG, Dow-Jones, LEXIS, OCLC First Search, and WESTLAW are available to law students for research. Special library collections include an extensive collection of materials on Latin American law, water law, and Indian law. The ratio of library volumes to faculty is 13,667 to 1 and to students is 863 to 1. The ratio of seats in the library to students is 1 to 1.

Faculty

The law school has 30 full-time and 55 part-time faculty members, of whom 36 are women. According to AAUP standards for Category I institutions, faculty salaries are average. About 47% of full-time faculty have a graduate law degree in addition to the J.D.; about 2% of part-time faculty have one. The ratio of full-time students to full-time faculty in an average class is 15 to 1; in a clinic, 7 to 1. The law school has a regular program of bringing visiting professors and other distinguished lecturers and visitors to campus. There is a chapter of the Order of the Coif; 15 faculty and 370 graduates are members.

Placement

Services available through: a separate law school placement center.

Services: extensive career counseling and direction, creative programming, and participation of faculty and alumni.

Special features: the college has a very active Career Services Office with 2 full-time attorneys on staff. The office takes a proactive approach to career services, educating, and assisting students.

Full-time job interviews:	70 employers
Summer job interviews:	110 employers
Placement by graduation:	65% of class
Placement within 9 months:	94% of class
Average starting salary:	$43,326 to $79,622

Areas of placement:

Private practice 2–10 attorneys	3%
Private practice 11–25 attorneys	8%
Private practice 26–50 attorneys	12%
Private practice 51–100 attorneys	15%
Judicial clerkships	22%
Government	17%
Business/industry	10%
Public interest	5%
LL.M. or Ph.D.	5%
Military	2%
Academic	1%

Students

About 50% of the student body are women; 29%, minorities; 5%, African American; 8%, Asian American; 12%, Hispanic; 4%, Native American; and 5%, foreign nationals. The majority of students come from Arizona (70%). The average age of entering students is 25; age range is 20 to 45. About 40% of students enter directly from undergraduate school, 22% have a graduate degree, and 60% have worked full-time prior to entering law school. About 1% drop out after the first year for academic or personal reasons; 98% remain to receive a law degree.

School of Law

Robert A. Leflar Law Center,
Waterman Hall
Fayetteville, AR 72701

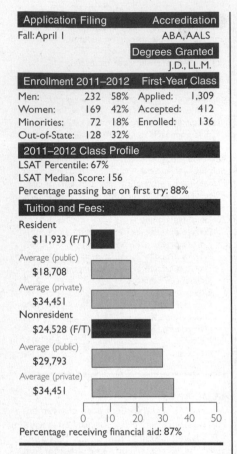

Application Filing	Accreditation
Fall: April 1	ABA, AALS
	Degrees Granted
	J.D., LL.M.

Enrollment 2011–2012		First-Year Class	
Men:	232 58%	Applied:	1,309
Women:	169 42%	Accepted:	412
Minorities:	72 18%	Enrolled:	136
Out-of-State:	128 32%		

2011–2012 Class Profile
LSAT Percentile: 67%
LSAT Median Score: 156
Percentage passing bar on first try: 88%

Tuition and Fees:

Resident
$11,933 (F/T)

Average (public)
$18,708

Average (private)
$34,451

Nonresident
$24,528 (F/T)

Average (public)
$29,793

Average (private)
$34,451

0 10 20 30 40 50
Percentage receiving financial aid: 87%

ADMISSIONS
In the fall of 2011 first-year class, 1309 applied, 412 were accepted, and 136 enrolled. Seven transfers enrolled. The median LSAT percentile of the most recent first-year class was 67; the median GPA was 3.5 on a scale of 4.0.

Requirements
Applicants must have a bachelor's degree and take the LSAT. The most important admission factors include state or country of residence, LSAT results, and GPA. No specific undergraduate courses are required. Candidates are not interviewed.

Procedure
The application deadline for fall entry is April 1. Applicants should submit an application form, LSAT results, and transcripts. Accepted students must submit a nonrefundable $75 preregistration fee, which is applied to the regular registration fee for the semester. Notification of the admissions decision is on a rolling basis. The law school uses the LSAC.

Special
The law school recruits minority and disadvantaged students by attending forums and career fairs; requesting candidate referral service reports via LSAC; and communicating with pre-law advisors and alumni. Requirements are different for out-of-state students in that index admission is granted to those nonresident applicants who have prediction indexes of 205 or above. If space permits, index admission is offered to other applicants. A small number of nonresidents who do not qualify for index admission may be admitted by the Admissions Committee. Transfer students must have one year of credit, must have attended an ABA-approved law school, and must contact the Associate Dean for Students at the school of law, indicating previous attendance at another school. Transfer students must complete the last 4 semesters at the University of Arkansas School of Law.

Costs
Tuition and fees for the 2011–2012 academic year are $10,565 for full-time in-state students and $23,160 for out-of-state students. On-campus room and board costs about $15,552 annually; books and supplies run $1,214.

Financial Aid
About 87% of current law students receive some form of aid. Awards are based on need and merit combined. The required financial statement is the FAFSA. The aid application deadline for fall entry is March 1. Special funds for minority or disadvantaged students exist. Several funds provide aid based on merit and need. First-year students are notified about their financial aid application at time of enrollment.

About the Law School
University of Arkansas School of Law was established in 1924 and is a public institution. The 345-acre campus is in a small town near the downtown area and in proximity to several Fortune 500 companies. The primary mission of the law school is to prepare students as lawyers who will provide professional service to their clients, who are interested in and capable of advancing legal process and reform, and who are prepared to fill the vital role of the lawyer as a

community leader. Students have access to federal, state, county, city, and local agencies, courts, correctional facilities, law firms, and legal aid organizations in the Fayetteville area. Duncan Avenue Apartments are available to upper-class and graduate students interested in living on campus. For students who choose to live off-campus, there are several apartments within walkng distance of the campus. All law school facilities are accessible to the physically disabled.

Calendar
The law school operates on a traditional semester basis. Courses for full-time students are offered days only and must be completed within 3 years. New full-time students are admitted in the fall. There is a 5-week summer session. Transferable summer courses are offered.

Programs
In addition to the J.D., the law school offers the LL.M. Students may take relevant courses in other programs and apply credit toward the J.D.; a maximum of 6 credits may be applied. The following joint degrees may be earned: J.D./M.A. (Juris Doctor/Master of Arts in International Law and Politics), J.D./M.B.A. (Juris Doctor/Master of Business Administration), and J.D./M.P.A. (Juris Doctor/Master of Public Administration).

Required
To earn the J.D., candidates must complete 90 total credits, of which 43 are for required courses. They must maintain a minimum GPA of 2.0 in the required courses. The following first-year courses are required of all students: Civil Procedure I and II, Contracts I and II, Criminal Law, Legal Research and Writing I and II, Property I and II, and Torts. Required upper-level courses consist of Constitutional Law, Legal Research and Writing III, and Professional Responsibility. The required orientation program for first-year students is a 3-day introduction to the study of law that includes an introduction to the library, law school and campus tours, and university resources and student life planning suggestions.

Phone: 479-575-3102
Fax: 479-575-3937
E-mail: *jkmiller@uark.edu*
Web: *law.uark.edu/*

Contact

James Miller, Associate Dean for Students, 479-575-3102 for general inquiries; Kattie Wing, Director, 479-575-3806 for financial aid information.

ARKANSAS

Electives

We offer seven clinics including civil, criminal, and immigration law. Students must have taken Basic Evidence, Civil Procedure, Criminal Procedure, Professional Responsibility, and Trial Advocacy. Additionally, students must have completed at least 48 credit hours and otherwise be elibible for licensing under Rule XV, Rules Governing Admission to the Bar. Seminars for 2 or 3 hours of credit are available to upper-level students. Seminars offered include Comparative Health Law, Police Discretion, and Entertainment Law. Faculty may hire research assistants. Students may earn up to 2 credits in independent research topics. Externship opportunities include: Judicial; Juvenile Justice; Corporate Counsel; Public Service; U.S. Attorney; Legislative; and Federal Public Defender. We offer the followig special lecture series: Hartman Hotz; H.L.A. Hart Society; Lawyer in the Library; and Pathways to the Profession. We participate in two study abroad summer programs: the Cambridge Study Abroad Program (Cambridge, England) and the St. Petersburg Summer Law Institute (St. Petersburg, Russia). We provide teaching assistants for first-year courses. Several scholarships are available for minority students. We have several special interest groups, including APALSA, BLSA, Environmental Law Society, Animal Law Society, and International Law Society. The most widely taken electives are Evidence, Business Organizations, and Criminal Procedure.

Graduation Requirements

In order to graduate, candidates must have a GPA of 2.0, must have completed the upper-division writing requirement, and must have 3 credits in skills courses.

Organizations

Students edit the folowing journals: *Arkansas Law Review*, *Journal of Food Law and Policy*, and the *Journal of Islamic Law and Culture*. The School of Law participates in a variety of national and regional moot court competitions, including ABA Moot Court, NYC Bar Association Moot Court, and Ben J. Altheimer Moot Court. Students also take part in other competitions, including ABA Client Counseling, ABA Negotiations, Jessup International Moot Court, APALSA Moot Court, and BLSA Trial Competition. The Women's Law Student Association, Arkansas Trial Lawyers Student Organization, and Christian Legal Society are a few of our law student organizations. Phi Alpha Delta, Phi Delta Phi, and Black Law Student Association are three local chapters of national associations at the school of law. Campus organizations include the Student Honor Council, Board of Advocates, and Student Bar Association.

Library

The law library contains 331,103 hard-copy volumes and 836,887 microform volume equivalents, and subscribes to 3,715 serial publications. Such online databases and networks as CALI, CIS Universe, Infotrac, Legal-Trac, LEXIS, Mathew Bender, OCLC First Search, WESTLAW, Wilsonline Indexes, Making of Modern Law, and Records and Briefs of the United States Supreme Court are available to law students for research. Special library collections include a growing collection of agricultural law materials developed on behalf of the law school's Agricultural and Food Law L.L.M. Program. The Young Law Library is a depository for federal documents, UN documents, and Arkansas State documents. The ratio of library volumes to faculty is 10,680 to 1 and to students is 822 to 1. The ratio of seats in the library to students is 1 to 1.

Faculty

The law school has 39 full-time and 34 part-time faculty members, of whom 28 are women. According to AAUP standards for Category I institutions, faculty salaries are below average. About 38% of full-time faculty have a graduate law degree in addition to the J.D. The ratio of full-time students to full-time faculty in an average clinic is 6 to 1.

Students

About 42% of the student body are women; 18%, minorities; 8%, African American; 2%, Asian American; 5%, Hispanic; and 2%, Native American. The majority of students come from Arkansas (68%). The average age of entering students is 23.

Placement

J.D.s awarded:	119
Services available through: a separate law school placement center and the university placement center.	
Full-time job interviews:	18 employers
Summer job interviews:	37 employers
Placement by graduation:	49% of class
Placement within 9 months:	95% of class
Areas of placement:	
Private practice 2–10 attorneys	30%
Private practice 11–25 attorneys	5%
Private practice 26–50 attorneys	4%
Private practice 51–100 attorneys	5%
Business/industry	21%
Government	12%
Judicial clerkships	6%
Public interest	4%
Academic	2%

UNIVERSITY OF ARKANSAS AT LITTLE ROCK

UALR William H. Bowen School of Law

1201 McMath Avenue
Little Rock, AR 72202-5142

Application Filing		Accreditation
Fall: April 15		ABA, AALS

		Degrees Granted
		J.D.

Enrollment 2011–2012		First-Year Class	
Men:	265 56%	Applied:	1,529
Women:	212 44%	Accepted:	475
Minorities:	72 15%	Enrolled:	145
Out-of-State:	119 25%		

2011–2012 Class Profile

LSAT Percentile: 60%
LSAT Median Score: 154
Percentage passing bar on first try: 83%

Tuition and Fees:

Resident
$12,177 (F/T)

Average (public)
$18,708

Average (private)
$34,451

Nonresident
$24,772 (F/T)

Average (public)
$29,793

Average (private)
$34,451

0 10 20 30 40 50

Percentage receiving financial aid: 85%

ADMISSIONS

In the fall of 2011 first-year class, 1529 applied, 475 were accepted, and 145 enrolled. Seven transfers enrolled. The median LSAT percentile of the most recent first-year class was 60; the median GPA was 3.3 on a scale of 4.0. The lowest LSAT percentile accepted was 26; the highest was 99.

Requirements

Applicants must have a bachelor's degree and take the LSAT. The most important admission factors include LSAT results, GPA, and life experience. No specific undergraduate courses are required. Candidates are not interviewed.

Procedure

The application deadline for fall entry is April 15. Applicants should submit an application form, LSAT results, transcripts, and a personal statement. Notification of the admissions decision is on a rolling basis. The law school uses the LSAC.

Special

The law school recruits minority and disadvantaged students through scholarships that take diversity of life experiences into account. Requirements are different for out-of-state students. Transfer students must have attended an ABA-approved law school, must have a personal statement, must have an official law school transcript showing completion of 20 semester hours, must have a letter of good standing stating class rank, must have an LSAT score, must have an official undergraduate transcript, must have a letter explaining the need to transfer, and must have a completed application.

Costs

Books and supplies run $1,800.

Financial Aid

About 85% of current law students receive some form of aid. The average annual amount of aid from all sources combined, including scholarships, loans, and work contracts, is $16,896; maximum, $20,058. Awards are based on need and merit combined. The required financial statement is the FAFSA. The aid application deadline for fall entry is March 1. Special funds for minority or disadvantaged students include scholarships based on diversity, including the Bowen Scholarship. First-year students are notified about their financial aid application at the time of admission application request.

About the Law School

University of Arkansas at Little Rock UALR William H. Bowen School of Law was established in 1975 and is a public institution. The 5-acre campus is in an urban area downtown, 6 miles from the main campus. The primary mission of the law school is to provide a high-quality legal education that equips students with the knowledge, skills, and ethical concepts to function as competent attorneys, public officials, business people, and other professionals, to think critically about the efficacy of the law and legal institutions, and to work for their improvement. Students have access to federal, state, county, city, and local agencies, courts, correctional facilities, law firms, and legal aid organizations in the Little Rock area. Facilities of special interest to law students include all branches of state government as well

as legal services and law firms. Housing for students consists of plentiful rental opportunities thoughout Little Rock along with privately owned law student housing adjacent to the law school. All law school facilities are accessible to the physically disabled.

Calendar

The law school operates on a traditional semester basis. Courses for full-time students are offered principally during the day, and must be completed within 6 years. For part-time students, courses are offered principally in the evenings, and must be completed within 6 years. New full- and part-time students are admitted in the fall. There is an 8-week summer session. Transferable summer courses are offered.

Programs

Students may take relevant courses in other programs and apply credit toward the J.D.; a maximum of 6 for the joint degree credits may be applied. The following joint degrees may be earned: J.D./ Pharm.D. (Juris Doctor/Doctor of Pharmacy), J.D./M.B.A. (Juris Doctor/Master of Business Administration), J.D./M.P.A. (Juris Doctor/Master of Public Administration), J.D./M.P.H. (Juris Doctor/Master of Public Health), J.D./M.P.S. (Juris Doctor/Master of Public Service), J.D./M.S.T. (Juris Doctor/Master of Science in Taxation), and J.D./M.D. (Juris Doctor/Medical Doctor).

Required

To earn the J.D., candidates must complete 90 total credits, of which 45 are for required courses. They must maintain a minimum GPA of 2.0 in the required courses. The following first-year courses are required of all students: Civil Procedure I and II, Contracts I and II, Criminal Law, Legal Research I and II, Property I and II, Reasoning, Writing, and Advocacy I and II, and Torts. Required upper-level courses consist of Constitutional Law, Evidence, Lawyering Skills I and II, and Legal Profession. The required orientation program for first-year students is 4 days long and covers the academic and personal skills needed to succeed in law school.

ARKANSAS

Electives

The UALR William H. Bowen School of Law offers concentrations in corporate law, criminal law, family law, internationl law, juveline law, labor law, litigation, securities law, tax law, and torts and insurance. In addition, of special curricular note are the 3 clinics, litigation (worth 6 hours), mediation (worth 4 hours), and tax (worth 4 hours). Upper-level students can choose from a number of seminar topics (worth 2 credits) as well as write their own independent paper (1 to 2 credits) under the supervision of a faculty member. Outside speakers participate in an annual symposium, and nationally notable speakers offer several lectures a year. The law school has a public interest externship program in which students earn academic credit working with government agencies, the state legislature, and judges. The law school accepts any ABA-accredited study-abroad program. A number of scholarships are available to students. Many factors are considered in the awarding of scholarships, including race, ethnicity, and background. An ongoing tutorial program directed by the associate dean and staffed by upper-level students who teach study skills is available to first-year students. An academic mentoring program is available to all first-year students. The most widely taken electives are Family Law, Debtor-Creditor, and Business Associations.

Graduation Requirements

In order to graduate, candidates must have a GPA of 2.0 and must have completed the upper-division writing requirement and the upper-level jurisprudential requirement, which can be fulfilled by a number of courses.

Organizations

Students edit the *University of Arkansas at Little Rock Law Review*. Other law reviews include the faculty-edited *Journal of Appellate Practice and Process*. Moot court competitions include First Amendment National Moot Court and ABA Young Lawyers National Moot Court Competition. Other competitions include the Henry Woods Trial Competition, National Trial Competition, an intraschool Moot Court Competition, and an Advocacy Slam. Law student organizations, local chapters of national associations, and campus organizations include Phi Alpha Delta, Phi Delta Phi, Delta Theta Phi, Black Law Students Association, The Federalist Society, American Bar Association, Community Outreach Opportunity League, Student Bar Association, and Pulaski County Bar-Law Student Division.

Library

The law library contains 320,407 hardcopy volumes and 593,296 microform volume equivalents, and subscribes to 4,626 serial publications. Such online databases and networks as CALI, CIS Universe, Infotrac, Legal-Trac, LEXIS, OCLC First Search, WESTLAW, Wilsonline Indexes, HeinOnline, LLMC Digital, BNA, Intelliconnect, and Lexis Congressional EBSCOhost, and others are available to law students for research. Special library collections include a federal documents depository, a state documents depository going back to 1993, Arkansas Supreme Court records and briefs for 1836–1926, and Arkansas legal materials. The ratio of library volumes to faculty is 11,443 to 1 and to students is 651 to 1. The ratio of seats in the library to students is 1 to 1.

Faculty

The law school has 27 full-time and 81 part-time faculty members, of whom 42 are women. About 11% of full-time faculty have a graduate law degree in addition to the J.D. The ratio of full-time students to full-time faculty in an average class is 12 to 1; in a clinic, 6 to 1. The law school has a regular program of bringing visiting professors and other distinguished lecturers and visitors to campus.

Students

About 44% of the student body are women; 15%, minorities; 10%, African American; 2%, Asian American; 4%, Hispanic; 1%, Native American; and 2%, international. The majority of students come from Arkansas (75%). The average age of entering students is 26; age range is 21 to 54. About 61% of students enter directly from undergraduate school, and 10% have a graduate degree. About 1% drop out after the first year for academic or personal reasons; 99% remain to receive a law degree.

Phone: 501-324-9903
Fax: 501-324-9909
E-mail: lawadm@ualr.edu
Web: ualr.edu/law

Contact

Director of Student Services, 501 569-3130 for financial aid information.

Placement	
J.D.s awarded:	151
Services available through: a separate law school placement center.	
Services: computer access to WESTLAW, lunch programs on various aspects of career planning, and a job search.	
Special features: the Symplicity online management system and membership in the Intercollegiate Job Bank.	
Full-time job interviews:	4 employers
Summer job interviews:	17 employers
Placement by graduation:	30% of class
Placement within 9 months:	91% of class
Average starting salary:	$39,000 to $65,000
Areas of placement:	
Private practice 2–10 attorneys	19%
Private practice 11–25 attorneys	16%
Private practice 51–100 attorneys	2%
Government	23%
Business/industry	22%
Judicial clerkships	6%
Academic	5%
Public interest	1%

School of Law

1420 North Charles Street
Baltimore, MD 21201-5779

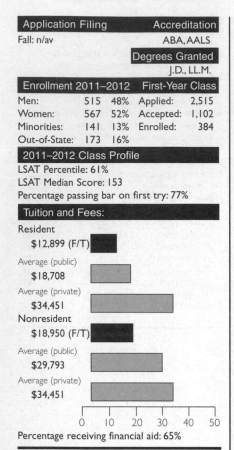

Application Filing	Accreditation
Fall: n/av	ABA, AALS
	Degrees Granted
	J.D., LL.M.

Enrollment 2011–2012		First-Year Class	
Men:	515 48%	Applied:	2,515
Women:	567 52%	Accepted:	1,102
Minorities:	141 13%	Enrolled:	384
Out-of-State:	173 16%		

2011–2012 Class Profile
LSAT Percentile: 61%
LSAT Median Score: 153
Percentage passing bar on first try: 77%

Tuition and Fees:

Resident
$12,899 (F/T)

Average (public)
$18,708

Average (private)
$34,451

Nonresident
$18,950 (F/T)

Average (public)
$29,793

Average (private)
$34,451

0   10   20   30   40   50

Percentage receiving financial aid: 65%

ADMISSIONS

In the fall of 2011 first-year class, 2515 applied, 1102 were accepted, and 384 enrolled. Fifteen transfers enrolled. The median LSAT percentile of the most recent first-year class was 61; the median GPA was 3.2 on a scale of 4.0. The lowest LSAT percentile accepted was 23; the highest was 93.

Requirements
Applicants must have a bachelor's degree and take the LSAT. The most important admission factors include work experience, GPA, and LSAT results. No specific undergraduate courses are required, and candidates are not interviewed.

Procedure
Applicants should submit an application form, a personal statement, 2 letters of recommendation, and resume. LSAT scores, transcripts, and letters of recommendation must come through LSAC. Notification of the admissions decision

is on a rolling basis. The law school uses the LSAC.

Special
The law school recruits minority and disadvantaged students by means of an on-campus minority law forum, recruiting at historically black colleges, recruiting minorities during visits to undergraduate institutions, and through the Baltimore Scholar Program. Requirements are different for out-of-state students. Transfer students must have one year of credits, attended an ABA-approved law school, a personal statement, files individually reviewed by committee.

Costs

Tuition and fees for the 2011–2012 academic year are $11,964 for full-time in-state students and $18,015 for out-of-state students. Tuition for part-time students is $11,892 for in-state students and $16,908 out-of-state.

Financial Aid

About 65% of current law students receive some form of aid. The average annual amount of aid from all sources combined, including scholarships, loans, and work contracts, is $18,000; maximum, $30,000. Awards are based on need and merit, along with need only for federal programs; scholarships are based on need and/or merit. Required financial statement is the FAFSA. The aid application deadline for fall entry is March 1. First-year students are notified about their financial aid application in May.

About the Law School

University of Baltimore School of Law was established in 1925 and is a public institution. The campus is located in an urban area in Baltimore. The primary mission of the law school is to draw together students and faculty from a variety of backgrounds in a common search for knowledge and understanding. Students have access to federal, state, county, city, and local agencies, courts, correctional facilities, law firms, and legal aid organizations in the Baltimore area. Area corporations and nonprofit organizations are also accessible. Facilities of special interest to law students consist of 2 small personal computer laboratories for student use and

online databases and networks. The entire campus is wireless. Housing for students is available off campus; a roommate referral service is also offered. Nearby, many apartments range from inexpensive studios to luxury apartment buildings. All law school facilities are accessible to the physically disabled.

Calendar

The law school operates on a traditional semester basis. Courses for full-time students are offered both day and evening and must be completed within 5 years. For part-time students, courses are offered both day and evening and must be completed within 6 years. New full- and part-time students are admitted in the fall. There is an 8-week summer session. Transferable summer courses are offered.

Programs

In addition to the J.D., the law school offers the LL.M. Students may take relevant courses in other programs and apply credit toward the J.D.; a maximum of 6 credits may be applied. The following joint degrees may be earned: J.D./Ph.D. (Juris Doctor/ Doctor of Philosophy in policy sciences), J.D./M.B.A. (Juris Doctor/ Master of Business Administration), J.D./M.P.A. (Juris Doctor/ Master of Public Administration), and J.D./M.S. (Juris Doctor/Master of Science in Criminal Justice and Negotiations).

Required
To earn the J.D., candidates must complete 90 total credits, of which 41 are for required courses. They must maintain a minimum GPA of 2.0 in the required courses. The following first-year courses are required of all students: Civil Procedure I and II, Contracts I and II, Criminal Law, Legal Analysis, Research, and Writing, Property, and Torts or Introduction to Lawyering/Torts. Required upper-level courses consist of 2 upper-level research and writing projects, an advocacy requirement, Constitutional Law II, Evidence, Legal Analysis, Research, and Writing III (Moot Court), and Professional Responsibility. Clinical courses are offered as part of upper-level elective courses. The required orientation program for first-year students is 3 days; students meet with faculty and peer advisers, attend case analysis and other seminars, and attend

Phone: 410-837-4459
Fax: 410-837-4450
E-mail: lwadmiss@ubmail.ubalt.edu;
jzavrotny@ubalt.edu
Web: law.ubalt.edu

Contact

Jeffrey Zavrotny, Director, 410-837-4454 for general inquiries; Marlene Telak, Program Administration, 410-837-4763 for financial aid information.

an Information Fair on school services and student activities.

Electives

The School of Law offers concentrations in corporate law, criminal law, family law, intellectual property law, internationl law, litigation, tax law, civil rights, estate planning, public and government law, and real estate practice. In addition, clinics offer the opportunity to work under the direct supervision of attorneys. Upper-level students undertake the representation of real clients in actual cases and perform all tasks necessary for proper representation. Students also earn credits in the Criminal Practice Clinic, Family Law Clinic, Appellate Advocacy Clinic, Civil Advocacy Clinic, Tax Clinic, Community Development Clinic, Immigrant Rights Clinic, and Family Mediation Clinic. Seminars are advanced classes that require independent research, writing, and discussion leadership by students. The Internship Program allows upper-level students to learn about the lawyering and judicial process by working closely with supervising attorneys and judges. Internships include the Attorney Practice Internship and Judicial Internship, which are open to any upper-level students in good standing. Special lecture series include the Liss Memorial Lectures, A.M. Law Series, Hoffberger Center for Professional Ethics, and the Center for International and Comparative Law. Study abroad is open to any student after the first year of study. The school offers a program in international comparative law in conjunction with the University of Aberdeen, Scotland; Curacao (Winter Intersession); and summer abroad in Haifa, Israel. First-year students may receive tutorial assistance through the Law Achievement Workshop, which consists of weekly tutorial sessions for almost every first-year class. Other tutorial programs are handled on an individual basis. Programs for minority students include the Law Achievement Workshop, Attorney Mentors, Exam Writing Workshop, Afro-American Lectures in Law, and Black Law Student Orientation. The most widely taken electives are Business Organizations; Criminal Procedure I, and Family Law.

Graduation Requirements

In order to graduate, candidates must have a GPA of 2.0, completed the upper-division writing requirement, and fulfilled the upper-level advocacy and perspective course requirements.

Organizations

Students edit *The University of Baltimore Law Review*, the *University of Baltimore Law Forum*, the *University of Baltimore Journal of Environmental Law,* the *University of Baltimore Intellectual Property Journal*, and the newspaper *Official Reporter*. Annually, teams compete at the American Trial Lawyers Association and Trial Advocacy and Client Counseling competitions, as well as the Client Negotiation Moot Court, Pace National Environmental Law Moot Court, Tax Moot Court, and Trial Advocacy competitions. Law student organizations include the Intellectual Property Legal Society, Christian Legal Society, and Criminal Law Association. There are local chapters of Phi Alpha Delta, Phi Delta Kappa, and Phi Delta Phi. Campus clubs and other organizations include BLSA, APALSA, and WBA.

Library

The law library contains 365,150 hardcopy volumes and 193,533 microform volume equivalents, and subscribes to 765 serial publications. Online databases and networks include CALI, CIS Universe, Legal-Trac, LEXIS, OCLC First Search, WESTLAW, and Wilsonline Indexes, which are available to law students for research. Special library collections include a U.S. government selective depository. The ratio of library volumes to faculty is 7,607 to 1 and to students is 337 to 1. The ratio of seats in the library to students is 1 to 3.

Faculty

The law school has 48 full-time and 92 part-time faculty members, of whom 48 are women. According to AAUP standards for Category I institutions, faculty salaries are above average. About 30% of full-time faculty have a graduate law degree in addition to the J.D. The ratio of full-time students to full-time faculty in an average class is 19 to 1; in a clinic, 6 to 1. The law school has a regular program of bringing visiting professors and other distinguished lecturers and visitors to campus.

Placement

J.D.s awarded:	292

Services available through: a separate law school placement center.

Services: some 20 different panels and workshops on job search techniques, specialty areas, and career opportunities.

Special features: University of Baltimore/ University of Maryland Public Interest Career Fair; Greater Washington Baltimore Public Service Career Fair, and EXPLOR, a summer legal experience program for first year students.

Full-time job interviews:	20 employers
Summer job interviews:	30 employers
Placement by graduation:	93% of class
Placement within 9 months:	94% of class
Average starting salary:	$27,500 to $145,000

Areas of placement:

Private practice 2–10 attorneys	18%
Private practice 11–25 attorneys	3%
Private practice 26–50 attorneys	3%
Private practice 51–100 attorneys	2%
Judicial clerkships	23%
Business/industry	18%
Government	13%
Public interest	5%
Academic	3%
Military	1%

Students

About 52% of the student body are women; 13%, minorities; 8%, African American; 5%, Asian American; 2%, Hispanic; and 1%, Native American. The majority of students come from Maryland (84%). The average age of entering students is 26; age range is 22 to 58. About 7% drop out after the first year for academic or personal reasons; 93% remain to receive a law degree.

UNIVERSITY OF CALIFORNIA

Hastings College of the Law

200 McAllister Street
San Francisco, CA 94102

Application Filing		Accreditation
Fall: March 1		ABA, AALS

Degrees Granted
J.D., LL.M., MSL

Enrollment 2011–2012		First-Year Class	
Men:	590 46%	Applied:	5,167
Women:	699 54%	Accepted:	1,791
Minorities:	490 38%	Enrolled:	414
Out-of-State:	180 14%		

2011–2012 Class Profile
LSAT Percentile: 86%
LSAT Median Score: 162
Percentage passing bar on first try: 76%

Tuition and Fees:

Resident
$40,836 (F/T)

Average (public)
$18,708

Average (private)
$34,451

Nonresident
$49,336 (F/T)

Average (public)
$29,793

Average (private)
$34,451

0   10   20   30   40   50

Percentage receiving financial aid: 91%

ADMISSIONS
In the fall of 2011 first-year class, 5167 applied, 1791 were accepted, and 414 enrolled. Forty-one transfers enrolled. The median LSAT percentile of the most recent first-year class was 86; the median GPA was 3.6 on a scale of 4.0. The lowest LSAT percentile accepted was 23; the highest was 99.

Requirements
Applicants must have a bachelor's degree and take the LSAT. The most important admission factors include academic achievement, LSAT results, and GPA. No specific undergraduate courses are required. Candidates are not interviewed.

Procedure
The application deadline for fall entry is March 1. Applicants should submit an application form, LSAT results, transcripts, a personal statement, and 2 letters of recommendation. Notification of the admissions decision is January through May. The law school uses the LSAC.

Special
The law school recruits minority and disadvantaged students by enrolling 20% of the class through the LEOP program, an alternative means of evaluating disadvantaged students, through specific outreach initiatives and the Candidate Referral Service, and through a holistic evaluation process. Requirements are different for out-of-state students. Transfer students must have one year of credit, must have a minimum GPA of 3, must have attended an ABA-approved law school, and must submit a personal statement.

Costs
On-campus room and board costs about $15,000 annually; books and supplies run $1,200.

Financial Aid
About 91% of current law students receive some form of aid. The average annual amount of aid from all sources combined, including scholarships, loans, and work contracts, is $36,064; maximum, $69,083. Awards are based on need and merit combined. Required financial statements are the FAFSA and the entering student financial aid supplement form. The aid application deadline for fall entry is March 1. First-year students are notified about their financial aid application as soon after acceptance as possible.

About the Law School
University of California Hastings College of the Law was established in 1878 and is a public institution. The campus is in an urban area in San Francisco. The primary mission of the law school is to prepare new members of the legal profession who are capable of and willing to serve all segments of the public as lawyers, judges, legislators, legal scholars, and in other roles in society. Students have access to federal, state, county, city, and local agencies, courts, correctional facilities, law firms, and legal aid organizations in the San Francisco area. Facilities of special interest to law students include the Public Interest Clearinghouse, the Public Law Research Institute, and the Land Conservation Institute. Housing for students is offered at McAllister Tower, which accommodates approximately 450 students. There are studios, 1-bedroom, and 2-bedroom units available. About 90% of

the law school facilities are accessible to the physically disabled.

Calendar
The law school operates on a traditional semester basis. Courses for full-time students are offered days only, and must be completed within 3 years. New full-time students are admitted in the fall. There is a 6-week summer session. Transferable summer courses are offered.

Programs
In addition to the J.D., the law school offers the LL.M. and M.S.L. Students may take relevant courses in other programs and apply credit toward the J.D.; a maximum of 6 units credits may be applied. The following joint degrees may be earned: J.D./M.A. (Juris Doctor/Master of Arts), J.D./M.B.A. (Juris Doctor/Master of Business Administration), J.D./M.P.H. (Juris Doctor/Master of Public Health), and J.D./M.P.P. (Juris Doctor/Master of Public Policy).

Required
To earn the J.D., candidates must complete 86 total credits, of which 34 are for required courses. They must maintain a minimum GPA of 2.0 in the required courses. The following first-year courses are required of all students: a statutory course, Civil Procedure, Constitutional Law I, Contracts, Criminal Law, Legal Writing and Research, Moot Court, Property, and Torts. Required upper-level courses consist of a professional skills course, Professional Responsibility, and a seminar or independent study with a substantial writing component. The required orientation program for first-year students is a 3-day program that includes mock classes taught by first-year faculty, assignments, and discussions of professional study habits, test-taking, diversity issues, and career opportunities.

Electives
The Hastings College of the Law offers concentrations in criminal law, intellectual property law, internationl law, litigation, tax law, public interest law, civil litigation, social justice lawyering, and health law. In addition, upper-level students may act as judicial externs for one of the state or federal courts. Students also

Phone: 415-565-4623
Fax: 415-581-8946
E-mail: admiss@uchastings.edu
Web: www.uchastings.edu

Contact

Greg Canada, Director of Admissions, 415-565-4885 for general inquiries; Linda Bisesi, Assistant Dean of Financial Aid, 415-565-4624 for financial aid information.

CALIFORNIA

may participate in a clinical seminar and gain practice experience under the supervision of an attorney. Clinics include Civil Justice, Civil Practice, Criminal Practice, Environmental Law, Workers' Rights, Immigration, and Local Government Law. Enrollment in seminars is limited to 24 second- and third-year students. Upper-level students whose academic work is of superior quality may conduct research under the supervision of a full-time faculty member. There are exchange programs with Leiden University, Austral University, Bocconi University, Bucerius Law School, Copenhagen University, IE Law School, International University of College of Turin, Waseds University, Peking University, University of Paris II, Freie University, and Central European University. The Legal Education Opportunity Program (LEOP) offers academic support to selected students with backgrounds that include some serious disadvantage that has been encountered and overcome. Incoming students have a special 1-week orientation introducing them to case briefing, legal writing, and analysis. Other programs for LEOP students include the First-Year Study Program for the California bar examination, which is taught by and for LEOP students. An exchange program in environmental law is offered with the Vermont Law School. The most widely taken electives are Constitutional Law, Evidence, and Criminal Procedure.

Graduation Requirements

In order to graduate, candidates must have a GPA of 2.0 and must have completed the upper-division writing requirement.

Organizations

Students edit the *Hastings Law Journal*, the *The Constitutional Law Quarterly*, *International and Comparative Law Review*, *Communications and Entertainment Law Journal*, *Race and Poverty*, *Women's Law Journal*, *Business Law Review*, and *North/Northwest Journal of Environmental Law and Policy*. The student newspaper is the *Hastings Law News*. Moot court competitions include the Giles Sutherland Rich Moot Court, National Appellate Advocacy, and the Frederick Douglass Moot Court. Two credit hours are awarded for participation. Among the

40 student organizations are the Associated Students of Hastings, La Raza Law Students Association, and the Black Law Students Association. There are local chapters of the National Lawyers Guild, Phi Delta Phi, and Amnesty International.

Library

The law library contains 707,264 hardcopy volumes and 71,568 microform volume equivalents, and subscribes to 7,858 serial publications. Such online databases and networks as CALI, CIS Universe, Legal-Trac, LEXIS, OCLC First Search, WESTLAW, Wilsonline Indexes, ABI/Inform, BNA Core, CCH Internet Tax Library, CCH Internet Business and Finance Library, HeinOnline, PsycINFO, and U.S. Supreme Court Records and Briefs are available to law students for research. Special library collections include a state and federal depository, a state and federal records and briefs collection, and documents of the U.S. Supreme Court, U.S. Court of Appeals for the Ninth Circuit, and California appellate courts. The ratio of library volumes to faculty is 11,788 to 1 and to students is 560 to 1. The ratio of seats in the library to students is 1 to 2.

Faculty

The law school has 60 full-time and 117 part-time faculty members, of whom 72 are women. About 28% of full-time faculty have a graduate law degree in addition to the J.D. The ratio of full-time students to full-time faculty in an average class is 21 to 1; in a clinic, 18 to 1. The law school has a regular program of bringing visiting professors and other distinguished lecturers and visitors to campus. There is a chapter of the Order of the Coif; 48 faculty and 1630 graduates are members.

Students

About 54% of the student body are women; 38%, minorities; 4%, African American; 19%, Asian American; and 10%, Hispanic. The majority of students come from California (86%). The average age of entering students is 25; age range is 20 to 58. About 8% of students have a graduate degree. About 2% drop out after the first year for academic or personal reasons; 98% remain to receive a law degree.

Placement

J.D.s awarded:	421
Services available through: a separate law school placement center.	
Special features: the center is a co-sponsor of an annual public interest and public service conference; it also conducts on-campus interviewing twice a year.	
Full-time job interviews:	200 employers
Summer job interviews:	225 employers
Placement by graduation:	61% of class
Placement within 9 months:	94% of class
Average starting salary:	$26,000 to $150,000
Areas of placement:	
Private practice 2–10 attorneys	14%
Private practice 11–25 attorneys	6%
Private practice 26–50 attorneys	4%
Private practice 51–100 attorneys	4%
Private practice 101–500 attorneys	45%
Business/industry	9%
Government	8%
Judicial clerkships	4%
Public interest	4%
Academic	2%

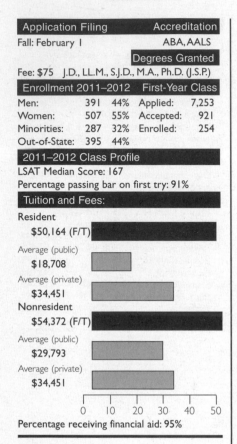

Application Filing	Accreditation
Fall: February 1	ABA, AALS

Degrees Granted

Fee: $75   J.D., LL.M., S.J.D., M.A., Ph.D. (J.S.P.)

Enrollment 2011–2012   First-Year Class

Men:	391	44%	Applied:	7,253
Women:	507	55%	Accepted:	921
Minorities:	287	32%	Enrolled:	254
Out-of-State:	395	44%		

2011–2012 Class Profile

LSAT Median Score: 167
Percentage passing bar on first try: 91%

Tuition and Fees:

Resident
$50,164 (F/T)

Average (public)
$18,708

Average (private)
$34,451

Nonresident
$54,372 (F/T)

Average (public)
$29,793

Average (private)
$34,451

0   10   20   30   40   50

Percentage receiving financial aid: 95%

ADMISSIONS

In the fall of 2011 first-year class, 7253 applied, 921 were accepted, and 254 enrolled. Sixty-five transfers enrolled. The median GPA of the most recent first-year class was 3.8. The lowest LSAT percentile accepted was 48; the highest was 100.

Requirements

Applicants must have a bachelor's degree and take the LSAT. The most important admission factors include life experience, LSAT results, and academic achievement. No specific undergraduate courses are required. Candidates are not interviewed.

Procedure

The application deadline for fall entry is February 1. Applicants should submit an application form, LSAT results, transcripts, a personal statement, a non-refundable application fee of $75 and 2 letters of recommendation. Notification of the admissions decision is from January to May. The law school uses the LSAC.

Special

The law school recruits minority and disadvantaged students by participating in outreach activities at a wide variety of institutions, including minority colleges and universities. The law school also actively recruits all admitted students, including those from underrepresented minority groups. Requirements are different for out-of-state students. Transfer students must have one year of credit, must have attended an ABA-approved law school, must submit a personal statement, and must be in the top 3%–5% at their current law school.

Costs

Books and supplies run $1,500.

Financial Aid

About 95% of current law students receive some form of aid. Awards are based on need and merit combined. The required financial statement is the FAFSA. The aid application deadline for fall entry is March 2. First-year students are notified about their financial aid application in early spring.

About the Law School

University of California at Berkeley School of Law was established in 1903 and is a public institution. The campus is in an urban area 12 miles east of San Francisco. The primary mission of the law school is to educate men and women not only for the practice of law, but also for all the varied roles lawyers perform in a modern society. Students have access to federal, state, county, city, and local agencies, courts, correctional facilities, law firms, and legal aid organizations in the Berkeley area. All other facilities of the Berkeley campus are available to law students. Housing for students is available at the law studio apartment complex, International House, and off campus. All law school facilities are accessible to the physically disabled.

Calendar

The law school operates on a traditional semester basis. Courses are offered days only, and must be completed within 3 years. New students are admitted in the fall. There is no summer session. Transferable summer courses are not offered.

Programs

In addition to the J.D., the law school offers the LL.M., S.J.D., M.A., and Ph.D. (J.S.P.). Students may take relevant courses in other programs and apply credit toward the J.D. The following joint degrees may be earned: J.D./M.A. (Juris Doctor/Master of Arts in Asian Studies or Jurisprudence), J.D./M.A.L.D. (Juris Doctor/Master of Arts in Law and Diplomacy), J.D./M.B.A. (Juris Doctor/Master of Business Administration), J.D./M.C.P. (Juris Doctor/Master of City and Regional Planning), J.D./M.J. (Juris Doctor/Master of Journalism), J.D./M.P.P. (Juris Doctor/Master of Public Policy), J.D./M.S.W. (Juris Doctor/Master of Social Work), and J.D./Ph.D. (Juris Doctor/Doctor of Philosophy in Jurisprudence).

Required

To earn the J.D., candidates must complete 85 total credits, of which 32 are for required courses. The following first-year courses are required of all students: Civil Procedure, Contracts, Criminal Law, Legal Writing, Research, and Advocacy, Property, and Torts. Required upper-level courses consist of Constitutional Law and Professional Responsibility. The required orientation program for first-year students consists of 2 days of basic material for new students, including the curriculum and services in August and 1 day in October for information regarding final exams, grading, and other matters.

Electives

The School of Law offers concentrations in corporate law, environmental law, intellectual property law, internationl law, law and technology, social justice/public interest, intellectual property, comparative legal studies, and law and economics. In addition, clinics, mostly open to second- and third-year students, include Death Penalty, International Human Rights Law, and Technology and Public Policy. Field work may be done at the East Bay Community Law Center and in the other clinics. Special lecture series are offered through various centers. Study abroad is available on a case-by-case basis. Special interest group programs include the Center for Social Justice and the Center for Law and Technology. The most widely taken electives are Evidence, Civil Procedures II, and Corporations.

Phone: 510-642-2274
Fax: 510-643-6222
E-mail: admissions@law.berkeley.edu
Web: www.law.berkeley.edu

Contact
Dennis Tominaga, Assistant Dean, 510-642-1568 for financial aid information.

CALIFORNIA

Graduation Requirements
In order to graduate, candidates must have completed the upper-division writing requirement.

Organizations
Students edit *The California Law Review, Berkeley Business Law Journal, Ecology Law Quarterly, Berkeley Technology Law Journal, Berkeley Journal of Employment and Labor Law, Berkeley Journal of International Law, Berkeley Women's Law Journal, African American Law and Policy Report, La Raza Law Journal, California Criminal Law Review,* and *Asian Law Journal.* The *Cross-Examiner* is the student newspaper. Annual moot court competitions are held at the school and include the McBaine and Jessup competitions. Law student organizations, local chapters of national associations, and campus organizations include the Asian Pacific American Law Students Association, Law Students of African Descent, La Raza, Federalist Society, National Lawyers Guild, Phi Alpha Delta, and the ABA-Law Student Division.

Library
The law library contains 875,000 hardcopy volumes and 188,598 microform volume equivalents, and subscribes to 8,200 serial publications. Such online databases and networks as CIS Universe, DIALOG, Legal-Trac, LEXIS, RLIN, and WESTLAW are available to law students for research. Special library collections include the Robbins Collection of ecclesiastical, foreign, comparative, and international law. The ratio of library volumes to faculty is 7,341 to 1 and to students is 790 to 1. The ratio of seats in the library to students is 1 to 2.

Faculty
The law school has 152 full-time and 38 part-time faculty members, of whom 69 are women. About 3% of full-time faculty have a graduate law degree in addition to the J.D. The ratio of full-time students to full-time faculty in an average class is 33 to 1; in a clinic, 13 to 1. The law school has a regular program of bringing visiting professors and other distinguished lecturers and visitors to campus. There is a chapter of the Order of the Coif; 8 faculty are members.

Students
About 55% of the student body are women; 32%, minorities; 6%, African American; 16%, Asian American; 13%, Hispanic; and 3%, Native American. The majority of students come from California (56%). The average age of entering students is 25; age range is 20 to 50. About 40% of students enter directly from undergraduate school, 14% have a graduate degree, and 60% have worked full-time prior to entering law school. About 1% drop out after the first year for academic or personal reasons; 98% remain to receive a law degree.

Placement

J.D.s awarded:	296

Services available through: a separate law school placement center and the university placement center.

Services: a searchable job database is available on the school's web site.

Special features: fall and spring on-campus interview programs, a career symposium for first year students, a mentor program, mock interviews, a speaker series on law specialties, as well as individual counseling sessions with counselors who have all practiced law themselves. Two full-time counselors focus on public interest/public sector careers, fellowships, and judicial clerkship advising.

Full-time job interviews:	30 employers
Summer job interviews:	200 employers
Placement within 9 months of graduation:	96% of class
Average starting salary:	$22,000 to $235,000
Areas of placement:	
Public interest	13%
Judicial clerkships	10%
Government	8%
Academic	3%
Business/industry	1%

School of Law

Martin Luther King, Jr. Hall
400 Mrak Hall Drive
Davis, CA 95616-5201

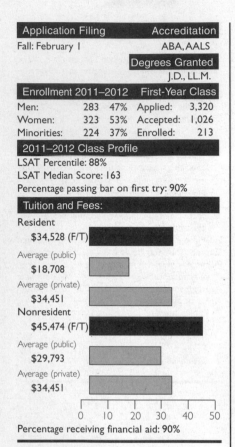

Application Filing	Accreditation
Fall: February 1	ABA, AALS
	Degrees Granted
	J.D., LL.M.

Enrollment 2011–2012			First-Year Class	
Men:	283	47%	Applied:	3,320
Women:	323	53%	Accepted:	1,026
Minorities:	224	37%	Enrolled:	213

2011–2012 Class Profile
LSAT Percentile: 88%
LSAT Median Score: 163
Percentage passing bar on first try: 90%

Tuition and Fees:

Resident
$34,528 (F/T)

Average (public)
$18,708

Average (private)
$34,451

Nonresident
$45,474 (F/T)

Average (public)
$29,793

Average (private)
$34,451

0   10   20   30   40   50

Percentage receiving financial aid: 90%

ADMISSIONS

In the fall of 2011 first-year class, 3320 applied, 1026 were accepted, and 213 enrolled. Eleven transfers enrolled. The median LSAT percentile of the most recent first-year class was 88; the median GPA was 3.5 on a scale of 4.0. The lowest LSAT percentile accepted was 52; the highest was 100.

Requirements

Applicants must have a bachelor's degree and take the LSAT. The most important admission factors include LSAT results. No specific undergraduate courses are required. Candidates are not interviewed.

Procedure

The application deadline for fall entry is February 1. Applicants should submit an application form, LSAT results, transcripts, a personal statement, and 2 letters of recommendation. Notification of the admissions decision is from January to April. The law school uses the LSAC.

Special

The law school recruits minority and disadvantaged students by means of visits to undergraduate campuses, the Candidate Referral Service, graduate/professional information days, LSAC forums, and various outreach programs and events. Requirements are different for out-of-state students in that they pay tuition not required of California residents. All admission requirements are the same; however, international applicants must provide a TOEFL score. Transfer students must have one year of credit, must have attended an ABA-approved law school, must submit a personal statement, and are usually in the top 5% to 10% of their first-year class.

Costs

Books and supplies run $1,014.

Financial Aid

About 90% of current law students receive some form of aid. The average annual amount of aid from all sources combined, including scholarships, loans, and work contracts, is $34,491; maximum, $51,439. Awards are based on need. Required financial statements are the FAFSA and Need Access. The aid application deadline for fall entry is March 2. First-year students are notified about their financial aid application once they have been admitted.

About the Law School

University of California at Davis School of Law was established in 1965 and is a public institution. The 5200-acre campus is in a small town 15 miles west of Sacramento. The primary mission of the law school is to be a nationally and internationally recognized leader in the development and dissemination of legal knowledge, as well as the training of students to become socially responsible lawyers committed to professional excellence and high ethical standards, and to promote public service through law reform and professional activities. Students have access to federal, state, county, city, and local agencies, courts, correctional facilities, law firms, and legal aid organizations in the Davis area. Facilities of special interest to law students include the instructional computer laboratory, the library, which allows 24-hour access, a day care co-op where care is provided by parents for children

12 months and younger, and wireless Internet access throughout the law school building and in the courtyard. Housing for students is available on and off campus through the ASUCD Community Housing Listing Service and a variety of community resource listings (e.g., newspapers); rental rates are reasonable and consistently lower than those in San Francisco and Los Angeles. All law school facilities are accessible to the physically disabled.

Calendar

The law school operates on a traditional semester basis. Courses for full-time students are offered days only, and must be completed within 3 years. There is no part-time program. New students are admitted in the fall. There is no summer session. Transferable summer courses are not offered.

Programs

In addition to the J.D., the law school offers the LL.M. Students may take relevant courses in other programs and apply credit toward the J.D.; a maximum of 10 semester units credits may be applied. The following joint degrees may be earned: J.D./M.A. (Juris Doctor/Master of Arts in most programs offered by UC Davis) and J.D./M.B.A. (Juris Doctor/Masters in Business Administration).

Required

To earn the J.D., candidates must complete 88 total credits, of which 33 are for required courses. They must maintain a minimum GPA of 2.0 in the required courses. The following first-year courses are required of all students: Civil Procedure, Constitutional Law, Criminal Law, Contracts, Introduction to Law, Legal Research and Legal Writing, Property, and Torts. Required upper-level courses consist of an advanced legal writing project, Professional Responsibility, and a skills requirement. The required orientation program for first-year students is an introductory week that includes meeting the Academic Assistance Program tutors, a tour of the law library, a photo session, class registration, a financial aid information session, dean's orientation, and social activities. The primary focus is a 1-unit course, Introduction to Law.

Phone: 530-752-6477
E-mail: admissions@lawucdavis.edu
Web: www.law.ucdavis.edu

Contact
Lawrence Gallardo, Financial Aid Director, 530-752-6573 for financial aid information.

CALIFORNIA

Electives
The School of Law offers concentrations in environmental law, international law, and a certificate program in public interest law; the law school provides for a number of specialized studies, including intellectual property and business law. In addition, clinics are open to upper-level students. Placements are available with selected public agencies, judges, and some private attorneys through such formal clinical programs as Administration of Criminal Justice (2 to 6 or 12 units), Civil Rights (2 to 6 units), and Employment Relations (2 to 6 units). Seminars for 2 or 3 credits, open to upper-level students, include areas of constitutional law, criminal law, and estate planning. An extensive array of seminars for 2 to 3 credits are open to upper-level students. Internships are available through clinics; additional opportunities are available in tax and public interest. In the second or third year, all students must complete a writing project (an individually authored work of rigorous intellectual effort). Special lecture series include Bodenheimer Lecture on the Family and Barrett Lecture on Constitutional Law. Exchange programs with China University of Political Science and Law, University College Dublin, and University of Copenhagen are available. The UCDC Law Program is a uniquely collaborative semester-long externship program in Washington, D.C., combining a weekly seminar with a full-time field placement, to offer law students an unparralleled opportunity to learn how federal statutes, regulations, and policies are made, changed, and understood in the nation's capital. From Introduction Week to the week of the bar exam, the Academic Success Program offers tutorial assistance, study aids, same practice exams, study and exam skills workshops, individual academic counseling, and study plan and learning styles assessments. All programs are designed to help students improve their academic performance in law school and the profession. The Academic Success Program is staffed by a Director and 14 to 16 second- and third-year law student tutors. Special interest group programs include the King Hall Pro Bono Program, the Public Interest Law Program, and the Environmental and Natural Resource Law Program. The most widely taken electives are Evidence, Business Association, and Trust Wills.

Graduation Requirements
In order to graduate, candidates must have a GPA of 2.0, and must have completed the upper-division writing requirement and the required course Professional Responsibility.

Organizations
Students edit the *UC Davis Law Review* and the newspaper *Advocate*. Moot court competitions held annually include the Moot Court Trial Competition, Client Counseling, and National Moot Court. Other competitions include the Frances Newall Carr Competition-Intraschool Mock Trial and National Negotiation Competition. Student organizations, local chapters of national associations, and campus organizations include the ABA-Law Student Division, Phi Alpha Delta, Phi Delta Phi, Tax Law Society, Advocates for the Rights of Children, Criminal Law Association, King Hall Legal Foundation, American Constitution Society, and the Federalist Society.

Library
The law library contains 302,516 hardcopy volumes and 768,833 microform volume equivalents, and subscribes to 4,249 serial publications. Such online databases and networks as CALI, CIS Universe, DIALOG, Legal-Trac, LEXIS, Mathew Bender, OCLC First Search, WESTLAW, California Digital Libraries, RIA Checkpoint, SSRN, HeinOnline, TRAC, MELVYL, CA Continuing Education of the Bar Online Publication, BNA & CCH Topical Online databases, and knowledge MOSAIC are available to law students for research. Special library collections include federal and California documents depositories. Special emphasis is in intellectual property environmental law, international law, and immigration and civil rights. The ratio of library volumes to faculty is 6,174 to 1 and to students is 499 to 1. The ratio of seats in the library to students is 1 to 1.

Faculty
The law school has 49 full-time and 14 part-time faculty members, of whom 28 are women. According to AAUP standards for Category I institutions, faculty salaries are above average. About 8% of full-time faculty have a graduate law degree in addition to the J.D. The ratio of students

Placement
J.D.s awarded:	191

Services available through: a separate law school placement center.
Special features: there is a career services library as well as career-related panels and presentations. UC Davis has its own internal Public Interest Program.

Full-time job interviews:	47 employers
Summer job interviews:	123 employers
Placement by graduation:	95% of class
Placement within 9 months:	98% of class
Average starting salary:	$30,000 to $125,000

Areas of placement:
Private practice 2–10 attorneys	15%
Private practice 11–25 attorneys	10%
Private practice 26–50 attorneys	3%
Private practice 51–100 attorneys	5%
Private practice 100+ attorneys	25%
Public interest	13%
Judicial clerkships	11%
Business/industry	8%
Government	7%
Academic	1%

to faculty in an average class is 35 to 1; in a clinic, 10 to 1. The law school has a regular program of bringing visiting professors and other distinguished lecturers and visitors to campus. There is a chapter of the Order of the Coif; 26 faculty and 502 graduates are members.

Students
About 53% of the student body are women; 37%, minorities; 2%, African American; 24%, Asian American; 7%, Hispanic; and 1%, Native American. The average age of entering students is 24; age range is 20 to 52. About 29% of students enter directly from undergraduate school, and 7% have a graduate degree. About 5% drop out after the first year for academic or personal reasons; 90% remain to receive a law degree.

UCLA School of Law

P.O. Box 951445
Los Angeles, CA 90095-1445

Application Filing	Accreditation
Fall: February 1	ABA, AALS
	Degrees Granted
Fee: $75	J.D., LL.M., S.J.D.

Enrollment 2011–2012		First-Year Class	
Men:	523 53%	Applied:	7,328
Women:	464 47%	Accepted:	1,471
Minorities:	286 29%	Enrolled:	321
Out-of-State:	316 32%		

2011–2012 Class Profile
LSAT Percentile: 96%
LSAT Median Score: 168
Percentage passing bar on first try: 86%

Tuition and Fees:

Resident
$44,922 (F/T)

Average (public)
$18,708

Average (private)
$34,451

Nonresident
$54,767 (F/T)

Average (public)
$29,793

Average (private)
$34,451

0 10 20 30 40 50

Percentage receiving financial aid: 90%

ADMISSIONS

In the fall of 2011 first-year class, 7328 applied, 1471 were accepted, and 321 enrolled. Forty transfers enrolled. The median LSAT percentile of the most recent first-year class was 96; the median GPA was 3.8 on a scale of 4.0. The lowest LSAT percentile accepted was 56; the highest was 100.

Requirements

Applicants must have a bachelor's degree and take the LSAT. No specific undergraduate courses are required. Candidates are not interviewed.

Procedure

The application deadline for fall entry is February 1. Applicants should submit an application form, LSAT results, transcripts, a personal statement, a nonrefundable application fee of $75, 2 letters of recommendation, and a resume. Notification of the admissions decision is on a rolling basis. The law school uses the LSAC.

Special

The law school recruits minority and disadvantaged students by means of visits to undergraduate schools, participation in LSAC forums, and programs arranged by law school administration and law student organizations. Requirements are different for out-of-state students. Transfer students must have one year of credit, must have attended an ABA-approved law school, and must submit a personal statement.

Costs

Books and supplies run $6,195.

Financial Aid

About 90% of current law students receive some form of aid. The average annual amount of aid from all sources combined, including scholarships, loans, and work contracts, is $48,676; maximum, $78,319. Awards are based on need and merit combined. Required financial statements are the FAFSA and the Need Access application (for those who want need-based aid). The aid application deadline for fall entry is March 2. Special funds for minority or disadvantaged students are available. First-year students are notified about their financial aid application once they are admitted and after their FAFSA and/or Need Access applications have been submitted.

About the Law School

University of California at Los Angeles UCLA School of Law was established in 1948 and is a public institution. The 419-acre campus is in an urban area. The primary mission of the law school is the training of attorneys who will attain high levels of professional excellence and integrity and who will exercise civic responsibility in myriad ways during long careers. Students have access to federal, state, county, city, and local agencies, courts, correctional facilities, law firms, and legal aid organizations in the Los Angeles area. There are many housing options open to UCLA law students, and the law school hosts a web-based service to help students with roommate searches. There are both university owned and privately owned apartments. About 99% of the law school facilities are accessible to the physically disabled.

Calendar

The law school operates on a traditional semester basis. Courses are offered days only, and must be completed within 5 years. New students are admitted in the fall. There is no summer session. Transferable summer courses are not offered.

Programs

In addition to the J.D., the law school offers the LL.M. and S.J.D. Students may take relevant courses in other programs and apply credit toward the J.D.; a maximum of 6 semester units credits may be applied. The following joint degrees may be earned: J.D./M.A. (Juris Doctor/Master of Arts in Afro-American studies), J.D./M.A. (Juris Doctor/Master of Arts in American Indian Studies), J.D./M.B.A. (Juris Doctor/Master of Business Administration), J.D./M.P.H. (Juris Doctor/Master of Public Health), J.D./M.P.P. (Juris Doctor/Master of Public Policy), J.D./M.S.W. (Juris Doctor/Master of Social Welfare), and J.D./Ph.D. (Juris Doctor/Doctor of Philosophy).

Required

To earn the J.D., candidates must complete 87 total credits, of which 35 are for required courses. They must maintain a minimum GPA of 2.0 in the required courses. The following first-year courses are required of all students: Civil Procedure, Constitutional Law I, Contracts, Criminal Law, Lawyering Skills, Property, and Torts. Required upper-level courses consist of Professional Responsibility and an upper-division writing course. The required orientation program for first-year students is a 5-day program designed to acquaint first-year students with classmates, professors, and deans, and with the study of law and how to handle a variety of administrative tasks. It incorporates panels, group discussions, and substantive sessions with law faculty as well as a formal convocation ceremony.

Electives

The UCLA School of Law offers concentrations in corporate law, criminal law, entertainment law, environmental law, family law, intellectual property law, internationl law, labor law, litigation, media law, securities law, sports law, and tax law. Academic specializations include critical race studies, public interest law and policy, business law

Phone: 310-825-2080
Fax: 310-206-7227
E-mail: *admissions@law.ucla.edu*
Web: *www.law.ucla.edu*

Contact

Karman Hsu, Director of Admissions, 310-825-2080 for general inquiries; Biljana Vuletic, 310-825-2459 for financial aid information.

CALIFORNIA

and policy, entertainment and media law, and law and philosophy. In addition, there are 30 clinical offerings, with 300 clinical spots for students, including the Criminal Defense Clinic, International Justice Clinic, and Sports and the Law. Credit ranges from 4 to 6 units. Seminars are offered to advanced students, and credit ranges from 2 to 4 units; seminars include, among others, Music and Industry Law, International Human Rights, and National Security in the Information Economy. Full-time, semester-long national and international externships are offered to students and are worth 13 units (11 units for the placement and 2 units for a related seminar or tutorial taught by a faculty member). Students can work as extern law clerks to a federal judge or in a government agency, public interest law firm, or nonprofit organization. Students can also propose new agency externships tailored to their academic goals. Directed research, for which students must produce original scholarship of publishable quality, is worth 1 to 5 units. Special lecture series include International Law Speaker Series, Critical Race Speaker Series, and Sexual Orientation Law Speaker Series. Students may spend one semester abroad through student exchange agreements with universities in several countries. The academic support program includes study groups led by academically successful second- and third-year students, exam and outlining workshops for all first-year students, individual academic counseling, and a summer program for 40 incoming first-year students. There are special sections in Constitutional Law, Evidence, Wills and Trusts, and Legal Analysis. Minority programs include Asian/Pacific Islander Law Students Association (APILSA), Black Law Students Association (BLSA), La Raza Law Students Association (La Raza), Native American Law Students Association (NALSA), and South Asian Law Students Association (SALSA). The most widely taken electives are Evidence, Constitutional Criminal Procedure, and Business Associations.

Graduation Requirements

In order to graduate, candidates must have a GPA of 2.0, must have completed the upper-division writing requirement, and must complete the first-year curriculum, 6 semesters of residence credit in regular session, and a course of study in professional responsibility.

Organizations

Students edit the *UCLA Law Review*. Other student-edited publications include the *Asian Pacific American Law Journal, Chicano/Latino Law Review, National Black Law Journal, Pacific Basin Law Journal, Entertainment Law Review, Journal of Environmental Law and Policy, Journal of Islamic and Near Eastern Law, Journal of Law and Technology, Dukeminier Awards: Best Sexual Orientation Law Review Articles, Women's Law Journal,* and the *Journal of International Law and Foreign Affairs.* Moot court competitions include the UCLA Moot Court Honors Program, Sexual Orientation Law Moot Court Competition, and Jessup International Law Moot Court Competition. Law student organizations include the Disability Law Society, Environmental Law Society, and Mock Trial Association. Local chapters of national organizations include the American Constitution Society, the Federalist Society, and many minority student organizations. Other campus clubs and organizations include Advocates for Children and Teens and Immigration Law Society.

Library

The law library contains 689,513 hardcopy volumes and 20,343 microform volume equivalents, and subscribes to 8,309 serial publications. Such online databases and networks as CALI, CIS Universe, DIALOG, Infotrac, Legal-Trac, LEXIS, Mathew Bender, OCLC First Search, RLIN, WESTLAW, Wilsonline Indexes, LLMC, Interam, HeinOnline, BNA Core, CCH IntelliConnect, Bloomberg, California Continuing Education of the Bar, Making of Modern Law, and more are available to law students for research. Special library collections include a U.S. government depository, a California depository, and an East Asian law collection. The ratio of library volumes to faculty is 5,345 to 1 and to students is 603 to 1. The ratio of seats in the library to students is 1 to 1.

Faculty

The law school has 111 full-time and 63 part-time faculty members, of whom 59 are women. About 7% of full-time faculty have a graduate law degree in addition to the J.D.; about 13% of part-time faculty have one. The ratio of full-time students

Placement	
J.D.s awarded:	342
Services available through: a separate law school placement center.	
Services: a twice-yearly on-campus interview program; the office hosts public interest, government, and small firm events as well.	
Special features: individual counseling and workshops on career planning and interviewing skills; online job listings can be accessed by students and alumni.	
Full-time job interviews:	34 employers
Summer job interviews:	197 employers
Placement by graduation:	86% of class
Placement within 9 months:	94% of class
Average starting salary:	$25,000 to $160,000
Areas of placement:	
Private practice 2–10 attorneys	11%
Private practice 11–25 attorneys	3%
Private practice 26–50 attorneys	2%
Private practice 51–100 attorneys	3%
Private Practice 101+ attorneys	39%
Government	10%
Business/industry	9%
Public interest	9%
Judicial clerkships	8%
Academic	6%
Military	1%

to full-time faculty in an average class is 11 to 1; in a clinic, 12 to 1. The law school has a regular program of bringing visiting professors and other distinguished lecturers and visitors to campus. There is a chapter of the Order of the Coif; 34 faculty are members.

Students

About 47% of the student body are women; 29%, minorities; 4%, African American; 15%, Asian American; 9%, Hispanic; and 2%, Native American. The majority of students come from California (68%). The average age of entering students is 25; age range is 18 to 47. About 26% of students enter directly from undergraduate school, and 7% have a graduate degree. About 2% drop out after the first year for academic or personal reasons; 98% remain to receive a law degree.

Law School

1111 East 60th Street
Chicago, IL 60637

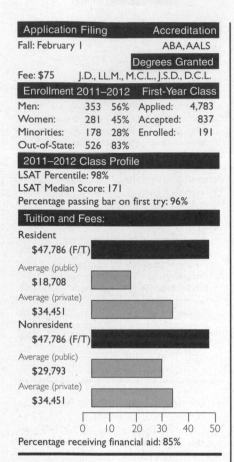

Application Filing	Accreditation
Fall: February 1	ABA, AALS

Degrees Granted	
Fee: $75	J.D., LL.M., M.C.L., J.S.D., D.C.L.

Enrollment 2011–2012		First-Year Class	
Men:	353 56%	Applied:	4,783
Women:	281 45%	Accepted:	837
Minorities:	178 28%	Enrolled:	191
Out-of-State:	526 83%		

2011–2012 Class Profile
LSAT Percentile: 98%
LSAT Median Score: 171
Percentage passing bar on first try: 96%

Tuition and Fees:

Resident
$47,786 (F/T)

Average (public)
$18,708

Average (private)
$34,451

Nonresident
$47,786 (F/T)

Average (public)
$29,793

Average (private)
$34,451

0   10   20   30   40   50
Percentage receiving financial aid: 85%

ADMISSIONS

In the fall of 2011 first-year class, 4783 applied, 837 were accepted, and 191 enrolled. Sixteen transfers enrolled. The median LSAT percentile of the most recent first-year class was 98; the median GPA was 3.9 on a scale of 4.0.

Requirements
Applicants must have a bachelor's degree and take the LSAT. No specific undergraduate courses are required. Candidates are interviewed.

Procedure
The application deadline for fall entry is February 1. Applicants should submit an application form, LSAT results, transcripts, a nonrefundable application fee of $75, 2 letters of recommendation, a personal statement, and a resume. Notification of the admissions decision is rolling starting in December. The law school uses the LSAC.

Special
The law school recruits minority and disadvantaged students by using the law school candidate referral service and outreach at law school forums, colleges, and minority fairs. Requirements are different for out-of-state students. Transfer students must have one year of credit, must have attended an ABA-approved law school, and must be planning to spend at least 2 years at the law school.

Costs

Tuition and fees for the 2011–2012 academic year are $47,502 for all full-time students. On-campus room and board costs about $13,590 annually.

Financial Aid

About 85% of current law students receive some form of aid. Awards are based on need and merit combined. The required financial statement is the FAFSA. The aid application deadline for fall entry is March 1. First-year students are notified about their financial aid application at time of acceptance.

About the Law School

University of Chicago Law School was established in 1902 and is a private institution. The 203-acre campus is in an urban area 7 miles from downtown Chicago. The primary mission of the law school is to train well-rounded, critical, and socially conscious thinkers and doers. Three cornerstones provide the foundation for Chicago's educational mission: the life of the mind, participatory learning, and interdisciplinary inquiry. Students have access to federal, state, county, city, and local agencies, courts, correctional facilities, law firms, and legal aid organizations in the Chicago area. The clinics involve more than 120 students each year and permit them to represent clients with real-world legal problems under the guidance of clinical faculty. Facilities of special interest to law students include the law quadrangle, made up of buildings surrounding a reflecting pool and housing the law library, classrooms, offices, the legal aid clinics, an auditorium, and a moot court room. Housing for students consists of dormitories and a variety of apartments and single-family homes located in nearby Hyde Park. About 90% of the law school

facilities are accessible to the physically disabled.

Calendar

The law school operates on a quarter basis. Courses are offered days only, and must be completed within 3-years. New students are admitted in the fall. There is no summer session. Transferable summer courses are not offered.

Programs

In addition to the J.D., the law school offers the LL.M., M.C.L., J.S.D., and D.C.L. Students may take relevant courses in other programs and apply credit toward the J.D.; a maximum of 12 credits may be applied.

Required
To earn the J.D., candidates must complete 105 total credits, of which 40 are for required courses. They must maintain a minimum GPA of 1.6 in the required courses. The following first-year courses are required of all students: an elective, Civil Procedure, Contracts, Criminal Law, Elements of the Law, Legal Research and Writing, Property, and Torts. Required upper-level courses consist of Professional Responsibility. The optional orientation program for first-year students consists of 3 days of presentations, tours, and social events, including a dinner, a Lake Michigan boat cruise, and a picnic.

Electives
The Law School offers concentrations in corporate law, criminal law, entertainment law, environmental law, family law, intellectual property law, internationl law, juvenile law, labor law, litigation, maritime law, media law, securities law, sports law, tax law, torts and insurance, law and economics, and law and philosophy. In addition, clinics available to second- and third-year students include the Mandel Legal Aid Clinic, the Institute for Justice Clinic on Entrepreneurship, and the Exoneration Project. Seventy-two seminars are open to second- and third-year law students. The Career Services Center helps students locate summer internships. Nearly all of first-year students and 97% of second-year students are employed during the summer. The Chicago Law Foundation, a student-run charitable

ILLINOIS

Phone: 773-702-9484
Fax: 773-834-0942
E-mail: admissions@law.uchicago.edu
Web: law.uchicago.edu

Contact

Admissions Office, 773-702-9484 for general inquiries; Ann Perry, 773-702-9484 for financial aid information.

organization, awards grants to students working in public-interest jobs during the summer. Also, the law school has funding available for public-interest work. Faculty-supervised research may be done in the individual research program for credit. Lectures, open to the law school community, occur several times a year in workshops such as Constitutional Law, International Law, and Law and Economics. Academic counselors, the Dean of Students, and the Associate Director of Student Affairs provide academic programming and counseling for students. The most widely taken electives are Evidence, Constitutional Law, and Corporations Law.

Graduation Requirements
In order to graduate, candidates must have a GPA of 1.7, and must have completed the upper-division writing requirement and a Professional Responsibility course.

Organizations

Students edit *The University of Chicago Law Review*, *The University of Chicago Legal Forum*, and *The Chicago Journal of International Law*. There are 4 faculty-edited journals: the *Supreme Court Review*, *Journal of Law and Economics*, *Journal of Legal Studies*, and *Law and Economics: Working Papers*. The student newspaper is *The Phoenix*. While first-year students have moot court practice in their Legal Research and Writing class, upper-level students participate in the Hinton Moot Court Program and selected outside moot court competitions. Other competitions include the annual trivia contest. The school has about 60 student organizations that include the Intellectual Property and Entertainment Law Society and the International Law Society. Local chapters of national associations include the Black Law Students Association, the Federalist Society, and the American Constitution Society. Other organizations include Habitat for Humanity, the Hemingway Society, and the Scales of Justice.

Library

The law library contains 672,456 hard-copy volumes and 11,712 microform volume equivalents, and subscribes to 6,212 serial publications. Such online databases and networks as CALI, CIS Universe, DIALOG, Dow-Jones, Infotrac, Legal-Trac, LEXIS, OCLC First Search, RLIN,

WESTLAW, HeinOnline, LLMC Digital, Bloomberg Law, CCH International, BNA-ALL, Access UN, Arbititration Law Online, and TRACFED are available to law students for research. Special library collections include a federal document depository and Supreme Court briefs and records. The ratio of library volumes to faculty is 12,905 to 1 and to students is 950 to 1. The ratio of seats in the library to students is 1 to 2.

Faculty

The law school has 70 full-time and 31 part-time faculty members, of whom 26 are women. According to AAUP standards for Category I institutions, faculty salaries are well above average. The ratio of full-time students to full-time faculty in an average class is 9 to 1; in a clinic, 10 to 1. The law school has a regular program of bringing visiting professors and other distinguished lecturers and visitors to campus. There is a chapter of the Order of the Coif.

Students

About 45% of the student body are women; 28%, minorities; 6%, African American; 9%, Asian American; 10%, Hispanic; and 1%, Native American. The average age of entering students is 24; age range is 21 to 42. About 38% of students enter directly from undergraduate school, 18% have a graduate degree, and 62% have worked full-time prior to entering law school. About 1% drop out after the first year for academic or personal reasons; 99% remain to receive a law degree.

Placement

J.D.s awarded:	198
Services available through: a separate law school placement center.	
Services: Seminars and publications.	
Special features: clerkship counseling, academic job market counseling, and individual interview coaching.	
Full-time job interviews:	200 employers
Summer job interviews:	400 employers
Placement by graduation:	95% of class
Placement within 9 months:	98% of class
Average starting salary:	$60,000 to $160,000
Areas of placement:	
Private practice 2–10 attorneys	3%
Private practice 11–25 attorneys	3%
Private practice 26–50 attorneys	1%
Private practice 51–100 attorneys	3%
Law firms 101–500+ attorneys	61%
Judicial clerkships	14%
Public interest	5%
Business/industry	4%
Government	3%
Academic	2%

College of Law

P.O. Box 210040
Cincinnati, OH 45221-0040

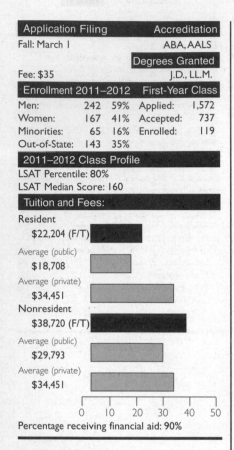

Application Filing	Accreditation
Fall: March 1	ABA, AALS

	Degrees Granted
Fee: $35	J.D., LL.M.

Enrollment 2011–2012		First-Year Class	
Men:	242 59%	Applied:	1,572
Women:	167 41%	Accepted:	737
Minorities:	65 16%	Enrolled:	119
Out-of-State:	143 35%		

2011–2012 Class Profile
LSAT Percentile: 80%
LSAT Median Score: 160

Tuition and Fees:

Resident
$22,204 (F/T)

Average (public)
$18,708

Average (private)
$34,451

Nonresident
$38,720 (F/T)

Average (public)
$29,793

Average (private)
$34,451

0   10   20   30   40   50

Percentage receiving financial aid: 90%

ADMISSIONS

In the fall of 2011 first-year class, 1572 applied, 737 were accepted, and 119 enrolled. The median LSAT percentile of the most recent first-year class was 80; the median GPA was 3.6 on a scale of 4.0. The lowest LSAT percentile accepted was 33; the highest was 97.

Requirements

Applicants must have a bachelor's degree and take the LSAT. The most important admission factors include GPA, LSAT results, and academic achievement. No specific undergraduate courses are required. Candidates are not interviewed.

Procedure

The application deadline for fall entry is March 1. Applicants should submit an application form, LSAT results, transcripts, a personal statement, TOEFL results (if applicable), a nonrefundable application fee of $35, and 2 letters of recommendation. Notification of the admissions decision is on a rolling basis. The law school uses the LSAC.

Special

The law school recruits minority and disadvantaged students. Requirements are different for out-of-state students. Transfer students must have one year of credit, must have attended an ABA-approved law school, must submit a personal statement, and must supply their class rank.

Costs

On-campus room and board costs about $10,914 annually.

Financial Aid

About 90% of current law students receive some form of aid. The maximum annual amount of aid from all sources combined, including scholarships, loans, and work contracts, is $57,056. Awards are based on need and merit. The required financial statement is the FAFSA. The aid application deadline for fall entry is March 1. First-year students are notified about their financial aid application within 4 weeks of acceptance.

About the Law School

University of Cincinnati College of Law was established in 1833 and is a public institution. The 473-acre campus is in an urban area in the Clifton area of Cincinnati. The primary mission of the law school is to provide students with an opportunity to equip themselves for effective and creative participation in the roles lawyers play in society. Students have access to federal, state, county, city, and local agencies, courts, correctional facilities, law firms, and legal aid organizations in the Cincinnati area. Students also have access to a variety of legal externships in Cincinnati and several clinical opportunities. Facilities of special interest to law students are the U.S. Court of Appeals for the Sixth Circuit and the District Court for the Southern District of Ohio; the 3000-plus members of the Cincinnati Bar Association; the more than 600 law firms; and the Legal Aid Society of Cincinnati. Housing for students is plentiful; most law students live off campus in housing within walking distance of campus. All law school facilities are accessible to the physically disabled.

Calendar

The law school operates on a traditional semester basis. Courses are offered days only. New students are admitted in the fall. There is no summer session. Transferable summer courses are offered.

Programs

In addition to the J.D., the law school offers the LL.M. Students may take relevant courses in other programs and apply credit toward the J.D.; a maximum of 8 credits may be applied. The following joint degrees may be earned: J.D./M.A. (Juris Doctor/Master of Arts in Women's Gender and Sexuality Studies), J.D./M.A.P.S. (Juris Doctor/Master of Arts in Political Science), J.D./M.B.A. (Juris Doctor/Master of Business Administration), J.D./M.C.P. (Juris Doctor/Master of Community Planning), and J.D./M.S.W. (Juris Doctor/Master of Social Work).

Required

To earn the J.D., candidates must complete 90 total credits, of which 36 are for required courses. They must maintain a minimum GPA of 2.0 in the required courses. The following first-year courses are required of all students: Advocacy, Civil Procedure I and II, Constitutional Law I and II, Contracts, Criminal Law, Introduction to Law, Legal Research and Writing, Property, and Torts. Required upper-level courses consist of a lawyering course, a seminar requirement, a writing requirement, and Legal Ethics, The required orientation program for first-year students is 1 week and includes the Introduction to Law course, registration, assignment of faculty and student advisers, a meeting with student advisers, a social event with upper-level students, information about the law library, and bar association membership opportunities.

Electives

The College of Law offers concentrations in corporate law, criminal law, environmental law, intellectual property law, internationl law, litigation, tax law, and international human rights. Clinics include Sixth Circuit, Domestic Violence, and Ohio Innocence Project. Seminar topics include corporate law, Constitutional law, and jurisprudence. An externship program is offered to 50 or 60 students and is worth 3 credit hours. Both judi-

Phone: 513-556-6805
Fax: 513-556-2391
E-mail: admissions@law.uc.edu
Web: www.law.uc.edu

Contact

Al Watson, Assistant Dean and Director of Admission, 513-556-6805 for general inquiries; Al Watson, Assistant Dean and Director of Admission, 513-556-6805 for financial aid information.

OHIO

cial and legal externships are available. Individual research projects are also available. Speakers can be heard at the Human Rights Institute, which invites international human rights scholars, the Center for Corporate Law, Institute for Law and Psychiatry, and the Corporate Law symposium. The college has a student exchange program with the University of Canterbury, Christchurch, New Zealand. An academic success program is also available. The most widely taken electives are Corporations, Wills, and Secured Transactions.

Graduation Requirements

In order to graduate, candidates must have a GPA of 2.0, must have completed the upper-division writing requirement, and must have completed the lawyering course.

Organizations

Students edit the *University of Cincinnati Law Review, Immigration and Nationality Law Review, Human Rights Quarterly,* and *Freedom Center Journal.* Students compete at the Jessup International Law Moot Court, the J. Braxton Craven, Jr. Memorial Moot Court, and the Giles Sutherland Rich Moot Court in patent law. Also, the College of Law hosts the National Product Liability Competition and participates in all other national competitions. Law student organizations and campus clubs include the ABA-Law Student Division, International Law Society, Intellectual Property Society. Student Bar Association, Moot Court, and Black Law Students Association. There are local chapters of Order of the Barristers and Order of the Coif.

Library

The law library contains 437,356 hardcopy volumes and 781,570 microform volume equivalents, and subscribes to 11,673 serial publications. Such online databases and networks as CALI, CIS Universe, LEXIS, OCLC First Search, WESTLAW, HeinOnline, WORLDCAT, BNA Direct, Bloomberg Law, CCH Intelliconnect, and others are available to law students for research. Special library collections include the Urban Morgan Human Rights Collection; the Segoe Collection on Land Use and Urban Planning; the Goldstein Collection on the Law

of Church and State; William J. Butler papers, Nathaniel R. Jones papers, records of the Ohio 1987 Merit Plan constitutional amendment campaign regarding judicial selection, and a selective depository for U.S. federal government. The ratio of library volumes to faculty is 12,927 to 1 and to students is 1,071 to 1. The ratio of seats in the library to students is 1 to 1.

Faculty

The law school has 28 full-time faculty members. According to AAUP standards for Category I institutions, faculty salaries are average. The ratio of full-time students to full-time faculty in an average class is 11 to 1. The law school has a regular program of bringing visiting professors and other distinguished lecturers and visitors to campus. There is a chapter of the Order of the Coif.

Students

About 41% of the student body are women; 16%, minorities; 7%, African American; 6%, Asian American; and 3%, Hispanic. The majority of students come from Ohio (65%). The average age of entering students is 25; age range is 21 to 38. About 60% of students enter directly from undergraduate school, 8% have a graduate degree, and 40% have worked full-time prior to entering law school. About 1% drop out after the first year for academic or personal reasons; 98% remain to receive a law degree.

Placement

J.D.s awarded:	120

Services available through: a separate law school placement center.

Special features: individual counseling and planning, annual meetings to update students' professional plan, Legal Externship Program for credit, and Volunteer Opportunity Program for transcript recognition.

Full-time job interviews:	8 employers
Summer job interviews:	24 employers
Placement within 9 months of graduation:	91% of class

Areas of placement:

Private practice 2–10 attorneys	10%
Private practice 11–25 attorneys	5%
Private practice 26–50 attorneys	4%
Private practice 51–100 attorneys	5%
Business/industry	17%
Academic	17%
Government	16%
Judicial clerkships	9%
Public interest	7%
Military	5%

UNIVERSITY OF COLORADO

Law School

Campus Box 403, Wolf Law Building
Boulder, CO 80309-0403

Application Filing	Accreditation
Fall: March 15	ABA, AALS

	Degrees Granted
Fee: $65	J.D., LL.M.

Enrollment 2011–2012		First-Year Class	
Men:	279 52%	Applied:	3,175
Women:	261 48%	Accepted:	956
Minorities:	119 22%	Enrolled:	163
Out-of-State:	297 55%		

2011–2012 Class Profile

LSAT Percentile: 90%
LSAT Median Score: 164
Percentage passing bar on first try: 94%

Tuition and Fees:

Resident
$31,044 (F/T)

Average (public)
$18,708

Average (private)
$34,451

Nonresident
$37,452 (F/T)

Average (public)
$29,793

Average (private)
$34,451

0 10 20 30 40 50

Percentage receiving financial aid: 99%

ADMISSIONS

In the fall of 2011 first-year class, 3175 applied, 956 were accepted, and 163 enrolled. Forty-two transfers enrolled. The median LSAT percentile of the most recent first-year class was 90; the median GPA was 3.6 on a scale of 4.0. The lowest LSAT percentile accepted was 48; the highest was 99.

Requirements

Applicants must have a bachelor's degree and take the LSAT. No specific undergraduate courses are required. Candidates are not interviewed.

Procedure

The application deadline for fall entry is March 15. Applicants should submit an application form, LSAT results, transcripts, a personal statement, a nonrefundable application fee of $65, 2 letters of recommendation, and résumé. Notification of the admissions decision is December through May. The law school uses the LSAC.

Special

The law school recruits minority and disadvantaged students by means of law school forums, candidate referral services through LSAC, partnerships with organizations on campus, and special outreach by faculty, staff, students, and alumni. Requirements are different for out-of-state students. Transfer students must have one year of credits, attended an ABA-approved law school, and have a personal statement.

Costs

Tuition and fees for the 2011–2012 academic year are $29,214 for full-time in-state students and $35,622 for out-of-state students. On-campus room and board costs about $18,092 annually; books and supplies run $1,998.

Financial Aid

About 99% of current law students receive some form of aid. The average annual amount of aid from all sources combined, including scholarships, loans, and work contracts, is $33,700; maximum, $60,000. Awards are based on need and merit, and loans are based on need. Scholarships are usually based on a combination of need and merit. Required financial statements are the FAFSA and tax returns. The aid application deadline for fall entry is April 1. Special funds for minority or disadvantaged students include need-based, merit, and scholarships that advance the diversity of the student body. First-year students are notified about their financial aid application at the time of the initial inquiry; information on financial aid is available on the web site, the Viewbook, and the Admitted Student Web Portal. Admitted students are encouraged to apply for financial aid as early as possible.

About the Law School

University of Colorado Law School was established in 1892 and is a public institution. The 873-acre campus is in a small town 30 miles northwest of Denver. The primary mission of the law school is to develop the skills, ethics, and habits of being an excellent lawyer, with a strong sense of the legal profession's greatest traditions, and to develop an equal dedication to public service. Students have access to federal, state, county, city, and local agencies, courts, correctional facilities, law

firms, and legal aid organizations in the Boulder area. Facilities of special interest to law students include the "green" Wolf Law Building, which contains all aspects of academic, administrative, clinical, research, career services, social, and audiovisual offerings for law students under one roof. Housing for students is primarily apartments, located about 10 minutes from the law school. Less expensive accommodations are available in nearby towns. All law school facilities are accessible to the physically disabled.

Calendar

The law school operates on a traditional semester basis. Courses are offered days only and must be completed within 7 years. New students are admitted in the fall. There is a 3- and 5-week summer session. Transferable summer courses are offered.

Programs

In addition to the J.D., the law school offers the LL.M. students the opportunity to take relevant courses in other programs and apply credit toward the J.D.; a maximum of varies credits may be applied. The following joint degrees may be earned: J.D./M.D. (Juris Doctor/Doctor of Medicine), J.D./Ph.D (Juris Doctor/Doctor of Philosophy in Environmental Science), J.D./M.B.A. (Juris Doctor/Master of Business Administration), J.D./M.P.A. (Juris Doctor/Master of Public Administration), J.D./M.S. (Juris Doctor/Master of Science in Environmental Science), J.D./M.S.T. (Juris Doctor/Master of Science, Telecommunications), and J.D./M.U.R.P. (Juris Doctor/Master of Urban and Regional Planning).

Required

To earn the J.D., candidates must complete 89 total credits, of which 38 are for required courses. The following first-year courses are required of all students: Appellate Court Advocacy, Civil Procedure, Constitutional Law, Contracts, Criminal Law, Legal Writing, Legislation and Regulation, Property, and Torts. Required upper-level courses consist of Evidence, Legal Ethics and Professionalism, Seminars include a practice requirement, and Professional Responsibility. The required orientation program for first-year students is 3 days, and includes a legal writing class, social

Phone: 303-492-7203
Fax: 303-492-2542
E-mail: lawadmin@colorado.edu
Web: www.colorado.edu/law

Contact

Admissions Office, 303-492-7203 for general inquiries; Kristine M. Jackson, Assistant Dean for Admission, 303-492-7203 for financial aid information.

COLORADO

activities, and an introduction to faculty, law school, and university facilities.

Electives

The Law School offers concentrations in corporate law, criminal law, environmental law, family law, intellectual property law, internationl law, juvenile law, labor law, litigation, media law, securities law, tax law, torts and insurance, natural resources, civil rights law, constitutional law, health/medicine law, Indian law, legal ethics, public interest law, and trial law. In addition, Clinics are available for either a year or 1 semester and a maximum of 14 credits may be awarded. Clinics include American Indian Law, Appellate Advocacy, Entrepreneurial Law, Juvenile Law, Wrongful Conviction, Civil Practice, Criminal Defense, Natural Resources Litigation, and Technology Law and Policy. A minimum of 1 seminar must be chosen from a variety of subjects. Externships allow students to earn up to 4 hours of academic credit for work in a governmental agency, private nonprofit institution, or a private law office. Independent study is permitted for 1 credit. Field work is offered through some seminars, externships, and clinics. Special no-credit lectures are offered to all students on a variety of topics. Students may study abroad in Oxford, England; St. Petersburg and Moscow, Russia; Dublin, Ireland; Paris, France; Barcelona, Spain; and Florence, Italy. A tutorial program is open to all first-year students who wish to participate. Students on academic probation are furnished with tutors. The most widely taken electives are Natural Resources and Environmental Law, Business Law, and Government and Public Law.

Graduation Requirements

In order to graduate, candidates must have a GPA of 72.0, and have completed the upper-division writing requirement.

Organizations

Students edit the *University of Colorado Law Review*, *Colorado Journal of International Environmental Law and Policy*, and the *Journal on Telecommunications and High Technology Law*. The most successful teams in the Rothgerber Moot Court Competition participate in the National Moot Court Competition. The school also competes in the Jessup Moot Court, held each year regionally, nationally, and internationally, and the Carrigan Cup Competition, an internal competition in which participants are selected for regional competitions leading to the national mock trial competition sponsored by the ABA. Other competitions deal with environmental law, American Indian law, and trademark law. There are local chapters of Phi Alpha Delta—Julius Caesar Chapter, American Bar Association Law Student Division, and ACLU. Law student organizations include Women's Law Caucus, Latino Law Students Association, and Environmental Law Society.

Library

The law library contains 888,178 hardcopy volumes and 1,653,416 microform volume equivalents, and subscribes to 4,587 serial publications. Online databases and networks include CIS Universe, DIALOG, Infotrac, Legal-Trac, LEXIS, Mathew Bender, OCLC First Search, WESTLAW, and Wilsonline Indexes. HeinOnline, BNA All, LLMC Digital, Digital Dissertation, and Factiva are also available to law students for research. Special library collections include a federal publications depository, Strengths in Environmental Law, Native American Law, and Constitutional Law. The ratio of library volumes to faculty is 16,448 to 1 and to students is 1,624 to 1. The ratio of seats in the library to students is 1 to 1.

Faculty

The law school has 50 full-time and 31 part-time faculty members, of whom 26 are women. According to AAUP standards for Category I institutions, faculty salaries are average. About 5% of full-time faculty have a graduate law degree in addition to the J.D. The ratio of full-time students to full-time faculty in an average class is 10 to 1; in a clinic, 9 to 1. The law school has a regular program of bringing visiting professors and other distinguished lecturers and visitors to campus. There is a chapter of the Order of the Coif; 15 faculty and 656 graduates are members.

Students

About 48% of the student body are women; 22%, minorities; 4%, African American; 6%, Asian American; 9%, Hispanic; and 3%, Native American. The majority of students come from Colorado (45%). The

Placement

J.D.s awarded:	176

Services available through: a separate law school placement center.

Services: access to computer career search resources; written documents providing job search information.

Special features: on-campus interview program; lunch-time informational sessions on job-seeking skills and various types of employment (traditional and nontraditional); Internet access to job postings, career workshops for law school graduates; a mock interview program, government/public interest career fair symposium series covering judicial, government, corporate, and private practice sectors; diversity hiring programs.

Full-time job interviews:	18 employers
Summer job interviews:	44 employers
Placement by graduation:	57% of class
Placement within 9 months:	83% of class
Average starting salary:	$49,594 to $86,359

Areas of placement:

Private practice 2–10 attorneys	14%
Private practice 11–25 attorneys	10%
Private practice 26–50 attorneys	5%
Private practice 51–100 attorneys	2%
Private practice 100+ attorneys	14%
Judicial clerkships	18%
Government	15%
Business/industry	15%
Public interest	3%
Academic	2%

average age of entering students is 25; age range is 21 to 53. About 44% of students enter directly from undergraduate school, 8% have a graduate degree, and 55% have worked full-time prior to entering law school. About 1% drop out after the first year for academic or personal reasons; 99% remain to receive a law degree.

UNIVERSITY OF CONNECTICUT

School of Law

55 Elizabeth Street
Hartford, CT 06105

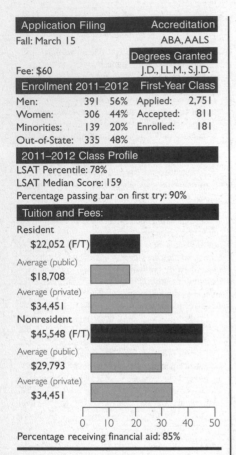

Application Filing	Accreditation
Fall: March 15	ABA, AALS

	Degrees Granted
Fee: $60	J.D., LL.M., S.J.D.

Enrollment 2011–2012		First-Year Class	
Men:	391 56%	Applied:	2,751
Women:	306 44%	Accepted:	811
Minorities:	139 20%	Enrolled:	181
Out-of-State:	335 48%		

2011–2012 Class Profile
LSAT Percentile: 78%
LSAT Median Score: 159
Percentage passing bar on first try: 90%

Tuition and Fees:
Resident $22,052 (F/T)
Average (public) $18,708
Average (private) $34,451
Nonresident $45,548 (F/T)
Average (public) $29,793
Average (private) $34,451

Percentage receiving financial aid: 85%

ADMISSIONS
In the fall of 2011 first-year class, 2751 applied, 811 were accepted, and 181 enrolled. Twelve transfers enrolled. The median LSAT percentile of the most recent first-year class was 78; the median GPA was 3.5 on a scale of 4.0.

Requirements
Applicants must have a bachelor's degree and take the LSAT. The most important admission factors include LSAT results, GPA, and writing ability. No specific undergraduate courses are required. Candidates are not interviewed.

Procedure
The application deadline for fall entry is March 15. Applicants should submit an application form, LSAT results, transcripts, a personal statement, a nonrefundable application fee of $60, 2 letters of recommendation, and a résumé. Notification of the admissions decision is December through May. The law school uses the LSAC.

Special
The law school recruits minority and disadvantaged students by attending recruiting fairs hosted by LSAC and HBCV as well as other minority majority institutions; hosting or co-hosting events such as balancing the scales and minority Law Day, and participating LSAC's discover law.org events. Minority Bar association and student organizations also host events aimed at recruiting and informing future minority law students. Requirements are different for out-of-state students. Transfer students must have one year of credit, have attended an ABA-approved law school, a personal statement, should be within the top 10% of their class, and must show compelling reasons for transfer.

Costs
Tuition and fees for the 2011–2012 academic year are $21,240 for full-time in-state students and $44,736 for out-of-state students. Tuition for part-time students is $14,800 for in-state students and $31,220 out-of-state. Books and supplies run $1,376.

Financial Aid
About 85% of current law students receive some form of aid. The average annual amount of aid from all sources combined, including scholarships, loans, and work contracts, is $30,641; maximum, $62,274. Awards are based on need. Required financial statements are the FAFSA and institutional financial aid application. The aid application deadline for fall entry is March 15. Special funds for minority or disadvantaged students include several grants that are awarded each year to entering students from economically, and educationally disadvantaged backgrounds who demonstrate promise. First-year students are notified about their financial aid application at time of acceptance.

About the Law School
University of Connecticut School of Law was established in 1921 and is a public institution. The 21-acre campus is in an urban area in Hartford Connecticut, 2 hours from New York and 1.5 hours from Boston. The primary mission of the law school is to provide a legal education of high quality, serve the state and the bar, and prepare students to practice law in any jurisdiction. Students have access to federal, state, county, city, and local agencies, courts, correctional facilities, law firms, and legal aid organizations in the Hartford area. Housing for students is ample and affordable in the surrounding areas; there are no on-campus housing facilities.

Calendar
The law school operates on a traditional semester basis. Courses for full-time students are offered both day and evening and days and evenings after the first year and must be completed within 5 years. For part-time students, courses are offered both day and evening and must be completed within 6 years. New full- and part-time students are admitted in the fall. There is a 4-week summer session. Transferable summer courses are offered.

Programs
In addition to the J.D., the law school offers the LL.M. and S.J.D. Students may take relevant courses in other programs and apply credit toward the J.D.; a maximum of 6 credits may be applied. The following joint degrees may be earned: J.D./M.B.A. (Juris Doctor/Master of Business Administration), J.D./L.L.M. (Juris Doctor/Master of Laws, Insurance Law), J.D./M.P.A. (Juris Doctor/Master of Public Affairs Administration), J.D./M.P.H. (Juris Doctor/Master of Public Health), and J.D./M.S.W. (Juris Doctor/Master of Social Work).

Required
To earn the J.D., candidates must complete 86 total credits, of which 36 are for required courses. They must maintain a minimum GPA of 2.3 in the required courses. The following first-year courses are required of all students: Civil Procedure, Contracts, Criminal Law, Lawyering Process, Statutory/Regulatory Class, Torts, Moot Court, Property, and Constitutional Law. Required upper-level courses consist of Legal Profession and the upper-class writing requirement. The required orientation program for first-year students is a 2-day event including presentations by the dean, faculty members, alumni, student services, financial aid, and career planning offices. In addition, the law school introduces students to practical lawyering and public service.

Phone: 860-570-5159
Fax: 860-570-5153
E-mail: admissions@law.uconn.edu
Web: www.law.uconn.edu

Contact

Karen DeMeola, Assistant Dean for Admissions, Student Finance, and Student Services, 860-570-5100 for general inquiries; Roberta Frick, Director of Financial Aid, 860-570-5147 for financial aid information.

CONNECTICUT

Placement

J.D.s awarded:	177

Services available through: a separate law school placement center.

Services: alumni mentor program, job bulletins, newsletter.

Special features: summer and permanent job résumé bank, presentations, workshops, seminars on career-related and job search projects.

Placement within 9 months of graduation:	86% of class
Average starting salary:	$15,000 to $160,000

Areas of placement:

Private practice 2–10 attorneys	16%
Private practice 11–25 attorneys	6%
Private practice 26–50 attorneys	4%
Private practice 51–100 attorneys	4%
Private practice 100–250 attorneys	6%
Business/industry	20%
Government	13%
Judicial clerkships	10%
Public interest	5%
Academic	3%
Military	1%

Electives

The School of Law offers concentrations in corporate law, criminal law, environmental law, family law, intellectual property law, internationl law, juvenile law, labor law, litigation, securities law, tax law, torts and insurance, legal theory, information technology law, property and land, child advocacy, and policy. In addition, clinics provide hands-on, practical training to upper-level students who earn up to 10 credits for their work; strong and widely recognized asylum and human rights, criminal law, appellate, child advocacy, immigration, intellectual property, and tax clinics are available. Seminars in a multitude of different substantive areas are available to upper-level students for typically 3 credits. Internships, research programs, and field work are available to upper-level students. Research positions are open to upper-level students under the direction of a faculty adviser. Special lecture series include Intellectual Property; Law Review Symposium; and various human rights, international, diversity, and insurance law series. Study abroad is open to upper-level students for 1 semester in various countries, including England, the Netherlands, Ireland, France, Germany, Israel, Italy, or Puerto Rico. Exchange programs in environmental law with the University of Vermont Law School and University of London are also available. Students having academic difficulty meet weekly with a faculty or student tutor to review case briefing, writing, legal analysis, and exam techniques. No credit is granted. An academic support program is offered for students that includes 1 minicourse designed to introduce case briefing, writing, and legal analysis. Special interest group programs include the Tax Law Certificate Program, the Intellectual Property Certificate Program, the Certificate in Law and Public Policy, and the Certificate in Human Rights. The most widely taken electives are Evidence, Intellectual Property, and International Law.

Graduation Requirements

In order to graduate, candidates must have a GPA of 2.3, and have completed the upper-division writing requirement.

Organizations

Students edit the *Connecticut Law Review*, *Connecticut Journal of International Law*, *Connecticut Insurance Law Journal*, *Connecticut Intellectual Property Notes*, and the *Public Interest Law Journal*, and the student newspaper, *Pro Se*. Moot court competitions include the Alva P. Loiselle, William H. Hastie, and Willem Vis International Moot Court. Other competitions include the National Appellate Advocacy Competition, Family Law Competition, Craven Competition, and National Moot Court Competition. A wide range of intellectual, political, social, and special interest organizations and activities are available to students, including the Student Bar Association, Black, Latino, South Asian, Asian, and Women's Law Students Associations, and Public Interest Law Group. Among many others, there are local chapters of the Federalist Society, the American Constitution Society, the National Lawyers Guild, the Tax Law Society, the Connecticut Alliance of International Lawyers, and the Intellectual Property and Technology Law Society.

Library

The law library contains 545,754 hardcopy volumes and 222,856 microform volume equivalents, and subscribes to 5,704 serial publications. Online databases and networks include CALI, CIS Universe, Infotrac, Legal-Trac, LEXIS, Mathew Bender, OCLC First Search, WESTLAW, Wilsonline Indexes. More than 200 others are available to law students for research. Special library collections include a federal depository, Connecticut materials, an international collection, and an insurance law collection. Recently, the library acquired federal depository, Connecticut materials, an international collection, and an insurance law collection. The ratio of library volumes to faculty is 12,404 to 1 and to students is 763 to 1. The ratio of seats in the library to students is 1 to 1.

Faculty

The law school has 59 full-time and 75 part-time faculty members, of whom 48 are women. According to AAUP standards for Category I institutions, faculty salaries are above average. About 33% of full-time faculty have a graduate law degree in addition to the J.D. The ratio of full-time students to full-time faculty in an average class is 11 to 1; in a clinic, 8 to 1. The law school has a regular program of bringing visiting professors and other distinguished lecturers and visitors to campus.

Students

About 44% of the student body are women; 20%, minorities; 3%, African American; 9%, Asian American; 7%, Hispanic; 1%, Native American; and 1%, other. The majority of students come from Connecticut (52%). The average age of entering students is 25; age range is 19 to 47. About 33% of students enter directly from undergraduate school, 9% have a graduate degree, and 67% have worked full-time prior to entering law school. About 1% drop out after the first year for academic or personal reasons; 95% remain to receive a law degree.

School of Law

300 College Park
Dayton, OH 45469-2760

Application Filing	Accreditation
Fall: May 1	ABA, AALS

	Degrees Granted
Fee: $50	J.D., LL.M., M.S.L.

Enrollment 2011–2012		First-Year Class	
Men:	282 57%	Applied:	1,751
Women:	206 41%	Accepted:	1,214
Minorities:	60 12%	Enrolled:	177
Out-of-State:	273 55%		

2011–2012 Class Profile
LSAT Percentile: 40%
LSAT Median Score: 149
Percentage passing bar on first try: 70%

Tuition and Fees:

Resident
$33,678 (F/T)

Average (public)
$18,708

Average (private)
$34,451

Nonresident
$33,678 (F/T)

Average (public)
$29,793

Average (private)
$34,451

0 10 20 30 40 50
Percentage receiving financial aid: 98%

ADMISSIONS

In the fall of 2011 first-year class, 1751 applied, 1214 were accepted, and 177 enrolled. Five transfers enrolled. The median LSAT percentile of the most recent first-year class was 40; the median GPA was 3.1 on a scale of 4.0. The lowest LSAT percentile accepted was 13; the highest was 94.

Requirements
Applicants must have a bachelor's degree and take the LSAT. The most important admission factors include LSAT results, GPA, and academic achievement. No specific undergraduate courses are required. Candidates are not interviewed.

Procedure
The application deadline for fall entry is May 1. Applicants should submit an application form, LSAT results, transcripts, a personal statement, a nonrefundable application fee of $50, 2 letters of recommendation, and an optional diversity statement. Notification of the admissions

decision is 4 to 6 weeks after receipt of a completed application. The law school uses the LSAC.

Special
The law school recruits minority and disadvantaged students by means of targeted mailings, recruiting at undergraduate schools, meeting with targeted student organizations, and some scholarship aid. Requirements are different for out-of-state students. Transfer students must have one year of credit, must have attended an ABA-approved law school, and must submit a personal statement.

Costs
Books and supplies run $1,500.

Financial Aid
About 98% of current law students receive some form of aid. The average annual amount of aid from all sources combined, including scholarships, loans, and work contracts, is $44,409; maximum, $50,178. Awards are based on need and merit combined. The required financial statement is the FAFSA. The aid application deadline for fall entry is March 1. Special funds for minority or disadvantaged students are available. First-year students are notified about their financial aid application at time of acceptance.

About the Law School
University of Dayton School of Law was established in 1974 and is a private institution. The 373-acre campus is in an urban area 1 mile south of downtown Dayton. The primary mission of the law school is to enroll a diverse group of women and men who are intellectually curious, who possess self-discipline, and who are well motivated, and to rigorously educate them in the substantive and procedural principles of public and private law. Students have access to federal, state, county, city, and local agencies, courts, correctional facilities, law firms, and legal aid organizations in the Dayton area. Area corporations regularly employ students in their legal departments; some students are interns with the Ohio Supreme Court. Housing for students is convenient and readily available both on campus and off campus. All law school facilities are accessible to the physically disabled.

Calendar
The law school operates on a traditional semester basis. Courses are offered both day and evening, and must be completed within 3 years. New students are admitted in the fall. There is a 6-week summer session. Transferable summer courses are offered.

Programs
In addition to the J.D., the law school offers the LL.M. and M.S.L. Students may take relevant courses in other programs and apply credit toward the J.D.; a maximum of 6 credits may be applied. The following joint degrees may be earned: J.D./M.B.A. (Juris Doctor/Master of Business Administration).

Required
To earn the J.D., candidates must complete 90 total credits, of which 79 are for required courses. They must maintain a minimum GPA of 2.2 in the required courses. The following first-year courses are required of all students: Civil Practice and Procedure, Contracts, Criminal Law, Criminial Procedure, Intra-session: Skills, Intra-session: Values and Ethics, Legal Profession I and II, Legislation, Real Property, and Torts I and II. Required upper-level courses consist of Business Organizations, Capstone Course/Clinical Experience, Commercial Transactions, Constitutional Law, Contracts II, Evidence for the Litigator or Fundamentals of Evidence, Externship, Intra-session: Skills Proficiency, Professional Responsibility, Real Property II, and Wills and Trusts. There is a required orientation program for first-year students.

Electives
The School of Law offers concentrations in corporate law, criminal law, litigation, tax law, intellectual property, patent law, and computer/cyberspace law. A 4-credit clinic studies lawyer decision making by placing students in the role of lawyer in real cases and by analyzing decisions made in that role. In field work and class sessions, students assume the responsibility of representing clients in a variety of legal matters under the supervision of professors while focusing on the role and skills of a lawyer, using simulation review and discussion and "case rounds" methodologies. A rigorous writing experience

Phone: 937-229-3555
Fax: 937-229-4194
E-mail: lawinfo@udayton.edu
Web: www.udayton.edu/law

Contact

Janet L. Hein, Assistant Dean, Director of Admissions, 937-229-3555 for financial aid information.

OHIO

is a key component. More than 30 elective seminars are offered in topics as varied as cybercrimes, employment, discrimination, entertainment law, law and education, and health care law. All students are required to participate in a 4-credit, semester-long externship with a court government office or agency, public-interest organization, or business, during which the student performs the tasks of a lawyer under the mentorship and direction of an on-site lawyer supervisor. Special lecture series include the Scholarly Symposia Series, Law and Technology Seminars, and Bankruptcy Seminars. Study-abroad includes a comparative law program offered during summer sessions in Italy and England. The Academic Success Program (ASP), a comparative academic support program, provides academic assistance to all students with workshops throughout the year on class preparation, case synthesis, and exam writing. A pre-orientation week-long intensisve preparation workshop is part of this program. The Road to Bar Passage Program provides guidance and support in the bar exam preparation process, including group informational meeting and individual bar exam counseling. The Minority Summer Judicial Clerkship Program, Minority Summer Extenship Program, and regional minority career fairs are available. The most widely taken electives are Evidence, Tax, and Corporations.

Graduation Requirements

In order to graduate, candidates must have a GPA of 2.2 and must have completed the upper-division writing requirement.

Organizations

Students edit the *University of Dayton Law Review*. Students typically participate in moot court competitions including bankruptcy law, patent law, and international law. There is a mock trial competition. Students also compete in the intercollegiate National Trial Competition. There are local chapters of Volunteer Student Law Project and the Intellectual Property Law Society. Local chapters of national organizations include Phi Alpha Delta, ACLU, and St. Thomas More Society. Campus organizations include Habitat for Humanity, Big Brothers/Big Sisters, and intramual sports teams.

Library

The law library contains 195,218 hardcopy volumes and 689,730 microform volume equivalents, and subscribes to 4,671 serial publications. Such online databases and networks as CALI, LEXIS, OCLC First Search, WESTLAW, and Ohio LINK are available to law students for research. The ratio of library volumes to faculty is 5,916 to 1 and to students is 399 to 1. The ratio of seats in the library to students is 1 to 1.

Faculty

The law school has 25 full-time and 21 part-time faculty members, of whom 13 are women. According to AAUP standards for Category IIA institutions, faculty salaries are above average. About 15% of full-time faculty have a graduate law degree in addition to the J.D. The ratio of full-time students to full-time faculty in an average class is 16 to 1; in a clinic, 6 to 1. The law school has a regular program of bringing visiting professors and other distinguished lecturers and visitors to campus.

Students

About 41% of the student body are women; 12%, minorities; 6%, African American; 3%, Asian American; 1%, Hispanic; and 2%, multicultural. The average age of entering students is 25; age range is 20 to 54. About 44% of students enter directly from undergraduate school, 3% have a graduate degree, and 50% have worked full-time prior to entering law school. About 1% drop out after the first year for academic or personal reasons; 80% remain to receive a law degree.

Placement

J.D.s awarded:	167
Services available through: a separate law school placement center.	
Full-time job interviews:	11 employers
Summer job interviews:	10 employers
Placement within 9 months of graduation:	86% of class
Average starting salary:	$19,700 to $135,000
Areas of placement:	
Private practice 2–10 attorneys	36%
Private practice 11–25 attorneys	3%
Private practice 26–50 attorneys	4%
Private practice 51–100 attorneys	3%
Business/industry	21%
Government	12%
Judicial clerkships	6%
Solo practice	6%
Academic	3%
Military	2%
Public interest	1%

Sturm College of Law

2255 East Evans Avenue
Denver, CO 80208

Application Filing	Accreditation
Fall: June 1	ABA, AALS
	Degrees Granted
Fee: $45	J.D., LL.M., M.S.L.A. and M.R.L.S.

Enrollment 2011–2012		First-Year Class	
Men:	480 51%	Applied:	2,425
Women:	466 49%	Accepted:	986
Minorities:	161 17%	Enrolled:	297
Out-of-State:	445 47%		

2011–2012 Class Profile

LSAT Percentile: 78%
LSAT Median Score: 159
Percentage passing bar on first try: 90%

Tuition and Fees:

Resident
$38,502 (F/T)

Average (public)
$18,708

Average (private)
$34,451

Nonresident
$38,502 (F/T)

Average (public)
$29,793

Average (private)
$34,451

0   10   20   30   40   50

Percentage receiving financial aid: 90%

ADMISSIONS

In the fall of 2011 first-year class, 2425 applied, 986 were accepted, and 297 enrolled. Sixteen transfers enrolled. The median LSAT percentile of the most recent first-year class was 78; the median GPA was 3.5 on a scale of 4.0. The lowest LSAT percentile accepted was 23; the highest was 98.

Requirements
Applicants must have a bachelor's degree and take the LSAT. Minimum acceptable GPA is 2.0 on a scale of 4.0. The most important admission factors include LSAT results and GPA. No specific undergraduate courses are required. Candidates are not interviewed.

Procedure
The application deadline for fall entry is June 1. Applicants should submit an application form, LSAT results, transcripts, a personal statement, a nonrefundable application fee of $45, 2 letters of recommendation, and a résumé. Notification

of the admissions decision is on a rolling basis. The law school uses the LSAC.

Special
The law school recruits minority and disadvantaged students by offering scholarships and working with student groups on recruitment and retention through the Office of Admissions. Requirements are different for out-of-state students. Transfer students must have one year of credits, attended an ABA-approved law school, and a personal statement.

Costs

Tuition and fees for the 2011–2012 academic year are $37,830 for all full-time students. Tuition for part-time students is $27,742 for in-state students and $27,742 out-of-state. On-campus room and board costs about $10,222 annually; books and supplies run $2,000.

Financial Aid

About 90% of current law students receive some form of aid. The average annual amount of aid from all sources combined, including scholarships, loans, and work contracts, is $42,331; maximum, $53,859. Awards are based on need and merit; award letters offer aid (scholarships, loans, work study) up to the cost of attendance. Required financial statement is the FAFSA. The aid application deadline for fall entry is open. Special funds for minority or disadvantaged students include a variety of scholarships to support members of these groups. First-year students are notified about their financial aid application at time of acceptance.

About the Law School

University of Denver Sturm College of Law was established in 1892 and is a private institution. The 33-acre campus is in an urban area 10 minutes from downtown Denver. The primary mission of the law school is to provide an excellent, innovative, technologically sophisticated program of legal education to a diverse student body of high academic quality. Students have access to federal, state, county, city, and local agencies, courts, correctional facilities, law firms, and legal aid organizations in the Denver area. Facilities of special interest to law students include The Frank H.

Ricketson Law Building. Housing for students consists of on-campus graduate student housing, as well as near campus neighborhood apartment complexes. All law school facilities are accessible to the physically disabled.

Calendar

The law school operates on a traditional semester basis. Courses for full-time students are offered both day and evening and must be completed within 7 years. For part-time students, courses are offered both day and evening and must be completed within 7 years. New full- and part-time students are admitted in the fall. There is an 11-week summer session. Transferable summer courses are offered.

Programs

In addition to the J.D., the law school offers the LL.M., M.S.L.A. and M.R.L.S. Students may take relevant courses in other programs and apply credit toward the J.D.; a maximum of 10 credits may be applied. The following joint degrees may be earned: J.D./M.A. (Juris Doctor/Master of Arts (in various disciplines)), J.D./M.B.A. (Juris Doctor/Master of Business Administration), J.D./M.I.M. (Juris Doctor/Master of International Management), J.D./G.S.I.S. (Juris Doctor/Master of International Studies), J.D./M.S.L.A. (Juris Doctor/Master of Science in Legal Administration), J.D./M.S.W. (Juris Doctor/Master of Social Work), and J.D./M.T. (Juris Doctor/Master of Taxation).

Required
To earn the J.D., candidates must complete 90 total credits, of which 40 are for required courses. They must maintain a minimum GPA of 2.3 in the required courses. The following first-year courses are required of all students: Civil Procedure, Contracts, Criminal Law, Lawyering Process, Property, and Torts. Required upper-level courses consist of Administrative Law, Constitutional Law, Evidence, and Legal Profession and Legal Writing. The required orientation program for first-year students consists of 3 days of programming focused on programs, facilities, student support organizations, and procedures.

Phone: 303-871-6135
Fax: 303-871-6992
E-mail: *admissions@law.du.edu*
Web: *www.law.du.edu*

Contact

Iain Davis, Assistant Dean of Admissions, 303-871-6128 for general inquiries; Kasia Palm, Director of Financial Aid, 303-871-6362 for financial aid information.

COLORADO

Electives

The Sturm College of Law offers concentrations in corporate law, environmental law, internationl law, and labor law. In addition, upper-level students receive 5–6 credit hours for a clinic. Clinics include Community Law, Civil Rights, Criminal Representation, Environmental Law, and Mediation/Arbitration. Seminars, offered to upper-level students, are worth 2 to 3 credit hours. Internships, open to upper-level students for 2–6 credits, are available in the offices of prosecutors; public defenders; the attorney general; and judicial, legislative, corporate, immigration, and natural resources agencies. Directed research may be undertaken under a professor's supervision. Research positions are open only to upper-level students for 2 to 3 credits. Students may elect to apply for study-abroad programs at other universities. The no-credit Academic Achievement Program is a tutorial program offered to first-year students. The most widely taken electives are Basic Tax, Corporations, and Trusts and Estates.

Graduation Requirements

In order to graduate, candidates must have a GPA of 2.3 and completed the upper-division writing requirement.

Organizations

Students edit the *University of Denver Law Journal*, *Water Court Reporter*, *Sports and Entertainment Law Journal*, *Transportation Law Journal*, *Denver Journal of International Law and Policy*, and the student newspaper, *The Writ*. Moot court competitions running through the school year include the Negotiations Competition, Jessup International Law Competition, and Hoffman Cup Trial Competition. Other competitions include the National Civil Trial Competition, American Trial Lawyers, and Tournament of Champions. Among the student organizations are the Christian Legal Society, Colorado Council of Mediators Organization, Entertainment Law Society, and Black Law Students Association. Chapters of national associations include Delta Theta Phi, Phi Alpha Delta, and Phi Delta Phi. There are more than 40 student organizations.

Library

The law library contains 241,077 hardcopy volumes and 178,930 microform volume equivalents, and subscribes to 6,932 serial publications. Online databases and networks include CALI, CIS Universe, Infotrac, Legal-Trac, LEXIS, Mathew Bender, OCLC First Search, WESTLAW, and Wilsonline Indexes, and are available to law students for research. Special library collections include a government document selective depository and the Hughes Memorial Library Collection. The ratio of library volumes to faculty is 3,257 to 1 and to students is 255 to 1. The ratio of seats in the library to students is 1 to 3.

Faculty

The law school has 74 full-time and 57 part-time faculty members, of whom 46 are women. According to AAUP standards for Category I institutions, faculty salaries are below average. About 30% of full-time faculty have a graduate law degree in addition to the J.D. The ratio of full-time students to full-time faculty in an average class is 20 to 1; in a clinic, 6 to 1. The law school has a regular program of bringing visiting professors and other distinguished lecturers and visitors to campus.

Students

About 49% of the student body are women; 17%, minorities; 2%, African American; 3%, Asian American; 8%, Hispanic; and 1%, Native American. The majority of students come from Colorado (53%). The average age of entering students is 26; age range is 20 to 53. About 8% of students have a graduate degree. About 5% drop out after the first year for academic or personal reasons; 98% remain to receive a law degree.

Placement

J.D.s awarded:	288

Services available through: a separate law school placement center.

Services: self-assessment and alternative careers, job-matching program, on-campus interviewing, and student development program.

Special features: out-of-town alumni networks, DU alumni links, individualized networking strategies, professional mentor program, local and national employer outreach, and specialized advising and programming on the private and public sector.

Full-time job interviews:	13 employers
Summer job interviews:	41 employers
Placement by graduation:	65% of class
Placement within 9 months:	91% of class
Average starting salary:	$25,000 to $160,000

Areas of placement:

Private practice 2–10 attorneys	20%
Private practice 11–25 attorneys	4%
Private practice 26–50 attorneys	4%
Private practice 51–100 attorneys	1%
Government	22%
Business/industry	19%
Judicial clerkships	9%
Public interest	7%
Academic	4%

School of Law

651 East Jefferson Avenue
Detroit, MI 48226

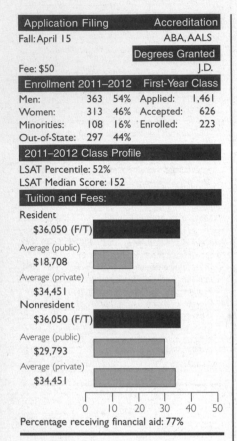

Application Filing		Accreditation
Fall: April 15		ABA, AALS
		Degrees Granted
Fee: $50		J.D.

Enrollment 2011–2012		First-Year Class	
Men:	363 54%	Applied:	1,461
Women:	313 46%	Accepted:	626
Minorities:	108 16%	Enrolled:	223
Out-of-State:	297 44%		

2011–2012 Class Profile

LSAT Percentile: 52%
LSAT Median Score: 152

Tuition and Fees:

Resident
$36,050 (F/T)

Average (public)
$18,708

Average (private)
$34,451

Nonresident
$36,050 (F/T)

Average (public)
$29,793

Average (private)
$34,451

0 10 20 30 40 50

Percentage receiving financial aid: 77%

ADMISSIONS

In the fall of 2011 first-year class, 1461 applied, 626 were accepted, and 223 enrolled. The median LSAT percentile of the most recent first-year class was 52; the median GPA was 3.2 on a scale of 4.0. The lowest LSAT percentile accepted was 15; the highest was 96.

Requirements
Applicants must have a bachelor's degree and take the LSAT. Minimum acceptable LSAT percentile is 15. The most important admission factors include academic achievement, LSAT results, and GPA. No specific undergraduate courses are required, and candidates are not interviewed.

Procedure
The application deadline for fall entry is April 15. Applicants should submit an application form, LSAT results, transcripts, a personal statement, TOEFL (may be required in some instances), a nonrefundable application fee of $50, 2 letters of recommendation, and a resume.

Notification of the admissions decision is on a rolling basis. The law school uses the LSAC.

Special
The law school recruits minority and disadvantaged students by hosting an annual informational fair for prospective students of color, by attending law fairs at colleges and universities targeted to reach students of color and by using the LSAC. Requirements are different for out-of-state students. Transfer students must have one year of credit, have a minimum GPA of 3.0, attended an ABA-approved law school, a personal statement, and be in good standing at his or her current law school.

Costs
Books and supplies run $1,950.

Financial Aid
About 77% of current law students receive some form of aid. Awards are based on need and merit. Scholarships are based on merit, while all other aid, except unsubsidized loans, is based on need. Required financial statement is the FAFSA. The aid application deadline for fall entry is April 1. First-year students are notified about their financial aid application at time of acceptance.

About the Law School
University of Detroit Mercy School of Law was established in 1912 and is a private institution. The 4-acre campus is located in an urban area in downtown Detroit. The primary mission of the law school is to provide a rigorous legal education that integrates theory, doctrine, and practice and emphasizes legal writing, ethics, and public service. Students have access to federal, state, county, city, and local agencies, courts, correctional facilities, law firms, and legal aid organizations in the Detroit area. The career services office provides a wide array of resources to enable students to obtain short- and long-term positions in these areas. A full range of extracurricular activities and organizations like the St. Thomas More Society, the Student Bar Association, the Black Law Students Association, and Phi Alpha Delta offer the chance to exercise leadership skills and perform community service. Housing for

students includes apartments and houses within walking distance or a short driving commute to the school. The law school assists students with housing needs. All law school facilities are accessible to the physically disabled.

Calendar
The law school operates on a traditional semester basis. Courses for full-time students are offered both day and evening and must be completed within 3 years. For part-time students, courses are offered both day and evening and must be completed within 5 years. New full- and part-time students are admitted in the fall. There is a 7-week summer session. Transferable summer courses are offered.

Programs
The following joint degrees may be earned: J.D./L.E.D. (Juris Doctor/Bachelor of Laws (Mexico)), J.D./J.D. (Juris Doctor/Juris Doctor (Canada)), and J.D./M.B.A. (Juris Doctor/Master of Business Administration).

Required
To earn the J.D., candidates must complete 90 total credits, of which 51 are for required courses. They must maintain a minimum GPA of 1.0 in the required courses. The following first-year courses are required of all students: Analytical Tools, Applied Legal Theory and Analysis, Civil Procedure, Contracts, Property, and Torts. Required upper-level courses consist of 1 clinic course, 2 law firm modules, Basic Federal Tax, Constitutional Law, Criminal Law, Evidence, International Law, Professional Responsibility, and upper-level writing course. All students must take clinical courses. The required orientation program for first-year students is a 4-day immersion program that includes presentations by faculty and administrators, alumni panel discussions, and an overview of the first-year curriculum.

Electives
The School of Law offers concentrations in corporate law, criminal law, entertainment law, environmental law, family law, intellectual property law, internationl law, juvenile law, labor law, litigation, tax law, health law, and constitutional law. In addition, several clinical opportunities are

Phone: 313-596-0264
866-428-1610 ext. 529
Fax: 313-596-0280
E-mail: udmlawao@udmercy.edu
Web: www.law.udmercy.edu

Contact

Associate Dean, Admissions and Student Affairs, 313-596-0264 for general inquiries; Denise Daniel, Financial Aid Coordinator, 313-596-0214 for financial aid information.

available for students including Immigration Law Clinic, Mobile Law Office, and Mediation Clinic, among others. The school of law offers seminars on selected law topics. A variety of clinical externships are available to upper-class students. Students with a GPA of 2.5 may work under the supervision of faculty attorneys in preparing cases for local civil and criminal courts, federal district courts, nonprofit legal agencies, and state and federal administrative courts. The clinic places students with such agencies as the Wayne County Prosecutor's Office, the U.S. Attorney's Office, the Attorney Grievance Commission, the American Civil Liberties Union, the City of Detroit Law Department, and local health care systems. Students may enroll to complete a research project of 1 to 2 credits. The law school holds an annual McElroy Lecture in Religion and Law and an Interfaith panel as well as frequent Dean's debates. UDM offers its International Opportunities Program in which students receive a $1,000 loan. The loan is forgiven after the student successfully completes one of 20 approved programs and returns to UDM the following semester. There is an academic support program. Minority and disadvantaged students who do not meet the standards of those currently being admitted, but who have strong qualifications that indicate possible success in law school may be admitted to the Special Summer Program (SSP). Students who successfully complete the SSP may matriculate with the fall class. Through a consortium with 2 other law schools, students interested in intellectual property may choose from a wide array of intellectual property law electives. The most widely taken electives are Trial Practice, Estates and Trusts, and Criminal Procedure.

Graduation Requirements

In order to graduate, candidates must have a GPA of 2.0 and completed the upper-division writing requirement.

Organizations

The primary law review is *The University of Detroit Mercy Law Review*. The student newspaper is *In Brief*. Moot court competitions include the Gallagher Competition, the G. Mennen Williams Annual Moot Court Competition, and the Professional Responsibility Competition. Law student organizations include Sports and

Entertainment Law Society, Student Animal Defense Fund, and Moot Court Board of Advocates. Local chapters of national associations include Phi Alpha Delta, Delta Theta Phi, and Black Law Students Association. Other clubs include the UDM Hockey Club, Women's Law Caucus, and St. Thomas More Society.

Library

The law library contains 392,744 hardcopy volumes and 197,510 microform volume equivalents, and subscribes to 3,026 serial publications. Online databases and networks include CALI, CIS Universe, DIALOG, Legal-Trac, LEXIS, Mathew Bender, OCLC First Search, WESTLAW, Wilsonline Indexes, and LANs, which are available to law students for research. Special library collections include English and Canadian Law, government documents, records, legal periodical indexes on CD-ROM, and several hundred databases in related fields. The ratio of library volumes to faculty is 4,316 to 1 and to students is 581 to 1. The ratio of seats in the library to students is 1 to 3.

Faculty

The law school has 52 full-time and 39 part-time faculty members, of whom 37 are women. About 12% of full-time faculty have a graduate law degree in addition to the J.D. The ratio of full-time students to full-time faculty in an average class is 17 to 1; in a clinic, 9 to 1. The law school has a regular program of bringing visiting professors and other distinguished lecturers and visitors to campus.

Students

About 46% of the student body are women; 16%, minorities; 10%, African American; 3%, Asian American; 2%, Hispanic; and 10%, Unknown. The majority of students come from Michigan (56%). The average age of entering students is 26; age range is 21 to 46. About 13% drop out after the first year for academic or personal reasons; 87% remain to receive a law degree.

Placement

J.D.s awarded:	210

Services available through: a separate law school placement center.

Special features: The Career Services Office operates on-campus interview programs in the fall and spring, provides seminars and individual advice on such topics as interviewing and résumé preparation, and sponsors the weekly "Lunch with a Lawyer" series and the Alumni Mentor Program. Students and alumni can access and apply to jobs online using UDM's web-based career services management database.

Placement within 9 months of graduation:	75% of class
Average starting salary:	$53,891
Areas of placement:	
Private practice 2–10 attorneys	16%
Private practice 11–25 attorneys	10%
Private practice 26–50 attorneys	1%
Private practice 51–100 attorneys	3%
Business/industry	25%
Government	12%
Judicial clerkships	6%
Public interest	5%
Academic	3%

Application Filing	Accreditation
Fall: March 15	ABA, AALS
	Degrees Granted
Fee: $30	J.D., LL.M., S.J.D.

Enrollment 2011–2012		First-Year Class	
Men:	577 55%	Applied:	3,201
Women:	467 45%	Accepted:	875
Minorities:	261 25%	Enrolled:	295
Out-of-State:	136 13%		

2011–2012 Class Profile

LSAT Median Score: 162
Percentage passing bar on first try: 89%

Tuition and Fees:

Resident
$18,710 (F/T)

Average (public)
$18,708

Average (private)
$34,451

Nonresident
$38,074 (F/T)

Average (public)
$29,793

Average (private)
$34,451

0 10 20 30 40 50

Percentage receiving financial aid: 94%

ADMISSIONS

In the fall of 2011 first-year class, 3201 applied, 875 were accepted, and 295 enrolled. Fifty-two transfers enrolled. The median GPA of the most recent first-year class was 3.64.

Requirements
Applicants must have a bachelor's degree and take the LSAT. No specific undergraduate courses are required and candidates are not interviewed.

Procedure
The application deadline for fall entry is March 15. Applicants should submit an application form, LSAT results, transcripts, a personal statement, a nonrefundable application fee of $30, 4 are recommended but not required letters of recommendation, and candidates are strongly encouraged to use the LSAC letter of recommendation option. Notification of the admissions decision is Between December and late April. The law school uses the LSAC.

Special
The law school recruits minority and disadvantaged students. The College of Law is represented at a large number of Law Day programs in Florida and other southern states. This activity is supplemented by individual campus visits and other visits to historically black colleges in Florida and the South. The law school actively seeks a diverse student body. Requirements are different for out-of-state students. Transfer students must have one year of credits, attended an ABA-approved law school, a personal statement, ranked in the top 1/3 of their class, and finished the required first-year curriculum.

Costs

On-campus room and board costs about $9,200 annually; books and supplies run $1,070.

Financial Aid

About 94% of current law students receive some form of aid. The average annual amount of aid from all sources combined, including scholarships, loans, and work contracts, is $25,969; maximum, $54,176. Awards are based on need and merit combined. Required financial statements are the FAFSA and and an additional application for merit/need-based scholarships and grants. The aid application deadline for fall entry is April 15. Special funds for minority or disadvantaged students are available, as are need-based grants. First-year students are notified about their financial aid application some time after acceptance, but prior to enrollment.

About the Law School

The University of Florida Fredric G. Levin College of Law was established in 1909 and is a public institution. The 2000-acre campus is in a suburban area of Gainesville, Florida. The primary mission of the law school is to offer excellence in educating professionals, advancing legal scholarship, serving the public, and fostering justice. Students have access to federal, state, county, city, and local agencies, courts, correctional facilities, law firms, and legal aid organizations in the Gainesville area. Recreational, athletic facilities of special interest to law students include an advocacy center (including a fully functional trial and appellate court room), law library, and 2 academic buildings, which offer

the latest in teaching technology. Housing for students is available in university dormitories, as well as family housing, and numerous nearby apartments. All law school facilities are accessible to the physically disabled.

Calendar

The law school operates on a traditional semester basis. Courses for full-time students are offered both day and evening and must be completed within 84 months. There is no part-time program. New full-time students are admitted in the fall. There is an 8-week summer session. Transferable summer courses are offered.

Programs

In addition to the J.D., the law school offers the LL.M. and S.J.D. Students may take relevant courses in other programs and apply credit toward the J.D.; a maximum of 6 credits may be applied. The following joint degrees may be earned: J.D./M.D. (Juris Doctor/Doctor of Medicine), J.D./Ph.D. (Juris Doctor/Doctor of Philosophy), J.D./M.A. (Juris Doctor/Master of Arts), J.D./M.B.A. (Juris Doctor/Master of Business Administration), and J.D./M.S. (Juris Doctor/Master of Science).

Required
To earn the J.D., candidates must complete 88 total credits, of which 34 are for required courses. They must maintain a minimum GPA of 2.0 in the required courses. The following first-year courses are required of all students: Appellate Advocacy, Civil Procedure, Constitutional Law, Contracts, Criminal Law, Introduction to Lawyering, Legal Research, Legal Research and Writing, Property, and Torts. Required upper-level courses consist of Advanced Writing requirement, Legal Drafting, and Professional Responsibility. The required orientation program for first-year students is a three-day comprehensive orientation to the profession and College of Law.

Electives
The Fredric G. Levin College of Law offers concentrations in criminal law, environmental law, family law, intellectual property law, internationl law, and estates and trust practice. In addition, clinics include a Child Welfare Clinic, Mediation Clinic,

Phone: 352-273-0890
877-429-1297
Fax: 352-392-4087
E-mail: madorno@law.ufl.edu
Web: http://www.law.ufl.edu

Contact
Michell Adorno, Assistant Dean of Admissions, 352-273-0890 for general inquiries; Carol Huber, Director of Financial Aid, 352-273-0620 for financial aid information.

FLORIDA

Criminal Clinic, and Conservation Clinic. The clinics are open to students who have completed at least 48 hours and Professional Responsibility. Seminiars covering a variety of legal topics are also offered, and open to students who have completed the first-year curriculum. A large number of externships are available with judges, prosecutor and defender's offices, and other governmental and nonprofit organizations as well as some "in-house counsel" positions. They are open to students who have completed the first-year curriculum. Special lecture series include Environmental and Land Use Law and Graduate Tax. Students may study abroad at Bar-Ilan University (Israel), John Wolfgang Goethe University (Germany), Leiden University (the Netherlands), Monash University (Australia), PUC-Rio (Brazil), Tel Aviv University (Israel), University of Montpellier (France), University of Cape Town (South Africa), University of Costa Rica, and University of Warsaw (Poland). First-semester students participate in the Academic Success Program. Academic Support workshops for students at risk of being placed on academic probation are available. The program is open to all students. The College's Office of Student Affairs offers programs, support, and services to minorities and diverse student groups. The most widely taken electives are Corporations, Evidence, and Estates and Trusts.

Graduation Requirements
In order to graduate, candidates must have a GPA of 2.0 and complete the upper-division writing requirement.

Organizations
Students edit the *Florida Review*, *Florida International Law Journal*, *Journal of Law and Public Policy*, *Florida Tax Review*, *Journal of Technology Law and Policy*, and the student newspaper, *The Docket*. Moot court competitions include ABA National Appellate Advocacy Competition, National Security Law Competition, and Duberstein Bankruptcy Competition. Other competitions include the Thomas Tang Moot Court Competition, St. Johns National Civic Rights Mock Trial Competition, the Robert Orseck Florida Bar Competition, and the Sutherland Cup. Law student organizations, local chapters of national associations, and campus organizations include the Association for Public Interest Law, John Marshall Bar Association, BLSA, Gaters for Alternative Dispute Association, International Law Society, American Bar Association-Law Student Division, Law College Council, Phi Alpha Delta, and Phi Delta Phi.

Library
The law library contains 643,282 hardcopy volumes and 318,270 microform volume equivalents, and subscribes to 7,526 serial publications. Online databases and networks include CALI, CIS Universe, Dow-Jones, Infotrac, Legal-Trac, LEXIS, Mathew Bender, OCLC First Search, RLIN, and WESTLAW. Wilsonline Indexes, BNA, CCH, HeinOnline, RIA, Fastcase, Tax Analysis, and Current Index to Legal Periodicals, are also available to law students for research. Special library collections include Tax collection, selective government document depository. The ratio of library volumes to faculty is 4,465 to 1 and to students is 312 to 1. The ratio of seats in the library to students is 1 to 1.

Faculty
The law school has 73 full-time and 61 part-time faculty members, of whom 62 are women. According to AAUP standards for Category I institutions, faculty salaries are average. About 28% of full-time faculty have a graduate law degree in addition to the J.D. The ratio of full-time students to full-time faculty in an average class is 24 to 1; in a clinic, 8 to 1. The law school has a regular program of bringing visiting professors and other distinguished lecturers and visitors to campus. There is a chapter of the Order of the Coif; 20 faculty and 1726 graduates are members.

Students
About 45% of the student body are women; 25%, minorities; 7%, African American; 7%, Asian American; 10%, Hispanic; and 1%, Native American. The majority of students come from Florida (87%). The average age of entering students is 23; age range is 20 to 41. About 51% of students enter directly from undergraduate school, and 11% have a graduate degree. About 2% drop out after the first year for academic or personal reasons; 98% remain to receive a law degree.

Placement
J.D.s awarded: 430
Services available through: a separate law school placement center.
Services: Mock interviews, off-campus recruiting units, online interview sign-up/ job listings available 24/7, pro bono-public interest law, career programs, career library, Shadow Program, Judicial Clerkship Program, Mentor Program, resume books.
Special features: Numerous employers typically interview on campus, fall and spring 4 full-time professionals are assigned to advise students and conduct programming and mock interviews.

Full-time job interviews:	26 employers
Summer job interviews:	64 employers
Placement by graduation:	51% of class
Placement within 9 months:	85% of class
Average starting salary:	$55,000 to $92,500

Areas of placement:
Private practice 2–10 attorneys	18%
Private practice 11–25 attorneys	8%
Private practice 26–50 attorneys	5%
Private practice 51–100 attorneys	4%
Government	15%
Business/industry	14%
Academic	7%
Judicial clerkships	6%
Public interest	6%

University of Florida **487**

School of Law

Hirsch Hall, 225 Herty Drive
Athens, GA 30602-6012

Application Filing	Accreditation
Fall: March 1	ABA, AALS
	Degrees Granted
Fee: $50	J.D., LL.M.

Enrollment 2011–2012		First-Year Class	
Men:	397 57%	Applied:	3,186
Women:	294 43%	Accepted:	814
Minorities:	138 20%	Enrolled:	225
Out-of-State:	207 30%		

2011–2012 Class Profile
LSAT Percentile: 90%
LSAT Median Score: 165
Percentage passing bar on first try: 99%

Tuition and Fees:

Resident
$17,624 (F/T)

Average (public)
$18,708

Average (private)
$34,451

Nonresident
$34,732 (F/T)

Average (public)
$29,793

Average (private)
$34,451

0 10 20 30 40 50

Percentage receiving financial aid: 90%

ADMISSIONS

In the fall of 2011 first-year class, 3186 applied, 814 were accepted, and 225 enrolled. Six transfer students enrolled. The median LSAT percentile of the most recent first-year class was 90; the median GPA was 3.6 on a scale of 4.0. The lowest LSAT percentile accepted was 40; the highest was 99.

Requirements
Applicants must take the LSAT. Minimum acceptable GPA is 2.0 on a scale of 4.0. The most important admission factors include character or personality, general background, and academic achievement. No specific undergraduate courses are required, and candidates are not interviewed.

Procedure
The application deadline for fall entry is March 1. Applicants should submit an application form, LSAT results, transcripts, personal statement, nonrefundable application fee of $50, and 2 letters of recommendation. Notification of the admissions decision is from October through August. The law school uses the LSAC.

Special
The law school recruits minority and disadvantaged students by means of the Candidate Referral Service of Law Services, LSAC Law Forums, and campus visitations. Requirements are different for out-of-state students. Transfer students must have one year of credits, attended an ABA-approved law school, personal statement, LSAC report, law school transcript, dean's certification letter, and 2 letters of recommendation.

Costs
On-campus room and board costs about $14,330 annually; books and supplies run $1,500.

Financial Aid
About 90% of current law students receive some form of aid. The average annual amount of aid from all sources combined, including scholarships, loans, and work contracts, is $60,000; maximum, $51,252. Awards are based on need and merit combined. Required financial statement is the FAFSA. The aid application deadline for fall entry is July 1. First-year students are notified about their financial aid application at time of acceptance.

About the Law School
University of Georgia School of Law was established in 1859 and is a public institution. The 1289-acre campus is located in a small town 65 miles northeast of Atlanta. Students have access to federal, state, county, city, and local agencies, courts, correctional facilities, law firms, and legal aid organizations in the Athens area. Students have access to the facilities of the University of Georgia. Facilities of special interest to law students are the Dean Rusk Center for International Law and Policy, the Institute for Continuing Legal Education, and the Institution for Continuing Judicial Education. Housing for students is available on campus for single students in residence halls; students with a spouse and/or children may live in University Village, an on-campus apartment complex. About 99% of the law school facilities are accessible to the physically disabled.

Calendar
The law school operates on a traditional semester basis. Courses for full-time students are offered days only and must be completed within 5 years. There is no part-time program. New full-time students are admitted in the fall. There is a 7-week summer session. Transferable summer courses are offered.

Programs
In addition to the J.D., the law school offers the LL.M. Students may take relevant courses in other programs and apply credit toward the J.D.; a maximum of 6 credits may be applied. The following joint degrees may be earned: J.D./M.B.A. (Juris Doctor/Master of Business Administration), J.D./M.Ed. (Juris Doctor/Master of Education in sports studies), J.D./M.H.P. (Juris Doctor/Master of Historic Preservation), J.D./M.P.A. (Juris Doctor/Master of Public Administration), and J.D./M.S.W. (Juris Doctor/Master of Social Work).

Required
To earn the J.D., candidates must complete 88 total credits, of which 36 are for required courses. They must maintain a minimum GPA of 2.0 in the required courses. The following first-year courses are required of all students: Civil Procedure, Contracts and Sales, Criminal Law, Legal Research and Writing, Property, and Torts. Required upper-level courses consist of Legal Profession. Students must complete at least 1 practical skills course. Courses satisfying this requirement include the 12 service learning clinics. The required orientation program for first-year students is a 2-day program that provides an introduction to the school's activities, programs, and requirements, to the case method and Socratic Method of teaching.

Electives
The School of Law offers concentrations in corporate law, criminal law, entertainment law, environmental law, family law, intellectual property law, internationl law, juvenile law, labor law, litigation, sports law, tax law, and torts and insurance. Clinics offered to the students include the Criminal Defense Clinic, the Prosecutorial Clinic, and the Land Use Clinic, all of which have varying credit amounts. Seminars, and supervised research and

Phone: 706-542-7060
Fax: 706-542-5556
E-mail: ugajd@uga.edu
Web: www.law.uga.edu

Contact

Paul Rollins, Director of Law Admissions, 706-542-7060 for general inquiries; Bonnie Joerschke, Director, Office of Student Financial Aid, 706-542-6147 for financial aid information.

GEORGIA

independent projects, are also open to upper-level students. Students may intern with the Civil Externship Clinic, the Public Interest Practicum, and the Global Internship Program. The Dean Rusk Center for International and Comparative Law provides research programs. Field work opportunities for students include Equal Justice Foundation Fellowships. Study abroad programs may be undertaken with permission and include the Georgia Law at Oxford, Brussels Seminar on Law and Institutions of the European Union and Community, and Georgia Law Summer Program in China. Several tutorial and mentoring programs are offered for no credit. The most widely taken electives are Constitutional Law I and II, Evidence, and Federal Income Tax.

Graduation Requirements

In order to graduate, candidates must have a GPA of 2.0 and complete the upper-division writing requirement.

Organizations

Students edit the *Georgia Law Review*, *Georgia Journal of International and Comparative Law*, and *Journal of Intellectual Property Law*. Annually, moot court teams participate in competitions, including the National and the Phillip C. Jessup Moot Courts and the ABA National Moot Court competitions. Other competitions are the American Trial Lawyers Association and National Mock Trial competitions. Law student organizations include the Environmental Law Association, Student Animal Legal Defense Fund, and Business Law Society. There are local chapters of Black Law Students Association, Phi Alpha Delta, and ABA-Law Student Division. Campus clubs and other organizations include Equal Justice Foundation, Women Law Students Association, and Student Bar Association.

Library

The law library contains 390,000 hardcopy volumes and 504,653 microform volume equivalents, and subscribes to 7,223 serial publications. Online databases and networks include CALI, CIS Universe, Legal-Trac, LEXIS, OCLC First Search, WESTLAW, and Wilsonline Indexes, which are available to law students for research. Special library collections include complete English and Canadian law collections and

a European Community depository library. The ratio of library volumes to faculty is 7,959 to 1 and to students is 549 to 1. The ratio of seats in the library to students is 1 to 1.

Faculty

The law school has 46 full-time and 22 part-time faculty members, of whom 21 are women. According to AAUP standards for Category I institutions, faculty salaries are average. About 18% of full-time faculty have a graduate law degree in addition to the J.D.; about 75% of part-time faculty have one. The ratio of full-time students to full-time faculty in an average class is 12 to 1. The law school has a regular program of bringing visiting professors and other distinguished lecturers and visitors to campus. There is a chapter of the Order of the Coif.

Placement

J.D.s awarded:	240

Services available through: a separate law school placement center.

Services: more than 20 separate informational programs, including forums on legal practice and settings, resume and cover letter writing, interviewing and other career-related topics; several initiatives matching more than 100 students with alumni for in-depth career advice, contacts information and experience; more than 6 days of mock interviews; more than 20 off-campus interview initiatives; fall and spring on-campus interview programs; online interview scheduling system, including a personal resume database; and video conference interviewing.

Special features: visiting career consultants, a career lecture series and videotaping of mock interviews, shadow programs, mentor programs, and 12 or more interviewing consortia.

Full-time job interviews:	59 employers
Summer job interviews:	59 employers
Placement by graduation:	91% of class
Placement within 9 months:	96% of class
Average starting salary:	$53,285 to $130,000

Areas of placement:

Private practice 2–10 attorneys	25%
Private practice 11–25 attorneys	7%
Private practice 26–50 attorneys	3%
Private practice 51–100 attorneys	4%
Government	18%
Judicial clerkships	14%
Business/industry	8%
Public interest	2%
Academic	1%

UNIVERSITY OF HAWAII AT MANOA

William S. Richardson School of Law

2515 Dole Street
Honolulu, HI 96822

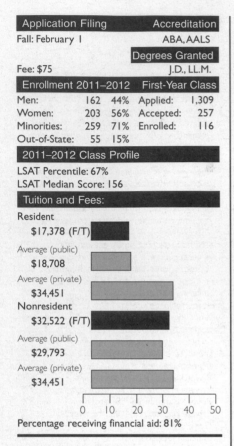

Application Filing		Accreditation
Fall: February 1		ABA, AALS
		Degrees Granted
Fee: $75		J.D., LL.M.

Enrollment 2011–2012			First-Year Class	
Men:	162	44%	Applied:	1,309
Women:	203	56%	Accepted:	257
Minorities:	259	71%	Enrolled:	116
Out-of-State:	55	15%		

2011–2012 Class Profile

LSAT Percentile: 67%
LSAT Median Score: 156

Tuition and Fees:

Resident
$17,378 (F/T)

Average (public)
$18,708

Average (private)
$34,451

Nonresident
$32,522 (F/T)

Average (public)
$29,793

Average (private)
$34,451

Percentage receiving financial aid: 81%

ADMISSIONS

In the fall of 2011 first-year class, 1309 applied, 257 were accepted, and 116 enrolled. Five transfers enrolled. The median LSAT percentile of the most recent first-year class was 67; the median GPA was 3.4 on a scale of 4.0. The lowest LSAT percentile accepted was 13; the highest was 95.

Requirements
Applicants must have a bachelor's degree and take the LSAT. The most important admission factors include academic achievement, LSAT results, and GPA. No specific undergraduate courses are required. Candidates are not interviewed.

Procedure
The application deadline for fall entry is February 1. Applicants should submit an application form, LSAT results, transcripts, TOEFL (if applicable), a nonrefundable application fee of $75, 2 letters of recommendation, and a resume. Notification of the admissions decision is by mid-March. The law school uses the LSAC.

Special
Requirements are different for out-of-state students. Transfer students must have one year of credit, must have attended an ABA-approved law school, and must submit 2 letters of recommendation, including one from a law professor, as well as a complete application.

Costs

Tuition and fees for the 2011–2012 academic year are $16,728 for full-time in-state students and $31,872 for out-of-state students. Tuition for part-time students is $12,546 for in-state students and $23,904 out-of-state. On-campus room and board costs about $12,543 annually; books and supplies run $1,170.

Financial Aid

About 81% of current law students receive some form of aid. The average annual amount of aid from all sources combined, including scholarships, loans, and work contracts, is $21,633; maximum, $48,007. Awards are based on need and merit. The required financial statement is the FAFSA. The aid application deadline for fall entry is March 1. Special funds for minority or disadvantaged students are available. These include grants from the Bishop Estate for Native Hawaiians. Native Hawaiians also qualify for resident tuition rates regardless of residency. First-year students are notified about their financial aid application in late March or early April.

About the Law School

University of Hawaii at Manoa William S. Richardson School of Law was established in 1973 and is a public institution. The campus is in an urban area 2 miles east of Honolulu. The primary mission of the law school is to provide a professional legal education to highly qualified and diverse students in a collaborative, multidisciplinary educational community that is committed to teaching, scholarship, public service, ethical responsibility, and the pursuit of social and economic justice, with a special responsibility to Hawaii. Students have access to federal, state, county, city, and local agencies, courts, correctional facilities, law firms, and legal aid organizations in the Honolulu area. Housing for students is very limited on campus; nearly all law students live off campus in nearby apartments and houses. All law school facilities are accessible to the physically disabled.

Calendar

The law school operates on a traditional semester basis. Courses for full-time students are offered both day and evening, and must be completed within 7 years. For part-time students, courses are offered evenings only, and must be completed within 7 years. New full- and part-time students are admitted in the fall. There is a 5-week summer session. Transferable summer courses are offered.

Programs

In addition to the J.D., the law school offers the LL.M. Students may take relevant courses in other programs and apply credit toward the J.D.; a maximum of 10 credits may be applied. The following joint degrees may be earned: J.D./Ph.D. (Juris Doctor/Doctor of Philosophy in psychology), J.D./M.A. (Juris Doctor/Master of Arts in Asian Studies), J.D./M.B.A. (Juris Doctor/Master of Business Administration), J.D./M.P.H. (Juris Doctor/Master of Public Health), J.D./M.S.W. (Juris Doctor/Master of Social Work), and J.D./M.U.R.P. (Juris Doctor/Master of Urban and Regional Planning).

Required
To earn the J.D., candidates must complete 89 total credits, of which 42 are for required courses. They must maintain a minimum GPA of 2.0 in the required courses. The following first-year courses are required of all students: Civil Procedure I and II, Contracts I and II, Criminal Justice, Legal Practice I and II, Real Property, and Torts. Required upper-level courses consist of a clinical experience, Constitutional Law I, pro bono legal service, Professional Responsibility, and second-year seminar. All students must take clinical courses. The required orientation program for first-year students introduces students to their classmates, faculty, and staff; previews the first-year curriculum; introduces academic regulations; and introduces the Hawaiian legal system.

Electives
The William S. Richardson School of Law offers concentrations in environmental law, Pacific Asian Legal Studies, and

Phone: 808-956-7966
Fax: 808-956-3813
E-mail: lawadm@hawaii.edu
Web: law.hawaii.edu

Contact
Director of Admissions and Special Projects, 808-956-5557 for general inquiries; Melissa K Skillings, Director of Financial Aid, 808-956-7966 for financial aid information.

HAWAII

Native Hawaiian Law. In addition, clinics for 3 or 4 credits each are assigned by lottery to upper-level students who meet the prerequisites. Clinics include Prosecution, Elder Law, and Native Hawaiian Rights. Upper-level students are offered a variety of seminars in advanced legal studies and Pacific-Asian Legal Studies for 1 to 3 credits per seminar. The required Second Year Seminar is offered for 4 credits. One externship per semester may be taken by upper-level students; a maximum of 2 externships may be taken for 2 credits each. Alternatively, a 14-credit externship in an approved Pacific Island jurisdiction may be taken. Under the directed studies program, any upper-level student may elect to conduct special research for 1 to 3 credits. Research can be repeated. Field work is linked to those clinics that include live client representation as well as actual court appearances under a special state Supreme Court rule. Special lecture series are offered for no credit; any student may attend. Annually, there is a Distinguished Fujiyama Visiting Professor, a George Johnson Visiting Scholar, and Jurist-in-Residence Program. There is also a Pacific Asian Legal Studies lecture series for visiting Asian legal scholars. Study abroad can be accomplished by special arrangement for varying credits or by a full-semester externship in certain Pacific Island jurisdictions for 14 credits. Tutorial programs are available and administered through the Student Bar Association for no credit. Special interest group programs, offered for no credit, include the Filipino Law Students Association, 'Ahahui 'O Hawai'i (a Native Hawaiian organization), Advocates for Public Interest Law, and the Pacific Asian Legal Studies Organization. The most widely taken electives are Evidence, Trusts and Estates, and Secured Transactions.

Graduation Requirements
In order to graduate, candidates must have a GPA of 2.0 and must have completed the upper-division writing requirement.

Organizations
Students edit the *University of Hawaii Law Review* and the *Asian Pacific Law Policy Journal*. Students participate in the annual Susan McKay Moot Court Competition, the Environmental Law Moot Court, and the Jessup International Moot Court competition. Other competitions

include Client Counseling. Law student organizations include the Student Bar Association, Environmental Law Society, and Hawaii Association of Women Law Students. Local chapters of national associations include the American Inns of Court, Phi Delta Phi, and Federalist Society.

Library
The law library contains 119,827 hardcopy volumes and 1,167,923 microform volume equivalents, and subscribes to 3,206 serial publications. Such online databases and networks as CALI, DIALOG, Legal-Trac, LEXIS, WESTLAW, and other online databases are available to law students for research. Special library collections include a partial federal government depository. The ratio of library volumes to faculty is 3,994 to 1 and to students is 328 to 1. The ratio of seats in the library to students is 1 to 1.

Faculty
The law school has 30 full-time and 26 part-time faculty members, of whom 27 are women. According to AAUP standards for Category I institutions, faculty salaries are average. About 23% of full-time faculty have a graduate law degree in addition to the J.D. The ratio of full-time students to full-time faculty in an average class is 11 to 1; in a clinic, 8 to 1. The law school has a regular program of bringing visiting professors and other distinguished lecturers and visitors to campus.

Students
About 56% of the student body are women; 71%, minorities; 2%, African American; 42%, Asian American; 6%, Hispanic; and 4%, Native American. The majority of students come from Hawaii (85%). The average age of entering students is 28; age range is 20 to 57. About 20% of students enter directly from undergraduate school, 22% have a graduate degree, and 69% have worked full-time prior to entering law school. About 5% drop out after the first year for academic or personal reasons; 95% remain to receive a law degree.

Placement
J.D.s awarded:	96

Services available through: a separate law school placement center and Law School Career Services Office.
Services: career information series.
Special features: nearly all placement activity is focused on the Hawaii market, as are on-campus interviews, since 95% of graduates remain in the state.

Full-time job interviews:	5 employers
Summer job interviews:	20 employers
Placement by graduation:	54% of class
Placement within 9 months:	80% of class
Average starting salary:	$42,000 to $70,000

Areas of placement:
Private practice 2–10 attorneys	12%
Private practice 11–25 attorneys	2%
Private practice 26–50 attorneys	8%
Private practice 51–100 attorneys	5%
Judicial clerkships	27%
Public interest	15%
Government	12%
Military	9%
Business/industry	2%
Academic	2%

UNIVERSITY OF HOUSTON

Law Center

100 Law Center
Houston, TX 77204-6060

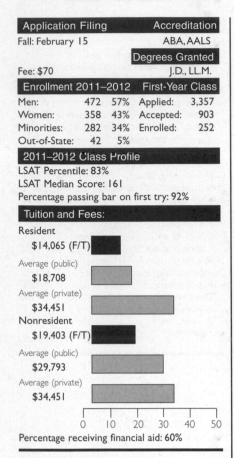

Application Filing	Accreditation
Fall: February 15	ABA, AALS

	Degrees Granted
Fee: $70	J.D., LL.M.

Enrollment 2011–2012		First-Year Class	
Men:	472 57%	Applied:	3,357
Women:	358 43%	Accepted:	903
Minorities:	282 34%	Enrolled:	252
Out-of-State:	42 5%		

2011–2012 Class Profile

LSAT Percentile: 83%
LSAT Median Score: 161
Percentage passing bar on first try: 92%

Tuition and Fees:

Resident
$14,065 (F/T)

Average (public)
$18,708

Average (private)
$34,451

Nonresident
$19,403 (F/T)

Average (public)
$29,793

Average (private)
$34,451

0   10   20   30   40   50

Percentage receiving financial aid: 60%

ADMISSIONS

In the fall of 2011 first-year class, 3357 applied, 903 were accepted, and 252 enrolled. Twenty-four transfer students enrolled. The median LSAT percentile of the most recent first-year class was 83; the median GPA was 3.4 on a scale of 4.0. The lowest LSAT percentile accepted was 27; the highest was 100.

Requirements
Applicants must have a bachelor's degree and take the LSAT. The most important admission factors include LSAT results, GPA, and general background. No specific undergraduate courses are required, and candidates are not interviewed.

Procedure
The application deadline for fall entry is February 15. Applicants should submit an application form, LSAT results, transcripts, personal statement, nonrefundable application fee of $70, résumé, the LSAC report, and letters of recommendation (2 required, no more than 3).

Notification of the admissions decision is December through July. The law school uses the LSAC.

Special
The law school recruits minority and disadvantaged students through a strong support system on campus, well-funded BLSA, HLSA, and ALSA organizations, and by visiting various colleges and hosting programs. Requirements are different for out-of-state students in that there is a 35% cap for nonresident students. Transfer students must have one year of credits, attended an ABA-approved law school, personal statement, and rank in the top of their first-year class.

Costs

Tuition and fees for the 2011–2012 academic year are $11,733 for full-time in-state students and $17,071 for out-of-state students. Tuition for part-time students is $7,822 for in-state students and $11,380 out-of-state. On-campus room and board costs about $4,900 annually; books and supplies run $600.

Financial Aid

About 60% of current law students receive some form of aid. The average annual amount of aid from all sources combined, including scholarships, loans, and work contracts, is $35,617; maximum, $44,164. Awards are based on need and merit. Need-based financial aid is handled by the University's Director of Financial Aid. Scholarships are handled by the Scholarship Committee. Required financial statement is the FAFSA. The aid application deadline for fall entry is April 1. First-year students are notified about their financial aid application on a rolling basis once their financial aid file is complete, but no earlier than mid-April.

About the Law School

University of Houston Law Center was established in 1947 and is a public institution. The 540-acre campus is located in an urban area 3 miles south of downtown Houston. The mission of the law school is to attract a social and ethnic diverse student body and expose them to an educational experience that will allow them to enter the legal profession in positions of responsibility. Students have access to

federal, state, county, city, and local agencies, courts, correctional facilities, law firms, and legal aid organizations in the Houston area. Special attention is given to accommodating students with disabilities. Housing for students is available, including those who are married. The majority of students live 15 to 20 minutes from campus. About 95% of the law school facilities are accessible to the physically disabled.

Calendar

The law school operates on a traditional semester basis. Courses for full-time students are offered both day (first-year courses are offered days only) and evening and must be completed within 4 years. For part-time students, courses are offered both day (first-year courses are offered evenings only) and evening and must be completed within 6 years. New full- and part-time students are admitted in the fall. There is a 5-week summer session. Transferable summer courses are offered.

Programs

In addition to the J.D., the law school offers the LL.M. Students may take relevant courses in other programs and apply credit toward the J.D.; a maximum of 12 to 15 hours depending credits may be applied. The following joint degrees may be earned: J.D./M.D. (Juris Doctor/Doctor of Medicine), J.D./Ph.D. (Juris Doctor/Doctor of Philosophy in Medical Humanities), J.D./M.A. (Juris Doctor/Master of Arts in History), J.D./M.B.A. (Juris Doctor/Master of Business Administration), J.D./M.P.H. (Juris Doctor/Master of Public Health), and J.D./M.S.W. (Juris Doctor/Master of Social Work).

Required
To earn the J.D., candidates must complete 90 total credits, of which 38 are for required courses. They must maintain a minimum GPA of 2.5 in the required courses. The following first-year courses are required of all students: Constitutional Law, Contracts, Criminal Law, Lawyering Skills and Strategies, Procedure, Property, Statutory Interpretation and Regulation, and Torts. Required upper-level courses consist of Practice-Skills Course, Professional Responsibility, and Senior Writing Requirement. The required orientation program for first-year students is 2 days of general information.

Phone: 713-743-2280
Fax: 713-743-2194
E-mail: lawadmissions@uh.edu
Web: www.law.uh.edu

Contact

Jamie Ann West Dillon, J.D., Assistant Dean, 713-743-2280 for general inquiries; Laura Neal, Financial Aid Counselor, 713-743-2269 for financial aid information.

TEXAS

Electives

The Law Center offers concentrations in corporate law, criminal law, environmental law, family law, intellectual property law, internationl law, labor law, litigation, tax law, and health law, consumer law, higher education law and governance, and law and computation. In addition, students may choose among 7 clinics, including Civil Practice, Consumer Law, Immigration Practice, Mediation, Transactional, Criminal Practice, and Health Law externships. Seminar courses are available in all areas. There are judicial internships at federal, state, district, county, and municipal levels. Research programs include the Health Law and Policy Institute; Institute for Intellectual Property and Information Law; Center for Environment, Energy and Natural Resources Law, Center for Children, Law and Policy; Blakely Advocacy Institute; Institute for Higher Education Law and Governance; Texas Innocence Network; and the Criminal Justice Institute. Lecture series include the Baker Botts Lecture and Katz-Kiley Lecture. Study Abroad may be done through the North American Consortium on Legal Education (NACLE). The Academic Enrichment Program provides tutorial assistance. The One-L Mentoring Program helps new students acclimate to a legal and life law school. The most widely taken electives are Commercial Transactions, Business Organizations, and Evidence.

Graduation Requirements

In order to graduate, candidates must have a GPA of 2.5 and complete the upper-division writing requirement.

Organizations

Students edit the *Houston Law Review, Houston Journal of International law, Houston Journal of Health Law and Policy, Houston Business and Tax Law Journal, Journal of Consumer and Commercial Law,* and the *Environmental and Energy Law and Policy Journal.* Additional publications include *Health Law News* and the student newspaper, *Legalese.* Intrascholarship competitions include the Blakely-Butler Moot Court Competition, Hippard Mock Trial Competition, Newhouse Mediation Competition, and the Hofheinz Tournament of Champions. Law student organizations include Advocates, Corporate and Taxation Law

Society, and the Energy and Environmental Law Society. The Law Center hosts local chapters of the ABA-Law Student Division, Phi Delta Phi, and Order of the Coif. Other organizations include the Student Bar Association, Black Law Students Association, Hispanic Law Students Association, Asian Law Students Association, Public Interest Law Organization, Outlaw (GLBT), and American Constitution Society for Law and Policy.

Library

The law library contains 554,954 hardcopy volumes and 1,665,443 microform volume equivalents, and subscribes to 2,329 serial publications. Online databases and networks include CALI, Legal-Trac, LEXIS, OCLC First Search, WESTLAW, and others are available to law students for research. Special library collections include a U.S. Government Depository, Mexican Law Collection, Admiralty and Maritime Law Collection, John R. Brown Archives, and Texas Supreme Court Briefs. The ratio of library volumes to faculty is 10,800 to 1 and to students is 600 to 1. The ratio of seats in the library to students is 1 to 1.

Faculty

The law school has 61 full-time and 146 part-time faculty members, of whom 61 are women. According to AAUP standards for Category I institutions, faculty salaries are average. About 20% of full-time faculty have a graduate law degree in addition to the J.D. The ratio of full-time students to full-time faculty in an average class is 11 to 1; in a clinic, 8 to 1. The law school has a regular program of bringing visiting professors and other distinguished lecturers and visitors to campus. There is a chapter of the Order of the Coif.

Students

About 43% of the student body are women; 34%, minorities; 7%, African American; 14%, Asian American; 10%, Hispanic; 1%, Native American; and 2%, Unknown. The majority of students come from Texas (95%). The average age of entering students is 25; age range is 21 to 47. About 33% of students enter directly from undergraduate school, and 12% have a graduate degree. About 2% drop out after the first year for academic or personal reasons; 97% remain to receive a law degree.

Placement

J.D.s awarded:	284

Services available through: a separate law school placement center.

Services: Public Interest/Public Sector Fellowship Program.

Special features: A comprehensive career education series is held every year and includes networking events, speaker panels, and mock interviews for first-year students. UHLC participates in 10 off-campus recruitment programs during the year.

Full-time job interviews:	27 employers
Summer job interviews:	97 employers
Placement by graduation:	82% of class
Placement within 9 months:	92% of class
Average starting salary:	$28,750 to $160,000

Areas of placement:

Private practice 2–10 attorneys	18%
Private practice 11–25 attorneys	11%
Private practice 26–50 attorneys	5%
Private practice 51–100 attorneys	3%
Private practice 100+ attorneys	15%
Business/industry	23%
Government	9%
Judicial clerkships	4%
Public interest	4%
Academic	2%
Military	1%

University of Houston   **493**

College of Law

P.O. Box 442321
Moscow, ID 83844-2321

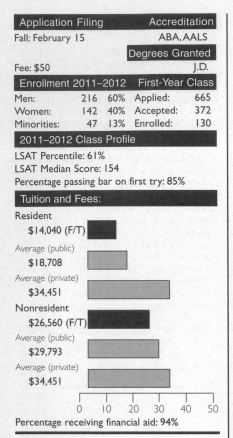

Application Filing	Accreditation
Fall: February 15	ABA, AALS

	Degrees Granted
Fee: $50	J.D.

Enrollment 2011–2012		First-Year Class	
Men:	216 60%	Applied:	665
Women:	142 40%	Accepted:	372
Minorities:	47 13%	Enrolled:	130

2011–2012 Class Profile

LSAT Percentile: 61%
LSAT Median Score: 154
Percentage passing bar on first try: 85%

Tuition and Fees:

Resident
$14,040 (F/T)

Average (public)
$18,708

Average (private)
$34,451

Nonresident
$26,560 (F/T)

Average (public)
$29,793

Average (private)
$34,451

0 10 20 30 40 50

Percentage receiving financial aid: 94%

ADMISSIONS

In the fall of 2011 first-year class, 665 applied, 372 were accepted, and 130 enrolled. Four transfers enrolled. The median LSAT percentile of the most recent first-year class was 61; the median GPA was 3.3 on a scale of 4.0. The lowest LSAT percentile accepted was 15; the highest was 93.

Requirements
Applicants must have a bachelor's degree and take the LSAT. The most important admission factors include state or country of residence, GPA, and LSAT results. No specific undergraduate courses are required. Candidates are not interviewed.

Procedure
The application deadline for fall entry is February 15. Applicants should submit an application form, LSAT results, transcripts, a personal statement, TOEFL (if applicable), a nonrefundable application fee of $50, and 2 letters of recommendation. LSAC registration is required. Notification of the admissions decision is early April.

Special
The law school recruits minority and disadvantaged students through scholarships, application workshops for undergraduate minority groups, and recruiting at colleges and universities with distinctive programs to serve minority populations. Requirements are different for out-of-state students. Transfer students must have one year of credit, must have attended an ABA-approved law school, must submit a personal statement and a letter of good standing, must rank in the top half of their class, and must have competitive LSAT results and GPA.

Costs

On-campus room and board costs about $9,264 annually; books and supplies run $1,474.

Financial Aid

About 94% of current law students receive some form of aid. The average annual amount of aid from all sources combined, including scholarships, loans, and work contracts, is $29,685. Awards are based on need and merit combined. Required financial statements are the FAFSA and University of Idaho special forms. The aid application deadline for fall entry is February 15. Special funds for minority or disadvantaged students are available. First-year students are notified about their financial aid application at time of acceptance.

About the Law School

University of Idaho College of Law was established in 1909 and is a public institution. The 1585-acre campus is in the small town of Moscow. The primary mission of the law school is to prepare students for careers in law, business, and public service. Students have access to federal, state, county, city, and local agencies, courts, correctional facilities, law firms, and legal aid organizations in the Moscow area. Facilities of special interest to law students include the law building, which recently underwent more than $1.5 million in renovations, including a new courtroom and new study carrels. Classrooms include smartboards, computer power

and data connections, and remote viewing between Moscow and Boise. Housing for students is available and includes many on- and off-campus options. All law school facilities are accessible to the physically disabled.

Calendar

The law school operates on a traditional semester basis. Courses for full-time students are offered days only, and must be completed within 84 months. New full-time students are admitted in the fall. There is an 8-week summer session. Transferable summer courses are offered.

Programs

Students may take relevant courses in other programs and apply credit toward the J.D.; a maximum of 6 credits may be applied. The following joint degrees may be earned: J.D./M.B.A. (Juris Doctor/ Master of Business Administration), J.D./M. Acct. (Juris Doctor/Master of Accountancy), J.D./M.S. (Juris Doctor/Master of Science in Accounting and Taxation), J.D./M.S. (Juris Doctor/Master of Science in Environmental Science), and J.D./M.S./ Ph.D. (Juris Doctor/Master of Science/ Doctor of Philosophy in Water).

Required
To earn the J.D., candidates must complete 90 total credits, of which 39 are for required courses. They must maintain a minimum GPA of 2.0 in the required courses. The following first-year courses are required of all students: Constitutional Law I, Contracts, Criminal Law, Introduction to Law and Procedure, Legal Research and Writing, Legislation and Regulation, Procedure II, Property, and Torts. Required upper-level courses consist of an upper-division writing requirement, Constitutional Law II, and Professional Responsibility. The pro bono program, which provides practical skills, is required. The required orientation program for first-year students is a 4-day program covering study skills and case briefings and culminating with students participating as witnesses and jurors in the upper-level Trial Advocacy mock trials. The program also includes a half-day Professionalism Workshop where current lawyers and judges discuss ethical issues with new students in small groups.

Phone: 208-885-2300
Fax: 208-885-5709
E-mail: cwells@uidaho.edu
Web: www.uidaho.edu/law

Contact

Carol Wells, Director of Admissions, 208-885-2300 for general inquiries; Dan Davenport, Director of Student Financial Aid, 208-885-6312 for financial aid information.

IDAHO

Placement

J.D.s awarded:	104

Services available through: an in-house career services director.

Services: a career services director who is a licensed attorney.

Special features: a career services director who is a licensed attorney.

Placement within 9 months of graduation:	75% of class
Average starting salary:	$33,000 to $160,000

Areas of placement:

Private practice 2–10 attorneys	22%
Private practice 11–25 attorneys	4%
Private practice 26–50 attorneys	1%
Judicial clerkships	22%
Business/industry	17%
Government	14%
Solo practitioner	5%
Public interest	4%
Academic	4%

Electives

The College of Law offers concentrations in corporate law, environmental law, litigation, and lawyering skills. There is also a Native American Law and Natural Resources Environmental Law emphasis. In addition, third-year students may participate in one of 6 live clinics, including 9th Circuit Appellate, Tribal and Immigration, Small Business, Domestic Violence, Victims' Rights, Tax, and General Practice, for a maximum of 8 credits. Upper-level students may choose from seminars in several subject areas, including corporate law, dispute resolution, and environmental law, for 1 to 3 credits. The College of Law offers an extensive externship program, awarding class credit for summer placements in various government agencies, nonprofit organizations, and judicial offices, for 1 to 8 credits. Any student may perform directed research upon a professor's approval for 1 to 2 credits. Third-year students may participate in the Semester-in-Practice program in Boise for up to 12 credits. The Sherman Bellwood Lectures bring learned individuals to the state of Idaho and the University of Idaho campus to allow students the opportunity to discuss, examine, and debate subjects related to the justice system. The speakers are prominent and highly regarded local, regional, and national leaders who cover a wide range of topics. Students may transfer in study-abroad credits earned through any ABA-approved study-abroad program. The College of Law has an Office of Academic Support run by a licensed attorney to assist students with their academic needs. Student organizations dedicated to promoting and supporting legal education among underrepresented groups include the Multicultural Law Caucus, Outlaw, Women's Law Caucus, the Black Law Students Association, and Latino Law Caucus. The most widely taken electives are in the areas of natural resources and water law and trial practice skills/clinics.

Graduation Requirements

In order to graduate, candidates must have a GPA of 2.0, must have completed the upper-division writing requirement, and must have completed 40 hours of law-related pro bono service.

Organizations

The *Idaho Law Review* is the primary law review. There is also the *University* of *Idaho Journal of Critical Studies* ("The Crit") and inter alia (student satire). Teams compete in the McNichols Moot Court competition, Duberstein Bankruptcy, and Environmental Law. Other competitions include the American Association for Justice Mock Trial competition. The Student Bar Association is the umbrella student government organization and coordinates the College of Law's 23 student organizations, including the Board of Student Advocates, Public Interest Law Group, and Environmental Law Society. Law student organizations, local chapters of national associations, and campus organizations include, among others, Phi Alpha Delta, American Civil Liberties Union, the Federalist Society, the Hunting and Fishing Club, Nontraditional Students Group, and Law School Support Association for spouses and partners of law students.

Library

The law library contains 254,602 hardcopy volumes and 103,774 microform volume equivalents, and subscribes to 6,000 serial publications. Such online databases and networks as CALI, CIS Universe, DIALOG, Infotrac, Legal-Trac, LEXIS, Mathew Bender, OCLC First Search, WESTLAW, Wilsonline Indexes, Proquest Newspapers, BNA Tax Management Library, EBSCO databases, GPO Access, CIAO, CILP, LLMC Digital, HeinOnline, IndexMaster, WorldCat Local, and many others are available to law students for research. Special library collections include archives of Idaho materials, Idaho Supreme Court records and briefs, and Clagett historical materials. The ratio of library volumes to faculty is 4,389 to 1 and to students is 74 to 1. The ratio of seats in the library to students is 1 to 1.

Faculty

The law school has 25 full-time and 33 part-time faculty members, of whom 31 are women. According to AAUP standards for Category 1 institutions, faculty salaries are well below average. About 46% of full-time faculty have a graduate law degree in addition to the J.D. The ratio of full-time students to full-time faculty in an average class is 14 to 1; in a clinic, 8 to 1. The law school has a regular program of bringing visiting professors and other distinguished lecturers and visitors to campus.

Students

About 40% of the student body are women; 13%, minorities; 2%, Asian American; 7%, Hispanic; and 2%, Native American. The average age of entering students is 27; age range is 21 to 59. About 3% drop out after the first year for academic or personal reasons; 97% remain to receive a law degree.

UNIVERSITY OF ILLINOIS
College of Law

504 East Pennsylvania Avenue
Champaign, IL 61820

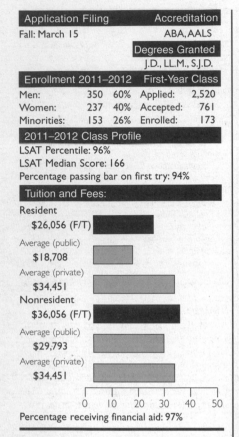

Application Filing	Accreditation
Fall: March 15	ABA, AALS

Degrees Granted
J.D., LL.M., S.J.D.

Enrollment 2011–2012			First-Year Class	
Men:	350	60%	Applied:	2,520
Women:	237	40%	Accepted:	761
Minorities:	153	26%	Enrolled:	173

2011–2012 Class Profile
LSAT Percentile: 96%
LSAT Median Score: 166
Percentage passing bar on first try: 94%

Tuition and Fees:

Resident
$26,056 (F/T)

Average (public)
$18,708

Average (private)
$34,451

Nonresident
$36,056 (F/T)

Average (public)
$29,793

Average (private)
$34,451

0   10   20   30   40   50

Percentage receiving financial aid: 97%

ADMISSIONS
In the fall of 2011 first-year class, 2520 applied, 761 were accepted, and 173 enrolled. Sixty transfers enrolled. The median LSAT percentile of the most recent first-year class was 96; the median GPA was 3.6 on a scale of 4.0. The lowest LSAT percentile accepted was 25; the highest was 99.

Requirements
Applicants must have a bachelor's degree and take the LSAT. The most important admission factors include character or personality, LSAT results, and GPA. No specific undergraduate courses are required. Candidates are not interviewed.

Procedure
The application deadline for fall entry is March 15. Applicants should submit an application form, LSAT results, transcripts, a personal statement, 2 letters of recommendation, and a resume. Notification of the admissions decision is on a rolling basis beginning in December. The law school uses the LSAC.

Special
The law school recruits minority and disadvantaged students by participating in recruiting fairs and visiting schools where there are a large number of minority students. Requirements are different for out-of-state students. Transfer students must have one year of credit, must have attended an ABA-approved law school, and must submit a personal statement.

Costs
Tuition and fees for the 2011–2012 academic year are $23,000 for full-time in-state students and $33,000 for out-of-state students. On-campus room and board costs about $11,000 annually; books and supplies run $1,800.

Financial Aid
About 97% of current law students receive some form of aid. The average annual amount of aid from all sources combined, including scholarships, loans, and work contracts, is $35,000; maximum, $48,218. Awards are based on need and merit. The required financial statement is the FAFSA. Special funds for minority or disadvantaged students are available. First-year students are notified about their financial aid application at the time application is made and again in a letter of acceptance.

About the Law School
University of Illinois College of Law was established in 1897 and is a public institution. The 710-acre campus is in an urban area 130 miles south of Chicago. The primary mission of the law school is to serve the state, nation, and the world as a leading center of legal education, legal scholarship, and public service. Students have access to federal, state, county, city, and local agencies, courts, correctional facilities, law firms, and legal aid organizations in the Champaign area. Housing for students is available throughout the Champaign-Urbana area. In addition, there are several graduate student dorms available to law students. All law school facilities are accessible to the physically disabled.

Calendar
The law school operates on a traditional semester basis. Courses are offered days only, and must be completed within 3 years. New students are admitted in the fall. There is a summer session. Transferable summer courses are not offered.

Programs
In addition to the J.D., the law school offers the LL.M. and S.J.D. Students may take relevant courses in other programs and apply credit toward the J.D.; a maximum of 12 credits may be applied. The following joint degrees may be earned: J.D./M.B.A. (Juris Doctor/ Master of Business Administration), J.D./M.C.S. (Juris Doctor/Master of Computer Science), J.D./M.D. (Juris Doctor/ Doctor of Medicine), J.D./D.V.M. (Juris Doctor/ Doctor of Veterinary Medicine), J.D./M.Ed. (Juris Doctor/ Master of Education), J.D./M.H.R.I.R. (Juris Doctor/Master of Human Resources and Industrial), J.D./M.S.Chem. (Juris Doctor/Master of Science in Chemistry), J.D./M.S.Journalism (Juris Doctor/Master Science in Journalism), J.D./M.S.N.R.E.S. (Juris Doctor/Master of Science in Natural Resources and Environment), J.D./M.U.P. (Juris Doctor/Master of Urban Planning), and J.D./Ph.D.Ed. (Juris Doctor/Doctor of Philosophy in Education).

Required
To earn the J.D., candidates must complete 90 total credits, of which 33 are for required courses. They must maintain a minimum GPA of 2.0 in the required courses. The following first-year courses are required of all students: Contracts, Civil Procedure, Constitutional Law I, Criminal Law, Introduction to Advocacy, Legal Research, Legal Writing and Analysis, Property and Torts. Required upper-level courses consist of Professional Responsibility and Upper-level Writing. The required orientation program for first-year students is a 2-day program filled with information and experiences designed to acclimate new students to the law school.

Electives
The College of Law offers concentrations in corporate law, criminal law, environmental law, family law, intellectual property law, international law, labor law, litigation, securities law, sports law, tax law, torts and insurance, and public interest law. In addition, clinics are open to second- and third-year students.

Phone: 217-244-6415
Fax: 217-244-1478
E mail: admissions@law.uiuc.edu
Web: www.law.uiuc.edu

Contact
Paul Pless, Assistant Dean for Admissions and Financial Aid, 217-244-6415 for general inquiries and financial aid information.

ILLINOIS

Numerous seminars are generally limited-enrollment classes to ensure more individualized experiences and are offered each semester to all second- and third-year students. The topics vary widely to ensure timely coverage of relevant issues. Externships offer students the opportunity to receive law credit for uncompensated work with a nonprofit organization, government agency, or a judge. Students may work as research assistants for faculty members. They may also participate in individual research projects under the supervision of a faculty member, which result in a substantial research paper and corresponding academic credit for scholarly work. Courses that involve interaction with live clients include externships, clinics, legislative projects, and appellate defender work. Additional field work is available through the Prisoner's Rights Research Project. The David C. Baum Memorial Lectures are presented twice each year by distinguished scholars in the areas of civil liberties and civil rights. The Paul M. Van Arsdell, Jr. Memorial Lecture is presented annually on litigation and the legal profession. The Carl Vacketta/Piper Rudnick Lecture is presented annually on government and public affairs. Students may receive credit for ABA-approved study-abroad programs. The Academic Assistance Program offers group programs and individual counseling and tutoring. There are 7 minority student organizations. There are also minority career fairs, numerous speakers and lectures, and a student-chaired diversity committee. The most widely taken electives are Trial Advocacy, Business Associations, and Evidence.

Graduation Requirements

In order to graduate, candidates must have a GPA of 2.0, must have completed the upper-division writing requirement, and must have 90 semester hours of passing grades, 56 hours earned from the College of Law, at least 4 full-time semesters at the College of Law, and passing grades in all required courses.

Organizations
Students edit *The University of Illinois Law Review, Elder Law Journal,* and the *Journal of Law, Technology, and Policy.* Law students write the highly regarded Illinois Law Update sections of the *Illinois Bar Journal* and the *Illinois Business*

Law Journal. Three moot court competitions are Frederick Green, Frederick Douglass, and Intellectual Property Moot Court competitions. Other competitions include ABA Negotiations, ABA Client Counseling competitions, and Trial Team. Law student organizations, local chapters of national associations, and campus clubs and organizations include Latino/Latina Law Students Association, Black Law Students Association, Street Law, American Association for Justice, Asian American Law Students Association, the Myra Bradwell Association for Women Law Students, the Student Bar Association, Public Interest Law Foundation, and Impact.

Library
The law library contains 615,739 hardcopy volumes and 928,746 microform volume equivalents. Such online databases and networks as CALI, CIS Universe, DIALOG, Dow-Jones, Infotrac, Legal-Trac, LEXIS, OCLC First Search, WESTLAW, Wilsonline Indexes, Making of Modern Law, and many others are available to law students for research. Special library collections include a federal government depository, a European Union depository, and an extensive collection of rare Anglo-American items. The ratio of library volumes to faculty is 15,393 to 1 and to students is 1,049 to 1. The ratio of seats in the library to students is 1 to 6.

Faculty
The law school has 40 full-time and 46 part-time faculty members, of whom 33 are women. According to AAUP standards for Category 1 institutions, faculty salaries are above average. About 10% of full-time faculty have a graduate law degree in addition to the J.D. The ratio of full-time students to full-time faculty in an average class is 12 to 1; in a clinic, 8 to 1. The law school has a regular program of bringing visiting professors and other distinguished lecturers and visitors to campus. There is a chapter of the Order of the Coif.

Students
About 40% of the student body are women; 26%, minorities; 8%, African American; 12%, Asian American; 6%, Hispanic; and 1%, Native American. The average age of entering students is 24; age range is 20 to 43. About 55% of students enter

Placement

J.D.s awarded:	222

Services available through: a separate law school placement center, the university placement center, and other college placement offices.

Special features: the Alumni-Student Job Search Conference, where more than 50 alumni provide counseling and programs for students about the job search process, and professional staff of 3 attorneys.

Full-time job interviews:	27 employers
Summer job interviews:	90 employers
Placement by graduation:	83% of class
Placement within 9 months:	98% of class

Areas of placement:

Private practice 2–10 attorneys	10%
Private practice 11–25 attorneys	7%
Private practice 26–50 attorneys	1%
Private practice 51–100 attorneys	3%
Private practice 100+ attorneys	35%
Business/industry	12%
Government	9%
Judicial clerkships	6%
Academic	3%
Military	2%
Public interest	1%

directly from undergraduate school, 25% have a graduate degree, and 35% have worked full-time prior to entering law school. About 2% drop out after the first year for academic or personal reasons; 98% remain to receive a law degree.

College of Law

320 Melrose Avenue
Iowa City, IA 52242

Application Filing		Accreditation
Fall: March 1		ABA, AALS

			Degrees Granted
Fee: $60			J.D., LL.M.

Enrollment 2011–2012		First-Year Class	
Men:	321 58%	Applied:	1,872
Women:	235 42%	Accepted:	729
Minorities:	100 19%	Enrolled:	180
Out-of-State:	280 49%		

2011–2012 Class Profile

LSAT Percentile: 82%
LSAT Median Score: 161
Percentage passing bar on first try: 94%

Tuition and Fees:

Resident
$26,348 (F/T)

Average (public)
$18,708

Average (private)
$34,451

Nonresident
$46,056 (F/T)

Average (public)
$29,793

Average (private)
$34,451

0 10 20 30 40 50

Percentage receiving financial aid: 94%

ADMISSIONS

In the fall of 2011 first-year class, 1872 applied, 729 were accepted, and 180 enrolled. Four transfers enrolled. The median LSAT percentile of the most recent first-year class was 82; the median GPA was 3.6 on a scale of 4.0.

Requirements

Applicants must have a bachelor's degree and take the LSAT. The most important admission factors include academic achievement and LSAT results. No specific undergraduate courses are required. Candidates are not interviewed.

Procedure

The application deadline for fall entry is March 1. Applicants should submit an application form, LSAT results, transcripts, personal statement, TOEFL (if applicable), a nonrefundable application fee of $60, and 2 letters of recommendation. Notification of the admissions decision is December through April. The law school uses the LSAC.

Special

The law school recruits minority and disadvantaged students through a minority prelaw seminar that is brought to potential applicants and prospects. The law school also supports Council on Legal Education Opportunity and The American Indian Pre-Law Summer Institute. Requirements are different for out-of-state students in that Iowa residents will have a slight advantage. Transfer students must have one year of credit, must have attended an ABA-approved law school, must submit a personal statement, and must have attended an ABA-approved law school and be in good academic standing at that law school.

Costs

Tuition and fees for the 2011–2012 academic year are $24,682 for full-time in-state students and $44,390 for out-of-state students. On-campus room and board costs about $8,750 annually; books and supplies run $2,300.

Financial Aid

About 94% of current law students receive some form of aid. The average annual amount of aid from all sources combined, including scholarships, loans, and work contracts, is $43,075; maximum, $62,783. Awards are based on need and merit combined. Required financial statements are the FAFSA, the student's federal tax returns, and Iowa's institutional form. The aid application deadline for fall entry is open. Special funds for minority or disadvantaged students are available. First-year students are notified about their financial aid application after admission.

About the Law School

University of Iowa College of Law was established in 1865 and is a public institution. The 1900-acre campus is in a small town 115 miles east of Des Moines, 30 miles south of Cedar Rapids. The primary mission of the law school is to challenge students to set high standards for themselves and to strive for the best professional education they can obtain, resulting in graduates that make a positive and significant impact on society. Students have access to federal, state, county, city, and local agencies, courts, correctional facilities, law firms, and legal aid organizations in the Iowa City area. Facilities

of special interest to law students include a law building that features state-of-the-art computer equipment, audiovisual technology, and 3 full-scale courtrooms. Housing for students is available in graduate family housing for married or single parent students. Otherwise, students live in apartments, duplexes, and other rental options off campus. All law school facilities are accessible to the physically disabled.

Calendar

The law school operates on a traditional semester basis. Courses are offered days only, and must be completed within 84 months. New students are admitted in the fall. There is an 11-week summer session. Transferable summer courses are offered.

Programs

In addition to the J.D., the law school offers the LL.M. Students may take relevant courses in other programs and apply credit toward the J.D.; a maximum of 6 credits may be applied. The following joint degrees may be earned: J.D./M.A. (Juris Doctor/Master of Arts in Urban and Regional Planning, Accounting, or Journalism), J.D./M.B.A. (Juris Doctor/Master of Business Administration), J.D./M.D. (Juris Doctor/Medical Doctor), J.D./M.H.A. (Juris Doctor/Master of Health Administration), J.D./M.P.H. (Juris Doctor/Master of Public Health), J.D./M.S. (Juris Doctor/Master of Civil and Environmental Engineering), J.D./M.S.W. (Juris Doctor/Master of Social Work), and J.D./Ph.D. (Juris Doctor/Doctorate of Higher Education).

Required

To earn the J.D., candidates must complete 84 total credits, of which 33 are for required courses. The following first-year courses are required of all students: Civil Procedure, Constitutional Law I, Contracts, Criminal Law, Introduction to Law and Legal Reasoning, Legal Analysis, Writing, and Research I and II, Property, and Torts. Required upper-level courses consist of Constitutional Law II and Professional Responsibility. In addition, all students must earn 4 upper-class writing units and complete a skills course. Though not required, approximately 33% of our law students participate in a clinic. The required orientation program for first-year students is 1 week; the 1-unit

Phone: 319-335-9095
Fax: 319-335-9646
E-mail: law-admissions@uiowa.edu
Web: www.law.uiowa.edu

Contact
College of Law Admissions Staff, 319-335-9095 for general inquiries; Susan Palmer, Director of Financial Aid, 319-335-9142 for financial aid information.

IOWA

course component covers an overview of the American legal system, legal education, the legal profession, and perspectives on law. The program component covers academic and other support services, bar requirements, dealing with stress, professional conduct standards, community service, and social events.

Electives

The College of Law offers concentrations in corporate law, criminal law, intellectual property law, international law, litigation, securities law, and tax law. In addition, the highly practical clinical law programs give students the opportunity to gain experience in many different areas of substantive law, including, but not limited to, civil rights, employment law, and criminal defense. Clinics are open to students in their second and third years for up to 15 credit hours and usually fulfill the need for field work. Semester seminars are offered in a variety of subject areas. The seminars are for 4 credits and upper-level writing units are awarded. If there is excess enrollment in the seminars, priority is given to third-year students and those seeking maximum credit. There are externship placements with a variety of outside agencies. They may be arranged in the summer or during the academic year. Credit for each externship varies and a maximum of 15 credits may be awarded under certain circumstances. Students may arrange an independent research project with faculty members in areas of mutual interest. Special guest lectures (by judges, professors, practitioners, politicians, and others) are open to students every semester. The college offers 5 study-abroad programs: the London Law Consortium (spring semester); the Summer Law Program in Comparative and International Law in Arcachon, France; a semester program at Catolica University in Lisbon, Portugal; an exchange program with Bucerius Law School in Hamburg, Germany; and a program with Radboud University in Nijmegen, The Netherlands. In addition, students may receive credit for study-abroad programs sponsored by other ABA-approved law schools. The Academic Achievement Program (AAP) presents a variety of workshops during the year, with an emphasis on the needs of first-year students. Also, faculty members provide mentoring for students who need special assistance. The writing resource center works with students individually to help

strengthen writing skills vital to the study and practice of law. Minority students are involved in all law school opportunities, as well as in the minority student organizations. Special interest programs include the Women in Law Conference, Journal of Gender, Race, and Justice Symposium, and Transnational and Contemporary Problems Symposium. The most widely taken electives are Clinics, Business Associations, and Evidence.

Graduation Requirements

In order to graduate, candidates must have a GPA of 2.1, must have completed the upper-division writing requirement, and must fulfill a practical skills requirement.

Organizations

Students edit the *Iowa Law Review*, the *Journal of Corporation Law*, *Transnational Law and Contemporary Problems*, and the *Journal of Gender, Race, and Justice*. Moot court competitions include the Baskerville Competition, whose winners comprise the Chicago Moot Court team, the Van Oosterhout, to select the National Moot Court team, and the Jessup International Law Competition. Additionally, the Stephenson Competition offers an intramural competition for students interested in trial advocacy. Winners become the school's representatives to regional and national competitions. Law student organizations, local chapters of national associations, and campus organizations include AALSA (Asian American Law Students Association), BLSA (Black Law Students Association), Equal Justice Foundation, Intellectual Property Law Society, OWLSS (Organization for Women Law Students and Staff), Phi Alpha Delta, Phi Delta Phi (Phids), the Federalist Society, and others.

Library

The law library contains 857,946 hardcopy volumes and 454,237 microform volume equivalents, and subscribes to 15,805 serial publications. Such online databases and networks as CIS Universe, DIALOG, Dow-Jones, Infotrac, Legal-Trac, LEXIS, Mathew Bender, OCLC First Search, RLIN, WESTLAW, and Wilsonline Indexes are available to law students for research. Special library collections include U.S. Government Printing Office and Iowa depositories as well as a United Nations collection and

a human rights collection. The ratio of library volumes to faculty is 19,065 to 1 and to students is 1,430 to 1. The ratio of seats in the library to students is 1 to 1.

Faculty

The law school has 48 full-time and 12 part-time faculty members, of whom 20 are women. According to AAUP standards for Category I institutions, faculty salaries are above average. About 8% of full-time faculty have a graduate law degree in addition to the J.D.; about 38% of part-time faculty have one. The ratio of full-time students to full-time faculty in an average class is 11 to 1; in a clinic, 7 to 1. The law school has a regular program of bringing visiting professors and other distinguished lecturers and visitors to campus. There is a chapter of the Order of the Coif; 48 faculty and 959 graduates are members.

Students

About 42% of the student body are women; 17%, minorities; 3%, African American; 7%, Asian American; 5%, Hispanic; and 1%, Native American. The average age of entering students is 24; age range is 21 to 49. About 9% of students have a graduate degree. About 2% drop out after the first year for academic or personal reasons; 96% remain to receive a law degree.

School of Law

205 Green Hall, 1535 West
15th Street
Lawrence, KS 66045

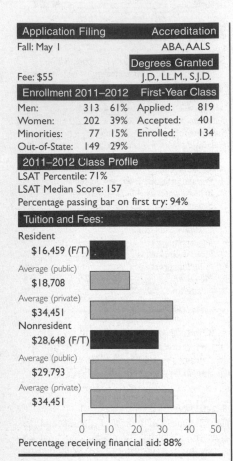

Application Filing		Accreditation
Fall: May 1		ABA, AALS
		Degrees Granted
Fee: $55		J.D., LL.M., S.J.D.

Enrollment 2011–2012		First-Year Class	
Men:	313 61%	Applied:	819
Women:	202 39%	Accepted:	401
Minorities:	77 15%	Enrolled:	134
Out-of-State:	149 29%		

2011–2012 Class Profile

LSAT Percentile: 71%
LSAT Median Score: 157
Percentage passing bar on first try: 94%

Tuition and Fees:

Resident
$16,459 (F/T)

Average (public)
$18,708

Average (private)
$34,451

Nonresident
$28,648 (F/T)

Average (public)
$29,793

Average (private)
$34,451

0   10   20   30   40   50

Percentage receiving financial aid: 88%

ADMISSIONS

In the fall of 2011 first-year class, 819 applied, 401 were accepted, and 134 enrolled. The median LSAT percentile of the most recent first-year class was 71; the median GPA was 3.5 on a scale of 4.0. The lowest LSAT percentile accepted was 18; the highest was 98.

Requirements

Applicants must have a bachelor's degree and take the LSAT. The most important admission factors are academic achievement, general background, and a letter of recommendation. No specific undergraduate courses are required. Candidates are not interviewed.

Procedure

The application deadline for fall entry is May 1. Applicants should submit an application form, LSAT results, transcripts, and a personal statement. International students must submit the TOEFL, a non-refundable application fee of $55, and 2 letters of recommendation. Notification of the admissions decision is on a rolling basis. The law school uses the LSAC.

Special

The law school recruits minority and disadvantaged students by means of recruiting in various geographic locations, at CLEO, and at PLSI. In addition, the law school hosts a diversity breakfast and uses the Law Services Candidate Referral System. Requirements are different for out-of-state students. Transfer students must have one year of credits, attended an ABA-approved law school, and a personal statement. No more than 30 hours from the student's previous law school can be transferred.

Costs

Tuition and fees for the 2011–2012 academic year are $15,602 for full-time in-state students and $27,790 for out-of-state students. On-campus room and board costs about $10,852 annually; books and supplies run $1,100.

Financial Aid

About 88% of current law students receive some form of aid. The average annual amount of aid from all sources combined, including scholarships, loans, and work contracts, is $24,344; maximum, $49,813. Awards are based on need and merit combined. Required financial statement is the FAFSA. The aid application deadline for fall entry is February 15. Special funds for minority or disadvantaged students consist of scholarships and financial aid. First-year students are notified about their financial aid application any point in time from acceptance through the time of enrollment.

About the Law School

University of Kansas School of Law was established in 1878 and is a public institution. The 1000-acre campus is located in a suburban area of Lawrence, Kansas. The primary mission of the law school is to prepare students to be outstanding members of the legal profession, well educated in the law, with a commitment to professional achievement and public service. Students have access to federal, state, county, city, and local agencies, courts, correctional facilities, law firms, and legal aid organizations in the Lawrence area. Facilities of special interest to law students include the Paul E. Wilson Defender Project, which allows students to advocate for wrongly convicted criminal defendents. Housing for students is available in a university residence hall or apartment complex. Apartments and houses are also available off campus, as is family student housing. All law school facilities are accessible to the physically disabled.

Calendar

The law school operates on a traditional semester basis. Courses for full-time students are offered days only and must be completed within 5 years. There is no part-time program. New full-time students are admitted in the fall and summer. There is a 5-week summer session. Transferable summer courses are offered.

Programs

In addition to the J.D., the law school offers the LL.M. and S.J.D. Students may take relevant courses in other programs and apply credit toward the J.D.; a maximum of 6 hours credits may be applied. The following joint degrees may be earned: J.D./M.A. (Juris Doctor/Master of Arts in East Asian languages), J.D./M.B.A. (Juris Doctor/Master of Business Administration), J.D./M.P.A. (Juris Doctor/Master of Public Administration), J.D./M.S. (Juris Doctor/Master of Science in health services), J.D./M.S.W. (Juris Doctor/Master of Social Work), and J.D./M.U.P. (Juris Doctor/Master of Urban Planning).

Required

To earn the J.D., candidates must complete 90 total credits, of which 37 to 38 are for required courses. They must maintain a minimum GPA of 2.0 in the required courses. The following first-year courses are required of all students: Civil Procedure, Contracts, Criminal Law, Introduction to Constitutional Law, Lawyering Skills I and II, Property, and Torts I. Required upper-level courses consist of Commercial Law I, Evidence, Professional Responsibility, Writing requirement, and Professional Skills requirement. The required orientation program for first-year students is a 5-day program that includes sessions on lawyering skills, ethics in the legal profession, a mock class, small group sessions, tours of the building, and practical issues.

Phone: 785-864-4378
866-220-3654
Fax: 785-864-5054
E-mail: admitlaw@ku.edu
Web: www.law.ku.edu

Contact

Steven Freedman, Assistant Dean of Admissions, 785-864-4378 for general inquiries; Brenda Maigaard, Director of Financial Aid, 785-864-5491 for financial aid information.

KANSAS

Electives

The School of Law offers concentrations in corporate law, criminal law, environmental law, family law, international law, juvenile law, labor law, litigation, media law, securities law, tax law, torts and insurance, agricultural law, civil rights law, constitutional law, energy law, industrial relations law, tribal law, and patent law. In addition, clinics are offered to second- and third-year students for 1 to 4 hours of credit. Clinics include Criminal Prosecution, the Paul E. Wilson Defender Project, and the Douglas County Legal Aid Clinic. Periodically, research workshops are offered for all students. Second- and third-year students may take advantage of available internship opportunities; usually no academic credit is awarded. Independent research seminars are available. Field work includes a judicial clerkship, an elder law externship, and a legislative clinic. Guest lecture programs are offered for no credit. Students may study at University College in London through the London Law Consortium, of which the University of Kansas is a member. Students may also study at the Summer Institute in Cambridge, England; Istanbul, Turkey; and Limerick, Ireland. There are other ABA-approved study-abroad programs that students may participate in. Tutorial programs are voluntary. The most widely taken electives are Business Associations I and II, Income Tax, and Family Law.

Graduation Requirements

In order to graduate, candidates must have a GPA of 2.0, completed the upper-division writing requirement, and Professional Skills requirement.

Organizations

Students edit the *Kansas Law Review, Kansas Journal of Law and Public Policy,* and the student newspaper, *Kansas Law Free Press.* Other publications include the *KU Law Magazine.* Students compete in the National Moot Court, Jessup International Moot Court, and Criminal Procedure Moot Court Competitions. Other competitions include the First Amendment Moot Court and the Stetson International Environmental Moot Court Competitions. Law student organizations, local chapters of national associations, and campus organizations include the International Law Society, Women in Law,

Public Interest Law Society, Traffic Court, Student Bar Association, the Federalist Society, Black Law Students Association, Phi Alpha Delta, and Native American Law Students Association.

Library

The law library contains 360,139 hardcopy volumes and 101,732 microform volume equivalents, and subscribes to 3,702 serial publications. Online databases and networks include CALI, LEXIS, WESTLAW, Wilsonline Indexes, RIA Checkpoint (Tax), BEP Journals, Environmental Law Reporter, Foreign Law Guide, CCH Intelliconnect, Elder Law Library Database, BNA ALL, Making of Modern Law, and HeinOnline, which are available to law students for research. Special library collections include selective government depositories for both state and federal documents, American judicial biographies, the International & Comparative Law Display, the Casad Collection, the Heller Collection, and the Hoeflich Rare Book Room. The ratio of library volumes to faculty is 9,234 to 1 and to students is 699 to 1. The ratio of seats in the library to students is 1 to 1.

Faculty

The law school has 35 full-time and 19 part-time faculty members, of whom 20 are women. According to AAUP standards for Category I institutions, faculty salaries are average. About 8% of full-time faculty have a graduate law degree in addition to the J.D. The ratio of full-time students to full-time faculty in an average class is 13 to 1; in a clinic, 8 to 1. The law school has a regular program of bringing visiting professors and other distinguished lecturers and visitors to campus. There is a chapter of the Order of the Coif; 16 faculty and 800 graduates are members.

Students

About 39% of the student body are women; 15%, minorities; 3%, African American; 3%, Asian American; 7%, Hispanic; and 2%, Native American. The majority of students come from Kansas (71%). The average age of entering students is 25; age range is 21 to 51. About 13% of students have a graduate degree. About 2% drop out after the first year for academic or personal reasons; 98% remain to receive a law degree.

Placement

J.D.s awarded:	168

Services available through: a separate law school placement center.

Special features: a mentoring program that matches current law students with practicing alumni, Legal Career Options Day.

Full-time job interviews:	15 employers
Summer job interviews:	67 employers
Placement by graduation:	55% of class
Placement within 9 months:	89% of class
Average starting salary:	$24,000 to $160,000

Areas of placement:

Private practice 2–10 attorneys	24%
Private practice 11–25 attorneys	11%
Private practice 26–50 attorneys	3%
Private practice 51–100 attorneys	3%
Private practice 101+ attorneys	17%
Government	18%
Business/industry	11%
Public interest	8%
Judicial clerkships	2%
Academic	2%

209 Law Building
Lexington, KY 40506-0048

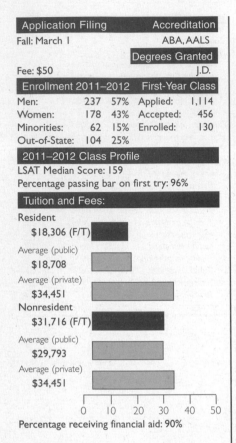

Application Filing		Accreditation
Fall: March 1		ABA, AALS
		Degrees Granted
Fee: $50		J.D.

Enrollment 2011–2012			First-Year Class	
Men:	237	57%	Applied:	1,114
Women:	178	43%	Accepted:	456
Minorities:	62	15%	Enrolled:	130
Out-of-State:	104	25%		

2011–2012 Class Profile
LSAT Median Score: 159
Percentage passing bar on first try: 96%

Tuition and Fees:

Resident
$18,306 (F/T)

Average (public)
$18,708

Average (private)
$34,451

Nonresident
$31,716 (F/T)

Average (public)
$29,793

Average (private)
$34,451

Percentage receiving financial aid: 90%

ADMISSIONS
In the fall of 2011 first-year class, 1114 applied, 456 were accepted, and 130 enrolled. Twelve transfers enrolled. The median GPA of the most recent first-year class was 3.57. The lowest LSAT percentile accepted was 30; the highest was 97.

Requirements
Applicants must have a bachelor's degree and take the LSAT. The most important admission factors include writing ability, LSAT results, and GPA. No specific undergraduate courses are required, and candidates are not interviewed.

Procedure
The application deadline for fall entry is March 1. Applicants should submit an application form, LSAT results, transcripts, personal statement, TOEFL (if a foreign student), nonrefundable application fee of $50, and 2 letters of recommendation. Notification of the admissions decision is weekly on a rolling basis. The law school uses the LSAC.

Special
The law school recruits minority and disadvantaged students by means of scholarships and stipends, visits to campuses, participation in CLEO, and general academic support offerings. Requirements are different for out-of-state students. Transfer students must have one year of credits, have a minimum GPA of 2.75, a personal statement, provide reasons for wanting to transfer (as transfers are not encouraged and applications are reviewed on a case-by-case basis).

Costs
Tuition and fees for the 2011–2012 academic year are $17,300 for full-time in-state students and $30,710 for out-of-state students. On-campus room and board costs about $11,460 annually; books and supplies run $900.

Financial Aid
About 90% of current law students receive some form of aid. The average annual amount of aid from all sources combined, including scholarships, loans, and work contracts, is $34,000; maximum, $47,200. Awards are based on need and merit, along with special funds available that have specific criteria that must be met by the applicants. Required financial statement is the FAFSA. The aid application deadline for fall entry is March 15. Special funds for minority or disadvantaged students include scholarships available through the combined efforts of the college's and university's administration. First-year students are notified about their financial aid application 1 week after acceptance for scholarships, and in May for loans.

About the Law School
University of Kentucky College of Law was established in 1908 and is a public institution. The 673-acre campus is located in an urban area walking distance to downtown Lexington. The primary mission of the law school is to provide a legal education to individuals so that they might render a high quality of professional service to Kentucky and the nation. Students have access to federal, state, county, city, and local agencies, courts, correctional facilities, law firms, and legal aid organizations in the Lexington area. Additional opportunities are available in state agencies and the state judicial system. Facilities of special interest to law students include a civil law clinic; students have their own clients and caseloads under the supervision of a former trial attorney. Housing for students is plentiful both on and off campus. Most law students choose off-campus housing, some of which are located across the street from the law school. All law school facilities are accessible to the physically disabled.

Calendar
The law school operates on a traditional semester basis. Courses for students are offered days only and must be completed within 3 to 4 years. There is no part-time program. New students are admitted in the fall. There is an 8-week summer session. Transferable summer courses are offered.

Programs
Students may take relevant courses in other programs and apply credit toward the J.D. a maximum of 6 credits may be applied. The following joint degrees may be earned: J.D./M.A. (Juris Doctor/Master of Arts in Diplomacy and International), J.D./M.B.A. (Juris Doctor/Master of Business Administration), and J.D./M.P.A. (Juris Doctor/Master of Public Administration).

Required
To earn the J.D., candidates must complete 90 total credits, of which 34 are for required courses. They must maintain a minimum GPA of 2.0 in the required courses. The following first-year courses are required of all students: Civil Procedure I and II, Constitutional Law I, Contracts and Sales I and II, Criminal Law, Legal Research and Writing, Property, and Torts. Required upper-level courses consist of Professional Responsibility and a seminar with a writing requirement. Students must also complete at least one professional skills class that includes clinic and externships. The required orientation program for first-year students is 2 days and includes an introduction to the community, to the case method, to the faculty, and to the current students.

Electives
The College of Law offers concentrations in corporate law, criminal law, environ-

Phone: 606-257-7938
Fax: 859-323-1061
E-mail: luwadmissions@email.uky.edu
Web: www.law.uky.edu

Contact

Jeanie Powell, Admissions Associate, 859-257-1678 for general inquiries; Student Financial Aid Office, 859-257-3172 for financial aid information.

KENTUCKY

mental law, family law, intellectual property law, international law, juvenile law, labor law, litigation, securities law, sports law, tax law, and torts and insurance. In addition, clinics include Prison Counsel for upper-level students, and Civil-Law Clinic for upper-level students. Numerous seminars are offered, including Gender Discrimination, Housing Law, and Intellectual Property. Third-year students may participate in internships with prosecutors and with state and federal judges. An Innocence Project with the state public defender's office is also offered. Independent research may be done on topics of special interest. Third-year students receive credits for clerking with judges in state district, circuit, and appellate division courts, or in either of 2 federal district courts. Third-year students also may work with local prosecutors and in the prison internship program. Study abroad is available via transient work at a number of ABA-approved law schools. Academic support is offered for all first-year students in the first semester and in later semesters for those in academic difficulty. An academic success program and tutorials are offered to minority students. The most widely taken electives are Evidence, Business Associations, and Tax.

Graduation Requirements

In order to graduate, candidates must have a GPA of 2.0 and complete the upper-division writing requirement.

Organizations

Students edit the *Kentucky Law Journal, KJEANRL*, and the newspaper *Week in Brief*. Students compete in the National Moot Court Competition, Jessup Competition, and First Amendment Moot Court Competition. Other competitions include the Trial Advocacy Competition, the Wilhelm Vis International Commercial Law Moot Court, and competitions in sports law, space law, and telecommunications law. Student organizations include the Student Bar Association, Black Law Students Association, and Women's Law Caucus. Other organizations include Intellectual Property Law Society, Health Law Society, and International Law Society. Henry Clay Inns of Court and several legal fraternities have local chapters.

Library

The law library contains 346,201 hardcopy volumes and 254,293 microform volume equivalents, and subscribes to 3,810 serial publications. Online databases and networks include CALI, CIS Universe, DIALOG, Dow-Jones, Legal-Trac, LEXIS, Mathew Bender, OCLC First Search, and WESTLAW, which are available to law students for research. Special library collections include human rights and mineral law and policy, as well as a selective government document depository. The ratio of library volumes to faculty is 20,000 to 1 and to students is 1,500 to 1. The ratio of seats in the library to students is 1 to 1.

Faculty

The law school has 24 full-time and 19 part-time faculty members, of whom 12 are women. According to AAUP standards for Category I institutions, faculty salaries are below average. About 25% of full-time faculty have a graduate law degree in addition to the J.D.; about 10% of part-time faculty have one. The ratio of full-time students to full-time faculty in an average class is 14 to 1; in a clinic, 8 to 1. The law school has a regular program of bringing visiting professors and other distinguished lecturers and visitors to campus. There is a chapter of the Order of the Coif; 23 faculty and 450 graduates are members.

Students

About 43% of the student body are women; 15%, minorities; 10%, African American; 3%, Asian American; and 2%, Hispanic. The majority of students come from Kentucky (75%). The average age of entering students is 23; age range is 21 to 50. About 3% drop out after the first year for academic or personal reasons; 95% remain to receive a law degree.

Placement

J.D.s awarded:	136
Services available through: a separate law school placement center and the university placement center.	
Services: a computer database on Kentucky law firms and numerous recruitment conferences and job fairs.	
Special features: individual attention from two formerly practicing attorneys who are UK Law graduates.	
Full-time job interviews:	50 employers
Summer job interviews:	50 employers
Placement by graduation:	67% of class
Placement within 9 months:	95% of class
Average starting salary:	$42,000 to $90,000
Areas of placement:	
Private practice 2–10 attorneys	27%
Private practice 11–25 attorneys	5%
Private practice 26–50 attorneys	3%
Private practice 51–100 attorneys	11%
Judicial clerkships	27%
Business/industry	11%
Government	9%
Public interest	5%
Military	1%
Academic	1%

UNIVERSITY OF LA VERNE

College of Law

320 East D Street
Ontario, CA 91764

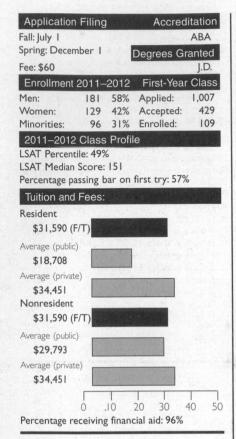

ADMISSIONS

In the fall of 2011 first-year class, 1007 applied, 429 were accepted, and 109 enrolled. Seven transfers enrolled. The median LSAT percentile of the most recent first-year class was 49; the median GPA was 3.3 on a scale of 4.3. The lowest LSAT percentile accepted was 33; the highest was 90.

Requirements

Applicants must have a bachelor's degree and take the LSAT. Minimum acceptable LSAT percentile is 33 and minimum acceptable GPA is 2.0 on a scale of 4.3. The most important admission factors include LSAT results, GPA, and general background. No specific undergraduate courses are required. Candidates are not interviewed.

Procedure

The application deadline for fall entry is July 1. Applicants should submit an application form, LSAT results, transcripts, and a nonrefundable application fee of $60. Notification of the admissions decision is 4 to 6 weeks after the application is received. The law school uses the LSAC.

Special

The law school recruits minority and disadvantaged students through minority outreach programs and CLEO. Requirements are different for out-of-state students. Transfer students must have one year of law school credits, a competitive LSAT score, and a letter of good standing.

Costs

On-campus room and board costs about $16,833 annually; books and supplies run $1,386.

Financial Aid

About 96% of current law students receive some form of aid. The average annual amount of aid from all sources combined, including scholarships, loans, and work contracts, is $35,556; maximum, $53,797. Awards are based on need and merit combined. The required financial statement is the FAFSA. The aid application deadline for fall entry is May 15. Special funds for minority or disadvantaged students are available. First-year students are notified about their financial aid application at the time of acceptance.

About the Law School

University of La Verne College of Law was established in 1970 and is a private institution. The 7-acre campus is in a suburban area of Southern California. The primary mission of the law school is to teach students to be effective legal professionals who use their skills and talents for the benefit of their communities, to imbue these students with pride in the legal profession, and to promote diversity within the law school community, accomplished by providing full- and part-time law programs with high academic standards. Students have access to federal, state, county, city, and local agencies, courts, correctional facilities, law firms, and legal aid organizations in the Ontario area. Housing for students is not available on campus, but there is a student housing network that enables students to connect with others who are also seeking housing.

Listings of housing options in the area are available.

Calendar

The law school operates on a traditional semester basis. Courses for full-time students are offered days only, and must be completed within 3 years. For part-time students, courses are offered both day and evening, and must be completed within 4 years. New full-time students are admitted in the fall. New part-time students are admitted in the fall and spring. There is an 8-week summer session. Transferable summer courses are offered.

Programs

Students may take relevant courses in other programs and apply credit toward the J.D. The following joint degrees may be earned: J.D./M.B.A. (Juris Doctor/Master of Business Administration) and J.D./M.P.A. (Juris Doctor/Master of Public Administration).

Required

To earn the J.D., candidates must complete 88 total credits, of which 60 are for required courses. They must maintain a minimum GPA of 2.0 in the required courses. The following first-year courses are required of all students: Civil Procedure, Contracts, Criminal Law, Legal Analysis and Writing, Legal Research I, Property, and Torts. Required upper-level courses consist of Appellate Advocacy, Business Organizations, Constitutional Law, Criminal Procedure, Evidence, Lawyering Skills Practicum, Professional Responsibility, and Wills and Trusts. The required orientation program for first-year students is a 2-day program, 7 hours total.

Electives

The College of Law offers concentrations in corporate law, criminal law, entertainment law, environmental law, family law, intellectual property law, international law, juvenile law, labor law, litigation, media law, securities law, sports law, tax law, and torts and insurance. In addition, clinics include the Disability Rights Legal Center (worth 3 to 6 units) and the Justice and Immigration Center (worth 6 units). There are also clinical externships. Seminars are open to upper division

Phone: 909-460-2001
877-858-4529
Fax: 909-460-2082
E-mail: lawadm@ulv.edu
Web: http://law.ulv.edu

Contact

Office of Admissions, 909-460-2001/877-858-4529 for general inquiries; Stephanie Stoval, Financial Aid Coordinator, 909-460-2006 for financial aid information.

CALIFORNIA

law students. Current seminar offerings are Law, Science, and Medicine, Philosophy and Law, Environmental Law and Policy, and Global Issues in Constitutional Law. Internships are available. Credit is given for study abroad programs. Tutorial programs include the Peer Assistance Support System (PASS), Graduate Mentor Program, and workshops. There is also an Academic Support Program. The most widely taken electives are Entertainment Law, Real Estate Law, and Sales.

Graduation Requirements

In order to graduate, candidates must have a GPA of 2.0.

Organizations

The primary law review is the *Journal of Juvenile Law*. Moot court competitions include Roger J. Traynor California Moot Court Competition, National Criminal Procedure Moot Competition, and Frederick Douglass National Moot Court Competition. Law student organizations include Student Bar Association, Delta Theta Phi Law Fraternity, and Hispanic National Bar Association. Campus clubs and other organizations include Law Review, Asian Pacific American Law Student Association, Black Law Students Association, Entertainment Law Society, J. Reuben Clark Society, and Moot Court.

Library

The law library contains 97,233 hardcopy volumes and 208,841 microform volume equivalents, and subscribes to 2,320 serial publications. Such online databases and networks as CALI, CIS Universe, Legal-Trac, LEXIS, WESTLAW, Wilsonline Indexes, VersusLaw, LLMC Digital, HeinOnline, Legal Scholarship Network, Berkeley Electronic Press, Philosopher's Index, CCH Legal Professional Library, RIA Checkpoint, BNA Core Plus Library, UN Treaty Database, and WorldTrade Law.net are available to law students for research. Special library collections include a selective federal and California depository library. The ratio of library volumes to faculty is 5,118 to 1 and to students is 674 to 1. The ratio of seats in the library to students is 1 to 1.

Faculty

The law school has 19 full-time and 12 part-time faculty members, of whom 13 are women. About 47% of full-time faculty have a graduate law degree in addition to the J.D. The ratio of full-time students to full-time faculty in an average class is 11 to 1. The law school has a regular program of bringing visiting professors and other distinguished lecturers and visitors to campus.

Students

About 42% of the student body are women; 31%, minorities; 3%, African American; 14%, Asian American; and 13%, Hispanic. The average age of entering students is 26; age range is 21 to 55. About 22% drop out after the first year for academic or personal reasons; 69% remain to receive a law degree.

Placement

J.D.s awarded:	66
Services available through: a separate law school placement center.	
Placement by graduation:	97% of class
Areas of placement:	
Private practice 2–10 attorneys	38%
Private practice 11–25 attorneys	5%
Private practice 26–50 attorneys	14%
Private practice 51–100 attorneys	14%
Business/industry	14%
Government	11%

UNIVERSITY OF LOUISVILLE

Louis D. Brandeis School of Law

University of Louisville Belknap
Campus-Wilson W. Wyatt Hall
Louisville, KY 40292

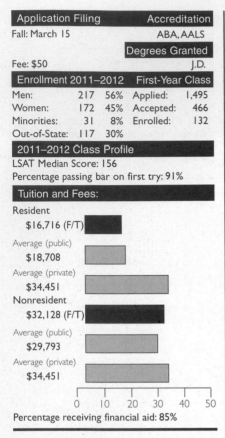

Application Filing	Accreditation
Fall: March 15	ABA, AALS
	Degrees Granted
Fee: $50	J.D.

Enrollment 2011–2012		First-Year Class	
Men:	217 56%	Applied:	1,495
Women:	172 45%	Accepted:	466
Minorities:	31 8%	Enrolled:	132
Out-of-State:	117 30%		

2011–2012 Class Profile
LSAT Median Score: 156
Percentage passing bar on first try: 91%

Tuition and Fees:

Resident
$16,716 (F/T)

Average (public)
$18,708

Average (private)
$34,451

Nonresident
$32,128 (F/T)

Average (public)
$29,793

Average (private)
$34,451

0   10   20   30   40   50

Percentage receiving financial aid: 85%

ADMISSIONS

In the fall of 2011 first-year class, 1495 applied, 466 were accepted, and 132 enrolled. Seven transfers enrolled. The median GPA of the most recent first-year class was 3.43. The lowest LSAT percentile accepted was 16; the highest was 99.

Requirements

Applicants must have a bachelor's degree and take the LSAT. Minimum acceptable GPA is 2.0 on a scale of 4.0. The most important admission factors include GPA, LSAT results, and graduate work. No specific undergraduate courses are required and candidates are not interviewed.

Procedure

The application deadline for fall entry is March 15. Applicants should submit an application form, LSAT results, transcripts, personal statement, nonrefundable application fee of $50, and 2 letters of recommendation. Notification of the admissions decision is on a rolling basis. The law school uses the LSAC.

Special

The law school recruits minority and disadvantaged students by sponsoring a minority prelaw day and attending minority fairs and programs at other schools. Requirements are different for out-of-state students. Transfer students must have one year of credit, attended an ABA-approved law school, personal statement, be in good standing, met entrance requirements for the school that they applied for initial admission, and be in the upper quarter of their law school class.

Costs

Books and supplies run $1,000.

Financial Aid

About 85% of current law students receive some form of aid. Awards are based on need and merit combined. Required financial statement is the FAFSA. The aid application deadline for fall entry is June 1. Special funds for minority or disadvantaged students are available. First-year students are notified about their financial aid application prior to enrollment, usually by May 15.

About the Law School

University of Louisville Louis D. Brandeis School of Law was established in 1846 and is a public institution. The campus is located in an urban area 4 miles south of downtown Louisville. The primary mission of the law school is to provide students with a quality legal education and prepare them for professional life through a curriculum that emphasizes fundamental lawyering skills and the development of professional values, while also affording students the opportunity to take advanced courses in a wide variety of specialty areas. Students have access to federal, state, county, city, and local agencies, courts, correctional facilities, law firms, and legal aid organizations in the Louisville area. Facilities of special interest to law students include the school's physical facility that provides students with a large, comfortable environment in which to attend class and study. Many student gathering places and study group rooms are available. Housing for students is available in a university dormitory and in affordable rental housing close to campus. All law school facilities are accessible to the physically disabled.

Calendar

The law school operates on a traditional semester basis. Courses for full-time students are offered days only and first-year students enroll in day only. Second- and third-year may take day and evening and must be completed within 5 years. For part-time students, courses are offered days only and first-year students enroll in day only. Second- and third-year students may take day and evening and must be completed within 6 years. New full- and part-time students are admitted in the fall. There is an 8-week summer session. Transferable summer courses are offered.

Programs

Students may take relevant courses in other programs and apply credit toward the J.D.; a maximum of 6 credits may be applied. The following joint degrees may be earned: J.D./M.A.H. (Juris Doctor/Master of Arts in Humanities), J.D./M.A.P.S. (Juris Doctor/Master of Arts in Political Science), J.D./M.B.A. (Juris Doctor/Master of Business Administration), J.D./M.Div. (Juris Doctor/Master of Divinity), J.D./M.S. (Juris Doctor/Master of Science in Bioethics), and J.D./M.S.S.W. (Juris Doctor/Master of Science in Social Work).

Required

To earn the J.D., candidates must complete 90 total credits, of which 44 are for required courses. They must maintain a minimum GPA of 2.0 in the required courses. The following first-year courses are required of all students: Basic Legal Skills, Civil Procedure, Contracts, Criminal Law, Legal Research, Property, and Torts. Required upper-level courses consist of 24 hours of core courses, a perspective course, a skill-based course, a writing requirement, Constitutional Law I and II, and Professional Responsibility. The required orientation program for first-year students is 2{1/2} days devoted to skills development and orientation to legal education and the profession. There is also time for social events.

Electives

The Louis D. Brandeis School of Law offers concentrations in corporate law, criminal law, entertainment law, environmental law, family law, intellectual property law, internationl law, juvenile

Phone: 502-852-6364
800-334-8634
Fax: 502-852-8971
E-mail: brandon.hamilton@louisville.edu
Web: www.law.louisville

Contact

Admission Office, 502-852-6364 for general inquiries; Brandon Hamilton, Assistant Dean for Admissions, 502-852-6364 for financial aid information.

KENTUCKY

law, labor law, litigation, securities law, sports law, tax law, torts and insurance, and disability law. In addition, there is a Law Clinic that focuses on the representation of low income clients in public housing and domestic violence cases. Law school students also participate in clinics hosted by the Louisville and Kentucky Bar Association. Clinical Externship, for upper-level students, provide the opportunity to perform law related work and gain practical experience with judges, clients through legal aid, Center for Women and Families, Public Defender's office, and the Internal Revenue Service, just to name a few. A wide variety of seminars are offered to second-, third, and fourth-year students in specialized fields of law. There are also several internships. All students are required to complete Legal Research, a 3-hour basic legal skills course, and a seminar that requires a substantial research paper. Special lecture series include the Brandeis and Harlan Lecture Series. Students may earn credit for participation in foreign study in an ABA-accredited program. Students with adequate language abilities may be foreign exchange students with several law schools throughout the world. The academic success program provides structured study groups for all first year students. A library of academic resources is also available. Academic counseling is required by those students who are on academic probation. The school has several minority recruiting activities each year and a number of scholarships for minority students. A diversity committee presents programs to the student body on topics such as gay/lesbian issues and women in politics. The most widely taken electives are Secured Transactions and Negotiable Instruments, and Business Organizations.

Graduation Requirements

In order to graduate, candidates must have a GPA of 2.0, complete the upper-division writing requirement, in addition to 30 hours of law-related public service at a placement approved by the school.

Organizations

Students edit *The University of Louisville Law Review, Journal of Law and Education*, and *Journal of Animal and Environmental Law*. Annually, students participate in the National Moot Court, the American Association of Trial Lawyers

Mock Trial, and the ABA Negotiation Competition. Other competitions include a Trial Advocacy Moot Court exercise in a student's first year and the Pirtle-Washer Moot Court in a student's second year. Law student organizations, local chapters of national associations, and campus organizations include the Student Bar Association, Environmental Law Society, International Law Society, Delta Theta Phi, Phi Alpha Delta, the Federalist Society, Lambda Law Caucus, Black Law Students Association, and Women's Law Caucus.

Library

The law library contains 417,747 hardcopy volumes and 190,390 microform volume equivalents, and subscribes to 5,200 serial publications. Online databases and networks include CALI, CIS Universe, DIALOG, LEXIS, OCLC First Search, WESTLAW, Wilsonline Indexes, as well as other extensive databases, which are available to law students for research. Special library collections include the Justice Brandeis papers, Justice Harlan papers, and a Supreme Court brief depository. The ratio of library volumes to faculty is 12,287 to 1 and to students is 960 to 1. The ratio of seats in the library to students is 1 to 1.

Faculty

The law school has 34 full-time and 9 part-time faculty members, of whom 18 are women. According to AAUP standards for Category I institutions, faculty salaries are below average. About 30% of full-time faculty have a graduate law degree in addition to the J.D. The ratio of full-time students to full-time faculty in an average class is 14 to 1; in a clinic, 9 to 1. The law school has a regular program of bringing visiting professors and other distinguished lecturers and visitors to campus.

Students

About 45% of the student body are women; 8%, minorities; 3%, African American; 3%, Asian American; and 2%, Hispanic. The majority of students come from Kentucky (70%). The average age of entering students is 26; age range is 21 to 54. About 5% drop out after the first year for academic or personal reasons; 95% remain to receive a law degree.

Placement

J.D.s awarded:	119

Services available through: a separate law school placement center.

Special features: participation in recruiting consortia in the southeast and Kentucky.

Full-time job interviews:	20 employers
Summer job interviews:	35 employers
Placement by graduation:	71% of class
Placement within 9 months:	95% of class
Average starting salary:	$37,000 to $103,000

Areas of placement:

Solo Practice	3%
Private practice 2–10 attorneys	28%
Private practice 11–25 attorneys	15%
Private practice 26–50 attorneys	9%
Private practice 51–100 attorneys	9%
Government	17%
Business/industry	15%
Judicial clerkships	5%
Academic	3%

School of Law

246 Deering Avenue
Portland, ME 04102

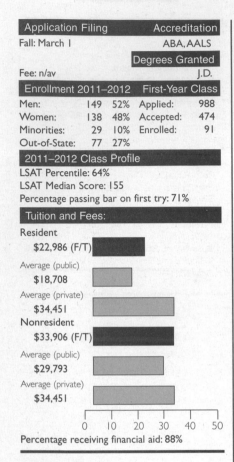

Application Filing	Accreditation
Fall: March 1	ABA, AALS

Degrees Granted
Fee: n/av	J.D.

Enrollment 2011–2012		First-Year Class	
Men:	149 52%	Applied:	988
Women:	138 48%	Accepted:	474
Minorities:	29 10%	Enrolled:	91
Out-of-State:	77 27%		

2011–2012 Class Profile
LSAT Percentile: 64%
LSAT Median Score: 155
Percentage passing bar on first try: 71%

Tuition and Fees:

Resident
$22,986 (F/T)

Average (public)
$18,708

Average (private)
$34,451

Nonresident
$33,906 (F/T)

Average (public)
$29,793

Average (private)
$34,451

0 10 20 30 40 50

Percentage receiving financial aid: 88%

ADMISSIONS
In the fall of 2011 first-year class, 988 applied, 474 were accepted, and 91 enrolled. Six transfers enrolled. The median LSAT percentile of the most recent first-year class was 64; the median GPA was 3.4 on a scale of 4.0.

Requirements
Applicants must have a bachelor's degree and take the LSAT. The most important admission factors include academic achievement. No specific undergraduate courses are required. Candidates are not interviewed.

Procedure
The application deadline for fall entry is March 1. Applicants should submit an application form, LSAT results, transcripts, TOEFL (for foreign educated applicants only), and a letter of recommendation. Notification of the admissions decision begins in December of each year. The law school uses the LSAC.

Special
The law school recruits minority and disadvantaged students through law school admissions forums, scholarship assistance, contacts with law school minority organizations, and mailings to minority candidates through Law Service's C.R.S. Requirements are different for out-of-state students. Transfer students must have one year of credits, attended an ABA-approved law school, and have superior academic credentials.

Costs
On-campus room and board costs about $10,908 annually; books and supplies run $5,714.

Financial Aid
About 88% of current law students receive some form of aid. The average annual amount of aid from all sources combined, including scholarships, loans, and work contracts, is $34,955; maximum, $50,000. Awards are based on need. Required financial statement is the FAFSA. The aid application deadline for fall entry is February 15. Special funds for minority or disadvantaged students are at the discretion of the law school. First-year students are notified about their financial aid application at time of acceptance.

About the Law School
University of Maine School of Law was established in 1962 and is a public institution. The campus is located in an urban area in Portland. The primary mission of the law school is to educate students to serve the public and private sectors with distinction; to contribute to the advancement of the law through scholarly and professional research and writing; and to engage in public services aimed at improving the legal system. Students have access to federal, state, county, city, and local agencies, courts, correctional facilities, law firms, and legal aid organizations in the Portland area. Portland is the major urban and legal center in the state. Facilities of special interest to law students are the Cumberland County Superior Court, the Maine Supreme Judicial Court, the U.S. Bankruptcy Court, and the Federal District Court. There is a privately-owned and operated student housing complex located less than five minutes from the Law School. There is also an abundance of affordable rental housing in and around Portland. All law school facilities are accessible to the physically disabled.

Calendar
The law school operates on a traditional semester basis. Courses for full-time students are offered days only and must be completed within 3 years. For part-time students, courses are offered days only and must be completed within 5 years. New full- and part-time students are admitted in the fall. There is a 7-week summer session. Transferable summer courses are offered.

Programs
Students may take relevant courses in other programs and apply credit toward the J.D.; a maximum of 6 credits may be applied. The following joint degrees may be earned: J.D./M.C.P (Juris Doctor/Master in Community Planning and Development), J.D./M.A. (Juris Doctor/Master of Arts in public policy and management), J.D./M.B.A. (Juris Doctor/Master of Science in Business Administration), and J.D./M.S. (Juris Doctor/Master of Science in Health Policy and Management).

Required
To earn the J.D., candidates must complete 90 total credits, of which 41 are for required courses. They must maintain a minimum GPA of 2.0 in the required courses. The following first-year courses are required of all students: Civil Procedure I and II, Constitutional Law I, Contracts I and II, Criminal Law, Legal Research and Writing I and II, Property, and Torts. Required upper-level courses consist of a Professional Skills course (e.g., Externship, Trial Practice, Clinic, Mediation Practicum, Estate, an independent writing requirement, and Professional Responsibility. Clinical courses are not required, but they are popular among our students and help satisfy the Professional Skills course requirement. The required orientation program for first-year students is 2 days. The first day includes mini-classes, then discussion with alumni on the same case, and small group discussions with faculty; the second day is information on university services, student organizations, and a session on professional responsibility.

MAINE

Phone: 207-780-4341
Fax: 207-780-4239
E-mail: *mainelaw@usm.maine.edu*
Web: *mainelaw.maine.edu*

Contact

Assistant Dean of Admissions, 207-780-4341 for general inquiries; Assistant Director Financial Aid (University of Southern Maine), 207-780-5250 for financial aid information.

Placement

J.D.s awarded:	90
Services available through: a separate law school placement center.	
Special features: personalized, individualized attention.	
Placement within 9 months of graduation:	80% of class
Average starting salary:	$47,000 to $ 73,000
Areas of placement:	
Private practice 2–10 attorneys	30%
Private practice 11–25 attorneys	2%
Private practice 26–50 attorneys	3%
Private practice 51–100 attorneys	2%
Business/industry	26%
Judicial clerkships	12%
Government	9%
Public interest	6%
Academic	1%

Electives

In addition, Maine Law offers an Integrated Clinical Education Program to third-year students and includes civil practice and criminal defense under the auspices of the Cumberland Legal Aid Clinic. This Clinic includes the General Practice Clinic, Prisoner Assistance Clinic (civil matters), transactional Intellectual Property Clinic, Criminal Law, and Family practicum's. All Clinics are open to third-year students and range from 3 to 6 credits. Students can also gain academic credit for work at many non-profit and government agencies through an extensive externship program. Maine Law offers 3-, 4-, and 6-credit externships to second- and third-year students at numerous host organizations that include local, state, and federal courts, government agencies, and various corporate and nonprofit/public interest entities. Seminars in commercial law, consumer law, constitutional law, intellectual property law and international law are open to second- and third-year students. The Frank M. Coffin Lecture on Law and Public Service is held annually, along with the Godfrey Distinguished Visiting Lecturer and the Deans Distinguished Lecture Series. The Student Bar Association and other student organizations also offer guest lectures. There is a 1-semester option at Dalhousie Law School in Halifax, Nova Scotia; the University of New Brunswick, Canada; University College, Galway, Ireland; University of Buckingham, England; Université du Maine, LeMans, France; or Cergy-Pontoise University in Paris, France. To facilitate success in law school we offer all first-year students the opportunity to take advantage of the Academic Support Program through which students are exposed to basic skills necessary to study law effectively and to strategies that enable students to make the most of their academic efforts and to minimize stress. The most widely taken electives are Trial Practice, Business Associations, and Evidence.

Graduation Requirements

In order to graduate, candidates must have a GPA of 2.0, completed the upper-division writing requirement, which may be fulfilled with Law Review, Ocean and Coastal Law Journal, Moot Court, or an independent writing project; taken Constitutional Law II, one course that places the law in a broader philosophic, historic,

or comparative context, and a course in professional responsibility.

Organizations

Students edit the *Maine Law Review, Ocean and Coastal Law Journal*. The second-year Moot Court Board is chosen by internal competition. Board members compete in a number of regional, national, and international competitions, such as the National Moot Court Competition, Jessup International, and the Trilateral Moot Court competition with Canadian law schools. Other competitions include the National Mock Trial Competition. Student organizations include the Student Bar Association, Black Law Students Association, the Maine Association, for Public Interest Law, Environmental Law Society, Maine Law and Technology Association and the Lesbian, Gay and Bisexual Law Caucus. Local chapters of national associations include the National Lawyers Guild, International Law Society, and the Federalist Society.

Library

The law library contains 302,287 hardcopy volumes and 138,833 microform volume equivalents, and subscribes to 5,691 serial publications. Online databases and networks include CALI, LEXIS, OCLC First Search, RLIN, WESTLAW, and Wils online Indexes, which are available to law students for research. Special library collections include EU and U.S. government publications depository. The ratio of library volumes to faculty is 18,893 to 1 and to students is 1,053 to 1. The ratio of seats in the library to students is 1 to 1.

Faculty

The law school has 16 full-time and 13 part-time faculty members, of whom 8 are women. About 30% of full-time faculty have a graduate law degree in addition to the J.D. The ratio of full-time students to full-time faculty in an average class is 18 to 1; in a clinic, 6 to 1. The law school has a regular program of bringing visiting professors and other distinguished lecturers and visitors to campus.

Students

About 48% of the student body are women; 10%, minorities; 1%, African American; 1%, Asian American; 4%, Hispanic;

and 3%, Native American. The majority of students come from Maine (73%). The average age of entering students is 27; age range is 21 to 52. About 24% of students enter directly from undergraduate school, 11% have a graduate degree, and 76% have worked full-time prior to entering law school. About 3% drop out after the first year for academic or personal reasons; 97% remain to receive a law degree.

Francis King Cary School of Law

500 West Baltimore Street
Baltimore, MD 21201

Application Filing		Accreditation
Fall: March 1		ABA, AALS
		Degrees Granted
		J.D.

Enrollment 2011–2012		First-Year Class	
Men:	373 45%	Applied:	3,747
Women:	458 55%	Accepted:	598
Minorities:	291 35%	Enrolled:	290
Out-of-State:	291 35%		

2011–2012 Class Profile

LSAT Percentile: 84%

LSAT Median Score: 160

Percentage passing bar on first try: 84%

Tuition and Fees:

Resident

n/av

Average (public)

$18,708

Average (private)

$34,451

Nonresident

n/av

Average (public)

$29,793

Average (private)

$34,451

Percentage receiving financial aid: 81%

ADMISSIONS

In the fall of 2011 first-year class, 3747 applied, 598 were accepted, and 290 enrolled. Twenty-nine transfer students enrolled. The median LSAT percentile of the most recent first-year class was 84; the median GPA was 3.6 on a scale of 4.0. The lowest LSAT percentile accepted was 20; the highest was 99.

Requirements

Applicants must have a bachelor's degree and take the LSAT. The most important admission factors include GPA, general background, and faculty recommendation. No specific undergraduate courses are required, and candidates are not interviewed.

Procedure

The application deadline for fall entry is March 1. Applicants should submit an application form, LSAT results, transcripts, a personal statement, and 2 letters of recommendation. Notification of the admissions decision is December through April. The law school uses the LSAC.

Special

The law school recruits minority and disadvantaged students by encouraging applications from African Americans and other students of color, and from disadvantaged persons who will enrich the law school and the profession. Requirements are different for out-of-state students. Transfer students must have one year of credit, have attended an ABA-approved law school, a personal statement, and have competitive academic credentials.

Costs

Tuition and fees for the 2011–2012 academic year are $23,744 for full-time in-state students and $35,022 for out-of-state students. Tuition for part-time students is $17,782 for in-state students and $26,250 out-of-state. On-campus room and board costs about $19,350 annually; books and supplies run $1,725.

Financial Aid

About 81% of current law students receive some form of aid. The average annual amount of aid from all sources combined, including scholarships, loans, and work contracts, is $27,061; maximum, $55,621. Awards are based on need and merit. The average financial package is $48,891, based on need. There are a limited number of merit scholarships awarded through the admissions process. Required financial statement is the FAFSA. The aid application deadline for fall entry is March 1. Special funds for minority or disadvantaged students consist of grants that are available for students whose enrollment would add significantly to student diversity. First-year students are notified about their financial aid application at time of acceptance.

About the Law School

University of Maryland Francis King Cary School of Law was established in 1816 and is a public institution. The 24-acre campus is located in an urban area adjacent to a revitalized cultural and arts district. The primary mission of the law school is to contribute to the achievement of a more just society by educating outstanding lawyers, advancing understanding of law and legal institutions, and enhancing access to justice. The school is a leader in clinical education and public service law. Students have access to federal, state, county, city, and local agencies, courts,

correctional facilities, law firms, and legal aid organizations in the Baltimore area. The law school is within walking distance of local and federal courts. Facilities of special interest to law students include classrooms on each of its four floors and more than 400 study seats. State-of-the-art technology is integrated throughout with wired and wireless networks, smart podiums in the classrooms and video conferencing capabilities in all three court-rooms. The law library has 97 computer workstations and 424 wired network connections. Housing for students consists of campus apartments; board is not offered. The university's Residence Life Office assists in finding off-campus housing. All law school facilities are accessible to the physically disabled.

Calendar

The law school operates on a traditional semester basis. Courses for full-time students are offered during the day only (for required courses), and must be completed within 7 years. For part-time students, courses are offered both day and evening and must be completed within 7 years. New full- and part-time students are admitted in the fall. There is a 7-week summer session. Transferable summer courses are offered.

Programs

Students may take relevant courses in other programs and apply credit toward the J.D.; a maximum of 32 credits may be applied. The following joint degrees may be earned: J.D./Pharm.D. (Juris Doctor/Doctor of Pharmacy), J.D./Ph.D. (Juris Doctor/Doctor of Philosophy in public policy), J.D./M.A. (Juris Doctor/Master of Arts in Criminal Justice), J.D./M.B.A. (Juris Doctor/Master of Business Administration), and J.D./M.S.W. (Juris Doctor/Master of Social Work).

Required

To earn the J.D., candidates must complete 85 total credits, of which 34 to 35 are for required courses. They must maintain a minimum GPA of 2.0 in the required courses. The following first-year courses are required of all students: Civil Procedure, Constitutional Law: Governance, Contracts, Criminal Law, Legal Analysis, Writing and Research (LAWR I), Legal Analysis, Writing and Research (LAWR II),

Phone: 410-706-7214
Fax: 410-706-7714
E-mail: admissions@law.umaryland.edu
Web: http://www.law.umaryland.edu

Contact

Michele Hayes, Director of Admissions, 410-706-3492 for general inquiries; Marilyn Heath, Student Financial Planning Coordinator 410-706-0873 for financial aid information.

MARYLAND

Property, and Torts. Required upper-level courses consist of Advanced Legal Research, Advanced Writing Requirement, Cardin Requirement, Constitutional Law: Individual Rights, and Legal Profession. All students must take clinical courses. The required orientation program for first-year students lasts 2 days. During that time, students receive instruction in case briefing, attend a sample class, are introduced to the web and technology-based law school systems, learn about the honor code, have lunch with faculty and deans, and meet with upper-class peer advisers.

Electives

The Francis King Cary School of Law offers concentrations in corporate law, criminal law, environmental law, family law, intellectual property law, international law, juvenile law, labor law, litigation, securities law, tax law, health care law, public interest law, mediation, constitutional law, jurisprudence/legal theory, legislation/public policy, and human and civil rights. In addition, the Clinical Law Program offers 20 legal clinics that operate in a wide range of practice areas such as environmental law, disability law, family law, mediation, youth, education, healthcare, and community development. Approximately 55 seminars are offered. Externships are available in public agencies and nonprofit organizations. Externships are coordinated with classroom discussion and a writing requirement. Research may be undertaken through 4 legal journals, through independent research/writing under faculty supervision, by acting as research assistants for faculty, and in courses and seminars. The Academic Achievement Program enlists the assistance of upper-level students who, as teaching fellows, work directly with first-year students. Mentoring and social support is provided through a wide variety of student groups. First-year students are eligible to join any of the more than 30 student groups, which include the Asian/Pacific American Law Students Association, Black Law Students Association, Latino Law Students Association, and the LGBT Law School Alliance. The most widely taken electives are Business, Environmental, and Health Law related courses.

Graduation Requirements

In order to graduate, candidates must have a GPA of 2.0, completed the upper-division writing requirement, and meet the residency requirements of 6 semesters of attendance for full-time students, and 8 semesters for part-time students.

Organizations

The primary law review is the *Maryland Law Review*. Other law reviews include *The Journal of Health Care Law and Policy*, *The Journal Business and Technology*, and the *University of Maryland Journal Race, Religion, Gender, and Class*. The student newspaper is *The Raven*. Moot court competitions include the Morris B. Myerowitz Competition, Jessup International Moot Court Competition, and Pace University National Environmental Law Moot Court Competition. Other competitions include Health Law Moot Court, Robert R. Merhige, Jr. National Environmental Negotiations Competition, American College of Trial Lawyers, and Association of Trial Lawyers of America. Law student organizations, local chapters of national associations, and campus organizations include the Maryland Environmental Law Society, Student Health Law Organization, American Constitution Society, Student Bar Association, Women's Bar Association (student chapter), Phi Alpha Delta, Criminal Law Association, International Law Society, and Business Law Society.

Library

The law library contains 353,820 hardcopy volumes and 141,718 microform volume equivalents, and subscribes to 3,780 serial publications. Online databases and networks include CALI, Infotrac, Legal-Trac, LEXIS, Mathew Bender, OCLC First Search, WESTLAW, and Wilsonline Indexes, which are available to law students for research. Special library collections include a partial federal government depository, African-Americans in the Law, and historical publications of the U.S. Civil Rights Commission. The ratio of library volumes to faculty is 6,318 to 1 and to students is 426 to 1. The ratio of seats in the library to students is 1 to 1.

Faculty

The law school has 56 full-time and 99 part-time faculty members, of whom 65 are women. According to AAUP standards for Category I institutions, faculty salaries are above average. About 25% of full-time faculty have a graduate law degree in addition to the J.D.; about 4% of part-time

Placement

J.D.s awarded:	254

Services available through: a separate law school placement center.

Services: job fairs, online jobs/internship listing database.

Special features: Career Development staff assists in developing job search strategies, facilitates year-round on-campus interviewing and other recruitment programs, and provides professional development workshops and seminars.

Full-time job interviews:	69 employers
Summer job interviews:	123 employers
Placement by graduation:	83% of class
Placement within 9 months:	98% of class
Average starting salary:	$61,498 to $150,000

Areas of placement:

Private practice 2–10 attorneys	12%
Private practice 11–25 attorneys	3%
Private practice 26–50 attorneys	4%
Private practice 51–100 attorneys	2%
Private practice 101–501+ attorneys	19%
Judicial clerkships	25%
Government	13%
Business/industry	10%
Public interest	5%
Academic	5%
Military	2%

faculty have one. The ratio of full-time students to full-time faculty in an average class is 12 to 1; in a clinic, 8 to 1. The law school has a regular program of bringing visiting professors and other distinguished lecturers and visitors to campus. There is a chapter of the Order of the Coif.

Students

About 55% of the student body are women; 36%, minorities; 14%, African American; 13%, Asian American; 8%, Hispanic; and 1%, Native American. The majority of students come from Maryland (65%). The average age of entering students is 25; age range is 20 to 56. About 35% of students enter directly from undergraduate school, 20% have a graduate degree, and 65% have worked full-time prior to entering law school. About 1% drop out after the first year for academic or personal reasons; 94% remain to receive a law degree.

UNIVERSITY OF MEMPHIS

Cecil C. Humphreys School of Law

1 North Front Street
Memphis, TN 38103-2189

Application Filing		Accreditation
Fall: March 1		ABA, AALS
		Degrees Granted
Fee: $25		J.D.

Enrollment 2011–2012		First-Year Class	
Men:	247 59%	Applied:	861
Women:	174 41%	Accepted:	302
Minorities:	59 14%	Enrolled:	144
Out-of-State:	42 10%		

2011–2012 Class Profile
LSAT Percentile: 64%
LSAT Median Score: 155
Percentage passing bar on first try: 93%

Tuition and Fees:

Resident
$15,570 (F/T)

Average (public)
$18,708

Average (private)
$34,451

Nonresident
$37,442 (F/T)

Average (public)
$29,793

Average (private)
$34,451

0 10 20 30 40 50

Percentage receiving financial aid: 84%

ADMISSIONS

In the fall of 2011 first-year class, 861 applied, 302 were accepted, and 144 enrolled. Two transfers enrolled. The median LSAT percentile of the most recent first-year class was 64; the median GPA was 3.4 on a scale of 4.0. The lowest LSAT percentile accepted was 8; the highest was 99.

Requirements
Applicants must have a bachelor's degree and take the LSAT. Minimum acceptable GPA is 2.0 on a scale of 4.0. The most important admission factors include LSAT results, GPA, and academic achievement. No specific undergraduate courses are required. Candidates are not interviewed.

Procedure
The application deadline for fall entry is March 1. Applicants should submit an application form, LSAT results, a personal statement, a recent TOEFL score (if applicable), a nonrefundable application fee of $25, and 3 letters of recommendation.

Notification of the admissions decision is from December to May. The law school uses the LSAC.

Special
Law school representatives attend graduate and professional fairs and national LSAC forums, and visit minority colleges and universities in the region. Diverse candidates from Tennessee are contacted by e-mail using LSAC. An on-campus diversity workshop is held in each semester. Requirements are different for out-of-state students in that they must submit a "Non-resident Addendum" explaining their interest in attending the University of Memphis. Transfer students must have one year of credit, must have attended an ABA-approved law school, and must submit a personal statement.

Costs

Tuition and fees for the 2011–2012 academic year are $13,942 for full-time in-state students and $35,814 for out-of-state students. Tuition for part-time students is $12,464 for in-state students and $33,000 out-of-state. On-campus room and board costs about $9,084 annually; books and supplies run $1,875.

Financial Aid

About 84% of current law students receive some form of aid. The average annual amount of aid from all sources combined, including scholarships, loans, and work contracts, is $26,128; maximum, $58,500. Awards are based on need and merit combined. The required financial statement is the FAFSA. The aid application deadline for fall entry is April 1. Special funds for minority or disadvantaged students are available. First-year students are notified about their financial aid application at time of acceptance.

About the Law School

University of Memphis Cecil C. Humphreys School of Law was established in 1962 and is a public institution. The 1160-acre campus is in downtown Memphis. The University of Memphis is a state-assisted law school committed to the education of its students, to the academic and scholarly accomplishments of its faculty and students, and to the improvement of the legal profession and the advancement of

justice in our community, state, and nation through principles of professional responsibility and equal opportunity. Students have access to federal, state, county, city, and local agencies, courts, correctional facilities, law firms, and legal aid organizations in the Memphis area. Housing for students consists of university-owned and -managed apartment-style units on the main campus. All law school facilities are accessible to the physically disabled.

Calendar

The law school operates on a traditional semester basis. Courses for full-time students are offered days only, must be completed within 6 years. For part-time students, courses are offered days only, and must be completed within 6 years. New full- and part-time students are admitted in the fall. There is a 7-week summer session. Transferable summer courses are offered.

Programs

Students may take relevant courses in other programs and apply credit toward the J.D.; a maximum of 30 credits may be applied. The following joint degrees may be earned: J.D./M.A. (Juris Doctor/Master of Political Science), J.D./M.B.A. (Juris Doctor/Master of Business Administration), and J.D./M.P.H. (Juris Doctor/Master of Public Health).

Required
To earn the J.D., candidates must complete 90 total credits, of which 61 are for required courses. They must maintain a minimum GPA of 2.0 in the required courses. The following first-year courses are required of all students: Civil Procedure I and II, Constitutional Law, Contracts I and II, Criminal Law, Legal Methods I and II, Property, and Torts I and II. Required upper-level courses consist of a skills course, Advanced Writing and Research, Evidence, and Professional Responsibility. All students must satisfy an upper-level skills requirement which could include a clinic. The required orientation program for first-year students consists of a 3-day program that takes place immediately before the beginning of fall classes.

Electives
The Cecil C. Humphreys School of Law offers concentrations in corporate law,

Phone: 901-678-5403
Fax: 901-678-0741
E-mail: *lawadmissions@memphis.edu*
Web: *http://www.memphis.edu/law*

Contact

Office of Law Admissions, 901-678-5403 for general inquiries; Debra Ann Brown, Assistant Director, Student Financial Aid, 901-678-4825, direct line 901-678-3737 for financial aid information.

TENNESSEE

criminal law, family law, intellectual property law, labor law, litigation, tax law, torts and insurance, commercial law, and real estate law. Clinics currently offered are Civil Litigation, Elder Law, Child and Family Litigation, and Small Business (worth 4 credit hours each) and are available to upper-class students as an elective. Seminar classes are available to second- or third-year students, and they are typically 2-credit courses. Many different seminar options are available. The seminar courses satisfy the upper-division research requirement. Externship credit is available with the U.S. Attorney's Office, Bankruptcy Court, National Labor Relations Board, public defenders, state appellate and federal district courts, and Memphis area legal services. Students can receive research credit for law review or seminars. An academic support program (ASP) for first-year students helps ease the transition to law school. Its 2 primary components are group presentations and individual tutorials for selected first-year courses. The Tennessee Institute for Pre-Law (TIP) is an alternative admission program for Tennessee residents and MS and AR border counties; candidates must meet diversity criteria. TIP is a 5-week summer program and is limited to 20 students. The most widely taken electives are Family Law, Remedies, and Trial Advocacy.

Graduation Requirements

In order to graduate, candidates must have a GPA of 2.0 and must have completed the upper-division writing requirement and skills course.

Organizations

The primary law review is *The University of Memphis Law Review*. Moot court competitions include Freshman Moot Court (first year) and Mock Trial Advanced Moot Court (second and third year). Other competitions include Frederick Douglass Moot Court, National Moot Court, ABA National Appellate Advocacy Competition, Duberstein Moot Court Competition, Wagner Moot Court, National Mock Trial, Thurgood Marshall Mock Trial, and the Public Action Law Society. Law student organizations, local chapters of national associations, and campus organizations include the Student Bar Association, The Association of Women Attorneys, and the Public Action Law Society. Phi Alpha Delta, the Federalist Society, the Black Law

Students Association, Public Action Law Society, Intellectual Property Law Society, and Sports and Entertainment Society are also on campus.

Library

The law library contains 274,162 hardcopy volumes and 107,229 microform volume equivalents, and subscribes to 1,705 serial publications. Such online databases and networks as CALI, Legal-Trac, LEXIS, OCLC First Search, WESTLAW, Wilsonline Indexes, CCH databases, and BNA databases are available to law students for research. The library is a select federal government documents depository. The ratio of library volumes to faculty is 10,967 to 1 and to students is 653 to 1. The ratio of seats in the library to students is 1 to 2.

Faculty

The law school has 24 full-time and 42 part-time faculty members, of whom 22 are women. About 26% of full-time faculty have a graduate law degree in addition to the J.D. The ratio of full-time students to full-time faculty in an average class is 20 to 1; in a clinic, 8 to 1.

Students

About 41% of the student body are women; 15%, minorities; 10%, African American; 2%, Asian American; 2%, Hispanic; and 1%, Native American. The majority of students come from Tennessee (90%). The average age of entering students is 25; age range is 21 to 46. About 66% of students enter directly from undergraduate school, 12% have a graduate degree, and 34% have worked full-time prior to entering law school. About 11% drop out after the first year for academic or personal reasons; 89% remain to receive a law degree.

Placement

J.D.s awarded:	123
Services available through: a separate law school placement center.	
Services: workshops, seminars, and nontraditional legal career advice.	
Special features: membership in regional, national, and minority law placement consortiums.	
Full-time job interviews:	9 employers
Summer job interviews:	22 employers
Placement by graduation:	48% of class
Placement within 9 months:	86% of class
Average starting salary:	$32,000 to $125,000
Areas of placement:	
Private practice 2–10 attorneys	29%
Private practice 11–25 attorneys	13%
Private practice 26–50 attorneys	1%
Private practice 51–100 attorneys	3%
Government	13%
Judicial clerkships	11%
Business/industry	6%
Academic	6%
Solo practice	6%
Public interest	3%

School of Law

P.O. Box 248087, 1311 Miller Drive
Coral Gables, FL 33124-8087

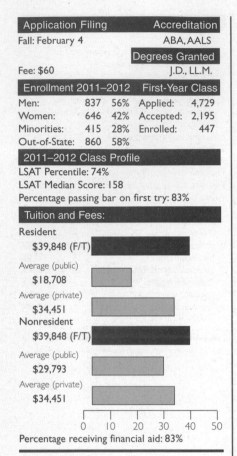

Application Filing	Accreditation
Fall: February 4	ABA, AALS
	Degrees Granted
Fee: $60	J.D., LL.M.

Enrollment 2011–2012		First-Year Class	
Men:	837 56%	Applied:	4,729
Women:	646 42%	Accepted:	2,195
Minorities:	415 28%	Enrolled:	447
Out-of-State:	860 58%		

2011–2012 Class Profile
LSAT Percentile: 74%
LSAT Median Score: 158
Percentage passing bar on first try: 83%

Tuition and Fees:

Resident
$39,848 (F/T)

Average (public)
$18,708

Average (private)
$34,451

Nonresident
$39,848 (F/T)

Average (public)
$29,793

Average (private)
$34,451

0 10 20 30 40 50

Percentage receiving financial aid: 83%

ADMISSIONS

In the fall of 2011 first-year class, 4729 applied, 2195 were accepted, and 447 enrolled. Nine transfers enrolled. The median LSAT percentile of the most recent first-year class was 74; the median GPA was 3.4 on a scale of 4.0. The lowest LSAT percentile accepted was 23; the highest was 98.

Requirements
Applicants must have a bachelor's degree and take the LSAT. No specific undergraduate courses are required, and candidates are not interviewed.

Procedure
The application deadline for fall entry is February 4. Applicants should submit an application form, LSAT results, TOEFL for foreign students, a nonrefundable application fee of $60, 2 letters of recommendation, and graduates from foreign institutions must submit transcript evaluations. All students must possess a bachelor's degree or its equivalent from a regionally accredited institution prior to the first day of classes. Notification of the admissions decision is on a rolling basis. The law school uses the LSAC.

Special
The law school recruits minority and disadvantaged students by means of a committee reviewing all files, sending information to prelaw advisers at historically minority institutions, hosting diversity admissions fairs, and participating in recruiting events at historically black schools and locations at schools where minority population is strong; also, current minority students contact newly admitted minority students. Requirements are different for out-of-state students. Transfer students must have one year of credit, have a minimum GPA of 3, have attended an ABA-approved law school, and have their LSAT and undergraduate performance reviewed.

Costs

Tuition and fees for the 2011–2012 academic year are $38,918 for all full-time students. Books and supplies run $1,200.

Financial Aid

About 83% of current law students receive some form of aid. The average annual amount of aid from all sources combined, including scholarships, loans, and work contracts, is $26,926; maximum, $63,555. Awards are based on need and merit, but the majority of scholarships are merit-based. Required financial statement is the FAFSA. The aid application deadline for fall entry is March 1. Special funds for minority or disadvantaged students include need-based scholarships and merit scholarships, both institutional and donor, including the Colson Scholarship Fund, Florida Bar Minority Scholarships, and the Spellman and Baker McKenzie scholarships. First-year students are notified about their financial aid application on a rolling basis as the files are complete.

About the Law School

University of Miami School of Law was established in 1926 and is a private institution. The 239-acre campus is located in an urban area 7 miles south of Miami. The primary mission of the law school is to teach students the craft as well as the theory of law, develop the research and writing skills necessary to the legal profession, and expose students to other skills necessary to develop a deep intellectual foundation for effective professional service, such as client counseling, fact investigation, and trial skills. Students have access to federal, state, county, city, and local agencies, courts, correctional facilities, law firms, and legal aid organizations in the Coral Gables area, and the legal institutions and firms of Miami, Fort Lauderdale, West Palm Beach, and the Florida Keys. Facilities of special interest to law students offer a broad variety of clinic and clerkship opportunities in Miami's vibrant legal and business communities, as well as numerous opportunities for practical community service experiences. Miami students also have access to the other libraries throughout the University of Miami academic community. Housing for students is limited on campus but is widely available off-campus. Roommate referral, apartment listings, and a relocation guide are supplied to admitted students. All law school facilities are accessible to the physically disabled.

Calendar

The law school operates on a traditional semester basis. Courses for full-time students are offered both day and evening with evening courses offered after the first year and must be completed within 5 years. There is no part-time program. New full-time students are admitted in the fall. There is an 8- to 9-week summer session. Transferable summer courses are offered.

Programs

In addition to the J.D., the law school offers the LL.M. Students may take relevant courses in other programs and apply credit toward the J.D.; a maximum of 6 credits may be applied. The following joint degrees may be earned: J.D./M.B.A. (Juris Doctor/Master of Business Administration), J.D./M.A. (Juris Doctor/Master of Communication), J.D./L.L.M. (Juris Doctor/Master of Laws in Taxation), J.D./M.A. (Juris Doctor/Master of Marine Affairs), J.D./M.M, (Juris Doctor/Master of Music Affairs), and J.D./M.P.H. (Juris Doctor/Master of Public Health).

FLORIDA

Contact

Therese Lambert, Director of Student Recruiting, 305-284-6746 for general inquiries; Wendi Owens, Associate Director of Financial Aid, 305-284-3115 for financial aid information.

Phone: 305-284-2523
Fax: 305-284-4400
E-mail: *admissions@law.miami.edu*
Web: *law.miami.edu*

Required

To earn the J.D., candidates must complete 88 total credits, of which 72 are for required courses. They must maintain a minimum GPA of 2.0 in the required courses. The following first-year courses are required of all students: a first-year elective, Civil Procedure I, Constitutional Law I, Contracts, Criminal Procedure, Elements, Legal Communication and Research I and II, Property, and Torts. Required upper-level courses consist of 2 seminars/workshops, Professional Responsibility, skills course, and upper-level writing. The required orientation program for first-year students is a week long formal program before classes begin. Students participate in panels and presentations, and lunches with faculty and current students.

Electives

The School of Law offers concentrations in corporate law, criminal law, entertainment law, environmental law, family law, international law, juvenile law, labor law, litigation, maritime law, securities law, sports law, tax law, and torts and insurance. In addition, a variety of clinics and hands-on legal training are offered through the Center for Ethics and Public Service, and various public interest programs, such as HOPE (Helping others through Pro Bono efforts), Street Law, and the Wrongful Convictions Project. The Children and Youth Law Clinic, the Health & Elder Clinic, and the Immigration Clinic are open to second- and third-year students. Seminars and workshops are typically 2 credits and limited to 20–25 students. Most seminars require some independent research and significant writing. Second- and third-year students are also able to take part in individual research projects. Special lecture series bring distinguished judges, scholars, and practicing attorneys from around the world to campus. Summer-based programs include Ultimate China, LEAP (London, English countyside, Amsterdam, and Paris), Greece, Italy, and Middle Europe. An intensive short-term workshop is offered with law students from the University of Leipzigin in Germany, and the University of Zurich in Switzerland. These competitive programs, which meet in Miami in the winter and their respective European cities in the spring, focus on cutting-edge international and comparative law. All first-year stu-

dents participate in the Legal Research and Writing program, a year-long program taught in small group settings. Additionally, the Academic Achievement program offers a variety of programs such as the writing center, Dean's Fellows, and Exam Workshops. The most widely taken electives are Litigation Skills and Clinical Program, Civil Procedure II, and Evidence.

Graduation Requirements

In order to graduate, candidates must have a GPA of 2.0, complete the upper-division writing requirement. Many offerings in the upper division require substantial papers.

Organizations

Student-edited publications include the *University of Miami Law Review; Inter-American Law Review; Business Law Review; International and Comparative Law Review; Psychology, Public Policy, and Law Journal*: the student newspaper *Res Ispa Loquitur*, the yearbook, *Amicus Curiae*, and *Tax Law Chronicle*. The Moot Court Board runs one of the nation's largest mock trial competitions, involving more than 200 experienced lawyers. This organization also sponsors several local, state, and regional moot court competitions, as well as negotiation and client counseling competitions. Other competitions include the International Moot Court. Law student organizations include Hispanic Law Students, Entertainment and Sports Law Society, and the Tax Law Society. Local chapters of national associations include the ABA-Law Student Division, Association of Trial Lawyers of America, and Phi Alpha Delta. Other campus organizations include Miami Law Woman and Society of Bar and Gavel.

Library

The law library contains 438,790 hardcopy volumes and 203,197 microform volume equivalents, and subscribes to 11,597 serial publications. Online databases and networks include CALI, CIS Universe, Legal-Trac, LEXIS, Mathew Bender, OCLC First Search, RLIN, WESTLAW, and Wilsonline Indexes, which are available to law students for research. Special library collections include Soia Mentschikoff Papers, Everglades Litigation Files, Federal Depository Selective Housing Site,

Placement

J.D.s awarded:	439
Services available through: a separate law school placement center.	
Services: off-campus interview programs/ job fairs.	
Special features: The Career Development Office (CDO) has a professional staff consisting of 11 attorneys.	
Full-time job interviews:	14 employers
Summer job interviews:	50 employers
Placement by graduation:	53% of class
Placement within 9 months:	84% of class
Average starting salary:	$30,000 to $160,000
Areas of placement:	
Private practice 2–10 attorneys	28%
Private practice 11–25 attorneys	22%
Private practice 26–50 attorneys	5%
Private practice 51–100 attorneys	6%
Government	11%
Business/industry	11%
Public interest	11%
Judicial clerkships	6%
Military	2%
Academic	1%
Unknown	1%

and Roman Law Collection. The ratio of library volumes to faculty is 2,322 to 1 and to students is 295 to 1. The ratio of seats in the library to students is 1 to 2.

Faculty

The law school has 82 full-time and 107 part-time faculty members, of whom 78 are women. According to AAUP standards for Category I institutions, faculty salaries are above average. The ratio of full-time students to full-time faculty in an average class is 13 to 1. The law school has a regular program of bringing visiting professors and other distinguished lecturers and visitors to campus. There is a chapter of the Order of the Coif; 55 faculty and 974 graduates are members.

Students

About 42% of the student body are women; 28%, minorities; 6%, African American; 3%, Asian American; 15%, Hispanic; and 1%, Native American. The majority of students come from Florida (42%). The average age of entering students is 24; age range is 20 to 49. About 48% of students enter directly from undergraduate school, and 52% have worked full-time prior to entering law school. About 2% drop out after the first year for academic or personal reasons; 98% remain to receive a law degree.

University of Miami   **515**

Law School

625 South State Street
Ann Arbor, MI 48109-1215

Application Filing	Accreditation
Fall: February 15	ABA, AALS

	Degrees Granted
Fee: $75	J.D., LL.M., M.C.L., S.J.D.

Enrollment 2011–2012		First-Year Class	
Men:	615 54%	Applied:	5,424
Women:	534 46%	Accepted:	1,162
Minorities:	241 21%	Enrolled:	359
Out-of-State:	873 76%		

2011–2012 Class Profile
LSAT Percentile: 96%
LSAT Median Score: 169
Percentage passing bar on first try: 94%

Tuition and Fees:

Resident
$46,838 (F/T)

Average (public)
$18,708

Average (private)
$34,451

Nonresident
$49,740 (F/T)

Average (public)
$29,793

Average (private)
$34,451

0 10 20 30 40 50

Percentage receiving financial aid: 93%

ADMISSIONS

In the fall of 2011 first-year class, 5424 applied, 1162 were accepted, and 359 enrolled. Sixty-five transfer students enrolled. The median LSAT percentile of the most recent first-year class was 96; the median GPA was 3.8 on a scale of 4.0.

Requirements

Applicants must have a bachelor's degree and take the LSAT. No specific undergraduate courses are required, and candidates are not interviewed.

Procedure

The application deadline for fall entry is February 15. Applicants should submit an application form, LSAT results, transcripts, a personal statement, a nonrefundable application fee of $75, 1 (although 3 are encouraged) letter of recommendation. Transcripts and LSAT results must be sent via LSAC. There is an optional supplemental essay. Notification of the admissions decision is on a rolling

basis from November. The law school uses the LSAC.

Special

The law school recruits minority and disadvantaged students by reaching out to student populations that are likely to consist of minority or economically disadvantaged students in significant concentrations. Specific means of recruiting include attending minority Law Days, writing to minority students who participate in the candidate referral service, and holding alumni receptions in various nationwide settings. The law school attempts to attract economically disadvantaged students by providing need-based financial aid packages, as well as some merit-based financial aid awards. Requirements are different for out-of-state students. Transfer students must have one year of credits, attended an ABA-approved law school, a personal statement, and typically must be in top 5% to 10% of their first-year class.

Costs

Tuition and fees for the 2011–2012 academic year are $46,586 for full-time in-state students and $49,496 for out-of-state students. On-campus room and board costs about $11,750 annually; books and supplies run $1,050.

Financial Aid

About 93% of current law students receive some form of aid. The average annual amount of aid from all sources combined, including scholarships, loans, and work contracts, is $50,422; maximum, $123,690. Awards are based on need and merit combined. Required financial statement is the FAFSA. The aid application deadline for fall entry is rolling. First-year students are notified about their financial aid application 3 to 5 working days from the admission date or the middle of February, whichever is later.

About the Law School

University of Michigan Law School was established in 1859 and is a public institution. The 2860-acre campus is located in a suburban area 45 miles west of Detroit. The primary mission of the law school is to provide professional training on the topic of law through an interdisciplinary approach with a practical focus. Its

graduates go on to practice in a wide variety of careers around the nation and globe. Students have access to federal, state, county, city, and local agencies, courts, correctional facilities, law firms, and legal aid organizations in the Ann Arbor area. Other resources come from the school's integration in an international university. Facilities of special interest to law students are a new state-of-the-art academic building. Student housing is available at the Lawyers Club; in university family housing; graduate dormitories; and other dormitories as resident advisers. Off-campus housing is also available. All law school facilities are accessible to the physically disabled.

Calendar

The law school operates on a traditional semester basis. Courses for full-time students are offered days only and must be completed within 5 years. There is no part-time program. New full-time students are admitted in the fall and summer. There is an 11-week summer session. Transferable summer courses are not offered.

Programs

In addition to the J.D., the law school offers the LL.M., M.C.L., and S.J.D. Students may take relevant courses in other programs and apply credit toward the J.D.; a maximum of 12 credits may be applied. The following joint degrees may be earned: J.D./M.A. (Juris Doctor/Master of Arts (various disciplines)), J.D./M.B.A. (Juris Doctor/Master of Business Administration), J.D./M.P.H. (Juris Doctor/Master of Public Health), J.D./M.P.P. (Juris Doctor/Master of Public Policy Studies), J.D./M.S.I. (Juris Doctor/Master of Science in Information), J.D./M.S. (Juris Doctor/Master of Science in Natural Resources), J.D./M.S.W. (Juris Doctor/Master of Science in Social Work), J.D./M.U.P (Juris Doctor/Master of Urban Planning), and J.D./Ph.D. (Juris Doctor/Doctor of Economics).

Required

To earn the J.D., candidates must complete 82 total credits, of which 32 are for required courses. They must maintain a minimum GPA of 2.0 in the required courses. The following first-year courses are required of all students: Civil Procedure, Contracts, Criminal Law,

Phone: 734-764-0537

Fax: 734-647-3218

E-mail: law.jd.admissions@umich.edu

Web: http://www.law.umich.edu

Contact

Sarah C. Zearfoss, Assistant Dean, Director, 734-764-0537 for general inquiries; Katherine Gottschalk, Assistant Dean for Financial Aid, 734-764-5289 for financial aid information.

Introduction to Constitutional Law, Legal Practice I and II, Legal Practice Skills, Property, and Torts. Required upper-level courses consist of a course meeting the professional responsibility requirement, a course that meets the upper-level writing requirement, and Transnational Law. The required orientation program for first-year students consists of 2 days of presentations by deans, faculty, and upper-class students. There is also tours; information about the school and Ann Arbor; and an introduction to the study of law. On the second day of orientation, new students, along with participating orientation leaders, administrators, and faculty, are brought to various sites in the Ann Arbor and Detroit area to engage in a community service project. The orientation also includes a Commitment to Integrity Ceremony, during which the new students are addressed by an esteemed judge or lawyer about issues related to ethics and professionalism and then pledge their commitment to comporting themselves professionally and with integrity during law school and throughtout their careers.

Electives

The Law School offers concentrations in corporate law, criminal law, entertainment law, environmental law, family law, intellectual property law, international law, juvenile law, labor law, litigation, securities law, sports law, tax law, torts and insurance, civil rights, feminist legal theory, law and literature, and asylum and refugee law. In addition, upper-class students may take clinical and externship courses for up to 12 hours of credit. Students may elect a civil or criminal concentration. These clinics include Child Advocacy Law Clinic, Criminal Appellate Clinic, Environmental Law Clinic, Urban Communities Clinic, Mediation, Pediatric Advocacy, Low Income Taxpayer, International Transactions, Innocence, and Human Trafficking. Students must take at least 1 seminar in their second or third year; most recently, 74 seminars were offered. Students may spend a full semester on an externship and earn up to 12 hours of credit for the term. As part of the externship requirement, students produce a significant research paper under the supervision of a Michigan Law faculty member, on a subject related to the substantive field of the externship. Under the supervision of a school faculty member, students may pursue up to a total of 6 hours of independent research. The

same variety that exists for the law school summer internships exists for pro bono legal work. Individual tutors are available to any students who request them. The most widely taken electives are Enterprise Organizations, Evidence, and Jurisdiction.

Graduation Requirements

In order to graduate, candidates must have a GPA of 2.0 and have completed the upper-division writing requirement.

Organizations

Students edit the *Michigan Law Review, Michigan Journal of International Law, University of Michigan Journal of Law Reform, Michigan Journal of Gender and Law, Michigan Journal of Race and Law, Michigan Telecommunications and Technology Law Review*, and the newspaper *Res Gestae*. Annual moot court competitions include the Henry M. Campbell Memorial, the Philip C. Jessup International Moot Court, and the Client Counseling Competition. Other competitions include the Sexual Orientation Moot Court, Child Advocacy Moot Court Competition, and National Environmental Moot Court. Law student organizations include the Black Law Student Association, Federalist Society, and Outlaws. There are local chapters of Phi Alpha Delta, Phi Delta Phi, ABA-Law Student Division, American Constitution Society, and American Civil Liberties Union.

Library

The law library contains 1,026,712 hardcopy volumes and 1,722,515 microform volume equivalents, and subscribes to 5,571 serial publications. Online databases and networks include CALI, CIS Universe, DIALOG, Infotrac, Legal-Trac, LEXIS, Mathew Bender, OCLC First Search, WESTLAW, and Wilsonline Indexes, which are available to law students for research. Special library collections include a depository for U.S. and European Union documents, all documents from U.N. and other supra-national authorities, as well as U.S. state and federal material. There are also extensive special collections in the fields of Roman law, canon law, comparative law, indigenous nations, trials, biography, and legal bibliography. The ratio of library volumes to faculty is 10,922 to 1 and to students is 894 to 1. The ratio of seats in the library to students is 1 to 1.

Placement

J.D.s awarded:	378

Services available through: a separate law school placement center.

Services: databases to assist in job searches and mailings.

Special features: A separate counselor dedicated to public interest placement, and access to an innovative nationwide database program that helps students and lawyers find permanent positions, internships, and postgraduate fellowships with nonprofit offices and government agencies.

Full-time job interviews:	441 employers
Summer job interviews:	441 employers
Placement by graduation:	96% of class
Placement within 9 months:	99% of class
Average starting salary:	$39,000 to $180,000

Areas of placement:

Private practice 2–10 attorneys	2%
Private practice 11–25 attorneys	2%
Private practice 26–50 attorneys	1%
Private practice 51–100 attorneys	2%
Unknown	57%
Judicial clerkships	11%
Public interest	9%
Government	7%
Business/industry	5%
Military	2%
Academic	1%

Faculty

The law school has 94 full-time and 36 part-time faculty members, of whom 43 are women. About 28% of full-time faculty have a graduate law degree in addition to the J.D.; about 25% of part-time faculty have one. The ratio of full-time students to full-time faculty in an average class is 13 to 1; in a clinic, 6 to 1. The law school has a regular program of bringing visiting professors and other distinguished lecturers and visitors to campus. There is a chapter of the Order of the Coif.

Students

About 46% of the student body are women; 21%, minorities; 3%, African American; 9%, Asian American; 5%, Hispanic; and 3%, unknown. The average age of entering students is 24; age range is 21 to 40. About 26% of students enter directly from undergraduate school, 12% have a graduate degree, and 69% have worked full-time prior to entering law school.

Law School

Application Filing	Accreditation
Fall: April 1	ABA, AALS

	Degrees Granted
Fee: $75	J.D., LL.M.

Enrollment 2011–2012   First-Year Class

Men:	421	56%	Applied:	3,546
Women:	331	44%	Accepted:	879
Minorities:	143	19%	Enrolled:	246
Out-of-State:	466	62%		

2011–2012 Class Profile

LSAT Percentile: 94%

LSAT Median Score: 167

Percentage passing bar on first try: 97%

Tuition and Fees:

Resident
    $34,817 (F/T)

Average (public)
    $18,708

Average (private)
    $34,451

Nonresident
    $43,385 (F/T)

Average (public)
    $29,793

Average (private)
    $34,451

0   10   20   30   40   50

Percentage receiving financial aid: 90%

ADMISSIONS

In the fall of 2011 first-year class, 3546 applied, 879 were accepted, and 246 enrolled. Thirty-one transfer students enrolled. The median LSAT percentile of the most recent first-year class was 94; the median GPA was 3.8 on a scale of 4.0.

Requirements

Applicants must have a bachelor's degree and take the LSAT. No specific undergraduate courses are required, and candidates are not interviewed.

Procedure

The application deadline for fall entry is April 1. Applicants should submit an application form, LSAT results, transcripts, personal statement, nonrefundable application fee of $75, and 2 letters of recommendation. Notification of the admissions decision is on a rolling basis. The law school uses the LSAC.

Special

The law school recruits minority and disadvantaged students by means of national recruitment, CLEO, Candidate Referral Service, the Legal Education Awareness Program and an annual summer LSAT Prep course hosted by the law school. Requirements are different for out-of-state students. Transfer students must have one year of credits, attended an ABA-approved law school, personal statement, meet credentials to be admitted as a first-year law student, and exhibit good standing with quality work at a comparable law school.

Costs

Books and supplies run $1,666.

Financial Aid

About 90% of current law students receive some form of aid. Awards are based on need and merit combined. Required financial statement is the FAFSA. The aid application deadline for fall entry is April 1. Special funds for minority or disadvantaged students are available. First-year students are notified about their financial aid application Students receive estimated financial aid and total cost of attendance upon admission and final notification in July.

About the Law School

University of Minnesota Law School was established in 1888 and is a public institution. The 446-acre campus is in an urban area in Minneapolis. The mission of the law school is to provide high quality legal education by educating men and women in the law principally through instruction leading to a J.D. degree and through other high quality programs, by contributing to knowledge of the legal order through the publication and other dissemination of scholarship, and by providing discipline-related public service, to the university, the state, the nation, and the international community, and to the legal profession in those fields in which it has a special expertise. Students have access to federal, state, county, city, and local agencies, courts, correctional facilities, law firms, and legal aid organizations in the Minneapolis area. Facilities of special interest to law students consist of the clinic law office, 2 courtrooms, 24-hour library access, a Career Center,

a bookstore, group study rooms, student publication and organization offices, café, and multiple lounge areas with an adjoining outdoor plaza. There is plenty of housing available for students, including apartments and efficiencies near campus. All law school facilities are accessible to the physically disabled.

Calendar

The law school operates on a traditional semester basis. Courses for full-time students are offered days only and must be completed within 5 years. There is no part-time program. New full-time students are admitted in the fall. There is an 8-week summer session. Transferable summer courses are offered.

Programs

In addition to the J.D., the law school offers the LL.M. Students may take relevant courses in other programs and apply credit toward the J.D.; a maximum of 6 credits may be applied. The following joint degrees may be earned: J.D./M.D. (Juris Doctor/Doctor of Medicine), J.D./Ph.D. (Juris Doctor/Doctor of Philosophy), J.D./M.A. (Juris Doctor/Master of Arts), J.D./M.B.S (Juris Doctor/Master of Biological Science), J.D./M.B.A (Juris Doctor/Master of Business Administration), J.D./M.B.T. (Juris Doctor/Master of Business Tax), J.D./M.Ed. (Juris Doctor/Master of Education), J.D./M.P.A. (Juris Doctor/Master of Public Affairs), J.D./M.P.H. (Juris Doctor/Master of Public Health), J.D./M.P.P. (Juris Doctor/Master of Public Policy), J.D./M.S. (Juris Doctor/Master of Science), and J.D./M.U.R.P. (Juris Doctor/Master of Urban Regional Planning).

Required

To earn the J.D., candidates must complete 88 total credits, of which 33 are for required courses. They must maintain a minimum GPA of 2.0 in the required courses. The following first-year courses are required of all students: Civil Procedure, Constitutional Law, Contracts, Criminal Law, Legal Research and Writing, Property, Statutory Interpretation, and Torts. Required upper-level courses consist of Legal Research & Writing and Professional Responsibility. Clinical courses are not required, but they are popular, with a 50% participation rate. The required orientation program for first-year students

Phone: 612-625-3487
Fax: 612-626-1874
E-mail: jdadmissions@umn.edu
Web: www.law.umn.edu

Contact

Nick Wallace, Director of Admissions, 612-625-3487 for general inquiries; Office of Admissions, 612-625-3487 for financial aid information.

MINNESOTA

consists of 3 days in which the entering class is introduced to each other and the law school faculty and staff.

Electives

The Law School offers concentrations in corporate law, criminal law, environmental law, international law, health law & bioethics, bioethics, human rights, and labor and employment. In addition, second- and third-year students may enroll in 24 separate clinics in such areas as bankruptcy, child advocacy, and civil practice. Through these clinics, students receive academic credit while also providing more than 18,000 hours of pro bono legal assistance to low income individuals in the Twin Cities each year. The Law School houses 10 research institutes: Human Rights Center, Institute on Race and Poverty, Corporate Institute, Institute for Law and Rationality, Institute for Law and Politics, Institute for Law and Economics, Institute for Crime and Public Policy, and Consortium on Law and Values in Health, Environment, and Life Sciences, Robina Institute of Criminal Law and Criminal Justice, Program in Law & History. The Judicial Externship Program places students with local, federal, and state court judges. There is a variety of endowed lecture programs that bring special speakers to the law school each year. In addition, the Minnesota Supreme Court and the U.S. Court of Appeals for the Eighth Circuit preside over special hearings at the Law School each year. Study abroad is available in France, Sweden, Germany, Ireland, the Netherlands, Uruguay, Italy, Spain and Brazil. A structured study group program is available to all first-year students. Student organizations include American Indian Law Student Association, Asian American Law Student Association, Black Law Student Association, Latino Law Students Alliance, and LAMBDA Law Student Association. The most widely taken electives are Business/Corporations, Tax, and Evidence.

Graduation Requirements

In order to graduate, candidates must have a GPA of 2.0 and complete the upper-division writing requirement.

Organizations

Students edit the *Minnesota Law Review, Law and Inequality: A Journal of Theory and Practice, Minnesota Journal of Global Trade,* and the *Minnesota Intellectual Property Review*. Moot court competitions include Jessup International Law, Giles S. Rich Intellectual Property Moot Court, and the William McGee Civil Rights Moot Court. Other competitions include National Moot Court, Wagner Labor Law Moot Court, Environmental Law Moot Court, ABA Moot Court, and Maynard Pirsig Moot Court. Law student organizations, local chapters of national associations, and campus organizations include Law Council, Black Law Students Association, Student Intellectual Property Law Association, the ABA, National Lawyers Guild, and Federalist Society.

Library

The law library contains 1,084,527 hardcopy volumes and 383,310 microform volume equivalents, and subscribes to 10,886 serial publications. Online databases and networks include CALI, CIS Universe, DIALOG, Dow-Jones, Infotrac, Legal-Trac, LEXIS, Mathew Bender, OCLC First Search, and WESTLAW. Wilsonline Indexes, ALEPH, University of Minnesota online catalog, BNA, Bloomberg Law, RIA Checkpoint, PACER, HeinOnline, LLMC Digital, Making of Modern Law, numerous titles from Cambridge University and Oxford University, Springer, and Wolters Kluwer are also available to law students for research. Special library collections include United Nations, European Union, International trade, human rights, American Indian Law, Scandinavian law, law and literature. Rare books include early English and American law, canon law trials, and the papers of Clarence Darrow. The ratio of library volumes to faculty is 16,423 to 1 and to students is 1,442 to 1. The ratio of seats in the library to students is 1 to 1.

Faculty

The law school has 66 full-time and 204 part-time faculty members, of whom 81 are women. About 42% of full-time faculty have a graduate law degree in addition to the J.D. The ratio of full-time students to full-time faculty in an average class is 11 to 1; in a clinic, 7 to 1. The law school has a regular program of bringing visiting professors and other distinguished lecturers and visitors to campus. There is a chapter of the Order of the Coif; 11 faculty are members.

Placement

J.D.s awarded:	281
Services available through: a separate law school placement center.	
Special features: extensive career programming, an alumni networking program for students, and listings of employers by type, size, and city.	
Full-time job interviews:	405 employers
Summer job interviews:	405 employers
Placement by graduation:	86% of class
Placement within 9 months:	98% of class
Areas of placement:	
Private practice 2–10 attorneys	14%
Private practice 11–25 attorneys	3%
Private practice 26–50 attorneys	2%
Private practice 51–100 attorneys	1%
Business/industry	16%
Judicial clerkships	15%
Government	11%
Public interest	11%
Academic	1%

Students

About 44% of the student body are women; 19%, minorities; 4%, African American; 7%, Asian American; 3%, Hispanic; and 1%, Native American. The majority of students come from Minnesota (38%). The average age of entering students is 25; age range is 21 to 41. About 71% of students enter directly from undergraduate school, and 11% have a graduate degree. About 6% drop out after the first year for academic or personal reasons; 99% remain to receive a law degree.

L.Q.C. Lamar Hall

P.O. Box 1848 Lamar Law Center
University, MS 38677

Application Filing		Accreditation
Fall: March 1		ABA, AALS
		Degrees Granted
		J.D.

Enrollment 2011–2012		First-Year Class
Men:	287 56%	Applied: 1,572
Women:	230 44%	Accepted: 482
Minorities:	72 14%	Enrolled: 173
Out-of-State:	62 12%	

2011–2012 Class Profile
LSAT Percentile: 64%
LSAT Median Score: 155
Percentage passing bar on first try: 93%

Tuition and Fees:

Resident
$11,293 (F/T)

Average (public)
$18,708

Average (private)
$34,451

Nonresident
$13,398 (F/T)

Average (public)
$29,793

Average (private)
$34,451

Percentage receiving financial aid: 75%

ADMISSIONS

In the fall of 2011 first-year class, 1572 applied, 482 were accepted, and 173 enrolled. The median LSAT percentile of the most recent first-year class was 64; the median GPA was 3.6 on a scale of 4.0. The lowest LSAT percentile accepted was 15; the highest was 99.

Requirements
Applicants must have a bachelor's degree and take the LSAT. The most important admission factors include state or country of residence, LSAT results, and GPA. No specific undergraduate courses are required. Candidates are not interviewed.

Procedure
The application deadline for fall entry is March 1. Applicants should submit an application form, LSAT results, transcripts, a personal statement, TOEFL (if applicable), and 2 letters of recommendation. Notification of the admissions

decision is no later than April 15. The law school uses the LSAC.

Special
The law school recruits minority and disadvantaged students by means of an extensive recruiting program aimed at historically black colleges and universities in Mississippi and in other states as well as participation in law school forums. Requirements are different for out-of-state students in that slightly higher credentials are required and the percentage of nonresidents admitted is limited. Transfer students must have one year of credit, must submit a personal statement, and must be transferring from a law school that is accredited by the ABA and AALS.

Costs
Books and supplies run $1,500.

Financial Aid
About 75% of current law students receive some form of aid. The average annual amount of aid from all sources combined, including scholarships, loans, and work contracts, is $10,000; maximum, $18,500. Awards are based on need and merit combined. Required financial statements are the CSS Profile and the FAFSA. Special funds for minority or disadvantaged students include tuition grants; some grants, based on both merit and need, exceed tuition. First-year students are notified about their financial aid application at time of acceptance.

About the Law School
University of Mississippi L.Q.C. Lamar Hall was established in 1854 and is a public institution. The 1900-acre campus is in a small town 80 miles southeast of Memphis. The primary mission of the law school is to provide a quality legal education that prepares graduates for the practice of law in the United States and for entry into government and public service or any profession in which a legal education is a helpful or necessary background. Students have access to federal, state, county, city, and local agencies, courts, correctional facilities, law firms, and legal aid organizations in the university area. Housing for students is primarily off campus and is described as adequate and

reasonably priced. All law school facilities are accessible to the physically disabled.

Calendar
The law school operates on a traditional semester basis. Courses are offered days only. New students are admitted in the fall and summer. There is an 8-week summer session. Transferable summer courses are offered.

Programs
Students may take relevant courses in other programs and apply credit toward the J.D.; a maximum of 6 credits may be applied. The following joint degrees may be earned: J.D./M.A. (Juris Doctor/Master of Arts in Taxation and in Accounting) and J.D./M.B.A. (Juris Doctor/Master of Business Administration).

Required
To earn the J.D., candidates must complete 90 total credits, of which 36 to 37 are for required courses. The following first-year courses are required of all students: Civil Procedure I, Constitutional Law, Contracts, Criminal Law, Legal Research and Writing I and II, Property, and Torts. Required upper-level courses consist of Legal Profession and a skills/writing course. The required orientation program for first-year students is a 2-day program incorporating an introduction to the study of law, professionalism, analytical and case-briefing skills, and exam-taking skills.

Electives
The L.Q.C. Lamar Hall offers concentrations in corporate law, criminal law, environmental law, family law, international law, juvenile law, labor law, litigation, tax law, and remote sensing and space law. In addition, the Civil Law Clinic, worth 4 credit hours, provides legal referral and assistance to indigent clients; also offered are the Criminal Appeals Clinic (4 hours credit) and Prosecutorial Externship (4 hours credit). Several seminars, including Constitutional Law, Bankruptcy Reorganization, and Family Law, are offered. Public Service Internships, awarding up to 6 hours of pass/fail credit, are offered to senior students with more than 60 hours, a GPA of 2.2, and the permission of the Director. Law students work with judges,

Phone: 662-915-6910
Fax: 662-915-1289
E-mail: bvinson@olemiss.edu
Web: www.law.olemiss.edu

Contact

Barbara Vinson, Director, Law Admissions, 662-915-6910 for general inquiries; Laura Diven-Brown, Director of Financial Aid, 662-915-5633 for financial aid information.

MISSISSIPPI

prosecuting attorneys, and public defenders under the Student Limited Practice Act. The Mississippi Law Research Institute, operated as an auxiliary program, offers students the opportunity to perform legal research. Students receive wages for their work but no law school credit. Field work opportunities are available. Special lectures include the Dunbar Lectures in Philosophy and the Law, the Currie Lectures, which relate law, religion, and the behavioral sciences, and the McClure Memorial Lectures in Law. Upper-class students may take 6 hours in the study-abroad program in Cambridge, England, where various courses are offered. All first-year students may take advantage of a tutorial program in which upper-class students serve as teaching assistants. The program is under the direction of the Legal Writing Director. Minority programs consist of the Minority Tuition Scholarship Program and those offered through the Black Law Students Association (BLSA). There are various active special interest organizations. The most widely taken electives are Wills and Estates, Mississippi Civil Practice, and Corporations.

Graduation Requirements

In order to graduate, candidates must have a GPA of 2.0 and must have completed the upper-division writing requirement.

Organizations

Student-edited publications include the *Mississippi Law Journal, Journal of Space Law, Mississippi Review of First Impressions*, and *The Advocate*, the School of Law yearbook. Moot court competitions include the Steen-Reynolds Competition in the fall semester and trial competitions and appellate competitions each semester. Other competitions include the National Moot Court, Douglass Moot Court, Student Trial, Craven Moot Court, Heidelberg, Woodliff Oral Advocacy, and Jessup International Law. Law student organizations, local chapters of national associations, and campus organizations include the Gorove Society of International Law, Law School Student Body Association, student divisions of ABA, Delta Theta Phi, and Phi Delta Phi, and other organizations such as Law Association for Women, Black Law Students Association, Environmental Law Society, and the American Constitution Society.

Library

The law library contains 336,487 hardcopy volumes and 172,860 microform volume equivalents, and subscribes to 2,017 serial publications. Such online databases and networks as CALI, CIS Universe, DIALOG, Infotrac, Legal-Trac, LEXIS, Mathew Bender, OCLC First Search, WESTLAW, mslawyer.com, HeinOnline, BNA Core Plus, CCH Business, Congressional Search, Disclosure, EBSCO host, IndexMaster, JSTOR, Social Science Research, and UM Online Database are available to law students for research. Special library collections include a depository of federal documents and a space law collection. The ratio of library volumes to faculty is 12,942 to 1 and to students is 651 to 1.

Faculty

The law school has 26 full-time and 16 part-time faculty members, of whom 15 are women. According to AAUP standards for Category I institutions, faculty salaries are well below average. About 12% of full-time faculty have a graduate law degree in addition to the J.D.; about 17% of part-time faculty have one. The ratio of full-time students to full-time faculty in an average class is 15 to 1; in a clinic, 7 to 1. The law school has a regular program of bringing visiting professors and other distinguished lecturers and visitors to campus. There is a chapter of the Order of the Coif; 9 faculty are members.

Students

About 44% of the student body are women; 14%, minorities; 11%, African American; 1%, Asian American; 1%, Hispanic; 1%, Native American; and 1%, multiracial. The majority of students come from Mississippi (88%). The average age of entering students is 23; age range is 21 to 44. About 75% of students enter directly from undergraduate school, 5% have a graduate degree, and 25% have worked full-time prior to entering law school. About 2% drop out after the first year for academic or personal reasons; 97% remain to receive a law degree.

Placement

J.D.s awarded:	153
Services available through: a separate law school placement center.	
Services: a course in general practice offers insight into establishing a solo practice.	
Special features: personalized service based on the small student body.	
Full-time job interviews:	18 employers
Summer job interviews:	39 employers
Placement by graduation:	66% of class
Placement within 9 months:	93% of class
Average starting salary:	$28,000 to $100,000
Areas of placement:	
Private practice 2–10 attorneys	28%
Private practice 11–25 attorneys	5%
Private practice 26–50 attorneys	7%
Private practice 51–100 attorneys	8%
Judicial clerkships	18%
Government	10%
Business/industry	6%
Public interest	4%
Military	2%
Academic	2%

UNIVERSITY OF MISSOURI

School of Law

103 Hulston Hall
Columbia, MO 65211

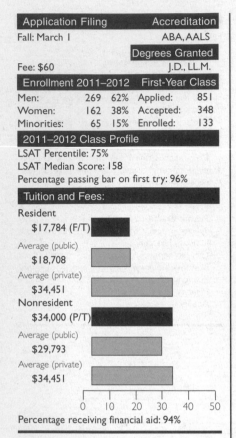

Application Filing	Accreditation
Fall: March 1	ABA, AALS
	Degrees Granted
Fee: $60	J.D., LL.M.

Enrollment 2011–2012			First-Year Class	
Men:	269	62%	Applied:	851
Women:	162	38%	Accepted:	348
Minorities:	65	15%	Enrolled:	133

2011–2012 Class Profile

LSAT Percentile: 75%
LSAT Median Score: 158
Percentage passing bar on first try: 96%

Tuition and Fees:

Resident
$17,784 (F/T)

Average (public)
$18,708

Average (private)
$34,451

Nonresident
$34,000 (P/T)

Average (public)
$29,793

Average (private)
$34,451

0 10 20 30 40 50

Percentage receiving financial aid: 94%

ADMISSIONS

In the fall of 2011 first-year class, 851 applied, 348 were accepted, and 133 enrolled. Nine transfers enrolled. The median LSAT percentile of the most recent first-year class was 75; the median GPA was 3.5 on a scale of 4.0.

Requirements

Applicants must have a bachelor's degree and take the LSAT. Minimum acceptable LSAT percentile is 27. The most important admission factors include LSAT results, GPA, and academic achievement. No specific undergraduate courses are required. Candidates are not interviewed.

Procedure

The application deadline for fall entry is March 1. Applicants should submit an application form, LSAT results, transcripts, a personal statement, a nonrefundable application fee of $60, and 2 letters of recommendation. For nonscholarship recipients, a first deposit of $250 is due in April; the second deposit of $250 is due in May. For scholarship recipients, the full $500 deposit is due in April. The deposits are credited toward tuition. Notification of the admissions decision is on a rolling basis from October. The law school uses the LSAC.

Special

The law school recruits minority and disadvantaged students by attending LSAC forums, as well as graduate and career fairs at schools, including historically black colleges and universities. Requirements are different for out-of-state students. Transfer students must have one year of credit, must have attended an ABA-approved law school, must submit a personal statement, and must have a B average or better in their first-year law school classes.

Costs

Tuition and fees for the 2011–2012 academic year are $16,644 for full-time in-state students. On-campus room and board costs about $8,932 annually; books and supplies run $1,624.

Financial Aid

About 94% of current law students receive some form of aid. The average annual amount of aid from all sources combined, including scholarships, loans, and work contracts, is $26,753; maximum, $46,802. Awards are based on need and merit combined. The required financial statement is the FAFSA. The aid application deadline for fall entry is March 1. Special funds for minority or disadvantaged students include need- and merit-based law school scholarships, ranging from $500 to full tuition. First-year students are notified about their financial aid application at time of acceptance.

About the Law School

University of Missouri School of Law was established in 1872 and is a public institution. The 1348-acre campus is in a suburban area in a college town approximately 125 miles west of St. Louis and 125 miles east of Kansas City. The primary mission of the law school is to be the school of choice for outstanding students, both from Missouri and other states. As a national leader in the field of dispute resolution, we seek to complement a strong traditional curriculum with an orientation toward lawyering as a problem-solving endeavor. We strive to foster a diverse faculty of nationally recognized scholars who are committed to effective teaching and to attract a student body with diverse experiences and views. We also strive to offer an intellectually rigorous and collegial environment for the study of law. Students have access to federal, state, county, city, and local agencies, courts, correctional facilities, law firms, and legal aid organizations in the Columbia area. Facilities of interest to students include the Center for the Study of Dispute Resolution and the trial practice program, which gives students hands-on learning experience. MU law students also have the opportunity to develop their legal skills in one of our five clinical programs, including one of the few criminal prosecution clinics in the country. There is also an online alumni mentoring network, which allows students to reach out to alumni with whom they are interested in establishing a relationship. Affordable housing is plentiful, with most students choosing to rent an apartment, townhouse, or condo. All law school facilities are accessible to the physically disabled.

Calendar

The law school operates on a traditional semester basis. Courses are offered days only. New students are admitted in the fall. There is an 8-week summer session. Transferable summer courses are offered.

Programs

In addition to the J.D., the law school offers the LL.M. Students may take relevant courses in other programs and apply credit toward the J.D.; a maximum of 6 credits may be applied. The following joint degrees may be earned: J.D./M.A. (Juris Doctor/Master of Arts in Economics), J.D./M.A. (Juris Doctor/Master of Arts in Journalism), J.D./M.A. or M.S. (Juris Doctor/Master of Arts or Master of Science in Human Development & Family Studies), J.D./M.B.A. (Juris Doctor/Master of Business Administration), J.D./M.H.A. (Juris Doctor/Master of Health Administration), J.D./M.L.S. (Juris Doctor/Master of Library & Information Science), J.D./M.P.A. (Juris Doctor/Master of Public Administration), J.D./M.S. (Juris Doctor/Master of Science in Personal Financial

Phone: 573-882-6042
888-685-2948
Fax: 573-882-9625
E-mail: heckm@missouri.edu
Web: www.law.missouri.edu

Contact
Michelle Heck, Director of Law Admissions, 573-882-6042 or 888-MULAW4U (685-2948) for general inquiries; Jeff Turnbull, Financial Aid Adviser, 573-882-1383 for financial aid information.

MISSOURI

Planning), and J.D./Ph.D. (Juris Doctor/ Doctor of Journalism).

Required
To earn the J.D., candidates must complete 89 total credits, of which 45 are for required courses. They must maintain a minimum GPA of 70.0 in the required courses. The following first-year courses are required of all students: Advocacy and Research, Civil Procedure I and II, Contracts I and II, Criminal Law, Lawyering, Legal Research and Writing, Property, and Torts. Required upper-level courses consist of completion of a writing requirement, Constitutional Law, Criminal Procedure, Evidence, and Professional Responsibility. The required orientation program for first-year students is a 3-day program consisting of interactive meetings with administration, faculty, alumni, and student organizations designed to acclimate students to the law school. It includes introductory sessions to their legal research and writing course, as well as a luncheon with alumni.

Electives
The School of Law offers concentrations in corporate law, criminal law, environmental law, family law, intellectual property law, international law, labor law, litigation, securities law, tax law, alternative dispute resolution, health care law, public law & policy, real estate law, estate planning, and electronic & commercial law. The most widely taken electives are Trial Practice, Business Organizations, and Estates and Trusts.

Graduation Requirements
In order to graduate, candidates must have a GPA of 77.5 and must have completed the upper-division writing requirement.

Organizations
Students edit the *Missouri Law Review*, the Journal of *Environmental and Sustainability Law*, and *Journal of Dispute Resolution*. Moot court competitions include the National Moot Court, ABA Moot Court, and the Polsinelli Shughart Fall Moot Court. Other competitions are Negotiation, Client Counseling, First Year Moot Court, Attorney General's Cup, and Mock Trial. Student organizations, local chapters of national associations, and campus organizations include the Board of Advocates, the Student Bar Association, the Women's Law Association, the Federalist Society, Phi Alpha Delta, the American Constitution Society for Law & Policy, the Black Law Students Association, the Non-Traditional Law Student Association, and the Association of Intellectual Property and Entertainment Law.

Library
The law library contains 421,208 hardcopy volumes and 112,921 microform volume equivalents, and subscribes to 2,635 serial publications. Such online databases and networks as CALI, DIALOG, Legal-Trac, LEXIS, OCLC First Search, WESTLAW, BNA-ALL, CCH Intelliconnect, HeinOnline, MOBIUS, Pro Quest, and Kluwer International are available to law students for research. Special library collections include U.S. and Missouri state documents, a nineteenth-century criminal trial collection, the Lloyd L. Gaines Digital Collection, and the Fratcher Rare Book Collection. The ratio of library volumes to faculty is 15,043 to 1 and to students is 977 to 1. The ratio of seats in the library to students is 1 to 1.

Faculty
The law school has 28 full-time and 20 part-time faculty members, of whom 17 are women. According to AAUP standards for Category I institutions, faculty salaries are average. The ratio of full-time students to full-time faculty in an average class is 13 to 1; in a clinic, 7 to 1. The law school has a regular program of bringing visiting professors and other distinguished lecturers and visitors to campus. There is a chapter of the Order of the Coif; 29 faculty are members.

Students
About 38% of the student body are women; 15%, minorities; 7%, African American; 2%, Asian American; 3%, Hispanic; and 3%, multicultural. The average age of entering students is 25; age range is 20 to 47. About 62% of students enter directly from undergraduate school, 12% have a graduate degree, and 38% have worked full-time prior to entering law school. About 11% drop out after the first year for academic or personal reasons; 89% remain to receive a law degree.

Placement

J.D.s awarded:	141

Services available through: a separate law school placement center, the university placement center, and Business and Public Administration Career Services.

Services: counseling on professional development and career growth; networking opportunities and development of networking skills; and long-distance interviewing and internships through video teleconferencing.

Special features: individual counseling for each student, an active and successful judicial clerkship committee, and active alumni support.

Full-time job interviews:	8 employers
Summer job interviews:	19 employers
Placement by graduation:	47% of class
Placement within 9 months:	82% of class
Average starting salary:	$12,000 to $120,000

Areas of placement:

Private practice 2–10 attorneys	22%
Private practice 11–25 attorneys	8%
Private practice 26–50 attorneys	3%
Private practice 51–100 attorneys	1%
Private practice 100+ attorneys	17%
Business/industry	19%
Government	15%
Public interest	7%
Judicial clerkships	5%
Academic	3%

School of Law

500 East 52nd Street
Kansas City, MO 64110-2499

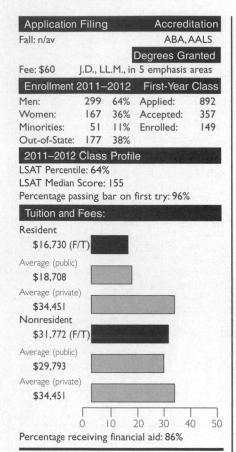

Application Filing	Accreditation
Fall: n/av	ABA, AALS

	Degrees Granted
Fee: $60	J.D., LL.M., in 5 emphasis areas

Enrollment 2011–2012		First-Year Class	
Men:	299 64%	Applied:	892
Women:	167 36%	Accepted:	357
Minorities:	51 11%	Enrolled:	149
Out-of-State:	177 38%		

2011–2012 Class Profile
LSAT Percentile: 64%
LSAT Median Score: 155
Percentage passing bar on first try: 96%

Tuition and Fees:

Resident
$16,730 (F/T)

Average (public)
$18,708

Average (private)
$34,451

Nonresident
$31,772 (F/T)

Average (public)
$29,793

Average (private)
$34,451

0 10 20 30 40 50

Percentage receiving financial aid: 86%

ADMISSIONS

In the fall of 2011 first-year class, 892 applied, 357 were accepted, and 149 enrolled. Sixteen transfers enrolled. The median LSAT percentile of the most recent first-year class was 64; the median GPA was 3.3 on a scale of 4.0. The lowest LSAT percentile accepted was 36; the highest was 96.

Requirements
Applicants must take the LSAT. Minimum acceptable GPA is 2.0 on a scale of 4.0. The most important admission factors include academic achievement, LSAT results, and personal interview. No specific undergraduate courses are required. Candidates are interviewed.

Procedure
Applicants should submit an application form, LSAT results, transcripts, a personal statement, a nonrefundable application fee of $60, 2 letters of recommendation, and two seat deposits totaling $500.

Notification of the admissions decision is on a rolling basis. The law school uses the LSAC.

Special
The law school recruits minority and disadvantaged students by means of minority recruitment, forums, personal letters, and telephone calls to potential applicants. Requirements are different for out-of-state students. Transfer students must have one year of credit, must have a minimum GPA of 2.3, must have attended an ABA-approved law school, and must submite a personal statement.

Costs

Tuition and fees for the 2011–2012 academic year are $15,438 for full-time in-state students and $30,480 for out-of-state students. Tuition for part-time students is $9,263 for in-state students and $18,288 out-of-state. On-campus room and board costs about $18,108 annually.

Financial Aid

About 86% of current law students receive some form of aid. The average annual amount of aid from all sources combined, including scholarships, loans, and work contracts, is $36,087; maximum, $78,965. Awards are based on need and merit combined. The required financial statement is the FAFSA. The aid application deadline for fall entry is March 1. Special funds for minority or disadvantaged students include scholarships and out-of-state tuition waivers. First-year students are notified about their financial aid application at time of acceptance.

About the Law School

University of Missouri-Kansas City School of Law was established in 1895 and is a public institution. The 93-acre campus is in an urban area in Kansas City. The primary mission of the law school is to be an urban, public law school that prepares men and women for the practice of law and for policy-forming functions in government, business, and community life, while providing a curriculum that offers a learning experience integrating academic theory with practical skills. Students have access to federal, state, county, city, and local agencies, courts, correctional facilities, law firms, and legal

aid organizations in the Kansas City area. Clerkship opportunities are available in the numerous nearby law firms and government agencies. Facilities of special interest to law students include "virtual office" suites shared by faculty and students, designed to foster the exchange of ideas and promote collegiality between faculty and students. The school has more than 121,000 square feet of space, including the E.E. "Tom" Thompson Courtroom, which is equipped with audiovisual equipment, used to augment the advocacy training program of the school. Digital classrooms with wireless computer access enhance the learning experience for students. The Leon E. Bloch Law Library is a modern facility that combines the traditions of print with electronic media. Housing for students is limited on campus, but a large selection of reasonably priced housing is available off campus. About 95% of the law school facilities are accessible to the physically disabled.

Calendar

The law school operates on a traditional semester basis. Courses for full-time students are offered both day and evening, and must be completed within 5 years. For part-time students, courses are offered both day and evening, and must be completed within 5 years. New full- and part-time students are admitted in the fall. There is a 7-week summer session. Transferable summer courses are offered.

Programs

In addition to the J.D., the law school offers the LL.M. in 5 emphasis areas. Students may take relevant courses in other programs and apply credit toward the J.D.; a maximum of 10 credits may be applied. The following joint degrees may be earned: J.D./M.B.A. (Juris Doctor/Master of Business Administration) and J.D./M.P.A (Juris Doctor/Master of Public Administration).

Required
To earn the J.D., candidates must complete 91 total credits, of which 51–54 are for required courses. They must maintain a minimum GPA of 2.0 in the required courses. The following first-year courses are required of all students: Civil Procedure I, Constitutional Law, Contracts I and II, Introduction to Law I and II,

Phone: 816-235-1644
Fax: 816-235-5276
E-mail: brooksdu@umkc.edu
Web: law.umkc.edu

Contact

Debbie Brooks, Associate Dean, 816-235-1672 for general inquiries; Linda Lawrence, Financial Aid Coordinator, 816-235-1236 for financial aid information.

MISSOURI

Property I and II, and Torts. Required upper-level courses consist of an advanced Torts course, Business Organizations, Civil Procedure II, Criminal Procedure I, Evidence, Federal Taxation, Jurisprudence course, Professional Responsibility, and Research and Writing requirement. All students must take clinical courses. The required orientation program for first-year students is a 2-day program that introduces students to all aspects of law school and legal study.

Electives

The School of Law offers concentrations in family law, international law, litigation, tax law, business and entrepreneurial law, urban, land use, and environmental law, and estates and trust planning. In addition, in-house clinics from 2 to 6 credit hours include child and family services, tax, and entrepreneurial law and practice. Seminars for 2 or 3 credit hours include Civil Rights Litigation, Gender and Justice, and Famous Trials. Internships from 2 to 6 credit hours include legal aid, public defender trial, prosecutor, and sports law. Research is conducted as part of the research and writing requirement for all students. Introduction to Law and Legal Processes, for 5 hours, requires all students to engage in research, case analysis, and synthesis, and Advanced Legal Writing, a 3-credit-hour course for upper-level students focuses on drafting seminars in corporate law and litigation. Credit may be given for independent study/research projects conducted under faculty supervision, and which may include empirical studies/data gathering. The Cohen, Gage, and Smith Lecture Series brings national speakers to the law school. Study abroad is possible in China, Ireland, and Wales. Structured study groups are offered in 1 substantive course in each first-year section. Trained upper-level study leaders model effective learning strategies and assist in writing/synthesis skills. An academic enrichment program, focusing on analytical, organization, and exam-writing skills, is offered. The Black Law Students Association, APILSA, and the National Hispanic Bar Association work closely with the law school in offering educational and cultural programs that enhance cultural diversity and sensitivity. The law school has more than 20 student groups in all interest areas that sponsor programs on a regular basis. The most widely taken electives are Family Law, Trial and Appellate Advocacy, and Estates and Trusts.

Graduation Requirements

In order to graduate, candidates must have a GPA of 2.0, and must have completed the upper-division writing requirement, the jurisprudential requirement, the advanced torts requirement, and the professional skills requirement.

Organizations

Students edit the *UMKC Law Review* and the *Journal of the American Academy of Matrimonial Lawyers*. Annual moot court competitions include the National Moot Court, Jessup International Law, and the National Appellate Advocacy Competition. Other competitions include the National Trial, Duberstein Bankruptcy Moot Court, Environmental Law, Frederick Douglass Moot Court, American Association for Justice Mock Trial, Client Counseling, and ABA Negotiation. Law student organizations include Public Interest Law Association, Business and Tax Society, and Environmental Law Society. Local chapters of national associations include Phi Alpha Delta, Theta Phi, Phi Delta Phi, and the Federalist Society.

Library

The law library contains 230,215 hardcopy volumes and 125,573 microform volume equivalents, and subscribes to 1,889 serial publications. Such online databases and networks as CALI, CIS Universe, DIALOG, Infotrac, Legal-Trac, LEXIS, Mathew Bender, OCLC First Search, WESTLAW, Wilsonline Indexes, OCLC Merlin, and INNOPAC are available to law students for research. Special library collections include a depository for federal, Missouri, and Kansas documents, an urban law collection, and a tax law concentration. The ratio of library volumes to faculty is 2,423 to 1 and to students is 494 to 1. The ratio of seats in the library to students is 1 to 1.

Faculty

The law school has 48 full-time and 47 part-time faculty members, of whom 29 are women. According to AAUP standards for Category I institutions, faculty salaries are below average. About 21% of full-time faculty have a graduate law degree in

Placement

J.D.s awarded:	154

Services available through: a separate law school placement center.

Services: career services, e-job bulletins, and the career services library.

Special features: support and resources for students interested in solo and small firm practice.

Summer job interviews:	21 employers
Placement by graduation:	19% of class
Placement within 9 months:	73% of class
Average starting salary:	$30,000 to $110,000

Areas of placement:

Private practice 2–10 attorneys	25%
Private practice 11–25 attorneys	8%
Private practice 26–50 attorneys	3%
Private practice 51–100 attorneys	3%
Business/industry	15%
Judicial clerkships	12%
Government	11%
Academic	2%

addition to the J.D. The ratio of full-time students to full-time faculty in an average class is 13 to 1; in a clinic, 6 to 1. The law school has a regular program of bringing visiting professors and other distinguished lecturers and visitors to campus.

Students

About 36% of the student body are women; 11%, minorities; 4%, African American; 3%, Asian American; 3%, Hispanic; and 1%, Native American. The majority of students come from Missouri (62%). The average age of entering students is 26; age range is 21 to 63. About 11% of students have a graduate degree. About 10% drop out after the first year for academic or personal reasons; 90% remain to receive a law degree.

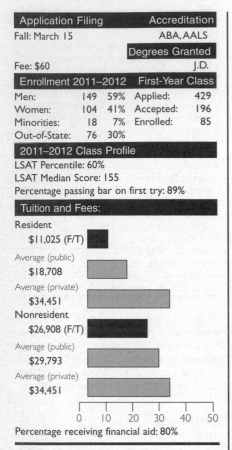

Application Filing	Accreditation
Fall: March 15	ABA, AALS
	Degrees Granted
Fee: $60	J.D.

Enrollment 2011–2012		First-Year Class	
Men:	149 59%	Applied:	429
Women:	104 41%	Accepted:	196
Minorities:	18 7%	Enrolled:	85
Out-of-State:	76 30%		

2011–2012 Class Profile
LSAT Percentile: 60%
LSAT Median Score: 155
Percentage passing bar on first try: 89%

Tuition and Fees:

Resident
$11,025 (F/T)

Average (public)
$18,708

Average (private)
$34,451

Nonresident
$26,908 (F/T)

Average (public)
$29,793

Average (private)
$34,451

0 10 20 30 40 50

Percentage receiving financial aid: 80%

ADMISSIONS

In the fall of 2011 first-year class, 429 applied, 196 were accepted, and 85 enrolled. Eleven transfers enrolled. The median LSAT percentile of the most recent first-year class was 60; the median GPA was 3.4 on a scale of 4.0. The lowest LSAT percentile accepted was 5; the highest was 92.

Requirements

Applicants must have a bachelor's degree and take the LSAT. The most important admission factors include academic achievement, life experience, and LSAT results. No specific undergraduate courses are required. Candidates are not interviewed.

Procedure

The application deadline for fall entry is March 15. Applicants should submit an application form, LSAT results, transcripts, TOEFL (if applicable), a nonrefundable application fee of $60, 3 letters of recommendation, and two personal statements. Notification of the admissions decision is April 15. The law school uses the LSAC.

Special

The law school recruits minority and disadvantaged students by means of special recruiting efforts aimed at Native American and other minority students. Requirements are different for out-of-state students. Transfer students must have one year of credit, must have a minimum GPA of 2, must have attended an ABA-approved law school, and must be in good standing.

Costs

On-campus room and board costs about $12,840 annually; books and supplies run $1,200.

Financial Aid

About 80% of current law students receive some form of aid. The average annual amount of aid from all sources combined, including scholarships, loans, and work contracts, is $23,800; maximum, $40,948. Awards are based on need. The required financial statement is the FAFSA. The aid application deadline for fall entry is February 15. Special funds for minority or disadvantaged students include Native American fee waivers and scholarships. First-year students are notified about their financial aid application at a time determined by the University Financial Aid Office.

About the Law School

University of Montana School of Law was established in 1911 and is a public institution. The campus is in the small town of Missoula, Montana. The primary mission of the law school is to teach a competency-based curriculum. Legal writing, trial practice, and clinical programs require students to demonstrate their abilities to apply highly technical legal knowledge to practical situations. Students have access to federal, state, county, city, and local agencies, courts, correctional facilities, law firms, and legal aid organizations in the Missoula area. Students in clinics benefit from natural resource groups and Native American tribal courts and governments. Facilities of special interest to law students include a computerized courtroom facility and first-year moot "law firms." Housing for students is available for students in university housing; apartments and houses are available for rent in the community. All law school facilities are accessible to the physically disabled.

Calendar

The law school operates on a traditional semester basis. Courses are offered days only, and must be completed within 3 years. New students are admitted in the fall. There is a 6-week summer session. Transferable summer courses are offered.

Programs

Students may take relevant courses in other programs and apply credit toward the J.D. The following joint degrees may be earned: J.D./M.B.A. (Juris Doctor/Master of Business Administration), J.D./M.P.A. (Juris Doctor/Master of Public Administration), and J.D./M.S. (Juris Doctor/Master of Science in Environmental Studies).

Required

To earn the J.D., candidates must complete 90 total credits, of which 58 are for required courses. They must maintain a minimum GPA of 2.0 in the required courses. The following first-year courses are required of all students: Civil Procedure I and II, Contracts I and II, Criminal Law and Procedure I, Lawyering, and Torts I and II. Required upper-level courses consist of Advanced Writing Component, Business Organizations, Clinical Training, Constitutional Law, Evidence, Federal Tax, Professional Responsibility, Property I and II, and Trial Practice. All students must take clinical courses. The required orientation program for first-year students is 5 days and includes concepts of jurisprudence, the role of lawyers in society, legal history, and other topics.

Electives

The School of Law offers concentrations in corporate law, criminal law, environmental law, family law, litigation, tax law, torts and insurance, and Indian law. In addition, clinics, field work, and internships include the Criminal Defense Clinic, Montana Legal Services, and Natural

Phone: 406-243-2698
Fax: 406-243-6601
E-mail: *lori.freeman@umontana.edu*
Web: *http://www.umt.edu/law*

Contact

Lori Freeman, Director of Admissions & Career Services, 406-243-2698 for general inquiries; Connie Bowman, 406-243-5524 for financial aid information.

MONTANA

Resource Clinic for 1 to 4 credit hours for third-year students. Seminars include Contemporary Problems in Constitutional Law, Problems in Estate Planning, and Problems in Indian Law Regulation for 2 credit hours each, and open to second- and third-year students. Independent study programs designed by law students and professors for 1 to 2 credit hours for third-year students and periodic law reform projects for second- and third-year students, for no credit hours, are available. Special lectures include the Blankenbaker Lecture in Ethics and the Judge William B. Jones and Judge Edward A. Tamm Judicial Lecture Series. Tutorial programs include the Academic Assistance Program. Minority programs are sponsored by the Native American Law Students Association. Periodic programs are offered by the Federalist Society, Women's Law Caucus, Phi Delta Phi, Student Bar Association, and 8 other student groups. The most widely taken electives are Environmental Law, Tax of Property Transactions, and Estate Planning.

Graduation Requirements

In order to graduate, candidates must have a GPA of 2.0 and must have completed the upper-division writing requirement.

Organizations

Students edit the *Montana Law Review* and the *Public Land and Resource Law Review*. Moot court competitions include National Moot Court Team, NALSA Moot Court Team, Pace Environmental Moot Court Team, and International Law Moot Court Team (Jessup). Other competitions include ATLA Trial Team, ABA Negotiations Team, and ABA Client Counseling Team. Student organizations include the Student Bar Association, Phi Delta Phi, and Women's Law Caucus. Local chapters of national organizations include American Trial Lawyers and ACLU.

Library

The law library contains 135,535 hardcopy volumes and 35,109 microform volume equivalents. Such online databases and networks as CALI, LEXIS, OCLC First Search, WESTLAW, MontLaw, HeinOnline, Law Library microfiche Consortium, BNA, CCH, and Making Modern Law are available to law students for research. The ratio of library volumes to faculty is 4,490 to 1 and to students is 674 to 1. The ratio of seats in the library to students is 1 to 1.

Faculty

The law school has 22 full-time and 16 part-time faculty members, of whom 15 are women. According to AAUP standards for Category I institutions, faculty salaries are well below average. The ratio of full-time students to full-time faculty in an average class is 19 to 1; in a clinic, 10 to 1. The law school has a regular program of bringing visiting professors and other distinguished lecturers and visitors to campus.

Students

About 41% of the student body are women; 7%, minorities; 1%, Asian American; 3%, Hispanic; and 3%, Native American. The majority of students come from Montana (70%). The average age of entering students is 28; age range is 21 to 45. About 20% of students enter directly from undergraduate school, and 15% have a graduate degree.

Placement

J.D.s awarded:	80
Services available through: a separate law school placement center.	
Special features: semiannual on-campus recruitment conferences.	
Full-time job interviews:	10 employers
Summer job interviews:	10 employers
Placement by graduation:	40% of class
Placement within 9 months:	88% of class
Average starting salary:	$47,369
Areas of placement:	
Private practice 2–10 attorneys	29%
Judicial clerkships	21%
Government	11%
Advanced degree program	11%
Public interest	8%
Business/industry	5%

College of Law

P.O. Box 830902
Lincoln, NE 68583-0902

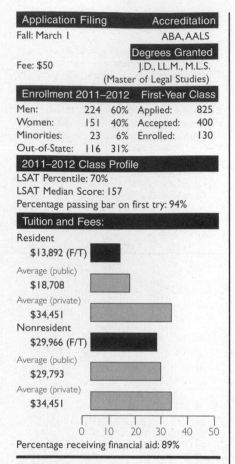

Application Filing	Accreditation
Fall: March 1	ABA, AALS
	Degrees Granted
Fee: $50	J.D., LL.M., M.L.S.
	(Master of Legal Studies)

Enrollment 2011–2012		First-Year Class	
Men:	224 60%	Applied:	825
Women:	151 40%	Accepted:	400
Minorities:	23 6%	Enrolled:	130
Out-of-State:	116 31%		

2011–2012 Class Profile
LSAT Percentile: 70%
LSAT Median Score: 157
Percentage passing bar on first try: 94%

Tuition and Fees:

Resident
$13,892 (F/T)

Average (public)
$18,708

Average (private)
$34,451

Nonresident
$29,966 (F/T)

Average (public)
$29,793

Average (private)
$34,451

0 10 20 30 40 50

Percentage receiving financial aid: 89%

ADMISSIONS

In the fall of 2011 first-year class, 825 applied, 400 were accepted, and 130 enrolled. Five transfers enrolled. The median LSAT percentile of the most recent first-year class was 70; the median GPA was 3.5 on a scale of 4.0. The lowest LSAT percentile accepted was 33; the highest was 99.

Requirements
Applicants must have a bachelor's degree and take the LSAT. The most important admission factors include LSAT results, GPA, and academic achievement. No specific undergraduate courses are required. Candidates are not interviewed.

Procedure
The application deadline for fall entry is March 1. Applicants should submit an application form, LSAT results, transcripts, a personal statement, a nonrefundable application fee of $50, and 2 letters of recommendation. Notification

of the admissions decision is on a rolling basis after December 1. The law school uses the LSAC.

Special
The law school recruits minority and disadvantaged students by sponsoring and attending events to promote the College of Law. Requirements are different for out-of-state students. Transfer students must have one year of credit, must have attended an ABA-approved law school, must submit a personal statement, and must be in good standing at the end of a full year of study and eligible to continue at their current law school. Other requirements may apply.

Costs
Tuition and fees for the 2011–2012 academic year are $10,788 for full-time in-state students and $26,862 for out-of-state students. On-campus room and board costs about $9,248 annually; books and supplies run $1,378.

Financial Aid
About 89% of current law students receive some form of aid. Awards are based on need and merit combined. Required financial statements are the FAFSA and institutional need-based grant form. The aid application deadline for fall entry is May 1. Special funds for minority or disadvantaged students include funds for opportunity scholarships for students who have overcome economic or educational disadvantages. First-year students are notified about their financial aid application at time of acceptance.

About the Law School
University of Nebraska-Lincoln College of Law was established in 1888 and is a public institution. The 339-acre campus is in a suburban area on the east campus of the University of Nebraska. The primary mission of the law school is to provide an excellent, affordable legal education with a balance between legal theory and professional skills in the atmosphere of a small law school. Students have access to federal, state, county, city, and local agencies, courts, correctional facilities, law firms, and legal aid organizations in the Lincoln area. As Lincoln is the state capital, the legislature, the State Supreme Court, and

the Court of Appeals are nearby, as are the Nebraska Attorney General's office and state agencies. Facilities of interest to students include the Shermon S. Welpton, Jr. courtroom, which is used for actual trials as well as practical skills training. Housing for students is available on and off campus. All law school facilities are accessible to the physically disabled.

Calendar
The law school operates on a traditional semester basis. Courses are offered days only, and must be completed within 3 years. New full-time students are admitted in the fall. There is a 5-week summer session. Transferable summer courses are offered.

Programs
In addition to the J.D., the law school offers the LL.M. and M.L.S. (Master of Legal Studies). Students may take relevant courses in other programs and apply credit toward the J.D.; a maximum of 6 credits may be applied. The following joint degrees may be earned: J.D./M.A. (Juris Doctor/Master of Arts in Psychology, Gerontology, Political Science, or Journalism), J.D./M.B.A. (Juris Doctor/Master of Business Administration), J.D./M.C.R.P. (Juris Doctor/Master of Community and Regional Planning), J.D./M.P.A. (Juris Doctor/Master of Professional Accountancy), and J.D./Ph.D (Juris Doctor/Doctor of Philosophy in Psychology and Educational Administration).

Required
To earn the J.D., candidates must complete 93 total credits, of which 45 are for required courses. They must maintain a minimum GPA of 2.0 in the required courses. The following first-year courses are required of all students: Civil Procedure, Contracts, Criminal Law, International Perspectives in the U.S. Legal System: Practicing Law in a Global Legal Environment, Legal Research and Writing, Property, and Torts. Required upper-level courses consist of Constitutional Law I, Legal Profession, a professional skills course, and a seminar with substantial writing requirement. The required orientation program for first-year students is 2 days prior to the beginning of the fall semester. Students listen to speakers, tour the college, meet faculty and upper-level students, and attend a legal writing class.

Phone: 402-472-8333
Fax: 402-472-5185
E-mail: *lawadm@unl.edu*
Web: *http://law.unl.edu*

Contact

Tracy Warren, Assistant Dean, 402-472-8333 for general inquiries; Glenda J. Pierce, Associate Dean, 402-472-2161 for financial aid information.

NEBRASKA

Students also participate in an orientation on professionalism and ethics with judges and attorneys.

Electives

The College of Law offers concentrations in corporate law, criminal law, entertainment law, environmental law, family law, intellectual property law, international law, juvenile law, labor law, litigation, securities law, sports law, tax law, torts and insurance, and students may design an individualized program of concentrated study in virtually any area. In addition, students who have obtained senior standing are eligible to take either a 6-credit hour civil or criminal clinic, 4-hour civil clinic, or 6-hour immigration clinic. Second- or third-year students must take a 3-credit-hour seminar with a substantial writing requirement. Externships are available for 1 to 3 credit hours. A 1- to 3-credit-hour research program in a selected field under the supervision of a faculty member is available to any upper-level student. With the approval of a sponsoring faculty member, students may register for 1 to 3 hours of externship credit to be earned in a field placement program. Each externship involves at least 40 hours of field experience for every credit hour earned. Special lecture series include many national and international speakers. The Academic Resource Program offers a non-credit skills class for first-year students to assist in developing such skills as note taking, case briefing, and exam taking. The most widely taken electives are Business Association, Evidence, and Wills and Trusts.

Graduation Requirements

In order to graduate, candidates must have a GPA of 2.0, must have completed the upper-division writing requirement, and must have taken Constitutional Law I and a professional skills course.

Organizations

Students edit the *Nebraska Law Review* and an online Nebraska Law Review Bulletin. Moot court competitions include the Fall Grether Moot Court Competition for second-year students, Allen Moot Court competition, and the Animal Law Competition. Other competitions include Client Counseling and National Trial. Student organizations include the Student Bar

Association, Women's Law Caucus, and Community Legal Education Project. Delta Theta Phi, ABA-Law Student Division, and Phi Alpha Delta have local chapters. Other organizations include the Multicultural Legal Society, Environmental and Agriculture Law Society, and Equal Justice Society.

Library

The law library contains 254,068 hardcopy volumes and 179,623 microform volume equivalents, and subscribes to 3,736 serial publications. Such online databases and networks as CALI, CIS Universe, Infotrac, Legal-Trac, LEXIS, Mathew Bender, OCLC First Search, WESTLAW, Wilsonline Indexes, Expanded Academic Index Full Text, EBSCO host, JSTOR, BNA, LLMC Digital, RIA Checkpoint, MOML, IFLP, ILP, and CCH IntelliConnect are available to law students for research. Special library collections include a selected federal government depository and the Great Plains Tax Library. The ratio of library volumes to faculty is 7,699 to 1 and to students is 609 to 1. The ratio of seats in the library to students is 1 to 1.

Faculty

The law school has 37 full-time and 28 part-time faculty members, of whom 4 are women. According to AAUP standards for Category I institutions, faculty salaries are average. About 21% of full-time faculty have a graduate law degree in addition to the J.D. The ratio of full-time students to full-time faculty in an average class is 12 to 1; in a clinic, 8 to 1. The law school has a regular program of bringing visiting professors and other distinguished lecturers and visitors to campus. There is a chapter of the Order of the Coif; 31 faculty and 794 graduates are members.

Students

About 40% of the student body are women; 6%, minorities; 1%, African American; 2%, Asian American; 2%, Hispanic; and 1%, Native American. The majority of students come from Nebraska (69%). The average age of entering students is 24; age range is 21 to 41. About 55% of students enter directly from undergraduate school, 5% have a graduate degree, and 43% have worked full-time prior to entering law school. About 6% drop out after the first year for academic or personal reasons; 94% remain to receive a law degree.

Placement

J.D.s awarded:	130
Services available through: a separate law school placement center.	
Services: regular presentations on practice areas and alternative legal careers.	
Special features: video conferencing capabilities and newly renovated interview facilities.	
Full-time job interviews:	15 employers
Summer job interviews:	24 employers
Placement by graduation:	74% of class
Placement within 9 months:	90% of class
Average starting salary:	$32,000 to $150,000
Areas of placement:	
Private practice 2–10 attorneys	38%
Private practice 11–25 attorneys	6%
Private practice 26–50 attorneys	3%
Private practice 51–100 attorneys	3%
Private practice 100+ attorneys	5%
Government	16%
Business/industry	16%
Judicial clerkships	7%
Academic	3%
Public interest	2%
Military	1%

University of Nebraska-Lincoln **529**

William S. Boyd School of Law

4505 Maryland Parkway, Box 451003
Las Vegas, NV 89154-1003

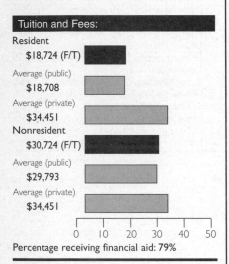

Application Filing		Accreditation	
Fall: March 15		ABA, AALS	
		Degrees Granted	
Fee: $50		J.D.	
Enrollment 2011–2012		First-Year Class	
Men:	261 53%	Applied:	1,737
Women:	227 47%	Accepted:	384
Minorities:	142 29%	Enrolled:	158
Out-of-State:	102 21%		

2011–2012 Class Profile
LSAT Median Score: 158
Percentage passing bar on first try: 85%

Tuition and Fees:

Resident
$18,724 (F/T)

Average (public)
$18,708

Average (private)
$34,451

Nonresident
$30,724 (F/T)

Average (public)
$29,793

Average (private)
$34,451

0   10   20   30   40   50

Percentage receiving financial aid: 79%

ADMISSIONS
In the fall of 2011 first-year class, 1737 applied, 384 were accepted, and 158 enrolled. Nineteen transfers enrolled. The median GPA of the most recent first-year class was 3.5.

Requirements
Applicants must have a bachelor's degree and take the LSAT. No specific undergraduate courses are required. Candidates are not interviewed.

Procedure
The application deadline for fall entry is March 15. Applicants should submit an application form, LSAT results, transcripts, a personal statement, a nonrefundable application fee of $50, a letter of recommendation, and a resume. Notification of the admissions decision is generally April. The law school uses the LSAC.

Special
The law school recruits minority and disadvantaged students through outreach to various individuals and community organizations to generate a large and diverse applicant pool. Requirements are not different for out-of-state students. Transfer students must have one year of credit, must have attended an ABA-approved law school, must submit a personal statement, and must undergo an admissions committee review.

Costs
Tuition and fees for the 2011–2012 academic year are $18,000 for full-time in-state students and $30,000 for out-of-state students. Books and supplies run $1,700.

Financial Aid
About 79% of current law students receive some form of aid. The maximum annual amount of aid from all sources combined, including scholarships, loans, and work contracts, is $34,860. Awards are based on need and merit combined. The required financial statement is the FAFSA. The aid application deadline for fall entry is February 1. First-year students are notified about their financial aid application on a rolling basis.

About the Law School
University of Nevada, Las Vegas William S. Boyd School of Law was established in 1998 and is a public institution. The 335-acre campus is in an urban area in one of the fastest growing metropolitan areas. The primary mission of the law school is to serve the State of Nevada and the national and international legal and academic communities through an innovative educational program that will train ethical and effective lawyers and leaders, and to stress community service and excellent scholarship. Students have access to federal, state, county, city, and local agencies, courts, correctional facilities, law firms, and legal aid organizations in the Las Vegas area. Facilities of special interest to law students include the Thomas and Mack Moot Court Facility, which supports the school's trial advocacy, Kids' Court, and appellate advocacy programs and provides a venue for judicial proceedings by state and federal courts, including the Nevada Supreme Court and the U.S. Court of Appeals for the Ninth Circuit. Housing

for students is not available on campus, but is abundantly available off campus. All law school facilities are accessible to the physically disabled.

Calendar
The law school operates on a traditional semester basis. Courses for full-time students are offered both day and evening, and must be completed within 5 years. For part-time students, courses are offered both day and evening, and must be completed within 6 years. New full- and part-time students are admitted in the fall. There is a 10-week summer session. Transferable summer courses are offered.

Programs
Students may take relevant courses in other programs and apply credit toward the J.D.; a maximum of 6 credits may be applied. The following joint degrees may be earned: J.D./M.B.A. (Juris Doctor/Master of Business Administration), J.D./M.S.W. (Juris Doctor/Master of Social Work), and J.D./Ph.D. (Juris Doctor/Doctor of Philosophy in Education).

Required
To earn the J.D., candidates must complete 89 total credits, of which 41 are for required courses. The following first-year courses are required of all students: Civil Procedure/Alternative Dispute Resolution I and II, Contracts I, Constitutional Law I, Criminal Law I, Introduction to Law, Lawyering Process I and II, Property I and II, and Torts. Required upper-level courses consist of Constitutional Law II, Lawyering Process III, and Professional Responsibility. The required orientation program for first-year students is Introduction to Law, a 1-week course.

Electives
The Capital Defense Clinic, Child Welfare Clinic, and Immigration Clinic, worth 1 to 6 credits each, afford students the opportunity to represent clients in real-life settings, under faculty supervision. Each clinic also has a classroom component. In the Child Welfare Clinic, students represent children, parents, or guardians in child protection, termination of parental rights, guardianship, and related matters that involve contested trials, administrative advocacy and sometimes cutting-edge

Phone: 702-895-2440
Fax: 702-895-2414
E-mail: request@law.unlv.edu
Web: www.law.unlv.edu

Contact

Nathan Neely, Director of Admissions and Financial Aid, 702-895-2440 for general inquiries; Christopher Kypunos, Associate Director, 702-895-3424 for financial aid information.

NEVADA

legal issues. In the Juvenile Justice Clinic, students represent children who have been charged in juvenile delinquency proceedings. In the Capital Defense Clinic, students represent defendants in Nevada death penalty cases, focusing primarily on preparing mitigating evidence and arguments. In the Immigration Clinic, students represent clients in a variety of matters involving immigration and immigrant rights. In the Education Clinic, students represent children and parents in education matters in the Clark County School System, such as special education, suspension, expulsion, and English as a Second Language. In the Criminal Appellate Clinic, students represent young convicted criminal defendants in state post-conviction appellate proceedings. Seminars include Bill of Rights in Law and History, Education Law and Policy, Natural Resources Field Seminar, Domestic Violence, Advanced Intellectual Practice, Death Penalty, and Gaming Policy Law. Government and Public Interest Externships, worth 1 to 12 credits, Judicial Externships, worth 3 to 6 credits, and Legislative Externships, worth 1 to 12 credits, are also offered. Research programs include Directed Readings, where students earn credit for completing readings under the supervision and approval of a faculty member for 1 credit, or Directed Research, where they research and write about a legal topic of their choice under faculty supervision, for 1 to 3 credits. The law school provides an Academic Success Program, a comprehensive network of presentations, activities, tutorials, and workshops designed to stimulate learning and amplify the classroom experience. This program, which supplements the required curriculum, supervises the Center for Academic Success and Enrichment, a student-operated mentoring, advising, and tutoring program. The most widely taken electives are Evidence, Criminal Procedure, and Wills, Trusts, and Estates.

Graduation Requirements

In order to graduate, candidates must have a GPA of 2.0, must have completed the upper-division writing requirement, and must have completed community service and writing requirements.

Organizations

Students edit the *Nevada Law Journal*. Moot Court Competitions include the ABA-LSD National Appellate Advocacy, Jessup International Law Moot Court Competition, and Bar Association of the City of New York National Moot Court Competition. Other competitions include the ABA-LSD Negotiation Competition, Clark County Client Counseling Competition, and Clark County Moot Court Competition. Law student organizations include the American Constitution Society, Federalist Society, and Phi Alpha Delta. Local chapters of national associations include the Student Bar Association, Minority Law Students Association, and Public Interest Law Association. Campus clubs include the Environmental Law Society, Sports and Entertainment Law Association, and Organizations of Woman Law Students.

Library

The law library contains 330,808 hardcopy volumes and 198,454 microform volume equivalents, and subscribes to 3,870 serial publications. Such online databases and networks as CALI, Infotrac, LegalTrac, LEXIS, Mathew Bender, OCLC First Search, and WESTLAW are available to law students for research. The ratio of library volumes to faculty is 4,411 to 1 and to students is 678 to 1. The ratio of seats in the library to students is 1 to 1.

Faculty

The law school has 52 full-time and 23 part-time faculty members, of whom 32 are women. According to AAUP standards for Category I institutions, faculty salaries are above average. About 19% of full-time faculty have a graduate law degree in addition to the J.D. The ratio of full-time students to full-time faculty in an average class is 14 to 1; in a clinic, 8 to 1. The law school has a regular program of bringing visiting professors and other distinguished lecturers and visitors to campus.

Students

About 47% of the student body are women; 29%, minorities; 6%, African American; 11%, Asian American; 10%, Hispanic; and 2%, Native American. The majority of students come from Nevada (79%). The average age of entering students is 27; age range is 21 to 73.

Placement

J.D.s awarded:	145

Services available through: a separate law school placement center.

Services: web-based recruiting and placement software programs accessible 24 hours a day to students and employers; Career Services Library and Resource Center; and judicial clerkship resource manual pertaining to hiring practices of the Nevada and federal judiciary.

Full-time job interviews:	8 employers
Summer job interviews:	35 employers
Placement by graduation:	78% of class
Placement within 9 months:	94% of class
Average starting salary:	$56,000 to $87,500

Areas of placement:

Private practice 2–10 attorneys	27%
Private practice 11–25 attorneys	6%
Private practice 26–50 attorneys	3%
Private practice 51–100 attorneys	3%
Private practice solo	16%
Judicial clerkships	16%
Business/industry	12%
Government	8%
Public interest	4%
Military	2%
Academic	2%

UNIVERSITY OF NEW HAMPSHIRE

School of Law

2 White Street
Concord, NH 03301

Application Filing		Accreditation
Fall: April 1		ABA

		Degrees Granted
Fee: $55		J.D., LL.M.

Enrollment 2011–2012		First-Year Class	
Men:	239 61%	Applied:	1,247
Women:	155 39%	Accepted:	627
Minorities:	75 19%	Enrolled:	146
Out-of-State:	343 87%		

2011–2012 Class Profile

LSAT Percentile: 63%
LSAT Median Score: 155
Percentage passing bar on first try: 82%

Tuition and Fees:

Resident
$39,990 (F/T)

Average (public)
$18,708

Average (private)
$34,451

Nonresident
$39,980 (F/T)

Average (public)
$29,793

Average (private)
$34,451

Percentage receiving financial aid: 92%

ADMISSIONS

In the fall of 2011 first-year class, 1247 applied, 627 were accepted, and 146 enrolled. Two transfers enrolled. The median LSAT percentile of the most recent first-year class was 63; the median GPA was 3.3 on a scale of 4.3. The lowest LSAT percentile accepted was 18; the highest was 97.

Requirements
Applicants must have a bachelor's degree and take the LSAT. The most important admission factors include academic achievement. No specific undergraduate courses are required. Candidates are interviewed.

Procedure
The application deadline for fall entry is April 1. Applicants should submit an application form, LSAT results, transcripts, a personal statement, TOEFL (if applicable), a nonrefundable application fee of $55, and 2 letters of recommendation. Notification of the admissions decision is on a rolling basis. The law school uses the LSAC.

Special
The law school recruits minority and disadvantaged students by participating in minority programs such as the Council on Legal Education Opportunity (CLEO) and the Puerto Rican Legal Defense Fund, actively recruiting self-identified minorities through the Law School Admission Council forums, and offering diversity scholarships. Students are also invited to submit a supplemental statement addressing their challenges and achievements. Requirements are different for out-of-state students. Transfer students must have one year of credit, must have a minimum GPA of 3, must have attended an ABA-approved law school, and must submit a personal statement.

Costs

Tuition and fees for the 2011–2012 academic year are $39,900 for all full-time students. Books and supplies run $1,200.

Financial Aid

About 92% of current law students receive some form of aid. The average annual amount of aid from all sources combined, including scholarships, loans, and work contracts, is $46,375; maximum, $56,644. Awards are based on need and merit combined. Required financial statements are the FAFSA and UNH application and tax return. The aid application deadline for fall entry is open. Special funds for minority or disadvantaged students include diversity scholarships that are available to members of groups currently underrepresented in the law center community. They are awarded based on academic and community involvement factors. First-year students are notified about their financial aid application on a rolling basis after application and acceptance.

About the Law School

University of New Hampshire School of Law was established in 1973 and is a private institution. The 1-acre campus is in a small town 70 miles north of Boston. The primary mission of the law school is to create a learning environment that produces highly capable, confident professionals who will serve clients, employers, and the public with integrity and excellence. Students have access to federal, state, county, city, and local agencies, courts, correctional facilities, law firms, and legal aid organizations in the Concord area. Housing for students is available around the school in residential neighborhoods. About 95% of the law school facilities are accessible to the physically disabled.

Calendar

The law school operates on a traditional semester basis. Courses are offered both day and evening, and must be completed within 3 years. New students are admitted in the fall. There is a 7-week summer session. Transferable summer courses are offered.

Programs

In addition to the J.D., the law school offers the LL.M. Students may take relevant courses in other programs and apply credit toward the J.D. The following joint degrees may be earned: J.D./M.B.A. (Juris Doctor/Master of Business), J.D./M.C.T. (Juris Doctor/Master of Commerce and Technology Law), J.D./M.I.C.L.J. (Juris Doctor/Master of International Criminal Law and Justice), J.D./M.I.P. (Juris Doctor/Master of Intellectual Property), and J.D./M.S.W. (Juris Doctor/Master of Social Work).

Required
To earn the J.D., candidates must complete 85 total credits, of which 39 are for required courses. They must maintain a minimum GPA of 2.0 in the required courses. The following first-year courses are required of all students: a legal perspective course, Civil Procedure, Constitutional Law, Contracts, Introduction to Legal Research and Information Literacy, Legal Analysis I and II, Property, and Torts. Required upper-level courses consist of Administrative Law, Criminal Procedure I, and Professional Responsibility. The required orientation program for first-year students is a 3-day program that includes an overview of the first year academic program, career services, academic support services, student organizations, and student advising, as well as social events.

Electives
The school offers concentrations in criminal law and intellectual property law. In addition, UNH operates 6 clinics in offices designed to emulate a state-of-the-art law office; second- and third-year students represent actual clients in a range of matters.

Phone: 603-228-9217
Fax: 603-229-0425
E-mail: admissions@law.unh.edu
Web: law.unh.edu/admissions/

Contact

Katie McDonald, Dean for Admissions, 603-513-5123 for general inquries; Susan Ahern, Director of Financial Aid, 603-513-5123 for financial aid information.

NEW HAMPSHIRE

Students receive either 4 or 5 credits. Clinics include the Intellectual Property and Business Transaction Clinic, Administrative Advocacy Clinic, Consumer and Commercial Law Clinic, Criminal Practice Clinic, Appellate Defender Program, and IP Amicus Clinic. Research seminars are offered in medical decision making, supreme court issues, and advanced legal research. Externships are available to students after the third semester. Externships are part time for 4 credits or full time for 12 credits. The school has a large number of regular placements, and students may design their own externship as long as it is appropriate for the number of credits and with an experienced practitioner who has committed to educating the student. Second- and third-year students may also take independent study with a specific faculty member for a maximum of 4 credits. Periodically, speakers are invited to the school to lecture on a variety of subjects, including civil rights, health law, patent law, and corporate law. Study abroad is possible through programs provided by ABA-approved schools. In addition, UNH sponsors the Intellectual Property Seminar Institute in Beijing, China (with Tsinghua University) and the eLaw Summer Institute in Cork, Ireland (with University College Cork). Computer tutorial programs are offered to all students. The Academic Success Program works with students individually and in small groups. Teaching assistants are available for individual consultation; all first-year courses have teaching assistants for discussion and explanation. Various student organizations bring in speakers, special programs, and conferences throughout the year. The most widely taken electives are Evidence, Business Associations, and Trademarks.

Graduation Requirements

In order to graduate, candidates must have a GPA of 2.0, must have completed the upper-division writing requirement, must have 6 full-time semesters of residency, must have offset all credits below C- with an equal number of credits of B- or above, and must have satisfied any terms of academic probation or financial obligation.

Organizations

Student-edited publications are *IDEA: The Journal of Law and Technology* and *Pierce Law Review*. The Annual Survey of New Hampshire Law, which publishes articles focusing on recent opinions of the New Hampshire Supreme Court, is a 4-credit, 2-semester course in which second-year students write articles and a third-year student serves as editor. Moot court competitions include the required appellate argument for second semester first-year students. Students annually enter the Giles Sutherland Rich Intellectual Property Moot Court, Saul Lefkowitz Moot Court Competition, National Health Law Competition, Association of Trial Lawyers of America, and Student Trial Advocacy Competition. Students enter legal essay writing contests on a volunteer basis. Law student organizations, local chapters of national associations and campus organizations include Student Intellectual Property Association, Women Law Students Association, Licensing Executive Society, Minority Law Students Association, Phi Alpha Delta, International Law Students Association, Student Bar Association, and Black Law Students Association.

Library

The law library contains 313,143 hardcopy volumes and 652,164 microform volume equivalents, and subscribes to 1,269 serial publications. Such online databases and networks as CALI, CIS Universe, Legal-Trac, LEXIS, OCLC First Search, and WESTLAW are available to law students for research. Special library collections include an intellectual property special collection, a repository for the World Intellectual Property Organization (WIPO), and a federal GPO selective depository. The ratio of library volumes to faculty is 4,015 to 1 and to students is 702 to 1. The ratio of seats in the library to students is 1 to 2.

Faculty

The law school has 21 full-time and 27 part-time faculty members, of whom 21 are women. According to AAUP standards for Category IIB institutions, faculty salaries are average. About 17% of full-time faculty have a graduate law degree in addition to the J.D. The ratio of full-time students to full-time faculty in an average class is 15 to 1; in a clinic, 4 to 1. The law school has a regular program of bringing visiting professors and other distinguished lecturers and visitors to campus.

Placement

J.D.s awarded:	167

Services available through: a separate law school placement center.

Services: video interviews and playbacks; workshops on information interviewing; career planning for students interested in intellectual property, business, public interest, and general practice; and externships for academic credit.

Special features: career services offers individualized service and programs that train all students in critical skills such as resume writing, interview skills, and networking.

Full-time job interviews:	8 employers
Summer job interviews:	8 employers
Placement by graduation:	83% of class
Placement within 9 months:	75% of class
Average starting salary:	$50,000 to $135,000

Areas of placement:

Private practice 2–10 attorneys	31%
Private practice 11–25 attorneys	6%
Private practice 26–50 attorneys	2%
Private practice 51–100 attorneys	13%
Private practice 101+ attorneys	8%
Business/industry	17%
Government	9%
Judicial clerkships	6%
Public interest	4%
Academic	1%

Students

About 39% of the student body are women; 19%, minorities; 4%, African American; 9%, Asian American; and 3%, Hispanic. The average age of entering students is 27; age range is 21 to 51. About 33% of students enter directly from undergraduate school, 17% have a graduate degree, and 67% have worked full-time prior to entering law school. About 8% drop out after the first year for academic or personal reasons; 90% remain to receive a law degree.

UNIVERSITY OF NEW MEXICO

School of Law

MSC11-6070, 1 University of
New Mexico
Albuquerque, NM 87131-0001

Application Filing

Fall: February 15

Accreditation

ABA, AALS

Degrees Granted

Fee: $50 — J.D.

Enrollment 2011–2012 / First-Year Class

Men:	190	52%	Applied:	942
Women:	172	51%	Accepted:	237
Minorities:	163	45%	Enrolled:	113

2011–2012 Class Profile

LSAT Median Score: 157
Percentage passing bar on first try: 86%

Tuition and Fees:

Resident
$14,482 (F/T)

Average (public)
$18,708

Average (private)
$34,451

Nonresident
$32,611 (F/T)

Average (public)
$29,793

Average (private)
$34,451

0   10   20   30   40   50

ADMISSIONS

In the fall of 2011 first-year class, 942 applied, 237 were accepted, and 113 enrolled. The median GPA of the most recent first-year class was 3.3.

Requirements

Applicants must have a bachelor's degree and take the LSAT. No specific undergraduate courses are required. Candidates are not interviewed.

Procedure

The application deadline for fall entry is February 15. Applicants should submit an application form, LSAT results, transcripts, a personal statement, a nonrefundable application fee of $50, a letter of recommendation, an LSAC report, and a resume. Notification of the admissions decision is on a rolling basis.

Special

Requirements are different for out-of-state students in that preference is given to New Mexico residents. Transfer students must have one year of credit, must have attended an ABA-approved law school, and must submit a personal statement and a letter from the dean of the previously attended school. The applicant must be in good academic standing.

Costs

Tuition and fees for the 2011–2012 academic year are $13,292 for full-time in-state students and $31,421 for out-of-state students. On-campus room and board costs about $8,068 annually; books and supplies run $1,126.

Financial Aid

Awards are based on need and merit combined. Required financial statements are the FAFSA and Need Access. The aid application deadline for fall entry is March 1. Special funds for minority or disadvantaged students include graduate fellowships, which are available through the Office of Graduate Studies. First-year students are notified about their financial aid application after acceptance.

About the Law School

University of New Mexico School of Law was established in 1947 and is a public institution. The 600-acre campus is in an urban area in the city of Albuquerque. The primary mission of the law school is to offer a legal education that combines training in legal doctrine, theory, and policy with the development of practical lawyering skills. Emphasis is placed on student-faculty interaction. Students have access to federal, state, county, city, and local agencies, courts, correctional facilities, law firms, and legal aid organizations in the Albuquerque area. Facilities of special interest to law students include Bratton Hall, which, in addition to housing classrooms, seminar rooms, and faculty, staff, and student organization offices, is home to the Utton Transboundary Resources Center, the American Indian Law Center, and the Law Practice Clinic. Housing for students consists of off-campus rental homes and apartments, where most students live, and 200 student family apartments. The university helps with finding housing. All law school facilities are accessible to the physically disabled.

Calendar

The law school operates on a traditional semester basis. Courses are offered days only, and must be completed within 3 years. New students are admitted in the fall. There is a 10-week summer session. Transferable summer courses are offered.

Programs

Students may take relevant courses in other programs and apply credit toward the J.D.; a maximum of 6 credits may be applied. The following joint degrees may be earned: J.D./M.A.L.A.S. (Juris Doctor/Master of Arts in Latin American Studies), J.D./M.B.A. (Juris Doctor/Master of Business Administration), and J.D./M.P.A. (Juris Doctor/Master of Public Administration).

Required

To earn the J.D., candidates must complete 86 total credits, of which 45 are for required courses. They must maintain a minimum GPA of 2.0 in the required courses. The following first-year courses are required of all students: Constitutional Law, Contracts I, Criminal Law, Elements of Legal Argumentation I and II, Historical Introduction to Law, Practicum, Property I, and Torts. Required upper-level courses consist of courses in legal research, professional responsibility, and writing. All students must take clinical courses. The required orientation program for first-year students lasts 2 days.

Electives

The School of Law offers concentrations in Indian law and natural resources and environmental law. Certificate programs are offered. In addition, UNM's Clinical Law Program is a requirement for the J.D. degree. Students, supervised by faculty members, may counsel and advise clients and appear in state, federal, and tribal courts in New Mexico. Judicial and law office externships are available. Individual research, worth from 1 to 3 credits, is available under faculty direction. Summer-abroad programs are available through the Guanajuato Summer Law Institute. Exchange programs are offered with schools in Mexico, Canada, and Australia. Tutorials are available for each substantive course to first-year students. The most widely taken electives are Criminal Procedure I, Civil Procedure II, and Evidence.

Phone: 505-277-0958
Fax: 505-277-9958
E-mail: campos@law.unm.edu
Web: http://lawschool.unm.edu

Contact

Assistant Director of Admissions, 505-277-1030 for general inquiries; Susan Mitchell, Assistant Dean for Admissions and Financial Aid, 505-277-0959 for financial aid information.

NEW MEXICO

Graduation Requirements

In order to graduate, candidates must have a GPA of 2.0, must have completed the upper-division writing requirement, and must have at least 3 full academic years in residence. An ethics course must be taken.

Organizations

The primary law review is the *New Mexico Law Review*, which is published 3 times a year. Students also edit the *Natural Resources Journal and Tribal Law Journal.* Moot court teams attend the Native American Law Student Association, Hispanic, and National Moot Court competitions. Other competitions include the Jessup Moot Court Competition and Health Law Moot Court Competition. Law student organizations include the Student Bar Association, Environmental Law Society, International Law Students Association, Mexican American Law Students Association, Black Law Students Association, and Native American Law Students Association. There are campus chapters of Phi Alpha Delta, Phi Delta Phi, and Association of Trial Lawyers of America/New Mexico.

Library

The law library contains 403,430 hard-copy volumes and 155,256 microform volume equivalents, and subscribes to 1,098 serial publications. Such online databases and networks as CALI, CIS Universe, Infotrac, Legal-Trac, LEXIS, OCLC First Search, WESTLAW, and Wils online Indexes are available to law students for research. Special library collections include a selective federal and New Mexico government document depository, an extensive collection of New Mexico appellate briefs and records, American Indian law, Mexican and Latin American law, and land-grant law documents, Water Policy Collection, and law school archives. The library is also home to the Governor Bruce King Archives and Reading Room. The ratio of library volumes to faculty is 10,616 to 1 and to students is 1,111 to 1. The ratio of seats in the library to students is 1 to 1.

Faculty

The law school has 34 full-time and 82 part-time faculty members, of whom 57 are women. According to AAUP standards for Category 1 institutions, faculty salaries are below average. About 9% of full-time faculty have a graduate law degree in addition to the J.D. The ratio of full-time students to full-time faculty in an average class is 11 to 1; in a clinic, 8 to 1. The law school has a regular program of bringing visiting professors and other distinguished lecturers and visitors to campus. There is a chapter of the Order of the Coif.

Students

About 51% of the student body are women; 45%, minorities; 2%, African American; 2%, Asian American; 28%, Hispanic; and 8%, Native American. The average age of entering students is 28; age range is 21 to 63.

Placement

J.D.s awarded:	108

Services available through: a separate law school placement center and the university placement center.

Services: various career fairs, externships, computer resources, practice area programs, mock interviews, support for students with disabilities, academic counseling from 2 full-time attorney-counselors, mentorship, and judicial clerkship programs.

Special features: a mentoring program between members of the State Bar of New Mexico and law students.

Full-time job interviews:	21 employers
Summer job interviews:	21 employers
Placement by graduation:	56% of class
Placement within 9 months:	91% of class
Average starting salary:	$24,000 to $130,000

Areas of placement:

Private practice 2–10 attorneys	33%
Private practice 11–25 attorneys	4%
Private practice 26–50 attorneys	6%
Private practice 51–100 attorneys	1%
Private practice 101–250 attorneys	1%
Government	19%
Judicial clerkships	14%
Public interest	10%
Academic	5%
Business/industry	2%

UNIVERSITY OF NORTH CAROLINA AT CHAPEL HILL

School of Law

Campus Box 3380,
Van Hecke-Wettach Hall
Chapel Hill, NC 27599-3380

Application Filing		Accreditation	
Fall: March 1		ABA, AALS	
		Degrees Granted	
Fee: $75		J.D.	

Enrollment 2011–2012		First-Year Class	
Men:	379 49%	Applied:	2,576
Women:	393 51%	Accepted:	462
Minorities:	216 28%	Enrolled:	248
Out-of-State:	232 30%		

2011–2012 Class Profile
LSAT Percentile: 88%
LSAT Median Score: 163
Percentage passing bar on first try: 90%

Tuition and Fees:

Resident
  $19,012 (F/T)

Average (public)
  $18,708

Average (private)
  $34,451

Nonresident
  $34,120 (F/T)

Average (public)
  $29,793

Average (private)
  $34,451

0   10   20   30   40   50

Percentage receiving financial aid: 87%

ADMISSIONS

In the fall of 2011 first-year class, 2576 applied, 462 were accepted, and 248 enrolled. Four transfers enrolled. The median LSAT percentile of the most recent first-year class was 88; the median GPA was 3.5 on a scale of 4.0. The lowest LSAT percentile accepted was 30; the highest was 99.

Requirements

Applicants must have a bachelor's degree and take the LSAT. The most important admission factors include academic achievement, LSAT results, and general background. No specific undergraduate courses are required. Candidates are not interviewed.

Procedure

The application deadline for fall entry is March 1. Applicants should submit an application form, LSAT results, transcripts, a personal statement, a nonrefundable application fee of $75, 2 letters of recommendation, and a resume.

Notification of the admissions decision is on a rolling basis from January. The law school uses the LSAC.

Special

The law school recruits minority and disadvantaged students by means of the Candidate Referral Service, a special open house for minority students, LSAC forums, and visits to colleges and universities with significant minority populations. Requirements are different for out-of-state students. Transfer students must have one year of credit, must have attended an ABA-approved law school, must submit a personal statement, and must have been originally admissible to UNC School of Law.

Costs

On-campus room and board costs about $10,570 annually; books and supplies run $1,150.

Financial Aid

About 87% of current law students receive some form of aid. The average annual amount of aid from all sources combined, including scholarships, loans, and work contracts, is $29,676; maximum, $55,364. Awards are based on need and merit combined. The required financial statement is the FAFSA. The aid application deadline for fall entry is March 1. Special funds for minority or disadvantaged students are available. First-year students are notified about their financial aid application at time of acceptance.

About the Law School

University of North Carolina at Chapel Hill School of Law was established in 1845 and is a public institution. The 700-acre campus is in a small town 23 miles northwest of Raleigh. The primary mission of the law school is to educate future practitioners and leaders of the bench and bar. Students have access to federal, state, county, city, and local agencies, courts, correctional facilities, law firms, and legal aid organizations in the Chapel Hill area. Housing for students is available in the residence hall for graduate and professional students located near the law school; there are also many apartments in the area. About 95% of the law school facilities are accessible to the physically disabled.

Calendar

The law school operates on a traditional semester basis. Courses for full-time students are offered days only, and must be completed within 5 years. New students are admitted in the fall. There is a 6-week summer session. Transferable summer courses are not offered.

Programs

Students may take relevant courses in other programs and apply credit toward the J.D.; a maximum of 6 credits may be applied. The following joint degrees may be earned: J.D./M.A.M.C. (Juris Doctor/Master of Arts in Mass Communication), J.D./M.A.S.A. (Juris Doctor/Master of Arts in Sports Administration), J.D./M.B.A. (Juris Doctor/Master of Business Administration), J.D./M.P.A. (Juris Doctor/Master of Public Administration), J.D./M.P.H. (Juris Doctor/Master of Public Health), J.D./M.P.P.S. (Juris Doctor/Master of Public Policy), J.D./M.R.P. (Juris Doctor/Master of Regional Planning), J.D./M.S.I.S. (Juris Doctor/Master of Science in Information Science), J.D./M.S.L.S. (Juris Doctor/Master of Science in Library Science), and J.D./M.S.W. (Juris Doctor/Master of Social Work).

Required

To earn the J.D., candidates must complete 86 total credits, of which 31 are for required courses. They must maintain a minimum GPA of 2.2 in the required courses. The following first-year courses are required of all students: Civil Procedure, Constitutional Law, Contracts, Criminal Law, Property, Research and Writing, and Torts. Required upper-level courses consist of a third-year seminar, a writing requirement, and Professional Responsibility. The required orientation program for first-year students is 3 days and includes an introduction to case study method and briefing and social activities.

Electives

The School of Law offers concentrations in corporate law, criminal law, environmental law, family law, intellectual property law, international law, juvenile law, labor law, litigation, media law, securities law, tax law, and torts and insurance. Third-year students may participate in the Criminal Law Clinic, Immigration/Human Rights Clinic, Civil Legal Assistance

Phone: 919-962-5109
Fax: 919-843-7939
E mail: law_admission@unc.edu
Web: http://www.law.unc.edu

Contact
Admissions Office, 919-962-5109 for general inquiries; 919-962-8396, for financial aid information.

NORTH CAROLINA

Clinic, and Community Development Law Clinic. Students may also participate in the Policy Clinic: Gender and Human Rights. Domestic Violence Law is a prerequisite. There are approximately 40 seminars offered to upper-level students for 3 credit hours; preference is given to third-year students, then second-year students. Research may be undertaken for no more than 3 credit hours and only with faculty permission. The law school has an externship program for third-year students. Students are placed by the school and also take a required class. Students may study in Lyon, France; Nijmegen, the Netherlands; Glasgow, Scotland; Mexico City, Mexico; or Manchester, England during the spring semester of the second or third year for 12 credit hours. Courses focus on international law. The LEAP program is a first-year academic support program for a select group of entering students. The most widely taken electives are Business Associations, Trusts and Estates, and Evidence.

Graduation Requirements
In order to graduate, candidates must have a GPA of 2.3, must have completed the upper-division writing requirement, and must have completed the second-year writing class and the seminar requirement in the third year.

Organizations
Students edit the *North Carolina Law Review*, *North Carolina Journal of International Law and Commercial Regulation*, *Journal of Online Technology*, *Banking Law Journal*, and *First Amendment Law Journal*. The Holderness Moot Court Bench consists of the negotiations team, client counseling team, invitational team, national team, constitutional team, and international team, and sponsors the annual Craven Moot Court competition. Other competitions include American Jurisprudence Award, Block Improvement, Burkan Memorial, Millard S. Breckenridge, Judge Heriot Clarkson, Chief Justice Walter Clark, Albert Coates, Investors Title Insurance, William T. Jayner, James William Morrow III, U.S. Law Week, and West Publishing Company. Law student organizations include Domestic Violence Advocacy Project, Environmental Law Project, and the Christian Society. Local chapters of national associations include American Civil Liberties Union, Black Law

Students Association, and Federalist Society. Campus clubs and other organizations include Hispanic/Latino Law Students Association, LAMBDA Law Students Association, and Trial Law Academy.

Library
The law library contains 540,098 hardcopy volumes and 42,241 microform volume equivalents, and subscribes to 1,466 serial publications. Such online databases and networks as CALI, Dow-Jones, Infotrac, Legal-Trac, LEXIS, Mathew Bender, OCLC First Search, WESTLAW, Wilsonline Indexes, ProQuest Congressional, Factiva, HeinOnline, CCH IntelliConnect, Making of the Modern Law, and Bloomberg Law are available to law students for research. Special library collections include Anglo-American legal materials. The ratio of library volumes to faculty is 12,560 to 1 and to students is 700 to 1. The ratio of seats in the library to students is 1 to 1.

Faculty
The law school has 43 full-time and 40 part-time faculty members, of whom 29 are women. The ratio of full-time students to full-time faculty in an average class is 18 to 1; in a clinic, 12 to 1. The law school has a regular program of bringing visiting professors and other distinguished lecturers and visitors to campus. There is a chapter of the Order of the Coif; 40 faculty are members.

Students
About 51% of the student body are women; 28%, minorities; 8%, African American; 6%, Asian American; 9%, Hispanic; and 1%, Native American. The majority of students come from North Carolina (70%). The average age of entering students is 23; age range is 21 to 53. About 32% of students enter directly from undergraduate school, and 9% have a graduate degree. About 3% drop out after the first year for academic or personal reasons; 95% remain to receive a law degree.

Placement
J.D.s awarded:	236
Services available through: a separate law school placement center and the university placement center.	
Special features: career services staff of nine professionals.	
Full-time job interviews:	13 employers
Summer job interviews:	65 employers
Placement by graduation:	70% of class
Placement within 9 months:	92% of class
Average starting salary:	$38,400 to $160,000
Areas of placement:	
Private practice 2–10 attorneys	22%
Private practice 11–25 attorneys	1%
Private practice 26–50 attorneys	3%
Private practice 51–100 attorneys	3%
Private practice 101+ attorneys	17%
Judicial clerkships	15%
Business/industry	14%
Government	12%
Public interest	11%
Academic	2%

UNIVERSITY OF NORTH DAKOTA

School of Law

Box 9003
Grand Forks, ND 58202

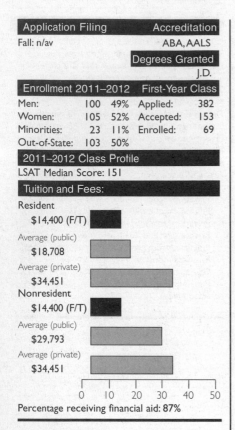

Application Filing		Accreditation
Fall: n/av		ABA, AALS
		Degrees Granted
		J.D.

Enrollment 2011–2012		First-Year Class	
Men:	100 49%	Applied:	382
Women:	105 52%	Accepted:	153
Minorities:	23 11%	Enrolled:	69
Out-of-State:	103 50%		

2011–2012 Class Profile
LSAT Median Score: 151

Tuition and Fees:

Resident
$14,400 (F/T)

Average (public)
$18,708

Average (private)
$34,451

Nonresident
$14,400 (F/T)

Average (public)
$29,793

Average (private)
$34,451

0 10 20 30 40 50

Percentage receiving financial aid: 87%

ADMISSIONS

In the fall of 2011 first-year class, 382 applied, 153 were accepted, and 69 enrolled. Three transfers enrolled. The median GPA of the most recent first-year class was 3.6.

Requirements

Applicants must have a bachelor's degree and take the LSAT. The most important admission factors include academic achievement, GPA, and LSAT results. No specific undergraduate courses are required. Candidates are not interviewed.

Procedure

Applicants should submit an application form and 2 letters of recommendation. Notification of the admissions decision is on a rolling basis. The law school uses the LSAC.

Special

The law school recruits minority and disadvantaged students as part of the school's philosophy of promoting diversity in the student body. Requirements are different for out-of-state students in that preference is given to qualified state residents, depending on the number of applications received. Transfer students must have a minimum GPA of 2 and must have attended an ABA-approved law school.

Financial Aid

About 87% of current law students receive some form of aid. The average annual amount of aid from all sources combined, including scholarships, loans, and work contracts, is $16,500; maximum, $37,800. Awards are based on need and merit combined. The required financial statement is the FAFSA. Check with the school for current application deadlines. Special funds for minority or disadvantaged students include Cultural Diversity Tuition Waivers. First-year students are notified about their financial aid application at time of acceptance.

About the Law School

University of North Dakota School of Law was established in 1899 and is a public institution. The campus is in a small town 320 miles northwest of Minneapolis-St. Paul. The primary mission of the law school is to provide education and training in legal analysis and the application of legal principles leading to professional competence. Students have access to federal, state, county, city, and local agencies, courts, correctional facilities, law firms, and legal aid organizations in the Grand Forks area. Housing for students is in residence halls, single-student apartments, family housing apartments, and a trailer court, all adjacent to the campus. About 95% of the law school facilities are accessible to the physically disabled.

Calendar

The law school operates on a traditional semester basis. Courses students are offered are days only, and must be completed within 5 years. New students are admitted in the fall. There is a 6-week summer session. Transferable summer courses are offered.

Programs

Students may take relevant courses in other programs and apply credit toward the J.D.; a maximum of 6 credits may be applied. The following joint degrees may be earned: J.D/M.P.A. (Juris Doctor/Master of Public Administration).

Required

To earn the J.D., candidates must complete 90 total credits, of which 34 are for required courses. They must maintain a minimum GPA of 2.0 in the required courses. The following first-year courses are required of all students: Brief Writing and Appellate Advocacy, Civil Procedure, Constitutional Law I and II, Contracts I and II, Criminal Law, Legal Process, Property I and II, and Torts I and II. Required upper-level courses consist of Professional Responsibility. The required orientation program for first-year students lasts 1 week.

Electives

Clinics conducted under the supervision of the Director of Legal Aid and other clinical instructors include a Civil Litigation Project and a Civil Rights Project. Internships are available with the North Dakota District Court, North Dakota Legislative Assembly, Grand Forks County States Attorney, and the Office of the Staff Judge Advocate at the Grand Forks Air Force Base. Various supervised research projects are available through the Special Projects Committee. Also, Central Legal Research employs second- and third-year students to work on current legal research questions. The Rocky Mountain Mineral Law Foundation, through grants, scholarships, seminars, and publications, promotes research in natural resources law. The Fode Lecture is a special lecture series. Students may receive credit for summer law study at the University of Oslo, Norway. The Canadian-American Law Institute encourages interchange among law students and faculty from North Dakota and several Canadian provinces. The most widely taken electives are bar courses, skills courses, and Trial Advocacy.

Phone: 701-777-2104
Fax: 701-777-2217
E-mail: linda.kohoutek@thor.law.und.noduk.edu
Web: http://www.law.und.nodak.edu

Contact

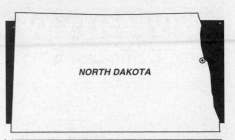

NORTH DAKOTA

Admissions and Records Associate, 701-777-2260 for general inquiries; Mark Brickson, Director of Career Services, 701-777-2269 for financial aid information.

Graduation Requirements

In order to graduate, candidates must have a GPA of 2.0, must have completed the upper-division writing requirement, must have completed Legal Process, Brief Writing, and Professional Responsibility, must have completed 2 significant writing projects, and must have completed the residency requirements of the last 4 semesters of study at the school.

Organizations

Students edit the *North Dakota Law Review* and the student newspaper, *Rhadamanthus*. The North Dakota Agricultural Law Institute serves the state's agricultural industry by publishing bulletins related to agriculture. Members of the Moot Court Association participate in an appellate moot court intraschool competition. During the past few years, members have also participated in the National Moot Court Competition, the Tulane Sports Law Competition, and various regional competitions. Student organizations, local chapters of national associations, and campus organizations include the Student Bar Association, Native American Law Students Association, Christian Law Students Society, Public Interest Law Students Association, Student Trial Lawyers Association, Law Women's Caucus, Phi Alpha Delta, Phi Delta Phi, and Order of the Coif.

Library

The law library contains 251,320 hardcopy volumes and 129,554 microform volume equivalents, and subscribes to 2,710 serial publications Such online databases and networks as DIALOG, LEXIS, WESTLAW, OCLC, ODIN, Internet, and CALI are available to law students for research. Special library collections include a Canadian collection, partial U.S. government documents depository, and a Norwegian law collection. The ratio of library volumes to faculty is 22,847 to 1 and to students is 1,257 to 1. The ratio of seats in the library to students is 1 to 1.

Faculty

The law school has 11 full-time and 16 part-time faculty members, of whom 13 are women. According to AAUP standards for Category I institutions, faculty salaries are well below average. About 36% of full-time faculty have a graduate law degree in addition to the J.D. There is a chapter of the Order of the Coif.

Students

About 52% of the student body are women; 11%, minorities; 1%, African American; 1%, Asian American; 2%, Hispanic; and 7%, Native American. The average age of entering students is 26; age range is 21 to 48. About 6% drop out after the first year for academic or personal reasons.

Placement

Services available through: a separate law school placement center.

Services: job board, on which full- and part-time positions are listed.

Special features: a job-seeking resource and reference library, files on individual firms or organizations, and files on job bulletins from over 80 other law schools around the nation. Internet, legal, and job-seeking sites are bookmarked from the school's web page.

Full-time job interviews:	6 employers
Summer job interviews:	10 employers
Placement by graduation:	60% of class
Placement within 9 months:	91% of class
Average starting salary:	$24,000 to $90,000

Areas of placement:

Private practice 2–10 attorneys	34%
Private practice 11–25 attorneys	7%
Private practice 26–50 attorneys	2%
Private practice 51–100 attorneys	9%
Judicial clerkships	15%
Government	14%
Public interest	8%
Business/industry	7%
Military	3%
Sole practitioner	1%

Notre Dame Law School

P.O. Box 780
Notre Dame, IN 46556-0780

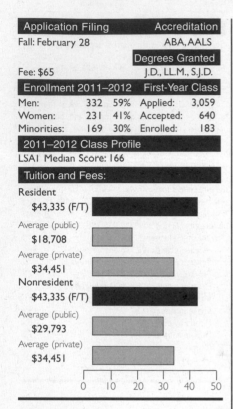

Application Filing	Accreditation
Fall: February 28	ABA, AALS

	Degrees Granted
Fee: $65	J.D., LL.M., S.J.D.

Enrollment 2011–2012			First-Year Class	
Men:	332	59%	Applied:	3,059
Women:	231	41%	Accepted:	640
Minorities:	169	30%	Enrolled:	183

2011–2012 Class Profile
LSAT Median Score: 166

Tuition and Fees:

Resident
$43,335 (F/T)

Average (public)
$18,708

Average (private)
$34,451

Nonresident
$43,335 (F/T)

Average (public)
$29,793

Average (private)
$34,451

0 10 20 30 40 50

ADMISSIONS

In the fall of 2011 first-year class, 3059 applied, 640 were accepted, and 183 enrolled. Eighteen transfers enrolled. The median GPA of the most recent first-year class was 3.7.

Requirements

Applicants must have a bachelor's degree and take the LSAT. No specific undergraduate courses are required, and candidates are not interviewed.

Procedure

The application deadline for fall entry is February 28. Applicants should submit an application form, LSAT results, transcripts, a personal statement, a nonrefundable application fee of $65, 2 letters of recommendation, and an optional essay. Notification of the admissions decision is on a rolling basis. The law school uses the LSAC.

Special

The law school recruits minority and disadvantaged students through admissions representatives attendance at LSAC forums and university law days across the country. Requirements are different for out-of-state students. Transfer students must have one year of credit, attended an ABA-approved law school, and include a personal statement.

Costs

Tuition and fees for the 2011–2012 academic year are $42,870 for all full-time students. On-campus room and board costs about $8,850 annually; books and supplies run $1,500.

Financial Aid

Awards are based on need and merit combined. Required financial statement is the FAFSA. The aid application deadline for fall entry is February 15. Special funds for minority or disadvantaged students include special grants. First-year students are notified about their financial aid application as soon as possible after financial documents are received.

About the Law School

University of Notre Dame Law School was established in 1869 and is a private institution. The 1250-acre campus is located in a small town north of South Bend. The primary mission of the law school is to educate a different kind of lawyer through the integration of faith and reason. The law school's goal is that the "Notre Dame Lawyer" should exemplify the legal profession at its best. Students have access to federal, state, county, city, and local agencies, courts, correctional facilities, law firms, and legal aid organizations in the Notre Dame area. Students also have access to the courts and legal aid clinics of South Bend, Chicago, and Michigan. Housing for students is available as is on-campus apartments for single and married students. Townhouses are available for graduate and law students. The University also assists students in finding off-campus housing.

Calendar

The law school operates on a traditional semester basis. Courses for full-time students are offered both day and evening. Most courses are offered during the day

and must be completed within 5 years. There is no part-time program. New full-time students are admitted in the fall. There is a 6-week summer session. Transferable summer courses are offered.

Programs

In addition to the J.D., the law school offers the L.M. and S.J.D. Students may take relevant courses in other programs and apply credit toward the J.D.; a maximum of 9 credits may be applied. The following joint degrees may be earned: J.D./M.A. (Juris Doctor/Master of Arts in English and other programs), J.D./M.B.A. (Juris Doctor/Master of Business Administration), and J.D./M.S. (Juris Doctor/Master of Science in Engineering).

Required

To earn the J.D., candidates must complete 90 total credits, of which 34 are for required courses. They must maintain a minimum GPA of 2.0 in the required courses. The following first-year courses are required of all students: Civil Procedure, Constitutional Law, Contracts, Criminal Law, Legal Research, Legal Writing, Property, and Torts. Required upper-level courses consist of Ethics and Jurisprudence. The required orientation program for first-year students is 2 days in length.

Electives

Clinical training is available through Legal Aid, Appellate Advocacy, Criminal Practice, Public Interest Practice, and Trial Advocacy programs. There are also special seminars offered in a variety of areas. Internships are available through the Public Defender and Prosecutor's offices. The Law School, as well as other academic departments, offer an array of programs. A study-abroad program allows students to take their second year or a summer session at the Law School's London campus. Tutorial programs are tailored to meet the needs of individual students. Diversity groups are actively involved in the law School, both at the regional and national levels. The most widely taken electives are International Law, Trial Advocacy, and Legal Aid Clinic.

Graduation Requirements

In order to graduate, candidates must have a GPA of 2.0 and completed the upper-division writing requirement.

Phone: 574-631-6626
Fax: 574-631-5474
E mail: lawadmit@nd.edu
Web: www.law.nd.edu

Contact

Director of Admissions and Financial Aid, 574-631-6626 for general inquiries and financial aid information.

INDIANA

Organizations

Students edit the *Notre Dame Law Review*, published 5 times a year. Other publications include *Journal of Legislation, Journal of College and University Law*, and the *Journal of Law, Ethics, and Public Policy*. Moot court competitions include the National, Regional, and Seventh Circuit Moot Court Competitions, as well as the Jessup Moot Court Competition. Additional competitions include the National Trial Competition and Client Counseling, Law student organizations, local chapters of national associations. Campus organizations include Phi Alpha Delta, Business Law Forum, Environmental Law Society, Black Law Students of Notre Dame, Hispanic Law Students Association, Asian Law Students Association, Native American Law Students Association, Federalist Society, Public Interest Law Forum, and Women's Law Forum.

Library

The law library contains 356,733 hard-copy volumes and 315,657 microform volume equivalents. Online databases and networks include CALI, CIS Universe, Infotrac, Legal-Trac, LEXIS, Mathew Bender, OCLC First Search, RLIN, WESTLAW, and Wilsonline Indexes, which are available to law students for research. The law school is a member of the Federal Depository Library System, and has several archival sets of personal papers, in addition to a collection of approximately 800 rare books. The ratio of library volumes to faculty is 6,731 to 1 and to students is 650 to 1.

Faculty

The law school has 61 full-time and 47 part-time faculty members, of whom 38 are women. The ratio of full-time students to full-time faculty in an average class is 25 to 1; in a clinic, 6 to 1. The law school has a regular program of bringing visiting professors and other distinguished lecturers and visitors to campus.

Students

About 41% of the student body are women; 30%, minorities; 6%, African American; 8%, Asian American; 12%, Hispanic; and 2%, Native American. The average age of entering students is 24; age range is 21 to 45. About 1% drop out after the first year for academic or personal reasons; 99% remain to receive a law degree.

Placement

J.D.s awarded:	172

Services available through: a separate law school placement center.
Services: conducting seminars and surveys, maintaining a library, and networking through a national alumni network.
Special features: summer funded fellowships for work in the public sector.

Andrew M. Coats Hall,
300 Timberdell Road
Norman, OK 73019

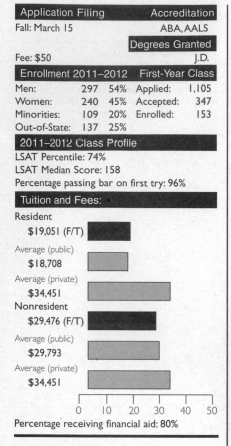

Application Filing			Accreditation
Fall: March 15			ABA, AALS
			Degrees Granted
Fee: $50			J.D.
Enrollment 2011–2012			**First-Year Class**
Men:	297	54%	Applied: 1,105
Women:	240	45%	Accepted: 347
Minorities:	109	20%	Enrolled: 153
Out-of-State:	137	25%	

2011–2012 Class Profile
LSAT Percentile: 74%
LSAT Median Score: 158
Percentage passing bar on first try: 96%

Tuition and Fees:

Resident
  $19,051 (F/T)

Average (public)
  $18,708

Average (private)
  $34,451

Nonresident
  $29,476 (F/T)

Average (public)
  $29,793

Average (private)
  $34,451

0   10   20   30   40   50

Percentage receiving financial aid: 80%

ADMISSIONS

In the fall of 2011 first-year class, 1105 applied, 347 were accepted, and 153 enrolled. Twenty transfers enrolled. The median LSAT percentile of the most recent first-year class was 74; the median GPA was 3.5 on a scale of 4.0.

Requirements
Applicants must have a bachelor's degree and take the LSAT. The most important admission factors include GPA, LSAT results, and character or personality. No specific undergraduate courses are required. Candidates are not interviewed.

Procedure
The application deadline for fall entry is March 15. Applicants should submit an application form, LSAT results, transcripts, a nonrefundable application fee of $50, and 2 letters of recommendation. Notification of the admissions decision is 2 to 6 weeks after packet completion. The law school uses the LSAC.

Special
The law school recruits minority and disadvantaged students through prelaw fairs and career days at undergraduate institutions, and through personal correspondence and contacts, LSAC forums, and CRS searches. Requirements are different for out-of-state students. Transfer students must have one year of credit and must have attended an ABA-approved law school.

Costs
On-campus room and board costs about $11,300 annually; books and supplies run $5,911.

Financial Aid
About 80% of current law students receive some form of aid. The average annual amount of aid from all sources combined, including scholarships, loans, and work contracts, is $24,936. Awards are based on need and merit combined. The required financial statement is the FAFSA. The aid application deadline for fall entry is March 1. Special funds for minority or disadvantaged students include money several donors have embarked for ethnic scholarships. First-year students are notified about their financial aid application at time of acceptance.

About the Law School
University of Oklahoma College of Law was established in 1909 and is a public institution. The 3905-acre campus is in a suburban area 20 miles south of Oklahoma City. The primary mission of the law school is to prepare qualified students to practice law or to use the law in their disciplines, to enable law graduates to remain qualified, and to promote further understanding of law and legal institutions. Students have access to federal, state, county, city, and local agencies, courts, correctional facilities, law firms, and legal aid organizations in the Norman area. Facilities of special interest to law students include three state-of-the-art courtrooms, the largest law library in the state, and a world class physical fitness center. Housing for students includes dormitories, off-campus apartments, and university-owned apartments for graduate and law students. All law school facilities are accessible to the physically disabled.

Calendar
The law school operates on a traditional semester basis. Courses are offered days only, and must be completed within 5 years. New students are admitted in the fall. There is an 8-week summer session. Transferable summer courses are offered.

Programs
The following joint degrees may be earned: J.D./M.B.A. (Juris Doctor/Master of Business Administration) and J.D./M.P.H. (Juris Doctor/Master of Public Health).

Required
To earn the J.D., candidates must complete 90 total credits, of which 41 are for required courses. They must maintain a minimum GPA of 4.0 in the required courses. The following first-year courses are required of all students: Civil Procedure I and II, Constitutional Law, Contracts, Criminal Law, Legal Research and Writing I and II, Property, and Torts I and II. Required upper-level courses consist of a graduation writing requirement, Criminal Procedure I, Evidence, and Professional Responsibility. No clinical courses are required, but many students participate in a clinical program. The required orientation program for first-year students is a 1-day orientation that provides a basic introduction to legal study and the OU Law Center.

Electives
The College of Law offers concentrations in corporate law, criminal law, entertainment law, environmental law, family law, international law, juvenile law, labor law, litigation, media law, securities law, sports law, tax law, torts and insurance, natural resources law, and Native American law. The Civil Clinic, Criminal Defense Clinic, and International Human Rights Clinic are available for 3 hours per semester. All students who have completed their first year of law studies may take seminars. Each semester several are offered for 2 credit hours each. There is no limit, though students generally take no more than 2 or 3. A federal Indian Law internship is available for 12 credit hours. Second- and third-year students may be research assistants for law professors for no credit while receiving an hourly wage. Field work includes extern placement. Enrichment programs include

Phone: 405-325-4728
Fax: 405-325-0502
E-mail: rlucas@ou.edu
Web: www.law.ou.edu

Contact
Becky Lucas, Administrative Assistant to Associate Dean, 405-325-4702 for general inquiries; University of Oklahoma-Main Office, 405-325-4521 for financial aid information.

OKLAHOMA
◉

the Henry Lecture Series and the Chair Professorship Series. A summer program is available at Brasenose College, Oxford University, Oxford, England. In addition, students have the opportunity to study abroad for a semester or full academic year after they have completed at least the first year of law studies and are in good academic standing. Students can create individual study programs at foreign law schools, and if approved by the College of Law and the American Bar Association, they can receive up to 30 hours of credit. Such study programs are particularly relevant to students who have an interest in international law or international business. A mandatory mentoring program for incoming students, given by upper class members, is provided to ease their integration into the law school environment. The Early Admission Program (EAP) of 15 to 20 students is a special admissions program designed to provide a small class environment, mentoring, and head start for students prior to joining the regular fall class. Minority law student organizations provide minority support programs to include retention, community activities, and graduation placement. The most widely taken electives are Corporations, Commercial Law, and Wills and Trusts.

Graduation Requirements
In order to graduate, candidates must have a GPA of 4.0 and must have completed the upper-division writing requirement.

Organizations
Students edit the *Oklahoma Law Review, American Indian Law Review*, and *Oklahoma Journal of Law and Technology*. Moot court competitions include the National Moot Court, ABA NAAC, Jessup International, and 15 others. The College of Law has mandatory first-year moot court competitions and voluntary upper-class moot court competitions. Law student organizations, local chapters of national associations, and campus organizations include BLSA, OAWL, Federalist Society, Student Bar Association, Phi Alpha Delta, Phi Delta Phi, J. Reuben Clark Society, and student components of ABA and OBA.

Library
The law library contains 373,066 hardcopy volumes and 81,235 microform volume equivalents, and subscribes to 4,389 serial publications. Such online databases and networks as CALI, CIS Universe, DIALOG, Dow-Jones, Infotrac, Legal-Trac, LEXIS, Mathew Bender, OCLC First Search, and WESTLAW are available to law students for research. Special library collections include the Native Peoples Collection, GPO Depository, and Oil and Gas Law Collection. The ratio of library volumes to faculty is 6,783 to 1 and to students is 695 to 1. The ratio of seats in the library to students is 1 to 1.

Faculty
The law school has 33 full-time and 15 part-time faculty members, of whom 18 are women. According to AAUP standards for Category I institutions, faculty salaries are below average. About 18% of full-time faculty have a graduate law degree in addition to the J.D. The ratio of full-time students to full-time faculty in an average class is 14 to 1; in a clinic, 10 to 1. The law school has a regular program of bringing visiting professors and other distinguished lecturers and visitors to campus. There is a chapter of the Order of the Coif; 36 faculty and 1282 graduates are members.

Students
About 45% of the student body are women; 20%, minorities; 4%, African American; 4%, Asian American; 4%, Hispanic; and 8%, Native American. The majority of students come from Oklahoma (75%). The average age of entering students is 25; age range is 22 to 48. About 50% of students enter directly from undergraduate school, 6% have a graduate degree, and 50% have worked full-time prior to entering law school. About 2% drop out after the first year for academic or personal reasons; 98% remain to receive a law degree.

Placement

J.D.s awarded:	177

Services available through: a separate law school placement center.
Special features: personal student counseling, on-campus seminars, mentoring by alumni, professional development workshops, and career development workshops.

Full-time job interviews:	9 employers
Summer job interviews:	39 employers
Placement by graduation:	98% of class
Placement within 9 months:	100% of class
Average starting salary:	$20,000 to $160,000

Areas of placement:

Private practice 2–10 attorneys	30%
Private practice 11–25 attorneys	9%
Private practice 26–50 attorneys	1%
Private practice 51–100 attorneys	3%
Business/industry	19%
Government	14%
Judicial clerkships	5%
Public interest	3%

UNIVERSITY OF OREGON

School of Law, William W. Knight Law Center

1515 Agate Street
Eugene, OR 97403-1221

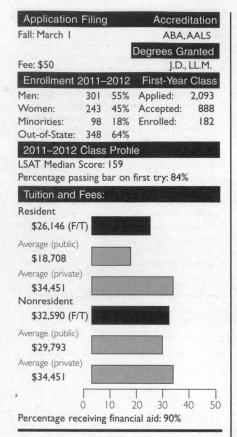

Application Filing		Accreditation
Fall: March 1		ABA, AALS
		Degrees Granted
Fee: $50		J.D., LL.M.

Enrollment 2011–2012		First-Year Class	
Men:	301 55%	Applied:	2,093
Women:	243 45%	Accepted:	888
Minorities:	98 18%	Enrolled:	182
Out-of-State:	348 64%		

2011–2012 Class Profile
LSAT Median Score: 159
Percentage passing bar on first try: 84%

Tuition and Fees:

Resident
$26,146 (F/T)

Average (public)
$18,708

Average (private)
$34,451

Nonresident
$32,590 (F/T)

Average (public)
$29,793

Average (private)
$34,451

Percentage receiving financial aid: 90%

ADMISSIONS

In the fall of 2011 first-year class, 2093 applied, 888 were accepted, and 182 enrolled. Seventeen transfers enrolled. The median GPA of the most recent first-year class was 3.34.

Requirements

Applicants must have a bachelor's degree and take the LSAT. No specific undergraduate courses are required.

Procedure

The application deadline for fall entry is March 1. Applicants should submit an application form, LSAT results, transcripts, a personal statement, TOEFL (if international), nonrefundable application fee of $50, 2 letters of recommendation, and résumé. Notification of the admissions decision is January through May. The law school uses the LSAC.

Special

The law school recruits minority and disadvantaged students in a variety of ways, in accordance with the law school's diversity plan. Requirements are different for out-of-state students. Transfer students must have one year of credits, attended an ABA-approved law school, and include a personal statement. The Admissions Committee considers each application on an individual basis.

Costs

On-campus room and board costs about $10,854 annually; books and supplies run $1,050.

Financial Aid

About 90% of current law students receive some form of aid. Awards are based on need and merit combined. Required financial statement is the FAFSA. Special funds are available for minority or disadvantaged students. Check the web site for additional scholarship information. First-year students are notified about their financial aid application soon after acceptance.

About the Law School

University of Oregon School of Law, William W. Knight Law Center was established in 1884 and is a public institution. The 295-acre campus is located in the small town of Eugene, Oregon. The primary mission of the law school is to offer a rigorous legal education with a curriculum that balances: basic intellectual and analytical skills for the practice of law; an introduction to advanced and frontier areas of law; knowledge of the persistent values of law; and opportunities to develop hands-on legal skills. Students have access to federal, state, county, city, and local agencies, courts, correctional facilities, law firms, and legal aid organizations in the Eugene area. The law school is aggressive in its commitment to nationwide networks that provide both summer and permanent employment. Housing for students is available in Eugene and the surrounding area. Law students are also eligible for special graduate student housing. All law school facilities are accessible to the physically disabled.

Calendar

The law school operates on a traditional semester basis. Courses for full-time students are offered both day and evening and must be completed within 3 years. There is no part-time program. New full-time students are admitted in the fall. There is an 8-week summer session. Transferable summer courses are offered.

Programs

In addition to the J.D., the law school offers the LL.M. Students may take relevant courses in other programs and apply credit toward the J.D.; a maximum of 5 semester credits may be applied. The following joint degrees may be earned: J.D./M.B.A. (Juris Doctor/Master of Business Administration), J.D./M.S. (Juris Doctor/Master of Science in International Studies), and J.D./M.S. or M.A. (Juris Doctor/Master of Science or Master of Arts).

Required

To earn the J.D., candidates must complete 85 total credits, of which 36 are for required courses. They must maintain a minimum GPA of 2.0 in the required courses. The following first-year courses are required of all students: Civil Procedure, Constitutional Law I, Contracts, Criminal Law, Legal Research and Writing, Property, and Torts. Required upper-level courses consist of a law school writing requirement, Constitutional Law II, and Legal Profession. Students are encouraged to participate in 1 of 7 clinics and/or skills training courses. The required orientation program for first-year students consists of a 3-day orientation and registration before the first day of classes. Orientation includes a convocation, small group sessions, peer advising sessions, a library tour, and an all-school picnic. Peer and faculty advising continues throughout the J.D. program.

Electives

The School of Law, William W. Knight Law Center offers concentrations in corporate law, criminal law, environmental law, family law, intellectual property law, international law, juvenile law, labor law, litigation, maritime law, securities law, tax law, torts and insurance, sustainable business law, ocean and coastal law, estate planning, public interest, public service law, Oregon Child Advocacy Project, and

Phone: 541-346-3852
800-825-6687
Fax: 541 346 3846
E-mail: *admissions@law.uoregon.edu*
Web: *www.law.uoregon.edu*

Contact
Office of Financial Aid, 1-800-760-6953 for financial aid information.

OREGON

Placement

J.D.s awarded:	178

Services available through: a separate law school placement center.

Services: a Career Services Library with more than 500 references, and information on fellowships, graduate and summer writing programs, and writing competitions.

Special features: online job postings and biweekly newsletter for students; bi-monthly bulletin for alumni.

Full-time job interviews:	15 employers
Summer job interviews:	42 employers
Placement by graduation:	58% of class
Placement within 9 months:	90% of class
Average starting salary:	$24,000 to $120,000

Areas of placement:

Private law firms of all sizes	45%
Government	16%
Judicial clerkships	14%
Business/industry	11%
Public interest	11%
Academic	4%
Military	1%

appropriate dispute resolution/conflict resolution. In addition, a variety of clinics are offered that include the Civil Practice Clinic, Criminal Defense Clinic, Criminal Prosecution Clinic, Domestic Violence Clinic, Environmental Law Clinic, Mediation Clinic, and the Small Business Clinic. A variety of seminars are also offered. Students have excellent opportunities for internships including the Federal Bankruptcy Court internship, Judicial internships, and the Legislative Issues Workshop. Faculty-supervised research may be done for school credit or for pay. Each year, the law school hosts symposia and lectures through the many programs, including the Wayne Morse Center for Law and Politics, Bowerman Center for Environmental Law, and the Center for Law and Entrepreneurship. A reciprocal student-abroad exchange has been established with the University of Adelaide in Australia. The Academic Choice for Excellence Program (ACE) is offered to all first-year students and addresses the needs of nontraditional law students. It provides tutorial assistance during the academic year. Law students are active in six multicultural organizations including the Minority Law Students Association (MLSA), and the Oregon State Bar Affirmative Action Program, which offers financial assistance through scholarships and loans. Additionally, the law school offers placement assistance and scholarships to ethnic minority students.

Graduation Requirements
In order to graduate, candidates must have a GPA of 2.0, and complete the upper-division writing requirement.

Organizations
Students edit the *Oregon Law Review*, the *Journal of Environmental Law*, and the *Oregon Review of International Law*. Other publications include the *Western Environmental Law Update*. Students compete in the Client Counseling Competition, Mock Trial Competition, and the Environmental Moot Court Competition. Other competitions include the National Corporate Law Moot Court Competition and the Technology Entrepreneurship Program (TEP). Student organizations include the Women's Law Forum, Outlaws (LGBT), and Land Air Water (LAW). Local chapters of national associations include the Black Law Student Association, Phi Alpha Delta,

and the American Constitution Society for Law and Policy. Campus clubs and organizations include Streetlaw, Run Club, and the Legal Ballers Association.

Library
The law library contains 205,324 hardcopy volumes and 185,420 microform volume equivalents, and subscribes to 1,055 serial publications. Online databases and networks include CALI, CIS Universe, DIALOG, Infotrac, Legal-Trac, LEXIS, Mathew Bender, OCLC First Search, and WESTLAW. Additional resources include Wilsonline Indexes, Internet, HeinOnline, BNA All, MOML, LLMC, casemaker, SSRN, ECCO, Oxdord, Serial Set, CCH Tax and Business, RIA, and ELR, which are available to law students for research. Special library collections include an Ocean and Coastal Law Library, a rare book collection, an Indian Law and culture collection, and a labor and employment collection, and a sustainable business collection. The ratio of library volumes to faculty is 6,222 to 1 and to students is 377 to 1. The ratio of seats in the library to students is 1 to 2.

Faculty
The law school has 33 full-time and 51 part-time faculty members, of whom 42 are women. According to AAUP standards for Category I institutions, faculty salaries are below average. About 27% of full-time faculty have a graduate law degree in addition to the J.D.; about 6% of part-time faculty have one. The ratio of full-time students to full-time faculty in an average class is 34 to 1; in a clinic, 8 to 1. The law school has a regular program of bringing visiting professors and other distinguished lecturers and visitors to campus. There is a chapter of the Order of the Coif; 28 faculty and 618 graduates are members.

Students
About 45% of the student body are women; 18%, minorities; 3%, African American; 10%, Asian American; 4%, Hispanic; 2%, Native American; and 1%, Unknown. The majority of students come from Oregon (36%). The average age of entering students is 26; age range is 21 to 56. About 8% of students have a graduate degree. About 1% drop out after the first year for academic or personal reasons; 99% remain to receive a law degree.

Law School

3501 Sansom Street
Philadelphia, PA 19104-6204

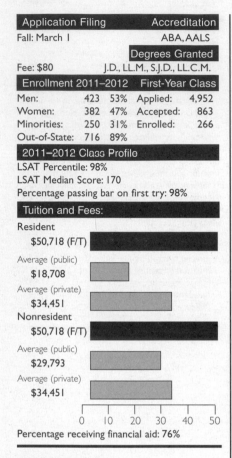

Application Filing	Accreditation
Fall: March 1	ABA, AALS

	Degrees Granted
Fee: $80	J.D., LL.M., S.J.D., LL.C.M.

Enrollment 2011–2012		First-Year Class	
Men:	423 53%	Applied:	4,952
Women:	382 47%	Accepted:	863
Minorities:	250 31%	Enrolled:	266
Out-of-State:	716 89%		

2011–2012 Class Profile
LSAT Percentile: 98%
LSAT Median Score: 170
Percentage passing bar on first try: 98%

Tuition and Fees:

Resident
$50,718 (F/T)

Average (public)
$18,708

Average (private)
$34,451

Nonresident
$50,718 (F/T)

Average (public)
$29,793

Average (private)
$34,451

Percentage receiving financial aid: 76%

ADMISSIONS

In the fall of 2011 first-year class, 4952 applied, 863 were accepted, and 266 enrolled. Twenty-three transfer students enrolled. The median LSAT percentile of the most recent first-year class was 98; the median GPA was 3.9 on a scale of 4.0.

Requirements
Applicants must have a bachelor's degree and take the LSAT. No specific undergraduate courses are required, and candidates are not interviewed.

Procedure
The application deadline for fall entry is March 1. Applicants should submit an application form, LSAT results, transcripts, personal statement, nonrefundable application fee of $80, 2 letters of recommendation, and a resume. Notification of the admissions decision is on a rolling basis. The law school uses the LSAC.

Special
The law school recruits minority and disadvantaged students through a diversity brochure, diversity page on web site with student contracts, and targeted college visits. Requirements are different for out-of-state students. Transfer students must have one year of credits, attended an ABA-approved law school (the school must be ABA- and AALS-approved), a personal statement, and complete a full-time first-year curriculum.

Costs

Tuition and fees for the 2011–2012 academic year are $47,600 for all full-time students. On-campus room and board costs about $13,392 annually; books and supplies run $1,300.

Financial Aid

About 76% of current law students receive some form of aid. The average annual amount of aid from all sources combined, including scholarships, loans, and work contracts, is $61,895; maximum, $65,610. Awards are based on need and merit combined. Required financial statements are the FAFSA and the institution's financial aid form. The aid application deadline for fall entry is March 1. First-year students are notified about their financial aid application shortly after acceptance.

About the Law School

University of Pennsylvania Law School was established in 1790 and is a private institution. The 260-acre campus is located in an urban area 2 miles from central Philadelphia. The primary mission of the law school is to provide a cross-disciplinary, globally focused legal education to prepare graduates to become leaders in the profession and society. Students have access to federal, state, county, city, and local agencies, courts, correctional facilities, law firms, and legal aid organizations in the Philadelphia area. The Pennsylvania Supreme Court is in Philadelphia, the federal courthouse headquarters, the U.S. District Court for the Eastern District of Pennsylvania, and the Court of Appeals for the Third Circuit. Facilities of special interest to law students include the National Constitution Center. Housing for students is available on and off-campus with the majority of law students living in off-campus housing.

The university also offers graduate housing one block from the law school. About 95% of the law school facilities are accessible to the physically disabled.

Calendar

The law school operates on a traditional semester basis. Courses for full-time students are offered both day and evening and must be completed within 3 years. There is no part-time program. New full-time students are admitted in the fall. There is no summer session. Transferable summer courses are not offered.

Programs

In addition to the J.D., the law school offers the LL.M., S.J.D., and LL.C.M. Students may take relevant courses in other programs and apply credit toward the J.D. a maximum of 12 credits may be applied. The following joint degrees may be earned: J.D./Ph.D. (Juris Doctor/Doctor of various disciplines), J.D./M.A. (Juris Doctor/Master of Arts (various disciplines), J.D./A.M. (Juris Doctor/Master of Arts in Islamic Studies), J.D./M.B.A. (Juris Doctor/Master of Business Administration), J.D./M.C.P. (Juris Doctor/Master of City and Regional Planning), J.D./M.S.Ed. (Juris Doctor/Master of Education), J.D./M.E.S. (Juris Doctor/Master of Environmental Studies), J.D./LL.M (Juris Doctor/Master of Laws), J.D./M.P.H. (Juris Doctor/Master of Public Health), J.D./M.P.A. (Juris Doctor/Master of Public Planning), J.D./M.S. (Juris Doctor/Master of Science (various disciplines)), J.D./M.S.S.P. (Juris Doctor/Master of Social Policy), and J.D./M.S.W. (Juris Doctor/Master of Social Work).

Required
To earn the J.D., candidates must complete 89 total credits, of which 24 are for required courses. The following first-year courses are required of all students: Civil Procedure, Constitutional Law, Contracts, Criminal Law, Legal Writing, and Torts. Required upper-level courses consist of Professional Responsibility. The required orientation program for first-year students lasts 2 days.

Phone: 215-898-7400
Fax: 215-898-9606
E mail: *admissions@law.upenn.edu*
Web: *www.law.upenn.edu*

Contact

Anthony Henry, Director, 215-898-7400 for financial aid information.

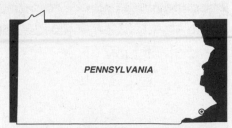

PENNSYLVANIA

Electives

The Law School offers concentrations in corporate law, criminal law, environmental law, family law, intellectual property law, international law, juvenile law, labor law, litigation, media law, securities law, tax law, torts and insurance, regulation of business, property and land development, perspectives on the law, law and the health services, constitutional law, courts and administration of justice, commercial law, urban and public interest law, clinical, professional responsibility, and co-curricular courses. In addition, clinics and extern programs are available for credit in law-related agencies outside of the school. The clinical program includes courses in litigation, civil practice, interdisciplinary child advocacy, public interest, entrepreneurship legal clinic, legislative process, transnational issues, mediation, and criminal defense. Seminars are available to second- and third-year students. First-year students enroll in 2 electives in regulatory/administrative law and 1 in perspectives. Each year a substantial number of students are employed as research assistants for faculty members. The school requires that all students complete 70 hours of service in public interest (pro bono). Penn Law has a partnership with the National Constitution Center that involves multiple events and lectures. Penn Law has programs in Hamburg, Germany; Tokyo, Japan; Beijing, China; Paris, France; Barcelona, Spain; Tel Aviv, Israel; a joint degree with Wharton's Lauder Institute, which involves study abroad, and Penn Law's Global Research seminar. A wide range of minority organizations host conferences and social events. Upper-level students provide mentoring. Student groups reflect the interests of students. The most widely taken electives are Corporations, Evidence, and Federal Income Tax.

Graduation Requirements

In order to graduate, candidates must complete the upper-division writing requirement.

Organizations

Students edit the *University of Pennsylvania Law Review*, the *University of Pennsylvania Journal of Business and Employment Law*, the *University of Pennsylvania*

Journal of Constitutional Law, University of Pennsylvania Journal of International Law, Journal of Law and Social Change, University of Pennsylvania East Asia Law Review and *Journal of Animal Law and Ethics*. The student Moot Court Board, made up of third-year students, administers the Moot Court Program, which holds a voluntary intramural competition for the Edwin R. Keedy Trophy. The school also participates in several competitions sponsored by bar associations or other law schools, including the Jessup International Moot Court Competition, the Frederick Douglass Moot Court Competition, and others. Penn Law has more than 90 student organizations with a broad spectrum of interests, including academic, recreational, and areas of diversity.

Library

The law library contains 1,134,376 hardcopy volumes and 240,852 microform volume equivalents, and subscribes to 3,867 serial publications. Online databases and networks include CALI, CIS Universe, Infotrac, Legal-Trac, LEXIS, OCLC First Search, WESTLAW, and Wilsonline Indexes, which are available to law students for research. Special library collections include foreign, international, and rare book collections, archives of the American Law Institute and the National Conference of Commissioners on Uniform State Laws, and the papers of Judge Bazelon and Bernard G. Segal. The ratio of library volumes to faculty is 6,673 to 1 and to students is 1,407 to 1. The ratio of seats in the library to students is 1 to 2.

Faculty

The law school has 83 full-time and 87 part-time faculty members, of whom 47 are women. According to AAUP standards for Category I institutions, faculty salaries are well above average. About 4% of full-time faculty have a graduate law degree in addition to the J.D. The ratio of full-time students to full-time faculty in an average class is 10 to 1; in a clinic, 7 to 1. The law school has a regular program of bringing visiting professors and other distinguished lecturers and visitors to campus. There is a chapter of the Order of the Coif; 26 graduates are members.

Placement

J.D.s awarded:	273

Services available through: a separate law school placement center.

Services: Placement library contains material on a wide variety of subjects and includes all major legal press. Many resources, including job postings, are available for students and alumni online.

Special features: Students work individually with counselors on their career searches. The office holds panel discussions and small-group meetings during the year to explore the practice of law and career opportunities. Additionally, first-year students work in small groups on issues such as resume writing and career opportunities,

Placement by graduation:	97% of class
Placement within 9 months:	98% of class
Average starting salary:	$48,450 to $152,000

Areas of placement:

Private practice 2–10 attorneys	2%
Private practice 11–25 attorneys	1%
Private practice 26–50 attorneys	2%
Private practice 51–100 attorneys	2%
Judicial clerkships	19%
Public interest	5%
Government	4%
Business/industry	3%
Academic	1%

Students

About 47% of the student body are women; 31%, minorities; 7%, African American; 15%, Asian American; and 4%, Hispanic. The majority of students come from Pennsylvania (11%). The average age of entering students is 24; age range is 20 to 41. About 37% of students enter directly from undergraduate school, 10% have a graduate degree, and 63% have worked full-time prior to entering law school. About 1% drop out after the first year for academic or personal reasons; 99% remain to receive a law degree.

School of Law

3900 Forbes Avenue
Pittsburgh, PA 15260

Application Filing	Accreditation
Fall: March 1	ABA, AALS

	Degrees Granted
Fee: $55	J.D., LL.M., S.J.D., M.S.L.

Enrollment 2011–2012			First-Year Class	
Men:	410	58%	Applied:	2,379
Women:	294	42%	Accepted:	869
Minorities:	113	16%	Enrolled:	230
Out-of-State:	282	40%		

2011–2012 Class Profile

LSAT Percentile: 78%

LSAT Median Score: 159

Percentage passing bar on first try: 84%

Tuition and Fees:

Resident

$28,734 (F/T)

Average (public)
$18,708

Average (private)
$34,451

Nonresident

$28,734 (F/T)

Average (public)
$29,793

Average (private)
$34,451

0   10   20   30   40   50

Percentage receiving financial aid: 85%

ADMISSIONS

In the fall of 2011 first-year class, 2379 applied, 869 were accepted, and 230 enrolled. Ten transfer students enrolled. The median LSAT percentile of the most recent first-year class was 78; the median GPA was 3.5 on a scale of 4.0. The lowest LSAT percentile accepted was 23; the highest was 97.

Requirements

Applicants must have a bachelor's degree and take the LSAT. The most important admission factors include LSAT results, GPA, and academic achievement. No specific undergraduate courses are required, and candidates are not interviewed.

Procedure

The application deadline for fall entry is March 1. Applicants should submit an application form, LSAT results, transcripts, personal statement, nonrefundable application fee of $55, and letters of recommendation (3 are suggested). Notification of the admissions decision is on a rolling basis. The law school uses the LSAC.

Costs

Tuition and fees for the 2011–2012 academic year are $27,892 for full-time in-state students and $34,666 for out-of-state students. On-campus room and board costs about $15,738 annually; books and supplies run $1,530.

Financial Aid

About 85% of current law students receive some form of aid. The average annual amount of aid from all sources combined, including scholarships, loans, and work contracts, is $10,000; maximum, $20,000. Awards are based on need and merit combined. Required financial statement is the FAFSA. The aid application deadline for fall entry is March 1. Special funds for minority or disadvantaged students include scholarships provided by the school and the university. First-year students are notified about their financial aid application at time of acceptance.

About the Law School

University of Pittsburgh School of Law was established in 1895 and is a public institution. The 132-acre campus is located in an urban area 3 miles from downtown Pittsburgh. The mission of the law school is to provide education, research, and public service to students who are entering the legal profession. Students have access to federal, state, county, city, and local agencies, courts, correctional facilities, law firms, and legal aid organizations in the Pittsburgh area. They also have access to the county law library. Facilities of special interest to students are the law library, classrooms, seminar rooms, courtroom complex, student lounge, student activities offices, meeting rooms, administrative offices, and computer laboratories and kiosks. Housing for students is in rental apartments that cost $700 to $800 and are available within 1 to 3 miles of the law school. On-campus housing is not available. All law school facilities are accessible to the physically disabled.

Calendar

The law school operates on a traditional semester basis. Courses for full-time students are offered days only and must be completed within 3 years. For part-time students, courses are offered days only and (flex-time students) and must be completed within 5 years. New full- and part-time students are admitted in the fall. There is no summer session. Transferable summer courses are not offered.

Programs

In addition to the J.D., the law school offers the LL.M., S.J.D., and M.S.L. Students may take relevant courses in other programs and apply credit toward the J.D.; a maximum of 6 credits may be applied. The following joint degrees may be earned: J.D./M.B.A. (Juris Doctor/ Master of Business Administration), J.D./M.P.A. (Juris Doctor/ Master of Public Administration), J.D./M.P.I.A. (Juris Doctor/ Master of Public and International Affairs), J.D./M.S. (Juris Doctor/ Master of Science in law and Public Management), J.D./M.A. (Juris Doctor/Master of Arts in Bioethics), J.D./M.P.H. (Juris Doctor/Master of Public Health), and J.D./M.S.W. (Juris Doctor/ Master of Social Work).

Required

To earn the J.D., candidates must complete 88 total credits, of which 34 are for required courses. They must maintain a minimum GPA of 2.0 in the required courses. The following first-year courses are required of all students: ADP: Legislation and Regulation, Civil Procedure, Constitutional Law, Contracts, Criminal Law, Lawyering, Legal Analysis and Writing, Pitt Law Academy, Property, and Torts. Required upper-level courses consist of a course relating to international or comparative law, a legal research course, and Legal Profession (ethics). The required orientation program for first-year students is conducted over a 2-day period including a formal program, diversity training, discussion groups, family and friends orientation, lunch, and a student activities fair.

Electives

The School of Law offers concentrations in corporate law, criminal law, environmental law, family law, intellectual property law, international law, litigation, tax law, torts and insurance, and health law. In addition, clinical offerings consist of the Tax Clinic, Family Law Clinic, Environmental Law Clinic, and Civil Practice Clinic, which includes Health Law and Elder Law. Second- and third-year students can choose from a variety of seminars, which

Phone: 412-648-1413
Fax: 412-648-1318
E mail: cmccall@pitt.edu
Web: www.pitt.law.edu

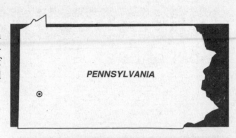

Contact

Charmaine C. McCall, Assistant Dean for Admission, 412-648-1413 for general inquiries; Meme Jeffries, Director of Financial Aid, 412-648-1415 for financial aid information.

can satisfy the upper-level writing requirement. Externship opportunities are available with 62 federal and state judges, 34 other judges throughout Pennsylvania, and 34 judges in other states. Students are also placed in 91 Pennsylvania and federal agencies and out-of-state agencies; including Legal Aid Societies, the Urban Redevelopment Authority, U.S. Attorneys, neighborhood legal services, public defenders, the National Labor Relations Board, hospitals, and housing authorities. Students can earn a full-semester's credits by completing a semester-long externship in Washington, D.C. The school sponsors annual lectures in the fields of health law, disability law, intellectual property law, ethics, law and social work, and lawyering for social change. The school is a sponsor of a summer study program in Zagreb, Croatia. The Center for International Legal Education will work individually with students interested in studying abroad at any location. A Law at Sea program, in which each student is required to take credits of law school courses, is also available. The Law School invites minority and other students to participate in the Mellon Legal Writing Program, which is designed to provide additional academic and social support for students confronting special challenges. The Law School has been co-sponsor of the CLEO (The Council for Legal Educational Opportunity) Institute. Student organizations sponsor programs reflecting the interests of the group, such as Sports and Entertainment Law, International Law, Environmental Law, Health Law, Business Law, and Family Law. The most widely taken electives are Federal Income Tax, Corporations, and Evidence.

Graduation Requirements

In order to graduate, candidates must have a GPA of 2.0, complete the upper-division writing requirement, a Legal Profession Ethics course, course relating to international or comparative law, and a legal research course.

Organizations

Students edit the *University of Pittsburgh Law Review, University of Pittsburgh Journal of Law and Commerce, Pittsburgh Journal of Technology*, the *Pittsburgh Tax Review,* and the *Pittsburgh Journal of Environmental* and *Public Health Law*. Moot court competitions include the Murray S. Love Trial Moot Court Competition,

the National Health Law Moot Court Competition, and the BMI/Cardoza Entertainment Law Moot Court Competition. Law student organizations include The Pitt Legal Income Sharing Foundation, Hispanic Law Society, and Pitt Law Women's Association. There are local chapters of the Black Law Student's Association, International Law Society, and Phi Alpha Delta.

Library

The law library contains 470,958 hardcopy volumes and 204,232 microform volume equivalents, and subscribes to 4,035 serial publications. Online databases and networks include CALI, CIS Universe, DIALOG, Dow-Jones, Infotrac, Legal-Trac, LEXIS, Mathew Bender, OCLC First Search, WESTLAW, and Wilsonline Indexes. In addition, more than 300 separate databases are available through the University of Pittsburgh Digital Library, and available to law students for research. Special library collections include international law, tax and labor law, health law, and a selective federal depository. The ratio of library volumes to faculty is 8,525 to 1 and to students is 664 to 1. The ratio of seats in the library to students is 1 to 2.

Faculty

The law school has 53 full-time and 108 part-time faculty members, of whom 51 are women. According to AAUP standards for Category I institutions, faculty salaries are average. About 24% of full-time faculty have a graduate law degree in addition to the J.D. The ratio of full-time students to full-time faculty in an average class is 15 to 1; in a clinic, 8 to 1. The law school has a regular program of bringing visiting professors and other distinguished lecturers and visitors to campus. There is a chapter of the Order of the Coif; 8 faculty are members.

Students

About 42% of the student body are women; 16%, minorities; 8%, African American; 4%, Asian American; and 2%, Hispanic. The majority of students come from Pennsylvania (60%). The average age of entering students is 24; age range is 20 to 59. About 46% of students enter directly from undergraduate school, 7% have a graduate degree, and 10% have worked full-time prior to entering law school. About 1% drop out after the first year for academic or personal reasons.

PENNSYLVANIA

Placement

J.D.s awarded:	254

Services available through: a separate law school placement center.

Services: training in computerized job searching, workshops, publication of a weekly student newsletter, online student and alumni job posting site, videotaped interviews, participation in job fairs, and programs focused on diversity in the legal profession.

Special features: an emphasis on exploring career options and long-range career planning and developing and refining job procurement and retention skills. The professional staff consists of many specialists.

Full-time job interviews:	7 employers
Summer job interviews:	30 employers
Placement by graduation:	48% of class
Placement within 9 months:	82% of class
Average starting salary:	$42,000 to $160,000

Areas of placement:

Private practice 2–10 attorneys	38%
Private practice 11–25 attorneys	6%
Private practice 26–50 attorneys	10%
Private practice 51–100 attorneys	3%
Business/industry	20%
Government	11%
Judicial clerkships	8%
Public interest	4%
Academic	2%
Military	1%

UNIVERSITY OF PUERTO RICO

School of Law

P.O. Box 23349, UPR Station
Rio Piedras, PR 00931-3349

Application Filing	Accreditation
Fall: February 15	ABA, AALS
	Degrees Granted
Fee: $20	J.D., LL.M.

Enrollment 2011–2012		First-Year Class	
Men:	307 43%	Applied:	422
Women:	401 52%	Accepted:	215
Minorities:	0 0%	Enrolled:	201
Out-of-State:	7 1%		

2011–2012 Class Profile
LSAT Percentile: 27%
LSAT Median Score: 146
Percentage passing bar on first try: 62%

Tuition and Fees:

Resident
$4,904 (F/T)

Average (public)
$18,708

Average (private)
$34,451

Nonresident
$4,904 (F/T)

Average (public)
$29,793

Average (private)
$34,451

0 10 20 30 40 50

Percentage receiving financial aid: 60%

ADMISSIONS
In the fall of 2011 first-year class, 422 applied, 215 were accepted, and 201 enrolled. Seventeen transfers enrolled. The median LSAT percentile of the most recent first-year class was 27; the median GPA was 3.6 on a scale of 4.0. The lowest LSAT percentile accepted was 2; the highest was 89.

Requirements
Applicants must have a bachelor's degree and take the LSAT. No specific undergraduate courses are required. Candidates are not interviewed.

Procedure
The application deadline for fall entry is February 15. Applicants should submit an application form, LSAT results, transcripts, EXADEP results, and a nonrefundable application fee of $20. Accepted students must pay a $45 seat deposit (credited toward tuition). Notification of the admissions decision is in April and May. The law school uses the LSAC.

Special
The law school recruits minority and disadvantaged students. Requirements are different for out-of-state students. Transfer students must have a minimum GPA of 3.3, must have attended an ABA-approved law school, and must have 12 approved credits.

Costs
On-campus room and board costs about $5,720 annually; books and supplies run $3,050.

Financial Aid
About 60% of current law students receive some form of aid. The average annual amount of aid from all sources combined, including scholarships, loans, and work contracts, is $10,500; maximum, $19,909. Awards are based on need and merit combined. The required financial statement is the FAFSA. The aid application deadline for fall entry is May 1. First-year students are notified about their financial aid application at time of acceptance.

About the Law School
University of Puerto Rico School of Law was established in 1913 and is a public institution. The 5-acre campus is in an urban area in metropolitan San Juan. The primary mission of the law school is to train competent lawyers and jurists with a strong sense of professional, ethical, and social responsibility. Students have access to federal, state, county, city, and local agencies, courts, correctional facilities, law firms, and legal aid organizations in the Rio Piedras area. Housing for students is available in dormitories on campus. About 95% of the law school facilities are accessible to the physically disabled.

Calendar
The law school operates on a traditional semester basis. Courses for full-time students are offered both day and evening, and must be completed within 6 semesters. For part-time students, courses are offered both day and evening, and must be completed within 8 semesters. New full- and part-time students are admitted in the fall. There is a 6-week summer session. Transferable summer courses are not offered.

Programs
In addition to the J.D., the law school offers the LL.M. Students may take relevant courses in other programs and apply credit toward the J.D.; a maximum of 6 credits may be applied. The following joint degrees may be earned: J.D./Lic. (Juris Doctor/dual degree program with the University of Barcelona), J.D./M.B.A. (Juris Doctor/Master of Business Administration), J.D./M.D. (Juris Doctor/Doctor of Medicine), and J.D./M.P.P. (Juris Doctor/Master of Public Policy).

Required
To earn the J.D., candidates must complete 92 total credits, of which 46 are for required courses. They must maintain a minimum GPA of 2.0 in the required courses. The following first-year courses are required of all students: Civil Procedure, Constitutional Law, Criminal Law, Family Law, Introduction to Law, Legal Research, Obligations and Contracts Law, Problems in International Law, Property, and Torts. Required upper-level courses consist of Business Associations and Corporations, Evidence, Legal Aid Clinic I and II, and Theory of Law. All students must take clinical courses. The required orientation program for first-year students lasts 1 week and includes information on financial aid, required courses, exchange programs, methods of study, and a brief introduction to law school.

Electives
All students are required to take clinics on civil, criminal, or federal law, worth 6 credits, and 2 2-credit seminars. During the summer an elective legal practice workshop is offered; it is worth 2 credits. Legal research in urban planning, housing, poverty, and related subjects is encouraged in a number of courses. There is a summer course in Barcelona, worth up to 6 credits, which is open to all students in good standing. There is also a double-degree program with the University of Barcelona, and programs with the University of Chile Law School; University of Ottawa, Canada; University of Palermo, Argentina; University of Arizona; University of Connecticut; and University of Antwerp, Belgium. The most widely taken electives are Bankruptcy, Taxation, and Criminology.

Phone: 787-999-9551
Fax: 787-999-9564
E-mail: aquinones@law.upr.edu

Contact

Director of Admissions, 787-999-9551 or 787-999-9553 for general inquiries; Michael Ayala, 787-999-9557 or 787-999-9563 for financial aid information.

PUERTO RICO

Graduation Requirements

In order to graduate, candidates must have a GPA of 2.0 and must have completed the upper-division writing requirement.

Organizations

Students edit the *University of Puerto Rico Law Review* and the newspaper *El Nuevo Jurista*. Moot court competitions include the Annual Pace University School of Law National Environmental, NACDL Katty Bennet Criminal Trial, and Philip C. Jessup International. Another competition is the Miguel Velazquez Annual Debate. Law student organizations include the Student Council, Derecho Pa Vieques, Phi Alpha Delta, the National Association of Law Students, and ABA-Law Student Division. Student representatives chosen by the student council serve on all law school committees, except the personnel committee.

Library

The law library contains 283,745 hardcopy volumes and 172,059 microform volume equivalents, and subscribes to 5,159 serial publications. Such online databases and networks as CALI, DIALOG, Infotrac, Legal-Trac, LEXIS, Mathew Bender, WESTLAW, Wilsonline Indexes, West Law Spain, HeinOnline, Index to Foreign Legal Periodicals, RIA Checkpoint, LexisNexis Argentina, Microjuris, JTS Online, Consulta Legislativa, and El Nuevo Dia are available to law students for research. Special library collections include extensive collections of Puerto Rico, Spain, Caribbean, Latin American, and comparative and international law, a U.S. GPO government depository, specialized European Communities Documentation Centre, and documents collections of former judges of the Supreme Court of Puerto Rico. The ratio of library volumes to faculty is 9,458 to 1 and to students is 396 to 1. The ratio of seats in the library to students is 1 to 1.

Faculty

The law school has 29 full-time and 48 part-time faculty members, of whom 27 are women. About 73% of full-time faculty have a graduate law degree in addition to the J.D.; about 40% of part-time faculty have one. The ratio of full-time students to full-time faculty in an average class is 15 to 1; in a clinic, 13 to 1. The law school has a regular program of bringing visiting professors and other distinguished lecturers and visitors to campus.

Students

About 52% of the student body are women. The majority of students come from Puerto Rico (99%). The average age of entering students is 24; age range is 20 to 54. About 81% of students enter directly from undergraduate school, and 19% have a graduate degree. About 5% drop out after the first year for academic or personal reasons; 95% remain to receive a law degree.

Placement

J.D.s awarded:	235
Services available through: a separate law school placement center.	
Special features: an annual job fair.	
Full-time job interviews:	1 employer
Placement within 9 months of graduation:	81% of class
Average starting salary:	$24,000 to $50,999
Areas of placement:	
Private practice 2–10 attorneys	15%
Private practice 11–25 attorneys	3%
Private practice 26–50 attorneys	22%
Business/industry	20%
Judicial clerkships	18%
Government	17%
Academic	5%

School of Law

28 Westhampton Way
Richmond, VA 23173

Application Filing		Accreditation
Fall: March 15		ABA, AALS
		Degrees Granted
Fee: $50		J.D.

Enrollment 2011–2012			First-Year Class	
Men:	246	54%	Applied:	2,371
Women:	211	46%	Accepted:	563
Minorities:	78	17%	Enrolled:	154
Out-of-State:	206	45%		

2011–2012 Class Profile

LSAT Percentile: 86%
LSAT Median Score: 162
Percentage passing bar on first try: 85%

Tuition and Fees:

Resident
$35,430 (F/T)

Average (public)
$18,708

Average (private)
$34,451

Nonresident
$35,430 (F/T)

Average (public)
$29,793

Average (private)
$34,451

0 10 20 30 40 50

Percentage receiving financial aid: 89%

ADMISSIONS

In the fall of 2011 first-year class, 2371 applied, 563 were accepted, and 154 enrolled. Twenty transfer students enrolled. The median LSAT percentile of the most recent first-year class was 86; the median GPA was 3.5 on a scale of 4.0. The lowest LSAT percentile accepted was 48; the highest was 99.

Requirements
Applicants must have a bachelor's degree and take the LSAT. The most important admission factors include academic achievement, LSAT results, and general background. No specific undergraduate courses are required, and candidates are not interviewed.

Procedure
The application deadline for fall entry is March 15. Applicants should submit an application form, LSAT results, transcripts, personal statement, nonrefundable application fee of $50, and 2 letters of recommendation. Notification of the admissions decision is April 1. The law school uses the LSAC.

Special
The law school recruits minority and disadvantaged students by attending minority law forums, being a Council for Legal Education Opportunity (CLEO) sponsor, being a CLEO Regional Summer Institute site, visiting historically black colleges and universities, and offering scholarships. Requirements are different for out-of-state students. Transfer students must have one year of credits, attended an ABA-approved law school, personal statement, and must be in good standing at an ABA-approved law school.

Costs

Tuition and fees for the 2011–2012 academic year are $35,430 for all full-time students. On-campus room and board costs about $9,590 annually; books and supplies run $1,400.

Financial Aid

About 89% of current law students receive some form of aid. The average annual amount of aid from all sources combined, including scholarships, loans, and work contracts, is $44,040; maximum, $51,210. Awards are based on need and merit. All admitted students must file the FAFSA by February 25. Required financial statement is the FAFSA. The aid application deadline for fall entry is February 25. First-year students are notified about their financial aid application April 1.

About the Law School

University of Richmond School of Law was established in 1870 and is a private institution. The 350-acre campus is located in a suburban area 2 miles west of Richmond. The primary mission of the law school is to train its graduates to practice law. Its relatively small size helps fashion a close and open relationship between students and faculty. Students have access to federal, state, county, city, and local agencies, courts, correctional facilities, law firms, and legal aid organizations in the Richmond area. Facilities of special interest to law students include the law library with a legal research and writing computer laboratory, and individualized study carrels that are electronically networked via students' personal computers to the Legal Information Center, a schoolwide computer system that gives instant access to the electronic age in law. Housing for students is available in a law dormitory with single rooms. Attractively priced apartments are available very close to the campus. All law school facilities are accessible to the physically disabled.

Calendar

The law school operates on a traditional semester basis. Courses for full-time students are offered days only and must be completed within 5 years. For part-time students, courses are offered days only and must be completed within 5 years. New full- and part-time students are admitted in the fall and summer. There are 3- and 8-week summer sessions. Transferable summer courses are offered.

Programs

Students may take relevant courses in other programs and apply credit toward the J.D.; a maximum of 9 credits may be applied. The following joint degrees may be earned: J.D./M.B.A. (Juris Doctor/Master of Business Administration), J.D./M.H.A. (Juris Doctor/Master of Health Administration), J.D./M.P.A. (Juris Doctor/Master of Public Administration), J.D./M.S.W. (Juris Doctor/Master of Social Work), and J.D./M.U.R.P. (Juris Doctor/Master of Urban and Regional Planning).

Required
To earn the J.D., candidates must complete 86 total credits, of which 38 are for required courses. The following first-year courses are required of all students: Civil Procedure, Constitutional Law, Contracts, Criminal Law, Lawyering Skills I and II, Legislation and Regulation, Property, and Torts. Required upper-level courses consist of Professional Responsibility, upper-level lawyering skills III and IV, and upper-level writing requirement. The required orientation program for first-year students lasts 3 days and includes network and computer training and an introduction to lawyering skills as well as the law school administration, faculty, staff, student organizations, and law student advisers.

Phone: 804-289-8189
Fax: 804-287-6516
E-mail: lawadmissions@richmond.edu
Web: law.richmond.edu

Contact

Michelle L. Rahman, Associate Dean, 804-289-8189 for general inquiries; C. Deffenbaugh, Director of Financial Aid, 804-289-8438 for financial aid information.

VIRGINIA

Electives

The School of Law offers concentrations in environmental law, family law, intellectual property law, juvenile law, torts and insurance, Intellectual Property Certification, Environmental Law Certification, and Family Law Certification. In addition, third-year students may participate in either the outplacement clinic or the school's in-house Children's Law Center, with Youth Advocacy and Mental Disabilities clinics. The outplacement clinic allows students to work in various legal offices in the community, which are complemented by a classroom component. The clinical programs, supervised by a staff attorney, allows students to represent clients in business, civil, criminal, and judicial matters. Students may also participate in the D.C. Summer Environmental Internship Program in Washington, D.C. Credit varies for these programs. The Special Lecture series includes the Allen Chair Lecture, Emroch Lecture, Austin Owen Lecture, and Legal Forum. There is also a study-abroad option. Students may study international law for 5 weeks at Emmanuel College in Cambridge, England, or for a semester at any one of 9 foreign universities with which the law school has an exchange program. There is an academic support program for all students. The most widely taken electives are Evidence, Corporations, and Criminal Procedure.

Graduation Requirements

In order to graduate, candidates must have a GPA of 2.2 and complete the upper-division writing requirement.

Organizations

Students edit the *University of Richmond Law Review, Journal of Law and Technology* (which is completely online), *Perspectives on Law and the Public Interest, Journal of International Law and Business, Journal of Law and Public Interest*, and the newspaper *Juris Publici*. Moot court teams attend the Appellate Advocacy Moot Court Competition in the fall and the Motions and Interscholastic Motions Competition in the spring as well as the Judge John R. Brown Admiralty Moot Court Competition. There are intramural competitions in both client counseling and negotiations. The winning teams enter respective ABA competitions. Annually, the National Environmental Negotiation Competition is entered. The school has hosted the ABA regional competition. Law student organizations include the Student Bar Association, Client Counseling and Negotiation Board, American Constitution Society, and Federalist Society for Law and Public Policy Studies. There are local chapters of ABA-Student Division, the Black Law Students Association, and Phi Alpha Delta. Additionally, there are intramural sports, including soccer and softball.

Library

The law library contains 425,122 hardcopy volumes and 204,393 microform volume equivalents, and subscribes to 4,503 serial publications. Online databases and networks include CALI, CIS Universe, DIALOG, Infotrac, Legal-Trac, LEXIS, Mathew Bender, OCLC First Search, WESTLAW, and Wilsonline Indexes. The school also subsribes to many other online databases, which are available to law students for research. Special library collections include a U.S. government documents depository, Robert R. Merhige, Jr. judicial papers, Tokyo war crimes tribunal, Blackwell N. Shelley bankruptcy opinions, and Virginia Supreme Court records and briefs digital collection. The ratio of library volumes to faculty is 8,852 to 1 and to students is 928 to 1. The ratio of seats in the library to students is 1 to 1.

Faculty

The law school has 46 full-time and 80 part-time faculty members, of whom 45 are women. About 47% of full-time faculty have a graduate law degree in addition to the J.D. The ratio of full-time students to full-time faculty in an average class is 12 to 1; in a clinic, 6 to 1. The law school has a regular program of bringing visiting professors and other distinguished lecturers and visitors to campus. There is a chapter of the Order of the Coif.

Students

About 46% of the student body are women; 17%, minorities; 8%, African American; 6%, Asian American; 1%, Hispanic; and 1%, Native American. The majority of students come from Virginia (55%). The average age of entering students is 24; age range is 20 to 50. About 51% of students enter directly from undergraduate school, 10% have a graduate degree, and 50% have worked full-time prior to entering law school. About 1% drop out after the first year for academic or personal reasons; 99% remain to receive a law degree.

Placement

J.D.s awarded:	166

Services available through: a separate law school placement center and the university placement center.

Services: programs on law practice areas, minority job and career fairs, specialty fairs, and job search programs with national speakers and specialty career fairs.

Special features: Individual attention available to all students with 4 professional staff members in career services office.

Placement by graduation:	62% of class
Placement within 9 months:	89% of class
Average starting salary:	$40,000 to $165,000

Areas of placement:

Private practice 2–10 attorneys	15%
Private practice 11–25 attorneys	7%
Private practice 26–50 attorneys	4%
Private practice 51–100 attorneys	1%
Business/industry	36%
Judicial clerkships	21%
Government	9%
Public interest	2%

University of Richmond   **553**

UNIVERSITY OF SAINT THOMAS

School of Law

1000 LaSalle Ave.
Minneapolis, MN 55403

Application Filing		Accreditation
Fall: July 1		ABA
		Degrees Granted
		J.D.

Enrollment 2011–2012			First-Year Class	
Men:	274	57%	Applied:	1,283
Women:	209	43%	Accepted:	711
Minorities:	68	14%	Enrolled:	171
Out-of-State:	217	45%		

2011–2012 Class Profile
LSAT Percentile: 67%
LSAT Median Score: 156
Percentage passing bar on first try: 91%

Tuition and Fees:

Resident
$34,898 (F/T)

Average (public)
$18,708

Average (private)
$34,451

Nonresident
$34,898 (F/T)

Average (public)
$29,793

Average (private)
$34,451

Percentage receiving financial aid: 99%

ADMISSIONS

In the fall of 2011 first-year class, 1283 applied, 711 were accepted, and 171 enrolled. Five transfers enrolled. The median LSAT percentile of the most recent first-year class was 67; the median GPA was 3.4 on a scale of 4.0. The lowest LSAT percentile accepted was 11; the highest was 98.

Requirements
Applicants must have a bachelor's degree and take the LSAT. The most important admission factors include academic achievement and general background. No specific undergraduate courses are required. Candidates are not interviewed.

Procedure
The application deadline for fall entry is July 1. Applicants should submit an application form, LSAT results, transcripts, a personal statement, and 2 letters of recommendation. Notification of the admissions decision is on a rolling basis. The law school uses the LSAC.

Special
The law school recruits minority and disadvantaged students through campus visits, advertising, direct mailings, participation in minority recruitment events, and a scholarship program. Requirements are different for out-of-state students. Transfer students must have one year of credit, must have attended an ABA-approved law school, and must submit a personal statement.

Costs

Tuition and fees for the 2011–2012 academic year are $34,599 for all full-time students. Books and supplies run $1,550.

Financial Aid

About 99% of current law students receive some form of aid. The average annual amount of aid from all sources combined, including scholarships, loans, and work contracts, is $45,547; maximum, $68,760. Awards are based on need and merit combined. The required financial statement is the FAFSA. The aid application deadline for fall entry is July 1. Special funds for minority or disadvantaged students include the Ciresi Scholarship. First-year students are notified about their financial aid application at time of acceptance.

About the Law School

University of Saint Thomas School of Law was established in 2001 and is a private institution. The 53-acre campus is in an urban area in downtown Minneapolis. The primary mission of the law school is to train lawyers dedicated to promoting excellence in professional preparation, knowledge creation and societal reform, and dedicated to service and community. Students have access to federal, state, county, city, and local agencies, courts, correctional facilities, law firms, and legal aid organizations in the Minneapolis area. Students have access to in-house corporate legal staff, and each student is assigned a mentor. Facilities of special interest to law students include the four-story atrium moot court room and chapel, modern technology throughout the law building, and the library's strong electronic collection. There is no on-campus housing, but the school offers assistance in finding housing. All law school facilities are accessible to the physically disabled.

Calendar

The law school operates on a traditional semester basis. Courses are offered both day and evening, and must be completed within 4 years. New students are admitted in the fall. There is a 7-week summer session. Transferable summer courses are offered.

Programs

Students may take relevant courses in other programs and apply credit toward the J.D.; a maximum of 6 credits may be applied. The following joint degrees may be earned: J.D./M.A.C.S. (Juris Doctor/Master of Arts in Catholic Studies), J.D./M.A.Ed. (Juris Doctor/Master of Arts in Educational Leadership), J.D./M.B.A. (Juris Doctor/Master of Business Administration), and J.D./M.S.W. (Juris Doctor/Master of Social Work).

Required
To earn the J.D., candidates must complete 88 total credits, of which 46 are for required courses. They must maintain a minimum GPA of 2.0 in the required courses. The following first-year courses are required of all students: Civil Procedure I, Constitutional Law, Contracts, Criminal Law, Foundations of Justice, Lawyering Skills I and II, Property, and Torts. Required upper-level courses consist of Business Associations, Evidence, Lawyering Skills III, Mentor Externship, Professional Responsibility, and Public Service Requirement. The required orientation program for first-year students is called "First Week," lasts five days, and includes a noncredit academic success course, a one-credit Foundation of Justice course, and a variety of optional social, spiritual service, and informational programs introducing students to UST and the Twin Cities legal system.

Electives
Clinics include Immigration Law (6 credits), Community Justice Project (6 credits), and Elder Law (6 credits). Seminars include Ethical Leadership in Corporate Practice (3 credits), Catholic Social Thought (2 credits), and Critical Perspectives on the Law: Race (2 credits). There is a Mentor Externship Program (2 credits) that combines mentor directed fieldwork with a contemporaneous faculty-led seminar (upper level). Supervised research

Phone: 651-962-4895
800-328-6819
Fax: 651-962-4876
E-mail: lawschool@stthomas.edu
Web: www.stthomas.edu/lawschool

Contact

Director of Admissions, 651-962-4895 for general inquiries; Chad Nosbusch, Director of Financial Aid, 651-962-4051 for financial aid information.

MINNESOTA

Services available through: a separate law school placement center.

Services: mock interviews; counseling on other application material preparation; and training in networking skills.

Full-time job interviews:	5 employers
Summer job interviews:	34 employers
Placement by graduation:	57% of class
Placement within 9 months:	88% of class

Areas of placement:

Private practice 2–10 attorneys	22%
Private practice 11–25 attorneys	5%
Private practice 26–50 attorneys	1%
Private practice 51–100 attorneys	2%
Business/industry	21%
Judicial clerkships	11%
Government	11%
Public interest	6%
Military	2%
Academic	2%

and writing (1 to 2 credits) is available. Field work includes District Court Judicial Externship (3 credits) and Business Law Externship (2 credits). Special lecture series include law journal symposia (2 per year). The school accepts credit from ABA-approved study-abroad programs and co-sponsors a summer program in Rome. Tutorial/remedial programs include a non-credit academic achievement program, study skills, advising, and a 2-credit bar skills course. There is a law firm-sponsored minority scholarship/mentor program; the Ciresi Scholarship for minority students; and the Minnesota Minority Clerkship Program in which UST students can participate. The family law student group partners with law firms and agencies to assist in adoptions. The most widely taken electives are Wills, Estates, and Trusts; Employment Law; and Criminal Procedure.

Graduation Requirements

In order to graduate, candidates must have a GPA of 2.0, must have completed the upper-division writing requirement, and must have completed public service (50 hours) and the Mentor Externship Program.

Organizations

Students edit the *University of St. Thomas Law Journal, Fides es Iustitia*, the student newspaper *Tommie Law News*, and the student organization published *Journal of Law and Public policy*. Moot court competitions include the National Advocacy Competition, Giles Sutherland Rich Memorial Moot Court Competition, and Philip C. Jessup International Law Moot Court Competition. Other competitions include ABA Negotiation Competition and AAJ Trial Advocacy Competition. Law student organizations include the Christian Legal Society, American Constitution Society, and Minnesota Justice Foundation. Local chapters of national associations are the Black Law Students Association, The Federalist Society, and Phi Alpha Delta legal fraternity. Other clubs include Environmental Law Society, Business and Corporate Law Society, and Criminal Law Society.

Library

The law library contains 218,238 hardcopy volumes and 889,735 microform volume equivalents, and subscribes to 3,492 serial publications. Such online databases and networks as CALI, CIS Universe, Infotrac, Legal-Trac, LEXIS, OCLC First Search, WESTLAW, Wilsonline Indexes, and other online databases are available to law students for research. The ratio of library volumes to faculty is 8,083 to 1 and to students is 454 to 1. The ratio of seats in the library to students is 1 to 1.

Faculty

The law school has 33 full-time and 64 part-time faculty members, of whom 31 are women. According to AAUP standards for Category I institutions, faculty salaries are average. About 21% of full-time faculty have a graduate law degree in addition to the J.D.; about 8% of part-time faculty have one. The ratio of full-time students to full-time faculty in an average class is 14 to 1; in a clinic, 7 to 1. The law school has a regular program of bringing visiting professors and other distinguished lecturers and visitors to campus.

Students

About 43% of the student body are women; 14%, minorities; 3%, African American; 5%, Asian American; 4%, Hispanic; and 1%, Native American. The majority of students come from Minnesota (55%). The average age of entering students is 25; age range is 21 to 54. About 37% of students enter directly from undergraduate school, 6% have a graduate degree, and 67% have worked full-time prior to entering law school. About 3% drop out after the first year for academic or personal reasons; 96% remain to receive a law degree.

UNIVERSITY OF SAN DIEGO

School of Law

5998 Alcala Park
San Diego, CA 92110

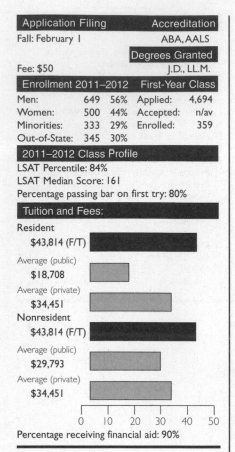

Application Filing	Accreditation
Fall: February 1	ABA, AALS
	Degrees Granted
Fee: $50	J.D., LL.M.

Enrollment 2011–2012		First-Year Class	
Men:	649 56%	Applied:	4,694
Women:	500 44%	Accepted:	n/av
Minorities:	333 29%	Enrolled:	359
Out-of-State:	345 30%		

2011–2012 Class Profile
LSAT Percentile: 84%
LSAT Median Score: 161
Percentage passing bar on first try: 80%

Tuition and Fees:

Resident
$43,814 (F/T)

Average (public)
$18,708

Average (private)
$34,451

Nonresident
$43,814 (F/T)

Average (public)
$29,793

Average (private)
$34,451

Percentage receiving financial aid: 90%

ADMISSIONS
In the fall of 2011 first-year class, 4694 applied and 359 enrolled. The median LSAT percentile of the most recent first-year class was 84; the median GPA was 3.3 on a scale of 4.0.

Requirements
Applicants must have a bachelor's degree and take the LSAT. The most important admission factors include academic achievement, GPA, and LSAT results. No specific undergraduate courses are required. Candidates are not interviewed.

Procedure
The application deadline for fall entry is February 1. Applicants should submit an application form, LSAT results, transcripts, a personal statement, and a nonrefundable application fee of $50. Notification of the admissions decision is January through mid-April. The law school uses the LSAC.

Special
The law school recruits minority and disadvantaged students by welcoming and respecting those whose lives are formed by different traditions, recognizing that diversity of viewpoint, background, and experience (including race, ethnicity, cultural diversity, gender, religion, age, socioeconomic status, and disability) among its student body is essential to the full and informed exchange of ideas and to the quality of legal education it seeks to provide. Requirements are different for out-of-state students. Transfer students must have one year of credit, must have attended an ABA-approved law school, must submit a personal statement, and should rank in the top quintile of the first-year class.

Costs
Tuition and fees for the 2011–2012 academic year are $43,600 for all full-time students. Tuition for part-time students is $31,440 for in-state students and $31,440 out-of-state. On-campus room and board costs about $18,440 annually; books and supplies run $1,447.

Financial Aid
About 90% of current law students receive some form of aid. The average annual amount of aid from all sources combined, including scholarships, loans, and work contracts, is $38,000; maximum, $57,100. Awards are based on need and merit combined. Required financial statements are the FAFSA and institutional application for accepted students. The aid application deadline for fall entry is March 2. Special funds for minority or disadvantaged are based on the applicant's academic promise, financial need, potential for service to the community, and contribution to the diversity of the student body. First-year students are notified about their financial aid application at time of acceptance.

About the Law School
University of San Diego School of Law was established in 1954 and is a private institution. The 180-acre campus is in an urban area 5 miles north of downtown San Diego. The primary mission of the law school is to foster an environment of stimulating and rigorous intellectual exchange between teacher and student in which teaching and learning engage the full attention of faculty and students while maintaining concern for the broader personal and moral development of the law student. Students have access to federal, state, county, city, and local agencies, courts, correctional facilities, law firms, and legal aid organizations in the San Diego area. Housing for students is available in safe and affordable accommodations near campus. The Admissions Office maintains a listing of students seeking roommates and other resources. About 90% of the law school facilities are accessible to the physically disabled.

Calendar
The law school operates on a traditional semester basis. Courses for full-time students are offered days only, and must be completed within 5 years. For part-time students, courses are offered evenings only, and must be completed within 5 years. New full- and part-time students are admitted in the fall. There is an 8-week summer session. Transferable summer courses are offered.

Programs
In addition to the J.D., the law school offers the LL.M. Students may take relevant courses in other programs and apply credit toward the J.D.; a maximum of 6 credits may be applied. The following joint degrees may be earned: J.D./I.M.B.A. (Juris Doctor/International Master of Business Administration), J.D./M.A. (Juris Doctor/Master of Arts in International Relations), and J.D./M.B.A. (Juris Doctor/Master of Business Administration).

Required
To earn the J.D., candidates must complete 85 total credits, of which 35 are for required courses. They must maintain a minimum GPA of 2.0 in the required courses. The following first-year courses are required of all students: Civil Procedure, Constitutional Law, Contracts, Criminal Law, Lawyering Skills I, Property, and Torts. Required upper-level courses consist of Professional Responsibility and Tax I. The required orientation program for first-year students is offered to incoming students, who attend a mandatory 2-day orientation. Many topics are presented for discussion including Socratic method, time management, and how to study for law school exams.

Phone: 619-260-4528
800-248-4873
Fax: 619-260-2718
E-mail: jdinfo@sandiego.edu
Web: law.sandiego.edu

Contact

Assistant Dean of Admissions and Financial Aid, 619-260-4528 for general inquiries; Carl J. Eging, Assistant Dean of Admissions, 619-260-4570 for financial aid information.

Electives

The School of Law offers concentrations in corporate law, criminal law, environmental law, family law, international law, labor law, litigation, tax law, torts and insurance, and public/children's advocacy. In addition, students may enroll for up to 10 credits of clinical field work. They represent clients in consumer, housing, family, and administrative matters. Several seminar courses are offered each semester. Internships are available in-house through the Clinical Education Program, as well as with local agencies, government offices, and law firms in a variety of areas. Research programs are available at the Center for Public Interest Law, Patient Advocacy Program, and the Children's Advocacy Institute. Special lecture series include the Nathanson Series and the Seigan Series. The Institute on International and Comparative Law sponsors the Summer Law Study Programs in England, France, Ireland, Italy, and Spain. Internships for credit are available in England and France. The Academic Support Program provides special services to students. A faculty member provides academic counseling and sets up study groups for each class. Minority programs include a Multicultural Law Day. Pro Bono Legal Advocates promote diversity in the bar and donate students' talent and time to clients who cannot afford a lawyer. The most widely taken electives are courses relevant to international law, environmental law, and corporate law.

Graduation Requirements

In order to graduate, candidates must have a GPA of 2.0 and must have completed the upper-division writing requirement.

Organizations

Students edit the *San Diego Law Review*, the *San Diego International Law Journal*, the newspaper *Motions*, the *Journal of Contemporary Legal Issues*, and *Legal Theory*. Moot court competitions include the Alumni Tort, Annual USD National Criminal Procedure Competition, and Jessup International Law. Other competitions include Advanced Trial Advocacy, Mock Trial, and Thomas More Constitutional Law. Student organizations, local chapters of national associations, and campus organizations include American Trial Lawyers Association, Pro Bono Legal Advocates, Women's Law Caucus, Student Bar Association, Environmental Law Society, International Law Society, Phi Delta Phi, and Phi Alpha Delta.

Library

The law library contains 529,802 hardcopy volumes and 226,282 microform volume equivalents, and subscribes to 6,250 serial publications. Such online databases and networks as CALI, CIS Universe, DIALOG, Dow-Jones, Infotrac, Legal-Trac, LEXIS, Mathew Bender, OCLC First Search, RLIN, WESTLAW, CCH, RIA, HeinOnline, LLMC, and Index Master are available to law students for research. Special library collections include state and federal depositories, tax collection, and California collection. The ratio of library volumes to faculty is 9,461 to 1 and to students is 461 to 1. The ratio of seats in the library to students is 1 to 2.

Faculty

The law school has 56 full-time and 39 part-time faculty members, of whom 23 are women. According to AAUP standards for Category 1 institutions, faculty salaries are above average. The ratio of full-time students to full-time faculty in an average class is 18 to 1. The law school has a regular program of bringing visiting professors and other distinguished lecturers and visitors to campus. There is a chapter of the Order of the Coif.

Students

About 44% of the student body are women; 29%, minorities; 3%, African American; 15%, Asian American; 10%, Hispanic; 1%, Native American; and 1%, foreign nationals. The majority of students come from California (70%). The average age of entering students is 24; age range is 21 to 52. About 8% of students have a graduate degree. About 2% drop out after the first year for academic or personal reasons; 85% remain to receive a law degree.

CALIFORNIA

Placement

J.D.s awarded:	333
Services available through: a separate law school placement center.	
Special features: panel discussions sponsored by the Alumni Association that focus on law practice, alternative careers, and law clerk training.	
Placement within 9 months of graduation:	97% of class
Average starting salary:	$35,000 to $160,000
Areas of placement:	
Private practice 2–10 attorneys	28%
Private practice 11–25 attorneys	14%
Private practice 26–50 attorneys	10%
Private practice 51–100 attorneys	11%
Business/industry	17%
Government	13%
Public interest	5%
Judicial clerkships	2%
Academic	2%
Military	1%

School of Law

2130 Fulton Street
San Francisco, CA 94117-1080

Application Filing	Accreditation
Fall: February 1	ABA, AALS

	Degrees Granted
Fee: $60	J.D., LL.M.

Enrollment 2011–2012			First-Year Class	
Men:	332	45%	Applied:	4,215
Women:	399	55%	Accepted:	1,603
Minorities:	285	39%	Enrolled:	246
Out-of-State:	154	21%		

2011–2012 Class Profile
LSAT Percentile: 70%
LSAT Median Score: 157
Percentage passing bar on first try: 85%

Tuition and Fees:

Resident
$40,544 (F/T)

Average (public)
$18,708

Average (private)
$34,451

Nonresident
$40,544 (F/T)

Average (public)
$29,793

Average (private)
$34,451

0 10 20 30 40 50

Percentage receiving financial aid: 85%

ADMISSIONS
In the fall of 2011 first-year class, 4215 applied, 1603 were accepted, and 246 enrolled. Six transfers enrolled. The median LSAT percentile of the most recent first-year class was 70; the median GPA was 3.4 on a scale of 4.0. The lowest LSAT percentile accepted was 13; the highest was 98.

Requirements
Applicants must have a bachelor's degree and take the LSAT. The most important admission factors include academic achievement, general background, and minority status. No specific undergraduate courses are required. Candidates are not interviewed.

Procedure
The application deadline for fall entry is February 1. Applicants should submit an application form, LSAT results, transcripts, a personal statement, a nonrefundable application fee of $60, 2 letters of recommendation, and optional diversity statement. Notification of the admissions decision is on a rolling basis. The law school uses the LSAC.

Special
The law school recruits minority and disadvantaged students by actively recruiting and targeting colleges with large populations of students of color. Requirements are different for out-of-state students. Transfer students must have one year of credit, must have attended an ABA-approved law school, and must submit a personal statement. The deadline for transfer is June 26.

Costs
Tuition and fees for the 2011–2012 academic year are $40,464 for all full-time students. Tuition for part-time students is $30,345 for in-state students and $30,345 out-of-state. On-campus room and board costs about $15,000 annually; books and supplies run $1,500.

Financial Aid
About 85% of current law students receive some form of aid. The maximum annual amount of aid from all sources combined, including scholarships, loans, and work contracts, is $61,204. Awards are based on need and merit combined. The required financial statement is the FAFSA. The aid application deadline for fall entry is February 15. Special funds for minority or disadvantaged students include the Academic Support Program, which provides two grants that vary in amounts up to $3,500, based on need. First-year students are notified about their financial aid application at time of acceptance.

About the Law School
University of San Francisco School of Law was established in 1912 and is a private institution. The 55-acre campus is in an urban area in the center of San Francisco. The primary mission of the law school is to educate students to be skilled lawyers with a social conscience and a global perspective, emphasizing analytical ability and other fundamental skills, along with full awareness of special obligations to society. Students have access to federal, state, county, city, and local agencies, courts, correctional facilities, law firms, and legal aid organizations in the San Francisco area. The law school is minutes away from federal, state, and municipal courts as well as cultural, social, and recreational resources in San Francisco and throughout the greater Bay Area. Facilities of special interest to law students include Kendrick Hall and the Dorraine Zief Library. The law library has numerous individual and group study rooms, as well as computer classrooms, laboratories, and specially designed training and research rooms. In Kendrick Hall the classrooms include power and data connections at every seat, and state-of-the-art equipment throughout the building. Housing for students is limited on campus; listings of off-campus accommodations also available. All law school facilities are accessible to the physically disabled.

Calendar
The law school operates on a traditional semester basis. Courses for full-time students are offered during the day, and sometimes in the evening, and must be completed within 5 years. For part-time students, courses are offered mostly in evenings, and must be completed within 5 years. New full- and part-time students are admitted in the fall. There is a 7-week summer session. Transferable summer courses are offered.

Programs
In addition to the J.D., the law school offers the LL.M. The following joint degrees may be earned: J.D./M.B.A. (Juris Doctor/ Master of Business Administration).

Required
To earn the J.D., candidates must complete 84 total credits, of which 48 are for required courses. They must maintain a minimum GPA of 2.3 in the required courses. The following first-year courses are required of all students: Civil Procedure I, Contracts I, Criminal Law (second-year part-time), Legal Research, Writing, and Analysis I and II, Property, and Torts. Required upper-level courses consist of Constitutional Law, Evidence, Legal Ethics, Professional Responsibility, and a professional skills requirement. The required orientation program for first-year students is a week long program that serves to welcome and inform incoming students. An introduction course provides essential initiation to first-year courses. Other

Phone: 415-422-6586
Fax: 415-422-5442
E-mail: lawadmissions@usfca.edu
Web: usfca.edu/law

Contact
Director of Admissions, 415-422-6586 for general inquiries; Jamal Collins, Law School Financial Aid Coordinator, 415-422-6210 for financial aid information.

CALIFORNIA

meetings and events cover important topics and social activities designed to ease the transition to the law school experience and environment.

Electives

The School of Law offers concentrations in corporate law, criminal law, environmental law, family law, intellectual property law, internationl law, juvenile law, labor law, litigation, maritime law, securities law, tax law, torts and insurance, and intellectual property (including entertainment, sports, and media law). In addition, clinical programs include International Human Rights Clinic (3 units), Criminal and Juvenile Justice Clinic (6 units), and the Child Advocacy Clinic (6 units). Seminars are offered in many subjects, including International Business and Civil Dispute Resolution (3 units), and Legal Ethics and the Practice of Law (3 units). The Clinical Internship and Judicial Externship programs give students the opportunity to earn academic credit while working in legal agencies (3 to 6 units) or with federal and state judges (3 to 12 units) throughout the San Francisco Bay Area. Students may earn 1 to 2 units of credit working on a directed research project, under the supervision of a full-time faculty member. USF offers three summer abroad study opportunities in Dublin, Prague, and Mexico. Academic support is available to select incoming students for the first semester based on admission criteria. All first-year students are eligible for academic support as needed after the first semester or when referred by a faculty member. Support is ongoing for those in need through a special second-year course, and in the final year through a series of bar preparation workshops. The Academic Support Program (ASP) was created to assist students of diverse backgrounds in succeeding in law school. The most widely taken electives are Corporations, Wills and Trusts, and Remedies.

Graduation Requirements

In order to graduate, candidates must have a GPA of 2.3 and must have completed the upper-division writing requirement.

Organizations
Students edit the *University of San Francisco Law Review* and the *University of San Francisco Maritime Law Journal*, 1 of only 2 maritime law reviews published in the United States. Student members of the Intellectual Property Law Association publish the *Intellectual Property Law Bulletin*. *The Forum* is the student newspaper. Students participate in the National Moot Court Competition, National Appellate Advocacy Competition, and Phillip C. Jessup International Law Competition. Other competitions include the Saul Lefkowitz Moot Court Competition, State Bar of California Environmental Negotiations Competition, San Francisco Trial Lawyers Association Mock Trial Competition, Judge John R. Brown Admiralty Moot Court Competition, Giles Sutherland Rich Memorial Moot Court Competition, and Roger J. Traynor California Moot Court Competition. Law student organizations, local chapters of national associations, and campus organizations include the Public Interest Law Foundation, the Sports and Entertainment Law Association, the International Law Society, the National Lawyers Guild, St. Thomas More Society, the Equal Justice Society, Pride Law Association, the Federalist Society, and the Law in Motion Service Program.

Library
The law library contains 148,872 hardcopy volumes and 190,326 microform volume equivalents, and subscribes to 1,957 serial publications. Such online databases and networks as CALI, CIS Universe, Infotrac, Legal-Trac, LEXIS, OCLC First Search, WESTLAW, Wilsonline Indexes, Innovative OPAC, Internet Legal Resources, BNA, LLMC, Ind Law, HeinOnline, Bloomberg, IntelliConnect Law, and China Law info are available to law students for research. Special library collections include California and federal government documents depository collections. The ratio of library volumes to faculty is 4,253 to 1 and to students is 206 to 1. The ratio of seats in the library to students is 1 to 2.

Faculty
The law school has 36 full-time and 76 part-time faculty members, of whom 39 are women. About 14% of full-time faculty have a graduate law degree in addition to the J.D.; about 8% of part-time faculty have one. The ratio of full-time students to full-time faculty in an average class is 41 to 1; in a clinic, 6 to 1. The law school has a regular program of bringing visiting

Placement	
J.D.s awarded:	207
Services available through: a separate law school placement center.	
Services: career seminars, on-campus interviewing, skills workshops, guest speakers, and alumni panels.	
Special features: Public Interest Law Program.	
Full-time job interviews:	21 employers
Summer job interviews:	47 employers
Placement within 9 months of graduation:	92% of class
Average starting salary:	$38,000 to $135,000
Areas of placement:	
Private practice 2–10 attorneys	32%
Private practice 11–25 attorneys	8%
Private practice 26–50 attorneys	6%
Private practice 51–100 attorneys	8%
Public interest	14%
Government	12%
Business/industry	12%
Judicial clerkships	4%

professors and other distinguished lecturers and visitors to campus.

Students
About 55% of the student body are women; 39%, minorities; 8%, African American; 12%, Asian American; 12%, Hispanic; 1%, Native American; and 6%, multiethnic. The majority of students come from California (79%). The average age of entering students is 27; age range is 20 to 54. About 19% of students enter directly from undergraduate school, and 5% have a graduate degree. About 10% drop out after the first year for academic or personal reasons; 90% remain to receive a law degree.

School of Law

701 South Main Street
Columbia, SC 29208

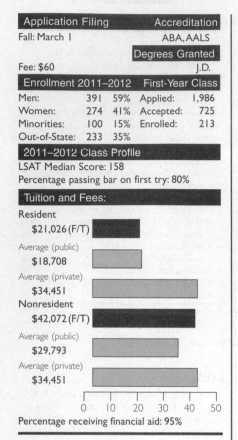

Application Filing		Accreditation	
Fall: March 1		ABA, AALS	
		Degrees Granted	
Fee: $60			J.D.
Enrollment 2011–2012		**First-Year Class**	
Men:	391 59%	Applied:	1,986
Women:	274 41%	Accepted:	725
Minorities:	100 15%	Enrolled:	213
Out-of-State:	233 35%		
2011–2012 Class Profile			
LSAT Median Score: 158			
Percentage passing bar on first try: 80%			

Tuition and Fees:

Resident
$21,026 (F/T)

Average (public)
$18,708

Average (private)
$34,451

Nonresident
$42,072 (F/T)

Average (public)
$29,793

Average (private)
$34,451

0   10   20   30   40   50

Percentage receiving financial aid: 95%

ADMISSIONS
In the fall of 2011 first-year class, 1986 applied, 725 were accepted, and 213 enrolled. Twenty-one transfers enrolled. The median GPA of the most recent first-year class was 3.5.

Requirements
Applicants must have a bachelor's degree and take the LSAT. No specific undergraduate courses are required.

Procedure
The application deadline for fall entry is March 1. Applicants should submit an application form, LSAT results, transcripts, a personal statement, a nonrefundable application fee of $60, 2 letters of recommendation, a personal statement, and a resume. Notification of the admissions decision is from mid-December to May. The law school uses the LSAC.

Special
The law school recruits minority and disadvantaged students through campus visits and e-mails, phone calls, and fee waivers. Requirements are different for out-of-state students. Transfer students must have one year of credit, must have attended an ABA-approved law school, must submit a personal statement, must be in good standing, and must be eligible to return to their current law school.

Costs
Books and supplies run $1,000.

Financial Aid
About 95% of current law students receive some form of aid. Awards are based on need and merit combined. The required financial statement is the FAFSA. The aid application deadline for fall entry is March 1. First-year students are notified about their financial aid application at time of acceptance.

About the Law School
University of South Carolina School of Law was established in 1867 and is a public institution. The campus is in downtown Columbia. The primary mission of the law school is to develop professional competence and responsibility. The school seeks to qualify its graduates for the highest opportunities in professional legal services and to instill a sense of perspective about what the law is capable of doing for the good of society. Students have access to federal, state, county, city, and local agencies, courts, correctional facilities, law firms, and legal aid organizations in the Columbia area. The U.S. Department of Justice's Legal Education Program has moved from Washington, D.C., to Columbia, and is affiliated with the law school. Housing for students is available in numerous apartments within commuting distance of the school. The university has apartments for married students near the campus. All law school facilities are accessible to the physically disabled.

Calendar
The law school operates on a traditional semester basis. Courses are offered days only, and must be completed within 3 years. New students are admitted in the fall. There is an 8-week summer session. Transferable summer courses are offered.

Programs
Students may take relevant courses in other programs and apply credit toward the J.D.; a maximum of 9 hours credits may be applied. The following joint degrees may be earned: J.D./I.M.B.A. (Juris Doctor/Master of International Business Administration), J.D./M.A. (Juris Doctor/Master of Arts in Criminal Justice), J.D./M.Acc. (Juris Doctor/Master of Accountancy), J.D./M.A.E. (Juris Doctor/Master of Arts in Economics), J.D./M.E.E.R.M. (Juris Doctor/Master of Earth and Environmental Resources), J.D./H.R.M. (Juris Doctor/Master of Human Resource Management), J.D./M.E.S. (Juris Doctor/Master of Environmental Science), J.D./M.H.A. (Juris Doctor/Master of Health Administration), J.D./M.P.A. (Juris Doctor/Master of Public Administration), J.D./M.P.A. (Juris Doctor/Master of Social Work), and J.D./M.S.W. (Juris Doctor/Master of Social Work).

Required
To earn the J.D., candidates must complete 90 total credits, of which 46 are for required courses. They must maintain a minimum GPA of 2.0 in the required courses. The following first-year courses are required of all students: Civil Procedure I, Constitutional Law I, Contracts I and II, Criminal Law, Introduction to Legal Profession, Legal Research, Legal Writing I and II, Property I and II, and Torts I and II. Required upper-level courses consist of a perspective course, a skills course, a writing requirement, and Professional Responsibility. The required orientation program for first-year students is 2 days before the start of classes.

Electives
The School of Law offers concentrations in corporate law, environmental law, internationl law, litigation, tax law, torts and insurance, business law, commercial law and bankruptcy, probate and estate planning, and real estate law. There are several types of clinics, usually for 3 credits hours. Clinics include Consumer Bankruptcy, Criminal Practice, Environmental Law, Federal Litigation, and Non-Profit Organizations. Students gain closely supervised training experience in the representation of clients. A number of seminars are offered each semester. All have limited enrollment, require a paper to be written, and are for 3 credit hours. In the area of research

Phone: 803-777-6605
Fax: 803-777-7751
E-mail: usclaw@law.sc.edu
Web: www.law.sc.edu

Contact

Assistant Dean of Admissions, 803-777-6605 for general inquiries; Assistant Dean of Admissions, 803-777-6605 for financial aid information.

SOUTH CAROLINA

programs, students may take the course Supervised Legal Research for 2 credit hours. It is independent study performed under the supervision of a faculty member and requires a research paper. Many upper-level students clerk for law firms, with state or federal government agencies, or with judges or the legislature during the school year. A special lecture series is open to all students. Study abroad is offered in London. First-year students are offered a tutorial program. A minority peer assistance tutorial program is also available. Special interest group programs include the Pro Bono Program, which provides opportunities for volunteer law students to obtain practical legal training. The most widely taken electives are litigation, business, and commercial law.

Graduation Requirements

In order to graduate, candidates must have a GPA of 2.0 and must have completed the upper-division writing requirement.

Organizations

The primary law review is the *South Carolina Law Review*; other law reviews are *ABA Real Property, Probate, and Trust Journal, The Southeastern Environmental Law Journal, Law Education Journal,* and *Journal of International Law and Business*. The school sponsors teams in the National, International, American Bar Association, and Labor Law Moot Court competitions as well as in the National Trial competitions. It also competes in the J. Woodrow Lewis Intramural Moot Court competition in appellate advocacy. Law student organizations, local chapters of national associations, and campus organizations include the Student Bar Association, Black Law Students Association, Women in Law, Phi Alpha Delta, Phi Delta Phi, Society of International Law, Wig and Robe, Federalist Society, American Constitution Society, Environmental Law Society, Public Interest Law Society, and Veterans in Law.

Library

The law library contains 562,559 hardcopy volumes and subscribes to 1,352 serial publications. Such online databases and networks as CALI, CIS Universe, DIALOG, Infotrac, Legal-Trac, LEXIS, OCLC First Search, WESTLAW, and Wilsonline Indexes are available to law students for research. Special library collections include a South Carolina legal history collection, a selective GPO depository, and SC appellate court records and briefs. The ratio of library volumes to faculty is 16,073 to 1 and to students is 845 to 1. The ratio of seats in the library to students is 1 to 1.

Faculty

The law school has 35 full-time and 18 part-time faculty members, of whom 18 are women. According to AAUP standards for Category I institutions, faculty salaries are below average. About 55% of full-time faculty have a graduate law degree in addition to the J.D. The ratio of full-time students to full-time faculty in an average class is 42 to 1; in a clinic, 12 to 1. The law school has a regular program of bringing visiting professors and other distinguished lecturers and visitors to campus. There is a chapter of the Order of the Coif; 19 faculty and 281 graduates are members.

Students

About 41% of the student body are women; 15%, minorities; 8%, African American; 2%, Asian American; and 2%, Hispanic. The majority of students come from South Carolina (65%). The average age of entering students is 24; age range is 20 to 45. About 8% of students have a graduate degree. About 3% drop out after the first year for academic or personal reasons; 97% remain to receive a law degree.

Placement

J.D.s awarded:	222

Services available through: a separate law school placement center.

Special features: free job opportunities postings on the web site, symplicity job listings and searchable web site of legal employers, and reciprocity with other law schools.

Full-time job interviews:	13 employers
Summer job interviews:	30 employers
Placement within 9 months of graduation:	89% of class
Average starting salary:	$30,000 to $160,000

Areas of placement:

Private practice 2–10 attorneys	21%
Private practice 11–25 attorneys	6%
Private practice 26–50 attorneys	2%
Private practice 51–100 attorneys	1%
Business/industry	5%
Judicial clerkships	25%
Government	17%
Private practice 100+ attorneys	9%
Public interest	3%
Military	2%
Academic	2%

School of Law

414 East Clark Street
Vermillion, SD 57069-2390

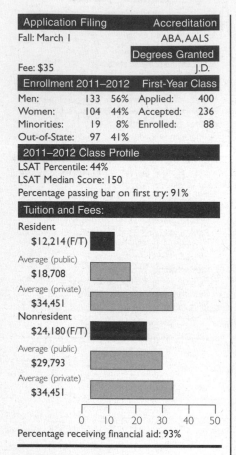

Application Filing		Accreditation	
Fall: March 1		ABA, AALS	
		Degrees Granted	
Fee: $35		J.D.	

Enrollment 2011–2012		First-Year Class	
Men:	133 56%	Applied:	400
Women:	104 44%	Accepted:	236
Minorities:	19 8%	Enrolled:	88
Out-of-State:	97 41%		

2011–2012 Class Profile

LSAT Percentile: 44%

LSAT Median Score: 150

Percentage passing bar on first try: 91%

Tuition and Fees:

Resident
$12,214 (F/T)

Average (public)
$18,708

Average (private)
$34,451

Nonresident
$24,180 (F/T)

Average (public)
$29,793

Average (private)
$34,451

0   10   20   30   40   50

Percentage receiving financial aid: 93%

ADMISSIONS
In the fall of 2011 first-year class, 400 applied, 236 were accepted, and 88 enrolled. Two transfers enrolled. The median LSAT percentile of the most recent first-year class was 44; the median GPA was 3.3 on a scale of 4.0. The lowest LSAT percentile accepted was 4; the highest was 83.

Requirements
Applicants must have a bachelor's degree and take the LSAT. The most important admission factors include GPA, LSAT results, and character or personality. No specific undergraduate courses are required. Candidates are not interviewed.

Procedure
The application deadline for fall entry is March 1. Applicants should submit an application form, a personal statement, transcripts, a nonrefundable application fee of $35, 2 letters of recommendation, and an LSAC report. Notification of the admissions decision is on a rolling basis.

Special
The law school recruits minority and disadvantaged students by mail solicitation and meeting in person with prospects. Requirements are different for out-of-state students. Transfer students must have one year of credit, must have attended an ABA-approved law school, must submit a personal statement, and must be in good standing at their present law school.

Costs
Tuition and fees for the 2011–2012 academic year are $6,304 for full-time in-state students and $18,270 for out-of-state students. Tuition for part-time students is $4,202 for in-state students and $12,180 out-of-state. On-campus room and board costs about $6,161 annually; books and supplies run $1,400.

Financial Aid
About 93% of current law students receive some form of aid. The average annual amount of aid from all sources combined, including scholarships, loans, and work contracts, is $24,538; maximum, $38,000. Awards are based on need and merit combined. The required financial statement is the FAFSA. First-year students are notified about their financial aid application at time of acceptance.

About the Law School
University of South Dakota School of Law was established in 1901 and is a public institution. The 216-acre campus is in a small town 50 miles south of Sioux Falls. The primary mission of the law school is to prepare students for the practice of law and to train professionally competent graduates capable of achieving their career goals and serving their profession. Students have access to federal, state, county, city, and local agencies, courts, correctional facilities, law firms, and legal aid organizations in the Vermillion area. Housing for students is described as adequate. All law school facilities are accessible to the physically disabled.

Calendar
The law school operates on a traditional semester basis. Courses for full-time students are offered days only, and must be completed within 6 semesters. For part-time students, courses are offered days only, and must be completed within 10 semesters. New full- and part-time students are admitted in the fall. There is no summer session. Transferable summer courses are not offered.

Programs
Students may take relevant courses in other programs and apply credit toward the J.D.; a maximum of 9 credits may be applied. The following joint degrees may be earned: J.D./M.A. (Juris Doctor/Master of Arts), J.D./M.B.A. (Juris Doctor/Master of Business Administration), J.D./M.P.A. (Juris Doctor/Master of Public Administration), J.D./M.P.Acc. (Juris Doctor/Master of Professional Accountancy), and J.D./M.S.A.S. (Juris Doctor/Master of Science in Administrative Studies).

Required
To earn the J.D., candidates must complete 90 total credits, of which 46 are for required courses. They must maintain a minimum GPA of 70.0 in the required courses. The following first-year courses are required of all students: Civil Procedure, Contracts, Criminal Law, Criminal Procedure, Fundamental Legal Skills, Property, and Torts. Required upper-level courses consist of Code Course (Commercial Law, Secured Transactions, or Federal), Constitutional Law, Evidence, Legal Profession, and Skills Course (Trial Techniques, Alternative Dispute Resolution, Legislation, or Negotiations). The required orientation program for first-year students lasts 5 days.

Electives
The School of Law offers concentrations in environmental law and Indian law. In addition, research programs, amounting to 1 or 2 hours of credit, are available for second- and third-year students. Externships are available for third-year students, and a federal judicial externship is available for second-year students. The most widely taken electives are Family Law, Commercial Law, and Trusts/Wills.

Graduation Requirements
In order to graduate, candidates must have a GPA of 70.0 and must have completed the upper-division writing requirement.

Phone: 605-677-5443
Fax: 605-677-5417
E-mail: *law.school@usd.edu*
Web: *www.usd.edu/law*

Contact
Jean Henriques, Admission Officer/Registrar, 605-677-5443 for general inquiries; University Financial Aid Office, 605-677-5446 for financial aid information.

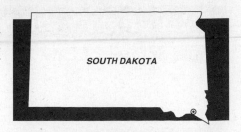

SOUTH DAKOTA

Organizations
The primary law review is the *South Dakota Law Review*. Other publications include the *Sustainable Development Law Journal*. Moot court competitions are the New York Bar, ABA, and Southern Illinois University Health Law Tournament. Other competitions include ABA-LSD Competitions (Negotiations, Client Counseling, Mediation) and the Robert R. Merhige, Jr., National Negotiation Competition. Law student organizations, local chapters of national associations, and campus organizations include Native American Law Students Association, Black Law Students Association, Federalist Society, Women in Law, R.D. Hurd Pro Bono Society, and Student Bar Association.

Library
The law library contains 213,077 hardcopy volumes and 46,922 microform volume equivalents, and subscribes to 280 serial publications. Such online databases and networks as CALI, CIS Universe, Infotrac, Legal-Trac, LEXIS, OCLC First Search, WESTLAW, BNA resources, RIA Tax resources, and HeinOnline are available to law students for research. Special library collections include a government documents depository collection, which is an extension of the main university library's collection. Other collections include reference, reserve, Indian law, and professional responsibility collections. The ratio of library volumes to faculty is 14,205 to 1 and to students is 1,044 to 1. The ratio of seats in the library to students is 1 to 1.

Faculty
The law school has 13 full-time faculty members, of whom 3 are women. According to AAUP standards for Category 1 institutions, faculty salaries are well below average. About 23% of full-time faculty have a graduate law degree in addition to the J.D. The law school has a regular program of bringing visiting professors and other distinguished lecturers and visitors to campus.

Students
About 44% of the student body are women; 8%, minorities; 1%, African American; 1%, Asian American; 1%, Hispanic; and 3%, Native American. The majority of students come from South Dakota (59%). The average age of entering students is 26; age range is 22 to 39. About 38% of students enter directly from undergraduate school, and 9% have a graduate degree. About 3% drop out after the first year for academic or personal reasons; 97% remain to receive a law degree.

Placement

J.D.s awarded:	53
Services available through: a separate law school placement center and the university placement center.	
Services: job postings available to alumni and non-legal field employment opportunities available through the university.	
Full-time job interviews:	10 employers
Summer job interviews:	21 employers
Placement by graduation:	41% of class
Placement within 9 months:	78% of class
Average starting salary:	$45,306 to $56,411
Areas of placement:	
Private practice 2–10 attorneys	29%
Private practice 11–25 attorneys	7%
Private practice 26–50 attorneys	2%
Judicial clerkships	27%
Enrolled in a full-time degree program	9%
Government	7%
Business/industry	7%
Public interest	7%
Academic	5%

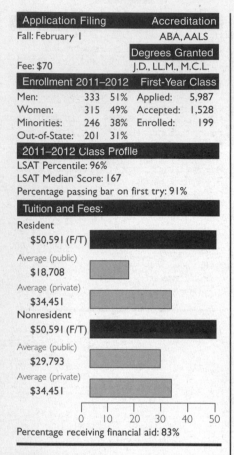

Application Filing	Accreditation
Fall: February 1	ABA, AALS
	Degrees Granted
Fee: $70	J.D., LL.M., M.C.L.

Enrollment 2011–2012		First-Year Class	
Men:	333 51%	Applied:	5,987
Women:	315 49%	Accepted:	1,528
Minorities:	246 38%	Enrolled:	199
Out-of-State:	201 31%		

2011–2012 Class Profile

LSAT Percentile: 96%
LSAT Median Score: 167
Percentage passing bar on first try: 91%

Tuition and Fees:

Resident
$50,591 (F/T)

Average (public)
$18,708

Average (private)
$34,451

Nonresident
$50,591 (F/T)

Average (public)
$29,793

Average (private)
$34,451

Percentage receiving financial aid: 83%

ADMISSIONS

In the fall of 2011 first-year class, 5987 applied, 1528 were accepted, and 199 enrolled. Twenty-four transfers enrolled. The median LSAT percentile of the most recent first-year class was 96; the median GPA was 3.7 on a scale of 4.0. The lowest LSAT percentile accepted was 52; the highest was 99.

Requirements

Applicants must have a bachelor's degree and take the LSAT. No specific undergraduate courses are required. Candidates are not interviewed.

Procedure

The application deadline for fall entry is February 1. Applicants should submit an application form, LSAT results, transcripts, a personal statement, a nonrefundable application fee of $70, and 2 letters of recommendation. Notification of the admissions decision is in the spring. The law school uses the LSAC.

Special

The law school recruits minority and disadvantaged students by means of mail outreach campaigns, school visits, and minority receptions; minority student organizations also help recruit and retain qualified candidates. Requirements are different for out-of-state students. Transfer students must have one year of credit, must have attended an ABA-approved law school, must submit a personal statement, and must be in the top 20% of their first-year class.

Costs

Tuition and fees for the 2011–2012 academic year are $48,832 for all full-time students. On-campus room and board costs about $21,915 annually; books and supplies run $1,664.

Financial Aid

About 83% of current law students receive some form of aid. The average annual amount of aid from all sources combined, including scholarships, loans, and work contracts, is $55,278; maximum, $75,884. Awards are based on need and merit combined. Required financial statements are the FAFSA and the law school financial aid application. The aid application deadline for fall entry is March 1. Special funds for minority or disadvantaged students consist of scholarships that are used in part to assist disadvantaged and minority students. First-year students are notified about their financial aid application at time of acceptance.

About the Law School

University of Southern California Gould School of Law was established in 1900 and is a private institution. The 226-acre campus is in an urban area 4 miles south of downtown Los Angeles. The primary mission of the law school is to offer an innovative, interdisciplinary, and interprofessional program focusing on the law as an expression of social values and as an instrument for implementing social goals. Students have access to federal, state, county, city, and local agencies, courts, correctional facilities, law firms, and legal aid organizations in the Los Angeles area. Facilities of special interest to law students include a computer laboratory, multimedia classrooms, large and high-tech library facilities, a spacious student cafe

and lounge, and clinical law offices. The USC campus features a 24-hour library, fitness center, specialty libraries, theaters, and restaurants. Housing for students consists of an on-campus apartment house designated for law students. All law school facilities are accessible to the physically disabled.

Calendar

The law school operates on a traditional semester basis. Courses are offered days only, and must be completed within 4 years. New students are admitted in the fall. There is no summer session. Transferable summer courses are not offered.

Programs

In addition to the J.D., the law school offers the LL.M. and M.C.L. Students may take relevant courses in other programs and apply credit toward the J.D.; a maximum of 12 credits may be applied. The following joint degrees may be earned: J.D./Pharm.D. (Juris Doctor/Doctor of Pharmacy), J.D./Ph.D. (Juris Doctor/ Doctor of Philosophy in Social Science), J.D./M.A. (Juris Doctor/Master of Arts (various disciplines)), J.D./M.C.M. (Juris Doctor/Master of Arts in Communication Management), J.D./M.B.A. (Juris Doctor/Master of Business Administration), J.D./M.B.T. (Juris Doctor/Master of Business Taxation), J.D./M.A.P. (Juris Doctor/ Master of Philosophy), J.D./M.P.A. (Juris Doctor/Master of Public Administration), J.D./M.P.P. (Juris Doctor/Master of Public Policy), J.D./M.R.E.D. (Juris Doctor/Master of Real Estate Development), J.D./M.S. (Juris Doctor/Master of Science in Gerontology), and J.D./M.S.W. (Juris Doctor/ Master of Social Work).

Required

To earn the J.D., candidates must complete 88 total credits, of which 35 are for required courses. They must maintain a minimum GPA of 2.6 in the required courses. The following first-year courses are required of all students: Civil Procedure, Constitutional Law, Contracts, Criminal Law, Law Language and Values, Legal Profession, Legal Research, Writing, and Advocacy, Property, and Torts I. Required upper-level courses consist of a writing requirement. The required orientation program for first-year students is a 2-day program that includes a

Phone: 213-740-2523
E-mail: admissions@law.usc.edu
Web: www.law.usc.edu

Contact

Chloe Reid, Associate Dean for Admissions, 213-740-2523 for general inquiries; Mary Bingham, Director of Financial Aid, 213-740-6314 for financial aid information.

CALIFORNIA

welcoming address, luncheon, financial aid counseling, meetings with second-year advisers assigned to incoming students, and a barbecue. A student-run mentor program for first-year students has year-round activities.

Electives

The Gould School of Law offers concentrations in corporate law, criminal law, entertainment law, environmental law, family law, intellectual property law, internationl law, juvenile law, labor law, litigation, media law, securities law, sports law, tax law, torts and insurance, public interest, constitutional law, and civil rights. In addition, in-house and simulated clinics are available for upper-level students. In-house clinics include the Post-Conviction Justice Project, Children's Legal Issues Clinic, Employer Legal Advice Clinic, Intellectual Property Clinic, the Immigration Clinic, and the Small Business Clinic. Seminars, available to upper-level students, are offered on many topics and facilitate intensive discussions in small groups. Internships, worth up to 4 credits, are available to upper-level students with government or public interest nonprofit organizations. Judicial externships allow students to clerk for a state or federal judge. The law school co-sponsors the Pacific Center for Health Policy and Ethics research program; Center for Communications Law and Policy; Center for the Study of Law and Politics; the Initiative and Referendum Institute; Center for Law, History, and Culture; Center for Law, Economics, and Organization; and Center for Law and Philosophy. Multiple opportunities for hands-on experience are available through clinical programs, internships and externships, and public interest placements. Special lecture series include the annual Roth Lecture, faculty workshops, and workshops sponsored by centers. The law school sponsors a semester exchange program with the University of Hong Kong and a dual degree program with the London School of Economics. Credit may be given for work done in other accredited law schools' study-abroad programs. Tutorials are arranged on a case-by-case basis. The school also offers a 5-part workshop on studying. An exam-taking skills course is offered to first-year students in the spring and upper-division students in the fall. Minority student organizations and minority

alumni associations collaborate on a range of social and educational programs as well as networking opportunities. Student-run organizations geared at specific areas of the legal profession include the Entertainment Law Society, International Law Society, Public Interest Law Foundation, and Government Law Organization. The most widely taken electives are Evidence, Business Organizations, and Tax.

Graduation Requirements

In order to graduate, candidates must have completed the upper-division writing requirement.

Organizations

Students edit the *Southern California Law Review*, *Southern California Interdisciplinary Law Journal*, and *Southern California Review of Law and Social Justice*. All first-year students participate in moot court competition; the 40 best advocates are selected to compete in their second year in the Hale Moot Court Honors Program. In addition, the best advocates from the Hale Moot Court Competition participate in numerous national competitions. Law student organizations, local chapters of national associations, and campus organizations include Women's Law Association, Phi Alpha Delta, Phi Delta Phi, La Raza Law Students Association, Public Interest Law Foundation, Entertainment Law Society, Street Law, and Order of the Coif.

Library

The law library contains 459,058 hard-copy volumes and 92,809 microform volume equivalents. Such online databases and networks as CALI, CIS Universe, Infotrac, Legal-Trac, LEXIS, Mathew Bender, OCLC First Search, WESTLAW, and Wilsonline Indexes are available to law students for research. Special library collections include a selected depository. Among the important holdings are health law/bioethics, law and economics, law and philosophy, law and social sciences, taxation, preventive law, and historic documents concerning President Lincoln. The ratio of library volumes to faculty is 8,585 to 1 and to students is 718 to 1. The ratio of seats in the library to students is 1 to 3.

Placement

J.D.s awarded:	207

Services available through: a separate law school placement center.

Services: lists of public interest contacts, counseling, a major on-campus placement program, videotaped practice interviews, and a 1-to-1 mentor program with graduates for first-year students in the second semester.

Special features: 1-on-1 counseling session for each first-year student; the Career Services Office's *Guide to Public Interest Law* for its students/graduates; and Alumni-Student Mock Interview Program.

Full-time job interviews:	15 employers
Summer job interviews:	94 employers
Placement by graduation:	83% of class
Placement within 9 months:	92% of class
Average starting salary:	$60,000 to $160,000

Areas of placement:

Private practice 2–10 attorneys	14%
Private practice 11–25 attorneys	3%
Private practice 26–50 attorneys	2%
Private practice 51–100 attorneys	5%
Government	11%
Business/industry	10%
Judicial clerkships	7%
Public interest	5%
Academic	4%

Faculty

The law school has 45 full-time and 56 part-time faculty members, of whom 39 are women. The ratio of full-time students to full-time faculty in an average class is 13 to 1. The law school has a regular program of bringing visiting professors and other distinguished lecturers and visitors to campus. There is a chapter of the Order of the Coif; 10 faculty are members.

Students

About 49% of the student body are women; 38%, minorities; 6%, African American; 19%, Asian American; 11%, Hispanic; and 1%, Native American. The majority of students come from California (69%). The average age of entering students is 23; age range is 19 to 40. About 65% of students enter directly from undergraduate school, 7% have a graduate degree, and 35% have worked full-time prior to entering law school. About 1% drop out after the first year for academic or personal reasons; 99% remain to receive a law degree.

College of Law

1505 W. Cumberland Avenue
Knoxville, TN 37996-1810

Application Filing		Accreditation	
Fall: February 15		ABA, AALS	
		Degrees Granted	
Fee: $15		J.D.	
Enrollment 2011–2012		First-Year Class	
Men:	275 56%	Applied:	1,277
Women:	212 44%	Accepted:	435
Minorities:	122 25%	Enrolled:	160
Out-of-State:	68 14%		

2011–2012 Class Profile

LSAT Percentile: 80%
LSAT Median Score: 160
Percentage passing bar on first try: 82%

Tuition and Fees:

Resident
$16,456 (F/T)

Average (public)
$18,708

Average (private)
$34,451

Nonresident
$35,200 (F/T)

Average (public)
$29,793

Average (private)
$34,451

0   10   20   30   40   50
Percentage receiving financial aid: 91%

ADMISSIONS

In the fall of 2011 first-year class, 1277 applied, 435 were accepted, and 160 enrolled. The median LSAT percentile of the most recent first-year class was 80; the median GPA was 3.5 on a scale of 4.0. The lowest LSAT percentile accepted was 11; the highest was 97.

Requirements

Applicants must have a bachelor's degree and take the LSAT. No specific undergraduate courses are required. Candidates are not interviewed.

Procedure

The application deadline for fall entry is February 15. Applicants should submit an application form, LSAT results, transcripts, a personal statement, a nonrefundable application fee of $15, 2 letters of recommendation, a personal statement, and an essay. The law school uses the LSAC.

Special

The law school recruits minority and disadvantaged students through on-campus visits, LSAC forums and on-campus workshops. Requirements are different for out-of-state students. Transfer students must have one year of credit, must have a minimum GPA of 2, must have attended an ABA-approved law school, and must submit a personal statement.

Costs

Tuition and fees for the 2011–2012 academic year are $14,044 for full-time in-state students and $32,488 for out-of-state students. On-campus room and board costs about $11,040 annually; books and supplies run $1,846.

Financial Aid

About 91% of current law students receive some form of aid. The average annual amount of aid from all sources combined, including scholarships, loans, and work contracts, is $26,039; maximum, $53,794. Awards are based on need and merit combined. The required financial statement is the FAFSA. The aid application deadline for fall entry is March 1. Special funds for minority or disadvantaged students consist of scholarships that are awarded on the basis of demonstrated financial need and merit. First-year students are notified about their financial aid application usually in January.

About the Law School

University of Tennessee College of Law was established in 1890 and is a public institution. The 417-acre campus is in an urban area in Knoxville. The primary mission of the law school is to be a preeminent state-supported law school where faculty, staff, and students devoted to teaching, scholarship, and service thrive. Students have access to federal, state, county, city, and local agencies, courts, correctional facilities, law firms, and legal aid organizations in the Knoxville area. The College of Law is located approximately 1 mile from downtown Knoxville law offices and courts. Facilities of special interest to law students include a law center, which houses civil and criminal clinics, a mediation program, the Center for Entrepreneurial Law, classrooms, law library, and faculty administrative offices. Housing

for students consists of many off-campus apartment complexes available to law students. Several apartment complexes are located within a 5-mile radius of the campus. All law school facilities are accessible to the physically disabled.

Calendar

The law school operates on a traditional semester basis. Courses are offered both day and evening, and must be completed within 5 years. New students are admitted in the fall. There is an 8-week summer session. Transferable summer courses are offered.

Programs

Students may take relevant courses in other programs and apply credit toward the J.D.; a maximum of 6 credits may be applied. The following joint degrees may be earned: J.D./M.B.A. (Juris Doctor/Master of Business Administration) and J.D./M.P.A. (Juris Doctor/Master of Public Administration).

Required

To earn the J.D., candidates must complete 89 total credits, of which 38 are for required courses. They must maintain a minimum GPA of 2.0 in the required courses. The following first-year courses are required of all students: Civil Procedure I and II, Contracts I and II, Criminal Law, Legal Process I and II, Property, and Torts I and II. Required upper-level courses consist of a perspective course, a planning and drafting course, an expository writing course, Constitutional Law I, and Legal Profession. The required orientation program for first-year students offers 4 days of mini-courses in Civil Litigation Process and Case Analysis and Briefing, includes panel discussions and guest speakers, and concludes with one regular class meeting in Criminal Law, Contracts, and Torts.

Electives

The College of Law offers concentrations in corporate law, business transactions, and advocacy and dispute resolution. Clinics include Advocacy (6 credit hours), Prosecutional Externship (6 credit hours), Business Clinic (6 credit hours), Public Defender (6 credit hours), Judicial Externship (4 credit hours), Domestic Violence

Phone: 865-974-4131
Fax: 865-974-1572
E-mail: lawadmit@utk.edu
Web: www.law.utk.edu

Contact

Carolyn Dossett, Senior Admission Specialist, 865-974-4131 for general inquiries; Janet Hatcher, Admissions and Financial Aid Advisor, 865-974-4131 for financial aid information.

TENNESSEE

Clinic (3 credit hours), Wills Clinic (3 credit hours), and Mediation Clinic (3 credit hours). A mediation clinic is open to all upper-division students for 3 hours of credit. Several special topic seminars are available for 2 hours credit. A prosecutorial externship is open to third-year students, who preferably have completed both Criminal Procedure I and II. Students receive 6 credit hours. There is a judicial externship, for 4 credits hours, and a public defender externship for 6 credit hours. They are open to third-year students. Field work is available through "for-credit" externships. Special lecture series include the Alumni Distinguished Lecture in Jurisprudence, the Charles Henderson Miller Lecture in Professional Responsibility, and the Speaker Series, which hosts nationally known speakers. Any student may study abroad through ABA-approved summer abroad programs. A maximum of 8 credit hours may be transferred. Students with a first-semester average below 2.0 are invited to participate, in the second semester, in tutorials in Contracts, Civil Procedure, and Torts. First-year students attend Law School Success Skills seminars on topics such as Managing Time and Energy in Law School and Outlining. The most widely taken electives are Trial Practice and Evidence.

Graduation Requirements

In order to graduate, candidates must have a GPA of 2.0, must have completed the upper-division writing and other upper-level requirements.

Organizations

Students edit the *Tennessee Law Review, Journal of Law and Policy*, and *Transactions: Tennessee Journal of Business Law*. Moot court competitions include the National Moot Court, National Trial, and Jerome Prince Evidence. Other competitions include the Jenkins Trial Advocates Prize Moot Court, Intellectual Property, Labor Law, and Jessup International Law. Law student organizations, local chapters of national associations, and campus organizations include the Student Bar Association, Christian Legal Society, Speaker Series, the American Bar Associations-Law Student Division, Association of Trial Lawyers of America-Student Chapter, Hamilton Barrett Chapter of the American Inns of Court, the Black Law Students Association, Phi Delta Phi, and Tennessee Innocence Project.

Library

The law library contains 597,882 hardcopy volumes and 54,365 microform volume equivalents, and subscribes to 791 serial publications. Such online databases and networks as CALI, CIS Universe, DIALOG, Dow-Jones, Infotrac, Legal-Trac, LEXIS, Mathew Bender, OCLC First Search, RLIN, WESTLAW, Wilsonline Indexes, CCH, Business and Finance Internet Library, CCH Health and Human Resources Internet Library, Historical Documents, Current Indexes to Legal Periodicals, HeinOnline, Treaties Agreements Online, LexisNexis, PAGER, LOIS, and RIA Checkpoint are available to law students for research. Special library collections include federal documents depository, Tennessee collection, and selected braille collection. The ratio of library volumes to faculty is 20,617 to 1 and to students is 1,228 to 1. The ratio of seats in the library to students is 1 to 1.

Faculty

The law school has 29 full-time and 36 part-time faculty members, of whom 26 are women. According to AAUP standards for Category 1 institutions, faculty salaries are below average. About 17% of full-time faculty have a graduate law degree in addition to the J.D. The ratio of full-time students to full-time faculty in an average class is 14 to 1; in a clinic, 8 to 1. The law school has a regular program of bringing visiting professors and other distinguished lecturers and visitors to campus. There is a chapter of the Order of the Coif.

Students

About 44% of the student body are women; 25%, minorities; 10%, African American; 4%, Asian American; and 6%, Hispanic. The majority of students come from Tennessee (86%). The average age of entering students is 23. About 65% of students enter directly from undergraduate school, 13% have a graduate degree, and 22% have worked full-time prior to entering law school. About 2% drop out after the first year for academic or personal reasons; 98% remain to receive a law degree.

Placement

J.D.s awarded:	133

Services available through: a separate law school placement center, and law students also may use the UTK placement center.

Services: off-campus recruiting events, including the Southeastern Minority Job Fair, the Southeastern Law Placement Consortium, Patent Law Interview Program, Nashville Bar Association Minority Clerkship Program, Mid-Atlantic Legal Recruiting Conference, the Equal Justice Works Career Fair, Spring Southeastern Legal Hiring Conference, Southeastern Intellectual Property Job Fair, and Tennessee Bar Association Diversity Job Fair.

Special features: individual advising sessions and small-group orientations.

Full-time job interviews:	4 employers
Summer job interviews:	29 employers
Placement by graduation:	54% of class
Placement within 9 months:	81% of class
Average starting salary:	$37,000 to $145,000

Areas of placement:

Private practice 2–10 attorneys	27%
Private practice 11–25 attorneys	4%
Private practice 26–50 attorneys	6%
Private practice 51–100 attorneys	16%
Government	13%
Business/industry	12%
Judicial clerkships	11%
Public interest	4%
Academic	4%
Military	3%

School of Law

727 East Dean Keeton Street
Austin, TX 78705

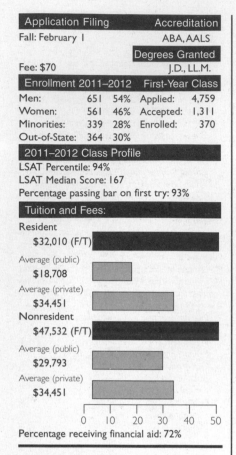

Application Filing			Accreditation
Fall: February 1			ABA, AALS

			Degrees Granted
Fee: $70			J.D., LL.M.

Enrollment 2011–2012		First-Year Class	
Men:	651 54%	Applied:	4,759
Women:	561 46%	Accepted:	1,311
Minorities:	339 28%	Enrolled:	370
Out-of-State:	364 30%		

2011–2012 Class Profile
LSAT Percentile: 94%
LSAT Median Score: 167
Percentage passing bar on first try: 93%

Tuition and Fees:

Resident
$32,010 (F/T)

Average (public)
$18,708

Average (private)
$34,451

Nonresident
$47,532 (F/T)

Average (public)
$29,793

Average (private)
$34,451

Percentage receiving financial aid: 72%

ADMISSIONS

In the fall of 2011 first-year class, 4759 applied, 1311 were accepted, and 370 enrolled. Nineteen transfer students enrolled. The median LSAT percentile of the most recent first-year class was 94; the median GPA was 3.7 on a scale of 4.0. The lowest LSAT percentile accepted was 36; the highest was 100.

Requirements
Applicants must have a bachelor's degree and take the LSAT. Minimum acceptable GPA is 2.2 on a scale of 4.0. No specific undergraduate courses are required. Candidates are interviewed.

Procedure
The application deadline for fall entry is February 1. Applicants should submit an application form, LSAT results, transcripts, personal statement, nonrefundable application fee of $70, registration with LSAC, and a résumé. Notification of the admissions decision is December to April. The law school uses the LSAC.

Special
The law school recruits minority and disadvantaged students through campus visits, law forums, special mailings, and phone calls. Requirements are different for out-of-state students in that Texas's state legislature limits nonresident enrollment to 35% of the entering class. Transfer students must have one year of credits, a minimum GPA of 2.20, attended an ABA-approved law school, personal statement, demonstrate good cause for the transfer, and have a strong academic record prior to and during law school.

Costs

On-campus room and board costs about $10,422 annually.

Financial Aid

About 72% of current law students receive some form of aid. The average annual amount of aid from all sources combined, including scholarships, loans, and work contracts, is $30,770; maximum, $45,170. Awards are based on need and merit combined. Required financial statement is the FAFSA. The aid application deadline for fall entry is March 31. First-year students are notified about their financial aid application at time of acceptance.

About the Law School

The University of Texas at Austin School of Law was established in 1883 and is a public institution. The 350-acre campus is located in an urban area within Austin. The primary mission of the law school is to educate students for the practice of law by advancing knowledge of the law as an institution to effect social change. Students have access to federal, state, county, city, and local agencies, courts, correctional facilities, law firms, and legal aid organizations in the Austin area. Facilities of special interest to law students include Townes Hall and Tarlton Law Library, which is housed in the Joseph D. Jamail Center for Legal Research, 2 connected buildings that house the law library, classrooms, seminar rooms, student organization areas, and other support facilities. Housing for students is available. Few students select on-campus housing. All law school facilities are accessible to the physically disabled.

Calendar

The law school operates on a traditional semester basis. Courses for full-time students are offered days only and must be completed within five years. There is no part-time program. New full-time students are admitted in the fall. There is a 10 1/2-week summer session. Transferable summer courses are offered.

Programs

In addition to the J.D., the law school offers the LL.M. Students may take relevant courses in other programs and apply credit toward the J.D.; a maximum of 12 credits may be applied. The following joint degrees may be earned: J.D./Ph.D. (Juris Doctor/Doctor of Philosophy (various disciplines), J.D./M.A. (Juris Doctor/Master of Arts (various disciplines)), J.D./M.B.A. (Juris Doctor/Master of Business Administration), J.D./M.P.A. (Juris Doctor/Master of Public Affairs), and J.D./M.S. (Juris Doctor/Master of Science (various disciplines)).

Required
To earn the J.D., candidates must complete 86 total credits, of which 38 are for required courses. They must maintain a minimum GPA of 1.9 in the required courses. The following first-year courses are required of all students: Civil Procedure, Constitutional Law I, Contracts, Criminal Law, Legal Research and Writing, Property, and Torts. Required upper-level courses consist of a writing seminar, Constitutional Law II, and Professional Responsibility. The required orientation program for first-year students is a 2-day program that familiarizes them with the physical facilities, rules, and procedures of the law school and the university. Students also attend a general welcome and social event.

Electives
The School of Law offers concentrations in corporate law, criminal law, entertainment law, family law, internationl law, juvenile law, labor law, litigation, maritime law, media law, securities law, tax law, torts and insurance, natural resources law, civil liberties, commercial law, and intellectual property law. In addition, Clinics are offered in Capital Punishment, Children's Rights, and Criminal Defense; students must have completed half of their degree.

Phone: 512-232-1200
Fax: 512-471-2765
E-mail: admissions@law.utexas.edu
Web: www.utexas.edu/law

Contact

Samuel Riley, Director for Admissions Programs, 512-232-1200 for general inquiries; Linda Alba, Financial Aid Counselor, 512-232-1130 for financial aid information.

Examples of 3 seminars are: Supreme Court litigation, Entertainment Law, and Class Action. Seminars are for upper-division students. Judicial internships are available with the Texas Supreme Court, the Texas Court of Criminal Appeals, and the Texas Court of Appeals through which a small number of students earn law school credit. Empirical legal research projects sponsored and directly supervised by a faculty member are available. An advanced student may also conduct individual research projects. The school has a semester-long exchange program with Queen Mary College and Westfield College, which are both colleges of the University of London. Up to 30 upper-class students enroll for 4 approved courses in international or comparative law. Students can create their own study abroad program as well. Students on scholastic probation and second-semester first-year students at risk of being placed on scholastic probation are assigned tutors. There are student organizations focusing on almost every area of the law. The most widely taken electives are Wills and Estates, Business Associations, and Federal Income Tax.

Graduation Requirements

In order to graduate, candidates must have a GPA of 1.9, complete the upper-division writing requirement, and 86 credit hours, of which 38 are required courses.

Organizations

Students edit the *Texas Law Review, Texas International Law Journal, American Journal of Criminal Law, The Review of Litigation,* the *Texas Forum on Civil Liberties and Civil Rights, Texas Environmental Law Journal, Texas Intellectual Property Law Journal, Texas Journal of Women and the Law, Texas Hispanic Journal of Law and Policy, Texas Review of Law and Politics, Texas Review of Entertainment and Sports Law,* and *Texas Oil and Gas Journal.* The Board of Advocates directs a range of moot court, mock trial, and client counseling contests, both interscholastic and intrascholastic. Law student organizations, local chapters of national associations, and campus organizations include the Student Bar Association, Thurgood Marshall Legal Society, Chicano/Hispanic Law Students Association, Public Interest Law Association and Board of Advocates.

Library

The law library contains 1,029,976 hardcopy volumes and 1,219,852 microform volume equivalents, and subscribes to 3,663 serial publications. Online databases and networks include CALI, CIS Universe, DIALOG, Dow-Jones, Infotrac, Legal-Trac, LEXIS, Mathew Bender, OCLC First Search, RLIN, WESTLAW, and Wilsonline Indexes, and are available to law students for research. In addition, the library also has numerous special collections. The ratio of library volumes to faculty is 12,560 to 1 and to students is 850 to 1. The ratio of seats in the library to students is 1 to 1.

Faculty

The law school has 82 full-time and 62 part-time faculty members, of whom 51 are women. According to AAUP standards for Category I institutions, faculty salaries are above average. About 19% of full-time faculty have a graduate law degree in addition to the J.D.; about 5% of part-time faculty have one. The ratio of full-time students to full-time faculty in an average class is 11 to 1; in a clinic, 8 to 1. The law school has a regular program of bringing visiting professors and other distinguished lecturers and visitors to campus. There is a chapter of the Order of the Coif; 58 graduates are members.

Students

About 46% of the student body are women; 28%, minorities; 5%, African American; 5%, Asian American; and 15%, Hispanic. The majority of students come from Texas (70%). The average age of entering students is 24; age range is 19 to 49. About 1% drop out after the first year for academic or personal reasons; 99% remain to receive a law degree.

Placement

J.D.s awarded:	382

Services available through: a separate law school placement center.

Services: Mentor Program/Directory, Judicial Clerkship Program, approximately 60 student programs/workshops per year.

Special features: Founding member of PSLawNet.org; use of Simplicity; host of largest public service job fair for law students in Texas (Public Service Career Day).

Full-time job interviews:	174 employers
Summer job interviews:	466 employers
Placement by graduation:	95% of class
Placement within 9 months:	99% of class
Average starting salary:	$47,000 to $134,100

Areas of placement:

Private practice 2–10 attorneys	11%
Private practice 11–25 attorneys	7%
Private practice 26–50 attorneys	4%
Private practice 51–100 attorneys	3%
Judicial clerkships	13%
Government	10%
Business/industry	9%
Public interest	5%
Military	1%
Academic	1%

David A. Clarke School of Law

4200 Connecticut Avenue, N.W.
Washington, DC 20008

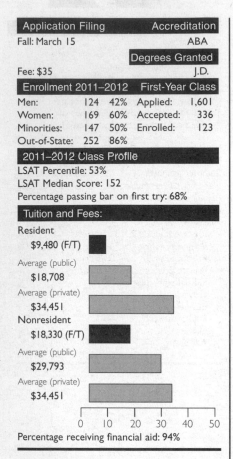

Application Filing		Accreditation
Fall: March 15		ABA
		Degrees Granted
Fee: $35		J.D.

Enrollment 2011–2012		First-Year Class	
Men:	124 42%	Applied:	1,601
Women:	169 60%	Accepted:	336
Minorities:	147 50%	Enrolled:	123
Out-of-State:	252 86%		

2011–2012 Class Profile

LSAT Percentile: 53%
LSAT Median Score: 152
Percentage passing bar on first try: 68%

Tuition and Fees:

Resident
$9,480 (F/T)

Average (public)
$18,708

Average (private)
$34,451

Nonresident
$18,330 (F/T)

Average (public)
$29,793

Average (private)
$34,451

0   10   20   30   40   50

Percentage receiving financial aid: 94%

ADMISSIONS

In the fall of 2011 first-year class, 1601 applied, 336 were accepted, and 123 enrolled. Three transfer students enrolled. The median LSAT percentile of the most recent first-year class was 53; the median GPA was 3.0 on a scale of 4.0. The lowest LSAT percentile accepted was 23; the highest was 88.

Requirements
Applicants must have a bachelor's degree and take the LSAT. The most important admission factors include general background, GPA, and LSAT results. No specific undergraduate courses are required. Candidates are interviewed.

Procedure
The application deadline for fall entry is March 15. Applicants should submit an application form, LSAT results, transcripts, personal statement, nonrefundable application fee of $35, 2 letters of recommendation, and a supplemental essay. Notification of the admissions decision is on a rolling basis. The law school uses the LSAC.

Special
The law school recruits minority and disadvantaged students by direct mail recruitment campaigns, such as LSAC; through visits to historically black and minority serving institutions; by maintaining contact with local community groups and organizations; holding Law Day and Open House programs; LSAC-sponsored minority program; and through advertising in school papers and local government periodicals. Requirements are different for out-of-state students. Transfer students must have one year of credits, a minimum GPA of 2, attended an ABA-approved law school, a personal statement, and good/satisfactory academic status.

Costs

Tuition and fees for the 2011–2012 academic year are $8,850 for full-time in-state students and $17,700 for out-of-state students.

Financial Aid

About 94% of current law students receive some form of aid. The average annual amount of aid from all sources combined, including scholarships, loans, and work contracts, is $36,792; maximum, $47,799. Awards are based on need and merit. Students may apply for non-need-based alternative loans with eligibility based on credit worthiness. Required financial statements are the FAFSA and NEED ACCESS required for institutional scholarships. The aid application deadline for fall entry is March 31. Special funds for minority or disadvantaged students are available through need-based named scholarships donated to the law school's scholarship fund for minority student awards. First-year students are notified about their financial aid application at time of acceptance.

About the Law School

University of the District of Columbia David A. Clarke School of Law was established in 1987 and is a public institution.

The campus is located in an urban area upper Northwest Washington, D.C. The mission of the law school is to represent the legal needs of low-income persons, particularly those who reside in the District of Columbia, while recruiting, enrolling, and training persons from racial, ethnic, or other population groups that have been traditionally underrepresented at the Bar. Students have access to federal, state, county, city, and local agencies, courts, correctional facilities, law firms, and legal aid organizations in the Washington area. Other resources include the Supreme Court, Capitol Hill, Library of Congress, and public interest groups and organizations. Facilities of special interest to law students include local and federal government offices, courts and administrative agencies, public interest organizations, and Capitol Hill. There is no on-campus housing. The School of Law assists incoming students with locating housing in the Washington, D.C. metropolitan area. All law school facilities are accessible to the physically disabled.

Calendar

The law school operates on a traditional semester basis. Courses for full-time students are offered both day and evening and must be completed within 5 years. For part-time students, courses are offered evenings only and must be completed within 5 years. New full- and part-time students are admitted in the fall. There is an 8- to 10-week summer session. Transferable summer courses are offered.

Programs

Required
To earn the J.D., candidates must complete 90 total credits, of which 75 are for required courses. They must maintain a minimum GPA of 2.0 in the required courses. The following first-year courses are required of all students: Civil Procedure I and II, Contracts I and II, Criminal Law, Criminal Procedure, Law and Justice, Lawyering Process I and II, and Torts I and II. Required upper-level courses consist of Clinic I and II, Constitutional Law I and II, Evidence, Moot Court, Professional Responsibility, and Property I and II. All students must take clinical courses. The required orientation program for

Phone: 202-274-7341
Fax: 202-274-5583
E-mail: vcanty@udc.edu; lawadmission@udc.edu
Web: www.law.udc.edu

Contact

Vivian W. Canty, Assistant Dean of Admission, 202-274-7341 for general inquiries; Nailah Williams, Financial Aid Director, 202-274-7337 for financial aid information.

DISTRICT
OF
COLUMBIA

first-year students begins in early to mid-August and lasts approximately 2 weeks. Students take two courses, Lawyering Process I and Law and Justice. There are other enrichment activities, such as student and faculty presentations, tours of the Supreme and D.C. Superior Courts, and a Dean's reception.

Electives

The David A. Clarke School of Law offers concentrations in public interest law. In addition, 8 clinics are offered in topics such as Small Business and Community Development, Government Accountability Project, Low-Income Tax, and Immigration Law. Seminars are offered each semester. An internship seminar is required of all students who do an internship. Internships with government or nonprofit agencies are offered for advanced students who have completed 14 credits of clinic and are in good standing. Students may be selected to be research assistants on faculty research projects. The clinics involve students in various forms of field work. In addition, the internship program provides full-time field work. Special lecture series include the Dean's Lecture Series. The Career Services Office and student organizations also plan guest speakers' visits and programs. Students may participate in study abroad programs sponsored by other law schools. The Academic Success Program provides small group and individual tutorials for students during the 3 years of law school. The Program requires students to examine the analytic processes needed to solve legal problems. It also provides counseling and tutoring for students whose GPA falls below 2.0. This program also sponsors workshops on time management, test-taking, and self-regulated learning. The most widely taken electives are Race and The Law, Business Organizations I, and Uniform Commercial Code.

Graduation Requirements

In order to graduate, candidates must have a GPA of 2.0 and complete the upper-division writing requirement.

Organizations

Students edit *The District of Columbia Law Review* and *The Advocate*, Law student organizations, local chapters of national associations, and campus

organizations include the UDC-DCSL Student Bar Association, Women's Law Society, Black Law Students Association, Negotiation Team Competition, Client Counseling, Oral Advocacy Team, Phi Alpha Delta, National Lawyers Guild, National Association of Public Interest Law, Sports and Entertainment Student Lawyers Association, Latino/a Law Students Association, and Gay and Lesbian Outlaw Student Association.

Library

The law library contains 257,000 hardcopy volumes and 114,989 microform volume equivalents, and subscribes to 1,585 serial publications. On-line databases and networks include CALI, Infotrac, Legal-Trac, LEXIS, Mathew Bender, OCLC First Search, WESTLAW, Wilsonline Indexes, and BNA and the Internet, which are available to law students for research. Special library collections include District of Columbia law and clinical legal practice materials. The ratio of library volumes to faculty is 12,850 to 1 and to students is 877 to 1. The ratio of seats in the library to students is 1 to 1.

Faculty

The law school has 20 full-time and 17 part-time faculty members, of whom 17 are women. About 10% of full-time faculty have a graduate law degree in addition to the J.D.; about 22% of part-time faculty have one. The ratio of full-time students to full-time faculty in an average class is 11 to 1; in a clinic, 8 to 1. The law school has a regular program of bringing visiting professors and other distinguished lecturers and visitors to campus.

Students

About 60% of the student body are women; 50%, minorities; 29%, African American; 8%, Asian American; 11%, Hispanic; 1%, Native American; and 1%, other. The majority of students come from District of Columbia (14%). The average age of entering students is 28; age range is 20 to 63. About 37% of students enter directly from undergraduate school, 12% have a graduate degree, and 45% have worked full-time prior to entering law school. About 5% drop out after the first year for academic or personal reasons; 91% remain to receive a law degree.

Placement

J.D.s awarded:	67

Services available through: a separate law school placement center.

Services: lists of judicial clerkships, fellowships, and writing competitions. In keeping with the school's mission, emphasis is placed on public sector careers.

Special features: personalized career counseling; guaranteed summer stipend for all qualifying first year students doing full time public interest work.

Full-time job interviews:	7 employers
Summer job interviews:	40 employers
Placement within 9 months of graduation:	85% of class
Average starting salary:	$37,000 to $66,000

Areas of placement:

Private practice 2–10 attorneys	29%
Government	21%
Business/industry	17%
Public interest	14%
Judicial clerkships	10%
Academic	5%

UNIVERSITY OF THE PACIFIC

McGeorge School of Law

3200 Fifth Avenue
Sacramento, CA 95817

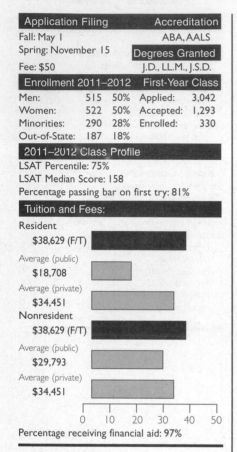

Application Filing			Accreditation
Fall: May 1			ABA, AALS
Spring: November 15			**Degrees Granted**
Fee: $50			J.D., LL.M., J.S.D.

Enrollment 2011–2012			First-Year Class	
Men:	515	50%	Applied:	3,042
Women:	522	50%	Accepted:	1,293
Minorities:	290	28%	Enrolled:	330
Out-of-State:	187	18%		

2011–2012 Class Profile
LSAT Percentile: 75%
LSAT Median Score: 158
Percentage passing bar on first try: 81%

Tuition and Fees:

Resident
$38,629 (F/T)
Average (public)
$18,708
Average (private)
$34,451
Nonresident
$38,629 (F/T)
Average (public)
$29,793
Average (private)
$34,451

0 10 20 30 40 50

Percentage receiving financial aid: 97%

ADMISSIONS

In the fall of 2011 first-year class, 3042 applied, 1293 were accepted, and 330 enrolled. Nine transfers enrolled. The median LSAT percentile of the most recent first-year class was 75; the median GPA was 3.4 on a scale of 4.3. The lowest LSAT percentile accepted was 44; the highest was 99.

Requirements
Applicants must have a bachelor's degree and take the LSAT. The most important admission factors include academic achievement, LSAT results, and general background. No specific undergraduate courses are required. Candidates are not interviewed.

Procedure
The application deadline for fall entry is May 1. Applicants should submit an application form, LSAT results, transcripts, a personal statement, a nonrefundable application fee of $50, and letters of rec-

ommendation (3 optional letters suggested). Notification of the admissions decision begins in January. The law school uses the LSAC.

Special
The law school recruits minority and disadvantaged students through recruiting events, publications, letters, contacts with McGeorge students, and scholarship and grant programs. Requirements are different for out-of-state students. Transfer students must have one year of credit and must submit a personal statement. Acceptance of transfer students is dependent upon space availability; preference is given to students with compelling reasons to request transfer.

Costs

Tuition and fees for the 2011–2012 academic year are $38,556 for all full-time students. Tuition for part-time students is $25,632 for in-state students and $25,632 for out-of-state. On-campus room and board costs about $9,738 annually; books and supplies run $1,600.

Financial Aid

About 97% of current law students receive some form of aid. The average annual amount of aid from all sources combined, including scholarships, loans, and work contracts, is $47,237; maximum, $61,687. Awards are based on need and merit combined. The required financial statement is the FAFSA. The aid application deadline for fall entry is open. Special funds for minority or disadvantaged students are available. Diversity factors are considered in the award of scholarships and grants. First-year students are notified about their financial aid application at time of acceptance.

About the Law School

University of the Pacific McGeorge School of Law was established in 1924 and is a private institution. The 13-acre campus is in a suburban area in Sacramento. The primary mission of the law school is to educate practice-ready graduates, able to represent clients skillfully and ethically, through a rigorous curriculum that unifies classroom study with development of professional skills. Students have access to federal, state, county, city,

and local agencies, courts, correctional facilities, law firms, and legal aid organizations in the Sacramento area. Facilities of special interest to law students include the trial courtroom, the LawLab equipped with computer technology, the "live-client" clinical facilities, the student center with food service, the library with ample study and computer areas, and recreational facilities. Housing for students consists of 158 on-campus apartments; housing off campus is readily available in the Sacramento area at a reasonable cost. About 95% of the law school facilities are accessible to the physically disabled.

Calendar

The law school operates on a traditional semester basis. Courses for full-time students are offered both day and evening, and must be completed within 4 years. For part-time students, courses are offered both day and evening, and must be completed within 5 years. New full- and part-time students are admitted in the fall. There is an 8-week summer session. Transferable summer courses are offered.

Programs

In addition to the J.D., the law school offers the LL.M. and J.S.D. Students may take relevant courses in other programs and apply credit toward the J.D.; a maximum of 30 credits may be applied. The following joint degrees may be earned: J.D./M.A. or M.S. (Juris Doctor/Master of Arts or Sciences), J.D./M.B.A. (Juris Doctor/Master of Business Administration), and J.D./M.P.P.A. (Juris Doctor/Master of Public Policy and Administration).

Required
To earn the J.D., candidates must complete 88 total credits, of which 59 are for required courses. They must maintain a minimum GPA of 2.3 in the required courses. The following first-year courses are required of all students: Civil Procedure, Contracts, Criminal Law, Legal Process, Property, and Torts. Required upper-level courses consist of Appellate and International Advocacy, Business Associations, Community Property, Constitutional Law, Criminal Procedure, Evidence, Professional Responsibility, Remedies, and Wills and Trusts. The required orientation program for first-year students is a 3-day program at the beginning

Phone: 916-739-7105
Fax: 916-739-7301
E-mail: *mcgeorge@pacific.edu*
Web: *www.mcgeorge.edu*

Contact

Mathiew H. Le, Associate Director of Admissions, 916-739-7105 for general inquiries; Joe Pinkas, Director of Financial Aid, 916-739-7158 for financial aid information.

CALIFORNIA

of the year that includes orientation classes, small group sessions, and social activities. First-year faculty provide special feedback programs, including practice examinations, throughout the first year.

Electives

The McGeorge School of Law offers concentrations in corporate law, criminal law, environmental law, family law, intellectual property law, internationl law, juvenile law, litigation, tax law, torts and insurance, public law, and policy and advocacy. In addition, on-campus clinics include Community Legal Services, which provides legal services for those not otherwise able to afford them; it is available to advanced students, carries a 2-semester commitment, and is worth 6 credits. Other campus-based clinics available to advanced students for 2 or 3 credits each semester are Administrative Adjudication Clinic, Parole Representation Clinic; Immigration Clinic, Bankruptcy Clinic, Business and Community Development Clinic, Civil Practice Clinic, Victims' Rights Clinic, and Legislative Process, Strategy and Ethics Clinic. A number of elective courses are in a seminar format with limited enrollment. Of particular interest are Advanced Intellectual Property; Negotiations and Settlement; California Law Revision; Reorganization, Recapitalization and Insolvency; and International Water Resources Law. More than 80 off-campus internships are available in nonprofit and local, state, and federal governmental offices and agencies. Internships are available to advanced students and are worth 2 or 3 credits per semester. Directed research, available as an elective for advanced students, is offered for 1 or 2 credits. Individual professors also have student research assistants. Additionally, the Research Pool undertakes research projects for practitioners. Lecture series such as the Distinguished Speaker's Series, Hefner Memorial Lecture Series, and Lou Ashe Symposium bring outstanding guest speakers to campus. The Institute on International Legal Studies includes a 3-week program in Salzburg, Austria, in cooperation with the University of Salzburg. International and comparative law courses are offered in public and commercial law fields. For more than a decade, Anthony M. Kennedy, Associate Justice of the U.S. Supreme Court, has co-taught "Fundamental Rights

in Europe and the U.S." McGeorge also has a Summer Institute in Suzhou, China, with courses and cultural visits in Chinese courts. Tutorial programs include the Skills Hour Program and the Practice Examination Program offered in the fall of the student's first year. A voluntary Minority Support Program provides a peer support and networking system as well as special orientation sessions, student-led discussion groups, and course review sessions. The most widely taken electives are Trial Advocacy, clinical offerings, and business courses.

Graduation Requirements

In order to graduate, candidates must have a GPA of 2.3 and must have completed the upper-division writing requirement.

Organizations

Students edit the *McGeorge Law Review* and the *Pacific McGeorge Global Business and Development Law Journal*. McGeorge teams compete in the National and ABA Moot Court competitions and the Philip Jessup International Moot Court Competition. Other competitions include Willem C. Viz International Commercial Arbitration in Vienna, San Diego Defense Lawyers, William Daniel Mock Trial, San Diego Consumer Attorneys Mock Trial, Michigan State Competition, ABA Texas Young Lawyers National Trial Competition Nationals, ATLA National Student Advocacy Competition Nationals, ABA Client Counseling, and ABA Negotiation. Law student organizations include the Student Bar Association, Public Legal Services Society, and Government Affairs Student Association. There are local chapters of ABA-Law Student Division and Phi Alpha Delta fraternity. Campus clubs and other organizations include Entertainment Law Society, Women's Caucus, and International Law Society.

Library

The law library contains 509,762 hardcopy volumes and 294,936 microform volume equivalents, and subscribes to 4,503 serial publications. Such online databases and networks as CALI, CIS Universe, Legal-Trac, LEXIS, Mathew Bender, OCLC First Search, RLIN, WEST-LAW, CCH,and BNA are available to law

students for research. Special library collections include California legal materials, California and U.S. documents depository, tax, international law, and water, and natural resources collections. The ratio of library volumes to faculty is 9,268 to 1 and to students is 492 to 1. The ratio of seats in the library to students is 1 to 1.

Faculty

The law school has 55 full-time and 57 part-time faculty members, of whom 42 are women. About 30% of full-time faculty have a graduate law degree in addition to the J.D.; about 11% of part-time faculty have one. The ratio of full-time students to full-time faculty in an average class is 16 to 1; in a clinic, 10 to 1. The law school has a regular program of bringing visiting professors and other distinguished lecturers and visitors to campus. There is a chapter of the Order of the Coif; 31 faculty and 712 graduates are members.

Students

About 50% of the student body are women; 28%, minorities; 3%, African American; 13%, Asian American; 9%, Hispanic; and 3%, Native American. The majority of students come from California (82%). The average age of entering students is 25; age range is 21 to 53. About 76% of students enter directly from undergraduate school, and 2% have a graduate degree. About 14% drop out after the first year for academic or personal reasons.

2801 West Bancroft Street, MS 507
Toledo, OH 43606-3390

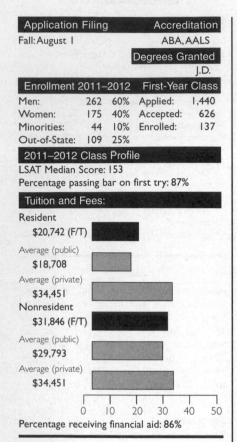

Application Filing	Accreditation
Fall: August 1	ABA, AALS

Degrees Granted
J.D.

Enrollment 2011–2012		First-Year Class	
Men:	262 60%	Applied:	1,440
Women:	175 40%	Accepted:	626
Minorities:	44 10%	Enrolled:	137
Out-of-State:	109 25%		

2011–2012 Class Profile
LSAT Median Score: 153
Percentage passing bar on first try: 87%

Tuition and Fees:

Resident
$20,742 (F/T)

Average (public)
$18,708

Average (private)
$34,451

Nonresident
$31,846 (F/T)

Average (public)
$29,793

Average (private)
$34,451

0   10   20   30   40   50

Percentage receiving financial aid: 86%

ADMISSIONS

In the fall of 2011 first-year class, 1440 applied, 626 were accepted, and 137 enrolled. Four transfers enrolled. The median GPA of the most recent first-year class was 3.3.

Requirements

Applicants must have a bachelor's degree and take the LSAT. Minimum acceptable LSAT percentile is 40 and minimum acceptable GPA is 1.8 on a scale of 4.0. The most important admission factors include LSAT results, GPA, and undergraduate curriculum. No specific undergraduate courses are required. Candidates are not interviewed.

Procedure

The application deadline for fall entry is August 1. Applicants should submit an application form, LSAT results, transcripts, a personal statement, and 2 letters of recommendation, and they should indicate preference for full- or part-time study. Notification of the admissions decision is on a rolling basis. The law school uses the LSAC.

Special

The law school recruits minority and disadvantaged students through Minority Preview Day, Minority Law Days, mailings, e-mails, and law forums. Requirements are different for out-of-state students. Transfer students must have attended an ABA-approved law school, must submit a personal statement, and must be in good standing at the previous school.

Costs

Tuition and fees for the 2011–2012 academic year are $19,118 for full-time in-state students and $30,222 for out-of-state students. Tuition for part-time students is $14,338 for in-state students and $22,667 out-of-state. Books and supplies run $2,000.

Financial Aid

About 86% of current law students receive some form of aid. The average annual amount of aid from all sources combined, including scholarships, loans, and work contracts, is $34,676; maximum, $70,793. Awards are based on need and merit combined. The required financial statement is the FAFSA. The aid application deadline for fall entry is July 1. First-year students are notified about their financial aid application at time of acceptance.

About the Law School

University of Toledo College of Law was established in 1906 and is a public institution. The 210-acre campus is in a suburban area west of downtown Toledo, adjacent to Ottawa Hills. The primary mission of the law school is to create a diverse intellectual environment that prepares students to engage in the legal practice of their choice, enhances the college's national and regional reputation for academic excellence, fosters a spirit of community, individual attention and professional values, and encourages participation in the life of the university, region, and state. Students have access to federal, state, county, city, and local agencies, courts, correctional facilities, law firms, and legal aid organizations in the Toledo area. Students are placed in prosecutor offices and public interest offices throughout the U.S. Facilities of special interest to law students include a state-of-the-art moot courtroom, which is available for trial practice and appellate advocacy programs, renovated classrooms, and wireless access throughout the law center. Numerous accommodations are located near the campus. The university assists students in finding housing. All law school facilities are accessible to the physically disabled.

Calendar

The law school operates on a traditional semester basis. Courses for full-time students are offered both day and evening, and must be completed within 5 years. For part-time students, courses are offered both day and evening, and must be completed within 6 years. New full- and part-time students are admitted in the fall. There is a 9-week summer session. Transferable summer courses are offered.

Programs

Students may take relevant courses in other programs and apply credit toward the J.D.; a maximum of 6 credits may be applied. The following joint degrees may be earned: J.D./M.A.C.J. (Juris Doctor/Master of Arts in Criminal Justice), J.D./M.B.A. (Juris Doctor/Master of Business Administration), J.D./M.P.A. (Juris Doctor/Master of Public Administration), and J.D./M.S.E. (Juris Doctor/Master of Science in Engineering).

Required

To earn the J.D., candidates must complete 89 total credits, of which 42 are for required courses. They must maintain a minimum GPA of 2.0 in the required courses. The following first-year courses are required of all students: Civil Procedure I, Constitutional Law I, Contracts I and II, Legal Research, Writing, and Appellate Advocacy I and II, Property I and II, and Torts. Required upper-level courses consist of Civil Procedure II, Constitutional Law II, Evidence, and Legal Ethics and Professional Responsibility. The required orientation program for first-year students lasts 2 days.

Phone: 419-530-4131
Fax: 419-530-4345
E-mail: *law admissions@utoledo.edu*
Web: *law.utoledo.edu*

Contact
Beth Solo, Assistant Director, 419-530-7929 for financial aid information.

OHIO

Electives
The College of Law offers concentrations in criminal law, environmental law, intellectual property law, international law, and labor law. Clinical programs include the College of Law Legal Clinic, Criminal Law Practice programs, the Domestic Violence Clinic, and the Dispute Resolution Clinic. These are offered to all upper-level students for 2 to 6 hours of credit. Internships are available anywhere in the U.S. through the Criminal Law Practice Program and the Public Service Externship Program. Individual research programs allow students to develop their own research projects, which are pursued in consultation with a faculty adviser. The Cannon Lecture Series and the Stranahan National Issues Forum have hosted individuals of national prominence who provide the college and general public with timely discussions of legal and policy issues. Teaching assistants and tutors are available. The most widely taken electives are Criminal Procedure, Business Associations, and Federal Taxation.

Graduation Requirements
In order to graduate, candidates must have a GPA of 2.0 and must have completed the upper-division writing requirement.

Organizations
Students edit the *University of Toledo Law Review* and the student newspaper, *No Holds Bar Review*. The Moot Court program helps build skills in the arts of brief writing and oral advocacy through participation in national and intraschool competitions, such as the Charles W. Faroff Intraschool Competition. Competitions are managed by a student Moot Court Board. Other competitions include Family Law, Constitutional Law, and Jessup International Law. Law student organizations, local chapters of national associations, and campus organizations include Student Bar Association, BLSA, Health Law Association, American Constitution Society, Federalist Society, HLSA, Delta Theta Phi, Phi Alpha Delta, Inns of Court, Environmental Law, Public Interest Law Association, Women Law Students Association, and Labor and Employment Law Association.

Library
The law library contains 360,833 hardcopy volumes and 137,340 microform volume equivalents, and subscribes to 3,371 serial publications. Such online databases and networks as CALI, CIS Universe, Legal-Trac, LEXIS, WESTLAW, Wilsonline Indexes, Ohio Capital Connection, CCH, and BNA are available to law students for research. Special library collections include significant holdings of primary materials for the United Kingdom, Canada, Australia, and New Zealand, and primary and secondary materials for studying international law. The library is a federal depository. The ratio of library volumes to faculty is 11,639 to 1 and to students is 730 to 1. The ratio of seats in the library to students is 1 to 1.

Faculty
The law school has 31 full-time faculty members, of whom 14 are women. According to AAUP standards for Category I institutions, faculty salaries are below average. About 20% of full-time faculty have a graduate law degree in addition to the J.D. The ratio of full-time students to full-time faculty in an average class is 13 to 1; in a clinic, 5 to 1. The law school has a regular program of bringing visiting professors and other distinguished lecturers and visitors to campus. There is a chapter of the Order of the Coif.

Students
About 40% of the student body are women; 10%, minorities; 4%, African American; 3%, Asian American; 3%, Hispanic; and 1%, Native American. The majority of students come from Ohio (75%). The average age of entering students is 26; age range is 20 to 57. About 11% drop out after the first year for academic or personal reasons; 89% remain to receive a law degree.

Placement

J.D.s awarded:	97

Services available through: a separate law school placement center.

Services: interviews using video conferencing equipment, mentor program, reciprocity with other law schools, and job fairs.

Special features: the O.P.D. Resource Library, the O.P.D. Student Handbook, mentor program for first-year students, and an alumni online network for all students.

Full-time job interviews:	3 employers
Summer job interviews:	12 employers
Placement by graduation:	61% of class
Placement within 9 months:	90% of class
Average starting salary:	$24,000 to $105,000

Areas of placement:

Private practice 2–10 attorneys	19%
Private practice 11–25 attorneys	3%
Private practice 26–50 attorneys	1%
Private practice 51–100 attorneys	1%
Business/industry	24%
Government	11%
Public interest	8%
Judicial clerkships	6%
Academic	5%
Military	1%

College of Law

3120 East Fourth Place
Tulsa, OK 74104-2499

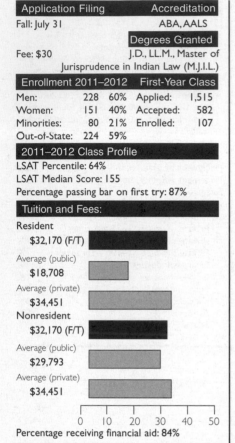

Application Filing	Accreditation
Fall: July 31	ABA, AALS

	Degrees Granted
Fee: $30	J.D., LL.M., Master of
	Jurisprudence in Indian Law (M.J.I.L.)

Enrollment 2011–2012		First-Year Class	
Men:	228 60%	Applied:	1,515
Women:	151 40%	Accepted:	582
Minorities:	80 21%	Enrolled:	107
Out-of-State:	224 59%		

2011–2012 Class Profile

LSAT Percentile: 64%
LSAT Median Score: 155
Percentage passing bar on first try: 87%

Tuition and Fees:

Resident
    $32,170 (F/T)

Average (public)
    $18,708

Average (private)
    $34,451

Nonresident
    $32,170 (F/T)

Average (public)
    $29,793

Average (private)
    $34,451

0   10   20   30   40   50

Percentage receiving financial aid: 84%

ADMISSIONS

In the fall of 2011 first-year class, 1515 applied, 582 were accepted, and 107 enrolled. Two transfers enrolled. The median LSAT percentile of the most recent first-year class was 64; the median GPA was 3.3 on a scale of 4.0. The lowest LSAT percentile accepted was 41; the highest was 92.

Requirements

Applicants must have a bachelor's degree and take the LSAT. The most important admission factors include LSAT results, GPA, and undergraduate curriculum. No specific undergraduate courses are required. Candidates are not interviewed.

Procedure

The application deadline for fall entry is July 31. Applicants should submit an application form, LSAT results, transcripts, a personal statement, a nonrefundable application fee of $30, and 2 letters of recommendation. Notification of the admissions decision is on an ongoing basis. The law school uses the LSAC.

Special

The law school recruits minority and disadvantaged students through CLEO, PLSI, an academic success program in summer, and recruitment at minority schools. Requirements are different for out-of-state students. Transfer students must have one year of credit, must have a minimum GPA of 2.6, must have attended an ABA-approved law school, and must submit a personal statement.

Costs

Tuition and fees for the 2011–2012 academic year are $31,836 for all full-time students. On-campus room and board costs about $7,578 annually; books and supplies run $1,500.

Financial Aid

About 84% of current law students receive some form of aid. The average annual amount of aid from all sources combined, including scholarships, loans, and work contracts, is $40,232; maximum, $68,073. Awards are based on need and merit combined. The required financial statement is the FAFSA. The aid application deadline for fall entry is open. Special funds for minority or disadvantaged students include scholarship awards. First-year students are notified about their financial aid application at time of acceptance.

About the Law School

University of Tulsa College of Law was established in 1923 and is a private institution. The 207-acre campus is in a suburban area 3 miles east of downtown Tulsa. The primary mission of the law school is to prepare students from diverse backgrounds to excel in the legal profession through an intellectually rigorous program that promotes the core values of excellence in scholarship, dedication to free inquiry, integrity of character, professionalism, and commitment to humanity. Students have access to federal, state, county, city, and local agencies, courts, correctional facilities, law firms, and legal aid organizations in the Tulsa area. Tribal courts and agencies are also accessible. Facilities of special interest to law students include Collins Fitness Center, Mabee Legal Information Center, and Boesche Legal Clinic. Housing for students is available in university apartments. Accommodations are available in non-university facilities at a reasonable cost. All law school facilities are accessible to the physically disabled.

Calendar

The law school operates on a traditional semester basis. Courses for full-time students are offered both day and evening, and must be completed within 7 years. For part-time students, courses are offered both day and evening, and must be completed within 7 years. New full- and part-time students are admitted in the fall and spring. There are 6- and 12-week summer sessions. Transferable summer courses are offered.

Programs

In addition to the J.D., the law school offers the LL.M. and Master of Jurisprudence in Indian Law (M.J.I.L.). Students may take relevant courses in other programs and apply credit toward the J.D.; a maximum of 6 credits may be applied. The following joint degrees may be earned: J.D./M.A. (Juris Doctor/Master of Arts), J.D./M.B.A. (Juris Doctor/Master of Business Administration), J.D./M.S. (Juris Doctor/Master of Science), J.D./M.S.F. (Juris Doctor/Master of Science in Finance), and J.D./M.Tax (Juris Doctor/ Master of Taxation).

Required

To earn the J.D., candidates must complete 88 total credits, of which 48–51 are for required courses. They must maintain a minimum GPA of 2.0 in the required courses. The following first-year courses are required of all students: Civil Procedure I and II, Constitutional Law, Contracts, Criminal Law and Administration, Dean's Seminar on Legal Profession, Legal Reasoning and Analysis, Legal Writing, Property, and Torts. Required upper-level courses consist of a skills course, a transnational course, a writing course, Constitutional Law II, Evidence, Legal Writing II, and Professional Responsibility. The required orientation program for first-year students starts 1 week before the beginning of other courses.

Phone: 918-631-2406
Fax: 918-631-3630
E-mail: april-fox@utulsa.edu
Web: www.law.utulsa.edu

Contact

April Fox, Dean of Admissions, 918-631-2709 for general inquiries; Kristi Emerson, Assistant Director of Financial Aid, 918-631-3325 for financial aid information.

OKLAHOMA

Electives

The College of Law offers concentrations in criminal law, environmental law, internationl law, Native American Law, sustainable energy and resources law, health law, and entrepreneurial law. Clinics include Immigrant Rights Project and the Social Enterprise and Economic Development (SEED) Law Project. At the University of Tulsa Boesche Legal Clinic, students represent underserved clients in a variety of civil cases. All students are supervised by a faculty member, and credit is offered. Numerous seminars are offered and have a limited enrollment. Through the college's Legal Internship Program, students may obtain practical experience gained under the supervision of practicing attorneys and the college. The Judicial Internships Program offers students supervised educational experience in the Oklahoma District Court, Oklahoma Court of Appeals, U.S. District Court, U.S. Magistrate's Office, U.S. Bankruptcy Court, and the Muskogee Creek Nation Tribal courts. Externships and internships with certificates are offered in health law and Indian law. Qualified students may pursue independent study in specific areas of the law under the supervision of law professors. Through the In-Residence Program, students meet and talk with scholars, alumni, practitioners, and judges in classes and lectures. Special lecture series include Legal Scholarship Symposium, Supreme Court Review, Buck Franklin Lecture, and the Hager Lecture. Summer institutes in law are offered in Ireland, Switzerland, China, and Argentina. Students also have the opportunity to study abroad in London for a semester. A first-year workshop focuses on study and exam skills and a third-year bar exam preparation program is available. The most widely taken electives are Basic Corporate Law, Evidence, and Administrative Law.

Graduation Requirements

In order to graduate, candidates must have a GPA of 2.0 and must have completed the upper-division writing requirement.

Organizations

Students edit the *Tulsa Law Review, Energy Law Journal: Year in Review*, published jointly with the ABA section of Environment, Energy, and Resources (SEER), and the newspaper *Dicta*. The TU Law Board of Advocates sponsors 7 moot court competitions, including the first-year Client Counseling (regional and national) and ABA Negotiation (regional and national). Other competitions include Native American law and health law competitions. Law student organizations, local chapters of national associations, and campus organizations include Native American Law Students Association, Black Law Students Association, Hispanic Law Students Association, ABA-Law Student Division, Delta Theta Phi, Phi Alpha Delta, and Phi Delta Phi.

Library

The law library contains 425,711 hardcopy volumes and 1,070,722 microform volume equivalents, and subscribes to 2,904 serial publications. Such online databases and networks as CALI, CIS Universe, DIALOG, Infotrac, Legal-Trac, LEXIS, Mathew Bender, OCLC First Search, and WESTLAW are available to law students for research. Special library collections include literature and information on energy, environmental law, Indian law, and international law. The ratio of library volumes to faculty is 14,190 to 1 and to students is 1,199 to 1. The ratio of seats in the library to students is 1 to 1.

Faculty

The law school has 28 full-time and 39 part-time faculty members, of whom 20 are women. About 29% of full-time faculty have a graduate law degree in addition to the J.D.; about 10% of part-time faculty have one. The ratio of full-time students to full-time faculty in an average class is 11 to 1; in a clinic, 8 to 1. The law school has a regular program of bringing visiting professors and other distinguished lecturers and visitors to campus. There is a chapter of the Order of the Coif; 4 faculty are members.

Placement

J.D.s awarded:	127
Services available through: a separate law school placement center, the university placement center, and reciprocity services with other law schools.	
Full-time job interviews:	3 employers
Summer job interviews:	10 employers
Placement by graduation:	58% of class
Placement within 9 months:	92% of class
Average starting salary:	$42,000 to $83,000
Areas of placement:	
Private practice 2–10 attorneys	31%
Private practice 11–25 attorneys	6%
Private practice 26–50 attorneys	3%
Private practice 51–100 attorneys	1%
Business/industry	21%
Government	16%
Public interest	6%
Academic	4%
Judicial clerkships	1%
Military	1%

Students

About 40% of the student body are women; 21%, minorities; 3%, African American; 1%, Asian American; 3%, Hispanic; and 11%, Native American. The average age of entering students is 26; age range is 21 to 53. About 40% of students enter directly from undergraduate school, 14% have a graduate degree, and 48% have worked full-time prior to entering law school. About 2% drop out after the first year for academic or personal reasons; 91% remain to receive a law degree.

S. J. Quinney College of Law

332 South 1400, East Room 101
Salt Lake City, UT 84112

Application Filing		Accreditation
Fall: February 15		ABA, AALS

		Degrees Granted
Fee: $60		J.D., LL.M.

Enrollment 2011–2012		First-Year Class	
Men:	231 58%	Applied:	1,230
Women:	167 42%	Accepted:	378
Minorities:	44 11%	Enrolled:	114
Out-of-State:	127 32%		

2011–2012 Class Profile
LSAT Percentile: 83%
LSAT Median Score: 161
Percentage passing bar on first try: 90%

Tuition and Fees:

Resident
$20,760 (F/T)

Average (public)
$18,708

Average (private)
$34,451

Nonresident
$39,410 (F/T)

Average (public)
$29,793

Average (private)
$34,451

0 10 20 30 40 50

Percentage receiving financial aid: 86%

ADMISSIONS

In the fall of 2011 first-year class, 1230 applied, 378 were accepted, and 114 enrolled. Twenty-six transfers enrolled. The median LSAT percentile of the most recent first-year class was 83; the median GPA was 3.5 on a scale of 4.0. The lowest LSAT percentile accepted was 21; the highest was 99.

Requirements
Applicants must have a bachelor's degree and take the LSAT. The most important admission factors include academic achievement, general background, and writing ability. No specific undergraduate courses are required, and candidates are not interviewed.

Procedure
The application deadline for fall entry is February 15. Applicants should submit an application form, LSAT results, transcripts, a personal statement, a nonrefundable application fee of $60, a letter of recommendation, a resume, and an LSAC report. Notification of the admissions decision is from February on.

Special
The law school recruits minority and disadvantaged students through extensive mailing to prospective applicants located through the Candidate Referral Service of LSAC and through special targeted recruitment programs. Council on Legal Opportunity fellows and Pre-Law Summer Institute fellows are recruited. Requirements are different for out-of-state students. Transfer students must have one year of credit, must have attended an ABA-approved law school, must submit a personal statement, and must be in the top 30% of the first-year class.

Costs

On-campus room and board costs about $9,108 annually; books and supplies run $1,916.

Financial Aid

About 86% of current law students receive some form of aid. The average annual amount of aid from all sources combined, including scholarships, loans, and work contracts, is $32,967; maximum, $60,968. Awards are based on need and merit combined. Required financial statements are the FAFSA and College of Law need-based scholarship application. The aid application deadline for fall entry is April 1. Special funds for minority or disadvantaged students include need and merit scholarships and CLEO fellowships. First-year students are notified about their financial aid application at time of acceptance.

About the Law School

University of Utah S. J. Quinney College of Law was established in 1913 and is a public institution. The 1535-acre campus is located in an urban area 2 miles east of downtown Salt Lake City. The primary mission of the law school is to achieve academic excellence in the professional education of lawyers, to advance knowledge through the dissemination of high-quality legal scholarship, and to perform public service to the university, the State of Utah, the nation, and the global community. Students have access to federal, state, county, city, and local agencies, courts, correctional facilities, law firms, and legal aid organizations in the Salt Lake City area. Students have access to the state capital. Facilities of special interest to law students include the library, which features individual study carrels with wireless connections to laptop computers and extensive computing and online facilities. Housing for students is abundant and affordable on and off campus in safe neighborhoods within walking distance of campus. All law school facilities are accessible to the physically disabled.

Calendar

The law school operates on a traditional semester basis. Courses are offered days only, and must be completed within 6 semesters. New students are admitted in the fall. There are summer sessions. Transferable summer courses are offered.

Programs

In addition to the J.D., the law school offers the LL.M. Students may take relevant courses in other programs and apply credit toward the J.D.; a maximum of 12 credits may be applied. The following joint degrees may be earned: J.D./M.B.A. (Juris Doctor/Master of Business Administration), J.D./M.P.A. (Juris Doctor/Master of Public Administration), J.D./M.P.P. (Juris Doctor/Master of Public Policy), and J.D./M.S.W. (Juris Doctor/Master of Social Work).

Required
To earn the J.D., candidates must complete 88 total credits, of which 40 are for required courses. They must maintain a minimum GPA of 2.5 in the required courses. The following first-year courses are required of all students: Civil Procedure, Constitutional Law, Contracts, Criminal Law, Legal Methods, Property, and Torts. Required upper-level courses consist of a skills course, an advanced legal writing course, Constitutional Law II, and Legal Profession. The required orientation program for first-year students is a 4-day course before classes begin to help students understand the role of law, the tasks of a lawyer, and the method of legal education and study.

Phone: 801-581-7479

800-444-8638 ext. 1-7479

Fax: 801-581-6897

E-mail: *aguilarr@law.utah.edu*

Web: *www.law.utah.edu*

Contact

Reyes Aguilar, Associate Dean, 801-581-7479 for general inquiries; Law School Financial Aid Counselor, 801-581-6211 for financial aid information.

UTAH

Electives

The S. J. Quinney College of Law offers concentrations in corporate law, criminal law, environmental law, family law, intellectual property law, internationl law, juvenile law, and litigation. In addition, live and simulation component clinics are offered in which students work at the offices of the county attorney, U.S. Attorney, federal defender, or Salt Lake legal defenders; civil, in which students represent actual clients from a public-interest law firm; or judicial, in which students act as law clerks to state and federal judges. There are also placements in environmental law, health law, and legislative and mediation program locations. In seminars, students perform closely supervised research, analysis, and writing, covering a wide array of topics. Students may spend a semester as full-time clerks in the judicial extern program as part of the judicial clinic. Numerous opportunities exist for students to be paid as research assistants for faculty, or to undertake directed research for credit or advanced legal research courses. Field placements with a public interest law office, Utah Legal Services, Legal Aid Society of Salt Lake, Legal Center for People with Disabilities, Catholic Community Services, and the ACLU are part of the clinical program. Special lecture series include the Leary Lecture, Fordham Debate, Distinguished Jurist in Residence, Law Review Symposium, the Natural Resources Law Forum, and the annual Wallace Stegnar Symposium. Study abroad is possible for upper-level students in the London Law Consortium, a 1-semester, ABA-approved program. The academic support program is available for eligible students and includes a legal process tutorial course, organized study groups, and academic counseling. The college sponsors a summer intern program, funded with private donations, for minority students. Selected students intern with major Salt Lake City law firms for 10 weeks following the completion of their first year and receive a $3000 stipend. The college has hosted and regularly recruits participants from the Council on Legal Education Opportunity Summer Institute and the Pre-Law Summer Institute. Special interest groups include the Utah Criminial Justice Center and the Global Justice Project. The most widely taken electives are Evidence, Criminal Procedure, and Business Organizations.

Graduation Requirements

In order to graduate, candidates must have a GPA of 2.5 and must complete the upper-division writing requirement.

Organizations

Students edit the *Utah Law Review, Journal of Law and Family Studies, Journal of Land Resources and Environmental Law*, and the newspaper, *Utah Law Forum*. Moot court competitions include the Annual National Moot Court, Pace University Environmental Law Moot Court, and Giles Rich Moot Court Competition. In addition, several writing and research competitions are offered in connection with scholarships and awards. Law student organizations include the Natural Resources Law Forum, Women's Law Caucus, and Minority Law Caucus. Local chapters of the Native American Law Student Association, Federalist Society, and American Constitution Society are represented on campus. Campus organizations include Phi Alpha Delta, Phi Delta Phi, and the International Law Society.

Library

The law library contains 255,657 hardcopy volumes and 630,657 microform volume equivalents, and subscribes to 4,500 serial publications. Online databases and networks include CALI, Infotrac, Legal-Trac, LEXIS, Mathew Bender, OCLC First Search, WESTLAW, and Wilsonline Indexes, which are available to law students for research. Special library collections include energy, environmental, and natural resources law, Utah historical legal collection, Utah government documents depository, and U.S. government documents depository. The ratio of library volumes to faculty is 4,479 to 1 and to students is 922 to 1. The ratio of seats in the library to students is 1 to 1.

Faculty

The law school has 45 full-time and 37 part-time faculty members, of whom 24 are women. According to AAUP standards for Category I institutions, faculty salaries are average. About 6% of full-time faculty have a graduate law degree in addition to the J.D. The ratio of full-time students to full-time faculty in an average class is 19 to 1; in a clinic, 8 to 1. The law school has a regular program of bringing visiting professors and other distinguished lecturers

Placement

J.D.s awarded:	134

Services available through: a separate law school placement center.

Special features: computer-maintained records of current and former students may be transmitted to prospective employers to facilitate both on- and off-campus recruiting. The Professional Development Office offers personal counseling, maintains a resource library, and sponsors seminars to aid students in their self-directed job search.

Full-time job interviews:	25 employers
Summer job interviews:	61 employers
Placement by graduation:	75% of class
Placement within 9 months:	91% of class
Average starting salary:	$40,000 to $133,000

Areas of placement:

Solo Practice	6%
Private practice 2–10 attorneys	30%
Private practice 11–25 attorneys	4%
Private practice 26–50 attorneys	8%
Private practice 51–100 attorneys	4%
Judicial clerkships	12%
Government	10%
Business/industry	10%
Public interest	4%
Military	4%
Academic	3%

and visitors to campus. There is a chapter of the Order of the Coif; 5 faculty and 14 graduates are members.

Students

About 42% of the student body are women; 11%, minorities; 1%, African American; 4%, Asian American; 4%, Hispanic; and 1%, Native American. The majority of students come from Utah (68%). The average age of entering students is 26; age range is 21 to 55. About 29% of students enter directly from undergraduate school, 9% have a graduate degree, and 69% have worked full-time prior to entering law school. About 1% drop out after the first year for academic or personal reasons; 97% remain to receive a law degree.

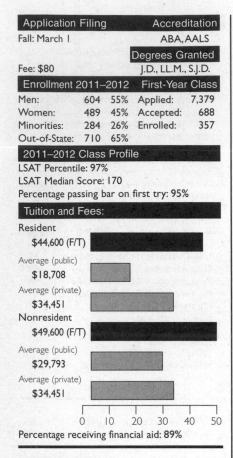

Application Filing	Accreditation
Fall: March 1	ABA, AALS

	Degrees Granted
Fee: $80	J.D., LL.M., S.J.D.

Enrollment 2011–2012		First-Year Class	
Men:	604 55%	Applied:	7,379
Women:	489 45%	Accepted:	688
Minorities:	284 26%	Enrolled:	357
Out-of-State:	710 65%		

2011–2012 Class Profile
LSAT Percentile: 97%
LSAT Median Score: 170
Percentage passing bar on first try: 95%

Tuition and Fees:

Resident
$44,600 (F/T)

Average (public)
$18,708

Average (private)
$34,451

Nonresident
$49,600 (F/T)

Average (public)
$29,793

Average (private)
$34,451

0   10   20   30   40   50

Percentage receiving financial aid: 89%

ADMISSIONS
In the fall of 2011 first-year class, 7379 applied, 688 were accepted, and 357 enrolled. Twelve transfer students enrolled. The median LSAT percentile of the most recent first-year class was 97; the median GPA was 3.9 on a scale of 4.0. The lowest LSAT percentile accepted was 40; the highest was 99.

Requirements
Applicants must have a bachelor's degree and take the LSAT. No specific undergraduate courses are required and candidates are not interviewed.

Procedure
The application deadline for fall entry is March 1. Applicants should submit an application form, LSAT results, transcripts, personal statement, nonrefundable application fee of $80, and 2 letters of recommendation. Notification of the admissions decision is by April 15. The law school uses the LSAC.

Special
The law school recruits minority and disadvantaged students through the Candidate Referral Service, Law Days, and student initiated outreach. Requirements are different for out-of-state students. Transfer students must have one year of credit, attended an ABA-approved law school, and a personal statement.

Costs
On-campus room and board costs about $15,466 annually; books and supplies run $5,334.

Financial Aid
About 89% of current law students receive some form of aid. The average annual amount of aid from all sources combined, including scholarships, loans, and work contracts, is $49,411. Awards are based on need and merit combined. Required financial statements are the FAFSA and institutional forms. The aid application deadline for fall entry is February 17. First-year students are notified about their financial aid application by January 1.

About the Law School
University of Virginia School of Law was established in 1819 and is a public institution. The 1135-acre campus is located in a suburban area 115 miles southwest of Washington D.C. and 70 miles west of Richmond. The primary mission of the law school is to help build a new dedication in society to the classical roles and skills of lawyering, and to foster an intellectual environment rich in the transmission of traditional values and character as well as immersed in new and creative legal thinking, analysis, and research. Students have access to federal, state, county, city, and local agencies, courts, correctional facilities, law firms, and legal aid organizations in the Charlottesville area. The Public Service Center and numerous student organizations offer pro bono opportunities and other practice situations. Facilities of special interest to law students include an extensive library, modern classrooms, moot court rooms, student organization offices, lounges, group study rooms, coffee facilities, and outdoor gardens and recreational areas. University housing is available for both single and married students; the Off-Grounds Housing Office

also helps students find off-campus accommodations. All law school facilities are accessible to the physically disabled.

Calendar
The law school operates on a traditional semester basis. Courses for full-time students are offered days only. There is no part-time program. New full-time students are admitted in the fall. There is no summer session. Transferable summer courses are not offered.

Programs
In addition to the J.D., the law school offers the LL.M. and S.J.D. Students may take relevant courses in other programs and apply credit toward the J.D.; a maximum of 12 credits may be applied. The following joint degrees may be earned: J.D./M.A. (Juris Doctor/Master of Arts (various disciplines)), J.D./M.B.A. (Juris Doctor/Master of Business Administration), J.D./M.A.L.D. (Juris Doctor/Master of Law and Diplomacy), J.D./M.P.A. (Juris Doctor/Master of Public Affairs), J.D./M.P.H. (Juris Doctor/Master of Public Health), J.D./M.S. (Juris Doctor/Master of Science in Accounting), and J.D./M.U.E.P. (Juris Doctor/Master of Urban and Environmental Planning).

Required
To earn the J.D., candidates must complete 86 total credits, of which 29 are for required courses. They must maintain a minimum GPA of 2.3 in the required courses. The following first-year courses are required of all students: Civil Procedure, Constitutional Law, Contracts, Criminal Law, Legal Research and Writing, Property, and Torts. Required upper-level courses consist of a professional ethics course and a professional skills course. The required orientation program for first-year students is two days.

Electives
The School of Law offers concentrations in corporate law, criminal law, environmental law, family law, intellectual property law, international law, juvenile law, labor law, litigation, media law, securities law, tax law, business organizations and finance, law and public service, commercial, constitutional, health, human rights and civil liberties, legal history, jurisprudence,

Phone: 434-924-7351
Fax: 434-982-2128
E-mail: lawadmit@virginia.edu
Web: www.law.virginia.edu

Contact

Anne Richard, Senior Assistant Dean for Admission, 434-924-7351 for general inquiries; Jennifer Hulvey, Director of Financial Aid, 434-924-7805 for financial aid information.

comparative law, race and law, and public policy and regulation. In addition, clinical offerings include employment, environmental law and conservation, human rights, patents, criminal practice, housing environment, child advocacy, and others. More than 90 seminar offerings are available each year, two-thirds taught by full-time faculty. A special program of seminars in ethical values is also offered. Students may work with local judges in the surrounding jurisdictions, in commonwealth attorneys' offices, and with public defenders. Students may also work with individual faculty on independent research projects and may also assist faculty in research and publication projects. There are numerous special lecture series held throughout the year, including the Contemporary Legal Thought series. Study abroad programs are available at University of Auckland, New Zealand; Tel Aviv University, Israel; Bucerius Law School, Hamburg, Germany; University of Nottingham, England; and Melbourne Law School, Australia and Waseda Law School, Japan. Students may also gain experience through the University of Virginia's Legal Assistance Society; the Post-Conviction Assistance Project; the John M. Olin Program in Law and Economics; the Center for Oceans Law and Policy; the Institute of Law Psychiatry, and Public Policy; the Center for Environmental Studies; the Center for National Security Law; and the Human Rights Study Project. The most widely taken electives are Corporations, Evidence, and Federal Income Tax.

Graduation Requirements

In order to graduate, candidates must have a GPA of 2.3, complete the upper-division writing requirement, professional ethics course, and a professional skills course.

Organizations

Students edit the *Virginia Law Review; Virginia Tax Review; Virginia Environmental Law Journal; Virginia Journal of International Law*, the oldest continuously published student-edited international law review in the country; *Journal of Law and Politics; Virginia Journal of Social Policy and the Law; Virginia Journal of Law and Technology; Virginia Sports and Entertainment Law Journal; Virginia Law and Business Review*; and

the newspaper *Virginia Law Weekly*. Students participate in in-house, intramural, and national competitions. More than 100 teams enter in the William Minor Lile Moot Court Competition. Law student organizations, local chapters of national associations, and campus organizations include the Federalist Society, American Constitution Society, Black Law Students Association, Phi Alpha Delta, Student Legal Forums include Public Interest Law Association, Environmental Law Forum, and John Basset Moore.

Library

The law library contains 873,981 hardcopy volumes and 278,125 microform volume equivalents, and subscribes to 4,892 serial publications. Online databases and networks include CALI, CIS Universe, Dow-Jones, Infotrac, Legal-Trac, LEXIS, OCLC First Search, RLIN, WESTLAW, and Wilsonline Indexes. Other resources are CCH, HeinOnline, Justis, LLMC Digital, RIA, SSRN, and PACER, which are available to law students for research. Special library collections include the Oceans Law Collection. The ratio of library volumes to faculty is 19,282 to 1 and to students is 800 to 1. The ratio of seats in the library to students is 1 to 1.

Faculty

The law school has 85 full-time and 100 part-time faculty members, of whom 41 are women. The ratio of full-time students to full-time faculty in an average class is 11 to 1. The law school has a regular program of bringing visiting professors and other distinguished lecturers and visitors to campus. There is a chapter of the Order of the Coif.

Students

About 45% of the student body are women; 26%, minorities; 7%, African American; 11%, Asian American; 5%, Hispanic; and 3%, Unknown. The majority of students come from Virginia (35%). The average age of entering students is 24; age range is 18 to 46. About 30% of students enter directly from undergraduate school, 14% have a graduate degree, and 70% have worked full-time prior to entering law school. About 1% drop out after the first year for academic or personal reasons; 99% remain to receive a law degree.

Placement

J.D.s awarded:	378

Services available through: a separate law school placement center.

Special features: Career counseling and assistance with job search, cover letters, resumes, and interviews, online information on employment opportunities in the public and private sector, and online interview sign-ups. There is also an active and extensive national alumni network.

Full-time job interviews:	121 employers
Summer job interviews:	581 employers
Placement by graduation:	98% of class
Placement within 9 months:	98% of class
Average starting salary:	$25,455 to $180,000

Areas of placement:

Private practice 2–10 attorneys	6%
Private practice 11–25 attorneys	1%
Private practice 51–100 attorneys	2%
Judicial clerkships	14%
Government	14%
Public interest	7%
Business/industry	3%
Academic	1%

UNIVERSITY OF WASHINGTON

School of Law

Box 353020
Seattle, WA 98195-3020

Application Filing	Accreditation
Fall: February 15	ABA, AALS

	Degrees Granted
Fee: $60	J.D., LL.M., Ph.D in Asian law

Enrollment 2011–2012		First-Year Class	
Men:	295 54%	Applied:	2,656
Women:	250 46%	Accepted:	586
Minorities:	114 21%	Enrolled:	182
Out-of-State:	191 35%		

2011–2012 Class Profile

LSAT Percentile: 90%
LSAT Median Score: 164
Percentage passing bar on first try: 84%

Tuition and Fees:

Resident
$25,780 (F/T)

Average (public)
$18,708

Average (private)
$34,451

Nonresident
$39,850 (F/T)

Average (public)
$29,793

Average (private)
$34,451

0   10   20   30   40   50

Percentage receiving financial aid: 85%

ADMISSIONS

In the fall of 2011 first-year class, 2656 applied, 586 were accepted, and 182 enrolled. Five transfer students enrolled. The median LSAT percentile of the most recent first-year class was 90; the median GPA was 3.7 on a scale of 4.0. The lowest LSAT percentile accepted was 49; the highest was 99.

Requirements

Applicants must have a bachelor's degree and take the LSAT. The most important admission factors include LSAT results, GPA, and academic achievement. No specific undergraduate courses are required and candidates are not interviewed.

Procedure

The application deadline for fall entry is February 15. Applicants should submit an application form, LSAT results, transcripts, personal statement, nonrefundable application fee of $60, 2 optional evaluations letters of recommendation, and a resume. Notification of the admissions decision is April 1. The law school uses the LSAC.

Special

The law school recruits minority and disadvantaged students through U.S. law fairs, Washington undergraduate schools, law forums, and personal referrals. Requirements are different for out-of-state students. Transfer students must have one year of credits, attended an ABA-approved law school, personal statement, attend an AALS-member law school, and a dean's letter of good standing.

Costs

On-campus room and board costs about $13,812 annually; books and supplies run $1,206.

Financial Aid

About 85% of current law students receive some form of aid. The average annual amount of aid from all sources combined, including scholarships, loans, and work contracts, is $30,000. Awards are based on need. Required financial statement is the FAFSA. The aid application deadline for fall entry is February 28. Special funds for minority or disadvantaged students include scholarships that are available from the school's privately donated scholarship funds, and awarded based on demonstrated financial need. First-year students are notified about their financial aid application in late spring for on-time applicants who have been admitted.

About the Law School

University of Washington School of Law was established in 1899 and is a public institution. The 20-acre campus is located in an urban area 3 miles from downtown Seattle. The mission of the law school is to serve and educate students to be leaders for the global common good. Students have access to federal, state, county, city, and local agencies, courts, correctional facilities, law firms, and legal aid organizations in the Seattle area. Of special interest to law students is a Center for Professional and Leadership Development, Center for Public Service Law Facilities, a new law school building, and a large law library. Housing for students is available for single and married students to a limited degree

in university housing. The Student Housing Affairs Office maintains listings of off-campus accommodations. All law school facilities are accessible to the physically disabled.

Calendar

The law school operates on a quarter basis. Courses for full-time students are offered days only and must be completed within 3 years. There is no part-time program. New full-time students are admitted in the fall. There is a 4-week summer session. Transferable summer courses are offered.

Programs

In addition to the J.D., the law school offers the LL.M. and Ph.D in Asian law. Students may take relevant courses in other programs and apply credit toward the J.D.; a maximum of 15 quarter credits may be applied.

Required

To earn the J.D., candidates must complete 135 quarters total credits, of which 49 are for required courses. The following first-year courses are required of all students: Civil Procedure, Comparative International Law, Constitutional Law, Contracts, Criminal Law, Legal Analysis, Research, Writing, Property, and Torts. Required upper-level courses consist of Advanced Writing, Professional Responsibility, and sixty hours of pro bono legal work. The required orientation program for first-year students is 8 days (4 days per week for 2 weeks prior to first regular class day).

Electives

The School of Law offers concentrations in environmental law, intellectual property law, internationl law, Asian law, alternative dispute resolution, public service, and health law. Clinics, open to second- and third-year students, are available in mediation, child advocacy, unemployment, criminal law, low-income taxpayer, immigration, refugee and immigrant advocacy law, and Indian law. Seminars, internships, and independent research programs are also open to second- and third-year students. Several study-abroad programs are coordinated by the law school, and students are eligible to pursue any

Phone: 206-543-4078
Fax: 206-543-5671
E-mail. luwudm@u.washington.edu
Web: www.law.washington.edu

Contact
Mathew Le, Director of Admissions and Financial Aid, 206-543-4078 for financial aid information.

WASHINGTON

ABA-approved study-abroad program. The law school offers peer tutoring through the Academic Support Program. The most widely taken electives are Trial Advocacy, Payment Systems, and Evidence.

Graduation Requirements

In order to graduate, candidates must complete the upper-division writing requirement and 8 quarters in residence.

Organizations
Students edit the *Washington Law Review, Pacific Rim and Policy Journal*, and the *Shidler Journal of Law, Commerce, and Technology*. Moot court competitions include the Jessup and International Jessup. Law student organizations include the Student Bar Association, Women's Law Caucus, and Minority Law Students Association. Other organizations include International Law Society, Innocence Project Northwest, and Public Interest Law Association. Local chapters of national associations include the ABA Law Student Division, ACLU, and Federalist Society.

Library
The law library contains 663,540 hardcopy volumes and 200,955 microform volume equivalents, and subscribes to 3,670 serial publications. Online databases and networks include CALI, CIS Universe, Dow-Jones, Infotrac, Legal-Trac, LEXIS, OCLC First Search, RLIN, WESTLAW, full Internet access; UW Information Navigator, and CD Law, which are available to law students for research. Special library collections include Japanese and other East Asian law materials. The library has been designated as a depository for U.S. government documents, Washington state materials, and Nuremburg trial documents. The ratio of library volumes to faculty is 51,978 to 1 and to students is 953 to 1. The ratio of seats in the library to students is 1 to 3.

Faculty
The law school has 51 full-time and 125 part-time faculty members, of whom 65 are women. According to AAUP standards for Category I institutions, faculty salaries are above average. About 25% of full-time faculty have a graduate law degree in addition to the J.D. The ratio of full-time

students to full-time faculty in an average class is 4 to 1. The law school has a regular program of bringing visiting professors and other distinguished lecturers and visitors to campus. There is a chapter of the Order of the Coif; 100 faculty and 19 graduates are members.

Students
About 46% of the student body are women; 21%, minorities; 2%, African American; 10%, Asian American; 6%, Hispanic; and 4%, Native American. The majority of students come from Washington (65%). The average age of entering students is 26; age range is 21 to 44. About 20% of students enter directly from undergraduate school, and 12% have a graduate degree. About 2% drop out after the first year for academic or personal reasons; 98% remain to receive a law degree.

Placement

J.D.s awarded:	182
Services available through: a separate law school placement center.	
Services: separate counseling service for public service law students.	
Special features: first-year student job workshops, first-year student mock interview program, and other career programs throughout the school year.	
Full-time job interviews:	9 employers
Summer job interviews:	51 employers
Placement within 9 months of graduation:	96% of class
Average starting salary:	$48,150 to $119,298
Areas of placement:	
Private practice 2–10 attorneys	18%
Private practice 11–25 attorneys	2%
Private practice 26–50 attorneys	5%
Private practice 51–100 attorneys	16%
Business/industry	15%
Judicial clerkships	14%
Government	14%
Public interest	7%
Military	3%
Academic	1%

School of Law

9920 S. LaCienega Blvd. #404
Inglewood, CA 90301-2902

Application Filing		Accreditation
Fall: open		no

	Degrees Granted
Fee: $55	J.D.

Enrollment 2011–2012		First-Year Class	
Men:	126 49%	Applied:	217
Women:	133 51%	Accepted:	118
Minorities:	78 30%	Enrolled:	104
Out-of-State:	0 0%		

2011–2012 Class Profile
LSAT Percentile: 31%
LSAT Median Score: 150
Percentage passing bar on first try: 25%

Tuition and Fees:

Resident
$23,330 (F/T)

Average (public)
$18,708

Average (private)
$34,451

Nonresident
n/av

Average (public)
$29,793

Average (private)
$34,451

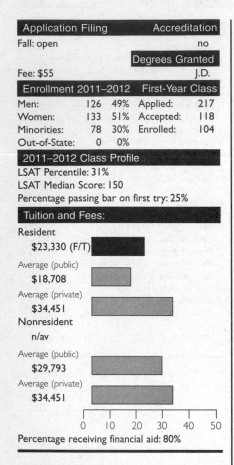

Percentage receiving financial aid: 80%

ADMISSIONS

In the fall of 2011 first-year class, 217 applied, 118 were accepted, and 104 enrolled. Seventeen transfers enrolled. The median LSAT percentile of the most recent first-year class was 31; the median GPA was 3.1 on a scale of 4.0. The lowest LSAT percentile accepted was 8; the highest was 98.

Requirements
Applicants must take the LSAT. Minimum acceptable LSAT percentile is 20 and minimum acceptable GPA is 2.0 on a scale of 4.0. The most important admission factors include LSAT results, GPA, and personal interview. No specific undergraduate courses are required. Candidates are not interviewed.

Procedure
The application deadline for fall entry is open. Applicants should submit an application form, LSAT results, transcripts, TOEFL (if applicable), and a nonrefundable application fee of $55. Notification of the admissions decision is as soon as a decision is made. The law school uses the LSAC.

Special
Requirements are different for out-of-state students. Transfer students must have attended an ABA-approved law school and be in good standing at the previous institution.

Costs

Tuition and fees for the 2011–2012 academic year are $22,680 for full-time in-state students. Books and supplies run $900.

Financial Aid

About 80% of current law students receive some form of aid. The average annual amount of aid from all sources combined, including scholarships, loans, and work contracts, is $18,382; maximum, $36,620. Awards are based on need and merit combined. The required financial statement is the FAFSA. The aid application deadline for fall entry is August 4. First-year students are notified about their financial aid application at time of acceptance.

About the Law School

University of West Los Angeles School of Law was established in 1966 and is a private institution. The 5-acre campus is in an urban area of west Los Angeles. The primary mission of the law school is to provide an opportunity for a legal education to non-traditional students. Housing for students is not available on campus, but is available in the surrounding neighborhoods. All law school facilities are accessible to the physically disabled.

Calendar

The law school operates on a traditional semester basis. Courses for full-time students are offered both day and evening, and must be completed within 3 years. For part-time students, courses are offered both day and evening, and must be completed within 4 years. New full- and part-time students are admitted in the fall, spring, and summer. There is an 8-week summer session. Transferable summer courses are offered.

Programs

Required
To earn the J.D., candidates must complete 85 total credits, of which 69 are for required courses. They must maintain a minimum GPA of 2.0 in the required courses. The following first-year courses are required of all students: Contracts I and II, Criminal Law, Introduction to Legal Study, Property I and II, and Torts I and II. Required upper-level courses consist of a lawyering skills practicum, an advanced legal writing course, Appellate Advocacy, Business Associations, Civil Procedure, Community Property, Constitutional Law I and II, Criminal Procedure, Ethical Lawyering, and Evidence I and II. The required orientation program for first-year students includes the Introduction to Legal Study course.

Electives
The most widely taken electives are Bankruptcy, Legal Aid, and Immigration Law.

Graduation Requirements
In order to graduate, candidates must have a GPA of 2.0, and must have completed the upper-division writing requirement and the Appellate Advocacy course.

Phone: 310-342-5210
Fax: 310-342-5295
E-mail: tsmith@uwla.edu
Web: uwla.edu

Contact
Associate Dean, 310-342-5210 for general inquiries; Danille Reeves, Financial Administrator, 310-342-5268 for financial aid information.

Organizations
Students edit the newspaper *The Brief*. Students participate in the Traynor and Ventura County Court of Appeals Moot Court Competitions. Law student organizations include Student Bar Association and Delta Theta Law Fraternity.

Library
The law library contains 27,500 hard-copy volumes and 15,000 microform volume equivalents. Such online databases and networks as CALI and WESTLAW are available to law students for research. The ratio of library volumes to faculty is 6,875 to 1 and to students is 106 to 1.

Faculty
The law school has 4 full-time and 37 part-time faculty members, of whom 10 are women. The ratio of full-time students to full-time faculty in an average class is 50 to 1.

Students
About 51% of the student body are women; 31%, minorities; 13%, African American; 9%, Asian American; 8%, Hispanic; and 1%, Native American. The majority of students come from California (100%). The age range of entering students is 25 to 39. About 10% drop out after the first year for academic or personal reasons; 90% remain to receive a law degree.

Placement	
J.D.s awarded:	50
Services available through: the university placement center.	
Special features: individual counseling for graduates and students, career fair, and speaker forums.	
Average starting salary:	$50,000 to $90,000
Areas of placement:	
Private practice 2–10 attorneys	38%
Private practice 11–25 attorneys	13%
Business/industry	13%
Public interest	13%

Law School

975 Bascom Mall
Madison, WI 53706

Application Filing	Accreditation
Fall: March 1	ABA, AALS

	Degrees Granted
Fee: $56	J.D., LL.M., S.J.D., M.L.I.

Enrollment 2011–2012		First-Year Class	
Men:	445 56%	Applied:	2,870
Women:	347 44%	Accepted:	741
Minorities:	166 21%	Enrolled:	242
Out-of-State:	317 40%		

2011–2012 Class Profile
LSAT Percentile: 88%
LSAT Median Score: 163
Percentage passing bar on first try: 100%

Tuition and Fees:

Resident
$19,684 (F/T)

Average (public)
$18,708

Average (private)
$34,451

Nonresident
$38,811 (F/T)

Average (public)
$29,793

Average (private)
$34,451

0   10   20   30   40   50
Percentage receiving financial aid: 85%

ADMISSIONS
In the fall of 2011 first-year class, 2870 applied, 741 were accepted, and 242 enrolled. Twenty-four transfers enrolled. The median LSAT percentile of the most recent first-year class was 88; the median GPA was 3.7 on a scale of 4.0.

Requirements
Applicants must have a bachelor's degree and take the LSAT. The most important admission factors include LSAT results, GPA, and state or country of residence. No specific undergraduate courses are required and candidates are not interviewed.

Procedure
The application deadline for fall entry is March 1. Applicants should submit an application form, LSAT results, transcripts, a personal statement, nonrefundable application fee of $56, 2 letters of recommendation, and a resume. Notification of the admissions decision is on a rolling basis. The law school uses the LSAC.

Special
The law school recruits minority and disadvantaged students through mailings, law school and graduate school days, minority career fairs, and a network of alumni and current students. Requirements are different for out-of-state students. Transfer students must have one year of credits, must have attended an ABA-approved law school, and must submit a personal statement. Due to enrollment pressures, transfer applications are accepted primarily on the basis of class rank in the transferring law school, or, if class rank is unavailable, on the basis of other evidence of academic performance.

Costs
On-campus room and board costs about $9,250 annually; books and supplies run $2,300.

Financial Aid
About 85% of current law students receive some form of aid. The average annual amount of aid from all sources combined, including scholarships, loans, and work contracts, is $29,331. Awards are based on need and merit combined. Required financial statements are the FAFSA and student tax form. The aid application deadline for fall entry is March 1. Special funds for minority or disadvantaged students include need- and merit-based scholarships with criteria preference for students from disadvantaged backgrounds.

About the Law School
University of Wisconsin Law School was established in 1868 and is a public institution. The 933-acre campus is located in an urban area in the middle of one of the world's leading research universities. The primary mission of the law school is to focus on helping its students understand how law both affects and is affected by every other institutional force in society. Students have access to federal, state, county, city, and local agencies, courts, correctional facilities, law firms, and legal aid organizations in the Madison area. All of the resources of the University of Wisconsin, including educational, cultural, and social opportunities, are available to law students. Housing for students in university graduate student housing is available; most students live in private rental property close to campus. All law

school facilities are accessible to the physically disabled.

Calendar
The law school operates on a traditional semester basis. Courses for full-time students are offered both day and evening, and must be completed within 6 years. For part-time students, courses are offered both day and evening, and must be completed within 6 years. New full- and part-time students are admitted in the fall. There is a 13-week summer session. Transferable summer courses are offered.

Programs
In addition to the J.D., the law school offers the LL.M., S.J.D., and M.L.I. Students may take relevant courses in other programs and apply credit toward the J.D.; a maximum of 6 credits may be applied. The following joint degrees may be earned: J.D./M.A. (Juris Doctor/Master of Arts) and J.D./Ph.D. (Juris Doctor/Doctor of Philosophy).

Required
To earn the J.D., candidates must complete 90 total credits, of which 40 are for required courses. They must maintain a minimum GPA of 2.0 in the required courses. The following first-year courses are required of all students: Civil Procedure I, Constitutional Law I, Contracts I, Criminal Procedure, Introduction to the Law, Legal Research and Writing, Property, and Torts. Required upper-level courses consist of Civil Procedure II (for Diploma Privilege), Constitutional Law II (for Diploma Privilege), Evidence (for Diploma Privilege), Legal Process, Legal Research & Writing II, Professional Responsibilities, and Trusts and Estates (for Diploma Privilege). An extensive selection of clinical courses is available for students who wish to participate. The required orientation program for first-year students is a 3-day program that includes a check-in with the Admissions Office staff, study skills workshop, informal gatherings, and student photos.

Electives
The law school offers concentrations in corporate law, criminal law, environmental law, family law, intellectual property law, internationl law, labor law, litigation, securities law, sports law, tax law, torts

Phone: 608-262-5914
Fax: 608-263-3191
E-mail: admissions@law.wisc.edu
Web: www.law.wisc.edu

Contact

Rebecca L. Scheller, Interim Assistant Dean, 608-262-5914 for general inquiries and financial aid information.

WISCONSIN

and insurance, and estate planning and community health. In addition, numerous seminars are available. Hands-on judicial interships are available with the Wisconsin Supreme Court, Wisconsin Court of Appeals, Federal District Court, and various county circuit courts. Directed reading and research is available to all second- and third-year students who want to focus on a specific area of research under a professor's guidance. Field work includes such programs as Midwest Enviornmental Advocates and the Center for Patient Partnerships. Tutorial programs and special interest group programs, including the Fairchild Lecture Series, the Robert W. Kastennmeier Lecture, and various group lectures, are offered. Study abroad is possible through the Germany, Holland, Italy, Chile, Peru, South Africa, United Kingdom, Brazil, France, and Asia programs. An individualized instruction service, offering courses on writing, study skills, test taking, time management, research papers, and other topics are available to all students. The Legal Education Opportunities Program is available for students of color. Many special interest programs are available. There are more than 30 special interest group programs, with more being created each year. The most widely taken electives are Business Organizations, Tax, and Administrative Law.

Graduation Requirements

In order to graduate, candidates must have a GPA of 2.0 and must have completed the upper-division writing requirement.

Organizations

Students edit the *Wisconsin Law Review, Wisconsin International Law Journal, Wisconsin Journal of Law, and Gender & Society*. Moot court competitions include Evan A. Evans Constitutional Law Competition, Philip C. Jessup International Law Moot Court Competition, and Saul Lefkowitz IP Moot Court. Law student organizations on campus include the Intellectual Property Students Association, Business and Tax Law Association, and Asian Pacific American/South Asian Law Students Association. Local chapters of national associations include American Constitution Society, Federalist Society, and National Lawyers Guild. Campus organizations include Black Law Student Association,

Indigenous Law Students Association, and Latino Law Students Association.

Library

The law library contains 467,966 hardcopy volumes and 174,057 microform volume equivalents, and subscribes to 6,518 serial publications. Online databases and networks include CIS Universe, DIALOG, Legal-Trac, LEXIS, OCLC First Search, RLIN, WESTLAW, Wilsonline Indexes, BNA Online, HeinOnline, CCH Intelliconnect, and Bloomberg Law, which are available to law students for research. Special library collections include criminal justice, foreign, and international law materials, and a federal depository. The ratio of library volumes to faculty is 4,119 to 1 and to students is 567 to 1. The ratio of seats in the library to students is 1 to 1.

Faculty

The law school has 57 full-time and 70 part-time faculty members, of whom 59 are women. According to AAUP standards for Category I institutions, faculty salaries are above average. The ratio of full-time students to full-time faculty in an average class is 11 to 1; in a clinic, 6 to 1. The law school has a regular program of bringing visiting professors and other distinguished lecturers and visitors to campus. There is a chapter of the Order of the Coif.

Students

About 44% of the student body are women; 21%, minorities; 6%, African American; 5%, Asian American; 7%, Hispanic; and 2%, Native American. The majority of students come from Wisconsin (60%). The average age of entering students is 24; age range is 20 to 46. About 42% of students enter directly from undergraduate school, and 7% have a graduate degree.

Placement

J.D.s awarded:	242

Services available through: a separate law school placement center and workshops on careers in various areas of the law, including nontraditional careers.

Services: information on diversity and opportunities, organizing employer visits, off-campus recruiting fairs, and participation in other national job fairs.

Special features: a pro bono project matching students with practitioners and mock interviews with practitioners.

Full-time job interviews:	15 employers
Summer job interviews:	49 employers
Placement by graduation:	78% of class
Placement within 9 months:	96% of class
Areas of placement:	
Private practice 2–10 attorneys	21%
Private practice 11–25 attorneys	3%
Private practice 26–50 attorneys	2%
Private practice 51–100 attorneys	2%
Government	22%
Solo practice	21%
Business/industry	10%
Public interest	9%
Judicial clerkships	5%
Academic	3%
Military	2%

University of Wisconsin   **587**

UNIVERSITY OF WYOMING

College of Law

Dept. 3035,
1000 East University Avenue
Laramie, WY 82071

Application Filing	Accreditation
Fall: March 1	ABA, AALS
	Degrees Granted
Fee: $50	J.D.

Enrollment 2011–2012			First-Year Class	
Men:	119	53%	Applied:	540
Women:	107	47%	Accepted:	242
Minorities:	32	14%	Enrolled:	69
Out-of-State:	120	53%		

2011–2012 Class Profile
LSAT Percentile: 56%
LSAT Median Score: 153

Tuition and Fees:

Resident
$13,095 (F/T)

Average (public)
$18,708

Average (private)
$34,451

Nonresident
$25,425 (F/T)

Average (public)
$29,793

Average (private)
$34,451

Percentage receiving financial aid: 95%

ADMISSIONS
In the fall of 2011 first-year class, 540 applied, 242 were accepted, and 69 enrolled. Seven transfer students enrolled. The median LSAT percentile of the most recent first-year class was 56; the median GPA was 3.4 on a scale of 4.0. The lowest LSAT percentile accepted was 15; the highest was 99.

Requirements
Applicants must have a bachelor's degree and take the LSAT. The most important admission factors include academic achievement, GPA, and LSAT results. No specific undergraduate courses are required, and candidates are not interviewed.

Procedure
The application deadline for fall entry is March 1. Applicants should submit an application form, LSAT results, transcripts, a personal statement, TOEFL (if applicable), and a nonrefundable application fee of $50. Notification of the admissions decision is on a rolling basis, beginning in December. The law school uses the LSAC.

Special
The law school recruits minority and disadvantaged students by soliciting applications, hosting a law day session for minority undergraduate students at the university, attending LSAC forums and regional recruiting events focused on minority students, and multicultural events. Requirements are different for out-of-state students. Transfer students must have one year of credits, must have a minimum GPA of 2, must have attended an ABA-approved law school, and must submit a personal statement.

Costs
Tuition and fees for the 2011–2012 academic year are $12,090 for full-time in-state students and $24,420 for out-of-state students. On-campus room and board costs about $10,851 annually; books and supplies run $1,200.

Financial Aid
About 95% of current law students receive some form of aid. The average annual amount of aid from all sources combined, including scholarships, loans, and work contracts, is $20,867; maximum, $26,722. Awards are based on need and merit combined. The required financial statement is the FAFSA. The aid application deadline for fall entry is March 1. Special funds for minority or disadvantaged students consist of minority graduate assistantships offered on a competitive basis. First-year students are notified about their financial aid application at time of acceptance.

About the Law School
University of Wyoming College of Law was established in 1920 and is a public institution. The 785-acre campus is located in a small town 45 miles from Cheyenne. The primary mission of the law school is to provide students with the knowledge and training necessary to meet the responsibilities of the legal profession; students must secure a broad and basic knowledge of law principles, understand the social and economic factors underlying these principles, and learn to judge the effectiveness of these principles in solving client and societal problems. Students have access to federal, state, county, city, and local agencies, courts, correctional facilities, law firms, and legal aid organizations in the Laramie area. Housing for students is available in a university residence hall for single students. Graduate and professional students are housed separately from undergraduates. The university also maintains 2-bedroom furnished apartments for married students. An ample supply of apartments and rental properties are available throughout the community. About 98% of the law school facilities are accessible to the physically disabled.

Calendar
The law school operates on a traditional semester basis. Courses for full-time students are offered days only, and must be completed within 3 years. There is no part-time program. New full-time students are admitted in the fall. There is no summer session. Transferable summer courses are not offered.

Programs
Students may take relevant courses in other programs and apply credit toward the J.D.; a maximum of 6 credits may be applied. The following joint degrees may be earned: J.D./M.A. (Juris Doctor/Master of Environment and National Resources), J.D./M.B.A. (Juris Doctor/Master of Business Administration), and J.D./M.P.A. (Juris Doctor/Master of Public Administration).

Required
To earn the J.D., candidates must complete 89 total credits, of which 38 are for required courses. They must maintain a minimum GPA of 2.0 in the required courses. The following first-year courses are required of all students: Appellate Advocacy, Civil Procedure I and II, Constitutional Law I, Contracts I and II, Criminal Law, Introduction to Law, Legal Writing and Research, Property I and II, and Torts I and II. Required upper-level courses consist of a skills course, Advanced Writing Requirement, Evidence, and Professional Responsibility. The required orientation program for first-year students is a 3-day program including lectures on legal analysis, legal reasoning, the study of law, and case briefing sessions.

Phone: 307-766-6416
Fax: 307-766-6417
E-mail: dburke@uwyo.edu
Web: uwyo.edu/law

Contact

N. Denise Burke, Assistant Dean, 307-766-6416 for general inquiries; Office of Student Financial Aid, 307-766-2116 for financial aid information.

WYOMING

Electives

The College of Law offers concentrations in corporate law, criminal law, environmental law, family law, international law, litigation, and tax law. In addition, Defender Aid, Legal Services, Prosecution Assistance, and Domestic Violence programs are available to third-year students. In order to graduate, the advanced writing and skills requirements must be fulfilled; a variety of seminars that meet these requirements are offered for credits. Seminars are offered in Health Law, Education Law, Federal Water Rights, White Collar Crime, and Energy Law & Policy. Second- and third-year students may participate in the externship program for 2 to 3 credit hours per semester. Externs are placed with the Wyoming Attorney General's Office, Wyoming Supreme Court, the U.S. District Court, Wyoming Supreme Court, State Department of the U.S. District Court, State Department of Revenue and Taxation, Wyoming state courts, U.S. Attorney's Office, state and federal public defenders, and various state agencies, including Environmental Quality Guardian, and nonprofits such as ACLI, Biodiversity Alliance, Innocence Project, and Western Resource Advocates. Individualized tutoring is available through the Academic Support Program. Minority enrichment programs and lectures are also available through the Academic Support Program. A retention program is offered each spring to first-year students who have GPAs near or below 2.0 after the first semester. The most widely taken electives are Business Organizations, Family Law, and Trusts and Estates.

Graduation Requirements

In order to graduate, candidates must have a GPA of 2.0 and must have completed the upper-division writing requirement and one skills course.

Organizations

Students edit the *Wyoming Law Review*. Moot court competitions include the National Moot Court, National Environmental Law Moot Court at Pace University, and Natural Resources Law Moot Court at the University of Denver. Other competitions include the National Client Counseling, the ATLA Student Trial Advocacy, and locally sponsored moot court and trial competitions. Law student organizations include the Potter Law Club, Natural Resources Law Forum, Women's Law Forum, Public Interest Law Forum, Sports Law Club, Students for Equal Justice, International Law Club, and J. Reuben Clark Law Society. There are local chapters of Phi Alpha Delta, Phi Delta Phi, and Delta Theta Phi. Campus clubs and other organizations include the Multicultural Students Organization, Associated Students of the University of Wyoming, and GLTB Organization.

Library

The law library contains 145,916 hardcopy volumes and 154,014 microform volume equivalents, and subscribes to 574 serial publications. Online databases and networks include CALI, CIS Universe, Infotrac, Legal-Trac, LEXIS, OCLC First Search, WESTLAW, and Wilsonline Indexes. HeinOnline, LLMC Digital, VersusLaw, Making of Modern Law, JSTOR, Legal Periodicals Retrospective, Foreign and International Law, U.N. Treaty Collection, U.S. Supreme Court Records and Briefs, CCH Tax Network, ELR, BNA Libraries, Fastcase, CVN Law School, and Oxford Reports and are available to law students for research. Special library collections include a selective government depository and a Roman Law collection. The ratio of library volumes to faculty is 14,008 to 1 and to students is 1,426 to 1. The ratio of seats in the library to students is 1 to 1.

Faculty

The law school has 17 full-time and 19 part-time faculty members, of whom 11 are women. According to AAUP standards for Category I institutions, faculty salaries are below average. About 10% of full-time faculty have a graduate law degree in addition to the J.D. The ratio of full-time students to full-time faculty in an average class is 11 to 1; in a clinic, 8 to 1. The law school has a regular program of bringing visiting professors and other distinguished lecturers and visitors to campus. There is a chapter of the Order of the Coif; 15 faculty and 222 graduates are members.

Students

About 49% of the student body are women; 13%, minorities; 1%, African American; 3%, Asian American; 2%, Hispanic; 1%, Native American; and 11%, self-identified with LSAC or on application as "Other." The majority of students come from the

Placement

J.D.s awarded:	75
Services available through: a separate law school placement center and the university placement center.	
Services: individual career counseling.	
Special features: online job database, on campus interviews, on campus job fairs, regional recruiting events, and access to subscription services.	
Full-time job interviews:	5 employers
Summer job interviews:	6 employers
Placement by graduation:	45% of class
Placement within 9 months:	79% of class
Average starting salary:	$36,000 to $120,000
Areas of placement:	
Private practice 2–10 attorneys	48%
Private practice 11–25 attorneys	9%
Private practice 51–100 attorneys	4%
Government	11%
Business/industry	11%
Public interest	8%
Judicial clerkships	4%
Private practice	4%
Military	2%

West (91%). The average age of entering students is 26; age range is 21 to 56. About 33% of students enter directly from undergraduate school and 11% have a graduate degree. About 2% drop out after the first year for academic or personal reasons; 93% remain to receive a law degree.

VALPARAISO UNIVERSITY

School of Law

Wesemann Hall,
656 S. Greenwich Street
Valparaiso, IN 46383-6493

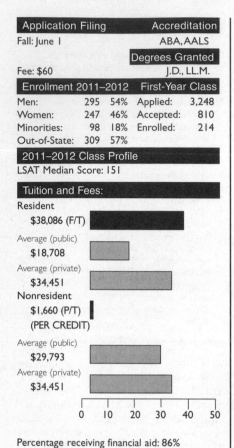

Application Filing	Accreditation
Fall: June 1	ABA, AALS
	Degrees Granted
Fee: $60	J.D., LL.M.

Enrollment 2011–2012		First-Year Class	
Men:	295 54%	Applied:	3,248
Women:	247 46%	Accepted:	810
Minorities:	98 18%	Enrolled:	214
Out-of-State:	309 57%		

2011–2012 Class Profile
LSAT Median Score: 151

Tuition and Fees:

Resident
$38,086 (F/T)

Average (public)
$18,708

Average (private)
$34,451

Nonresident
$1,660 (P/T)
(PER CREDIT)

Average (public)
$29,793

Average (private)
$34,451

0   10   20   30   40   50

Percentage receiving financial aid: 86%

ADMISSIONS

In the fall of 2011 first-year class, 3248 applied, 810 were accepted, and 214 enrolled. Four transfers enrolled. The median GPA of the most recent first-year class was 3.5.

Requirements

Applicants must have a bachelor's degree and take the LSAT. The most important admission factors include academic achievement, general background, and LSAT results. No specific undergraduate courses are required. Candidates are not interviewed.

Procedure

The application deadline for fall entry is June 1. Applicants should submit an application form, LSAT results, transcripts, a personal statement, the TOEFL (international applicants), a nonrefundable application fee of $60, and 2 letters of recommendation. Notification of the admissions decision is on a rolling basis. The law school uses the LSAC.

Special

The law school recruits minority and disadvantaged students through recruitment mailings and relationship building. Requirements are different for out-of-state students. Transfer students must have one year of credits, a minimum GPA of 2.0, attended an ABA-approved law school, a personal statement, and have their application reviewed by the admissions committee.

Costs

Tuition and fees for the 2011–2012 academic year are $37,240 for full-time in-state students. On-campus room and board costs about $7,700 annually; books and supplies run $1,200.

Financial Aid

About 86% of current law students receive some form of aid. The average annual amount of aid from all sources combined, including scholarships, loans, and work contracts, is $20,500; maximum, $42,318. Awards are based on need and merit combined. Required financial statement is the FAFSA. The aid application deadline for fall entry is March 1. First-year students are notified about their financial aid application at time of acceptance.

About the Law School

Valparaiso University School of Law was established in 1879 and is a private institution. The 310-acre campus is located in a suburban area 55 miles southeast of Chicago in northwest Indiana. The primary mission of the law school is to foster a learning environment; to maintain a community of teacher-scholars committed to excellence in legal research and publication that will shape the development of the law; and to embody an interaction between demands of the law and the Lutheran heritage of Valparaiso University. Students have access to federal, state, county, city, and local agencies, courts, correctional facilities, law firms, and legal aid organizations in the Valparaiso area. Valparaiso is the county seat of Porter County. Students also have access to charitable and community organizations for volunteer/pro bono work in Porter and Lake counties, Indiana, and Cook County, Illinois (Chicago). Facilities of special interest to law students are Wesemann Hall, which houses classrooms, a courtroom, and an administrative complex, and Heritage Hall, which is listed on the National Register of Historic Places, and houses the law clinic. Housing for students includes limited on-campus apartments; local apartments and large apartment complexes; and modest lakeside summer homes and cottages available for rent. The Admissions Office provides assistance in locating housing. About 75% of the law school facilities are accessible to the physically disabled.

Calendar

The law school operates on a traditional semester basis. Courses for full-time students are offered both day and evening and must be completed within 7 years. For part-time students, courses are offered both day and evening and must be completed within 7 years. New full- and part-time students are admitted in the fall. There is an 8-week summer session. Transferable summer courses are offered.

Programs

In addition to the J.D., the law school offers the LL.M. The following joint degrees may be earned: J.D./M.A.C.S. (Juris Doctor/Master of Arts in Chinese Studies), J.D./M.A.L.S. (Juris Doctor/Master of Arts in Liberal Studies), J.D./M.A. (Juris Doctor/Master of Arts in psychology and clinical mental), J.D./M.B.A. (Juris Doctor/Master of Business Administration), J.D./M.S.I.C.P. (Juris Doctor/Master of International Commerce and Policy), and J.D./M.S.S.A. (Juris Doctor/Master of Science in Sports Administration).

Required

To earn the J.D., candidates must complete 90 total credits, of which 57 are required courses. They must maintain a minimum GPA of 2.0 in the required courses. The following first-year courses are required of all students: Civil Procedure, Constitutional Law I, Contracts, Criminal Law, Legal Research, Legal Writing, Property, and Torts. Required upper-level courses consist of Business Associations, Constitutional Law II, Evidence, a seminar, Legal Profession, 1 of 3 administrative courses,

Phone: 219-465-7821
888-VALPOLAW (825-7652)
Fax: 219-465-7808
E-mail: law.admissions@valpo.edu
Web: www.valpo.edu/law

Contact

Director of Admissions, 219-465-7829 for general inquiries; Financial Aid, 219-465-7818 for financial aid information.

INDIANA

1 of 3 code courses, 1 of 4 advanced writing courses, 1 of 5 perspective courses, and 1 of 3 property courses. Third-year (and some second-year) law students in Indiana are permitted to represent clients in court, under faculty supervision. The law clinic is available to third-year students and handles civil, criminal, tax, sports law, juvenile, and mediation law matters. The required orientation program for first-year students is 2 or 3 days preceding the start of the fall semester. Formal registration and meetings with current students, deans, and faculty advisers are included.

Electives

Clinics are available to third-year students for 2 or 3 credits a semester for a maximum of 12 credit hours. A seminar is required of all third-year students not on the *Law Review*, and a substantial paper is required. Second- and third-year students may also participate in up to 9 credit hours of an extern program. The law school supports 72 externship programs. Students may assist faculty with current representation or in research assistantships in which they work one-on-one with a professor in his or her area of current interest and research. No credit is given for the 20 hours of pro bono public service. Special lecture series include the Monsanto Annual Lecture on Tort Law Reform, the annual Seegers Lecture Series, the Distinguished Visitors Program, and the annual Tabor Institute on Legal Ethics. There is a summer study-abroad program that takes place in Cambridge, England. There is also a voluntary Academic Success Program; no credit is given and participation is by invitation only. Other tutorials are led by first-year faculty with student tutors available for individual consultation. The Hispanic Law Students Association, Black Law Students Association, and Multicultural Law Students Association sponsor minority programming. Special interest group programs include the Intellectual Property Association, Health Law Association, Sports and Entertainment Law Association, Coalition for Choice, Jus Vitae, Equal Justice Alliance, Third World Legal Studies, International Law, Pastoral Ministry, ATLA, and ABA/LSD. The most widely taken electives are Trusts and Estates, Federal Income Tax, and business and commercial law courses.

Graduation Requirements

In order to graduate, candidates must have a GPA of 2.0, completed the upper-division writing requirement, and have completed the pro bono service requirement of 20 hours, for which no grade or credit is given.

Organizations

Students edit the *Valparaiso University Law Review*. The student newspaper is *The Forum*. Moot court teams are sent annually to the Environmental Moot Court held at Pace University, the Giles Sutherland Rich Moot Court (1995 National Champions), and the Jessup International Moot Court. Other annual competitions are the Negotiations, the National Mock Trial, Association of Trial Lawyers of America, and Client Counseling. Law student organizations include the Midwest Environmental Law Caucus and Christian Legal Society. Local chapters of national associations include Delta Theta Phi, Phi Alpha Delta, and Phi Delta Phi. Other groups are Just Democracy and Law Spouses Association.

Library

The law library contains 332,337 hardcopy volumes and 936,822 microform volume equivalents, and subscribes to 2,371 serial publications. Online databases and networks include CALI, CIS Universe, DIALOG, Infotrac, Legal-Trac, LEXIS, OCLC First Search, WESTLAW, and Wilsonline Indexes, which are available to law students for research. Special library collections include a U.S. Government Printing Office Depository, a Readex United Nations basic law library collection, and briefs from the Indiana Supreme Court and Indiana Court of Appeals. The ratio of library volumes to faculty is 8,982 to 1 and to students is 613 to 1. The ratio of seats in the library to students is 1 to 2.

Faculty

The law school has 37 full-time and 40 part-time faculty members, of whom 27 are women. According to AAUP standards for Category IIA institutions, faculty salaries are average. About 23% of full-time faculty members have a graduate law degree in addition to the J.D. The ratio of full-time students to full-time faculty in an average class is 17 to 1; in a clinic, 9 to 1. The law school has a regular program

Placement

J.D.s awarded:	150

Services available through: a separate law school placement center.

Services: annually participate in job fairs, write articles for students, and hold numerous seminars and workshops. Focus on personalized counseling through meeting with 1 of 3 professional counselors. Host professional Career Day where alumni and practitioners in a wide variety of legal practice areas come to the school to provide 1-on-1 counseling to students.

Special features: member of NACD and Chicago Area Law School Consortium; Administer Loan Repayment Assistance Program and Public Interest Scholarship.

Full-time job interviews:	16 employers
Summer job interviews:	33 employers
Placement by graduation:	39% of class
Placement within 9 months:	88% of class
Average starting salary:	$35,000 to $140,000

Areas of placement:

Law firms	56%
Government	16%
Business/industry	14%
Judicial clerkships	7%
Public interest	4%
Academic	1%

of bringing visiting professors and other distinguished lecturers and visitors to campus.

Students

About 46% of the student body are women; 18%, minorities; 5%, African American; 2%, Asian American; 5%, Hispanic; and 6%, international and multiracial. The majority of students come from Indiana (43%). The average age of entering students is 25; age range is 20 to 55. About 56% of students enter directly from undergraduate school, and 8% have a graduate degree. About 15% drop out after the first year for academic or personal reasons; 86% remain to receive a law degree.

VANDERBILT UNIVERSITY

Vanderbilt Law School

131 21st Avenue South
Nashville, TN 37203

Application Filing	Accreditation
Fall: March 15	ABA, AALS

	Degrees Granted
Fee: $50	J.D., LL.M., Ph.D. in Law and Economics

Enrollment 2011–2012   First-Year Class

Men:	319	54%	Applied:	3,987
Women:	267	46%	Accepted:	1,193
Minorities:	111	19%	Enrolled:	194

2011–2012 Class Profile
LSAT Percentile: 97%
LSAT Median Score: 169
Percentage passing bar on first try: 93%

Tuition and Fees:

Resident
$46,148 (F/T)

Average (public)
$18,708

Average (private)
$34,451

Nonresident
$46,148 (F/T)

Average (public)
$29,793

Average (private)
$34,451

0   10   20   30   40   50
Percentage receiving financial aid: 85%

ADMISSIONS
In the fall of 2011 first-year class, 3987 applied, 1193 were accepted, and 194 enrolled. Thirty transfers enrolled. The median LSAT percentile of the most recent first-year class was 97; the median GPA was 3.7 on a scale of 4.0.

Requirements
Applicants must have a bachelor's degree and take the LSAT. No specific undergraduate courses are required. Candidates are interviewed.

Procedure
The application deadline for fall entry is March 15. Applicants should submit an application form, LSAT results, transcripts, a personal statement, TOEFL (if applicable), a nonrefundable application fee of $50, and 2 letters of recommendation. Notification of the admissions decision is on a rolling basis. The law school uses the LSAC.

Special
The law school recruits minority and disadvantaged students by means of on-campus recruiting, general mailings, consortium recruiting events, and LSAC forums. Requirements are different for out-of-state students. Transfer students must have one year of credit, must have attended an ABA-approved law school, and must submit a personal statement.

Costs
Tuition and fees for the 2011–2012 academic year are $45,750 for all full-time students. Books and supplies run $1,788.

Financial Aid
About 85% of current law students receive some form of aid. The maximum annual amount of aid from all sources combined, including scholarships, loans, and work contracts, is $68,664. Awards are based on need and merit combined. Required financial statements are the FAFSA and Need Access. The aid application deadline for fall entry is February 15. First-year students are notified about their financial aid application after acceptance.

About the Law School
Vanderbilt University Vanderbilt Law School was established in 1874 and is a private institution. The 330-acre campus is in an urban area 1.5 miles west of downtown Nashville. The primary mission of the law school is to educate effective lawyers in a wide range of professional areas. Students have access to federal, state, county, city, and local agencies, courts, correctional facilities, law firms, and legal aid organizations in the Nashville area. Housing for students includes a variety of options near the campus. All law school facilities are accessible to the physically disabled.

Calendar
The law school operates on a traditional semester basis. Courses are offered days only, and must be completed within 3 years. New students are admitted in the fall. There is no summer session. Transferable summer courses are not offered.

Programs
In addition to the J.D., the law school offers the LL.M. and Ph.D. in Law and Economics. Students may take relevant courses in other programs and apply credit toward the J.D.; a maximum of 6 credits may be applied. The following joint degrees may be earned: J.D./M.A. (Juris Doctor/Master of Arts), J.D./M.B.A. (Juris Doctor/Master of Business Administration), J.D./D.I.V. (Juris Doctor/Master of Divinity), J.D./M.D. (Juris Doctor/Doctor of Medicine), J.D./M.P.P. (Juris Doctor/Master of Public Policy), J.D./M.T.S. (Juris Doctor/Master of Theological Studies), J.D./Ph.D. (Juris Doctor/Doctor of Philosophy), and LL.M./M.A. (Master of Laws/Master of Arts in Latin American Studies).

Required
To earn the J.D., candidates must complete 88 total credits, of which 38 are for required courses. They must maintain a minimum GPA of 2.0 in the required courses. The following first-year courses are required of all students: Civil Procedure, Constitutional Law, Contracts, Criminal Law, Legal Research and Writing I and II, Life of the Law, Property, Regulatory State, and Torts. Required upper-level courses consist of a seminar, a skills course, and Professional Responsibility. The required orientation program for first-year students consists of a comprehensive 5-day orientation, including a 1-credit course surveying the U.S. legal system and legal education.

Electives
The Vanderbilt Law School offers concentrations in corporate law, criminal law, entertainment law, environmental law, family law, intellectual property law, internationl law, juvenile law, labor law, litigation, media law, securities law, sports law, tax law, torts and insurance, and law and social behavior. Clinic offerings include business law, child and family law, civil practice, criminal practice, domestic violence, intellectual property and the arts, international law practice, and juvenile practice. Students may also pursue externships that provide valuable experience

Phone: 615-322-6452
Fax: 615-322-1531
E-mail: admissions@law.vanderbilt.edu
Web: law.vanderbilt.edu

Contact

G. Todd Morton, Assistant Dean and Dean of Admissions, 615-322-6452 for general inquiries; Richelle Acker, Associate Director of Admissions, 615-322-6452 for financial aid information.

while gaining academic credit. Eighteen seminars were recently offered to second- and third-year students. Research programs consist of faculty research assistantships. Students can gain valuable professional experience in nonprofits, government agencies, and other organizations around the world supported by various stipend opportunities, including the Legal Aid Society and Public Interest Stipend Fund. Students gain experience and academic credits through individual externship placements. An array of speakers, academic conferences, and symposia are held each year, including student-initiated events funded by the Hyatt Student Activities Fund. Students may participate in summer study-abroad programs sponsored by ABA-accredited law schools. Vanderbilt offers a "Summer in Venice" study-abroad program. Special writing assistance is available for first-year students who need tutoring. Legal writing workshops are offered for second- and third-year students. A bar preparation seminar is offered for third-year students.

Graduation Requirements

In order to graduate, candidates must have a GPA of 2.0 and must have completed the upper-division writing requirement.

Organizations

Students edit the *Vanderbilt Law Review, Journal of Transnational Law, the Vanderbilt Journal of Entertainment and Technology Law,* the *Journal of Risk and Uncertainty*, and the newspaper *VLS-VENT*. Organizations that participate in moot court competitions are the National Moot Court Team, the Jessup International Moot Court Team, and the Traveling Moot Court Team. Law student organizations include the Vanderbilt Bar Association, Environmental Law Society, and Isocratic Society. There are local chapters of ABA-Law Student Division and Phi Alpha Delta.

Library

The law library contains 491,027 hardcopy volumes and 757,763 microform volume equivalents, and subscribes to 1,122 serial publications. Such online databases and networks as CALI, CIS Universe, DIALOG, Infotrac, Legal-Trac, LEXIS, Mathew Bender, OCLC First Search, WESTLAW, and Wilsonline Indexes are available to law students for research. Special library collections include Stumpf Collection (Jurisprudence and Bioethics) and a selected depository. The ratio of library volumes to faculty is 10,447 to 1 and to students is 838 to 1. The ratio of seats in the library to students is 1 to 2.

Faculty

The law school has 47 full-time and 71 part-time faculty members, of whom 42 are women. About 11% of full-time faculty have a graduate law degree in addition to the J.D. The ratio of full-time students to full-time faculty in an average class is 13 to 1; in a clinic, 7 to 1. The law school has a regular program of bringing visiting professors and other distinguished lecturers and visitors to campus. There is a chapter of the Order of the Coif.

Students

About 46% of the student body are women; 19%, minorities; 8%, African American; 5%, Asian American; and 4%, Hispanic. The average age of entering students is 23; age range is 19 to 40. About 40% of students enter directly from undergraduate school, 9% have a graduate degree, and 60% have worked full-time prior to entering law school.

Placement

J.D.s awarded:	198
Services available through: a separate law school placement center.	
Special features: etiquette dinner, mock interview program, public service initiative, and speakers series.	
Full-time job interviews:	320 employers
Summer job interviews:	320 employers
Placement by graduation:	96% of class
Placement within 9 months:	96% of class
Average starting salary:	$50,000 to $160,000
Areas of placement:	
Private practice 2–10 attorneys	5%
Private practice 11–25 attorneys	5%
Private practice 26–50 attorneys	3%
Private practice 51–100 attorneys	4%
Private practice 100+ attorneys	34%
Judicial clerkships	18%
Government	14%
Public interest	8%
Business/industry	6%
Military	2%

VERMONT LAW SCHOOL

P.O. Box 96, Chelsea Street
South Royalton, VT 05068-0096

Application Filing	Accreditation
Fall: March 1	ABA, AALS

	Degrees Granted
Fee: $60	J.D., LL.M., M.E.L.P. (Master of Environmental Law and Policy)

Enrollment 2011–2012		First-Year Class	
Men:	284 50%	Applied:	1,020
Women:	282 50%	Accepted:	704
Minorities:	57 10%	Enrolled:	151
Out-of-State:	481 85%		

2011–2012 Class Profile
LSAT Percentile: 64%
LSAT Median Score: 154

Tuition and Fees:

Resident
$40,420 (F/T)

Average (public)
$18,708

Average (private)
$34,451

Nonresident
$40,420 (F/T)

Average (public)
$29,793

Average (private)
$34,451

0 10 20 30 40 50

Percentage receiving financial aid: 85%

ADMISSIONS
In the fall of 2011 first-year class, 1020 applied, 704 were accepted, and 151 enrolled. One transfer enrolled. The median LSAT percentile of the most recent first-year class was 64; the median GPA was 3.3 on a scale of 4.0.

Requirements
Applicants must have a bachelor's degree and take the LSAT. The most important admission factors are academic achievement, character or personality, and LSAT results. No specific undergraduate courses are required. Candidates are interviewed.

Procedure
The application deadline for fall entry is March 1. Applicants should submit an application form, a personal statement, a nonrefundable application fee of $60, 2 letters of recommendation, and 2 essay questions. Notification of the admissions decision is on a rolling basis. The law school uses the LSAC.

Special
The law school recruits minority and disadvantaged students through the Council on Legal Education Opportunity (CLEO) program, direct mail through the Candidate Referral Service (CRS), and through participation in college minority student events and a diversity scholarship program. Requirements are different for out-of-state students. Transfer students must submit a personal statement and be in good academic standing and eligible to return to the school from which they are transferring.

Costs
Tuition and fees for the 2011–2012 academic year are $39,995 for all full-time students. Tuition for part-time students is $43,468 for in-state students and $43,468 out-of-state. Books and supplies run $1,500.

Financial Aid
About 85% of current law students receive some form of aid. The average annual amount of aid from all sources combined, including scholarships, loans, and work contracts, is $34,000; maximum, $61,480. Awards are based on need and merit combined. Required financial statement is the FAFSA. The aid application deadline for fall entry is March 1. Special funds for minority or disadvantaged students include the Debevoise Family Scholarship Fund, which provides grants to qualified diverse applicants from traditionally underrepresented groups with demonstrated financial need. First-year students are notified about their financial aid application as early as possible after acceptance (usually late March) Merit awards are included in packet with acceptance letter.

About the Law School
Vermont Law School was established in 1972 and is independent. The 13-acre campus is located in a small town 70 miles southeast of Burlington. The primary mission of the law school is to provide a thorough understanding of the nature and function of law in society and to equip graduates to serve their communities in positions of leadership and responsibility. The school believes lawyers should be liberally educated, ethical, competent, and committed to improving the law and its administration. Students have access to federal, state, county, city, and local agencies, courts, correctional facilities, law firms, and legal aid organizations in the South Royalton area. The South Royalton Legal Clinic is located on campus. Facilities of special interest to law students include a modern library and classroom building. Nearby Hanover, New Hampshire, home of Dartmouth College, is a source of student cultural and social life. Child care is available on campus. Housing for students is available in private houses, apartments, or rooms in the community or nearby towns. Rental units are plentiful; the law school provides students with a listing. About 75% of the law school facilities are accessible to the physically disabled.

Calendar
The law school operates on a traditional semester basis. Courses for full-time students are offered days only and must be completed within 4 years. There is no part-time program. New full-time students are admitted in the fall.

Programs
In addition to the J.D., the law school offers the LL.M. and M.E.L.P. (Master of Environmental Law and Policy). Students may take relevant courses in other programs and apply credit toward the J.D.; a maximum of 9 credits may be applied.

Required
To earn the J.D., candidates must complete 87 total credits, of which 52 are for required courses. They must maintain a minimum GPA of 2.2 in the required courses. The following first-year courses are required of all students: Civil Procedure I and II, Constitutional Law I and II, Contracts, Criminal Law, Legal Reasoning, Property, Research, Torts, and Writing. Required upper-level courses consist of 1 perspective elective, 1 skills or clinical elective, advanced writing project, Appellate Advocacy, and Legal Profession. All students must take clinical courses. The required orientation program for first-year students is 5 days of lectures and workshops on the legal process, court systems, and sources of law, and the analysis and briefing of cases. It also includes an orientation to the law library, its resources and support systems, and meetings with faculty advisers.

Phone: 802-831-1239
888-277-5985
Fax: 802-831-1174
E-mail: admiss@vermontlaw.edu
Web: www.vermontlaw.edu

Contact

Kathy Hartman, Associate Dean for Enrollment Management, 802-831-1232 or 888-277-5985 for general inquiries; Cathy Mullins, Director of Financial Aid, 802-831-1235 or 888-277-5985 for financial aid information.

Electives

The Vermont Law School offers concentrations in corporate law, criminal law, environmental law, family law, international law, labor law, and general practice; alternative dispute resolution; land use and real estate; and traditionally disadvantaged groups. In addition, clinics are open to second and third-year students, but enrollment is limited. Clinics are Semester in Practice, Legislation Clinic, Environmental and Natural Resources Law Clinic, and South Royalton Legal Clinic. About 20 seminars are offered annually on various topics to second- and third-year students. Faculty-supervised internships are open to second- and third-year students. Credit varies and placement can be in a variety of legal settings, including private practice, government, nonprofit agencies, the judiciary, and businesses. Faculty-supervised research programs are open to second- and third-year students and culminate in a major piece of legal writing. Special lecture series include the Waterman Lectures and other lectures arranged by faculty and student organizations. There is an exchange program with McGill University, Faculty of Law in Montreal, University of Paris (France), and University of Trento (Italy). Tutorial programs and the Program for Academic Success are offered. Workshops on topics such as time and stress management, case briefing, and exam taking are held. Minority programs are offered through the Coalition for Diversity, BALSA, APALSA, NLALSA, Native American Law Society, and the Office of the Dean of Student Services and Diversity. Special interest group programs are offered through the Alliance, Animal Law League, Environmental Law Society, and other groups. The most widely taken electives are Environmental Law, Corporations, and Estates.

Graduation Requirements

In order to graduate, candidates must have a GPA of 2.2, complete the upper-division writing requirement, and Legal Profession course; 1 perspective elective; 1 skills elective.

Organizations

Students edit the *Vermont Law Review*, the *Environmental Law Journal*, a literary journal *Hearsay*, and the newspaper, *The Forum*. Moot court competitions include the annual Thomas M. Debevoise Moot Court, with finals argued before the Vermont Supreme Court, the annual Douglas M. Costle Environmental Moot Court, and various regional and national moot court competitions. Student organizations include the Jewish Students Group, Guardians ad Litem, and Coalition for Diversity. There are local chapters of Amnesty International, Association of Trial Lawyers of America, and Equal Justice Foundation. Campus clubs include the Barrister Bookshop, Law Partners, and Chamber Music Group.

Library

The law library contains 255,118 hardcopy volumes and 123,387 microform volume equivalents, and subscribes to 1,856 serial publications. Online databases and networks include CALI, CIS Universe, DIALOG, Infotrac, Legal-Trac, LEXIS, OCLC First Search, WESTLAW, ECON-ET, and EPIC, which are available to law students for research. Special library collections include environmental law, historic preservation, and alternative dispute resolution. The ratio of library volumes to faculty is 4,307 to 1 and to students is 448 to 1. The ratio of seats in the library to students is 1 to 5.

Faculty

The law school has 59 full-time and 14 part-time faculty members, of whom 32 are women. About 20% of full-time faculty have a graduate law degree in addition to the J.D.; about 15% of part-time faculty have one. The ratio of full-time students to full-time faculty in an average class is 10 to 1; in a clinic, 6 to 1. The law school has a regular program of bringing visiting professors and other distinguished lecturers and visitors to campus.

Students

About 50% of the student body are women; 10%, minorities; 3%, African American; 3%, Asian American; 3%, Hispanic; and 1%, Native American. The majority of students come from Vermont (15%). The average age of entering students is 26; age range is 22 to 56. About 28% of students enter directly from undergraduate school, 10% have a graduate degree, and 75% have worked full-time prior to entering law school. About 8% drop out after the first year for academic or personal reasons; 92% remain to receive a law degree.

Placement

J.D.s awarded:	175

Services available through: a separate law school placement center.
Services: travel stipend for interview.
Special features: Letters of application are prepared for students from an employer database, leading to computerized matching of student interests and employers. Services are characterized by individual attention, with particularly strong public interest and environmental employer listings.

Full-time job interviews:	17 employers
Summer job interviews:	35 employers
Placement by graduation:	66% of class
Placement within 9 months:	96% of class
Average starting salary:	$30,000 to $160,000

Areas of placement:

Private practice 2–10 attorneys	15%
Private practice 11–25 attorneys	6%
Private practice 26–50 attorneys	4%
Private practice 51–100 attorneys	4%
Private practice 100+ attorneys	6%
Business/industry	19%
Judicial clerkships	15%
Government	15%
Public interest	15%
Military	1%
Academic	1%

VILLANOVA UNIVERSITY

School of Law

299 North Spring Mill Road
Villanova, PA 19085

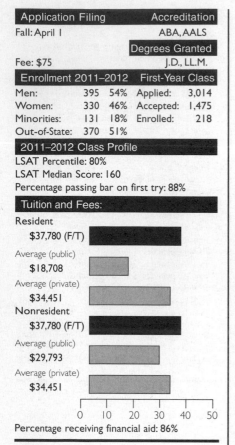

Application Filing			Accreditation
Fall: April 1			ABA, AALS
			Degrees Granted
Fee: $75			J.D., LL.M.

Enrollment 2011–2012			First-Year Class	
Men:	395	54%	Applied:	3,014
Women:	330	46%	Accepted:	1,475
Minorities:	131	18%	Enrolled:	218
Out-of-State:	370	51%		

2011–2012 Class Profile
LSAT Percentile: 80%
LSAT Median Score: 160
Percentage passing bar on first try: 88%

Tuition and Fees:

Resident
$37,780 (F/T)

Average (public)
$18,708

Average (private)
$34,451

Nonresident
$37,780 (F/T)

Average (public)
$29,793

Average (private)
$34,451

0 10 20 30 40 50

Percentage receiving financial aid: 86%

ADMISSIONS

In the fall of 2011 first-year class, 3014 applied, 1475 were accepted, and 218 enrolled. Thirty-six transfer students enrolled. The median LSAT percentile of the most recent first-year class was 80; the median GPA was 3.6 on a scale of 4.0. The lowest LSAT percentile accepted was 44; the highest was 97.

Requirements
Applicants must have a bachelor's degree and take the LSAT. The most important admission factors include GPA and LSAT results. No specific undergraduate courses are required, and candidates are not interviewed.

Procedure
The application deadline for fall entry is April 1. Applicants should submit an application form, LSAT results, transcripts, a personal statement, a nonrefundable application fee of $75, 2 or 3 are suggested letters of recommendation, and deposits are required of students after acceptance. Notification of the admissions decision is on a rolling basis beginning in December. The law school uses the LSAC.

Special
The law school recruits minority and disadvantaged students at LSAC forums, through outreach programs offered by various minority student groups on campus through the Deirdre Bailey Leadership Scholarships and by targeted mailings and targeted college visits. Requirements are different for out-of-state students. Transfer students must have one year of credits, attended an ABA-approved law school, and a personal statement.

Costs

Tuition and fees for the 2011–2012 academic year are $37,390 for all full-time students. Books and supplies run $1,400.

Financial Aid

About 86% of current law students receive some form of aid. The average annual amount of aid from all sources combined, including scholarships, loans, and work contracts, is $46,604; maximum, $88,845. Awards are based on need and merit combined. Required financial statement is the FAFSA. The aid application deadline for fall entry is March 1. There are special funds for minority or disadvantaged students. Our diversity scholarships are the Deidre L. Bailey Leadership Scholarship and the Minority Alumni Society Book Scholarship. First-year students are notified about their financial aid application at time of acceptance.

About the Law School

Villanova University School of Law was established in 1953 and is a private institution. The 250-acre campus is located in a suburban area 15 miles west of Philadelphia. The mission of Villanova University School of Law is a commitment to educating students in a community rooted in a tradition of respect for human dignity, academic freedom, academic excellence, and inclusion. Students have access to federal, state, county, city, and local agencies, courts, correctional facilities, law firms, and legal aid organizations in the Villanova area. They also have access to the numerous colleges and universities in the Philadelphia area. The Law School is housed with state-of-the-art technology, including wireless network access and instructional technology available in every classroom, along with a computer lab containing twenty-five workstations. The law school building also houses a spacious library with many comfortable and inviting workspaces for student use. There is a coffee bar/study space adjacent to the library. On-campus housing is not available. The Admissions Office assists students in finding housing. About 98% of the law school facilities are accessible to the physically disabled.

Calendar

The law school operates on a traditional semester basis. Courses for full-time students are offered and majority of courses are offered during the day and must be completed within 3 years. There is no part-time program. New full-time students are admitted in the fall. There is no summer session. Transferable summer courses are not offered.

Programs

In addition to the J.D., the law school offers the LL.M. The following joint degrees may be earned: J.D./M.B.A. (Juris Doctor/Master of Business Administration), J.D./LL.M. (Juris Doctor/Master of Law in International Studies), J.D./LL.M. (Juris Doctor/Master of Law in Taxation), and J.D./M.P.A. (Juris Doctor/Master of Public Administration).

Required
To earn the J.D., candidates must complete 88 total credits, of which 43 are for required courses. The following first-year courses are required of all students: Civil Procedure I and II, Constitutional Law l, Contracts I and II, Criminial Law, Legal Research, Legal Writing, Analysis, Oral Advocacy, Property, and Torts. Required upper-level courses consist of a practical skills writing course, a research paper course, Appellate Advocacy, Constitutional Law, and Legal Profession. A wide variety of clinics, practicum's, and externships is available. Students are encouraged, but not required, to take advantage of these opportunities. The required orientation program for first-year students is a 2 1/2 day course, which includes meetings with faculty advisors; an introduction to Legal Analysis, Research and Reasoning; and a reception.

Phone: 610-519-7010
Fax: 610-519-6291
E-mail: *admissions@law.villanova.edu*
Web: *http://www.law.villanova.edu*

Contact

Amy Ellis, Senior Admissions Administrator, 610-519-7010 for general inquiries; Felicia Hamilton, Assistant Director of Financial Aid, 610-519-7015 for financial aid information.

PENNSYLVANIA

Electives

The Villanova University School of Law does not offer concentrations, but suggests curricula for a broad range of specialties. In addition, clinics, open to second- and third- year students, include Farmworker Legal Aid, Federal Tax, Civil Justice, Asylum, Refugee, and Emigrant Services, and Advance Advocacy. Seminars, also open to second- and third- year students, give students 2 credits of intensive learning, research, and writing, working closely with a faculty member in a small group setting. Internships/externships include the U.S. Attorney's Office (Eastern District of Pennsylvania, Delaware), EPA, IRS, NLRB, various District Attorney's and judge's offices, Legal Aid, the U.S. Department of Justice (Antitrust Division), Volunteer Lawyers for the Arts and Defenders. Research assistantships with faculty members are available. Two practicums are offered: a Capital Defense Practicum, in which students work representing death row inmates, and a Mediation Practicum, in which students are trained for, and then handle, mediations for the courts and public interest agencies. Special lecture series include Donald A. Giannella Memorial Lecture, Law Review Symposium, Environmental Law Symposium, Sports and Entertainment Law Symposium, Symposium on Law and Catholic Social Thought and the Law, and Martin Luther King, Jr. lectures. Villanova offers a summer program in Rome, Italy. The school also accepts up to 6 credits from an accredited American Law summer program abroad, provided it meets the standards of the school. Academic support is provided after the first semester to students at risk and to upper level students with identified learning issues or who are at risk of failing the bar exam. In support of its minority students and diversity, an active Minority Alumni Society, a minority mentoring program, several affinity groups including BLSA, LALSA, and APALSA, and a joint student/faculty/staff committee charged with fostering inclusiveness. The most widely taken electives are Business Organizations, Evidence, and Trial Practice.

Graduation Requirements

In order to graduate, candidates must have a GPA of 2.0, complete the upper-division writing requirement, as well as Constitutional Law I and II, upper level Appellate Advocacy and Legal Professional. The upper-division writing requirement currently consists of a research paper course and a practical writing course.

Organizations

Law students publish the *Villanova Law Review, Villanova Environmental Law Journal,* and *Villanova Sports and Entertainment Law Journal.* Annually, the school sponsors the Reimel Moot Court Competition and students participate in numerous outside moot court competitions, including Jessup Law and the Thurgood Marshall Moot Court Competitions. In addition to moot court competitions, the school enters teams in several mock trial competitions each year. The students are selected through an audition process and must enroll in a trial competition course to be eligible to compete. Law student organizations, local chapters of national associations, and campus organizations include Women's Law Caucus, Public Interest Fellowship Program, Outlaw, Student Bar Association, Black Law Students Association (BLSA), Phi Alpha Delta, Phi Delta Phi, the Justinian Society, and the Federalist Society.

Library

The law library contains 358,613 hardcopy volumes and 1,177,420 microform volume equivalents, and subscribes to 944 serial publications. Online databases and networks include CALI, CIS Universe, DIALOG, Infotrac, Legal-Trac, LEXIS, Mathew Bender, OCLC First Search, and WESTLAW. Other resources include CCH IntelliConnect, RIA Checkpoint, Social Science Research network, HeinOnline, TRAC, and BNA Tax, which are available to law students for research. Special library collections include a government documents depository. The ratio of library volumes to faculty is 5,352 to 1 and to students is 485 to 1. The ratio of seats in the library to students is 1 to 2.

Faculty

The law school has 52 full-time and 65 part-time faculty members, of whom 39 are women. About 29% of full-time faculty have a graduate law degree in addition to the J.D. The ratio of full-time students to full-time faculty in an average class is 17 to 1; in a clinic, 7 to 1. The law school has

Placement

J.D.s awarded:	233

Services available through: a separate law school placement center.

Services: sponsors career seminars and job fairs and maintains a career development and research library as well as alumni networking opportunities.

Special features: 3 attorney-advisers and one specialist on staff, interview programs, public interest job fairs, minority job fairs, and geographic location job fairs.

Full-time job interviews:	18 employers
Summer job interviews:	47 employers
Placement within 9 months of graduation:	80% of class
Average starting salary:	$30,000 to $160,000

Areas of placement:

Private practice 2–10 attorneys	20%
Private practice 11–25 attorneys	6%
Private practice 26–50 attorneys	5%
Private practice 51–100 attorneys	5%
Private practice 101+ attorneys	19%
Judicial clerkships	15%
Business/industry	15%
Government	8%
Public interest	4%
Academic	3%

a regular program of bringing visiting professors and other distinguished lecturers and visitors to campus. There is a chapter of the Order of the Coif; 35 faculty and 821 graduates are members.

Students

About 46% of the student body are women; 18%, minorities; 3%, African American; 6%, Asian American; 7%, Hispanic; and 5%, Unknown ethnicity. The majority of students come from Pennsylvania (49%). The average age of entering students is 23; age range is 21 to 37. About 53% of students enter directly from undergraduate school, and 3% have a graduate degree. About 1% drop out after the first year for academic or personal reasons; 92% remain to receive a law degree.

School of Law

P.O. Box 7206
Winston-Salem, NC 27109

Application Filing		Accreditation	
Fall: March 15		ABA, AALS	
		Degrees Granted	
Fee: $60		J.D., LL.M., S.J.D.	

Enrollment 2011–2012		First-Year Class	
Men:	303 58%	Applied:	2,633
Women:	220 42%	Accepted:	948
Minorities:	110 21%	Enrolled:	185
Out-of-State:	282 54%		

2011–2012 Class Profile

LSAT Percentile: 93%
LSAT Median Score: 163
Percentage passing bar on first try: 95%

Tuition and Fees:

Resident
$38,756 (F/T)

Average (public)
$18,708

Average (private)
$34,451

Nonresident
n/av

Average (public)
$29,793

Average (private)
$34,451

Percentage receiving financial aid: 78%

ADMISSIONS

In the fall of 2011 first-year class, 2633 applied, 948 were accepted, and 185 enrolled. Fourteen transfers enrolled. The median LSAT percentile of the most recent first-year class was 93; the median GPA was 3.6 on a scale of 4.0. The lowest LSAT percentile accepted was 40; the highest was 98.

Requirements

Applicants must have a bachelor's degree and take the LSAT. The most important admission factors include academic achievement, GPA, and LSAT results. No specific undergraduate courses are required. Candidates are interviewed.

Procedure

The application deadline for fall entry is March 15. Applicants should submit an application form, LSAT results, transcripts, a personal statement, a nonrefundable application fee of $60, and 2 letters of recommendation. A dean's

certification is required prior to matriculation. Notification of the admissions decision is on a rolling basis. The law school uses the LSAC.

Special

The law school recruits minority and disadvantaged students through collaboration with the Black Law Students Association (BLSA), as well as Latino and pan Asian organizations, who call accepted minority candidates to discuss the school and answer questions. These groups and the school sponsor a minority recruitment day where students visit the campus, meet with enrolled students, and attend a mock class and a moot court presentation. Also, the Career Services Office works with major law firms in the state to place minority candidates for summer employment and to expedite consideration of minority applicants. Requirements are different for out-of-state students. Transfer students must have one year of credit, must have attended an ABA-approved law school, must submit a personal statement, and must have a letter of good standing from the dean of the law school and an official transcript of first-year grades.

Costs

Tuition and fees for the 2011–2012 academic year are $37,940 for full-time in-state students. Books and supplies run $1,400.

Financial Aid

About 78% of current law students receive some form of aid. The average annual amount of aid from all sources combined, including scholarships, loans, and work contracts, is $20,000; maximum, $37,940. Awards are based on need and merit combined. The required financial statement is the FAFSA. The aid application deadline for fall entry is May 1. Special funds for minority or disadvantaged students include full-tuition scholarships that are awarded in each entering class and for which all candidates are eligible. First-year students are notified about their financial aid application at time of acceptance.

About the Law School

Wake Forest University School of Law was established in 1894 and is a private

institution. The 340-acre campus is in a suburban area in Winston-Salem, North Carolina. The primary mission of the law school is to graduate students eligible and qualified to practice law. Students have access to federal, state, county, city, and local agencies, courts, correctional facilities, law firms, and legal aid organizations in the Winston-Salem area. Clinical placements are with the district attorney, U.S. attorney, Legal Aid, private practitioners, U.S. bankruptcy judge, and public defender. Housing for students is available in approximately 6000 apartment units that are within a 3-mile radius of the campus. All law school facilities are accessible to the physically disabled.

Calendar

The law school operates on a traditional semester basis. Courses are offered days only, and must be completed within 3 years. New students are admitted in the fall. There is a 5-week summer session. Transferable summer courses are offered.

Programs

In addition to the J.D., the law school offers the LL.M. and S.J.D. Students may take relevant courses in other programs and apply credit toward the J.D.; a maximum of 7 credits may be applied. The following joint degrees may be earned: J.D./M.A. (Juris Doctor/Master of Arts in Bioethics), J.D./M.A. (Juris Doctor/Master of Arts in Religion), J.D./M.B.A. (Juris Doctor/Masters of Business Administration), and J.D./M.Div. (Juris Doctor/Master of Divinity).

Required

To earn the J.D., candidates must complete 89 total credits, of which 41 are for required courses. They must maintain a minimum GPA of 73.0 in the required courses. The following first-year courses are required of all students: Civil Procedure I and II, Constitutional Law I, Contracts I and II, Criminal Law I, Legal Research and Writing I and II, Property, and Torts. Required upper-level courses consist of a practical skills course, a writing requirement, Constitutional Law II, Evidence, Legislation and Administrative Law, Legal Research and Writing III, and Professional Responsibility. All students may take clinics in addition to the skills courses. The required orientation program

Phone: 336-758-5437
Fax: 336-758-3930
E-mail: *lawadmissions@wfu.edu*
Web: *law.wfu.edu*

Contact
R. Jay Shively, J.D., Assistant Dean for Admissions and Financial Aid, 336-758-5437 for general inquiries.

NORTH CAROLINA

for first-year students is a 1-week program before the beginning of classes devoted to the basics of legal analysis, writing, and research.

Electives

The School of Law offers concentrations in corporate law, family law, internationl law, labor law, litigation, securities law, tax law, torts and insurance, and clinical law. Clinics include the Appellate Advocacy Clinic, which represents low-income clients in all sorts of appeals, both civil and criminial; the Community Law and Business Clinic, available to law and graduate business students; the Elder Law Clinic, created by the School of Law and Wake Forest's School of Medicine; the Innocence and Justice Clinic, which gives students the opportunity to review and investigate all types of innocence claims and pursue litigation when appropriate; and the Litigation Clinic. The Constitutional Lecture Series is an annual program featuring an address by a nationally prominent figure in the field of Constitutional law. Three 5-week summer programs are offered, one in London, England; one in Vienna, Austria; and the other in Venice, Italy. Enrollment is open to all students depending on availability. A tutorial program is offered to first-year students through the Dean's Office. The most widely taken electives are Federal Tax, Decendents' Estates, and Business Organizations.

Graduation Requirements

In order to graduate, candidates must have a GPA of 73.0, must have completed the upper-division writing requirement, and must have written a paper or a brief to the satisfaction of the instructor in a course approved by the faculty.

Organizations
Students edit the *Wake Forest Law Review, Journal of Business Intellectual Property Law, Journal of Law and Policy,* the student newspaper *The Hearsay,* and *The Jurist,* an alumni magazine published in the spring and fall of each year. Moot court competitions include the Marshall Competition in Chicago, National Moot Court Competition, and Jessup International Moot Court Competition. Student organizations include ABA-Law Student Division, Environmental Law Society, and

the BLSA/Latino/Pan-Asian associations. There is a local chapter of the Inns of Court.

Library
The law library contains 423,007 hardcopy volumes and 1,416,489 microform volume equivalents. Such online databases and networks as CALI, CIS Universe, Infotrac, Legal-Trac, LEXIS, OCLC First Search, WESTLAW, Wilsonline Indexes, Index to Foreign Legal Periodicals (1985–present), Index to Legal Periodicals and Books (1908–present), LEGAL TRAC, Lexis, Westlaw, AudioCaseFiles, BNA Web, CALI Lessons, CCH IntelliConnect, Climate Wire, CQ Electronic Library, Environment and Energy Daily, FastCase, Foreign Law Guide, Greenwire, HeinOnline, Landletter, LLMC-Digital, ProQuest Congressional, ProQuest Statistical Datasets, RIA Checkpoint, Treaties and International Agreements Online, and U.N. Treaty Collection are available to law students for research. Special library collections include a U.S. government documents depository. The ratio of seats in the library to students is 1 to 1.

Faculty
The law school has 48 full-time and 17 part-time faculty members, of whom 25 are women. According to AAUP standards for Category IIA institutions, faculty salaries are well above average. The ratio of full-time students to full-time faculty in an average class is 10 to 1; in a clinic, 10 to 1. The law school has a regular program of bringing visiting professors and other distinguished lecturers and visitors to campus. There is a chapter of the Order of the Coif.

Students
About 42% of the student body are women; 21%, minorities; 9%, African American; 4%, Asian American; 6%, Hispanic; 2%, Native American; and 1%, Native Hawaiian/Pacific Islander. The average age of entering students is 24; age range is 20 to 47. About 50% of students enter directly from undergraduate school, 50% have a graduate degree, and 50% have worked full-time prior to entering law school. About 3% drop out after the first year for academic or personal reasons; 94% remain to receive a law degree.

Placement

J.D.s awarded:	159
Services available through: a separate law school placement center.	
Special features: the Career Services Office sponsors an employment fair that targets small North Carolina legal employers, the Southeastern Minority Job Fair, and regional job fairs in Chicago, New York, Washington D.C., Texas, and Southern California.	
Full-time job interviews:	50 employers
Placement within 9 months of graduation:	96% of class
Average starting salary:	$73,000 to $145,000
Areas of placement:	
Private practice 2–10 attorneys	28%
Private practice 11–25 attorneys	9%
Private practice 26–50 attorneys	7%
Private practice 51–100 attorneys	14%
Judicial clerkships	12%
Public interest	12%
Business/industry	11%
Government	8%
Academic	2%

WASHBURN UNIVERSITY

School of Law

1700 SW College Avenue
Topeka, KS 66621

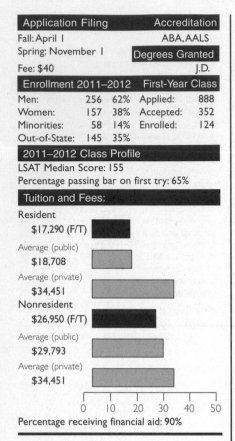

Application Filing	Accreditation
Fall: April 1	ABA, AALS
Spring: November 1	**Degrees Granted**
Fee: $40	J.D.

Enrollment 2011–2012		First-Year Class	
Men:	256 62%	Applied:	888
Women:	157 38%	Accepted:	352
Minorities:	58 14%	Enrolled:	124
Out-of-State:	145 35%		

2011–2012 Class Profile
LSAT Median Score: 155
Percentage passing bar on first try: 65%

Tuition and Fees:

Resident
$17,290 (F/T)

Average (public)
$18,708

Average (private)
$34,451

Nonresident
$26,950 (F/T)

Average (public)
$29,793

Average (private)
$34,451

0 10 20 30 40 50

Percentage receiving financial aid: 90%

ADMISSIONS

In the fall of 2011 first-year class, 888 applied, 352 were accepted, and 124 enrolled. Seven transfers enrolled. The median GPA of the most recent first-year class was 3.2. The lowest LSAT percentile accepted was 25; the highest was 75.

Requirements
Applicants must have a bachelor's degree and take the LSAT. The most important admission factors include LSAT results, GPA, and academic achievement. No specific undergraduate courses are required. Candidates are not interviewed.

Procedure
The application deadline for fall entry is April 1. Applicants should submit an application form, LSAT results, transcripts, a personal statement, a nonrefundable application fee of $40, a letter of recommendation (1 is required, 2 or 3 recommended), a personal statement, plus a credential evaluation (if for a foreign bachelor's degree). Notification of the admissions decision is November to May. The law school uses the LSAC.

Special
The law school recruits minority and disadvantaged students through CRS mailings; CLEO; law school forums in Chicago, Atlanta, Houston and accompanying workshops; law fairs at many colleges and universities; events in conjunction with BLSA, HALSA, AALSA, and NALSA; scholarships (merit); through efforts with HBCU and Hispanic colleges and universities, and events cospondored with LSAC for diversity outreach. Requirements are different for out-of-state students. Transfer students must have one year of credits, have a minimum GPA of 2.5, attended an ABA-approved law school, a personal statement, present a copy of the LSAC report, official undergraduate degree transcript, a letter of good standing from the dean of the law school, an official transcript of law school grades, law school class rank, and 1 letter of recommendation from a law school professor.

Costs

Tuition and fees for the 2011–2012 academic year are $17,220 for full-time in-state students and $26,880 for out-of-state students. On-campus room and board costs about $9,261 annually; books and supplies run $2,500.

Financial Aid

About 90% of current law students receive some form of aid. The average annual amount of aid from all sources combined, including scholarships, loans, and work contracts, is $32,832. Awards are based on need and merit, along with federal loans up to $20,500, which have no need or merit base. Factors that could increase the total award amount include number of dependents and other unusual expenses. All admitted applicants are automatically considered for academic scholarships. Required financial statement is the FAFSA. The aid application deadline for fall entry is June 1. Special funds for minority or disadvantaged students include need and academic scholarships. First-year students are notified about their financial aid application at time of acceptance.

About the Law School

Washburn University School of Law was established in 1903 and is a public institution. The 160-acre campus is located in an urban area 60 miles west of Kansas City. The primary mission of the law school is to provide a foundation in the theory, doctrine, and practice of law with a strong emphasis on professionalism in an atmosphere of

cooperation and congeniality. Students have access to federal, state, county, city, and local agencies, courts, correctional facilities, law firms, and legal aid organizations in the Topeka area. Located in the capital city of Kansas, the law school provides students direct access to clerkship, internship, and externship experiences. The Kansas Judicial Center, Capitol and state office buildings are located only minutes from the law school, providing students unique opportunities to meet and interact with key community and state leaders. Facilities of special interest to law students include a 4-story library, 1 computer laboratory, high-speed wireless network throughout the building, group study rooms, individual study carrels, and a special collections room. The state-of-the-art courtroom is regularly used for state administrative law hearings and occasional sittings by the Kansas Court of Appeals and the U.S. Tenth Circuit Court of Appeals. Housing for students is available on campus, but most students live in the many reasonably priced houses and apartments near the campus. About 90% of the law school facilities are accessible to the physically disabled.

Calendar

The law school operates on a traditional semester basis. Courses for full-time students are offered both day and evening and must be completed within 7 years. There is no part-time program. New full-time students are admitted in the fall and spring. There is a 6-week summer session. Transferable summer courses are offered.

Programs

The following joint degrees may be earned: J.D./M.B.A. (Juris Doctor/Master of Business Administration) and J.D./M.S.W. (Juris Doctor/Master of Social Work).

Required
To earn the J.D., candidates must complete 90 total credits, of which 44 are for required courses. They must maintain a minimum GPA of 2.0 in the required courses. The following first-year courses are required of all students: Civil Procedure I, Constitutional Law I, Contracts I and II, Criminal Law, Property, Criminal Procedure and Torts. Required upper-level courses consist of Evidence, Professional Responsibility, a writing requirement, an oral presentation requirement, Constitutional Law II, Secured Transactions, Perspectives on Law course—students choose from 27 listed, and a skills course. The required orientation program for

Contact

Karla Whitaker, Director of Admissions, 785-670-1706 or 800-WASHLAW (800-927-4529) for general inquiries; Janessa Akin, Scholarships, 800-927-4529 for financial aid information.

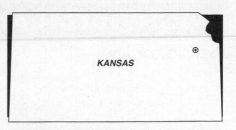

KANSAS

first-year students is 1 week and contains an intensive academic component as well as administrative and social events.

Electives

The School of Law offers concentrations in corporate law, environmental law, family law, internationl law, litigation, tax law, torts and insurance, certificates in tax law, family law, natural resources law, advocacy, estate planning, transactional law, international, comparative law, and law and government. In addition, Law Clinic may be taken as a one-semester elective for 4 to 5 credit hours by students with 60 or more credit hours and upon completion of prerequisite courses. In-house, live client opportunities exist in the areas of Family Law, Juvenile Law, Civil Law, Criminal Defense, Native American, and Transactional Law. A Directed Clinical Internship is available by permission for 1 to 3 credit hours after successful completion of Law Clinic. Second- or third-year students may take seminars for 2 to 3 credit hours in areas such as civil liberties, civil rights, constitutional litigation, family law, negotiation and settlement, and natural resources. Informal internships (part-time professional librarian positions) may be available in the law library for those with an MLS degree working toward a J.D. Research may be done as a student option through the Advanced Legal Research course for 2 credit hours or Directed Research for 1 to 3 credit hours. Students who have completed one year of study are eligible to enroll in the Externship Program. This program enables students to work outside of the law school for course credit. Students may apply 2 to 4 hours of externship course credit toward graduation. Placements are available in the Kansas Legislature, state agencies, the Kansas Judiciary, and in corporations. Special lecture series include the Foulson and Siefkin LLP Law Journal Lecture Series. A 65-credit-hour summer program, with various courses in comparative law, is conducted at the University of the West Indies in Barbados each year. A full semester program is also available at Maastricht University in the Netherlands. Every first-year student participates in a small study group facilited by an upper-division student. Groups meet weekly to collaborate on understanding their first-year course, write practice exams, and engage in other law school success-related activities. All prospective bar takers are invited to participate in a variety of bar preparation and bar exam practice programs. At risk second- and third- year students receive one-on-one help from the academic success program director

and from a faculty member chosen by the student. Minority programs include active chapters of Black (BLSA), Asian (AALSA), Hispanic (HALSA), and Native American (NALSA), law student associations; supporting institution of CLEO program; Women's Legal Forum; and Gay/Straight Legal Alliance. Special interest group programs are offered at the Business Transactional Law Center, Children and Family Law Center, Center for Excellence in Advocacy, and Center for Law and Government. The most widely taken electives are Business Associations, Civil Procedure II, and Decendents' Estates.

Graduation Requirements

In order to graduate, candidates must have a GPA of 2.0, completed the upper-division writing requirement, and upper-level oral presentation.

Organizations

The primary law review is the *Washburn Law Journal*. Students also solicit articles for and edit *The ABA Family Law Quarterly*. Students participate in numerous moot court competitions each year, including the Evan A. Evans Constitutional Moot Court Competition; Herbert Wechsler National Criminal Law Moot Court Competition; and the John J. Gibbons National Criminal Procedure Moot Court Competition. Other competitions include the Pace Environmental Law Competition, Domenick Gabriella National Family Law Competition, and J. Buberstein Bankruptcy. Law student organizations, local chapters of national associations, and campus clubs and organizations include The Washburn Association of Public Interest Lawyers, J. Reuben Clark Law Society, American Bar Association Student Division, Veterans Legal Association of Washburn, Washburn Tax Law Society, Equal Justice Works, Phi Alpha Delta and Phi Delta Phi legal fraternities, and Washburn Law Volunteer Society.

Library

The law library contains 406,398 hardcopy volumes and 183,232 microform volume equivalents, and subscribes to 4,250 serial publications. Online databases and networks include CALI, CIS Universe, Infotrac, Legal-Trac, LEXIS, OCLC First Search, WESTLAW, and Wilsonline Indexes. HeinOnline, Pacer, Marcive, Index Master, Gale Ready Reference Shelf, Foreign Law Guide, UN Treaty Collect, Access UN, and CCH Internet Research Network, serials solution, BNA's Law School Professional Information Center, and Making of Modern Law, Fastcase, RISE of American Law, RIA

Placement

J.D.s awarded:	142
Services available through: a separate law school placement center.	
Services: presentations and panel discussions by employers, alumni, and practitioners (e.g., U.S. Attorney's Office, Judicial Clerkships, alternative careers, diversity issues).	
Special features: coordinated meetings with all first-year students; on-campus interview and resume collection service.	
Full-time job interviews:	12 employers
Summer job interviews:	32 employers
Placement within 9 months of graduation:	92% of class
Average starting salary:	$30,000 to $115,000
Areas of placement:	
Private practice 2-10 attorneys	28%
Private practice 11-25 attorneys	4%
Private practice 26-50 attorneys	2%
Government	19%
Public interest	11%
Business/industry	10%
Judicial clerkships	6%
Military	3%
Academic	2%

Tax Research, and Proquest Legislative Insight are also available to law students for research. Special library collections include U.S. documents, Kansas documents, U.S. Supreme Court autographs. The ratio of library volumes to faculty is 13,547 to 1 and to students is 913 to 1. The ratio of seats in the library to students is 1 to 1.

Faculty

The law school has 33 full-time and 51 part-time faculty members, of whom 33 are women. According to AAUP standards for Category IIA institutions, faculty salaries are average. About 30% of full-time faculty have a graduate law degree in addition to the J.D. The ratio of full-time students to full-time faculty in an average class is 13 to 1; in a clinic, 8 to 1. The law school has a regular program of bringing visiting professors and other distinguished lecturers and visitors to campus.

Students

About 38% of the student body are women; 14%, minorities; 4%, African American; 2%, Asian American; 4%, Hispanic; 3%, Native American; and 1%, Native Hawaiian or other Pacific Islander. The majority of students come from Kansas (65%). The average age of entering students is 26; age range is 21 to 44. About 47% of students enter directly from undergraduate school, and 8% have a graduate degree. About 4% drop out after the first year for academic or personal reasons; 94% remain to receive a law degree.

School of Law

Lewis Hall
Lexington, VA 24450

Application Filing	Accreditation
Fall: March 1	ABA, AALS

Degrees Granted
J.D., LL.M.

Enrollment 2011–2012		First-Year Class	
Men:	214 54%	Applied:	3,972
Women:	181 46%	Accepted:	964
Minorities:	55 14%	Enrolled:	121
Out-of-State:	328 83%		

2011–2012 Class Profile
LSAT Percentile: 90%
LSAT Median Score: 164

Tuition and Fees:

Resident
$41,947 (F/T)

Average (public)
$18,708

Average (private)
$34,451

Nonresident
$41,947 (F/T)

Average (public)
$29,793

Average (private)
$34,451

0 10 20 30 40 50

Percentage receiving financial aid: 95%

ADMISSIONS

In the fall of 2011 first-year class, 3972 applied, 964 were accepted, and 121 enrolled. Forty-one transfer students enrolled. The median LSAT percentile of the most recent first-year class was 90; the median GPA was 3.7 on a scale of 4.0. The lowest LSAT percentile accepted was 44; the highest was 100.

Requirements
Applicants must have a bachelor's degree and take the LSAT. No specific undergraduate courses are required. Candidates are interviewed.

Procedure
The application deadline for fall entry is March 1. Applicants should submit an application form, LSAT results, transcripts, and 2 letters of recommendation. Notification of the admissions decision is by April 1. The law school uses the LSAC.

Special
The law school recruits minority and disadvantaged students through regional law forums sponsored by LSAC and college-sponsored forums, interviews at institutions with a substantial proportion of minority students, and by direct mail. Requirements are different for out-of-state students. Transfer students must have attended an ABA-approved law school.

Costs

On-campus room and board costs about $17,713 annually; books and supplies run $2,425.

Financial Aid

About 95% of current law students receive some form of aid. The average annual amount of aid from all sources combined, including scholarships, loans, and work contracts, is $47,742; maximum, $57,102. Awards are based on need and merit combined. Required financial statement is the FAFSA. The aid application deadline for fall entry is February 15. First-year students are notified about their financial aid application at time of acceptance.

About the Law School

Washington and Lee University School of Law was established in 1849 and is a private institution. The 322-acre campus is located in a small town 3 hours southwest of Washington, D.C. The mission of the law school is to provide a rigorous, writing-intensive, and personalized legal education to each student as preparation for the legal profession in an atmosphere of mutual respect, collegiality, and appreciation for each person's dignity, and to inculcate a sense of the responsibility placed on lawyers and the ethical obligations of law practice. Students have access to federal, state, county, city, and local agencies, courts, correctional facilities, law firms, and legal aid organizations in the Lexington area. Housing for students includes on-campus apartments adjacent to the law school building for single students, and private apartments, rooms, and houses in Lexington and the surrounding area. All law school facilities are accessible to the physically disabled.

Calendar

The law school operates on a traditional semester basis. Courses for full-time students are offered days only and must be completed within 6 semesters. There is no part-time program. New full-time students are admitted in the fall. There is no summer session. Transferable summer courses are not offered.

Programs

In addition to the J.D., the law school offers the LL.M. The following joint degrees may be earned: J.D./M.H.A. (Juris Doctor/Master of Health Administration).

Required
To earn the J.D., candidates must complete 85 total credits, of which 45 are for required courses. They must maintain a minimum GPA of 1.0 in the required courses. The following first-year courses are required of all students: American Public Law Process, Civil Procedure, Contracts, Criminal Law, Legal Writing, Professional Responsibility, Property, Torts, and Transnational Law. Required upper-level courses consist of Constitutional Law, Evidence, Law Related Services, The Legal Profession, and Skills Immersion. The required orientation program for first-year students is 5 days and includes social activities for the entire student body, introduction to the case method and case briefing techniques, introduction to legal research, an honor system orientation, and a university orientation.

Electives
Various clinics, open to second- and third-year students, provide direct service to miners seeking black lung benefits, to clients facing the death penalty, and to lower-income clients in the region. Seminars, available to upper-level students, are offered in a variety of areas. Upper-level students may perform internships with judges or prosecutors during the academic year or with government or nonprofit employers in the summer. Independent research projects may be undertaken by second- or third-year students. The Frances Lewis Law Center sponsors research fellowships for third-year students. Bain and Shepherd Fellowships provide stipends to support collaborative research projects between students and faculty. Special lecture series include the annual

Phone: 540-458#8503
Fax: 540-458-8586
E-mail: luwadm@wlu.edu
Web: www.wlu.edu

Contact
Cynthia Hintze, Assistant Director of Financial Aid, 540-458-8032 for financial aid information.

VIRGINIA

John Randolph Tucker Lecture and visiting lectures sponsored by the Frances Lewis Law Center and other law student organizations in areas of special interest to their members. The school offers no summer session but may accept credit for courses taken in programs offered by other ABA-approved law schools. The school offers exchange programs with Bucerius Law School in Hamburg, Germany; Trinity College Dublin in Dublin, Ireland; the University of Copenhagen in Denmark; and the University of Western Ontario in Ontario, Canada. Tutorials are offered to upper-class students in a variety of fields. The Academic Support Program offers a series of programs introducing the case method and legal analysis, and provides continuing academic support throughout the year. Special interest group programs include Women Law Students Organization, Black Law Students Association, Christian Legal Society, and Gay Law. The most widely taken electives are Federal Income Tax, Close Business Arrangements, and Criminal Procedure.

Graduation Requirements
In order to graduate, candidates must have a GPA of 2.0 and complete the upper-division writing requirement.

Organizations
Students edit the *Washington and Lee Law Review, German Law Journal, Journal of Energy, Climate and the Environment, Journal of Civil Rights and Social Justice,* and the newspaper *Law News.* Moot court competitions include Robert J. Grey, Jr. Negotiation Competition, John W. Davis Moot Court, and Jessup International Law Moot Court. Other competitions include National Mock Trial, Client Counseling, Mediation, Negotiation, and Arbitration competitions. Law student organizations, local chapters of national associations, and campus organizations include American Constitution Society, Federalist Society, National Lawyers Guild, Environmental Law Society, Intellectual Property and Technology Law Society, International Law Society, Public Interest Law Students Association, and Asian American Law Society.

Library
The law library contains 472,707 hardcopy volumes and 1,274,234 microform volume equivalents, and subscribes to 3,053 serial publications. Online databases and networks include CIS Universe, DIALOG, Dow-Jones, Infotrac, Legal-Trac, LEXIS, Mathew Bender, OCLC First Search, RLIN, WESTLAW, Wilsonline Indexes, and CIS Serial Set, which are available to law students for research. Special library collections include the Bankruptcy Revision Act 1978 (committee papers), the John W. Davis Collection of Records and Briefs, the Impeachment of President Nixon (committee papers), and the Lewis F. Powell, Jr. Archives. The ratio of library volumes to faculty is 12,440 to 1 and to students is 1,197 to 1. The ratio of seats in the library to students is 1 to 1.

Faculty
The law school has 38 full-time and 25 part-time faculty members, of whom 17 are women. About 29% of full-time faculty have a graduate law degree in addition to the J.D. The ratio of full-time students to full-time faculty in an average class is 10 to 1; in a clinic, 9 to 1. The law school has a regular program of bringing visiting professors and other distinguished lecturers and visitors to campus. There is a chapter of the Order of the Coif; 38 faculty and 376 graduates are members.

Students
About 46% of the student body are women; 14%, minorities; 8%, African American; 3%, Asian American; 3%, Hispanic; and 2%, Unknown. The majority of students come from Virginia (17%). The average age of entering students is 23; age range is 21 to 36. About 41% of students enter directly from undergraduate school, 12% have a graduate degree, and 59% have worked full-time prior to entering law school. About 2% drop out after the first year for academic or personal reasons; 98% remain to receive a law degree.

Placement

J.D.s awarded:	130

Services available through: a separate law school placement center.
Services: advice on networking, and programs on specific practice areas, (e.g., corporate law, small firms, prosecution).
Special features: one-on-one work with students on resumes, cover letters, job search advice; preparation for practice program mock interviews with alumni and faculty; interviews via videoconferencing; job fairs in New York, Chicago, Atlanta, Dallas, Boston, and Southern California.

Full-time job interviews:	8 employers
Summer job interviews:	35 employers
Placement by graduation:	89% of class
Placement within 9 months:	94% of class
Average starting salary:	$26,000 to $160,000

Areas of placement:

Private practice 2-10 attorneys	12%
Private practice 26-50 attorneys	2%
Private practice 51-100 attorneys	5%
Private practice 101+ attorneys	14%
Judicial clerkships	21%
Government	21%
Public interest	9%
Academic	9%
Business/industry	7%

School of Law

Box 1120, One Brookings Drive
St. Louis, MO 63130

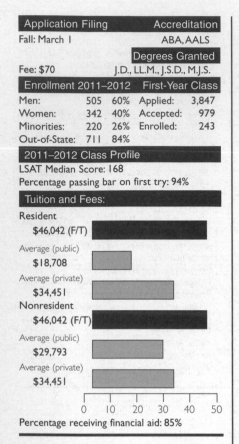

Application Filing		Accreditation	
Fall: March 1		ABA, AALS	
		Degrees Granted	
Fee: $70		J.D., LL.M., J.S.D., M.J.S.	

Enrollment 2011–2012		First-Year Class	
Men:	505 60%	Applied:	3,847
Women:	342 40%	Accepted:	979
Minorities:	220 26%	Enrolled:	243
Out-of-State:	711 84%		

2011–2012 Class Profile
LSAT Median Score: 168
Percentage passing bar on first try: 94%

Tuition and Fees:

Resident
$46,042 (F/T)

Average (public)
$18,708

Average (private)
$34,451

Nonresident
$46,042 (F/T)

Average (public)
$29,793

Average (private)
$34,451

Percentage receiving financial aid: 85%

ADMISSIONS

In the fall of 2011 first-year class, 3847 applied, 979 were accepted, and 243 enrolled. Forty Three transfers enrolled. The median GPA of the most recent first-year class was 3.7.

Requirements
Applicants must have a bachelor's degree and take the LSAT. Minimum acceptable GPA is 2.0 on a scale of 4.0. The most important admission factors include LSAT results, GPA, and academic achievement. No specific undergraduate courses are required. Candidates are not interviewed.

Procedure
The application deadline for fall entry is March 1. Applicants should submit an application form, LSAT results, transcripts, a nonrefundable application fee of $70, 2 letters of recommendation, and resume. Notification of the admissions decision is April. The law school uses the LSAC.

Special
The law school recruits minority and disadvantaged students through specific mailings, scholarship programs, and visitation programs. Requirements are different for out-of-state students. Transfer students must have one year of credit, must have attended an ABA-approved law school, and must submit a letter of good standing from their previous institution.

Costs

Tuition and fees for the 2011–2012 academic year are $45,350 for all full-time students. Books and supplies run $2,000.

Financial Aid

About 85% of current law students receive some form of aid. The average annual amount of aid from all sources combined, including scholarships, loans, and work contracts, is $51,830; maximum, $66,600. Awards are based on merit. The required financial statement is the FAFSA. The aid application deadline for fall entry is March 1. First-year students are notified about their financial aid application between the time of acceptance and enrollment.

About the Law School

Washington University in St. Louis School of Law was established in 1867 and is a private institution. The 169-acre campus is in a suburban area in St. Louis. An education at Washington University Law provides the opportunity to combine outstanding teaching and a mastery of fundamentals necessary for the practice of law. Students have access to federal, state, county, city, and local agencies, courts, correctional facilities, law firms, and legal aid organizations in the St. Louis area. Students have access to agencies and organizations in Washington D.C. and New York through clinical education opportunities. Housing is plentiful in the neighborhoods surrounding campus. The Admissions Office provides assistance through postings and Housing Day events. All law school facilities are accessible to the physically disabled.

Calendar

The law school operates on a traditional semester basis. Courses are offered days only. New students are admitted in the fall. There is no summer session. Transferable summer courses are offered.

Programs

In addition to the J.D., the law school offers the LL.M., J.S.D., and M.J.S. Students may take relevant courses in other programs and apply credit toward the J.D.; a maximum of 9 credits may be applied. The following joint degrees may be earned: J.D./M.A. (Juris Doctor/Master of Arts in East Asian Studies), J.D./M.A. (Juris Doctor/Master of International Affairs), J.D./M.A. (Juris Doctor/Master of Islamic and Near Eastern Studies), J.D./M.A. (Juris Doctor/Master of Jewish Studies), J.D./M.A. (Juris Doctor/Master of Political Economy and Public Policy), J.D./M.B.A. (Juris Doctor/Master of Business Administration), J.D./M.S. (Juris Doctor/Master of Science in Biology), and J.D./M.S.W. (Juris Doctor/Master of Social Work).

Required
To earn the J.D., candidates must complete 86 total credits, of which 37 are for required courses. They must maintain a minimum GPA of 79.0 in the required courses. The following first-year courses are required of all students: Civil Procedure, Constitutional Law I, Contracts, Criminal Law, Legal Practice I, Legal Practice II: Advocacy, Legal Research Methodologies I & II, Negotiations, Property, and Torts. Required upper-level courses consist of an additional writing seminar, an applied lawyering/professional skills course, and Professional Responsibility-Legal Profession. The required orientation program for first-year students runs for 5 days and focuses on academic, social, and administrative components of the school. It is modeled as an introduction to the profession.

Electives
The School of Law offers concentrations in corporate law, criminal law, environmental law, family law, intellectual property law, international law, juvenile law, labor law, litigation, securities law, tax law, and torts and insurance. In addition, clinics are offered for 3 to 10 credit hours, including Congressional Clinic in Washington, D.C., Civil Justice Clinic, and Interdisciplinary Environmental Clinic. Seminars include White Collar Crime Seminar, Biomedical

Phone: 314-935-4525
Fax: 314-935-8778
E-mail: admiss@wulaw.wustl.edu
Web: law.wustl.edu

Contact
Admissions Office, 314-935-4525 for general inquiries; JoAnn Eckrich, Director of Financial Aid, 314-935-4605 for financial aid information.

MISSOURI

Research Law + Policy Seminar, and Racial Profiling Seminar. Students may participate in research programs after the first year. Field work is performed as part of the clinics; 9 clinics are offered. Special lectures include the Tyrrell Williams Memorial Lectures and the Public Interest Speakers Series. Students may study abroad in Germany, London, South Africa, the Netherlands, and Singapore. Tutorial programs are available on an individual basis. The Black Law Students Association organizes student study groups and visiting minority speakers. The most widely taken electives are Evidence, Corporations, and Federal Income Tax.

Graduation Requirements
In order to graduate, candidates must have a GPA of 79.0 and must have completed the upper-division writing requirement.

Organizations
Students edit *The Washington University Law Quarterly, Journal of Law and Policy*, and the *Global Studies Law Review*. The student newspaper is *The Devil's Advocate*. Moot court competitions include the Wiley Rutledge Moot Court program held in the fall and spring, Environmental Moot Court, and the Jessup International Law Moot Court. Other competitions include National Mock Trial, Intellectual Property Moot Court, National Client Counseling, Negotiation, and Intramural Client Counseling. Student organizations include the Student Bar Association, Environmental Law Society, and International Law Society. The Federalist Society, Phi Alpha Delta, and Phi Delta Phi have local chapters. There are numerous other campus organizations.

Library
The law library contains 705,730 hardcopy volumes and 1,481,896 microform volume equivalents, and subscribes to 6,285 serial publications. Such online databases and networks as CALI, CIS Universe, DIALOG, Infotrac, Legal-Trac, LEXIS, Mathew Bender, OCLC First Search, WESTLAW, Wilsonline Indexes, Index to Foreign Legal Periodicals, LawInfoChina, BNA Core Plus Package, 3 CCH Internet Research Network Libraries, Aspen Treatises Online, Oceana Constitutions of the World, and other legal information databases are available to law students for research. Special library collections include a depository for federal and Missouri government documents, and Chinese and Japanese law collections. The ratio of library volumes to faculty is 13,069 to 1 and to students is 807 to 1. The ratio of seats in the library to students is 1 to 2.

Faculty
The law school has 67 full-time and 77 part-time faculty members, of whom 55 are women. The ratio of full-time students to full-time faculty in an average class is 11 to 1; in a clinic, 8 to 1. The law school has a regular program of bringing visiting professors and other distinguished lecturers and visitors to campus. There is a chapter of the Order of the Coif.

Students
About 40% of the student body are women; 26%, minorities; 11%, African American; 9%, Asian American; 2%, Hispanic; and 1%, Native American. The average age of entering students is 23; age range is 21 to 59. About 3% drop out after the first year for academic or personal reasons; 97% remain to receive a law degree.

Placement
J.D.s awarded:	323

Services available through: a separate law school placement center.
Services: video conferencing for individual interviews, networking receptions, extensive programming, and job fairs.
Special features: personalized services of 7 professionals who are experienced in the legal field.
Areas of placement:

Private practice 2-10 attorneys	9%
Private practice 11-25 attorneys	4%
Private practice 26-50 attorneys	4%
Private practice 51-100 attorneys	5%
Private practice 100+ attorneys	24%
Government	17%
Business/industry	12%
Judicial clerkships	8%
Public interest	6%
Academic	4%

Law School

471 West Palmer Street
Detroit, MI 48202

Application Filing	Accreditation
Fall: March 15	ABA, AALS

	Degrees Granted
Fee: $50	J.D., LL.M.

Enrollment 2011–2012		First-Year Class	
Men:	330 58%	Applied:	1,123
Women:	240 42%	Accepted:	517
Minorities:	103 18%	Enrolled:	181
Out-of-State:	68 12%		

2011–2012 Class Profile
LSAT Percentile: 70%
LSAT Median Score: 157

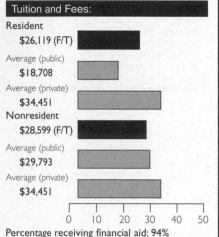

Tuition and Fees:

Resident
$26,119 (F/T)

Average (public)
$18,708

Average (private)
$34,451

Nonresident
$28,599 (F/T)

Average (public)
$29,793

Average (private)
$34,451

0   10   20   30   40   50

Percentage receiving financial aid: 94%

ADMISSIONS

In the fall of 2011 first-year class, 1123 applied, 517 were accepted, and 181 enrolled. One transfer student enrolled. The median LSAT percentile of the most recent first-year class was 70; the median GPA was 3.4 on a scale of 4.0. The lowest LSAT percentile accepted was 18; the highest was 99.

Requirements

Applicants must have a bachelor's degree and take the LSAT. The most important admission factors include a letter of recommendation, GPA, and the LSAT results. No specific undergraduate courses are required, and candidates are not interviewed.

Procedure

The application deadline for fall entry is March 15. Applicants should submit an application form, LSAT results, transcripts, a personal statement, a nonrefundable application fee of $50, and 2 letters of recommendation. Notification of the admissions decision is on a rolling basis. The law school uses the LSAC.

Special

The law school recruits minority and disadvantaged students by hosting Diversity Law Day, recruiting at historically black colleges and universities, and at hispanic service institutions. In addition, the school also participates in the LSAC Discover Law Program. Requirements are different for out-of-state students. Transfer students must have one year of credits, attended an ABA-approved law school, a personal statement, official transcripts sent from their current law school and their undergraduate institution, a letter of good standing submitted from the dean, and submit a copy of the LSAC report.

Costs

Tuition and fees for the 2011–2012 academic year are $24,572 for full-time in-state students and $27,002 for out-of-state students. Tuition for part-time students is $13,105 for in-state students and $14,401 out-of-state. On-campus room and board costs about $8,696 annually; books and supplies run $1,600.

Financial Aid

About 94% of current law students receive some form of aid. The average annual amount of aid from all sources combined, including scholarships, loans, and work contracts, is $32,438; maximum, $51,087. Awards are based on need and merit combined. Required financial statement is the FAFSA. The aid application deadline for fall entry is June 30. First-year students are notified about their financial aid application at the time of acceptance in most cases.

About the Law School

Wayne State University Law School was established in 1927 and is a public institution. The campus is located in an urban area in Detroit. The primary mission of the law school is to promote excellence in teaching, in scholarly research, and provide service to the community, the bench, and to the bar. Students have access to federal, state, county, city, and local agencies, courts, correctional facilities, law firms, and legal aid organizations in the Detroit area. Facilities of special interest to law students are four connected buildings, which house classrooms, seminar rooms, a moot court room, the law library, offices for faculty and student groups, a student lounge, and a 250-seat auditorium that can be used as either a trial or appellate courtroom. Classrooms are set up for multimedia presentations, and wireless Internet access is available throughout. There is housing available for students on or nearby the campus and throughout the metropolitan area. All law school facilities are accessible to the physically disabled.

Calendar

The law school operates on a traditional semester basis. Courses for full-time students are offered both day and evening and must be completed within 5 years. For part-time students, courses are offered both day and evening and must be completed within 6 years. New full- and part-time students are admitted in the fall. There is a 6 1/2-week summer session. Transferable summer courses are offered.

Programs

In addition to the J.D., the law school offers the LL.M. Students may take relevant courses in other programs and apply credit toward the J.D.; a maximum of 16 credits may be applied. The following joint degrees may be earned: J.D./M.A. (Juris Doctor/Master of Arts (various disciplines)) and J.D./M.B.A. (Juris Doctor/Master of Business Administration).

Required

To earn the J.D., candidates must complete 86 total credits, of which 35 are for required courses. They must maintain a minimum GPA of 2.0 in the required courses. The following first-year courses are required of all students: Civil Procedure A, Constitutional Law I, Contracts, Criminal Law, Legal Research and Writing, Property, The Regulatory State, and Torts. Required upper-level courses consist of Civil Procedure B and Professional Responsibility and the Legal Profession. The required orientation program for first-year students is a 3-day program introducing sources of law and the structure of the court system; the development of the law through the common law process; the relationship between statutes and case law; reading, analyzing, and synthesizing

Phone: 313-577-3937
Fax: 313-993-8129
E-mail: emjackson@wayne.edu
Web: www.law.wayne.edu

Contact

Ericka M. Jackson, Assistant Dean of Admissions, 313-577-3937 for general inquiries; Diedre Moore, Assistant Director of Financial Aid, 313-577-5142 for financial aid information.

case law; citation to provide authority and attribution; and professionalism.

Electives

Clinical experience is offered through a range of clinics, including the Child Advocacy Clinic, Disablility Law Clinic, and the Criminal Appellate Practice Program. There are 20 to 25 seminars. Second- and third-year students may receive 1 to 3 credits through internships with distinguished judges and a variety of governmental and nonprofit agencies. Special lecture series include the I. Goodman Cohen Lecture in Trial Advocacy, Driker Forum for Excellence in the Law, Biennial Keith Lecture, and Bernard Gottfried Memorial Labor Law Symposium. There are summer exchange programs in England and the Netherlands. The Intellectual Property Law Institute, a consortium with 2 local law schools, offers additional intellectual property courses to law students. The most widely taken electives are Evidence, Corporations, and Trusts and Estates.

Graduation Requirements

In order to graduate, candidates must have a GPA of 2.0 and completed the upper-division writing requirement.

Organizations

Students edit *The Wayne State Law Review, The Journal of Law in Society*, and the newspaper *The Advocate*. Moot court competitions include the New York City Bar National Moot Court, Jessup International Moot Court Competitions. Law student organizations include Student Board of Governors, Black Law Students Association, and Sports and Entertainment Law Society. There are local chapters of the National Lawyers Guild, the Federalist Socicty, and Phi Delta. Other organizations include the St. Thomas More Society, the Outlaws, and the Wayne Intellectual Property Student Association.

Library

The law library contains 630,196 hardcopy volumes and 225,401 microform volume equivalents, and subscribes to 5,061 serial publications. Online databases and networks include CALI, CIS Universe, DIALOG, Dow-Jones, Infotrac, Legal-Trac, LEXIS, OCLC First Search, WESTLAW, Access UN, BNA, CCH Intelliconnect, CIAO, CQ Researcher, Ebrary, EISIL, HeinOnline, IBFD, JSTOR, LSN, LLMC Digital, MOML, PACER, and RIA Checkpoint, which are available to law students for research. Special library collections include a U.S. government document depository, Michigan Supreme Court records and briefs, Michigan Probate Court opinions, and Michigan Superfund Sites Collection. The ratio of library volumes to faculty is 7,002 to 1 and to students is 1,105 to 1. The ratio of seats in the library to students is 1 to 2.

Faculty

The law school has 47 full-time and 43 part-time faculty members, of whom 30 are women. According to AAUP standards for Category 1 institutions, faculty salaries are average. About 21% of full-time faculty have a graduate law degree in addition to the J.D.; about 7% of part-time faculty have one. The ratio of full-time students to full-time faculty in an average class is 25 to 1; in a clinic, 6 to 1. The law school has a regular program of bringing visiting professors and other distinguished lecturers and visitors to campus. There is a chapter of the Order of the Coif; 36 faculty and 700 graduates are members.

Students

About 42% of the student body are women; 18%, minorities; 6%, African American; 8%, Asian American; 3%, Hispanic; and 1%, Native American. The majority of students come from Michigan (88%). The average age of entering students is 25; age range is 19 to 52. About 48% of students enter directly from undergraduate school, and 74% have a graduate degree. About 3% drop out after the first year for academic or personal reasons; 97% remain to receive a law degree.

Placement

J.D.s awarded:	124
Services available through: a separate law school placement center.	
Services: a full placement service that provides career counseling.	
Full-time job interviews:	63 employers
Summer job interviews:	63 employers
Placement within 9 months of graduation:	86% of class
Average starting salary:	$42,500 to $105,000
Areas of placement:	
Private practice 2-10 attorneys	24%
Private practice 11-25 attorneys	14%
Private practice 26-50 attorneys	17%
Private practice 51-100 attorneys	3%
Business/industry	18%
Government	9%
Judicial clerkships	5%
Public interest	5%

Application Filing		Accreditation	
Fall: March 1		ABA, AALS	
		Degrees Granted	
Fee: $50			J.D.
Enrollment 2011–2012		**First-Year Class**	
Men:	270 63%	Applied:	1,107
Women:	157 37%	Accepted:	506
Minorities:	51 12%	Enrolled:	141
Out-of-State:	128 30%		

2011–2012 Class Profile
LSAT Percentile: 60%
LSAT Median Score: 154
Percentage passing bar on first try: 78%

Tuition and Fees:

Resident
$16,420 (F/T)

Average (public)
$18,708

Average (private)
$34,451

Nonresident
$31,358 (F/T)

Average (public)
$29,793

Average (private)
$34,451

0 10 20 30 40 50

Percentage receiving financial aid: 86%

ADMISSIONS

In the fall of 2011 first-year class, 1107 applied, 506 were accepted, and 141 enrolled. Three transfers enrolled. The median LSAT percentile of the most recent first-year class was 60; the median GPA was 3.4 on a scale of 4.0. The lowest LSAT percentile accepted was 33; the highest was 97.

Requirements
Applicants must have a bachelor's degree and take the LSAT. The most important admission factors include LSAT results, academic achievement, and GPA. No specific undergraduate courses are required. Candidates are not interviewed.

Procedure
The application deadline for fall entry is March 1. Applicants should submit an application form, LSAT results, transcripts, a nonrefundable application fee of $50, 3 letters of recommendation, and a personal statement. Notification of the admissions decision is on a rolling basis. The law school uses the LSAC.

Special
The law school recruits minority and disadvantaged students through mailings, Minority Law Day, forums, and personal contacts from the school's Graduate Assistant for Minority Recruitment. Requirements are different for out-of-state students in that preference is given to West Virginia residents. Transfer students must have one year of credit, must have a minimum GPA of 2.5, and must have attended an ABA-approved law school.

Costs

Books and supplies run $2,400.

Financial Aid

About 86% of current law students receive some form of aid. The average annual amount of aid from all sources combined, including scholarships, loans, and work contracts, is $21,984; maximum, $38,490. Awards are based on need and merit combined. The required financial statement is the FAFSA. The aid application deadline for fall entry is March 1. Special funds for minority or disadvantaged students include scholarships, and vocational-rehabilitation is offered to disabled and disadvantaged students. First-year students are notified about their financial aid application at the time of application.

About the Law School

West Virginia University College of Law was established in 1878 and is a public institution. The 1000-acre campus is in a small town 77 miles south of Pittsburgh, Pennsylvania. The primary mission of the law school is to prepare students for the practice of law and for public leadership through a curriculum that stresses basic legal principles, lawyering skills, and the responsibilities of the legal profession. Students have access to federal, state, county, city, and local agencies, courts, correctional facilities, law firms, and legal aid organizations in the Morgantown area. Facilities of special interest to law students are the Leo Carlin Computer Laboratory; the Marlyn E. Lugar Courtroom, a combination courtroom-auditorium; a mini-courtroom; 3 conference-seminar rooms; 1 large courtroom; the law library; the Meredith Career Services Center with placement interview rooms; a student lounge; and a child-care cooperative. Housing for students is available for both single and married students. The university housing office helps students find off-campus housing. All law school facilities are accessible to the physically disabled.

Calendar

The law school operates on a traditional semester basis. Courses for full-time students are offered days only, and must be completed within 6 years. For part-time students, courses are offered days only, and must be completed within 6 years. New full- and part-time students are admitted in the fall. There is no summer session. Transferable summer courses are not offered.

Programs

The following joint degrees may be earned: J.D./M.B.A. (Juris Doctor/Master of Business Administration) and J.D./M.P.A. (Juris Doctor/Master of Public Administration).

Required
To earn the J.D., candidates must complete 91 total credits, of which 37 are for required courses. They must maintain a minimum GPA of 2.2 in the required courses. The following first-year courses are required of all students: Civil Procedure Jurisdiction, Civil Procedure Rules, Constitutional Law, Contracts I, Criminal Law, Legal Research and Writing I and II, Professional Responsibility, Property I, and Torts. Required upper-level courses consist of a clinic, a business drafting course, a seminar, Appellate Advocacy, 2 perspective courses, and Trial advocacy. The required orientation program for first-year students is a 2-day program featuring large group discussion and mini-classes covering introduction to legal analysis, legal writing, note taking, class participation, and law school exam taking; student panels on first-year life; and a presentation about services available to law students including counseling, financial aid information, and a computer workshop for interested students. During the first semester, there are three one-hour programs: state bar license, class preparation, and final exam taking.

Phone: 304-293-5301

Fax: 304-293-6891

E-mail: wvulaw.Admissions@mail.wvu.edu

Web: law.wvu.edu

Contact

Admissions Office, 304-293-5304 for general inquiries; Eric Meadows, Financial Counselor, 304-293-5302 for financial aid information.

WEST VIRGINIA

Electives

The law school has no concentrations, but it has a full curriculum in all subjects except juvenile law and maritime law. Approved upper-class students may earn 14 credit hours in a civil legal clinic. There is also an immigration clinic for 5 credit hours. The most widely taken electives are Business Organizations, Evidence, and Wealth Transfers.

Graduation Requirements

In order to graduate, candidates must have a GPA of 2.2, must have completed the upper-division writing requirement, and must satisfactorily complete all first-year requirements, the seminar and the perspectives course requirements, and the capstone/practicum requirement.

Organizations

Students edit the *West Virginia Law Review*, the fourth oldest legal journal in the United States; the *Journal of College and University Law* in conjunction with the National Association of College and University Attorneys; and the newspaper *On-Point*. Moot court competitions include the Moot Court Board, Baker Cup Competition, Marlyn E. Lugar Trial Association Mock Trial Competition, and Gourley Cup Trial Competition. The law school sends 2- to 6-person teams to 5 outside appellate advocacy competitions and 2- to 5-person teams to several outside trial advocacy competitions. Law student organizations, local chapters of national associations, and campus clubs and organizations include the Black Law Students Association, Women's Law Caucus, Public Interest Advocates, Environmental Law Society, Labor and Employment Law Association, Student Bar Association, National Lawyers Guild, Energy Law Club, and Phi Delta Phi.

Library

The law library contains 347,393 hardcopy volumes and 550,200 microform volume equivalents, and subscribes to 1,070 serial publications. Such online databases and networks as CALI, CIS Universe, Legal-Trac, LEXIS, OCLC First Search, WESTLAW, and Wilsonline Indexes are available to law students for research. Special library collections include a rare book room, government documents collection, and the Baker Collection. The ratio

of library volumes to faculty is 18,284 to 1 and to students is 734 to 1. The ratio of seats in the library to students is 1 to 2.

Faculty

The law school has 34 full-time and 25 part-time faculty members, of whom 20 are women. According to AAUP standards for Category I institutions, faculty salaries are below average. About 80% of full-time faculty have a graduate law degree in addition to the J.D. The ratio of full-time students to full-time faculty in an average class is 12 to 1; in a clinic, 10 to 1. The law school has a regular program of bringing visiting professors and other distinguished lecturers and visitors to campus. There is a chapter of the Order of the Coif; 4 faculty are members.

Students

About 37% of the student body are women; 12%, minorities; 5%, African American; 2%, Asian American; 2%, Hispanic; and 1%, Native American. The majority of students come from West Virginia (70%). The average age of entering students is 24; age range is 21 to 44. About 48% of students enter directly from undergraduate school, 5% have a graduate degree, and 52% have worked full-time prior to entering law school. About 1% drop out after the first year for academic or personal reasons; 99% remain to receive a law degree.

Placement

J.D.s awarded:	125

Services available through: a separate law school placement center and the university placement center.

Services: workshops on interviewing, resume writing, alternative jobs, working in a small firm, and finding a judicial clerkship.

Special features: the college has a close working relationship with the West Virginia State Bar.

Full-time job interviews:	25 employers
Summer job interviews:	30 employers
Placement by graduation:	65% of class
Placement within 9 months:	92% of class

Areas of placement:

Private practice 2-10 attorneys	25%
Private practice 11-25 attorneys	5%
Private practice 26-50 attorneys	16%
Private practice 51-100 attorneys	3%
Business/industry	24%
Judicial clerkships	13%
Government	10%
Public interest	4%
Military	2%

School of Law

1215 Wilbraham Road
Springfield, MA 01119

Application Filing	Accreditation
Fall: March 15	ABA, AALS

	Degrees Granted
Fee: $50	J.D., LL.M.

Enrollment 2011–2012			First-Year Class	
Men:	208	47%	Applied:	1,170
Women:	230	53%	Accepted:	593
Minorities:	48	11%	Enrolled:	106
Out-of-State:	254	58%		

2011–2012 Class Profile
LSAT Percentile: 56%
LSAT Median Score: 153
Percentage passing bar on first try: 75%

Tuition and Fees:
Resident
$38,240 (F/T)

Average (public)
$18,708

Average (private)
$34,451

Nonresident
$38,240 (F/T)

Average (public)
$29,793

Average (private)
$34,451

0   10   20   30   40   50

Percentage receiving financial aid: 72%

ADMISSIONS
In the fall of 2011 first-year class, 1170 applied, 593 were accepted, and 106 enrolled. Two transfer students enrolled. The median LSAT percentile of the most recent first-year class was 56; the median GPA was 3.2 on a scale of 4.0. The lowest LSAT percentile accepted was 33; the highest was 93.

Requirements
Applicants must have a bachelor's degree and take the LSAT. The most important admission factors for students are academic achievement, life experience, and character or personality. No specific undergraduate courses are required, and candidates are not interviewed.

Procedure
The application deadline for fall entry is March 15. Applicants should submit an application form, LSAT results, transcripts, a personal statement, a nonrefundable application fee of $50, 2 letters of recommendation, a CAS report, and resume. Notification of the admissions decision is on a rolling basis. The law school uses the LSAC.

Special
The law school recruits minority and disadvantaged students by means of Law Services forums, attendance at historically black college recruiting events, mailings through the Candidate Referral Service, and scholarships. Requirements are different for out-of-state students. Transfer students must have one year of credit and a personal statement.

Costs
Tuition and fees for the 2011–2012 academic year are $36,826 for all full-time students. Tuition for part-time students is $27,620 for in-state students and $27,620 out-of-state. Books and supplies run $1,528.

Financial Aid
About 72% of current law students receive some form of aid. The average annual amount of aid from all sources combined, including scholarships, loans, and work contracts, is $51,643; maximum, $58,399. Awards are based on need and merit combined. Required financial statements are the FAFSA, the college financial aid application, and tax returns with W2 statements for returning law students. The aid application deadline for fall entry is rolling. Special funds for minority or disadvantaged students include awards for those who have overcome educational, cultural, economic, or physical barriers to achieve success at the undergraduate level. First-year students are notified about their financial aid application at time of acceptance.

About the Law School
Western New England University School of Law was established in 1919 and is a private institution. The 215-acre campus is located in a suburban area 25 miles north of Hartford, 90 miles west of Boston. The primary mission of the law school is to provide a practical and effective legal education in a humane and supportive environment, in which faculty and students work together in a rigorous yet rewarding educational process. Students have access to federal, state, county, city, and local agencies, courts, correctional facilities, law firms, and legal aid organizations in the Springfield area. Students have opportunities to work for federal and state judges, government agencies, and public interest organizations arranged through the internship program, or by individual students. Facilities of special interest to law students include a 490,000 volume law library that contains computer laboratories exclusively for student use; a moot court room used for law trial simulation classes, moot court competitions, and semiannual visits by the Massachusetts appeals court; and the Healthful Living Center, a state-of-the-art athletic and recreation facility. There is limited on-campus housing for law students. However, a variety of housing for students is available in Springfield. All law school facilities are accessible to the physically disabled.

Calendar
The law school operates on a traditional semester basis. Courses for full-time students are offered both day and evening and must be completed within 4 years. For part-time students, courses are offered both day and evening and must be completed within 5 years. New full- and part-time students are admitted in the fall. There is a 7-week summer session. Transferable summer courses are offered.

Programs
In addition to the J.D., the law school offers the LL.M. The following joint degrees may be earned: J.D./M.S.A. (Juris Doctor/Master of Accounting), J.D./M.B.A. (Juris Doctor/Master of Business Administration), J.D./M.R.P. (Juris Doctor/Master of Regional Planning), and J.D./M.S.W. (Juris Doctor/Master of Social Work).

Required
To earn the J.D., candidates must complete 88 total credits, of which 46 are for required courses. They must maintain a minimum GPA of 70.0 in the required courses. The following first-year courses are required of all students: Criminal Law, Constitutional Law, Contracts, Lawyering Process, Civil Procedure, Property, and Torts. Required upper-level courses consist of Business Organizations, Income Tax, Evidence, Legal Profession, Practical

Phone: 413-782-1406
800-782-6665
Fax: 413-796-2067
E-mail: *admissions@law.wnec.edu*
Web: *www.law.wnec.edu*

Contact

Associate Dean for External Affairs, 413-782-1406 or 800-782-6665 for general inquiries; Sandra Belanger, Financial Aid Specialist, 413-796-2080 for financial aid information.

MASSACHUSETTS

Skills Elective, and Qualified Writing Elective. The required orientation program for first-year students is a 3-day program where students meet faculty members, administrators, and representatives of various student organizations, and attend Lawyering Process Orientation sessions.

Electives

The School of Law offers concentrations in corporate law, criminal law, internationl law, public interest law, real estate, estate planning, and gender and sexuality law. In addition, upper-level students may enroll in the Legal Services Clinic, Criminal Law Clinic, the Consumer Protection Clinic, the Small Business Clinic, the Real Estate Practicum, and the International Human Rights Clinic. There are a number of limited enrollment upper-level courses offered in a broad range of subject areas. Each is a 3-credit course designed to satisfy the upper-class writing requirement. Internships are available with the Massachusetts State Attorney, Connecticut State Attorney, Western Massachusetts Legal Services, Federal Judicial, U.S. Attorney, and the Internal Revenue Service's Regional Counsel Office. In independent study programs, a student may engage in advanced legal research under the supervision of 2 faculty members. Special lecture series include the Clason Lecture Series, events at the Legislative Institute, and a speaker series sponsored by the Law and Business Center for Advanced Entrepreneurship. Students may take summer programs offered by other ABA-accredited law schools. Students may study in tutorials with a faculty member on a mutually agreed upon subject. Remedial programs consist of a Legal Education Assistance Program, which is voluntary and available to all students. The goal of the program is to provide additional assistance in legal research, writing, reasoning, and examination-taking skills. The Multi-Cultural Law Students Association (MCLSA) provides support and mentoring. Special interest group programs include the ABA Tax Challenge. The most widely taken electives are Criminal Procedure: Investigation, Trusts and Estates, and Trial Methods.

Graduation Requirements

In order to graduate, candidates must have a GPA of 70.0 and completed the upper-division writing requirement.

Organizations

Students edit the *Western New England Law Review* and *Lex Brevis*, the student newspaper. Teams are annually sent to the National Moot Court, Jessup Moot Court International Law Competition, and Frederick Douglass Moot Court Competition. Other competitions include the ABA National Trial Competition and the ABA National Negotiation Competition. Law student organizations include local chapters of national associations, as well as Phi Alpha Delta, ABA-Law Student Division, and Equal Justice Works. Campus organizations are the Multi-Cultural Law Students Association, Women's Law Association, and OUTlaw (Gay/Lesbian/Bisexual/Straight Alliance). Other organizations include International Law Society, Environmental Law Coalition, and Federalist Society.

Library

The law library contains 375,070 hardcopy volumes and 235,661 microform volume equivalents, and subscribes to 801 serial publications. On-line databases and networks include CALI, CIS Universe, DIALOG, Infotrac, Legal-Trac, LEXIS, OCLC First Search, WESTLAW, and Wilsonline Indexes, which are available to law students for research. Special library collections include a selective federal government document depository, publications of Massachusetts Continuing Legal Education, Inc., and a law and popular culture, print, video, and audio collection. The ratio of library volumes to faculty is 10,716 to 1 and to students is 673 to 1. The ratio of seats in the library to students is 1 to 2.

Faculty

The law school has 38 full-time and 36 part-time faculty members, of whom 22 are women. About 18% of full-time faculty have a graduate law degree in addition to the J.D.; about 5% of part-time faculty have one. The ratio of full-time students

Placement

J.D.s awarded:	173

Services available through: a separate law school placement center.

Services: advice on judicial clerkships, fellowships, LL.M. programs, alternative careers, and practice in various areas of the law.

Special features: networking functions, videotaped individual mock interviews, various panels and workshops presented on conducting a job search and on career options, a weekly Career Services newsletter containing part- and full-time job listings for students and alumni, articles of interest, and notices of writing competitions, summer study, study abroad, fellowships, clerkships, and internships. The school is an active member of 2 law school placement consortia, 1 state and 1 regional.

Full-time job interviews:	4 employers
Summer job interviews:	10 employers
Placement within 9 months of graduation:	82% of class
Average starting salary:	$26,000 to $103,000

Areas of placement:

Private practice 2-10 attorneys	20%
Private practice 11-25 attorneys	1%
Private practice 26-50 attorneys	2%
Private practice 51-100 attorneys	16%
Business/industry	26%
Government	16%
Judicial clerkships	7%
Public interest	6%
Private practice solo or unknown size	5%
Academic	3%

to full-time faculty in an average class is 18 to 1; in a clinic, 8 to 1. The law school has a regular program of bringing visiting professors and other distinguished lecturers and visitors to campus.

Students

About 53% of the student body are women; 11%, minorities; 4%, African American; 4%, Asian American; and 3%, Hispanic. The majority of students come from Massachusetts (42%). The average age of entering students is 25; age range is 21 to 47. About 36% of students enter directly from undergraduate school, and 6% have a graduate degree. About 9% drop out after the first year for academic or personal reasons; 91% remain to receive a law degree.

WESTERN STATE UNIVERSITY

College of Law

1111 North State College Blvd
Fullerton, CA 92831

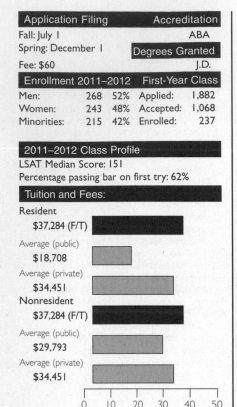

Application Filing		Accreditation
Fall: July 1		ABA
Spring: December 1		Degrees Granted
Fee: $60		J.D.

Enrollment 2011–2012			First-Year Class	
Men:	268	52%	Applied:	1,882
Women:	243	48%	Accepted:	1,068
Minorities:	215	42%	Enrolled:	237

2011–2012 Class Profile
LSAT Median Score: 151
Percentage passing bar on first try: 62%

Tuition and Fees:

Resident
$37,284 (F/T)

Average (public)
$18,708

Average (private)
$34,451

Nonresident
$37,284 (F/T)

Average (public)
$29,793

Average (private)
$34,451

0   10   20   30   40   50

Percentage receiving financial aid: 93%

ADMISSIONS

In the fall of 2011 first-year class, 1882 applied, 1068 were accepted, and 237 enrolled. Eleven transfers enrolled. The median GPA of the most recent first-year class was 3.1.

Requirements

Applicants must have a bachelor's degree and take the LSAT. Minimum acceptable GPA is 2.3 on a scale of 4.0. The most important admission factors include LSAT results, GPA, and writing ability. No specific undergraduate courses are required. Candidates are interviewed.

Procedure

The application deadline for fall entry is July 1. Applicants should submit an application form, LSAT results, transcripts, a personal statement, a nonrefundable application fee of $60, and 2 letters of recommendation. Additional items are required for transfer and international applicants. Notification of the admissions

decision is 2 weeks after a decision is made. The law school uses the LSAC.

Special

The law school recruits minority and disadvantaged students through diversity recruiting and scholarships. Requirements are different for out-of-state students. Transfer students must have a minimum GPA of 2.3, a personal statement, and a letter of standing at an accredited law school.

Costs

Tuition and fees for the 2011–2012 academic year are $36,994 for all full-time students. Tuition for part-time students is $24,740 for in-state students and $24,740 out-of-state. Books and supplies run $1,500.

Financial Aid

About 93% of current law students receive some form of aid. The average annual amount of aid from all sources combined, including scholarships, loans, and work contracts, is $43,572; maximum, $62,116. Awards are based on need and merit combined. Required financial statements are the FAFSA and an institutional application. The aid application deadline for fall entry is March 2. First-year students are notified about their financial aid application at time of acceptance.

About the Law School

Western State University College of Law was established in 1966 and is a private institution. The 4-acre campus is in a suburban area midway between Los Angeles and San Diego. The primary mission of the law school is to provide the highest quality legal education, based on an innovative program of studies designed to develop the tools of careful legal analysis and to foster a broad understanding of law, law practice, and legal theory. Students have access to federal, state, county, city, and local agencies, courts, correctional facilities, law firms, and legal aid organizations in the Fullerton area. Facilities of special interest to law students include county, state, city, and federal agencies, courts, correctional facilities, law firms, and legal aid organizations. Housing for students is widely available in a university environment adjacent to Western State and

California State University of Fullerton. About 98% of the law school facilities are accessible to the physically disabled.

Calendar

The law school operates on a traditional semester basis. Courses for full-time students are offered days only, and must be completed within 5 years. For part-time students, courses are offered both day and evening, and must be completed within 6 years. New full-time students are admitted in the fall. New part-time students are admitted in the fall and spring. There is an 8-week summer session. Transferable summer courses are offered.

Programs

Required

To earn the J.D., candidates must complete 88 total credits, of which 69 are for required courses. They must maintain a minimum GPA of 2.0 in the required courses. The following first-year courses are required of all students: Civil Procedure I and II, Contracts, Criminal Law, Criminal Procedure, Legal Writing and Research, and Torts I and II. Required upper-level courses consist of an advanced professional skills course, Business Associations I and II, Community Property, Constitutional Law I and II, Estates, Evidence I and II, Federal Income Tax Law, Property I and II, Professional Responsibility, Remedies, and Sales. The required orientation program for first-year students is a 1-week program called Introduction to Legal Methods.

Electives

The College of Law offers concentrations in corporate law and criminal law. In addition, all students are eligible for the Immigration Law Clinic (5 credits) once prerequisites have been met. Research programs are available to all students for up to 3 credits. All students are eligible for externships (worth 5 to 8 credits) once prerequisites have been met. Study abroad is available to all students for a maximum of 6 credits. Non-credit tutorial and remedial programs are available to all students. There is a wide array of academic support programs available to all students.

Phone: 714-459-1101
800-978-4529
Fax: 714-441-1748
E-mail: adm@wsulaw.edu
Web: wsulaw.edu

Contact

Donna Espinoza, Director of Student Finance, 714-459-1120 for financial aid information.

CALIFORNIA

Graduation Requirements

In order to graduate, candidates must have a GPA of 2.0, must have completed the upper-division writing requirement, and must have completed advanced professional skills courses for 6 credits.

Organizations

Students edit the *Western State University Law Review*. Moot Court competitions include the Roger J. Traynor California Moot Court Competition (Sponsored by Witkin Institute), National Juvenile Law Moot Court Competition (Whittier Law School), and Herbert J. Wechsler National Criminal Law Moot Court Competition (SUNY Buffalo School of Law). Law student organizations and campus organizations include Business Law Association. Local chapters of national associations include The Federalist Society, Black Law Students Association, and Christian Legal Society. Other campus organizations include Phi Alpha Delta, Student Bar Association, and Women's Law Association.

Library

The law library contains 206,201 hardcopy volumes and 99,172 microform volume equivalents, and subscribes to 2,948 serial publications. Such online databases and networks as CALI, DIALOG, Infotrac, Legal-Trac, LEXIS, WESTLAW, Wilsonline Indexes, HeinOnline, BNA, Intelliconnect, Foreign Law Grads, LexisNexis Congressional, and LLMC are available to law students for research. Special library collections include WSU archives. The ratio of library volumes to faculty is 9,047 to 1 and to students is 536 to 1. The ratio of seats in the library to students is 1 to 1.

Faculty

The law school has 28 full-time and 19 part-time faculty members, of whom 18 are women. About 24% of full-time faculty have a graduate law degree in addition to the J.D. The ratio of full-time students to full-time faculty in an average clinic is 10 to 1. The law school has a regular program of bringing visiting professors and other distinguished lecturers and visitors to campus.

Students

About 48% of the student body are women; 42%, minorities; 5%, African American; 16%, Asian American; 16%, Hispanic; and 1%, Native American. The average age of entering students is 26; age range is 21 to 62.

Placement

J.D.s awarded:	105
Services available through: a separate law school placement center.	
Special features: public service program, externship program, online job listings, and alumni mentors.	
Full-time job interviews:	10 employers
Summer job interviews:	10 employers
Placement within 9 months of graduation:	74% of class
Average starting salary:	$29,000 to $160,000
Areas of placement:	
Private practice 2-10 attorneys	58%
Private practice 11-25 attorneys	9%
Private practice 26-50 attorneys	3%
Private practice 51-100 attorneys	4%
Business/industry	9%
Government	7%
Academic	4%
Public interest	2%

Whittier Law School

3333 Harbor Blvd.
Costa Mesa, CA 92626

Application Filing	Accreditation
Fall: August 1	ABA, AALS

	Degrees Granted
Fee: $60	J.D., LL.M.

Enrollment 2011–2012		First-Year Class	
Men:	361 51%	Applied:	2,245
Women:	345 48%	Accepted:	1,247
Minorities:	367 52%	Enrolled:	275
Out-of-State:	134 19%		

2011–2012 Class Profile
LSAT Percentile: 52%
LSAT Median Score: 152
Percentage passing bar on first try: 56%

Tuition and Fees:

Resident
$39,140 (F/T)

Average (public)
$18,708

Average (private)
$34,451

Nonresident
$39,140 (F/T)

Average (public)
$29,793

Average (private)
$34,451

0 10 20 30 40 50

Percentage receiving financial aid: 93%

ADMISSIONS

In the fall of 2011 first-year class, 2245 applied, 1247 were accepted, and 275 enrolled. Twenty transfers enrolled. The median LSAT percentile of the most recent first-year class was 52; the median GPA was 3.0 on a scale of 4.0. The lowest LSAT percentile accepted was 15; the highest was 95.

Requirements
Applicants must have a bachelor's degree and take the LSAT. Minimum acceptable GPA is 2.0 on a scale of 4.0. The most important admission factors include academic achievement, GPA, and LSAT results. No specific undergraduate courses are required. Candidates are not interviewed.

Procedure
The application deadline for fall entry is August 1. Applicants should submit an application form, LSAT results, transcripts, TOEFL (if applicable), a nonrefundable application fee of $60, 2 letters of recommendation, and a personal statement; if foreign, the applicant must have his/her foreign degree reviewed by an evaluation service approved by the school. Moreover, transcripts must be presented at matriculation. Notification of the admissions decision is as decisions are made. The law school uses the LSAC.

Special
The law school recruits minority and disadvantaged students by means of extensive fall recruiting, mass mailings targeted at minority groups, and diversity scholarships. Requirements are different for out-of-state students. Transfer students must have one year of credit and must have attended an ABA-approved law school.

Costs

Books and supplies run $1,656.

Financial Aid

About 93% of current law students receive some form of aid. The average annual amount of aid from all sources combined, including scholarships, loans, and work contracts, is $51,796; maximum, $64,552. Awards are based on need and merit combined. The required financial statement is the FAFSA. The aid application deadline for fall entry is May 1. Special funds for minority or disadvantaged students are available. First-year students are notified about their financial aid application at time of acceptance.

About the Law School

Whittier College Whittier Law School was established in 1966 and is a private institution. The 15-acre campus is in a suburban area of Costa Mesa, California. Whittier Law School provides a practical legal education, emphasizing experiential learning for the student. Students have access to federal, state, county, city, and local agencies, courts, correctional facilities, law firms, and legal aid organizations in the Costa Mesa area. Facilities of special interest to law students include approximately 150 law firms that exist within a 5-mile radius of campus. Orange County courts provide abundant opportunities for externships, clerkships, and other opportunities for students. Housing for students is not available on campus, but is available and affordable in surrounding areas. The

Office of Student Affairs assists students seeking housing accommodations. All law school facilities are accessible to the physically disabled.

Calendar

The law school operates on a traditional semester basis. Courses for full-time students are offered both day and evening, and must be completed within 7 years. For part-time students, courses are offered both day and evening, and must be completed within 7 years. New full- and part-time students are admitted in the fall. There is an 8-week summer session. Transferable summer courses are offered.

Programs

In addition to the J.D., the law school offers the LL.M. Students may take relevant courses in other programs and apply credit toward the J.D.; a maximum of 6 credits may be applied.

Required
To earn the J.D., candidates must complete 87 total credits, of which 53 are for required courses. They must maintain a minimum GPA of 2.5 in the required courses. The following first-year courses are required of all students: Civil Procedure, Contracts I and II, Criminal Law, Legal Writing I and II, Real Property I and II, and Torts I and II. Required upper-level courses consist of Business Associations, Constitutional Law I and II, Criminal Procedure, Evidence, Legal Analysis Workshop, Professional Responsibility, and Professional Skills I and II. The required orientation program for first-year students is a 3-day program that includes introductions to and presentations by faculty, the administration, the library, the financial aid office, and student organizations.

Electives
The Whittier Law School offers concentrations in corporate law, criminal law, environmental law, family law, intellectual property law, international law, juvenile law, and litigation. In addition, clinics are offered to upper division students for up to 10 units of credit. The Children's Rights Clinic offers 10 law students per semester the opportunity to provide pro bono legal assistance to children in selected cases on

Phone: 714-444-4141, ext. 123
800-808-8188
Fax: 714-444-0250
E-mail: info@law.whittier.edu
Web: law.whittier.edu

Contact

Tom McColl, Assistant Dean of Admissions and Financial Aid, 714-444-4141, ext. 123 for general inquiries; Jennifer Pham, Director of Financial Aid, 714-444-4141, ext. 203 for financial aid information.

CALIFORNIA

such matters as guardianship, custody, and adoption, under faculty supervision. The Special Education Clinic affords the same number of students the opportunity to assist special-needs children to request services from local school districts, in mediation sessions and administrative hearings. The Family Violence Clinic is designed to provide holistic legal services, combining the law with mental health, counseling, and other social services. Assistance is provided at several local shelter locations and up to 10 students can participate each term. The Legal Policy Clinic is a "clientless" clinic permitting students to advocate legal positions in the student's area of interest. Seminars are available including First Amendment, Advanced Torts, Natural Resources, Reproductive Technology, Information Privacy Seminar, and Adoption. Internships are permitted after the completion of the first year curriculum. Students can earn up to 6 units working at the offices of county, state, city, and federal agencies and courts, such as the City Attorney's office, District Attorney's office, Department of Corporations, and the public defender's office. Placements are also available with various public and private nonprofit legal entities. Students may take up to 3 units of independent study each semester with a full-time professor. Special lecture series include International Law, Health Law, and Center for Children's Fellow Program. Summer-abroad programs are offered in Israel, Spain, China, the Netherlands, and France. Exchange programs are available at the University of Paris, the University of Catabria, and the University of Seville. Students are also permitted to enroll in ABA-approved study-abroad programs sponsored by other law schools for a maximum credit of 6 units. Each semester during the first year of law school, students are invited to attend extensive skills and exam writing workshops. In addition, teaching assistants are available in most first year classes for 1-on-1 tutorials. The Academic Success Program is structured to meet the needs of individuals in mastering writing and other skills. Each semester during the first year of law school, students are required to attend weekly small group sessions and lectures on skills, including exam writing skills. These sessions are taught by the director of the program and by full-time professors. Special interest group programs include International Law, Environmental

Law, Center for Children's Rights, and Intellectual Property. The most widely taken electives are Criminal Procedure, Evidence, and Wills and Trusts.

Graduation Requirements

In order to graduate, candidates must have a GPA of 2.5 and must have completed the upper-division writing requirement.

Organizations

Students edit the *Whittier Law Review,* the *Whittier Journal of Child and Family Advocacy,* and the student newspaper, *The Zealous Advocate.* Moot court teams are sent to the National Moot Court, National Criminal Procedure, and Jessup International Moot Court competitions, among others. The law school also hosts the National Juvenile Law and Sonnenberg First Year Moot Court competitions. Law student organizations, local chapters of national associations, and campus organizations include the Alternative Dispute Resolution Group, Asian and Pacific Islander Law Students Association, Trial Advocacy Honors Board, Delta Theta Phi, Phi Alpha Delta, Phi Delta Phi, the Middle Eastern Law Students Organization, and Black Law Students Associations, and the Women's Law Association.

Library

The law library contains 682,290 hardcopy volumes and 141,361 microform volume equivalents, and subscribes to 2,165 serial publications. Such online databases and networks as CALI, DIALOG, Infotrac, Legal-Trac, LEXIS, Mathew Bender, WESTLAW, Wilsonline Indexes, JSTOR, HeinOnline, New York Times, and others are available to law students for research. Special library collections include a federal and a California state depository. The ratio of library volumes to faculty is 21,321 to 1 and to students is 1,034 to 1. The ratio of seats in the library to students is 1 to 54.

Faculty

The law school has 36 full-time and 30 part-time faculty members, of whom 33 are women. About 28% of full-time faculty have a graduate law degree in addition to the J.D.; about 5% of part-time faculty have one. The ratio of full-time students

Placement

J.D.s awarded:	128

Services available through: a separate law school placement center.

Services: the Career Development Offices offers a mentor program, mock interviews, informational programs, a comprehensive library of directories and other materials, online job postings, information on financing through grants, fellowships and federal programs, and formal on-campus recruiting programs.

Special features: member of Law School Career Advisors of Southern California (LSCA), a group of 11 law schools that sponsors career programs.

Full-time job interviews:	10 employers
Summer job interviews:	20 employers
Placement by graduation:	43% of class
Placement within 9 months:	84% of class
Average starting salary:	$27,000 to $120,000
Areas of placement:	
Private practice 2-10 attorneys	40%
Private practice 11-25 attorneys	1%
Private practice 26-50 attorneys	6%
Business/industry	31%
Public interest	6%
Academic	6%
Government	5%
Judicial clerkships	1%

to full-time faculty in an average class is 22 to 1; in a clinic, 8 to 1. The law school has a regular program of bringing visiting professors and other distinguished lecturers and visitors to campus.

Students

About 48% of the student body are women; 52%, minorities; 3%, African American; 18%, Asian American; 21%, Hispanic; and 1%, Native American. The majority of students come from California (81%). The average age of entering students is 27; age range is 20 to 54. About 70% of students enter directly from undergraduate school. About 31% drop out after the first year for academic or personal reasons; 69% remain to receive a law degree.

Widener University School of Law

4601 Concord Pike, P.O. Box 7474
Wilmington, DE 19803-0474

Application Filing	Accreditation
Fall: May 15	ABA, AALS
	Degrees Granted
Fee: $60	J.D., LL.M., S.J.D., M.J. (Master of Jurisprudence), D.L. (Doctor of Laws)

Enrollment 2011–2012		First-Year Class	
Men:	531 56%	Applied:	2,039
Women:	419 44%	Accepted:	918
Minorities:	152 16%	Enrolled:	313
Out-of-State:	798 84%		

2011–2012 Class Profile
LSAT Percentile: 52%
LSAT Median Score: 152
Percentage passing bar on first try: 88%

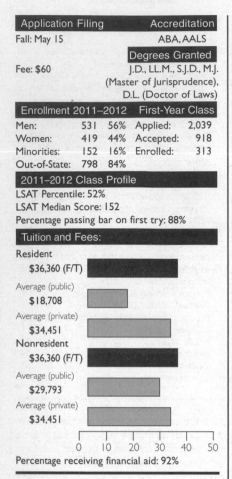

Tuition and Fees:

Resident
$36,360 (F/T)

Average (public)
$18,708

Average (private)
$34,451

Nonresident
$36,360 (F/T)

Average (public)
$29,793

Average (private)
$34,451

Percentage receiving financial aid: 92%

ADMISSIONS

In the fall of 2011 first-year class, 2039 applied, 918 were accepted, and 313 enrolled. Two transfer students enrolled. The median LSAT percentile of the most recent first-year class was 52; the median GPA was 3.1 on a scale of 4.0. The lowest LSAT percentile accepted was 14; the highest was 96.

Requirements

Applicants must have a bachelor's degree and take the LSAT. The most important admission factors include LSAT results, GPA, and academic achievement. No specific undergraduate courses are required. Candidates are not interviewed.

Procedure

The application deadline for fall entry is May 15. Applicants should submit their application form, LSAT results, transcripts, and a nonrefundable application fee of $60. Also strongly recommended are letters of recommendation and a personal statement. Notification of the admissions decision is on a rolling basis. The law school uses the LSAC.

Special

The law school recruits minority and disadvantaged students at programs sponsored by colleges and universities across the country. The application also encourages applicants to submit a personal statement. The admissions committee may also consider relevant such factors as a history of economic or educational disadvantage, cultural or language differences, disability, and whether they believe the admission of the student would help correct underrepresentation of a particular minority or disadvantaged group in the legal profession. Requirements are different for out-of-state students. Transfer students must have one year of credit, attended an ABA-approved law school, and submit a certified transcript and letter of good standing. A maximum of 35 qualified credits will be accepted in transfer. Transfer candidates must be in the top-third of their law school class.

Costs

On-campus room and board costs about $5,050 annually; books and supplies cost about $1,350.

Financial Aid

Approximately 92% of current law students receive some form of aid. The average annual amount of aid from all sources combined, including scholarships, loans, and work contracts, is $42,141; maximum, $54,977. Awards are based on merit. Required financial statement is the FAFSA. The aid application deadline for fall entry is open. Special funds include merit scholarships, which are available to majority, minority, and disadvantaged students. Widener scholar loans are offered to students maintaining a satisfactory GPA. First-year students are notified about their financial aid application at time of acceptance.

About the Law School

Widener University School of Law was established in 1971 and is a private institution. The 34-acre campus is in a suburban area in Delaware, 3 miles from downtown Wilmington. The primary mission of the law school is to give students a strong foundation in the law, encouraging them to be lifelong learners who are actively engaged in its development. Students have access to federal, state, county, city, and local agencies, courts, correctional facilities, law firms, and legal aid organizations in the Wilmington area. In addition, students have access to the numerous resources available at the university's main campus. Facilities of special interest to law students include extensive clinical and skills programs, moot court rooms, extensive law library, audiovisual centers, computer laboratory, student lounge areas, private study/conference rooms, and recreational facilities. Housing for students consists of residence halls and townhouse apartments. Area apartments are widely available. All law school facilities are accessible to the physically disabled.

Calendar

The law school operates on a traditional semester basis. Courses for full-time students are offered days only. Evening classes are offered on a space-available basis to full-time students and must be completed within 7 years. For part-time students, courses are offered both day and evening. Some elective courses are offered on Saturdays and must be completed within 7 years. New full- and part-time students are admitted in the fall. There is a 7-week summer session. Transferable summer courses are offered.

Programs

In addition to the J.D., the law school offers the LL.M., S.J.D., M.J. (Master of Jurisprudence), and D.L. (Doctor of Laws). Students may take relevant courses in other programs and apply credit toward the J.D.; a maximum of 9 credits may be applied. The following joint degrees can be earned: J.D./M.B.A. (Juris Doctor/Master of Business Administration), J.D./M.M.P. (Juris Doctor/Master of Marine Policy), J.D./Psy.D. (Juris Doctor/Master of Psychology in Law), and J.D./M.P.H. (Juris Doctor/Master of Public Health).

Required

To earn the J.D., candidates must complete 88 total credits, of which 57 are for required courses. They must maintain a minimum GPA of 2.0 in the required courses. The following first-year courses are required of all students: Civil Procedure, Constitutional Law I, Contracts, Criminal Law, Legal Methods I/Analysis, Legal Methods II/Advocacy, Property I and II, and Torts. Required upper-level courses consist of Administrative Law, Business Organizations, Constitutional Law II, Criminal Procedure, Evidence, Federal Income Tax, Legal Methods II, Professional Responsibility, Sales and Leases, Skill Requirement, and Writing Requirement. Two skills classes are required. The required orientation program for first-year students

Phone: 302-477-2703
1-888-WIDENER
Fax: 302-477-2224
E-mail: *law.admissions@law.widener.edu*

Contact
Assistant Dean for Admissions, 302-477-2703 for general inquiries; Eleanor Kelly, Director of Financial Aid, 302-477-2272 for financial aid information.

DELAWARE

is 1-week and includes an introduction to law course, individual case briefing and legislative analysis, and informational sessions on information technology, the legal information center, stress management, student organizations, meet the faculty, financial aid, and character and fitness to practice law.

Electives
The Widener University School of Law offers concentrations in corporate law, criminal law, environmental law, litigation, health law, and technology and law. In addition, clinics for up to 8 credits include Environmental Law, Family Law, Consumer Bankruptcy, Veterans Affairs, and Criminal Defense. Clinical education also includes a comprehensive trial advocacy training program. Seminars are offered in a variety of specialized areas to all upper-level students. Students may take part in externships with legislative and state agencies, district attorneys, public defenders, legal aid societies, and state and local courts. All students must complete a major research paper or directed research project. The Law School's law journals, moot court, and trial advocacy programs, and the many institutes and organizations help provide additional opportunities for scholarly research. Field work opportunities include the Wolcott Fellowship Program, which each academic year places students as part-time clerks for the Delaware Supreme Court. The Francis G. Pileggi Distinguished Lecture in Law is an annual lecture series featuring practitioners, judges, academicians, and distinguished experts in corporate law, and held for the benefit of the Delaware bench and bar and Widener students. Study-abroad programs are offered at Macquarie University in Sydney, Australia, the University of Nairobi in Kenya, the University of Lausanne in Lausanne Switzerland, the University of Venice in Italy, and the southwest University of Political Science and Law in Chongqing, China. The Academic Support Program provides a comprehensive series focusing on basic examination skills, study and outlining skills, and time management. The content of the program varies for each academic level. An intensive Legal Analysis course and an Advanced Analytical Applications course are offered for some second-year students. Specialized programs for minority students are offered through the Career Development Office, the Black Law Students Association, and the Minority Law Students Association. The Delaware Community Foundation Fellowship provides an opportunity to explore the area of trusts and estates, and the Chad-

wick Constitutional Education Fellowship involves work with high school students in the area of constitutional law. Wills and Trusts, Family Law, and Trial Advocacy are the most widely taken electives.

Graduation Requirements
In order to graduate, candidates must have a GPA of 2.0, have completed the upper-division writing requirement, skills requirements, Professionalism Day, and Introduction to Law.

Organizations
The primary law reviews are *Delaware Journal of Corporate Law* and *The Widener Law Review*. Other law reviews include the *Widener Journal of Law, Economics and Race*. The student newspaper is *The Law Forum*. The Health Institute publishes the *Newsletter of the Society of Health Care Attorneys*. The Moot Court Honor Society sponsors the G. Fred DiBona Competition and the Delaware-Harrisburg Moot Court Competition, and hosts the Ruby R. Vale Interschool Corporate Moot Court Competition. The Moe Levine Trial Advocacy Honor Society sponsors the Hugh B. Pearce Trial Competition. Law student organizations, local chapters of national associations, and campus organizations include the Student Bar Association, ADR Society, Black Law Students Association, ACLU, ATLA, Phi Alpha Delta, Rugby Club, Women's Law Caucus, and Health Law Society.

Library
The law library contains 236,011 hard-copy volumes, 374,833 microform volume equivalents, and subscribes to 6,655 serial publications. Online databases and networks include CALI, Legal-Trac, LEXIS, Mathew Bender, OCLC First Search, WESTLAW, and Wilsonline Indexes. Full text sources Online, Proquest, UN Treaty Collection, HeinOnline, CCH Research Network, RIA Checkpoint, BNA All, Constitutions of the Countries of the World, JSTOR, WorldCat, EBSO, and LLMC Digital are also available to law students for research. Special library collections include state and federal depository materials, U.S. Supreme Court records and briefs, CIS congressional library, corporate law, law and government, and health law collections. Recently, the Special library collections acquired state and federal depository materials, U.S. Supreme Court records and briefs, CIS congressional library, corporate law, law and government, and health law collections. The ratio of library volumes to faculty is 3,933 to 1 and

Placement
J.D.s awarded:	248

Services available through: a separate law school placement center.

Services: career resource library that includes books, directories, and periodicals, videotapes; lists of area judges and firms.

Special features: Alumni-student mentor program; mock interview program featuring alumni employers; online job board, free faxing, photocopying and telephone usage; videotaped mock interviews; career panels on various career options, professionalism programming and specialized Job Fairs for diverse students. All professional staff possess J.D. degrees.

Full-time job interviews:	14 employers
Summer job interviews:	22 employers
Placement by graduation:	57% of class
Placement within 9 months:	88% of class
Average starting salary:	$32,000 to $150,000

Areas of placement:

Private practice 2-10 attorneys	19%
Private practice 11-25 attorneys	12%
Private practice 26-50 attorneys	3%
Private practice 51-100 attorneys	4%
Private practice 100+ attorneys	8%
Business/industry	23%
Judicial clerkships	16%
Government	9%
Public interest	3%
Academic	2%
Military	1%

to students is 247 to 1. The ratio of seats in the library to students is 1 to 2.

Faculty
The law school has 62 full-time and 44 part-time faculty members, of whom 44 are women. About 23% of full-time faculty have a graduate law degree in addition to the J.D.; about 16% of part-time faculty have one. The ratio of full-time students to full-time faculty in an average class is 10 to 1; in a clinic, 10 to 1. The law school has a regular program of bringing visiting professors and other distinguished lecturers and visitors to campus.

Students
About 44% of the student body are women; 16%, minorities; 7%, African American; 5%, Asian American; 3%, Hispanic; and 1%, Native American. The majority of students come from Delaware (16%). The average age of entering students is 24; age range is 20 to 67. About 33% of students enter directly from undergraduate school. About 28% drop out after the first year for academic or personal reasons; 80% remain to receive a law degree.

Widener University School of Law

3800 Vartan Way, P.O. Box 69381
Harrisburg, PA 17106-9381

Application Filing	Accreditation
Fall: May 15	ABA, AALS

	Degrees Granted
Fee: $60	J.D.

Enrollment 2011–2012		First-Year Class	
Men:	240 52%	Applied:	908
Women:	221 48%	Accepted:	624
Minorities:	46 10%	Enrolled:	183
Out-of-State:	143 31%		

2011–2012 Class Profile

LSAT Percentile: 44%
LSAT Median Score: 150
Percentage passing bar on first try: 92%

Tuition and Fees:

Resident
$33,540 (F/T)

Average (public)
$18,708

Average (private)
$34,451

Nonresident
$33,540 (F/T)

Average (public)
$29,793

Average (private)
$34,451

0 10 20 30 40 50

Percentage receiving financial aid: 90%

ADMISSIONS

In the fall of 2011 first-year class, 908 applied, 624 were accepted, and 183 enrolled. One transfer student enrolled. The median LSAT percentile of the most recent first-year class was 44; the median GPA was 3.2 on a scale of 4.0. The lowest LSAT percentile accepted was 15; the highest was 81.

Requirements

Applicants must have a bachelor's degree and take the LSAT. The most important admission factors include LSAT results, GPA, and academic achievement. No specific undergraduate courses are required, and candidates are not interviewed.

Procedure

The application deadline for fall entry is May 15. Applicants should submit an application form, LSAT results, transcripts, nonrefundable application fee of $60, letters of recommendation (strongly suggested, but not required), and a personal statement (highly encouraged). Notification of the admissions decision is on a rolling basis. The law school uses the LSAC.

Special

The law school recruits minority and disadvantaged students through programs sponsored by colleges and universities across the country. Additionally, applicants are encouraged to submit a personal statement detailing why they believe their admission would help to correct under representation of a particular minority or disadvantaged group in the legal profession. Requirements are different for out-of-state students. Transfer students must have one year of credits, attended an ABA-approved law school, submit a certified transcript and letter of good standing, and be in the top third of their law school class.

Costs

Books and supplies run $1,200.

Financial Aid

About 90% of current law students receive some form of aid. The average annual amount of aid from all sources combined, including scholarships, loans, and work contracts, is $37,585; maximum, $50,570. Awards are based on need and merit. A number of substantial scholarships are awarded to outstanding applicants and continuing students. Required financial statement is the FAFSA. The aid application deadline for fall entry is open. Special funds for minority, or disadvantaged students include merit scholarships available to majority, minority, and disadvantaged students, and deferred tuition. First-year students are notified about their financial aid application at time of acceptance.

About the Law School

Widener University School of Law was established in 1989 and is a private institution. The 25-acre campus is located in a rural area 7 miles from the capital. The primary mission of the law school is to offer students a dynamic environment from which to enter the legal profession; to encourage students to actively engage in the development of the law. Widener Law gives students a strong foundation in the fundamental theories and principles of law. Students have access to federal, state, county, city, and local agencies, courts, correctional facilities, law firms, and legal aid organizations in the Harrisburg area, as well as numerous resources at the university's main campus. Facilities of special interest to law students include extensive clinical and skills programs, moot court rooms, extensive law library, computer laboratory, lounge areas, and student dining center. Housing for students is available in several apartment complexes within walking distance of campus, including a modern apartment complex adjacent to campus. About 90% of the law school facilities are accessible to the physically disabled.

Calendar

The law school operates on a traditional semester basis. Courses for full-time students are offered days only and must be completed within 6 years. For part-time students, courses are offered both day and evening and must be completed within 6 years. New full- and part-time students are admitted in the fall. There is a 7-week summer session. Transferable summer courses are offered.

Programs

Students may take relevant courses in other programs and apply credit toward the J.D.; a maximum of 9 credits may be applied. The following joint degrees may be earned: J.D./M.S.L.S. (Juris Doctor/Master of Science in Library Science).

Required

To earn the J.D., candidates must complete 88 total credits, of which 66 are for required courses. They must maintain a minimum GPA of 2.0 in the required courses. The following first-year courses are required of all students: Civil Procedure I and II, Contracts I and II, Legal Methods I and II, Property I and II, and Torts I and II. Required upper-level courses consist of Skills Requirement, Administrative Law, Business Organizations, Constitutional Law, Criminal Law, Criminal Procedure, Evidence, Federal Income Tax, Professional Responsibility, Sales and Leases, Secured Transactions, Wills and Trusts, and Writing Requirement. The required orientation program for first-year students is a 1-week orientation that includes an introduction to law course and informational sessions on

Phone: 717-541-3903
1-888-WIDENER
Fax: 717-541-3999
E-mail: *law.admissions@law.widener.edu*
Web: *law.widener.edu*

Contact

Director for Admissions, 717-541-3903 for general inquiries; Eleanor Kelly, Director of Financial Aid, 302-477-2273 for financial aid information.

PENNSYLVANIA

information technology, the legal information center, stress management, student organizations, meet the faculty, financial aid, and character and fitness to practice law.

Electives

The Widener University School of Law offers concentrations in environmental law and Law and Government. In the Harrisburg Civil Law Clinic, students represent clients in a myriad of civil litigation areas. A variety of seminars are offered in specialized topic areas to upper-level students. Students may take part in extensive externship opportunities with legislative and state agencies, district attorneys, public defenders, legal aid societies, and state and local courts. All students must complete a major research paper in a seminar or directed research. Special lecture series are provided by the Law and Government Institute and the Career Development Office. Study-abroad programs are available at Macquarie University in Sydney, Australia, the University of Nairobi in Kenya, the University of Lausanne in Lausanne, Switzerland, the University of Venice, Italy, and the Southwest University of Political Science and Law in Chongqing, China. Widener has an Academic Support Program that provides a comprehensive program focusing on basic examination skills, studying and outlining skills, and time management. An Intensive Legal Analysis course is offered for some first-year students. Specialized programs for minority students are provided through the Career Development Office, the Black Law Students Association, and the Minority Law Students Association. The most widely taken electives are Family Law, Sports Law, and Trial Advocacy.

Graduation Requirements

In order to graduate, candidates must have a GPA of 2.0, complete the upper-division writing requirement, skills requirement, Professionalism Day, and Introduction to Law.

Organizations

Students edit the *Widener Law Journal*, and *Widener Journal of Law, Economics & Race*. Moot court competitions for students include the Burton Wexler First Amendment Competition, Jerome

Prince Evidence Competition, and Jessup International Law Competition. Other competitions include the Buffalo Invitational Trial Advocacy Competition, National Trial Competition, Evan Gorley Trial Advocacy Competition, and the American Association for Justice Trial Advocacy Competition. Law student organizations include the Student Bar Association, Black Law Students Association, and Minority Law Students Association. There are local chapters of ATLA, Phi Alpha Delta, and the National Association of Public Interest Law. Campus clubs include St. Thomas More Society, Sports and Entertainment Law Society, and Criminal Law Society.

Library

The law library contains 258,433 hardcopy volumes and 332,319 microform volume equivalents, and subscribes to 6,026 serial publications. Online databases and networks include CALI, CIS Universe, Legal-Trac, LEXIS, Mathew Bender, OCLC First Search, and WESTLAW. Other resources include Wilsonline Indexes, Full text sources Online, PROQUEST, UN Treaty Collection, HeinOnline, CCH Research Network, RIA Checkpoint, BNA All, constitutions of the countries of the world, JSTOR, world cat, LLMC Digital, and EBSCO Host, which are available to law students for research. Special library collections include state and federal depository materials, U.S. Supreme Court records and briefs, CIS Congressional library, corporate law, law and government, health law collections. The ratio of library volumes to faculty is 8,614 to 1 and to students is 560 to 1. The ratio of seats in the library to students is 1 to 2.

Faculty

The law school has 30 full-time and 30 part-time faculty members, of whom 23 are women. About 30% of full-time faculty have a graduate law degree in addition to the J.D.; about 18% of part-time faculty have one. The ratio of full-time students to full-time faculty in an average class is 19 to 1; in a clinic, 10 to 1. The law school has a regular program of bringing visiting professors and other distinguished lecturers and visitors to campus.

Placement

J.D.s awarded:	106

Services available through: a separate law school placement center.

Services: career resource library that includes books, directories, and periodicals, lists of area judges and firms.

Special features: Alumni-student mentor program; online job board; free faxing, photocopying, and telephone usage; videotaped mock interviews; career panels on various career options and professionalism programming; specialized for diverse students; and a weekly e-mail alumni employment newsletter. All professional staff possess J.D. degrees.

Full-time job interviews:	16 employers
Summer job interviews:	28 employers
Placement by graduation:	64% of class
Placement within 9 months:	97% of class
Average starting salary:	$35,000 to $135,000

Areas of placement:

Private practice 2-10 attorneys	30%
Private practice 11-25 attorneys	3%
Private practice 26-50 attorneys	3%
Government	21%
Business/industry	17%
Judicial clerkships	14%
Public interest	6%
Academic	2%
Military	1%

Students

About 48% of the student body are women; 10%, minorities; 3%, African American; 2%, Asian American; and 2%, Hispanic. The majority of students come from Pennsylvania (69%). The average age of entering students is 23; age range is 21 to 51. About 35% of students enter directly from undergraduate school, 12% have a graduate degree, and 52% have worked full-time prior to entering law school. About 13% drop out after the first year for academic or personal reasons; 87% remain to receive a law degree.

WILLAMETTE UNIVERSITY

College of Law

245 Winter Street S.E.
Salem, OR 97301

Application Filing			Accreditation
Fall: March 1			ABA, AALS

			Degrees Granted
Fee: $50			J.D., LL.M.

Enrollment 2011–2012		First-Year Class	
Men:	241 58%	Applied:	1,092
Women:	173 39%	Accepted:	538
Minorities:	75 18%	Enrolled:	141
Out-of-State:	n/av		

2011–2012 Class Profile
LSAT Percentile: 64%
LSAT Median Score: 155
Percentage passing bar on first try: 72%

Tuition and Fees:

Resident
$29,680 (F/T)

Average (public)
$18,708

Average (private)
$34,451

Nonresident
$29,680 (F/T)

Average (public)
$29,793

Average (private)
$34,451

Percentage receiving financial aid: 98%

ADMISSIONS

In the fall of 2011 first-year class, 1092 applied, 538 were accepted, and 141 enrolled. Eight transfer students enrolled. The median LSAT percentile of the most recent first-year class was 64; the median GPA was 3.2 on a scale of 4.0.

Requirements

Applicants must have a bachelor's degree and take the LSAT. The most important admission factors include LSAT results, GPA, and academic achievement. No specific undergraduate courses are required, and candidates are not interviewed.

Procedure

The application deadline for fall entry is March 1. Applicants should submit an application form, LSAT results, transcripts, personal statement, nonrefundable application fee of $50, 2 letters of recommendation, and a resume. Notification of the admissions decision is between January and May. The law school uses the LSAC.

Special

The law school recruits minority and disadvantaged students. The College of Law has a Coordinator for Multicultural Affairs whose principal responsibility is the recruitment and retention of students of color. Requirements are different for out-of-state students. Transfer students must have a minimum GPA of 2.29, have attended an ABA-approved law school, personal statement, be in good standing academically, and eligible to return to their current law school.

Costs

Tuition and fees for the 2011–2012 academic year are $29,600 for all full-time students. Tuition for part-time students is $32,460 for in-state students and $32,460 out-of-state. Books and supplies run $1,450.

Financial Aid

About 98% of current law students receive some form of aid. The average annual amount of aid from all sources combined, including scholarships, loans, and work contracts, is $46,625. Awards are based on need and merit combined. Required financial statement is the FAFSA. The aid application deadline for fall entry is March 1. First-year students are notified about their financial aid application approximately 2 weeks after acceptance.

About the Law School

Willamette University College of Law was established in 1883 and is a private institution. The 65-acre campus is located in an urban area in Salem, the capital of Oregon, which is 45 miles from Portland. The primary mission of the law school is to provide academic and professional excellence in a supportive environment that maximizes a student's potential. Students have access to federal, state, county, city, and local agencies, courts, correctional facilities, law firms, and legal aid organizations in the Salem area. The college is within walking distance of several courts and their libraries and virtually all state agencies and departments. Housing for students is available in afforable apartments and houses located near the campus. All law school facilities are accessible to the physically disabled.

Calendar

The law school operates on a traditional semester basis. Courses for full-time students are offered days only and must be completed within 3 years. For part-time students, courses are offered days only. New full-time students are admitted in the fall. There is a 7-week summer session. Transferable summer courses are offered.

Programs

In addition to the J.D., the law school offers the LL.M. Students may take relevant courses in other programs and apply credit toward the J.D.; a maximum of 6 credits may be applied. The following joint degrees may be earned: J.D./M.B.A. (Juris Doctor/Master of Business Administration).

Required

To earn the J.D., candidates must complete 90 total credits, of which 40 are for required courses. They must maintain a minimum GPA of 2.3 in the required courses. The following first-year courses are required of all students: an elective course, Civil Procedure, Constitutional Law I, Contracts I and II, Criminal Law, Legal Research and Writing, Property, and Torts. Required upper-level courses consist of Constitutional Law II, Evidence, and Professional Responsibility. The required orientation program for first-year students lasts 3 days and consists of an introduction to the law program and to legal research and writing.

Electives

The College of Law offers concentrations in corporate law, criminal law, environmental law, family law, internationl law, labor law, litigation, tax law, torts and insurance, dispute resolution, law and government, commercial law, and estate planning. In addition, the school offers several clincs. In the Civil Practice Clinic, students represent clients in actual cases and transactions under the close supervision of faculty. Seminars are offered to second- and third-year students on such topics as First Amendment law, American Indian law, Global Sustainability, Human

Phone: 503-370-6282
Fax: 503-370-6087
E-mail: law-admission@willamette.edu
Web: www.willamette.edu/wucl

Contact

Carolyn Dennis, Director of Admissions, 503-370-6282 for general inquiries; Katy Wilson, Senior Financial Aid Counselor, 503-370-6273 for financial aid information.

OREGON

Rights, and Advanced Topics in Conflict Theory. Students receive academic credit while working in a close mentoring relationship with attorneys in the courts, the state legislature, state agencies, non-profits, and legal departments of private companies. All first-year students are required to take a yearlong legal research and writing course. There is an Annual Lecture Series, Dispute Resolution Series, and Paulus Lecture Series. A Summer in China study program is offered to second- and third-year students. In addition, individual students, with ABA approval, may spend a semester at a leading new law school in Quito, Ecuador or Hamburg, Germany. Special student assistants are available for students in legal research and writing. The College of Law has an active multicultural law student organization that, among other activities, sponsors a Martin Luther King event involving the community at large. The college offers simulation courses on negotiations, mediation, arbitration, interviewing and counseling, and trial practice. The most widely taken electives are various simulation courses and seminars.

Graduation Requirements

In order to graduate, candidates must have a GPA of 2.3, and complete the upper-division writing requirement.

Organizations

Students edit the *Willamette Law Review, Willamette Journal of International Law & Dispute Resolution*, and the *Willamette Law Online* (a student run/edited online service providing case summaries and law updates). Students participate in a number of moot court competitions, including the National Appellate Competition, the International Law Competition, and the ATLA Trial Competition. Other moot court competitions students participate in include the Environmental Appellate Competition, Negotiation Competition, and Criminal Law Competition. Law student organizations include the Multi-Cultural Law Students Association, International Law Society, and Women's Law Caucus. There are local chapters of Phi Alpha Delta and Phi Delta Phi. Campus clubs and other organizations include the Public Interest Law Society, Environmental Law Society, and Willamette Lambda Legal Organization.

Library

The law library contains 300,000 hardcopy volumes and 156,872 microform volume equivalents, and subscribes to 1,618 serial publications. Online databases and networks include CALI, CIS Universe, Legal-Trac, LEXIS, Mathew Bender, OCLC First Search, WESTLAW, Wilsonline Indexes, and Summit, which are available to law students for research. Special library collections include a federal depository, Public International Law, and tax and labor collections. The ratio of library volumes to faculty is 10,000 to 1 and to students is 706 to 1. The ratio of seats in the library to students is 1 to 1.

Faculty

The law school has 31 full-time and 29 part-time faculty members, of whom 17 are women. About 19% of full-time faculty have a graduate law degree in addition to the J.D.; about 17% of part-time faculty have one. The ratio of full-time students to full-time faculty in an average class is 14 to 1; in a clinic, 8 to 1. The law school has a regular program of bringing visiting professors and other distinguished lecturers and visitors to campus.

Students

About 39% of the student body are women; 18%, minorities; 1%, African American; 7%, Asian American; 6%, Hispanic; and 2%, Native American. The average age of entering students is 25; age range is 21 to 55. About 4% drop out after the first year for academic or personal reasons; 96% remain to receive a law degree.

Placement

J.D.s awarded:	130

Services available through: a separate law school placement center.

Services: attorney-student extensive mentor program; public interest clerkship stipends; public interest loan repayment program for graduates; and a fellowship program for minority students through the Oregon State Bar.

Special features: Career and Professional Development services web site includes a C.S. calendar, events, information, as well as job postings; coordinated effort for joint degree. Students with Atkinson Graduate School of Management; and specialty law attorney panels and career workshops.

Placement within 9 months of graduation:	87% of class
Average starting salary:	$16,000 to $120,000

Areas of placement:

Solo Practice	5%
Private practice 2-10 attorneys	56%
Private practice 11-25 attorneys	3%
Private practice 26-50 attorneys	1%
Private practice 51-100 attorneys	3%
Business/industry	16%
Government	8%
Judicial clerkships	4%
Public interest	4%

WILLIAM MITCHELL COLLEGE OF LAW

875 Summit Avenue
St. Paul, MN 55105-3076

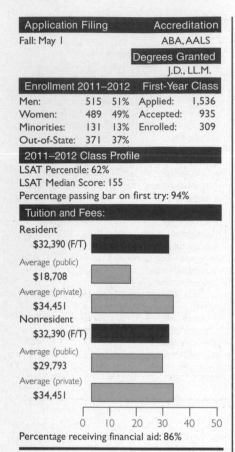

Application Filing		Accreditation
Fall: May 1		ABA, AALS

Degrees Granted
J.D., LL.M.

Enrollment 2011–2012		First-Year Class	
Men:	515 51%	Applied:	1,536
Women:	489 49%	Accepted:	935
Minorities:	131 13%	Enrolled:	309
Out-of-State:	371 37%		

2011–2012 Class Profile
LSAT Percentile: 62%
LSAT Median Score: 155
Percentage passing bar on first try: 94%

Tuition and Fees:

Resident
$32,390 (F/T)

Average (public)
$18,708

Average (private)
$34,451

Nonresident
$32,390 (F/T)

Average (public)
$29,793

Average (private)
$34,451

0 10 20 30 40 50

Percentage receiving financial aid: 86%

ADMISSIONS

In the fall of 2011 first-year class, 1536 applied, 935 were accepted, and 309 enrolled. Thirteen transfers enrolled. The median LSAT percentile of the most recent first-year class was 62; the median GPA was 3.4 on a scale of 4.0. The lowest LSAT percentile accepted was 11; the highest was 99.

Requirements
Applicants must have a bachelor's degree and take the LSAT. The most important admission factors include academic achievement, LSAT results, and writing ability. No specific undergraduate courses are required. Candidates are not interviewed.

Procedure
The application deadline for fall entry is May 1. Applicants should submit an application form, LSAT results, transcripts, a personal statement, TOEFL (if applicable), 2 letters of recommendation, and

a resume. Notification of the admissions decision is on a rolling basis. The law school uses the LSAC.

Special
The law school recruits minority and disadvantaged students through a general policy of admissions that encourages diversity in the student body and on-campus visits. Requirements are different for out-of-state students. Transfer students must have one year of credit, must have a minimum GPA of 2.5, must have attended an ABA-approved law school, must submit a personal statement, and must submit a letter of good standing from the dean of the previously attended school. 24 credits must by completed at William Mitchell.

Costs

Tuition and fees for the 2011–2012 academic year are $32,340 for all full-time students. Tuition for part-time students is $23,400 for in-state students and $23,400 out-of-state. Books and supplies run $1,550.

Financial Aid

About 86% of current law students receive some form of aid. The average annual amount of aid from all sources combined, including scholarships, loans, and work contracts, is $45,996; maximum, $54,460. Awards are based on need and merit combined. The required financial statement is the FAFSA. The aid application deadline for fall entry is March 15. Special funds for minority or disadvantaged students include many named scholarships. First-year students are notified about their financial aid application at time of acceptance.

About the Law School

William Mitchell College of Law was established in 1900 and is a private institution. The 7-acre campus is in an urban area of St. Paul. The primary mission of the law school is to provide a demanding legal education so engaged with the profession that graduates have an enduring advantage as they meet the challenges of an increasingly complex world. Students have access to federal, state, county, city, local agencies, courts, correctional facilities, law firms, and legal aid organizations in the St. Paul area. There are numerous

corporations and nonprofit organizations in the Twin Cities metropolitan area providing opportunities and resources for students. Facilities of special interest to law students are the Warren E. Burger Library, high-tech classrooms, 4 high-tech courtrooms, student center with comfortable areas for individual and group study as well as socializing outside the classroom, and a wireless network, which has been expanded to include all classrooms and common areas. Housing for students is available in the neighborhood and elsewhere in Minneapolis-St. Paul. About 99% of the law school facilities are accessible to the physically disabled.

Calendar

The law school operates on a traditional semester basis. Courses for full-time students are offered both day and evening, and must be completed within 6 years. For part-time students, courses are offered both day and evening, and must be completed within 6 years. New full- and part-time students are admitted in the fall. There is a 7-week summer session. Transferable summer courses are offered.

Programs

In addition to the J.D., the law school offers the LL.M. Students may take relevant courses in other programs and apply credit toward the J.D.; a maximum of 9 credits may be applied. The following joint degrees may be earned: J.D./M.S (Juris Doctor/Master of Science in Community Health).

Required
To earn the J.D., candidates must complete 86 total credits, of which 46 are for required courses. They must maintain a minimum GPA of 2.0 in the required courses. The following first-year courses are required of all students: Civil Procedure, Contracts, Property I and II, Torts I and II, and Writing and Representation: Advice and Persuasion. Required upper-level courses consist of a skills course, Advanced Research and Writing, Constitutional Law-Liberties, Constitutional Law-Powers, Perspectives on the Legal Profession, Professional Responsibility, two statutory courses, and Writing and Representation: Advocacy. Clinical courses are offered, but not required. The required orientation program for

Phone: 651-290-6343
888-WMCL-LAW
Fax: 651-290-6414
E-mail: *admissions@wmitchell.edu*
Web: *www.wmitchell.edu*

Contact

Kendra Dane, Assistant Dean and Director, 651-290-6476 for general inquiries; Patty Harris, Director of Financial Aid, 651-290-6358 for financial aid information.

first-year students lasts 2 days and covers an introduction to law school, tours, the first class, and writing and representation. There is an optional four-day orientation that covers academic skills.

Electives

The law school offers concentrations in corporate law, criminal law, family law, intellectual property law, internationl law, labor law, litigation, tax law, torts and insurance, commercial law, property law, estates law, government, and ADR. In addition, there are 11 clinics available including Civil Advocacy, Business Law, and Immigration Law. Seminars are available in several areas. Externships are also available. Independent research projects are available for 1 to 4 credits. Special lecture series include the Public Square Lecture Series and the National Security Forum. Study abroad consists of summer programs in London, Malta, Chile, Turkey, and the Czech Republic. Minority programs are provided by the Black Law Students Association, Jewish Law Students Association, Asian Law Students Association, Latino Law Students Association, and Native American Law Students Association. The college also has an Office of Multicultural Affairs which, among other things, offers services and support to traditionally underrepresented populations. Special interest group programs are provided by the Student Intellectual Property Association, Christian Law Society, National Lawyers Guild, Minnesota Justice Foundation, Women Law Students Association, Health Law Society, Italian American Bar Association, Federalist Society, and Outlaw. The most widely taken electives are Evidence, Business-Agency, Partnerships, Limited Liability Companies, and Family Law.

Graduation Requirements

In order to graduate, candidates must have a GPA of 2.0 and must have completed the upper-division writing requirement.

Organizations

The primary law review is the *William Mitchell Law Review* and the student newspaper is the *Opinion*. Teams participate in the William E. McGee National Civil Rights Moot Court, New York City Bar/ACTL National Moot Court, and Phil-

ip C. Jessup International Moot Court. Other competitions include Cardozo BMI Moot Court Competition and Saul Lefkowitz Moot Court Competititon. Law student organizations, local chapters of national associations, and campus organizations include Association for International Law, Health Law Society, Women's Law Student Association, American Constitution Society, Federalist Society, Black Law Students Association, Delta Theta Phi, Hockey Club, and William Mitchell Families Organization.

Library

The law library contains 355,102 hardcopy volumes and 155,379 microform volume equivalents, and subscribes to 809 serial publications. Such online databases and networks as CALI, CIS Universe, Infotrac, Legal-Trac, LEXIS, OCLC First Search, WESTLAW, Wilsonline Indexes, Worldcat, HeinOnline, RIA Checkpoint, CCH Intelliconnect, EBSCO, Gale Collections, Access UN, BNA Online, LexisNexis Congressional, and Readex Serial Set are also available to law students for research. Special library collections include a selective federal depository library. The ratio of library volumes to faculty is 8,871 to 1 and to students is 354 to 1. The ratio of seats in the library to students is 1 to 2.

Faculty

The law school has 36 full-time and 229 part-time faculty members, of whom 113 are women. About 11% of full-time faculty have a graduate law degree in addition to the J.D. The ratio of full-time students to full-time faculty in an average class is 20 to 1; in a clinic, 4 to 1. The law school has a regular program of bringing visiting professors and other distinguished lecturers and visitors to campus.

Students

About 49% of the student body are women; 13%, minorities; 2%, African American; 6%, Asian American; 3%, Hispanic; and 1%, Native American. The majority of students come from Minnesota (63%). The average age of entering students is 24; age range is 19 to 63. About 34% of students enter directly from undergraduate school, and 7% have a graduate degree. About 8% drop out after the first year for academic or personal reasons; 91% remain to receive a law degree.

Placement

J.D.s awarded:	282

Services available through: a separate law school placement center and Career and Professional Development Office.

Services: career programs, resource library, out-of-state job-search resources, online resources on the web site, on campus interviews, mock interviews, and student assessments.

Special features: career development staff members who provide legal experience as well as career development experience.

Full-time job interviews:	10 employers
Summer job interviews:	43 employers
Placement within 9 months of graduation:	97% of class
Average starting salary:	$20,000 to $200,000

Areas of placement:

Private practice 2-10 attorneys	25%
Private practice 11-25 attorneys	9%
Private practice 26-50 attorneys	3%
Private practice 51-100 attorneys	9%
Business/industry	24%
Judicial clerkships	10%
Government	6%
Public interest	3%
Academic	1%

Yale Law School

P.O. Box 208329
New Haven, CT 06520-8215

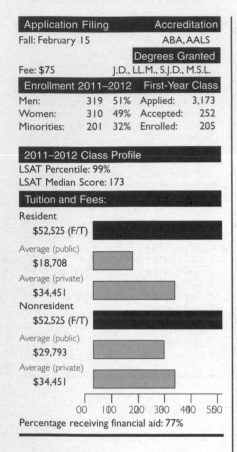

Application Filing		Accreditation
Fall: February 15		ABA, AALS
		Degrees Granted
Fee: $75		J.D., LL.M., S.J.D., M.S.L.

Enrollment 2011–2012		First-Year Class	
Men:	319 51%	Applied:	3,173
Women:	310 49%	Accepted:	252
Minorities:	201 32%	Enrolled:	205

2011–2012 Class Profile
LSAT Percentile: 99%
LSAT Median Score: 173

Tuition and Fees:

Resident
$52,525 (F/T)

Average (public)
$18,708

Average (private)
$34,451

Nonresident
$52,525 (F/T)

Average (public)
$29,793

Average (private)
$34,451

00 100 200 300 400 500

Percentage receiving financial aid: 77%

ADMISSIONS

In the fall of 2011 first-year class, 3173 applied, 252 were accepted, and 205 enrolled. The median LSAT percentile of the most recent first-year class was 99; the median GPA was 3.9 on a scale of 4.0. The lowest LSAT percentile accepted was 80; the highest was 99.

Requirements
Applicants must have a bachelor's degree and take the LSAT. No specific undergraduate courses are required. Candidates are not interviewed.

Procedure
The application deadline for fall entry is February 15. Applicants should submit an application form, LSAT results, transcripts, a personal statement, a nonrefundable application fee of $75, 2 letters of recommendation, and a 250-word essay. The law school uses the LSAC.

Special
The law school recruits minority and disadvantaged students by means of Candidate Referral Services through LSAC. Requirements are different for out-of-state students. Transfer students must have one year of credit, have attended an ABA-approved law school, a personal statement, and have a weighted average grade of not less than B.

Costs

Tuition and fees for the 2011–2012 academic year are $50,275 for all full-time students. Books and supplies cost $1,100.

Financial Aid

About 77% of current law students receive some form of aid. The average annual amount of aid from all sources combined, including scholarships, loans, and work contracts, is $52,164; maximum, $72,675. Awards are based on need. Required financial statements are the FAFSA and Need Access. The aid application deadline for fall entry is March 15. First-year students are notified about their financial aid application at time of acceptance.

About the Law School

Yale University / Yale Law School was established in 1801 and is a private institution. The campus is in an urban area in New Haven, on the block bounded by Grove, High, Wall, and York Streets. The primary mission of the law school is to train lawyers and leaders in the public and private sectors, and to encourage research in the law. Students have access to federal, state, county, city, and local agencies, courts, correctional facilities, law firms, and legal aid organizations in the New Haven area. Facilities of special interest to law students include: a renovated law library and computer facility; the Jerome W. Frank Legal Services Organization; the Orville H. Shell, Jr. Center for International Human Rights; the Center for the Study of Corporate Law, and numerous endowed lecture programs that bring distinguished speakers from around the world. Housing for students includes off-campus housing. Some family housing is available from the university. The university also has a housing office that assists students in locating housing.

Calendar

The law school operates on a traditional semester basis. Courses for full-time students are offered days only and must be completed within 6 terms. New full-time students are admitted in the fall. There is no summer session and transferable summer courses are not offered.

Programs

In addition to the J.D., the law school offers the LL.M., S.J.D., and M.S.L. Students may take relevant courses in other programs and apply credit toward the J.D.; a maximum of 12 credits may be applied. The following joint degrees may be earned: J.D./M.D. (Juris Doctor/Doctor of Medicine), J.D./Ph.D. (Juris Doctor/Doctor of Philosophy), J.D./M.A. (Juris Doctor/Master of Arts), J.D./M.A.R. (Juris Doctor/Master of Arts in religion), J.D./M.B.A. (Juris Doctor/Master of Business Administration), J.D./M.Div. (Juris Doctor/Master of Divinity), and J.D./M.E.S. (Juris Doctor/Master of Environmental Studies).

Required
To earn the J.D., candidates must complete 83 total credits, of which 21 are for required courses. The following first-year courses are required of all students: Constitutional Law, Contracts, Procedure, and Torts. Required upper-level courses consist of a supervised analytic writing paper and a substantial paper, Criminal Law and Administration, and Professional Responsibility Legal Ethics. The optional orientation program for first-year students consists of a weekend gathering prior to registration, at which life at the law school and in New Haven is discussed.

Electives
The Yale Law School offers concentrations in corporate law, criminal law, entertainment law, environmental law, family law, intellectual property law, internationl law, juvenile law, labor law, litigation, media law, securities law, sports law, tax law, torts and insurance, administrative law, constitutional law, comparative law, legal history, torts, criminal procedure, bankruptcy, law and economics, employment discrimination, property, health, antitrust, evidence, and international business. In addition, clinical opportunities are offered through many clinics including Community and

Phone: 203-432-4995
E-mail: *admissions.law@yale.edu*
Web: *www.law.yale.edu*

Contact
Dean of Admissions, 203-432-4995 for general inquiries; Jill Stone, Director of Financial Aid, 203-432-1688 for financial aid information.

CONNECTICUT

Economic Development, Complex Federal Litigation, and the Allard K. Lowenstein International Human Rights Law Clinic. In addition to the many seminars offered during the fall and spring terms, students may submit proposals for research and legislative drafting seminars. Research programs and independent reading may be undertaken after the first term with faculty permissions. Numerous special lecture series are held annually, including the Timothy B. Atkeson Environmental Practitioner in Residence; the Cover Lecture in Law and Religion; the Ralph Gregory Elliot First Amendment Lecture; the Preiskel/Silverman Program on the Practicing Lawyer and the Public Interest; and the Robert L. Bernstein Lecture in International Human Rights. In the second term, students may begin participation in programs managed primarily by students under the supervision of a faculty adviser. These include the Capital Defense Project, the Domestic Violence Temporary Restraining Order Project, the Greenhaven Prison Project, Street Law, Thomas Swan Barristers' Union, Morris Tyler Moot Court of Appeals, and numerous reviews and journals.

Graduation Requirements
In order to graduate, candidates must have completed the upper-division writing requirement.

Organizations
Student-edited publications include the *Yale Law Journal, Yale Journal of International Law, Yale Journal of Law and Feminism, Yale Journal of Law and Humanities, Yale Journal on Regulation, Yale Human Rights and Development Law Journal, Yale Law and Policy Review,* and *Yale Journal of Health Policy, Law, and Ethics.* Moot court competitions include the Thurman Arnold Appellate Competition Prize, the Benjamin N. Cardozo Prize, and the John Fletcher Caskey prize. Other competitions or prizes include the Albom, Brody, Burkan Memorial, Cohen, Connecticut Attorneys' Title Insurance Company, Cullen, Egger, Emerson, Gherini, Gruter, Jewell, Khosla, Lemkin, Massey, Miller, Munson, Olin, Parker, Peres, Porter, Robbins Memorial, Scharps, Townsend, Wang, and Wayland. Law student organizations include the Asia Law Forum, the Initiative for Public Interest Law at Yale, and the Yale Law and Technology Society. There are local chapters of the Black Law Students Association, the Federalist Society, and the American Constitution Society.

Library
The law library contains 1,294,682 hardcopy volumes and 321,732 microform volume equivalents, and subscribes to 34,773 serial publications. Online databases and networks include CALI, CIS Universe, DIALOG, Dow-Jones, Infotrac, Legal-Trac, LEXIS, Mathew Bender, OCLC First Search, RLIN, WESTLAW, Wilsonline Indexes, ORBIS (Yale University catalog), and MORRIS (Yale Law School catalog), which are available to law students for research. Special library collections include a 200,000-volume foreign and international law collection and a rare book collection of 20,000 volumes. The ratio of library volumes to faculty is 19,918 to 1 and to students is 1,874 to 1. The ratio of seats in the library to students is 1 to 1.

Faculty
The law school has 65 full-time and 54 part-time faculty members, of whom 28 are women. According to AAUP standards for Category I institutions, faculty salaries are well above average. The ratio of full-time students to full-time faculty in an average class is 8 to 1. The law school has a regular program of bringing distinguished professors, lecturers, and visitors to campus.

Students
About 49% of the student body are women; and 32%, minorities. The majority of students come from foreign countries (4%). The average age of entering students is 24. About 20% of students enter directly from undergraduate school.

Placement
J.D.s awarded:	201

Services available through: a separate law school placement center.
Services: judicial clerkship counseling and programs, public interest counseling and programs, career counseling, publications, recruiting events, resource library.
Special features: a professional counseling staff, comprehensive individual career counseling, a program resource library, publications, and recruiting events.

Benjamin N. Cardozo School of Law

55 Fifth Avenue
New York, NY 10003

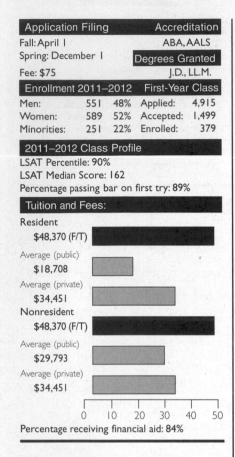

Application Filing	Accreditation
Fall: April 1	ABA, AALS
Spring: December 1	**Degrees Granted**
Fee: $75	J.D., LL.M.

Enrollment 2011–2012		First-Year Class	
Men:	551 48%	Applied:	4,915
Women:	589 52%	Accepted:	1,499
Minorities:	251 22%	Enrolled:	379

2011–2012 Class Profile
LSAT Percentile: 90%
LSAT Median Score: 162
Percentage passing bar on first try: 89%

Tuition and Fees:

Resident
$48,370 (F/T)

Average (public)
$18,708

Average (private)
$34,451

Nonresident
$48,370 (F/T)

Average (public)
$29,793

Average (private)
$34,451

0   10   20   30   40   50

Percentage receiving financial aid: 84%

ADMISSIONS
In the fall of 2011 first-year class, 4915 applied, 1499 were accepted, and 379 enrolled. Forty-five transfers enrolled. The median LSAT percentile of the most recent first-year class was 90; the median GPA was 3.6 on a scale of 4.0.

Requirements
Applicants must have a bachelor's degree and take the LSAT. The most important admission factors include academic achievement, LSAT results, and general background. No specific undergraduate courses are required. Candidates are not interviewed.

Procedure
The application deadline for fall entry is April 1. Applicants should submit an application form, LSAT results, transcripts, a personal statement, a nonrefundable application fee of $75, and 2 letters of recommendation. A resume is also recommended. Notification of the admissions decision is on a rolling basis. The law school uses the LSAC.

Special
The law school recruits minority and disadvantaged students by means of special mailings, attendance at law fairs and receptions, a brochure designed for minority applicants, and an on-campus visitation program. Requirements are different for out-of-state students. Transfer students must have one year of credit, must have attended an ABA-approved law school, and must submit a personal statement.

Costs
Tuition and fees for the 2011–2012 academic year are $40,788 for full-time in-state students and $47,800 for out-of-state students. On-campus room and board costs about $18,650 annually.

Financial Aid
About 84% of current law students receive some form of aid. The average annual amount of aid from all sources combined, including scholarships, loans, and work contracts, is $51,481; maximum, $72,938. Awards are based on need and merit combined. The required financial statement is the FAFSA. The aid application deadline for fall entry is April 15. Special funds for minority or disadvantaged students are available. First-year students are notified about their financial aid application at time of acceptance.

About the Law School
Yeshiva University Benjamin N. Cardozo School of Law was established in 1976 and is a private institution. The campus is in an urban area in the heart of Greenwich Village in lower Manhattan. The primary mission of the law school is to enhance the student's understanding of the legal profession and of the ethical dilemmas and professional responsibilities for a lawyer in today's society. Students have access to federal, state, county, city, and local agencies, courts, correctional facilities, law firms, and legal aid organizations in the New York City area. Students benefit from the school's proximity to city, state, and federal offices. Organizations within proximity of the law school include the New York Stock Exchange, American Stock Exchange, the United Nations, as well as many of New York's cultural institutions. Housing for students is available in a residence hall located one block from the law school. The office maintains apartment

listings and circulates a roommate newsletter. All law school facilities are accessible to the physically disabled.

Calendar
The law school operates on a traditional semester basis. Courses for full-time students are offered days only, and must be completed within 5 years. For part-time students, courses are offered days only, and must be completed within 5 years. New full-time students are admitted in the fall and spring. New part-time students are admitted in the summer. There is a 13-week summer session. Transferable summer courses are not offered.

Programs
In addition to the J.D., the law school offers the LL.M. Students may take relevant courses in other programs and apply credit toward the J.D.; a maximum of 2 credits may be applied. The following joint degrees may be earned: J.D./M.P.H. (Juris Doctor/Master of Public Health), J.D./M.S.B. (Juris Doctor/Master of Science in Bioethics), and J.D./M.S.W (Juris Doctor/Master of Social Work).

Required
To earn the J.D., candidates must complete 84 total credits, of which 55 are for required courses. They must maintain a minimum GPA of 2.4 in the required courses. The following first-year courses are required of all students: Civil Procedure, Constitutional Law, Contracts, Criminal Law, Elements of the Law, Legal Writing I and II, Property, and Torts. Required upper-level courses consist of Advanced Legal Research, distribution requirements, Professional Responsibility, and upper-level writing requirement. The required orientation program for first-year students is held over 7 days. The first two days consist of programs to introduce students to Cardozo, as well as social gatherings. Over the next five days, students have introductory law school classes in the morning, followed by afternoon programming designed to introduce students to the legal profession and legal ethics.

Electives
The Benjamin N. Cardozo School of Law offers concentrations in corporate law, criminal law, entertainment law, family

Phone: 212-790-0274
Fax: 212-790-0482
E-mail: *lawinfo@yu.edu*
Web: *www.cardozo.yu.edu/*

Contact

David G. Martinidez, Associate Dean, 212-790-0274 for general inquiries; Kahryn Tuman, Director of Student Finance, 212-790-0392 for financial aid information.

NEW YORK

law, intellectual property law, internationl law, litigation, media law, tax law, communications law, commercial law, constitutional law and rights, property and real estate law, and dispute resolution. In addition, clinics, open to second- and third year students include the Innocence Project, Mediation Clinic, and Human Rights and Genocide Clinic. Special courses and seminars are offered in human rights and children, intellectual property and globalization, and multicultural dispute resolution. A wide variety of internships and externships is offered during the academic year including a full-time internship with the Manhattan District Attorney's Office. Research assistants are hired by professors. Students also have the option to conduct their own research under the supervision of a faculty member. Field work opportunities include the Alexander Fellows Program. Cardozo hosts numerous lectures including the Uri and Caroline Bauer Memorial Lecture, the Jacob Burns Institute for Advanced Legal Studies, and the Distinguished Lecture in Intellectual Property Law. Cardozo offers summer programs at Oxford in Comparative Corporate Governance and Mediation and Democratic Dialogue in Budapest. Cardozo students also have the opportunity to spend a semester in Hamburg, Germany, Budapest, Hungary, Tel Aviv, Israel, Amsterdam, the Netherlands, Hong Kong, and Bilbao, Spain. In addition, Cardozo also offers short-term intensive programs abroad scheduled during winter breaks. Seminars have been recently held in Japan, Rwanda, India, and China. Minority programs include activities of the Minority Law Student Association and Outlaw. Panels and outside speakers are sponsored by such institutes as the Howard M. Squadron Program in Law, Media, and Society, the Samuel and Ronnie Heyman Center on Corporate Governance, the Kukin Program for Conflict Resolution, the Floersheimer Center for Constitutional Democracy, Cardozo Center for Public Service Law, and the Program in Family Law, Policy, and Bioethics. The most widely taken electives are Copyright, Corporations, and Evidence.

Graduation Requirements

In order to graduate, candidates must have a GPA of 2.4, and must have completed the upper-division writing requirement and the Advanced Legal Research and Professional Responsibility courses, and must have fulfilled distribution requirements.

Organizations

Students edit the *Cardozo Law Review, Arts and Entertainment Law Journal, Cardozo Journal of Law and Gender, Cardozo Journal of International and Comparative Law, Cardozo Journal of Conflict Resolution, The Cardozo Public Law, Policy, and Ethics Journal, Law and Literature, New York Real Estate Reports*, and the newspaper *The Cardozo Dispatch*. Cardozo students compete in numerous moot court competitions including the Pepperdine University School of Law National Entertainment and Law Moot Court Competition, the Appellate Lawyers Association Moot Court Competition, and the Wechsler First Amendment Moot Court Competition at American University. Cardozo's Moot Court Honor Society hosts the national Cardozo BMI Entertainment and Communications Law Moot Court Competition and the Monrad G. Paulsen Intramural Moot Court Competition. Law student organizations, local chapters of national associations, and campus organizations include the Intellectual Property Law Society, Public Interest Law Students Association, the Federalist Society, Minority Law Students Alliance, Cardozo Women Law Students Associations, and Outlaw.

Library

The law library contains 579,289 hardcopy volumes, 1,338,310 microform volume equivalents, and subscribes to 7,918 serial publications. Online databases and networks include CALI, Legal-Trac, LEXIS, OCLC First Search, WESTLAW, and Wilsonline Indexes are available to law students for research. Special library collections include the Louis and Ida Shlansky Family Foundation Library of Jewish and Israeli Law and a U.S. government depository. The ratio of library volumes to faculty is 9,830 to 1 and to students is 500 to 1. The ratio of seats in the library to students is 1 to 2.

Faculty

The law school has 58 full-time and 107 part-time faculty members, of whom 64 are women. About 16% of full-time faculty have a graduate law degree in addition to the J.D.; about 16% of part-time faculty have one. The ratio of full-time students to full-time faculty in an average class is 15 to 1; in a clinic, 16 to 1. The law school has a regular program of bringing visiting

Placement

J.D.s awarded:	380

Services available through: a separate law school placement center. The Office of Career Services offers access to a national jobs database, computerized databases for student and alumni use, and an online registration system for on-campus recruitment.

Special features: six full-time counselors provide comprehensive advice on interviewing and resume writing. Career Services coordinates a myriad of programs, including the Practice Area Symposium during which students learn about different areas of law, the Mentor/Mentee Program through which students are paired with alumni mentors, and the Public Sector Law Expo, which provides information about summer public sector opportunities.

Full-time job interviews:	21 employers
Summer job interviews:	59 employers
Placement by graduation:	71% of class
Placement within 9 months:	93% of class
Average starting salary:	$50,000 to $160,000

Areas of placement:

Private practice 2-10 attorneys	32%
Private practice 11-25 attorneys	8%
Private practice 26-50 attorneys	7%
Private practice 51-100 attorneys	5%
Private practice 101-500+ attorneys	5%
Business/industry	19%
Government	14%
Public interest	12%
Judicial clerkships	6%
Military	1%
Academic	1%

professors and other distinguished lecturers and visitors to campus. There is a chapter of the Order of the Coif; 11 faculty and 515 graduates are members.

Students

About 52% of the student body are women; 22%, minorities; 5%, African American; 4%, Asian American; and 7%, Hispanic. The average age of entering students is 24; age range is 20 to 44. About 36% of students enter directly from undergraduate school, and 10% have a graduate degree. About 7% drop out after the first year for academic or personal reasons; 93% remain to receive a law degree.

CHAPTER 16

Law Schools Not Approved by the ABA

AN OVERVIEW

Although the vast majority of law school students attend institutions approved by the American Bar Association, a distinct minority attend schools that have not received ABA accreditation. Applicants frequently wonder whether it will make a difference if they attend a nonapproved school. The answer to this question requires an understanding of what it means for a law school to be accredited.

For nearly a century, the American Bar Association has developed educational standards for law schools, reviewed institutional adherence to those standards, and approved law schools that complied with the standards. The standards themselves have evolved out of the crucible of experience with input from legal educators, practitioners, and judges. The standards, while sometimes mystifying to those who do not understand legal education, represent well-reasoned statements of policy aimed at assuring that individuals who enter the practice of law undertake a rigorous curriculum in an intellectually demanding setting. Over the years the ABA approval process has established and maintained a basic set of standards for entry into the practice of law that is accepted by bar licensing authorities, practitioners, and the courts.

Recognizing the value of the accreditation process in upholding the quality of legal education and ultimately the legal profession, most states require candidates for the bar examination to have graduated from an ABA-approved law school. Some other states certify graduates of law schools located in the state but not approved by the ABA to sit for the bar exam in that state. It is virtually impossible for graduates of a nonapproved law school to take the bar outside the state where they attended law school.

The non-ABA schools generally fall into three groups: new schools seeking ABA approval, state-approved schools, and unapproved schools. New law schools seeking ABA accreditation must go through an initial review and provisional accreditation before becoming fully approved. During this period of several years the school undergoes strict scrutiny, and students who enroll run the risk that the institution may never meet ABA standards. In recent years, more than a few such schools have dissolved when they could not secure ABA approval. If this happens, students may lose all their law school credits, and, worse, find that they cannot take a bar examination anywhere. On the other hand, if the school gains ABA approval, the risk will turn out to have been worthwhile.

The differences between state-approved and unapproved schools may seem murky. In most states where graduates of non-ABA schools can take the bar, there are only one or two non-ABA schools. Whether these schools are accredited by a state accrediting agency or whether the graduates simply are certified by the bar examiners is probably immaterial to most students. In California, however, the distinction does have ramifications. Significantly, that state has the largest number of lawyers as well as the largest number of non-ABA schools. In California, the state approves law schools using a procedure similar to but different from the ABA. State-approved law schools are treated within the state much like ABA schools; outside California the graduates of these schools usually will be considered like graduates of any other non-ABA approved school. Schools in California that have not been approved by either the state or the ABA represent a separate group within that state, and graduates face additional restrictions on (but not prohibition from) bar admission.

Why would you choose to attend a non-ABA law school? The most common reason might be that you do not gain admission to an ABA school. There is definitely a pecking order among law schools from elite schools like Harvard or Yale down to the unapproved schools. Generally, the more prestigious the law school, the more competitive it will be, and, conversely, the lower the school's perceived ranking, the less stringent will be the admission standards. Legal educators frequently warn prelaw students to beware of law school rankings because they often are based on reputations decades old rather than the current state of legal education at the schools. Rankings also overlook distinctions among schools that make different schools the best choice for different students. In this sense you should evaluate the quality of education at an unapproved school the same way you would evaluate an approved school. The point here is that some students whose traditional qualifications (such as undergraduate GPA and LSAT percentile) will not get them into an approved school may be able to secure a seat at an unapproved one. Some candidates may decide not to attend law school at all if they are not accepted at an ABA school; others may want a law degree so much that they select one of the non-ABA institutions.

A second reason that some students give for attending an unapproved school is cost. Because they are not bound by ABA requirements, non-ABA schools frequently rely heavily on part-time instructors, who cost less than full-time professors. In addition, non-ABA schools may provide more spartan facilities (the library, for example). This bargain basement approach to education can mean tuition savings for students.

Those considering attending an unapproved law school should consider also the educational experience they will receive. Since many such schools provide a bare bones education, applicants should scrutinize the academic program of the school at least as carefully as they would that of an ABA-approved school. While many non-ABA schools have existed for many years and maintain sound local reputations, other schools have less than solid foundations.

A final consideration that anyone contemplating attending a non-ABA-approved law school should address involves the career opportunities available to graduates. Not only is the bar passage rate lower at some non-ABA schools, thereby limiting career opportunities, but also the placement patterns of the graduates may be significantly different. The bottom line is that anyone considering law school should carefully investigate and research all aspects of each potential school before applying.

PROFILES OF SELECTED LAW SCHOOLS

Brief profiles of selected law schools not approved by the ABA appear on the following pages. The pros and cons of such law schools are discussed above. Only schools responding to our request for current information are included here.

Each profile begins with the name of the law school, its address and phone and fax numbers, and e-mail and Web addresses if provided. The capsule of basic information about the law school presents the following information.

Application Filing Fall and spring application deadlines and the application fee are given.

Accreditation Any professional accreditation is noted. (See **Abbreviations and Degrees** on page iv).

Degrees Granted Degrees are nearly always limited to the J.D.

Enrollment Enrollment breakdowns for a recent year include men, women, minorities, and out-of-state students.

First-Year Class The applied, accepted, and enrolled figures refer to the number of students applying for a recent year entering class.

Class Profile This section includes the median LSAT percentile and the median LSAT score of freshmen in a recent year entering class, as well as the percentage of a recent graduating class that passed the bar on the first attempt.

Tuition and Fees Tuition and Fees figures given here are annual amounts, unless otherwise indicated. Because tuition charges change periodically, it is important to check with the school for current figures. This section also features the percentage of current students receiving financial aid.

Contact The person or position to whom inquiries should be directed is given, along with appropriate phone numbers.

3745 W. Chapman Avenue, #250
Orange, CA 92868

Phone: 714-772-9000
Fax: 714-634-3330
E-mail: americanclaw@yahoo.com
Web: www.aclaw.com

Application Filing	Accreditation
Fall: August 30	no
Spring: January 20	
Fee: $25	Degrees Granted
	J.D.

Enrollment 2011–2012			First-Year Class	
Men:	51	58%	Applied:	32
Women:	37	42%	Accepted:	24
Minorities:	62	70%	Enrolled:	24
Out-of-State:	9	10%		

2011–2012 Class Profile
LSAT Percentile: 67%
LSAT Median Score: n/av
Percentage passing bar on first try: 22%

Tuition and Fees:

Resident
$ 400 (P/T) (PER CREDIT)

Average (public)
$18,708

Average (private)
$34,451

Nonresident
$ 400 (P/T) (PER CREDIT)

Average (public)
$29,793

Average (private)
$34,451

0 10 20 30 40 50
Percentage receiving financial aid: 80%

Contact
Waleed Akleh, Dean, 714-772-9000 for general inquiries and financial aid information.

Laurence Drivon School of Law

6650 Inglewood
Stockton, CA 95207

Phone: 209-478-0800 ext. 5
Fax: 209-235-2889
E-mail: lawadmission@humphreys.edu
Web: www.humphreys.edu

Application Filing	Accreditation
Fall: July 1	no
	Degrees Granted
Fee: $35	J.D.

Enrollment 2011–2012			First-Year Class	
Men:	33	38%	Applied:	83
Women:	53	62%	Accepted:	41
Minorities:	20	23%	Enrolled:	29

2011–2012 Class Profile
LSAT Percentile: 27%
LSAT Median Score: 145
Percentage passing bar on first try: 50%

Tuition and Fees:

Resident
$8,937 (P/T)

Average (public)
$18,708

Average (private)
$34,451

Nonresident
$8,937 (P/T)

Average (public)
$29,793

Average (private)
$34,451

0 10 20 30 40 50
Percentage receiving financial aid: 81%

Contact
Santa Lopez, Admissions Officer, 209-478-0800 for general inquiries; Judi Johnstone, 209-478-0800, ext. 3 for financial aid information.

Lincoln Law School of Sacramento

3140 J Street
Sacramento, CA 95816

Phone: 916-446-1275
Fax: 916-446-5641
E-mail: info@lincolnlaw.edu
Web: www.lincolnlaw.edu

Application Filing	Accreditation
Fall: June 15	no
Spring: November 15	
Fee: $50	Degrees Granted
	J.D.

Enrollment 2011–2012			First-Year Class	
Men:	115	48%	Applied:	140
Women:	125	52%	Accepted:	125
Minorities:	77	32%	Enrolled:	105

2011–2012 Class Profile
LSAT Percentile: 35%
LSAT Median Score: 148
Percentage passing bar on first try: 46%

Tuition and Fees:

Resident
$10,120 (P/T)

Average (public)
$18,708

Average (private)
$34,451

Nonresident
n/av

Average (public)
$29,793

Average (private)
$34,451

0 10 20 30 40 50

Contact
Melissa Fuller, Assistant Registrar, 916-446-1275 for financial aid information.

MONTEREY COLLEGE OF LAW

100 Col. Durham Street
Seaside, CA 93955

Phone: 831-582-4000
Fax: 831-582-4095
E-mail: *wlariviere@montereylaw.edu*
Web: *www.montereylaw.edu*

Application Filing	Accreditation
Fall: May 1	no

Degrees Granted	
Fee: $75	J.D., M.L.S.

Enrollment 2011–2012		First-Year Class	
Men:	39 46%	Applied:	72
Women:	45 47%	Accepted:	48
Minorities:	31 37%	Enrolled:	37
Out-of-State:	4 5%		

2011–2012 Class Profile
LSAT Percentile: 47%
Percentage passing bar on first try: 37%

Tuition and Fees:
Resident
n/av

Average (public)
$18,708

Average (private)
$34,451

Nonresident
n/av

Average (public)
$29,793

Average (private)
$34,451

Percentage receiving financial aid: 30%

Contact
Dean of Admissions and Placement, 831-582-4000 for general inquiries.

SAN FRANCISCO LAW SCHOOL

20 Haight Street
San Francisco, CA 94102

Phone: 415-626-5550, ext.123
Fax: 415-626-5584
E-mail: *admitadmin@sfls.edu*
Web: *www.sfls.edu*

Application Filing	Accreditation
Fall: June 15	no

Degrees Granted	
Fee: $75	J.D.

Enrollment 2011–2012		First-Year Class	
Men:	62 52%	Applied:	82
Women:	58 48%	Accepted:	45
Minorities:	60 50%	Enrolled:	28
Out-of-State:	1 1%		

2011–2012 Class Profile
LSAT Percentile: 33%
LSAT Median Score: 147

Tuition and Fees:
Resident
$ 525 (P/T)

Average (public)
$18,708

Average (private)
$34,451

Nonresident
n/av

Average (public)
$29,793

Average (private)
$34,451

Percentage receiving financial aid: 40%

Contact
Registrar, 415-626-5550, ext. 123 for general inquiries; Jane Gamp, 415-626-5550, ext. 121 for financial aid information.

SANTA BARBARA AND VENTURA COLLEGES OF LAW

Santa Barbara College of Law

20 East Victoria Street
Santa Barbara, CA 93101

Phone: 805-966-0010
Fax: 805-966-7181
E-mail: *admits@venturalaw.edu*
Web: *www.santabarbaralaw.edu*

Application Filing	Accreditation
Fall: n/av	no

Degrees Granted	
	J.D.

Enrollment 2011–2012		First-Year Class	
Men:	45 43%	Applied:	n/av
Women:	60 59%	Accepted:	n/av
Minorities:	17 16%	Enrolled:	n/av

2011–2012 Class Profile
LSAT Percentile: 40%
LSAT Median Score: 149
Percentage passing bar on first try: 61%

Tuition and Fees:

Resident
$4,825 (P/T)

Average (public)
$18,708

Average (private)
$34,451

Nonresident
$4,825 (P/T)

Average (public)
$29,793

Average (private)
$34,451

Percentage receiving financial aid: 25%

Contact
Director of Admissions, 805-966-0010 ext. 18 for general inquiries.

TRINITY INTERNATIONAL UNIVERSITY

Trinity Law School

2200 North Grand Avenue
Santa Ana, CA 92705

Phone: 714-796-7100
Fax: 714-796-7190
E-mail: *tls@tiu.edu*
Web: *www.tiu.edu/law/*

Application Filing	Accreditation
Fall: May 1	no
Spring: December 1	**Degrees Granted**
Fee: $35	J.D.

Enrollment 2011–2012		First-Year Class	
Men:	103 44%	Applied:	256
Women:	132 56%	Accepted:	134
Minorities:	141 60%	Enrolled:	90
Out-of-State:	2 1%		

2011–2012 Class Profile
LSAT Percentile: 37%
LSAT Median Score: 147

Tuition and Fees:

Resident
    $9,300 (F/T)

Average (public)
    $18,708

Average (private)
    $34,451

Nonresident
    $9,300 (F/T)

Average (public)
    $29,793

Average (private)
    $34,451

0 10 20 30 40 50
Percentage receiving financial aid: 78%

Contact
Jennifer Tracy, 714-796-7121 for financial aid and information

---

UNIVERSITY OF NORTHERN CALIFORNIA

Lorenzo Patino School of Law

1012 J Street
Sacramento, CA 95814

Phone: 916-441-4485
Fax: 916-441-0175
E-mail: *registrarunclawschool@gmail.com*

Application Filing	Accreditation
Fall: n/av	no
	Degrees Granted
	J.D.

Enrollment 2011–2012		First-Year Class	
Men:	23 38%	Applied:	78
Women:	37 0%	Accepted:	75
Minorities:	0 0%	Enrolled:	75

2011–2012 Class Profile
LSAT Percentile: n/av
LSAT Median Score: n/av
Percentage passing bar on first try: n/av

Tuition and Fees:

Resident
    $2,700 (F/T)

Average (public)
    $18,708

Average (private)
    $34,451

Nonresident
    $1,875 (F/T)

Average (public)
    $29,793

Average (private)
    $34,451

0 10 20 30 40 50

Contact
Registrar's Office, (916) 441-4485 for general inquiries.

WILLIAM HOWARD TAFT UNIVERSITY

Taft Law School

3700 S. Susan Street
Santa Ana, CA 92704

Phone: 714-850-4800
Fax: 714-708-2082
E-mail: *admissions@taftu.edu*
Web: *taftu.edu*

Application Filing	Accreditation
Fall:	no
Spring:	**Degrees Granted**
	J.D., LL.M.

Enrollment 2011–2012		First-Year Class	
Men:	150 63%	Applied:	0
Women:	90 37%	Accepted:	0
Minorities:	82 34%	Enrolled:	0
Out-of-State:	144 60%		

2011–2012 Class Profile
LSAT Percentile: n/av
LSAT Median Score: n/av
Percentage passing bar on first try: 50%

Tuition and Fees:

Resident
    $7,920 (F/T)

Average (public)
    $18,708

Average (private)
    $34,451

Nonresident
    $7,920 (F/T)

Average (public)
    $29,793

Average (private)
    $34,451

0 10 20 30 40 50
Percentage receiving financial aid: n/av

Contact
Director of Student Services, 714-850-4800 or 800-882-4555 for general inquiries; Tina Saxon, Financial Director, 800-882-4555 for financial aid information.

INDEX

Entries set in roman type are law schools approved by the American Bar Association.
Entries set in italic type are law schools not approved by the American Bar Association.

NOTES